Lanterns in Hand

MADELINE MUNRO

First Published in 2003 by
Whareama Press
PO Box 203, Tunbridge Wells, Kent, TN3 0WL

British Library Cataloguing in Publication data.

A catalogue record for this book is available from the British Library.

ISBN 0-9544821-0-7

Typeset by Tradespools, Frome, Somerset
Printed and bound by Antony Rowe Ltd, Chippenham, Wiltshire

Some of the poems in this collection have appeared in Ambit, The Frogmore Papers, Helix, The Independent (Daily Poem), Jersey Eisteddfod Competition, Lancaster Literature Festival Anthology, Links, Macmillan Education: The unicorn and lions (school anthology), National Poetry Competition 1988 Prizewinners, Outposts, South East Arts anthologies, Scotland Alive Series, Stand, Sunday Telegraph Magazine (Cheltenham Festival 1st=), Understanding, University Tutorial Press: Changing Islands (school anthology), Virago New Poets, Yorick Pamphlet Poets (S.E.Arts financial support) and been broadcast on Radio 3 and Radio Kent.

For Marion

Contents

I

The Chant

Say, Frock, frock; Janet, Janet.
Her mother's plan, the chant,
to put away the morning's dread
along the two mile road to school;
hold down the fear at night
past empty Tomashogle,
bare on the upper field,
unlit, and harbouring fright
before the darker edge of trees.
Frock, frock; Janet, Janet.
Round to the turn, the bend,
and then clear sight of home.

Tuesday, the market day
at Inverness. He had been
asked. Tonight her father
would bring home, under his arm,
the frock, maybe a box with something
more, and want his slippers
while it was unwrapped.
Now there was Janet, safe
in the byre, soft black
of the Jersey round the eyes -
and she could lead her like
a dog, for summer holidays
rope-haltered to Newmill.

Frock, frock; Janet, Janet.

What can we chant now to lift the dark?

Lamps

Before the dark we rushed to organise
the lamps, brought paraffin in cans,
and grumbled when the funnel slipped, oil
running its engine smell across the dresser top.
With screwed-up newspaper, quick puff and blow,
we shone the globes, trimmed wicks, set lanterns
and the candles out, then pumped the fickle Tilley,
new-fangled with its priming meths, its mantle -
dust at a touch. But more of ritual still
to watch at Uncle Fred's while Wakle
brought the tall Aladdin lamp, to wait
agog the magic hum, see spread the small
blue circling flame, witness the startling
breaking of that new white light.

Winter Work

The short cold afternoon had gone when
lanterns in hand we followed Uncle Fred
to 'feed the beasts': he guarding child
as we hoisted and hauled, intent, like working
men, with hook or fork or four-pronged graip
to keep the turnip cutters fed. Iron-hard,
the handles rose and fell, while underneath
the wire-net baskets caught, clean-sliced
or diced, the frosted, earth-cold crop.
Docile, loose-chained, the cows ranked first,
the favoured two-to-a-stall, kept apart
from the mob, the knee-deep hordes, boxing
and bullying, heads thrusting for space where
each load brought was shaken and tipped
into the wall-long trough. Absorbed
in the world of byre and fold, barn and
shed, we filled haiks with hay, spread straw
for the night-long beds; and if Fred,
who had spoken when I was born of 'another
soul come to suffer', dwelt then, as we gave
the last look round, on freedom and chains
and ultimate ends, we stood secure in the
heavy air, content in the goodness
of giving. Latching the doors, next in our thoughts
was supper with 'youma' and fresh turn-over
bread from Asher's van, and which of the six
small fancy cakes would be our final pick.

Afed

When Afed found batteries dead
In cycle lamps, he slung
A lantern from the handlebars; then led
Us on our road along the four miles home.

Wind caught the flame, blackening
The globe, but some rough flicker
Stayed ahead. Last one behind came pedalling
Hard, eyes on Afed, chased by the dark.

The few known lights from farms
Marked off the miles and drew
Us on, round to the Quarry Brae, past
Paterson's, where we got off to walk.

There, winds in the hollow passed
On through the heavy trees,
Dark rootless oceans; lost, then held,
Straining the night, topped by the pricking stars.

But it was Spring, drenched clean
With new living cold, still bright,
When coughing and bent, too spent to come,
He turned to wave back from Bognie cross-roads.

Your hands look cold, Afed.
Maybe you should have gloves.
We'd watched winter and wet soak up the dread
Of Mayday auctions and of leaving Newmill.

Black Polls fed off their feet;
The heavy-headed corn
Fallen in August rain after the fretting heat
Dank and sodden: these surfeitings gone.

His boots by the kitchen grate
Gathered remorse and griefs.
Tired, roughened hands blurred delicate
On the fiddle's slackening strings.

Then funeral clothes; a factious will:
The old betrayals. And even Mam,
Lured to the spoil, could half-forget till
Finding his favourite garden place,

She stood by the flowering currant
Bush, and wept to look
At the narcissi, sweet paper-whites, blowing
His light among the bolder daffodils.

Wakle

Auldearn to Nairn on the Bluebird bus
With Wakle, and the eyes' first shock
Of the northern sea, wonder of waves, vast
Ocean clean, the sky far out, the links
Greener than dreams, sporting the tiny
Summer booth with Morganti's own ice-cream.

Dapper as any clerk, Wakle, in navy
Serge, stepped from his rough cocoon,
The laundry collar starched to a stiff
White butterfly.

                 First sea, first bike,
First watch, first fountain pen, we list
His wifeless epitaph; white silky ankle
Socks (with one thick band of blue)
Angora gloves, fur mitts and Christmas
Shopping sprees, on *Eve night*, last stop
At Cumming's for a taxi home, clasping
Some clever winding toy - the dancing *jigger* man,
Boy on the swing - books, torch, a cheap
Net stocking, ready packed, (trite gesture
To the Santa myth) and all the other treats -
Cake, candied fruits, half whisky, one port wine.

Parcels laid safe, Wakle nipped off;
Came down from the unmade den, the cigarette ends,
Restored to his hodden working suit,
Hard, leather-laces boots, and the battered
Grease-patched hat. Tin pail in hand,
He bent at the treacle barrel, mixing

16

A drink for the bull - that maharajah
Prisoner, consuming the heavy darkness
In his dayless, night-long shed.

My Father

My father - who can boast like this? -
Once brought in testicles of calves
To roast on the shovel of the
Best bronze fireside set.

We lacked the full disgust of Mam's
Ripe rage but furtive lurked around
The orgy. They said he was good
As a vet at cutting calves.

We were more ravaged by that other
Sacrifice, when cows and stirks dehorned,
Pruned raw with some crude secateurs
Or saw, filed from the surgery.

Blood, horror, flies, clogged in my sister's
Head - little girl's rage matched giant's.
He won. How could he know, he said,
She really was his girl.

Savage, ill-educated beast
Causing such hurt - and yet
He fed us, clad us, never once
Struck one of us. One night he played.

He slipped on the kitchen floor we'd
Rubbed till it shone like glass. He laughed.
We spun him around and around.
Fifteen stone felled and brought to ground.

Late August coming from Newmill
We'd find two kitchen dressers all
Festooned with apples. Tiered temples
of scent. A windfall welcome home.

Wet days he drove us in style
To school, sang *Daisy, Daisy* at
The schoolhouse gate. Daisy was handsome.
Daisy was terror. Daisy had lovers
...... and, oh, if she heard!

Sixty when I was born, he was
Never young. But only real old age
Robbed him of roar, gave him
An easier, unaccustomed tearfulness.

Past eighty, leaning on two sticks,
He'd work the dogs once more at
Sheepdog trial tricks; or grieve
With Kaffir by a flock of rams.

We washed, shaved and tended him, fetched
Slippers, doctor, bible. The future
Lessened the past, wore down that
Stubbornness, let in some kind of love.

You're a good lass, he told my sister
Not long before he died.
It was a father's blessing
From the last of Abraham's kind.

They filled the farmyard at his funeral.
We wept with the crowd who sang
The Lord's My Shepherd - felt proud
On reading *North East Breeder Dies.*

What neighbours said away from us
Is hard to know. Perhaps they mocked
His big man airs but that day sensed
A milestone gone, scanned new horizons

Where, even on the land, professionals brought
Push-button ease to cruelty;
Switched off the daylight; recorded
And reduced mass crimes to microfilm.

Kaffir - a highly intelligent collie with a split black and white face

And Bobby Danced

Some summers came hot.

Down by the burn we set the stage
For blanket washing day.

Black cast-iron pot already there,
Inside rusted to ochre-red.

We scoured the pot, raked out
The claggy ash and dammed the burn.

Sharp wood smoke rose, shimmered
Through steam, and the pummelling began.

We were carriers, tramplers, manglers; then, bored,
We played with sawdust at the porridge making game.

And once the heat pressed closer
Till the dusk was taut with thunder.

Some elemental charge possessed our lambs,
Three petted Blackface bottle-feds.

Out-capering all Bobby sprang clear,
Skipped high on the washing table.

By the cauldron set on the heavy stones
We watched convulsed in the last red glow.

Soon great, slow drops, releasing
Rain, brought in the dark, ended the game.

Beyond the storm loomed school; September
Sales. But Hector, Sandy and poor dancing Bobby

Trusted, no doubt, that always we should
Call their soft mouths to the gate.

Milking Time

Pressed warm against the cows' soft flanks
Sometimes we tilted heads to eye
The weird gargantuan webs looping
The rafters; grey, ragged sheets
Draping the deepier dustier dark
Of frightened hermit spiders.

                    Crick
In the neck, we'd turn to the cats;
Tease them by aiming cheeky jets
At the waiting, anxious, time-marking
Line, till baleful, bedraggled they
Broke up parade, licked insult
Away, then sulked back, one by one,
To malign us.

                    Stripping the teats
We'd edge our palms, scuff from the froth
Odd hard-dung flecks and fallen bits,
Fling to the wall the muck-caked stool,
Slosh amends to the cats, and swing
Fast down *the pass* to strain our pails
Into the large milk bowls.

                    Byre smells
Seeped into hair and skin, came
with us to school to the smart town kids
Whose education lacked our lore
Strong healthy words like *sharn* and *strang*.

Now exiled in prim, pasteurised ways
We view strange farms from stranger
Camp site splatterings. We frown
As we double-rinse our cups at stray
Specks of grass on the plastic ware.
At the barbed wire fence we stretch
Across to stroke the cows; feel once
Again soft sides, warm simple folds
That then, too safely, held our heads.

Deaths

Sometimes a cow lost
all the strength to rise, day
upon day sunk adamant
in her damp misery
until we, too, accepted
there would be no miracle.

And then the other stricken days
the knackery arrived,
grey lorry with pulley
and rope, to take away
a mare, still young, the fever
cropped in the summer grass.

And stuck in my head, one stifling
day, the pass stuffy with smells
of last year's straw, old sacks,
and lack of air, watching
a hen, caught in the throes
of something like the staggers;

cruel burlesque of rise and fall;
lesson in death
the slow, indifferent struggle,
the squeezing out
of life, wrung
to the last half jerk.

Laiken Days

Even now we get uptight before our guests
arrive. Can't cope in that smooth,
casual way. Hang-up from Laiken days
when *people to tea* began the uphill push
of getting ready. Charlie dragooned
to lug out carpets to the little field
where we joined in, grasping an end
till holding knuckles tore, to make
the winter's dust shake out in waves,
brushing with brooms and beating with sticks,
leaving the summer grass to all the blame.
Windows with fly spots cleaned, candle grease scraped
from round the stairs, Brasso to knobs, Zebo
to grates, steel of the kitchen range scratch-emeried
bright as the black; and towards the end our mother
flushed at baking. Last scurryings
to throw some water at the back-door big slate slab
where all the hens had been, round to the front
to rub the wettened steps with some hard
whiting block; a last quick wash and change
and they came rolling in.

Nice in the summer when they'd gone
to stand by the burn's worn stepping stone
watching the shallow water flow.

                    In winter, through,
lights disappearing through the dark
left a small emptiness we took with us to bed.

The Fly Catchers

They grew around the edges of the bog
and by the old Drum road, well overgrown
by then, the leaf-curled butterwort, fly catchers,
unsocial little flowers, not quite as rare
as the scented orchids we might want to press,
but always their violet innocence
flawed by those specks of irksome
flies, motes in the eye.

Tiny, two-faced insectivore, no one
had told us of your acid baths, your
rosette appetite - though scientists
have learnt to copy something
from your Venus tricks. Out-timing bees
in orchards they can shower the trees
with phantom sex, and as the summers pass
watch crops of seedless apples swell.

11

We hung them round the kitchen
unrolling almost gleefully the sticky
pale brown paper strips, tackily
spread with some smooth syrup
glue. And as the streamers dried
to black we reckoned numbers, smug
as the hardened trapper.

Hands that now
lightly brush away a fly, lift spiders
out and spare a wasp, have grown more
thoughtful.

Yet what have we come to, drawn
by what? Perhaps no more than misfits
in the scheme of things, minds
strained skew-whiff from when
(for all the heartache of the cattle floats)
we sat quite happily to eat.

Again

Cruets, ashets, dishes, decanters,
dressers, wine-red velvet chairs,
summer surprises, wanted or not,
arrived at night from the May farm sales;
over the big stone, over the bridge,
bumped along on a rollicking swell,
rolling away our ready fears of cattle floats
that ferried out (with foul mouthed
fallen-morning shouts) the press-ganged loads
and left the empty stalls.

Glennie came, then, in some such way,
small for a collie, yet vaguely touched
with the tense Alsatian face.
Though eager for work, he quivered for love.
He had landed in luck. 'You'll spoil that dog,'
our father said. 'Stupid to *darling* a dog'.
And Glennie's was not a favoured head
where his hand would rest. With one more throw
of the dealer's dice, Glennie had gone
to be cattleman's dog at Craiggie.

Markets, sellings, disasters, deaths
made partings the dark core of life;
so great was the rejoicing of lost and found
when rumpling up one Sunday's sloth,
Glennie rushed through the back-door porch
and hurtled straight to our arms.

Short sore reprieve of less than a day:
months passed before we came to hear
how the runaway fared. He had not made good.
Nor had they known
from what sickness or pining he died.

Tonight in the rising dark, again
a small shape stirs by that pool
where were-men drag their prey.
We watch with tethered hearts. Inscrutable
patrols, age-old and unassuaged,
close in, scenting the winds for love.

Stones

The Stone Field opposite the Laiken road
was named from the *cromlech* set below the Ord.
As distinct to our eyes as Ailsa Craig, the boulder
was just tall as a man on its highest side
with the girth, maybe, of a farmyard stack.

Up at New Arr stones blossomed like yarrow.
When Robbie Willox took the lease, all his last
strength was heaped there, too, high views
of the firth for sustenance. Beyond New Arr,
and at The Drum, the broken, small stone-cottages.

Halfway to school at Littlemill, familiar
as our reading books, two raw stone bridges
we could dawdle round, hauling our bodies
off our feet, to stare below at the Muckle Burn,
let the world pull down, into its darkened flow.

We were bred in granite country, edging the colder hills.

Mice in the Cream

A mouse in the wide milk basin
Put the morning at odds; fur and tail
In the stretch of cream - waste
Of the last night's milking - set the loss
Beyond strict common sense, since
Again the cows stood waiting and,
Dogs to ducks, plenty would run
To the overspill.

                    Now, further
Each day from all of that, mornings
We drag uneasily from sleep,
For they are always there, first thing,
Lodged in their weight, the old mistakes,
The missing out, the finished, doused
Wrong-running dreams - mice in the cream.

Poor mice, back then we hardly saw -
Or cared - that you were drawn
Into a heavy drowning.

The Ord Walk

We took apples with us - the early
Beauty of Bath. Our mother wanted
to go, as she had as a child,
over the Hill of the Ord
to Geddes School. We knew
the sawdust bog across the road,
strewn still with slivers and spelks
of crumbling planks
pale in their rottenness, old
sawmill remnants from the First World War:
then on and up
further for us than ever before,
the roughening bracken
holding a freak September heat.
But whether we grew too tired
and slow, or over-complained,
we didn't that day, or ever
with her, go all the way.

For what, in a bothersome sun,
could it mean to us? Impossible
to picture her with Ada Aird,
two restless, racing girls
at Ada's father's school,
or the album's earnest boys,
Walter and Fred, pushing uphill
to the drumming *r*s, the scratchy
slates and the inky copperplate.

At the top we paused, like travellers
at a cottage gate. A woman
smiled and spoke; and brought us
water, Adam's wine, the afternoon's
unburdening. We turned back home
by Rait, stared at the ruined walls
where a lord took his sword
in feuding rage - or so they said -
to a daughter's hands
as she hung there,
poised for her lover's arms.
Then by the dipper and Winewell,
our mother's childhood home;
its doors familiar to her once,
shut hard against us three.

For all the trudging later years
that must have been
her last long 'pleasure' walk.

Returning now on our own pilgrimage
- as old as she was then -
we find, quite strange to us, The Ord
green forested, restored
as she that day ·
had tried to tell us it had been
before our time.

Prisoners

Little had touched us of the war
except, perhaps, the daily news
and one bad raid on Aberdeen
when Marion was there. It raised
excitement, then, when V-day past
the still-held prisoners were sent
round farms, and two or three were due
with us for threshing day. I felt
each footfall would send shivers
through our heads. But it was not
that way. Agog from school
I heard how these young, distinguished men
had come with the greatest courtesy
to leave their coats indoors. Mid-day,
Charlie had seen them at the burn
washing their hands and sprucing up
before they came to eat. They'd lined
potatoes round their plates
with unabashed precision. One,
glimpsing the piano through a door,
had intimated he could play.
He knew Beethoven off by heart - brought quiet
with the Moonlight's opening bars.

Next time they came (as harvest help) we saw them
for ourselves. By then, the local men
were at their ease, using their names
and kind enough, but relishing
the ribald jeer at Goering, Goebbels,
Rommel (made to run). The vanquished
held their dignity. The tallest one,

refined and very pale, had been on
submarines: I can't remember where
the others served, but the handsomest,
who'd charmed my mother when he played,
shone in my sister's eyes. Leaving,
he asked if he might visit us.
Unsure, my mother could not quite
agree. Neighbours might view this
as some treachery. Perhaps, too,
she wondered where it all would end. Karl.
At times my sister talks about him still.

Seasons

Snow on the Clunas hills. Autumn
after summer gone, the last of the windfalls
neglected in the garden, left
like the straggle of obdurate leaves
loose on the trees. The first storm
to come, felt one night in the waiting dusk
or later in the darker winds
as we closed the door on all outside,
glad of the cattle fed, came in
to the ease of fire and light
and the kitchen table laid.
Slow hours of peering out. Morning
with every handle stone, the byre
strange with its skylight white.
Outside the day turned arctic
bright - a picture show - or bringing
the snow again in driving sweeps
across the hill at Asher's. A wilder night
of *bloving*. Surely, at last,
the road to school impassable.

                    Then winter, too,
gone stale, its hardships overstayed.
Under the larch tree cattle huddling still
in April sleet.

                But soon the Achavelgin moor
seething with frogs; smoke from the burning whin
incense of early summer, the outlined black remains
whatever sacrifice. Small primroses

around Slagachorrie road and in the glen; and then
by every road the June wild roses
Dresden pale, while our bog blazed
with marigold and buttercup.
We popped unopened foxglove bells
like tiny blown-up paperbags, stayed quiet
while broom pods burst themselves.

Out from the town the summer's end
carried stray wisps of teasing sound
from the last remaining roundabouts.
The Games gone by, already the nights
were closing in.

              Alone in the little field
the red-beaded rowan shone with the words
of the old song, our mother's rosary.

Cups

We brought them out today, the china
Cups, our mother's best, for visitors,
The handles held uncertainly, drinking
Our tea at first as though from some fine
Objet d'art - delicate, brittle.

In Laiken days, with roughened hands
We set them out with confidence, questioned,
Maybe, her 'different' taste, but used them
More as we did best clothes - special, familiar.

Later, we washed them, one by one,
With even greater care, holding them up
To see a hand show through, slowly
Arranged them on display, sliding
Still further back the broken ones,
Letting the painted berries shine
Through the sideboard glass, hanging
From tiny garlands
In separate dark blue pairs.

Easter Thoughts

(on a coach returning from Sauze d'Oulx to Milan)

In death
My mother lost the grace
She could take on;
Clay face reduced
To mediaeval size
Mouth shrunken
Old beyond aged;
Denied the soft, flushed look
So often shown
In welcome
Or in goodbye wave
Hand shading her eyes against the sun.

Tick tocking pendulum
Dredges my thought
Now we have left the mountains
In their last white folds,
Dropped to the valleys,
Down
To showers of new cowslips
Eager, though tightly prim,
To taste the first, fresh sweetness
Of that callous swindler, Spring.

Nae Kingdom

He wha has gi'en sall tak awa
   an' a' that's green
   an' fu' o' sang
sall pass.
The drocht sall seep.
   The win's sough
   it winna hear
   an' the place
   it sall na ken.

The flesh is nocht but the grass,
   nor bides the sap
   tae feed the pride
     o' man.
Sin maun bear deith.
   The deid stour
   taks but its ain
   whan the years
   sall crine awa.

Nocht but the Spirit is spirit.
   Nocht o' the flesh,
   nocht but the Word
     sall bide
for aye and aye.
   I hae heard
   but havna kent.
   I hae seen
   but no' divined.

An' I'm sweir, sweir, tae cam auld,
   sair for the flesh,
   the grass
      the stour
Spirit an' Word
   whaur sall he seek
   wha kens
   nae kingdom
   within?

II

Zermatt, Easter '86

We saw now why the last in line
had called - a pig's head
above us there, like an animal Christ
with the pallor of human death.

It was stuck on some post
or door where the huts
slope down at Zmütt, just off
the piste, below the restaurant.

I did go back to stare
but kept my mind away from
all of that, and from the red
that trailed along the snow.

Klein Matterhorn, Garten, Swarzee -
the challenge of two black runs.
Time here to prop up skis,
grab our mid-day lounge in the sun.

A Walkman went the rounds,
Rachmaninov. A dentist in the group
was set to memorise
this hefty score for piano.

Then someone pointed out,
edging the wooden terrace,
hutch upon hutch - rabbits,
quiet by the bragging chatter.

That night the chalet talk
went on for hours. Gaddafi bombed.
The unwhite outer world brought back,
knocking at every door.

He had it coming, a young American
pronounced. The arguments flared on,
then out. Burning with mountain sun,
we turned our thoughts to morning.

Out of the broken quiet, left
like a child's last words
in the drift to sleep, *The poor pig,*
what a day it must have had.

Girl with Rats

Growing chilled
in the sunless precinct
we roll up our posters
of pathetic naked hens
and walk with the folded trestle
to her flat for tea.

The talk moves on to festivals,
her singing; ley lines,
dowsing and healing;
the psychic or not.
Auras, she feels,
perhaps anyone can see.

Before we leave
we want to meet her pets.
She lets them perch
one on each shouder -
a collar
of moving rats.

I stare
at the long-nosed faces
the bare, segmented tails,
try to distinguish
which one is timid
which one bold.

But still the old revulsions rise:
dark shapes that bolt in shadow
through a wall; vermin
they lunged at,
yelling with pitchforks
on a threshing day.

She lifts her arms
to rearrange them
carefully
holds them
beneath
the intellectual face.

Snails...... and more so slugs

They came out in the dusk.
It was not easy to walk,
even on stone,
without crudely smashing
some spiralling shell.

Anxious,
we trailed with our torches
inspecting young plants,
shone beams on snails,
considering them.

Night upon night
we tipped slugs from leaves
brought them in cartons,
antlers astir, to forage
in wilder greenery.

Laughable folly,
futile as hope:
dahlias and asters
stricken by morning
were sullied to rags.

To try beer
seemed the optional, half
moral strategy: let them
choose to get drunk,
topple and drown.

We expected, of course,
the first squeamish guilt:
heavy slugs
lay like whales
wrecked by disaster.

Rank after days
the death trays were cleared,
heaped
odd-sized shreds
of discoloured rubber.

Now big winds
blow through the trees.
The reddened brambles
gleam with black.

Our summer has come to little.

Foie Gras

[The Revd. Sydney Smith's idea of heaven *eating pâtés de foie gras to the sound of trumpets* is often quoted and has passed into the literary tradition of our country.]

It could be hard sometimes
to escape the lost goose.
Once you caught his eye and spoke
he could attach himself to you.

Tamed till he craved for
human company, he'd coax
two schoolboys on a lakeside bench
to let him perch between them.

Perhaps, by some small field gate, others waited;
pictured the awkward lift to flight;
longed for him flat-footed, neck
outstretched, hurrying to greet them.

Or had they brought him furtively
to be with his kind, their nerves
on edge with this follower, each day
becoming more than was ever meant?

But he went, too, from the lakes.
After the summer holiday, only
the waterfowl, or lunchtime children
ravelling rumours of harm.

******

On this clear forest day one goose
flies overhead. The grating cry
fades into distances
our lives will never reach.

Feelings, vague as the memories
of old homesicknesses, stories
we know that we once read,
blur in the mind - The Goose Girl

unmasked as the virtuous
princess; The Snow Goose
healing the loneness
of hunchback and child.-

Now with their jangled noise
more follow, wild geese,
arrowing forward, straining
towards their heaven.

They are guided far
from the fanfares,
the gleaming,
funnelled trumpets.

Ear-rings

She had stopped
to stare at sheep.
Each year the tags
grew larger
hung from ears
like numbered bars
on hotel keys.
And every tail
docked to extremity.
She wondered
if in winter
they felt cold
(their udders so exposed)
or sensed
their loss of privacy.
The boldest came
to stamp a foot
challenge
the Shepherd parables.

She had quite liked
ear-rings
ivory flowers
and plastic shapes
small metal
Chinese letters
pearls and mother of pearl
and diamond paste
to clip on hopefully.
Odd ones she'd lost.
Pierced ears for her

had seemed taboo -
like paint on fleece
or inked tattoos
or the curled tongues
presented one by one
for wafer bread
or the soiled communion cup
passing from lip to lip.

Sheep

With the early Christmas cards, already five
of flocks with shepherd, in a winter sunset scene.
Joseph Farquharson R.A. - had he been alive -
could celebrate. My thoughts fix on our video screen:

sheep brought through his quiet fields and gate
to truck on their tight-limbed road to Spain or Greece
or where men hoist on chains each floundering weight
by one thin leg - before the knife's release.

But who at Christmas, or at any time,
makes room for sullied images - the festive twinned
with savagery, the virgin birth and shepherd mime
challenged as doubtful history? Minds opened

suffocate in tides of upturned heresy,
like fish Christ hauled to air in Galilee.

The White Bull

This bull has been redesigned with surgeons'
craft, penis rerouted to his side.
Daubed with some Judas colour, he lords around
among the cows, becomes a full-time guide

with marker pen. The herds will never see
the other bull that fathers each one's calf,
floods the syringe. The stars' destiny
for bulls: performing while technicians laugh,

or vaseline-blind on knees with banderilla
barbs that rouse the sun-filled cheers. Taurus.
At school a white bull pictured with Europa
in a field of flowers. What could we know of Zeus?

We thought of the Jersey bull we stroked through open bars,
his great head weighted gently on small supporting hands.

The Cage Farmer's Boy

"Father, I fear your trade;
Surely it's wrong!
Little birds limed and made
Captive life-long."
                    Thomas Hardy

Father, calves are bleeding,
Whitening in the dark.
Their prisons hold no blue sky.
No pastures hung with lark.

Father, pigs lie pilloried
Great mothers pinned in place,
And wind and sun, the nourishers,
Smirch evil on your face.

Father, hens were given
Legs and flapping wings.
You say that through the blunted beaks
The crated choir still sings.

Father, the abattoirs,
Nightmares in my head:
Blind, mindless hands that butcher
Behind the blindfold fed.

Father, you lift your eyes
Up to the Easter hill.
Your arms reach out towards the lambs:
The April cries rise chill.

Father, I fear your trade,
Row on piled-on row.
The cages stretch to Heaven.
The rage will fall below.

Luck

Bedraggled feathers are not easy
on the eye. Yet here was this little hen
being washed in a bowl, the woman
cupping her hands, spilling
the water over the bird, gently
as with a newborn child. There was no struggle.
The towel wrap, the soft blow-dry
were beauty salon pleasures. And the finished,
fluffed-up, white creation
stayed content in the holding hands. She was
keeping close to love, close to luck.

With Suki

I

The old dog is breathing.
I hold her head against me
without words, both of us glad
of the life still there. Each night
is slowly stiffening her
to what we know will come.
Behind the half-drawn curtains
an angered housefly
pesters about the window
in the morning's winter sun.
Today by the edge of trees
the last pink dahlia has bent
towards the ground, but two small
salvias, poker straight, keep
to their living red like truth.

II

As children we made it fun
to rush with a dog upstairs,
command it in rising tones
to look at itself in our
narrow wardrobe mirror. Some
would hesitate uncomfortably
then bristle and growl
at the enemy ahead. It was
a game not often played
since, anyhow, most dogs
soon learn to turn away from
their reflections, the unknown
that is always there.

Afternoon

[*I have wasted my life.* James Wright: Lying in a Hammock at William Duffy's Farm in Pine Island, Minnesota]

It was a trick of the sunlight
through the trees.
The long reflections
in the shallow pool
made us believe
the water reached
to some fictitious depth.

The sun lay flat
on the harvest fields.
A Constable day,
we said
though the rolled-up
moonscape bales
would hardly fit.

There was a mouse
in our trip-trap
when we came back home,
boxed tail to nose,
sweated in plastic.
We had meant
not to feel guilty.

We took it
back to the fields.
There was no chance to study
the circle eyes
cartoonists squiggle.

It sprang from its terror
into an earth-cold stubble.

Dark had already
sealed the wood.
The night sounds
waited.
Lost into distance
a cattle beast called,
and called again.

III

The Meeting

She is quite ordinary,
well set in middle age,
and he the healer, charmer

(perhaps guru) is measuring energy.
Step by step away from her
his hand moves on the air,

follows the unseen
till the room
can not contain her.

Half doubting, half not,
peeved, perhaps,
at her auric share

I, the newcomer,
return to basics,
rub palms together,

draw hands apart,
strain to feel something,
grapple with ether,

start and restart,
confess to the class
I find nothing there.

And with me now
he searches and shrugs -
moves to another.

Small moment of truth.
He is dowsing for happiness.
There is no well here.

But up on the hills,
with no subtle energies,
I could outwalk this seer.

Woman with Bag

All through the long freak summer
she was out on Silkham Road.
The woman with the shopping bag
trudged up and down
and round by Eastlands Way.

Like the constant weather map,
the awkward coat
and flattened cap,
even the bag,
kept an unchanging shape.

That she was out of kilter
caught the eye
where the coloured houses -
yellow and blue and green -
blistered in the heat.

Sometimes her husband
trailed behind
and she would want to know
what man it was
who always tried to follow.

We saw them last in town,
on some street bench - preoccupied together -
he, in the late sun, colourless
but she, among stale commuters,
brown as a mountain peasant.

Come winter, sometimes we thought
of how it must be for her
in that perplexing home -
where she would walk,
what she would carry.

On The Way Out

The girl in the specs shop
has six rings in one ear.
I could worship her youth
her solicitous charm
but my thoughts snag
on rituals
and spoilings
and notions of harm.

******

Sweet - not yet - sixteen
from across the way
serves in the village shop
a.m. Sunday
blonded hair
midriff bare
navel adorned
with a brooch-like pin.

The little girl
who came with her dolls
sang the Tommy Thumb song
crusading now
for teenage tribal.

She smiles across
from the serious till
propped up
on her how-many inches heels.

Mary Magdalene

(Donatello: The Penitent Magdalen)

He had cast out the seven
Devils: the rags of her suffering
Dropped at his feet.
                              But without
Love the healing could not last.
And coming in the morning's
Dark she found the stone rolled
Back.
                    Her weeping brought him near
To comfort her - until the spoken
Touch me not.
                              Again
She knew that there was none
To help; the old infirmity
The fearful sepulchre of self.

Prayer before Conception (or Negative)

This child
who was never conceived
and never born
will not hear in the night
the cry of the hunted,
the triumph of fear,
or lost
between stars and abattoirs,
the desolate call
of the unmothered calf.

He will not suffer
the breaking of body
or the breaking of mind;
be called
to the killing fields;
search for the self
in self
or in others;
seal up
the unspillable tears.

He will not fear
the crush of the millions,
watch the numberless starving
cross the horizon;
stare out
at the empty seas,

or turn to the cliffs
where sheep
with their sun-scorched eyes
come stumbling.

He will not bend
to spoon-feed the old
waiting for death,
nor watch himself
grow old,
puzzle to know
the faces tending him,
or who he is,
his hands a stranger's
dark-veined against the sheet.

Polaroid

Stay where you are.
The Sunday's pola sonic toy
whirrs out its unformed print.
The instant grows from ghost
to real, held by an outer edge.

We want ourselves caught
happy in the sunlit garden,
to find this unmet self before us
looking good, bask
in a little flattery.
We know it lasts less true
than half-kept dreams
where we rush on a darkened
journey, vague and afraid,
or watch uneasily in sleep
some impossible wagon-shape
move through the sky, or weep.

They come up grinning now
- our likenesses -
beneath the ailing apple tree.
And somewhere near
the restless cracking
from the practice range
beyond the firethorn hedge.

The Black-Eyed Beans

The eyes of the black-eyed beans
   whisper
where I left them,
little secret presences
   set close
in a crowd.

When soaked the eyes become
   brown faces
white helmeted -
Hanuman monkeys
   sacred
to Vishnu.

The image grows
   till
shape and colour
blur - boring then
   common
as haricot.

And when, forgotten, the pan
   burns dry
the charred remains
show blacker punishment
   for being
ordinary.

[For stealing the rare mango fruit the Hanuman monkey was cast into the
fire, but managed to escape with its life, only its face and limbs being
scorched.]

A Brief History of Evolution

Funny things toes
Little amputees
Funny things knees

Funny our eyes
Enjoying green grass
Blue dome of the sky

But that's not truth
- The dome, I mean, -
Old Atlas myth

Star-gazers today
Speak in equations
Hawking believes $S=kA$

Funny things genes -
The long-life one
Too late for me

That's for the brave
New century
Being 31 at 93

Funny ...... computers
Cleverer than me
(Grammar-check I)

And monster fears
In cybernetics: robots
Out-thinking creator man

Tyrannus late 21stC
Using dumb humans
Like chimpanzees

Funny not knowing
How it will be
World without me

A Bad Poem

This is a bad poem. I have no mind
for anything but generalities. I want to make
big statements about a bad world. *To generalize
is to be an idiot*. - Blake - though along with
The Tyger, The Lamb and The Sick Rose
come *Mercy, Pity, Peace, and Love* -
and reams of sermonising.

Burns, Wordsworth, Arnold, left us
more of the stuff: *man's inhumanity
to man* (and beast), *getting and spending*,
fear that *the world. . . so beautiful. . . has neither
joy, nor love. . . nor peace, nor help for pain*.
You all know who said what - quote (or half-quote)
line upon line - with Auden's
Not to be born is the best for man.

Yeats (too early for the Tamworth pigs) told us
that man alone waits death with dread and hope.
This is a bad poem. I can stray here
from bad to macabre. Last night
lines in a quirky song
slipped into a science debate. A smile.
*If the Ju-ju had meant us not to eat people
He wouldn't have made us of meat*.
Cannibals (Polynesian) call man
the long pig. Same taste. Reassuring
for surgeons appealing for hearts.

Larkin caught us with cheerless generalities:
Get out as early as you can -
and some few contradictions: Days

are to be happy in. I try. Abandon
the stricken earth, the stolen
fractured sky. Late in the year
three giant sunflowers,
nine feet tall, are nearly out -
a kind of mantra. Turned to the sun
their faces grow, hour by hour.

* Two Tamworth pigs became newspaper, radio and TV celebrities when
they escaped from a slaughterhouse. They fascinated the public in this
country and around the world as they dodged their hunters for several
days, even swimming across a river. Finally captured, a national
newspaper bought them and placed them in an animal sanctuary.

Time Travel

Time can run backwards.

Strange – though our minds may go
To a year when the summer winds
Teased along boulevards,
Or a night of driving snow
That filled the moor road home.

But those who were waiting then
Can only be as dreams.
They cannot touch our hands,
Or lead us in.
Nor can we choose again,
Start afresh on the road not taken.

STRIKER

The Greatest Goalscorers of
the Decade in British Football

STRIKER

The Greatest Goalscorers of the Decade in British Football

JASON WOOLGAR

ROBERT HALE · LONDON

Photoset in North Wales by
Derek Doyle & Associates, Mold, Flintshire.
Printed and bound in Great Britain by
Mackays of Chatham.

Contents

Player Profiles

Records

Acknowledgements

As you will note from the extended lists that follow I am greatly indebted to a vast number of people who have kindly assisted me with this book. I would firstly like to thank the multitude of football supporters without whose help I could not possibly have completed what turned out to be a mammoth task. Many thanks also to the various players, associations and football clubs who have all provided invaluable assistance. I have below individually acknowledged every contributor including the various football clubs that provided programmes and information.

My apologies to any who have been inadvertently omitted and also to those who assisted with players that do not actually appear in this publication. I did originally intend to include a greater number of players but, due to size restrictions, was not able to do so.

My research has included far too many programmes, magazines, newspapers and club histories to individually mention each, however I have frequently referred to various editions of the following:

The Rothmans Football Yearbook (Jack Rollin)
The Guinness Soccer Who's Who (Jack Rollin)
Soccer Who's Who (Jack Rollin)
The Football Club Directory (Tony Williams)
Football League Players Records 1946-92 (Barry J.Hugman)
FA Carling Premiership – The Players 1993/94 (Barry J.Hugman)
The 1996-97 Official PFA Footballers Factfile (Barry J.Hugman)
The European Football Yearbook (Mike Hammond)
NASL (Colin Jose)

Finally I would like to pay special thanks to Kim Sykes, Elaine Woolgar, Barry Woolgar, Karen Woolgar and Steve Avis who all made significant contributions in the completion of this book. Especially to Elaine Woolgar who has checked the enclosed more times than is healthy!

The following all provided assistance above and beyond....

Juan Pedro Adrados – Spain
Mervyn D.Baker – Europe
Graham Blackwood – Heart of Midlothian
Jean Calvert – Bradford City
Gabriele Crocco – Italy
Gareth M.Davies – Wrexham & Wales
David Downs – Reading
George W.Forster – Sunderland
Cyril George – Celtic & Scotland
Marshall Gillespie – Northern Ireland
Richard Harnwell – Stockport County
Colin Jose – North American Soccer League & Major League Soccer
Walter Morandell – Italy
Fred Ollier – Arsenal
Terry O'Neill – Europe
Paul Rhodes – Luton Town
John Taylor – Rangers
Sylvain Vernisse – France
Darren White – Sheffield United
Adrian Wood – Wycombe Wanderers

SUPPORTERS
Aberdeen: Peter Cogle, Colin Massie – **Aldershot:** David Walton, Peter Ward
Arsenal: Dennis Cooper, Derek Howell, Joe Waters
Aston Villa: Graham Carlin, Dave Hodges, Mark Lench, Anthony Stirk
Birmingham City: Darren Shaw, Andy Vant – **Blackpool:** Roger Harrison, Paul Lavery
Bolton Wanderers: A.Cooke, Michael Unsworth – **Bradford City:** I.Bates, Terry Frost
Brighton & Hove Albion: Derek Bryant, Charles Sargeant
Bristol Rovers: Keith Brookman, Mike Jay, Roger Tilbury
Cambridge United: Andrew Pincher – **Cardiff City:** M.Adams, Alan Jenkins
Carlisle United: Nick Hadkiss, David Steele – **Chelsea:** David Brown, Scott Cheshire
Chester City: George Guest, John Hughes, R.Prince, C.Sumner
Clydebank: Stuart Scott – **Colchester United:** Michael Middleton
Coventry City: D.Mobley, J.Moore – **Crewe Alexandra:** Harold Finch
Crystal Palace: Paul Firmage, Ian King – **Darlington:** Frank Tweddle
Derby County: Tony Billings – **Doncaster Rovers:** John Coyle
Dumbarton: Jim McAllister – **Dundee United:** P.Rundo – **East Fife:** Andrew Wilkie

Everton: Mike Thornton – **France:** Jean Paul Barreau – **General:** Barry J.Hugman
Germany: Dr Ulf Leinweber, Gerhard Jung, Michael Freyberg, Seebauer Hans-Jurgen
Gillingham: Roger Triggs, Andy Wells – **Greece:** Theodore Mantzouranis
Hartlepool United: Dave Green, Gordon Small – **Hereford United:** Lawrence Appelby
Holland: Wim Moorman – **Huddersfield Town:** David Bell, Paul Whiteley
Hull City: Colin Davenport, C.Elton, Ray Tuplin – **Ipswich Town:** Colin Foster, V.Kemp
Leeds United: Malcolm Macdonald, Richard Nunn, Steve Owen
Leicester City: Robert Lee, Bob Staniforth, P.Taylor
Lincoln City: Donald Nannestad, Gary Parle
Liverpool: Malcolm Bird, David Prole, Alex Twells – **Luton Town:** Brian Ellis
Manchester City: Dennis Chapman, Derek Crompton – **Mansfield Town:** R.Shaw, Paul Taylor
Middlesbrough: Nigel Gibb, D.Slasor – **Millwall:** Bernie Kingman – **Morton:** D.Smith
Motherwell: Terry Willoughby – **Newcastle United:** Paul Joannou, Bill Swann
Newport County: Tony Ambrosen – **Norway:** Geir Juva
Nottingham Forest: E.Collins, Andy Johnson
Oldham Athletic: Tim Clarke, Garth Dykes, Peter Windle – **Partick Thistle:** John Norman
Plymouth Argyle: Fred Lee, S.Tomlin – **Portsmouth:** Len Bone, Colin Morris
Queens Park Rangers: David Rolph, Dennis Samuels – **Reading:** Bryan Horsnell
Republic of Ireland: Niall MacSweeney, Sean Creedon – **Rotherham United:** Barrie Dalby
Scarborough: Steve Adamson – **Scunthorpe United:** Vic Duke, Michael Norton
Sheffield United: David Burkinshaw, Andrew Kirkham
Sheffield Wednesday: Mick Grayson, Mick Renshaw
Shrewsbury Town: A.Nicholas, Richard Stocken
Southampton: Derek Buckle, Norman Gannaway, Ken Prior, Richard Walker
Southend United: Dave Goody, Martin Smith – **Spain:** Jose Andres Estalrich
St Mirren: John Byrne – **Sunderland:** Brian Leng – **Swansea City:** Colin Jones
Swindon Town: Alan Harding, David Johnson, Mike Skinner, Andy Tyrer
Tranmere Rovers: Bernard Jones, G.Upton – **Turkey:** Alexander Graham – **Watford:** Trevor Jones
West Bromwich Albion: Robert Aiken, Tony Matthews
Wolverhampton Wanderers: Ulf Brennmo, D.Roft
York City: David Batters, Malcolm Ferguson

FOOTBALL CLUBS

Aberdeen, Arsenal, Aston Villa, FC Barcelona, Bari, Barnsley (M.Spinks & C.Patzelt), Birmingham City (Angela Ramsay & Allan Robson), Blackburn Rovers (Keith Whittaker), Bolton Wanderers (Simon Marland), Brentford (Eric White & Lee Doyle), Bristol City, Burnley, Bury, Cambridge United (Becky Pope), Cardiff City (Jim Finney), Carlisle United, Celtic (Alan H.Smith), Chelsea (Carole Phair), Chester City, Clyde (John Taylor), Colchester United, Coventry City (Mike Williams), Crewe Alexandra, Crystal Palace, Dagenham & Redbridge (Tony Middleton), Darlington, Derby County, Derry City (Jim Roddy), Doncaster Rovers, Dundee (Dave Forbes), Enfield, Everton, Falkirk (Jim Hendry), Fulham (Emma Hawkey), Gillingham (Joy Lavender & J.Radbourne), Hartlepool United (Frank Baggs), Heart of Midlothian (L.Porteous & Brian Whittaker), Hereford United (Joan Fennessy & Marcella), Hibernian (Mike Stevenson), Huddersfield Town, Hull City, Ipswich Town (Mike Noye), Kansas City Wizards, Leeds United (Bob Baldwin), Leicester City (Paul Mace), Lincoln City, Liverpool (Carole Timms), Luton Town (Simon Oxley), Manchester City (Joanne Parker), Manchester United (Cliff Butler), Mansfield Town, Olympique de Marseille, Middlesbrough (David Allan & Barry Fry), Millwall (David Sullivan), Motherwell (J.Swinburne), Nagoya Grampus Eight (Shinji Ogura), AS Nancy-Lorraine, Newcastle United, Northampton Town, Norwich City, Nottingham Forest, Oldham Athletic (A.Hardy), Oxford United (Roy Grant), Plymouth Argyle (Jill Page), Portsmouth (Joanne Foster), Port Vale (Margaret Moran Smith), Preston North End, Purfleet, Queens Park Rangers, Rangers (Douglas Cumming, Brian Main & Bob Reilly), Reading, Real Sociedad (Andoni Traola), Rotherham United (Dave Nicholls), Sampdoria, Scarborough, Scunthorpe United, Sheffield United, Sheffield Wednesday (Roger Oldfield), Shrewsbury Town (Mike Thomas), FC Sion (Paul-Andre Dubosson), Southampton (Sarah Carmichael & Kim Lawford), Southend United (Diana Mclaughlin & Christine Owen), St Mirren (Alastair MacLachlan), Stoke City (Tony Tams), Sunderland (Sara Barwick), Swansea City, Swindon Town (Jon Pollard), Telford United (Clair Finnigan), Torquay United, Tottenham Hotspur, Tranmere Rovers (Janet Ratcliffe), Watford (Gabriela Lang & Ed Coan), West Bromwich Albion (Kate Evans), West Ham United, Wimbledon (Reg Davis), Wolverhampton Wanderers (Lorraine Hennessy), Wrexham (Geraint Parry)

ASSOCIATIONS AND COMPANIES

The F.A.Premier League (Mike Foster & Neil Harrison)
The Football Association (David Barber)
The Football League (Jonathan Hargreaves & Lorna Parnell)
Scottish Football Association (J.Farry & David Findlay)
The Football Association of Wales (Ceri Stennett)
Irish Football Association (Jim Boyce)
The Football Association of Ireland (Audrey Magee)
French Football Federation (D.Corcelle)
Spanish Football Federation (Gerardo Gonzalez Otero)
Japanese Football Association (T.Ito)
The Association of Football Statisticians (Ray Spiller)
Sports Projects Ltd (Bernard Gallagher)
World Soccer (Keir Radnedge)

Acknowledgements

Kicker-Sportmagazin
Huddersfield Examiner (Mel Booth)
Crawley Observer (Simon Milham)
JMS Photography (J.Sumpter)

PLAYERS
John Aldridge, Gary Bannister, Eric Cantona, Tony Cottee, Kenny Dalglish, Les Ferdinand, Ryan Giggs, Keith Houchen, Mark Hughes, Matthew Le Tissier, Gary Lineker, Ally McCoist, Alan Shearer, Bernie Slaven, Frank Stapelton.

Introduction

Who is the best striker in British football? A simple enough question perhaps, but one that I have heard debated with no less fervour and contention than the perennial 'name your England team' poser.

To actually answer such a question is of course an impossibility for who could state that the prolific Ian Rush is of greater ability than say Eric Cantona, merely because he has scored more goals. At best we can accurately determine exactly how many goals each player has scored and this was my original intention when I began my research five years ago.

I quickly realized that accomplishing this would be no easy task and that it was nigh on impossible to ascertain definitive records. In the very beginning the Football League informed me that they have never maintained a record of goals, only appearance details, and that all information pertaining to goals scored is kept by each club. At first glance this does not seem to be a problem until you discover that numerous teams have not kept entirely accurate records, fires seem to have accounted for those of others and in one famous case a particularly over-zealous official receiver took every record and promptly destroyed them!

The other major difficulty encountered is what actually constitutes a goal. On numerous occasions I have seen a newspaper report cite an own-goal only to later notice that the club have very generously awarded it to their player. Despite this generosity I decided that as the clubs themselves are the only official source available if they have credited a player with a goal, however dubious, it must stand. As no other authoritative records exist I had very little choice in this matter and though many goals remain debatable the knowledge that they have all been officially awarded by each club will have to suffice.

The problem has now eased slightly with the introduction, in 1992, of the Premier League, which became the first British organization to adjudicate on the scorers of controversial goals. However, their adjudications are not complete, none were made for the 1995/96 season, and affect only those players in the highest echelon. A case could certainly now be made, with all matches televized, for the formation of an official panel to rule on all dubious goals in the entire English and Scottish Leagues. Although there is an obvious need for such a panel I would only like to see it used to adjudicate on the more controversial or difficult decisions. To follow the unsatisfactory Italian system, whereby own-goals are awarded for the slightest deflections, would be a mistake.

As far as the actual selection of players was concerned, although the vast majority picked themselves, the final choice was of course a personal one. The only selection criterion used, and then only in the loosest sense, was that every player must have scored the majority of their goals within the last ten seasons. I have not, however, chosen players purely on their goal-scoring ability as an obvious distinction exists between great goalscorers and the scorers of great goals. All players therefore fall within at least one, the more talented within both, of the following categories. They are either prolific goalscorers or outstandingly creative players who score remarkable goals and also provide team-mates with numerous opportunities.

I am certain that not everyone will agree with my final choice but this, as even Gareth Davies (who lobbied for just about every Welshman's inclusion) will concede, was an impossible task. The preponderance of players was chosen three years ago and I did originally select more than 100. Unfortunately due to the book's size I had to reduce this number considerably and it would be true to say that many are slightly unfortunate not to feature, having missed out by the narrowest of margins. My apologies therefore if you consider your favourite player to be a notable absentee – perhaps next time.

The various record tables are included as useful guides only and are not intended to be used as definitive proof that one player is superior to another. Although they can assist in identifying the best goalscoring records they can never be used to judge an entire career, as far too many variables have to be taken into account.

The length of a career, and the various injuries suffered throughout it, are two of the more important aspects to be examined. The vast majority of players, John Aldridge is a notable exception, score considerably fewer goals as they get older. A good example of this would be Ian Rush who, a few seasons ago would have been in the top three as far as matches per goals were concerned but who now finds himself in 12th place. In contrast Robbie Fowler tops most of the goalscoring tables simply because he has not yet experienced the levelling out periods that the majority of careers eventually encompass.

The calibre of opposition is another factor to be considered. Is it, for instance, correct to assume that scoring goals in the Premier League is more difficult than in the lower divisions? Although the defenders in the top flight are certainly of a higher standard than their lower league counterparts so too are the team-mates helping to create goalscoring opportunities. Equally apparent are the differentials in standards between countries. Many players, on paper at least, have enhanced their careers by playing a lower standard of football abroad, whilst others have seen their goalscoring records decimated after joining some of Europe's finest teams.

Aside from the vagaries of form and luck, two unquantifiable features, a player's goalscoring record will also be greatly determined by the position in which he is regularly employed. As the tactical lines blur and are redefined between midfield and attacking formations so many of the enclosed would no longer be classified as out and out strikers. Some have been used in wide positions, limiting their scoring potential, whilst others have been deployed in that now very fashionable withdrawn role behind one or two orthodox strikers. Many, towards the twilight of their careers, have taken up deeper roles dropping back into midfield or even defence and others have only spasmodically been used up front. David Platt, for example, has not been assigned a conventional forward's role for a number of years.

Penalties also have a bearing on the number of goals a player will score and although I do not subscribe to the theory that penalties falsely inflate a player's career record, believing instead that it takes a special type of skill to continually score from the penalty spot, they can certainly enhance it. It is therefore a small matter of regret that you will not find penalties listed separately in this publication. Unfortunately it was not practical to include them as they were not possible to obtain for many foreign teams and I am always reluctant to include information for certain players and not for others.

As far as exclusions are concerned I should perhaps also mention that this publication contains only matches played for league clubs. Appearances made in the FA Cup whilst playing non-league football are not included.

Far outweighing these small points are the unique foreign details that this book contains. I have for the first time reproduced the complete career records of many of the British and Irish players who have played abroad. You will now be able to see exactly how Gary Lineker fared in Spain and Japan and even how Mick Quinn and Gordon Davies performed in Greece and Norway respectively.

All information includes the entire 1996–97 season and although I have made every effort to ensure 100% accuracy it is probable, perhaps even inevitable in a book of this size, that some small errors might have gone undetected. If you do notice such an occurrence I would be pleased to hear from you. I would add that all goals have been checked with at least two sources and the majority have either been confirmed by each individual club or by a supporter of that club.

As the plethora of acknowledgements will testify the vast majority of supporters, clubs and associations have been extremely helpful. However a very small number of foreign teams and national organizations have been less so and I would therefore be particularly happy to hear from anyone with information appertaining to Turkey, South Africa, China or Hong Kong, the countries from which I received the least assistance.

Despite my relative lack of success with these countries I trust that this publication will go some way to eradicating many of the vagaries which persistently confuse the career records of the game's leading players. During my extensive research I have not only added new and previously unpublished material but have also corrected many of the errors that yearbooks and magazines continue to perpetuate.

As far as my original question is concerned I do not think that any number of statistics can prove that one player is better than another. Football is much more than a game of statistics – it is a game of fleeting moments and it is the players who can consistently produce these brief capsules of brilliance that earn the right to be called the best. Such players are the catalysts of excellence without which no team can aspire to greatness. They are the majesty amid the mundane and add the beauty to the beautiful game.

Jason Woolgar
Surrey
July 1997

Official Tournaments and Abbreviations

Abbreviation	Tournament
Lge Cup	League Cup*
AW Shield	Auto Windscreens Shield
A Trophy	Autoglass Trophy
LD Cup	Leyland Daf Cup
SV Trophy	Sherpa Van Trophy
FR Trophy	Freight Rover Trophy
AM Cup	Associate Members Cup
FL Trophy	Football League Trophy
FLG Cup	Football League Group Cup
AS Cup	Anglo-Scottish Cup
AI Cup	Anglo-Italian Cup
ZDS Cup	Zenith Data Systems Cup
Simod Cup	Simod Cup
FM Cup	Full Members Cup
ZDSC Cup	Zenith Data Systems Challenge Cup
MCC Trophy	Mercantile Centenary Credit Trophy
SSS Cup	Screen Sport Super Cup
FA C/S	FA Charity Shield
Eur Cup	European Cup
ECW Cup	European Cup Winners Cup
UEFA Cup	UEFA Cup
ES Cup	European Super Cup
WCC	World Club Championship
IT Cup	Inter-Toto Cup
WC	World Cup
WCQ	World Cup Qualifier
EC	European Championships
ECQ	European Championships Qualifier
HC	Home International Championship
RC	Rous Cup
US	United States Cup
KC	Kirin Cup
UC	Umbro Cup
LTDF	Le Tournoi de France
F	Friendly

* Incorporating Milk Cup 81/82–85/86, Littlewoods Cup 86/87–89/90, Rumbelows Cup 90/91–91/92, Coca–Cola Cup 92/93–96/97

Unless otherwise stated an asterisk is used to denote that extra time was played.

British and Irish International Venues

England
Wembley – London
Old Trafford – Manchester
Elland Road – Leeds

Northern Ireland
Windsor Park – Belfast

Scotland
Hampden Park – Glasgow
Ibrox Park – Glasgow
Celtic Park – Glasgow
Pittodrie – Aberdeen
Rugby Park – Kilmarnock

Wales
Racecourse – Wrexham
Ninian Park – Cardiff
Vetch Field – Swansea
Cardiff Arms Park – Cardiff
(National Stadium)

Republic of Ireland
Lansdowne Road – Dublin
Tolka – Dublin
Dalymount Park – Dublin
Royal Society Showground – Dublin
Anfield – Liverpool

Premier League Amendments to Goalscorers 1992–97

The introduction of the FA Premier League in 1992 also saw the instigation of an official panel to adjudicate on controversial goals. The following players have had goals deducted, or credited, by this panel. If a goal has been deducted it will not subsequently appear in this publication. Only those decisions affecting the players included in this book are listed below.

SEASON 1992–93

-1 Lee Chapman	Leeds United away to Ipswich Town	03/10/92
-1 Lee Chapman	Leeds United away to Sheffield Wednesday	04/05/93
-1 Dean Saunders	Aston Villa away to Sheffield United	27/01/93

SEASON 1993–94

-1 Les Ferdinand	Queens Park Rangers at home to Blackburn Rovers	06/11/93
-1 Mark Hughes	Manchester United away to Tottenham Hotspur	15/01/94
-1 Dean Saunders	Aston Villa away to Southampton	30/04/94
+1 Teddy Sheringham	Tottenham Hotspur away to Sheffield United	11/09/93

SEASON 1994–95

-1 Stan Collymore	Nottingham Forest away to Manchester City	08/10/94
-1 Alan Smith	Arsenal at home to Manchester City	20/08/94

SEASON 1995–96
No amendments made

SEASON 1996–97

-1 Andy Cole	Manchester United at home to Coventry City	01/03/97
-1 Dion Dublin	Coventry City at home to West Ham United	22/03/97

STRIKER

The Greatest Goalscorers of
the Decade in British Football

TONY ADCOCK

Born: 27/02/63 – Bethnal Green
Height: 5.10
Weight: 11.09 (96–97)

Clubs
Colchester United: **1981–87** – Matches: **233+21** – Goals: **112**
Manchester City: **1987–88** – Matches: **18+4** – Goals: **9**
Northampton Town: **1988–89** – Matches: **83** – Goals: **34**
Bradford City: **1989–91** – Matches: **36+6** – Goals: **6**
Northampton Town: **1991** – Matches: **38+1** – Goals: **12**
Peterborough United: **1992–94** – Matches: **124+7** – Goals: **41**
Luton Town: **1994–95** – Matches: **0+3** – Goals: **0**
Colchester United: **1995–97** – Matches: **82+13** – Goals: **31**

SEASON 1980–81

Colchester United – League Division Three

1	02/05/81	Carlisle United	Home	League	1–0	

SEASON 1981–82

League Division Four

Sub+1	29/08/81	Hartlepool United	Away	League	3–1		
2	01/09/81	Gillingham	Home	Lge Cup	2–0		
3	04/09/81	Tranmere Rovers	Home	League	4–0		
Sub+2	12/09/81	Sheffield United	Away	League	0–1		
4	15/09/81	Gillingham	Away	Lge Cup	1–1		
5	18/09/81	Torquay United	Home	League	3–0	2 Goals	(2)
6	22/09/81	Aldershot	Home	League	1–1		
7	26/09/81	Bradford City	Away	League	1–2		
8	28/09/81	Port Vale	Away	League	1–2		
9	02/10/81	Northampton Town	Home	League	5–1		
10	06/10/81	Cambridge United	Home	Lge Cup	3–1		
11	11/10/81	Rochdale	Away	League	2–1		
12	16/10/81	York City	Home	League	4–0		
13	20/10/81	Hereford United	Home	League	4–0		
14	24/10/81	Halifax Town	Away	League	2–0		
15	27/10/81	Cambridge United	Away	Lge Cup	2–3*		
16	30/10/81	Wigan Athletic	Home	League	1–2		
Sub+3	02/11/81	Mansfield Town	Away	League	3–1		
17	07/11/81	Hull City	Away	League	3–2		
Sub+4	10/11/81	Tranmere Rovers	Away	Lge Cup	0–1		
18	13/11/81	Scunthorpe United	Home	League	2–1		
19	21/11/81	Newport County	Home	FA Cup	2–0	1 Goal	(3)
20	28/11/81	Darlington	Away	League	2–1		
21	04/12/81	Blackpool	Home	League	2–1		
Sub+5	26/12/81	AFC Bournemouth	Away	League	1–1		
Sub+6	04/01/81	Newcastle United	Away	FA Cup	1–1		
22	16/01/82	Bury	Home	League	1–1	1 Goal	(4)
23	18/01/82	Newcastle United	Home	FA Cup	3–4*		
24	23/01/82	Hartlepool United	Home	League	3–3		
Sub+7	30/01/82	Torquay United	Away	League	0–1		
25	06/02/82	Sheffield United	Home	League	5–2		
26	09/02/82	Aldershot	Away	League	1–1		
Sub+8	14/02/82	Northampton Town	Away	League	2–1		
27	19/02/82	Bradford City	Home	League	1–2		
28	26/02/82	Rochdale	Home	League	3–2	2 Goals	(6)
29	02/03/82	Tranmere Rovers	Away	League	1–2		
Sub+9	10/03/82	Hereford United	Away	League	2–2		
Sub+10	12/03/82	Halifax Town	Home	League	1–1		
30	16/03/82	Mansfield Town	Home	League	0–1		
31	26/03/82	Hull City	Home	League	2–0		
32	02/04/82	Scunthorpe United	Away	League	1–2		

33	10/04/82	AFC Bournemouth	Home	League	1–2		
Sub+11	24/04/82	Darlington	Home	League	1–0		
34	27/04/82	Peterborough United	Home	League	1–1		
35	01/05/82	Bury	Away	League	3–4		
36	03/05/82	Port Vale	Home	League	1–0		
37	07/05/82	Stockport County	Home	League	0–1		
38	15/05/82	Crewe Alexandra	Away	League	3–1		

SEASON 1982–83

League Division Four

39	13/08/82	Southend United	Home	FL Trophy	3–1		
40	21/08/82	Orient	Away	FL Trophy	2–0		
41	06/10/82	Southampton	Home	Lge Cup	0–0		
42	10/10/82	Swindon Town	Away	League	0–3		
43	15/10/82	Darlington	Home	League	2–2		
Sub+12	13/11/82	Tranmere Rovers	Away	League	4–2	1 Goal	(7)
Sub+13	20/11/82	Torquay United	Home	FA Cup	0–2		
Sub+14	27/11/82	Bristol City	Away	League	2–0		
Sub+15	11/12/82	Hull City	Away	League	0–3		
Sub+16	28/12/82	Aldershot	Home	League	0–0		
44	01/01/83	Torquay United	Away	League	0–2		
45	03/01/83	Hartlepool United	Home	League	4–1	2 Goals	(9)
46	07/01/83	Hereford United	Home	League	3–2	1 Goal	(10)
47	14/01/83	Halifax Town	Away	League	0–4		
48	21/01/83	Crewe Alexandra	Home	League	4–3	3 Goals	(13)
49	05/02/83	Blackpool	Away	League	2–1	1 Goal	(14)
50	15/02/83	Wimbledon	Away	League	1–2	1 Goal	(15)
51	18/02/83	Swindon Town	Home	League	1–0		
52	26/02/83	Darlington	Away	League	3–1	2 Goals	(17)
53	01/03/83	Northampton Town	Home	League	3–1	1 Goal	(18)
54	05/03/83	Chester City	Away	League	1–1	1 Goal	(19)
55	12/03/83	Bury	Home	League	2–1		
56	19/03/83	Mansfield Town	Away	League	1–1		
57	25/03/83	Tranmere Rovers	Home	League	3–3	1 Goal	(20)
58	01/04/83	Peterborough United	Home	League	1–0		
59	02/04/83	Aldershot	Away	League	1–0		
60	09/04/83	York City	Away	League	0–3		
61	12/04/83	Port Vale	Home	League	1–2	1 Goal	(21)
62	15/04/83	Scunthorpe United	Home	League	5–1	2 Goals	(23)
63	22/04/83	Stockport County	Away	League	0–3		
64	26/04/83	Rochdale	Away	League	1–2		
65	29/04/83	Bristol City	Home	League	3–1		
66	02/05/83	Hartlepool United	Away	League	4–1		
67	13/05/83	Torquay United	Home	League	1–0		

SEASON 1983–84

League Division Four

68	27/08/83	Darlington	Away	League	2–0	1 Goal	(24)
69	30/08/83	Reading	Home	Lge Cup	3–2	2 Goals	(26)
70	03/09/83	Blackpool	Home	League	2–1	1 Goal	(27)
71	06/09/83	Bristol City	Home	League	0–0		
72	09/09/83	Stockport County	Away	League	0–0		
73	14/09/83	Reading	Away	Lge Cup	3–4*	1 Goal	(28)
74	17/09/83	Rochdale	Home	League	4–0	2 Goals	(30)
75	24/09/83	Chesterfield	Away	League	1–1		
76	26/09/83	Tranmere Rovers	Away	League	1–2	1 Goal	(31)
77	01/10/83	Chester City	Home	League	1–0	1 Goal	(32)
78	04/10/83	Swansea City	Away	Lge Cup	1–1	1 Goal	(33)
79	07/10/83	York City	Away	League	0–3		
80	15/10/83	Northampton Town	Home	League	2–2		
81	18/10/83	Bury	Home	League	1–0	1 Goal	(34)
82	22/10/83	Swindon Town	Away	League	1–2	1 Goal	(35)
83	25/10/83	Swansea City	Home	Lge Cup	1–0	1 Goal	(36)
84	29/10/83	Crewe Alexandra	Home	League	2–0	2 Goals	(38)
85	01/11/83	Doncaster Rovers	Away	League	3–3	1 Goal	(39)
86	05/11/83	Reading	Home	League	3–0	1 Goal	(40)
87	08/11/83	Manchester United	Home	Lge Cup	0–2		
88	12/11/83	Mansfield Town	Away	League	0–0		
89	19/11/83	Torquay United	Away	FA Cup	2–1		
90	26/11/83	Torquay United	Away	League	1–2		
91	03/12/83	Hartlepool United	Home	League	6–0		
92	10/12/83	Wealdstone	Home	FA Cup	4–0		
93	17/12/83	Halifax Town	Home	League	4–1	1 Goal	(41)

94	26/12/83	Peterborough United	Away	League	0–2		
95	27/12/83	Aldershot	Home	League	4–1	2 Goals	(43)
96	02/01/84	Wrexham	Home	League	1–1	1 Goal	(44)
97	07/01/84	Charlton Athletic	Home	FA Cup	0–1		
98	14/01/84	Darlington	Home	League	2–1	2 Goals	(46)
99	28/01/84	Stockport County	Home	League	1–1	1 Goal	(47)
100	04/02/84	Chester City	Away	League	4–1		
101	11/02/84	Chesterfield	Home	League	2–0	1 Goal	(48)
102	14/02/84	Doncaster Rovers	Home	League	1–1		
103	18/02/84	Crewe Alexandra	Away	League	1–1		
104	21/02/84	Wimbledon	Home	AM Cup	2–1	2 Goals	(50)
105	25/02/84	Swindon Town	Home	League	0–0		
106	03/03/84	Bury	Away	League	1–1	1 Goal	(51)
107	13/03/84	Southend United	Home	AM Cup	0–2		
108	17/03/84	York City	Home	League	1–3		
Sub+17	24/03/84	Northampton Town	Away	League	1–3		
109	31/03/84	Bristol City	Away	League	1–4		
Sub+18	07/04/84	Tranmere Rovers	Home	League	0–1		
110	14/04/84	Hartlepool United	Away	League	0–0		
111	17/04/84	Rochdale	Away	League	0–0		
112	21/04/84	Peterborough United	Home	League	1–1	1 Goal	(52)
113	23/04/84	Aldershot	Away	League	1–5	1 Goal	(53)
114	28/04/84	Torquay United	Home	League	3–0	1 Goal	(54)
115	01/05/84	Blackpool	Away	League	2–3	1 Goal	(55)
116	05/05/84	Wrexham	Away	League	2–0		
117	07/05/84	Hereford United	Home	League	3–0	1 Goal	(56)
118	11/05/84	Halifax Town	Away	League	1–4		

SEASON 1984–85

League Division Four

119	25/08/84	Southend United	Home	League	3–3	3 Goals	(59)
120	28/08/84	Gillingham	Away	Lge Cup	2–3		
121	31/08/84	Scunthorpe United	Away	Lge Cup	2–2	1 Goal	(60)
122	04/09/84	Gillingham	Home	Lge Cup	0–2		
123	08/09/84	Blackpool	Home	League	1–1	1 Goal	(61)
124	15/09/84	Bury	Away	League	3–4	1 Goal	(62)
125	19/09/84	Mansfield Town	Away	League	1–0		
126	22/09/84	Aldershot	Home	League	2–0	2 Goals	(64)
127	29/09/84	Northampton Town	Away	League	3–1	1 Goal	(65)
128	02/10/84	Torquay United	Home	League	2–1		
129	13/10/84	Darlington	Away	League	0–4		
130	16/10/84	Exeter City	Home	League	3–4	1 Goal	(66)
131	20/10/84	Chester City	Away	League	2–1	2 Goals	(68)
132	23/10/84	Stockport County	Home	League	3–0		
133	26/10/84	Halifax Town	Home	League	1–3	1 Goal	(69)
134	03/11/84	Chesterfield	Away	League	1–1	1 Goal	(70)
135	06/11/84	Tranmere Rovers	Away	League	1–3		
136	09/11/84	Hartlepool United	Home	League	1–0	1 Goal	(71)
137	17/11/84	Southend United	Away	FA Cup	2–2		
138	21/11/84	Southend United	Home	FA Cup	3–2*	1 Goal	(72)
139	24/11/84	Rochdale	Away	League	1–1		
140	01/12/84	Peterborough United	Home	League	3–1	1 Goal	(73)
141	08/12/84	Gillingham	Home	FA Cup	0–5		
142	15/12/84	Swindon Town	Away	League	1–2	1 Goal	(74)
143	21/12/84	Crewe Alexandra	Away	League	4–1	1 Goal	(75)
144	26/12/84	Hereford United	Home	League	2–2	1 Goal	(76)
145	28/12/84	Port Vale	Home	League	3–2		
146	01/01/85	Wrexham	Away	League	2–2		
147	23/01/85	Gillingham	Away	FR Trophy	2–2	1 Goal	(77)
148	26/01/85	Bury	Home	League	1–0		
149	29/01/85	Southend United	Away	League	5–2	1 Goal	(78)
150	01/02/85	Northampton Town	Home	League	4–1	1 Goal	(79)
151	05/02/85	Gillingham	Home	FR Trophy	2–0	2 Goals	(81)
152	22/02/85	Chesterfield	Home	League	3–1	3 Goals	(84)
Sub+19	10/05/85	Crewe Alexandra	Home	League	4–1		

SEASON 1985–86

League Division Four

153	17/08/85	Stockport County	Home	League	3–1	1 Goal	(85)
154	21/08/85	Millwall	Home	Lge Cup	2–3		
155	24/08/85	Wrexham	Away	League	1–2		

156	27/08/85	Aldershot	Home	League	4–0	1 Goal	(86)
157	31/08/85	Torquay United	Away	League	1–2	1 Goal	(87)
158	03/09/85	Millwall	Away	Lge Cup	1–4		
159	06/09/85	Halifax Town	Home	League	3–1	2 Goals	(89)
160	14/09/85	Tranmere Rovers	Away	League	4–3		
161	17/09/85	Cambridge United	Home	League	4–1	3 Goals	(92)
162	21/09/85	Orient	Away	League	2–1		
163	27/09/85	Port Vale	Home	League	1–0		
164	01/10/85	Burnley	Away	League	2–0	1 Goal	(93)
165	04/10/85	Exeter City	Home	League	1–1		
166	12/10/85	Mansfield Town	Away	League	1–2		
167	18/10/85	Scunthorpe United	Home	League	1–1		
168	22/10/85	Southend United	Away	League	4–2		
169	26/10/85	Northampton Town	Home	League	0–2		
170	02/11/85	Hereford United	Away	League	0–2		
171	06/11/85	Chester City	Away	League	0–4		
172	08/11/85	Rochdale	Home	League	0–1		
173	16/11/85	Wycombe Wanderers	Away	FA Cup	0–2		
174	23/11/85	Preston North End	Away	League	2–3	1 Goal	(94)
175	14/12/85	Hartlepool United	Away	League	1–4		
176	20/12/85	Wrexham	Home	League	5–2	2 Goals	(96)
177	28/12/85	Aldershot	Away	League	1–1		
178	01/01/86	Swindon Town	Away	League	1–2		
179	03/01/86	Hereford United	Home	League	4–1		
180	11/01/86	Torquay United	Home	League	0–0		
181	14/01/86	Southend United	Home	FR Trophy	4–1	1 Goal	(97)
182	17/01/86	Stockport County	Away	League	1–1		
183	21/01/86	Northampton Town	Away	FR Trophy	1–2		
184	24/01/86	Tranmere Rovers	Home	League	1–2		
185	31/01/86	Halifax Town	Away	League	2–2	1 Goal	(98)
186	04/02/86	Southend United	Home	League	2–0	1 Goal	(99)
187	01/03/86	Port Vale	Away	League	1–1		
188	08/03/86	Exeter City	Away	League	2–2	1 Goal	(100)
189	14/03/86	Mansfield Town	Home	League	0–0		
190	22/03/86	Northampton Town	Away	League	0–1		

SEASON 1986–87

League Division Four

191	23/08/86	Lincoln City	Away	League	1–3	1 Goal	(101)
192	26/08/86	Peterborough United	Home	Lge Cup	0–0		
193	29/08/86	Exeter City	Home	League	1–1		
194	03/09/86	Peterborough United	Away	Lge Cup	0–2		
195	05/09/86	Tranmere Rovers	Away	League	4–3	1 Goal	(102)
196	12/09/86	Torquay United	Home	League	3–0		
197	16/09/86	Hartlepool United	Home	League	2–1	2 Goals	(104)
198	20/09/86	Rochdale	Away	League	0–1		
199	15/11/86	Bishop's Stortford	Away	FA Cup	1–1		
200	18/11/86	Bishop's Stortford	Home	FA Cup	2–0	1 Goal	(105)
201	21/11/86	Scunthorpe United	Away	League	2–5		
202	25/11/86	Peterborough United	Home	FR Trophy	2–1		
203	28/11/86	Halifax Town	Home	League	3–1	1 Goal	(106)
204	06/12/86	Aldershot	Away	FA Cup	2–3		
205	09/12/86	Aldershot	Away	FR Trophy	2–4		
206	13/12/86	Preston North End	Home	League	0–2		
207	20/12/86	Swansea City	Away	League	2–1		
208	26/12/86	Cambridge United	Home	League	1–2		
209	27/12/86	Aldershot	Away	League	0–1		
210	01/01/87	Northampton Town	Away	League	2–3	2 Goals	(108)
211	03/01/87	Scunthorpe United	Home	League	1–0	1 Goal	(109)
212	10/01/87	Lincoln City	Home	League	2–0		
213	17/01/87	Exeter City	Away	League	0–2		
214	23/01/87	Tranmere Rovers	Home	League	1–1		
215	26/01/87	Gillingham	Away	FR Trophy	0–2		
216	31/01/87	Torquay United	Away	League	1–3	1 Goal	(110)
217	06/02/87	Hartlepool United	Away	League	0–1		
218	13/02/87	Rochdale	Home	League	2–0		
219	21/02/87	Peterborough United	Away	League	0–2		
220	27/02/87	Hereford United	Home	League	2–0		
Sub+20	03/03/87	Wolverhampton Wanderers	Away	League	0–2		
Sub+21	06/03/87	Stockport County	Home	League	5–1		
221	14/03/87	Cardiff City	Away	League	2–0		
222	17/03/87	Crewe Alexandra	Home	League	2–1		
223	20/03/87	Southend United	Home	League	1–2		
224	28/03/87	Wrexham	Away	League	1–0		

225	03/04/87	Orient	Away	League	0–1		
226	10/04/87	Burnley	Home	League	1–0	1 Goal	(111)
227	17/04/87	Northampton Town	Home	League	3–1		
228	24/04/87	Swansea City	Home	League	2–1	1 Goal	(112)
229	29/04/87	Halifax Town	Away	League	0–0		
230	04/05/87	Aldershot	Home	League	0–1		
231	09/05/87	Preston North End	Away	League	0–1		
232	14/05/87	Wolverhampton Wanderers	Home	Lge P/O	0–2		
233	17/05/87	Wolverhampton Wanderers	Away	Lge P/O	0–0		

SEASON 1987–88

Manchester City – League Division Two

Sub+1	15/08/87	Plymouth Argyle	Home	League	2–1		
1	31/08/87	Aston Villa	Away	League	1–1		
2	05/09/87	Blackburn Rovers	Home	League	1–2		
3	22/09/87	Wolverhampton Wanderers	Home	Lge Cup	1–2	1 Goal	(1)
Sub+2	26/09/87	Leeds United	Away	League	0–2		
Sub+3	06/10/87	Wolverhampton Wanderers	Away	Lge Cup	2–0		
Sub+4	04/11/87	Middlesbrough	Home	League	1–1		
4	07/11/87	Huddersfield Town	Home	League	10–1	3 Goals	(4)
5	10/11/87	Plymouth Argyle	Home	Simod Cup	6–2	3 Goals	(7)
6	14/11/87	Reading	Away	League	2–0		
7	17/11/87	Watford	Home	Lge Cup	3–1		
8	21/11/87	Birmingham City	Home	League	3–0		
9	28/11/87	West Bromwich Albion	Away	League	1–1	1 Goal	(8)
10	01/12/87	AFC Bournemouth	Away	League	2–0		
11	05/12/87	Crystal Palace	Home	League	1–3		
12	12/12/87	Millwall	Away	League	1–0	1 Goal	(9)
13	16/12/87	Chelsea	Home	Simod Cup	0–2		
14	19/12/87	Oldham Athletic	Home	League	1–2		
15	02/01/87	Shrewsbury Town	Home	League	1–3		
16	09/01/88	Huddersfield Town	Away	FA Cup	2–2		
17	12/01/88	Huddersfield Town	Home	FA Cup	0–0*		
18	16/01/88	Plymouth Argyle	Away	League	2–3		

Northampton Town – League Division Three

1	27/01/88	Preston North End	Home	League	0–1		
2	30/01/88	Wigan Athletic	Home	League	1–1	1 Goal	(1)
3	06/02/88	Doncaster Rovers	Home	League	1–0	1 Goal	(2)
4	13/02/88	Bury	Away	League	0–0		
5	20/02/88	Chester City	Home	League	2–0	1 Goal	(3)
6	27/02/88	Bristol City	Away	League	2–2	1 Goal	(4)
7	02/03/88	Southend United	Home	League	4–0	1 Goal	(5)
8	05/03/88	Chesterfield	Away	League	2–0		
9	11/03/88	Rotherham United	Home	League	0–0		
10	19/03/88	Aldershot	Home	League	1–1	1 Goal	(6)
11	26/03/88	Grimsby Town	Away	League	2–2		
12	02/04/88	Fulham	Home	League	3–2	1 Goal	(7)
13	04/04/88	Gillingham	Away	League	2–1	1 Goal	(8)
14	10/04/88	Mansfield Town	Home	League	2–0		
15	15/04/88	Brighton & Hove Albion	Away	League	0–3		
16	23/04/88	York City	Away	League	2–2		
17	30/04/88	Blackpool	Home	League	3–3	1 Goal	(9)
18	02/05/88	Sunderland	Away	League	1–3	1 Goal	(10)

SEASON 1988–89

League Division Three

19	27/08/88	Mansfield Town	Away	League	1–1		
20	30/08/88	Colchester United	Away	Lge Cup	0–0		
21	03/09/88	Brentford	Home	League	1–0		
22	05/09/88	Colchester United	Home	Lge Cup	5–0	2 Goals	(12)
23	10/09/88	Notts County	Away	League	1–0		
24	17/09/88	Chesterfield	Home	League	3–0	3 Goals	(15)
25	20/09/88	Sheffield United	Away	League	0–4		
26	24/09/88	Bristol Rovers	Home	League	1–2	1 Goal	(16)
27	27/09/88	Charlton Athletic	Home	Lge Cup	1–1		
28	01/10/88	Aldershot	Home	League	6–0	2 Goals	(18)
29	04/10/88	Blackpool	Away	League	1–3		
30	08/10/88	Huddersfield Town	Home	League	1–3		
31	11/10/88	Charlton Athletic	Away	Lge Cup	1–2		
32	15/10/88	Swansea City	Away	League	0–1		
33	22/10/88	Bristol City	Home	League	1–3		
34	25/10/88	Fulham	Away	League	2–3	1 Goal	(19)

Striker

35	29/10/88	Reading	Home	League	1–3		
36	05/11/88	Wigan Athletic	Away	League	3–1	1 Goal	(20)
37	08/11/88	Port Vale	Home	League	1–3		
38	12/11/88	Cardiff City	Away	League	0–1		
39	19/11/88	Swansea City	Away	FA Cup	1–3		
40	22/11/88	Cambridge United	Home	SV Trophy	1–1		
41	26/11/88	Bolton Wanderers	Away	League	1–2		
42	04/12/88	Wolverhampton Wanderers	Home	League	3–1	1 Goal	(21)
43	18/12/88	Gillingham	Home	League	1–2		
44	21/12/88	Peterborough United	Away	SV Trophy	2–0	1 Goal	(22)
45	26/12/88	Southend United	Away	League	1–2	1 Goal	(23)
46	31/12/88	Chester City	Away	League	1–2		
47	02/01/89	Preston North End	Home	League	1–0		
48	07/01/89	Bury	Home	League	2–0		
49	14/01/89	Brentford	Away	League	0–2		
50	17/01/89	Southend United	Home	SV Trophy	2–1		
51	21/01/89	Notts County	Home	League	1–3	1 Goal	(24)
52	28/01/89	Chesterfield	Away	League	1–1		
53	04/02/89	Aldershot	Away	League	1–5		
54	11/02/89	Blackpool	Home	League	4–2	1 Goal	(25)
55	18/02/89	Huddersfield Town	Away	League	2–1		
56	21/02/89	Wolverhampton Wanderers	Away	SV Trophy	1–3*		
57	25/02/89	Swansea City	Home	League	1–0		
58	28/02/89	Fulham	Home	League	2–1		
59	04/03/89	Bristol City	Away	League	1–3		
60	11/03/89	Wigan Athletic	Home	League	1–1	1 Goal	(26)
61	15/03/89	Reading	Away	League	1–1		
62	18/03/89	Mansfield Town	Home	League	2–1		
63	25/03/89	Preston North End	Away	League	2–3	1 Goal	(27)
64	27/03/89	Southend United	Home	League	2–2	1 Goal	(28)
65	01/04/89	Gillingham	Away	League	0–1		
66	04/04/89	Bury	Away	League	1–0		
67	08/04/89	Chester City	Home	League	0–2		
68	15/04/89	Sheffield United	Home	League	1–2		
69	22/04/89	Bristol Rovers	Away	League	1–1	1 Goal	(29)
70	29/04/89	Cardiff City	Home	League	3–0		
71	01/05/89	Port Vale	Away	League	2–1		
72	06/05/89	Wolverhampton Wanderers	Away	League	2–3		
73	13/05/89	Bolton Wanderers	Home	League	2–3	1 Goal	(30)

SEASON 1989–90

League Division Three

74	19/08/89	Walsall	Away	League	0–1		
75	22/08/89	Mansfield Town	Away	Lge Cup	1–1	1 Goal	(31)
76	26/08/89	Swansea City	Away	League	1–1		
77	02/09/89	Bristol City	Home	League	2–0	1 Goal	(32)
78	05/09/89	Mansfield Town	Home	Lge Cup	0–2		
79	09/09/89	Wigan Athletic	Away	League	0–0		
80	16/09/89	Shrewsbury Town	Home	League	2–1	1 Goal	(33)
81	23/09/89	Crewe Alexandra	Away	League	1–2		
82	26/09/89	Cardiff City	Away	League	3–2	1 Goal	(34)
83	30/09/89	Bury	Home	League	0–1		

Bradford City – League Division Two

1	07/10/89	Brighton & Hove Albion	Home	League	2–0	1 Goal	(1)
2	14/10/89	Newcastle United	Away	League	0–1		
3	18/10/89	Ipswich Town	Home	League	1–0	1 Goal	(2)
4	21/10/89	Sunderland	Away	League	0–1		
5	28/10/89	Leeds United	Home	League	0–1		
6	31/10/89	Oldham Athletic	Away	League	2–2		
7	04/11/89	Plymouth Argyle	Away	League	1–1		
8	11/11/89	Hull City	Home	League	2–3		
9	18/11/89	Sheffield United	Away	League	1–1		
10	25/11/89	AFC Bournemouth	Home	League	1–0		
11	28/11/89	Stoke City	Away	ZDS Cup	1–2		
Sub+1	02/12/89	Port Vale	Away	League	2–3		
12	16/12/89	Watford	Away	League	2–7		
13	26/12/89	Middlesbrough	Home	League	0–1		
14	30/12/89	West Bromwich Albion	Home	League	2–0		
15	01/01/90	Blackburn Rovers	Away	League	2–2		
16	13/01/90	Wolverhampton Wanderers	Home	League	1–1		
17	20/01/90	Portsmouth	Away	League	0–3		
18	03/02/90	Barnsley	Home	League	0–0		
19	10/02/90	Leicester City	Away	League	1–1	1 Goal	(3)

20	17/02/90	Oxford United	Home	League	1–2		
21	24/02/90	AFC Bournemouth	Away	League	0–1		
Sub+2	03/03/90	Sheffield United	Home	League	1–4	1 Goal	(4)
Sub+3	06/03/90	Swindon Town	Away	League	1–3		
22	10/03/90	Stoke City	Home	League	1–0		
23	14/03/90	West Bromwich Albion	Away	League	0–2		
24	17/03/90	Brighton & Hove Albion	Away	League	1–2		
25	05/05/90	Plymouth Argyle	Home	League	0–1		
26	07/05/90	Oldham Athletic	Home	League	1–1	1 Goal	(5)

SEASON 1990–91

League Division Three

Sub+4	25/08/90	Tranmere Rovers	Home	League	1–2		
27	03/10/90	Chester City	Home	League	2–1		
28	06/10/90	Brentford	Home	League	0–1		
29	27/10/90	Wigan Athletic	Home	League	2–1		
30	30/10/90	Tottenham Hotspur	Away	Lge Cup	1–2		
31	03/11/90	Rotherham United	Away	League	2–0		
32	07/11/90	Huddersfield Town	Home	LD Cup	1–1		
33	10/11/90	Preston North End	Home	League	2–1		
Sub+5	20/11/90	Shrewsbury Town	Away	FA Cup	1–2		
Sub+6	22/12/90	Shrewsbury Town	Home	League	2–4		
34	28/12/90	Southend United	Away	League	1–1		
35	01/01/91	Bury	Home	League	3–1		
36	05/01/91	Birmingham City	Away	League	1–1	1 Goal	(6)

Northampton Town – League Division Four

1	12/01/91	Maidstone United	Home	League	2–0	1 Goal	(1)
2	19/01/91	Hereford United	Home	League	3–0		
3	26/01/91	Aldershot	Home	League	2–1	1 Goal	(2)
4	01/02/91	Scarborough	Home	League	0–2		
5	05/02/91	Peterborough United	Away	League	0–1		
6	15/02/91	York City	Home	League	2–1		
7	23/02/91	Wrexham	Away	League	2–0		
8	02/03/91	Rochdale	Away	League	1–1		
9	05/03/91	Scunthorpe United	Away	League	0–3		
10	23/03/91	Chesterfield	Home	League	2–0		
11	26/03/91	Torquay United	Away	League	0–0		
12	30/03/91	Scunthorpe United	Home	League	2–1		
13	01/04/91	Cardiff City	Away	League	0–1		
14	06/04/91	Gillingham	Home	League	2–1		
Sub+1	09/04/91	Stockport County	Away	League	0–2		
15	16/04/91	Torquay United	Home	League	1–4	1 Goal	(3)
16	20/04/91	Walsall	Away	League	3–3		
17	27/04/91	Darlington	Home	League	0–3		
18	30/04/91	Lincoln City	Home	League	1–1		
19	07/05/91	Blackpool	Away	League	1–2		
20	11/05/91	Hartlepool United	Away	League	1–3		

SEASON 1991–92

League Division Four

21	17/08/91	Halifax Town	Home	League	1–0		
22	20/08/91	Leyton Orient	Away	Lge Cup	0–5		
23	12/10/91	Scarborough	Away	League	1–2	1 Goal	(4)
24	15/10/91	Chesterfield	Home	League	1–1	1 Goal	(5)
25	19/10/91	Scunthorpe United	Home	League	0–1		
26	26/10/91	Gillingham	Away	League	1–3		
27	02/11/91	Rotherham United	Away	League	0–1		
28	05/11/91	Mansfield Town	Home	League	1–2	1 Goal	(6)
29	09/11/91	Lincoln City	Home	League	1–0	1 Goal	(7)
30	15/11/91	Crawley Town	Away	FA Cup	2–4	1 Goal	(8)
31	20/11/91	Reading	Away	A Trophy	2–0	1 Goal	(9)
32	23/11/91	Cardiff City	Away	League	2–3		
33	30/11/91	Burnley	Home	League	1–2		
34	03/12/91	Leyton Orient	Home	A Trophy	1–2		
35	07/12/91	Scarborough	Home	League	3–2	1 Goal	(10)
36	21/12/91	Chesterfield	Away	League	2–1		
37	26/12/91	Halifax Town	Home	League	4–0	2 Goals	(12)
38	28/12/91	Wrexham	Home	League	1–1		

Peterborough United – League Division Three

Sub+1	01/01/92	Bury	Home	League	0–0		
1	11/01/92	Fulham	Home	League	4–1	2 Goals	(2)

2	18/01/92	Huddersfield Town	Away	League	0–0		
3	01/02/92	Reading	Home	League	5–3		
4	08/02/92	Hartlepool United	Away	League	1–0		
5	15/02/92	Stockport County	Home	League	3–2	2 Goals	(4)
6	22/02/92	Fulham	Away	League	1–0	1 Goal	(5)
7	29/02/92	Bolton Wanderers	Home	League	1–0	1 Goal	(6)
8	03/03/92	Huddersfield Town	Home	League	2–0		
9	07/03/92	AFC Bournemouth	Away	League	2–1		
10	10/03/92	Chester City	Away	League	4–2	1 Goal	(7)
11	14/03/92	Shrewsbury Town	Home	League	1–0		
12	21/03/92	Bradford City	Away	League	1–2		
13	24/03/92	Bolton Wanderers	Away	League	1–2		
14	28/03/92	Darlington	Home	League	1–1		
15	31/03/92	Birmingham City	Home	League	2–3		
16	03/04/92	Wigan Athletic	Away	League	0–3		
17	08/04/92	AFC Bournemouth	Home	League	2–0		
18	11/04/92	West Bromwich Albion	Home	League	0–0		
19	18/04/92	Exeter City	Away	League	2–2		
20	21/04/92	Swansea City	Home	League	3–1		
21	25/04/92	Leyton Orient	Away	League	2–1		
22	28/04/92	Torquay United	Away	League	2–2		
23	02/05/92	Brentford	Home	League	0–1		
24	11/05/92	Huddersfield Town	Home	Lge P/O	2–2		
25	14/05/92	Huddersfield Town	Away	Lge P/O	2–1		
26	24/05/92	Stockport County	Wembley	Lge P/O	2–1		

SEASON 1992–93

Football League Division One

27	15/08/92	Derby County	Home	League	1–0		
28	18/08/92	Barnet	Home	Lge Cup	4–0	2 Goals	(9)
29	22/08/92	Southend United	Away	League	1–0	1 Goal	(10)
30	29/08/92	Notts County	Home	League	1–3		
Sub+2	01/09/92	Tranmere Rovers	Home	AI Cup	0–0		
31	05/09/92	Wolverhampton Wanderers	Away	League	3–4		
32	12/09/92	West Ham United	Home	League	1–3	1 Goal	(11)
33	15/09/92	Millwall	Home	League	0–0		
34	19/09/92	Barnsley	Away	League	2–1	1 Goal	(12)
35	23/09/92	Leicester City	Away	Lge Cup	0–2		
36	26/09/92	Newcastle United	Home	League	0–1		
37	03/10/92	Grimsby Town	Away	League	3–1	1 Goal	(13)
38	06/10/92	Leicester City	Home	Lge Cup	2–1		
39	10/10/92	Brentford	Home	League	0–0		
40	18/10/92	Leicester City	Away	League	2–0		
41	24/10/92	Luton Town	Home	League	2–3	1 Goal	(14)
42	30/10/92	Tranmere Rovers	Away	League	1–1		
43	03/11/92	Watford	Away	League	2–1		
44	07/11/92	Sunderland	Home	League	5–2	2 Goals	(16)
45	14/11/92	Kingstonian	Away	FA Cup	1–1	1 Goal	(17)
46	21/11/92	Bristol Rovers	Home	League	1–1	1 Goal	(18)
47	25/11/92	Kingstonian	Home	FA Cup	9–1+	2 Goals	(20)
48	29/11/92	Swindon Town	Home	League	3–3	2 Goals	(22)
49	04/12/92	Kingstonian	Home	FA Cup	1–0#		
50	09/12/92	Plymouth Argyle	Away	FA Cup	2–3		
51	12/12/92	Portsmouth	Home	League	1–1		
52	19/12/92	Bristol City	Away	League	1–0		
53	28/12/92	Charlton Athletic	Home	League	1–1		
54	09/01/93	Barnsley	Home	League	1–1		
55	16/01/93	Newcastle United	Away	League	0–3		
56	22/01/93	Birmingham City	Away	League	0–2		
57	27/01/93	Millwall	Away	League	0–4		
Sub+3	30/01/93	Southend United	Home	League	1–0		
58	06/02/93	Derby County	Away	League	3–2	1 Goal	(23)
59	09/02/93	West Ham United	Away	League	1–2		
60	13/02/93	Wolverhampton Wanderers	Home	League	2–3	1 Goal	(24)
61	21/02/93	Notts County	Away	League	0–1		
62	27/02/93	Brentford	Away	League	1–0		
63	06/03/93	Grimsby Town	Home	League	1–0	1 Goal	(25)
64	09/03/93	Birmingham City	Home	League	2–1		
65	13/03/93	Sunderland	Away	League	0–3		
66	16/03/93	Cambridge United	Away	League	2–2	2 Goals	(27)
67	20/03/93	Oxford United	Home	League	1–1		
68	24/03/93	Bristol Rovers	Away	League	1–3		
69	27/03/93	Watford	Home	League	0–0		
70	03/04/93	Swindon Town	Away	League	0–1		

71	06/04/93	Portsmouth	Away	League	0–4		
72	10/04/93	Cambridge United	Home	League	1–0		
73	12/04/93	Charlton Athletic	Away	League	1–0		
74	20/04/93	Oxford United	Away	League	1–2		
75	24/04/93	Leicester City	Home	League	3–0	1 Goal	(28)
76	01/05/93	Luton Town	Away	League	0–0		
77	08/05/93	Tranmere Rovers	Home	League	1–1		

+ Match replayed after the Kingstonian goalkeeper (Blake) was struck by a missile and had
to be substituted
Played behind closed doors

SEASON 1993–94

Football League Division One

78	14/08/93	Leicester City	Away	League	1–2		
79	17/08/93	Barnsley	Home	League	4–1	1 Goal	(29)
80	21/08/93	Notts County	Home	League	1–1		
81	28/08/93	Southend United	Away	League	0–3		
82	04/09/93	Grimsby Town	Home	League	1–2		
83	11/09/93	Derby County	Away	League	0–2		
Sub+4	14/09/93	West Bromwich Albion	Away	AI Cup	1–3		
Sub+5	18/09/93	Oxford United	Home	League	3–1		
Sub+6	21/09/93	Barnsley	Away	Lge Cup	1–1		
Sub+7	25/09/93	Millwall	Home	League	0–0		
84	02/10/93	Sunderland	Away	League	0–2		
85	05/10/93	Barnsley	Home	Lge Cup	3–1		
86	09/10/93	Portsmouth	Home	League	2–2	1 Goal	(30)
87	16/10/93	West Bromwich Albion	Away	League	0–3		
88	23/10/93	Birmingham City	Home	League	1–0		
89	26/10/93	Blackpool	Away	Lge Cup	2–2	1 Goal	(31)
90	30/10/93	Middlesbrough	Away	League	1–1		
91	02/11/93	Bolton Wanderers	Away	League	1–1		
92	06/11/93	Tranmere Rovers	Home	League	0–0		
93	09/11/93	Blackpool	Home	Lge Cup	2–1		
94	20/11/93	Charlton Athletic	Home	League	0–1		
95	27/11/93	Bristol City	Home	League	0–2		
96	30/11/93	Portsmouth	Home	Lge Cup	0–0		
97	03/12/93	Tranmere Rovers	Away	League	1–2	1 Goal	(32)
98	11/12/93	Barnsley	Away	League	0–1		
99	15/12/93	Portsmouth	Away	Lge Cup	0–1		
100	19/12/93	Leicester City	Home	League	1–1	1 Goal	(33)
101	27/12/93	Luton Town	Home	League	0–0		
102	28/12/93	Watford	Away	League	1–2	1 Goal	(34)
103	01/01/94	Wolverhampton Wanderers	Home	League	0–1		
104	08/01/94	Tottenham Hotspur	Home	FA Cup	1–1		
105	15/01/94	West Bromwich Albion	Home	League	2–0		
106	19/01/94	Tottenham Hotspur	Away	FA Cup	1–1+		
107	22/01/94	Portsmouth	Away	League	2–0	2 Goals	(36)
108	01/02/94	Crystal Palace	Away	League	2–3		
109	05/02/94	Birmingham City	Away	League	0–0		
110	12/02/94	Middlesbrough	Home	League	1–0		
111	19/02/94	Stoke City	Home	League	1–1		
112	22/02/94	Notts County	Away	League	1–2		
113	02/03/94	Nottingham Forest	Away	League	0–2		
114	05/03/94	Southend United	Home	League	3–1	1 Goal	(37)
115	08/03/94	Grimsby Town	Away	League	2–3	1 Goal	(38)
116	12/03/94	Oxford United	Away	League	2–1		
117	16/03/94	Derby County	Home	League	2–2		
118	22/03/94	Millwall	Away	League	0–1		
119	26/03/94	Sunderland	Home	League	1–3	1 Goal	(39)
120	29/03/94	Crystal Palace	Home	League	1–1		
121	02/04/94	Luton Town	Away	League	0–2		
122	05/04/94	Watford	Home	League	3–4	2 Goals	(41)
123	09/04/94	Wolverhampton Wanderers	Away	League	1–1		
124	16/04/94	Bolton Wanderers	Home	League	2–3		

+ AET Tottenham Hotspur won 5–4 on penalties

SEASON 1994–95

Luton Town – Football League Division One

Sub+1	31/12/94	Notts County	Away	League	1–0		
Sub+2	02/01/95	Charlton Athletic	Home	League	0–1		
Sub+3	07/01/95	Bristol Rovers	Home	FA Cup	1–1		

SEASON 1995–96

Colchester United – Football League Division Three

1	12/08/95	Plymouth Argyle	Home	League	2–1		
2	15/08/95	Bristol City	Home	Lge Cup	2–1	1 Goal	(1)
3	19/08/95	Barnet	Away	League	1–1	1 Goal	(2)
4	22/08/95	Bristol City	Away	Lge Cup	1–2+		
5	26/08/95	Lincoln City	Home	League	3–0		
6	29/08/95	Cambridge United	Away	League	1–3	1 Goal	(3)
7	02/09/95	Gillingham	Away	League	1–0	1 Goal	(4)
8	09/09/95	Chester City	Home	League	1–2		
9	12/09/95	Preston North End	Home	League	2–2		
10	16/09/95	Darlington	Away	League	2–2		
11	23/09/95	Hereford United	Home	League	2–0		
12	26/09/95	Torquay United	Home	AW Shield	5–2	3 Goals	(7)
13	30/09/95	Scunthorpe United	Away	League	0–1		
14	07/10/95	Hartlepool United	Home	League	4–1	1 Goal	(8)
15	14/10/95	Rochdale	Away	League	1–1		
16	21/10/95	Northampton Town	Home	League	1–0		
17	28/10/95	Cardiff City	Away	League	2–1	2 Goals	(10)
18	31/10/95	Fulham	Away	League	1–1		
19	04/11/95	Exeter City	Home	League	1–1		
20	11/11/95	Gravesend & Northfleet Unt	Away	FA Cup	0–2		
21	18/11/95	Doncaster Rovers	Away	League	2–3	1 Goal	(11)
22	25/11/95	Mansfield Town	Home	League	1–3	1 Goal	(12)
23	28/11/95	Oxford United	Away	AW Shield	2–1	1 Goal	(13)
24	09/12/95	Hereford United	Away	League	1–1		
25	16/12/95	Scunthorpe United	Home	League	2–1		
26	23/12/95	Bury	Away	League	0–0		
27	26/12/95	Leyton Orient	Home	League	0–0		
28	01/01/96	Torquay United	Away	League	3–2		
29	09/01/96	Peterborough United	Away	AW Shield	2–3		
30	20/01/96	Plymouth Argyle	Away	League	1–1		
31	30/01/96	Wigan Athletic	Away	League	0–2		
32	03/02/96	Lincoln City	Away	League	0–0		
33	06/02/96	Scarborough	Home	League	1–1		
34	10/02/96	Wigan Athletic	Home	League	1–2	1 Goal	(14)
35	17/02/96	Preston North End	Away	League	0–2		
36	24/02/96	Darlington	Home	League	1–1	1 Goal	(15)
37	27/02/96	Chester City	Away	League	1–1		
38	02/03/96	Leyton Orient	Away	League	1–0	1 Goal	(16)
39	09/03/96	Bury	Home	League	1–0		
40	16/03/96	Scarborough	Away	League	0–0		
41	19/03/96	Cambridge United	Home	League	2–1	1 Goal	(17)
42	23/03/96	Torquay United	Home	League	3–1		
43	06/04/96	Cardiff City	Home	League	1–0		
44	08/04/96	Northampton Town	Away	League	1–2		
45	13/04/96	Fulham	Home	League	2–2		
46	16/04/96	Gillingham	Home	League	1–1		
47	20/04/96	Exeter City	Away	League	2–2		
Sub+1	15/05/96	Plymouth Argyle	Away	Lge P/O	1–3		

+ AET Bristol City won 5–3 on penalties

SEASON 1996–97

Football League Division Three

48	17/08/96	Hartlepool United	Home	League	0–2		
49	20/08/96	West Bromwich Albion	Home	Lge Cup	2–3		
50	24/08/96	Rochdale	Away	League	0–0		
51	27/08/96	Darlington	Away	League	1–1		
52	31/08/96	Hereford United	Home	League	1–1		
Sub+2	03/09/96	West Bromwich Albion	Away	Lge Cup	3–1		
Sub+3	07/09/96	Fulham	Away	League	1–3		
53	10/09/96	Brighton & Hove Albion	Home	League	2–0		
54	14/09/96	Hull City	Home	League	1–1		
55	17/09/96	Huddersfield Town	Away	Lge Cup	1–1	1 Goal	(18)
56	21/09/96	Leyton Orient	Away	League	1–1		
57	24/09/96	Huddersfield Town	Home	Lge Cup	0–2*		
58	28/09/96	Doncaster Rovers	Home	League	2–2	1 Goal	(19)
59	01/10/96	Carlisle United	Away	League	0–3		
Sub+4	12/10/96	Wigan Athletic	Home	League	3–1	1 Goal	(20)
Sub+5	19/10/96	Northampton Town	Away	League	1–2		
Sub+6	02/11/96	Cardiff City	Home	League	1–1		
Sub+7	16/11/96	Wycombe Wanderers	Home	FA Cup	1–2		

60	19/11/96	Scunthorpe United	Home	League	1–1		
Sub+8	30/11/96	Lincoln City	Home	League	7–1	1 Goal	(21)
Sub+9	20/12/96	Cambridge United	Home	League	2–2	1 Goal	(22)
Sub+10	26/12/96	Brighton & Hove Albion	Away	League	1–1		
61	07/01/97	Millwall	Away	AW Shield	3–2*	2 Goals	(24)
62	11/01/97	Doncaster Rovers	Away	League	0–0		
63	14/01/97	Fulham	Home	League	2–1		
64	18/01/97	Carlisle United	Home	League	1–1	1 Goal	(25)
65	25/01/97	Exeter City	Away	League	3–0		
66	28/01/97	Brentford	Away	AW Shield	1–0		
67	31/01/97	Torquay United	Home	League	2–0	2 Goals	(27)
68	04/02/97	Leyton Orient	Home	League	2–1		
69	08/02/97	Cardiff City	Away	League	2–1	1 Goal	(28)
70	14/02/97	Chester City	Home	League	0–0		
71	18/02/97	Northampton Town	Home	AW Shield	2–1		
72	22/02/97	Scunthorpe United	Away	League	1–2		
73	28/02/97	Scarborough	Home	League	1–3	1 Goal	(29)
74	07/03/97	Cambridge United	Away	League	0–1		
75	11/03/97	Peterborough United	Away	AW Shield	0–2		
76	14/03/97	Mansfield Town	Home	League	2–1	1 Goal	(30)
77	18/03/97	Peterborough United	Home	AW Shield	3–0*		
78	21/03/97	Rochdale	Home	League	1–0		
Sub+11	29/03/97	Hartlepool United	Away	League	0–1		
79	31/03/97	Darlington	Home	League	0–3		
Sub+12	05/04/97	Hereford United	Away	League	0–1		
Sub+13	08/04/97	Wigan Athletic	Away	League	0–1		
80	11/04/97	Swansea City	Home	League	3–1		
81	15/04/97	Hull City	Away	League	2–1	1 Goal	(31)
82	20/04/97	Carlisle United	Wembley	AW Shield	0–0+		

+ AET Carlisle United won 4–3 on penalties

APPEARANCES AND GOALS PER SEASON

SEASON 80–81	GAMES	GOALS
League	1	0
TOTAL	**1**	**0**

SEASON 81–82	GAMES	GOALS
League	31+9	5
FA Cup	2+1	1
League Cup	4+1	0
TOTAL	**37+11**	**6**

SEASON 82–83	GAMES	GOALS
League	26+4	17
FA Cup	0+1	0
League Cup	1	0
Football League Trophy	2	0
TOTAL	**29+5**	**17**

SEASON 83–84	GAMES	GOALS
League	41+2	26
FA Cup	3	0
League Cup	5	5
Associate Members Cup	2	2
TOTAL	**51+2**	**33**

SEASON 84–85	GAMES	GOALS
League	27+1	24
FA Cup	3	1
League Cup	2	0
Freight Rover Trophy	2	3
TOTAL	**34+1**	**28**

SEASON 85–86	GAMES	GOALS
League	33	15
FA Cup	1	0
League Cup	2	0
Freight Rover Trophy	2	1
TOTAL	**38**	**16**

SEASON 86–87	**GAMES**	**GOALS**
League	33+2	11
League Play–offs	2	0
FA Cup	3	1
League Cup	2	0
Freight Rover Trophy	3	0
TOTAL	**43+2**	**12**

SEASON 87–88	**GAMES**	**GOALS**
League	30+3	15
FA Cup	2	0
League Cup	2+1	1
Simod Cup	2	3
TOTAL	**36+4**	**19**

SEASON 88–89	**GAMES**	**GOALS**
League	46	17
FA Cup	1	0
League Cup	4	2
Sherpa Van Trophy	4	1
TOTAL	**55**	**20**

SEASON 89–90	**GAMES**	**GOALS**
League	33+3	8
League Cup	2	1
Zenith Data Systems Cup	1	0
TOTAL	**36+3**	**9**

SEASON 90–91	**GAMES**	**GOALS**
League	28+3	4
FA Cup	0+1	0
League Cup	1	0
Leyland Daf Cup	1	0
TOTAL	**30+4**	**4**

SEASON 91–92	**GAMES**	**GOALS**
League	37+1	14
League Play–offs	3	0
FA Cup	1	1
League Cup	1	0
Autoglass Trophy	2	1
TOTAL	**44+1**	**16**

SEASON 92–93	**GAMES**	**GOALS**
League	44+1	16
FA Cup	4	3
League Cup	3	2
Anglo–Italian Cup	0+1	0
TOTAL	**51+2**	**21**

SEASON 93–94	**GAMES**	**GOALS**
League	40+2	12
FA Cup	2	0
League Cup	5+1	1
Anglo–Italian Cup	0+1	0
TOTAL	**47+4**	**13**

SEASON 94–95	**GAMES**	**GOALS**
League	0+2	0
FA Cup	0+1	0
TOTAL	**0+3**	**0**

SEASON 95–96	**GAMES**	**GOALS**
League	41	12
League Play–offs	0+1	0
FA Cup	1	0
League Cup	2	1
Auto Windscreens Shield	3	4
TOTAL	**47+1**	**17**

SEASON 96–97	**GAMES**	**GOALS**
League	26+10	11
FA Cup	0+1	0
League Cup	3+1	1
Auto Windscreens Shield	6	2
TOTAL	**35+12**	**14**

CAREER APPEARANCES AND GOALS

COMPETITION	GAMES	TOTAL	GOALS
League	517+43	560	207
League Play–offs	5+1	6	0
FA Cup	23+5	28	7
League Cup	39+4	43	14
Football League Trophy	2	2	0
Associate Members Cup	2	2	2
Freight Rover Trophy	7	7	4
Simod Cup	2	2	3
Sherpa Van Trophy	4	4	1
Zenith Data Systems Cup	1	1	0
Leyland Daf Cup	1	1	0
Autoglass Trophy	2	2	1
Auto Windscreens Shield	9	9	6
Anglo–Italian Cup	0+2	2	0
TOTAL	**614+55**	**669**	**245**

HAT-TRICKS

Colchester United

1	3	Crewe Alexandra	21/01/83	Home	League	4–3
2	3	Southend United	25/08/84	Home	League	3–3
3	3	Chesterfield	22/02/85	Home	League	3–1
4	3	Cambridge United	17/09/85	Home	League	4–1

Manchester City

1	3	Huddersfield Town	07/11/87	Home	League	10–1
2	3	Plymouth Argyle	10/11/87	Home	Simod Cup	6–2

Northampton Town

1	3	Chesterfield	17/09/88	Home	League	3–0

Colchester United

1	3	Torquay United	26/09/95	Home	AW Shield	5–2

League: 6
Simod Cup: 1
Auto Windscreens Shield: 1
TOTAL: 8

HONOURS

Winners medals
None

Runner-up medals
Auto Windscreens Shield: 96/97
Promoted to Football League Division One: 91/92

JOHN ALDRIDGE

Born: 18/09/58 – Liverpool
Height: 5.11
Weight: 12.03 (96–97)

Clubs
Newport County: **1979–84** – Matches: **198+15** – Goals: **90**
Oxford United: **1984–87** – Matches: **138+3** – Goals: **90**
Liverpool: **1987–89** – Matches: **89+15** – Goals: **63**
Real Sociedad: **1989–91** – Matches: **75** – Goals: **40**
Tranmere Rovers: **1991–97** – Matches: **265+15** – Goals: **169**

Country
Republic of Ireland: **1986–96** – Matches: **58+11** – Goals: **19**

SEASON 1979–80

Newport County – League Division Four

Sub+1	29/09/79	Lincoln City	Home	League	1–1
1	02/10/79	Northampton Town	Away	League	2–3

Sub+2	06/10/79	Halifax Town	Away	League	1–2		
2	09/10/79	Aldershot	Home	League	4–2	2 Goals	(2)
3	13/10/79	Tranmere Rovers	Home	League	2–0	1 Goal	(3)
4	20/10/79	Scunthorpe United	Home	League	3–1	2 Goals	(5)
5	23/10/79	Portsmouth	Away	League	2–0		
6	27/10/79	Wigan Athletic	Home	League	3–2		
7	03/11/79	Port Vale	Away	League	0–2		
8	06/11/79	Portsmouth	Home	League	4–3	1 Goal	(6)
9	10/11/79	Crewe Alexandra	Home	League	1–1		
10	17/11/79	Stockport County	Away	League	5–0	3 Goals	(9)
11	24/11/79	Portsmouth	Away	FA Cup	0–1		
12	01/12/79	Darlington	Home	League	4–0		
13	08/12/79	Hartlepool United	Away	League	0–0		
14	15/12/79	Scunthorpe United	Home	League	2–1		
15	21/12/79	Peterborough United	Home	League	1–1		
16	26/12/79	Torquay United	Away	League	0–2		
17	29/12/79	Walsall	Home	League	0–1		
18	01/01/80	Hereford United	Home	League	1–0		
19	12/01/80	York City	Away	League	1–2	1 Goal	(10)
20	18/01/80	Huddersfield Town	Home	League	2–2		
21	22/01/80	Cardiff City	Home	Welsh Cup	2–0	1 Goal	(11)
22	26/01/80	AFC Bournemouth	Home	League	0–0		
Sub+3	16/02/80	Lincoln City	Away	League	1–2		
23	22/02/80	Tranmere Rovers	Away	League	2–0		
24	26/02/80	Doncaster Rovers	Home	League	2–1		
25	08/03/80	Wigan Athletic	Away	League	1–0		
26	04/03/80	Wrexham	Away	Welsh Cup	1–0		
27	14/03/80	Halifax Town	Home	League	5–2	1 Goal	(12)
28	22/03/80	Crewe Alexandra	Away	League	3–0		
29	25/03/80	Merthyr Tydfil	Home	Welsh Cup	3–1	1 Goal	(13)
30	29/03/80	Stockport County	Home	League	3–1		
31	05/04/80	Torquay United	Home	League	3–0		
32	07/04/80	Hereford United	Away	League	2–0		
33	08/04/80	Peterborough United	Away	League	1–0		
34	12/04/80	Rochdale	Home	League	1–0		
35	19/04/80	Darlington	Away	League	1–1		
36	22/04/80	Bradford City	Away	League	0–3		
37	26/04/80	Hartlepool United	Home	League	1–0	1 Goal	(14)
38	29/04/80	Rochdale	Away	League	0–2		
39	03/05/80	Walsall	Away	League	4–2	2 Goals	(16)
40	06/05/80	Shrewsbury Town	Home	Welsh Cup	2–1		
41	12/05/80	Shrewsbury Town	Away	Welsh Cup	3–0		

SEASON 1980–81

League Division Three

42	09/08/80	Hereford United	Away	Lge Cup	0–1		
43	12/08/80	Hereford United	Home	Lge Cup	5–0	2 Goals	(18)
44	16/08/80	Burnley	Away	League	1–1	1 Goal	(19)
45	19/08/80	Charlton Athletic	Home	League	1–2		
46	23/08/80	Millwall	Home	League	2–1		
47	26/08/80	Notts County	Home	Lge Cup	1–1		
48	30/08/80	Carlisle United	Away	League	4–1	1 Goal	(20)
49	02/09/80	Notts County	Away	Lge Cup	0–2		
50	06/09/80	Gillingham	Away	League	2–3		
51	13/09/80	Oxford United	Home	League	0–1		
52	16/09/80	Crusaders FC Belfast	Home	ECW Cup	4–0	1 Goal	(21)
53	20/09/80	Chesterfield	Away	League	2–3		
54	27/09/80	Plymouth Argyle	Home	League	0–2		
55	01/10/80	Crusaders FC Belfast	Away	ECW Cup	0–0		
Sub+4	11/10/80	Portsmouth	Home	League	2–1		
Sub+5	14/10/80	Sheffield United	Away	League	0–2		
56	18/10/80	Walsall	Away	League	0–1		
57	22/10/80	SK Haugar Haugesund	Away	ECW Cup	0–0		
58	25/10/80	Huddersfield Town	Home	League	3–2		
59	28/10/80	Fulham	Home	League	2–1	1 Goal	(22)
60	01/11/80	Blackpool	Away	League	4–2	1 Goal	(23)
61	04/11/80	SK Haugar Haugesund	Home	ECW Cup	6–0	1 Goal	(24)
62	08/11/80	Hull City	Home	League	4–0		
63	11/11/80	Charlton Athletic	Away	League	0–3		
64	15/11/80	Burnley	Home	League	1–2		
Sub+6	22/11/80	Plymouth Argyle	Away	FA Cup	0–2		
65	24/11/80	Worcester City	Away	Welsh Cup	3–2	1 Goal	(25)
66	03/12/80	Chester	Away	League	1–1		
67	06/12/80	Barnsley	Home	League	0–0		

68	13/12/80	Chester	Home	League	1–1		
Sub+7	31/03/81	Hereford United	Home	Welsh Cup	1–1		
Sub+8	04/04/81	Blackpool	Home	League	3–1	2 Goals	(27)
69	07/04/81	Walsall	Home	League	1–1		
70	18/04/81	Exeter City	Home	League	2–1		
71	20/04/81	Swindon Town	Away	League	1–1		
72	25/04/81	Colchester United	Home	League	1–0	1 Goal	(28)
Sub+9	05/05/81	Carlisle United	Home	League	4–0		
73	07/05/81	Hull City	Away	League	1–3		

SEASON 1981–82

League Division Three

74	29/08/81	Chesterfield	Home	League	1–0		
75	02/09/81	Torquay United	Away	Lge Cup	3–2	1 Goal	(29)
76	04/09/81	Southend United	Away	League	4–0	1 Goal	(30)
77	12/09/81	Oxford United	Home	League	3–2	1 Goal	(31)
78	15/09/81	Torquay United	Home	Lge Cup	0–0		
79	19/09/81	Bristol City	Away	League	1–2	1 Goal	(32)
80	23/09/81	Reading	Away	League	1–2	1 Goal	(33)
81	26/09/81	Preston North End	Home	League	1–1		
82	29/09/81	Brentford	Home	League	0–1		
83	03/10/81	Lincoln City	Away	League	2–2		
84	24/10/81	Portsmouth	Away	League	0–0		
85	07/11/81	Walsall	Away	League	1–3		
86	14/11/81	Plymouth Argyle	Home	League	0–1		
87	21/11/81	Colchester United	Away	FA Cup	0–2		
88	26/12/81	Chester	Home	League	0–1		
89	28/12/81	Gillingham	Away	League	1–1		
90	02/01/82	Reading	Home	League	3–1	2 Goals	(35)
Sub+10	23/01/82	Chesterfield	Away	League	0–1		
91	30/01/82	Bristol City	Home	League	1–1		
Sub+11	13/02/82	Lincoln City	Home	League	0–0		
Sub+12	20/02/82	Brentford	Away	League	0–2		
92	27/02/82	Doncaster Rovers	Away	League	2–0	1 Goal	(36)
93	07/03/82	Fulham	Home	League	1–3		
94	09/03/82	Millwall	Away	League	0–1		
95	13/03/82	Portsmouth	Home	League	1–1		
96	16/03/82	Bristol Rovers	Home	League	1–1		
97	20/03/82	Carlisle United	Away	League	2–2	1 Goal	(37)
98	27/03/82	Walsall	Home	League	2–2		
99	30/03/82	Huddersfield Town	Away	League	0–2		
100	02/04/82	Plymouth Argyle	Away	League	2–1		
101	10/04/82	Chester	Away	League	2–0	2 Goals	(39)
102	12/04/82	Gillingham	Home	League	4–2		
103	17/04/82	Wimbledon	Home	League	0–0		
104	24/04/82	Exeter City	Away	League	0–1		
Sub+13	04/05/82	Preston North End	Away	League	1–2		
105	08/05/82	Swindon Town	Away	League	1–1	1 Goal	(40)
106	11/05/82	Southend United	Home	League	3–2		
107	15/05/82	Huddersfield Town	Home	League	1–0		
108	18/05/82	Swindon Town	Home	League	1–0		

SEASON 1982–83

League Division Three

109	14/08/82	Torquay United	Home	FL Trophy	0–1		
Sub+14	18/08/82	Exeter City	Home	FL Trophy	5–1		
Sub+15	21/08/82	Bristol City	Away	FL Trophy	4–1		
110	11/09/82	Bradford city	Away	League	2–4	1 Goal	(41)
111	14/09/82	Exeter City	Home	Lge Cup	6–0	1 Goal	(42)
112	18/09/82	Huddersfield Town	Home	League	2–1	2 Goals	(44)
113	25/09/82	Portsmouth	Away	League	2–1	1 Goal	(45)
114	28/09/82	Brentford	Away	League	0–2		
115	02/10/82	Lincoln City	Home	League	1–0		
116	05/10/82	Everton	Home	Lge Cup	0–2		
117	09/10/82	Bristol Rovers	Home	League	2–0		
118	16/10/82	Orient	Away	League	5–1	1 Goal	(46)
119	19/10/82	Preston North End	Away	League	0–0		
120	23/10/82	Southend United	Home	League	1–1		
121	27/10/82	Everton	Away	Lge Cup	2–2		
122	30/10/82	Wigan Athletic	Away	League	1–0	1 Goal	(47)
123	02/11/82	Sheffield United	Home	League	3–1	1 Goal	(48)
124	06/11/82	Reading	Away	League	2–4		
125	13/11/82	AFC Bournemouth	Home	League	5–1	3 Goals	(51)

126	20/11/82	Enfield	Away	FA Cup	0–0		
127	23/11/82	Enfield	Home	FA Cup	4–2	1 Goal	(52)
128	30/11/82	Cardiff City	Home	Welsh Cup	1–0		
129	04/12/82	Gillingham	Home	League	2–1		
130	11/12/82	Orient	Home	FA Cup	1–0		
131	18/12/82	Walsall	Home	League	1–1		
132	27/12/82	Cardiff City	Away	League	2–3		
133	28/12/82	Oxford United	Home	League	1–2		
134	01/01/83	Exeter City	Away	League	1–0		
135	08/01/83	Everton	Home	FA Cup	1–1		
136	11/01/83	Everton	Away	FA Cup	1–2	1 Goal	(53)
137	15/01/83	Doncaster Rovers	Home	League	1–2	1 Goal	(54)
138	19/01/83	Wrexham	Away	Welsh Cup	1–4	1 Goal	(55)
139	22/01/83	Plymouth Argyle	Away	League	4–2		
140	26/01/83	Chester City	Away	FL Trophy	0–0+		
141	29/01/83	Bradford City	Home	League	1–1		
142	01/02/83	Chesterfield	Away	League	1–3		
143	06/02/83	Brentford	Home	League	0–0		
144	15/02/83	Preston North End	Home	League	3–0		
145	19/02/83	Bristol Rovers	Away	League	3–1	1 Goal	(56)
146	26/02/83	Orient	Home	League	4–1	1 Goal	(57)
147	01/03/83	Sheffield United	Away	League	0–2		
148	04/03/83	Southend United	Away	League	4–1	1 Goal	(58)
149	12/03/83	Wigan Athletic	Home	League	1–0	1 Goal	(59)
150	19/03/83	Reading	Home	League	1–0		
151	23/03/83	Lincoln City	Away	League	4–1		
152	26/03/83	AFC Bournemouth	Away	League	1–0		
153	02/04/83	Oxford United	Away	League	3–0	1 Goal	(60)
154	04/04/83	Cardiff City	Home	League	1–0	1 Goal	(61)
155	09/04/83	Gillingham	Away	League	0–2		
156	16/04/83	Portsmouth	Home	League	0–3		
157	23/04/83	Walsall	Away	League	1–2		
158	30/04/83	Wrexham	Home	League	4–0		
159	02/05/83	Millwall	Away	League	0–3		
160	07/05/83	Huddersfield Town	Away	League	0–1		
161	14/05/83	Exeter City	Home	League	1–1		

+ AET Chester City won 5–4 on penalties

SEASON 1983–84

League Division Three

162	27/08/83	Bristol Rovers	Home	League	2–1	1 Goal	(62)
163	31/08/83	Torquay United	Home	Lge Cup	2–3	1 Goal	(63)
164	03/09/83	Wimbledon	Away	League	0–6		
165	06/09/83	Burnley	Away	League	0–2		
166	10/09/83	Bradford City	Home	League	4–3	1 Goal	(64)
167	14/09/83	Torquay United	Away	Lge Cup	0–1		
168	17/09/83	Walsall	Away	League	2–3		
169	24/09/83	Scunthorpe United	Home	League	1–1		
170	27/09/83	Preston North End	Home	League	1–1	1 Goal	(65)
171	01/10/83	Rotherham United	Away	League	1–0	1 Goal	(66)
172	08/10/83	Orient	Home	League	0–0		
173	15/10/83	Bolton Wanderers	Away	League	3–2		
174	18/10/83	Lincoln City	Home	League	1–0	1 Goal	(67)
175	22/10/83	Exeter City	Away	League	2–1	2 Goals	(69)
176	29/10/83	Port Vale	Home	League	2–1	1 Goal	(70)
177	01/11/83	Millwall	Away	League	1–1	1 Goal	(71)
178	05/11/83	Southend United	Home	League	1–1	1 Goal	(72)
179	12/11/83	Hull City	Away	League	0–0		
180	20/11/83	Poole Town	Away	FA Cup	0–0		
181	22/11/83	Poole Town	Home	FA Cup	3–0	1 Goal	(73)
182	03/12/83	Wigan Athletic	Home	League	5–3	3 Goals	(76)
183	10/12/83	Harrow Borough	Away	FA Cup	3–1	2 Goals	(78)
184	17/12/83	Sheffield United	Home	League	0–2		
185	26/12/83	AFC Bournemouth	Away	League	1–1		
186	27/12/83	Plymouth Argyle	Home	League	2–0	2 Goals	(80)
187	31/12/83	Brentford	Away	League	0–2		
188	07/01/84	Plymouth Argyle	Away	FA Cup	2–2	2 Goals	(82)
189	10/01/84	Plymouth Argyle	Home	FA Cup	0–1		
190	14/01/84	Bristol Rovers	Away	League	0–4		
191	17/01/84	Lex XI	Home	Welsh Cup	6–0	3 Goals	(85)
192	22/01/84	Walsall	Home	League	3–1	2 Goals	(87)
193	04/02/84	Rotherham United	Home	League	1–4	1 Goal	(88)
194	07/02/84	Wrexham	Home	Welsh Cup	0–1		

195	10/02/84	Scunthorpe United	Away	League	3–3		
196	14/02/84	Millwall	Home	League	1–1	1 Goal	(89)
197	25/02/84	Exeter City	Home	League	1–0	1 Goal	(90)
198	17/03/84	Orient	Away	League	2–2		

Oxford United – League Division Three

Sub+1	07/04/84	Walsall	Away	League	1–0		
1	20/04/84	Bolton Wanderers	Home	League	5–0	1 Goal	(1)
Sub+2	21/04/84	Bristol Rovers	Away	League	1–1	1 Goal	(2)
2	28/04/84	Newport County	Away	League	1–1	1 Goal	(3)
3	02/05/84	Wigan Athletic	Home	League	0–0		
4	05/05/84	Exeter City	Home	League	1–1		
5	07/05/84	Orient	Away	League	2–1	1 Goal	(4)
Sub+3	12/05/84	Rotherham United	Home	League	3–2		

SEASON 1984–85

League Division Two

6	25/08/84	Huddersfield Town	Away	League	3–0	1 Goal	(5)
7	29/08/84	Hereford United	Away	Lge Cup	2–2		
8	01/09/84	Portsmouth	Home	League	1–1		
9	05/09/84	Hereford United	Home	Lge Cup	5–3	2 Goals	(7)
10	08/09/84	Wimbledon	Away	League	3–1	1 Goal	(8)
11	15/09/84	Fulham	Home	League	3–2	2 Goals	(10)
12	19/09/84	Wolverhampton Wanderers	Home	League	3–1	2 Goals	(12)
13	22/09/84	Grimsby Town	Away	League	2–1		
14	25/09/84	Blackburn Rovers	Away	Lge Cup	1–1		
15	29/09/84	Carlisle United	Home	League	4–0	1 Goal	(13)
16	06/10/84	Manchester City	Away	League	0–1		
17	10/10/84	Blackburn Rovers	Home	Lge Cup	3–1		
18	13/10/84	Brighton & Hove Albion	Home	League	2–1	1 Goal	(14)
19	20/10/84	Sheffield United	Home	League	5–1	1 Goal	(15)
20	27/10/84	Birmingham City	Away	League	0–0		
21	31/10/84	Arsenal	Home	Lge Cup	3–2	1 Goal	(16)
22	03/11/84	Blackburn Rovers	Home	League	2–1		
23	10/11/84	Shrewsbury Town	Away	League	2–2	2 Goals	(18)
24	17/11/84	Oldham Athletic	Away	League	0–0		
25	20/11/84	Ipswich Town	Away	Lge Cup	1–2		
26	24/11/84	Leeds United	Home	League	5–2	3 Goals	(21)
27	01/12/84	Notts County	Away	League	0–2		
28	08/12/84	Charlton Athletic	Home	League	5–0	1 Goal	(22)
29	22/12/84	Portsmouth	Away	League	1–2		
30	26/12/84	Cardiff City	Home	League	4–0	2 Goals	(24)
31	29/12/84	Crystal Palace	Home	League	5–0	1 Goal	(25)
32	01/01/85	Middlesbrough	Away	League	1–0		
33	05/01/85	Shrewsbury Town	Away	FA Cup	2–0	1 Goal	(26)
34	30/01/85	Blackburn Rovers	Home	FA Cup	0–1		
35	02/02/85	Carlisle United	Away	League	1–0		
36	05/02/85	Crystal Palace	Away	League	0–1		
37	19/02/85	Fulham	Away	League	0–1		
38	23/02/85	Blackburn Rovers	Away	League	1–1		
39	02/03/85	Birmingham City	Home	League	0–3		
40	09/03/85	Sheffield United	Away	League	1–1		
41	13/03/85	Wimbledon	Home	League	4–0	2 Goals	(28)
42	16/03/85	Brighton & Hove Albion	Away	League	0–0		
43	23/03/85	Manchester City	Home	League	3–0	2 Goals	(30)
44	30/03/85	Grimsby Town	Home	League	1–0		
45	02/04/85	Barnsley	Away	League	0–3		
46	06/04/85	Cardiff City	Away	League	2–0	1 Goal	(31)
47	08/04/85	Middlesbrough	Home	League	1–0		
48	13/04/85	Wolverhampton Wanderers	Away	League	2–1		
49	17/04/85	Huddersfield Town	Home	League	3–0	1 Goal	(32)
50	20/04/85	Oldham Athletic	Home	League	5–2	3 Goals	(35)
51	24/04/85	Shrewsbury Town	Home	League	1–0		
52	27/04/85	Leeds United	Away	League	0–1		
53	04/05/85	Notts County	Home	League	1–1		
54	07/05/85	Charlton Athletic	Away	League	3–3	1 Goal	(36)
55	11/05/85	Barnsley	Home	League	4–0	2 Goals	(38)

SEASON 1985–86

League Division One

56	17/08/85	West Bromwich Albion	Away	League	1–1		
57	26/08/85	Birmingham City	Away	League	1–3	1 Goal	(39)
58	31/08/85	Sheffield Wednesday	Home	League	0–1		

59	03/09/85	Coventry City	Away	League	2–5		
60	07/09/85	Manchester United	Away	League	0–3		
61	14/09/85	Liverpool	Home	League	2–2	1 Goal	(40)
62	18/09/85	Shrewsbury Town	Home	FM Cup	3–0		
63	21/09/85	Newcastle United	Away	League	0–3		
64	25/09/85	Northampton Town	Home	Lge Cup	2–1		
65	28/09/85	Manchester City	Home	League	1–0		
66	02/10/85	Leicester City	Away	League	4–4	2 Goals	(42)
67	05/10/85	Everton	Away	League	0–2		
68	08/10/85	Northampton Town	Away	Lge Cup	2–0	2 Goals	(44)
69	12/10/85	Luton Town	Home	League	1–1		
70	19/10/85	Chelsea	Home	League	2–1	1 Goal	(45)
71	22/10/85	Fulham	Away	FM Cup	2–0		
72	02/11/85	Aston Villa	Away	League	0–2		
73	06/11/85	Stoke City	Away	FM Cup	1–0	1 Goal	(46)
74	09/11/85	West Ham United	Home	League	1–2	1 Goal	(47)
75	16/11/85	Arsenal	Away	League	1–2		
76	19/11/85	Norwich City	Home	Lge Cup	3–1	1 Goal	(48)
77	23/11/85	Ipswich Town	Home	League	4–3	3 Goals	(51)
78	01/12/85	Nottingham Forest	Away	League	1–1		
79	04/12/85	Chelsea	Home	FM Cup	1–4	1 Goal	(52)
80	07/12/85	Tottenham Hotspur	Away	League	1–5	1 Goal	(53)
81	14/12/85	West Bromwich Albion	Home	League	2–2	1 Goal	(54)
82	17/12/85	Chelsea	Away	FM Cup	1–0		
83	26/12/85	Southampton	Home	League	3–0	1 Goal	(55)
84	01/01/86	Queens Park Rangers	Away	League	1–3		
85	04/01/86	Tottenham Hotspur	Home	FA Cup	1–1		
86	08/01/86	Tottenham Hotspur	Away	FA Cup	1–2	1 Goal	(56)
87	11/01/86	Manchester United	Home	League	1–3		
88	18/01/86	Sheffield Wednesday	Away	League	1–2		
89	22/01/86	Portsmouth	Home	Lge Cup	3–1		
90	25/01/86	Coventry City	Home	League	0–1		
91	01/02/86	Birmingham City	Home	League	0–1		
92	08/02/86	Chelsea	Away	League	4–1	1 Goal	(57)
93	12/02/86	Aston Villa	Away	Lge Cup	2–2	2 Goals	(59)
94	01/03/86	Manchester City	Away	League	3–0	2 Goals	(61)
95	12/03/86	Aston Villa	Home	Lge Cup	2–1		
96	15/03/86	Luton Town	Away	League	2–1	1 Goal	(62)
97	19/03/86	Newcastle United	Home	League	1–2	1 Goal	(63)
98	22/03/86	Liverpool	Away	League	0–6		
99	29/03/86	Queens Park Rangers	Home	League	3–3	2 Goals	(65)
100	01/04/86	Southampton	Away	League	1–1	1 Goal	(66)
101	05/04/86	Aston Villa	Home	League	1–1		
102	09/04/86	Watford	Home	League	1–1	1 Goal	(67)
103	12/04/86	West Ham United	Away	League	1–3		
104	20/04/86	Queens Park Rangers	Wembley	Lge Cup	3–0		
105	26/04/86	Ipswich Town	Away	League	2–3	1 Goal	(68)
106	30/04/86	Everton	Home	League	1–0		
107	03/05/86	Nottingham Forest	Home	League	1–2		
108	05/05/86	Arsenal	Home	League	3–0	1 Goal	(69)

SEASON 1986–87

League Division One

109	23/08/86	Watford	Away	League	0–3		
110	25/08/86	Chelsea	Home	League	1–1		
111	30/08/86	West Ham United	Home	League	0–0		
112	02/09/86	Everton	Away	League	1–3		
113	06/09/86	Aston Villa	Away	League	2–1	1 Goal	(70)
114	13/09/86	Manchester City	Home	League	0–0		
115	20/09/86	Arsenal	Away	League	0–0		
116	24/09/86	Gillingham	Home	Lge Cup	6–0	4 Goals	(74)
117	27/09/86	Charlton Athletic	Home	League	3–2	2 Goals	(76)
118	04/10/86	Sheffield Wednesday	Away	League	1–6	1 Goal	(77)
119	07/10/86	Gillingham	Away	Lge Cup	1–1	1 Goal	(78)
120	11/10/86	Coventry City	Home	League	2–0	2 Goals	(80)
121	18/10/86	Liverpool	Away	League	0–4		
122	25/10/86	Nottingham Forest	Home	League	2–1	1 Goal	(81)
123	29/10/86	Sheffield United	Home	Lge Cup	3–1	1 Goal	(82)
124	01/11/86	Newcastle United	Away	League	0–0		
125	08/11/86	Manchester United	Home	League	2–0	1 Goal	(83)
126	15/11/86	Queens Park Rangers	Away	League	1–1		
127	18/11/86	West Ham United	Away	Lge Cup	0–1		
128	22/11/86	Tottenham Hotspur	Home	League	2–4		
129	29/11/86	Norwich City	Away	League	1–2	1 Goal	(84)

130	06/12/86	Luton Town	Home	League	4–2	3 Goals	(87)
131	14/12/86	Leicester City	Away	League	0–2		
132	20/12/86	Aston Villa	Home	League	2–2	1 Goal	(88)
133	26/12/86	Wimbledon	Away	League	1–1	1 Goal	(89)
134	27/12/86	Queens Park Rangers	Home	League	0–1		
135	01/01/87	Southampton	Home	League	3–1	1 Goal	(90)
136	03/01/87	Manchester City	Away	League	0–1		
137	10/01/87	Aldershot	Away	FA Cup	0–3		
138	24/01/87	Watford	Home	League	1–3		

Liverpool – League Division One

Sub+1	21/02/87	Aston Villa	Away	League	2–2		
1	28/02/87	Southampton	Home	League	1–0	1 Goal	(1)
Sub+2	10/03/87	Arsenal	Away	League	1–0		
Sub+3	18/03/87	Queens Park Rangers	Home	League	2–1		
Sub+4	22/03/87	Tottenham Hotspur	Away	League	0–1		
Sub+5	28/03/87	Wimbledon	Home	League	1–2		
Sub+6	18/04/87	Nottingham Forest	Home	League	3–0		
Sub+7	02/05/87	Coventry City	Away	League	0–1		
Sub+8	04/05/87	Watford	Home	League	1–0		
2	09/05/87	Chelsea	Away	League	3–3	1 Goal	(2)

SEASON 1987–88

League Division One

3	15/08/87	Arsenal	Away	League	2–1	1 Goal	(3)
4	29/08/87	Coventry City	Away	League	4–1	1 Goal	(4)
5	05/09/87	West Ham United	Away	League	1–1	1 Goal	(5)
6	12/09/87	Oxford United	Home	League	2–0	1 Goal	(6)
7	15/09/87	Charlton Athletic	Home	League	3–2	1 Goal	(7)
8	20/09/87	Newcastle United	Away	League	4–1	1 Goal	(8)
9	23/09/87	Blackburn Rovers	Away	Lge Cup	1–1		
10	29/09/87	Derby County	Home	League	4–0	3 Goals	(11)
11	03/10/87	Portsmouth	Home	League	4–0	1 Goal	(12)
12	06/10/87	Blackburn Rovers	Home	Lge Cup	1–0	1 Goal	(13)
13	17/10/87	Queens Park Rangers	Home	League	4–0	1 Goal	(14)
14	24/10/87	Luton Town	Away	League	1–0		
15	28/10/87	Everton	Away	Lge Cup	0–1		
16	01/11/87	Everton	Home	League	2–0		
17	04/11/87	Wimbledon	Away	League	1–1		
18	15/11/87	Manchester United	Away	League	1–1	1 Goal	(15)
19	21/11/87	Norwich City	Home	League	0–0		
20	24/11/87	Watford	Home	League	4–0	1 Goal	(16)
21	28/11/87	Tottenham Hotspur	Away	League	2–0		
22	06/12/87	Chelsea	Home	League	2–1	1 Goal	(17)
23	12/12/87	Southampton	Away	League	2–2		
24	19/12/87	Sheffield Wednesday	Home	League	1–0		
25	26/12/87	Oxford United	Away	League	3–0	1 Goal	(18)
26	28/12/87	Newcastle United	Home	League	4–0	2 Goals	(20)
27	01/01/88	Coventry City	Home	League	4–0	1 Goal	(21)
28	09/01/88	Stoke City	Away	FA Cup	0–0		
29	12/01/88	Stoke City	Home	FA Cup	1–0		
30	16/01/88	Arsenal	Home	League	2–0	1 Goal	(22)
31	23/01/88	Charlton Athletic	Away	League	2–0		
32	31/01/88	Aston Villa	Away	FA Cup	2–0		
33	06/02/88	West Ham United	Home	League	0–0		
34	13/02/88	Watford	Away	League	4–1	1 Goal	(23)
35	21/02/88	Everton	Away	FA Cup	1–0		
36	27/02/88	Portsmouth	Away	League	2–0		
37	26/03/88	Wimbledon	Home	League	2–1	1 Goal	(24)
38	02/04/88	Nottingham Forest	Away	League	1–2	1 Goal	(25)
39	04/04/88	Manchester United	Home	League	3–3		
40	09/04/88	Nottingham Forest	Neutral	FA Cup	2–1	2 Goals	(27)
41	13/04/88	Nottingham Forest	Home	League	5–0	2 Goals	(29)
42	20/04/88	Norwich City	Away	League	0–0		
43	23/04/88	Tottenham Hotspur	Home	League	1–0		
44	30/04/88	Chelsea	Away	League	1–1		
45	02/05/88	Southampton	Home	League	1–1	1 Goal	(30)
46	09/05/88	Luton Town	Home	League	1–1	1 Goal	(31)
47	14/05/88	Wimbledon	Wembley	FA Cup	0–1		

SEASON 1988–89

League Division One

48	20/08/88	Wimbledon	Wembley	FA C/S	2–0	2 Goals	(33)

49	27/08/88	Charlton Athletic	Away	League	3–0	3 Goals	(36)
50	03/09/88	Manchester United	Home	League	1–0		
51	10/09/88	Aston Villa	Away	League	1–1		
52	17/09/88	Tottenham Hotspur	Home	League	1–1		
53	24/09/88	Southampton	Away	League	3–1	1 Goal	(37)
54	28/09/88	Walsall	Home	Lge Cup	1–0		
55	01/10/88	Newcastle United	Home	League	1–2		
Sub+9	22/10/88	Coventry City	Home	League	0–0		
Sub+10	26/10/88	Nottingham Forest	Away	League	1–2		
56	29/10/88	West Ham United	Away	League	2–0		
57	02/11/88	Arsenal	Home	Lge Cup	1–1		
58	05/11/88	Middlesbrough	Home	League	3–0	1 Goal	(38)
59	09/11/88	Arsenal	Away	Lge Cup	0–0*		
60	12/11/88	Millwall	Home	League	1–1		
61	19/11/88	Queens Park Rangers	Away	League	1–0	1 Goal	(39)
Sub+11	23/11/88	Arsenal	Away	Lge Cup	2–1	1 Goal	(40)
Sub+12	26/11/88	Wimbledon	Home	League	1–1		
62	30/11/88	West Ham United	Away	Lge Cup	1–4	1 Goal	(41)
63	04/12/88	Arsenal	Away	League	1–1		
64	11/12/88	Everton	Home	League	1–1		
65	01/01/89	Manchester United	Away	League	1–3		
66	03/01/89	Aston Villa	Home	League	1–0		
67	07/01/89	Carlisle United	Away	FA Cup	3–0		
Sub+13	14/01/89	Sheffield Wednesday	Away	League	2–2	1 Goal	(42)
68	21/01/89	Southampton	Home	League	2–0	1 Goal	(43)
69	29/01/89	Millwall	Away	FA Cup	2–0	1 Goal	(44)
70	04/02/89	Newcastle United	Away	League	2–2	1 Goal	(45)
71	18/02/89	Hull City	Away	FA Cup	3–2	2 Goals	(47)
72	01/03/89	Charlton Athletic	Home	League	2–0	1 Goal	(48)
73	11/03/89	Middlesbrough	Away	League	4–0	1 Goal	(49)
74	14/03/89	Luton Town	Home	League	5–0	3 Goals	(52)
75	18/03/89	Brentford	Home	FA Cup	4–0		
76	22/03/89	Coventry City	Away	League	3–1	1 Goal	(53)
77	26/03/89	Tottenham Hotspur	Away	League	2–1	1 Goal	(54)
78	29/03/89	Derby County	Home	League	1–0		
79	01/04/89	Norwich City	Away	League	1–0		
80	08/04/89	Sheffield Wednesday	Home	League	5–1		
81	11/04/89	Millwall	Away	League	2–1	1 Goal	(55)
82	03/05/89	Everton	Away	League	0–0		
83	07/05/89	Nottingham Forest	Neutral	FA Cup	3–1	2 Goals	(57)
84	10/05/89	Nottingham Forest	Home	League	1–0	1 Goal	(58)
85	13/05/89	Wimbledon	Away	League	2–1	1 Goal	(59)
86	16/05/89	Queens Park Rangers	Home	League	2–0	1 Goal	(60)
87	20/05/89	Everton	Wembley	FA Cup	3–2*	1 Goal	(61)
88	23/05/89	West Ham United	Home	League	5–1	1 Goal	(62)
89	26/05/89	Arsenal	Home	League	0–2		

SEASON 1989–90

League Division One

Sub+14	26/08/89	Luton Town	Away	League	0–0		
Sub+15	12/09/89	Crystal Palace	Home	League	9–0	1 Goal	(63)

Real Sociedad – Spanish League Division One

1	24/09/89	CA Osasuna	Home	League	1–0		
2	01/10/89	Real Oviedo	Away	League	0–5		
3	04/10/89	Atletico Madrileno	Away	Sp Cup	2–2	2 Goals	(2)
4	08/10/89	CD Castellon	Home	League	2–0		
5	15/10/89	RCD Mallorca	Away	League	0–0		
6	21/10/89	FC Barcelona	Home	League	2–2	2 Goals	(4)
7	25/10/89	Atletico Madrileno	Home	Sp Cup	3–2	1 Goal	(5)
8	04/11/89	Real Madrid	Home	League	2–1	1 Goal	(6)
9	08/11/89	CE Sabadell FC	Away	Sp Cup	1–0		
10	12/11/89	CD Tenerife	Home	League	1–0		
11	19/11/89	RC Celta Vigo	Away	League	0–0		
12	26/11/89	CD Logrones	Home	League	1–0		
13	29/11/89	CE Sabadell FC	Home	Sp Cup	3–2	1 Goal	(7)
14	10/12/89	Sporting Gijon	Home	League	1–2		
15	17/12/89	Valencia CF	Away	League	1–3		
16	30/12/89	Cadiz CF	Home	League	2–0	1 Goal	(8)
17	07/01/90	CD Malaga	Away	League	2–0	1 Goal	(9)
18	10/01/90	FC Barcelona	Home	Sp Cup	0–1		
19	13/01/90	Sevilla FC	Home	League	2–1	1 Goal	(10)
20	21/01/90	Athletic Bilbao	Home	League	0–0		
21	24/01/90	FC Barcelona	Away	Sp Cup	3–3	2 Goals	(12)

22	04/02/90	CA Osasuna	Away	League	1–1	1 Goal	(13)
23	11/02/90	Real Oviedo	Home	League	1–1	1 Goal	(14)
24	14/02/90	CD Castellon	Away	League	2–0	1 Goal	(15)
25	18/02/90	RCD Mallorca	Home	League	2–0	1 Goal	(16)
26	24/02/90	FC Barcelona	Away	League	2–2	2 Goals	(18)
27	04/03/90	AD Rayo Vallecano	Home	League	4–1	2 Goals	(20)
28	11/03/90	Real Madrid	Away	League	0–3		
29	07/04/90	Atletico Madrid	Home	League	0–0		
30	15/04/90	Sporting Gijon	Away	League	0–0		
31	21/04/90	Valencia CF	Home	League	2–2	1 Goal	(21)
32	25/04/90	Cadiz CF	Away	League	0–1		
33	29/04/90	CD Malaga	Home	League	1–1		
34	06/05/90	Sevilla FC	Away	League	1–0	1 Goal	(22)

SEASON 1990–91

Spanish League Division One

35	02/09/90	Real Zaragoza	Home	League	1–0	1 Goal	(23)
36	09/09/90	Cadiz CF	Away	League	1–1		
37	16/09/90	Real Burgos	Away	League	0–2		
38	19/09/90	Lausanne Sports	Away	UEFA Cup	2–3		
39	23/09/90	CD Logrones	Home	League	2–0	2 Goals	(25)
40	29/09/90	Real Oviedo	Away	League	1–2		
41	03/10/90	Lausanne Sports	Home	UEFA Cup	1–0	1 Goal	(26)
42	07/10/90	Real Madrid	Home	League	1–1		
43	14/10/90	RCD Espanol	Away	League	0–1		
44	20/10/90	Valencia CF	Home	League	1–0	1 Goal	(27)
45	24/10/90	FK Partizan Beograd	Home	UEFA Cup	1–0		
46	28/10/90	Real Betis	Away	League	1–1		
47	04/11/90	Real Valladolid	Home	League	1–1		
48	07/11/90	FK Partizan Beograd	Away	UEFA Cup	0–1+		
49	18/11/90	CD Tenerife	Away	League	0–2		
50	25/11/90	Athletic Bilbao	Home	League	0–1		
51	02/12/90	CA Osasuna	Away	League	1–3	1 Goal	(28)
52	09/12/90	Sporting Gijon	Home	League	1–0		
53	16/12/90	Atletico Madrid	Away	League	0–4		
54	30/12/90	FC Barcelona	Home	League	1–1		
55	06/01/91	CD Castellon	Away	League	1–1	1 Goal	(29)
56	13/01/91	Sevilla FC	Home	League	1–1	1 Goal	(30)
57	19/01/91	RCD Mallorca	Away	League	1–2	1 Goal	(31)
58	27/01/91	Real Zaragoza	Away	League	1–1		
59	03/02/91	Cadiz CF	Home	League	0–0		
60	06/02/91	Sporting Gijon	Home	Sp Cup	1–1		
61	10/02/91	Real Burgos	Home	League	3–1	1 Goal	(32)
62	24/02/91	CD Logrones	Away	League	0–0		
63	27/02/91	Sporting Gijon	Away	Sp Cup	0–1		
64	03/03/91	Real Oviedo	Home	League	3–1	1 Goal	(33)
65	10/03/91	Real Madrid	Away	League	3–2	1 Goal	(34)
66	17/03/91	RCD Espanol	Home	League	0–0		
67	31/03/91	Real Betis	Home	League	1–0	1 Goal	(35)
68	14/04/91	CD Tenerife	Home	League	1–3	1 Goal	(36)
69	20/04/91	Athletic Bilbao	Away	League	1–2		
70	28/04/91	CA Osasuna	Home	League	1–1	1 Goal	(37)
71	12/05/91	Atletico Madrid	Home	League	2–1	1 Goal	(38)
72	18/05/91	FC Barcelona	Away	League	3–1	2 Goals	(40)
73	26/05/91	CD Castellon	Home	League	1–1		
74	02/06/91	Sevilla FC	Away	League	0–1		
75	09/06/91	RCD Mallorca	Home	League	0–0		

+ AET FK Partizan Beograd won 5–4 on penalties

SEASON 1991–92

Tranmere Rovers – League Division Two

1	17/08/91	Brighton & Hove Albion	Away	League	2–0	2 Goals	(2)
2	20/08/91	Halifax Town	Away	Lge Cup	4–3	3 Goals	(5)
3	23/08/91	Bristol Rovers	Home	League	2–2	1 Goal	(6)
4	27/08/91	Halifax Town	Home	Lge Cup	4–3	2 Goals	(8)
5	31/08/91	Grimsby Town	Away	League	2–2	1 Goal	(9)
6	03/09/91	Charlton Athletic	Home	League	2–2		
7	07/09/91	Newcastle United	Home	League	3–2		
8	14/09/91	Bristol City	Away	League	2–2		
9	17/09/91	Middlesbrough	Away	League	0–1		
10	21/09/91	Barnsley	Home	League	2–1	1 Goal	(10)
11	25/09/91	Chelsea	Away	Lge Cup	1–1	1 Goal	(11)

12	28/09/91	Blackburn Rovers	Away	League	0–0		
13	01/10/91	Newcastle United	Away	ZDS Cup	6–6+	3 Goals	(14)
14	04/10/91	Southend United	Home	League	1–1		
15	08/10/91	Chelsea	Home	Lge Cup	3–1	1 Goal	(15)
16	12/10/91	Oxford United	Away	League	0–1		
17	18/10/91	Cambridge United	Home	League	1–2	1 Goal	(16)
18	22/10/91	Grimsby Town	Home	ZDS Cup	5–1	3 Goals	(19)
19	26/10/91	Wolverhampton Wanderers	Away	League	1–1		
20	29/10/91	Leeds United	Away	Lge Cup	1–3	1 Goal	(20)
21	02/11/91	Derby County	Away	League	1–0	1 Goal	(21)
22	05/11/91	Millwall	Home	League	2–1	1 Goal	(22)
23	08/11/91	Plymouth Argyle	Home	League	1–0	1 Goal	(23)
24	16/11/91	Runcorn	Away	FA Cup	3–0#	2 Goals	(25)
25	22/11/91	Swindon Town	Home	League	0–0		
26	26/11/91	Middlesbrough	Away	ZDS Cup	1–0	1 Goal	(26)
27	30/11/91	Ipswich Town	Away	League	0–4		
28	07/12/91	York City	Away	FA Cup	1–1		
29	10/12/91	Nottingham Forest	Home	ZDS Cup	0–2		
30	13/12/91	Port Vale	Away	League	1–1		
31	17/12/91	York City	Home	FA Cup	2–1	1 Goal	(27)
32	26/12/91	Sunderland	Home	League	1–0		
33	28/12/91	Grimsby Town	Home	League	1–1	1 Goal	(28)
34	01/01/92	Watford	Away	League	0–0		
35	04/01/92	Oxford United	Away	FA Cup	1–3		
36	31/01/92	Cambridge United	Away	League	0–0		
37	08/02/92	Wolverhampton Wanderers	Home	League	4–3	1 Goal	(29)
38	11/02/92	Sunderland	Away	League	1–1	1 Goal	(30)
39	21/02/92	Ipswich Town	Home	League	0–1		
40	29/02/92	Portsmouth	Away	League	0–2		
41	06/03/92	Port Vale	Home	League	2–1	1 Goal	(31)
42	11/03/92	Millwall	Away	League	3–0	2 Goals	(33)
43	14/03/92	Derby County	Home	League	4–3	3 Goals	(36)
44	17/03/92	Swindon Town	Away	League	0–2		
45	21/03/92	Plymouth Argyle	Away	League	0–1		
46	27/03/92	Leicester City	Home	League	1–2		
47	31/03/92	Bristol City	Home	League	2–2		
48	04/04/92	Newcastle United	Away	League	3–2	2 Goals	(38)
49	07/04/92	Portsmouth	Home	League	2–0		
50	10/04/92	Middlesbrough	Home	League	1–2		
51	15/04/92	Leicester City	Away	League	0–1		
52	18/04/92	Barnsley	Away	League	1–1		
53	20/04/92	Blackburn Rovers	Home	League	2–2		
54	25/04/92	Southend United	Away	League	1–1		
55	28/04/92	Charlton Athletic	Away	League	1–0	1 Goal	(39)
56	02/05/92	Oxford United	Home	League	1–2	1 Goal	(40)

+ AET Tranmere Rovers won 3–2 on penalties
# Played at Tranmere Rovers

SEASON 1992–93

Football League Division One

57	15/08/92	Cambridge United	Home	League	2–0	1 Goal	(41)
58	19/08/92	Blackpool	Home	Lge Cup	3–0	2 Goals	(43)
59	22/08/92	Sunderland	Away	League	0–1		
60	25/08/92	Blackpool	Away	Lge Cup	0–4		
61	28/08/92	Bristol Rovers	Home	League	2–1		
62	01/09/92	Peterborough United	Away	AI Cup	0–0		
63	05/09/92	Luton Town	Away	League	3–3	1 Goal	(44)
64	12/09/92	Grimsby Town	Home	League	1–1		
65	15/09/92	Wolverhampton Wanderers	Home	AI Cup	2–1	2 Goals	(46)
66	18/09/92	Charlton Athletic	Home	League	0–0		
67	26/09/92	Oxford United	Away	League	2–1		
68	29/09/92	Notts County	Home	League	3–1	1 Goal	(47)
69	03/10/92	Bristol City	Home	League	3–0	2 Goals	(49)
70	10/10/92	Newcastle United	Away	League	0–1		
71	17/10/92	Birmingham City	Home	League	4–0	2 Goals	(51)
72	24/10/92	Watford	Away	League	2–3		
73	30/10/92	Peterborough United	Home	League	1–1		
74	03/11/92	Southend United	Home	League	3–0	1 Goal	(52)
75	07/11/92	Leicester City	Away	League	1–0		
76	11/11/92	AC Reggiana	Away	AI Cup	0–0		
77	14/11/92	Brentford	Home	League	3–2		
78	21/11/92	Portsmouth	Away	League	0–4		
79	24/11/92	US Cremonese	Home	AI Cup	1–2		

80	28/11/92	Derby County	Away	League	2–1	2 Goals	(54)
81	04/12/92	West Ham United	Home	League	5–2	3 Goals	(57)
82	16/12/92	Cosenza Calcio	Home	AI Cup	2–1		
83	19/12/92	Wolverhampton Wanderers	Home	League	3–0	3 Goals	(60)
84	26/12/92	Millwall	Home	League	1–1		
85	28/12/92	Barnsley	Away	League	1–3		
86	02/01/93	Oldham Athletic	Away	FA Cup	2–2	1 Goal	(61)
87	09/01/93	Charlton Athletic	Away	League	2–2	1 Goal	(62)
88	12/01/93	Oldham Athletic	Home	FA Cup	3–0		
89	15/01/93	Oxford United	Home	League	4–0	2 Goals	(64)
90	13/02/93	Luton Town	Home	League	0–2		
91	20/02/93	Bristol Rovers	Away	League	0–1		
Sub+1	24/04/93	Birmingham City	Away	League	0–0		
92	01/05/93	Watford	Home	League	2–1	2 Goals	(66)
93	04/05/93	Sunderland	Home	League	2–1		
94	08/05/93	Peterborough United	Away	League	1–1		
95	16/05/93	Swindon Town	Away	Lge P/O	1–3		
96	19/05/93	Swindon Town	Home	Lge P/O	3–2		

SEASON 1993–94

Football League Division One

97	14/08/93	Crystal Palace	Away	League	0–0		
98	21/08/93	Leicester City	Home	League	1–0		
99	24/08/93	Charlton Athletic	Away	League	1–3		
100	28/08/93	Grimsby Town	Away	League	0–0		
101	31/08/93	Sunderland	Away	AI Cup	0–2		
102	04/09/93	Notts County	Home	League	3–1	1 Goal	(67)
103	11/09/93	Stoke City	Away	League	2–1		
104	14/09/93	Luton Town	Home	League	4–1	1 Goal	(68)
105	18/09/93	Barnsley	Home	League	0–3		
106	21/09/93	Oxford United	Home	Lge Cup	5–1	2 Goals	(70)
107	25/09/93	Oxford United	Home	League	2–0		
108	26/10/93	Grimsby Town	Home	Lge Cup	4–1	2 Goals	(72)
109	13/11/93	Sunderland	Home	League	4–1	1 Goal	(73)
110	27/11/93	Birmingham City	Away	League	3–0	2 Goals	(75)
111	30/11/93	Oldham Athletic	Home	Lge Cup	3–0	1 Goal	(76)
112	03/12/93	Peterborough United	Home	League	2–1	1 Goal	(77)
113	11/12/93	Luton Town	Away	League	1–0	1 Goal	(78)
114	19/12/93	Crystal Palace	Home	League	0–1		
115	27/12/93	Wolverhampton Wanderers	Home	League	1–1		
116	16/01/94	Nottingham Forest	Home	League	1–2	1 Goal	(79)
117	23/01/94	Bolton Wanderers	Away	League	1–2		
118	26/01/94	Nottingham Forest	Away	Lge Cup	1–1		
119	29/01/94	Nottingham Forest	Home	Lge Cup	2–0		
120	05/02/94	Bristol City	Away	League	0–2		
121	11/02/94	Portsmouth	Home	League	3–1	1 Goal	(80)
122	16/02/94	Aston Villa	Home	Lge Cup	3–1	1 Goal	(81)
123	23/02/94	Leicester City	Away	League	1–1		
124	27/02/94	Aston Villa	Away	Lge Cup	1–3+	1 Goal	(82)
125	05/03/94	Grimsby Town	Home	League	1–2		
126	12/03/94	Barnsley	Away	League	0–1		
127	15/03/94	Stoke City	Home	League	2–0	2 Goals	(84)
128	19/03/94	Oxford United	Away	League	0–1		
129	25/03/94	Southend United	Home	League	1–1	1 Goal	(85)
130	29/03/94	Derby County	Home	League	4–0	2 Goals	(87)
131	02/04/94	Wolverhampton Wanderers	Away	League	1–2	1 Goal	(88)
132	04/04/94	Middlesbrough	Home	League	4–0	1 Goal	(89)
133	09/04/94	Watford	Away	League	2–1	1 Goal	(90)
134	16/04/94	West Bromwich Albion	Away	League	3–1		
135	23/04/94	Millwall	Home	League	3–2	2 Goals	(92)
136	26/04/94	Charlton Athletic	Home	League	2–0	1 Goal	(93)
137	30/04/94	Sunderland	Away	League	2–3	1 Goal	(94)
138	08/05/94	Birmingham City	Home	League	1–2		
139	15/05/94	Leicester City	Home	Lge P/O	0–0		
140	18/05/94	Leicester City	Away	Lge P/O	1–2		

+ AET Aston Villa won 5–4 on penalties

SEASON 1994–95

Football League Division One

141	13/08/94	Stoke City	Away	League	0–1		
142	20/08/94	Swindon Town	Home	League	3–2	2 Goals	(96)
143	24/08/94	AC Venezia	Home	AI Cup	2–2	1 Goal	(97)

144	27/08/94	Grimsby Town	Away	League	1–2	1 Goal	(98)
145	30/08/94	Luton Town	Home	League	4–2	3 Goals	(101)
146	03/09/94	Sheffield United	Home	League	2–1	1 Goal	(102)
147	10/09/94	Wolverhampton Wanderers	Away	League	0–2		
148	14/09/94	Portsmouth	Away	League	1–1		
149	17/09/94	Millwall	Home	League	3–1	1 Goal	(103)
150	20/09/94	Brentford	Home	Lge Cup	1–0		
151	24/09/94	Sunderland	Home	League	1–0		
152	27/09/94	Brentford	Away	Lge Cup	0–0		
153	01/10/94	Burnley	Away	League	1–1	1 Goal	(104)
154	04/10/94	Ascoli Calcio	Home	AI Cup	0–1		
155	08/10/94	Middlesbrough	Away	League	1–0	1 Goal	(105)
156	15/10/94	West Bromwich Albion	Home	League	3–1	3 Goals	(108)
157	22/10/94	Watford	Away	League	0–2		
158	26/10/94	Norwich City	Home	Lge Cup	1–1	1 Goal	(109)
159	29/10/94	Port Vale	Home	League	1–1		
160	01/11/94	Barnsley	Home	League	6–1	4 Goals	(113)
161	09/11/94	Norwich City	Away	Lge Cup	2–4		
162	03/12/94	Watford	Home	League	2–1		
163	06/12/94	Notts County	Away	League	0–1		
164	10/12/94	Swindon Town	Away	League	2–2		
165	17/12/94	Stoke City	Home	League	0–1		
Sub+2	29/01/95	Wimbledon	Home	FA Cup	0–2		
Sub+3	25/02/95	Burnley	Home	League	4–1	1 Goal	(114)
Sub+4	05/03/95	Sunderland	Away	League	1–0		
166	07/03/95	Sheffield United	Away	League	0–2		
167	11/03/95	Grimsby Town	Home	League	2–0	1 Goal	(115)
168	18/03/95	Luton Town	Away	League	0–2		
169	25/03/95	Millwall	Away	League	1–2		
170	01/04/95	Portsmouth	Home	League	4–2	2 Goals	(117)
171	08/04/95	Bristol City	Away	League	1–0	1 Goal	(118)
172	14/04/95	Bolton Wanderers	Home	League	1–0		
173	17/04/95	Derby County	Away	League	0–5		
174	21/04/95	Southend United	Home	League	0–2		
175	30/04/95	West Bromwich Albion	Away	League	1–5	1 Goal	(119)
176	03/05/95	Wolverhampton Wanderers	Home	League	1–1	1 Goal	(120)
177	07/05/95	Middlesbrough	Home	League	1–1		
178	14/05/95	Reading	Home	Lge P/O	1–3		
179	17/05/95	Reading	Away	Lge P/O	0–0		

SEASON 1995–96

Football League Division One

180	12/08/95	Wolverhampton Wanderers	Home	League	2–2	1 Goal	(121)
181	19/08/95	Sheffield United	Away	League	2–0	2 Goals	(123)
182	26/08/95	Huddersfield Town	Home	League	3–1	1 Goal	(124)
183	29/08/95	Barnsley	Away	League	1–2	1 Goal	(125)
184	09/09/95	Charlton Athletic	Home	League	0–0		
185	12/09/95	West Bromwich Albion	Home	League	2–2	1 Goal	(126)
186	16/09/95	Stoke City	Away	League	0–0		
187	19/09/95	Oldham Athletic	Home	Lge Cup	1–0	1 Goal	(127)
188	23/09/95	Portsmouth	Away	League	2–0		
189	30/09/95	Watford	Home	League	2–3	1 Goal	(128)
190	07/10/95	Luton Town	Home	League	1–0	1 Goal	(129)
191	14/10/95	Millwall	Away	League	2–2		
192	21/10/95	Southend United	Home	League	3–0		
193	24/10/95	Birmingham City	Away	Lge Cup	1–1		
194	29/10/95	Norwich City	Away	League	1–1		
195	04/11/95	Derby County	Home	League	5–1	2 Goals	(131)
196	08/11/95	Birmingham City	Home	Lge Cup	1–3*	1 Goal	(132)
197	19/11/95	Leicester City	Away	League	1–0		
198	22/11/95	Port Vale	Home	League	2–1	2 Goals	(134)
199	25/11/95	Grimsby Town	Home	League	0–1		
200	02/12/95	Luton Town	Away	League	2–3		
201	16/12/95	Watford	Away	League	0–3		
202	23/12/95	Birmingham City	Away	League	0–1		
203	26/12/95	Oldham Athletic	Home	League	2–0	2 Goals	(136)
204	01/01/96	Reading	Away	League	0–1		
205	06/01/96	Queens Park Rangers	Home	FA Cup	0–2		
206	13/01/96	Sheffield United	Home	League	1–1		
207	20/01/96	Wolverhampton Wanderers	Away	League	1–2	1 Goal	(137)
208	30/01/96	Sunderland	Away	League	0–0		
209	03/02/96	Huddersfield Town	Away	League	0–1		
210	10/02/96	Barnsley	Home	League	1–3	1 Goal	(138)
211	17/02/96	West Bromwich Albion	Away	League	1–1		

212	20/02/96	Crystal Palace	Home	League	2–3	1 Goal	(139)
213	24/02/96	Stoke City	Home	League	0–0		
214	03/03/96	Oldham Athletic	Away	League	2–1	1 Goal	(140)
215	09/03/96	Birmingham City	Home	League	2–2	1 Goal	(141)
216	12/03/96	Crystal Palace	Away	League	1–2		
217	16/03/96	Ipswich Town	Away	League	2–1	1 Goal	(142)
218	23/03/96	Reading	Home	League	2–1	1 Goal	(143)
219	30/03/96	Southend United	Away	League	0–2		
220	02/04/96	Millwall	Home	League	2–2	1 Goal	(144)
221	06/04/96	Norwich City	Home	League	1–1	1 Goal	(145)
222	08/04/96	Derby County	Away	League	2–6	1 Goal	(146)
223	13/04/96	Leicester City	Home	League	1–1		
224	17/04/96	Ipswich Town	Home	League	5–2	1 Goal	(147)
225	20/04/96	Port Vale	Away	League	1–1		
226	27/04/96	Grimsby Town	Away	League	1–1	1 Goal	(148)
227	30/04/96	Charlton Athletic	Away	League	0–0		
228	05/05/96	Sunderland	Home	League	2–0	1 Goal	(149)

SEASON 1996–97

Football League Division One

229	17/08/96	Southend United	Away	League	1–1		
230	21/08/96	Shrewsbury Town	Away	Lge Cup	2–0	1 Goal	(150)
231	23/08/96	Grimsby Town	Home	League	3–2	2 Goals	(152)
232	27/08/96	Port Vale	Home	League	2–0		
233	31/08/96	Bradford City	Away	League	0–1		
234	03/09/96	Shrewsbury Town	Home	Lge Cup	1–1		
235	07/09/96	Birmingham City	Home	League	1–0	1 Goal	(153)
236	10/09/96	Huddersfield Town	Away	League	1–0	1 Goal	(154)
237	14/09/96	Swindon Town	Away	League	1–2	1 Goal	(155)
238	17/09/96	Oldham Athletic	Away	Lge Cup	2–2	1 Goal	(156)
239	21/09/96	West Bromwich Albion	Home	League	2–3	1 Goal	(157)
240	24/09/96	Oldham Athletic	Home	Lge Cup	0–1		
241	28/09/96	Norwich City	Away	League	1–1	1 Goal	(158)
242	01/10/96	Oxford United	Home	League	0–0		
243	04/10/96	Portsmouth	Home	League	4–3		
244	12/10/96	Sheffield United	Away	League	0–0		
245	15/10/96	Bolton Wanderers	Away	League	0–1		
246	20/10/96	Queens Park Rangers	Home	League	2–3	1 Goal	(159)
Sub+5	26/10/96	Ipswich Town	Away	League	2–0		
Sub+6	29/10/96	Charlton Athletic	Home	League	4–0	1 Goal	(160)
Sub+7	02/11/96	Crystal Palace	Home	League	1–3		
247	15/11/96	Oldham Athletic	Home	League	1–1	1 Goal	(161)
248	23/11/96	Manchester City	Away	League	2–1		
249	30/11/96	Ipswich Town	Home	League	3–0	2 Goals	(163)
250	03/12/96	Reading	Away	League	0–2		
251	07/12/96	Stoke City	Away	League	0–2		
252	14/12/96	Barnsley	Away	League	0–3		
Sub+8	21/12/96	Wolverhampton Wanderers	Home	League	0–2		
253	26/12/96	Huddersfield Town	Home	League	1–1		
254	01/01/97	West Bromwich Albion	Away	League	2–1	2 Goals	(165)
255	10/01/97	Swindon Town	Home	League	2–1		
256	14/01/97	Carlisle United	Away	FA Cup	0–1		
257	18/01/97	Oxford United	Away	League	1–2	1 Goal	(166)
Sub+9	22/02/97	Crystal Palace	Away	League	1–0		
Sub+10	28/02/97	Stoke City	Home	League	0–0		
258	04/03/97	Oldham Athletic	Away	League	2–1		
259	08/03/97	Wolverhampton Wanderers	Away	League	2–3	1 Goal	(167)
260	15/03/97	Barnsley	Home	League	1–1		
Sub+11	18/03/97	Manchester City	Home	League	1–1		
261	22/03/97	Grimsby Town	Away	League	0–0		
262	28/03/97	Southend United	Home	League	3–0	1 Goal	(168)
Sub+12	31/03/97	Port Vale	Away	League	1–2		
263	04/04/97	Bradford City	Home	League	3–0		
Sub+13	12/04/97	Portsmouth	Away	League	3–1		
Sub+14	15/04/97	Birmingham City	Away	League	0–0		
Sub+15	19/04/97	Sheffield United	Home	League	1–1		
264	26/04/97	Queens Park Rangers	Away	League	0–2		
265	04/05/97	Bolton Wanderers	Home	League	2–2	1 Goal	(169)

INTERNATIONAL APPEARANCES – REPUBLIC OF IRELAND

1	26/03/86	Wales	Lansdowne Road	0–1	F
2	23/04/86	Uruguay	Lansdowne Road	1–1	F
3	25/05/86	Iceland	Reykjavik	2–1	F

4	27/05/86	Czechoslovakia	Reykjavik	1–0	F		
5	10/09/86	Belgium	Brussels	2–2	ECQ		
6	15/10/86	Scotland	Lansdowne Road	0–0	ECQ		
7	12/11/86	Poland	Warsaw	0–1	F		
8	18/02/87	Scotland	Hampden Park	1–0	ECQ		
9	01/04/87	Bulgaria	Sofia	1–2	ECQ		
10	29/04/87	Belgium	Lansdowne Road	0–0	ECQ		
11	23/05/87	Brazil	Lansdowne Road	1–0	F		
12	28/05/87	Luxembourg	Luxembourg	2–0	ECQ		
13	14/10/87	Bulgaria	Lansdowne Road	2–0	ECQ		
14	22/05/88	Poland	Lansdowne Road	3–0	F		
15	01/06/88	Norway	Oslo	0–0	F		
16	12/06/88	England	Stuttgart	1–0	EC		
17	15/06/88	USSR	Hanover	1–1	EC		
18	18/06/88	Holland	Gelsenkirchen	0–1	EC		
19	14/09/88	Northern Ireland	Windsor Park	0–0	WCQ		
20	19/10/88	Tunisia	Lansdowne Road	4–0	F	1 Goal	(1)
21	16/11/88	Spain	Seville	0–2	WCQ		
Sub 22	07/02/89	France	Dalymount Park	0–0	F		
23	08/03/89	Hungary	Budapest	0–0	WCQ		
Sub 24	28/05/89	Malta	Lansdowne Road	2–0	WCQ		
25	04/06/89	Hungary	Lansdowne Road	2–0	WCQ		
26	06/09/89	West Germany	Lansdowne Road	1–1	F		
27	11/10/89	Northern Ireland	Lansdowne Road	3–0	WCQ		
28	15/11/89	Malta	Valletta	2–0	WCQ	2 Goals	(3)
Sub 29	16/05/90	Finland	Lansdowne Road	1–1	F		
30	27/05/90	Turkey	Izmir	0–0	F		
31	11/06/90	England	Cagliari	1–1	WC		
32	17/06/90	Egypt	Palermo	0–0	WC		
33	21/06/90	Holland	Palermo	1–1	WC		
34	25/06/90	Romania	Genoa	0–0+	WC		
35	30/06/90	Italy	Rome	0–1	WC		
36	17/10/90	Turkey	Lansdowne Road	5–0	ECQ	3 Goals	(6)
37	14/11/90	England	Lansdowne Road	1–1	ECQ		
38	27/03/91	England	Wembley	1–1	ECQ		
39	01/05/91	Poland	Lansdowne Road	0–0	ECQ		
Sub 40	11/09/91	Hungary	Gyor	2–1	F		
41	13/11/91	Turkey	Istanbul	3–1	ECQ		
Sub 42	19/02/92	Wales	RS Showground	0–1	F		
Sub 43	25/03/92	Switzerland	Lansdowne Road	2–1	F	1 Goal	(7)
Sub 44	29/04/92	USA	Lansdowne Road	4–1	F		
45	26/05/92	Albania	Lansdowne Road	2–0	WCQ	1 Goal	(8)
46	04/06/92	Italy	Boston	0–2	USC		
Sub 47	07/06/92	Portugal	Boston	2–0	USC		
48	09/09/92	Latvia	Lansdowne Road	4–0	WCQ	3 Goals	(11)
49	14/10/92	Denmark	Copenhagen	0–0	WCQ		
50	18/11/92	Spain	Seville	0–0	WCQ		
51	28/04/93	Denmark	Lansdowne Road	1–1	WCQ		
52	26/05/93	Albania	Tirana	2–1	WCQ		
53	09/06/93	Latvia	Riga	2–0	WCQ	1 Goal	(12)
54	16/06/93	Lithuania	Vilnius	1–0	WCQ		
55	08/09/93	Lithuania	Lansdowne Road	2–0	WCQ	1 Goal	(13)
56	17/11/93	Northern Ireland	Windsor Park	1–1	WCQ		
57	05/06/94	Czech Republic	Lansdowne Road	1–3	F		
Sub 58	18/06/94	Italy	New York	1–0	WC		
Sub 59	24/06/94	Mexico	Florida	1–2	WC	1 Goal	(14)
60	28/06/94	Norway	New York	0–0	WC		
61	07/09/94	Latvia	Riga	3–0	ECQ	2 Goals	(16)
62	16/11/94	Northern Ireland	Windsor Park	4–0	ECQ	1 Goal	(17)
63	26/04/95	Portugal	Lansdowne Road	1–0	ECQ		
64	03/06/95	Liechtenstein	Eschen	0–0	ECQ		
65	11/10/95	Latvia	Lansdowne Road	2–1	ECQ		
66	15/11/95	Portugal	Lisbon	0–3	ECQ	2 Goals	(19)
67	13/12/95	Holland	Anfield	0–2	ECQ		
68	27/03/96	Russia	Lansdowne Road	0–2	F		
Sub 69	09/10/96	Macedonia	Lansdowne Road	3–0	WCQ		

+ AET Republic of Ireland won 5–4 on penalties

APPEARANCES AND GOALS PER SEASON

SEASON 79–80	GAMES	GOALS
League	35+3	14
FA Cup	1	0
Welsh Cup	5	2
TOTAL	**41+3**	**16**

SEASON 80–81	GAMES	GOALS
League	23+4	7
FA Cup	0+1	0
League Cup	4	2
European Cup Winners Cup	4	2
Welsh Cup	1+1	1
TOTAL	**32+6**	**12**

SEASON 81–82	GAMES	GOALS
League	32+4	11
FA Cup	1	0
League Cup	2	1
TOTAL	**35+4**	**12**

SEASON 82–83	GAMES	GOALS
League	41	17
FA Cup	5	2
League Cup	3	1
Football League Trophy	2+2	0
Welsh Cup	2	1
TOTAL	**53+2**	**21**

SEASON 83–84	GAMES	GOALS
League	33+3	24
FA Cup	5	5
League Cup	2	1
Welsh Cup	2	3
TOTAL	**42+3**	**33**

SEASON 84–85	GAMES	GOALS
League	42	30
FA Cup	2	1
League Cup	6	3
TOTAL	**50**	**34**

SEASON 85–86	GAMES	GOALS
League	39	23
FA Cup	2	1
League Cup	7	5
Full Members Cup	5	2
TOTAL	**53**	**31**

SEASON 86–87	GAMES	GOALS
League	27+8	17
FA Cup	1	0
League Cup	4	6
TOTAL	**32+8**	**23**

SEASON 87–88	GAMES	GOALS
League	36	26
FA Cup	6	2
League Cup	3	1
TOTAL	**45**	**29**

SEASON 88–89	GAMES	GOALS
League	31+4	21
FA Cup	6	6
League Cup	4+1	2
FA Charity Shield	1	2
TOTAL	**42+5**	**31**

SEASON 89–90	GAMES	GOALS
League	0+2	1
Spanish League	28	16
Spanish Cup	6	6
TOTAL	**34+2**	**23**

SEASON 90–91	GAMES	GOALS
Spanish League	35	17
Spanish Cup	2	0
UEFA Cup	4	1
TOTAL	**41**	**18**

SEASON 91–92	GAMES	GOALS
League	43	22
FA Cup	4	3
League Cup	5	8
Zenith Data Systems Cup	4	7
TOTAL	**56**	**40**

SEASON 92–93	GAMES	GOALS
League	29+1	21
League Play–offs	2	0
FA Cup	2	1
League Cup	2	2
Anglo–Italian Cup	5	2
TOTAL	**40+1**	**26**

SEASON 93–94	GAMES	GOALS
League	34	21
League Play–offs	2	0
League Cup	7	7
Anglo–Italian Cup	1	0
TOTAL	**44**	**28**

SEASON 94–95	GAMES	GOALS
League	31+2	24
League Play–offs	2	0
FA Cup	0+1	0
League Cup	4	1
Anglo–Italian Cup	2	1
TOTAL	**39+3**	**26**

SEASON 95–96	GAMES	GOALS
League	45	27
FA Cup	1	0
League Cup	3	2
TOTAL	**49**	**29**

SEASON 96–97	GAMES	GOALS
League	32+11	18
FA Cup	1	0
League Cup	4	2
TOTAL	**37+11**	**20**

CAREER APPEARANCES AND GOALS

COMPETITION	GAMES	TOTAL	GOALS
League	553+42	595	324
League Play–offs	6	6	0
FA Cup	37+2	39	21
League Cup	60+1	61	44
Football League Trophy	2+2	4	0
Full Members Cup	5	5	2
Zenith Data Systems Cup	4	4	7
Anglo–Italian Cup	8	8	3
Welsh Cup	10+1	11	7
FA Charity Shield	1	1	2
European Cup Winners Cup	4	4	2
UEFA Cup	4	4	1
Spanish League	63	63	33
Spanish Cup	8	8	6
Internationals	58+11	69	19
TOTAL	**823+59**	**882**	**471**

HAT-TRICKS

Newport County

1	3	Stockport County	17/11/79	Away	League	5–0
2	3	AFC Bournemouth	13/11/82	Home	League	5–1
3	3	Wigan Athletic	03/12/83	Home	League	5–3
4	3	Lex XI	17/01/84	Home	Welsh Cup	6–0

Oxford United

1	3	Leeds United	24/11/84	Home	League	5–2
2	3	Oldham Athletic	20/04/85	Home	League	5–2

3	3	Ipswich Town	23/11/85	Home	League	4–3
4	4	Gillingham	24/09/86	Home	Lge Cup	6–0
5	3	Luton Town	06/12/86	Home	League	4–2

Liverpool

1	3	Derby County	29/09/87	Home	League	4–0
2	3	Charlton Athletic	27/08/88	Away	League	3–0
3	3	Luton Town	14/03/89	Home	League	5–0

Tranmere Rovers

1	3	Halifax Town	20/08/91	Away	Lge Cup	4–3
2	3	Newcastle United	01/10/91	Away	ZDS Cup	6–6
3	3	Grimsby Town	22/10/91	Home	ZDS Cup	5–1
4	3	Derby County	14/03/92	Home	League	4–3
5	3	West Ham United	04/12/92	Home	League	5–2
6	3	Wolverhampton Wanderers	19/12/92	Home	League	3–0
7	3	Luton Town	30/08/94	Home	League	4–2
8	3	West Bromwich Albion	15/10/94	Home	League	3–1
9	4	Barnsley	01/11/94	Home	League	6–1

Republic of Ireland

1	3	Turkey	17/10/90	Lansdowne Road	ECQ	5–0
2	3	Latvia	09/09/92	Lansdowne Road	WCQ	4–0

League: 16
League Cup: 2
Zenith Data Systems Cup: 2
Welsh Cup: 1
International: 2
TOTAL: 23

HONOURS

Winners medals
League Division One Championship: 87/88
League Division Two Championship: 84/85
FA Cup: 88/89
League Cup: 85/86
FA Charity Shield: 88/89
Welsh Cup: 79/80

Runner-up medals
League Division One Championship: 86/87, 88/89
FA Cup: 87/88
Promoted to League Division Three: 79/80
Promoted to League Division Two: 83/84*

* Played eight (5+3/4) League matches in the Oxford United team that won the
League Division Three Championship.
Played two (0+2/1) League matches in the Liverpool team that won the 1989/90
League Division One Championship.

CLIVE ALLEN

Born: 20/05/61 – London
Height: 5.10
Weight: 12.03 (95–96)

Clubs
Queens Park Rangers: **1978–80** – Matches: **49+6** – Goals: **34**
Arsenal: **1980** – No Competitive Matches
Crystal Palace: **1980–81** – Matches: **29** – Goals: **11**
Queens Park Rangers: **1981–84** – Matches: **98+4** – Goals: **49**
Tottenham Hotspur: **1984–88** – Matches: **129+11** – Goals: **85**
Girondins de Bordeaux: **1988–89** – Matches: **23**– Goals: **14**
Manchester City: **1989–91** – Matches: **42+26** – Goals: **21**
Chelsea: **1991–92** – Matches: **22+2** – Goals: **9**
West Ham United: **1992–94** – Matches: **46+4** – Goals: **21**

Millwall: **1994–95** – Matches: **12+1** – Goals: **0**
Carlisle United: **1995** – Matches: **3** – Goals: **0**

Country
England: **1984–88** – Matches: **4+1** – Goals: **0**

SEASON 1978–79

Queens Park Rangers – League Division One

Sub+1	04/11/78	Chelsea	Home	League	0–0		
Sub+2	30/12/78	Leeds United	Home	League	1–4		
Sub+3	24/02/79	Southampton	Home	League	0–1		
Sub+4	20/03/79	Aston Villa	Away	League	1–3	1 Goal	(1)
Sub+5	03/04/79	Bristol City	Away	League	0–2		
Sub+6	13/04/79	Norwich City	Home	League	0–0		
1	28/04/79	Coventry City	Home	League	5–1	3 Goals	(4)
2	04/05/79	Leeds United	Away	League	3–4		
3	07/05/79	Birmingham City	Home	League	1–3		
4	11/05/79	Ipswich Town	Home	League	0–4		

SEASON 1979–80

League Division Two

5	18/08/79	Bristol Rovers	Home	League	2–0	1 Goal	(5)
6	22/08/79	Cardiff City	Away	League	0–1		
7	25/08/79	Leicester City	Home	League	1–4	1 Goal	(6)
8	28/08/79	Bradford City	Home	Lge Cup	2–1		
9	01/09/79	Notts County	Away	League	0–1		
10	05/09/79	Bradford City	Away	Lge Cup	2–0		
11	08/09/79	Fulham	Home	League	3–0	1 Goal	(7)
12	15/09/79	Swansea City	Away	League	2–1		
13	22/09/79	West Ham United	Home	League	3–0	2 Goals	(9)
14	25/09/79	Mansfield Town	Away	Lge Cup	3–0	1 Goal	(10)
15	29/09/79	Oldham Athletic	Away	League	0–0		
16	06/10/79	Watford	Away	League	2–1	1 Goal	(11)
17	09/10/79	Cardiff City	Home	League	3–0	2 Goals	(13)
18	13/10/79	Preston North End	Home	League	1–1		
19	20/10/79	Sunderland	Away	League	0–3		
20	27/10/79	Burnley	Home	League	7–0	2 Goals	(15)
21	30/10/79	Wolverhampton Wanderers	Home	Lge Cup	1–1	1 Goal	(16)
22	03/11/79	Bristol Rovers	Away	League	3–1	1 Goal	(17)
23	06/11/79	Wolverhampton Wanderers	Away	Lge Cup	0–1		
24	10/11/79	Luton Town	Away	League	1–1	1 Goal	(18)
25	17/11/79	Shrewsbury Town	Home	League	2–1		
26	24/11/79	Charlton Athletic	Home	League	4–0	2 Goals	(20)
27	01/12/79	Cambridge United	Away	League	1–2		
28	08/12/79	Wrexham	Home	League	2–2		
29	15/12/79	Newcastle United	Away	League	2–4		
30	18/12/79	Chelsea	Home	League	2–2	2 Goals	(22)
31	29/12/79	Leicester City	Away	League	0–2		
32	01/01/80	Birmingham City	Away	League	1–2	1 Goal	(23)
33	05/01/80	Watford	Home	FA Cup	1–2		
34	12/01/80	Notts County	Home	League	1–3	1 Goal	(24)
35	19/01/80	Fulham	Away	League	2–0		
36	02/02/80	Swansea City	Home	League	3–2	1 Goal	(25)
37	09/02/80	West Ham United	Away	League	1–2		
38	12/02/80	Orient	Home	League	0–0		
39	16/02/80	Oldham Athletic	Home	League	4–3	2 Goals	(27)
40	23/02/80	Preston North End	Away	League	3–0	1 Goal	(28)
41	01/03/80	Sunderland	Home	League	0–0		
42	08/03/80	Burnley	Away	League	3–0	1 Goal	(29)
43	14/03/80	Watford	Home	League	1–1		
44	22/03/80	Luton Town	Home	League	2–2		
45	05/04/80	Birmingham City	Home	League	1–1		
46	08/04/80	Orient	Away	League	1–1	1 Goal	(30)
47	12/04/80	Cambridge United	Home	League	2–2	1 Goal	(31)
48	19/04/80	Charlton Athletic	Away	League	2–2	2 Goals	(33)
49	03/05/80	Wrexham	Away	League	3–0	1 Goal	(34)

SEASON 1980–81

Arsenal – League Division One
No Competitive Matches

Crystal Palace – League Division One

1	16/08/80	Liverpool	Away	League	0–3		
2	19/08/80	Tottenham Hotspur	Home	League	3–4		
3	23/08/80	Middlesbrough	Home	League	5–2	3 Goals	(3)
4	26/08/80	Bolton Wanderers	Away	Lge Cup	3–0		
5	30/08/80	Wolverhampton Wanderers	Away	League	0–2		
6	02/09/80	Bolton Wanderers	Home	Lge Cup	2–1	1 Goal	(4)
7	06/09/80	Coventry City	Away	League	1–3	1 Goal	(5)
8	13/09/80	Ipswich Town	Home	League	1–2		
9	20/09/80	Everton	Away	League	0–5		
10	24/09/80	Tottenham Hotspur	Away	Lge Cup	0–0		
11	27/09/80	Aston Villa	Home	League	0–1		
12	30/09/80	Tottenham Hotspur	Home	Lge Cup	1–3	1 Goal	(6)
13	04/10/80	West Bromwich Albion	Home	League	0–1		
14	11/10/80	Sunderland	Away	League	0–1		
15	18/10/80	Leicester City	Home	League	2–1	1 Goal	(7)
16	21/10/80	Southampton	Home	League	3–2		
17	25/10/80	Leeds United	Away	League	0–1		
18	06/12/80	Nottingham Forest	Away	League	0–3		
19	13/12/80	Norwich City	Home	League	4–1	2 Goals	(9)
20	20/12/80	Southampton	Away	League	2–4	1 Goal	(10)
21	26/12/80	Arsenal	Home	League	2–2		
22	27/12/80	Brighton & Hove Albion	Away	League	2–3		
23	17/01/81	Wolverhampton Wanderers	Home	League	0–0		
24	31/01/81	Middlesbrough	Away	League	0–2		
25	07/02/81	Ipswich Town	Away	League	2–3		
26	17/02/81	Coventry City	Home	League	0–3		
27	21/02/81	Aston Villa	Away	League	1–2		
28	28/02/81	Everton	Home	League	2–3	1 Goal	(11)
29	20/04/81	Arsenal	Away	League	2–3		

SEASON 1981–82

Queens Park Rangers – League Division Two

1	29/08/81	Wrexham	Away	League	3–1	2 Goals	(2)
2	01/09/81	Luton Town	Home	League	1–2		
3	05/09/81	Newcastle United	Home	League	3–0		
4	12/09/81	Grimsby Town	Away	League	1–2		
5	19/09/81	Crystal Palace	Home	League	1–0		
6	22/09/81	Oldham Athletic	Away	League	0–2		
7	26/09/81	Derby County	Away	League	1–3		
8	03/10/81	Blackburn Rovers	Home	League	2–0	1 Goal	(3)
9	06/10/81	Portsmouth	Home	Lge Cup	5–0		
10	10/10/81	Norwich City	Home	League	2–0		
11	18/10/81	Orient	Away	League	1–1		
12	24/10/81	Leicester City	Home	League	2–0		
13	31/10/81	Charlton Athletic	Away	League	2–1	1 Goal	(4)
14	10/11/81	Bristol City	Home	Lge Cup	3–0	1 Goal	(5)
15	14/11/81	Sheffield Wednesday	Away	League	3–1		
16	21/11/81	Shrewsbury Town	Away	League	1–2		
17	24/11/81	Oldham Athletic	Home	League	0–0		
Sub+1	26/12/81	Chelsea	Home	League	0–2		
18	16/01/82	Wrexham	Home	League	1–1		
19	18/01/82	Middlesbrough	Away	FA Cup	3–2*		
20	23/01/82	Blackpool	Away	FA Cup	0–0		
21	26/01/82	Blackpool	Home	FA Cup	5–1	4 Goals	(9)
22	30/01/82	Crystal Palace	Away	League	0–0		
23	06/02/82	Grimsby Town	Home	League	1–0		
24	09/02/82	Cambridge United	Away	League	0–1		
25	13/02/82	Grimsby Town	Home	FA Cup	3–1	1 Goal	(10)
26	16/02/82	Blackburn Rovers	Away	League	1–2	1 Goal	(11)
27	20/02/82	Derby County	Home	League	3–0		
28	27/02/82	Norwich City	Away	League	1–0		
29	06/03/82	Leicester City	Home	FA Cup	1–0	1 Goal	(12)
30	13/03/82	Leicester City	Away	League	2–3		
31	20/03/82	Charlton Athletic	Home	League	4–0	3 Goals	(15)
32	27/03/82	Rotherham United	Away	League	0–1		
33	29/03/82	Sheffield Wednesday	Home	League	2–0		
34	03/04/82	West Bromwich Albion	Neutral	FA Cup	1–0	1 Goal	(16)
35	06/04/82	Orient	Home	League	3–0		
36	10/04/82	Chelsea	Away	League	1–2		
37	12/04/82	Watford	Home	League	0–0		
38	17/04/82	Shrewsbury Town	Home	League	2–1	1 Goal	(17)
39	24/04/82	Cardiff City	Away	League	2–1	1 Goal	(18)
40	01/05/82	Bolton Wanderers	Home	League	7–1	1 Goal	(19)

41	05/05/82	Newcastle United	Away	League	4–0	1 Goal	(20)
42	08/05/82	Barnsley	Away	League	0–3		
43	11/05/82	Luton Town	Away	League	2–3		
44	15/05/82	Cambridge United	Home	League	2–1	1 Goal	(21)
45	22/05/82	Tottenham Hotspur	Wembley	FA Cup	1–1*		

SEASON 1982–83

League Division Two

46	02/10/82	Burnley	Home	League	3–2	1 Goal	(22)
47	05/10/82	Rotherham United	Away	Lge Cup	1–2		
48	09/10/82	Barnsley	Away	League	1–0	1 Goal	(23)
49	16/10/82	Shrewsbury Town	Home	League	4–0	1 Goal	(24)
50	23/10/82	Middlesbrough	Away	League	1–2	1 Goal	(25)
51	26/10/82	Rotherham United	Home	Lge Cup	0–0		
52	30/10/82	Bolton Wanderers	Home	League	1–0		
53	06/11/82	Rotherham United	Away	League	0–0		
54	13/11/82	Blackburn Rovers	Home	League	2–2	1 Goal	(26)
55	20/11/82	Cambridge United	Away	League	4–1	2 Goals	(28)
56	27/11/82	Carlisle United	Home	League	1–0		
57	04/12/82	Leeds United	Away	League	1–0	1 Goal	(29)
58	11/12/82	Grimsby Town	Home	League	4–0		
59	18/12/82	Wolverhampton Wanderers	Away	League	0–4		
60	27/12/82	Chelsea	Home	League	1–2		
61	29/12/82	Charlton Athletic	Away	League	3–1		
62	03/01/83	Derby County	Away	League	0–2		
63	08/01/83	West Bromwich Albion	Away	FA Cup	2–3		
64	15/01/83	Newcastle United	Home	League	2–0		
65	22/01/83	Crystal Palace	Away	League	3–0	2 Goals	(31)
66	05/02/83	Oldham Athletic	Home	League	1–0		
67	19/02/83	Barnsley	Home	League	3–0		
68	26/02/83	Shrewsbury Town	Away	League	0–0		
69	05/03/83	Middlesbrough	Home	League	6–1	3 Goals	(34)
70	12/03/83	Bolton Wanderers	Away	League	2–3		
Sub+2	22/03/83	Charlton Athletic	Home	League	5–1		
Sub+3	04/04/83	Chelsea	Away	League	2–0		
71	10/05/83	Burnley	Away	League	1–2		

SEASON 1983–84

League Division One

72	27/08/83	Manchester United	Away	League	1–3	1 Goal	(35)
73	29/08/83	Southampton	Away	League	0–0		
74	03/09/83	Aston Villa	Home	League	2–1		
75	06/09/83	Watford	Home	League	1–1		
76	17/09/83	Sunderland	Home	League	3–0	1 Goal	(36)
77	24/09/83	Wolverhampton Wanderers	Away	League	4–0	2 Goals	(38)
78	01/10/83	Arsenal	Home	League	2–0		
79	04/10/83	Crewe Alexandra	Home	Lge Cup	8–1	1 Goal	(39)
80	15/10/83	Ipswich Town	Away	League	2–0		
81	22/10/83	Liverpool	Home	League	0–1		
82	25/10/83	Crewe Alexandra	Away	Lge Cup	0–3		
83	29/10/83	Norwich City	Away	League	3–0		
84	05/11/83	Luton Town	Home	League	0–1		
85	09/11/83	Ipswich Town	Away	Lge Cup	2–3		
Sub+4	03/03/84	Luton Town	Away	League	0–0		
86	07/03/84	Sunderland	Away	League	0–1		
87	10/03/84	Coventry City	Home	League	2–1	1 Goal	(40)
88	17/03/84	Watford	Away	League	0–1		
89	24/03/84	Southampton	Home	League	4–0	1 Goal	(41)
90	31/03/84	West Ham United	Away	League	2–2	2 Goals	(43)
91	07/04/84	Ipswich Town	Home	League	1–0	1 Goal	(44)
92	14/04/84	Birmingham City	Away	League	2–0		
93	21/04/84	Leicester City	Home	League	2–0		
94	23/04/84	Stoke City	Away	League	2–1	1 Goal	(45)
95	28/04/84	Tottenham Hotspur	Home	League	2–1	1 Goal	(46)
96	05/05/84	Notts County	Away	League	3–0	3 Goals	(49)
97	07/05/84	West Bromwich Albion	Home	League	1–1		
98	12/05/84	Everton	Away	League	1–3		

SEASON 1984–85

Tottenham Hotspur – League Division One

| 1 | 25/08/84 | Everton | Away | League | 4–1 | 2 Goals | (2) |
| 2 | 27/08/84 | Leicester City | Home | League | 2–2 | | |

3	01/09/84	Norwich City	Home	League	3–1		
4	04/09/84	Sunderland	Away	League	0–1		
5	08/09/84	Sheffield Wednesday	Away	League	1–2		
6	15/09/84	Queens Park Rangers	Home	League	5–0	2 Goals	(4)
7	19/09/84	Sporting Clube de Braga	Away	UEFA Cup	3–0		
Sub+1	24/10/84	Club Brugge KV	Away	UEFA Cup	1–2	1 Goal	(5)
8	27/10/84	Stoke City	Home	League	4–0	2 Goals	(7)
9	31/10/84	Liverpool	Home	Lge Cup	1–0	1 Goal	(8)
10	03/11/84	West Bromwich Albion	Home	League	2–3		
11	07/11/84	Club Brugge KV	Home	UEFA Cup	3–0	1 Goal	(9)
12	10/11/84	Nottingham Forest	Away	League	2–1		
13	17/11/84	Ipswich Town	Away	League	3–0	1 Goal	(10)
14	21/11/84	Sunderland	Away	Lge Cup	0–0		
15	24/11/84	Chelsea	Home	League	1–1		
16	28/11/84	TJ Bohemians CDK Praha	Home	UEFA Cup	2–0		
17	01/12/84	Coventry City	Away	League	1–1		
18	05/12/84	Sunderland	Home	Lge Cup	1–2		
Sub+2	01/01/85	Arsenal	Away	League	2–1		

SEASON 1985–86

League Division One

19	02/10/85	Southampton	Home	SSS Cup	2–1		
20	30/11/85	Aston Villa	Away	League	2–1		
21	03/12/85	Liverpool	Away	SSS Cup	0–2		
22	07/12/85	Oxford United	Home	League	5–1	2 Goals	(12)
23	10/12/85	Portsmouth	Away	Lge Cup	0–1		
24	14/12/85	Watford	Away	League	0–1		
25	17/12/85	Southampton	Away	SSS Cup	3–1	1 Goal	(13)
26	21/12/85	Ipswich Town	Home	League	2–0	1 Goal	(14)
27	26/12/85	West Ham United	Home	League	1–0		
28	28/12/85	Chelsea	Away	League	0–2		
29	01/01/86	Arsenal	Away	League	0–0		
30	04/01/86	Oxford United	Away	FA Cup	1–1		
Sub+3	08/01/86	Oxford United	Home	FA Cup	2–1	1 Goal	(15)
Sub+4	11/01/86	Nottingham Forest	Home	League	0–3		
31	14/01/86	Liverpool	Home	SSS Cup	0–3		
32	18/01/86	Manchester City	Home	League	0–2		
33	25/01/86	Notts County	Away	FA Cup	1–1	1 Goal	(16)
34	29/01/86	Notts County	Home	FA Cup	5–0	1 Goal	(17)
35	01/02/86	Everton	Away	League	0–1		
36	05/02/86	Everton	Home	SSS Cup	0–0		
Sub+5	08/03/86	West Bromwich Albion	Home	League	5–0		
Sub+6	31/03/86	West Ham United	Away	League	1–2		
37	05/04/86	Leicester City	Away	League	4–1		
38	12/04/86	Luton Town	Away	League	1–1	1 Goal	(18)
39	16/04/86	Birmingham City	Home	League	2–0		
40	19/04/86	Manchester United	Home	League	0–0		
41	26/04/86	Queens Park Rangers	Away	League	5–2	2 Goals	(20)
42	03/05/86	Aston Villa	Home	League	4–2	2 Goals	(22)
43	05/05/86	Southampton	Home	League	5–3	1 Goal	(23)

SEASON 1986–87

League Division One

44	23/08/86	Aston Villa	Away	League	3–0	3 Goals	(26)
45	25/08/86	Newcastle United	Home	League	1–1	1 Goal	(27)
46	30/08/86	Manchester City	Home	League	1–0		
47	02/09/86	Southampton	Away	League	0–2		
48	06/09/86	Arsenal	Away	League	0–0		
49	13/09/86	Chelsea	Home	League	1–3	1 Goal	(28)
50	20/09/86	Leicester City	Away	League	2–1	2 Goals	(30)
51	23/09/86	Barnsley	Away	Lge Cup	3–2	1 Goal	(31)
52	27/09/86	Everton	Home	League	2–0	2 Goals	(33)
Sub+7	08/10/86	Barnsley	Home	Lge Cup	5–3	1 Goal	(34)
53	11/10/86	Liverpool	Away	League	1–0	1 Goal	(35)
54	18/10/86	Sheffield Wednesday	Home	League	1–1	1 Goal	(36)
55	25/10/86	Queens Park Rangers	Away	League	0–2		
56	29/10/86	Birmingham City	Home	Lge Cup	5–0	2 Goals	(38)
57	01/11/86	Wimbledon	Home	League	1–2		
58	08/11/86	Norwich City	Away	League	1–2		
59	15/11/86	Coventry City	Home	League	1–0	1 Goal	(39)
60	22/11/86	Oxford United	Away	League	4–2	2 Goals	(41)
61	26/11/86	Cambridge United	Away	Lge Cup	3–1	1 Goal	(42)
62	29/11/86	Nottingham Forest	Home	League	2–3	2 Goals	(44)

63	07/12/86	Manchester United	Away	League	3–3	1 Goal	(45)
64	13/12/86	Watford	Home	League	2–1		
65	20/12/86	Chelsea	Away	League	2–0	2 Goals	(47)
66	26/12/86	West Ham United	Home	League	4–0	2 Goals	(49)
67	27/12/86	Coventry City	Away	League	3–4	2 Goals	(51)
68	01/01/87	Charlton Athletic	Away	League	2–0		
69	04/01/87	Arsenal	Home	League	1–2		
70	10/01/87	Scunthorpe United	Home	FA Cup	3–2		
71	24/01/87	Aston Villa	Home	League	3–0		
72	27/01/87	West Ham United	Away	Lge Cup	1–1	1 Goal	(52)
73	31/01/87	Crystal Palace	Home	FA Cup	4–0	1 Goal	(53)
74	02/02/87	West Ham United	Home	Lge Cup	5–0	3 Goals	(56)
75	08/02/87	Arsenal	Away	Lge Cup	1–0	1 Goal	(57)
76	14/02/87	Southampton	Home	League	2–0		
77	21/02/87	Newcastle United	Home	FA Cup	1–0	1 Goal	(58)
78	25/02/87	Leicester City	Home	League	5–0	2 Goals	(60)
79	01/03/87	Arsenal	Home	Lge Cup	1–2*	1 Goal	(61)
80	04/03/87	Arsenal	Home	Lge Cup	1–2	1 Goal	(62)
81	07/03/87	Queens Park Rangers	Home	League	1–0	1 Goal	(63)
82	14/03/87	Wimbledon	Away	FA Cup	2–0		
83	22/03/87	Liverpool	Home	League	1–0		
84	25/03/87	Newcastle United	Away	League	1–1		
85	28/03/87	Luton Town	Away	League	1–3		
86	04/04/87	Norwich City	Home	League	3–0	3 Goals	(66)
87	07/04/87	Sheffield Wednesday	Away	League	1–0	1 Goal	(67)
88	11/04/87	Watford	Neutral	FA Cup	4–1	1 Goal	(68)
89	15/04/87	Manchester City	Away	League	1–1		
90	18/04/87	Charlton Athletic	Home	League	1–0	1 Goal	(69)
91	20/04/87	West Ham United	Away	League	1–2	1 Goal	(70)
Sub+8	22/04/87	Wimbledon	Away	League	2–2		
92	25/04/87	Oxford United	Home	League	3–1		
93	04/05/87	Manchester United	Home	League	4–0	1 Goal	(71)
94	09/05/87	Watford	Away	League	0–1		
95	16/05/87	Coventry City	Wembley	FA Cup	2–3*	1 Goal	(72)

SEASON 1987–88

League Division One

96	15/08/87	Coventry City	Away	League	1–2		
97	19/08/87	Newcastle United	Home	League	3–1	1 Goal	(73)
98	22/08/87	Chelsea	Home	League	1–0		
99	29/08/87	Watford	Away	League	1–1	1 Goal	(74)
100	01/09/87	Oxford United	Home	League	3–0	1 Goal	(75)
101	05/09/87	Everton	Away	League	0–0		
102	12/09/87	Southampton	Home	League	2–1	1 Goal	(76)
103	19/09/87	West Ham United	Away	League	1–0		
104	03/10/87	Sheffield Wednesday	Home	League	2–0		
Sub+9	18/10/87	Arsenal	Home	League	1–2		
105	24/10/87	Nottingham Forest	Away	League	0–3		
106	28/10/87	Aston Villa	Away	Lge Cup	1–2		
107	31/10/87	Wimbledon	Home	League	0–3		
Sub+10	04/11/87	Portsmouth	Away	League	0–0		
108	14/11/87	Queens Park Rangers	Home	League	1–1		
109	21/11/87	Luton Town	Away	League	0–2		
110	28/11/87	Liverpool	Home	League	0–2		
111	13/12/87	Charlton Athletic	Home	League	0–1		
112	20/12/87	Derby County	Away	League	2–1	1 Goal	(77)
113	26/12/87	Southampton	Away	League	1–2		
114	01/01/88	Watford	Home	League	2–1	1 Goal	(78)
115	02/01/88	Chelsea	Away	League	0–0		
116	09/01/88	Oldham Athletic	Away	FA Cup	4–2	2 Goals	(80)
117	16/01/88	Coventry City	Home	League	2–2	2 Goals	(82)
118	23/01/88	Newcastle United	Away	League	0–2		
119	30/01/88	Port Vale	Away	FA Cup	1–2		
120	13/02/88	Oxford United	Away	League	0–0		
121	23/02/88	Manchester United	Home	League	1–1	1 Goal	(83)
122	27/02/88	Sheffield Wednesday	Away	League	3–0	1 Goal	(84)
123	01/03/88	Derby County	Home	League	0–0		
124	06/03/88	Arsenal	Away	League	1–2	1 Goal	(85)
125	09/03/88	Everton	Home	League	2–1		
126	12/03/88	Norwich City	Home	League	1–3		
127	19/03/88	Wimbledon	Away	League	0–3		
Sub+11	23/04/88	Liverpool	Away	League	0–1		
128	02/05/88	Charlton Athletic	Away	League	1–1		
129	04/05/88	Luton Town	Home	League	2–1		

SEASON 1988–89

Girondins de Bordeaux – French League Division One

1	16/07/88	AJ Auxerre	Home	League	2–0		
2	26/07/88	Montpellier HCS	Home	League	2–1	1 Goal	(1)
3	13/08/88	FC Sochaux	Away	League	1–1	1 Goal	(2)
4	17/08/88	AS Saint–Etienne	Home	League	5–0	1 Goal	(3)
5	20/08/88	Toulouse FC	Away	League	1–1	1 Goal	(4)
6	27/08/88	RC Strasbourg	Home	League	2–0	2 Goals	(6)
7	03/09/88	OGC Nice	Away	League	0–1		
8	07/09/88	Dnepr Dnepropetrovsk	Away	UEFA Cup	1–1		
9	10/09/88	Olympique de Marseille	Home	League	0–0		
10	14/09/88	Paris Saint–Germain	Away	League	1–1		
11	21/09/88	RC Lens	Home	League	4–1	1 Goal	(7)
12	05/10/88	Dnepr Dnepropetrovsk	Home	UEFA Cup	2–1		
13	08/10/88	FC Metz	Away	League	0–3		
14	08/11/88	Ujpesti Dozsa Budapest	Home	UEFA Cup	1–0		
15	19/02/89	RC Strasbourg	Away	League	2–3	1 Goal	(8)
16	22/02/89	OGC Nice	Home	League	2–0	1 Goal	(9)
17	25/02/89	AS Beauvais–oise	Neutral	Fr Cup	1–1+	1 Goal	(10)
18	11/03/89	Olympique de Marseille	Away	League	2–2		
19	18/03/89	Stade Lavallois de Laval	Home	League	2–1		
20	01/04/89	Matra Racing Paris	Home	League	3–2	1 Goal	(11)
21	12/04/89	FC Metz	Home	League	4–1	1 Goal	(12)
22	20/05/89	SM Caen	Home	League	2–3	1 Goal	(13)
23	31/05/89	AJ Auxerre	Away	League	1–1	1 Goal	(14)

+ AET AS Beauvais–oise won 3–2 on penalties

SEASON 1989–90

Manchester City – League Division One

1	19/08/89	Liverpool	Away	League	1–3		
2	23/08/89	Southampton	Home	League	1–2		
3	26/08/89	Tottenham Hotspur	Home	League	1–1		
4	30/08/89	Coventry City	Away	League	1–2		
5	09/09/89	Queens Park Rangers	Home	League	1–0	1 Goal	(1)
Sub+1	14/10/89	Arsenal	Away	League	0–4		
Sub+2	22/10/89	Aston Villa	Home	League	0–2		
6	25/10/89	Norwich City	Home	Lge Cup	3–1	1 Goal	(2)
7	28/10/89	Chelsea	Away	League	1–1	1 Goal	(3)
8	04/11/89	Crystal Palace	Home	League	3–0	1 Goal	(4)
9	11/11/89	Derby County	Away	League	0–6		
10	18/11/89	Nottingham Forest	Home	League	0–3		
11	22/11/89	Coventry City	Home	Lge Cup	0–1		
12	25/11/89	Charlton Athletic	Away	League	1–1	1 Goal	(5)
13	02/12/89	Liverpool	Home	League	1–4	1 Goal	(6)
14	09/12/89	Southampton	Away	League	1–2	1 Goal	(7)
15	17/12/89	Everton	Away	League	0–0		
Sub+3	26/12/89	Norwich City	Home	League	1–0	1 Goal	(8)
16	30/12/89	Millwall	Home	League	2–0		
17	01/01/90	Sheffield Wednesday	Away	League	0–2		
18	06/01/90	Millwall	Home	FA Cup	0–0		
19	09/01/90	Millwall	Away	FA Cup	1–1*		
20	13/01/90	Tottenham Hotspur	Away	League	1–1		
21	15/01/90	Millwall	Away	FA Cup	1–3		
Sub+4	10/02/90	Wimbledon	Home	League	1–1		
Sub+5	10/03/90	Arsenal	Home	League	1–1		
22	17/03/90	Luton Town	Away	League	1–1	1 Goal	(9)
23	21/03/90	Chelsea	Home	League	1–1		
24	01/04/90	Aston Villa	Away	League	2–1		
25	07/04/90	Millwall	Away	League	1–1		
26	11/04/90	Queens Park Rangers	Away	League	3–1	1 Goal	(10)
27	14/04/90	Sheffield Wednesday	Home	League	2–1		
28	16/04/90	Norwich City	Away	League	1–0		
Sub+6	28/04/90	Derby County	Home	League	0–1		
Sub+7	05/05/90	Crystal Palace	Away	League	2–2	1 Goal	(11)

SEASON 1990–91

League Division One

Sub+8	25/08/90	Tottenham Hotspur	Away	League	1–3		
Sub+9	08/09/90	Sheffield United	Away	League	1–1		
Sub+10	15/09/90	Norwich City	Home	League	2–1		
Sub+11	22/09/90	Chelsea	Away	League	1–1		
29	26/09/90	Torquay United	Away	Lge Cup	4–0	1 Goal	(12)

Sub+12	29/09/90	Wimbledon	Away	League	1–1		
Sub+13	06/10/90	Coventry City	Home	League	2–0	1 Goal	(13)
30	10/10/90	Torquay United	Home	Lge Cup	0–0		
Sub+14	20/10/90	Derby County	Away	League	1–1		
Sub+15	30/10/90	Arsenal	Home	Lge Cup	1–2		
Sub+16	03/11/90	Sunderland	Away	League	1–1	1 Goal	(14)
Sub+17	11/11/90	Leeds United	Home	League	2–3		
Sub+18	24/11/90	Liverpool	Away	League	2–2		
Sub+19	06/01/91	Burnley	Away	FA Cup	1–0		
Sub+20	13/01/91	Everton	Away	League	0–2		
31	19/01/91	Sheffield United	Home	League	2–0		
32	22/01/91	Sheffield United	Away	ZDS Cup	2–0		
Sub+21	26/01/91	Port Vale	Away	FA Cup	2–1	1 Goal	(15)
33	02/02/91	Norwich City	Away	League	2–1		
34	09/02/91	Chelsea	Home	League	2–1		
35	16/02/91	Notts County	Away	FA Cup	0–1		
36	20/02/91	Leeds United	Away	ZDS Cup	0–2*		
Sub+22	02/03/91	Queens Park Rangers	Away	League	0–1		
37	05/03/91	Luton Town	Home	League	3–0	1 Goal	(16)
38	09/03/91	Liverpool	Home	League	0–3		
39	16/03/91	Wimbledon	Home	League	1–1		
40	23/03/91	Coventry City	Away	League	1–3	1 Goal	(17)
41	30/03/91	Southampton	Home	League	3–3	1 Goal	(18)

SEASON 1991–92

League Division One

Sub+23	06/10/91	Notts County	Away	League	3–1	2 Goals	(20)
42	08/10/91	Chester City	Away	Lge Cup	3–0	1 Goal	(21)
Sub+24	16/11/91	Manchester United	Home	League	0–0		
Sub+25	30/11/91	Wimbledon	Home	League	0–0		
Sub+26	03/12/91	Middlesbrough	Away	Lge Cup	1–2		

Chelsea – League Division One

1	07/12/91	Sheffield Wednesday	Away	League	0–3		
2	10/12/91	Crystal Palace	Away	ZDS Cup	1–0		
3	15/12/91	Manchester United	Home	League	1–3	1 Goal	(1)
4	21/12/91	Oldham Athletic	Home	League	4–2	2 Goals	(3)
5	26/12/91	Notts County	Away	League	0–2		
6	28/12/91	Luton Town	Away	League	0–2		
7	01/01/92	Manchester City	Home	League	1–1	1 Goal	(4)
8	04/01/92	Hull City	Away	FA Cup	2–0		
9	11/01/92	Tottenham Hotspur	Home	League	2–0	1 Goal	(5)
10	18/01/92	Wimbledon	Away	League	2–1	1 Goal	(6)
11	21/01/92	Southampton	Away	ZDS Cup	0–2		
12	26/01/92	Everton	Home	FA Cup	1–0	1 Goal	(7)
13	29/01/92	Southampton	Home	ZDS Cup	1–3		
14	01/02/92	Liverpool	Away	League	2–1		
15	08/02/92	Crystal Palace	Home	League	1–1		
16	12/02/92	Southampton	Home	League	1–1		
17	15/02/92	Sheffield United	Home	FA Cup	1–0		
18	22/02/92	Nottingham Forest	Away	League	1–1	1 Goal	(8)
19	26/02/92	Manchester United	Away	League	1–1		
20	29/02/92	Sheffield Wednesday	Home	League	0–3		
21	09/03/92	Sunderland	Home	FA Cup	1–1	1 Goal	(9)
Sub+1	14/03/92	Coventry City	Home	League	0–1		
Sub+2	18/03/92	Sunderland	Away	FA Cup	1–2		
22	21/03/92	Sheffield United	Home	League	1–2		

West Ham United – League Division One

1	04/04/92	Chelsea	Away	League	1–2	1 Goal	(1)
2	11/04/92	Norwich City	Home	League	4–0		
3	14/04/92	Southampton	Home	League	0–1		
4	20/04/92	Crystal Palace	Home	League	0–2		

SEASON 1992–93

Football League Division One

5	16/08/92	Barnsley	Away	League	1–0	1 Goal	(2)
6	22/08/92	Charlton Athletic	Home	League	0–1		
7	29/08/92	Newcastle United	Away	League	0–2		
8	02/09/92	Bristol Rovers	Home	AI Cup	2–2		
9	05/09/92	Watford	Home	League	2–1	1 Goal	(3)
10	12/09/92	Peterborough United	Away	League	3–1		
11	15/09/92	Bristol City	Away	League	5–1	2 Goals	(5)

12	20/09/92	Derby County	Home	League	1–1		
13	23/09/92	Crewe Alexandra	Home	Lge Cup	0–0		
14	27/09/92	Portsmouth	Away	League	1–0	1 Goal	(6)
15	30/09/92	Southend United	Away	AI Cup	3–0		
16	04/10/92	Wolverhampton Wanderers	Away	League	0–0		
17	07/10/92	Crewe Alexandra	Away	Lge Cup	0–2		
18	11/10/92	Sunderland	Home	League	6–0		
19	17/10/92	Bristol Rovers	Away	League	4–0	1 Goal	(7)
20	24/10/92	Swindon Town	Home	League	0–1		
21	31/10/92	Cambridge United	Away	League	1–2		
22	03/11/92	Grimsby Town	Away	League	1–1		
23	07/11/92	Notts County	Home	League	2–0	1 Goal	(8)
24	11/11/92	US Cremonese	Away	AI Cup	0–2		
25	15/11/92	Millwall	Away	League	1–2		
26	21/11/92	Oxford United	Home	League	5–3	1 Goal	(9)
27	24/11/92	AC Reggiana	Home	AI Cup	2–0	2 Goals	(11)
28	28/11/92	Birmingham City	Home	League	3–1	2 Goals	(13)
29	04/12/92	Tranmere Rovers	Away	League	2–5	1 Goal	(14)
30	08/12/92	Cosenza Calcio	Away	AI Cup	1–0	1 Goal	(15)
31	12/12/92	Southend United	Home	League	2–0	1 Goal	(16)
32	16/12/92	SC Pisa	Home	AI Cup	0–0		
33	20/12/92	Brentford	Away	League	0–0		
34	26/12/92	Charlton Athletic	Away	League	1–1		
35	28/12/92	Luton Town	Home	League	2–2		
36	02/01/93	West Bromwich Albion	Away	FA Cup	2–0	1 Goal	(17)
37	10/01/93	Derby County	Away	League	2–0		
38	16/01/93	Portsmouth	Home	League	2–0		
Sub+1	02/05/93	Swindon Town	Away	League	3–1	1 Goal	(18)
Sub+2	08/05/93	Cambridge United	Home	League	2–0	1 Goal	(19)

SEASON 1993–94

Premier League

39	14/08/93	Wimbledon	Home	League	0–2		
40	17/08/93	Leeds United	Away	League	0–1		
41	21/08/93	Coventry City	Away	League	1–1		
42	25/08/93	Sheffield Wednesday	Home	League	2–0	2 Goals	(21)
43	28/08/93	Queens Park Rangers	Home	League	0–4		
44	01/09/93	Manchester United	Away	League	0–3		
Sub+3	09/02/94	Notts County	Home	FA Cup	1–0*		
45	12/02/94	Manchester City	Away	League	0–0		
46	19/02/94	Kidderminster Harriers	Away	FA Cup	1–0		
Sub+4	14/03/94	Luton Town	Home	FA Cup	0–0		

Millwall – Football League Division One

Sub+1	26/03/94	Watford	Away	League	0–2	
1	30/03/94	Luton Town	Home	League	2–2	
2	02/04/94	Portsmouth	Away	League	2–2	
3	06/04/94	Sunderland	Home	League	2–1	
4	09/04/94	Crystal Palace	Away	League	0–1	
5	17/04/94	Nottingham Forest	Home	League	2–2	
6	20/04/94	Wolverhampton Wanderers	Home	League	1–0	
7	23/04/94	Tranmere Rovers	Away	League	2–3	
8	26/04/94	Luton Town	Away	League	1–1	
9	30/04/94	Bristol City	Home	League	0–0	
10	03/05/94	Barnsley	Away	League	1–0	
11	08/05/94	Grimsby Town	Away	League	0–0	
12	18/05/94	Derby County	Home	Lge P/O	1–3	

SEASON 1994–95

Football League Division One
No Competitive Matches

SEASON 1995–96

Carlisle United – Football League Division Two

1	23/09/95	Hull City	Home	League	2–0	
2	30/09/95	Walsall	Away	League	1–2	
3	07/10/95	Notts County	Home	League	0–0	

INTERNATIONAL APPEARANCES – ENGLAND

Sub 1	10/06/84	Brazil	Rio de Janeiro	2–0	F
2	13/06/84	Uruguay	Montevideo	0–2	F

3	17/06/84	Chile	Santiago	0–0	F
4	29/04/87	Turkey	Izmir	0–0	ECQ
5	17/02/88	Israel	Tel Aviv	0–0	F

APPEARANCES AND GOALS PER SEASON

SEASON 78–79	GAMES	GOALS
League	4+6	4
TOTAL	**4+6**	**4**

SEASON 79–80	GAMES	GOALS
League	39	28
FA Cup	1	0
League Cup	5	2
TOTAL	**45**	**30**

SEASON 80–81	GAMES	GOALS
League	25	9
League Cup	4	2
TOTAL	**29**	**11**

SEASON 81–82	GAMES	GOALS
League	36+1	13
FA Cup	7	7
League Cup	2	1
TOTAL	**45+1**	**21**

SEASON 82–83	GAMES	GOALS
League	23+2	13
FA Cup	1	0
League Cup	2	0
TOTAL	**26+2**	**13**

SEASON 83–84	GAMES	GOALS
League	24+1	14
League Cup	3	1
TOTAL	**27+1**	**15**

SEASON 84–85	GAMES	GOALS
League	12+1	7
League Cup	3	1
UEFA Cup	3+1	2
TOTAL	**18+2**	**10**

SEASON 85–86	GAMES	GOALS
League	16+3	9
FA Cup	3+1	3
League Cup	1	0
Screen Sport Super Cup	5	1
TOTAL	**25+4**	**13**

SEASON 86–87	GAMES	GOALS
League	38+1	33
FA Cup	6	4
League Cup	8+1	12
TOTAL	**52+2**	**49**

SEASON 87–88	GAMES	GOALS
League	31+3	11
FA Cup	2	2
League Cup	1	0
TOTAL	**34+3**	**13**

SEASON 88–89	GAMES	GOALS
French League	19	13
French Cup	1	1
UEFA Cup	3	0
TOTAL	**23**	**14**

SEASON 89–90	GAMES	GOALS
League	23+7	10
FA Cup	3	0
League Cup	2	1
TOTAL	**28+7**	**11**

SEASON 90–91	GAMES	GOALS
League	8+12	4
FA Cup	1+2	1
League Cup	2+1	2
Zenith Data Systems Cup	2	0
TOTAL	**13+15**	**7**

SEASON 91–92	GAMES	GOALS
League	19+4	10
FA Cup	4+1	2
League Cup	1+1	1
Zenith Data Systems Cup	3	0
TOTAL	**27+6**	**13**

SEASON 92–93	GAMES	GOALS
League	25+2	14
FA Cup	1	1
League Cup	2	0
Anglo–Italian Cup	6	3
TOTAL	**34+2**	**18**

SEASON 93–94	GAMES	GOALS
League	18+1	2
League Play–offs	1	0
FA Cup	1+2	0
TOTAL	**20+3**	**2**

SEASON 94–95
No Competitive Matches

SEASON 95–96	GAMES	GOALS
League	3	0
TOTAL	**3**	**0**

CAREER APPEARANCES GAMES AND GOALS

COMPETITION	GAMES	TOTAL	GOALS
League	344+44	388	181
League Play–offs	1	1	0
FA Cup	30+6	36	20
League Cup	36+3	39	23
Screen Sport Super Cup	5	5	1
Zenith Data Systems Cup	5	5	0
Anglo–Italian Cup	6	6	3
UEFA Cup	6+1	7	2
French League	19	19	13
French Cup	1	1	1
Internationals	4+1	5	0
TOTAL	**457+55**	**512**	**244**

HAT-TRICKS

Queens Park Rangers

1	3	Coventry City	28/04/79	Home	League	5–1

Crystal Palace

1	3	Middlesbrough	23/08/80	Home	League	5–2

Queens Park Rangers

1	4	Blackpool	26/01/82	Home	FA Cup	5–1
2	3	Charlton Athletic	20/03/82	Home	League	4–0
3	3	Middlesbrough	05/03/83	Home	League	6–1
4	3	Notts County	05/05/84	Away	League	3–0

Tottenham Hotspur

1	3	Aston Villa	23/08/86	Away	League	3–0
2	3	West Ham United	02/02/87	Home	Lge Cup	5–0
3	3	Norwich City	04/04/87	Home	League	3–0

League: 7
FA Cup: 1
League Cup: 1
TOTAL: 9

HONOURS

Winners medals
League Division Two Championship: 82/83

Runner-up medals
FA Cup: 81/82, 86/87
Football League Division One Championship: 92/93

CHRIS ARMSTRONG

Born: 19/06/71 – Newcastle
Height: 6.0
Weight: 13.03 (96–97)

Clubs
Wrexham: **1989–91** – Matches: **52+28** – Goals: **18**
Millwall: **1991–92** – Matches: **14+20** – Goals: **7**
Crystal Palace: **1992–95** – Matches: **136** – Goals: **58**
Tottenham Hotspur: **1995–96** – Matches: **60** – Goals: **28**

Country
England: England B

SEASON 1989–90

Wrexham – League Division Four

Sub+1	29/08/89	Wigan Athletic	Away	Lge Cup	0–5		
1	04/11/89	Hartlepool United	Away	League	0–3		
Sub+2	11/11/89	Grimsby Town	Home	League	0–1		
Sub+3	26/12/89	Doncaster Rovers	Away	League	2–2		
Sub+4	30/12/89	Gillingham	Away	League	0–1		
2	01/01/90	Scunthorpe United	Home	League	0–0		
3	06/01/90	Peterborough United	Home	League	2–1		
4	12/01/90	Southend United	Away	League	1–2		
5	15/01/90	Worcester City	Away	Welsh Cup	1–0		
6	20/01/90	Scarborough	Home	League	0–2		
Sub+5	26/01/90	Halifax Town	Away	League	2–4		
7	03/02/90	Lincoln City	Away	League	0–1		
8	06/02/90	Rhyl	Home	Welsh Cup	1–1		
Sub+6	13/02/90	Rochdale	Home	League	1–1		
Sub+7	17/02/90	Chesterfield	Away	League	0–3		
Sub+8	21/02/90	Rhyl	Away	Welsh Cup	2–0		
Sub+9	24/02/90	Exeter City	Home	League	1–1		
9	03/03/90	Peterborough United	Away	League	1–3		
Sub+10	21/03/90	Barry Town	Away	Welsh Cup	1–0		
Sub+11	24/03/90	Colchester United	Home	League	3–2		
Sub+12	27/03/90	Aldershot	Away	League	0–1		
Sub+13	07/04/90	Maidstone United	Home	League	4–2		
Sub+14	16/04/90	Doncaster Rovers	Home	League	0–0		
10	21/04/90	Burnley	Away	League	3–2	2 Goals	(2)
11	24/04/90	Gillingham	Home	League	2–1	1 Goal	(3)
12	28/04/90	Grimsby Town	Away	League	1–5		
Sub+15	05/04/90	Hartlepool United	Home	League	1–2		
Sub+16	13/05/90	Hereford United	Neutral	Welsh Cup	1–2		

SEASON 1990–91

League Division Four

Sub+17	25/08/90	Peterborough United	Home	League	0–0		
Sub+18	01/09/90	Doncaster Rovers	Away	League	1–3		
Sub+19	15/09/90	Blackpool	Away	League	1–4		
Sub+20	22/09/90	Darlington	Home	League	1–1	1 Goal	(4)
13	25/09/90	Everton	Home	Lge Cup	0–5		
14	29/09/90	Chesterfield	Home	League	1–1	1 Goal	(5)
15	03/10/90	Lyngby	Away	ECW Cup	1–0	1 Goal	(6)
16	05/10/90	Cardiff City	Away	League	0–1		
17	09/10/90	Everton	Away	Lge Cup	0–6		

18	13/10/90	Scarborough	Home	League	1–2		
19	16/10/90	Torquay United	Away	League	0–1		
20	20/10/90	Hartlepool United	Home	League	2–2		
21	23/10/90	Manchester United	Away	ECW Cup	0–3		
22	27/10/90	Gillingham	Away	League	3–2	1 Goal	(7)
23	31/10/90	Maidstone United	Away	League	2–0	1 Goal	(8)
24	03/11/90	Burnley	Home	League	2–4	2 Goals	(10)
25	07/11/90	Manchester United	Home	ECW Cup	0–2		
26	09/11/90	Northampton Town	Away	League	0–1		
27	13/11/90	Worcester City	Home	Welsh Cup	3–1		
Sub+21	17/11/90	Halifax Town	Away	FA Cup	2–3		
28	24/11/90	Scunthorpe United	Home	League	1–0		
29	27/11/90	Peterborough United	Home	LD Cup	3–3	2 Goals	(12)
30	01/12/90	Carlisle United	Home	League	3–0	1 Goal	(13)
31	07/12/90	Scarborough	Away	League	2–4	1 Goal	(14)
32	15/12/90	Rochdale	Away	League	0–2		
33	18/12/90	Cambridge United	Away	LD Cup	0–1		
34	21/12/90	Walsall	Away	League	0–1		
35	26/12/90	Hereford United	Home	League	1–2		
36	29/12/90	York City	Home	League	0–4		
Sub+22	04/01/91	Stockport County	Away	League	0–2		
37	09/01/91	Ammanford	Away	Welsh Cup	5–0	1 Goal	(15)
38	12/01/91	Doncaster Rovers	Home	League	2–1		
39	19/01/91	Peterborough United	Away	League	2–2	1 Goal	(16)
40	26/01/91	Blackpool	Home	League	0–1		
Sub+23	19/02/91	Stroud	Away	Welsh Cup	2–1	1 Goal	(17)
Sub+24	21/02/91	Brentford	Away	LD Cup	0–0+		
41	23/02/91	Northampton Town	Home	League	0–2		
Sub+25	02/03/91	Carlisle United	Away	League	0–2		
42	09/03/91	Rochdale	Home	League	2–1		
43	16/03/91	Chesterfield	Away	League	1–2		
44	22/03/91	Cardiff City	Home	League	1–0		
45	26/03/91	Halifax Town	Away	League	0–2		
46	01/04/91	Walsall	Home	League	1–1		
47	03/04/91	Hereford United	Home	Welsh Cup	1–1		
48	06/04/91	York City	Away	League	0–0		
49	09/04/91	Maidstone United	Home	League	2–2		
Sub+26	13/04/91	Lincoln City	Home	League	2–2		
50	16/04/91	Stockport County	Home	League	1–3	1 Goal	(18)
51	20/04/91	Hartlepool United	Away	League	1–2		
Sub+27	24/04/91	Hereford United	Away	Welsh Cup	2–1		
Sub+28	27/04/91	Torquay United	Home	League	2–1		
52	04/05/91	Gillingham	Home	League	3–0		

+ AET Brentford won 3–0 on penalties

SEASON 1991–92

Millwall – League Division Two

Sub+1	17/08/91	Middlesbrough	Away	League	0–1		
Sub+2	24/08/91	Sunderland	Home	League	4–1		
Sub+3	04/09/91	Brighton & Hove Albion	Home	League	1–2		
1	07/09/91	Cambridge United	Home	League	1–2		
Sub+4	14/09/91	Oxford United	Away	League	2–2		
Sub+5	17/09/91	Bristol City	Away	League	2–2		
Sub+6	21/09/91	Newcastle United	Home	League	2–1		
2	25/09/91	Swindon Town	Home	Lge Cup	2–2	1 Goal	(1)
Sub+7	28/09/91	Barnsley	Away	League	2–0		
Sub+8	08/10/91	Swindon Town	Away	Lge Cup	1–3		
Sub+9	19/10/91	Ipswich Town	Away	League	0–0		
Sub+10	22/10/91	Plymouth Argyle	Away	ZDS Cup	0–4		
3	26/10/91	Derby County	Home	League	1–2		
4	29/10/91	Watford	Away	League	2–0		
5	02/11/91	Portsmouth	Home	League	1–1	1 Goal	(2)
6	05/11/91	Tranmere Rovers	Away	League	1–2		
Sub+11	23/11/91	Grimsby Town	Away	League	1–1		
7	30/11/91	Bristol Rovers	Home	League	0–1		
Sub+12	07/12/91	Leicester City	Away	League	1–1		
Sub+13	26/12/91	Watford	Home	League	0–4		
Sub+14	04/01/92	Huddersfield Town	Away	FA Cup	4–0		
Sub+15	15/02/92	Grimsby Town	Home	League	1–1		
Sub+16	22/02/92	Bristol Rovers	Away	League	2–3	1 Goal	(3)
Sub+17	26/02/92	Charlton Athletic	Home	League	1–0		
Sub+18	29/02/92	Leicester City	Home	League	2–0		
Sub+19	07/03/92	Charlton Athletic	Away	League	0–1		

Sub+20	21/03/92	Port Vale	Home	League	1–0		
8	25/04/92	Blackburn Rovers	Away	League	1–2	1 Goal	(4)
9	02/05/92	Southend United	Home	League	2–0	1 Goal	(5)

SEASON 1992–93

Football League Division One

10	15/08/92	Watford	Away	League	1–3		
11	18/08/92	Leyton Orient	Away	Lge Cup	2–2		
12	22/08/92	Oxford United	Home	League	3–1	1 Goal	(6)
13	26/08/92	Leyton Orient	Home	Lge Cup	3–0	1 Goal	(7)
14	29/08/92	Barnsley	Away	League	0–0		

Crystal Palace – Premier League

1	02/09/92	Manchester United	Away	League	0–1		
2	05/09/92	Aston Villa	Away	League	0–3		
3	12/09/92	Oldham Athletic	Home	League	2–2	2 Goals	(2)
4	19/09/92	Everton	Away	League	2–0	2 Goals	(4)
5	26/09/92	Southampton	Home	League	1–2		
6	03/10/92	Coventry City	Away	League	2–2		
7	17/10/92	Manchester City	Home	League	0–0		
8	24/10/92	Ipswich Town	Away	League	2–2	1 Goal	(5)
9	02/11/92	Arsenal	Home	League	1–2		
10	07/11/92	Chelsea	Away	League	1–3		
11	21/11/92	Nottingham Forest	Home	League	1–1	1 Goal	(6)
12	28/11/92	Liverpool	Away	League	0–5		
13	05/12/92	Sheffield United	Home	League	2–0	1 Goal	(7)
14	12/12/92	Queens Park Rangers	Away	League	3–1	1 Goal	(8)
15	20/12/92	Leeds United	Home	League	1–0		
16	26/12/92	Wimbledon	Home	League	2–0		
17	28/12/92	Middlesbrough	Away	League	1–0		
18	02/01/93	Hartlepool United	Away	FA Cup	0–1		
19	09/01/93	Everton	Home	League	0–2		
20	16/01/93	Southampton	Away	League	0–1		
21	27/01/93	Norwich City	Away	League	2–4	1 Goal	(9)
22	30/01/93	Tottenham Hotspur	Home	League	1–3		
23	02/02/93	Blackburn Rovers	Away	League	2–1	1 Goal	(10)
24	10/02/93	Aston Villa	Home	League	1–0		
25	20/02/93	Sheffield Wednesday	Away	League	1–2	1 Goal	(11)
26	27/02/93	Coventry City	Home	League	0–0		
27	03/03/93	Nottingham Forest	Away	League	1–1		
28	15/03/93	Chelsea	Home	League	1–1	1 Goal	(12)
29	20/03/93	Sheffield United	Away	League	1–0		
30	23/03/93	Liverpool	Home	League	1–1	1 Goal	(13)
31	12/04/93	Middlesbrough	Home	League	4–1	1 Goal	(14)
32	17/04/93	Leeds United	Away	League	0–0		
33	21/04/93	Manchester United	Home	League	0–2		
34	01/05/93	Ipswich Town	Home	League	3–1	1 Goal	(15)
35	05/05/93	Manchester City	Away	League	0–0		
36	08/05/93	Arsenal	Away	League	0–3		

SEASON 1993–94

Football League Division One

37	14/08/93	Tranmere Rovers	Home	League	0–0		
38	21/08/93	Bristol City	Away	League	0–2		
39	24/08/93	Nottingham Forest	Home	League	2–0		
40	28/08/93	Portsmouth	Home	League	5–1	3 Goals	(18)
41	31/08/93	Birmingham City	Away	League	4–2	2 Goals	(20)
42	01/09/93	Charlton Athletic	Away	AI Cup	1–4		
43	08/09/93	Millwall	Home	AI Cup	3–0	1 Goal	(21)
44	12/09/93	Sunderland	Home	League	1–0	1 Goal	(22)
45	18/09/93	West Bromwich Albion	Away	League	4–1	1 Goal	(23)
46	05/10/93	Charlton Athletic	Away	Lge Cup	1–0	1 Goal	(24)
47	17/10/93	Wolverhampton Wanderers	Home	League	1–1		
48	23/10/93	Derby County	Away	League	1–3	1 Goal	(25)
49	26/10/93	Everton	Away	Lge Cup	2–2		
50	30/10/93	Grimsby Town	Home	League	1–0		
51	02/11/93	Luton Town	Home	League	3–2		
52	06/11/93	Notts County	Away	League	2–3	2 Goals	(27)
53	10/11/93	Everton	Home	Lge Cup	1–4		
54	20/11/93	Barnsley	Away	League	3–1	1 Goal	(28)
55	24/11/93	Bolton Wanderers	Away	League	0–1		
56	28/11/93	Watford	Away	League	3–1		
57	05/12/93	Notts County	Home	League	1–2	1 Goal	(29)

58	08/12/93	Leicester City	Away	League	1–1		
59	11/12/93	Birmingham City	Home	League	2–1		
60	19/12/93	Tranmere Rovers	Away	League	1–0		
61	27/12/93	Oxford United	Away	League	3–1	2 Goals	(31)
62	29/12/93	Southend United	Home	League	1–0		
63	01/01/94	Millwall	Away	League	0–3		
64	08/01/94	Wolverhampton Wanderers	Away	FA Cup	0–1		
65	15/01/94	Wolverhampton Wanderers	Away	League	0–2		
66	22/01/94	Leicester City	Home	League	2–1	1 Goal	(32)
67	01/02/94	Peterborough United	Home	League	3–2	1 Goal	(33)
68	05/02/94	Derby County	Home	League	1–1		
69	12/02/94	Grimsby Town	Away	League	1–1		
70	19/02/94	Nottingham Forest	Away	League	1–1		
71	22/02/94	Bristol City	Home	League	4–1	2 Goals	(35)
72	25/02/94	Bolton Wanderers	Home	League	1–1		
73	05/03/94	Portsmouth	Away	League	1–0		
74	12/03/94	West Bromwich Albion	Home	League	1–0		
75	16/03/94	Sunderland	Away	League	0–1		
76	20/03/94	Charlton Athletic	Home	League	2–0	1 Goal	(36)
77	23/03/94	Middlesbrough	Home	League	0–1		
78	26/03/94	Stoke City	Away	League	2–0		
79	02/04/94	Oxford United	Home	League	2–1	1 Goal	(37)
80	06/04/94	Southend United	Away	League	2–1	1 Goal	(38)
81	09/04/94	Millwall	Home	League	1–0	1 Goal	(39)
82	16/04/94	Luton Town	Away	League	1–0		
83	23/04/94	Barnsley	Home	League	1–0		
84	01/05/94	Middlesbrough	Away	League	3–2	1 Goal	(40)
85	08/05/94	Watford	Home	League	0–2		

SEASON 1994–95

Premier League

86	20/08/94	Liverpool	Home	League	1–6	1 Goal	(41)
87	24/08/94	Norwich City	Away	League	0–0		
88	27/08/94	Aston Villa	Away	League	1–1		
89	30/08/94	Leeds United	Home	League	1–2		
90	10/09/94	Manchester City	Away	League	1–1		
91	17/09/94	Wimbledon	Home	League	0–0		
92	20/09/94	Lincoln City	Away	Lge Cup	0–1		
93	24/09/94	Chelsea	Home	League	0–1		
94	01/10/94	Arsenal	Away	League	2–1		
95	04/10/94	Lincoln City	Home	Lge Cup	3–0	1 Goal	(42)
96	08/10/94	West Ham United	Away	League	0–1		
97	15/10/94	Newcastle United	Home	League	0–1		
98	22/10/94	Everton	Home	League	1–0		
99	25/10/94	Wimbledon	Away	Lge Cup	1–0	1 Goal	(43)
100	29/10/94	Leicester City	Away	League	1–0		
101	02/11/94	Coventry City	Away	League	4–1		
102	05/11/94	Ipswich Town	Home	League	3–0	1 Goal	(44)
103	19/11/94	Manchester United	Away	League	0–3		
104	26/11/94	Southampton	Home	League	0–0		
105	30/11/94	Aston Villa	Home	Lge Cup	4–1	2 Goals	(46)
106	03/12/94	Sheffield Wednesday	Away	League	0–1		
107	11/12/94	Liverpool	Away	League	0–0		
108	17/12/94	Norwich City	Home	League	0–1		
109	26/12/94	Queens Park Rangers	Home	League	0–0		
110	27/12/94	Tottenham Hotspur	Away	League	0–0		
111	31/12/94	Blackburn Rovers	Home	League	0–1		
112	02/01/95	Nottingham Forest	Away	League	0–1		
113	08/01/95	Lincoln City	Home	FA Cup	5–1	1 Goal	(47)
114	11/01/95	Manchester City	Home	Lge Cup	4–0	1 Goal	(48)
115	14/01/95	Leicester City	Home	League	2–0		
116	21/01/95	Everton	Away	League	1–3		
117	25/01/95	Manchester United	Home	League	1–1		
118	28/01/95	Nottingham Forest	Away	FA Cup	2–1	1 Goal	(49)
119	04/02/95	Ipswich Town	Away	League	2–0		
120	18/02/95	Watford	Away	FA Cup	0–0		
121	25/02/95	Arsenal	Home	League	0–3		
122	14/03/95	Sheffield Wednesday	Home	League	2–1	1 Goal	(50)
123	18/03/95	Wimbledon	Away	League	0–2		
124	22/03/95	Wolverhampton Wanderers	Away	FA Cup	4–1	2 Goals	(52)
125	01/04/95	Manchester City	Home	League	2–1	1 Goal	(53)
126	04/04/95	Aston Villa	Home	League	0–0		
127	09/04/95	Manchester United	Neutral	FA Cup	2–2*	1 Goal	(54)
128	12/04/95	Manchester United	Neutral	FA Cup	0–2		

129	14/04/95	Tottenham Hotspur	Home	League	1–1	1 Goal	(55)
130	17/04/95	Queens Park Rangers	Away	League	1–0		
131	20/04/95	Blackburn Rovers	Away	League	1–2		
132	29/04/95	Nottingham Forest	Home	League	1–2		
133	03/05/95	Southampton	Away	League	1–3		
134	06/05/95	West Ham United	Home	League	1–0	1 Goal	(56)
135	09/05/95	Leeds United	Away	League	1–3	1 Goal	(57)
136	14/05/95	Newcastle United	Away	League	2–3	1 Goal	(58)

SEASON 1995–96

Tottenham Hotspur – Premier League

1	19/08/95	Manchester City	Away	League	1–1		
2	23/08/95	Aston Villa	Home	League	0–1		
3	26/08/95	Liverpool	Home	League	1–3		
4	30/08/95	West Ham United	Away	League	1–1		
5	09/09/95	Leeds United	Home	League	2–1		
6	16/09/95	Sheffield Wednesday	Away	League	3–1		
7	20/09/95	Chester City	Home	Lge Cup	4–0	2 Goals	(2)
8	25/09/95	Queens Park Rangers	Away	League	3–2		
9	30/09/95	Wimbledon	Home	League	3–1		
10	04/10/95	Chester City	Away	Lge Cup	3–1		
11	22/10/95	Everton	Away	League	1–1	1 Goal	(3)
12	25/10/95	Coventry City	Away	Lge Cup	2–3	1 Goal	(4)
13	29/10/95	Newcastle United	Home	League	1–1	1 Goal	(5)
14	04/11/95	Coventry City	Away	League	3–2		
15	18/11/95	Arsenal	Home	League	2–1	1 Goal	(6)
16	21/11/95	Middlesbrough	Away	League	1–0	1 Goal	(7)
17	25/11/95	Chelsea	Away	League	0–0		
18	02/12/95	Everton	Home	League	0–0		
19	09/12/95	Queens Park Rangers	Home	League	1–0		
20	16/12/95	Wimbledon	Away	League	1–0		
21	23/12/95	Bolton Wanderers	Home	League	2–2	1 Goal	(8)
22	26/12/95	Southampton	Away	League	0–0		
23	30/12/95	Blackburn Rovers	Away	League	1–2		
24	01/01/96	Manchester United	Home	League	4–1	2 Goals	(10)
25	06/01/96	Hereford United	Away	FA Cup	1–1		
26	13/01/96	Manchester City	Home	League	1–0	1 Goal	(11)
27	17/01/96	Hereford United	Home	FA Cup	5–1	2 Goals	(13)
28	21/01/96	Aston Villa	Away	League	1–2		
29	27/01/96	Wolverhampton Wanderers	Home	FA Cup	1–1		
30	03/02/96	Liverpool	Away	League	0–0		
31	07/02/96	Wolverhampton Wanderers	Away	FA Cup	2–0		
32	12/02/96	West Ham United	Home	League	0–1		
33	24/02/96	Sheffield Wednesday	Home	League	1–0	1 Goal	(14)
34	28/02/96	Nottingham Forest	Away	FA Cup	2–2	2 Goals	(16)
35	09/03/96	Nottingham Forest	Home	FA Cup	1–1+		
36	16/03/96	Blackburn Rovers	Home	League	2–3	1 Goal	(17)
37	20/03/96	Bolton Wanderers	Away	League	3–2	1 Goal	(18)
38	24/03/96	Manchester United	Away	League	0–1		
39	30/03/96	Coventry City	Home	League	3–1		
40	06/04/96	Nottingham Forest	Away	League	1–2	1 Goal	(19)
41	08/04/96	Middlesbrough	Home	League	1–1	1 Goal	(20)
42	15/04/96	Arsenal	Away	League	0–0		
43	27/04/96	Chelsea	Home	League	1–1	1 Goal	(21)
44	02/05/96	Leeds United	Away	League	3–1	1 Goal	(22)
45	05/05/96	Newcastle United	Away	League	1–1		

+ AET Nottingham Forest won 3–1 on penalties

SEASON 1996–97

Premier League

46	17/08/96	Blackburn Rovers	Away	League	2–0	2 Goals	(24)
47	21/08/96	Derby County	Home	League	1–1		
48	24/08/96	Everton	Home	League	0–0		
49	07/09/96	Newcastle United	Home	League	1–2		
50	14/09/96	Southampton	Away	League	1–0	1 Goal	(25)
51	17/09/96	Preston North End	Away	Lge Cup	1–1		
52	12/10/96	Aston Villa	Home	League	1–0		
53	19/10/96	Middlesbrough	Away	League	3–0		
54	23/10/96	Sunderland	Home	Lge Cup	2–1	1 Goal	(26)
55	26/10/96	Chelsea	Away	League	1–3	1 Goal	(27)
56	02/11/96	West Ham United	Home	League	1–0	1 Goal	(28)
57	16/11/96	Sunderland	Home	League	2–0		

58	24/11/96	Arsenal	Away	League	1–3
59	27/11/96	Bolton Wanderers	Away	Lge Cup	1–6
60	02/12/96	Liverpool	Home	League	0–2

APPEARANCES AND GOALS PER SEASON

SEASON 89–90	GAMES	GOALS
League	10+12	3
League Cup	0+1	0
Welsh Cup	2+3	0
TOTAL	**12+16**	**3**

SEASON 90–91	GAMES	GOALS
League	30+8	10
FA Cup	0+1	0
League Cup	2	0
Leyland Daf Cup	2+1	2
Welsh Cup	3+2	2
European Cup Winners Cup	3	1
TOTAL	**40+12**	**15**

SEASON 91–92	GAMES	GOALS
League	8+17	4
FA Cup	0+1	0
League Cup	1+1	1
Zenith Data Systems Cup	0+1	0
TOTAL	**9+20**	**5**

SEASON 92–93	GAMES	GOALS
League	38	16
FA Cup	1	0
League Cup	2	1
TOTAL	**41**	**17**

SEASON 93–94	GAMES	GOALS
League	43	23
FA Cup	1	0
League Cup	3	1
Anglo–Italian Cup	2	1
TOTAL	**49**	**25**

SEASON 94–95	GAMES	GOALS
League	40	8
FA Cup	6	5
League Cup	5	5
TOTAL	**51**	**18**

SEASON 95–96	GAMES	GOALS
League	36	15
FA Cup	6	4
League Cup	3	3
TOTAL	**45**	**22**

SEASON 96–97	GAMES	GOALS
League	12	5
League Cup	3	1
TOTAL	**15**	**6**

CAREER APPEARANCES AND GOALS

COMPETITION	GAMES	TOTAL	GOALS
League	217+37	254	84
FA Cup	14+2	16	9
League Cup	19+2	21	12
Leyland Daf Cup	2+1	3	2
Zenith Data Systems Cup	0+1	1	0
Anglo–Italian Cup	2	2	1
Welsh Cup	5+5	10	2
European Cup Winners Cup	3	3	1
TOTAL	**262+48**	**310**	**111**

HAT-TRICKS

Crystal Palace

1	3	Portsmouth	28/08/93	Home	League	5–1

League: 1
TOTAL: 1

HONOURS

Winners medals
Football League Division One Championship: 93/94

Runner-up medals
Welsh Cup: 89/90

GARY BANNISTER

Born: 22/07/60 – Warrington
Height: 5.8
Weight: 11.10 (95–96)

Clubs
Coventry City: **1978–81** – Matches: **21+5** – Goals: **3**
Detroit Express: **1980** – Matches: **14+8** – Goals: **10**
Sheffield Wednesday: **1981–84** – Matches: **142+1** – Goals: **65**
Queens Park Rangers: **1984–88** – Matches: **172** – Goals: **72**
Coventry City: **1988–90** – Matches: **44+4** – Goals: **13**
West Bromwich Albion: **1990–92** – Matches: **68+13** – Goals: **20**
Oxford United (loan): **1992** – Matches: **7+3** – Goals: **2**
Nottingham Forest: **1992–93** – Matches: **32+5** – Goals: **10**
Stoke City: **1993–94** – Matches: **12+6** – Goals: **2**
Hong Kong Rangers: **1994** – No Competitive Matches
Lincoln City: **1994–95** – Matches: **29+5** – Goals: **8**
Darlington: **1995–96** – Matches: **48+3** – Goals: **11**

Country
England: Under 21

SEASON 1978–79

Coventry City – League Division One

Sub+1	26/08/78	Norwich City	Home	League	4–1		
1	30/08/78	Chester	Away	Lge Cup	1–2		
2	18/11/78	Norwich City	Away	League	0–1		
3	21/11/78	Derby County	Home	League	4–2		
4	05/05/79	Wolverhampton Wanderers	Home	League	3–0	1 Goal	(1)

SEASON 1979–80

League Division One

5	08/12/79	Arsenal	Away	League	1–3		
Sub+2	09/02/80	Manchester City	Home	League	0–0		
6	15/03/80	Everton	Away	League	1–1		
7	22/03/80	Leeds United	Away	League	0–0		
8	29/03/80	Wolverhampton Wanderers	Home	League	1–3		
Sub+3	26/04/80	Manchester United	Away	League	1–2		
9	03/05/80	Arsenal	Home	League	0–1		

Detroit Express – North American Soccer League – Season 1980

1	10/05/80	Atlanta Chiefs	Home	League	3–0	1 Goal	(1)
2	17/05/80	Chicago Sting	Away	League	2–3		
3	25/05/80	Minnesota Kicks	Away	League	2–4		
Sub+1	31/05/80	Vancouver Whitecaps	Home	League	0–1		
Sub+2	05/06/80	Toronto Blizzard	Away	League	2–1	1 Goal	(2)
Sub+3	08/06/80	Tulsa Roughnecks	Away	League	1–0		
Sub+4	11/06/80	San Jose Earthquakes	Home	League	0–1+		
4	17/06/80	Dallas Tornado	Home	League	5–1	1 Goal	(3)
5	28/06/80	San Diego Sockers	Home	League	1–0+		
6	04/07/80	Houston Hurricane	Home	League	2–0	1 Goal	(4)
7	06/07/80	Houston Hurricane	Away	League	3–4+	2 Goals	(6)
8	09/07/80	Fort Lauderdale Strikers	Away	League	1–3		
9	12/07/80	New York Cosmos	Home	League	1–0+		
10	19/07/80	Rochester Lancers	Home	League	2–1		
Sub+5	23/07/80	Chicago Sting	Home	League	1–2+	1 Goal	(7)
11	26/07/80	Dallas Tornado	Away	League	1–2		
Sub+6	02/08/80	San Jose Earthquakes	Away	League	1–3		

Sub+7	06/08/80	San Diego Sockers	Away	League	0–1		
Sub+8	09/08/80	California Surf	Home	League	1–2		
12	13/08/80	Tampa Bay Rowdies	Away	League	2–3	1 Goal	(8)
13	16/08/80	Philadelphia Fury	Away	League	3–2*	2 Goals	(10)
14	24/08/80	Fort Lauderdale Strikers	Home	League	3–2		

* Sudden–death overtime
+ Decided on penalties

SEASON 1980–81

League Division One

10	02/09/80	Manchester United	Home	Lge Cup	1–0		
Sub+4	18/10/80	Norwich City	Home	League	0–1		
11	25/10/80	Tottenham Hotspur	Away	League	1–4		
12	27/12/80	Stoke City	Away	League	2–2		
13	03/01/81	Leeds United	Away	FA Cup	1–1		
14	06/01/81	Leeds United	Home	FA Cup	1–0		
15	17/02/81	Crystal Palace	Away	League	3–0	1 Goal	(2)
16	21/02/81	Everton	Away	League	0–3		
17	07/03/81	Brighton & Hove Albion	Away	League	1–4	1 Goal	(3)
18	14/03/81	Leicester City	Home	League	4–1		
19	21/03/81	Sunderland	Away	League	0–3		
Sub+5	04/04/81	Leeds United	Away	League	0–3		
20	11/04/81	Manchester United	Home	League	0–2		
21	18/04/81	Stoke City	Home	League	2–2		

SEASON 1981–82

Sheffield Wednesday – League Division Two

1	29/08/81	Blackburn Rovers	Away	League	1–0		
2	05/09/81	Crystal Palace	Home	League	1–0	1 Goal	(1)
3	08/09/81	Rotherham United	Home	League	2–0		
4	12/09/81	Luton Town	Away	League	3–0	1 Goal	(2)
5	19/09/81	Derby County	Home	League	1–1		
6	22/09/81	Barnsley	Away	League	0–1		
7	26/09/81	Grimsby Town	Away	League	1–0		
8	03/10/81	Wrexham	Home	League	0–3		
9	07/10/81	Blackburn Rovers	Away	Lge Cup	1–1		
10	10/10/81	Cardiff City	Home	League	2–1		
11	17/10/81	Charlton Athletic	Away	League	0–3		
12	24/10/81	Oldham Athletic	Home	League	2–1	1 Goal	(3)
13	27/10/81	Blackburn Rovers	Home	Lge Cup	1–2	1 Goal	(4)
14	31/10/81	Leicester City	Away	League	0–0		
15	07/11/81	Orient	Away	League	0–3		
16	14/11/81	Queens Park Rangers	Home	League	1–3	1 Goal	(5)
17	21/11/81	Cambridge United	Away	League	2–1	1 Goal	(6)
18	24/11/81	Barnsley	Home	League	2–2		
19	28/11/81	Watford	Home	League	3–1	1 Goal	(7)
20	05/12/81	Chelsea	Away	League	1–2	1 Goal	(8)
21	02/01/82	Coventry City	Away	FA Cup	1–3		
22	16/01/82	Blackburn Rovers	Home	League	2–2		
23	19/01/82	Crystal Palace	Away	League	2–1	1 Goal	(9)
24	30/01/82	Derby County	Away	League	1–3	1 Goal	(10)
25	03/02/82	Norwich City	Away	League	3–2	2 Goals	(12)
26	06/02/82	Luton Town	Home	League	3–3	1 Goal	(13)
27	13/02/82	Wrexham	Away	League	1–0	1 Goal	(14)
28	16/02/82	Bolton Wanderers	Home	League	0–1		
29	20/02/82	Grimsby Town	Home	League	1–1	1 Goal	(15)
30	24/02/82	Newcastle United	Away	League	0–1		
31	27/02/82	Cardiff City	Away	League	2–0	1 Goal	(16)
32	02/03/82	Shrewsbury Town	Home	League	0–0		
33	06/03/82	Charlton Athletic	Home	League	1–1		
34	13/03/82	Oldham Athletic	Away	League	3–0	1 Goal	(17)
35	20/03/82	Leicester City	Home	League	2–0	1 Goal	(18)
36	27/03/82	Orient	Home	League	2–0		
37	29/03/82	Queens Park Rangers	Away	League	0–2		
38	10/04/82	Shrewsbury Town	Away	League	1–0	1 Goal	(19)
39	12/04/82	Newcastle United	Home	League	2–1		
40	17/04/82	Cambridge United	Home	League	2–1		
41	24/04/82	Watford	Away	League	0–4		
42	01/05/82	Chelsea	Home	League	0–0		
43	04/05/82	Rotherham United	Away	League	2–2	2 Goals	(21)
44	08/05/82	Bolton Wanderers	Away	League	1–3		
45	15/05/82	Norwich City	Home	League	2–1	1 Goal	(22)

SEASON 1982–83

League Division Two

No	Date	Opponent	Venue	Competition	Score	Goals	
46	28/08/82	Middlesbrough	Home	League	3–1	1 Goal	(23)
47	04/09/82	Charlton Athletic	Away	League	3–0	1 Goal	(24)
48	07/09/82	Bolton Wanderers	Home	League	3–1		
49	11/09/82	Leeds United	Home	League	2–3	1 Goal	(25)
50	18/09/82	Queens Park Rangers	Away	League	2–0	1 Goal	(26)
51	25/09/82	Chelsea	Home	League	3–2	1 Goal	(27)
52	28/09/82	Carlisle United	Away	League	2–4		
53	02/10/82	Blackburn Rovers	Away	League	3–2	2 Goals	(29)
54	04/10/82	Bristol City	Away	Lge Cup	1–2		
55	09/10/82	Wolverhampton Wanderers	Home	League	0–0		
56	16/10/82	Cambridge United	Away	League	2–2	2 Goals	(31)
57	23/10/82	Grimsby Town	Home	League	2–0		
58	26/10/82	Bristol City	Home	Lge Cup	1–1		
59	30/10/82	Leicester City	Away	League	2–0		
60	06/11/82	Derby County	Home	League	2–0	2 Goals	(33)
61	09/11/82	Crystal Palace	Away	Lge Cup	2–1	1 Goal	(34)
62	13/11/82	Shrewsbury Town	Away	League	0–1		
63	20/11/82	Burnley	Home	League	1–1		
64	27/11/82	Fulham	Away	League	0–1		
65	30/11/82	Barnsley	Home	Lge Cup	1–0		
66	04/12/82	Oldham Athletic	Home	League	1–1	1 Goal	(35)
67	11/12/82	Crystal Palace	Away	League	0–2		
68	18/12/82	Newcastle United	Home	League	1–1		
69	27/12/82	Barnsley	Away	League	0–0		
70	28/12/82	Rotherham United	Home	League	0–1		
71	01/01/83	Burnley	Away	League	1–4		
72	03/01/83	Charlton Athletic	Home	League	5–4	1 Goal	(36)
73	08/01/83	Southend United	Away	FA Cup	0–0		
74	11/01/83	Southend United	Home	FA Cup	2–2*		
75	15/01/83	Middlesbrough	Away	League	1–1		
76	18/01/83	Arsenal	Away	Lge Cup	0–1		
77	22/01/83	Carlisle United	Home	League	1–1		
78	24/01/83	Southend United	Home	FA Cup	2–1		
79	29/01/83	Torquay United	Away	FA Cup	3–2		
80	26/02/83	Cambridge United	Home	League	3–1		
81	01/03/83	Wolverhampton Wanderers	Away	League	0–1		
82	05/03/83	Grimsby Town	Away	League	1–1		
83	12/03/83	Burnley	Away	FA Cup	1–1	1 Goal	(37)
84	26/03/83	Shrewsbury Town	Home	League	0–0		
85	02/04/83	Rotherham United	Away	League	3–0	2 Goals	(39)
86	04/04/83	Barnsley	Home	League	0–1		
87	09/04/83	Bolton Wanderers	Away	League	2–0	1 Goal	(40)
88	16/04/83	Brighton & Hove Albion	Neutral	FA Cup	1–2		
89	19/04/83	Queens Park Rangers	Home	League	0–1		
90	23/04/83	Oldham Athletic	Away	League	1–1	1 Goal	(41)
91	27/04/83	Leeds United	Away	League	2–1	1 Goal	(42)
92	30/04/83	Fulham	Home	League	2–1		
93	02/05/83	Chelsea	Away	League	1–1	1 Goal	(43)
94	07/05/83	Newcastle United	Away	League	1–2		
95	14/05/83	Crystal Palace	Home	League	2–1	1 Goal	(44)

SEASON 1983–84

League Division Two

No	Date	Opponent	Venue	Competition	Score	Goals	
96	27/08/83	Swansea City	Away	League	1–0		
97	29/08/83	Derby County	Away	League	1–1	1 Goal	(45)
98	03/09/83	Carlisle United	Home	League	2–0	1 Goal	(46)
99	06/09/83	Cambridge United	Home	League	1–0		
100	10/09/83	Charlton Athletic	Away	League	1–1		
101	17/09/83	Chelsea	Home	League	2–1		
102	24/09/83	Oldham Athletic	Away	League	3–1		
103	01/10/83	Blackburn Rovers	Home	League	4–2	1 Goal	(47)
104	04/10/83	Darlington	Home	Lge Cup	3–0	1 Goal	(48)
105	08/10/83	Leeds United	Home	League	3–1		
106	15/10/83	Portsmouth	Away	League	1–0		
107	22/10/83	Brighton & Hove Albion	Away	League	3–1	1 Goal	(49)
108	25/10/83	Darlington	Away	Lge Cup	4–2	2 Goals	(51)
109	29/10/83	Huddersfield Town	Home	League	0–0		
110	05/11/83	Barnsley	Home	League	2–0		
111	08/11/83	Preston North End	Away	Lge Cup	2–0		
112	11/11/83	Fulham	Away	League	1–1		
113	19/11/83	Newcastle United	Home	League	4–2	1 Goal	(52)

114	26/11/83	Crystal Palace	Away	League	0–1		
115	30/11/83	Stoke City	Away	Lge Cup	1–0	1 Goal	(53)
116	03/12/83	Shrewsbury Town	Home	League	1–1		
117	10/12/83	Manchester City	Away	League	2–1		
118	17/12/83	Cardiff City	Home	League	5–2	1 Goal	(54)
119	26/12/83	Grimsby Town	Away	League	0–1		
120	31/12/83	Carlisle United	Away	League	1–1		
121	02/01/84	Oldham Athletic	Home	League	3–0	1 Goal	(55)
122	07/01/84	Barnsley	Home	FA Cup	1–0		
123	14/01/84	Swansea City	Home	League	6–1		
124	17/01/84	Liverpool	Home	Lge Cup	2–2		
125	21/01/84	Chelsea	Away	League	2–3	1 Goal	(56)
126	25/01/84	Liverpool	Away	Lge Cup	0–3		
127	30/01/84	Coventry City	Home	FA Cup	3–2	1 Goal	(57)
128	04/02/84	Blackburn Rovers	Away	League	0–0		
129	11/02/84	Charlton Athletic	Home	League	4–1	1 Goal	(58)
130	18/02/84	Oxford United	Away	FA Cup	3–0	2 Goals	(60)
131	25/02/84	Brighton & Hove Albion	Home	League	2–1	1 Goal	(61)
132	03/03/84	Barnsley	Away	League	1–0		
133	07/03/84	Fulham	Home	League	1–1		
134	11/03/84	Southampton	Home	FA Cup	0–0		
135	17/03/84	Cambridge United	Away	League	2–1	1 Goal	(62)
136	20/03/84	Southampton	Away	FA Cup	1–5		
137	31/03/84	Leeds United	Away	League	1–1	1 Goal	(63)
138	07/04/84	Portsmouth	Home	League	2–0		
Sub+1	28/04/84	Crystal Palace	Home	League	1–0		
139	01/05/84	Huddersfield Town	Away	League	1–0		
140	05/05/84	Shrewsbury Town	Away	League	1–2	1 Goal	(64)
141	07/05/84	Manchester City	Home	League	0–0		
142	12/05/84	Cardiff City	Away	League	2–0	1 Goal	(65)

SEASON 1984–85

Queens Park Rangers – League Division One

1	25/08/84	West Bromwich Albion	Home	League	3–1		
2	28/08/84	Watford	Away	League	1–1	1 Goal	(1)
3	01/09/84	Liverpool	Away	League	1–1		
4	08/09/84	Nottingham Forest	Home	League	3–0	1 Goal	(2)
5	15/09/84	Tottenham Hotspur	Away	League	0–5		
6	18/09/84	KR Reykjavik	Away	UEFA Cup	3–0	1 Goal	(3)
7	22/09/84	Newcastle United	Home	League	5–5	1 Goal	(4)
8	25/09/84	York City	Away	Lge Cup	4–2	2 Goals	(6)
9	29/09/84	Southampton	Away	League	1–1		
10	02/10/84	KR Reykjavik	Home	UEFA Cup	4–0	3 Goals	(9)
11	06/10/84	Luton Town	Home	League	2–3	1 Goal	(10)
12	09/10/84	York City	Home	Lge Cup	4–1	2 Goals	(12)
13	13/10/84	Ipswich Town	Away	League	1–1		
14	20/10/84	Coventry City	Home	League	2–1		
15	24/10/84	FK Partizan Beograd	Home	UEFA Cup	6–2	2 Goals	(14)
16	27/10/84	Norwich City	Away	League	0–2		
17	30/10/84	Aston Villa	Home	Lge Cup	1–0		
18	03/11/84	Sunderland	Away	League	0–3		
19	07/11/84	KF Partizan Beograd	Away	UEFA Cup	0–4		
20	10/11/84	Sheffield Wednesday	Home	League	0–0		
21	17/11/84	Arsenal	Away	League	0–1		
22	20/11/84	Southampton	Away	Lge Cup	1–1		
23	24/11/84	Aston Villa	Home	League	2–0	1 Goal	(15)
24	27/11/84	Southampton	Home	Lge Cup	0–0*		
25	01/12/84	Leicester City	Away	League	0–4		
26	04/12/84	Stoke City	Home	League	2–0	1 Goal	(16)
27	08/12/84	Everton	Home	League	0–0		
28	12/12/84	Southampton	Home	Lge Cup	4–0		
29	15/12/84	Manchester United	Away	League	0–3		
30	21/12/84	Liverpool	Home	League	0–2		
31	26/12/84	Chelsea	Home	League	2–2	1 Goal	(17)
32	29/12/84	Stoke City	Away	League	2–0		
33	01/01/85	West Ham United	Away	League	3–1	1 Goal	(18)
34	05/01/85	Doncaster Rovers	Away	FA Cup	0–1		
35	12/01/85	Tottenham Hotspur	Home	League	2–2	2 Goals	(20)
36	23/01/85	Ipswich Town	Away	Lge Cup	0–0		
37	26/01/85	West Bromwich Albion	Away	League	0–0		
38	28/01/85	Ipswich Town	Home	Lge Cup	1–2	1 Goal	(21)
39	02/02/85	Southampton	Home	League	0–4		
40	09/02/85	Nottingham Forest	Away	League	0–2		
41	23/02/85	Sunderland	Home	League	1–0		

42	02/03/85	Norwich City	Home	League	2–2		
43	09/03/85	Coventry City	Away	League	0–3		
44	16/03/85	Ipswich Town	Home	League	3–0	1 Goal	(22)
45	23/03/85	Luton Town	Away	League	0–2		
46	30/03/85	Watford	Home	League	2–0		
47	06/04/85	Chelsea	Away	League	0–1		
48	08/04/85	West Ham United	Home	League	4–2	2 Goals	(24)
49	13/04/85	Newcastle United	Away	League	0–1		
50	20/04/85	Arsenal	Home	League	1–0		
51	23/04/85	Sheffield Wednesday	Away	League	1–3		
52	27/04/85	Aston Villa	Away	League	2–5	2 Goals	(26)
53	04/05/85	Leicester City	Home	League	4–3	1 Goal	(27)
54	06/05/85	Everton	Away	League	0–2		
55	11/05/85	Manchester United	Home	League	1–3	1 Goal	(28)

SEASON 1985–86

League Division One

56	17/08/85	Ipswich Town	Home	League	1–0		
57	20/08/85	West Ham United	Away	League	1–3		
58	24/08/85	Aston Villa	Away	League	2–1	2 Goals	(30)
59	27/08/85	Nottingham Forest	Home	League	2–1	1 Goal	(31)
60	31/08/85	Newcastle United	Away	League	1–3		
61	03/09/85	Arsenal	Home	League	0–1		
62	07/09/85	Everton	Home	League	3–0	2 Goals	(33)
63	14/09/85	Watford	Away	League	0–2		
64	21/09/85	Luton Town	Away	League	0–2		
65	24/09/85	Hull City	Home	Lge Cup	3–0	1 Goal	(34)
66	28/09/85	Birmingham City	Home	League	3–1	1 Goal	(35)
67	05/10/85	Liverpool	Home	League	2–1	1 Goal	(36)
68	07/10/85	Hull City	Away	Lge Cup	5–1		
69	12/10/85	Manchester United	Away	League	0–2		
70	19/10/85	Manchester City	Home	League	0–0		
71	26/10/85	Southampton	Away	League	0–3		
72	29/10/85	Watford	Away	Lge Cup	1–0		
73	02/11/85	Sheffield Wednesday	Home	League	1–1		
74	09/11/85	West Bromwich Albion	Away	League	1–0		
75	16/11/85	Leicester City	Home	League	2–0		
76	23/11/85	Tottenham Hotspur	Away	League	1–1		
77	25/11/85	Nottingham Forest	Home	Lge Cup	3–1	1 Goal	(37)
78	30/11/85	Coventry City	Home	League	0–2		
79	07/12/85	West Ham United	Home	League	0–1		
80	28/12/85	Arsenal	Away	League	1–3	1 Goal	(38)
81	01/01/86	Oxford United	Home	League	3–1		
82	11/01/86	Everton	Away	League	3–4	2 Goals	(40)
83	13/01/86	Carlisle United	Away	FA Cup	0–1		
84	18/01/86	Newcastle United	Home	League	3–1		
85	22/01/86	Chelsea	Home	Lge Cup	1–1		
86	29/01/86	Chelsea	Away	Lge Cup	2–0*		
87	01/02/86	Nottingham Forest	Away	League	0–4		
88	08/02/86	Manchester City	Away	League	0–2		
89	12/02/86	Liverpool	Home	Lge Cup	1–1		
90	22/02/86	Luton Town	Home	League	1–1		
91	05/03/86	Liverpool	Away	Lge Cup	2–2		
92	15/03/86	Manchester United	Home	League	1–0		
93	19/03/86	Chelsea	Away	League	1–1		
94	22/03/86	Watford	Home	League	2–1		
95	29/03/86	Oxford United	Away	League	3–3		
96	31/03/86	Chelsea	Home	League	6–0	3 Goals	(43)
97	08/04/86	Sheffield Wednesday	Away	League	0–0		
98	12/04/86	West Bromwich Albion	Home	League	1–0	1 Goal	(44)
99	14/04/86	Leicester City	Away	League	4–1	1 Goal	(45)
100	20/04/86	Oxford United	Wembley	Lge Cup	0–3		
101	26/04/86	Tottenham Hotspur	Home	League	2–5	1 Goal	(46)

SEASON 1986–87

League Division One

102	23/08/86	Southampton	Away	League	1–5		
103	26/08/86	Watford	Home	League	3–2	1 Goal	(47)
104	30/08/86	Aston Villa	Home	League	1–0	1 Goal	(48)
105	03/09/86	Newcastle United	Away	League	2–0	1 Goal	(49)
106	20/09/86	Manchester City	Away	League	0–0		
107	23/09/86	Blackburn Rovers	Home	Lge Cup	2–1		
108	27/09/86	Leicester City	Home	League	0–1		

109	04/10/86	Norwich City	Away	League	0–1		
110	07/10/86	Blackburn Rovers	Away	Lge Cup	2–2	1 Goal	(50)
111	11/10/86	Wimbledon	Home	League	2–1	1 Goal	(51)
112	18/10/86	Nottingham Forest	Away	League	0–1		
113	25/10/86	Tottenham Hotspur	Home	League	2–0		
114	28/10/86	Charlton Athletic	Away	Lge Cup	0–1		
115	01/11/86	Luton Town	Away	League	0–1		
116	08/11/86	Liverpool	Home	League	1–3	1 Goal	(52)
117	15/11/86	Oxford United	Home	League	1–1		
118	22/11/86	Manchester United	Away	League	0–1		
119	29/11/86	Sheffield Wednesday	Home	League	2–2	1 Goal	(53)
120	06/12/86	Arsenal	Away	League	1–3	1 Goal	(54)
121	13/12/86	Charlton Athletic	Home	League	0–0		
122	20/12/86	West Ham United	Away	League	1–1		
123	26/12/86	Coventry City	Home	League	3–1	1 Goal	(55)
124	27/12/86	Oxford United	Away	League	1–0		
125	10/01/87	Leicester City	Home	FA Cup	5–2		
126	24/01/87	Southampton	Home	League	2–1	1 Goal	(56)
127	31/01/87	Luton Town	Away	FA Cup	1–1		
128	04/02/87	Luton Town	Home	FA Cup	2–1		
129	14/02/87	Newcastle United	Home	League	2–1		
130	28/02/87	Manchester City	Home	League	1–0		
131	21/02/87	Leeds United	Away	FA Cup	1–2		
132	07/03/87	Tottenham Hotspur	Away	League	0–1		
133	14/03/87	Nottingham Forest	Home	League	3–1	1 Goal	(57)
134	18/03/87	Liverpool	Away	League	1–2		
135	21/03/87	Wimbledon	Away	League	1–1		
136	25/03/87	Leicester City	Away	League	1–4		
137	28/03/87	Norwich City	Home	League	1–1		
138	06/04/87	Watford	Away	League	3–0	3 Goals	(60)
139	11/04/87	Luton Town	Home	League	2–2		
140	18/04/87	Chelsea	Home	League	1–1	1 Goal	(61)
141	20/04/87	Coventry City	Away	League	0–4	1 Goal	(62)
142	25/04/87	Manchester United	Away	League	1–1		

SEASON 1987–88

League Division One

143	15/08/87	West Ham United	Away	League	3–0	1 Goal	(63)
144	19/08/87	Derby County	Home	League	1–1	1 Goal	(64)
145	22/08/87	Arsenal	Home	League	2–0		
146	29/08/87	Southampton	Away	League	1–0		
147	02/09/87	Everton	Home	League	1–0		
148	05/09/87	Charlton Athletic	Away	League	1–0		
149	12/09/87	Chelsea	Home	League	3–1	3 Goals	(67)
150	19/09/87	Oxford United	Away	League	0–2		
151	23/09/87	Millwall	Home	Lge Cup	2–1	1 Goal	(68)
152	26/09/87	Luton Town	Home	League	2–0		
153	03/10/87	Wimbledon	Away	League	2–1	1 Goal	(69)
154	06/10/87	Millwall	Away	Lge Cup	0–0		
155	17/10/87	Liverpool	Away	League	0–4		
156	24/10/87	Portsmouth	Home	League	2–1		
157	27/10/87	Bury	Home	Lge Cup	0–1		
158	21/11/87	Newcastle United	Home	League	1–1		
159	28/11/87	Sheffield Wednesday	Away	League	1–3	1 Goal	(70)
160	05/12/87	Manchester United	Home	League	0–2		
161	13/12/87	Nottingham Forest	Away	League	0–4		
162	18/12/87	Coventry City	Home	League	1–2		
163	26/12/87	Chelsea	Away	League	1–1		
164	28/12/87	Oxford United	Home	League	3–2		
165	01/01/88	Southampton	Home	League	3–0	1 Goal	(71)
166	02/01/88	Arsenal	Away	League	0–0		
167	09/01/88	Yeovil Town	Away	FA Cup	3–0		
168	16/01/88	West Ham United	Home	League	0–1		
169	30/01/88	West Ham United	Home	FA Cup	3–2	1 Goal	(72)
170	06/02/88	Charlton Athletic	Home	League	2–0		
171	13/02/88	Everton	Away	League	0–2		
172	20/02/88	Luton Town	Home	FA Cup	1–1		

Coventry City – League Division One

1	12/03/88	Southampton	Away	League	2–1		
2	15/03/88	Luton Town	Home	League	4–0	1 Goal	(1)
3	19/03/88	Derby County	Home	League	0–3		
4	26/03/88	Newcastle United	Away	League	2–2		
Sub+1	09/04/88	Charlton Athletic	Home	League	0–0		

5	30/04/88	Portsmouth	Home	League	1–0		
6	02/05/88	Arsenal	Away	League	1–1		
7	07/05/88	Queens Park Rangers	Home	League	0–0		

SEASON 1988–89

League Division One

8	03/09/88	Everton	Home	League	0–1		
9	10/09/88	Sheffield Wednesday	Away	League	2–1		
10	17/09/88	Charlton Athletic	Home	League	3–0	1 Goal	(2)
11	24/09/88	Wimbledon	Away	League	1–0	1 Goal	(3)
12	27/09/88	AFC Bournemouth	Away	Lge Cup	4–0	1 Goal	(4)
13	01/10/88	Middlesbrough	Home	League	3–4		
14	08/10/88	Newcastle United	Away	League	3–0		
15	11/10/88	AFC Bournemouth	Home	Lge Cup	3–1		
16	15/10/88	Millwall	Home	League	0–0		
17	22/10/88	Liverpool	Away	League	0–0		
18	29/10/88	Arsenal	Away	League	0–2		
19	02/11/88	Nottingham Forest	Away	Lge Cup	2–3	1 Goal	(5)
20	05/11/88	West Ham United	Home	League	1–1		
21	12/11/88	Luton Town	Home	League	1–0		
Sub+2	17/12/88	Derby County	Home	League	0–2		
22	26/12/88	Southampton	Away	League	2–2	1 Goal	(6)
23	31/12/88	Everton	Away	League	1–3	1 Goal	(7)
24	04/02/89	Middlesbrough	Away	League	1–1		
25	11/02/89	Newcastle United	Home	League	1–2		
26	11/03/89	West Ham United	Away	League	1–1		
27	18/03/89	Tottenham Hotspur	Home	League	1–1	1 Goal	(8)
28	22/03/89	Liverpool	Home	League	1–3	1 Goal	(9)
29	25/03/89	Charlton Athletic	Away	League	0–0		
Sub+3	15/04/89	Luton Town	Away	League	2–2		
30	22/04/89	Queens Park Rangers	Home	League	0–3		
31	29/04/89	Manchester United	Away	League	1–0	1 Goal	(10)
32	13/05/89	Aston Villa	Away	League	1–1	1 Goal	(11)

SEASON 1989–90

League Division One

33	19/08/89	Everton	Home	League	2–0	1 Goal	(12)
34	22/08/89	Arsenal	Away	League	0–2		
35	26/08/89	Crystal Palace	Away	League	1–0		
36	30/08/89	Manchester City	Home	League	2–1		
37	09/09/89	Millwall	Away	League	1–4		
38	16/09/89	Luton Town	Home	League	1–0	1 Goal	(13)
39	19/09/89	Grimsby Town	Away	Lge Cup	1–3		
40	23/09/89	Chelsea	Away	League	0–1		
41	30/09/89	Sheffield Wednesday	Away	League	0–0		
42	04/10/89	Grimsby Town	Home	Lge Cup	3–0		
43	14/10/89	Nottingham Forest	Home	League	0–2		
Sub+4	18/11/89	Aston Villa	Away	League	1–4		
44	13/01/90	Crystal Palace	Home	League	1–0		

West Bromwich Albion – League Division Two

1	10/03/90	Blackburn Rovers	Away	League	1–2		
2	14/03/90	Bradford City	Home	League	2–0		
3	17/03/90	Watford	Home	League	2–0		
4	20/03/90	Wolverhampton Wanderers	Away	League	1–2		
5	24/03/90	Stoke City	Home	League	1–1		
6	31/03/90	Hull City	Away	League	2–0		
7	04/04/90	West Ham United	Home	League	1–3		
8	07/04/90	Middlesbrough	Home	League	0–0		
9	11/04/90	Newcastle United	Away	League	1–2		
10	14/04/90	Brighton & Hove Albion	Away	League	3–0	1 Goal	(1)
11	16/04/90	Plymouth Argyle	Home	League	0–3		
12	28/04/90	Barnsley	Away	League	2–2		
13	05/05/90	Ipswich Town	Home	League	1–3	1 Goal	(2)

SEASON 1990–91

League Division Two

14	25/08/90	Portsmouth	Away	League	1–1		
15	29/08/90	Bristol City	Home	Lge Cup	2–2	1 Goal	(3)
16	01/09/90	Ipswich Town	Home	League	1–2	1 Goal	(4)
17	05/09/90	Bristol City	Away	Lge Cup	0–1*		
18	08/09/90	Oxford United	Away	League	3–1	1 Goal	(5)

19	15/09/90	Bristol City	Home	League	2–1	1 Goal	(6)
20	22/09/90	Hull City	Away	League	1–1		
21	29/09/90	Oldham Athletic	Home	League	0–0		
22	02/10/90	Plymouth Argyle	Away	League	0–2		
23	06/10/90	Millwall	Away	League	1–4		
24	13/10/90	Brighton & Hove Albion	Home	League	1–1		
25	20/10/90	Barnsley	Home	League	1–1		
26	22/10/90	Port Vale	Away	League	2–1	1 Goal	(7)
27	27/10/90	Newcastle United	Away	League	1–1		
28	03/11/90	Bristol Rovers	Home	League	3–1		
29	06/11/90	Middlesbrough	Home	League	0–1		
30	10/11/90	Notts County	Away	League	3–4	2 Goals	(9)
31	17/11/90	Blackburn Rovers	Home	League	2–0	1 Goal	(10)
32	21/11/90	Barnsley	Home	ZDS Cup	3–5	1 Goal	(11)
33	24/11/90	Sheffield Wednesday	Home	League	1–2		
34	01/12/90	West Ham United	Away	League	1–3		
35	05/12/90	Watford	Home	League	1–1		
Sub+1	15/12/90	Portsmouth	Home	League	0–0		
Sub+2	22/12/90	Swindon Town	Away	League	1–2		
36	26/12/90	Charlton Athletic	Home	League	1–0		
37	29/12/90	Wolverhampton Wanderers	Home	League	1–1	1 Goal	(12)
38	01/01/91	Leicester City	Away	League	1–2		
39	05/01/91	Woking	Home	FA Cup	2–4		
40	12/01/91	Ipswich Town	Away	League	0–1		
41	19/01/91	Oxford United	Home	League	2–0	1 Goal	(13)
42	02/02/91	Bristol City	Away	League	0–2		
43	16/02/91	Blackburn Rovers	Away	League	3–0		
44	19/02/91	Middlesbrough	Away	League	2–3	2 Goals	(15)
45	23/02/91	Notts County	Home	League	2–2	2 Goals	(17)
46	02/03/91	West Ham United	Home	League	0–0		
47	09/03/91	Sheffield Wednesday	Away	League	0–1		
48	13/03/91	Plymouth Argyle	Home	League	1–2		
49	16/03/91	Oldham Athletic	Away	League	1–2		
50	20/03/91	Brighton & Hove Albion	Away	League	0–2		
51	23/03/91	Millwall	Home	League	0–1		
52	01/04/91	Swindon Town	Home	League	2–1		
53	06/04/91	Wolverhampton Wanderers	Away	League	2–2		
54	10/04/91	Hull City	Home	League	1–1		
55	13/04/91	Leicester City	Home	League	2–1		
Sub+3	20/04/91	Barnsley	Away	League	1–1		
Sub+4	27/04/91	Port Vale	Home	League	1–1		
Sub+5	04/05/91	Newcastle United	Home	League	1–1		
Sub+6	11/05/91	Bristol Rovers	Away	League	1–1		

SEASON 1991–92

League Division Three

56	17/08/91	Exeter City	Home	League	6–3		
57	20/08/91	Swindon Town	Away	Lge Cup	0–2		
Sub+7	28/08/91	Swindon Town	Home	Lge Cup	2–2		
58	31/08/91	Wigan Athletic	Home	League	1–1		
59	03/09/91	Fulham	Away	League	0–0		
60	14/09/91	Stockport County	Home	League	1–0		
Sub+8	05/11/91	Hartlepool United	Away	League	0–0		
Sub+9	09/11/91	Reading	Away	League	2–1		
Sub+10	04/12/91	Lincoln City	Away	A Trophy	2–1		
Sub+11	09/12/91	Leyton Orient	Away	FA Cup	1–2		
Sub+12	22/12/91	Darlington	Home	League	3–1		
61	04/01/92	Torquay United	Away	League	0–1		
62	11/01/92	AFC Bournemouth	Home	League	4–0	2 Goals	(19)
63	14/01/92	Exeter City	Home	A Trophy	0–1		
64	18/01/92	Leyton Orient	Away	League	1–1		
65	25/01/92	Swansea City	Home	League	2–3		
Sub+13	12/02/92	Stoke City	Away	League	0–1		
66	03/03/92	Leyton Orient	Home	League	1–3	1 Goal	(20)
67	06/03/92	Swansea City	Away	League	0–0		
68	11/03/92	Hartlepool United	Home	League	1–2		

Oxford United (loan) – League Division Two

Sub+1	21/03/92	Portsmouth	Home	League	2–1		
Sub+2	28/03/92	Bristol City	Away	League	1–1	1 Goal	(1)
Sub+3	01/04/92	Millwall	Away	League	1–2		
1	04/04/92	Wolverhampton Wanderers	Home	League	1–0		
2	11/04/92	Derby County	Away	League	2–2		
3	15/04/92	Middlesbrough	Away	League	1–2		

4	18/04/92	Bristol Rovers	Home	League	2–2		
5	20/04/92	Plymouth Argyle	Away	League	1–3	1 Goal	(2)
6	25/04/92	Ipswich Town	Home	League	1–1		
7	02/05/92	Tranmere Rovers	Away	League	2–1		

SEASON 1992–93

Nottingham Forest – Premier League

Sub+1	22/08/92	Oldham Athletic	Away	League	3–5	2 Goals	(2)
1	29/08/92	Manchester City	Home	League	0–2		
2	31/08/92	Norwich City	Away	League	1–3		
3	05/09/92	Blackburn Rovers	Away	League	1–4	1 Goal	(3)
4	12/09/92	Sheffield Wednesday	Home	League	1–2	1 Goal	(4)
5	21/09/92	Coventry City	Home	League	1–1		
6	23/09/92	Stockport County	Away	Lge Cup	3–2	1 Goal	(5)
7	26/09/92	Chelsea	Away	League	0–0		
8	03/10/92	Manchester City	Away	League	2–2		
9	07/10/92	Stockport County	Home	Lge Cup	2–1		
10	17/10/92	Arsenal	Home	League	0–1		
11	21/10/92	Middlesbrough	Home	League	1–0		
Sub+2	31/10/92	Ipswich Town	Home	League	0–1		
12	21/11/92	Crystal Palace	Away	League	1–1	1 Goal	(6)
13	28/11/92	Southampton	Home	League	1–2		
Sub+3	02/12/92	Tottenham Hotspur	Home	Lge Cup	2–0		
Sub+4	05/12/92	Leeds United	Away	League	4–1		
14	09/01/93	Coventry City	Away	League	1–0		
15	16/01/93	Chelsea	Home	League	3–0	2 Goals	(8)
16	23/01/93	Middlesbrough	Home	FA Cup	1–1		
17	27/01/93	Manchester United	Away	League	0–2		
18	30/01/93	Oldham Athletic	Home	League	2–0		
19	03/02/93	Middlesbrough	Away	FA Cup	3–0	1 Goal	(9)
20	06/02/93	Liverpool	Away	League	0–0		
21	13/02/93	Arsenal	Away	FA Cup	0–2		
22	20/02/93	Middlesbrough	Away	League	2–1		
23	24/02/93	Queens Park Rangers	Home	League	1–0		
Sub+5	03/03/93	Crystal Palace	Home	League	1–1		
24	13/03/93	Everton	Away	League	0–3		
25	17/03/93	Norwich City	Home	League	0–3		
26	21/03/93	Leeds United	Home	League	1–1		
27	24/03/93	Southampton	Away	League	2–1		
28	04/04/93	Aston Villa	Home	League	0–1		
29	07/04/93	Blackburn Rovers	Home	League	1–3		
30	10/04/93	Queens Park Rangers	Away	League	3–4	1 Goal	(10)
31	12/04/93	Tottenham Hotspur	Home	League	2–1		
32	17/04/93	Wimbledon	Away	League	0–1		

SEASON 1993–94

Stoke City – Football League Division One

1	14/08/93	Millwall	Home	League	1–2		
Sub+1	11/09/93	Tranmere Rovers	Home	League	1–2		
Sub+2	03/11/93	Sunderland	Home	League	1–0		
Sub+3	16/11/93	Padova Calcio	Away	AI Cup	0–3		
Sub+4	20/11/93	Notts County	Away	League	0–2		
Sub+5	27/11/93	Luton Town	Away	League	2–6		
2	04/12/93	Watford	Home	League	2–0	1 Goal	(1)
3	11/12/93	Middlesbrough	Home	League	3–1	1 Goal	(2)
4	19/12/93	Millwall	Away	League	0–2		
5	26/12/93	Birmingham City	Home	League	2–1		
6	29/12/93	Charlton Athletic	Away	League	0–2		
7	01/01/94	Derby County	Home	League	2–1		
8	03/01/94	Bristol City	Away	League	0–0		
9	08/01/94	Bath City	Home	FA Cup	0–0		
10	09/01/94	Oldham Athletic	Home	FA Cup	0–1		
11	12/02/94	Barnsley	Away	League	0–3		
12	12/03/94	Nottingham Forest	Home	League	0–1		
Sub+6	23/04/94	Notts County	Home	League	0–0		

Hong Kong Rangers
No Competitive Matches

SEASON 1994–95

Lincoln City – Football League Division Three

Sub+1	17/09/94	Exeter City	Away	League	0–1	

1	20/09/94	Crystal Palace	Home	Lge Cup	1–0		
2	24/09/94	Hartlepool United	Away	League	3–0		
3	01/10/94	Northampton Town	Home	League	2–2		
4	04/10/94	Crystal Palace	Away	Lge Cup	0–3*		
5	08/10/94	Carlisle United	Home	League	1–1	1 Goal	(1)
6	15/10/94	Bury	Away	League	0–2		
7	17/10/94	Doncaster Rovers	Away	AW Shield	0–1		
8	22/10/94	Scarborough	Home	League	2–0	1 Goal	(2)
9	29/10/94	Hereford United	Away	League	3–0		
10	05/11/94	Barnet	Home	League	1–2		
11	12/11/94	Hull City	Away	FA Cup	1–0	1 Goal	(3)
12	19/11/94	Fulham	Away	League	1–1	1 Goal	(4)
13	26/11/94	Gillingham	Home	League	1–1		
Sub+2	10/12/94	Walsall	Home	League	1–1		
Sub+3	17/12/94	Torquay United	Away	League	1–2		
14	26/12/94	Scunthorpe United	Away	League	0–2		
15	27/12/94	Darlington	Home	League	3–1		
16	31/12/94	Chesterfield	Away	League	0–1		
Sub+4	08/01/95	Huddersfield Town	Home	FA Cup	1–0		
Sub+5	21/02/95	Colchester United	Home	League	2–0	1 Goal	(5)
17	25/02/95	Northampton Town	Away	League	1–3		
18	04/03/95	Hartlepool United	Home	League	3–0	1 Goal	(6)
19	11/03/95	Mansfield Town	Away	League	2–6		
20	18/03/95	Rochdale	Home	League	2–2		
21	25/03/95	Preston North End	Home	League	1–1		
22	01/04/95	Wigan Athletic	Away	League	1–0		
23	04/04/95	Barnet	Away	League	1–2		
24	08/04/95	Chesterfield	Home	League	0–1		
25	11/04/95	Fulham	Home	League	2–0		
26	15/04/95	Darlington	Away	League	0–0		
27	17/04/95	Scunthorpe United	Home	League	3–3		
28	22/04/95	Colchester United	Away	League	2–1	1 Goal	(7)
29	06/05/95	Carlisle United	Away	League	3–1	1 Goal	(8)

SEASON 1995–96

Darlington – Football League Division Three

1	12/08/95	Exeter City	Away	League	1–0		
2	19/08/95	Rochdale	Home	League	0–1		
3	23/08/95	Crewe Alexandra	Away	Lge Cup	0–4		
4	26/08/95	Leyton Orient	Away	League	1–1		
5	29/08/95	Fulham	Home	League	1–1		
6	02/09/95	Cardiff City	Home	League	0–1		
7	05/09/95	Crewe Alexandra	Home	Lge Cup	1–1		
8	09/09/95	Hartlepool United	Away	League	1–1		
9	12/09/95	Mansfield Town	Away	League	2–2	1 Goal	(1)
10	16/09/95	Colchester United	Home	League	2–2	1 Goal	(2)
11	23/09/95	Scarborough	Home	League	1–2		
12	30/09/95	Barnet	Away	League	1–1	1 Goal	(3)
13	07/10/95	Lincoln City	Home	League	2–0		
14	14/10/95	Gillingham	Home	League	1–0	1 Goal	(4)
15	21/10/95	Cambridge United	Away	League	1–0		
16	24/10/95	Rochdale	Away	AW Shield	2–5		
17	28/10/95	Plymouth Argyle	Home	League	2–2		
18	31/10/95	Wigan Athletic	Home	League	2–1		
19	04/11/95	Bury	Away	League	0–0		
Sub+1	07/11/95	Lincoln City	Home	AW Shield	0–1		
20	11/11/95	Hartlepool United	Away	FA Cup	4–2	1 Goal	(5)
21	18/11/95	Scunthorpe United	Home	League	0–0		
22	25/11/95	Chester City	Away	League	1–4		
23	02/12/95	Rochdale	Away	FA Cup	2–2		
24	09/12/95	Scarborough	Away	League	2–1	1 Goal	(6)
25	12/12/95	Rochdale	Home	FA Cup	0–1		
26	16/12/95	Barnet	Home	League	1–1		
27	23/12/95	Torquay United	Away	League	1–0	1 Goal	(7)
28	06/01/96	Northampton Town	Home	League	1–2		
29	30/01/96	Preston North End	Home	League	1–2		
30	17/02/96	Mansfield Town	Home	League	1–1	1 Goal	(8)
31	20/02/96	Cardiff City	Away	League	2–0		
32	24/02/96	Colchester United	Away	League	1–1		
Sub+2	27/02/96	Hartlepool United	Home	League	1–0		
33	02/03/96	Doncaster Rovers	Away	League	2–1	1 Goal	(9)
34	05/03/96	Fulham	Away	League	2–2		
35	09/03/96	Torquay United	Home	League	1–2		
36	16/03/96	Preston North End	Away	League	1–1	1 Goal	(10)

37	23/03/96	Hereford United	Home	League	1–0	
38	30/03/96	Lincoln City	Home	League	3–2	
39	02/04/96	Gillingham	Away	League	0–0	
Sub+3	06/04/96	Plymouth Argyle	Away	League	1–0	
40	08/04/96	Cambridge United	Home	League	0–0	
41	13/04/96	Wigan Athletic	Away	League	1–1	
42	20/04/96	Bury	Home	League	4–0	
43	23/04/96	Hereford United	Away	League	1–0	
44	27/04/96	Chester City	Home	League	3–1	
45	04/05/96	Scunthorpe United	Away	League	3–3	1 Goal (11)
46	12/05/96	Hereford United	Away	Lge P/O	2–1	
47	15/05/96	Hereford United	Home	Lge P/O	2–1	
48	25/05/96	Plymouth Argyle	Wembley	Lge P/O	0–1	

APPEARANCES AND GOALS PER SEASON

SEASON 78–79	GAMES	GOALS
League	3+1	1
League Cup	1	0
TOTAL	**4+1**	**1**

SEASON 79–80	GAMES	GOALS
League	5+2	0
North American Soccer League	14+8	10
TOTAL	**19+10**	**10**

SEASON 80–81	GAMES	GOALS
League	9+2	2
FA Cup	2	0
League Cup	1	0
TOTAL	**12+2**	**2**

SEASON 81–82	GAMES	GOALS
League	42	21
FA Cup	1	0
League Cup	2	1
TOTAL	**45**	**22**

SEASON 82–83	GAMES	GOALS
League	39	20
FA Cup	6	1
League Cup	5	1
TOTAL	**50**	**22**

SEASON 83–84	GAMES	GOALS
League	36+1	14
FA Cup	5	3
League Cup	6	4
TOTAL	**47+1**	**21**

SEASON 84–85	GAMES	GOALS
League	42	17
FA Cup	1	0
League Cup	8	5
UEFA Cup	4	6
TOTAL	**55**	**28**

SEASON 85–86	GAMES	GOALS
League	36	16
FA Cup	1	0
League Cup	9	2
TOTAL	**46**	**18**

SEASON 86–87	GAMES	GOALS
League	34	15
FA Cup	4	0
League Cup	3	1
TOTAL	**41**	**16**

SEASON 87–88	GAMES	GOALS
League	31+1	9
FA Cup	3	1
League Cup	3	1
TOTAL	**37+1**	**11**

SEASON 88–89	GAMES	GOALS
League	22+2	8
League Cup	3	2
TOTAL	**25+2**	**10**

SEASON 89–90	GAMES	GOALS
League	23+1	4
League Cup	2	0
TOTAL	**25+1**	**4**

SEASON 90–91	GAMES	GOALS
League	38+6	13
FA Cup	1	0
League Cup	2	1
Zenith Data Systems Cup	1	1
TOTAL	**42+6**	**15**

SEASON 91–92	GAMES	GOALS
League	18+7	5
FA Cup	0+1	0
League Cup	1+1	0
Autoglass Trophy	1+1	0
TOTAL	**20+10**	**5**

SEASON 92–93	GAMES	GOALS
League	27+4	8
FA Cup	3	1
League Cup	2+1	1
TOTAL	**32+5**	**10**

SEASON 93–94	GAMES	GOALS
League	10+5	2
FA Cup	2	0
Anglo–Italian Cup	0+1	0
TOTAL	**12+6**	**2**

SEASON 94–95	GAMES	GOALS
League	25+4	7
FA Cup	1+1	1
League Cup	2	0
Auto Windscreens Shield	1	0
TOTAL	**29+5**	**8**

SEASON 95–96	GAMES	GOALS
League	39+2	10
League Play–offs	3	0
FA Cup	3	1
League Cup	2	0
Auto Windscreens Shield	1+1	0
TOTAL	**48+3**	**11**

CAREER APPEARANCES AND GOALS

COMPETITION	GAMES	TOTAL	GOALS
League	479+38	517	172
League Play–offs	3	3	0
FA Cup	33+2	35	8
League Cup	52+2	54	19
Zenith Data Systems Cup	1	1	1
Autoglass Trophy	1+1	2	0
Anglo–Italian Cup	0+1	1	0
Auto Windscreens Shield	2+1	3	0
UEFA Cup	4	4	6
North American Soccer League	14+8	22	10
TOTAL	**589+53**	**642**	**216**

HAT-TRICKS

Queens Park Rangers

1	3	KR Reykjavik	02/10/84	Home	UEFA Cup	4–0
2	3	Chelsea	31/03/86	Home	League	6–0
3	3	Watford	06/04/87	Away	League	3–0
4	3	Chelsea	12/09/87	Home	League	3–1

League: 3
UEFA Cup: 1
TOTAL: 4

HONOURS

Winners medals
None

Runner-up medals
League Cup: 85/86
League Division Two Championship: 83/84

JOHN BARNES

Born: 07/11/63 – Jamaica, West Indies
Height: 5.11
Weight: 12.07 (96–97)

Clubs
Watford: **1981–87** – Matches: **295+1** – Goals: **85**
Liverpool: **1987–97** – Matches: **403+4** – Goals: **108**

Country
England: **1983–95** – Matches: **65+14** – Goals: **11**

SEASON 1981–82

Watford – League Division Two

Sub+1	05/09/81	Oldham Athletic	Home	League	1–1		
1	12/09/81	Chelsea	Away	League	3–1		
2	19/09/81	Rotherham United	Home	League	1–0		
3	22/09/81	Wrexham	Away	League	1–0		
4	26/09/81	Luton Town	Away	League	1–4		
5	03/10/81	Barnsley	Home	League	3–1	1 Goal	(1)
6	06/10/81	Grimsby Town	Away	Lge Cup	0–1		
7	10/10/81	Orient	Home	League	3–0	2 Goals	(3)
8	17/10/81	Cambridge United	Away	League	2–1		
9	24/10/81	Norwich City	Home	League	3–0	1 Goal	(4)
10	27/10/81	Grimsby Town	Home	Lge Cup	3–1		
11	31/10/81	Shrewsbury Town	Away	League	2–0	1 Goal	(5)
12	07/11/81	Bolton Wanderers	Away	League	0–2		
13	10/11/81	Lincoln City	Home	Lge Cup	2–2		
14	14/11/81	Cardiff City	Home	League	0–0		
15	21/11/81	Blackburn Rovers	Home	League	3–2		
16	01/12/81	Queens Park Rangers	Home	Lge Cup	4–1		
17	02/01/82	Manchester United	Home	FA Cup	1–0		
18	09/01/82	Oldham Athletic	Away	League	1–1		
19	16/01/82	Newcastle United	Home	League	2–3		
20	18/01/82	Ipswich Town	Away	Lge Cup	1–2	1 Goal	(6)
21	23/01/82	West Ham United	Home	FA Cup	2–0		
22	26/01/82	Derby County	Home	League	6–1	1 Goal	(7)
23	30/01/82	Rotherham United	Away	League	2–1	1 Goal	(8)
24	06/02/82	Chelsea	Home	League	1–0		
25	09/02/82	Barnsley	Away	League	0–0		
26	13/02/82	Leicester City	Away	FA Cup	0–2		
27	20/02/82	Luton Town	Home	League	1–1		
28	27/02/82	Orient	Away	League	3–1		
29	06/03/82	Cambridge United	Home	League	0–0		
30	09/03/82	Queens Park Rangers	Home	League	4–0		
31	13/03/82	Norwich City	Away	League	2–4	1 Goal	(9)
32	16/03/82	Grimsby Town	Away	League	2–0	1 Goal	(10)
33	20/03/82	Shrewsbury Town	Home	League	3–1		
34	27/03/82	Bolton Wanderers	Home	League	3–0		
35	03/04/82	Cardiff City	Away	League	0–2		
36	09/04/82	Crystal Palace	Home	League	1–1	1 Goal	(11)
37	12/04/82	Queens Park Rangers	Away	League	0–0		
38	17/04/82	Blackburn Rovers	Away	League	2–1		
39	24/04/82	Sheffield Wednesday	Home	League	4–0	1 Goal	(12)
40	27/04/82	Crystal Palace	Away	League	3–0		
41	04/05/82	Wrexham	Home	League	2–0		
42	08/05/82	Leicester City	Home	League	3–1	2 Goals	(14)
43	15/05/82	Derby County	Away	League	2–3		

SEASON 1982–83

League Division One

44	14/08/82	Orient	Home	FL Trophy	4–1		
45	17/08/82	Colchester United	Home	FL Trophy	2–1		
46	21/08/82	Southend United	Away	FL Trophy	4–1		
47	28/08/82	Everton	Home	League	2–0		
48	31/08/82	Southampton	Away	League	4–1		
49	04/09/82	Manchester City	Away	League	0–1		
50	07/09/82	Swansea City	Home	League	2–1		
51	11/09/82	West Bromwich Albion	Home	League	3–0		
52	18/09/82	Nottingham Forest	Away	League	0–2		
53	25/09/82	Sunderland	Home	League	8–0		
54	02/10/82	Birmingham City	Away	League	1–1		
55	05/10/82	Bolton Wanderers	Away	Lge Cup	2–1		
56	09/10/82	Norwich City	Home	League	2–2		
57	16/10/82	Aston Villa	Away	League	0–3		
58	23/10/82	Coventry City	Home	League	0–0		
59	26/10/82	Bolton Wanderers	Home	Lge Cup	2–1		
60	30/10/82	Notts County	Away	League	2–3	1 Goal	(15)
61	06/11/82	Tottenham Hotspur	Away	League	1–0		
62	10/11/82	Nottingham Forest	Away	Lge Cup	3–7		
63	13/11/82	Stoke City	Home	League	1–0	1 Goal	(16)
64	20/11/82	Brighton & Hove Albion	Home	League	4–1	1 Goal	(17)
65	27/11/82	Arsenal	Away	League	4–2	2 Goals	(19)
66	04/12/82	Manchester United	Home	League	0–1		
67	08/12/82	Reading	Away	FL Trophy	3–5	2 Goals	(21)
68	11/12/82	Liverpool	Away	League	1–3		
69	18/12/82	Ipswich Town	Home	League	2–1		
70	27/12/82	Luton Town	Away	League	0–1		
71	29/12/82	West Ham United	Home	League	2–1		
72	01/01/83	Brighton & Hove Albion	Away	League	1–1		
73	03/01/83	Manchester City	Home	League	2–0		
74	08/01/83	Plymouth Argyle	Home	FA Cup	2–0		
75	15/01/83	Everton	Away	League	0–1		
76	22/01/83	Southampton	Home	League	2–0		
77	29/01/83	Fulham	Home	FA Cup	1–1		
78	01/02/83	Fulham	Away	FA Cup	2–1	1 Goal	(22)
79	06/02/83	Swansea City	Away	League	3–1	1 Goal	(23)
80	19/02/83	Aston Villa	Away	FA Cup	1–4		
81	26/02/83	Aston Villa	Home	League	2–1		
82	02/03/83	Norwich City	Away	League	0–3		
83	05/03/83	Coventry City	Away	League	1–0		
84	12/03/83	Notts County	Home	League	5–3	1 Goal	(24)
85	19/03/83	Tottenham Hotspur	Home	League	0–1		
86	22/03/83	Birmingham City	Home	League	2–1		
87	26/03/83	Stoke City	Away	League	0–4		
88	02/04/83	West Ham United	Away	League	1–2		
89	04/04/83	Luton Town	Home	League	5–2	1 Goal	(25)
90	09/04/83	West Bromwich Albion	Away	League	3–1	1 Goal	(26)
91	16/04/83	Nottingham Forest	Home	League	1–3		
92	23/04/83	Manchester United	Away	League	0–2		
93	30/04/83	Arsenal	Home	League	2–1	1 Goal	(27)
94	02/05/83	Sunderland	Away	League	2–2		
95	07/05/83	Ipswich Town	Away	League	1–3		
96	14/05/83	Liverpool	Home	League	2–1		

SEASON 1983–84

League Division One

97	27/08/83	Coventry City	Home	League	2–3	1 Goal	(28)
98	30/08/83	Ipswich Town	Home	League	2–2		
99	03/09/83	Birmingham City	Away	League	0–2		
100	06/09/83	Queens Park Rangers	Away	League	1–1	1 Goal	(29)
101	10/09/83	Notts County	Home	League	3–1	1 Goal	(30)
102	14/09/83	1.FC Kaiserslautern	Away	UEFA Cup	1–3		
103	17/09/83	Stoke City	Away	League	4–0	2 Goals	(32)
104	24/09/83	Tottenham Hotspur	Home	League	2–3		
105	28/09/83	1.FC Kaiserslautern	Home	UEFA Cup	3–0		
106	01/10/83	West Bromwich Albion	Away	League	0–2		
107	04/10/83	Huddersfield Town	Away	Lge Cup	1–2	1 Goal	(33)
108	15/10/83	Norwich City	Home	League	1–3		
109	19/10/83	Levski–Spartak Sofija	Home	UEFA Cup	1–1		
110	25/10/83	Huddersfield Town	Home	Lge Cup	2–2		
111	28/10/83	West Ham United	Home	League	0–0		

112	02/11/83	Levski–Spartak Sofija	Away	UEFA Cup	3–1*		
113	05/11/83	Leicester City	Home	League	3–3		
114	12/11/83	Sunderland	Away	League	0–3		
115	19/11/83	Manchester United	Away	League	1–4		
116	23/11/83	TJ Sparta CKD Praha	Home	UEFA Cup	2–3		
117	26/11/83	Luton Town	Home	League	3–2		
118	03/12/83	Wolverhampton Wanderers	Away	League	5–0		
119	07/12/83	TJ Sparta CKD Praha	Away	UEFA Cup	0–4		
120	10/12/83	Nottingham Forest	Home	League	3–2		
121	17/12/83	Arsenal	Away	League	1–3		
122	26/12/83	Aston Villa	Home	League	3–2	1 Goal	(34)
123	27/12/83	Southampton	Away	League	0–1		
124	31/12/83	Birmingham City	Home	League	1–0		
125	02/01/84	Tottenham Hotspur	Away	League	3–2	1 Goal	(35)
126	07/01/84	Luton Town	Away	FA Cup	2–2	1 Goal	(36)
127	10/01/84	Luton Town	Home	FA Cup	4–3*	1 Goal	(37)
128	14/01/84	Coventry City	Away	League	2–1		
129	21/01/84	Stoke City	Home	League	2–0		
130	28/01/84	Charlton Athletic	Away	FA Cup	2–0		
131	01/02/84	Liverpool	Away	League	0–3		
132	04/02/84	West Bromwich Albion	Home	League	3–1		
133	11/02/84	Notts County	Away	League	5–3		
134	18/02/84	Brighton & Hove Albion	Home	FA Cup	3–1		
135	21/02/84	West Ham United	Away	League	4–2	2 Goals	(39)
136	25/02/84	Everton	Home	League	4–4	2 Goals	(41)
137	03/03/84	Leicester City	Away	League	1–4		
138	10/03/84	Birmingham City	Away	FA Cup	3–1	2 Goals	(43)
139	17/03/84	Queens Park Rangers	Home	League	1–0		
140	20/03/84	Sunderland	Home	League	2–1		
141	24/03/84	Ipswich Town	Away	League	0–0		
142	31/03/84	Liverpool	Home	League	0–2		
143	07/04/84	Norwich City	Away	League	1–6		
144	14/04/84	Plymouth Argyle	Neutral	FA Cup	1–0		
145	17/04/84	Manchester United	Home	League	0–0		
146	21/04/84	Aston Villa	Away	League	1–2		
147	24/04/84	Southampton	Home	League	1–1		
148	28/04/84	Luton Town	Away	League	2–1		
149	12/05/84	Arsenal	Home	League	2–1		
150	19/05/84	Everton	Wembley	FA Cup	0–2		

SEASON 1984–85

League Division One

151	25/08/84	Manchester United	Away	League	1–1		
152	01/09/84	Arsenal	Home	League	3–4		
153	05/09/84	Leicester City	Away	League	1–1		
154	08/09/84	West Ham United	Away	League	0–2		
155	15/09/84	Aston Villa	Home	League	3–3	1 Goal	(44)
156	22/09/84	Norwich City	Away	League	2–3		
157	25/09/84	Cardiff City	Home	Lge Cup	3–1	3 Goals	(47)
158	29/09/84	Everton	Home	League	4–5	1 Goal	(48)
159	06/10/84	Coventry City	Home	League	0–1		
160	09/10/84	Cardiff City	Away	Lge Cup	0–1		
161	13/10/84	Chelsea	Away	League	3–2	1 Goal	(49)
162	20/10/84	Luton Town	Away	League	2–3		
163	27/10/84	Newcastle United	Home	League	3–3		
164	31/10/84	Leeds United	Away	Lge Cup	4–0		
165	03/11/84	Ipswich Town	Away	League	3–3	1 Goal	(50)
166	10/11/84	Sunderland	Home	League	3–1		
167	17/11/84	Sheffield Wednesday	Home	League	1–0	1 Goal	(51)
168	20/11/84	West Bromwich Albion	Home	Lge Cup	4–1		
169	24/11/84	Stoke City	Away	League	3–1		
170	01/12/84	Nottingham Forest	Home	League	2–0		
171	08/12/84	West Bromwich Albion	Away	League	1–2	1 Goal	(52)
172	15/12/84	Tottenham Hotspur	Home	League	1–2		
173	22/12/84	Arsenal	Away	League	1–1		
174	26/12/84	Southampton	Away	League	2–1		
175	29/12/84	Leicester City	Home	League	4–1	1 Goal	(53)
176	01/01/85	Liverpool	Home	League	1–1		
177	05/01/85	Sheffield United	Home	FA Cup	5–0		
178	23/01/85	Sunderland	Home	Lge Cup	0–1		
179	02/02/85	Everton	Away	League	0–4		
180	24/02/85	Sheffield Wednesday	Away	League	1–1		
181	02/03/85	Newcastle United	Away	League	1–3		
182	09/03/85	Luton Town	Away	FA Cup	0–1		

183	16/03/85	Chelsea	Home	League	1–3		
184	19/03/85	Luton Town	Home	League	3–0		
185	23/03/85	Coventry City	Away	League	1–3		
186	30/03/85	Queens Park Rangers	Away	League	0–2		
187	02/04/85	West Ham United	Home	League	5–0	1 Goal	(54)
188	06/04/85	Southampton	Home	League	1–1		
189	13/04/85	Norwich City	Home	League	2–0	1 Goal	(55)
190	16/04/85	Ipswich Town	Home	League	3–1	1 Goal	(56)
191	24/04/85	Aston Villa	Away	League	1–1		
192	27/04/85	Stoke City	Home	League	2–0		
193	04/05/85	Nottingham Forest	Away	League	1–1		
194	07/05/85	West Bromwich Albion	Home	League	0–2		
195	11/05/85	Tottenham Hotspur	Away	League	5–1	1 Goal	(57)
196	13/05/85	Manchester United	Home	League	5–1		
197	17/05/85	Liverpool	Away	League	3–4	1 Goal	(58)

SEASON 1985–86

League Division One

198	17/08/85	Tottenham Hotspur	Away	League	0–4		
199	20/08/85	Birmingham City	Home	League	3–0	2 Goals	(60)
200	24/08/85	West Bromwich Albion	Home	League	5–1		
201	26/08/85	Sheffield Wednesday	Away	League	1–2		
202	31/08/85	Coventry City	Home	League	3–0		
203	04/09/85	Leicester City	Away	League	2–2		
204	07/09/85	Liverpool	Away	League	1–3		
205	14/09/85	Queens Park Rangers	Home	League	2–0		
206	21/09/85	Nottingham Forest	Away	League	2–3		
207	24/09/85	Crewe Alexandra	Away	Lge Cup	3–1		
208	28/09/85	Chelsea	Home	League	3–1	1 Goal	(61)
209	05/10/85	Southampton	Away	League	1–3		
210	09/10/85	Crewe Alexandra	Home	Lge Cup	3–2	1 Goal	(62)
211	12/10/85	Manchester City	Home	League	3–2	1 Goal	(63)
212	19/10/85	Everton	Away	League	1–4		
213	26/10/85	Oxford United	Home	League	2–2		
214	29/10/85	Queens Park Rangers	Home	Lge Cup	0–1		
215	02/11/85	Newcastle United	Away	League	1–1		
216	09/11/85	Aston Villa	Home	League	1–1		
217	16/11/85	West Ham United	Away	League	1–2		
218	23/11/85	Luton Town	Home	League	1–2		
219	30/11/85	Manchester United	Away	League	1–1		
220	28/12/85	Leicester City	Home	League	2–1		
221	01/01/86	Ipswich Town	Away	League	0–0		
222	04/01/86	Coventry City	Away	FA Cup	3–1		
223	12/01/86	Liverpool	Home	League	2–3		
224	18/01/86	Coventry City	Away	League	2–0	2 Goals	(65)
225	25/01/86	Manchester City	Away	FA Cup	1–1		
226	01/02/86	Sheffield Wednesday	Home	League	2–1	1 Goal	(66)
227	03/02/86	Manchester City	Home	FA Cup	0–0*		
228	06/02/86	Manchester City	Away	FA Cup	3–1	1 Goal	(67)
229	05/03/86	Bury	Home	FA Cup	1–1	1 Goal	(68)
230	08/03/86	Bury	Away	FA Cup	3–0		
231	11/03/86	Liverpool	Away	FA Cup	0–0		
232	15/03/86	Manchester City	Away	League	1–0		
233	17/03/86	Liverpool	Home	FA Cup	1–2*	1 Goal	(69)
234	22/03/86	Queens Park Rangers	Away	League	1–2		
235	29/03/86	Ipswich Town	Home	League	0–0		
236	31/03/86	Arsenal	Away	League	2–0	1 Goal	(70)
237	01/04/86	Arsenal	Home	League	3–0		
238	05/04/86	Newcastle United	Home	League	4–1		
239	09/04/86	Oxford United	Away	League	1–1		
240	12/04/86	Aston Villa	Away	League	1–4		
241	15/04/86	Everton	Home	League	0–2		
242	19/04/86	West Ham United	Home	League	0–2		
243	21/04/86	Nottingham Forest	Home	League	1–1	1 Goal	(71)
244	26/04/86	Luton Town	Away	League	2–3		
245	29/04/86	Southampton	Home	League	1–1		
246	03/05/86	Manchester United	Home	League	1–1		
247	05/05/86	Chelsea	Away	League	5–1		

SEASON 1986–87

League Division One

| 248 | 23/08/86 | Oxford United | Home | League | 3–0 | 1 Goal | (72) |
| 249 | 26/08/86 | Queens Park Rangers | Away | League | 2–3 | 1 Goal | (73) |

250	30/08/86	Nottingham Forest	Away	League	1–1		
251	06/09/86	Wimbledon	Home	League	0–1		
252	23/09/86	Rochdale	Home	Lge Cup	1–1		
253	27/09/86	Coventry City	Away	League	0–1		
254	04/10/86	West Ham United	Home	League	2–2		
255	07/10/86	Rochdale	Away	Lge Cup	1–2	1 Goal	(74)
256	11/10/86	Arsenal	Away	League	1–3		
257	18/10/86	Aston Villa	Home	League	4–2		
258	25/10/86	Everton	Away	League	2–3		
259	29/10/86	West Ham United	Home	Lge Cup	2–3		
260	01/11/86	Chelsea	Away	League	0–0		
261	08/11/86	Charlton Athletic	Home	League	4–1		
262	15/11/86	Newcastle United	Away	League	2–2		
263	22/11/86	Leicester City	Home	League	5–1	1 Goal	(75)
264	26/11/86	Manchester City	Away	FM Cup	0–1		
265	29/11/86	Southampton	Away	League	1–3		
266	06/12/86	Liverpool	Home	League	2–0	1 Goal	(76)
267	13/12/86	Tottenham Hotspur	Away	League	1–2		
268	19/12/86	Norwich City	Home	League	1–1	1 Goal	(77)
269	26/12/86	Luton Town	Away	League	2–0		
270	27/12/86	Newcastle United	Home	League	1–0	1 Goal	(78)
271	01/01/87	Manchester City	Home	League	1–1	1 Goal	(79)
272	03/01/87	Wimbledon	Away	League	1–2		
273	10/01/87	Maidstone United	Home	FA Cup	3–1		
274	24/01/87	Oxford United	Away	League	3–1	1 Goal	(80)
275	01/02/87	Chelsea	Home	FA Cup	1–0		
276	07/02/87	Nottingham Forest	Home	League	1–1	1 Goal	(81)
277	14/02/87	Manchester United	Away	League	1–3		
278	21/02/87	Walsall	Away	FA Cup	1–1		
279	24/02/87	Walsall	Home	FA Cup	4–4*	2 Goals	(83)
280	28/02/87	Sheffield Wednesday	Away	League	1–0		
281	02/03/87	Walsall	Away	FA Cup	1–0		
282	08/03/87	Everton	Home	League	2–1		
283	14/03/87	Arsenal	Away	FA Cup	3–1	1 Goal	(84)
284	21/03/87	Arsenal	Home	League	2–0		
285	25/03/87	Aston Villa	Away	League	1–1		
286	04/04/87	Charlton Athletic	Away	League	3–4		
287	06/04/87	Queens Park Rangers	Home	League	0–3		
288	11/04/87	Tottenham Hotspur	Neutral	FA Cup	1–4		
289	14/04/87	Chelsea	Home	League	3–1		
290	21/04/87	Luton Town	Home	League	2–0	1 Goal	(85)
291	25/04/87	Leicester City	Away	League	2–1		
292	30/04/87	Coventry City	Home	League	2–3		
293	02/05/87	Southampton	Home	League	1–1		
294	04/05/87	Liverpool	Away	League	0–1		
295	09/05/87	Tottenham Hotspur	Home	League	1–0		

SEASON 1987–88

Liverpool – League Division One

1	15/08/87	Arsenal	Away	League	2–1		
2	29/08/87	Coventry City	Away	League	4–1		
3	05/09/87	West Ham United	Away	League	1–1		
4	12/09/87	Oxford United	Home	League	2–0	1 Goal	(1)
5	15/09/87	Charlton Athletic	Home	League	3–2		
6	20/09/87	Newcastle United	Away	League	4–1		
7	23/09/87	Blackburn Rovers	Away	Lge Cup	1–1		
8	29/09/87	Derby County	Home	League	4–0		
9	03/10/87	Portsmouth	Home	League	4–0		
10	06/10/87	Blackburn Rovers	Home	Lge Cup	1–0		
11	17/10/87	Queens Park Rangers	Home	League	4–0	2 Goals	(3)
12	24/10/87	Luton Town	Away	League	1–0		
13	28/10/87	Everton	Away	Lge Cup	0–1		
14	01/11/87	Everton	Home	League	2–0		
15	04/11/87	Wimbledon	Away	League	1–1		
16	15/11/87	Manchester United	Away	League	1–1		
17	21/11/87	Norwich City	Home	League	0–0		
18	24/11/87	Watford	Home	League	4–0	1 Goal	(4)
19	28/11/87	Tottenham Hotspur	Away	League	2–0		
20	06/12/87	Chelsea	Home	League	2–1		
21	12/12/87	Southampton	Away	League	2–2	2 Goals	(6)
22	19/12/87	Sheffield Wednesday	Home	League	1–0		
23	26/12/87	Oxford United	Away	League	3–0	1 Goal	(7)
24	28/12/87	Newcastle United	Home	League	4–0		
25	01/01/88	Coventry City	Home	League	4–0		

26	09/01/88	Stoke City	Away	FA Cup	0–0		
27	12/01/88	Stoke City	Home	FA Cup	1–0		
28	16/01/88	Arsenal	Home	League	2–0		
29	23/01/88	Charlton Athletic	Away	League	2–0	1 Goal	(8)
30	31/01/88	Aston Villa	Away	FA Cup	2–0	1 Goal	(9)
31	06/02/88	West Ham United	Home	League	0–0		
32	13/02/88	Watford	Away	League	4–1	1 Goal	(10)
33	21/02/88	Everton	Away	FA Cup	1–0		
34	27/02/88	Portsmouth	Away	League	2–0	2 Goals	(12)
35	05/03/88	Queens Park Rangers	Away	League	1–0	1 Goal	(13)
36	13/03/88	Manchester City	Away	FA Cup	4–0	1 Goal	(14)
37	16/03/88	Derby County	Away	League	1–1		
38	20/03/88	Everton	Away	League	0–1		
39	26/03/88	Wimbledon	Home	League	2–1	1 Goal	(15)
40	02/04/88	Nottingham Forest	Away	League	1–2		
41	04/04/88	Manchester United	Home	League	3–3		
42	09/04/88	Nottingham Forest	Neutral	FA Cup	2–1		
43	13/04/88	Nottingham Forest	Home	League	5–0		
44	30/04/88	Chelsea	Away	League	1–1	1 Goal	(16)
45	02/05/88	Southampton	Home	League	1–1		
46	07/05/88	Sheffield Wednesday	Away	League	5–1	1 Goal	(17)
47	09/05/88	Luton Town	Home	League	1–1		
48	14/05/88	Wimbledon	Wembley	FA Cup	0–1		

SEASON 1988–89

League Division One

49	20/08/88	Wimbledon	Wembley	FA C/S	2–0		
50	27/08/88	Charlton Athletic	Away	League	3–0		
51	29/08/88	Nottingham Forest	Home	MCC Trophy	4–1	1 Goal	(18)
52	03/09/88	Manchester United	Home	League	1–0		
53	10/09/88	Aston Villa	Away	League	1–1		
54	08/10/88	Luton Town	Away	League	0–1		
55	12/10/88	Walsall	Away	Lge Cup	3–1	1 Goal	(19)
56	22/10/88	Coventry City	Home	League	0–0		
57	26/10/88	Nottingham Forest	Away	League	1–2		
58	29/10/88	West Ham United	Away	League	2–0		
59	02/11/88	Arsenal	Home	Lge Cup	1–1	1 Goal	(20)
60	05/11/88	Middlesbrough	Home	League	3–0		
61	09/11/88	Arsenal	Away	Lge Cup	0–0*		
62	12/11/88	Millwall	Home	League	1–1		
63	04/12/88	Arsenal	Away	League	1–1	1 Goal	(21)
64	11/12/88	Everton	Home	League	1–1		
65	17/12/88	Norwich City	Home	League	0–1		
66	26/12/88	Derby County	Away	League	1–0		
67	01/01/89	Manchester United	Away	League	1–3	1 Goal	(22)
68	03/01/89	Aston Villa	Home	League	1–0		
69	07/01/89	Carlisle United	Away	FA Cup	3–0	1 Goal	(23)
70	14/01/89	Sheffield Wednesday	Away	League	2–2		
71	21/01/89	Southampton	Home	League	2–0		
72	29/01/89	Millwall	Away	FA Cup	2–0		
73	04/02/89	Newcastle United	Away	League	2–2		
74	18/02/89	Hull City	Away	FA Cup	3–2	1 Goal	(24)
75	01/03/89	Charlton Athletic	Home	League	2–0		
76	11/03/89	Middlesbrough	Away	League	4–0		
77	14/03/89	Luton Town	Home	League	5–0		
78	18/03/89	Brentford	Home	FA Cup	4–0	1 Goal	(25)
79	22/03/89	Coventry City	Away	League	3–1	1 Goal	(26)
80	26/03/89	Tottenham Hotspur	Away	League	2–1		
81	29/03/89	Derby County	Home	League	1–0	1 Goal	(27)
82	01/04/89	Norwich City	Away	League	1–0		
83	08/04/89	Sheffield Wednesday	Home	League	5–1	1 Goal	(28)
84	11/04/89	Millwall	Away	League	2–1	1 Goal	(29)
85	03/05/89	Everton	Away	League	0–0		
86	07/05/89	Nottingham Forest	Neutral	FA Cup	3–1		
87	10/05/89	Nottingham Forest	Home	League	1–0		
88	13/05/89	Wimbledon	Away	League	2–1	1 Goal	(30)
89	16/05/89	Queens Park Rangers	Home	League	2–0		
90	20/05/89	Everton	Wembley	FA Cup	3–2*		
91	23/05/89	West Ham United	Home	League	5–1	1 Goal	(31)
92	26/05/89	Arsenal	Home	League	0–2		

SEASON 1989–90

League Division One

| 93 | 12/08/89 | Arsenal | Wembley | FA C/S | 1–0 | | |

94	19/08/89	Manchester City	Home	League	3–1	1 Goal	(32)
95	23/08/89	Aston Villa	Away	League	1–1	1 Goal	(33)
96	26/08/89	Luton Town	Away	League	0–0		
97	09/09/89	Derby County	Away	League	3–0	1 Goal	(34)
98	12/09/89	Crystal Palace	Home	League	9–0	1 Goal	(35)
99	16/09/89	Norwich City	Home	League	0–0		
100	19/09/89	Wigan Athletic	Home	Lge Cup	5–2	1 Goal	(36)
101	23/09/89	Everton	Away	League	3–1	1 Goal	(37)
102	14/10/89	Wimbledon	Away	League	2–1		
103	21/10/89	Southampton	Away	League	1–4		
104	25/10/89	Arsenal	Away	Lge Cup	0–1		
105	29/10/89	Tottenham Hotspur	Home	League	1–0	1 Goal	(38)
106	04/11/89	Coventry City	Home	League	0–1		
107	11/11/89	Queens Park Rangers	Away	League	2–3	2 Goals	(40)
108	19/11/89	Millwall	Away	League	2–1	1 Goal	(41)
109	26/11/89	Arsenal	Home	League	2–1	1 Goal	(42)
110	29/11/89	Sheffield Wednesday	Away	League	0–2		
111	09/12/89	Aston Villa	Home	League	1–1		
112	30/12/89	Charlton Athletic	Home	League	1–0	1 Goal	(43)
113	01/01/90	Nottingham Forest	Away	League	2–2		
114	06/01/90	Swansea City	Away	FA Cup	0–0		
115	09/01/90	Swansea City	Home	FA Cup	8–0	2 Goals	(45)
116	13/01/90	Luton Town	Home	League	2–2	1 Goal	(46)
117	20/01/90	Crystal Palace	Away	League	2–0		
118	28/01/90	Norwich City	Away	FA Cup	0–0		
119	31/01/90	Norwich City	Home	FA Cup	3–1	1 Goal	(47)
120	03/02/90	Everton	Home	League	2–1	1 Goal	(48)
121	10/02/90	Norwich City	Away	League	0–0		
122	17/02/90	Southampton	Home	FA Cup	3–0		
123	03/03/90	Millwall	Home	League	1–0		
124	11/03/90	Queens Park Rangers	Away	FA Cup	2–2	1 Goal	(49)
125	14/03/90	Queens Park Rangers	Home	FA Cup	1–0		
126	18/03/90	Manchester United	Away	League	2–1	2 Goals	(51)
127	21/03/90	Tottenham Hotspur	Away	League	0–1		
128	31/03/90	Southampton	Home	League	3–2	1 Goal	(52)
129	03/04/90	Wimbledon	Home	League	2–1		
130	08/04/90	Crystal Palace	Neutral	FA Cup	3–4*	1 Goal	(53)
131	11/04/90	Charlton Athletic	Away	League	4–0	1 Goal	(54)
132	14/04/90	Nottingham Forest	Home	League	2–2		
133	18/04/90	Arsenal	Away	League	1–1	1 Goal	(55)
134	21/04/90	Chelsea	Home	League	4–1		
135	28/04/90	Queens Park Rangers	Home	League	2–1	1 Goal	(56)
136	01/05/90	Derby County	Home	League	1–0		
137	05/05/90	Coventry City	Away	League	6–1	3 Goals	(59)

SEASON 1990–91

League Division One

138	18/08/90	Manchester United	Wembley	FA C/S	1–1	1 Goal	(60)
139	25/08/90	Sheffield United	Away	League	3–1	1 Goal	(61)
140	28/08/90	Nottingham Forest	Home	League	2–0		
141	01/09/90	Aston Villa	Home	League	2–1		
142	08/09/90	Wimbledon	Away	League	2–1	1 Goal	(62)
143	16/09/90	Manchester United	Home	League	4–0	1 Goal	(63)
144	22/09/90	Everton	Away	League	3–2	1 Goal	(64)
145	25/09/90	Crewe Alexandra	Home	Lge Cup	5–1	1 Goal	(65)
146	29/09/90	Sunderland	Away	League	1–0		
147	06/10/90	Derby County	Home	League	2–0		
148	09/10/90	Crewe Alexandra	Away	Lge Cup	4–1		
149	20/10/90	Norwich City	Away	League	1–1		
150	27/10/90	Chelsea	Home	League	2–0		
151	04/11/90	Tottenham Hotspur	Away	League	3–1		
152	24/11/90	Manchester City	Home	League	2–2		
153	02/12/90	Arsenal	Away	League	0–3		
154	15/12/90	Sheffield United	Home	League	2–0	1 Goal	(66)
155	22/12/90	Southampton	Home	League	3–2		
156	26/12/90	Queens Park Rangers	Away	League	1–1	1 Goal	(67)
157	30/12/90	Crystal Palace	Away	League	0–1		
158	01/01/91	Leeds United	Home	League	3–0	1 Goal	(68)
159	05/01/91	Blackburn Rovers	Away	FA Cup	1–1		
160	08/01/91	Blackburn Rovers	Home	FA Cup	3–0		
161	12/01/91	Aston Villa	Away	League	0–0		
162	19/01/91	Wimbledon	Home	League	1–1	1 Goal	(69)
163	26/01/91	Brighton & Hove Albion	Home	FA Cup	2–2		
164	30/01/91	Brighton & Hove Albion	Away	FA Cup	3–2*		

165	03/02/91	Manchester United	Away	League	1–1		
166	09/02/91	Everton	Home	League	3–1		
167	17/02/91	Everton	Home	FA Cup	0–0		
168	20/02/91	Everton	Away	FA Cup	4–4*	1 Goal	(70)
169	23/02/91	Luton Town	Away	League	1–3		
170	27/02/91	Everton	Away	FA Cup	0–1		
171	03/03/91	Arsenal	Home	League	0–1		
172	09/03/91	Manchester City	Away	League	3–0	1 Goal	(71)
173	16/03/91	Sunderland	Home	League	2–1		
174	23/03/91	Derby County	Away	League	7–1	2 Goals	(73)
175	01/04/91	Southampton	Away	League	0–1		
176	09/04/91	Coventry City	Home	League	1–1		
177	13/04/91	Leeds United	Away	League	5–4	2 Goals	(75)
178	20/04/91	Norwich City	Home	League	3–0	1 Goal	(76)
179	23/04/91	Crystal Palace	Home	League	3–0	1 Goal	(77)
180	04/05/91	Chelsea	Away	League	2–4		
181	06/05/91	Nottingham Forest	Away	League	1–2		
182	11/05/91	Tottenham Hotspur	Home	League	2–0		

SEASON 1991–92

League Division One

183	17/08/91	Oldham Athletic	Home	League	2–1	1 Goal	(78)
184	21/08/91	Manchester City	Away	League	1–2		
185	06/01/92	Crewe Alexandra	Away	FA Cup	4–0	3 Goals	(81)
186	11/01/92	Luton Town	Home	League	2–1		
187	18/01/92	Oldham Athletic	Away	League	3–2		
188	08/03/92	Aston Villa	Home	FA Cup	1–0		
189	11/03/92	West Ham United	Home	League	1–0		
190	14/03/92	Crystal Palace	Away	League	0–1		
191	18/03/92	Genoa	Home	UEFA Cup	1–2		
192	21/03/92	Tottenham Hotspur	Home	League	2–1		
193	05/04/92	Portsmouth	Neutral	FA Cup	1–1		
194	13/04/92	Portsmouth	Neutral	FA Cup	0–0+		
195	18/04/92	Leeds United	Home	League	0–0		
196	20/04/92	Arsenal	Away	League	0–4		
197	22/04/92	Nottingham Forest	Away	League	1–1		
198	26/04/92	Manchester United	Home	League	2–0		
199	02/05/92	Sheffield Wednesday	Away	League	0–0		

+ AET Liverpool won 3–1 on penalties

SEASON 1992–93

Premier League

Sub+1	23/11/92	Queens Park Rangers	Away	League	1–0		
200	28/11/93	Crystal Palace	Home	League	5–0		
201	01/12/92	Crystal Palace	Home	Lge Cup	1–1		
202	07/12/92	Everton	Away	League	1–2		
203	13/12/92	Blackburn Rovers	Home	League	2–1		
204	16/12/92	Crystal Palace	Away	Lge Cup	1–2		
205	19/12/92	Coventry City	Away	League	1–5		
206	28/12/92	Manchester City	Home	League	1–1		
207	03/01/93	Bolton Wanderers	Away	FA Cup	2–2		
208	09/01/93	Aston Villa	Home	League	1–2	1 Goal	(82)
209	13/01/93	Bolton Wanderers	Home	FA Cup	0–2		
210	16/01/93	Wimbledon	Away	League	0–2		
211	31/01/93	Arsenal	Away	League	1–0	1 Goal	(83)
212	06/02/93	Nottingham Forest	Home	League	0–0		
213	10/02/93	Chelsea	Away	League	0–0		
214	13/02/93	Southampton	Away	League	1–2		
215	20/02/93	Ipswich Town	Home	League	0–0		
216	27/02/93	Sheffield Wednesday	Away	League	1–1		
217	06/03/93	Manchester United	Home	League	1–2		
218	10/03/93	Queens Park Rangers	Home	League	1–0		
219	13/03/93	Middlesbrough	Away	League	2–1		
220	20/03/93	Everton	Home	League	1–0		
221	23/03/93	Crystal Palace	Away	League	1–1		
222	03/04/93	Blackburn Rovers	Away	League	1–4		
223	10/04/93	Oldham Athletic	Home	League	1–0		
224	12/04/93	Manchester City	Away	League	1–1		
225	17/04/93	Coventry City	Home	League	4–0		
226	21/04/93	Leeds United	Home	League	2–0	1 Goal	(84)
227	01/05/93	Norwich City	Away	League	0–1		
228	05/05/93	Oldham Athletic	Away	League	2–3		
229	08/05/93	Tottenham Hotspur	Home	League	6–2	2 Goals	(86)

SEASON 1993–94

Premier League

Sub+2	21/11/93	Newcastle United	Away	League	0–3		
230	28/11/93	Aston Villa	Home	League	2–1		
231	01/12/93	Wimbledon	Home	Lge Cup	1–1		
232	04/12/93	Sheffield Wednesday	Away	League	1–3		
233	08/12/93	Queens Park Rangers	Home	League	3–2	1 Goal	(87)
234	11/12/93	Swindon Town	Home	League	2–2	1 Goal	(88)
235	14/12/93	Wimbledon	Away	Lge Cup	2–2+		
236	18/12/93	Tottenham Hotspur	Away	League	3–3		
Sub+3	01/01/94	Ipswich Town	Away	League	2–1		
237	04/01/94	Manchester United	Home	League	3–3		
238	15/01/94	Oldham Athletic	Away	League	3–0		
239	19/01/94	Bristol City	Away	FA Cup	1–1		
240	22/01/94	Manchester City	Home	League	2–1		
241	25/01/94	Bristol City	Home	FA Cup	0–1		
242	05/02/94	Norwich City	Away	League	2–2	1 Goal	(89)
243	14/02/94	Southampton	Away	League	2–4		
244	19/02/94	Leeds United	Away	League	0–2		
245	25/02/94	Coventry City	Home	League	1–0		
246	05/03/94	Blackburn Rovers	Away	League	0–2		
247	13/03/94	Everton	Home	League	2–1		
248	19/03/94	Chelsea	Home	League	2–1		
249	26/03/94	Arsenal	Away	League	0–1		
250	29/03/94	Manchester United	Away	League	0–1		
251	02/04/94	Sheffield United	Home	League	1–2		
252	04/04/94	Wimbledon	Away	League	1–1		
253	09/04/94	Ipswich Town	Home	League	1–0		
254	16/04/94	Newcastle United	Home	League	0–2		
255	23/04/94	West Ham United	Away	League	2–1		
256	30/04/94	Norwich City	Home	League	0–1		
257	07/05/94	Aston Villa	Away	League	1–2		

+ AET Wimbledon won 4–3 on penalties

SEASON 1994–95

Premier League

258	20/08/94	Crystal Palace	Away	League	6–1		
259	28/08/94	Arsenal	Home	League	3–0		
260	31/08/94	Southampton	Away	League	2–0	1 Goal	(90)
261	10/09/94	West Ham United	Home	League	0–0		
262	17/09/94	Manchester United	Away	League	0–2		
263	21/09/94	Burnley	Home	Lge Cup	2–0		
264	24/09/94	Newcastle United	Away	League	1–1		
265	01/10/94	Sheffield Wednesday	Home	League	4–1		
266	08/10/94	Aston Villa	Home	League	3–2		
267	15/10/94	Blackburn Rovers	Away	League	2–3	1 Goal	(91)
268	22/10/94	Wimbledon	Home	League	3–0	1 Goal	(92)
269	25/10/94	Stoke City	Home	Lge Cup	2–1		
270	29/10/94	Ipswich Town	Away	League	3–1	1 Goal	(93)
271	31/10/94	Queens Park Rangers	Away	League	1–2	1 Goal	(94)
272	05/11/94	Nottingham Forest	Home	League	1–0		
273	09/11/94	Chelsea	Home	League	3–1		
274	21/11/94	Everton	Away	League	0–2		
275	26/11/94	Tottenham Hotspur	Home	League	1–1		
276	11/12/94	Crystal Palace	Home	League	0–0		
277	18/12/94	Chelsea	Away	League	0–0		
278	26/12/94	Leicester City	Away	League	2–1		
279	28/12/94	Manchester City	Home	League	2–0		
280	31/12/94	Leeds United	Away	League	2–0		
281	02/01/95	Norwich City	Home	League	4–0		
282	07/01/95	Birmingham City	Away	FA Cup	0–0		
283	11/01/95	Arsenal	Home	Lge Cup	1–0		
284	24/01/95	Everton	Home	League	0–0		
285	28/01/95	Burnley	Away	FA Cup	0–0		
286	04/02/95	Nottingham Forest	Away	League	1–1		
287	07/02/95	Burnley	Home	FA Cup	1–0	1 Goal	(95)
288	11/02/95	Queens Park Rangers	Home	League	1–1		
289	15/02/95	Crystal Palace	Home	Lge Cup	1–0		
290	19/02/95	Wimbledon	Home	FA Cup	1–1		
291	25/02/95	Sheffield Wednesday	Away	League	2–1	1 Goal	(96)
292	28/02/95	Wimbledon	Away	FA Cup	2–0	1 Goal	(97)
293	04/03/95	Newcastle United	Home	League	2–0		

294	08/03/95	Crystal Palace	Away	Lge Cup	1–0		
295	11/03/95	Tottenham Hotspur	Home	FA Cup	1–2		
296	19/03/95	Manchester United	Home	League	2–0		
297	02/04/95	Bolton Wanderers	Wembley	Lge Cup	2–1		
298	05/04/95	Southampton	Home	League	3–1		
299	09/04/95	Leeds United	Home	League	0–1		
300	12/04/95	Arsenal	Away	League	1–0		
301	14/04/95	Manchester City	Away	League	1–2		
302	17/04/95	Leicester City	Home	League	2–0		
303	29/04/95	Norwich City	Away	League	2–1		
304	02/05/95	Wimbledon	Away	League	0–0		
305	06/05/95	Aston Villa	Away	League	0–2		
306	10/05/95	West Ham United	Away	League	0–3		
307	14/05/95	Blackburn Rovers	Home	League	2–1	1 Goal	(98)

SEASON 1995–96

Premier League

308	19/08/95	Sheffield Wednesday	Home	League	1–0		
309	21/08/95	Leeds United	Away	League	0–1		
310	26/08/95	Tottenham Hotspur	Away	League	3–1	2 Goals	(100)
311	30/08/95	Queens Park Rangers	Home	League	1–0		
312	09/09/95	Wimbledon	Away	League	0–1		
313	12/09/95	Spartak–Alania Vladikavkaz	Away	UEFA Cup	2–1		
314	16/09/95	Blackburn Rovers	Home	League	3–0		
315	23/09/95	Bolton Wanderers	Home	League	5–2		
316	26/09/95	Spartak–Alania Vladikavkaz	Home	UEFA Cup	0–0		
317	04/10/95	Sunderland	Away	Lge Cup	1–0		
318	14/10/95	Coventry City	Home	League	0–0		
319	17/10/95	Brondby IF	Away	UEFA Cup	0–0		
320	22/10/95	Southampton	Away	League	3–1		
321	25/10/95	Manchester City	Home	Lge Cup	4–0		
322	28/10/95	Manchester City	Home	League	6–0		
323	31/10/95	Brondby IF	Home	UEFA Cup	0–1		
324	04/11/95	Newcastle United	Away	League	1–2		
325	18/11/95	Everton	Home	League	1–2		
326	22/11/95	West Ham United	Away	League	0–0		
327	25/11/95	Middlesbrough	Away	League	1–2		
328	29/11/95	Newcastle United	Home	Lge Cup	0–1		
329	02/12/95	Southampton	Home	League	1–1		
330	09/12/95	Bolton Wanderers	Away	League	1–0		
331	17/12/95	Manchester United	Home	League	2–0		
332	23/12/95	Arsenal	Home	League	3–1		
333	30/12/95	Chelsea	Away	League	2–2		
334	01/01/96	Nottingham Forest	Home	League	4–2		
335	06/01/96	Rochdale	Home	FA Cup	7–0		
336	13/01/96	Sheffield Wednesday	Away	League	1–1		
337	20/01/96	Leeds United	Home	League	5–0		
338	31/01/96	Aston Villa	Away	League	2–0		
339	03/02/96	Tottenham Hotspur	Home	League	0–0		
340	11/02/96	Queens Park Rangers	Away	League	2–1		
341	18/02/96	Shrewsbury Town	Away	FA Cup	4–0		
342	24/02/96	Blackburn Rovers	Away	League	3–2		
343	28/02/96	Charlton Athletic	Home	FA Cup	2–1		
344	03/03/96	Aston Villa	Home	League	3–0		
345	10/03/96	Leeds United	Away	FA Cup	0–0		
346	13/03/96	Wimbledon	Home	League	2–2		
347	16/03/96	Chelsea	Home	League	2–0		
348	20/03/96	Leeds United	Home	FA Cup	3–0		
349	23/03/96	Nottingham Forest	Away	League	0–1		
350	31/03/96	Aston Villa	Neutral	FA Cup	3–0		
351	03/04/96	Newcastle United	Home	League	4–3		
352	06/04/96	Coventry City	Away	League	0–1		
353	08/04/96	West Ham United	Home	League	2–0	1 Goal	(101)
354	16/04/96	Everton	Away	League	1–1		
355	27/04/96	Middlesbrough	Home	League	1–0		
356	01/05/96	Arsenal	Away	League	0–0		
357	11/05/96	Manchester United	Wembley	FA Cup	0–1		

SEASON 1996–97

Premier League

358	17/08/96	Middlesbrough	Away	League	3–3	1 Goal	(102)
359	19/08/96	Arsenal	Home	League	2–0		
360	24/08/96	Sunderland	Home	League	0–0		

361	04/09/96	Coventry City	Away	League	1–0		
362	07/09/96	Southampton	Home	League	2–1		
363	12/09/96	MYPA–47	Away	ECW Cup	1–0		
364	15/09/96	Leicester City	Away	League	3–0		
365	21/09/96	Chelsea	Home	League	5–1	1 Goal	(103)
366	26/09/96	MYPA–47	Home	ECW Cup	3–1	1 Goal	(104)
367	29/09/96	West Ham United	Away	League	2–1		
368	12/10/96	Manchester United	Away	League	0–1		
369	17/10/96	FC Sion	Away	ECW Cup	2–1	1 Goal	(105)
370	23/10/96	Charlton Athletic	Away	Lge Cup	1–1		
371	27/10/96	Derby County	Home	League	2–1		
372	31/10/96	FC Sion	Home	ECW Cup	6–3	1 Goal	(106)
373	03/11/96	Blackburn Rovers	Away	League	0–3		
374	13/11/96	Charlton Athletic	Home	Lge Cup	4–1		
375	16/11/96	Leeds United	Away	League	2–0		
376	20/11/96	Everton	Home	League	1–1		
377	23/11/96	Wimbledon	Home	League	1–1		
378	27/11/96	Arsenal	Home	Lge Cup	4–2		
379	02/12/96	Tottenham Hotspur	Away	League	2–0		
380	07/12/96	Sheffield Wednesday	Home	League	0–1		
381	14/12/96	Middlesbrough	Home	League	5–1		
382	17/12/96	Nottingham Forest	Home	League	4–2		
383	23/12/96	Newcastle United	Away	League	1–1		
384	26/12/96	Leicester City	Home	League	1–1		
385	29/12/96	Southampton	Away	League	1–0	1 Goal	(107)
386	01/01/97	Chelsea	Away	League	0–1		
387	04/01/97	Burnley	Home	FA Cup	1–0		
388	11/01/97	West Ham United	Home	League	0–0		
389	26/01/97	Chelsea	Away	FA Cup	2–4		
390	01/02/97	Derby County	Away	League	1–0		
391	19/02/97	Leeds United	Home	League	4–0		
392	22/02/97	Blackburn Rovers	Home	League	0–0		
393	02/03/97	Aston Villa	Away	League	0–1		
394	06/03/97	SK Brann	Away	ECW Cup	1–1		
395	10/03/97	Newcastle United	Home	League	4–3		
396	15/03/97	Nottingham Forest	Away	League	1–1		
397	20/03/97	SK Brann	Home	ECW Cup	3–0		
398	24/03/97	Arsenal	Away	League	2–1		
399	06/04/97	Coventry City	Home	League	1–2		
400	10/04/97	Paris Saint–Germain	Away	ECW Cup	0–3		
401	13/04/97	Sunderland	Away	League	2–1		
402	16/04/97	Everton	Away	League	1–1		
403	19/04/97	Manchester United	Home	League	1–3	1 Goal	(108)
Sub+4	11/05/97	Sheffield Wednesday	Away	League	1–1		

INTERNATIONAL APPEARANCES – ENGLAND

Sub 1	28/05/83	Northern Ireland	Windsor Park	0–0	HC		
Sub 2	12/06/83	Australia	Sydney	0–0	F		
3	15/06/83	Australia	Brisbane	1–0	F		
4	19/06/83	Australia	Melbourne	1–1	F		
5	21/09/83	Denmark	Wembley	0–1	ECQ		
Sub 6	16/11/83	Luxembourg	Luxembourg	4–0	ECQ		
Sub 7	29/02/84	France	Paris	0–2	F		
8	26/05/84	Scotland	Hampden Park	1–1	HC		
9	02/06/84	USSR	Wembley	0–2	F		
10	10/06/84	Brazil	Rio de Janeiro	2–0	F	1 Goal	(1)
11	13/06/84	Uruguay	Montevideo	0–2	F		
12	17/06/84	Chile	Santiago	0–0	F		
13	12/09/84	East Germany	Wembley	1–0	F		
14	17/10/84	Finland	Wembley	5–0	WCQ		
15	14/11/84	Turkey	Istanbul	8–0	WCQ	2 Goals	(3)
16	27/02/85	Northern Ireland	Windsor Park	1–0	WCQ		
17	01/05/85	Romania	Bucharest	0–0	WCQ		
18	22/05/85	Finland	Helsinki	1–1	WCQ		
19	25/05/85	Scotland	Hampden Park	0–1	RC		
Sub 20	06/06/85	Italy	Mexico City	1–2	F		
21	09/06/85	Mexico	Mexico City	0–1	F		
Sub 22	12/06/85	West Germany	Mexico City	3–0	F		
Sub 23	16/06/85	USA	Los Angeles	5–0	F		
Sub 24	11/09/85	Romania	Wembley	1–1	WCQ		
Sub 25	26/02/86	Israel	Tel Aviv	2–1	F		
Sub 26	17/05/86	Mexico	Los Angeles	3–0	F		
Sub 27	24/05/86	Canada	Vancouver	1–0	F		
Sub 28	22/06/86	Argentina	Mexico City	1–2	WC		

29	10/09/86	Sweden	Stockholm	0–1	F		
Sub 30	29/04/87	Turkey	Izmir	0–0	ECQ		
31	19/05/87	Brazil	Wembley	1–1	RC		
32	09/09/87	West Germany	Dusseldorf	1–3	F		
33	14/10/87	Turkey	Wembley	8–0	ECQ	2 Goals	(5)
34	11/11/87	Yugoslavia	Belgrade	4–1	ECQ	1 Goal	(6)
35	17/02/88	Israel	Tel Aviv	0–0	F		
36	23/03/88	Holland	Wembley	2–2	F		
37	21/05/88	Scotland	Wembley	1–0	RC		
38	24/05/88	Colombia	Wembley	1–1	RC		
39	28/05/88	Switzerland	Lausanne	1–0	F		
40	12/06/88	Republic of Ireland	Stuttgart	0–1	EC		
41	15/06/88	Holland	Dusseldorf	1–3	EC		
42	18/06/88	USSR	Frankfurt	1–3	EC		
43	19/10/88	Sweden	Wembley	0–0	WCQ		
44	08/02/89	Greece	Athens	2–1	F	1 Goal	(7)
45	08/03/89	Albania	Tirana	2–0	WCQ	1 Goal	(8)
46	03/06/89	Poland	Wembley	3–0	WCQ	1 Goal	(9)
47	07/06/89	Denmark	Copenhagen	1–1	F		
48	06/09/89	Sweden	Solna	0–0	WCQ		
49	15/11/89	Italy	Wembley	0–0	F		
50	28/03/90	Brazil	Wembley	1–0	F		
51	15/05/90	Denmark	Wembley	1–0	F		
52	22/05/90	Uruguay	Wembley	1–2	F	1 Goal	(10)
53	02/06/90	Tunisia	Tunis	1–1	F		
54	11/06/90	Republic of Ireland	Cagliari	1–1	WC		
55	16/06/90	Holland	Cagliari	0–0	WC		
56	21/06/90	Egypt	Cagliari	1–0	WC		
57	26/06/90	Belgium	Bologna	1–0*	WC		
58	01/07/90	Cameroon	Naples	3–2*	WC		
59	12/09/90	Hungary	Wembley	1–0	F		
60	17/10/90	Poland	Wembley	2–0	ECQ		
61	06/02/91	Cameroon	Wembley	2–0	F		
62	27/03/91	Republic of Ireland	Wembley	1–1	ECQ		
63	01/05/91	Turkey	Izmir	1–0	ECQ		
64	21/05/91	USSR	Wembley	3–1	F		
65	25/05/91	Argentina	Wembley	2–2	F		
66	25/03/92	Czechoslovakia	Prague	2–2	F		
67	03/06/92	Finland	Helsinki	2–1	F		
68	17/02/93	San Marino	Wembley	6–0	WCQ		
69	31/03/93	Turkey	Izmir	2–0	WCQ		
70	28/04/93	Holland	Wembley	2–2	WCQ	1 Goal	(11)
71	29/05/93	Poland	Katowice	1–1	WCQ		
72	09/06/93	USA	Boston	0–2	USC		
73	19/06/93	Germany	Detroit	1–2	USC		
74	07/09/94	USA	Wembley	2–0	F		
75	12/10/94	Romania	Wembley	1–1	F		
76	16/11/94	Nigeria	Wembley	1–0	F		
77	29/03/95	Uruguay	Wembley	0–0	F		
78	08/06/95	Sweden	Elland Road	3–3	UC		
Sub 79	06/09/95	Colombia	Wembley	0–0	F		

APPEARANCES AND GOALS PER SEASON

SEASON 81–82	GAMES	GOALS
League	35+1	13
FA Cup	3	0
League Cup	5	1
TOTAL	**43+1**	**14**

SEASON 82–83	GAMES	GOALS
League	42	10
FA Cup	4	1
League Cup	3	0
Football League Trophy	4	2
TOTAL	**53**	**13**

SEASON 83–84	GAMES	GOALS
League	39	11
FA Cup	7	4
League Cup	2	1
UEFA Cup	6	0
TOTAL	**54**	**16**

SEASON 84–85	GAMES	GOALS
League	40	12
FA Cup	2	0
League Cup	5	3
TOTAL	**47**	**15**

SEASON 85–86	GAMES	GOALS
League	39	9
FA Cup	8	3
League Cup	3	1
TOTAL	**50**	**13**

SEASON 86–87	GAMES	GOALS
League	37	10
FA Cup	7	3
League Cup	3	1
Full Members Cup	1	0
TOTAL	**48**	**14**

SEASON 87–88	GAMES	GOALS
League	38	15
FA Cup	7	2
League Cup	3	0
TOTAL	**48**	**17**

SEASON 88–89	GAMES	GOALS
League	33	8
FA Cup	6	3
League Cup	3	2
Mercantile Centenary Credit Trophy	1	1
FA Charity Shield	1	0
TOTAL	**44**	**14**

SEASON 89–90	GAMES	GOALS
League	34	22
FA Cup	8	5
League Cup	2	1
FA Charity Shield	1	0
TOTAL	**45**	**28**

SEASON 90–91	GAMES	GOALS
League	35	16
FA Cup	7	1
League Cup	2	0
FA Charity Shield	1	1
TOTAL	**45**	**18**

SEASON 91–92	GAMES	GOALS
League	12	1
FA Cup	4	3
UEFA Cup	1	0
TOTAL	**17**	**4**

SEASON 92–93	GAMES	GOALS
League	26+1	5
FA Cup	2	0
League Cup	2	0
TOTAL	**30+1**	**5**

SEASON 93–94	GAMES	GOALS
League	24+2	3
FA Cup	2	0
League Cup	2	0
TOTAL	**28+2**	**3**

SEASON 94–95	GAMES	GOALS
League	38	7
FA Cup	6	2
League Cup	6	0
TOTAL	**50**	**9**

SEASON 95–96	GAMES	GOALS
League	36	3
FA Cup	7	0
League Cup	3	0
UEFA Cup	4	0
TOTAL	**50**	**3**

SEASON 96–97	GAMES	GOALS
League	34+1	4
FA Cup	2	0
League Cup	3	0
European Cup Winners Cup	7	3
TOTAL	**46+1**	**7**

CAREER APPEARANCES AND GOALS

COMPETITION	GAMES	TOTAL	GOALS
League	542+5	547	149
FA Cup	82	82	27
League Cup	47	47	10
Football League Trophy	4	4	2
Mercantile Centenary Credit Trophy	1	1	1
Full Members Cup	1	1	0
FA Charity Shield	3	3	1
UEFA Cup	11	11	0
European Cup Winners Cup	7	7	3
Internationals	65+14	79	11
TOTAL	**763+19**	**782**	**204**

HAT-TRICKS

Watford

1	3	Cardiff City	25/09/84	Home	Lge Cup	3–1

Liverpool

1	3	Coventry City	05/05/90	Away	League	6–1
2	3	Crewe Alexandra	06/01/92	Away	FA Cup	4–0

League: 1
FA Cup: 1
League Cup: 1
TOTAL: 3

HONOURS

Winners medals
League Division One Championship: 87/88, 89/90
FA Cup: 88/89
League Cup: 94/95
FA Charity Shield: 88/89, 89/90, 90/91

Runner-up medals
League Division One Championship: 82/83, 88/89, 90/91
League Division Two Championship: 81/82
FA Cup: 83/84, 87/88, 95/96

PETER BEARDSLEY

Born: 18/01/61 – Newcastle
Height: 5.8
Weight: 11.07 (96–97)

Clubs
Carlisle United: **1979–82** – Matches: **116+12** – Goals: **29**
Vancouver Whitecaps: **1981–83** – Matches: **81** – Goals: **29**
Manchester United: **1982** – Matches: **1** – Goals: **0**
Newcastle United: **1983–87** – Matches: **163+1** – Goals: **61**
Liverpool: **1987–91** – Matches: **160+15** – Goals: **59**
Everton: **1991–93** – Matches: **95** – Goals: **32**
Newcastle United: **1993–97** – Matches: **159+3** – Goals: **58**

Country
England: **1986–96** – Matches: **46+13** – Goals: **9**

SEASON 1979–80

Carlisle United – League Division Three

1	21/08/79	Blackburn Rovers	Home	League	1–1
2	25/08/79	Bury	Home	League	1–0

3	08/09/79	Gillingham	Home	League	1–2		
4	15/09/79	Reading	Away	League	0–2		
5	18/09/79	Rotherham United	Home	League	3–1		
6	22/09/79	Exeter City	Away	League	2–1		
7	29/09/79	Chester	Home	League	2–2	1 Goal	(1)
8	02/10/79	Rotherham United	Away	League	1–4		
9	06/10/79	Wimbledon	Home	League	1–1		
10	10/10/79	Blackburn Rovers	Away	League	2–1		
11	13/10/79	Hull City	Away	League	0–2		
12	20/10/79	Barnsley	Home	League	3–1		
13	23/10/79	Mansfield Town	Home	League	1–1		
14	27/10/79	Oxford United	Away	League	0–1		
15	03/11/79	Southend United	Home	League	4–0		
Sub+1	10/11/79	Plymouth Argyle	Away	League	2–4		
Sub+2	07/12/79	Colchester United	Away	League	1–1	1 Goal	(2)
16	15/12/79	Sheffield Wednesday	Home	FA Cup	3–0	1 Goal	(3)
17	21/12/79	Grimsby Town	Home	League	0–2		
18	26/12/79	Chesterfield	Away	League	2–3		
19	05/01/80	Bradford City	Home	FA Cup	3–2		
20	12/01/80	Millwall	Home	League	4–0	1 Goal	(4)
21	19/01/80	Gillingham	Away	League	1–1	1 Goal	(5)
22	26/01/80	Wrexham	Home	FA Cup	0–0		
23	29/01/80	Wrexham	Away	FA Cup	1–3		
24	09/02/80	Exeter City	Home	League	4–1	1 Goal	(6)
25	20/02/80	Chester	Away	League	0–1		
26	23/02/80	Hull City	Home	League	3–2		
27	26/02/80	Sheffield Wednesday	Home	League	0–2		
28	01/03/80	Barnsley	Away	League	1–1	1 Goal	(7)
29	04/03/80	Bury	Away	League	2–0		
30	11/03/80	Swindon Town	Away	League	0–0		
31	14/03/80	Wimbledon	Away	League	0–0		
32	18/03/80	Blackpool	Home	League	2–0		
33	22/03/80	Plymouth Argyle	Home	League	2–1	1 Goal	(8)
34	29/03/80	Sheffield United	Away	League	2–0		
35	04/04/80	Grimsby Town	Away	League	0–2		
36	05/04/80	Chesterfield	Home	League	0–2		
37	07/04/80	Blackpool	Away	League	1–2		
38	12/04/80	Swindon Town	Home	League	2–1		
39	15/04/80	Reading	Home	League	3–3	1 Goal	(9)
40	26/04/80	Colchester United	Home	League	2–0		
41	03/05/80	Sheffield Wednesday	Away	League	0–0		

SEASON 1980–81

League Division Three

42	02/08/80	Blackpool	Home	AS Cup	1–2		
43	05/08/80	Blackburn Rovers	Home	AS Cup	1–4		
44	09/08/80	Rochdale	Home	Lge Cup	2–0		
45	12/08/80	Rochdale	Away	Lge Cup	1–1		
Sub+3	16/08/80	Sheffield United	Home	League	0–3		
Sub+4	19/08/80	Huddersfield Town	Away	League	1–1		
Sub+5	26/08/80	Charlton Athletic	Home	Lge Cup	1–2		
46	30/08/80	Newport County	Home	League	1–4		
47	02/09/80	Charlton Athletic	Away	Lge Cup	1–2		
48	06/09/80	Plymouth Argyle	Away	League	1–4		
Sub+6	13/09/80	Gillingham	Home	League	0–0		
Sub+7	16/09/80	Millwall	Home	League	2–1		
Sub+8	20/09/80	Oxford United	Away	League	2–1	1 Goal	(10)
49	27/09/80	Chesterfield	Home	League	2–6		
Sub+9	30/09/80	Millwall	Away	League	0–3		
50	04/10/80	Walsall	Away	League	3–4		
51	07/10/80	Barnsley	Home	League	2–2		
52	11/10/80	Brentford	Home	League	1–2	1 Goal	(11)
53	18/10/80	Swindon Town	Away	League	1–1		
54	21/10/80	Hull City	Away	League	1–0		
55	28/10/80	Blackpool	Home	League	2–0		
56	01/11/80	Portsmouth	Away	League	1–2	1 Goal	(12)
57	04/11/80	Barnsley	Away	League	1–3		
58	08/11/80	Fulham	Home	League	2–2		
59	11/11/80	Huddersfield Town	Home	League	1–1		
60	15/11/80	Sheffield United	Away	League	2–2		
61	22/11/80	Workington	Away	FA Cup	0–0		
62	29/11/80	Exeter City	Away	League	0–2		
63	01/12/80	Workington	Home	FA Cup	4–1	2 Goals	(14)
64	06/12/80	Colchester United	Home	League	4–0	2 Goals	(16)

65	13/12/80	Walsall	Home	FA Cup	3–0	2 Goals	(18)
66	20/12/80	Charlton Athletic	Away	League	1–2		
67	26/12/80	Burnley	Home	League	3–2	1 Goal	(19)
68	27/12/80	Rotherham United	Away	League	0–3		
69	03/01/81	Mansfield Town	Away	FA Cup	2–2		
70	06/01/81	Mansfield Town	Home	FA Cup	2–1	1 Goal	(20)
71	10/01/81	Reading	Away	League	1–3		
72	24/01/81	Bristol City	Home	FA Cup	1–1		
73	28/01/81	Bristol City	Away	FA Cup	0–5		
74	31/01/81	Chester	Home	League	3–0		
75	07/02/81	Gillingham	Away	League	1–0		
76	10/02/81	Reading	Home	League	0–0		
77	14/02/81	Plymouth Argyle	Home	League	2–0	1 Goal	(21)
78	21/02/81	Chesterfield	Away	League	0–1		
79	28/02/81	Oxford United	Home	League	0–0		
80	07/03/81	Walsall	Home	League	1–1		
81	14/03/81	Brentford	Away	League	1–1		
82	17/03/81	Swindon Town	Home	League	2–1		
83	21/03/81	Hull City	Home	League	2–0	1 Goal	(22)
84	28/03/81	Blackpool	Away	League	1–0	1 Goal	(23)
85	31/03/81	Exeter City	Home	League	1–1		
86	04/04/81	Portsmouth	Home	League	0–0		
87	11/04/81	Fulham	Away	League	3–2	1 Goal	(24)
88	18/04/81	Rotherham United	Home	League	0–1		
89	21/04/81	Burnley	Away	League	3–0		
90	25/04/81	Charlton Athletic	Home	League	1–2		

Vancouver Whitecaps – North American Soccer League – Season 1981

1	02/05/81	Seattle Sounders	Home	League	2–3		
2	08/05/81	Edmonton Drillers	Away	League	2–3*		
3	16/05/81	Seattle Sounders	Away	League	3–1	1 Goal	(1)
4	23/05/81	California Surf	Home	League	5–1		
5	27/05/81	Portland Timbers	Home	League	2–0	1 Goal	(2)
6	31/05/81	Los Angeles Aztecs	Away	League	2–0		
7	06/06/81	Calgary Boomers	Home	League	2–3+	1 Goal	(3)
8	10/06/81	Chicago Sting	Home	League	3–1	1 Goal	(4)
9	14/06/81	Fort Lauderdale Strikers	Home	League	0–1		
10	17/06/81	Minnesota Kicks	Away	League	2–0		
11	20/06/81	Tampa Bay Rowdies	Away	League	3–1		
12	24/06/81	Dallas Tornado	Away	League	3–2*		
13	27/06/81	Edmonton Drillers	Home	League	3–2		
14	01/07/81	San Jose Earthquakes	Away	League	5–1	3 Goals	(7)
15	04/07/81	Portland Timbers	Away	League	3–2*		
16	08/07/81	Tulsa Roughnecks	Home	League	3–2+		
17	12/07/81	Chicago Sting	Away	League	1–2*		
18	18/07/81	Toronto Blizzard	Home	League	2–0		
19	24/07/81	Calgary Boomers	Away	League	2–3		
20	30/07/81	Tulsa Roughnecks	Away	League	2–3	1 Goal	(8)
21	01/08/81	Montreal Manic	Away	League	1–2	1 Goal	(9)
22	05/08/81	Dallas Tornado	Home	League	2–0		
23	08/08/81	San Diego Sockers	Home	League	0–1		
24	12/08/81	Seattle Sounders	Home	League	5–0		
25	16/08/81	Edmonton Drillers	Away	League	5–4	3 Goals	(12)
26	19/08/81	San Jose Earthquakes	Home	League	3–1	1 Goal	(13)
27	23/08/81	Tampa Bay Rowdies	Away	Lge P/O	1–4		
28	26/08/81	Tampa Bay Rowdies	Home	Lge P/O	0–1		

* Sudden–death overtime
+ Decided on penalties

SEASON 1981–82

Carlisle United – League Division Three

91	12/09/81	Southend United	Home	League	3–2		
92	15/09/81	Bury	Home	Lge Cup	2–1*		
93	19/09/81	Lincoln City	Away	League	0–0		
94	22/09/81	Chesterfield	Away	League	0–1		
95	26/09/81	Oxford United	Home	League	2–1	1 Goal	(25)
96	29/09/81	Burnley	Home	League	1–0		
97	03/10/81	Brentford	Away	League	2–1		
98	06/10/81	Bristol City	Home	Lge Cup	0–0		
99	10/10/81	Swindon Town	Away	League	1–2	1 Goal	(26)
100	17/10/81	Plymouth Argyle	Home	League	3–1		
101	20/10/81	Huddersfield Town	Away	League	1–2		
102	24/10/81	Walsall	Home	League	2–1	1 Goal	(27)

103	27/10/81	Bristol City	Away	Lge Cup	1–2		
104	31/10/81	Newport County	Away	League	0–2		
105	03/11/81	Doncaster Rovers	Home	League	2–0		
106	14/11/81	Portsmouth	Away	League	2–1		
107	21/11/81	Darlington	Away	FA Cup	2–2		
108	24/11/81	Darlington	Home	FA Cup	3–1	1 Goal	(28)
109	28/11/81	Gillingham	Home	League	2–0		
110	19/12/81	Bristol Rovers	Away	League	1–0		
111	09/01/82	Bishop Auckland	Home	FA Cup	1–0+		
112	23/01/82	Huddersfield Town	Home	FA Cup	2–3		
Sub+10	30/01/82	Lincoln City	Home	League	1–0		
113	02/02/82	Preston North End	Home	League	1–0		
Sub+11	06/02/82	Southend United	Away	League	1–1		
114	09/02/82	Chesterfield	Home	League	3–0		
115	13/02/82	Brentford	Home	League	1–0		
Sub+12	20/02/82	Oxford United	Away	League	1–2		
116	27/02/82	Swindon Town	Home	League	1–1	1 Goal	(29)

+ Played at Workington

Vancouver Whitecaps – North American Soccer League – Season 1982

29	03/04/82	San Diego Sockers	Away	League	0–1		
30	07/04/82	Toronto Blizzard	Home	League	1–3	1 Goal	(14)
31	17/04/82	Seattle Sounders	Home	League	2–1		
32	24/04/82	Portland Timbers	Home	League	2–1*	1 Goal	(15)
33	02/05/82	Portland Timbers	Away	League	0–5		
34	05/05/82	San Jose Earthquakes	Away	League	0–2		
35	08/05/82	Edmonton Drillers	Home	League	3–1	1 Goal	(16)
36	12/05/82	Montreal Manic	Home	League	2–1+		
37	16/05/82	Edmonton Drillers	Away	League	2–3+	2 Goals	(18)
38	29/05/82	Portland Timbers	Home	League	1–0		
39	02/06/82	San Jose Earthquakes	Away	League	2–1		
40	05/06/82	Jacksonville Tea Men	Home	League	4–2	1 Goal	(19)
41	16/06/82	Tampa Bay Rowdies	Home	League	3–0		
42	19/06/82	Chicago Sting	Away	League	3–2+		
43	23/06/82	New York Cosmos	Away	League	2–3	1 Goal	(20)
44	26/06/82	Tampa Bay Rowdies	Away	League	5–2		
45	03/07/82	New York Cosmos	Home	League	1–0		
46	05/08/82	Fort Lauderdale Strikers	Home	League	4–1		
47	11/08/82	Edmonton Drillers	Home	League	2–1		
48	14/08/82	Edmonton Drillers	Away	League	0–1		
49	18/08/82	Seattle Sounders	Away	League	2–1		
50	21/08/82	San Diego Sockers	Home	League	1–2		
51	25/08/82	San Diego Sockers	Away	Lge P/O	1–5		
52	28/08/82	San Diego Sockers	Home	Lge P/O	1–0		
53	02/09/82	San Diego Sockers	Away	Lge P/O	1–2		

* Sudden–death overtime
+ Decided on penalties

SEASON 1982–83

Manchester United – League Division One

| 1 | 06/10/82 | AFC Bournemouth | Home | Lge Cup | 2–0 | | |

Vancouver Whitecaps – North American Soccer League – Season 1983

54	22/05/83	Golden Bay Earthquakes	Away	League	1–2		
55	27/05/83	Chicago Sting	Home	League	3–1		
56	01/06/83	Tulsa Roughnecks	Home	League	2–1*		
57	05/06/83	Toronto Blizzard	Away	League	3–2+	1 Goal	(21)
58	08/06/83	Chicago Sting	Away	League	2–0	1 Goal	(22)
59	11/06/83	Montreal Manic	Away	League	4–1		
60	20/06/83	Seattle Sounders	Home	League	2–1	2 Goals	(24)
61	22/06/83	San Diego Sockers	Away	League	1–0*		
62	26/06/83	Tampa Bay Rowdies	Home	League	4–1		
63	29/06/83	New York Cosmos	Away	League	0–3		
64	03/07/83	San Diego Sockers	Home	League	3–0	1 Goal	(25)
65	07/07/83	Montreal Manic	Home	League	5–3	1 Goal	(26)
66	10/07/83	New York Cosmos	Home	League	2–0		
67	13/07/83	Toronto Blizzard	Away	League	0–1+		
68	17/07/83	Golden Bay Earthquakes	Home	League	2–1		
69	20/07/83	Montreal Manic	Home	League	0–1		
70	24/07/83	Team America	Away	League	2–0	1 Goal	(27)
71	27/07/83	Team America	Home	League	1–0+		
72	30/07/83	Tulsa Roughnecks	Away	League	1–2*		

73	13/08/83	Seattle Sounders	Away	League	3–2+		
74	18/08/83	San Diego Sockers	Home	League	3–0		
75	24/08/83	Golden Bay Earthquakes	Home	League	2–1		
76	28/08/83	Seattle Sounders	Home	League	3–2*		
77	31/08/83	Golden Bay Earthquakes	Away	League	0–3		
78	03/09/83	San Diego Sockers	Away	League	5–4+	1 Goal	(28)
79	08/09/83	Toronto Blizzard	Home	Lge P/O	1–0		
80	12/09/83	Toronto Blizzard	Away	Lge P/O	3–4	1 Goal	(29)
81	15/09/83	Toronto Blizzard	Home	Lge P/O	0–1		

* Sudden–death overtime
+ Decided on penalties

SEASON 1983–84

Newcastle United – League Division Two

Sub+1	24/09/83	Barnsley	Away	League	1–1		
1	01/10/83	Portsmouth	Home	League	4–2		
2	05/10/83	Oxford United	Home	Lge Cup	1–1		
3	08/10/83	Charlton Athletic	Home	League	2–1		
4	16/10/83	Swansea City	Away	League	2–1		
5	19/10/83	Cardiff City	Away	League	2–0	1 Goal	(1)
6	26/10/83	Oxford United	Away	Lge Cup	1–2		
7	29/10/83	Manchester City	Home	League	5–0	3 Goals	(4)
8	05/11/83	Fulham	Home	League	3–2		
9	12/11/83	Chelsea	Away	League	0–4		
10	19/11/83	Sheffield Wednesday	Away	League	2–4		
11	26/11/83	Cambridge United	Home	League	2–1	1 Goal	(5)
12	03/12/83	Derby County	Away	League	2–3		
13	10/12/83	Huddersfield Town	Home	League	5–2	1 Goal	(6)
14	17/12/83	Brighton & Hove Albion	Away	League	1–0		
15	26/12/83	Blackburn Rovers	Home	League	1–1		
16	27/12/83	Carlisle United	Away	League	1–3		
17	02/01/84	Barnsley	Home	League	1–0		
18	06/01/84	Liverpool	Away	FA Cup	0–4		
19	21/01/84	Crystal Palace	Away	League	1–3	1 Goal	(7)
20	04/02/84	Portsmouth	Away	League	4–1	2 Goals	(9)
21	11/02/84	Grimsby Town	Home	League	0–1		
22	18/02/84	Manchester City	Away	League	2–1	1 Goal	(10)
23	25/02/84	Cardiff City	Home	League	3–1		
24	03/03/84	Fulham	Away	League	2–2	1 Goal	(11)
25	10/03/84	Chelsea	Home	League	1–1		
26	17/03/84	Middlesbrough	Home	League	3–1	1 Goal	(12)
27	24/03/84	Shrewsbury Town	Away	League	2–2		
28	28/03/84	Leeds United	Home	League	1–0		
29	31/03/84	Swansea City	Home	League	2–0	1 Goal	(13)
30	07/04/84	Charlton Athletic	Away	League	3–1	1 Goal	(14)
31	14/04/84	Sheffield Wednesday	Home	League	0–1		
32	20/04/84	Blackburn Rovers	Away	League	1–1		
33	23/04/84	Carlisle United	Home	League	5–1	2 Goals	(16)
34	28/04/84	Cambridge United	Away	League	0–1		
35	05/05/84	Derby County	Home	League	4–0	2 Goals	(18)
36	07/05/84	Huddersfield Town	Away	League	2–2	1 Goal	(19)
37	12/05/84	Brighton & Hove Albion	Home	League	3–1	1 Goal	(20)

SEASON 1984–85

League Division One

38	25/08/84	Leicester City	Away	League	3–2		
39	27/08/84	Sheffield Wednesday	Home	League	2–1	1 Goal	(21)
40	01/09/84	Aston Villa	Home	League	3–0	1 Goal	(22)
41	04/09/84	Arsenal	Away	League	0–2		
42	08/09/84	Manchester United	Away	League	0–5		
43	15/09/84	Everton	Home	League	2–3	1 Goal	(23)
44	22/09/84	Queens Park Rangers	Away	League	5–5		
45	26/09/84	Bradford City	Home	Lge Cup	3–1		
46	29/09/84	West Ham United	Home	League	1–1	1 Goal	(24)
47	06/10/84	Ipswich Town	Home	League	3–0		
48	10/10/84	Bradford City	Away	Lge Cup	1–0		
49	13/10/84	Coventry City	Away	League	1–1	1 Goal	(25)
50	20/10/84	Nottingham Forest	Home	League	1–1		
51	27/10/84	Watford	Away	League	3–3	1 Goal	(26)
52	30/10/84	Ipswich Town	Away	Lge Cup	1–1		
53	03/11/84	Luton Town	Away	League	2–2	1 Goal	(27)
54	07/11/84	Ipswich Town	Home	Lge Cup	1–2		

55	10/11/84	Chelsea	Home	League	2–1		
56	18/11/84	Liverpool	Home	League	0–2		
57	24/11/84	Southampton	Away	League	0–1		
58	08/12/84	Tottenham Hotspur	Away	League	1–3		
59	15/12/84	Norwich City	Home	League	1–1		
60	29/12/84	Arsenal	Home	League	1–3	1 Goal	(28)
61	01/01/85	Sunderland	Home	League	3–1	3 Goals	(31)
62	06/01/85	Nottingham Forest	Away	FA Cup	1–1		
63	09/01/85	Nottingham Forest	Home	FA Cup	1–3*		
64	02/02/85	West Ham United	Away	League	1–1		
65	09/02/85	Manchester United	Home	League	1–1	1 Goal	(32)
66	16/02/85	Chelsea	Away	League	0–1		
67	23/02/85	Luton Town	Home	League	1–0		
68	02/03/85	Watford	Home	League	3–1		
69	09/03/85	Nottingham Forest	Away	League	0–0		
70	20/03/85	Leicester City	Home	League	1–4	1 Goal	(33)
71	23/03/85	Ipswich Town	Away	League	1–1		
72	30/03/85	Sheffield Wednesday	Away	League	2–4	1 Goal	(34)
73	06/04/85	West Bromwich Albion	Home	League	1–0	1 Goal	(35)
74	08/04/85	Sunderland	Away	League	0–0		
75	13/04/85	Queens Park Rangers	Home	League	1–0		
76	17/04/85	Coventry City	Home	League	0–1		
77	20/04/85	Liverpool	Away	League	1–3		
78	27/04/85	Southampton	Home	League	2–1		
79	04/05/85	Stoke City	Away	League	1–0		
80	06/05/85	Tottenham Hotspur	Home	League	2–3	2 Goals	(37)
81	11/05/85	Norwich City	Away	League	0–0		

SEASON 1985–86

League Division One

82	17/08/85	Southampton	Away	League	1–1	1 Goal	(38)
83	21/08/85	Luton Town	Home	League	2–2	1 Goal	(39)
84	24/08/85	Liverpool	Home	League	1–0		
85	26/08/85	Coventry City	Away	League	2–1		
86	31/08/85	Queens Park Rangers	Home	League	3–1	1 Goal	(40)
87	04/09/85	Manchester United	Away	League	0–3		
88	07/09/85	Tottenham Hotspur	Away	League	1–5		
89	14/09/85	West Bromwich Albion	Home	League	4–1		
90	21/09/85	Oxford United	Home	League	3–0	1 Goal	(41)
91	25/09/85	Barnsley	Home	Lge Cup	0–0		
92	28/09/85	Arsenal	Away	League	0–0		
93	05/10/85	West Ham United	Home	League	1–2		
94	12/10/85	Ipswich Town	Away	League	2–2	1 Goal	(42)
95	19/10/85	Nottingham Forest	Home	League	0–3		
96	26/10/85	Aston Villa	Away	League	2–1	1 Goal	(43)
97	30/10/85	Oxford United	Away	Lge Cup	1–3		
98	02/11/85	Watford	Home	League	1–1		
99	09/11/85	Birmingham City	Away	League	1–0		
100	16/11/85	Chelsea	Home	League	1–3		
101	23/11/85	Manchester City	Away	League	0–1		
102	30/11/85	Leicester City	Home	League	2–1	1 Goal	(44)
103	07/12/85	Luton Town	Away	League	0–2		
104	14/12/85	Southampton	Home	League	2–1	1 Goal	(45)
105	21/12/85	Liverpool	Away	League	1–1	1 Goal	(46)
106	26/12/85	Sheffield Wednesday	Away	League	2–2	1 Goal	(47)
107	01/01/86	Everton	Home	League	2–2	1 Goal	(48)
108	04/01/86	Brighton & Hove Albion	Home	FA Cup	0–2		
109	11/01/86	West Bromwich Albion	Away	League	1–1		
110	18/01/86	Queens Park Rangers	Away	League	1–3		
111	01/02/86	Coventry City	Home	League	3–2	1 Goal	(49)
112	08/02/86	Nottingham Forest	Away	League	2–1	2 Goals	(51)
113	01/03/86	Arsenal	Home	League	1–0		
114	15/03/86	Ipswich Town	Home	League	3–1	1 Goal	(52)
115	19/03/86	Oxford United	Away	League	2–1	1 Goal	(53)
116	22/03/86	Tottenham Hotspur	Home	League	2–2		
117	29/03/86	Everton	Away	League	0–1		
118	31/03/86	Sheffield Wednesday	Home	League	4–1	1 Goal	(54)
119	05/04/86	Watford	Away	League	1–4		
120	09/04/86	Aston Villa	Home	League	2–2		
121	12/04/86	Birmingham City	Home	League	4–1	2 Goals	(56)
122	16/04/86	Manchester United	Home	League	2–4		
123	19/04/86	Chelsea	Away	League	1–1		
124	21/04/86	West Ham United	Away	League	1–8		

| 125 | 26/04/86 | Manchester City | Home | League | 3–1 |
| 126 | 03/05/86 | Leicester City | Away | League | 0–2 |

SEASON 1986–87

League Division One

127	23/08/86	Liverpool	Home	League	0–2		
128	25/08/86	Tottenham Hotspur	Away	League	1–1	1 Goal	(57)
129	30/08/86	Luton Town	Away	League	0–0		
130	23/09/86	Bradford City	Away	Lge Cup	0–2		
131	27/09/86	Norwich City	Away	League	0–2		
132	04/10/86	Southampton	Away	League	1–4		
133	08/10/86	Bradford City	Home	Lge Cup	1–0		
134	11/10/86	Manchester City	Home	League	3–1		
135	18/10/86	Arsenal	Home	League	1–2		
136	25/10/86	Aston Villa	Away	League	0–2		
137	01/11/86	Oxford United	Home	League	0–0		
138	08/11/86	Leicester City	Away	League	1–1		
139	15/11/86	Watford	Home	League	2–2		
140	22/11/86	Chelsea	Away	League	3–1	1 Goal	(58)
141	30/11/86	West Ham United	Home	League	4–0		
142	03/12/86	Everton	Away	FM Cup	2–5		
143	06/12/86	Charlton Athletic	Away	League	1–1		
144	13/12/86	Nottingham Forest	Home	League	3–2	1 Goal	(59)
145	21/12/86	Sheffield Wednesday	Away	League	0–2		
146	26/12/86	Everton	Home	League	0–4		
147	27/12/86	Watford	Away	League	0–1		
148	01/01/87	Manchester United	Away	League	1–4		
149	21/01/87	Northampton Town	Home	FA Cup	2–1		
150	24/01/87	Liverpool	Away	League	0–2		
151	07/02/87	Luton Town	Home	League	2–2		
152	14/02/87	Queens Park Rangers	Away	League	1–2		
153	21/02/87	Tottenham Hotspur	Away	FA Cup	0–1		
154	28/02/87	Wimbledon	Away	League	1–3	1 Goal	(60)
155	07/03/87	Aston Villa	Home	League	2–1	1 Goal	(61)
156	21/03/87	Manchester City	Away	League	0–0		
157	25/03/87	Tottenham Hotspur	Home	League	1–1		
158	28/03/87	Southampton	Home	League	2–0		
159	04/04/87	Leicester City	Home	League	2–0		
160	08/04/87	Norwich City	Home	League	4–1		
161	11/04/87	Oxford United	Away	League	1–1		
162	14/04/87	Arsenal	Away	League	1–0		
163	18/04/87	Manchester United	Home	League	2–1		

SEASON 1987–88

Liverpool – League Division One

1	15/08/87	Arsenal	Away	League	2–1		
2	29/08/87	Coventry City	Away	League	4–1	1 Goal	(1)
3	05/09/87	West Ham United	Away	League	1–1		
4	12/09/87	Oxford United	Home	League	2–0		
5	15/09/87	Charlton Athletic	Home	League	3–2		
6	20/09/87	Newcastle United	Away	League	4–1		
7	23/09/87	Blackburn Rovers	Away	Lge Cup	1–1		
8	29/09/87	Derby County	Home	League	4–0	1 Goal	(2)
9	03/10/87	Portsmouth	Home	League	4–0	1 Goal	(3)
10	06/10/87	Blackburn Rovers	Home	Lge Cup	1–0		
11	17/10/87	Queens Park Rangers	Home	League	4–0		
12	24/10/87	Luton Town	Away	League	1–0		
13	28/10/87	Everton	Away	Lge Cup	0–1		
14	01/11/87	Everton	Home	League	2–0	1 Goal	(4)
15	04/11/87	Wimbledon	Away	League	1–1		
16	15/11/87	Manchester United	Away	League	1–1		
17	21/11/87	Norwich City	Home	League	0–0		
18	24/11/87	Watford	Home	League	4–0		
19	06/12/87	Chelsea	Home	League	2–1		
20	12/12/87	Southampton	Away	League	2–2		
21	19/12/87	Sheffield Wednesday	Home	League	1–0		
22	26/12/87	Oxford United	Away	League	3–0		
23	28/12/87	Newcastle United	Home	League	4–0		
24	01/01/88	Coventry City	Home	League	4–0	2 Goals	(6)
25	09/01/88	Stoke City	Away	FA Cup	0–0		
26	12/01/88	Stoke City	Home	FA Cup	1–0	1 Goal	(7)
27	16/01/88	Arsenal	Home	League	2–0	1 Goal	(8)
28	23/01/88	Charlton Athletic	Away	League	2–0	1 Goal	(9)

29	31/01/88	Aston Villa	Away	FA Cup	2–0	1 Goal	(10)
30	06/02/88	West Ham United	Home	League	0–0		
31	13/02/88	Watford	Away	League	4–1	2 Goals	(12)
32	21/02/88	Everton	Away	FA Cup	1–0		
33	27/02/88	Portsmouth	Away	League	2–0		
34	05/03/88	Queens Park Rangers	Away	League	1–0		
35	13/03/88	Manchester City	Away	FA Cup	4–0	1 Goal	(13)
36	16/03/88	Derby County	Away	League	1–1		
37	20/03/88	Everton	Away	League	0–1		
38	26/03/88	Wimbledon	Home	League	2–1		
Sub+1	02/04/88	Nottingham Forest	Away	League	1–2		
39	04/04/88	Manchester United	Home	League	3–3	1 Goal	(14)
40	09/04/88	Nottingham Forest	Neutral	FA Cup	2–1		
41	13/04/88	Nottingham Forest	Home	League	5–0	1 Goal	(15)
42	20/04/88	Norwich City	Away	League	0–0		
43	23/04/88	Tottenham Hotspur	Home	League	1–0	1 Goal	(16)
Sub+2	30/04/88	Chelsea	Away	League	1–1		
44	02/05/88	Southampton	Home	League	1–1		
45	07/05/88	Sheffield Wednesday	Away	League	5–1	2 Goals	(18)
46	14/05/88	Wimbledon	Wembley	FA Cup	0–1		

SEASON 1988–89

League Division One

47	20/08/88	Wimbledon	Wembley	FA C/S	2–0		
48	27/08/88	Charlton Athletic	Away	League	3–0		
49	29/08/88	Nottingham Forest	Home	MCC Trophy	4–1		
50	03/09/88	Manchester United	Home	League	1–0		
Sub+3	10/09/88	Aston Villa	Away	League	1–1		
51	17/09/88	Tottenham Hotspur	Home	League	1–1	1 Goal	(19)
52	20/09/88	Arsenal	Away	MCC Trophy	1–2		
53	24/09/88	Southampton	Away	League	3–1	1 Goal	(20)
54	28/09/88	Walsall	Home	Lge Cup	1–0		
55	01/10/88	Newcastle United	Home	League	1–2		
56	08/10/88	Luton Town	Away	League	0–1		
57	12/10/88	Walsall	Away	Lge Cup	3–1		
58	22/10/88	Coventry City	Home	League	0–0		
59	26/10/88	Nottingham Forest	Away	League	1–2		
60	29/10/88	West Ham United	Away	League	2–0	1 Goal	(21)
61	02/11/88	Arsenal	Home	Lge Cup	1–1		
62	05/11/88	Middlesbrough	Home	League	3–0	1 Goal	(22)
63	09/11/88	Arsenal	Away	Lge Cup	0–0*		
64	12/11/88	Millwall	Home	League	1–1		
65	19/11/88	Queens Park Rangers	Away	League	1–0		
66	23/11/88	Arsenal	Away	Lge Cup	2–1		
67	26/11/88	Wimbledon	Home	League	1–1		
68	30/11/88	West Ham United	Away	Lge Cup	1–4		
69	04/12/88	Arsenal	Away	League	1–1		
70	11/12/88	Everton	Home	League	1–1		
71	17/12/88	Norwich City	Home	League	0–1		
72	26/12/88	Derby County	Away	League	1–0		
73	01/01/89	Manchester United	Away	League	1–3		
74	03/01/89	Aston Villa	Home	League	1–0		
75	07/01/89	Carlisle United	Away	FA Cup	3–0		
76	14/01/89	Sheffield Wednesday	Away	League	2–2		
77	21/01/89	Southampton	Home	League	2–0		
Sub+4	04/02/89	Newcastle United	Away	League	2–2		
78	18/02/89	Hull City	Away	FA Cup	3–2		
79	01/03/89	Charlton Athletic	Home	League	2–0	1 Goal	(23)
80	11/03/89	Middlesbrough	Away	League	4–0	1 Goal	(24)
81	14/03/89	Luton Town	Home	League	5–0	1 Goal	(25)
82	18/03/89	Brentford	Home	FA Cup	4–0	2 Goals	(27)
83	22/03/89	Coventry City	Away	League	3–1		
84	26/03/89	Tottenham Hotspur	Away	League	2–1	1 Goal	(28)
85	29/03/89	Derby County	Home	League	1–0		
86	01/04/89	Norwich City	Away	League	1–0		
87	08/04/89	Sheffield Wednesday	Home	League	5–1	2 Goals	(30)
88	11/04/89	Millwall	Away	League	2–1		
89	03/05/89	Everton	Away	League	0–0		
90	07/05/89	Nottingham Forest	Neutral	FA Cup	3–1		
91	10/05/89	Nottingham Forest	Home	League	1–0		
92	16/05/89	Queens Park Rangers	Home	League	2–0		
93	20/05/89	Everton	Wembley	FA Cup	3–2*		
Sub+5	23/05/89	West Ham United	Home	League	5–1		
Sub+6	26/05/89	Arsenal	Home	League	0–2		

SEASON 1989–90

League Division One

94	12/08/89	Arsenal	Wembley	FA C/S	1–0	1 Goal	(31)
95	19/08/89	Manchester City	Home	League	3–1	1 Goal	(32)
96	23/08/89	Aston Villa	Away	League	1–1		
97	26/08/89	Luton Town	Away	League	0–0		
98	09/09/89	Derby County	Away	League	3–0	1 Goal	(33)
99	12/09/89	Crystal Palace	Home	League	9–0	1 Goal	(34)
100	16/09/89	Norwich City	Home	League	0–0		
101	19/09/89	Wigan Athletic	Home	Lge Cup	5–2	1 Goal	(35)
102	23/09/89	Everton	Away	League	3–1		
103	04/10/89	Wigan Athletic	Away	Lge Cup	3–0+		
104	14/10/89	Wimbledon	Away	League	2–1	1 Goal	(36)
105	21/10/89	Southampton	Away	League	1–4	1 Goal	(37)
Sub+7	25/10/89	Arsenal	Away	Lge Cup	0–1		
106	29/10/89	Tottenham Hotspur	Home	League	1–0		
107	04/11/89	Coventry City	Home	League	0–1		
108	11/11/89	Queens Park Rangers	Away	League	2–3		
Sub+8	26/11/89	Arsenal	Home	League	2–1		
109	29/11/89	Sheffield Wednesday	Away	League	0–2		
110	02/12/89	Manchester City	Away	League	4–1	1 Goal	(38)
111	09/12/89	Aston Villa	Home	League	1–1	1 Goal	(39)
112	16/12/89	Chelsea	Away	League	5–2	1 Goal	(40)
113	23/12/89	Manchester United	Home	League	0–0		
114	26/12/89	Sheffield Wednesday	Home	League	2–1		
Sub+9	30/12/89	Charlton Athletic	Home	League	1–0		
115	01/01/90	Nottingham Forest	Away	League	2–2		
116	06/01/90	Swansea City	Away	FA Cup	0–0		
117	09/01/90	Swansea City	Home	FA Cup	8–0	1 Goal	(41)
118	13/01/90	Luton Town	Home	League	2–2		
119	20/01/90	Crystal Palace	Away	League	2–0	1 Goal	(42)
120	28/01/90	Norwich City	Away	FA Cup	0–0		
121	31/01/90	Norwich City	Home	FA Cup	3–1	1 Goal	(43)
122	03/02/90	Everton	Home	League	2–1	1 Goal	(44)
123	10/02/90	Norwich City	Away	League	0–0		
124	17/02/90	Southampton	Home	FA Cup	3–0	1 Goal	(45)
125	03/03/90	Millwall	Home	League	1–0		
126	11/03/90	Queens Park Rangers	Away	FA Cup	2–2		
127	14/03/90	Queens Park Rangers	Home	FA Cup	1–0	1 Goal	(46)
128	18/03/90	Manchester United	Away	League	2–1		
129	21/03/90	Tottenham Hotspur	Away	League	0–1		
130	31/03/90	Southampton	Home	League	3–2		
131	08/04/90	Crystal Palace	Neutral	FA Cup	3–4*		

+ Played at Liverpool

SEASON 1990–91

League Division One

132	18/08/90	Manchester United	Wembley	FA C/S	1–1		
133	28/08/90	Nottingham Forest	Home	League	2–0	1 Goal	(47)
134	01/09/90	Aston Villa	Home	League	2–1	1 Goal	(48)
135	16/09/90	Manchester United	Home	League	4–0	3 Goals	(51)
136	22/09/90	Everton	Away	League	3–2	2 Goals	(53)
137	25/09/90	Crewe Alexandra	Home	Lge Cup	5–1		
138	29/09/90	Sunderland	Away	League	1–0		
139	06/10/90	Derby County	Home	League	2–0	1 Goal	(54)
140	20/10/90	Norwich City	Away	League	1–1		
141	27/10/90	Chelsea	Home	League	2–0		
142	31/10/90	Manchester United	Away	Lge Cup	1–3		
Sub+10	04/11/90	Tottenham Hotspur	Away	League	3–1	1 Goal	(55)
143	10/11/90	Luton Town	Home	League	4–0	1 Goal	(56)
144	17/11/90	Coventry City	Away	League	1–0	1 Goal	(57)
145	24/11/90	Manchester City	Home	League	2–2		
146	15/12/90	Sheffield United	Home	League	2–0		
Sub+11	26/01/91	Brighton & Hove Albion	Home	FA Cup	2–2		
Sub+12	30/01/91	Brighton & Hove Albion	Away	FA Cup	3–2*		
Sub+13	09/02/91	Everton	Home	League	3–1		
Sub+14	17/02/91	Everton	Home	FA Cup	0–0		
147	20/02/91	Everton	Away	FA Cup	4–4*	2 Goals	(59)
148	23/02/91	Luton Town	Away	League	1–3		
149	27/02/91	Everton	Away	FA Cup	0–1		
150	03/03/91	Arsenal	Home	League	0–1		
151	09/03/91	Manchester City	Away	League	3–0		

152	16/03/91	Sunderland	Home	League	2–1		
153	23/03/91	Derby County	Away	League	7–1		
154	30/03/91	Queens Park Rangers	Home	League	1–3		
155	01/04/91	Southampton	Away	League	0–1		
156	09/04/91	Coventry City	Home	League	1–1		
157	13/04/91	Leeds United	Away	League	5–4		
158	20/04/91	Norwich City	Home	League	3–0		
159	23/04/91	Crystal Palace	Home	League	3–0		
160	04/05/91	Chelsea	Away	League	2–4		
Sub+15	11/05/91	Tottenham Hotspur	Home	League	2–0		

SEASON 1991–92

Everton – League Division One

1	17/08/91	Nottingham Forest	Away	League	1–2		
2	20/08/91	Arsenal	Home	League	3–1		
3	24/08/91	Manchester United	Home	League	0–0		
4	28/08/91	Sheffield Wednesday	Away	League	1–2		
5	31/08/91	Liverpool	Away	League	1–3		
6	03/09/91	Norwich City	Home	League	1–1		
7	07/09/91	Crystal Palace	Home	League	2–2	1 Goal	(1)
8	14/09/91	Sheffield United	Away	League	1–2	1 Goal	(2)
9	17/09/91	Manchester City	Away	League	1–0	1 Goal	(3)
10	21/09/91	Coventry City	Home	League	3–0	3 Goals	(6)
11	24/09/91	Watford	Home	Lge Cup	1–0	1 Goal	(7)
12	28/09/91	Chelsea	Away	League	2–2	1 Goal	(8)
13	01/10/91	Oldham Athletic	Home	ZDS Cup	3–2		
14	05/10/91	Tottenham Hotspur	Home	League	3–1		
15	08/10/91	Watford	Away	Lge Cup	2–1	1 Goal	(9)
16	19/10/91	Aston Villa	Home	League	0–2		
17	26/10/91	Queens Park Rangers	Away	League	1–3		
18	30/10/91	Wolverhampton Wanderers	Home	Lge Cup	4–1	1 Goal	(10)
19	02/11/91	Luton Town	Away	League	1–0		
20	16/11/91	Wimbledon	Home	League	2–0		
21	23/11/91	Notts County	Home	League	1–0		
22	27/11/91	Leicester City	Away	ZDS Cup	1–2	1 Goal	(11)
23	30/11/91	Leeds United	Away	League	0–1		
24	04/12/91	Leeds United	Home	Lge Cup	1–4		
25	07/12/91	West Ham United	Home	League	4–0	1 Goal	(12)
26	14/12/91	Oldham Athletic	Away	League	2–2		
27	21/12/91	Arsenal	Away	League	2–4		
28	26/12/91	Sheffield Wednesday	Home	League	0–1		
29	28/12/91	Liverpool	Home	League	1–1		
30	01/01/92	Southampton	Away	League	2–1	1 Goal	(13)
31	04/01/92	Southend United	Home	FA Cup	1–0	1 Goal	(14)
32	11/01/92	Manchester United	Away	League	0–1		
33	19/01/92	Nottingham Forest	Home	League	1–1		
34	26/01/92	Chelsea	Away	FA Cup	0–1		
35	02/02/92	Aston Villa	Away	League	0–0		
36	08/02/92	Queens Park Rangers	Home	League	0–0		
37	23/02/92	Leeds United	Home	League	1–1		
38	29/02/92	West Ham United	Away	League	2–0		
39	07/03/92	Oldham Athletic	Home	League	2–1	2 Goals	(16)
40	10/03/92	Wimbledon	Away	League	0–0		
41	14/03/92	Luton Town	Home	League	1–1		
42	17/03/92	Notts County	Away	League	0–0		
43	21/03/92	Norwich City	Away	League	3–4	1 Goal	(17)
44	01/04/92	Southampton	Home	League	0–1		
45	04/04/92	Crystal Palace	Away	League	0–2		
46	11/04/92	Sheffield United	Home	League	0–2		
47	18/04/92	Coventry City	Away	League	1–0		
48	20/04/92	Manchester City	Home	League	1–2		
49	25/04/92	Tottenham Hotspur	Away	League	3–3	2 Goals	(19)
50	02/05/92	Chelsea	Home	League	2–1	1 Goal	(20)

SEASON 1992–93

Premier League

51	15/08/92	Sheffield Wednesday	Home	League	1–1		
52	19/08/92	Manchester United	Away	League	3–0	1 Goal	(21)
53	22/08/92	Norwich City	Away	League	1–1	1 Goal	(22)
54	25/08/92	Aston Villa	Home	League	1–0		
55	29/08/92	Wimbledon	Home	League	0–0		
56	05/09/92	Tottenham Hotspur	Away	League	1–2	1 Goal	(23)
57	12/09/92	Manchester United	Home	League	0–2		

58	15/09/92	Blackburn Rovers	Away	League	3–2		
59	19/09/92	Crystal Palace	Home	League	0–2		
60	17/10/92	Coventry City	Home	League	1–1		
61	24/10/92	Arsenal	Away	League	0–2		
62	28/10/92	Wimbledon	Home	Lge Cup	0–0		
63	07/11/92	Nottingham Forest	Away	League	1–0		
64	10/11/92	Wimbledon	Away	Lge Cup	1–0	1 Goal	(24)
65	21/11/92	Chelsea	Home	League	0–1		
66	28/11/92	Ipswich Town	Away	League	0–1		
67	02/12/92	Chelsea	Home	Lge Cup	2–2	1 Goal	(25)
68	07/12/92	Liverpool	Home	League	2–1	1 Goal	(26)
69	12/12/92	Sheffield United	Away	League	0–1		
70	16/12/92	Chelsea	Away	Lge Cup	0–1		
71	19/12/92	Southampton	Home	League	2–1	1 Goal	(27)
72	26/12/92	Middlesbrough	Home	League	2–2	1 Goal	(28)
73	28/12/92	Queens Park Rangers	Away	League	2–4		
74	02/01/93	Wimbledon	Away	FA Cup	0–0		
75	09/01/93	Crystal Palace	Away	League	2–0	1 Goal	(29)
76	12/01/93	Wimbledon	Home	FA Cup	1–2		
77	16/01/93	Leeds United	Home	League	2–0		
78	26/01/93	Wimbledon	Away	League	3–1		
79	30/01/93	Norwich City	Home	League	0–1		
80	06/02/93	Sheffield Wednesday	Away	League	1–3		
81	10/02/93	Tottenham Hotspur	Home	League	1–2		
82	20/02/93	Aston Villa	Away	League	1–2	1 Goal	(30)
83	27/02/93	Oldham Athletic	Home	League	2–2	1 Goal	(31)
84	03/03/93	Blackburn Rovers	Home	League	2–1		
85	07/03/93	Coventry City	Away	League	1–0		
86	10/03/93	Chelsea	Away	League	1–2		
87	13/03/93	Nottingham Forest	Home	League	3–0		
88	20/03/93	Liverpool	Away	League	0–1		
89	24/03/93	Ipswich Town	Home	League	3–0		
90	10/04/93	Middlesbrough	Away	League	2–1		
91	12/04/93	Queens Park Rangers	Home	League	3–5		
92	17/04/93	Southampton	Away	League	0–0		
93	01/05/93	Arsenal	Home	League	0–1		
94	04/05/93	Sheffield United	Home	League	0–2		
95	08/05/93	Manchester City	Away	League	5–2	1 Goal	(32)

SEASON 1993–94

Newcastle United – Premier League

1	18/09/93	Swindon Town	Away	League	2–2		
2	22/09/93	Notts County	Home	Lge Cup	4–0		
3	25/09/93	West Ham United	Home	League	2–0		
4	02/10/93	Aston Villa	Away	League	2–0		
5	05/10/93	Notts County	Away	Lge Cup	7–1	1 Goal	(1)
6	16/10/93	Queens Park Rangers	Home	League	1–2		
7	24/10/93	Southampton	Away	League	1–2		
8	27/10/93	Wimbledon	Away	Lge Cup	2–1		
9	30/10/93	Wimbledon	Home	League	4–0	3 Goals	(4)
10	08/11/93	Oldham Athletic	Away	League	3–1	1 Goal	(5)
11	21/11/93	Liverpool	Home	League	3–0		
12	24/11/93	Sheffield United	Home	League	4–0	2 Goals	(7)
13	27/11/93	Arsenal	Away	League	1–2	1 Goal	(8)
14	04/12/93	Tottenham Hotspur	Away	League	2–1	2 Goals	(10)
15	11/12/93	Manchester United	Home	League	1–1		
16	18/12/93	Everton	Away	League	2–0	1 Goal	(11)
17	22/12/93	Leeds United	Home	League	1–1		
18	28/12/93	Chelsea	Away	League	0–1		
19	01/01/94	Manchester City	Home	League	2–0		
20	04/01/94	Norwich City	Away	League	2–1	1 Goal	(12)
21	08/01/94	Coventry City	Home	FA Cup	2–0	1 Goal	(13)
22	16/01/94	Queens Park Rangers	Away	League	2–1	1 Goal	(14)
23	22/01/94	Southampton	Home	League	1–2		
24	29/01/94	Luton Town	Home	FA Cup	1–1	1 Goal	(15)
25	09/02/94	Luton Town	Away	FA Cup	0–2		
26	12/02/94	Wimbledon	Away	League	2–4	2 Goals	(17)
27	19/02/94	Blackburn Rovers	Away	League	0–1		
28	23/02/94	Coventry City	Home	League	4–0		
29	05/03/94	Sheffield Wednesday	Away	League	1–0		
30	12/03/94	Swindon Town	Home	League	7–1	2 Goals	(19)
31	19/03/94	West Ham United	Away	League	4–2		
32	23/03/94	Ipswich Town	Home	League	2–0		
33	29/03/94	Norwich City	Home	League	3–0	1 Goal	(20)

34	01/04/94	Leeds United	Away	League	1–1		
35	04/04/94	Chelsea	Home	League	0–0		
36	09/04/94	Manchester City	Away	League	1–2		
37	16/04/94	Liverpool	Away	League	2–0		
38	23/04/94	Oldham Athletic	Home	League	3–2	1 Goal	(21)
39	27/04/94	Aston Villa	Home	League	5–1	2 Goals	(23)
40	30/04/94	Sheffield United	Away	League	0–2		
41	07/05/94	Arsenal	Home	League	2–0	1 Goal	(24)

SEASON 1994–95

Premier League

42	21/08/94	Leicester City	Away	League	3–1	1 Goal	(25)
43	13/09/94	Royal Antwerp FC	Away	UEFA Cup	5–0		
44	18/09/94	Arsenal	Away	League	3–2	2 Goals	(27)
45	21/09/94	Barnsley	Home	Lge Cup	2–1		
46	24/09/94	Liverpool	Home	League	1–1		
47	27/09/94	Royal Antwerp FC	Home	UEFA Cup	5–2	1 Goal	(28)
48	01/10/94	Aston Villa	Away	League	2–0		
49	09/10/94	Blackburn Rovers	Home	League	1–1		
50	15/10/94	Crystal Palace	Away	League	1–0	1 Goal	(29)
51	18/10/94	Athletic Bilbao	Home	UEFA Cup	3–2	1 Goal	(30)
52	22/10/94	Sheffield Wednesday	Home	League	2–1		
53	26/10/94	Manchester United	Home	Lge Cup	2–0		
54	29/10/94	Manchester United	Away	League	0–2		
55	01/11/94	Athletic Bilbao	Away	UEFA Cup	0–1		
56	05/11/94	Queens Park Rangers	Home	League	2–1	1 Goal	(31)
57	07/11/94	Nottingham Forest	Away	League	0–0		
58	19/11/94	Wimbledon	Away	League	2–3	1 Goal	(32)
59	26/11/94	Ipswich Town	Home	League	1–1		
60	30/11/94	Manchester City	Away	Lge Cup	1–1		
61	03/12/94	Tottenham Hotspur	Away	League	2–4		
62	10/12/94	Leicester City	Home	League	3–1		
63	17/12/94	Coventry City	Away	League	0–0		
64	02/01/95	Manchester City	Home	League	0–0		
65	08/01/95	Blackburn Rovers	Home	FA Cup	1–1		
66	21/01/95	Sheffield Wednesday	Away	League	0–0		
67	25/01/95	Wimbledon	Home	League	2–1		
68	28/01/95	Swansea City	Home	FA Cup	3–0		
69	01/02/95	Everton	Home	League	2–0	1 Goal	(33)
70	04/02/95	Queens Park Rangers	Away	League	0–3		
71	11/02/95	Nottingham Forest	Home	League	2–1		
72	19/02/95	Manchester City	Home	FA Cup	3–1		
73	25/02/95	Aston Villa	Home	League	3–1	2 Goals	(35)
74	28/02/95	Ipswich Town	Away	League	2–0		
75	04/03/95	Liverpool	Away	League	0–2		
76	19/03/95	Arsenal	Home	League	1–0	1 Goal	(36)
77	22/03/95	Southampton	Away	League	1–3		
78	01/04/95	Chelsea	Away	League	1–1		
79	08/04/95	Norwich City	Home	League	3–0	2 Goals	(38)
80	14/04/95	Everton	Away	League	0–2		
81	17/04/95	Leeds United	Home	League	1–2		
82	29/04/95	Manchester City	Away	League	0–0		
83	03/05/95	Tottenham Hotspur	Home	League	3–3	1 Goal	(39)
84	08/05/95	Blackburn Rovers	Away	League	0–1		
85	14/05/95	Crystal Palace	Home	League	3–2		

SEASON 1995–96

Premier League

86	19/08/95	Coventry City	Home	League	3–0	1 Goal	(40)
87	22/08/95	Bolton Wanderers	Away	League	3–1		
88	27/08/95	Sheffield Wednesday	Away	League	2–0	1 Goal	(41)
89	30/08/95	Middlesbrough	Home	League	1–0		
90	16/09/95	Manchester City	Home	League	3–1	1 Goal	(42)
91	14/10/95	Queens Park Rangers	Away	League	3–2		
92	21/10/95	Wimbledon	Home	League	6–1		
93	25/10/95	Stoke City	Away	Lge Cup	4–0	2 Goals	(44)
94	29/10/95	Tottenham Hotspur	Away	League	1–1		
95	04/11/95	Liverpool	Home	League	2–1		
96	08/11/95	Blackburn Rovers	Home	League	1–0		
97	18/11/95	Aston Villa	Away	League	1–1		
98	25/11/95	Leeds United	Home	League	2–1	1 Goal	(45)
99	29/11/95	Liverpool	Away	Lge Cup	1–0		
100	03/12/95	Wimbledon	Away	League	3–3		

101	09/12/95	Chelsea	Away	League	0–1		
102	16/12/95	Everton	Home	League	1–0		
103	23/12/95	Nottingham Forest	Home	League	3–1		
104	27/12/95	Manchester United	Away	League	0–2		
105	02/01/96	Arsenal	Home	League	2–0		
106	07/01/96	Chelsea	Away	FA Cup	1–1		
107	10/01/96	Arsenal	Away	Lge Cup	0–2		
108	14/01/96	Coventry City	Away	League	1–0		
109	17/01/96	Chelsea	Home	FA Cup	2–2+	1 Goal	(46)
110	20/01/96	Bolton Wanderers	Home	League	2–1	1 Goal	(47)
111	03/02/96	Sheffield Wednesday	Home	League	2–0		
112	10/02/96	Middlesbrough	Away	League	2–1		
113	21/02/96	West Ham United	Away	League	0–2		
114	24/02/96	Manchester City	Away	League	3–3		
115	04/03/96	Manchester United	Home	League	0–1		
116	18/03/96	West Ham United	Home	League	3–0		
117	23/03/96	Arsenal	Away	League	0–2		
118	03/04/96	Liverpool	Away	League	3–4		
119	06/04/96	Queens Park Rangers	Home	League	2–1	2 Goals	(49)
120	08/04/96	Blackburn Rovers	Away	League	1–2		
121	14/04/96	Aston Villa	Home	League	1–0		
122	17/04/96	Southampton	Home	League	1–0		
123	29/04/96	Leeds United	Away	League	1–0		
124	02/05/96	Nottingham Forest	Away	League	1–1	1 Goal	(50)
125	05/05/96	Tottenham Hotspur	Home	League	1–1		

+ AET Chelsea won 4–2 on penalties

SEASON 1996–97

Premier League

126	11/08/96	Manchester United	Wembley	FA C/S	0–4		
Sub+1	17/08/96	Everton	Away	League	0–2		
127	04/09/96	Sunderland	Away	League	2–1	1 Goal	(51)
128	07/09/96	Tottenham Hotspur	Away	League	2–1		
129	10/09/96	Halmstads BK	Home	UEFA Cup	4–0	1 Goal	(52)
130	14/09/96	Blackburn Rovers	Home	League	2–1		
131	21/09/96	Leeds United	Away	League	1–0		
132	12/10/96	Derby County	Away	League	1–0		
133	15/10/96	Ferencvarosi TC	Away	UEFA Cup	2–3		
134	20/10/96	Manchester United	Home	League	5–0		
135	23/10/96	Oldham Athletic	Home	Lge Cup	1–0	1 Goal	(53)
136	26/10/96	Leicester City	Away	League	0–2		
137	29/10/96	Ferencvarosi TC	Home	UEFA Cup	4–0		
138	03/11/96	Middlesbrough	Home	League	3–1	2 Goals	(55)
139	16/11/96	West Ham United	Home	League	1–1	1 Goal	(56)
140	19/11/96	FC Metz	Away	UEFA Cup	1–1	1 Goal	(57)
141	23/11/96	Chelsea	Away	League	1–1		
142	27/11/96	Middlesbrough	Away	Lge Cup	1–3		
143	30/11/96	Arsenal	Home	League	1–2		
144	03/12/96	FC Metz	Home	UEFA Cup	2–0		
145	09/12/96	Nottingham Forest	Away	League	0–0		
146	17/12/96	Coventry City	Away	League	1–2		
147	23/12/96	Liverpool	Home	League	1–1		
148	26/12/96	Blackburn Rovers	Away	League	0–1		
149	28/12/96	Tottenham Hotspur	Home	League	7–1		
150	01/01/97	Leeds United	Home	League	3–0		
151	05/01/97	Charlton Athletic	Away	FA Cup	1–1		
152	11/01/97	Aston Villa	Away	League	2–2		
153	15/01/97	Charlton Athletic	Home	FA Cup	2–1*		
154	18/01/97	Southampton	Away	League	2–2		
155	26/01/97	Nottingham Forest	Home	FA Cup	1–2		
156	29/01/97	Everton	Home	League	4–1		
Sub+2	01/03/97	Southampton	Home	League	0–1		
157	10/03/97	Liverpool	Away	League	3–4		
158	15/03/97	Coventry City	Home	League	4–0	1 Goal	(58)
159	18/03/97	AS Monaco	Away	UEFA Cup	0–3		
Sub+3	11/05/97	Nottingham Forest	Home	League	5–0		

INTERNATIONAL APPEARANCES – ENGLAND

Sub 1	29/01/86	Egypt	Cairo	4–0	F		
2	26/02/86	Israel	Tel Aviv	2–1	F		
3	26/03/86	USSR	Tbilisi	1–0	F		
4	17/05/86	Mexico	Los Angeles	3–0	F	1 Goal	(1)

Sub 5	24/05/86	Canada	Vancouver	1–0	F		
Sub 6	03/06/86	Portugal	Monterrey	0–1	WC		
7	11/06/86	Poland	Monterrey	3–0	WC		
8	18/06/86	Paraguay	Mexico City	3–0	WC		
9	22/06/86	Argentina	Mexico City	1–2	WC	1 Goal	(2)
10	15/10/86	Northern Ireland	Wembley	3–0	ECQ		
11	12/11/86	Yugoslavia	Wembley	2–0	ECQ		
12	18/02/87	Spain	Madrid	4–2	F		
13	01/04/87	Northern Ireland	Windsor Park	2–0	ECQ		
14	19/05/87	Brazil	Wembley	1–1	RC		
15	23/05/87	Scotland	Hampden Park	0–0	RC		
16	09/09/87	West Germany	Dusseldorf	1–3	F		
17	14/10/87	Turkey	Wembley	8–0	ECQ	1 Goal	(3)
18	11/11/87	Yugoslavia	Belgrade	4–1	ECQ	1 Goal	(4)
19	17/02/88	Israel	Tel Aviv	0–0	F		
20	23/03/88	Holland	Wembley	2–2	F		
21	27/04/88	Hungary	Budapest	0–0	F		
22	21/05/88	Scotland	Wembley	1–0	RC		
23	24/05/88	Colombia	Wembley	1–1	RC	1 Goal	(5)
24	28/05/88	Switzerland	Lausanne	1–0	F		
25	12/06/88	Republic of Ireland	Stuttgart	0–1	EC		
26	15/06/88	Holland	Dusseldorf	1–3	EC		
27	14/09/88	Denmark	Wembley	1–0	F		
28	19/10/88	Sweden	Wembley	0–0	WCQ		
29	16/11/88	Saudi Arabia	Riyadh	1–1	F		
Sub 30	08/02/89	Greece	Athens	2–1	F		
Sub 31	08/03/89	Albania	Tirana	2–0	WCQ		
32	26/04/89	Albania	Wembley	5–0	WCQ	2 Goals	(7)
33	03/06/89	Poland	Wembley	3–0	WCQ		
34	07/06/89	Denmark	Copenhagen	1–1	F		
35	06/09/89	Sweden	Solna	0–0	WCQ		
36	11/10/89	Poland	Katowice	0–0	WCQ		
37	15/11/89	Italy	Wembley	0–0	F		
38	28/03/90	Brazil	Wembley	1–0	F		
Sub 39	22/05/90	Uruguay	Wembley	1–2	F		
Sub 40	02/06/90	Tunisia	Tunis	1–1	F		
41	11/06/90	Republic of Ireland	Cagliari	1–1	WC		
Sub 42	21/06/90	Egypt	Cagliari	1–0	WC		
Sub 43	01/07/90	Cameroon	Naples	3–2*	WC		
44	04/07/90	West Germany	Turin	1–1+	WC		
45	07/07/90	Italy	Bari	1–2	WC		
Sub 46	17/10/90	Poland	Wembley	2–0	ECQ	1 Goal	(8)
47	14/11/90	Republic of Ireland	Lansdowne Road	1–1	ECQ		
48	27/03/91	Republic of Ireland	Wembley	1–1	ECQ		
Sub 49	21/05/91	USSR	Wembley	3–1	F		
50	09/03/94	Denmark	Wembley	1–0	F		
51	17/05/94	Greece	Wembley	5–0	F	1 Goal	(9)
52	22/05/94	Norway	Wembley	0–0	F		
53	16/11/94	Nigeria	Wembley	1–0	F		
54	15/02/95	Republic of Ireland	Lansdowne Road	Aba	F		
55	29/03/95	Uruguay	Wembley	0–0	F		
56	02/06/95	Japan	Wembley	2–1	UC		
57	08/06/95	Sweden	Elland Road	3–3	UC		
Sub 58	12/12/95	Portugal	Wembley	1–1	F		
Sub 59	23/05/96	China	Beijing	3–0	F		

+ AET West Germany won 4–3 on penalties

APPEARANCES AND GOALS PER SEASON

SEASON 79–80	GAMES	GOALS
League	37+2	8
FA Cup	4	1
TOTAL	**41+2**	**9**

SEASON 80–81	GAMES	GOALS
League	37+6	10
FA Cup	7	5
League Cup	3+1	0
Anglo–Scottish Cup	2	0
North American Soccer League	26	13
North American Soccer League Play–offs	2	0
TOTAL	**77+7**	**28**

SEASON 81–82	**GAMES**	**GOALS**
League	19+3	4
FA Cup	4	1
League Cup	3	0
North American Soccer League	22	7
North American Soccer League Play-offs	3	0
TOTAL	**51+3**	**12**

SEASON 82–83	**GAMES**	**GOALS**
League Cup	1	0
North American Soccer League	25	8
North American Soccer League Play-offs	3	1
TOTAL	**29**	**9**

SEASON 83–84	**GAMES**	**GOALS**
League	34+1	20
FA Cup	1	0
League Cup	2	0
TOTAL	**37+1**	**20**

SEASON 84–85	**GAMES**	**GOALS**
League	38	17
FA Cup	2	0
League Cup	4	0
TOTAL	**44**	**17**

SEASON 85–86	**GAMES**	**GOALS**
League	42	19
FA Cup	1	0
League Cup	2	0
TOTAL	**45**	**19**

SEASON 86–87	**GAMES**	**GOALS**
League	32	5
FA Cup	2	0
League Cup	2	0
Full Members Cup	1	0
TOTAL	**37**	**5**

SEASON 87–88	**GAMES**	**GOALS**
League	36+2	15
FA Cup	7	3
League Cup	3	0
TOTAL	**46+2**	**18**

SEASON 88–89	**GAMES**	**GOALS**
League	33+4	10
FA Cup	5	2
League Cup	6	0
Mercantile Centenary Credit Trophy	2	0
FA Charity Shield	1	0
TOTAL	**47+4**	**12**

SEASON 89–90	**GAMES**	**GOALS**
League	27+2	10
FA Cup	8	4
League Cup	2+1	1
FA Charity Shield	1	1
TOTAL	**38+3**	**16**

SEASON 90–91	**GAMES**	**GOALS**
League	24+3	11
FA Cup	2+3	2
League Cup	2	0
FA Charity Shield	1	0
TOTAL	**29+6**	**13**

SEASON 91–92	**GAMES**	**GOALS**
League	42	15
FA Cup	2	1
League Cup	4	3
Zenith Data Systems Cup	2	1
TOTAL	**50**	**20**

SEASON 92–93	**GAMES**	**GOALS**
League	39	10
FA Cup	2	0
League Cup	4	2
TOTAL	**45**	**12**

SEASON 93–94	**GAMES**	**GOALS**
League	35	21
FA Cup	3	2
League Cup	3	1
TOTAL	**41**	**24**

SEASON 94–95	**GAMES**	**GOALS**
League	34	13
FA Cup	3	0
League Cup	3	0
UEFA Cup	4	2
TOTAL	**44**	**15**

SEASON 95–96	**GAMES**	**GOALS**
League	35	8
FA Cup	2	1
League Cup	3	2
TOTAL	**40**	**11**

SEASON 96–97	**GAMES**	**GOALS**
League	22+3	5
FA Cup	3	0
League Cup	2	1
UEFA Cup	6	2
FA Charity Shield	1	0
TOTAL	**34+3**	**8**

CAREER APPEARANCES AND GOALS

COMPETITION	GAMES	TOTAL	GOALS
League	566+26	592	201
FA Cup	58+3	61	22
League Cup	49+2	51	10
Anglo–Scottish Cup	2	2	0
Full Members Cup	1	1	0
Mercantile Centenary Credit Trophy	2	2	0
Zenith Data Systems Cup	2	2	1
FA Charity Shield	4	4	1
UEFA Cup	10	10	4
North American Soccer League	73	73	28
North American Soccer League Play–offs	8	8	1
Internationals	46+13	59	9
TOTAL	**821+44**	**865**	**277**

HAT-TRICKS

Vancouver Whitecaps

1	3	San Jose Earthquakes	01/07/81	Away	League	5–1
2	3	Edmonton Drillers	16/08/81	Away	League	5–4

Newcastle United

1	3	Manchester City	29/10/83	Home	League	5–0
2	3	Sunderland	01/01/85	Home	League	3–1

Liverpool

1	3	Manchester United	16/09/90	Home	League	4–0

Everton

1	3	Coventry City	21/09/91	Home	League	3–0

Newcastle United

1	3	Wimbledon	30/10/93	Home	League	4–0

League: 5
North American Soccer League: 2
TOTAL: 7

HONOURS

Winners medals
League Division One Championship: 87/88, 89/90
FA Cup: 88/89
FA Charity Shield: 88/89, 89/90, 90/91

Runner-up medals
Premier League Championship: 95/96, 96/97
League Division One Championship: 88/89, 90/91
FA Cup: 87/88
FA Charity Shield: 96/97
Promoted to League Division One: 83/84

GARY BENNETT

Born: 20/09/62 – Liverpool
Height: 5.11
Weight: 12.00 (96–97)

Clubs
Wigan Athletic: **1984–85**– Matches: **14+11** – Goals: **4**
Chester City: **1985–88** – Matches: **133+22** – Goals: **47**
Southend United: **1988–90** – Matches: **43+7** – Goals: **10**
Chester City: **1990–92** – Matches: **88+10** – Goals: **19**
Wrexham: **1992–95** – Matches: **159+1** – Goals: **109**
Tranmere Rovers: **1995–96** – Matches: **30+3** – Goals: **9**
Preston North End: **1996–97** – Matches: **16+9** – Goals: **6**
Wrexham: **1997** – Matches: **15+1** – Goals: **5**

SEASON 1984–85

Wigan Athletic – League Division Three

Sub+1	19/10/84	Cambridge United	Away	League	1–1		
1	23/10/84	Bristol Rovers	Home	League	1–0		
2	27/10/84	Orient	Home	League	4–2		
3	03/11/84	Swansea City	Away	League	2–2		
4	06/11/84	AFC Bournemouth	Away	League	0–1		
Sub+2	01/12/84	Hull City	Home	League	1–1		
5	08/12/84	Northwich Victoria	Home	FA Cup	2–1		
Sub+3	12/01/85	Bradford City	Away	League	2–4		
Sub+4	29/01/85	Wrexham	Away	FR Trophy	2–2		
Sub+5	02/02/85	York City	Away	League	0–2		
Sub+6	09/02/85	Millwall	Home	League	0–1		
Sub+7	16/02/85	Lincoln City	Away	League	0–1		
6	09/03/85	Cambridge United	Home	League	3–3	1 Goal	(1)
7	17/03/85	Walsall	Home	League	1–2		
Sub+8	20/04/85	Derby County	Home	League	2–0		
Sub+9	23/04/85	Bristol City	Home	League	2–2	1 Goal	(2)
Sub+10	27/04/85	Hull City	Away	League	1–3		
8	30/04/85	Swansea City	Home	League	2–0	1 Goal	(3)
9	03/05/85	Doncaster Rovers	Home	League	5–2		
10	06/05/85	Preston North End	Away	League	5–2		
11	08/05/85	Lincoln City	Away	FR Trophy	3–1	1 Goal	(4)
12	11/05/85	Rotherham United	Home	League	2–1		
Sub+11	13/05/85	Reading	Home	League	1–1		
13	20/05/85	Mansfield Town	Away	FR Trophy	1–1+		
14	01/06/85	Brentford	Wembley	FR Trophy	3–1		

+ AET Wigan Athletic won 3–1 on penalties

SEASON 1985–86

Chester City – League Division Four

1	24/08/85	Peterborough United	Away	League	0–3	
2	26/08/85	Hartlepool United	Home	League	1–1	
3	28/08/85	Tranmere Rovers	Away	Lge Cup	3–1	
4	31/08/85	Tranmere Rovers	Away	League	3–2	
5	04/09/85	Tranmere Rovers	Home	Lge Cup	0–0	

6	07/09/85	Hereford United	Home	League	1–0		
7	14/09/85	Torquay United	Away	League	3–0		
8	21/09/85	Crewe Alexandra	Home	League	4–0	2 Goals	(2)
9	25/09/85	Coventry City	Home	Lge Cup	1–2		
10	28/09/85	Stockport County	Away	League	2–2	2 Goals	(4)
11	02/10/85	Mansfield Town	Home	League	1–0		
12	05/10/85	Burnley	Home	League	4–0	1 Goal	(5)
13	19/10/85	Swindon Town	Home	League	0–1		
14	22/10/85	Northampton Town	Away	League	2–2		
15	26/10/85	Wrexham	Away	League	1–1		
16	02/11/85	Aldershot	Home	League	1–0		
17	06/11/85	Colchester United	Home	League	4–0		
18	09/11/85	Exeter City	Away	League	3–1		
19	23/11/85	Orient	Home	League	3–0		
20	16/11/85	Bury	Away	FA Cup	0–2		
21	29/11/85	Southend United	Away	League	1–1		
22	07/12/85	Aldershot	Away	League	1–1		
23	14/12/85	Scunthorpe United	Home	League	1–1		
24	21/12/85	Peterborough United	Home	League	2–1	1 Goal	(6)
25	26/12/85	Cambridge United	Away	League	2–3	1 Goal	(7)
26	01/01/86	Port Vale	Home	League	4–1	1 Goal	(8)
27	08/01/86	Hartlepool United	Away	League	1–1		
28	11/01/86	Tranmere Rovers	Home	League	1–0		
29	17/01/86	Halifax Town	Away	League	2–1		
30	20/01/86	Rochdale	Away	FR Trophy	0–1		
31	22/01/86	Wigan Athletic	Home	FR Trophy	0–2		
32	25/01/86	Torquay United	Home	League	3–1	1 Goal	(9)
33	01/02/86	Hereford United	Away	League	2–0	2 Goals	(11)
34	05/02/86	Northampton Town	Home	League	2–3		
35	15/02/86	Rochdale	Home	League	1–1		
36	22/02/86	Crewe Alexandra	Away	League	2–2		
37	01/03/86	Stockport County	Home	League	1–2		
38	04/03/86	Mansfield Town	Away	League	0–0		
39	08/03/86	Burnley	Away	League	0–1		
Sub+1	15/03/86	Preston North End	Home	League	2–0		
Sub+2	22/03/86	Wrexham	Home	League	2–1	1 Goal	(12)
40	29/03/86	Port Vale	Away	League	1–1		
41	31/03/86	Cambridge United	Home	League	1–1		
42	04/04/86	Colchester United	Away	League	3–2		
43	08/04/86	Swindon Town	Away	League	2–4		
Sub+3	12/04/86	Exeter City	Home	League	2–1		
44	26/04/86	Southend United	Home	League	2–0	1 Goal	(13)
45	29/04/86	Rochdale	Away	League	2–1		
46	03/05/86	Scunthorpe United	Away	League	0–2		

SEASON 1986–87

League Division Three

47	23/08/86	Carlisle United	Home	League	2–2		
48	27/08/86	Derby County	Away	Lge Cup	1–0		
49	30/08/86	Bury	Away	League	1–1		
Sub+4	03/09/86	Derby County	Home	Lge Cup	1–2*	1 Goal	(14)
50	06/09/86	Fulham	Home	League	2–2	1 Goal	(15)
51	13/09/86	Swindon Town	Away	League	1–1		
Sub+5	16/09/86	AFC Bournemouth	Away	League	0–2		
52	27/09/86	Darlington	Away	League	0–1		
Sub+6	18/10/86	Mansfield Town	Home	League	1–1		
Sub+7	21/10/86	York City	Away	League	1–1		
Sub+8	25/10/86	Bolton Wanderers	Away	League	1–1		
53	01/11/86	Walsall	Home	League	0–0		
Sub+9	04/11/86	Rotherham United	Away	League	0–3		
Sub+10	08/11/86	Brentford	Home	League	1–1	1 Goal	(16)
54	15/11/86	Rotherham United	Home	FA Cup	1–1	1 Goal	(17)
55	18/11/86	Rotherham United	Away	FA Cup	1–1*		
56	22/11/86	Bristol Rovers	Home	League	3–1	2 Goals	(19)
57	24/11/86	Rotherham United	Home	FA Cup	1–0		
58	29/11/86	Middlesbrough	Away	League	2–1		
59	02/12/86	Crewe Alexandra	Away	FR Trophy	2–1	1 Goal	(20)
60	06/12/86	Doncaster Rovers	Home	FA Cup	3–1	1 Goal	(21)
61	14/12/86	Port Vale	Away	League	1–2		
62	16/12/86	Preston North End	Home	FR Trophy	1–1	1 Goal	(22)
63	19/12/86	Chesterfield	Home	League	1–1	1 Goal	(23)
64	26/12/86	Wigan Athletic	Away	League	2–2	2 Goals	(25)
65	27/12/86	Blackpool	Home	League	1–4		
66	10/01/87	Wrexham	Away	FA Cup	2–1	2 Goals	(27)

67	21/01/87	Lincoln City	Home	FR Trophy	1–1+	1 Goal	(28)
68	24/01/87	Fulham	Away	League	5–0	1 Goal	(29)
69	31/01/87	Sheffield Wednesday	Home	FA Cup	1–1		
70	04/02/87	Sheffield Wednesday	Away	FA Cup	1–3	1 Goal	(30)
71	07/02/87	AFC Bournemouth	Home	League	2–2	1 Goal	(31)
72	10/02/87	Bolton Wanderers	Away	FR Trophy	2–1	1 Goal	(32)
73	14/02/87	Gillingham	Away	League	2–1		
74	17/02/87	Notts County	Home	League	1–2	1 Goal	(33)
75	21/02/87	Darlington	Home	League	6–0	2 Goals	(35)
76	27/02/87	Doncaster Rovers	Away	League	1–1		
77	07/03/87	Bolton Wanderers	Home	League	0–0		
78	14/03/87	Mansfield Town	Away	League	3–2		
79	18/03/87	York City	Home	League	2–1		
80	08/04/87	Mansfield Town	Away	FR Trophy	0–2		
81	11/04/87	Rotherham United	Home	League	1–0		
82	15/04/87	Mansfield Town	Home	FR Trophy	1–0		
83	18/04/87	Notts County	Away	League	1–1		
Sub+11	02/05/87	Middlesbrough	Home	League	1–2		
84	04/05/87	Blackpool	Away	League	0–1		
85	06/05/87	Carlisle United	Away	League	2–0	1 Goal	(36)
86	09/05/87	Port Vale	Home	League	1–2		

+ AET Chester City won 5–4 on penalties

SEASON 1987–88

League Division Three

87	22/08/87	Southend United	Away	League	2–2		
88	26/08/87	Blackpool	Home	Lge Cup	1–0		
89	29/08/87	York City	Home	League	1–0		
90	31/08/87	Rotherham United	Away	League	2–5		
91	05/09/87	Aldershot	Home	League	4–1	1 Goal	(37)
92	12/09/87	Blackpool	Away	League	1–0		
93	16/09/87	Fulham	Home	League	1–2		
94	19/09/87	Grimsby Town	Home	League	1–0		
95	26/09/87	Sunderland	Away	League	2–0		
96	29/09/87	Gillingham	Away	League	1–0		
97	03/10/87	Notts County	Home	League	1–2		
98	13/10/87	Carlisle United	Away	SV Trophy	1–2		
99	17/10/87	Bristol Rovers	Away	League	2–2	1 Goal	(38)
100	20/10/87	Brentford	Away	League	1–1		
101	24/10/87	Mansfield Town	Home	League	0–2		
102	28/10/87	Blackpool	Home	SV Trophy	2–1	1 Goal	(39)
103	31/10/87	Preston North End	Away	League	1–1		
Sub+12	07/11/87	Walsall	Home	League	1–1		
Sub+13	14/11/87	Runcorn	Home	FA Cup	0–1		
104	21/11/87	Bristol City	Away	League	2–2		
105	28/11/87	Chesterfield	Home	League	1–1		
106	05/12/87	Doncaster Rovers	Home	League	1–1		
107	12/12/87	Brighton & Hove Albion	Away	League	0–1		
108	18/12/87	Bury	Away	League	4–4	1 Goal	(40)
109	26/12/87	Sunderland	Home	League	1–2		
110	28/12/87	Wigan Athletic	Away	League	0–1		
111	01/01/88	York City	Away	League	0–2		
112	02/01/88	Blackpool	Home	League	1–1	1 Goal	(41)
Sub+14	09/01/88	Southend United	Home	League	1–1		
113	30/01/88	Rotherham United	Home	League	1–0		
114	06/02/88	Aldershot	Away	League	1–4		
115	13/02/88	Wigan Athletic	Home	League	1–0		
116	20/02/88	Northampton Town	Away	League	0–2		
117	27/02/88	Notts County	Away	League	0–1		
118	02/03/88	Gillingham	Home	League	3–1		
119	05/03/88	Bristol Rovers	Home	League	0–3		
120	11/03/88	Doncaster Rovers	Away	League	2–2	2 Goals	(43)
121	19/03/88	Preston North End	Home	League	1–0	1 Goal	(44)
122	26/03/88	Mansfield Town	Away	League	2–1	1 Goal	(45)
123	02/04/88	Walsall	Away	League	0–1		
124	04/04/88	Bristol City	Home	League	1–0	1 Goal	(46)
125	09/04/88	Port Vale	Away	League	1–1		
126	15/04/88	Fulham	Away	League	0–1		
127	23/04/88	Brentford	Home	League	1–1		
128	30/04/88	Chesterfield	Away	League	0–0		
129	02/05/88	Brighton & Hove Albion	Home	League	2–2		
130	07/05/88	Bury	Away	League	1–0	1 Goal	(47)

SEASON 1988–89

League Division Three

131	27/08/88	Blackpool	Home	League	1–1		
132	30/08/88	Bolton Wanderers	Away	Lge Cup	0–1		
Sub+15	07/09/88	Bolton Wanderers	Home	Lge Cup	3–1		
Sub+16	17/09/88	Sheffield United	Away	League	1–6		
Sub+17	28/09/88	Nottingham Forest	Away	Lge Cup	0–6		
Sub+18	05/10/88	Brentford	Home	League	3–2		
Sub+19	12/10/88	Nottingham Forest	Home	Lge Cup	0–4		
Sub+20	15/10/88	Cardiff City	Home	League	0–0		
Sub+21	22/10/88	Bristol Rovers	Away	League	1–4		
Sub+22	29/10/88	Aldershot	Away	League	1–1		
133	05/11/88	Swansea City	Home	League	3–1		

Southend United – League Division Three

1	12/11/88	Notts County	Away	League	1–1		
2	19/11/88	Bristol City	Away	FA Cup	1–3		
3	22/11/88	Lincoln City	Home	SV Trophy	2–1		
4	26/11/88	Chester City	Away	League	4–2	1 Goal	(1)
5	02/12/88	Port Vale	Home	League	1–1		
6	10/12/88	Wigan Athletic	Away	League	0–3		
7	17/12/88	Sheffield United	Away	League	2–1		
8	26/12/88	Northampton Town	Home	League	2–1		
9	31/12/88	Bristol City	Home	League	1–2	1 Goal	(2)
10	02/01/89	Huddersfield Town	Away	League	2–3		
11	13/01/89	Fulham	Home	League	0–0		
12	28/01/89	Aldershot	Home	League	1–1		
13	03/02/89	Preston North End	Home	League	2–1		
14	11/02/89	Mansfield Town	Away	League	0–4		
15	10/03/89	Wolverhampton Wanderers	Home	League	3–1		
16	18/03/89	Bolton Wanderers	Away	League	0–0		
17	25/03/89	Huddersfield Town	Home	League	2–4		
18	04/04/89	Blackpool	Home	League	2–1		
Sub+1	22/04/89	Cardiff City	Away	League	0–2		

SEASON 1989–90

League Division Four

19	19/08/89	York City	Home	League	2–0		
20	22/08/89	Colchester United	Away	Lge Cup	4–3	1 Goal	(3)
21	26/08/89	Wrexham	Away	League	3–3	1 Goal	(4)
22	29/08/89	Colchester United	Home	Lge Cup	2–1	1 Goal	(5)
23	01/09/89	Hartlepool United	Home	League	3–0		
24	09/09/89	Aldershot	Away	League	5–0	1 Goal	(6)
25	15/09/89	Torquay United	Home	League	1–0	1 Goal	(7)
26	20/09/89	Tottenham Hotspur	Away	Lge Cup	0–1		
27	22/09/89	Doncaster Rovers	Away	League	1–0		
28	26/09/89	Gillingham	Away	League	0–5		
29	30/09/89	Lincoln City	Home	League	2–0		
30	04/10/89	Tottenham Hotspur	Home	Lge Cup	3–2*	2 Goals	(9)
31	07/10/89	Scarborough	Home	League	1–0		
32	14/10/89	Hereford United	Away	League	3–0		
33	21/10/89	Maidstone United	Home	League	0–1		
34	28/10/89	Chesterfield	Away	League	1–1		
35	31/10/89	Burnley	Home	League	3–2	1 Goal	(10)
Sub+2	26/12/89	Colchester United	Home	League	0–2		
36	30/12/89	Exeter City	Home	League	1–2		
37	01/01/90	Rochdale	Away	League	1–0		
38	06/01/90	Carlisle United	Away	League	0–3		
39	12/01/90	Wrexham	Home	League	2–1		
40	17/01/90	Northampton Town	Home	LD Cup	2–1		
41	20/01/90	York City	Away	League	1–2		
Sub+3	30/01/90	Walsall	Away	LD Cup	1–4		
Sub+4	02/02/90	Doncaster Rovers	Home	League	2–0		
Sub+5	06/02/90	Torquay United	Away	League	0–3		
Sub+6	13/02/90	Hartlepool United	Away	League	1–1		
Sub+7	16/02/90	Scunthorpe United	Home	League	0–0		
42	09/03/90	Gillingham	Home	League	2–0		
43	17/03/90	Scarborough	Away	League	1–1		

Chester City – League Division Three

1	31/03/90	Bolton Wanderers	Home	League	2–0		
2	07/04/90	Bristol Rovers	Away	League	1–2		
3	14/04/90	Northampton Town	Home	League	0–1		
4	16/04/90	Wigan Athletic	Away	League	0–1		

5	20/04/90	Tranmere Rovers	Home	League	2–2		
6	24/04/90	Blackpool	Away	League	3–1		
7	28/04/90	Rotherham United	Home	League	2–0	1 Goal	(1)
8	05/05/90	Huddersfield Town	Away	League	1–4		

SEASON 1990–91

League Division Three

9	25/08/90	Bury	Away	League	1–2		
10	28/08/90	Preston North End	Away	Lge Cup	0–2		
Sub+1	01/09/90	Exeter City	Home	League	1–2		
11	04/09/90	Preston North End	Home	Lge Cup	5–0		
12	08/09/90	Brentford	Away	League	1–0		
13	15/09/90	Leyton Orient	Home	League	2–0	1 Goal	(2)
14	18/09/90	Stoke City	Home	League	1–1		
15	21/09/90	Cambridge United	Away	League	1–1		
16	25/09/90	Arsenal	Home	Lge Cup	0–1		
17	29/09/90	Huddersfield Town	Home	League	1–2		
18	03/10/90	Bradford City	Away	League	1–2		
19	06/10/90	Tranmere Rovers	Away	League	2–1		
20	09/10/90	Arsenal	Away	Lge Cup	0–5		
21	13/10/90	Grimsby Town	Home	League	1–2		
22	20/10/90	Shrewsbury Town	Home	League	3–2	1 Goal	(3)
23	23/10/90	Preston North End	Away	League	0–0		
24	27/10/90	Crewe Alexandra	Away	League	3–1		
25	03/11/90	Bolton Wanderers	Home	League	0–2		
26	06/11/90	Wigan Athletic	Away	LD Cup	0–4		
27	10/11/90	Birmingham City	Home	League	0–1		
28	17/11/90	Doncaster Rovers	Home	FA Cup	2–2	1 Goal	(4)
29	20/11/90	Doncaster Rovers	Away	FA Cup	2–1*		
30	24/11/90	Swansea City	Away	League	0–1		
31	27/11/90	Bury	Home	LD Cup	2–0		
32	01/12/90	AFC Bournemouth	Home	League	0–0		
Sub+2	15/12/90	Mansfield Town	Away	League	0–1		
33	17/12/90	Leek Town	Home	FA Cup	4–0		
34	29/12/90	Fulham	Away	League	1–4		
Sub+3	12/01/91	Exeter City	Away	League	1–1		
Sub+4	02/02/91	Stoke City	Away	League	3–2		
Sub+5	16/03/91	Huddersfield Town	Away	League	1–1		
35	20/03/91	Grimsby Town	Away	League	0–2		
Sub+6	23/03/91	Tranmere Rovers	Home	League	0–2		
36	25/03/91	Cambridge United	Home	League	0–2		
37	30/03/91	Rotherham United	Home	League	1–2		
38	02/04/91	Southend United	Away	League	1–1		
39	06/04/91	Fulham	Home	League	1–0		
Sub+7	20/04/91	Shrewsbury Town	Away	League	0–1		
40	23/04/91	Swansea City	Home	League	2–1	1 Goal	(5)

SEASON 1991–92

League Division Three

41	17/08/91	Fulham	Home	League	2–0	1 Goal	(6)
42	20/08/91	Lincoln City	Home	Lge Cup	1–0		
43	23/08/91	Wigan Athletic	Away	League	1–2		
44	28/08/91	Lincoln City	Away	Lge Cup	3–4*	1 Goal	(7)
45	31/08/91	Swansea City	Home	League	2–0		
Sub+8	04/09/91	Huddersfield Town	Away	League	0–2		
Sub+9	07/09/91	AFC Bournemouth	Home	League	0–1		
46	14/09/91	Bradford City	Away	League	1–1		
47	17/09/91	Birmingham City	Away	League	2–3		
48	21/09/91	West Bromwich Albion	Home	League	1–2		
49	25/09/91	Manchester City	Away	Lge Cup	1–3	1 Goal	(8)
50	28/09/91	Torquay United	Away	League	2–3		
51	05/10/91	Stoke City	Home	League	0–0		
52	08/10/91	Manchester City	Home	Lge Cup	0–3+		
53	12/10/91	Leyton Orient	Away	League	0–1		
54	18/10/91	Stockport County	Away	League	4–0	3 Goals	(11)
55	26/10/91	Bolton Wanderers	Home	League	0–1		
56	02/11/91	Preston North End	Home	League	3–2		
57	16/11/91	Guiseley	Home	FA Cup	1–0		
Sub+10	19/11/91	Crewe Alexandra	Away	A Trophy	1–2		
58	23/11/91	Reading	Home	League	2–2		
59	30/11/91	Exeter City	Away	League	0–0		
60	07/12/91	Crewe Alexandra	Away	FA Cup	0–2		
61	14/12/91	Shrewsbury Town	Home	League	1–4		

62	26/12/91	Swansea City	Away	League	0–3		
63	28/12/91	Fulham	Away	League	2–2		
64	01/01/92	Huddersfield Town	Home	League	0–0		
65	04/01/92	Darlington	Home	League	2–5		
66	07/01/92	Darlington	Home	A Trophy	2–1	1 Goal	(12)
67	11/01/92	Hartlepool United	Away	League	0–1		
68	18/01/92	Brentford	Home	League	1–1		
69	21/01/92	Rotherham United	Away	A Trophy	0–3		
70	08/02/92	Bolton Wanderers	Away	League	0–0		
71	11/02/92	Exeter City	Home	League	5–2		
72	15/02/92	Shrewsbury Town	Away	League	2–2		
73	18/02/92	Wigan Athletic	Home	League	1–0		
74	22/02/92	Hartlepool United	Home	League	2–0		
75	25/02/92	Bury	Away	League	2–1	1 Goal	(13)
76	29/02/92	Darlington	Away	League	1–1		
77	03/03/92	Brentford	Away	League	0–2		
78	07/03/92	Bury	Home	League	3–1	2 Goals	(15)
79	10/03/92	Peterborough United	Home	League	2–4		
80	14/03/92	Preston North End	Away	League	3–0	2 Goals	(17)
81	24/03/92	Stockport County	Home	League	3–2	1 Goal	(18)
82	28/03/92	Reading	Away	League	0–0		
83	31/03/92	Bradford City	Home	League	0–0		
84	03/04/92	AFC Bournemouth	Away	League	0–2		
85	11/04/92	Birmingham City	Home	League	0–1		
86	18/04/92	West Bromwich Albion	Away	League	1–1		
87	20/04/92	Torquay United	Home	League	2–0		
88	25/04/92	Stoke City	Away	League	1–0	1 Goal	(19)

+ Match played at Edgeley Park, Stockport County

SEASON 1992–93

Wrexham – Football League Division Three

1	25/08/92	Bury	Away	Lge Cup	3–4	2 Goals	(2)
2	29/08/92	York City	Home	League	0–4		
3	01/09/92	Gillingham	Away	League	1–4		
4	05/09/92	Doncaster Rovers	Away	League	1–1		
5	12/09/92	Shrewsbury Town	Home	League	2–0		
6	15/09/92	Torquay United	Away	League	1–1		
7	26/09/92	Barnet	Home	League	2–3	1 Goal	(3)
8	03/10/92	Hereford United	Away	League	1–1		
9	10/10/92	Bury	Home	League	4–2	3 Goals	(6)
10	17/10/92	Carlisle United	Away	League	2–0		
11	24/10/92	Northampton Town	Home	League	0–1		
12	28/10/92	Llanidloes	Away	Welsh Cup	3–0		
13	30/10/92	Colchester United	Away	League	4–2	2 Goals	(8)
14	03/11/92	Scunthorpe United	Home	League	0–2		
15	07/11/92	Lincoln City	Away	League	0–0		
16	14/11/92	Crewe Alexandra	Away	FA Cup	1–6	1 Goal	(9)
17	21/11/92	Halifax Town	Home	League	1–0		
18	24/11/92	Hereford United	Away	Welsh Cup	3–2	1 Goal	(10)
19	28/11/92	Walsall	Away	League	1–1	1 Goal	(11)
20	08/12/92	Crewe Alexandra	Away	A Trophy	3–0	2 Goals	(13)
21	12/12/92	Scarborough	Home	League	4–1	2 Goals	(15)
22	15/12/92	Stoke City	Home	A Trophy	0–2		
23	18/12/92	Cardiff City	Away	League	2–1		
24	26/12/92	Crewe Alexandra	Away	League	1–0	1 Goal	(16)
25	28/12/92	Chesterfield	Home	League	5–4	1 Goal	(17)
26	02/01/93	Shrewsbury Town	Away	League	1–0		
27	09/01/93	Torquay United	Home	League	4–2	1 Goal	(18)
28	12/01/93	Leyton Orient	Away	A Trophy	1–4		
29	23/01/93	Walsall	Home	League	3–1		
30	06/02/93	Merthyr Tydfil	Home	Welsh Cup	1–0	1 Goal	(19)
31	13/02/93	Doncaster Rovers	Away	League	1–1		
32	20/02/93	Gillingham	Home	League	2–0	1 Goal	(20)
33	27/02/93	Bury	Away	League	1–3		
34	06/03/93	Hereford United	Home	League	2–0	1 Goal	(21)
35	09/03/93	Darlington	Away	League	1–1		
36	13/03/93	Lincoln City	Home	League	2–0		
37	16/03/93	Cardiff City	Away	Welsh Cup	0–2		
38	20/03/93	Scunthorpe United	Away	League	0–0		
39	26/03/93	Halifax Town	Away	League	1–0		
40	02/04/93	Darlington	Home	League	1–1		
Sub+1	17/04/93	Cardiff City	Home	League	0–2		
41	24/04/93	Carlisle United	Home	League	3–1		

| 42 | 27/04/93 | Northampton Town | Home | League | 2–0 | 2 Goals | (23) |
| 43 | 08/05/93 | Colchester United | Home | League | 4–3 | | |

SEASON 1993–94

Football League Division Two

44	14/08/93	Rotherham United	Home	League	3–3	2 Goals	(25)
45	17/08/93	Crewe Alexandra	Away	Lge Cup	1–0		
46	21/08/93	Swansea City	Away	League	1–3		
47	24/08/93	Crewe Alexandra	Home	Lge Cup	3–3	1 Goal	(26)
48	28/08/93	Blackpool	Home	League	2–3	1 Goal	(27)
49	31/08/93	Fulham	Away	League	0–0		
50	04/09/93	Stockport County	Away	League	0–1		
51	11/09/93	Reading	Home	League	3–2	1 Goal	(28)
52	14/09/93	Hull City	Home	League	3–0	3 Goals	(31)
53	18/09/93	Exeter City	Away	League	0–5		
54	21/09/93	Nottingham Forest	Home	Lge Cup	3–3	2 Goals	(33)
55	25/09/93	Barnet	Home	League	4–0	2 Goals	(35)
56	28/09/93	Shrewsbury Town	Home	A Trophy	3–1	1 Goal	(36)
57	02/10/93	Port Vale	Away	League	0–3		
58	06/10/93	Nottingham Forest	Away	Lge Cup	1–3		
59	09/10/93	Cambridge United	Home	League	1–1	1 Goal	(37)
60	16/10/93	Brentford	Away	League	1–2	1 Goal	(38)
61	23/10/93	Cardiff City	Home	League	3–1	1 Goal	(39)
62	27/10/93	Carno	Home	Welsh Cup	6–1	3 Goals	(42)
63	30/10/93	Plymouth Argyle	Away	League	1–1	1 Goal	(43)
64	13/11/93	Walsall	Home	FA Cup	1–1		
65	20/11/93	Hartlepool United	Away	League	2–1	1 Goal	(44)
66	23/11/93	Walsall	Away	FA Cup	0–2		
67	27/11/93	York City	Home	League	1–1	1 Goal	(45)
68	04/12/93	Colchester United	Home	A Trophy	0–1		
69	07/12/93	Cardiff City	Home	Welsh Cup	0–2		
70	11/12/93	Swansea City	Home	League	3–2	1 Goal	(46)
71	17/12/93	Rotherham United	Away	League	1–2	1 Goal	(47)
72	27/12/93	Burnley	Away	League	1–2		
73	01/01/94	Bradford City	Away	League	0–1		
74	03/01/94	Leyton Orient	Home	League	4–2	2 Goals	(49)
75	15/01/94	Brentford	Home	League	1–2	1 Goal	(50)
76	22/01/94	Cambridge United	Away	League	2–2	1 Goal	(51)
77	05/02/94	Cardiff City	Away	League	1–5		
78	12/02/94	Huddersfield Town	Home	League	3–1		
79	08/03/94	Stockport County	Home	League	0–1		
80	12/03/94	Exeter City	Home	League	1–1	1 Goal	(52)
81	15/03/94	Hull City	Away	League	0–0		
82	19/03/94	Barnet	Away	League	2–1	1 Goal	(53)
83	22/03/94	Bristol Rovers	Home	League	3–2	1 Goal	(54)
84	26/03/94	Port Vale	Home	League	2–1	2 Goals	(56)
85	29/03/94	Leyton Orient	Away	League	2–2	1 Goal	(57)
86	02/04/94	Burnley	Home	League	1–0	1 Goal	(58)
87	04/04/94	Bristol Rovers	Away	League	1–3		
88	09/04/94	Bradford City	Home	League	0–3		
89	12/04/94	Huddersfield Town	Away	League	0–3		
90	16/04/94	Brighton & Hove Albion	Home	League	1–3		
91	23/04/94	AFC Bournemouth	Away	League	2–1	2 Goals	(60)
92	26/04/94	Plymouth Argyle	Home	League	0–3		
93	30/04/94	Hartlepool United	Home	League	2–0	1 Goal	(61)
94	07/05/94	York City	Away	League	1–1	1 Goal	(62)

SEASON 1994–95

Football League Division Two

95	13/08/94	AFC Bournemouth	Home	League	2–0	1 Goal	(63)
96	15/08/94	Doncaster Rovers	Away	Lge Cup	4–2	1 Goal	(64)
97	20/08/94	Shrewsbury Town	Away	League	2–2	2 Goals	(66)
98	23/08/94	Doncaster Rovers	Home	Lge Cup	1–1		
99	27/08/94	Brighton & Hove Albion	Home	League	2–1	2 Goals	(68)
100	30/08/94	Cardiff City	Away	League	0–0		
101	10/09/94	Crewe Alexandra	Home	League	1–0		
102	13/09/94	Bradford City	Home	League	0–1		
103	17/09/94	Bristol Rovers	Away	League	2–4		
104	20/09/94	Coventry City	Home	Lge Cup	1–2		
105	24/09/94	Blackpool	Away	League	1–2		
106	27/09/94	Crewe Alexandra	Away	AW Shield	0–0		
107	01/10/94	Birmingham City	Home	League	1–1		
108	05/10/94	Coventry City	Away	Lge Cup	2–3	1 Goal	(69)

109	08/10/94	Cambridge United	Away	League	2–1	2 Goals	(71)
110	15/10/94	Hull City	Home	League	2–2	1 Goal	(72)
111	18/10/94	Mansfield Town	Home	AW Shield	2–0	2 Goals	(74)
112	22/10/94	Oxford United	Home	League	3–2		
113	30/10/94	Chester City	Away	League	1–1		
114	01/11/94	Huddersfield Town	Away	League	1–2		
115	05/11/94	Wycombe Wanderers	Home	League	4–1	3 Goals	(77)
116	08/11/94	Newtown	Away	Welsh Cup	1–1	1 Goal	(78)
117	12/11/94	Stockport County	Home	FA Cup	1–0		
118	15/11/94	Newtown	Home	Welsh Cup	2–0	1 Goal	(79)
119	19/11/94	Plymouth Argyle	Away	League	1–4		
120	26/11/94	Swansea City	Home	League	4–1		
121	29/11/94	Bradford City	Home	AW Shield	6–1	3 Goals	(82)
122	03/12/94	Rotherham United	Home	FA Cup	5–2	1 Goal	(83)
123	10/12/94	Shrewsbury Town	Home	League	0–1		
124	16/12/94	AFC Bournemouth	Away	League	3–1	1 Goal	(84)
125	20/12/94	Connahs Quay Nomads	Home	Welsh Cup	4–0	2 Goals	(86)
126	26/12/94	Stockport County	Away	League	1–1	1 Goal	(87)
127	27/12/94	Peterborough United	Home	League	3–3	2 Goals	(89)
128	07/01/95	Ipswich Town	Home	FA Cup	2–1	1 Goal	(90)
129	10/01/95	Carlisle United	Away	AW Shield	1–2	1 Goal	(91)
130	14/01/95	Leyton Orient	Home	League	4–1	3 Goals	(94)
131	24/01/95	Bangor City	Away	Welsh Cup	2–2		
132	28/01/95	Manchester United	Away	FA Cup	2–5		
133	31/01/95	Bangor City	Home	Welsh Cup	1–0		
134	04/02/95	Swansea City	Away	League	0–0		
135	07/02/95	York City	Away	League	1–0	1 Goal	(95)
136	11/02/95	Huddersfield Town	Home	League	1–2	1 Goal	(96)
137	14/02/95	Chester City	Home	League	2–2	1 Goal	(97)
138	18/02/95	Leyton Orient	Away	League	1–1		
139	21/02/95	Plymouth Argyle	Home	League	3–1	2 Goals	(99)
140	25/02/95	Birmingham City	Away	League	2–5	2 Goals	(101)
141	04/03/95	Blackpool	Home	League	0–1		
142	07/03/95	Brentford	Home	League	0–0		
143	11/03/95	Brighton & Hove Albion	Away	League	0–4		
144	14/03/95	Rotherham United	Home	League	3–1	1 Goal	(102)
145	18/03/95	Cardiff City	Home	League	0–3		
146	21/03/95	Crewe Alexandra	Away	League	3–1	1 Goal	(103)
147	25/03/95	Bristol Rovers	Home	League	1–1		
148	30/03/95	Merthyr Tydfil	Home	Welsh Cup	3–1	1 Goal	(104)
149	01/04/95	Bradford City	Away	League	1–1	1 Goal	(105)
150	04/04/95	Oxford United	Away	League	0–0		
151	08/04/95	York City	Home	League	1–1		
152	11/04/95	Wycombe Wanderers	Away	League	0–3		
153	15/04/95	Peterborough United	Away	League	0–1		
154	17/04/95	Stockport County	Home	League	1–0		
155	22/04/95	Rotherham United	Away	League	1–0	1 Goal	(106)
156	29/04/95	Hull City	Away	League	2–3		
157	03/05/95	Merthyr Tydfil	Away	Welsh Cup	1–0	1 Goal	(107)
158	06/05/95	Cambridge United	Home	League	0–1		
159	21/05/95	Cardiff City	Neutral	Welsh Cup	2–1	2 Goals	(109)

SEASON 1995–96

Tranmere Rovers – Football League Division One

1	12/08/95	Wolverhampton Wanderers	Home	League	2–2		
2	19/08/95	Sheffield United	Away	League	2–0		
3	26/08/95	Huddersfield Town	Home	League	3–1		
4	29/08/95	Barnsley	Away	League	1–2		
5	09/09/95	Charlton Athletic	Home	League	0–0		
6	12/09/95	West Bromwich Albion	Home	League	2–2	1 Goal	(1)
7	16/09/95	Stoke City	Away	League	0–0		
8	19/09/95	Oldham Athletic	Home	Lge Cup	1–0		
9	23/09/95	Portsmouth	Away	League	2–0	1 Goal	(2)
10	30/09/95	Watford	Home	League	2–3	1 Goal	(3)
11	04/10/95	Oldham Athletic	Away	Lge Cup	3–1		
12	07/10/95	Luton Town	Home	League	1–0		
13	14/10/95	Millwall	Away	League	2–2	1 Goal	(4)
14	21/10/95	Southend United	Home	League	3–0	1 Goal	(5)
15	24/10/95	Birmingham City	Away	Lge Cup	1–1		
16	29/10/95	Norwich City	Away	League	1–1		
17	04/11/95	Derby County	Home	League	5–1	1 Goal	(6)
18	08/11/95	Birmingham City	Home	Lge Cup	1–3*		
19	19/11/95	Leicester City	Away	League	1–0		
20	22/11/95	Port Vale	Home	League	2–1		

21	25/11/95	Grimsby Town	Home	League	0–1		
22	02/12/95	Luton Town	Away	League	2–3	1 Goal	(7)
23	09/12/95	Portsmouth	Home	League	1–2		
24	16/12/95	Watford	Away	League	0–3		
25	23/12/95	Birmingham City	Away	League	0–1		
26	26/12/95	Oldham Athletic	Home	League	2–0		
27	01/01/96	Reading	Away	League	0–1		
28	17/02/96	West Bromwich Albion	Away	League	1–1		
29	20/02/96	Crystal Palace	Home	League	2–3	1 Goal	(8)
30	24/02/96	Stoke City	Home	League	0–0		
Sub+1	03/03/96	Oldham Athletic	Away	League	2–1		
Sub+2	12/03/96	Crystal Palace	Away	League	1–2		
Sub+3	16/03/96	Ipswich Town	Away	League	2–1	1 Goal	(9)

Preston North End – Football League Division Three

1	30/03/96	Scarborough	Away	League	2–1	1 Goal	(1)
2	02/04/96	Torquay United	Home	League	1–0		
3	06/04/96	Doncaster Rovers	Home	League	1–0		
4	08/04/96	Mansfield Town	Away	League	0–0		
5	13/04/96	Northampton Town	Home	League	0–3		
Sub+1	16/04/96	Cambridge United	Away	League	1–2		
Sub+2	20/04/96	Leyton Orient	Away	League	2–0		
Sub+3	04/05/96	Exeter City	Home	League	2–0		

SEASON 1996–97

Football League Division Two

Sub+4	01/10/96	Watford	Away	League	0–1		
Sub+5	12/10/96	Stockport County	Away	League	0–1		
6	15/10/96	Walsall	Away	League	0–1		
7	19/10/96	Shrewsbury Town	Home	League	2–1	1 Goal	(2)
8	26/10/96	Gillingham	Away	League	1–1		
9	29/10/96	Burnley	Home	League	1–1		
10	02/11/96	Rotherham United	Home	League	0–0		
11	09/12/96	Chesterfield	Away	AW Shield	2–0	1 Goal	(3)
Sub+6	13/12/96	Blackpool	Home	League	3–0	2 Goals	(5)
12	21/12/96	Brentford	Away	League	0–0		
13	28/12/96	Bristol City	Home	League	0–2		
Sub+7	11/01/97	Millwall	Away	League	2–3		
14	18/01/97	Watford	Home	League	1–1	1 Goal	(6)
15	25/01/97	Burnley	Away	League	2–1		
16	01/02/97	Chesterfield	Home	League	0–1		
Sub+8	08/02/97	Rotherham United	Away	League	1–0		
Sub+9	11/02/97	AFC Bournemouth	Away	League	0–2		

Wrexham – Football League Division Two

1	01/03/97	Burnley	Home	League	0–0		
Sub+1	09/03/97	Chesterfield	Away	FA Cup	0–1		
2	12/03/97	Luton Town	Home	League	2–1	2 Goals	(2)
3	15/03/97	York City	Home	League	0–0		
4	18/03/97	Preston North End	Away	League	1–2	1 Goal	(3)
5	22/03/97	Plymouth Argyle	Away	League	1–0		
6	25/03/97	Brentford	Home	League	0–2		
7	28/03/97	Millwall	Home	League	3–3	1 Goal	(4)
8	31/03/97	Bristol Rovers	Away	League	0–2		
9	05/04/97	Walsall	Home	League	1–2		
10	08/04/97	Rotherham United	Home	League	1–0		
11	12/04/97	Shrewsbury Town	Away	League	1–0	1 Goal	(5)
12	15/04/97	Bristol City	Away	League	1–2		
13	19/04/97	Watford	Home	League	3–1		
14	22/04/97	Crewe Alexandra	Home	League	1–1		
15	26/04/97	AFC Bournemouth	Away	League	1–2		

APPEARANCES AND GOALS PER SEASON

SEASON 84–85	GAMES	GOALS
League	10+10	3
FA Cup	1	0
Freight Rover Trophy	3+1	1
TOTAL	**14+11**	**4**

SEASON 85–86	GAMES	GOALS
League	40+3	13
FA Cup	1	0
League Cup	3	0
Freight Rover Trophy	2	0
TOTAL	**46+3**	**13**

SEASON 86–87	GAMES	GOALS
League	26+7	13
FA Cup	7	5
League Cup	1+1	1
Freight Rover Trophy	6	4
TOTAL	**40+8**	**23**

SEASON 87–88	GAMES	GOALS
League	41+2	10
FA Cup	0+1	0
League Cup	1	0
Sherpa Van Trophy	2	1
TOTAL	**44+3**	**11**

SEASON 88–89	GAMES	GOALS
League	18+6	2
FA Cup	1	0
League Cup	1+3	0
Sherpa Van Trophy	1	0
TOTAL	**21+9**	**2**

SEASON 89–90	GAMES	GOALS
League	28+5	5
League Cup	4	4
Leyland Daf Cup	1+1	0
TOTAL	**33+6**	**9**

SEASON 90–91	GAMES	GOALS
League	23+7	3
FA Cup	3	1
League Cup	4	0
Leyland Daf Cup	2	0
TOTAL	**32+7**	**4**

SEASON 91–92	GAMES	GOALS
League	40+2	11
FA Cup	2	0
League Cup	4	2
Autoglass Trophy	2+1	1
TOTAL	**48+3**	**14**

SEASON 92–93	GAMES	GOALS
League	34+1	16
FA Cup	1	1
League Cup	1	2
Autoglass Trophy	3	2
Welsh Cup	4	2
TOTAL	**43+1**	**23**

SEASON 93–94	GAMES	GOALS
League	41	32
FA Cup	2	0
League Cup	4	3
Autoglass Trophy	2	1
Welsh Cup	2	3
TOTAL	**51**	**39**

SEASON 94–95	GAMES	GOALS
League	45	29
FA Cup	4	2
League Cup	4	2
Auto Windscreens Shield	4	6
Welsh Cup	8	8
TOTAL	**65**	**47**

SEASON 95–96	GAMES	GOALS
League	31+6	10
League Cup	4	0
TOTAL	**35+6**	**10**

SEASON 96–97	GAMES	GOALS
League	25+6	9
FA Cup	0+1	0
Auto Windscreens Shield	1	1
TOTAL	**26+7**	**10**

CAREER APPEARANCES AND GOALS

COMPETITION	GAMES	TOTAL	GOALS
League	402+55	457	156
FA Cup	22+2	24	9
League Cup	31+4	35	14
Freight Rover Trophy	11+1	12	5
Sherpa Van Trophy	3	3	1
Leyland Daf Cup	3+1	4	0
Autoglass Trophy	7+1	8	4
Auto Windscreens Shield	5	5	7
Welsh Cup	14	14	13
TOTAL	**498+64**	**562**	**209**

HAT-TRICKS

Chester City

1	3	Stockport County	18/10/91	Away	League	4–0

Wrexham

1	3	Bury	10/10/92	Home	League	4–2
2	3	Hull City	14/09/93	Home	League	3–0
3	3	Carno	27/10/93	Home	Welsh Cup	6–1
4	3	Wycombe Wanderers	05/11/94	Home	League	4–1
5	3	Bradford City	29/11/94	Home	AW Shield	6–1
6	3	Leyton Orient	14/01/95	Home	League	4–1

League: 5
Auto Windscreens Shield: 1
Welsh Cup: 1
TOTAL: 7

HONOURS

Winners medals
Freight Rover Trophy: 84/85
Welsh Cup: 94/95

Runner-up medals
Football League Division Three Championship: 92/93
League Division Four Championship: 85/86
Promoted to Football League Division Two: 95/96*

* Played eight (5+3/1) League matches in the Preston North End team that won the
Football League Division Three Championship.

LUTHER BLISSETT

Born: 01/02/58 – Jamaica, West Indies
Height: 5.11
Weight: 12.03 (93–94)

Clubs
Watford: **1976–83** – Matches: **273+25** – Goals: **117**
Milan AC: **1983–84** – Matches: **39**– Goals: **6**
Watford: **1984–88** – Matches: **139+18** – Goals: **57**
AFC Bournemouth: **1988–91** – Matches: **142** – Goals: **61**
Watford: **1991–92** – Matches: **39+9** – Goals: **12**
West Bromwich Albion (loan): **1992** – Matches: **3** – Goals: **1**
Bury: **1993–94** – Matches: **10+3** – Goals: **2**
Derry City (loan): **1993** – Matches: **4** – Goals: **1**
Mansfield Town (loan): **1994** – Matches: **4+1** – Goals: **1**

Country
England: **1982–84** – Matches: **8+6** – Goals: **3**

SEASON 1975–76

Watford – League Division Four

Sub+1	03/04/76	Barnsley	Home	League	1–0		
Sub+2	06/04/76	Bradford City	Home	League	3–0		
1	17/04/76	Swansea City	Home	League	2–1	1 Goal	(1)

Striker

SEASON 1976–77

League Division Four

Sub+3	04/09/76	Cambridge United	Away	League	0–4		
Sub+4	18/09/76	Rochdale	Away	League	1–3		
Sub+5	02/04/77	Workington	Home	League	2–0		
2	14/05/77	Darlington	Home	League	1–1		

SEASON 1977–78

League Division Four

3	06/09/77	Grimsby Town	Home	League	1–0	1 Goal	(2)
4	10/09/77	Huddersfield Town	Home	League	2–0		
5	14/09/77	Reading	Away	League	3–1	1 Goal	(3)
6	17/09/77	Barnsley	Away	League	0–1		
7	24/09/77	Darlington	Home	League	2–1	1 Goal	(4)
8	27/09/77	AFC Bournemouth	Home	League	2–1		
9	01/10/77	Rochdale	Away	League	3–2		
Sub+6	15/10/77	Aldershot	Away	League	0–1		
Sub+7	22/10/77	Newport County	Home	League	2–0		
10	25/10/77	West Bromwich Albion	Away	Lge Cup	0–1		
11	29/10/77	Crewe Alexandra	Home	League	5–2		
12	05/11/77	Hartlepool United	Away	League	2–1		
13	12/11/77	Scunthorpe United	Home	League	4–1		
Sub+8	19/11/77	Southend United	Away	League	0–1		
14	26/11/77	Hendon	Home	FA Cup	2–0		
Sub+9	27/12/77	Torquay United	Away	League	3–2		
Sub+10	31/12/77	Wimbledon	Away	League	3–1		
Sub+11	02/01/78	Hartlepool United	Home	League	1–0		
15	07/01/78	West Ham United	Away	FA Cup	0–1		
16	21/01/78	York City	Away	League	4–0	1 Goal	(5)
Sub+12	28/01/78	Doncaster Rovers	Home	League	6–0		
Sub+13	11/02/78	Barnsley	Home	League	0–0		
Sub+14	03/03/78	Swansea City	Away	League	3–3		
17	07/03/78	Reading	Home	League	1–0		
Sub+15	11/03/78	Aldershot	Home	League	1–0		
Sub+16	14/03/78	Huddersfield Town	Away	League	0–1		
18	17/03/78	Newport County	Away	League	2–2		
19	24/03/78	Crewe Alexandra	Away	League	2–2		
Sub+17	28/03/78	Northampton Town	Away	League	2–0		
Sub+18	01/04/78	Wimbledon	Home	League	2–0		
Sub+19	08/04/78	Scunthorpe United	Away	League	1–0		
Sub+20	15/04/78	Southend United	Home	League	1–1		
20	18/04/78	Darlington	Away	League	0–0		
Sub+21	22/04/78	Halifax Town	Away	League	1–1		
21	25/04/78	Brentford	Home	League	1–1	1 Goal	(6)
22	29/04/78	Southport	Home	League	3–2	1 Goal	(7)

SEASON 1978–79

League Division Three

Sub+22	26/08/78	Peterborough United	Home	League	1–2		
Sub+23	29/08/78	Newcastle United	Home	Lge Cup	2–1	2 Goals	(9)
23	02/09/78	Gillingham	Away	League	3–2	1 Goal	(10)
24	09/09/78	Swansea City	Home	League	0–2		
25	13/09/78	Lincoln City	Away	League	5–0	2 Goals	(12)
26	16/09/78	Bury	Away	League	2–1		
27	23/09/78	Oxford United	Home	League	4–2		
28	26/09/78	Rotherham United	Away	League	1–2	1 Goal	(13)
29	30/09/78	Tranmere Rovers	Home	League	4–0		
30	04/10/78	Manchester United	Away	Lge Cup	2–1	2 Goals	(15)
31	07/10/78	Chester	Away	League	1–2	1 Goal	(16)
32	14/10/78	Brentford	Home	League	2–0	1 Goal	(17)
33	17/10/78	Carlisle United	Home	League	2–1		
34	21/10/78	Chesterfield	Away	League	2–0	1 Goal	(18)
35	28/10/78	Exeter City	Home	League	1–0	1 Goal	(19)
36	04/11/78	Hull City	Away	League	0–4		
37	08/11/78	Exeter City	Away	Lge Cup	2–0		
38	11/11/78	Gillingham	Home	League	1–0		
39	18/11/78	Peterborough United	Away	League	1–0	1 Goal	(20)
40	02/12/78	Mansfield Town	Home	League	1–1		
41	09/12/78	Plymouth Argyle	Away	League	1–1		
42	13/12/78	Stoke City	Away	Lge Cup	0–0		
43	16/12/78	Southend United	Home	FA Cup	1–1		
44	30/12/78	Swindon Town	Home	League	2–0	2 Goals	(22)

45	06/01/79	Lincoln City	Home	League	2–0	2 Goals	(24)
46	09/01/79	Stoke City	Home	Lge Cup	3–1	2 Goals	(26)
47	17/01/79	Nottingham Forest	Away	Lge Cup	1–3	1 Goal	(27)
48	20/01/79	Bury	Home	League	3–3	2 Goals	(29)
49	27/01/79	Oxford United	Away	League	1–1		
50	30/01/79	Nottingham Forest	Home	Lge Cup	0–0		
51	03/02/79	Rotherham United	Home	League	2–2		
52	10/02/79	Tranmere Rovers	Away	League	1–1	1 Goal	(30)
53	24/02/79	Brentford	Away	League	3–3	1 Goal	(31)
54	03/03/79	Chesterfield	Home	League	2–0		
55	20/03/79	Swansea City	Away	League	2–3		
56	24/03/79	Blackpool	Away	League	1–1		
57	27/03/79	Walsall	Home	League	3–1	2 Goals	(33)
58	31/03/79	Sheffield Wednesday	Home	League	1–0		
59	02/04/79	Southend United	Away	League	0–1		
60	07/04/79	Mansfield Town	Away	League	3–0		
61	13/04/79	Colchester United	Home	League	0–3		
62	14/04/79	Shrewsbury Town	Away	League	1–1		
63	17/04/79	Southend United	Home	League	2–0		
64	21/04/79	Swindon Town	Away	League	0–2		
65	24/04/79	Carlisle United	Away	League	0–1		
66	28/04/79	Plymouth Argyle	Home	League	2–2		
67	02/05/79	Chester	Home	League	1–0		
68	05/05/79	Sheffield Wednesday	Away	League	3–2	1 Goal	(34)
69	14/05/79	Hull City	Home	League	4–0	1 Goal	(35)

SEASON 1979–80

League Division Two

70	01/08/79	Colchester United	Away	Lge Cup	0–2		
71	14/08/79	Colchester United	Home	Lge Cup	2–1		
72	18/08/79	Leicester City	Away	League	0–2		
73	21/08/79	Swansea City	Home	League	0–0		
74	25/08/79	Cambridge United	Away	League	2–2	1 Goal	(36)
75	01/09/79	West Ham United	Home	League	2–0	2 Goals	(38)
76	08/09/79	Bristol Rovers	Away	League	1–1		
77	15/09/79	Cardiff City	Home	League	1–1		
78	22/09/79	Chelsea	Away	League	0–2		
79	29/09/79	Charlton Athletic	Home	League	2–1		
80	06/10/79	Queens Park Rangers	Home	League	1–2		
81	09/10/79	Swansea City	Away	League	0–1		
82	13/10/79	Orient	Away	League	0–1		
83	20/10/79	Newcastle United	Home	League	2–0	1 Goal	(39)
84	27/10/79	Wrexham	Away	League	0–3		
85	03/11/79	Leicester City	Home	League	1–3		
86	10/11/79	Shrewsbury Town	Away	League	0–1		
87	17/11/79	Birmingham City	Home	League	1–0		
88	24/11/79	Fulham	Away	League	0–0		
89	01/12/79	Notts County	Home	League	2–1	1 Goal	(40)
90	08/12/79	Burnley	Away	League	0–1		
91	15/12/79	Sunderland	Home	League	1–1		
92	21/12/79	Preston North End	Away	League	2–1		
93	26/12/79	Luton Town	Home	League	0–1		
94	29/12/79	Cambridge United	Home	League	0–0		
95	05/01/80	Queens Park Rangers	Away	FA Cup	2–1		
96	12/01/80	West Ham United	Away	League	1–1		
Sub+24	19/01/80	Bristol Rovers	Home	League	0–0		
97	26/01/80	Harlow Town	Home	FA Cup	4–3		
98	02/02/80	Cardiff City	Away	League	0–1		
99	09/02/80	Chelsea	Home	League	2–3	1 Goal	(41)
100	16/02/80	Wolverhampton Wanderers	Away	FA Cup	3–0	1 Goal	(42)
101	19/02/80	Oldham Athletic	Away	League	1–1		
102	23/02/80	Orient	Home	League	0–3		
103	26/02/80	Charlton Athletic	Away	League	0–0		
104	01/03/80	Newcastle United	Away	League	2–0		
105	08/03/80	Arsenal	Home	FA Cup	1–2		
106	14/03/80	Queens Park Rangers	Away	League	1–1	1 Goal	(43)
107	18/03/80	Wrexham	Home	League	3–1	2 Goals	(45)
108	22/03/80	Shrewsbury Town	Home	League	0–1		
109	29/03/80	Birmingham City	Away	League	0–2		
110	05/04/80	Luton Town	Away	League	0–1		
111	07/04/80	Oldham Athletic	Home	League	1–0		
112	09/04/80	Preston North End	Home	League	0–0		
113	12/04/80	Notts County	Away	League	2–1	1 Goal	(46)
114	19/04/80	Fulham	Home	League	4–0		

| 115 | 26/04/90 | Sunderland | Away | League | 0–5 | | |
| Sub+25 | 03/05/90 | Burnley | Home | League | 4–0 | | |

SEASON 1980–81

League Division Two

116	09/08/80	Millwall	Home	Lge Cup	2–1		
117	12/08/80	Millwall	Away	Lge Cup	2–0	1 Goal	(47)
118	16/08/80	Swansea City	Home	League	2–1		
119	19/08/80	Luton Town	Away	League	0–1		
120	23/08/80	Cambridge United	Away	League	1–3		
121	26/08/80	Southampton	Away	Lge Cup	0–4		
122	30/08/80	Bristol City	Home	League	1–0		
123	02/09/80	Southampton	Home	Lge Cup	7–1*		
124	06/09/80	Shrewsbury Town	Away	League	1–2		
125	13/09/80	Preston North End	Home	League	2–1		
126	20/09/80	West Ham United	Away	League	2–3		
127	23/09/80	Sheffield Wednesday	Away	Lge Cup	2–1		
128	27/09/80	Chelsea	Home	League	2–3		
129	04/10/80	Cardiff City	Away	League	0–1		
130	07/10/80	Derby County	Home	League	1–1		
131	11/10/80	Wrexham	Home	League	1–0		
132	18/10/80	Grimsby Town	Away	League	1–1		
133	25/10/80	Oldham Athletic	Home	League	2–1	2 Goals	(49)
134	28/10/80	Nottingham Forest	Home	Lge Cup	4–1	1 Goal	(50)
135	01/11/80	Newcastle United	Away	League	1–2		
136	04/11/80	Bristol Rovers	Away	League	1–3		
137	08/11/80	Bolton Wanderers	Home	League	3–1		
138	11/11/80	Luton Town	Home	League	0–1		
139	22/11/80	Blackburn Rovers	Home	League	1–1	1 Goal	(51)
140	29/11/80	Sheffield Wednesday	Away	League	0–1		
141	02/12/80	Coventry City	Home	Lge Cup	2–2		
142	06/12/80	Notts County	Home	League	2–0		
143	09/12/80	Coventry City	Away	Lge Cup	0–5		
144	13/12/80	Derby County	Away	League	1–1	1 Goal	(52)
145	16/12/80	Swansea City	Away	League	0–1		
146	20/12/80	Grimsby Town	Home	League	3–1		
147	26/12/80	Orient	Away	League	1–1	1 Goal	(53)
148	27/12/80	Queens Park Rangers	Home	League	1–1		
149	03/01/81	Colchester United	Home	FA Cup	1–0		
150	10/01/81	Blackburn Rovers	Away	League	0–0		
151	17/01/81	Bristol City	Away	League	0–0		
152	24/01/81	Wolverhampton Wanderers	Home	FA Cup	1–1		
153	27/01/81	Wolverhampton Wanderers	Away	FA Cup	1–2		
154	31/01/81	Cambridge United	Home	League	0–0		
155	07/02/81	Preston North End	Away	League	1–2		
156	14/02/81	Shrewsbury Town	Home	League	1–0		
157	21/02/81	Chelsea	Away	League	1–0		
158	28/02/81	West Ham United	Home	League	1–2		
159	07/03/81	Cardiff City	Home	League	4–2	1 Goal	(54)
160	21/03/81	Bristol Rovers	Home	League	3–1	1 Goal	(55)
161	28/03/81	Oldham Athletic	Away	League	1–2		
162	04/04/81	Newcastle United	Home	League	0–0		
163	11/04/81	Bolton Wanderers	Away	League	1–2		
164	17/04/81	Orient	Home	League	2–0		
165	18/04/81	Queens Park Rangers	Away	League	0–0		
166	25/04/81	Notts County	Away	League	2–1	2 Goals	(57)
167	02/05/81	Sheffield Wednesday	Home	League	2–1	1 Goal	(58)
168	04/05/81	Wrexham	Away	League	1–0	1 Goal	(59)

SEASON 1981–82

League Division Two

169	15/08/81	Reading	Home	FLG Cup	4–1	1 Goal	(60)
170	19/08/81	Oxford United	Away	FLG Cup	4–2	1 Goal	(61)
171	22/08/81	Aldershot	Away	FLG Cup	1–1		
172	29/08/81	Newcastle United	Away	League	1–0		
173	01/09/81	Grimsby Town	Home	League	0–2		
174	05/09/81	Oldham Athletic	Home	League	1–1		
175	22/09/81	Wrexham	Away	League	1–0		
176	26/09/81	Luton Town	Away	League	1–4		
177	03/10/81	Barnsley	Home	League	3–1		
178	06/10/81	Grimsby Town	Away	Lge Cup	0–1		
179	10/10/81	Orient	Home	League	3–0		
180	17/10/81	Cambridge United	Away	League	2–1	2 Goals	(63)

181	24/10/81	Norwich City	Home	League	3–0	1 Goal	(64)
182	27/10/81	Grimsby Town	Home	Lge Cup	3–1	1 Goal	(65)
183	31/10/81	Shrewsbury Town	Away	League	2–0		
184	07/11/81	Bolton Wanderers	Away	League	0–2		
185	10/11/81	Lincoln City	Home	Lge Cup	2–2	1 Goal	(66)
186	14/11/81	Cardiff City	Home	League	0–0		
187	21/11/81	Blackburn Rovers	Home	League	3–2		
188	25/11/81	Lincoln City	Away	Lge Cup	3–2		
189	28/11/81	Sheffield Wednesday	Away	League	1–3		
190	01/12/81	Queens Park Rangers	Home	Lge Cup	4–1	1 Goal	(67)
191	05/12/81	Charlton Athletic	Home	League	2–2		
192	08/12/81	Burnley	Away	FLG Cup	1–2	1 Goal	(68)
193	12/12/81	Leicester City	Away	League	1–1		
194	02/01/82	Manchester United	Home	FA Cup	1–0		
195	09/01/82	Oldham Athletic	Away	League	1–1		
196	16/01/82	Newcastle United	Home	League	2–3		
197	18/01/82	Ipswich Town	Away	Lge Cup	1–2		
198	23/01/82	West Ham United	Home	FA Cup	2–0		
199	26/01/82	Derby County	Home	League	6–1	1 Goal	(69)
200	30/01/82	Rotherham United	Away	League	2–1		
201	06/02/82	Chelsea	Home	League	1–0	1 Goal	(70)
202	09/02/82	Barnsley	Away	League	0–0		
203	13/02/82	Leicester City	Away	FA Cup	0–2		
204	20/02/82	Luton Town	Home	League	1–1		
205	27/02/82	Orient	Away	League	3–1	2 Goals	(72)
206	06/03/82	Cambridge United	Home	League	0–0		
207	09/03/82	Queens Park Rangers	Home	League	4–0	1 Goal	(73)
208	13/03/82	Norwich City	Away	League	2–4		
209	16/03/82	Grimsby Town	Away	League	2–0		
210	20/03/82	Shrewsbury Town	Home	League	3–1	2 Goals	(75)
211	27/03/82	Bolton Wanderers	Home	League	3–0	2 Goals	(77)
212	03/04/82	Cardiff City	Away	League	0–2		
213	09/04/82	Crystal Palace	Home	League	1–1		
214	12/04/82	Queens Park Rangers	Away	League	0–0		
215	17/04/82	Blackburn Rovers	Away	League	2–1	1 Goal	(78)
216	24/04/82	Sheffield Wednesday	Home	League	4–0	2 Goals	(80)
217	27/04/82	Crystal Palace	Away	League	3–0	2 Goals	(82)
218	01/05/82	Charlton Athletic	Away	League	1–1		
219	04/05/82	Wrexham	Home	League	2–0		
220	08/05/82	Leicester City	Home	League	3–1	1 Goal	(83)
221	15/05/82	Derby County	Away	League	2–3	1 Goal	(84)

SEASON 1982–83

League Division One

222	14/08/82	Orient	Home	FL Trophy	4–1		
223	17/08/82	Colchester United	Home	FL Trophy	2–1	1 Goal	(85)
224	21/08/82	Southend United	Away	FL Trophy	4–1	1 Goal	(86)
225	28/08/82	Everton	Home	League	2–0		
226	31/08/82	Southampton	Away	League	4–1		
227	04/09/82	Manchester City	Away	League	0–1		
228	07/09/82	Swansea City	Home	League	2–1	1 Goal	(87)
229	11/09/82	West Bromwich Albion	Home	League	3–0	2 Goals	(89)
230	18/09/82	Nottingham Forest	Away	League	0–2		
231	25/09/82	Sunderland	Home	League	8–0	4 Goals	(93)
232	02/10/82	Birmingham City	Away	League	1–1	1 Goal	(94)
233	05/10/82	Bolton Wanderers	Away	Lge Cup	2–1		
234	09/10/82	Norwich City	Home	League	2–2		
235	16/10/82	Aston Villa	Away	League	0–3		
236	23/10/82	Coventry City	Home	League	0–0		
237	26/10/82	Bolton Wanderers	Home	Lge Cup	2–1	1 Goal	(95)
238	30/10/82	Notts County	Away	League	2–3	1 Goal	(96)
239	06/11/82	Tottenham Hotspur	Away	League	1–0		
240	10/11/82	Nottingham Forest	Away	Lge Cup	3–7		
241	13/11/82	Stoke City	Home	League	1–0		
242	20/11/82	Brighton & Hove Albion	Home	League	4–1	2 Goals	(98)
243	27/11/82	Arsenal	Away	League	4–2		
244	04/12/82	Manchester United	Home	League	0–1		
245	08/12/82	Reading	Away	FL Trophy	3–5	1 Goal	(99)
246	11/12/82	Liverpool	Away	League	1–3		
247	27/12/82	Luton Town	Away	League	0–1		
248	29/12/82	West Ham United	Home	League	2–1		
249	01/01/83	Brighton & Hove Albion	Away	League	1–1		
250	03/01/83	Manchester City	Home	League	2–0		
251	08/01/83	Plymouth Argyle	Home	FA Cup	2–0	1 Goal	(100)

252	15/01/83	Everton	Away	League	0–1		
253	22/01/83	Southampton	Home	League	2–0	1 Goal	(101)
254	29/01/83	Fulham	Home	FA Cup	1–1		
255	01/02/83	Fulham	Away	FA Cup	2–1		
256	06/02/83	Swansea City	Away	League	3–1	2 Goals	(103)
257	19/02/83	Aston Villa	Away	FA Cup	1–4	1 Goal	(104)
258	26/02/83	Aston Villa	Home	League	2–1	1 Goal	(105)
259	02/03/83	Norwich City	Away	League	0–3		
260	05/03/83	Coventry City	Away	League	1–0		
261	12/03/83	Notts County	Home	League	5–3	3 Goals	(108)
262	19/03/83	Tottenham Hotspur	Home	League	0–1		
263	22/03/83	Birmingham City	Home	League	2–1	2 Goals	(110)
264	26/03/83	Stoke City	Away	League	0–4		
265	02/04/83	West Ham United	Away	League	1–2		
266	04/04/83	Luton Town	Home	League	5–2	2 Goals	(112)
267	09/04/83	West Bromwich Albion	Away	League	3–1		
268	16/04/83	Nottingham Forest	Home	League	1–3	1 Goal	(113)
269	23/04/83	Manchester United	Away	League	0–2		
270	30/04/83	Arsenal	Home	League	2–1	1 Goal	(114)
271	02/05/83	Sunderland	Away	League	2–2	2 Goals	(116)
272	07/05/83	Ipswich Town	Away	League	1–3		
273	14/05/83	Liverpool	Home	League	2–1	1 Goal	(117)

SEASON 1983–84

Milan AC – Italian League Division One

1	21/08/83	Arezzo US	Away	It Cup	0–0		
2	24/08/83	AC Padova	Away	It Cup	2–0		
3	28/08/83	Rimini Calcio	Home	It Cup	3–1		
4	31/08/83	Atalanta BC	Away	It Cup	2–0		
5	04/09/83	AS Roma	Home	It Cup	1–1		
6	11/09/83	US Avellino	Away	League	0–4		
7	18/09/83	Hellas–Verona AC	Home	League	4–2	1 Goal	(1)
8	25/09/83	AS Roma	Away	League	1–3		
9	02/10/83	Catania Calcio	Home	League	2–1		
10	09/10/83	Juventus FC	Away	League	1–2		
11	23/10/83	Sampdoria UC	Home	League	2–1		
12	30/10/83	SS Lazio	Home	League	4–1	1 Goal	(2)
13	06/11/83	Internazionale Milano	Away	League	0–2		
14	20/11/83	AC Fiorentina	Home	League	2–2		
15	27/11/83	SSC Napoli	Away	League	0–0		
16	04/12/83	Genoa 1893	Home	League	1–0		
17	11/12/83	Ascoli Calcio	Away	League	4–2		
18	18/12/83	Torino Calcio	Home	League	0–1		
19	31/12/83	SC Pisa	Away	League	0–0		
20	08/01/84	Udinese Calcio	Home	League	3–3	1 Goal	(3)
21	15/01/84	US Avellino	Home	League	1–0		
22	22/01/84	Hellas–Verona	Away	League	1–1		
23	29/01/84	AS Roma	Home	League	1–1		
24	08/02/84	LR Vicenza	Away	It Cup	1–0		
25	12/02/84	Catania Calcio	Away	League	1–1		
26	19/02/84	Juventus FC	Home	League	0–3		
27	22/02/84	LR Vicenza	Home	It Cup	2–1	1 Goal	(4)
28	26/02/84	Sampdoria UC	Away	League	1–1		
29	11/03/84	SS Lazio	Away	League	0–0		
30	18/03/84	Internazionale Milano	Home	League	0–0		
31	25/03/84	AC Fiorentina	Away	League	2–2		
32	01/04/84	SSC Napoli	Home	League	0–2		
33	15/04/84	Genoa 1893	Away	League	0–2		
34	21/04/84	Ascoli Calcio	Home	League	0–0		
35	29/04/84	Torino Calcio	Away	League	2–1	1 Goal	(5)
36	06/05/84	SC Pisa	Home	League	2–1	1 Goal	(6)
37	13/05/84	Udinese Calcio	Away	League	2–1		
38	07/06/84	AS Roma	Away	It Cup	1–1		
39	10/06/84	AS Roma	Home	It Cup	1–2		

SEASON 1984–85

Watford – League Division One

1	25/08/84	Manchester United	Away	League	1–1		
2	28/08/84	Queens Park Rangers	Home	League	1–1		
Sub+1	01/09/84	Arsenal	Home	League	3–4	1 Goal	(1)
Sub+2	05/09/84	Leicester City	Away	League	1–1		
3	08/09/84	West Ham United	Away	League	0–2		
4	15/09/84	Aston Villa	Home	League	3–3	1 Goal	(2)

5	22/09/84	Norwich City	Away	League	2–3		
6	25/09/84	Cardiff City	Home	Lge Cup	3–1		
7	29/09/84	Everton	Home	League	4–5		
Sub+3	06/10/84	Coventry City	Home	League	0–1		
8	09/10/84	Cardiff City	Away	Lge Cup	0–1		
9	13/10/84	Chelsea	Away	League	3–2		
10	20/10/84	Luton Town	Away	League	2–3	1 Goal	(3)
11	27/10/84	Newcastle United	Home	League	3–3	2 Goals	(5)
12	31/10/84	Leeds United	Away	Lge Cup	4–0		
13	03/11/84	Ipswich Town	Away	League	3–3	2 Goals	(7)
14	10/11/84	Sunderland	Home	League	3–1		
15	17/11/84	Sheffield Wednesday	Home	League	1–0		
16	20/11/84	West Bromwich Albion	Home	Lge Cup	4–1	1 Goal	(8)
17	24/11/84	Stoke City	Away	League	3–1	1 Goal	(9)
18	01/12/84	Nottingham Forest	Home	League	2–0		
19	08/12/84	West Bromwich Albion	Away	League	1–2		
20	15/12/84	Tottenham Hotspur	Home	League	1–2		
21	22/12/84	Arsenal	Away	League	1–1		
22	26/12/84	Southampton	Away	League	2–1	2 Goals	(11)
23	29/12/84	Leicester City	Home	League	4–1		
24	01/01/85	Liverpool	Home	League	1–1	1 Goal	(12)
25	05/01/85	Sheffield United	Home	FA Cup	5–0	4 Goals	(16)
26	23/01/85	Sunderland	Home	Lge Cup	0–1		
27	26/01/85	Grimsby Town	Away	FA Cup	3–1	2 Goals	(18)
28	02/02/85	Everton	Away	League	0–4		
29	24/02/85	Sheffield Wednesday	Away	League	1–1		
30	02/03/85	Newcastle United	Away	League	1–3		
31	04/03/85	Luton Town	Away	FA Cup	0–0		
32	06/03/85	Luton Town	Home	FA Cup	2–2*		
33	09/03/85	Luton Town	Away	FA Cup	0–1		
34	12/03/85	Sunderland	Away	League	1–1	1 Goal	(19)
35	16/03/85	Chelsea	Home	League	1–3	1 Goal	(20)
36	19/03/85	Luton Town	Home	League	3–0	2 Goals	(22)
37	23/03/85	Coventry City	Away	League	1–3	1 Goal	(23)
38	30/03/85	Queens Park Rangers	Away	League	0–2		
39	02/04/85	West Ham United	Home	League	5–0	2 Goals	(25)
40	06/04/85	Southampton	Home	League	1–1		
41	13/04/85	Norwich City	Home	League	2–0		
42	16/04/85	Ipswich Town	Home	League	3–1		
43	24/04/85	Aston Villa	Away	League	1–1		
44	27/04/85	Stoke City	Home	League	2–0	1 Goal	(26)
45	04/05/85	Nottingham Forest	Away	League	1–1		
46	07/05/85	West Bromwich Albion	Home	League	0–2		
47	11/05/85	Tottenham Hotspur	Away	League	5–1	1 Goal	(27)
48	13/05/85	Manchester United	Home	League	5–1	1 Goal	(28)

SEASON 1985–86

League Division One

49	17/08/85	Tottenham Hotspur	Away	League	0–4		
50	20/08/85	Birmingham City	Home	League	3–0		
51	24/08/85	West Bromwich Albion	Home	League	5–1		
52	26/08/85	Sheffield Wednesday	Away	League	1–2	1 Goal	(29)
53	31/08/85	Coventry City	Home	League	3–0		
Sub+4	07/09/85	Liverpool	Away	League	1–3		
54	14/09/85	Queens Park Rangers	Home	League	2–0	1 Goal	(30)
55	21/09/85	Nottingham Forest	Away	League	2–3		
56	24/09/85	Crewe Alexandra	Away	Lge Cup	3–1	1 Goal	(31)
57	28/09/85	Chelsea	Home	League	3–1	1 Goal	(32)
58	05/10/85	Southampton	Away	League	1–3		
59	09/10/85	Crewe Alexandra	Home	Lge Cup	3–2		
60	12/10/85	Manchester City	Home	League	3–2	1 Goal	(33)
Sub+5	19/10/85	Everton	Away	League	1–4		
61	26/10/85	Oxford United	Home	League	2–2		
62	29/10/85	Queens Park Rangers	Home	Lge Cup	0–1		
63	02/11/85	Newcastle United	Away	League	1–1		
64	09/11/85	Aston Villa	Home	League	1–1		
65	30/11/85	Manchester United	Away	League	1–1		
66	07/12/85	Birmingham City	Away	League	2–1	1 Goal	(34)
67	14/12/85	Tottenham Hotspur	Home	League	1–0	1 Goal	(35)
68	22/12/85	West Bromwich Albion	Away	League	1–3		
69	28/12/85	Leicester City	Home	League	2–1		
Sub+6	29/04/86	Southampton	Home	League	1–1		
70	03/05/86	Manchester United	Home	League	1–1	1 Goal	(36)
71	05/05/86	Chelsea	Away	League	5–1		

SEASON 1986–87

League Division One

72	23/08/86	Oxford United	Home	League	3–0	1 Goal	(37)
73	26/08/86	Queens Park Rangers	Away	League	2–3		
74	30/08/86	Nottingham Forest	Away	League	1–1	1 Goal	(38)
75	06/09/86	Wimbledon	Home	League	0–1		
76	13/09/86	Norwich City	Away	League	3–1	1 Goal	(39)
77	16/09/86	Manchester United	Home	League	1–0		
78	20/09/86	Sheffield Wednesday	Home	League	0–1		
79	27/09/86	Coventry City	Away	League	0–1		
80	04/10/86	West Ham United	Home	League	2–2	1 Goal	(40)
81	07/10/86	Rochdale	Away	Lge Cup	2–1		
82	11/10/86	Arsenal	Away	League	1–3		
83	18/10/86	Aston Villa	Home	League	4–2		
84	25/10/86	Everton	Away	League	2–3		
85	08/11/86	Charlton Athletic	Home	League	4–1	1 Goal	(41)
86	15/11/86	Newcastle United	Away	League	2–2	1 Goal	(42)
87	22/11/86	Leicester City	Home	League	5–1		
88	26/11/86	Manchester City	Away	FM Cup	0–1		
89	29/11/86	Southampton	Away	League	1–3		
90	03/01/87	Wimbledon	Away	League	1–2		
91	24/01/87	Oxford United	Away	League	3–1		
92	01/02/87	Chelsea	Home	FA Cup	1–0	1 Goal	(43)
93	07/02/87	Nottingham Forest	Home	League	1–1		
94	14/02/87	Manchester United	Away	League	1–3		
95	24/02/87	Walsall	Home	FA Cup	4–4*	1 Goal	(44)
96	28/02/87	Sheffield Wednesday	Away	League	1–0	1 Goal	(45)
97	02/03/87	Walsall	Away	FA Cup	1–0		
98	08/03/87	Everton	Home	League	2–1	1 Goal	(46)
99	14/03/87	Arsenal	Away	FA Cup	3–1	2 Goals	(48)
100	21/03/87	Arsenal	Home	League	2–0	1 Goal	(49)
101	25/03/87	Aston Villa	Away	League	1–1		
102	28/03/87	West Ham United	Away	League	0–1		
103	04/04/87	Charlton Athletic	Away	League	3–4	1 Goal	(50)
104	06/04/87	Queens Park Rangers	Home	League	0–3		
105	11/04/87	Tottenham Hotspur	Neutral	FA Cup	1–4		
106	14/04/87	Chelsea	Home	League	3–1	1 Goal	(51)
107	18/04/87	Manchester City	Away	League	2–1		
108	21/04/87	Luton Town	Home	League	2–0		
109	25/04/87	Leicester City	Away	League	2–1		
110	30/04/87	Coventry City	Home	League	2–3		
111	02/05/87	Southampton	Home	League	1–1		
112	04/05/87	Liverpool	Away	League	0–1		
113	09/05/87	Tottenham Hotspur	Home	League	1–0		

SEASON 1987–88

League Division One

114	15/08/87	Wimbledon	Home	League	1–0	1 Goal	(52)
115	19/08/87	Nottingham Forest	Away	League	0–1		
116	22/08/87	Manchester United	Away	League	0–2		
117	29/08/87	Tottenham Hotspur	Home	League	1–1		
118	05/09/87	Norwich City	Home	League	0–1		
Sub+7	19/09/87	Portsmouth	Home	League	0–0		
Sub+8	22/09/87	Darlington	Away	Lge Cup	3–0		
Sub+9	26/09/87	Chelsea	Home	League	0–3		
119	06/10/87	Darlington	Home	Lge Cup	8–0	1 Goal	(53)
120	17/10/87	Southampton	Away	League	0–1		
Sub+10	03/11/87	Swindon Town	Home	Lge Cup	4–2		
121	21/11/87	Oxford United	Away	League	1–1	1 Goal	(54)
122	24/11/87	Liverpool	Away	League	0–4		
123	28/11/87	Arsenal	Home	League	2–0	1 Goal	(55)
124	05/12/87	Derby County	Away	League	1–1		
125	12/12/87	Luton Town	Home	League	0–1		
126	26/12/87	Sheffield Wednesday	Home	League	1–3		
127	12/01/88	Hull City	Away	FA Cup	2–2*		
128	16/01/88	Wimbledon	Away	League	2–1		
129	18/01/88	Hull City	Home	FA Cup	1–0		
130	23/01/88	Nottingham Forest	Home	League	0–0		
131	30/01/88	Coventry City	Away	FA Cup	1–0		
Sub+11	06/02/88	Norwich City	Away	League	0–0		
Sub+12	13/02/88	Liverpool	Home	League	1–4	1 Goal	(56)
Sub+13	20/02/88	Port Vale	Away	FA Cup	0–0		

Sub+14	23/02/88	Port Vale	Home	FA Cup	2–0
Sub+15	27/02/88	Coventry City	Home	League	0–1
Sub+16	05/03/88	Southampton	Home	League	0–1
132	12/03/88	Wimbledon	Away	FA Cup	1–2
133	19/03/88	West Ham United	Away	League	0–1
134	26/03/88	Everton	Home	League	1–2
Sub+17	29/03/88	Chelsea	Away	League	1–1
Sub+18	01/04/88	Queens Park Rangers	Home	League	0–1
135	04/04/88	Charlton Athletic	Away	League	0–1

SEASON 1988–89

League Division Two

136	04/10/88	Oldham Athletic	Home	League	3–1	1 Goal	(57)
137	08/10/88	Leeds United	Away	League	1–0		
138	11/10/88	Leicester City	Home	Lge Cup	2–2		
139	22/10/88	Stoke City	Away	League	0–2		

AFC Bournemouth – League Division Two

1	26/11/88	Barnsley	Away	League	2–5	1 Goal	(1)
2	29/11/88	Hull City	Home	League	5–1	4 Goals	(5)
3	03/12/88	Blackburn Rovers	Home	League	2–1	1 Goal	(6)
4	10/12/88	Plymouth Argyle	Away	League	1–1	1 Goal	(7)
5	17/12/88	Walsall	Home	League	2–1	1 Goal	(8)
6	26/12/88	Leicester City	Away	League	1–0		
7	31/12/88	Watford	Away	League	0–1		
8	02/01/89	Brighton & Hove Albion	Home	League	2–1	1 Goal	(9)
9	07/01/89	Blackpool	Away	FA Cup	1–0	1 Goal	(10)
10	14/01/89	Hull City	Away	League	0–4		
11	21/01/89	Sunderland	Home	League	0–1		
12	28/01/89	Hartlepool United	Away	FA Cup	1–1	1 Goal	(11)
13	31/01/89	Hartlepool United	Home	FA Cup	5–2		
14	04/02/89	West Bromwich Albion	Home	League	2–1		
15	11/02/89	Birmingham City	Away	League	1–0		
16	18/02/89	Manchester United	Home	FA Cup	1–1		
17	22/02/89	Manchester United	Away	FA Cup	0–1		
18	25/02/89	Portsmouth	Home	League	1–0		
19	28/02/89	Oldham Athletic	Home	League	2–2	2 Goals	(13)
20	04/03/89	Crystal Palace	Away	League	3–2		
21	11/03/89	Bradford City	Home	League	3–0	2 Goals	(15)
22	14/03/89	Ipswich Town	Away	League	1–3	1 Goal	(16)
23	18/03/89	Swindon Town	Home	League	2–3	1 Goal	(17)
24	25/03/89	Chelsea	Away	League	0–2		
25	27/03/89	Leicester City	Home	League	2–1	1 Goal	(18)
26	01/04/89	Leeds United	Away	League	0–3		
27	04/04/89	Walsall	Away	League	1–1		
28	08/04/89	Watford	Home	League	0–1		
29	11/04/89	Shrewsbury Town	Away	League	0–1		
30	15/04/89	Stoke City	Home	League	0–1		
31	22/04/89	Oxford United	Away	League	1–3		
32	29/04/89	Barnsley	Home	League	3–2	2 Goals	(20)
33	01/05/89	Blackburn Rovers	Away	League	0–2		
34	06/05/89	Manchester City	Away	League	3–3	1 Goal	(21)
35	13/05/89	Plymouth Argyle	Home	League	0–0		

SEASON 1989–90

League Division Two

36	19/08/89	Brighton & Hove Albion	Away	League	1–2		
37	22/08/89	West Bromwich Albion	Home	League	1–1		
38	26/08/89	Hull City	Home	League	5–4	1 Goal	(22)
39	02/09/89	Ipswich Town	Away	League	1–1		
40	09/09/89	Newcastle United	Home	League	2–1		
41	16/09/89	Middlesbrough	Away	League	1–2	1 Goal	(23)
42	19/09/89	Crewe Alexandra	Away	Lge Cup	1–0		
43	23/09/89	Blackburn Rovers	Home	League	2–4	1 Goal	(24)
44	26/09/89	Port Vale	Home	League	1–0	1 Goal	(25)
45	30/09/89	Oxford United	Away	League	2–1		
46	03/10/89	Crewe Alexandra	Home	Lge Cup	0–0		
47	07/10/89	Sunderland	Away	League	2–3	1 Goal	(26)
48	14/10/89	Oldham Athletic	Home	League	2–0		
49	17/10/89	Watford	Away	League	2–2	1 Goal	(27)
50	21/10/89	Portsmouth	Home	League	0–1		
51	24/10/89	Sunderland	Away	Lge Cup	1–1		

52	01/11/89	West Ham United	Home	League	1–1	1 Goal	(28)
53	04/11/89	Leeds United	Away	League	0–3		
54	07/11/89	Sunderland	Home	Lge Cup	0–1		
55	11/11/89	Sheffield United	Home	League	0–1		
56	18/11/89	Stoke City	Home	League	2–1		
57	25/11/89	Bradford City	Away	League	0–1		
58	28/11/89	Chelsea	Home	ZDS Cup	2–3*	1 Goal	(29)
59	02/12/89	Brighton & Hove Albion	Home	League	0–2		
60	05/12/89	Swindon Town	Away	League	3–2	2 Goals	(31)
61	09/12/89	West Bromwich Albion	Away	League	2–2	2 Goals	(33)
62	16/12/89	Barnsley	Home	League	2–1	1 Goal	(34)
63	26/12/89	Leicester City	Away	League	1–2		
64	30/12/89	Wolverhampton Wanderers	Away	League	1–3		
65	01/01/90	Plymouth Argyle	Home	League	2–2		
66	06/01/90	Sheffield United	Away	FA Cup	0–2		
67	13/01/90	Hull City	Away	League	4–1	1 Goal	(35)
68	20/01/90	Ipswich Town	Home	League	3–1	3 Goals	(38)
69	03/02/90	Blackburn Rovers	Away	League	1–1		
70	10/02/90	Middlesbrough	Home	League	2–2		
71	24/02/90	Bradford City	Home	League	1–0		
72	28/02/90	Newcastle United	Away	League	0–3		
73	03/03/90	Stoke City	Away	League	0–0		
74	06/03/90	Oxford United	Home	League	0–1		
75	10/03/90	Port Vale	Away	League	1–1		
76	17/03/90	Sunderland	Home	League	0–1		
77	20/03/90	Oldham Athletic	Away	League	0–4		
78	24/03/90	Watford	Home	League	0–0		
79	31/03/90	Portsmouth	Away	League	1–2		
80	03/04/90	Wolverhampton Wanderers	Home	League	1–1		
81	07/04/90	Swindon Town	Home	League	1–2	1 Goal	(39)
82	11/04/90	West Ham United	Away	League	1–4		
83	14/04/90	Plymouth Argyle	Away	League	0–1		
84	17/04/90	Leicester City	Home	League	2–3		
85	21/04/90	Barnsley	Away	League	1–0		
86	28/04/90	Sheffield United	Away	League	2–4	1 Goal	(40)
87	05/05/90	Leeds United	Home	League	0–1		

SEASON 1990–91

League Division Three

88	25/08/90	Brentford	Away	League	0–0		
89	28/08/90	Birmingham City	Away	Lge Cup	1–0	1 Goal	(41)
90	01/09/90	Bury	Home	League	1–1		
91	04/09/90	Birmingham City	Home	Lge Cup	1–1	1 Goal	(42)
92	08/09/90	Wigan Athletic	Away	League	0–2		
93	15/09/90	Stoke City	Home	League	1–1	1 Goal	(43)
94	18/09/90	Bradford City	Home	League	3–1	1 Goal	(44)
95	22/09/90	Exeter City	Away	League	0–2		
96	25/09/90	Millwall	Home	Lge Cup	0–0		
97	29/09/90	Fulham	Home	League	3–0	1 Goal	(45)
98	02/10/90	Reading	Away	League	1–2		
99	05/10/90	Southend United	Away	League	1–2		
100	10/10/90	Millwall	Away	Lge Cup	1–2		
101	20/10/90	Crewe Alexandra	Home	League	1–1	1 Goal	(46)
102	23/10/90	Huddersfield Town	Away	League	3–1	1 Goal	(47)
103	27/10/90	Preston North End	Away	League	0–0		
104	30/10/90	Tranmere Rovers	Home	League	1–0		
105	03/11/90	Shrewsbury Town	Home	League	3–2	1 Goal	(48)
106	05/11/90	Gillingham	Home	LD Cup	0–0		
107	10/11/90	Rotherham United	Home	League	4–2	3 Goals	(51)
108	17/11/90	Gillingham	Home	FA Cup	2–1		
109	24/11/90	Birmingham City	Away	League	0–0		
110	01/12/90	Chester City	Away	League	0–0		
111	08/12/90	Hayes	Home	FA Cup	1–0		
112	11/12/90	Maidstone United	Away	LD Cup	1–3		
113	14/12/90	Swansea City	Home	League	1–0	1 Goal	(52)
114	22/12/90	Grimsby Town	Away	League	0–5		
115	26/12/90	Mansfield Town	Home	League	0–0		
116	29/12/90	Leyton Orient	Home	League	2–2		
117	01/01/91	Bolton Wanderers	Away	League	1–4	1 Goal	(53)
118	05/01/91	Chester City	Away	FA Cup	3–2		
119	12/01/91	Bury	Away	League	4–2	1 Goal	(54)
120	19/01/91	Brentford	Home	League	2–0		
121	26/01/91	Portsmouth	Away	FA Cup	1–5		

122	02/02/91	Bradford City	Away	League	0–3		
123	05/02/91	Exeter City	Home	League	2–1	1 Goal	(55)
124	16/02/91	Birmingham City	Home	League	1–2		
125	23/02/91	Rotherham United	Away	League	1–1		
126	27/02/91	Stoke City	Away	League	3–1	1 Goal	(56)
127	02/03/91	Chester City	Home	League	1–0	1 Goal	(57)
128	05/03/91	Wigan Athletic	Home	League	0–3		
129	09/03/91	Swansea City	Away	League	2–1		
130	16/03/91	Fulham	Away	League	1–1		
131	18/03/91	Tranmere Rovers	Away	League	0–1		
132	23/03/91	Southend United	Home	League	3–1	1 Goal	(58)
133	30/03/91	Mansfield Town	Away	League	1–1		
134	02/04/91	Grimsby Town	Home	League	2–1		
135	06/04/91	Leyton Orient	Away	League	0–2		
136	13/04/91	Bolton Wanderers	Home	League	1–1		
137	16/04/91	Cambridge United	Home	League	0–1		
138	20/04/91	Crewe Alexandra	Away	League	2–0	2 Goals	(60)
139	24/04/91	Cambridge United	Away	League	0–4		
140	27/04/91	Huddersfield Town	Home	League	3–1	1 Goal	(61)
141	02/05/91	Preston North End	Home	League	0–0		
142	11/05/91	Shrewsbury Town	Away	League	1–3		

SEASON 1991–92

Watford – League Division Two

Sub+1	17/08/91	Wolverhampton Wanderers	Home	League	0–2		
1	20/08/91	Southend United	Home	Lge Cup	2–0	1 Goal	(1)
2	24/08/91	Newcastle United	Away	League	2–2	1 Goal	(2)
3	28/08/91	Southend United	Away	Lge Cup	1–1		
4	31/08/91	Cambridge United	Home	League	1–3	1 Goal	(3)
5	03/09/91	Barnsley	Away	League	3–0	1 Goal	(4)
6	07/09/91	Middlesbrough	Home	League	1–2		
7	14/09/91	Brighton & Hove Albion	Away	League	1–0		
8	17/09/91	Blackburn Rovers	Away	League	0–1		
9	21/09/91	Charlton Athletic	Home	League	2–0		
10	24/09/91	Everton	Away	Lge Cup	1–1		
11	28/09/91	Swindon Town	Away	League	1–3		
Sub+2	02/10/91	Southend United	Away	ZDS Cup	0–1		
12	05/10/91	Grimsby Town	Home	League	2–0		
13	08/10/91	Everton	Home	Lge Cup	1–2		
14	12/10/91	Bristol City	Away	League	0–1		
15	19/10/91	Southend United	Home	League	1–2		
16	26/10/91	Plymouth Argyle	Away	League	1–0		
17	29/10/91	Millwall	Home	League	0–2		
18	02/11/91	Sunderland	Away	League	1–3		
19	06/11/91	Oxford United	Home	League	2–0		
20	09/11/91	Leicester City	Home	League	0–1		
21	16/11/91	Bristol Rovers	Away	League	1–1	1 Goal	(5)
22	23/11/91	Portsmouth	Home	League	2–1	2 Goals	(7)
23	30/11/91	Port Vale	Away	League	1–2		
24	07/12/91	Derby County	Home	League	1–2	1 Goal	(8)
25	22/12/91	Barnsley	Home	League	1–1		
Sub+3	29/12/91	Cambridge United	Away	League	1–0		
26	01/01/92	Tranmere Rovers	Home	League	0–0		
27	04/01/92	Swindon Town	Away	FA Cup	2–3	2 Goals	(10)
28	11/01/92	Newcastle United	Home	League	2–2		
29	18/01/92	Wolverhampton Wanderers	Away	League	0–3		
30	24/01/92	Tranmere Rovers	Away	League	1–1		
31	01/02/92	Southend United	Away	League	0–1		
32	08/02/92	Plymouth Argyle	Home	League	1–0	1 Goal	(11)
33	22/02/92	Port Vale	Home	League	0–0		
34	29/02/92	Derby County	Away	League	1–3		
35	07/03/92	Ipswich Town	Home	League	0–1		
36	11/03/92	Oxford United	Away	League	0–0		
37	14/03/92	Sunderland	Home	League	1–0		
38	17/03/92	Ipswich Town	Away	League	2–1		
Sub+4	28/03/92	Bristol Rovers	Home	League	1–0		
Sub+5	04/04/92	Middlesbrough	Away	League	2–1		
Sub+6	11/04/92	Blackburn Rovers	Home	League	2–1		
Sub+7	18/04/92	Charlton Athletic	Away	League	1–1		
39	20/04/92	Swindon Town	Home	League	0–0		
Sub+8	25/04/92	Grimsby Town	Away	League	1–0		
Sub+9	02/05/92	Bristol City	Home	League	5–2	1 Goal	(12)

SEASON 1992–93

West Bromwich Albion (loan) – Football League Division Two

1	24/10/92	Rotherham United	Home	League	2–2		
2	03/11/92	Hartlepool United	Home	League	3–1	1 Goal	(1)
3	07/11/92	Leyton Orient	Away	League	0–2		

SEASON 1993–94

Bury – Football League Division Three

1	14/08/93	Northampton Town	Home	League	0–0		
2	17/08/93	Bolton Wanderers	Away	Lge Cup	2–0	1 Goal	(1)
3	21/08/93	Scunthorpe United	Away	League	1–1		
4	24/08/93	Bolton Wanderers	Home	Lge Cup	0–2+		
5	28/08/93	Crewe Alexandra	Home	League	1–0		
6	31/08/93	Preston North End	Away	League	1–3		
7	04/09/93	Shrewsbury Town	Away	League	0–1		
8	11/09/93	Wycombe Wanderers	Home	League	1–2	1 Goal	(2)
9	18/09/93	Lincoln City	Away	League	2–2		
10	25/09/93	Colchester United	Away	League	1–4		
Sub+1	09/10/93	Wigan Athletic	Home	League	3–0		

+ AET Bolton Wanderers won 3–0 on penalties

Derry City (loan) – Republic of Ireland – League Division One

1	17/10/93	Galway United	Away	League	1–2	1 Goal	(1)
2	24/10/93	Limerick	Home	League	0–0		
3	31/10/93	Limerick	Away	League	1–0		
4	07/11/93	Cobh Ramblers	Away	League	3–1		

Bury – Football League Division Three

| Sub+2 | 30/11/93 | Carlisle United | Away | A Trophy | 1–2 | | |

Mansfield Town (loan) – Football League Division Three

Sub+1	01/01/94	Torquay United	Away	League	0–1		
1	03/01/94	Chesterfield	Home	League	1–2		
2	15/01/94	Carlisle United	Home	League	0–1		
3	18/01/94	Hereford United	Home	League	2–1	1 Goal	(1)
4	22/01/94	Scarborough	Away	League	1–1		

Bury – Football League Division Three

| Sub+3 | 19/03/94 | Colchester United | Home | League | 0–1 | | |

INTERNATIONAL APPEARANCES – ENGLAND

Sub 1	13/10/82	West Germany	Wembley	1–2	F		
2	15/12/82	Luxembourg	Wembley	9–0	ECQ	3 Goals	(3)
3	23/02/83	Wales	Wembley	2–1	HC		
Sub 4	30/03/83	Greece	Wembley	0–0	ECQ		
5	27/04/83	Hungary	Wembley	2–0	ECQ		
6	28/05/83	Northern Ireland	Windsor Park	0–0	HC		
Sub 7	01/06/83	Scotland	Wembley	2–0	HC		
8	12/06/83	Australia	Sydney	0–0	F		
Sub 9	19/06/83	Australia	Melbourne	1–1	F		
Sub 10	21/09/83	Denmark	Wembley	0–1	ECQ		
11	12/10/83	Hungary	Budapest	3–0	ECQ		
Sub 12	02/05/84	Wales	Racecourse	0–1	HC		
13	26/05/84	Scotland	Hampden Park	1–1	HC		
14	02/06/84	USSR	Wembley	0–2	F		

APPEARANCES AND GOALS PER SEASON

SEASON 75–76	GAMES	GOALS
League	1+2	1
TOTAL	**1+2**	**1**

SEASON 76–77	GAMES	GOALS
League	1+3	0
TOTAL	**1+3**	**0**

SEASON 77–88	GAMES	GOALS
League	17+16	6
FA Cup	2	0
League Cup	1	0
TOTAL	**20+16**	**6**

SEASON 78–79	GAMES	GOALS
League	40+1	21
FA Cup	1	0
League Cup	6+1	7
TOTAL	**47+2**	**28**

SEASON 79–80	GAMES	GOALS
League	40+2	10
FA Cup	4	1
League Cup	2	0
TOTAL	**46+2**	**11**

SEASON 80–81	GAMES	GOALS
League	42	11
FA Cup	3	0
League Cup	8	2
TOTAL	**53**	**13**

SEASON 81–82	GAMES	GOALS
League	40	19
FA Cup	3	0
League Cup	6	3
Football League Group Cup	4	3
TOTAL	**53**	**25**

SEASON 82–83	GAMES	GOALS
League	41	27
FA Cup	4	2
League Cup	3	1
Football League Trophy	4	3
TOTAL	**52**	**33**

SEASON 83–84	GAMES	GOALS
Italian League	30	5
Italian Cup	9	1
TOTAL	**39**	**6**

SEASON 84–85	GAMES	GOALS
League	38+3	21
FA Cup	5	6
League Cup	5	1
TOTAL	**48+3**	**28**

SEASON 85–86	GAMES	GOALS
League	20+3	7
League Cup	3	1
TOTAL	**23+3**	**8**

SEASON 86–87	GAMES	GOALS
League	35	11
FA Cup	5	4
League Cup	1	0
Full Members Cup	1	0
TOTAL	**42**	**15**

SEASON 87–88	GAMES	GOALS
League	17+8	4
FA Cup	4+2	0
League Cup	1+2	1
TOTAL	**22+12**	**5**

SEASON 88–89	GAMES	GOALS
League	33	20
FA Cup	5	2
League Cup	1	0
TOTAL	**39**	**22**

SEASON 89–90	GAMES	GOALS
League	46	18
FA Cup	1	0
League Cup	4	0
Zenith Data Systems Cup	1	1
TOTAL	**52**	**19**

SEASON 90–91	GAMES	GOALS
League	45	19
FA Cup	4	0
League Cup	4	2
Leyland Daf Cup	2	0
TOTAL	**55**	**21**

SEASON 91–92	GAMES	GOALS
League	34+8	9
FA Cup	1	2
League Cup	4	1
Zenith Data Systems Cup	0+1	0
TOTAL	**39+9**	**12**

SEASON 92–93	GAMES	GOALS
League	3	1
TOTAL	**3**	**1**

SEASON 93–94	GAMES	GOALS
League	12+3	2
League Cup	2	1
Autoglass Trophy	0+1	0
Irish League	4	1
TOTAL	**18+4**	**4**

CAREER APPEARANCES AND GOALS

COMPETITION	GAMES	TOTAL	GOALS
League	505+49	554	207
FA Cup	42+2	44	17
League Cup	51+3	54	20
Football League Group Cup	4	4	3
Football League Trophy	4	4	3
Full Members Cup	1	1	0
Zenith Data Systems Cup	1+1	2	1
Leyland Daf Cup	2	2	0
Autoglass Trophy	0+1	1	0
Italian League	30	30	5
Italian Cup	9	9	1
Irish League	4	4	1
Internationals	8+6	14	3
TOTAL	**661+62**	**723**	**261**

HAT-TRICKS

Watford

1	4	Sunderland	25/09/82	Home	League	8–0
2	3	Notts County	12/03/83	Home	League	5–3
3	4	Sheffield United	05/01/85	Home	FA Cup	5–0

AFC Bournemouth

1	4	Hull City	29/11/88	Home	League	5–1
2	3	Ipswich Town	20/01/90	Home	League	3–1
3	3	Rotherham United	10/11/90	Home	League	4–2

England

1	3	Luxembourg	15/12/82	Wembley	ECQ	9–0

League: 5
FA Cup: 1
International: 1
TOTAL: 7

HONOURS

Winners medals
League Division Four Championship: 77/78

Runner-up medals
League Division One Championship: 82/83

League Division Two Championship: 81/82
League Division Three Championship: 78/79
Italian Cup: 83/84

MARK BRIGHT

Born: 06/06/62 – Stoke
Height: 6.0
Weight: 12.12 (96–97)

Clubs
Port Vale: **1982–84** – Matches: **21+13** – Goals: **11**
Leicester City: **1984–86** – Matches: **30+17** – Goals: **6**
Crystal Palace: **1986–92** – Matches: **282+4** – Goals: **113**
Sheffield Wednesday: **1992–97** – Matches: **148+22** – Goals: **70**
Millwall (loan): **1996–97** – Matches: **4** – Goals: **1**
FC Sion: **1997** – No Competitive Matches
Charlton Athletic: **1997** – Matches: **4+2** – Goals: **2**

SEASON 1981–82

Port Vale – League Division Four

Sub+1	01/05/82	York City	Home	League	0–0		
1	15/05/82	Torquay United	Home	League	2–0		

SEASON 1982–83

League Division Four

Sub+2	09/10/82	Hereford United	Home	League	2–0	1 Goal	(1)

SEASON 1983–84

League Division Three

2	27/08/83	Scunthorpe United	Home	League	0–0		
3	31/08/83	Wrexham	Home	Lge Cup	3–1		
4	26/09/83	Wigan Athletic	Home	Lge Cup	1–1		
5	01/10/83	Walsall	Away	League	0–2		
Sub+3	03/10/83	Manchester United	Home	Lge Cup	0–1		
Sub+4	14/10/83	Orient	Away	League	0–3		
6	31/10/83	Plymouth Argyle	Home	League	0–1		
Sub+5	19/11/83	Lincoln City	Home	FA Cup	1–2	1 Goal	(2)
Sub+6	31/12/83	Hull City	Away	League	0–1		
Sub+7	02/01/84	AFC Bournemouth	Home	League	2–1		
Sub+8	21/01/84	Wimbledon	Home	League	2–0	1 Goal	(3)
Sub+9	04/02/84	Walsall	Home	League	0–2		
7	11/02/84	Bradford City	Away	League	2–2		
Sub+10	14/02/84	Plymouth Argyle	Away	League	0–3		
Sub+11	18/02/84	Newport County	Home	League	4–2	1 Goal	(4)
8	22/02/84	Hereford United	Away	AM Cup	1–0		
9	25/02/84	Bolton Wanderers	Away	League	0–2		
10	10/03/84	Oxford United	Away	League	0–2		
11	13/03/84	Bristol Rovers	Away	AM Cup	0–2		
12	19/03/84	Southend United	Away	League	2–1	1 Goal	(5)
13	31/03/84	Wigan Athletic	Away	League	0–3		
Sub+12	02/04/84	Rotherham United	Home	League	2–3		
Sub+13	14/04/84	Gillingham	Away	League	1–1	1 Goal	(6)
14	17/04/84	Scunthorpe United	Away	League	1–1		
15	21/04/84	Preston North End	Home	League	1–1		
16	24/04/84	Sheffield United	Away	League	1–3	1 Goal	(7)
17	28/04/84	Burnley	Home	League	2–3	1 Goal	(8)
18	05/05/84	AFC Bournemouth	Away	League	1–1	1 Goal	(9)
19	07/05/84	Hull City	Home	League	1–0	1 Goal	(10)
20	12/05/84	Lincoln City	Away	League	2–3	1 Goal	(11)
21	14/05/84	Millwall	Home	League	1–0		

SEASON 1984–85

Leicester City – League Division One

1	25/08/84	Newcastle United	Home	League	2–3		
Sub+1	05/09/84	Watford	Home	League	1–1		

Sub+2	08/09/84	Ipswich Town	Home	League	2–1	
Sub+3	22/09/84	West Bromwich Albion	Home	League	2–1	
2	26/09/84	Brentford	Home	Lge Cup	4–2	
3	29/09/84	Chelsea	Away	League	0–3	
Sub+4	06/10/84	West Ham United	Away	League	1–3	
Sub+5	09/10/84	Brentford	Away	Lge Cup	2–0	
Sub+6	13/10/84	Arsenal	Home	League	1–4	
Sub+7	20/10/84	Sheffield Wednesday	Away	League	0–5	
Sub+8	23/02/85	Everton	Home	League	1–2	
Sub+9	09/03/85	Sheffield Wednesday	Home	League	3–1	
Sub+10	16/03/85	Arsenal	Away	League	0–2	
Sub+11	23/03/85	West Ham United	Home	League	1–0	
Sub+12	30/03/85	West Bromwich Albion	Away	League	0–2	
Sub+13	06/04/85	Liverpool	Home	League	0–1	
Sub+14	13/04/85	Tottenham Hotspur	Home	League	1–2	
Sub+15	11/05/85	Luton Town	Away	League	0–4	

SEASON 1985–86

League Division One

4	17/08/85	Everton	Home	League	3–1	2 Goals	(2)
5	21/08/85	Manchester City	Away	League	1–1		
6	24/08/85	Oxford United	Away	League	0–5		
7	28/08/85	Chelsea	Home	League	0–0		
8	31/08/85	Arsenal	Away	League	0–1		
9	04/09/85	Watford	Home	League	2–2	1 Goal	(3)
10	08/09/85	Nottingham Forest	Home	League	0–3		
11	14/09/85	West Ham United	Away	League	0–3		
12	21/09/85	Birmingham City	Away	League	1–2		
13	25/09/85	Derby County	Away	Lge Cup	0–2		
14	28/09/85	Ipswich Town	Home	League	1–0		
15	02/10/85	Oxford United	Home	League	4–4		
16	06/10/85	Coventry City	Away	League	0–3		
17	09/10/85	Derby County	Home	Lge Cup	1–1		
18	12/10/85	West Bromwich Albion	Home	League	2–2		
19	19/10/85	Sheffield Wednesday	Home	League	2–3		
20	26/10/85	Tottenham Hotspur	Away	League	3–1	1 Goal	(4)
21	02/11/85	Liverpool	Away	League	0–1		
22	09/11/85	Southampton	Home	League	2–2		
23	16/11/85	Queens Park Rangers	Away	League	0–2		
Sub+16	14/12/85	Everton	Away	League	2–1		
Sub+17	26/12/85	Aston Villa	Home	League	3–1	1 Goal	(5)
24	28/12/85	Watford	Away	League	1–2		
25	01/01/86	Luton Town	Away	League	1–3	1 Goal	(6)
26	04/01/86	Bristol Rovers	Away	FA Cup	1–3		
27	11/01/86	West Ham United	Home	League	0–1		
28	14/04/86	Queens Park Rangers	Home	League	1–4		

SEASON 1986–87

League Division One

29	23/08/86	Luton Town	Home	League	1–1		
30	30/08/86	Wimbledon	Away	League	0–1		

Crystal Palace – League Division Two

1	15/11/86	Ipswich Town	Home	League	3–3	1 Goal	(1)
2	22/11/86	Oldham Athletic	Away	League	0–1		
3	29/11/86	Sunderland	Home	League	2–0	1 Goal	(2)
4	06/12/86	Portsmouth	Away	League	0–2		
5	13/12/86	Hull City	Home	League	5–1		
6	20/12/86	Huddersfield Town	Away	League	2–1	2 Goals	(4)
7	26/12/86	Brighton & Hove Albion	Home	League	2–0		
8	27/12/86	Ipswich Town	Away	League	0–3		
9	01/01/87	West Bromwich Albion	Away	League	2–1	1 Goal	(5)
10	03/01/87	Derby County	Home	League	1–0		
11	11/01/87	Nottingham Forest	Home	FA Cup	1–0		
12	24/01/87	Barnsley	Home	League	0–1		
13	31/01/87	Tottenham Hotspur	Away	FA Cup	0–4		
14	07/02/87	Stoke City	Away	League	1–3		
15	14/02/87	Bradford City	Home	League	1–1		
16	21/02/87	Reading	Away	League	0–1		
17	28/02/87	Blackburn Rovers	Home	League	2–0		
18	14/03/87	Birmingham City	Home	League	6–0		
19	17/03/87	Sheffield United	Away	League	0–1		

20	21/03/87	Leeds United	Home	League	1–0		
21	24/03/87	Shrewsbury Town	Away	League	0–0		
22	28/03/87	Millwall	Away	League	1–0	1 Goal	(6)
23	04/04/87	Grimsby Town	Away	League	1–0	1 Goal	(7)
24	11/04/87	Plymouth Argyle	Home	League	0–0		
25	18/04/87	West Bromwich Albion	Home	League	1–1		
26	20/04/87	Brighton & Hove Albion	Away	League	0–2		
27	25/04/87	Oldham Athletic	Home	League	2–1	1 Goal	(8)
28	02/05/87	Sunderland	Away	League	0–1		
29	04/05/87	Portsmouth	Home	League	1–0		
30	09/05/87	Hull City	Away	League	0–3		

SEASON 1987–88

League Division Two

31	15/08/87	Huddersfield Town	Away	League	2–2	2 Goals	(10)
32	22/08/87	Hull City	Home	League	2–2		
33	29/08/87	Barnsley	Away	League	1–2	1 Goal	(11)
34	01/09/87	Middlesbrough	Home	League	3–1	2 Goals	(13)
35	05/09/87	Birmingham City	Away	League	6–0	1 Goal	(14)
36	08/09/87	West Bromwich Albion	Home	League	4–1	2 Goals	(16)
37	12/09/87	Leicester City	Home	League	2–1		
38	15/09/87	Sheffield United	Away	League	1–1		
39	19/09/87	Reading	Away	League	3–2	1 Goal	(17)
40	26/09/87	Ipswich Town	Home	League	1–2		
41	03/10/87	Shrewsbury Town	Away	League	0–2		
42	06/10/87	Newport County	Away	Lge Cup	2–0	1 Goal	(18)
43	10/10/87	Millwall	Home	League	1–0	1 Goal	(19)
44	21/10/87	Aston Villa	Away	League	1–4		
45	24/10/87	Swindon Town	Home	League	2–1	1 Goal	(20)
46	28/10/87	Manchester United	Away	Lge Cup	1–2		
47	31/10/87	Bradford City	Away	League	0–2		
48	03/11/87	Plymouth Argyle	Home	League	5–1		
49	07/11/87	AFC Bournemouth	Away	League	3–2	2 Goals	(22)
50	11/11/87	Oxford United	Away	Simod Cup	0–1		
51	14/11/87	Stoke City	Home	League	2–0	1 Goal	(23)
52	21/11/87	Blackburn Rovers	Away	League	0–2		
53	28/11/87	Leeds United	Home	League	3–0	1 Goal	(24)
54	05/12/87	Manchester City	Away	League	3–1	2 Goals	(26)
Sub+1	09/01/88	Newcastle United	Away	FA Cup	0–1		
55	16/01/88	Huddersfield Town	Home	League	2–1		
56	23/01/88	Middlesbrough	Away	League	2–1		
57	29/01/88	Oldham Athletic	Away	League	0–1		
58	06/02/88	Birmingham City	Home	League	3–0	1 Goal	(27)
59	13/02/88	West Bromwich Albion	Away	League	0–1		
60	27/02/88	Shrewsbury Town	Home	League	1–2		
61	05/03/88	Oldham Athletic	Home	League	3–1		
62	12/03/88	Millwall	Away	League	1–1		
63	19/03/88	Bradford City	Home	League	1–1		
64	27/03/88	Swindon Town	Away	League	2–2	1 Goal	(28)
65	02/04/88	AFC Bournemouth	Home	League	3–0	1 Goal	(29)
66	04/04/88	Stoke City	Away	League	1–1	1 Goal	(30)
67	09/04/88	Aston Villa	Home	League	1–1		
68	23/04/88	Plymouth Argyle	Away	League	3–1	2 Goals	(32)
69	30/04/88	Blackburn Rovers	Home	League	2–0	1 Goal	(33)
70	02/05/88	Leeds United	Away	League	0–1		
71	07/05/88	Manchester City	Home	League	2–0		

SEASON 1988–89

League Division Two

72	30/08/88	Chelsea	Home	League	1–1		
73	03/09/88	Watford	Home	League	0–2		
74	10/09/88	Walsall	Away	League	0–0		
75	17/09/88	Shrewsbury Town	Home	League	1–1		
76	20/09/88	Sunderland	Away	League	1–1		
77	24/09/88	Portsmouth	Away	League	1–1		
78	27/09/88	Swindon Town	Away	Lge Cup	2–1	1 Goal	(34)
79	01/10/88	Plymouth Argyle	Home	League	4–1	1 Goal	(35)
80	04/10/88	Ipswich Town	Home	League	2–0	1 Goal	(36)
81	08/10/88	Blackburn Rovers	Away	League	4–5	1 Goal	(37)
82	12/10/88	Swindon Town	Home	Lge Cup	2–0		
83	15/10/88	Bradford City	Away	League	1–0		
84	22/10/88	Hull City	Home	League	3–1		
85	25/10/88	Oxford United	Home	League	1–0		

86	29/10/88	Stoke City	Away	League	1–2	1 Goal	(38)
87	01/11/88	Bristol City	Away	Lge Cup	1–4		
88	05/11/88	Barnsley	Home	League	1–1	1 Goal	(39)
89	12/11/88	AFC Bournemouth	Away	League	0–2		
90	19/11/88	Leicester City	Home	League	4–2	1 Goal	(40)
91	22/11/88	Walsall	Home	Simod Cup	4–2		
92	26/11/88	West Bromwich Albion	Away	League	3–5		
93	03/12/88	Manchester City	Home	League	0–0		
94	10/12/88	Birmingham City	Away	League	1–0		
95	13/12/88	Southampton	Away	Simod Cup	2–1		
96	17/12/88	Leeds United	Home	League	0–0		
97	26/12/88	Brighton & Hove Albion	Away	League	1–3		
98	30/12/88	Oldham Athletic	Away	League	3–2		
99	02/01/89	Walsall	Home	League	4–0	3 Goals	(43)
100	07/01/89	Stoke City	Away	FA Cup	0–1		
101	10/01/89	Luton Town	Home	Simod Cup	4–1	3 Goals	(46)
102	14/01/89	Chelsea	Away	League	0–1		
103	21/01/89	Swindon Town	Home	League	2–1	2 Goals	(48)
104	28/01/89	Middlesbrough	Away	Simod Cup	3–2		
105	04/02/89	Ipswich Town	Away	League	2–1		
106	11/02/89	Blackburn Rovers	Home	League	2–2	1 Goal	(49)
107	22/02/89	Nottingham Forest	Away	Simod Cup	1–3		
108	25/02/89	Bradford City	Home	League	2–0	2 Goals	(51)
109	01/03/89	Oxford United	Away	League	0–1		
110	04/03/89	AFC Bournemouth	Home	League	2–3		
111	11/03/89	Barnsley	Away	League	1–1		
112	18/03/89	Sunderland	Home	League	1–0	1 Goal	(52)
113	24/03/89	Watford	Away	League	1–0		
114	27/03/89	Brighton & Hove Albion	Home	League	2–1	1 Goal	(53)
115	01/04/89	Shrewsbury Town	Away	League	1–2		
116	05/04/89	Leeds United	Away	League	2–1		
117	08/04/89	Oldham Athletic	Home	League	2–0	1 Goal	(54)
118	11/04/89	Hull City	Away	League	1–0		
119	15/04/89	Portsmouth	Home	League	2–0	1 Goal	(55)
120	22/04/89	Plymouth Argyle	Away	League	2–0	2 Goals	(57)
121	25/04/89	Swindon Town	Away	League	0–1		
122	29/04/89	West Bromwich Albion	Home	League	1–0		
123	01/05/89	Manchester City	Away	League	1–1		
124	06/05/89	Leicester City	Away	League	2–2		
125	09/05/89	Stoke City	Home	League	1–0		
126	13/05/89	Birmingham City	Home	League	4–1		
127	21/05/89	Swindon Town	Away	Lge P/O	0–1		
128	24/05/89	Swindon Town	Home	Lge P/O	2–0	1 Goal	(58)
129	31/05/89	Blackburn Rovers	Away	Lge P/O	1–3		
130	03/06/89	Blackburn Rovers	Home	Lge P/O	3–0*		

SEASON 1989–90

League Division One

131	19/08/89	Queens Park Rangers	Away	League	0–2		
132	22/08/89	Manchester United	Home	League	1–1		
133	26/08/89	Coventry City	Home	League	0–1		
134	09/09/89	Wimbledon	Home	League	2–0		
135	12/09/89	Liverpool	Away	League	0–9		
136	16/09/89	Southampton	Away	League	1–1		
137	19/09/89	Leicester City	Home	Lge Cup	1–2		
138	23/09/89	Nottingham Forest	Home	League	1–0		
139	30/09/89	Everton	Home	League	2–1		
140	04/10/89	Leicester City	Away	Lge Cup	3–2*	1 Goal	(59)
141	14/10/89	Derby County	Away	League	1–3		
142	21/10/89	Millwall	Home	League	4–3	2 Goals	(61)
143	24/10/89	Nottingham Forest	Home	Lge Cup	0–0		
144	28/10/89	Aston Villa	Away	League	1–2		
145	01/11/89	Nottingham Forest	Away	Lge Cup	0–5		
146	04/11/89	Manchester City	Away	League	0–3		
147	11/11/89	Luton Town	Home	League	1–1	1 Goal	(62)
148	18/11/89	Tottenham Hotspur	Home	League	2–3	2 Goals	(64)
149	25/11/89	Sheffield Wednesday	Away	League	2–2		
150	27/11/89	Luton Town	Home	ZDS Cup	4–1	2 Goals	(66)
151	02/12/89	Queens Park Rangers	Home	League	0–3		
152	09/12/89	Manchester United	Away	League	2–1	2 Goals	(68)
153	16/12/89	Charlton Athletic	Away	League	2–1	1 Goal	(69)
154	19/12/89	Charlton Athletic	Home	ZDS Cup	2–0		
155	26/12/89	Chelsea	Home	League	2–2		
156	30/12/89	Norwich City	Home	League	1–0		

157	01/01/90	Arsenal	Away	League	1–4		
158	06/01/90	Portsmouth	Home	FA Cup	2–1		
159	13/01/90	Coventry City	Away	League	0–1		
160	20/01/90	Liverpool	Home	League	0–2		
161	27/01/90	Huddersfield Town	Home	FA Cup	4–0	1 Goal	(70)
162	03/02/90	Nottingham Forest	Away	League	1–3		
163	10/02/90	Southampton	Home	League	3–1		
164	13/02/90	Swindon Town	Home	ZDS Cup	1–0		
165	17/02/90	Rochdale	Home	FA Cup	1–0		
166	21/02/90	Chelsea	Home	ZDS Cup	0–2		
167	24/02/90	Sheffield Wednesday	Home	League	1–1	1 Goal	(71)
168	03/03/90	Tottenham Hotspur	Away	League	1–0		
169	24/03/90	Aston Villa	Home	League	1–0		
170	31/03/90	Millwall	Away	League	2–1	1 Goal	(72)
171	04/04/90	Norwich City	Away	League	0–2		
172	08/04/90	Liverpool	Neutral	FA Cup	4–3*	1 Goal	(73)
173	14/04/90	Arsenal	Home	League	1–1		
174	16/04/90	Chelsea	Away	League	0–3		
175	21/04/90	Charlton Athletic	Home	League	2–0	1 Goal	(74)
176	28/04/90	Luton Town	Away	League	0–1		
177	02/05/90	Wimbledon	Away	League	1–0	1 Goal	(75)
178	05/05/90	Manchester City	Home	League	2–2		
179	12/05/90	Manchester United	Wembley	FA Cup	3–3*		
180	17/05/90	Manchester United	Wembley	FA Cup	0–1		

SEASON 1990–91

League Division One

Sub+2	01/09/90	Sheffield United	Home	League	1–0		
Sub+3	15/09/90	Nottingham Forest	Home	League	2–2		
Sub+4	22/09/90	Tottenham Hotspur	Away	League	1–1		
181	25/09/90	Southend United	Home	Lge Cup	8–0	3 Goals	(78)
182	29/09/90	Derby County	Away	League	2–0	1 Goal	(79)
183	06/10/90	Leeds United	Home	League	1–1		
184	09/10/90	Southend United	Away	Lge Cup	2–1		
185	20/10/90	Everton	Away	League	0–0		
186	27/10/90	Wimbledon	Home	League	4–3	1 Goal	(80)
187	30/10/90	Leyton Orient	Home	Lge Cup	0–0		
188	03/11/90	Manchester United	Away	League	0–2		
189	07/11/90	Leyton Orient	Away	Lge Cup	1–0	1 Goal	(81)
190	10/11/90	Arsenal	Home	League	0–0		
191	17/11/90	Queens Park Rangers	Away	League	2–1		
192	24/11/90	Southampton	Away	League	3–2	1 Goal	(82)
193	27/11/90	Southampton	Away	Lge Cup	0–2		
194	01/12/90	Coventry City	Home	League	2–1	1 Goal	(83)
195	08/12/90	Chelsea	Away	League	1–2		
196	16/12/90	Luton Town	Home	League	1–0	1 Goal	(84)
197	18/12/90	Bristol Rovers	Home	ZDS Cup	2–1		
198	22/12/90	Manchester City	Away	League	2–0		
199	26/12/90	Sunderland	Home	League	2–1	1 Goal	(85)
200	30/12/90	Liverpool	Home	League	1–0	1 Goal	(86)
201	01/01/91	Aston Villa	Away	League	0–2		
202	06/01/91	Nottingham Forest	Home	FA Cup	0–0		
203	12/01/91	Sheffield United	Away	League	1–0	1 Goal	(87)
204	19/01/91	Norwich City	Home	League	1–3	1 Goal	(88)
205	21/01/91	Nottingham Forest	Away	FA Cup	2–2*		
206	28/01/91	Nottingham Forest	Away	FA Cup	0–3		
207	02/02/91	Nottingham Forest	Away	League	1–0		
208	16/02/91	Queens Park Rangers	Home	League	0–0		
209	18/02/91	Brighton & Hove Albion	Away	ZDS Cup	2–0*	1 Goal	(89)
210	23/02/91	Arsenal	Away	League	0–4		
211	26/02/91	Luton Town	Home	ZDS Cup	3–1		
212	02/03/91	Coventry City	Away	League	1–3		
213	05/03/91	Norwich City	Away	ZDS Cup	1–1		
214	09/03/91	Southampton	Home	League	2–1		
215	16/03/91	Derby County	Home	League	2–1		
216	19/03/91	Norwich City	Home	ZDS Cup	2–0	1 Goal	(90)
217	23/03/91	Leeds United	Away	League	2–1		
218	30/03/91	Sunderland	Away	League	1–2		
219	01/04/91	Manchester City	Home	League	1–3		
220	07/04/91	Everton	Wembley	ZDS Cup	4–1*		
221	13/04/91	Aston Villa	Home	League	0–0		
222	17/04/91	Tottenham Hotspur	Home	League	1–0		
223	11/05/91	Manchester United	Home	League	3–0		

SEASON 1991–92

League Division One

224	24/08/91	Manchester City	Away	League	2–3	1 Goal	(91)
225	27/08/91	Wimbledon	Home	League	3–2	1 Goal	(92)
226	31/08/91	Sheffield United	Home	League	2–1		
227	04/09/91	Aston Villa	Away	League	1–0		
228	07/09/91	Everton	Away	League	2–2	1 Goal	(93)
229	14/09/91	Arsenal	Home	League	1–4	1 Goal	(94)
230	17/09/91	West Ham United	Home	League	2–3		
231	21/09/91	Oldham Athletic	Away	League	3–2	1 Goal	(95)
232	25/09/91	Hartlepool United	Away	Lge Cup	1–1	1 Goal	(96)
233	28/09/91	Queens Park Rangers	Home	League	2–2	1 Goal	(97)
234	01/10/91	Leeds United	Home	League	1–0	1 Goal	(98)
235	05/10/91	Sheffield Wednesday	Away	League	1–4	1 Goal	(99)
236	08/10/91	Hartlepool United	Home	Lge Cup	6–1	2 Goals	(101)
237	19/10/91	Coventry City	Away	League	2–1	1 Goal	(102)
238	22/10/91	Southend United	Home	ZDS Cup	4–0	1 Goal	(103)
239	26/10/91	Chelsea	Home	League	0–0		
240	29/10/91	Birmingham City	Away	Lge Cup	1–1		
241	02/11/91	Liverpool	Away	League	2–1		
242	16/11/91	Southampton	Home	League	1–0		
243	19/11/91	Birmingham City	Home	Lge Cup	1–1*		
244	23/11/91	Nottingham Forest	Away	League	1–5		
245	26/11/91	Queens Park Rangers	Away	ZDS Cup	3–2		
246	30/11/91	Manchester United	Home	League	1–3		
247	03/12/91	Birmingham City	Home	Lge Cup	2–1		
248	07/12/91	Norwich City	Away	League	3–3		
249	10/12/91	Chelsea	Home	ZDS Cup	0–1		
250	17/12/91	Swindon Town	Away	Lge Cup	1–0		
251	22/12/91	Tottenham Hotspur	Home	League	1–2		
252	26/12/91	Wimbledon	Away	League	1–1		
253	28/12/91	Sheffield United	Away	League	1–1		
254	01/01/92	Notts County	Home	League	1–0		
255	04/01/92	Leicester City	Away	FA Cup	0–1		
256	08/01/92	Nottingham Forest	Home	Lge Cup	1–1		
257	11/01/92	Manchester City	Home	League	1–1	1 Goal	(104)
258	18/01/92	Leeds United	Away	League	1–1		
259	01/02/92	Coventry City	Home	League	0–1		
260	05/02/92	Nottingham Forest	Away	Lge Cup	2–4	1 Goal	(105)
261	08/02/92	Chelsea	Away	League	1–1		
262	16/02/92	Tottenham Hotspur	Away	League	1–0		
263	22/02/92	Manchester United	Away	League	0–2		
264	25/02/92	Luton Town	Home	League	1–1	1 Goal	(106)
265	29/02/92	Norwich City	Home	League	3–4	2 Goals	(108)
266	03/03/92	Nottingham Forest	Home	League	0–0		
267	07/03/92	Luton Town	Away	League	1–1		
268	11/03/92	Southampton	Away	League	0–1		
269	14/03/92	Liverpool	Home	League	1–0		
270	21/03/92	Aston Villa	Home	League	0–0		
271	28/03/92	Notts County	Away	League	3–2	1 Goal	(109)
272	04/04/92	Everton	Home	League	2–0	1 Goal	(110)
273	11/04/92	Arsenal	Away	League	1–4		
274	18/04/92	Oldham Athletic	Home	League	0–0		
275	20/04/92	West Ham United	Away	League	2–0	1 Goal	(111)
276	25/04/92	Sheffield Wednesday	Home	League	1–1	1 Goal	(112)
277	02/05/92	Queens Park Rangers	Away	League	0–1		

SEASON 1992–93

Premier League

278	15/08/92	Blackburn Rovers	Home	League	3–3	1 Goal	(113)
279	25/08/92	Sheffield Wednesday	Home	League	1–1		
280	29/08/92	Norwich City	Home	League	1–2		
281	02/09/92	Manchester United	Away	League	0–1		
282	05/09/92	Aston Villa	Away	League	0–3		

Sheffield Wednesday – Premier League

1	12/09/92	Nottingham Forest	Away	League	2–1		
2	19/09/92	Norwich City	Away	League	0–1		
3	23/09/92	Hartlepool United	Home	Lge Cup	3–0	1 Goal	(1)
4	27/09/92	Tottenham Hotspur	Home	League	2–0	1 Goal	(2)
5	03/10/92	Liverpool	Away	League	0–1		
6	06/10/92	Hartlepool United	Away	Lge Cup	2–2	1 Goal	(3)
7	17/10/92	Oldham Athletic	Home	League	2–1	1 Goal	(4)

8	24/10/92	Middlesbrough	Away	League	1–1	1 Goal	(5)
9	27/10/92	Leicester City	Home	Lge Cup	7–1	2 Goals	(7)
10	31/10/92	Blackburn Rovers	Home	League	0–0		
11	08/11/92	Sheffield United	Away	League	1–1		
12	21/11/92	Ipswich Town	Home	League	1–1		
13	28/11/92	Wimbledon	Away	League	1–1		
14	02/12/92	Queens Park Rangers	Home	Lge Cup	4–0	1 Goal	(8)
15	05/12/92	Aston Villa	Home	League	1–2	1 Goal	(9)
16	12/12/92	Leeds United	Away	League	1–3		
17	19/12/92	Queens Park Rangers	Home	League	1–0	1 Goal	(10)
18	26/12/92	Manchester United	Home	League	3–3	1 Goal	(11)
19	28/12/92	Southampton	Away	League	2–1		
20	10/01/93	Norwich City	Home	League	1–0		
21	13/01/93	Cambridge United	Away	FA Cup	2–1	1 Goal	(12)
22	16/01/93	Tottenham Hotspur	Away	League	2–0	1 Goal	(13)
23	19/01/93	Ipswich Town	Away	Lge Cup	1–1		
24	24/01/93	Sunderland	Home	FA Cup	1–0	1 Goal	(14)
Sub+1	23/02/93	Manchester City	Away	League	2–1		
25	27/02/93	Liverpool	Home	League	1–1		
26	03/03/93	Coventry City	Away	League	0–1		
27	08/03/93	Derby County	Away	FA Cup	3–3		
28	10/03/93	Ipswich Town	Away	League	1–0		
29	14/03/93	Blackburn Rovers	Home	Lge Cup	2–1	1 Goal	(15)
30	17/03/93	Derby County	Home	FA Cup	1–0		
31	20/03/93	Aston Villa	Away	League	0–2		
32	24/03/93	Wimbledon	Home	League	1–1	1 Goal	(16)
33	03/04/93	Sheffield United	Wembley	FA Cup	2–1	1 Goal	(17)
Sub+2	10/04/93	Manchester United	Away	League	1–2		
34	12/04/93	Southampton	Home	League	5–2	1 Goal	(18)
35	18/04/93	Arsenal	Wembley	Lge Cup	1–2		
36	21/04/93	Sheffield United	Home	League	1–1		
37	01/05/93	Middlesbrough	Home	League	2–3		
38	06/05/93	Arsenal	Home	League	1–0	1 Goal	(19)
39	08/05/93	Blackburn Rovers	Away	League	0–1		
40	11/05/93	Queens Park Rovers	Away	League	1–3	1 Goal	(20)
41	15/05/93	Arsenal	Wembley	FA Cup	1–1*		
42	20/05/93	Arsenal	Wembley	FA Cup	1–2*		

SEASON 1993–94

Premier League

Sub+3	14/08/93	Liverpool	Away	League	0–2		
Sub+4	18/08/93	Aston Villa	Home	League	0–0		
Sub+5	21/08/93	Arsenal	Home	League	0–1		
Sub+6	25/08/93	West Ham United	Away	League	0–2		
43	28/08/93	Chelsea	Away	League	1–1	1 Goal	(21)
44	01/09/93	Norwich City	Home	League	3–3	1 Goal	(22)
45	13/09/93	Newcastle United	Away	League	2–4		
46	18/09/93	Southampton	Home	League	2–0		
47	21/09/93	Bolton Wanderers	Away	Lge Cup	1–1		
48	25/09/93	Blackburn Rovers	Away	League	1–1		
49	02/10/93	Manchester United	Home	League	2–3	1 Goal	(23)
50	06/10/93	Bolton Wanderers	Home	Lge Cup	1–0	1 Goal	(24)
51	16/10/93	Wimbledon	Home	League	2–2		
52	23/10/93	Sheffield United	Away	League	1–1		
53	26/10/93	Middlesbrough	Away	Lge Cup	1–1		
54	30/10/93	Leeds United	Home	League	3–3	1 Goal	(25)
55	06/11/93	Ipswich Town	Away	League	4–1	1 Goal	(26)
56	27/11/93	Manchester City	Away	League	3–1		
57	01/12/93	Queens Park Rangers	Away	Lge Cup	2–1		
58	04/12/93	Liverpool	Home	League	3–1	1 Goal	(27)
59	08/12/93	Aston Villa	Away	League	2–2		
60	12/12/93	Arsenal	Away	League	0–1		
61	18/12/93	West Ham United	Home	League	5–0	1 Goal	(28)
62	27/12/93	Everton	Away	League	2–0	1 Goal	(29)
63	29/12/93	Swindon Town	Home	League	3–3	1 Goal	(30)
64	01/01/94	Queens Park Rangers	Away	League	2–1	1 Goal	(31)
65	03/01/94	Tottenham Hotspur	Home	League	1–0	1 Goal	(32)
66	08/01/94	Nottingham Forest	Home	FA Cup	1–1	1 Goal	(33)
67	11/01/94	Wimbledon	Away	Lge Cup	2–1	1 Goal	(34)
68	15/01/94	Wimbledon	Away	League	1–2		
69	19/01/94	Nottingham Forest	Away	FA Cup	2–0		
70	22/01/94	Sheffield United	Home	League	3–1	1 Goal	(35)
71	05/02/94	Tottenham Hotspur	Away	League	3–1	2 Goals	(37)
72	09/02/94	Chelsea	Home	FA Cup	1–3*	1 Goal	(38)

73	13/02/94	Manchester United	Away	Lge Cup	0–1		
74	25/02/94	Norwich City	Away	League	1–1		
75	02/03/94	Manchester United	Home	Lge Cup	1–4		
76	05/03/94	Newcastle United	Home	League	0–1		
77	12/03/94	Southampton	Away	League	1–1		
78	16/03/94	Manchester United	Away	League	0–5		
79	20/03/94	Blackburn Rovers	Home	League	1–2		
80	30/03/94	Chelsea	Home	League	3–1		
81	02/04/94	Everton	Home	League	5–1	2 Goals	(40)
82	04/04/94	Swindon Town	Away	League	1–0		
83	09/04/94	Queens Park Rangers	Home	League	3–1	2 Goals	(42)
84	16/04/94	Coventry City	Away	League	1–1		
85	23/04/94	Ipswich Town	Home	League	5–0	1 Goal	(43)
86	30/04/94	Oldham Athletic	Away	League	0–0		
87	03/05/94	Leeds United	Away	League	2–2		
88	07/05/94	Manchester City	Home	League	1–1		

SEASON 1994–95

Premier League

89	20/08/94	Tottenham Hotspur	Home	League	3–4		
90	31/08/94	Norwich City	Home	League	0–0		
91	17/09/94	Manchester City	Home	League	1–1		
92	21/09/94	Bradford City	Home	Lge Cup	2–1		
93	26/09/94	Leeds United	Home	League	1–1	1 Goal	(44)
94	01/10/94	Liverpool	Away	League	1–4		
95	04/10/94	Bradford City	Away	Lge Cup	1–1		
96	08/10/94	Manchester United	Home	League	1–0		
97	16/10/94	Ipswich Town	Away	League	2–1	1 Goal	(45)
98	22/10/94	Newcastle United	Away	League	1–2		
99	26/10/94	Southampton	Home	Lge Cup	1–0		
100	29/10/94	Chelsea	Home	League	1–1	1 Goal	(46)
101	02/11/94	Blackburn Rovers	Home	League	0–1		
102	06/11/94	Arsenal	Away	League	0–0		
103	19/11/94	West Ham United	Home	League	1–0		
104	03/12/94	Crystal Palace	Home	League	1–0		
105	10/12/94	Tottenham Hotspur	Away	League	1–3		
106	17/12/94	Queens Park Rangers	Home	League	0–2		
107	26/12/94	Everton	Away	League	4–1	1 Goal	(47)
108	28/12/94	Coventry City	Home	League	5–1	2 Goals	(49)
109	31/12/94	Leicester City	Away	League	1–0		
110	02/01/95	Southampton	Home	League	1–1		
111	07/01/95	Gillingham	Away	FA Cup	2–1	1 Goal	(50)
112	14/01/95	Chelsea	Away	League	1–1		
Sub+7	21/01/95	Newcastle United	Home	League	0–0		
113	23/01/95	West Ham United	Away	League	2–0	1 Goal	(51)
114	30/01/95	Wolverhampton Wanderers	Home	FA Cup	0–0		
115	04/02/95	Arsenal	Home	League	3–1	1 Goal	(52)
116	08/02/95	Wolverhampton Wanderers	Away	FA Cup	1–1+	1 Goal	(53)
117	12/02/95	Blackburn Rovers	Away	League	1–3		
118	18/02/95	Aston Villa	Home	League	1–2	1 Goal	(54)
119	25/02/95	Liverpool	Home	League	1–2		
120	04/03/95	Leeds United	Away	League	1–0		
121	08/03/95	Norwich City	Away	League	0–0		
122	11/03/95	Wimbledon	Home	League	0–1		
123	14/03/95	Crystal Palace	Away	League	1–2		
124	18/03/95	Manchester City	Away	League	2–3		
125	01/04/95	Nottingham Forest	Home	League	1–7	1 Goal	(55)
Sub+8	08/04/95	Leicester City	Home	League	1–0		
Sub+9	17/04/95	Everton	Home	League	0–0		
126	29/04/95	Southampton	Away	League	0–0		
127	07/05/95	Manchester United	Away	League	0–1		
Sub+10	14/05/95	Ipswich Town	Home	League	4–1	1 Goal	(56)

+ AET Wolverhampton Wanderers won 4–3 on penalties

SEASON 1995–96

Premier League

128	08/07/95	Gornik Zabrze	Home	IT Cup	3–2+	1 Goal	(57)
129	15/07/95	Karlsruhe	Away	IT Cup	1–1	1 Goal	(58)
130	22/07/95	AGF Aarhus	Home	IT Cup	3–1+	2 Goals	(60)
131	19/08/95	Liverpool	Away	League	0–1		
132	23/08/95	Blackburn Rovers	Home	League	2–1		
133	27/08/95	Newcastle United	Home	League	0–2		

134	30/08/95	Wimbledon	Away	League	2–2		
135	09/09/95	Queens Park Rangers	Away	League	3–0	2 Goals	(62)
136	16/09/95	Tottenham Hotspur	Home	League	1–3		
137	19/09/95	Crewe Alexandra	Away	Lge Cup	2–2		
Sub+11	23/09/95	Manchester United	Home	League	0–0		
Sub+12	30/09/95	Leeds United	Away	League	0–2		
138	04/10/95	Crewe Alexandra	Home	Lge Cup	5–2	3 Goals	(65)
139	15/10/95	Middlesbrough	Home	League	0–1		
140	21/10/95	Coventry City	Away	League	1–0		
Sub+13	25/10/95	Millwall	Away	Lge Cup	2–0		
Sub+14	28/10/95	West Ham United	Home	League	0–1		
141	04/11/95	Chelsea	Away	League	0–0		
Sub+15	21/11/95	Arsenal	Away	League	2–4		
142	25/11/95	Everton	Away	League	2–2	2 Goals	(67)
143	29/11/95	Arsenal	Away	Lge Cup	1–2		
144	04/12/95	Coventry City	Home	League	4–3	1 Goal	(68)
145	09/12/95	Manchester United	Away	League	2–2	1 Goal	(69)
146	16/12/95	Leeds United	Home	League	6–2	1 Goal	(70)
147	23/12/95	Southampton	Home	League	2–2		
Sub+16	26/12/95	Nottingham Forest	Away	League	0–1		
Sub+17	01/01/96	Bolton Wanderers	Home	League	4–2		
Sub+18	13/01/96	Liverpool	Home	League	1–1		
Sub+19	20/01/96	Blackburn Rovers	Away	League	0–3		
148	03/02/96	Newcastle United	Away	League	0–2		
Sub+20	10/02/96	Wimbledon	Home	League	2–1		
Sub+21	17/02/96	Queens Park Rangers	Home	League	1–3		

+ Played at Millmoor Ground, Rotherham United

SEASON 1996–97

Premier League

Sub+22	02/09/96	Leicester City	Home	League	2–1		

Millwall (loan) – Football League Division Two

1	14/12/96	AFC Bournemouth	Away	League	1–1	1 Goal	(1)
2	18/12/96	Luton Town	Home	League	0–1		
3	26/12/96	Peterborough United	Home	League	0–2		
4	07/01/97	Colchester United	Home	AW Shield	2–3*		

FC Sion – Swiss League Division One
No Competitive Matches

Charlton Athletic – Football League Division One

Sub+1	09/04/97	Huddersfield Town	Home	League	2–1		
Sub+2	12/04/97	Barnsley	Away	League	0–4		
1	19/04/97	Portsmouth	Home	League	2–1	2 Goals	(2)
2	25/04/97	Bolton Wanderers	Away	League	1–4		
3	01/05/97	Bradford City	Away	League	0–1		
4	04/05/97	Sheffield United	Home	League	0–0		

APPEARANCES AND GOALS PER SEASON

SEASON 81–82	GAMES	GOALS
League	1+1	0
TOTAL	**1+1**	**0**

SEASON 82–83	GAMES	GOALS
League	0+1	1
TOTAL	**0+1**	**1**

SEASON 83–84	GAMES	GOALS
League	17+9	9
FA Cup	0+1	1
League Cup	1+1	0
Associate Members Cup	2	0
TOTAL	**20+11**	**10**

SEASON 84–85	GAMES	GOALS
League	2+14	0
League Cup	1+1	0
TOTAL	**3+15**	**0**

SEASON 85–86	GAMES	GOALS
League	22+2	6
FA Cup	1	0
League Cup	2	0
TOTAL	**25+2**	**6**

SEASON 86–87	GAMES	GOALS
League	30	8
FA Cup	2	0
TOTAL	**32**	**8**

SEASON 87–88	GAMES	GOALS
League	38	24
FA Cup	0+1	0
League Cup	2	1
Simod Cup	1	0
TOTAL	**41+1**	**25**

SEASON 88–89	GAMES	GOALS
League	46	20
League Play-offs	4	1
FA Cup	1	0
League Cup	3	1
Simod Cup	5	3
TOTAL	**59**	**25**

SEASON 89–90	GAMES	GOALS
League	36	12
FA Cup	6	2
League Cup	4	1
Zenith Data Systems Cup	4	2
TOTAL	**50**	**17**

SEASON 90–91	GAMES	GOALS
League	29+3	9
FA Cup	3	0
League Cup	5	4
Zenith Data Systems Cup	6	2
TOTAL	**43+3**	**15**

SEASON 91–92	GAMES	GOALS
League	42	17
FA Cup	1	0
League Cup	8	4
Zenith Data Systems Cup	3	1
TOTAL	**54**	**22**

SEASON 92–93	GAMES	GOALS
League	33+2	12
FA Cup	7	3
League Cup	7	6
TOTAL	**47+2**	**21**

SEASON 93–94	GAMES	GOALS
League	36+4	19
FA Cup	3	2
League Cup	7	2
TOTAL	**46+4**	**23**

SEASON 94–95	GAMES	GOALS
League	33+4	11
FA Cup	3	2
League Cup	3	0
TOTAL	**39+4**	**13**

SEASON 95–96	GAMES	GOALS
League	15+10	7
League Cup	3+1	3
Inter-Toto Cup	3	4
TOTAL	**21+11**	**14**

SEASON 96–97	GAMES	GOALS
League	7+3	3
Auto Windscreens Shield	1	0
TOTAL	**8+3**	**3**

CAREER APPEARANCES AND GOALS

COMPETITION	GAMES	TOTAL	GOALS
League	387+53	440	158
League Play–offs	4	4	1
FA Cup	27+2	29	10
League Cup	46+3	49	22
Associate Members Cup	2	2	0
Simod Cup	6	6	3
Zenith Data Systems Cup	13	13	5
Auto Windscreens Shield	1	1	0
Inter–Toto Cup	3	3	4
TOTAL	**489+58**	**547**	**203**

HAT-TRICKS

Crystal Palace

1	3	Walsall	02/01/89	Home	League	4–0
2	3	Luton Town	10/01/89	Home	Simod Cup	4–1
3	3	Southend United	25/09/90	Home	Lge Cup	8–0

Sheffield Wednesday

1	3	Crewe Alexandra	04/10/95	Home	Lge Cup	5–2

League: 1
League Cup: 2
Simod Cup: 1
TOTAL: 4

HONOURS

Winners medals
Zenith Data Systems Cup: 90/91

Runner-up medals
FA Cup: 89/90, 92/93
League Cup: 92/93
Promoted to League Division One: 88/89
Promoted to League Division Three: 82/83

STEVE BULL

Born: 28/03/65 – Tipton
Height: 5.11
Weight: 12.11 (96–97)

Clubs
West Bromwich Albion: **1985–86** – Matches: **5+4** – Goals: **3**
Wolverhampton Wanderers: **1986–97** – Matches: **501+4** – Goals: **291**

Country
England: **1989–90** – Matches: **5+8** – Goals: **4**

SEASON 1985–86

West Bromwich Albion – League Division One

Sub+1	23/10/85	Crystal Palace	Home	FM Cup	2–1	
Sub+2	13/11/85	Chelsea	Home	FM Cup	2–2+	
Sub+3	12/04/86	Queens Park Rangers	Away	League	0–1	

+ AET Chelsea won 5–4 on penalties

SEASON 1986–87

League Division Two

1	06/09/86	Reading	Away	League	1–1		
2	13/09/86	Ipswich Town	Home	League	3–4	2 Goals	(2)
Sub+4	20/09/86	Brighton & Hove Albion	Away	League	0–2		
3	24/09/86	Derby County	Away	Lge Cup	1–4	1 Goal	(3)

| 4 | 07/10/86 | Derby County | Home | Lge Cup | 0–1 | |
| 5 | 21/10/86 | Millwall | Away | FM Cup | 0–2 | |

Wolverhampton Wanderers – League Division Four

1	22/11/86	Wrexham	Home	League	0–3	
2	29/11/86	Lincoln City	Away	League	0–3	
3	02/12/86	Cardiff City	Away	FR Trophy	1–0	1 Goal (1)
4	13/12/86	Hartlepool United	Away	League	1–0	1 Goal (2)
5	16/12/86	AFC Bournemouth	Home	FR Trophy	4–3	2 Goals (4)
6	20/12/86	Southend United	Home	League	1–2	1 Goal (5)
7	26/12/86	Hereford United	Away	League	0–2	
8	27/12/86	Exeter City	Home	League	2–2	1 Goal (6)
9	01/01/87	Peterborough United	Home	League	0–3	
10	03/01/87	Wrexham	Away	League	0–0	
11	10/01/87	Cambridge United	Away	League	0–0	
12	24/01/87	Cardiff City	Away	League	2–0	1 Goal (7)
13	26/01/87	Hereford United	Home	FR Trophy	0–1	
14	31/01/87	Crewe Alexandra	Home	League	2–3	
15	07/02/87	Stockport County	Home	League	3–1	1 Goal (8)
16	14/02/87	Burnley	Away	League	5–2	
17	17/02/87	Aldershot	Home	League	3–0	
18	21/02/87	Northampton Town	Home	League	1–1	
19	28/02/87	Preston North End	Away	League	2–2	
20	03/03/87	Colchester United	Home	League	2–0	1 Goal (9)
21	07/03/87	Orient	Away	League	1–3	1 Goal (10)
22	14/03/87	Swansea City	Home	League	4–0	
23	17/03/87	Halifax Town	Away	League	4–3	
24	21/03/87	Tranmere Rovers	Away	League	1–0	
25	28/03/87	Scunthorpe United	Home	League	1–0	1 Goal (11)
26	04/04/87	Torquay United	Home	League	1–0	
27	11/04/87	Rochdale	Away	League	3–0	
28	18/04/87	Peterborough United	Away	League	1–0	1 Goal (12)
29	20/04/87	Hereford United	Home	League	1–0	
30	24/04/87	Southend United	Away	League	0–1	
31	02/05/87	Lincoln City	Home	League	3–0	2 Goals (14)
32	04/05/87	Exeter City	Away	League	3–1	1 Goal (15)
33	09/05/87	Hartlepool United	Home	League	4–1	3 Goals (18)
34	14/05/87	Colchester United	Away	Lge P/O	2–0	1 Goal (19)
35	17/05/87	Colchester United	Home	Lge P/O	0–0	
36	22/05/87	Aldershot	Home	Lge P/O	0–2	
37	25/05/87	Aldershot	Away	Lge P/O	0–1	

SEASON 1987–88

League Division Four

38	15/08/87	Scarborough	Away	League	2–2	1 Goal (20)
39	18/08/87	Notts County	Home	Lge Cup	3–0	
40	22/08/87	Halifax Town	Home	League	0–1	
41	25/08/87	Notts County	Away	Lge Cup	2–1	2 Goals (22)
42	29/08/87	Hereford United	Away	League	2–1	1 Goal (23)
43	31/08/87	Scunthorpe United	Home	League	4–1	2 Goals (25)
44	05/09/87	Cardiff City	Away	League	2–3	1 Goal (26)
45	12/09/87	Crewe Alexandra	Home	League	2–2	1 Goal (27)
46	16/09/87	Peterborough United	Away	League	1–1	1 Goal (28)
47	19/09/87	Stockport County	Away	League	2–0	
48	22/09/87	Manchester City	Away	Lge Cup	2–1	1 Goal (29)
49	26/09/87	Torquay United	Home	League	1–2	1 Goal (30)
50	29/09/87	Rochdale	Home	League	2–0	1 Goal (31)
51	03/10/87	Bolton Wanderers	Away	League	0–1	
52	06/10/87	Manchester City	Home	Lge Cup	0–2	
53	10/10/87	Carlisle United	Away	League	1–0	1 Goal (32)
54	17/10/87	Tranmere Rovers	Home	League	3–0	1 Goal (33)
55	20/10/87	Cambridge United	Home	League	3–0	1 Goal (34)
56	24/10/87	Darlington	Away	League	2–2	
57	26/10/87	Swansea City	Away	SV Trophy	1–1	1 Goal (35)
58	03/11/87	Swansea City	Away	League	2–1	1 Goal (36)
59	07/11/87	Burnley	Home	League	3–0	
60	14/11/87	Cheltenham Town	Home	FA Cup	5–1	3 Goals (39)
61	21/11/87	Colchester United	Away	League	1–0	
62	24/11/87	Bristol City	Home	SV Trophy	3–1	2 Goals (41)
63	28/11/87	Wrexham	Home	League	0–2	
64	19/12/87	Leyton Orient	Home	League	2–0	2 Goals (43)
65	28/12/87	Exeter City	Home	League	3–0	
66	01/01/88	Hereford United	Home	League	2–0	2 Goals (45)
67	02/01/88	Crewe Alexandra	Away	League	2–0	

68	09/01/88	Bradford City	Away	FA Cup	1–2		
69	16/01/88	Stockport County	Home	League	1–1		
70	19/01/88	Brentford	Home	SV Trophy	4–0	3 Goals	(48)
71	30/01/88	Scunthorpe United	Away	League	1–0		
72	06/02/88	Cardiff City	Home	League	1–4	1 Goal	(49)
73	09/02/88	Peterborough United	Home	SV Trophy	4–2	2 Goals	(51)
74	13/02/88	Exeter City	Away	League	4–2	3 Goals	(54)
75	16/02/88	Halifax Town	Away	League	1–2		
76	19/02/88	Scarborough	Home	League	0–0		
77	23/02/88	Torquay United	Away	League	0–0		
78	27/02/88	Bolton Wanderers	Home	League	4–0	2 Goals	(56)
79	01/03/88	Rochdale	Away	League	1–0		
80	04/03/88	Tranmere Rovers	Away	League	0–3		
81	08/03/88	Torquay United	Home	SV Trophy	1–0	1 Goal	(57)
82	12/03/88	Carlisle United	Home	League	3–1		
83	22/03/88	Peterborough United	Home	League	0–1		
84	26/03/88	Darlington	Home	League	5–3	3 Goals	(60)
85	02/04/88	Burnley	Away	League	3–0	1 Goal	(61)
86	04/04/88	Colchester United	Home	League	2–0	2 Goals	(63)
87	10/04/88	Cambridge United	Away	League	1–1		
88	12/04/88	Notts County	Away	SV Trophy	1–1	1 Goal	(64)
89	19/04/88	Notts County	Home	SV Trophy	3–0	2 Goals	(66)
90	23/04/88	Swansea City	Home	League	2–0	1 Goal	(67)
91	26/04/88	Newport County	Away	League	3–1	2 Goals	(69)
92	30/04/88	Wrexham	Away	League	2–4		
93	02/05/88	Hartlepool United	Home	League	2–0	2 Goals	(71)
94	07/05/88	Leyton Orient	Away	League	2–0		
95	29/05/88	Burnley	Wembley	SV Trophy	2–0		

SEASON 1988–89

League Division Three

96	27/08/88	Bury	Away	League	1–3		
97	30/08/88	Birmingham City	Home	Lge Cup	3–2	2 Goals	(73)
98	03/09/88	Reading	Home	League	2–1		
99	06/09/88	Birmingham City	Away	Lge Cup	0–1*		
100	10/09/88	Chesterfield	Away	League	3–0		
101	17/09/88	Notts County	Home	League	0–0		
102	20/09/88	Aldershot	Home	League	1–0	1 Goal	(74)
103	24/09/88	Swansea City	Away	League	5–2	2 Goals	(76)
104	01/10/88	Port Vale	Home	League	3–3	2 Goals	(78)
105	05/10/88	Fulham	Away	League	2–2		
106	08/10/88	Sheffield United	Away	League	0–2		
107	15/10/88	Wigan Athletic	Home	League	2–1	1 Goal	(79)
108	22/10/88	Bolton Wanderers	Away	League	2–1	1 Goal	(80)
109	25/10/88	Blackpool	Home	League	2–1		
110	29/10/88	Gillingham	Away	League	3–1	1 Goal	(81)
111	05/11/88	Southend United	Home	League	3–0	1 Goal	(82)
112	08/11/88	Bristol City	Away	League	1–0		
113	12/11/88	Huddersfield Town	Home	League	4–1	2 Goals	(84)
114	19/11/88	Grimsby Town	Away	FA Cup	0–1		
115	26/11/88	Preston North End	Home	League	6–0	4 Goals	(88)
116	30/11/88	Hereford United	Away	SV Trophy	2–2	1 Goal	(89)
117	04/12/88	Northampton Town	Away	League	1–3		
118	13/12/88	Port Vale	Home	SV Trophy	5–1	4 Goals	(93)
119	17/12/88	Mansfield Town	Home	League	6–2	3 Goals	(96)
120	26/12/88	Bristol Rovers	Away	League	0–0		
121	31/12/88	Brentford	Away	League	2–2	1 Goal	(97)
122	02/01/89	Chester City	Home	League	3–1	1 Goal	(98)
123	10/01/89	Cardiff City	Home	League	2–0	1 Goal	(99)
124	14/01/89	Reading	Away	League	2–0		
125	21/01/89	Chesterfield	Home	League	1–0		
126	24/01/89	Bristol City	Home	SV Trophy	3–0	3 Goals	(102)
127	29/01/89	Notts County	Away	League	1–1		
128	04/02/89	Port Vale	Away	League	0–0		
129	11/02/89	Fulham	Home	League	5–2	3 Goals	(105)
130	21/02/89	Northampton Town	Home	SV Trophy	3–1		
131	28/02/89	Blackpool	Away	League	2–0	1 Goal	(106)
132	04/03/89	Bolton Wanderers	Home	League	1–0	1 Goal	(107)
133	10/03/89	Southend United	Away	League	1–3		
134	14/03/89	Gillingham	Home	League	6–1	1 Goal	(108)
135	18/03/89	Bury	Home	League	4–0	3 Goals	(111)
136	22/03/89	Hereford United	Away	SV Trophy	2–0	1 Goal	(112)
137	25/03/89	Chester City	Away	League	1–1		
138	27/03/89	Bristol Rovers	Home	League	0–1		

139	01/04/89	Mansfield Town	Away	League	1–3	1 Goal	(113)
140	04/04/89	Cardiff City	Away	League	1–1		
141	08/04/89	Brentford	Home	League	2–0	1 Goal	(114)
142	12/04/89	Torquay United	Away	SV Trophy	2–1	2 Goals	(116)
143	15/04/89	Aldershot	Away	SV Trophy	2–1	1 Goal	(117)
144	18/04/89	Torquay United	Home	SV Trophy	0–2		
145	22/04/89	Swansea City	Home	League	1–1		
146	29/04/89	Huddersfield Town	Away	League	0–0		
147	01/05/89	Bristol City	Home	League	2–0	2 Goals	(119)
148	06/05/89	Northampton Town	Home	League	3–2	1 Goal	(120)
149	09/05/89	Sheffield United	Home	League	2–2	1 Goal	(121)
150	13/05/89	Preston North End	Away	League	3–3		

SEASON 1989–90

League Division Two

151	19/08/89	Middlesbrough	Away	League	2–4		
152	22/08/89	Lincoln City	Home	Lge Cup	1–0		
153	26/08/89	Bradford City	Home	League	1–1	1 Goal	(122)
154	30/08/89	Lincoln City	Away	Lge Cup	2–0	1 Goal	(123)
155	03/09/89	Swindon Town	Away	League	1–3		
156	09/09/89	Stoke City	Home	League	0–0		
157	12/09/89	Brighton & Hove Albion	Home	League	2–4	1 Goal	(124)
158	20/09/89	Aston Villa	Away	Lge Cup	1–2		
159	23/09/89	Plymouth Argyle	Home	League	1–0		
160	26/09/89	Barnsley	Away	League	2–2	2 Goals	(126)
161	30/09/89	Portsmouth	Home	League	5–0	2 Goals	(128)
162	04/10/89	Aston Villa	Home	Lge Cup	1–1	1 Goal	(129)
163	07/10/89	Sheffield United	Home	League	1–2		
164	15/10/89	West Bromwich Albion	Away	League	2–1	1 Goal	(130)
165	17/10/89	Port Vale	Home	League	2–0	1 Goal	(131)
166	21/10/89	Leeds United	Away	League	0–1		
167	28/10/89	Oldham Athletic	Home	League	1–1		
168	01/11/89	Leicester City	Away	League	0–0		
169	04/11/89	West Ham United	Home	League	1–0	1 Goal	(132)
170	07/11/89	Sheffield United	Away	ZDS Cup	0–1		
171	11/11/89	Sunderland	Away	League	1–1		
172	09/12/89	Brighton & Hove Albion	Away	League	1–1		
173	16/12/89	Oxford United	Away	League	2–2		
174	26/12/89	Hull City	Home	League	1–2	1 Goal	(133)
175	30/12/89	AFC Bournemouth	Home	League	3–1		
176	01/01/90	Newcastle United	Away	League	4–1	4 Goals	(137)
177	06/01/90	Sheffield Wednesday	Home	FA Cup	1–2	1 Goal	(138)
178	13/01/90	Bradford City	Away	League	1–1	1 Goal	(139)
179	20/01/90	Swindon Town	Home	League	2–1		
180	03/02/90	Plymouth Argyle	Away	League	1–0		
181	10/02/90	Ipswich Town	Home	League	2–1	1 Goal	(140)
182	17/02/90	Stoke City	Away	League	0–2		
183	24/02/90	Watford	Home	League	1–1	1 Goal	(141)
184	03/03/90	Blackburn Rovers	Away	League	3–2		
185	06/03/90	Portsmouth	Away	League	3–1	1 Goal	(142)
186	10/03/90	Barnsley	Home	League	1–1	1 Goal	(143)
187	17/03/90	Sheffield United	Away	League	0–3		
188	20/03/90	West Bromwich Albion	Home	League	2–1	1 Goal	(144)
189	24/03/90	Port Vale	Away	League	1–3		
190	31/03/90	Leeds United	Home	League	1–0		
191	03/04/90	AFC Bournemouth	Away	League	1–1		
192	10/04/90	Leicester City	Home	League	5–0	3 Goals	(147)
193	14/04/90	Newcastle United	Home	League	0–1		
194	16/04/90	Hull City	Away	League	0–2		
195	21/04/90	Oxford United	Home	League	2–0	1 Goal	(148)
196	28/04/90	Sunderland	Home	League	0–1		
197	03/05/90	Oldham Athletic	Away	League	1–1		
198	05/05/90	West Ham United	Away	League	0–4		

SEASON 1990–91

League Division Two

199	25/08/90	Oldham Athletic	Home	League	2–3	2 Goals	(150)
200	28/08/90	Port Vale	Away	League	2–1	1 Goal	(151)
201	01/09/90	Brighton & Hove Albion	Away	League	1–1		
202	08/09/90	Bristol Rovers	Home	League	1–1		
203	15/09/90	West Ham United	Away	League	1–1	1 Goal	(152)
204	18/09/90	Swindon Town	Away	League	0–1		
205	22/09/90	Plymouth Argyle	Home	League	3–1	2 Goals	(154)

206	25/09/90	Hull City	Away	Lge Cup	0–0		
207	29/09/90	Oxford United	Away	League	1–1		
208	02/10/90	Charlton Athletic	Home	League	3–0	2 Goals	(156)
209	06/10/90	Bristol City	Home	League	4–0	3 Goals	(159)
210	09/10/90	Hull City	Home	Lge Cup	1–1*		
211	13/10/90	Notts County	Away	League	1–1		
212	20/10/90	Hull City	Away	League	2–1	1 Goal	(160)
213	23/10/90	Middlesbrough	Home	League	1–0	1 Goal	(161)
214	27/10/90	Blackburn Rovers	Home	League	2–3		
215	03/11/90	Portsmouth	Away	League	0–0		
216	10/11/90	Newcastle United	Home	League	2–1		
217	17/11/90	Leicester City	Away	League	0–1		
218	24/11/90	Barnsley	Away	League	1–1		
219	27/11/90	Leicester City	Away	ZDS Cup	1–0	1 Goal	(162)
220	01/12/90	Ipswich Town	Home	League	2–2	2 Goals	(164)
221	15/12/90	Oldham Athletic	Away	League	1–4		
222	18/12/90	Leeds United	Home	ZDS Cup	1–2		
223	22/12/90	Millwall	Home	League	4–1	1 Goal	(165)
224	26/12/90	Sheffield Wednesday	Away	League	2–2	1 Goal	(166)
225	29/12/90	West Bromwich Albion	Away	League	1–1		
226	01/01/91	Watford	Home	League	0–0		
227	05/01/91	Cambridge United	Home	FA Cup	0–1		
228	12/01/91	Brighton & Hove Albion	Home	League	2–3	1 Goal	(167)
229	19/01/91	Bristol Rovers	Away	League	1–1		
230	02/02/91	West Ham United	Home	League	2–1	1 Goal	(168)
231	23/02/91	Newcastle United	Away	League	0–0		
232	26/02/91	Port Vale	Home	League	3–1	2 Goals	(170)
233	02/03/91	Ipswich Town	Away	League	0–0		
234	05/03/91	Leicester City	Home	League	2–1	1 Goal	(171)
235	09/03/91	Barnsley	Home	League	0–5		
236	12/03/91	Charlton Athletic	Away	League	0–1		
237	16/03/91	Oxford United	Home	League	3–3	3 Goals	(174)
238	19/03/91	Notts County	Home	League	0–2		
239	23/03/91	Bristol City	Away	League	1–1		
240	30/03/91	Sheffield Wednesday	Home	League	3–2	1 Goal	(175)
241	03/04/91	Millwall	Away	League	1–2		
242	06/04/91	West Bromwich Albion	Home	League	2–2		
243	09/04/91	Plymouth Argyle	Away	League	0–1		
244	13/04/91	Watford	Away	League	1–3		
245	16/04/91	Swindon Town	Home	League	1–2		
246	20/04/91	Hull City	Home	League	0–0		

SEASON 1991–92

League Division Two

247	17/08/91	Watford	Away	League	2–0	1 Goal	(176)
248	24/08/91	Charlton Athletic	Home	League	1–1	1 Goal	(177)
249	31/08/91	Brighton & Hove Albion	Away	League	3–3	1 Goal	(178)
250	03/09/91	Port Vale	Home	League	0–2		
251	07/09/91	Oxford United	Home	League	3–1	1 Goal	(179)
252	14/09/91	Newcastle United	Away	League	2–1	1 Goal	(180)
253	17/09/91	Cambridge United	Away	League	1–2	1 Goal	(181)
254	21/09/91	Swindon Town	Home	League	2–1	1 Goal	(182)
255	24/09/91	Shrewsbury Town	Home	Lge Cup	6–1	2 Goals	(184)
256	28/09/91	Southend United	Away	League	2–0		
257	01/10/91	Grimsby Town	Away	ZDS Cup	0–1		
258	05/10/91	Barnsley	Home	League	1–2		
259	12/10/91	Middlesbrough	Away	League	0–0		
260	19/10/91	Leicester City	Away	League	0–3		
261	26/10/91	Tranmere Rovers	Home	League	1–1		
262	30/10/91	Everton	Away	Lge Cup	4–1	1 Goal	(185)
263	05/11/91	Bristol Rovers	Home	League	2–3	2 Goals	(187)
264	09/11/91	Derby County	Home	League	2–3		
265	16/11/91	Millwall	Away	League	1–2		
266	23/11/91	Ipswich Town	Home	League	1–2		
267	26/11/91	Grimsby Town	Home	League	2–1		
268	21/12/91	Port Vale	Away	League	1–1		
269	26/12/91	Blackburn Rovers	Home	League	0–0		
270	28/12/91	Brighton & Hove Albion	Home	League	2–0	1 Goal	(188)
271	01/01/92	Grimsby Town	Away	League	2–0		
272	04/01/92	Nottingham Forest	Away	FA Cup	0–1		
273	15/01/92	Charlton Athletic	Away	League	2–0	1 Goal	(189)
274	18/01/92	Watford	Home	League	3–0	1 Goal	(190)
275	01/02/92	Leicester City	Away	League	1–0	1 Goal	(191)
276	08/02/92	Tranmere Rovers	Home	League	3–4	1 Goal	(192)

277	22/02/92	Portsmouth	Away	League	0–0		
278	29/02/92	Sunderland	Home	League	0–1		
279	07/03/92	Bristol City	Home	League	1–1	1 Goal	(193)
280	11/03/92	Bristol Rovers	Away	League	1–1	1 Goal	(194)
281	14/03/92	Plymouth Argyle	Home	League	1–0		
282	17/03/92	Bristol City	Away	League	0–2		
283	21/03/92	Derby County	Away	League	2–1	1 Goal	(195)
284	28/03/92	Millwall	Home	League	0–0		
285	31/03/92	Newcastle United	Home	League	6–2	1 Goal	(196)
286	04/04/92	Oxford United	Away	League	0–1		
287	07/04/92	Ipswich Town	Away	League	1–2		
288	11/04/92	Cambridge United	Home	League	2–1		
289	14/04/92	Blackburn Rovers	Away	League	2–1	1 Goal	(197)
290	18/04/92	Swindon Town	Away	League	0–1		
291	20/04/92	Southend United	Home	League	3–1	1 Goal	(198)
292	26/04/92	Barnsley	Away	League	0–2		
293	02/05/92	Middlesbrough	Home	League	1–2		

SEASON 1992–93

Football League Division One

294	15/08/92	Brentford	Away	League	2–0	1 Goal	(199)
295	18/08/92	Leicester City	Home	League	3–0	1 Goal	(200)
296	22/08/92	Swindon Town	Home	League	2–2		
297	29/08/92	Oxford United	Away	League	0–0		
298	01/09/92	Barnsley	Away	League	1–0		
299	05/09/92	Peterborough United	Home	League	4–3	1 Goal	(201)
300	13/09/92	Leicester City	Away	League	0–0		
301	15/09/92	Tranmere Rovers	Away	AI Cup	1–2		
302	19/09/92	Watford	Home	League	2–2	2 Goals	(203)
303	22/09/92	Notts County	Away	Lge Cup	2–3	1 Goal	(204)
304	27/09/92	Birmingham City	Away	League	4–0		
305	30/09/92	Peterborough United	Home	AI Cup	2–0	1 Goal	(205)
306	04/10/92	West Ham United	Home	League	0–0		
307	07/10/92	Notts County	Home	Lge Cup	0–1		
308	10/10/92	Southend United	Away	League	1–1		
309	17/10/92	Portsmouth	Home	League	1–1		
310	25/10/92	Millwall	Away	League	0–2		
311	31/10/92	Derby County	Home	League	0–2		
312	03/11/92	Sunderland	Away	League	0–2		
313	07/11/92	Bristol Rovers	Home	League	5–1	2 Goals	(207)
314	14/11/92	Notts County	Away	League	2–2	1 Goal	(208)
315	22/11/92	Charlton Athletic	Home	League	2–1		
316	28/11/92	Grimsby Town	Home	League	2–1		
317	05/12/92	Cambridge United	Away	League	1–1	1 Goal	(209)
318	12/12/92	Luton Town	Home	League	1–2		
319	19/12/92	Tranmere Rovers	Away	League	0–3		
320	26/12/92	Newcastle United	Away	League	1–2		
321	28/12/92	Bristol City	Home	League	0–0		
322	02/01/93	Watford	Away	FA Cup	4–1	1 Goal	(210)
323	09/01/93	Watford	Away	League	1–3		
324	17/01/93	Birmingham City	Home	League	2–1		
325	24/01/93	Bolton Wanderers	Home	FA Cup	0–2		
326	27/01/93	Barnsley	Home	League	1–0		
327	30/01/93	Swindon Town	Away	League	0–1		
328	06/02/93	Brentford	Home	League	1–2		
329	27/02/93	Southend United	Home	League	1–1	1 Goal	(211)
330	06/03/93	West Ham United	Away	League	1–3	1 Goal	(212)
331	09/03/93	Notts County	Home	League	3–0	2 Goals	(214)
332	13/03/93	Bristol Rovers	Away	League	1–1	1 Goal	(215)
333	20/03/93	Cambridge United	Home	League	1–2	1 Goal	(216)
334	03/04/93	Grimsby Town	Away	League	1–1		
335	07/04/93	Luton Town	Away	League	1–1	1 Goal	(217)

SEASON 1993–94

Football League Division One

336	14/08/93	Bristol City	Home	League	3–1	2 Goals	(219)
337	22/08/93	Birmingham City	Away	League	2–2		
338	25/08/93	Millwall	Home	League	2–0	1 Goal	(220)
339	28/08/93	Middlesbrough	Home	League	2–3		
Sub+1	31/08/93	Stoke City	Home	AI Cup	3–3	1 Goal	(221)
340	05/09/93	West Bromwich Albion	Away	League	2–3	1 Goal	(222)
341	25/09/93	Grimsby Town	Away	League	0–2		
342	30/10/93	Southend United	Away	League	1–1		

343	02/11/93	Notts County	Home	League	3–0	1 Goal	(223)
344	07/11/93	Derby County	Away	League	4–0	3 Goals	(226)
345	10/11/93	Nottingham Forest	Home	League	1–1		
346	13/11/93	Barnsley	Home	League	1–1		
347	27/11/93	Leicester City	Away	League	2–2	2 Goals	(228)
348	05/12/93	Derby County	Home	League	2–2	1 Goal	(229)
349	11/12/93	Watford	Home	League	2–0	1 Goal	(230)
350	18/12/93	Bristol City	Away	League	1–2		
351	27/12/93	Tranmere Rovers	Away	League	1–1	1 Goal	(231)
352	28/12/93	Oxford United	Home	League	2–1		
353	01/01/94	Peterborough United	Away	League	1–0		
354	03/01/94	Bolton Wanderers	Home	League	1–0		
355	08/01/94	Crystal Palace	Home	FA Cup	1–0		
356	15/01/94	Crystal Palace	Home	League	2–0		
357	23/01/94	Nottingham Forest	Away	League	0–0		
358	29/01/94	Port Vale	Away	FA Cup	2–0		
359	16/04/94	Notts County	Away	League	2–0		
360	20/04/94	Millwall	Away	League	0–1		
361	23/04/94	Luton Town	Home	League	1–0		
362	30/04/94	Barnsley	Away	League	0–2		
363	03/05/94	Sunderland	Home	League	1–1	1 Goal	(232)
364	08/05/94	Leicester City	Home	League	1–1		

SEASON 1994–95

Football League Division One

365	13/08/94	Reading	Home	League	1–0		
366	10/09/94	Tranmere Rovers	Home	League	2–0		
367	13/09/94	Southend United	Home	League	5–0	1 Goal	(233)
368	17/09/94	Burnley	Away	League	1–0	1 Goal	(234)
369	20/09/94	Chesterfield	Away	Lge Cup	3–1	2 Goals	(236)
370	24/09/94	Portsmouth	Away	League	2–1		
371	27/09/94	Chesterfield	Home	Lge Cup	1–1		
372	01/10/94	Port Vale	Home	League	2–1		
373	05/10/94	AC Venezia	Away	AI Cup	1–2		
374	08/10/94	Swindon Town	Away	League	2–3		
375	15/10/94	Grimsby Town	Home	League	2–1		
376	22/10/94	Millwall	Home	League	3–3	2 Goals	(238)
377	26/10/94	Nottingham Forest	Home	Lge Cup	2–3		
378	30/10/94	Stoke City	Away	League	1–1	1 Goal	(239)
379	01/11/94	Bristol City	Away	League	5–1		
380	05/11/94	Luton Town	Home	League	2–3		
381	04/12/94	Millwall	Away	League	0–1		
382	10/12/94	Notts County	Home	League	1–0	1 Goal	(240)
383	18/12/94	Reading	Away	League	2–4	1 Goal	(241)
384	28/12/94	Charlton Athletic	Home	League	2–0	1 Goal	(242)
385	25/02/95	Port Vale	Away	League	4–2	1 Goal	(243)
386	05/03/95	Portsmouth	Home	League	1–0	1 Goal	(244)
387	08/03/95	Sunderland	Home	League	1–0		
388	11/03/95	Crystal Palace	Away	FA Cup	1–1		
389	15/03/95	West Bromwich Albion	Away	League	0–2		
390	22/03/95	Crystal Palace	Home	FA Cup	1–4		
391	24/03/95	Burnley	Home	League	2–0	1 Goal	(245)
392	01/04/95	Southend United	Away	League	1–0	1 Goal	(246)
393	04/04/95	Luton Town	Away	League	3–3		
394	08/04/95	Barnsley	Home	League	0–0		
395	12/04/95	Derby County	Away	League	3–3		
396	15/04/95	Charlton Athletic	Away	League	2–3	2 Goals	(248)
397	17/04/95	Oldham Athletic	Home	League	2–1		
398	22/04/95	Sheffield United	Away	League	3–3	1 Goal	(249)
399	29/04/95	Grimsby Town	Away	League	0–0		
400	03/05/95	Tranmere Rovers	Away	League	1–1	1 Goal	(250)
401	07/05/95	Swindon Town	Home	League	1–1		
402	14/05/95	Bolton Wanderers	Home	Lge P/O	2–1	1 Goal	(251)
403	17/05/95	Bolton Wanderers	Away	Lge P/O	0–2		

SEASON 1995–96

Football League Division One

404	12/08/95	Tranmere Rovers	Away	League	2–2	1 Goal	(252)
405	20/08/95	West Bromwich Albion	Home	League	1–1		
406	26/08/95	Sunderland	Away	League	0–2		
407	30/08/95	Derby County	Home	League	3–0		
408	02/09/95	Leicester City	Away	League	0–1		
409	09/09/95	Grimsby Town	Home	League	4–1	2 Goals	(254)

410	13/09/95	Norwich City	Home	League	0–2		
411	16/09/95	Southend United	Away	League	1–2		
412	20/09/95	Fulham	Home	Lge Cup	2–0		
413	23/09/95	Luton Town	Home	League	0–0		
Sub+2	14/10/95	Stoke City	Home	League	1–4		
414	21/10/95	Watford	Away	League	1–1		
415	25/10/95	Charlton Athletic	Home	Lge Cup	0–0		
416	28/10/95	Sheffield United	Home	League	1–0	1 Goal	(255)
417	04/11/95	Barnsley	Away	League	0–1		
Sub+3	08/11/95	Charlton Athletic	Away	Lge Cup	2–1*		
Sub+4	12/11/95	Charlton Athletic	Home	League	0–0		
418	18/11/95	Oldham Athletic	Home	League	1–3		
419	22/11/95	Crystal Palace	Away	League	2–3		
420	25/11/95	Huddersfield Town	Away	League	1–2	1 Goal	(256)
421	29/11/95	Coventry City	Home	Lge Cup	2–1		
422	03/12/95	Ipswich Town	Home	League	2–2		
423	10/12/95	Luton Town	Away	League	3–2	1 Goal	(257)
424	16/12/95	Port Vale	Home	League	0–1		
425	26/12/95	Millwall	Home	League	1–1	1 Goal	(258)
426	30/12/95	Portsmouth	Home	League	2–2	1 Goal	(259)
427	06/01/96	Birmingham City	Away	FA Cup	1–1	1 Goal	(260)
428	10/01/96	Aston Villa	Away	Lge Cup	0–1		
429	13/01/96	West Bromwich Albion	Away	League	0–0		
430	17/01/96	Birmingham City	Home	FA Cup	2–1	1 Goal	(261)
431	20/01/96	Tranmere Rovers	Home	League	2–1	1 Goal	(262)
432	27/01/96	Tottenham Hotspur	Away	FA Cup	1–1		
433	03/02/96	Sunderland	Home	League	3–0		
434	07/02/96	Tottenham Hotspur	Home	FA Cup	0–2		
435	10/02/96	Derby County	Away	League	0–0		
436	17/02/96	Norwich City	Away	League	3–2	2 Goals	(264)
437	21/02/96	Leicester City	Home	League	2–3	1 Goal	(265)
438	24/02/96	Southend United	Home	League	2–0		
439	02/03/96	Millwall	Away	League	1–0	1 Goal	(266)
440	05/02/96	Birmingham City	Away	League	0–2		
441	09/03/96	Reading	Home	League	1–1		
442	12/03/96	Grimsby Town	Away	League	0–3		
443	16/03/96	Portsmouth	Away	League	2–0		
444	23/03/96	Birmingham City	Home	League	3–2	1 Goal	(267)
445	30/03/96	Watford	Home	League	3–0		
446	03/04/96	Stoke City	Away	League	0–2		
447	06/04/96	Sheffield United	Away	League	1–2		
448	08/04/96	Barnsley	Home	League	2–2	1 Goal	(268)
449	13/04/96	Oldham Athletic	Away	League	0–0		
450	20/04/96	Crystal Palace	Home	League	0–2		
451	27/04/96	Huddersfield Town	Home	League	0–0		
452	30/04/96	Reading	Away	League	0–3		
453	05/05/96	Charlton Athletic	Away	League	1–1		

SEASON 1996–97

Football League Division One

454	17/08/96	Grimsby Town	Away	League	3–1	3 Goals	(271)
455	20/08/96	Swindon Town	Away	Lge Cup	0–2		
456	24/08/96	Bradford City	Home	League	1–0	1 Goal	(272)
457	28/08/96	Queens Park Rangers	Home	League	1–1		
458	31/08/96	Norwich City	Away	League	0–1		
459	04/09/96	Swindon Town	Home	Lge Cup	1–0		
460	06/09/96	Charlton Athletic	Home	League	1–0		
461	10/09/96	Oxford United	Away	League	1–1		
462	15/09/96	West Bromwich Albion	Away	League	4–2	1 Goal	(273)
463	21/09/96	Sheffield United	Home	League	1–2		
464	27/09/96	Swindon Town	Away	League	2–1		
465	02/10/96	Bolton Wanderers	Home	League	1–2		
466	05/10/96	Reading	Home	League	0–1		
467	13/10/96	Southend United	Away	League	1–1	1 Goal	(274)
468	15/10/96	Portsmouth	Away	League	2–0	2 Goals	(276)
469	19/10/96	Port Vale	Home	League	0–1		
470	27/10/96	Manchester City	Away	League	1–0	1 Goal	(277)
471	30/10/96	Huddersfield Town	Home	League	0–0		
472	02/11/96	Barnsley	Home	League	3–3	1 Goal	(278)
473	17/11/96	Birmingham City	Home	League	1–2	1 Goal	(279)
474	23/11/96	Crystal Palace	Away	League	3–2		
475	01/12/96	Manchester City	Home	League	3–0		
476	07/12/96	Ipswich Town	Away	League	0–0		

477	14/12/96	Oldham Athletic	Home	League	0–1		
478	21/12/96	Tranmere Rovers	Away	League	2–0	1 Goal	(280)
479	26/12/96	Oxford United	Home	League	3–1		
480	28/12/96	Charlton Athletic	Away	League	0–0		
481	04/01/97	Portsmouth	Home	FA Cup	1–2		
482	12/01/97	West Bromwich Albion	Home	League	2–0		
483	18/01/97	Bolton Wanderers	Away	League	0–3		
484	24/01/97	Sheffield United	Away	League	3–2	1 Goal	(281)
485	29/01/97	Swindon Town	Home	League	1–0	1 Goal	(282)
486	01/02/97	Stoke City	Home	League	2–0	2 Goals	(284)
487	08/02/97	Huddersfield Town	Away	League	2–0	1 Goal	(285)
488	15/02/97	Crystal Palace	Home	League	0–3		
489	22/02/97	Barnsley	Away	League	3–1	1 Goal	(286)
490	01/03/97	Ipswich Town	Home	League	0–0		
491	04/03/97	Birmingham City	Away	League	2–1	1 Goal	(287)
492	08/03/97	Tranmere Rovers	Home	League	3–2	2 Goals	(289)
493	15/03/97	Oldham Athletic	Away	League	2–3	1 Goal	(290)
494	18/03/97	Stoke City	Away	League	0–1		
495	22/03/97	Bradford City	Away	League	1–2		
496	19/04/97	Southend United	Home	League	4–1	1 Goal	(291)
497	23/04/97	Grimsby Town	Home	League	1–1		
498	27/04/97	Port Vale	Away	League	2–1		
499	04/05/97	Portsmouth	Home	League	0–1		
500	10/05/97	Crystal Palace	Away	Lge P/O	1–3		
501	14/05/97	Crystal Palace	Home	Lge P/O	2–1		

INTERNATIONAL APPEARANCES – ENGLAND

Sub 1	27/05/89	Scotland	Hampden Park	2–0	RC	1 Goal	(1)
Sub 2	07/06/89	Denmark	Copenhagen	1–1	F		
3	13/12/89	Yugoslavia	Wembley	2–1	F		
4	25/04/90	Czechoslovakia	Wembley	4–2	F	2 Goals	(3)
Sub 5	15/05/90	Denmark	Wembley	1–0	F		
Sub 6	22/05/90	Uruguay	Wembley	1–2	F		
Sub 7	02/06/90	Tunisia	Tunis	1–1	F	1 Goal	(4)
Sub 8	11/06/90	Republic of Ireland	Cagliari	1–1	WC		
Sub 9	16/06/90	Holland	Cagliari	0–0	WC		
10	21/06/90	Egypt	Cagliari	1–0	WC		
Sub 11	26/06/90	Belgium	Bologna	1–0*	WC		
12	12/09/90	Hungary	Wembley	1–0	F		
13	17/10/90	Poland	Wembley	2–0	ECQ		

APPEARANCES AND GOALS PER SEASON

SEASON 85–86	GAMES	GOALS
League	0+1	0
Full Members Cup	0+2	0
TOTAL	**0+3**	**0**

SEASON 86–87	GAMES	GOALS
League	32+1	17
League Play–offs	4	1
League Cup	2	1
Full Members Cup	1	0
Freight Rover Trophy	3	3
TOTAL	**42+1**	**22**

SEASON 87–88	GAMES	GOALS
League	44	34
FA Cup	2	3
League Cup	4	3
Sherpa Van Trophy	8	12
TOTAL	**58**	**52**

SEASON 88–89	GAMES	GOALS
League	45	37
FA Cup	1	0
League Cup	2	2
Sherpa Van Trophy	7	11
TOTAL	**55**	**50**

SEASON 89–90	GAMES	GOALS
League	42	24
FA Cup	1	1
League Cup	4	2
Zenith Data Systems Cup	1	0
TOTAL	**48**	**27**

SEASON 90–91	GAMES	GOALS
League	43	26
FA Cup	1	0
League Cup	2	0
Zenith Data Systems Cup	2	1
TOTAL	**48**	**27**

SEASON 91–92	GAMES	GOALS
League	43	20
FA Cup	1	0
League Cup	2	3
Zenith Data Systems Cup	1	0
TOTAL	**47**	**23**

SEASON 92–93	GAMES	GOALS
League	36	16
FA Cup	2	1
League Cup	2	1
Anglo–Italian Cup	2	1
TOTAL	**42**	**19**

SEASON 93–94	GAMES	GOALS
League	27	14
FA Cup	2	0
Anglo–Italian Cup	0+1	1
TOTAL	**29+1**	**15**

SEASON 94–95	GAMES	GOALS
League	31	16
League Play–offs	2	1
FA Cup	2	0
League Cup	3	2
Anglo–Italian Cup	1	0
TOTAL	**39**	**19**

SEASON 95–96	GAMES	GOALS
League	42+2	15
FA Cup	4	2
League Cup	4+1	0
TOTAL	**50+3**	**17**

SEASON 96–97	GAMES	GOALS
League	43	23
League Play–offs	2	0
FA Cup	1	0
League Cup	2	0
TOTAL	**48**	**23**

CAREER APPEARANCES AND GOALS

COMPETITION	GAMES	TOTAL	GOALS
League	428+4	432	242
League Play–offs	8	8	2
FA Cup	17	17	7
League Cup	27+1	28	14
Full Members Cup	1+2	3	0
Freight Rover Trophy	3	3	3
Sherpa Van Trophy	15	15	23
Zenith Data Systems Cup	4	4	1
Anglo–Italian Cup	3+1	4	2
Internationals	5+8	13	4
TOTAL	**511+16**	**527**	**298**

HAT-TRICKS

Wolverhampton Wanderers

1	3	Hartlepool United	09/05/87	Home	League	4–1
2	3	Cheltenham Town	14/11/87	Home	FA Cup	5–1

3	3	Brentford	19/01/88	Home	SV Trophy	4–0
4	3	Exeter City	13/02/88	Away	League	4–2
5	3	Darlington	26/03/88	Home	League	5–3
6	4	Preston North End	26/11/88	Home	League	6–0
7	4	Port Vale	13/12/88	Home	SV Trophy	5–1
8	3	Mansfield Town	17/12/88	Home	League	6–2
9	3	Bristol City	24/01/89	Home	SV Trophy	3–0
10	3	Fulham	11/02/89	Home	League	5–2
11	3	Bury	18/03/89	Home	League	4–0
12	4	Newcastle United	01/01/90	Away	League	4–1
13	3	Leicester City	10/04/90	Home	League	5–0
14	3	Bristol City	06/10/90	Home	League	4–0
15	3	Oxford United	16/03/91	Home	League	3–3
16	3	Derby County	07/11/93	Away	League	4–0
17	3	Grimsby Town	17/08/96	Away	League	3–1

League: 13
FA Cup: 1
Sherpa Van Trophy: 3
TOTAL: 17

HONOURS

Winners medals
League Division Three Championship: 88/89
League Division Four Championship: 87/88
Sherpa Van Trophy: 87/88

Runner-up medals
None

ERIC CANTONA

Born: 24/05/66 – Nimes, France
Height: 6.2
Weight: 14.03 (96–97)

Clubs
AJ Auxerre: **1983–85** – Matches: **10+5** – Goals: **2**
FC Martigues: **1985–86** – Matches: **16** – Goals: **4**
AJ Auxerre: **1986–88** – Matches: **78+1** – Goals: **27**
Olympique de Marseille: **1988** – Matches: **22** – Goals: **6**
Girondins de Bordeaux: **1989** – Matches: **12** – Goals: **6**
Montpellier HSC: **1989–90** – Matches: **39** – Goals: **12**
Olympique de Marseille: **1990–91** – Matches: **19+2** – Goals: **9**
Nimes Olympique: **1991** – Matches: **16** – Goals: **2**
Leeds United: **1992** – Matches: **25+10** – Goals: **14**
Manchester United: **1992–97** – Matches: **184+1** – Goals: **82**

Country
France: **1987–95** – Matches: **45** – Goals: **20**

SEASON 1983–84

AJ Auxerre – French League Division One

1	05/11/83	AS Nancy–Lorraine	Home	League	4–0
2	18/11/83	RC Lens	Home	League	4–0

SEASON 1984–85

French League Division One

Sub+1	15/03/85	Paris Saint–Germain FC	Home	League	2–1		
Sub+2	26/03/85	SC Bastia	Home	League	3–1		
3	14/05/85	FC Rouen	Away	League	2–1	1 Goal	(1)
4	24/05/85	Racing Club Paris	Home	League	1–0		
5	28/05/85	RC Strasbourg	Away	League	1–1	1 Goal	(2)

SEASON 1985–86

French League Division One

6	16/07/85	Stade Lavallois de Laval	Away	League	0–0		
7	19/07/85	Olympique de Marseille	Home	League	2–0		
8	26/07/85	Le Havre AC	Away	League	3–3		
Sub+3	02/08/85	Brest–Amorique	Home	League	1–2		
9	09/08/85	AS Nancy–Lorraine	Away	League	0–1		
Sub+4	16/08/85	Paris Saint–Germain FC	Home	League	0–1		
Sub+5	02/10/85	Milan AC	Away	UEFA Cup	0–3		
10	05/10/85	AS Monaco	Away	League	0–1		

FC Martigues – French League Division Two

1	19/10/85	Montceau–Les–Mines	Home	League	2–0	1 Goal	(1)
2	26/10/85	Istres SF	Away	League	3–1		
3	02/11/85	AS Cannes	Home	League	1–1		
4	09/11/85	CS Thonon	Away	League	1–3	1 Goal	(2)
5	23/11/85	AS Red Star 93	Home	League	2–1		
6	29/11/85	Nimes Olympique	Home	League	1–1		
7	15/12/85	FC Grasse	Neutral	Fr Cup	5–0		
8	02/02/86	Olympique Lyonnais	Away	League	0–0		
9	08/02/86	Club Omnisport Le Puy	Home	League	1–0		
10	01/03/86	Montpellier HSC	Home	League	2–1		
11	08/03/86	FC Grenoble	Away	League	2–1	1 Goal	(3)
12	16/03/86	Olympique Ales	Home	League	1–0	1 Goal	(4)
13	22/03/86	Montceau–Les–Mines	Away	League	0–2		
14	25/03/86	Entente Chaumontaise Ath	Away	League	1–2		
15	29/03/86	Istres SF	Home	League	1–0		
16	09/04/86	AS Cannes	Away	League	1–1		

SEASON 1986–87

AJ Auxerre – French League Division One

1	05/08/86	AS Nancy–Lorraine	Away	League	1–1		
2	08/08/86	Paris Saint–Germain FC	Home	League	1–2		
3	12/08/86	RC Lens	Away	League	1–1		
4	15/08/86	AS Monaco	Home	League	1–3		
5	22/08/86	Toulouse FC	Away	League	0–2		
6	26/08/86	Stade Lavallois de Laval	Home	League	1–1		
7	29/08/86	Olympique de Marseille	Away	League	1–1		
8	03/09/86	Brest Armorique	Away	League	0–0		
9	13/09/86	AS Saint–Etienne	Home	League	3–0	1 Goal	(1)
10	20/09/86	FC Metz	Away	League	1–0	1 Goal	(2)
11	24/09/86	FC Nantes	Home	League	1–0		
12	04/10/86	Lille OSC	Away	League	1–1		
13	17/10/86	SC Toulon	Home	League	2–0		
14	24/10/86	OGC Nice	Away	League	0–2		
15	31/10/86	Racing Club de Paris	Home	League	2–0		
16	07/11/86	Stade Rennais FC de Rennes	Away	League	3–1	1 Goal	(3)
17	29/11/86	Le Havre AC	Home	League	1–0	1 Goal	(4)
18	05/12/86	Paris Saint–Germain FC	Away	League	0–1		
19	14/12/86	RC Lens	Home	League	3–1	2 Goals	(6)
20	17/12/86	AS Monaco	Away	League	0–2		
21	21/12/86	Toulouse FC	Home	League	2–1		
Sub+1	27/02/87	Stade Lavallois de Laval	Away	League	2–0		
22	07/03/87	Olympique de Marseille	Home	League	0–0		
23	11/03/87	Brest Armorique	Home	League	1–0	1 Goal	(7)
24	14/03/87	AS Saint–Etienne	Away	League	1–1		
25	20/03/87	Chamois Niortais de Niort	Neutral	Fr Cup	2–0	2 Goals	(9)
26	24/03/87	FC Metz	Home	League	0–0		
27	28/03/87	FC Nantes	Away	League	1–0	1 Goal	(10)
28	01/04/87	Baume–Les–Dames	Neutral	Fr Cup	5–0	2 Goals	(12)
29	04/04/87	Lille OSC	Home	League	1–0		
30	11/04/87	SC Toulon	Away	League	1–1		
31	17/04/87	OGC Nice	Home	League	2–0	1 Goal	(13)
32	21/04/87	Lille OSC	Away	Fr Cup	0–3		
33	02/05/87	Racing Club Paris	Away	League	0–3		
34	06/05/87	Lille OSC	Home	Fr Cup	0–0		
35	09/05/87	Stade Rennais FC de Rennes	Home	League	1–0	1 Goal	(14)
36	15/05/87	Girondins de Bordeaux	Away	League	0–2		
37	22/05/87	FC Sochaux	Home	League	0–0		
38	29/05/87	Le Havre AC	Away	League	4–1	2 Goals	(16)
39	05/06/87	AS Nancy–Lorraine	Home	League	4–2	1 Goal	(17)

SEASON 1987–88

French League Division One

40	18/07/87	AS Cannes	Away	League	0–0		
41	25/07/87	Girondins de Bordeaux	Home	League	1–3	1 Goal	(18)
42	01/08/87	SC Toulon	Away	League	0–0		
43	08/08/87	Lille OSC	Home	League	2–1	1 Goal	(19)
44	15/08/87	Brest Armorique	Away	League	1–1		
45	19/08/87	Stade Lavallois de Laval	Home	League	1–1		
46	12/09/87	FC Metz	Home	League	0–1		
47	17/09/87	Panathinaikos AO Athina	Away	UEFA Cup	0–2		
48	20/09/87	Racing Matra	Away	League	0–1		
49	26/09/87	Olympique de Marseille	Away	League	1–0		
50	30/09/87	Panathinaikos AO Athina	Home	UEFA Cup	3–2	1 Goal	(20)
51	03/10/87	RC Lens	Home	League	2–0		
52	07/10/87	Le Havre AC	Away	League	2–1	1 Goal	(21)
53	17/10/87	Montpellier HSC	Home	League	1–1		
54	24/10/87	Toulouse FC	Away	League	0–0		
55	31/10/87	Paris Saint–Germain FC	Home	League	3–0	1 Goal	(22)
56	07/11/87	Chamois Niortais de Niort	Away	League	0–0		
57	11/11/87	AS Monaco	Home	League	0–0		
58	21/11/87	Girondins de Bordeaux	Away	League	0–0		
59	28/11/87	SC Toulon	Home	League	0–0		
60	05/12/87	Lille OSC	Away	League	1–0	1 Goal	(23)
61	12/12/87	Brest Armorique	Home	League	4–0	1 Goal	(24)
62	19/12/87	Stade Lavallois de Laval	Away	League	0–0		
63	20/02/88	AS Saint–Etienne	Home	League	0–1		
64	27/02/88	FC Nantes	Away	League	0–0		
65	05/03/88	OGC Nice	Home	League	2–0	1 Goal	(25)
66	12/03/88	US Valenciennes–Anzin	Neutral	Fr Cup	2–0		
67	19/03/88	FC Metz	Away	League	0–1		
68	26/03/88	Racing Matra	Home	League	3–0		
69	30/03/88	FC Nantes	Home	Fr Cup	1–0		
70	02/04/88	Olympique de Marseille	Home	League	2–0	1 Goal	(26)
71	05/04/88	FC Nantes	Away	Fr Cup	0–0		
72	19/04/88	Lille OSC	Away	Fr Cup	0–1		
73	23/04/88	Lille OSC	Home	Fr Cup	2–1	1 Goal	(27)
74	30/04/88	Montpellier HSC	Away	League	2–2		
75	07/05/88	Toulouse FC	Home	League	0–2		
76	14/05/88	Paris Saint–Germain FC	Away	League	1–1		
77	21/05/88	Chamois Niortais de Niort	Home	League	1–3		
78	27/05/88	AS Monaco	Away	League	2–3		

SEASON 1988–89

Olympique de Marseille – French League Division One

1	16/07/88	Montpellier HSC	Home	League	1–1		
2	23/07/88	Lille OSC	Away	League	1–2		
3	27/07/88	FC Sochaux	Home	League	0–0		
4	06/08/88	OGC Nice	Home	League	3–2		
5	12/08/88	AS Saint–Etienne	Away	League	0–0		
6	17/08/88	Matra Racing Paris	Home	League	2–0	1 Goal	(1)
7	20/08/88	RC Strasbourg	Away	League	3–2	2 Goals	(3)
8	27/08/88	Stade Lavallois de Laval	Away	League	1–0		
9	03/09/88	RC Lens	Home	League	5–2	2 Goals	(5)
10	10/09/88	Girondins de Bordeaux	Away	League	0–0		
11	17/09/88	AS Cannes	Home	League	2–1		
12	21/09/88	FC Nantes	Away	League	1–1		
13	01/10/88	FC Metz	Home	League	3–2		
14	08/10/88	AS Monaco	Away	League	0–3		
15	15/10/88	SM Caen	Home	League	4–2	1 Goal	(6)
16	29/10/88	Paris Saint–Germain FC	Away	League	0–0		
17	05/11/88	SC Toulon	Home	League	1–0		
18	12/11/88	AJ Auxerre	Away	League	0–1		
19	03/12/88	FC Sochaux	Away	League	0–0		
20	10/12/88	Toulouse FC	Home	League	3–1		
21	13/12/88	OGC Nice	Away	League	2–2		
22	17/12/88	AS Saint–Etienne	Home	League	2–0		

Girondins de Bordeaux – French League Division One

1	19/02/89	RC Strasbourg	Away	League	2–3	1 Goal	(1)
2	22/02/89	OGC Nice	Home	League	2–0		
3	25/02/89	AS Beauvais–oise	Neutral	Fr Cup	1–1+		
4	18/03/89	Stade Lavallois de Laval	Home	League	2–1		
5	25/03/89	RC Lens	Away	League	2–0	1 Goal	(2)

6	01/04/89	Matra Racing Paris	Home	League	3–2		
7	12/04/89	FC Metz	Home	League	4–1	2 Goals	(4)
8	21/04/89	FC Nantes	Away	League	0–1		
9	06/05/89	AS Cannes	Home	League	0–0		
10	13/05/89	AS Monaco	Away	League	2–4	1 Goal	(5)
11	20/05/89	SM Caen	Home	League	2–3	1 Goal	(6)
12	31/05/89	AJ Auxerre	Away	League	1–1		

+ AET AS Beauvais–oise won 3–2 on penalties

SEASON 1989–90

Montpellier HSC – French League Division One

1	02/08/89	Girondins de Bordeaux	Home	League	1–2		
2	05/08/89	Paris Saint–Germain FC	Away	League	1–2	1 Goal	(1)
3	12/08/89	AJ Auxerre	Home	League	1–0		
4	19/08/89	Olympique de Marseille	Away	League	0–2		
5	26/08/89	Olympique Lyonnais	Home	League	2–0		
6	30/08/89	FC Nantes	Away	League	1–1		
7	09/09/89	Toulouse FC	Home	League	1–0		
8	16/09/89	OGC Nice	Away	League	0–3		
9	23/09/89	FC Metz	Home	League	1–2		
10	30/09/89	Racing Paris 1	Home	League	2–0	1 Goal	(2)
11	04/10/89	FC Sochaux	Away	League	1–3		
12	14/10/89	SC Toulon	Home	League	3–0		
13	21/10/89	Lille OSC	Away	League	0–1		
14	08/11/89	Brest Armorique	Home	League	1–1	1 Goal	(3)
15	11/11/89	AS Monaco	Away	League	0–1		
16	25/11/89	FG Mulhouse	Home	League	3–3	1 Goal	(4)
17	03/12/89	Girondins de Bordeaux	Away	League	0–2		
18	10/12/89	Paris Saint–Germain FC	Home	League	2–0		
19	17/12/89	AJ Auxerre	Away	League	1–2		
20	04/02/90	Olympique de Marseille	Home	League	1–1		
21	11/02/90	Olympique Lyonnais	Away	League	1–3		
22	17/02/90	Istres SF	Neutral	Fr Cup	1–0		
23	21/02/90	FC Nantes	Home	League	2–1		
24	25/02/90	Toulouse FC	Away	League	0–0		
25	03/03/90	OGC Nice	Home	League	1–0		
26	10/03/90	Louhans–Cuiseaux	Home	Fr Cup	5–1	3 Goals	(7)
27	15/03/90	FC Metz	Home	League	1–0		
28	24/03/90	Racing Paris 1	Away	League	0–0		
29	30/03/90	FC Sochaux	Home	League	2–0	2 Goals	(9)
30	07/04/90	SC Toulon	Away	League	0–3		
31	11/04/90	FC Nantes	Home	Fr Cup	2–0		
32	14/04/90	Lille OSC	Home	League	5–0	1 Goal	(10)
33	21/04/90	AS Saint–Etienne	Away	League	0–1		
34	28/04/90	SM Caen	Home	League	5–1	1 Goal	(11)
35	02/05/90	Olympique Avignon	Away	Fr Cup	1–0		
36	05/05/90	Brest Armorique	Away	League	1–1		
37	12/05/90	AS Monaco	Home	League	0–0		
38	26/05/90	AS Saint–Etienne	Away	Fr Cup	1–0	1 Goal	(12)
39	02/06/90	Racing Paris 1	Neutral	Fr Cup	2–1*		

SEASON 1990–91

Olympique de Marseille – French League Division One

1	21/07/90	OGC Nice	Home	League	1–0		
2	27/07/90	FC Metz	Away	League	2–0		
3	04/08/90	SM Caen	Home	League	2–1	2 Goals	(2)
4	11/08/90	Olympique Lyonnais	Away	League	2–2	1 Goal	(3)
5	18/08/90	Lille OSC	Home	League	2–0		
6	29/08/90	Girondins de Bordeaux	Home	League	2–0		
7	08/09/90	Paris–Saint–Germain FC	Home	League	2–1	1 Goal	(4)
8	15/09/90	Toulouse FC	Away	League	2–0		
9	18/09/90	KS Dinamo Tirane	Home	Eur Cup	5–1	1 Goal	(5)
10	22/09/90	AS Cannes	Home	League	0–1		
11	28/09/90	AS Monaco	Away	League	3–1		
12	03/10/90	KS Dinamo Tirane	Away	Eur Cup	0–0		
13	06/10/90	AS Saint–Etienne	Home	League	3–1	2 Goals	(7)
14	20/10/90	FC Sochaux	Away	League	1–2		
15	25/10/90	KKS Lech Poznan	Away	Eur Cup	2–3		
16	28/10/90	Brest–Armorique	Home	League	3–1	1 Goal	(8)
Sub+1	27/01/91	FC Nantes	Home	League	6–0		
Sub+2	01/02/91	Girondins de Bordeaux	Away	League	1–1		
17	24/02/91	AS Cannes	Away	League	0–0		

| 18 | 15/03/91 | AS Saint–Etienne | Away | League | 1–1 | 1 Goal | (9) |
| 19 | 23/03/91 | FC Sochaux | Home | League | 0–0 | | |

SEASON 1991–92

Nimes Olympique – French League Division One

1	27/07/91	Toulouse FC	Home	League	2–2	1 Goal	(1)
2	31/07/91	AS Saint–Etienne	Away	League	0–3		
3	03/08/91	RC Lens	Home	League	0–2		
4	10/08/91	AJ Auxerre	Away	League	0–0		
5	17/08/91	FC Nantes	Home	League	0–0		
6	14/09/91	Le Havre AC	Home	League	1–0		
7	21/09/91	AS Monaco	Away	League	1–1		
8	28/09/91	Olympique Lyonnais	Home	League	2–1		
9	05/10/91	Montpellier HSC	Away	League	0–0		
10	19/10/91	Lille OSC	Home	League	1–0	1 Goal	(2)
11	26/10/91	Paris Saint–Germain FC	Away	League	0–2		
12	02/11/91	Stade Rennais FC	Home	League	1–2		
13	09/11/91	SC Toulon	Away	League	0–5		
14	16/11/91	SM Caen	Home	League	0–1		
15	23/11/91	FC Metz	Away	League	0–4		
16	07/12/91	AS Saint–Etienne	Home	League	1–1		

Leeds United – League Division One

Sub+1	08/02/92	Oldham Athletic	Away	League	0–2		
1	23/02/92	Everton	Away	League	1–1		
Sub+2	29/02/92	Luton Town	Home	League	2–0	1 Goal	(1)
Sub+3	03/03/92	Aston Villa	Home	League	0–0		
Sub+4	07/03/92	Tottenham Hotspur	Away	League	3–1		
Sub+5	11/03/92	Queens Park Rangers	Away	League	1–4		
2	14/03/92	Wimbledon	Home	League	5–1	1 Goal	(2)
3	22/03/92	Arsenal	Away	League	1–1		
4	28/03/92	West Ham United	Home	League	0–0		
5	04/04/92	Manchester City	Away	League	0–4		
Sub+6	11/04/92	Chelsea	Home	League	3–0	1 Goal	(3)
Sub+7	18/04/92	Liverpool	Away	League	0–0		
Sub+8	20/04/92	Coventry City	Home	League	2–0		
Sub+9	26/04/92	Sheffield United	Away	League	3–2		
6	02/05/92	Norwich City	Home	League	1–1		

SEASON 1992–93

Premier League

7	08/08/92	Liverpool	Wembley	FA C/S	4–3	3 Goals	(6)
8	15/08/92	Wimbledon	Home	League	2–1		
9	19/08/92	Aston Villa	Away	League	1–1		
10	22/08/92	Middlesbrough	Away	League	1–4	1 Goal	(7)
11	25/08/92	Tottenham Hotspur	Home	League	5–0	3 Goals	(10)
12	29/08/92	Liverpool	Home	League	2–2		
13	01/09/92	Oldham Athletic	Away	League	2–2	2 Goals	(12)
14	06/09/92	Manchester United	Away	League	0–2		
15	13/09/92	Aston Villa	Home	League	1–1		
16	16/09/92	VFB Stuttgart	Away	Eur Cup	0–3		
17	26/09/92	Everton	Home	League	2–0		
18	30/09/92	VFB Stuttgart	Home	Eur Cup	4–1+	1 Goal	(13)
19	03/10/92	Ipswich Town	Away	League	2–4		
20	09/10/92	VFB Stuttgart	Neutral	Eur Cup	2–1		
21	17/10/92	Sheffield United	Home	League	3–1		
22	21/10/92	Rangers	Away	Eur Cup	1–2		
Sub+10	31/10/92	Coventry City	Home	League	2–2		
23	04/11/92	Rangers	Home	Eur Cup	1–2	1 Goal	(14)
24	07/11/92	Manchester City	Away	League	0–4		
25	10/11/92	Watford	Away	Lge Cup	1–2		

+ Leeds United awarded match 3–0 after VFB Stuttgart fielded an ineligible player

Manchester United – Premier League

Sub+1	06/12/92	Manchester City	Home	League	2–1		
1	12/12/92	Norwich City	Home	League	1–0		
2	19/12/92	Chelsea	Away	League	1–1	1 Goal	(1)
3	26/12/92	Sheffield Wednesday	Away	League	3–3	1 Goal	(2)
4	28/12/92	Coventry City	Home	League	5–0	1 Goal	(3)
5	05/01/93	Bury	Home	FA Cup	2–0		
6	09/01/93	Tottenham Hotspur	Home	League	4–1	1 Goal	(4)
7	27/01/93	Nottingham Forest	Home	League	2–0		

8	30/01/93	Ipswich Town	Away	League	1–2		
9	06/02/93	Sheffield United	Home	League	2–1	1 Goal	(5)
10	08/02/93	Leeds United	Away	League	0–0		
11	20/02/93	Southampton	Home	League	2–1		
12	27/02/93	Middlesbrough	Home	League	3–0	1 Goal	(6)
13	14/03/93	Aston Villa	Home	League	1–1		
14	20/03/93	Manchester City	Away	League	1–1	1 Goal	(7)
15	24/03/93	Arsenal	Home	League	0–0		
16	05/04/93	Norwich City	Away	League	3–1	1 Goal	(8)
17	10/04/93	Sheffield Wednesday	Home	League	2–1		
18	12/04/93	Coventry City	Away	League	1–0		
19	17/04/93	Chelsea	Home	League	3–0	1 Goal	(9)
20	21/04/93	Crystal Palace	Away	League	2–0		
21	03/05/93	Blackburn Rovers	Home	League	3–1		
22	09/05/93	Wimbledon	Away	League	2–1		

SEASON 1993–94

Premier League

23	07/08/93	Arsenal	Wembley	FA C/S	1–1+		
24	28/08/93	Southampton	Away	League	3–1	1 Goal	(10)
25	01/09/93	West Ham United	Home	League	3–0	1 Goal	(11)
26	11/09/93	Chelsea	Away	League	0–1		
27	15/09/93	Kispest Honved	Away	Eur Cup	3–2	1 Goal	(12)
28	19/09/93	Arsenal	Home	League	1–0	1 Goal	(13)
29	25/09/93	Swindon Town	Home	League	4–2	1 Goal	(14)
30	29/09/93	Kispest Honved	Home	Eur Cup	2–1		
31	02/10/93	Sheffield Wednesday	Away	League	3–2		
32	16/10/93	Tottenham Hotspur	Home	League	2–1		
33	20/10/93	Galatasaray SK	Home	Eur Cup	3–3	1 Goal	(15)
34	23/10/93	Everton	Away	League	1–0		
35	30/10/93	Queens Park Rangers	Home	League	2–1	1 Goal	(16)
36	03/11/93	Galatasaray SK	Away	Eur Cup	0–0		
37	07/11/93	Manchester City	Away	League	3–2	2 Goals	(18)
38	20/11/93	Wimbledon	Home	League	3–1		
39	24/11/93	Ipswich Town	Home	League	0–0		
40	27/11/93	Coventry City	Away	League	1–0	1 Goal	(19)
41	30/11/93	Everton	Home	Lge Cup	2–0		
42	04/12/93	Norwich City	Home	League	2–2		
43	07/12/93	Sheffield United	Away	League	3–0	1 Goal	(20)
44	11/12/93	Newcastle United	Away	League	1–1		
45	19/12/93	Aston Villa	Home	League	3–1	2 Goals	(22)
46	26/12/93	Blackburn Rovers	Home	League	1–1		
47	29/12/93	Oldham Athletic	Away	League	5–2	1 Goal	(23)
48	01/01/94	Leeds United	Home	League	0–0		
49	04/01/94	Liverpool	Away	League	3–3		
50	09/01/94	Sheffield United	Away	FA Cup	1–0		
51	12/01/94	Portsmouth	Home	Lge Cup	2–2	1 Goal	(24)
52	15/01/94	Tottenham Hotspur	Away	League	1–0		
53	22/01/94	Everton	Away	League	1–0		
54	26/01/94	Portsmouth	Away	Lge Cup	1–0		
55	30/01/94	Norwich City	Away	FA Cup	2–0	1 Goal	(25)
56	05/02/94	Queens Park Rangers	Away	League	3–2	1 Goal	(26)
57	13/02/94	Sheffield Wednesday	Home	Lge Cup	1–0		
58	20/02/94	Wimbledon	Away	FA Cup	3–0	1 Goal	(27)
59	26/02/94	West Ham United	Away	League	2–2		
60	12/03/94	Charlton Athletic	Home	FA Cup	3–1		
61	16/03/94	Sheffield Wednesday	Home	League	5–0	2 Goals	(29)
62	19/03/94	Swindon Town	Away	League	2–2		
63	22/03/94	Arsenal	Away	League	2–2		
64	27/03/94	Aston Villa	Wembley	Lge Cup	1–3		
65	30/03/94	Liverpool	Home	League	1–0		
66	23/04/94	Manchester City	Home	League	2–0	2 Goals	(31)
67	27/04/94	Leeds United	Away	League	2–0		
68	01/05/94	Ipswich Town	Away	League	2–1	1 Goal	(32)
69	04/05/94	Southampton	Home	League	2–0		
70	08/05/94	Coventry City	Home	League	0–0		
71	14/05/94	Chelsea	Wembley	FA Cup	4–0	2 Goals	(34)

+ Manchester United won 5–4 on penalties

SEASON 1994–95

Premier League

72	15/08/94	Blackburn Rovers	Wembley	FA C/S	2–0	1 Goal	(35)
73	31/08/94	Wimbledon	Home	League	3–0	1 Goal	(36)

74	11/09/94	Leeds United	Away	League	1–2	1 Goal	(37)
75	17/09/94	Liverpool	Home	League	2–0		
76	24/09/94	Ipswich Town	Away	League	2–3	1 Goal	(38)
77	01/10/94	Everton	Home	League	2–0		
78	15/10/94	West Ham United	Home	League	1–0	1 Goal	(39)
79	23/10/94	Blackburn Rovers	Away	League	4–2	1 Goal	(40)
80	29/10/94	Newcastle United	Home	League	2–0		
81	06/11/94	Aston Villa	Away	League	2–1		
82	10/11/94	Manchester City	Home	League	5–0	1 Goal	(41)
83	19/11/94	Crystal Palace	Home	League	3–0	1 Goal	(42)
84	23/11/94	IFK Goteborg	Away	Eur Cup	1–3		
85	26/11/94	Arsenal	Away	League	0–0		
86	03/12/94	Norwich City	Home	League	1–0	1 Goal	(43)
87	07/12/94	Galatasaray SK	Home	Eur Cup	4–0		
88	17/12/94	Nottingham Forest	Home	League	1–2	1 Goal	(44)
89	26/12/94	Chelsea	Away	League	3–2	1 Goal	(45)
90	28/12/94	Leicester City	Home	League	1–1		
91	31/12/94	Southampton	Away	League	2–2		
92	03/01/95	Coventry City	Home	League	2–0	1 Goal	(46)
93	09/01/95	Sheffield United	Away	FA Cup	2–0	1 Goal	(47)
94	15/01/95	Newcastle United	Away	League	1–1		
95	22/01/95	Blackburn Rovers	Home	League	1–0	1 Goal	(48)
96	25/01/95	Crystal Palace	Away	League	1–1		

SEASON 1995–96

Premier League

97	01/10/95	Liverpool	Home	League	2–2	1 Goal	(49)
98	03/10/95	York City	Away	Lge Cup	3–1		
99	21/10/95	Chelsea	Away	League	4–1		
100	28/10/95	Middlesbrough	Home	League	2–0		
101	04/11/95	Arsenal	Away	League	0–1		
102	18/11/95	Southampton	Home	League	4–1		
103	22/11/95	Coventry City	Away	League	4–0		
104	27/11/95	Nottingham Forest	Away	League	1–1	1 Goal	(50)
105	02/12/95	Chelsea	Home	League	1–1		
106	09/12/95	Sheffield Wednesday	Home	League	2–2	2 Goals	(52)
107	17/12/95	Liverpool	Away	League	0–2		
108	24/12/95	Leeds United	Away	League	1–3		
109	27/12/95	Newcastle United	Home	League	2–0		
110	30/12/95	Queens Park Rangers	Home	League	2–1		
111	01/01/96	Tottenham Hotspur	Away	League	1–4		
112	06/01/96	Sunderland	Home	FA Cup	2–2	1 Goal	(53)
113	13/01/96	Aston Villa	Home	League	0–0		
114	16/01/96	Sunderland	Away	FA Cup	2–1		
115	22/01/96	West Ham United	Away	League	1–0	1 Goal	(54)
116	27/01/96	Reading	Away	FA Cup	3–0	1 Goal	(55)
117	03/02/96	Wimbledon	Away	League	4–2	2 Goals	(57)
118	10/02/96	Blackburn Rovers	Home	League	1–0		
119	18/02/96	Manchester City	Home	FA Cup	2–1	1 Goal	(58)
120	21/02/96	Everton	Home	League	2–0		
121	25/02/96	Bolton Wanderers	Away	League	6–0		
122	04/03/96	Newcastle United	Away	League	1–0	1 Goal	(59)
123	11/03/96	Southampton	Home	FA Cup	2–0	1 Goal	(60)
124	16/03/96	Queens Park Rangers	Away	League	1–1	1 Goal	(61)
125	20/03/96	Arsenal	Home	League	1–0	1 Goal	(62)
126	24/03/96	Tottenham Hotspur	Home	League	1–0	1 Goal	(63)
127	31/03/96	Chelsea	Neutral	FA Cup	2–1		
128	06/04/96	Manchester City	Away	League	3–2	1 Goal	(64)
129	08/04/96	Coventry City	Home	League	1–0	1 Goal	(65)
130	13/04/96	Southampton	Away	League	1–3		
131	17/04/96	Leeds United	Home	League	1–0		
132	28/04/96	Nottingham Forest	Home	League	5–0	1 Goal	(66)
133	05/05/96	Middlesbrough	Away	League	3–0		
134	11/05/96	Liverpool	Wembley	FA Cup	1–0	1 Goal	(67)

SEASON 1996–97

Premier League

135	11/08/96	Newcastle United	Wembley	FA C/S	4–0	1 Goal	(68)
136	17/08/96	Wimbledon	Away	League	3–0	1 Goal	(69)
137	21/08/96	Everton	Home	League	2–2		
138	25/08/96	Blackburn Rovers	Home	League	2–2		
139	04/09/96	Derby County	Away	League	1–1		
140	07/09/96	Leeds United	Away	League	4–0	1 Goal	(70)

141	11/09/96	Juventus FC	Away	Eur Cup	0–1		
142	14/09/96	Nottingham Forest	Home	League	4–1	2 Goals	(72)
143	21/09/96	Aston Villa	Away	League	0–0		
144	25/09/96	SK Rapid Wien	Home	Eur Cup	2–0		
145	29/09/96	Tottenham Hotspur	Home	League	2–0		
146	12/10/96	Liverpool	Home	League	1–0		
147	16/10/96	Fenerbahce SK	Away	Eur Cup	2–0	1 Goal	(73)
148	20/10/96	Newcastle United	Away	League	0–5		
149	26/10/96	Southampton	Away	League	3–6		
150	30/10/96	Fenerbahce SK	Home	Eur Cup	0–1		
151	02/11/96	Chelsea	Home	League	1–2		
152	16/11/96	Arsenal	Home	League	1–0		
153	20/11/96	Juventus FC	Home	Eur Cup	0–1		
154	23/11/96	Middlesbrough	Away	League	2–2		
155	30/11/96	Leicester City	Home	League	3–1		
156	04/12/96	SK Rapid Wien	Away	Eur Cup	2–0	1 Goal	(74)
157	08/12/96	West Ham United	Away	League	2–2		
158	18/12/96	Sheffield Wednesday	Away	League	1–1		
159	21/12/96	Sunderland	Home	League	5–0	2 Goals	(76)
160	26/12/96	Nottingham Forest	Away	League	4–0		
161	28/12/96	Leeds United	Home	League	1–0	1 Goal	(77)
162	01/01/97	Aston Villa	Home	League	0–0		
163	05/01/97	Tottenham Hotspur	Home	FA Cup	2–0		
164	12/01/97	Tottenham Hotspur	Away	League	2–1		
165	18/01/97	Coventry City	Away	League	2–0		
166	25/01/97	Wimbledon	Home	FA Cup	1–1		
167	29/01/97	Wimbledon	Home	League	2–1		
168	01/02/97	Southampton	Home	League	2–1	1 Goal	(78)
169	04/02/97	Wimbledon	Away	FA Cup	0–1		
170	01/03/97	Coventry City	Home	League	3–1		
171	05/03/97	FC Porto	Home	Eur Cup	4–0	1 Goal	(79)
172	08/03/97	Sunderland	Away	League	1–2		
173	15/03/97	Sheffield Wednesday	Home	League	2–0		
174	19/03/97	FC Porto	Away	Eur Cup	0–0		
175	22/03/97	Everton	Away	League	2–0	1 Goal	(80)
176	05/04/97	Derby County	Home	League	2–3	1 Goal	(81)
177	09/04/97	Borussia Dortmund	Away	Eur Cup	0–1		
178	12/04/97	Blackburn Rovers	Away	League	3–2	1 Goal	(82)
179	19/04/97	Liverpool	Away	League	3–1		
180	23/04/97	Borussia Dortmund	Home	Eur Cup	0–1		
181	03/05/97	Leicester City	Away	League	2–2		
182	05/05/97	Middlesbrough	Home	League	3–3		
183	08/05/97	Newcastle United	Home	League	0–0		
184	11/05/97	West Ham United	Home	League	2–0		

INTERNATIONAL APPEARANCES – FRANCE

1	12/08/87	West Germany	Berlin	1–2	F	1 Goal	(1)
2	14/10/87	Norway	Paris	1–1	ECQ		
3	18/11/87	East Germany	Paris	0–1	F		
4	27/01/88	Israel	Tel Aviv	1–1	F		
5	23/03/88	Spain	Bordeaux	2–1	F		
6	16/08/89	Sweden	Malmo	4–2	F	2 Goals	(3)
7	05/09/89	Norway	Oslo	1–1	WCQ		
8	11/10/89	Scotland	Paris	3–0	WCQ	1 Goal	(4)
9	18/11/89	Cyprus	Toulouse	2–0	WCQ		
10	21/01/90	Kuwait	Kazma	1–0	F		
11	24/01/90	East Germany	Kazma	3–0	F	2 Goals	(6)
12	28/02/90	West Germany	Montpellier	2–1	F	1 Goal	(7)
13	28/03/90	Hungary	Budapest	3–1	F	2 Goals	(9)
14	15/08/90	Poland	Paris	0–0	F		
15	05/09/90	Iceland	Reykjavik	2–1	ECQ	1 Goal	(10)
16	13/10/90	Czechoslovakia	Paris	2–1	ECQ		
17	20/02/91	Spain	Paris	3–1	ECQ		
18	30/03/91	Albania	Paris	5–0	ECQ		
19	12/10/91	Spain	Seville	2–1	ECQ		
20	20/11/91	Iceland	Paris	3–1	ECQ	2 Goals	(12)
21	19/02/92	England	Wembley	0–2	F		
22	25/03/92	Belgium	Paris	3–3	F		
23	27/05/92	Switzerland	Lausanne	1–2	F		
24	05/06/92	Holland	Lens	1–1	F		
25	10/06/92	Sweden	Stockholm	1–1	EC		
26	14/06/92	England	Malmo	0–0	EC		
27	17/06/92	Denmark	Malmo	1–2	EC		
28	14/10/92	Austria	Paris	2–0	WCQ	1 Goal	(13)

29	14/11/92	Finland	Paris	2–1	WCQ	1 Goal	(14)
30	17/02/93	Israel	Tel Aviv	4–0	WCQ	1 Goal	(15)
31	28/04/93	Sweden	Paris	2–1	WCQ	2 Goals	(17)
32	28/07/93	Russia	Caen	3–1	F	1 Goal	(18)
33	22/08/93	Sweden	Solna	1–1	WCQ		
34	08/09/93	Finland	Tampere	2–0	WCQ		
35	13/10/93	Israel	Paris	2–3	WCQ		
36	17/11/93	Bulgaria	Paris	1–2	WCQ	1 Goal	(19)
37	16/02/94	Italy	Naples	1–0	F		
38	26/05/94	Australia	Kobe	1–0	F	1 Goal	(20)
39	29/05/94	Japan	Tokyo	4–1	F		
40	17/08/94	Czech Republic	Bordeaux	2–2	F		
41	07/09/94	Slovakia	Bratislava	0–0	EC		
42	08/10/94	Romania	St Etienne	0–0	EC		
43	16/11/94	Poland	Zabrze	0–0	EC		
44	13/12/94	Azerbaijan	Trabzon	2–0	EC		
45	18/01/95	Holland	Utrecht	0–1	F		

APPEARANCES AND GOALS PER SEASON

SEASON 83–84	**GAMES**	**GOALS**
French League	2	0
TOTAL	**2**	**0**

SEASON 84–85	**GAMES**	**GOALS**
French League	3+2	2
TOTAL	**3+2**	**2**

SEASON 85–86	**GAMES**	**GOALS**
French League	20+2	4
French Cup	1	0
UEFA Cup	0+1	0
TOTAL	**21+3**	**4**

SEASON 86–87	**GAMES**	**GOALS**
French League	35+1	13
French Cup	4	4
TOTAL	**39+1**	**17**

SEASON 87–88	**GAMES**	**GOALS**
French League	32	8
French Cup	5	1
UEFA Cup	2	1
TOTAL	**39**	**10**

SEASON 88–89	**GAMES**	**GOALS**
French League	33	12
French Cup	1	0
TOTAL	**34**	**12**

SEASON 89–90	**GAMES**	**GOALS**
French League	33	8
French Cup	6	4
TOTAL	**39**	**12**

SEASON 90–91	**GAMES**	**GOALS**
French League	16+2	8
European Cup	3	1
TOTAL	**19+2**	**9**

SEASON 91–92	**GAMES**	**GOALS**
League	6+9	3
French League	16	2
TOTAL	**22+9**	**5**

SEASON 92–93	**GAMES**	**GOALS**
League	33+2	15
FA Cup	1	0
League Cup	1	0
European Cup	5	2
FA Charity Shield	1	3
TOTAL	**41+2**	**20**

SEASON 93–94	GAMES	GOALS
League	34	18
FA Cup	5	4
League Cup	5	1
European Cup	4	2
FA Charity Shield	1	0
TOTAL	**49**	**25**

SEASON 94–95	GAMES	GOALS
League	21	12
FA Cup	1	1
European Cup	2	0
FA Charity Shield	1	1
TOTAL	**25**	**14**

SEASON 95–96	GAMES	GOALS
League	30	14
FA Cup	7	5
League Cup	1	0
TOTAL	**38**	**19**

SEASON 96–97	GAMES	GOALS
League	36	11
FA Cup	3	0
European Cup	10	3
FA Charity Shield	1	1
TOTAL	**50**	**15**

CAREER APPEARANCES AND GOALS

COMPETITION	GAMES	TOTAL	GOALS
League	160+11	171	73
FA Cup	17	17	10
League Cup	7	7	1
FA Charity Shield	4	4	5
European Cup	24	24	8
UEFA Cup	2+1	3	1
French League	190+7	197	57
French Cup	17	17	9
Internationals	45	45	20
TOTAL	**466+19**	**485**	**184**

HAT-TRICKS

Montpellier HSC

1	3	Louhans–Cuiseaux	10/03/90	Home	Fr Cup	5–1

Leeds United

1	3	Liverpool	08/08/92	Wembley	FA C/S	4–3
2	3	Tottenham Hotspur	25/08/92	Home	League	5–0

League: 1
FA Charity Shield: 1
French Cup: 1
TOTAL: 3

HONOURS

Winners medals
Premier League Championship: 92/93, 93/94, 95/96, 96/97
League Division One Championship: 91/92
FA Cup: 93/94, 95/96
FA Charity Shield: 92/93, 93/94, 94/95, 96/97
French League Division One Championship: 88/89, 90/91
French Cup: 89/90

Runner-up medals
Premier League Championship: 94/95
League Cup: 93/94

TONY CASCARINO

Born: 01/09/62 – Orpington
Height: 6.2
Weight: 13.12 (95–96)

Clubs
Gillingham: **1982–87** – Matches: **257+12** – Goals: **110**
Millwall: **1987–90** – Matches: **128** – Goals: **49**
Aston Villa: **1990–91** – Matches: **50+4** – Goals: **12**
Celtic: **1991–92** – Matches: **16+14** – Goals: **4**
Chelsea: **1992–94** – Matches: **39+6** – Goals: **8**
Olympique de Marseille: **1994–96** – Matches: **105** – Goals: **70**
AS Nancy–Lorraine: **1996–97** – Matches: **11+2** – Goals: **6**

Country
Republic of Ireland: **1985–97** – Matches: **35+35** – Goals: **16**

SEASON 1981–82

Gillingham – League Division Three

1	02/02/82	Burnley	Away	League	0–1		
2	06/02/82	Chester	Away	League	0–0		
Sub+1	09/02/82	Brentford	Home	League	1–1		
Sub+2	13/02/82	Wimbledon	Home	League	6–1	1 Goal	(1)
Sub+3	20/02/82	Exeter City	Away	League	1–1		
Sub+4	27/02/82	Plymouth Argyle	Home	League	3–2	1 Goal	(2)
3	06/03/82	Huddersfield Town	Away	League	0–2		
4	09/03/82	Portsmouth	Away	League	0–1		
5	12/03/82	Millwall	Home	League	1–1	1 Goal	(3)
6	16/03/82	Southend United	Home	League	2–0		
7	20/03/82	Swindon Town	Away	League	1–0		
8	27/03/82	Bristol City	Home	League	2–0		
9	31/03/82	Oxford United	Away	League	1–1		
Sub+5	03/04/82	Doncaster Rovers	Away	League	1–1		
10	06/04/82	Chesterfield	Home	League	3–2		
11	10/04/82	Fulham	Home	League	2–0		
12	12/04/82	Newport County	Away	League	2–4		
13	17/04/82	Walsall	Away	League	0–1		
14	01/05/82	Bristol City	Away	League	1–2		
15	04/05/82	Lincoln City	Home	League	1–0	1 Goal	(4)
16	08/05/82	Oxford United	Home	League	2–1		
17	11/05/82	Fulham	Away	League	0–0		
18	15/05/82	Chesterfield	Away	League	3–1	1 Goal	(5)
19	18/05/82	Reading	Home	League	2–1		

SEASON 1982–83

League Division Three

20	28/08/82	Oxford United	Home	League	0–1		
21	31/08/82	Orient	Home	Lge Cup	3–0	2 Goals	(7)
22	04/09/82	Exeter City	Away	League	2–2	1 Goal	(8)
23	07/09/82	Bristol Rovers	Away	League	1–2		
24	11/09/82	Millwall	Home	League	1–0	1 Goal	(9)
25	14/09/82	Orient	Away	Lge Cup	0–2		
26	18/09/82	Wrexham	Away	League	0–1		
27	25/09/82	Walsall	Home	League	3–0	1 Goal	(10)
28	28/09/82	Reading	Home	League	1–0	1 Goal	(11)
29	02/10/82	Sheffield United	Away	League	2–0		
30	05/10/82	Oldham Athletic	Home	Lge Cup	2–0	1 Goal	(12)
31	09/10/82	Preston North End	Home	League	2–1	1 Goal	(13)
32	16/10/82	Cardiff City	Away	League	0–1		
33	19/10/82	Orient	Home	League	4–0		
34	23/10/82	AFC Bournemouth	Away	League	1–0		
35	27/10/82	Oldham Athletic	Away	Lge Cup	0–1		
36	06/11/82	Portsmouth	Away	League	0–1		
37	09/11/82	Tottenham Hotspur	Home	Lge Cup	2–4		
38	13/11/82	Doncaster Rovers	Home	League	1–1		

39	20/11/82	Dagenham	Home	FA Cup	1–0	1 Goal	(14)
40	27/11/82	Wigan Athletic	Home	League	0–2		
41	04/12/82	Newport County	Away	League	1–2		
42	11/12/82	Northampton Town	Home	FA Cup	1–1		
Sub+6	14/12/82	Northampton Town	Away	FA Cup	2–3		
43	18/12/82	Plymouth Argyle	Away	League	0–2		
44	27/12/82	Southend United	Home	League	1–0		
45	28/12/82	Brentford	Away	League	1–1		
46	01/01/83	Lincoln City	Home	League	0–2		
47	03/01/83	Bradford City	Away	League	1–1		
48	08/01/83	Exeter City	Home	League	4–4		
49	15/01/83	Oxford United	Away	League	1–1		
50	22/01/83	Wrexham	Home	League	1–1		
51	30/01/83	Millwall	Away	League	1–4	1 Goal	(15)
52	05/02/83	Walsall	Away	League	0–0		
53	15/02/83	Chesterfield	Home	League	3–1	1 Goal	(16)
Sub+7	19/03/83	Portsmouth	Home	League	1–0		
54	25/03/83	Doncaster Rovers	Away	League	2–0	1 Goal	(17)
55	01/04/83	Southend United	Away	League	1–1	1 Goal	(18)
56	02/04/83	Brentford	Home	League	2–2	1 Goal	(19)
57	09/04/83	Newport County	Home	League	2–0		
58	16/04/83	Reading	Away	League	0–0		
59	23/04/83	Plymouth Argyle	Home	League	2–1	2 Goals	(21)
60	30/04/83	Wigan Athletic	Away	League	2–2		
61	03/05/83	Bradford City	Home	League	3–0	1 Goal	(22)
62	07/05/83	Bristol Rovers	Home	League	1–0	1 Goal	(23)
63	14/05/83	Lincoln City	Away	League	1–3	1 Goal	(24)

SEASON 1983–84

League Division Three

Sub+8	06/09/83	Bolton Wanderers	Home	League	2–0		
Sub+9	10/09/83	Plymouth Argyle	Away	League	1–1		
64	12/09/83	Chelsea	Away	Lge Cup	0–4		
65	17/09/83	Oxford United	Home	League	2–3		
66	24/09/83	AFC Bournemouth	Away	League	0–2		
67	01/10/83	Brentford	Home	League	4–2		
68	08/10/83	Preston North End	Home	League	2–0		
69	15/10/83	Burnley	Away	League	3–2	1 Goal	(25)
70	18/10/83	Exeter City	Home	League	3–1		
71	22/10/83	Wigan Athletic	Away	League	2–1		
72	24/10/83	Orient	Away	League	1–1	1 Goal	(26)
73	29/10/83	Millwall	Home	League	3–3		
74	05/11/83	Lincoln City	Home	League	2–0		
75	12/11/83	Walsall	Away	League	1–3	1 Goal	(27)
76	10/12/83	Chelmsford City	Home	FA Cup	6–1		
Sub+10	31/12/83	Wimbledon	Home	League	0–1		
Sub+11	07/01/84	Brentford	Home	FA Cup	5–3	1 Goal	(28)
77	14/01/84	Sheffield United	Home	League	4–2		
78	28/01/84	Everton	Away	FA Cup	0–0		
79	31/01/84	Everton	Home	FA Cup	0–0*		
80	04/02/84	Brentford	Away	League	3–2	1 Goal	(29)
81	06/02/84	Everton	Home	FA Cup	0–3		
82	11/02/84	AFC Bournemouth	Home	League	2–1		
83	14/02/84	Bradford City	Home	League	0–0		
84	19/02/84	Millwall	Away	League	2–2	1 Goal	(30)
85	25/02/84	Wigan Athletic	Home	League	3–0	1 Goal	(31)
86	28/02/84	Millwall	Away	AM Cup	3–4*	2 Goals	(33)
87	03/03/84	Exeter City	Away	League	0–0		
88	07/03/84	Lincoln City	Away	League	0–4		
89	10/03/84	Walsall	Home	League	1–3	1 Goal	(34)
90	13/03/84	Oxford United	Away	League	1–0		
91	17/03/84	Preston North End	Away	League	2–2		
92	24/03/84	Burnley	Home	League	0–1		
Sub+12	27/03/84	Newport County	Away	League	0–1		
93	31/03/84	Orient	Home	League	3–1	1 Goal	(35)
94	07/04/84	Bolton Wanderers	Away	League	1–0	1 Goal	(36)
95	11/04/84	Bradford City	Away	League	2–3		
96	14/04/84	Port Vale	Home	League	1–1		
97	17/04/84	Hull City	Away	League	0–0		
98	20/04/84	Southend United	Away	League	1–3		
99	01/05/84	Plymouth Argyle	Home	League	2–1		
100	05/05/84	Newport County	Home	League	4–1	2 Goals	(38)
101	07/05/84	Wimbledon	Away	League	3–1	1 Goal	(39)
102	12/05/84	Scunthorpe United	Home	League	1–1		

SEASON 1984–85

League Division Three

103	25/08/84	Newport County	Home	League	1–1	1 Goal	(40)
104	28/08/84	Colchester United	Home	Lge Cup	3–2		
105	01/09/84	Orient	Away	League	4–2	1 Goal	(41)
106	04/09/84	Colchester United	Away	Lge Cup	2–0		
107	08/09/84	Cambridge United	Home	League	3–0	1 Goal	(42)
108	15/09/84	Wigan Athletic	Away	League	1–0	1 Goal	(43)
109	18/09/84	Hull City	Away	League	0–2		
110	22/09/84	Walsall	Home	League	3–0	2 Goals	(45)
111	25/09/84	Leeds United	Home	Lge Cup	1–2	1 Goal	(46)
112	29/09/84	Swansea City	Away	League	1–0		
113	02/10/84	Plymouth Argyle	Home	League	3–3	1 Goal	(47)
114	06/10/84	Millwall	Home	League	1–4		
115	10/10/84	Leeds United	Away	Lge Cup	2–3	1 Goal	(48)
116	13/10/84	Bristol City	Away	League	0–2		
117	20/10/84	Brentford	Away	League	2–5		
118	23/10/84	Reading	Home	League	4–1	2 Goals	(50)
119	27/10/84	Bradford City	Home	League	2–2	1 Goal	(51)
120	03/11/84	York City	Away	League	1–7		
121	06/11/84	Burnley	Away	League	1–0		
122	10/11/84	Rotherham United	Home	League	2–1		
123	17/11/84	Windsor & Eton	Home	FA Cup	2–1	1 Goal	(52)
124	24/11/84	Bolton Wanderers	Away	League	2–1		
125	01/12/84	Preston North End	Home	League	4–0	1 Goal	(53)
126	08/12/84	Colchester United	Away	FA Cup	5–0	1 Goal	(54)
127	15/12/84	Lincoln City	Away	League	0–2		
128	22/12/84	Doncaster Rovers	Away	League	1–0		
129	26/12/84	Derby County	Home	League	3–2		
130	29/12/84	Bristol Rovers	Home	League	4–1		
131	02/02/85	Swansea City	Home	League	1–1		
132	05/02/85	Colchester United	Away	FR Trophy	0–2		
133	23/02/85	York City	Home	League	1–0		
134	26/02/85	Hull City	Home	League	1–0		
135	02/03/85	Bradford City	Away	League	1–1		
136	09/03/85	Brentford	Home	League	2–0		
137	12/03/85	Newport County	Away	League	3–0	1 Goal	(55)
138	16/03/85	Bristol City	Home	League	1–3	1 Goal	(56)
139	19/03/85	Plymouth Argyle	Away	League	1–1		
140	23/03/85	Millwall	Away	League	1–2		
141	29/03/85	Burnley	Home	League	1–1		
142	02/04/85	Cambridge United	Away	League	2–1		
143	09/04/85	AFC Bournemouth	Home	League	3–2		
144	13/04/85	Rotherham United	Away	League	0–1		
145	16/04/85	Walsall	Away	League	1–0	1 Goal	(57)
146	20/04/85	Bolton Wanderers	Home	League	2–3		
147	27/04/85	Preston North End	Away	League	0–0		
148	04/05/85	Lincoln City	Home	League	3–2		
149	07/05/85	Bristol Rovers	Away	League	2–3		
150	11/05/85	Doncaster Rovers	Home	League	2–1	1 Goal	(58)
151	14/05/85	Reading	Away	League	2–0	1 Goal	(59)
152	17/05/85	Wigan Athletic	Home	League	5–1		

SEASON 1985–86

League Division Three

153	17/08/85	Lincoln City	Away	League	0–1		
154	20/08/85	Southend United	Away	Lge Cup	1–1		
155	24/08/85	Darlington	Home	League	1–1		
156	26/08/85	Bristol City	Away	League	2–1	2 Goals	(61)
157	31/08/85	Bolton Wanderers	Home	League	2–1	1 Goal	(62)
158	03/09/85	Southend United	Home	Lge Cup	2–0	2 Goals	(64)
159	07/09/85	Notts County	Away	League	1–1		
160	14/09/85	Chesterfield	Home	League	1–1	1 Goal	(65)
161	17/09/85	Wigan Athletic	Home	League	2–0		
162	21/09/85	Bury	Away	League	2–1		
163	24/09/85	Portsmouth	Home	Lge Cup	1–3	1 Goal	(66)
164	28/09/85	York City	Home	League	1–2		
165	01/10/85	Plymouth Argyle	Away	League	0–3		
166	05/10/85	Blackpool	Away	League	2–2	1 Goal	(67)
167	07/10/85	Portsmouth	Away	Lge Cup	1–2		
168	12/10/85	Cardiff City	Home	League	2–0		
169	19/10/85	AFC Bournemouth	Away	League	3–2	2 Goals	(69)
170	02/11/85	Newport County	Away	League	1–1		

171	06/11/85	Rotherham United	Away	League	1–1		
172	09/11/85	Walsall	Home	League	5–2	1 Goal	(70)
173	16/11/85	Northampton Town	Home	FA Cup	3–0	1 Goal	(71)
174	23/11/85	Wolverhampton Wanderers	Away	League	3–1		
175	30/11/85	Doncaster Rovers	Home	League	4–0		
176	07/12/85	Bognor Regis	Home	FA Cup	6–1	2 Goals	(73)
177	14/12/85	Bristol Rovers	Away	League	0–1		
178	20/12/85	Darlington	Away	League	2–3	1 Goal	(74)
179	28/12/85	Bristol City	Home	League	1–1	1 Goal	(75)
180	01/01/86	Reading	Away	League	2–1		
181	04/01/86	Derby County	Home	FA Cup	1–1		
182	11/01/86	Bolton Wanderers	Away	League	1–0		
183	13/01/86	Derby County	Away	FA Cup	1–3		
184	18/01/86	Lincoln City	Home	League	2–0		
185	22/01/86	Derby County	Away	FR Trophy	2–0	1 Goal	(76)
186	25/01/86	Chesterfield	Away	League	1–1		
187	29/01/86	Brentford	Home	FR Trophy	1–1		
188	01/02/86	Notts County	Home	League	4–0		
189	08/02/86	AFC Bournemouth	Home	League	2–0	1 Goal	(77)
190	15/02/86	Wigan Athletic	Away	League	3–3		
191	22/02/86	Bury	Home	League	1–0		
192	24/02/86	Cambridge United	Home	FR Trophy	2–0		
193	01/03/86	York City	Away	League	0–2		
194	04/03/86	Plymouth Argyle	Home	League	1–1	1 Goal	(78)
195	08/03/86	Blackpool	Home	League	2–2	1 Goal	(79)
196	15/03/86	Cardiff City	Away	League	1–1	1 Goal	(80)
197	18/03/86	Brentford	Home	League	1–2		

SEASON 1986–87

League Division Three

198	23/08/86	Newport County	Away	League	2–1		
199	25/08/86	Northampton Town	Home	Lge Cup	1–0		
200	30/08/86	Bristol City	Home	League	1–1		
201	03/09/86	Northampton Town	Away	Lge Cup	2–2	2 Goals	(82)
202	06/09/86	Rotherham United	Away	League	1–0		
203	13/09/86	Middlesbrough	Home	League	0–0		
204	16/09/86	York City	Home	League	2–0		
205	24/09/86	Oxford United	Away	Lge Cup	0–6		
206	27/09/86	Brentford	Home	League	2–0		
207	30/09/86	Mansfield Town	Away	League	0–1		
208	04/10/86	Bury	Home	League	1–0		
209	07/10/86	Oxford United	Home	Lge Cup	1–1	1 Goal	(83)
210	15/10/86	Chester City	Away	League	1–1	1 Goal	(84)
211	18/10/86	Carlisle United	Home	League	1–0		
212	21/10/86	Darlington	Away	League	1–1		
213	25/10/86	Port Vale	Away	League	2–1		
214	01/11/86	Chesterfield	Home	League	3–0		
215	04/11/86	Blackpool	Home	League	2–1		
216	07/11/86	Doncaster Rovers	Away	League	0–2		
217	15/11/86	Kettering Town	Away	FA Cup	3–0		
218	22/11/86	Notts County	Home	League	3–1	1 Goal	(85)
219	24/11/86	Notts County	Away	FR Trophy	5–0	2 Goals	(87)
220	29/11/86	Wigan Athletic	Away	League	1–3		
221	02/12/86	AFC Bournemouth	Away	League	2–0		
222	06/12/86	Chelmsford City	Home	FA Cup	2–0	2 Goals	(89)
223	13/12/86	Bolton Wanderers	Away	League	0–3		
224	16/12/86	Northampton Town	Home	FR Trophy	1–0		
225	19/12/86	Bristol Rovers	Home	League	4–1	2 Goals	(91)
226	03/01/87	Notts County	Away	League	1–3	1 Goal	(92)
227	19/01/87	Wigan Athletic	Away	FA Cup	1–2		
228	26/01/87	Colchester United	Home	FR Trophy	2–0	1 Goal	(93)
229	03/02/87	Rotherham United	Home	League	1–0		
230	07/02/87	York City	Away	League	1–2		
231	10/02/87	Port Vale	Away	FR Trophy	3–3+	1 Goal	(94)
232	14/02/87	Chester City	Home	League	1–2		
233	17/02/87	Newport County	Home	League	1–1		
234	21/02/87	Brentford	Away	League	2–3	1 Goal	(95)
235	28/02/87	Mansfield Town	Home	League	2–0	1 Goal	(96)
236	03/03/87	Chesterfield	Away	League	0–1		
237	07/03/87	Port Vale	Home	League	0–0		
238	10/03/87	Bristol City	Away	FR Trophy	0–2		
239	14/03/87	Carlisle United	Away	League	4–2	1 Goal	(97)
240	17/03/87	Darlington	Home	League	4–1	3 Goals	(100)
241	21/03/87	AFC Bournemouth	Home	League	2–1		

242	28/03/87	Bury	Away	League	0–1		
243	04/04/87	Doncaster Rovers	Home	League	2–1	1 Goal	(101)
244	11/04/87	Blackpool	Away	League	1–0		
245	18/04/87	Walsall	Away	League	0–1		
246	20/04/87	Fulham	Home	League	4–1	2 Goals	(103)
247	22/04/87	Bristol City	Away	League	0–2		
248	25/04/87	Bristol Rovers	Away	League	1–0	1 Goal	(104)
249	28/04/87	Middlesbrough	Away	League	0–3		
250	02/05/87	Wigan Athletic	Home	League	0–0		
251	04/05/87	Swindon Town	Away	League	1–1		
252	09/05/87	Bolton Wanderers	Home	League	1–0	1 Goal	(105)
253	14/05/87	Sunderland	Home	Lge P/O	3–2	3 Goals	(108)
254	17/05/87	Sunderland	Away	Lge P/O	3–4*	2 Goals	(110)
255	22/05/87	Swindon Town	Home	Lge P/O	1–0		
256	25/05/87	Swindon Town	Away	Lge P/O	1–2		
257	29/05/87	Swindon Town	Away	Lge P/O	0–2		

+ AET Gillingham won 5–4 on penalties

SEASON 1987–88

Millwall – League Division Two

1	15/08/87	Middlesbrough	Away	League	1–1		
2	18/08/87	Leyton Orient	Away	Lge Cup	1–1		
3	22/08/87	Barnsley	Home	League	3–1	1 Goal	(1)
4	25/08/87	Leyton Orient	Home	Lge Cup	1–0		
5	01/09/87	Birmingham City	Home	League	3–1		
6	05/09/87	Bradford City	Away	League	1–3		
7	12/09/87	Ipswich Town	Home	League	2–1		
8	16/09/87	Manchester City	Away	League	0–4		
9	19/09/87	Sheffield United	Away	League	2–1		
10	23/09/87	Queens Park Rangers	Away	Lge Cup	1–2		
11	26/09/87	West Bromwich Albion	Home	League	2–0	1 Goal	(2)
12	29/09/87	Oldham Athletic	Away	League	0–0		
13	03/10/87	Swindon Town	Home	League	2–2		
14	06/10/87	Queens Park Rangers	Home	Lge Cup	0–0		
15	10/10/87	Crystal Palace	Away	League	0–1		
16	17/10/87	Shrewsbury Town	Home	League	4–1	1 Goal	(3)
17	20/10/87	Plymouth Argyle	Away	League	2–1	1 Goal	(4)
18	31/10/87	Huddersfield Town	Away	League	1–2		
19	03/11/87	AFC Bournemouth	Home	League	1–2	1 Goal	(5)
20	07/11/87	Aston Villa	Away	League	2–1	1 Goal	(6)
21	10/11/87	West Ham United	Away	Simod Cup	2–1	1 Goal	(7)
22	14/11/87	Leeds United	Home	League	3–1	3 Goals	(10)
23	21/11/87	Stoke City	Away	League	2–1	2 Goals	(12)
24	28/11/87	Hull City	Home	League	2–0		
25	01/12/87	Reading	Home	League	3–0	2 Goals	(14)
26	05/12/87	Blackburn Rovers	Away	League	1–2	1 Goal	(15)
27	01/01/88	Leicester City	Home	League	1–0		
28	02/01/88	Ipswich Town	Away	League	1–1	1 Goal	(16)
29	09/01/88	Arsenal	Away	FA Cup	0–2		
30	13/01/88	Norwich City	Home	Simod Cup	2–3	2 Goals	(18)
31	16/01/88	Middlesbrough	Home	League	2–1		
32	06/02/88	Bradford City	Home	League	0–1		
33	09/02/88	Birmingham City	Away	League	0–1		
34	13/02/88	Reading	Away	League	3–2		
35	20/02/88	Oldham Athletic	Home	League	1–1	1 Goal	(19)
36	27/02/88	Swindon Town	Away	League	1–0	1 Goal	(20)
37	05/03/88	Shrewsbury Town	Away	League	0–0		
38	12/03/88	Crystal Palace	Home	League	1–1		
39	19/03/88	Huddersfield Town	Home	League	4–1	1 Goal	(21)
40	02/04/88	Aston Villa	Home	League	2–1		
41	06/04/88	Leeds United	Away	League	2–1	1 Goal	(22)
42	09/04/88	Plymouth Argyle	Home	League	3–2	1 Goal	(23)
43	19/04/88	AFC Bournemouth	Away	League	2–1		
44	30/04/88	Stoke City	Home	League	2–1		
45	02/05/88	Hull City	Away	League	1–0		
46	07/05/88	Blackburn Rovers	Home	League	1–4		

SEASON 1988–89

League Division One

47	27/08/88	Aston Villa	Away	League	2–2	2 Goals	(25)
48	03/09/88	Derby County	Home	League	1–0		
49	10/09/88	Charlton Athletic	Away	League	3–0	1 Goal	(26)

50	17/09/88	Everton	Home	League	2–1	2 Goals	(28)
51	24/09/88	Norwich City	Away	League	2–2	1 Goal	(29)
52	27/09/88	Gillingham	Home	Lge Cup	3–0		
53	01/10/88	Queens Park Rangers	Home	League	3–2	2 Goals	(31)
54	11/10/88	Gillingham	Away	Lge Cup	3–1		
55	15/10/88	Coventry City	Away	League	0–0		
56	22/10/88	Nottingham Forest	Home	League	2–2		
57	29/10/88	Middlesbrough	Away	League	2–4	1 Goal	(32)
58	02/11/88	Aston Villa	Away	Lge Cup	1–3		
59	05/11/88	Luton Town	Home	League	3–1		
60	12/11/88	Liverpool	Away	League	1–1		
61	19/11/88	Newcastle United	Home	League	4–0	1 Goal	(33)
62	26/11/88	Southampton	Away	League	2–2		
63	29/11/88	Leeds United	Home	Simod Cup	2–0	1 Goal	(34)
64	03/12/88	West Ham United	Home	League	0–1		
65	10/12/88	Tottenham Hotspur	Away	League	0–2		
66	17/12/88	Sheffield Wednesday	Home	League	1–0		
67	20/12/88	Everton	Away	Simod Cup	0–2		
68	26/12/88	Wimbledon	Away	League	0–1		
69	31/12/88	Derby County	Away	League	1–0		
70	02/01/89	Charlton Athletic	Home	League	1–0		
71	07/01/89	Luton Town	Home	FA Cup	3–2	1 Goal	(35)
72	14/01/89	Manchester United	Away	League	0–3		
73	22/01/89	Norwich City	Home	League	2–3	1 Goal	(36)
74	29/01/89	Liverpool	Home	FA Cup	0–2		
75	04/02/89	Queens Park Rangers	Away	League	2–1	1 Goal	(37)
76	11/02/89	Arsenal	Home	League	1–2		
77	21/02/89	Middlesbrough	Home	League	2–0		
78	25/02/89	Coventry City	Home	League	1–0	1 Goal	(38)
79	28/02/89	Arsenal	Away	League	0–0		
80	11/03/89	Luton Town	Away	League	2–1		
81	18/03/89	Aston Villa	Home	League	2–0		
82	25/03/89	Everton	Away	League	1–1		
83	27/03/89	Wimbledon	Home	League	0–1		
84	01/04/89	Sheffield Wednesday	Away	League	0–3		
85	08/04/89	Manchester United	Home	League	0–0		
86	11/04/89	Liverpool	Home	League	1–2		
87	22/04/89	West Ham United	Away	League	0–3		
88	29/04/89	Tottenham Hotspur	Home	League	0–5		
89	03/05/89	Nottingham Forest	Away	League	1–4		
90	06/05/89	Newcastle United	Away	League	1–1		
91	13/05/89	Southampton	Home	League	1–1		

SEASON 1989–90

League Division One

92	19/08/89	Southampton	Away	League	2–1	1 Goal	(39)
93	22/08/89	Charlton Athletic	Home	League	2–2		
94	26/08/89	Nottingham Forest	Home	League	1–0		
95	29/08/89	Wimbledon	Away	League	2–2	1 Goal	(40)
96	09/09/89	Coventry City	Home	League	4–1		
97	16/09/89	Manchester United	Away	League	1–5		
98	19/09/89	Stoke City	Away	Lge Cup	0–1		
99	23/09/89	Sheffield Wednesday	Home	League	2–0	1 Goal	(41)
100	30/09/89	Norwich City	Home	League	0–1		
101	03/10/89	Stoke City	Home	Lge Cup	2–0*	1 Goal	(42)
102	14/10/89	Everton	Away	League	1–2		
103	21/10/89	Crystal Palace	Away	League	3–4	1 Goal	(43)
104	23/10/89	Tranmere Rovers	Away	Lge Cup	2–3		
105	28/10/89	Luton Town	Home	League	1–1		
106	04/11/89	Chelsea	Away	League	0–4		
107	11/11/89	Arsenal	Home	League	1–2		
108	19/11/89	Liverpool	Home	League	1–2		
109	25/11/89	Queens Park Rangers	Away	League	0–0		
110	02/12/89	Southampton	Home	League	2–2	1 Goal	(44)
111	09/12/89	Charlton Athletic	Away	League	1–1		
112	13/12/89	Swindon Town	Away	ZDS Cup	1–2		
113	16/12/89	Aston Villa	Home	League	2–0	1 Goal	(45)
114	26/12/89	Tottenham Hotspur	Away	League	1–3	1 Goal	(46)
115	30/12/89	Manchester City	Away	League	0–2		
116	01/01/90	Derby County	Home	League	1–1		
117	06/01/90	Manchester City	Away	FA Cup	0–0		
118	09/01/90	Manchester City	Home	FA Cup	1–1*		
119	13/01/90	Nottingham Forest	Away	League	1–3		
120	15/01/90	Manchester City	Home	FA Cup	3–1		

121	20/01/90	Wimbledon	Home	League	0–0		
122	27/01/90	Cambridge United	Home	FA Cup	1–1	1 Goal	(47)
123	30/01/90	Cambridge United	Away	FA Cup	0–1*		
124	03/02/90	Sheffield Wednesday	Away	League	1–1		
125	10/02/90	Manchester United	Home	League	1–2		
126	17/02/90	Coventry City	Away	League	1–3	1 Goal	(48)
127	24/02/90	Queens Park Rangers	Home	League	1–2	1 Goal	(49)
128	03/03/90	Liverpool	Away	League	0–1		

Aston Villa – League Division One

1	17/03/90	Derby County	Away	League	1–0		
2	20/03/90	Queens Park Rangers	Away	League	1–1		
3	24/03/90	Crystal Palace	Away	League	0–1		
4	01/04/90	Manchester City	Home	League	1–2		
5	11/04/90	Arsenal	Away	League	1–0		
6	14/04/90	Chelsea	Home	League	1–0		
7	17/04/90	Manchester United	Away	League	0–2		
8	21/04/90	Millwall	Home	League	1–0		
9	28/04/90	Norwich City	Home	League	3–3	1 Goal	(1)
10	05/05/90	Everton	Away	League	3–3	1 Goal	(2)

SEASON 1990–91

League Division One

11	25/08/90	Southampton	Home	League	1–1	1 Goal	(3)
12	01/09/90	Liverpool	Away	League	1–2		
13	05/09/90	Manchester City	Away	League	1–2		
14	08/09/90	Coventry City	Home	League	2–1	1 Goal	(4)
15	15/09/90	Derby County	Away	League	2–0		
16	19/09/90	FC Banik OKD Ostrava	Home	UEFA Cup	3–1		
Sub+1	06/10/90	Sunderland	Home	League	3–0		
Sub+2	09/10/90	Barnsley	Away	Lge Cup	1–0		
17	20/10/90	Wimbledon	Away	League	0–0		
18	24/10/90	Internazionale Milano	Home	UEFA Cup	2–0		
19	27/10/90	Leeds United	Home	League	0–0		
20	31/10/90	Millwall	Home	Lge Cup	2–0	1 Goal	(5)
21	03/11/90	Chelsea	Away	League	0–1		
22	07/11/90	Internazionale Milano	Away	UEFA Cup	0–3		
23	10/11/90	Nottingham Forest	Home	League	1–1		
24	17/11/90	Norwich City	Away	League	0–2		
25	24/11/90	Luton Town	Away	League	0–2		
Sub+3	01/12/90	Sheffield United	Home	League	2–1		
26	15/12/90	Southampton	Away	League	1–1		
27	23/12/90	Arsenal	Home	League	0–0		
28	26/12/90	Everton	Away	League	0–1		
29	29/12/90	Manchester United	Away	League	1–1		
30	01/01/91	Crystal Palace	Home	League	2–0		
31	05/01/91	Wimbledon	Home	FA Cup	1–1		
32	09/01/91	Wimbledon	Away	FA Cup	0–1*		
33	12/01/91	Liverpool	Home	League	0–0		
34	16/01/91	Leeds United	Away	Lge Cup	1–4		
35	19/01/91	Coventry City	Away	League	1–2		
36	02/02/91	Derby County	Home	League	3–2	1 Goal	(6)
37	23/02/91	Nottingham Forest	Away	League	2–2	1 Goal	(7)
38	02/03/91	Sheffield United	Away	League	1–2		
39	09/03/91	Luton Town	Home	League	1–2	1 Goal	(8)
40	16/03/91	Tottenham Hotspur	Home	League	3–2		
41	23/03/91	Sunderland	Away	League	3–1	2 Goals	(10)
42	30/03/91	Everton	Home	League	2–2		
43	03/04/91	Arsenal	Away	League	0–5		
44	06/04/91	Manchester United	Home	League	1–1	1 Goal	(11)
45	10/04/91	Queens Park Rangers	Away	League	1–2		
46	13/04/91	Crystal Palace	Away	League	0–0		
47	20/04/91	Wimbledon	Home	League	1–2		
Sub+4	23/04/91	Manchester City	Home	League	1–5		
48	04/05/91	Leeds United	Away	League	2–5		
49	08/05/91	Norwich City	Home	League	2–1		
50	11/05/91	Chelsea	Home	League	2–2	1 Goal	(12)

SEASON 1991–92

Celtic – Scottish League Premier Division

1	10/08/91	Dundee United	Away	League	4–3		
2	13/08/91	Dunfermline Athletic	Away	League	3–1		
3	17/08/91	Falkirk	Home	League	4–1		

4	31/08/91	Rangers	Home	League	0–2		
5	03/09/91	Airdrieonians	Away	S Lge Cup	0–0+		
6	07/09/91	St Mirren	Home	League	0–0		
7	14/09/91	St Johnstone	Away	League	0–1		
8	18/09/91	KFC Germinal Ekeren	Home	UEFA Cup	2–0		
Sub+1	28/09/91	Hibernian	Away	League	1–1		
Sub+2	01/10/91	KFC Germinal Ekeren	Away	UEFA Cup	1–1		
Sub+3	05/10/91	Heart of Midlothian	Home	League	3–1	1 Goal	(1)
Sub+4	12/10/91	Dundee United	Home	League	4–1		
Sub+5	19/10/91	Falkirk	Away	League	3–4		
9	22/10/91	Neuchatel Xamax	Away	UEFA Cup	1–5		
Sub+6	30/10/91	St Johnstone	Home	League	4–0		
Sub+7	02/11/91	Rangers	Away	League	1–1	1 Goal	(2)
Sub+8	06/11/91	Neuchatel Xamax	Home	UEFA Cup	1–0		
Sub+9	09/11/91	Aberdeen	Home	League	2–1		
Sub+10	16/11/91	Heart of Midlothian	Away	League	1–3		
Sub+11	20/11/91	Motherwell	Home	League	2–2		
10	23/11/91	Airdrieonians	Away	League	3–0	1 Goal	(3)
11	30/11/91	Dunfermline Athletic	Home	League	1–0		
12	04/12/91	Hibernian	Home	League	0–0		
13	07/12/91	Dundee United	Away	League	1–1		
14	14/12/91	St Mirren	Home	League	4–0		
Sub+12	28/12/91	Aberdeen	Away	League	2–2	1 Goal	(4)
15	01/01/92	Rangers	Home	League	1–3		
16	04/01/92	Heart of Midlothian	Home	League	1–2		
Sub+13	11/01/92	Motherwell	Away	League	0–0		
Sub+14	25/01/92	Montrose	Home	S Cup	6–0		

+ AET Airdrieonians won 4–2 on penalties

Chelsea – League Division One

1	08/02/92	Crystal Palace	Home	League	1–1	1 Goal	(1)
2	12/02/92	Southampton	Home	League	1–1		
3	15/02/92	Sheffield United	Home	FA Cup	1–0		
4	22/02/92	Nottingham Forest	Away	League	1–1		
5	29/02/92	Sheffield Wednesday	Home	League	0–3		
6	11/03/92	Norwich City	Away	League	1–0		
7	14/03/92	Coventry City	Home	League	0–1		
8	18/03/92	Sunderland	Away	FA Cup	1–2		
9	28/03/92	Manchester City	Away	League	0–0		
10	04/04/92	West Ham United	Home	League	2–1	1 Goal	(2)
11	11/04/92	Leeds United	Away	League	0–3		
12	25/04/92	Arsenal	Home	League	1–1		
13	02/05/92	Everton	Away	League	1–2		

SEASON 1992–93

Premier League

14	21/02/93	Blackburn Rovers	Away	League	0–2		
Sub+1	10/03/93	Everton	Home	League	2–1		
15	15/03/93	Crystal Palace	Away	League	1–1		
16	20/03/93	Tottenham Hotspur	Home	League	1–1	1 Goal	(3)
17	24/03/93	Leeds United	Away	League	1–1		
18	03/04/93	Middlesbrough	Home	League	4–0		
19	06/04/93	Ipswich Town	Away	League	1–1		
20	01/05/93	Coventry City	Home	League	2–1	1 Goal	(4)
21	08/05/93	Sheffield United	Away	League	2–4		

SEASON 1993–94

Premier League

22	14/08/93	Blackburn Rovers	Home	League	1–2		
23	17/08/93	Wimbledon	Away	League	1–1		
24	21/08/93	Ipswich Town	Away	League	0–1		
25	25/08/93	Queens Park Rangers	Home	League	2–0	1 Goal	(5)
26	28/08/93	Sheffield Wednesday	Home	League	1–1		
27	01/09/93	Tottenham Hotspur	Away	League	1–1	1 Goal	(6)
28	11/09/93	Manchester United	Home	League	1–0		
29	25/09/93	Liverpool	Home	League	1–0		
30	16/10/93	Norwich City	Home	League	1–2		
Sub+2	23/10/93	Aston Villa	Away	League	0–1		
31	26/10/93	Manchester City	Away	Lge Cup	0–1		
32	30/10/93	Oldham Athletic	Home	League	0–1		
33	06/11/93	Leeds United	Away	League	1–4		
Sub+3	27/11/93	Sheffield United	Away	League	0–1		

Sub+4	05/12/93	Blackburn Rovers	Away	League	0–2		
34	11/12/93	Ipswich Town	Home	League	1–1		
Sub+5	02/04/94	Southampton	Home	League	2–0		
35	04/04/94	Newcastle United	Away	League	0–0		
36	09/04/94	Luton Town	Wembley	FA Cup	2–0		
37	13/04/94	Queens Park Rangers	Away	League	1–1		
38	30/04/94	Manchester City	Away	League	2–2	1 Goal	(7)
39	04/05/94	Coventry City	Home	League	1–2	1 Goal	(8)
Sub+6	14/05/94	Manchester United	Wembley	FA Cup	0–4		

SEASON 1994–95

Olympique de Marseille – French League Division Two

1	30/07/94	UC Le Mans 72	Home	League	2–3	1 Goal	(1)
2	03/08/94	AS Saint–Brieuc	Away	League	2–1	1 Goal	(2)
3	06/08/94	CS Sedan–Ardennes	Home	League	2–0	1 Goal	(3)
4	13/08/94	AS Nancy–Lorraine	Away	League	1–1	1 Goal	(4)
5	20/08/94	Olympique Ales	Home	League	1–0	1 Goal	(5)
6	27/08/94	Charleville–Mezieres	Home	League	3–1	2 Goals	(7)
7	31/08/94	Chamois Niortais de Niort	Away	League	3–0		
8	03/09/94	Amiens SC	Home	League	5–0	2 Goals	(9)
9	09/09/94	AS Red Star 93	Away	League	1–2		
10	13/09/94	PAE Olympiakos	Away	UEFA Cup	2–1		
11	17/09/94	US Dunkerque	Home	League	5–1	3 Goals	(12)
12	21/09/94	FC Perpignan	Away	League	0–0		
13	24/09/94	Stade Lavallois de Laval	Home	League	5–0	3 Goals	(15)
14	27/09/94	PAE Olympiakos	Home	UEFA Cup	3–0	2 Goals	(17)
15	30/09/94	En Avant Guingamp	Away	League	1–1	1 Goal	(18)
16	09/10/94	Toulouse FC	Home	League	1–0	1 Goal	(19)
17	14/10/94	Nimes Olympique	Away	League	1–0	1 Goal	(20)
18	18/10/94	FC Sion	Away	UEFA Cup	0–2		
19	28/10/94	US Valenciennes–Anzin	Away	League	1–3	1 Goal	(21)
20	01/11/94	FC Sion	Home	UEFA Cup	3–1		
21	05/11/94	AS Beauvais–oise	Home	League	3–1	1 Goal	(22)
22	11/11/94	FC Gueugnon	Away	League	0–0		
23	19/11/94	FC Mulhouse	Home	League	3–0	1 Goal	(23)
24	26/11/94	SCO Angers	Away	League	1–1		
25	29/11/94	Chamois Niortais de Niort	Away	Fr Lge Cup	0–1*		
26	03/12/94	AS Saint–Brieuc	Home	League	2–0		
27	17/12/94	Olympique Ales	Home	Fr Cup	0–0+		
28	06/01/95	AS Nancy–Lorraine	Home	League	0–2#		
29	14/01/95	FC Sochaux–Montbeliard	Away	Fr Cup	0–0++		
30	21/01/95	Olympique Ales	Away	League	1–1	1 Goal	(24)
31	04/02/95	OGC Nice	Away	Fr Cup	1–0	1 Goal	(25)
32	08/02/95	Chamois Niortais de Niort	Home	League	1–0	1 Goal	(26)
33	11/02/95	Amiens SC	Away	League	2–1		
34	18/02/95	AS Beauvais–oise	Home	Fr Cup	2–0*	1 Goal	(27)
35	25/02/95	AS Red Star 93	Home	League	3–0	1 Goal	(28)
36	04/03/95	US Dunkerque	Away	League	2–2	2 Goals	(30)
37	18/03/95	LB Chateauroux	Home	Fr Cup	2–0	1 Goal	(31)
38	21/03/95	Stade Lavallois de Laval	Away	League	3–1	1 Goal	(32)
39	24/03/95	En Avant Guingamp	Home	League	0–1		
40	01/04/95	Toulouse FC	Away	League	2–0		
41	08/04/95	Nimes Olympique	Home	League	2–1	1 Goal	(33)
42	11/04/95	Paris Saint–Germain	Away	Fr Cup	0–2		
43	15/04/95	LB Chateauroux	Away	League	0–0		
44	21/04/95	ASOA Valence	Home	League	1–0		
45	29/04/95	AS Beauvais–oise	Away	League	1–2		
46	06/05/95	FC Gueugnon	Home	League	3–0	1 Goal	(34)
47	20/05/95	FC Mulhouse	Away	League	1–0		
48	27/05/95	SCO Angers	Home	League	3–1	1 Goal	(35)
49	31/05/95	UC Le Mans 72	Away	League	2–0	1 Goal	(36)

+ AET Olympique de Marseille won 5–4 on penalties
# Match awarded to Olympique de Marseille after crowd trouble
++ AET Olympique de Marseille won 5–4 on penalties

SEASON 1995–96

French League Division Two

50	19/07/95	UC Le Mans 72	Home	League	3–1	3 Goals	(39)
51	26/07/95	Stade Athletique Epinal	Away	League	0–2		
52	29/07/95	SCO Angers	Home	League	0–0		
53	05/08/95	CS Louhans–Cuiseaux	Away	League	1–3		

54	09/08/95	Amiens SC	Home	League	2–0	1 Goal	(40)
55	12/08/95	Perpignan FC	Away	League	2–0	1 Goal	(41)
56	19/08/95	US Dunkerque	Home	League	0–0		
57	26/08/95	SM Caen	Away	League	0–2		
58	09/09/95	FC Mulhouse	Away	League	0–2		
59	16/09/95	Stade Lavallois de Laval	Home	League	5–0	3 Goals	(44)
60	23/09/95	Olympique Ales	Away	League	0–0		
61	14/10/95	Stade Poitiers	Home	League	3–0	1 Goal	(45)
62	21/10/95	LB Chateauroux	Home	League	1–0		
63	24/10/95	Perpignan FC	Away	Fr Lge Cup	1–0	1 Goal	(46)
64	29/10/95	AS Red Star 93	Away	League	2–2		
65	04/11/95	Chamois Niortais de Niort	Home	League	2–1		
66	10/11/95	ASOA Valence	Away	League	2–0	1 Goal	(47)
67	18/11/95	Charleville–Mezieres	Home	League	4–0	2 Goals	(49)
68	25/11/95	FC Sochaux–Montbeliard	Away	League	0–1		
69	03/12/95	FC Eschirolles	Neutral	Fr Cup	4–1	1 Goal	(50)
70	17/12/95	Lempdes	Neutral	Fr Cup	8–1	1 Goal	(51)
71	06/01/96	AS Saint–Etienne	Home	Fr Lge Cup	2–0	1 Goal	(52)
72	10/01/96	SCO Angers	Away	League	1–1	1 Goal	(53)
73	13/01/96	Endoume–Marseille	Away	Fr Cup	2–0		
74	20/01/96	Louhans–Cuisseaux	Home	League	2–0	1 Goal	(54)
75	27/01/96	Amiens SC	Away	League	2–1		
76	30/01/96	En Avant Guingamp	Away	Fr Lge Cup	0–1		
77	03/02/96	Stade Pontivy	Neutral	Fr Cup	2–0		
78	07/02/96	Perpignan FC	Home	League	5–1	3 Goals	(57)
79	10/02/96	US Dunkerque	Away	League	2–1	1 Goal	(58)
80	17/02/96	SM Caen	Home	League	1–0	1 Goal	(59)
81	24/02/96	SS Blenod	Away	Fr Cup	2–0		
82	27/02/96	FC Toulouse	Away	League	0–0		
83	02/03/96	FC Mulhouse	Home	League	1–0		
84	08/03/96	Stade Lavallois	Away	League	3–1	2 Goals	(61)
85	13/03/96	Olympique Ales	Home	League	4–0	1 Goal	(62)
86	16/03/96	Lille OSC	Home	Fr Cup	1–0		
87	23/03/96	FC 56 Lorient	Away	League	1–0		
88	30/03/96	AS Nancy–Lorraine	Home	League	2–0	2 Goals	(64)
89	09/04/96	Stade Poitiers	Away	League	0–0		
90	13/04/96	AJ Auxerre	Home	Fr Cup	1–1+		
91	19/04/96	LB Chateauroux	Away	League	2–4	1 Goal	(65)
92	24/04/96	AS Red Star 93	Home	League	2–1	2 Goals	(67)
93	27/04/96	Chamois Niortais de Niort	Away	League	0–0		
94	03/05/96	ASOA Valence	Home	League	2–2	1 Goal	(68)
95	10/05/96	Charleville–Mezieres	Away	League	1–3	1 Goal	(69)
96	17/05/96	FC Sochaux–Montbeliard	Home	League	4–1	1 Goal	(70)

+ AET AJ Auxerre won 3–1 on penalties

SEASON 1996–97

French League Division One

97	09/08/96	Olympique Lyonnais	Home	League	3–1		
98	16/08/96	Le Havre AC	Away	League	1–1		
99	24/08/96	FC Metz	Home	League	1–2		
100	06/09/96	SC Bastia	Away	League	0–2		
101	14/09/96	OGC Nice	Home	League	1–0		
102	12/10/96	SM Caen	Home	League	0–1		
103	19/10/96	AS Nancy–Lorraine	Away	League	0–0		
104	25/10/96	FC Nantes	Home	League	0–1		
105	02/11/96	Montpellier HSC	Away	League	0–2		

AS Nancy–Lorraine – French League Division One

1	14/12/96	Olympique Lyonnais	Home	League	2–3		
2	20/12/96	Le Havre AC	Away	League	3–1	3 Goals	(3)
3	17/01/97	FC Sochaux–Montbeliard	Away	Fr Cup	1–3*		
4	25/01/97	FC Metz	Home	League	2–3		
5	01/02/97	AJ Auxerre	Away	League	0–1		
6	14/02/97	Stade Rennais FC	Home	League	1–0		
7	22/02/97	SC Bastia	Away	League	0–2		
8	08/03/97	OGC Nice	Home	League	1–0	1 Goal	(4)
9	13/03/97	Lille OSC	Away	League	0–2		
Sub+1	26/03/97	Olympique de Marseille	Away	League	1–4	1 Goal	(5)
Sub+2	16/04/97	SM Caen	Away	League	1–1		
10	03/05/97	Montpellier HSC	Away	League	1–1		
11	24/05/97	AS Cannes	Away	League	1–0	1 Goal	(6)

INTERNATIONAL APPEARANCES – REPUBLIC OF IRELAND

1	11/09/85	Switzerland	Bern	0–0	WCQ		
2	16/10/85	USSR	Moscow	0–2	WCQ		
3	13/11/85	Denmark	Lansdowne Road	1–4	WCQ		
4	22/05/88	Poland	Lansdowne Road	3–0	F	1 Goal	(1)
Sub 5	01/06/88	Norway	Oslo	0–0	F		
Sub 6	15/06/88	USSR	Hanover	1–1	EC		
Sub 7	18/06/88	Holland	Gelsenkirchen	0–1	EC		
8	14/09/88	Northern Ireland	Windsor Park	0–0	WCQ		
9	19/10/88	Tunisia	Lansdowne Road	4–0	F	2 Goals	(3)
10	16/11/88	Spain	Seville	0–2	WCQ		
11	07/02/89	France	Dalymount Park	0–0	F		
12	08/03/89	Hungary	Budapest	0–0	WCQ		
13	26/04/89	Spain	Lansdowne Road	1–0	WCQ		
14	28/05/89	Malta	Lansdowne Road	2–0	WCQ		
15	04/06/89	Hungary	Lansdowne Road	2–0	WCQ	1 Goal	(4)
Sub 16	06/09/89	West Germany	Lansdowne Road	1–1	F		
17	11/10/89	Northern Ireland	Lansdowne Road	3–0	WCQ	1 Goal	(5)
18	15/11/89	Malta	Valletta	2–0	WCQ		
19	28/03/90	Wales	Lansdowne Road	1–0	F		
20	16/05/90	Finland	Lansdowne Road	1–1	F		
21	27/05/90	Turkey	Izmir	0–0	F		
22	11/06/90	England	Cagliari	1–1	WC		
23	17/06/90	Egypt	Palermo	0–0	WC		
Sub 24	21/06/90	Holland	Palermo	1–1	WC		
Sub 25	25/06/90	Romania	Genoa	0–0+	WC		
Sub 26	30/06/90	Italy	Rome	0–1	WC		
Sub 27	12/09/90	Morocco	Lansdowne Road	1–0	F		
Sub 28	17/10/90	Turkey	Lansdowne Road	5–0	ECQ		
Sub 29	14/11/90	England	Lansdowne Road	1–1	ECQ	1 Goal	(6)
Sub 30	27/03/91	England	Wembley	1–1	ECQ		
Sub 31	01/05/91	Poland	Lansdowne Road	0–0	ECQ		
Sub 32	22/05/91	Chile	Lansdowne Road	1–1	F		
33	02/06/91	USA	Massachusetts	1–1	F	1 Goal	(7)
34	16/10/91	Poland	Poznan	3–3	ECQ	1 Goal	(8)
35	13/11/91	Turkey	Istanbul	3–1	ECQ	1 Goal	(9)
36	19/02/92	Wales	RS Showground	0–1	F		
37	25/03/92	Switzerland	Lansdowne Road	2–1	F		
Sub 38	29/04/92	USA	Lansdowne Road	4–1	F	1 Goal	(10)
39	17/02/93	Wales	Tolka Park	2–1	F		
Sub 40	31/03/93	Northern Ireland	Lansdowne Road	3–0	WCQ		
Sub 41	28/04/93	Denmark	Lansdowne Road	1–1	WCQ		
Sub 42	26/05/93	Albania	Tirana	2–1	WCQ	1 Goal	(11)
Sub 43	09/06/93	Latvia	Riga	2–0	WCQ		
Sub 44	08/09/93	Lithuania	Lansdowne Road	2–0	WCQ		
Sub 45	13/10/93	Spain	Lansdowne Road	1–3	WCQ		
Sub 46	17/11/93	Northern Ireland	Windsor Park	1–1	WCQ		
47	23/03/94	Russia	Lansdowne Road	0–0	F		
Sub 48	24/05/94	Bolivia	Lansdowne Road	1–0	F		
49	29/05/94	Germany	Hannover	2–0	F	1 Goal	(12)
50	05/06/94	Czech Republic	Lansdowne Road	1–3	F		
Sub 51	04/07/94	Holland	Orlando	0–2	WC		
Sub 52	07/09/94	Latvia	Riga	3–0	ECQ		
Sub 53	29/03/95	Northern Ireland	Lansdowne Road	1–1	ECQ		
Sub 54	26/04/95	Portugal	Lansdowne Road	1–0	ECQ		
Sub 55	03/06/95	Liechtenstein	Eschen	0–0	ECQ		
Sub 56	11/06/95	Austria	Lansdowne Road	1–3	ECQ		
Sub 57	06/09/95	Austria	Vienna	1–3	ECQ		
Sub 58	15/11/95	Portugal	Lisbon	0–3	ECQ		
59	13/12/95	Holland	Anfield	0–2	ECQ		
Sub 60	27/03/96	Russia	Lansdowne Road	0–2	F		
61	29/05/96	Portugal	Lansdowne Road	0–1	F		
Sub 62	02/06/96	Croatia	Lansdowne Road	2–2	F		
63	04/06/96	Holland	Rotterdam	1–3	F		
Sub 64	31/08/96	Liechtenstein	Eschen	5–0	WCQ		
65	09/10/96	Macedonia	Lansdowne Road	3–0	WCQ	2 Goals	(14)
66	10/11/96	Iceland	Lansdowne Road	0–0	WCQ		
67	11/02/97	Wales	Cardiff Arms Park	0–0	Fr		
68	02/04/97	Macedonia	Skopje	2–3	WCQ		
Sub 69	30/04/97	Romania	Bucharest	0–1	WCQ		
Sub 70	21/05/97	Liechtenstein	Lansdowne Road	5–0	WCQ	2 Goals	(16)

+ AET Republic of Ireland won 5–4 on penalties

APPEARANCES AND GOALS PER SEASON

SEASON 81–82	GAMES	GOALS
League	19+5	5
TOTAL	**19+5**	**5**

SEASON 82–83	GAMES	GOALS
League	37+1	15
FA Cup	2+1	1
League Cup	5	3
TOTAL	**44+2**	**19**

SEASON 83–84	GAMES	GOALS
League	33+4	12
FA Cup	4+1	1
League Cup	1	0
Associate Members Cup	1	2
TOTAL	**39+5**	**15**

SEASON 84–85	GAMES	GOALS
League	43	16
FA Cup	2	2
League Cup	4	2
Freight Rover Trophy	1	0
TOTAL	**50**	**20**

SEASON 85–86	GAMES	GOALS
League	34	14
FA Cup	4	3
League Cup	4	3
Freight Rover Trophy	3	1
TOTAL	**45**	**21**

SEASON 86–87	GAMES	GOALS
League	43	16
League Play–offs	5	5
FA Cup	3	2
League Cup	4	3
Freight Rover Trophy	5	4
TOTAL	**60**	**30**

SEASON 87–88	GAMES	GOALS
League	39	20
FA Cup	1	0
League Cup	4	0
Simod Cup	2	3
TOTAL	**46**	**23**

SEASON 88–89	GAMES	GOALS
League	38	13
FA Cup	2	1
League Cup	3	0
Simod Cup	2	1
TOTAL	**45**	**15**

SEASON 89–90	GAMES	GOALS
League	38	11
FA Cup	5	1
League Cup	3	1
Zenith Data Systems Cup	1	0
TOTAL	**47**	**13**

SEASON 90–91	GAMES	GOALS
League	33+3	9
FA Cup	2	0
League Cup	2+1	1
UEFA Cup	3	0
TOTAL	**40+4**	**10**

SEASON 91–92	GAMES	GOALS
League	11	2
FA Cup	2	0
UEFA Cup	2+2	0
Scottish League	13+11	4
Scottish Cup	0+1	0
Scottish League Cup	1	0
TOTAL	**29+14**	**6**

SEASON 92–93	GAMES	GOALS
League	8+1	2
TOTAL	**8+1**	**2**

SEASON 93–94	GAMES	GOALS
League	16+4	4
FA Cup	1+1	0
League Cup	1	0
TOTAL	**18+5**	**4**

SEASON 94–95	GAMES	GOALS
French League	38	31
French Cup	6	3
French League Cup	1	0
UEFA Cup	4	2
TOTAL	**49**	**36**

SEASON 95–96	GAMES	GOALS
French League	37	30
French Cup	7	2
French League Cup	3	2
TOTAL	**47**	**34**

SEASON 96–97	GAMES	GOALS
French League	19+2	6
French Cup	1	0
TOTAL	**20+2**	**6**

CAREER APPEARANCES AND GOALS

COMPETITION	GAMES	TOTAL	GOALS
League	392+18	410	139
League Play–offs	5	5	5
FA Cup	28+3	31	11
League Cup	31+1	32	13
Associate Members Cup	1	1	2
Freight Rover Trophy	9	9	5
Simod Cup	4	4	4
Zenith Data Systems Cup	1	1	0
UEFA Cup	9+2	11	2
Scottish League	13+11	24	4
Scottish Cup	0+1	1	0
Scottish League Cup	1	1	0
French League	94+2	96	67
French Cup	14	14	5
French League Cup	4	4	2
Internationals	35+35	70	16
TOTAL	**641+73**	**714**	**275**

HAT-TRICKS

Gillingham

1	3	Darlington	17/03/87	Home	League	4–1
2	3	Sunderland	14/05/87	Home	Lge P/O	3–2

Millwall

1	3	Leeds United	14/11/87	Home	League	3–1

Olympique de Marseille

1	3	US Dunkerque	17/09/94	Home	League	5–1
2	3	Stade Lavallois	24/09/94	Home	League	5–0
3	3	UC Le Mans 72	19/07/95	Home	League	5–1
4	3	Stade Lavallois	16/09/95	Home	League	5–0
5	3	Perpignan FC	07/02/96	Home	League	5–1

AS Nancy–Lorraine

1	3	Le Havre AC	20/12/96	Away	League	3–1

League: 2
League Play–offs: 1
French League: 6
TOTAL: 9

HONOURS

Winners medals
League Division Two Championship: 87/88
French League Division Two Championship: 94/95

Runner-up medals
FA Cup: 93/94
League Division One Championship: 89/90
French League Division Two Championship: 95/96

LEE CHAPMAN

Born: 05/12/59 – Lincoln
Height: 6.2
Weight: 13.00 (95–96)

Clubs
Stoke City: **1979–82** – Matches: **103+4** – Goals: **38**
Plymouth Argyle (loan): **1978** – Matches: **3+1** – Goals: **0**
Arsenal: **1982–83** – Matches: **17+11** – Goals: **6**
Sunderland: **1983–84** – Matches: **16+1** – Goals: **4**
Sheffield Wednesday: **1984–88** – Matches: **183+4** – Goals: **79**
Chamois Niortais de Niort: **1988** – Matches: **10** – Goals: **3**
Nottingham Forest: **1988–89** – Matches: **71** – Goals: **27**
Leeds United: **1990–93** – Matches: **169+4** – Goals: **80**
Portsmouth: **1993** – Matches: **6** – Goals: **2**
West Ham United: **1993–94** – Matches: **43+8** – Goals: **11**
Southend United (loan): **1995** – Matches: **1** – Goals: **1**
Ipswich Town: **1995–96** – Matches: **14+11** – Goals: **1**
Leeds United (loan): **1996** – Matches: **2** – Goals: **0**
Swansea City: **1996** – Matches: **7** – Goals: **4**

Country
England: Under 21 & England B

SEASON 1978–79

Stoke City – League Division Two
No Competitive Matches

Plymouth Argyle (loan) – League Division Three

1	09/12/78	Watford	Home	League	1–1		
2	16/12/78	Chesterfield	Home	League	1–1		
3	26/12/78	Brentford	Away	League	1–2		
Sub+1	30/12/78	Gillingham	Away	League	0–2		

SEASON 1979–80

Stoke City – League Division One

1	02/10/79	Swindon Town	Away	Lge Cup	1–2	1 Goal	(1)
Sub+1	01/12/79	Southampton	Away	League	1–3		
Sub+2	12/01/80	Ipswich Town	Home	League	0–1		
2	02/02/80	Bristol City	Home	League	1–0		
3	09/02/80	Crystal Palace	Away	League	1–0	1 Goal	(2)
4	16/02/80	Manchester United	Home	League	1–1		
5	23/02/80	Middlesbrough	Away	League	3–1		
6	01/03/80	Arsenal	Home	League	2–3	1 Goal	(3)
7	08/03/80	Derby County	Away	League	2–2		
8	15/03/80	Norwich City	Home	League	2–1		
9	18/03/80	Everton	Away	League	0–2		
10	22/03/80	Wolverhampton Wanderers	Away	League	0–3		
11	29/03/80	Aston Villa	Home	League	2–0	1 Goal	(4)
12	01/04/80	Liverpool	Away	League	0–1		
13	05/04/80	Manchester City	Home	League	0–0		
Sub+3	08/04/80	Leeds United	Away	League	0–3		
14	12/04/80	Southampton	Home	League	1–2		
15	19/04/80	Bolton Wanderers	Away	League	1–2		

SEASON 1980–81

League Division One

16	16/08/80	Norwich City	Away	League	1–5			
17	20/08/80	West Bromwich Albion	Home	League	0–0			
18	23/08/80	Ipswich Town	Home	League	2–2	1 Goal	(5)
19	27/08/80	Manchester City	Home	Lge Cup	1–1	1 Goal	(6)
20	30/08/80	Nottingham Forest	Away	League	0–5		
21	03/09/80	Manchester City	Away	Lge Cup	0–3		
22	06/09/80	Leeds United	Home	League	3–0		
23	13/09/80	Arsenal	Away	League	0–2		
24	20/09/80	Manchester City	Away	League	2–1	1 Goal	(7)
25	27/09/80	Middlesbrough	Home	League	1–0		
26	04/10/80	Tottenham Hotspur	Home	League	2–3		
27	08/10/80	Leicester City	Away	League	1–1	1 Goal	(8)
28	11/10/80	Southampton	Away	League	2–1		
29	18/10/80	Brighton & Hove Albion	Home	League	0–0		
30	22/10/80	Manchester United	Home	League	1–2		
31	25/10/80	Birmingham City	Away	League	1–1		
32	01/11/80	Liverpool	Home	League	2–2	1 Goal	(9)
33	08/11/80	Sunderland	Away	League	0–0		
34	15/11/80	Norwich City	Home	League	3–1	3 Goals	(12)
35	22/11/80	Crystal Palace	Home	League	1–0		
36	25/11/80	West Bromwich Albion	Away	League	0–0		
37	29/11/80	Wolverhampton Wanderers	Away	League	0–1		
38	06/12/80	Everton	Home	League	2–2	1 Goal	(13)
39	13/12/80	Manchester United	Away	League	2–2	1 Goal	(14)
40	20/12/80	Leicester City	Home	League	1–0	1 Goal	(15)
41	26/12/80	Aston Villa	Away	League	0–1		
42	03/01/81	Wolverhampton Wanderers	Home	FA Cup	2–2	1 Goal	(16)
43	06/01/81	Wolverhampton Wanderers	Away	FA Cup	1–2		
44	10/01/81	Crystal Palace	Away	League	1–1		
45	31/01/81	Ipswich Town	Away	League	0–4		
46	07/02/81	Arsenal	Home	League	1–1		
47	14/02/81	Leeds United	Away	League	3–1	3 Goals	(19)
48	18/02/81	Nottingham Forest	Home	League	1–2		
49	21/02/81	Middlesbrough	Away	League	1–3		
50	11/03/81	Tottenham Hotspur	Away	League	2–2		
51	14/03/81	Southampton	Home	League	1–2		
52	18/03/81	Manchester City	Home	League	2–1		
53	21/03/81	Brighton & Hove Albion	Away	League	1–1		
54	28/03/81	Birmingham City	Home	League	0–0		
55	03/04/81	Liverpool	Away	League	0–3		
56	11/04/81	Sunderland	Home	League	2–0	1 Goal	(20)
57	18/04/81	Coventry City	Away	League	2–2	1 Goal	(21)
58	20/04/81	Aston Villa	Home	League	1–1		
59	25/04/81	Everton	Away	League	1–0		
60	02/05/81	Wolverhampton Wanderers	Home	League	3–2		

SEASON 1981–82

League Division One

61	29/08/81	Arsenal	Away	League	1–0	1 Goal	(22)
62	02/09/81	Coventry City	Home	League	4–0	2 Goals	(24)
63	05/09/81	Manchester City	Home	League	1–3	1 Goal	(25)
64	12/09/81	West Ham United	Away	League	2–3		
65	19/09/81	Nottingham Forest	Home	League	1–2		
66	23/09/81	Aston Villa	Away	League	2–2		
67	26/09/81	Middlesbrough	Away	League	2–3	1 Goal	(26)
68	03/10/81	Everton	Home	League	3–1	2 Goals	(28)
69	07/10/81	Manchester City	Away	Lge Cup	0–2		
70	10/10/81	Tottenham Hotspur	Away	League	0–2		
71	17/10/81	Swansea City	Home	League	1–2		
72	24/10/81	Birmingham City	Home	League	1–0	1 Goal	(29)
73	28/10/81	Manchester City	Home	Lge Cup	2–0+	1 Goal	(30)
74	31/10/81	Brighton & Hove Albion	Away	League	0–0		
75	07/11/81	Southampton	Home	League	0–2		
76	14/11/81	West Bromwich Albion	Away	League	2–1	1 Goal	(31)
77	21/11/81	Ipswich Town	Home	League	2–0	1 Goal	(32)
78	24/11/81	Coventry City	Away	League	0–3		
79	28/11/81	Wolverhampton Wanderers	Away	League	0–2		
80	05/12/81	Leeds United	Home	League	1–2		
81	02/01/81	Norwich City	Home	FA Cup	0–1		
82	09/01/82	Manchester City	Away	League	1–1		
83	20/01/82	Arsenal	Home	League	0–1		

84	23/01/82	Manchester United	Home	League	0–3		
85	30/01/82	Nottingham Forest	Away	League	0–0		
86	06/02/82	West Ham United	Home	League	2–1	1 Goal	(33)
87	10/02/82	Sunderland	Away	League	2–0		
88	13/02/82	Everton	Away	League	0–0		
89	20/02/82	Middlesbrough	Home	League	2–0	1 Goal	(34)
90	27/02/82	Tottenham Hotspur	Home	League	0–2		
91	06/03/82	Swansea City	Away	League	0–3		
92	09/03/82	Liverpool	Home	League	1–5		
93	13/03/82	Birmingham City	Away	League	1–2	1 Goal	(35)
94	20/03/82	Brighton & Hove Albion	Home	League	0–0		
95	10/04/82	Sunderland	Home	League	0–1		
96	13/04/82	Liverpool	Away	League	0–2		
97	17/04/82	Ipswich Town	Away	League	0–2		
98	24/04/82	Wolverhampton Wanderers	Home	League	2–1	1 Goal	(36)
99	26/04/82	Notts County	Away	League	1–3	1 Goal	(37)
100	01/05/82	Leeds United	Away	League	0–0		
101	05/05/82	Aston Villa	Home	League	1–0		
102	08/05/82	Notts County	Home	League	2–2		
Sub+4	15/05/82	Manchester United	Away	League	0–2		
103	20/05/82	West Bromwich Albion	Home	League	3–0	1 Goal	(38)

+ AET Manchester City won 9–8 on penalties

SEASON 1982–83

Arsenal – League Division One

1	28/08/82	Stoke City	Away	League	1–2		
2	31/08/82	Norwich City	Home	League	1–1		
3	04/09/82	Liverpool	Home	League	0–2		
4	07/09/82	Brighton & Hove Albion	Away	League	0–1		
5	11/09/82	Coventry City	Away	League	2–0	1 Goal	(1)
6	15/09/82	Spartak Moskva	Away	UEFA Cup	2–3	1 Goal	(2)
7	18/09/82	Notts County	Home	League	2–0		
8	25/09/82	Manchester United	Away	League	0–0		
9	29/09/82	Spartak Moskva	Home	UEFA Cup	2–5	1 Goal	(3)
10	02/10/82	West Ham United	Home	League	2–3		
Sub+1	23/10/82	Nottingham Forest	Away	League	0–3		
Sub+2	30/10/82	Birmingham City	Home	League	0–0		
Sub+3	09/11/82	Everton	Away	Lge Cup	1–1		
11	13/11/82	Everton	Home	League	1–1		
Sub+4	20/11/82	Swansea City	Away	League	2–1	1 Goal	(4)
Sub+5	23/11/82	Everton	Home	Lge Cup	3–0		
12	04/12/82	Manchester City	Away	League	1–2		
Sub+6	18/12/82	Sunderland	Away	League	0–3		
Sub+7	28/12/82	Southampton	Away	League	2–2	1 Goal	(5)
Sub+8	01/01/83	Swansea City	Home	League	2–1		
13	03/01/83	Liverpool	Away	League	1–3		
Sub+9	09/04/83	Coventry City	Home	League	2–1		
Sub+10	16/04/83	Manchester United	Neutral	FA Cup	1–2		
14	20/04/83	Norwich City	Away	League	1–3		

SEASON 1983–84

League Division One

15	24/09/83	Norwich City	Home	League	3–0	1 Goal	(6)
16	01/10/83	Queens Park Rangers	Away	League	0–2		
17	15/10/83	Coventry City	Home	League	0–1		
Sub+11	26/11/83	Leicester City	Away	League	0–3		

Sunderland – League Division One

1	31/12/83	Luton Town	Home	League	2–0		
2	02/01/84	Coventry City	Away	League	1–2		
3	07/01/84	Bolton Wanderers	Away	FA Cup	3–0	1 Goal	(1)
4	14/01/84	Norwich City	Away	League	0–3		
5	28/01/84	Birmingham City	Home	FA Cup	1–2		
6	08/02/84	Tottenham Hotspur	Away	League	0–3		
7	11/02/84	Southampton	Away	League	1–1	1 Goal	(2)
8	18/02/84	Nottingham Forest	Home	League	1–1		
9	25/02/84	Manchester United	Away	League	1–2	1 Goal	(3)
10	03/03/84	Arsenal	Home	League	2–2		
11	07/03/84	Queens Park Rangers	Home	League	1–0		
12	17/03/84	Wolverhampton Wanderers	Away	League	0–0		
13	20/03/84	Watford	Away	League	1–2		
14	24/03/84	Aston Villa	Home	League	0–1		

15	31/03/84	Stoke City	Away	League	1–2		
Sub+1	07/05/84	Notts County	Home	League	0–0		
16	12/05/84	Leicester City	Away	League	2–0	1 Goal	(4)

SEASON 1984–85

Sheffield Wednesday – League Division One

1	25/08/84	Nottingham Forest	Home	League	3–1		
2	27/08/84	Newcastle United	Away	League	1–2	1 Goal	(1)
3	01/09/84	Stoke City	Away	League	1–2		
4	04/09/84	Southampton	Home	League	2–1		
5	08/09/84	Tottenham Hotspur	Home	League	2–1		
6	15/09/84	West Bromwich Albion	Away	League	2–2		
7	22/09/84	Ipswich Town	Home	League	2–2	1 Goal	(2)
8	25/09/84	Huddersfield Town	Home	Lge Cup	3–0	1 Goal	(3)
9	29/09/84	Liverpool	Away	League	2–0		
10	06/10/84	Sunderland	Home	League	2–2	1 Goal	(4)
11	09/10/84	Huddersfield Town	Away	Lge Cup	1–2		
12	13/10/84	Luton Town	Away	League	2–1	1 Goal	(5)
13	20/10/84	Leicester City	Home	League	5–0		
14	27/10/84	Coventry City	Away	League	0–1		
15	30/10/84	Fulham	Home	Lge Cup	3–2		
16	03/11/84	Norwich City	Home	League	1–2		
17	10/11/84	Queens Park Rangers	Away	League	0–0		
18	17/11/84	Watford	Away	League	0–1		
19	20/11/84	Luton Town	Home	Lge Cup	4–2		
20	25/11/84	Arsenal	Home	League	2–1	1 Goal	(6)
21	01/12/84	Everton	Away	League	1–1		
22	08/12/84	Chelsea	Home	League	1–1		
23	15/12/84	West Ham United	Away	League	0–0		
24	22/12/84	Stoke City	Home	League	2–1	1 Goal	(7)
25	26/12/84	Aston Villa	Home	League	1–1		
26	29/12/84	Southampton	Away	League	3–0	2 Goals	(9)
27	01/01/85	Manchester United	Away	League	2–1		
28	05/01/85	Fulham	Away	FA Cup	3–2	2 Goals	(11)
29	12/01/85	West Bromwich Albion	Home	League	2–0	1 Goal	(12)
30	26/01/85	Oldham Athletic	Home	FA Cup	5–1	1 Goal	(13)
31	28/01/85	Chelsea	Away	Lge Cup	1–1		
32	30/01/85	Chelsea	Home	Lge Cup	4–4*	1 Goal	(14)
33	02/02/85	Liverpool	Home	League	1–1		
34	06/02/85	Chelsea	Away	Lge Cup	1–2		
35	24/02/85	Watford	Home	League	1–1		
36	09/03/85	Leicester City	Away	League	1–3		
37	16/03/85	Luton Town	Home	League	1–1		
38	20/03/85	Nottingham Forest	Away	League	0–0		
39	30/03/85	Newcastle United	Home	League	4–2	2 Goals	(16)
40	03/04/85	Norwich City	Away	League	1–1		
41	06/04/85	Aston Villa	Away	League	0–3		
42	09/04/85	Manchester United	Home	League	1–0	1 Goal	(17)
43	13/04/85	Ipswich Town	Away	League	2–1	1 Goal	(18)
44	16/04/85	Sunderland	Away	League	0–0		
45	23/04/85	Queens Park Rangers	Home	League	3–1		
46	27/04/85	Arsenal	Away	League	0–1		
47	04/05/85	Everton	Home	League	0–1		
48	11/05/85	West Ham United	Home	League	2–1	2 Goals	(20)
49	14/05/85	Tottenham Hotspur	Away	League	0–2		

SEASON 1985–86

League Division One

50	17/08/85	Chelsea	Home	League	1–1		
51	21/08/85	Nottingham Forest	Away	League	1–0		
Sub+1	24/08/85	Manchester City	Away	League	3–1		
Sub+2	26/08/85	Watford	Home	League	2–1	1 Goal	(21)
52	31/08/85	Oxford United	Away	League	1–0		
53	03/09/85	Everton	Home	League	1–5		
54	07/09/85	West Ham United	Home	League	2–2	1 Goal	(22)
55	14/09/85	Arsenal	Away	League	0–1		
56	21/09/85	Tottenham Hotspur	Away	League	1–5	1 Goal	(23)
57	25/09/85	Brentford	Away	Lge Cup	2–2	2 Goals	(25)
58	28/09/85	Luton Town	Home	League	3–2	1 Goal	(26)
59	05/10/85	Birmingham City	Away	League	2–0		
60	15/10/85	Brentford	Home	Lge Cup	2–0	1 Goal	(27)
61	12/10/85	Coventry City	Home	League	2–2	1 Goal	(28)
62	19/10/85	Leicester City	Away	League	3–2	1 Goal	(29)

63	26/10/85	West Bromwich Albion	Home	League	1–0	1 Goal	(30)
64	29/10/85	Swindon Town	Away	Lge Cup	0–1		
65	02/11/85	Queens Park Rangers	Away	League	1–1		
66	09/11/85	Manchester United	Home	League	1–0	1 Goal	(31)
67	16/11/85	Aston Villa	Away	League	1–1		
68	23/11/85	Southampton	Home	League	2–1	1 Goal	(32)
69	30/11/85	Ipswich Town	Away	League	1–2		
70	07/12/85	Nottingham Forest	Home	League	2–1		
71	14/12/85	Chelsea	Away	League	1–2		
72	21/12/85	Manchester City	Home	League	3–2		
73	26/12/85	Newcastle United	Home	League	2–2		
Sub+3	13/01/86	West Bromwich Albion	Home	FA Cup	2–2		
74	16/01/86	West Bromwich Albion	Away	FA Cup	3–2	1 Goal	(33)
75	25/01/86	Orient	Home	FA Cup	5–0	1 Goal	(34)
76	01/02/86	Watford	Away	League	1–2		
77	22/02/86	Tottenham Hotspur	Home	League	1–2		
78	26/02/86	Derby County	Away	FA Cup	1–1		
79	05/03/86	Derby County	Home	FA Cup	2–0		
80	08/03/86	Birmingham City	Home	League	5–1	1 Goal	(35)
81	12/03/86	West Ham United	Home	FA Cup	2–1		
82	15/03/86	Coventry City	Away	League	1–0		
83	18/03/86	Leicester City	Home	League	1–0		
84	05/04/86	Everton	Neutral	FA Cup	1–2*		
85	08/04/86	Queens Park Rangers	Home	League	0–0		
86	13/04/86	Manchester United	Away	League	2–0		
87	16/04/86	Arsenal	Home	League	2–0		

SEASON 1986–87

League Division One

88	23/08/86	Charlton Athletic	Away	League	1–1		
89	25/08/86	Everton	Home	League	2–2		
90	30/08/86	Chelsea	Home	League	2–0		
91	02/09/86	Arsenal	Away	League	0–2		
92	06/09/86	Newcastle United	Away	League	3–2		
93	13/09/86	Leicester City	Home	League	2–2	2 Goals	(37)
94	20/09/86	Watford	Away	League	1–0		
95	23/09/86	Stockport County	Home	Lge Cup	3–0		
96	27/09/86	West Ham United	Home	League	2–2		
97	04/10/86	Oxford United	Home	League	6–1	1 Goal	(38)
98	11/10/86	Manchester United	Away	League	1–3		
99	18/10/86	Tottenham Hotspur	Away	League	1–1		
100	25/10/86	Coventry City	Home	League	2–2	2 Goals	(40)
101	28/10/86	Everton	Away	Lge Cup	0–4		
102	01/11/86	Nottingham Forest	Away	League	2–3	2 Goals	(42)
103	08/11/86	Southampton	Home	League	3–1	2 Goals	(44)
104	16/11/86	Liverpool	Away	League	1–1	1 Goal	(45)
105	22/11/86	Luton Town	Home	League	1–0		
106	25/11/86	Portsmouth	Home	FM Cup	0–1		
107	29/11/86	Queens Park Rangers	Away	League	2–2	1 Goal	(46)
108	06/12/86	Aston Villa	Home	League	2–1	1 Goal	(47)
109	13/12/86	Wimbledon	Away	League	0–3		
110	21/12/86	Newcastle United	Home	League	2–0	1 Goal	(48)
111	26/12/86	Manchester City	Away	League	0–1		
112	27/12/86	Liverpool	Home	League	0–1		
113	01/01/87	Norwich City	Home	League	1–1		
114	03/01/87	Leicester City	Away	League	1–6		
115	17/01/87	Everton	Away	League	0–2		
116	24/01/87	Charlton Athletic	Home	League	1–1		
117	26/01/87	Derby County	Home	FA Cup	1–0		
118	31/01/87	Chester City	Away	FA Cup	1–1	1 Goal	(49)
119	04/02/87	Chester City	Home	FA Cup	3–1	1 Goal	(50)
120	07/02/87	Chelsea	Away	League	0–2		
121	25/02/87	West Ham United	Away	FA Cup	2–0	1 Goal	(51)
122	28/02/87	Watford	Home	League	0–1		
123	07/03/87	Coventry City	Away	League	0–1		
124	14/03/87	Coventry City	Home	FA Cup	0–3		
125	21/03/87	Manchester United	Home	League	1–0		
126	24/03/87	West Ham United	Away	League	2–0	1 Goal	(52)
127	28/03/87	Oxford United	Away	League	1–2	1 Goal	(53)
128	07/04/87	Tottenham Hotspur	Home	League	0–1		
129	14/04/87	Nottingham Forest	Home	League	2–3	1 Goal	(54)
130	18/04/87	Norwich City	Away	League	0–1		
131	20/04/87	Manchester City	Home	League	2–1	1 Goal	(55)
132	22/04/87	Southampton	Away	League	1–1	1 Goal	(56)

133	25/04/87	Luton Town	Away	League	0–0		
134	02/05/87	Queens Park Rangers	Home	League	7–1		
135	04/05/87	Aston Villa	Away	League	2–1	1 Goal	(57)
136	09/05/87	Wimbledon	Home	League	0–2		

SEASON 1987–88

League Division One

137	15/08/87	Chelsea	Away	League	1–2	1 Goal	(58)
138	18/08/87	Oxford United	Home	League	1–1	1 Goal	(59)
139	22/08/87	Newcastle United	Home	League	0–1		
140	29/08/87	Everton	Away	League	0–4		
141	31/08/87	Coventry City	Home	League	0–3		
142	05/09/87	Southampton	Away	League	1–1	1 Goal	(60)
143	12/09/87	Watford	Home	League	2–3	1 Goal	(61)
144	19/09/87	Derby County	Away	League	2–2		
145	22/09/87	Shrewsbury Town	Away	Lge Cup	1–1		
146	26/09/87	Charlton Athletic	Home	League	2–0	2 Goals	(63)
147	03/10/87	Tottenham Hotspur	Away	League	0–2		
148	06/10/87	Shrewsbury Town	Home	Lge Cup	2–1		
149	10/10/87	Manchester United	Home	League	2–4		
150	17/10/87	Nottingham Forest	Away	League	0–3		
151	24/10/87	Norwich City	Home	League	1–0		
152	27/10/87	Barnsley	Away	Lge Cup	2–1		
Sub+4	10/11/87	AFC Bournemouth	Home	Simod Cup	2–0		
153	14/11/87	Luton Town	Home	League	0–2		
154	18/11/87	Aston Villa	Away	Lge Cup	2–1	1 Goal	(64)
155	28/11/87	Queens Park Rangers	Home	League	3–1		
156	01/12/87	Stoke City	Home	Simod Cup	0–1		
157	05/12/87	Arsenal	Away	League	1–3		
158	12/12/87	Wimbledon	Home	League	1–0	1 Goal	(65)
159	19/12/87	Liverpool	Away	League	0–1		
160	26/12/87	Watford	Away	League	3–1	1 Goal	(66)
161	28/12/87	Derby County	Home	League	2–1	1 Goal	(67)
162	01/01/88	Everton	Home	League	1–0		
163	02/01/88	Newcastle United	Away	League	2–2	1 Goal	(68)
164	09/01/88	Everton	Home	FA Cup	1–1		
165	13/01/88	Everton	Away	FA Cup	1–1*	1 Goal	(69)
166	20/01/88	Arsenal	Home	Lge Cup	0–1		
167	25/01/88	Everton	Away	FA Cup	1–1*	1 Goal	(70)
168	27/01/88	Everton	Home	FA Cup	0–5		
169	06/02/88	Southampton	Home	League	2–1	1 Goal	(71)
170	13/02/88	Coventry City	Away	League	0–3		
171	20/02/88	Charlton Athletic	Away	League	1–3	1 Goal	(72)
172	27/02/88	Tottenham Hotspur	Home	League	0–3		
173	05/03/88	Nottingham Forest	Home	League	0–1		
174	12/03/88	Manchester United	Away	League	1–4	1 Goal	(73)
175	19/03/88	Portsmouth	Home	League	1–0		
176	26/03/88	Norwich City	Away	League	3–0	1 Goal	(74)
177	02/04/88	West Ham United	Home	League	2–1		
178	05/04/88	Luton Town	Away	League	2–2	1 Goal	(75)
179	13/04/88	Oxford United	Away	League	3–0	2 Goals	(77)
180	23/04/88	Queens Park Rangers	Away	League	1–1		
181	30/04/88	Arsenal	Home	League	3–3	1 Goal	(78)
182	03/05/88	Wimbledon	Away	League	1–1	1 Goal	(79)
183	07/05/88	Liverpool	Home	League	1–5		

SEASON 1988–89

Chamois Niortais de Niort – French League Division Two

1	16/07/88	Istres SF	Home	League	3–1		
2	23/07/88	Cercle Dijon Football	Away	League	1–1	1 Goal	(1)
3	27/07/88	Montceau–Les–Mines	Home	League	1–1		
4	30/07/88	Olympique Ales	Away	League	1–1		
5	06/08/88	Stade Rodez	Away	League	1–2		
6	12/08/88	Clermont–Ferrand	Home	League	2–1	1 Goal	(2)
7	17/08/88	SC Etoile Bastia	Away	League	1–2		
8	20/08/88	Orleans	Home	League	1–1		
9	27/08/88	Club Omnisport Le Puy	Away	League	1–1		
10	10/09/88	Cuiseaux–Louhans	Away	League	1–2	1 Goal	(3)

Nottingham Forest – League Division One

1	22/10/88	Millwall	Away	League	2–2		
2	26/10/88	Liverpool	Home	League	2–1		
3	29/10/88	Newcastle United	Away	League	1–0	1 Goal	(1)

4	02/11/88	Coventry City	Home	Lge Cup	3–2		
5	06/11/88	Arsenal	Home	League	1–4		
6	12/11/88	West Ham United	Away	League	3–3		
7	19/11/88	Coventry City	Home	League	0–0		
8	26/11/88	Charlton Athletic	Away	League	1–0		
9	30/11/88	Leicester City	Away	Lge Cup	0–0		
10	03/12/88	Middlesbrough	Home	League	2–2	2 Goals	(3)
11	10/12/88	Southampton	Away	League	1–1		
12	14/12/88	Leicester City	Home	Lge Cup	2–1	1 Goal	(4)
13	18/12/88	Wimbledon	Home	League	0–1		
14	26/12/88	Manchester United	Away	League	0–2		
15	31/12/88	Sheffield Wednesday	Away	League	3–0		
16	02/01/89	Everton	Home	League	2–0		
17	07/01/89	Ipswich Town	Home	FA Cup	3–0	1 Goal	(5)
18	10/01/89	Chelsea	Away	Simod Cup	4–1	1 Goal	(6)
19	15/01/89	Tottenham Hotspur	Away	League	2–1		
20	18/01/89	Queens Park Rangers	Home	Lge Cup	5–2	4 Goals	(10)
21	21/01/89	Aston Villa	Home	League	4–0		
22	24/01/89	Ipswich Town	Away	Simod Cup	3–1		
23	28/01/89	Leeds United	Home	FA Cup	2–0	1 Goal	(11)
24	04/02/89	Luton Town	Away	League	3–2		
25	11/02/89	Queens Park Rangers	Home	League	0–0		
26	15/02/89	Bristol City	Home	Lge Cup	1–1		
27	19/02/89	Watford	Away	FA Cup	3–0	1 Goal	(12)
28	22/02/89	Crystal Palace	Home	Simod Cup	3–1		
29	26/02/89	Bristol City	Away	Lge Cup	1–0*		
30	11/03/89	Arsenal	Away	League	3–1		
31	15/03/89	Newcastle United	Home	League	1–1		
32	18/03/89	Manchester United	Away	FA Cup	1–0		
33	22/03/89	Tottenham Hotspur	Home	League	1–2		
34	25/03/89	Derby County	Away	League	2–0	1 Goal	(13)
35	27/03/89	Manchester United	Home	League	2–0	1 Goal	(14)
36	01/04/89	Wimbledon	Away	League	1–4		
37	05/04/89	Norwich City	Home	League	2–0		
38	09/04/89	Luton Town	Wembley	Lge Cup	3–1		
39	12/04/89	Southampton	Home	League	3–0		
40	22/04/89	Middlesbrough	Away	League	4–3	2 Goals	(16)
41	30/04/89	Everton	Wembley	Simod Cup	4–3*	2 Goals	(18)
42	07/05/89	Liverpool	Neutral	FA Cup	1–3		
43	10/05/89	Liverpool	Away	League	0–1		
44	13/05/89	Charlton Athletic	Home	League	4–0		
45	15/05/89	Coventry City	Away	League	2–2		
46	18/05/89	West Ham United	Home	League	1–2	1 Goal	(19)

SEASON 1989–90

League Division One

47	19/08/89	Aston Villa	Home	League	1–1		
48	23/08/89	Norwich City	Away	League	1–1	1 Goal	(20)
49	26/08/89	Millwall	Away	League	0–1		
50	30/08/89	Derby County	Home	League	2–1		
51	09/09/89	Chelsea	Away	League	2–2	2 Goals	(22)
52	20/09/89	Huddersfield Town	Home	Lge Cup	1–1		
53	16/09/89	Arsenal	Home	League	1–2		
54	23/09/89	Crystal Palace	Away	League	0–1		
55	30/09/89	Charlton Athletic	Home	League	2–0	1 Goal	(23)
56	03/10/89	Huddersfield Town	Away	Lge Cup	3–3*		
57	14/10/89	Coventry City	Away	League	2–0		
58	21/10/89	Wimbledon	Away	League	3–1		
59	24/10/89	Crystal Palace	Away	Lge Cup	0–0		
60	28/10/89	Queens Park Rangers	Home	League	2–2	1 Goal	(24)
61	01/11/89	Crystal Palace	Home	Lge Cup	5–0		
62	04/11/89	Sheffield Wednesday	Home	League	0–1		
63	12/11/89	Manchester United	Away	League	0–1		
64	18/11/89	Manchester City	Away	League	3–0		
65	22/11/89	Everton	Home	Lge Cup	1–0	1 Goal	(25)
66	25/11/89	Everton	Home	League	1–0		
67	29/11/89	Manchester City	Home	ZDS Cup	3–2		
68	02/12/89	Aston Villa	Away	League	1–2	1 Goal	(26)
69	09/12/89	Norwich City	Home	League	0–1		
70	17/12/89	Southampton	Home	League	2–0	1 Goal	(27)
71	22/12/89	Aston Villa	Away	ZDS Cup	1–2		

Leeds United – League Division Two

1	13/01/90	Blackburn Rovers	Away	League	2–1	1 Goal	(1)

2	20/01/90	Stoke City	Home	League	2–0		
3	04/02/90	Swindon Town	Away	League	2–3		
4	10/02/90	Hull City	Home	League	4–3		
5	17/02/90	Ipswich Town	Away	League	2–2	2 Goals	(3)
6	24/02/90	West Bromwich Albion	Home	League	2–2	1 Goal	(4)
7	03/03/90	Watford	Away	League	0–1		
8	07/03/90	Port Vale	Home	League	0–0		
9	10/03/90	Oxford United	Away	League	4–2	2 Goals	(6)
10	17/03/90	West Ham United	Home	League	3–2	2 Goals	(8)
11	20/03/90	Sunderland	Away	League	1–0		
12	24/03/90	Portsmouth	Home	League	2–0	1 Goal	(9)
13	31/03/90	Wolverhampton Wanderers	Away	League	0–1		
14	07/04/90	Bradford City	Home	League	1–1		
15	10/04/90	Plymouth Argyle	Away	League	1–1	1 Goal	(10)
16	13/04/90	Oldham Athletic	Away	League	1–3		
17	16/04/90	Sheffield United	Home	League	4–0	1 Goal	(11)
18	21/04/90	Brighton & Hove Albion	Away	League	2–2		
19	25/04/90	Barnsley	Home	League	1–2		
20	28/04/90	Leicester City	Home	League	2–1		
21	05/05/90	AFC Bournemouth	Away	League	1–0	1 Goal	(12)

SEASON 1990–91

League Division One

22	25/08/90	Everton	Away	League	3–2		
23	28/08/90	Manchester United	Home	League	0–0		
24	01/09/90	Norwich City	Home	League	3–0	2 Goals	(14)
25	08/09/90	Luton Town	Away	League	0–1		
26	15/09/90	Tottenham Hotspur	Home	League	0–2		
27	23/09/90	Sheffield United	Away	League	2–0		
28	26/09/90	Leicester City	Away	Lge Cup	0–1		
29	29/09/90	Arsenal	Home	League	2–2	1 Goal	(15)
30	06/10/90	Crystal Palace	Away	League	1–1		
31	10/10/90	Leicester City	Home	Lge Cup	3–0		
32	20/10/90	Queens Park Rangers	Home	League	2–3	1 Goal	(16)
33	27/10/90	Aston Villa	Away	League	0–0		
34	31/10/90	Oldham Athletic	Home	Lge Cup	2–0	1 Goal	(17)
35	03/11/90	Nottingham Forest	Home	League	3–1	1 Goal	(18)
36	11/11/90	Manchester City	Away	League	3–2	1 Goal	(19)
37	17/11/90	Derby County	Home	League	3–0	1 Goal	(20)
38	24/11/90	Coventry City	Away	League	1–1	1 Goal	(21)
39	27/11/90	Queens Park Rangers	Away	Lge Cup	3–0	1 Goal	(22)
40	01/12/90	Southampton	Home	League	2–1		
41	08/12/90	Manchester United	Away	League	1–1		
42	16/12/90	Everton	Home	League	2–0		
43	23/12/90	Sunderland	Away	League	1–0		
44	26/12/90	Chelsea	Home	League	4–1	2 Goals	(24)
45	29/12/90	Wimbledon	Home	League	3–0	1 Goal	(25)
46	01/01/91	Liverpool	Away	League	0–3		
47	06/01/91	Barnsley	Away	FA Cup	1–1		
48	09/01/91	Barnsley	Home	FA Cup	4–0	1 Goal	(26)
49	12/01/91	Norwich City	Away	League	0–2		
50	16/01/91	Aston Villa	Home	Lge Cup	4–1	2 Goals	(28)
51	19/01/91	Luton Town	Home	League	2–1		
52	22/01/91	Derby County	Away	ZDS Cup	2–1	1 Goal	(29)
53	27/01/91	Arsenal	Away	FA Cup	0–0		
54	29/01/91	Arsenal	Home	FA Cup	1–1*	1 Goal	(30)
55	02/02/91	Tottenham Hotspur	Away	League	0–0		
56	10/02/91	Manchester United	Away	Lge Cup	1–2		
57	13/02/91	Arsenal	Away	FA Cup	0–0*		
58	16/02/91	Arsenal	Home	FA Cup	1–2	1 Goal	(31)
59	20/02/91	Manchester City	Home	ZDS Cup	2–0*		
60	24/02/91	Manchester United	Home	Lge Cup	0–1		
61	02/03/91	Southampton	Away	League	0–2		
62	09/03/91	Coventry City	Home	League	2–0		
63	17/03/91	Arsenal	Away	League	0–2		
64	19/03/91	Everton	Home	ZDS Cup	3–3	2 Goals	(33)
65	21/03/91	Everton	Away	ZDS Cup	1–3*		
66	23/03/91	Crystal Palace	Home	League	1–2		
67	30/03/91	Chelsea	Away	League	2–1		
68	02/04/91	Sunderland	Home	League	5–0	2 Goals	(35)
69	06/04/91	Wimbledon	Away	League	1–0	1 Goal	(36)
70	10/04/91	Manchester City	Home	League	1–2		
71	13/04/91	Liverpool	Home	League	4–5	3 Goals	(39)
72	17/04/91	Queens Park Rangers	Away	League	0–2		

73	23/04/91	Derby County	Away	League	1–0		
74	04/05/91	Aston Villa	Home	League	5–2	2 Goals	(41)
75	08/05/91	Sheffield United	Home	League	2–1		
76	11/05/91	Nottingham Forest	Away	League	3–4	2 Goals	(43)

SEASON 1991–92

League Division One

77	20/08/91	Nottingham Forest	Home	League	1–0		
78	24/08/91	Sheffield Wednesday	Home	League	1–1		
79	28/08/91	Southampton	Away	League	4–0		
80	31/08/91	Manchester United	Away	League	1–1	1 Goal	(44)
81	03/09/91	Arsenal	Home	League	2–2	1 Goal	(45)
82	07/09/91	Manchester City	Home	League	3–0		
83	14/09/91	Chelsea	Away	League	1–0		
84	18/09/91	Coventry City	Away	League	0–0		
85	21/09/91	Liverpool	Home	League	1–0		
86	24/09/91	Scunthorpe United	Away	Lge Cup	0–0		
87	28/09/91	Norwich City	Away	League	2–2		
88	01/10/91	Crystal Palace	Away	League	0–1		
89	05/10/91	Sheffield United	Home	League	4–3		
90	08/10/91	Scunthorpe United	Home	Lge Cup	3–0	1 Goal	(46)
91	19/10/91	Notts County	Away	League	4–2	1 Goal	(47)
92	26/10/91	Oldham Athletic	Home	League	1–0		
93	29/10/91	Tranmere Rovers	Home	Lge Cup	3–1	2 Goals	(49)
94	02/11/91	Wimbledon	Away	League	0–0		
95	16/11/91	Queens Park Rangers	Home	League	2–0		
96	24/11/91	Aston Villa	Away	League	4–1	2 Goals	(51)
97	30/11/91	Everton	Home	League	1–0		
98	04/12/91	Everton	Away	Lge Cup	4–1	1 Goal	(52)
99	07/12/91	Luton Town	Away	League	2–0		
100	14/12/91	Tottenham Hotspur	Home	League	1–1		
101	22/12/91	Nottingham Forest	Away	League	0–0		
102	26/12/91	Southampton	Home	League	3–3		
103	29/12/91	Manchester United	Home	League	1–1		
104	01/01/92	West Ham United	Away	League	3–1	2 Goals	(54)
105	08/01/92	Manchester United	Home	Lge Cup	1–3		
106	12/01/92	Sheffield Wednesday	Away	League	6–1	3 Goals	(57)
107	15/01/92	Manchester United	Home	FA Cup	0–1		
108	29/02/92	Luton Town	Home	League	2–0	1 Goal	(58)
109	03/03/92	Aston Villa	Home	League	0–0		
110	07/03/92	Tottenham Hotspur	Away	League	3–1		
111	11/03/92	Queens Park Rangers	Away	League	1–4		
112	14/03/92	Wimbledon	Home	League	5–1	3 Goals	(61)
113	22/03/92	Arsenal	Away	League	1–1	1 Goal	(62)
114	28/03/92	West Ham United	Home	League	0–0		
115	04/04/92	Manchester City	Away	League	0–4		
116	11/04/92	Chelsea	Home	League	3–0	1 Goal	(63)
117	18/04/92	Liverpool	Away	League	0–0		
118	20/04/92	Coventry City	Home	League	2–0		
119	26/04/92	Sheffield United	Away	League	3–2		
120	02/05/92	Norwich City	Home	League	1–1		

SEASON 1992–93

Premier League

121	08/08/92	Liverpool	Wembley	FA C/S	4–3		
122	15/08/92	Wimbledon	Home	League	2–1	2 Goals	(65)
123	19/08/92	Aston Villa	Away	League	1–1		
124	22/08/92	Middlesbrough	Away	League	1–4		
125	25/08/92	Tottenham Hotspur	Home	League	5–0	1 Goal	(66)
126	29/08/92	Liverpool	Home	League	2–2	1 Goal	(67)
127	01/09/92	Oldham Athletic	Away	League	2–2		
128	06/09/92	Manchester United	Away	League	0–2		
129	13/09/92	Aston Villa	Home	League	1–1		
130	16/09/92	VFB Stuttgart	Away	Eur Cup	0–3		
131	19/09/92	Southampton	Away	League	1–1		
132	22/09/92	Scunthorpe United	Home	Lge Cup	4–1	1 Goal	(68)
133	26/09/92	Everton	Home	League	2–0	1 Goal	(69)
134	30/09/92	VFB Stuttgart	Home	Eur Cup	4–1+	1 Goal	(70)
135	03/10/92	Ipswich Town	Away	League	2–4		
136	09/10/92	VFB Stuttgart	Neutral	Eur Cup	2–1		
137	17/10/92	Sheffield United	Home	League	3–1	1 Goal	(71)
138	21/10/92	Rangers	Away	Eur Cup	1–2		
139	24/10/92	Queens Park Rangers	Away	League	1–2		

140	27/10/92	Scunthorpe United	Away	Lge Cup	2–2	1 Goal	(72)
141	31/10/92	Coventry City	Home	League	2–2	1 Goal	(73)
142	04/11/92	Rangers	Home	Eur Cup	1–2		
Sub+1	07/11/92	Manchester City	Away	League	0–4		
143	10/11/92	Watford	Away	Lge Cup	1–2		
144	21/11/92	Arsenal	Home	League	3–0	1 Goal	(74)
145	29/11/92	Chelsea	Away	League	0–1		
146	05/12/92	Nottingham Forest	Home	League	1–4		
147	12/12/92	Sheffield Wednesday	Home	League	3–1	1 Goal	(75)
148	20/12/92	Crystal Palace	Away	League	0–1		
149	26/12/92	Blackburn Rovers	Away	League	1–3		
150	28/12/92	Norwich City	Home	League	0–0		
151	02/01/93	Charlton Athletic	Home	FA Cup	1–1		
152	09/01/93	Southampton	Home	League	2–1	1 Goal	(76)
153	13/01/93	Charlton Athletic	Away	FA Cup	3–1		
154	16/01/93	Everton	Away	League	0–2		
155	25/01/93	Arsenal	Away	FA Cup	2–2	1 Goal	(77)
156	03/02/93	Arsenal	Home	FA Cup	2–3*		
157	06/02/93	Wimbledon	Away	League	0–1		
158	08/02/93	Manchester United	Home	League	0–0		
159	13/02/93	Oldham Athletic	Home	League	2–0	1 Goal	(78)
160	20/02/93	Tottenham Hotspur	Away	League	0–4		
Sub+2	24/02/93	Arsenal	Away	League	0–0		
Sub+3	27/02/93	Ipswich Town	Home	League	1–0		
Sub+4	13/03/93	Manchester City	Home	League	1–0		
161	21/03/93	Nottingham Forest	Away	League	1–1		
162	24/03/93	Chelsea	Home	League	1–1		
163	10/04/93	Blackburn Rovers	Home	League	5–2	1 Goal	(79)
164	14/04/93	Norwich City	Away	League	2–4	1 Goal	(80)
165	17/04/93	Crystal Palace	Home	League	0–0		
166	21/04/93	Liverpool	Away	League	0–2		
167	01/05/93	Queens Park Rangers	Home	League	1–1		
168	04/05/93	Sheffield Wednesday	Away	League	1–1		
169	08/05/93	Coventry City	Away	League	3–3		

+ Leeds United awarded match 3–0 after VFB Stuttgart fielded an ineligible player

SEASON 1993–94

Portsmouth – Football League Division One

1	14/08/93	Oxford United	Away	League	2–3	2 Goals	(2)
2	17/08/93	Charlton Athletic	Home	League	1–2		
3	21/08/93	Luton Town	Home	League	1–0		
4	24/08/93	Grimsby Town	Away	League	1–1		
5	28/08/93	Crystal Palace	Away	League	1–5		
6	14/09/93	Oxford United	Away	AI Cup	2–0		

West Ham United – Premier League

1	18/09/93	Blackburn Rovers	Away	League	2–0	1 Goal	(1)
2	22/09/93	Chesterfield	Home	Lge Cup	5–1	2 Goals	(3)
3	25/09/93	Newcastle United	Away	League	0–2		
4	02/10/93	Chelsea	Home	League	1–0		
5	05/10/93	Chesterfield	Away	Lge Cup	2–0		
6	16/10/93	Aston Villa	Home	League	0–0		
7	23/10/93	Norwich City	Away	League	0–0		
8	27/10/93	Nottingham Forest	Away	Lge Cup	1–2		
9	01/11/93	Manchester City	Home	League	3–1	1 Goal	(4)
10	06/11/93	Liverpool	Away	League	0–2		
11	20/11/93	Oldham Athletic	Home	League	2–0		
12	24/11/93	Arsenal	Home	League	0–0		
13	29/11/93	Southampton	Away	League	2–0	1 Goal	(5)
14	04/12/93	Wimbledon	Away	League	2–1	2 Goals	(7)
15	08/12/93	Leeds United	Home	League	0–1		
16	11/12/93	Coventry City	Home	League	3–2		
17	18/12/93	Sheffield Wednesday	Away	League	0–5		
18	27/12/93	Ipswich Town	Away	League	1–1	1 Goal	(8)
19	28/12/93	Tottenham Hotspur	Home	League	1–3		
20	01/01/94	Everton	Away	League	1–0		
21	03/01/94	Sheffield United	Home	League	0–0		
22	08/01/94	Watford	Home	FA Cup	2–1		
23	15/01/94	Aston Villa	Away	League	1–3		
24	24/01/94	Norwich City	Home	League	3–3		
25	29/01/94	Notts County	Away	FA Cup	1–1		
26	09/02/94	Notts County	Home	FA Cup	1–0*	1 Goal	(9)
27	12/02/94	Manchester City	Away	League	0–0		

28	19/02/94	Kidderminster Harriers	Away	FA Cup	1–0	1 Goal	(10)
29	25/02/94	Manchester United	Home	League	2–2	1 Goal	(11)
30	05/03/94	Swindon Town	Away	League	1–1		
31	14/03/94	Luton Town	Home	FA Cup	0–0		
32	19/03/94	Newcastle United	Home	League	2–4		
33	23/03/94	Luton Town	Away	FA Cup	2–3		
34	26/03/94	Chelsea	Away	League	0–2		
35	28/03/94	Sheffield United	Away	League	2–3		
Sub+1	23/04/94	Liverpool	Home	League	1–2		
Sub+2	27/04/94	Blackburn Rovers	Home	League	1–2		
Sub+3	03/05/94	Queens Park Rangers	Away	League	0–0		
Sub+4	07/05/94	Southampton	Home	League	3–3		

SEASON 1994–95

Premier League

36	20/08/94	Leeds United	Home	League	0–0		
37	24/08/94	Manchester City	Away	League	0–3		
Sub+5	27/08/94	Norwich City	Away	League	0–1		
Sub+6	17/09/94	Aston Villa	Home	League	1–0		
Sub+7	20/09/94	Walsall	Away	Lge Cup	1–2		
38	25/09/94	Arsenal	Home	League	0–2		
39	02/10/94	Chelsea	Away	League	2–1		
40	05/10/94	Walsall	Home	Lge Cup	2–0		
41	08/10/94	Crystal Palace	Home	League	1–0		
42	22/10/94	Southampton	Home	League	2–0		
Sub+8	29/10/94	Tottenham Hotspur	Away	League	1–3		
43	01/11/94	Everton	Away	League	0–1		

Southend United (loan) – Football League Division One

1	14/01/95	Grimsby Town	Away	League	1–4	1 Goal	(1)

Ipswich Town – Premier League

Sub+1	21/01/95	Chelsea	Home	League	2–2		
1	28/01/95	Blackburn Rovers	Away	League	1–4		
2	04/02/95	Crystal Palace	Home	League	0–2		
3	22/02/95	Manchester City	Away	League	0–2		
4	25/02/95	Southampton	Home	League	2–1	1 Goal	(1)
5	28/02/95	Newcastle United	Home	League	0–2		
6	04/03/95	Manchester United	Away	League	0–9		
7	08/03/95	Tottenham Hotspur	Away	League	0–3		
Sub+2	20/03/95	Norwich City	Away	League	0–3		
8	05/04/95	Leeds United	Away	League	0–4		
Sub+3	11/04/95	Queens Park Rangers	Home	League	0–1		
Sub+4	15/04/95	Arsenal	Away	League	1–4		
Sub+5	17/04/95	West Ham United	Home	League	1–1		
Sub+6	06/05/95	Coventry City	Home	League	2–0		
Sub+7	09/05/95	Everton	Home	League	0–1		
9	14/05/95	Sheffield Wednesday	Away	League	1–4		

SEASON 1995–96

Football League Division One

Sub+8	12/08/95	Birmingham City	Away	League	1–3		
10	26/08/95	West Bromwich Albion	Away	League	0–0		
11	30/08/95	Stoke City	Home	League	4–1		
12	05/09/95	AC Reggiana	Home	AI Cup	2–1		
Sub+9	09/09/95	Huddersfield Town	Away	League	1–2		
Sub+10	12/09/95	Oldham Athletic	Away	League	1–1		
13	19/09/95	Stockport County	Away	Lge Cup	1–1		
Sub+11	23/09/95	Charlton Athletic	Home	League	1–5		
14	08/11/95	Foggia Calcio	Away	AI Cup	1–0		

Leeds United (loan) – Premier League

1	13/01/96	West Ham United	Home	League	2–0		
2	20/01/96	Liverpool	Away	League	0–5		

Swansea City – Football League Division Two

1	30/03/96	Bradford City	Away	League	1–5	1 Goal	(1)
2	02/04/96	Peterborough United	Home	League	0–0		
3	06/04/96	Wrexham	Home	League	1–3		
4	09/04/96	AFC Bournemouth	Away	League	1–3	1 Goal	(2)
5	13/04/96	Brighton & Hove Albion	Home	League	2–1	1 Goal	(3)
6	20/04/96	Wycombe Wanderers	Away	League	1–0	1 Goal	(4)
7	27/04/96	Notts County	Away	League	0–4		

APPEARANCES AND GOALS PER SEASON

SEASON 78–79	GAMES	GOALS
League	3+1	0
TOTAL	**3+1**	**0**

SEASON 79–80	GAMES	GOALS
League	14+3	3
League Cup	1	1
TOTAL	**15+3**	**4**

SEASON 80–81	GAMES	GOALS
League	41	15
FA Cup	2	1
League Cup	2	1
TOTAL	**45**	**17**

SEASON 81–82	GAMES	GOALS
League	40+1	16
FA Cup	1	0
League Cup	2	1
TOTAL	**43+1**	**17**

SEASON 82–83	GAMES	GOALS
League	12+7	3
FA Cup	0+1	0
League Cup	0+2	0
UEFA Cup	2	2
TOTAL	**14+10**	**5**

SEASON 83–84	GAMES	GOALS
League	17+2	4
FA Cup	2	1
TOTAL	**19+2**	**5**

SEASON 84–85	GAMES	GOALS
League	40	15
FA Cup	2	3
League Cup	7	2
TOTAL	**49**	**20**

SEASON 85–86	GAMES	GOALS
League	29+2	10
FA Cup	6+1	2
League Cup	3	3
TOTAL	**38+3**	**15**

SEASON 86–87	GAMES	GOALS
League	41	19
FA Cup	5	3
League Cup	2	0
Full Members Cup	1	0
TOTAL	**49**	**22**

SEASON 87–88	GAMES	GOALS
League	37	19
FA Cup	4	2
League Cup	5	1
Simod Cup	1+1	0
TOTAL	**47+1**	**22**

SEASON 88–89	GAMES	GOALS
League	30	8
FA Cup	5	3
League Cup	7	5
Simod Cup	4	3
French League	10	3
TOTAL	**56**	**22**

SEASON 89–90	GAMES	GOALS
League	39	19
League Cup	5	1
Zenith Data Systems Cup	2	0
TOTAL	**46**	**20**

SEASON 90–91	GAMES	GOALS
League	38	21
FA Cup	6	3
League Cup	7	4
Zenith Data Systems Cup	4	3
TOTAL	**55**	**31**

SEASON 91–92	GAMES	GOALS
League	38	16
FA Cup	1	0
League Cup	5	4
TOTAL	**44**	**20**

SEASON 92–93	GAMES	GOALS
League	36+4	13
FA Cup	4	1
League Cup	3	2
European Cup	5	1
FA Charity Shield	1	0
TOTAL	**49+4**	**17**

SEASON 93–94	GAMES	GOALS
League	31+4	9
FA Cup	6	2
League Cup	3	2
Anglo–Italian Cup	1	0
TOTAL	**41+4**	**13**

SEASON 94–95	GAMES	GOALS
League	17+10	2
League Cup	1+1	0
TOTAL	**18+11**	**2**

SEASON 95–96	GAMES	GOALS
League	11+4	4
League Cup	1	0
Anglo–Italian Cup	2	0
TOTAL	**14+4**	**4**

CAREER APPEARANCES AND GOALS

COMPETITION	GAMES	TOTAL	GOALS
League	514+38	552	196
FA Cup	44+2	46	21
League Cup	54+3	57	27
Full Members Cup	1	1	0
Simod Cup	5+1	6	3
Zenith Data Systems Cup	6	6	3
Anglo–Italian Cup	3	3	0
FA Charity Shield	1	1	0
European Cup	5	5	1
UEFA Cup	2	2	2
French League	10	10	3
TOTAL	**645+44**	**689**	**256**

HAT-TRICKS

Stoke City

1	3	Norwich City	15/11/80	Home	League	3–1
2	3	Leeds United	14/02/81	Away	League	3–1

Nottingham Forest

1	4	Queens Park Rangers	18/01/89	Home	Lge Cup	5–2

Leeds United

1	3	Liverpool	13/04/91	Home	League	4–5
2	3	Sheffield Wednesday	12/01/92	Away	League	6–1
3	3	Wimbledon	14/03/92	Home	League	5–1

League: 5
League Cup: 1
TOTAL: 6

HONOURS

Winners medals
League Division One Championship: 91/92
League Division Two Championship: 89/90
League Cup: 88/89
Simod Cup: 88/89
FA Charity Shield: 92/93

Runner-up medals
None

ANDY COLE

Born: 15/10/71 – Nottingham
Height: 5.11
Weight: 11.02 (96–97)

Clubs
Arsenal: **1990–91** – Matches: **0+2** – Goals: **0**
Fulham (loan): **1991** – Matches: **15** – Goals: **4**
Bristol City: **1992–93** – Matches: **49** – Goals: **25**
Newcastle United: **1993–95** – Matches: **83+1** – Goals: **68**
Manchester United: **1995–97** – Matches: **72+17** – Goals: **32**

Country
England: **1995–97** – Matches: **0+2** – Goals: **0**

SEASON 1990–91

Arsenal – League Division One

Sub+1	29/12/90	Sheffield United	Home	League	4–1	

SEASON 1991–92

League Division One

Sub+2	10/08/91	Tottenham Hotspur	Wembley	FA C/S	0–0	

Fulham (loan) – League Division Three

1	07/09/91	Swansea City	Home	League	3–0		
2	14/09/91	Stoke City	Away	League	2–2	1 Goal	(1)
3	17/09/91	Bury	Away	League	1–3		
4	21/09/91	Leyton Orient	Home	League	2–1		
5	27/09/91	AFC Bournemouth	Away	League	0–0		
6	05/10/91	Brentford	Home	League	0–1		
7	12/10/91	Bradford City	Away	League	4–3		
8	19/10/91	Bolton Wanderers	Away	League	3–0	1 Goal	(2)
9	23/10/91	Maidstone United	Away	A Trophy	6–2		
10	26/10/91	Preston North End	Home	League	1–0		
11	02/11/91	Hull City	Home	League	0–0		
12	06/11/91	Huddersfield Town	Away	League	1–3		
13	09/11/91	Hartlepool United	Away	League	0–2		
14	20/11/91	Gillingham	Home	A Trophy	2–0	1 Goal	(3)
15	23/11/91	Stockport County	Home	League	1–2	1 Goal	(4)

Bristol City (loan) – League Division Two

1	14/03/92	Cambridge United	Home	League	1–2		
2	17/03/92	Wolverhampton Wanderers	Home	League	2–0		
3	21/03/92	Sunderland	Away	League	3–1	1 Goal	(1)
4	28/03/92	Oxford United	Home	League	1–1		
5	31/03/92	Tranmere Rovers	Away	League	2–2	1 Goal	(2)
6	04/04/92	Leicester City	Home	League	2–1	1 Goal	(3)
7	07/04/92	Middlesbrough	Home	League	1–1	1 Goal	(4)
8	11/04/92	Millwall	Away	League	3–2	1 Goal	(5)
9	18/04/92	Ipswich Town	Home	League	2–1	1 Goal	(6)
10	20/04/92	Portsmouth	Away	League	0–1		
11	25/04/92	Derby County	Home	League	1–2		
12	02/05/92	Watford	Away	League	2–5	2 Goals	(8)

SEASON 1992–93

Bristol City – Football League Division One

13	15/08/92	Portsmouth	Home	League	3–3	1 Goal	(9)
14	18/08/92	Cardiff City	Away	Lge Cup	0–1		
15	22/08/92	Luton Town	Away	League	3–0	1 Goal	(10)
16	25/08/92	Cardiff City	Home	Lge Cup	5–1	3 Goals	(13)
17	29/08/92	Sunderland	Home	League	0–0		
18	01/09/92	Watford	Home	AI Cup	1–0		
19	15/09/92	West Ham United	Home	League	1–5		
20	03/10/92	Tranmere Rovers	Away	League	0–3		
21	07/10/92	Sheffield United	Away	Lge Cup	1–4	1 Goal	(14)
22	10/10/92	Charlton Athletic	Home	League	2–1		
23	17/10/92	Cambridge United	Away	League	1–2	1 Goal	(15)
24	24/10/92	Leicester City	Home	League	2–1	1 Goal	(16)
25	31/10/92	Brentford	Away	League	1–5	1 Goal	(17)
26	04/11/92	Millwall	Away	League	1–4	1 Goal	(18)
27	07/11/92	Birmingham City	Home	League	3–0	1 Goal	(19)
28	11/11/92	Cosenza Calcio	Home	AI Cup	0–2		
29	14/11/92	Grimsby Town	Away	League	1–2	1 Goal	(20)
30	17/11/92	Swindon Town	Home	League	2–2		
31	24/11/92	SC Pisa	Away	AI Cup	3–4		
32	28/11/92	Notts County	Home	League	1–0		
33	05/12/92	Watford	Away	League	0–0		
34	13/12/92	Bristol Rovers	Away	League	0–4		
35	16/12/92	US Cremonese	Away	AI Cup	2–2	1 Goal	(21)
36	19/12/92	Peterborough United	Home	League	0–1		
37	26/12/92	Oxford United	Home	League	1–1		
38	28/12/92	Wolverhampton Wanderers	Away	League	0–0		
39	09/01/93	Newcastle United	Home	League	1–2		
40	16/01/93	Barnsley	Away	League	1–2	1 Goal	(22)
41	19/01/93	Luton Town	Away	FA Cup	0–2		
42	27/01/93	West Ham United	Away	League	0–2		
43	30/01/93	Luton Town	Home	League	0–0		
44	06/02/93	Portsmouth	Away	League	3–2		
45	10/02/93	Southend United	Away	League	1–1	1 Goal	(23)
46	20/02/93	Sunderland	Away	League	0–0		
47	27/02/93	Charlton Athletic	Away	League	1–2	1 Goal	(24)
48	06/03/93	Tranmere Rovers	Home	League	1–3	1 Goal	(25)
49	09/03/93	Millwall	Home	League	0–1		

Newcastle United – Football League Division One

Sub+1	13/03/93	Swindon Town	Away	League	1–2		
1	20/03/93	Notts County	Home	League	4–0	1 Goal	(1)
2	23/03/93	Watford	Away	League	0–1		
3	28/03/93	Birmingham City	Home	League	2–2	1 Goal	(2)
4	03/04/93	Cambridge United	Away	League	3–0	1 Goal	(3)
5	07/04/93	Barnsley	Home	League	6–0	3 Goals	(6)
6	10/04/93	Wolverhampton Wanderers	Away	League	0–1		
7	17/04/93	Millwall	Away	League	2–1	1 Goal	(7)
8	25/04/93	Sunderland	Home	League	1–0		
9	04/05/93	Grimsby Town	Away	League	2–0	1 Goal	(8)
10	06/05/93	Oxford United	Home	League	2–1	1 Goal	(9)
11	09/05/93	Leicester City	Home	League	7–1	3 Goals	(12)

SEASON 1993–94

Premier League

12	14/08/93	Tottenham Hotspur	Home	League	0–1		
13	18/08/93	Coventry City	Away	League	1–2		
14	21/08/93	Manchester United	Away	League	1–1	1 Goal	(13)
15	25/08/93	Everton	Home	League	1–0		
16	29/08/93	Blackburn Rovers	Home	League	1–1	1 Goal	(14)
17	31/08/93	Ipswich Town	Away	League	1–1	1 Goal	(15)
18	13/09/93	Sheffield Wednesday	Home	League	4–2	2 Goals	(17)
19	18/09/93	Swindon Town	Away	League	2–2		
20	22/09/93	Notts County	Home	Lge Cup	4–0	3 Goals	(20)
21	25/09/93	West Ham United	Home	League	2–0	2 Goals	(22)
22	02/10/93	Aston Villa	Away	League	2–0	1 Goal	(23)
23	05/10/93	Notts County	Away	Lge Cup	7–1	3 Goals	(26)
24	16/10/93	Queens Park Rangers	Home	League	1–2		
25	24/10/93	Southampton	Away	League	1–2	1 Goal	(27)
26	30/10/93	Wimbledon	Home	League	4–0	1 Goal	(28)
27	08/11/93	Oldham Athletic	Away	League	3–1	2 Goals	(30)

28	21/11/93	Liverpool	Home	League	3–0	3 Goals	(33)
29	24/11/93	Sheffield United	Home	League	4–0	1 Goal	(34)
30	27/11/93	Arsenal	Away	League	1–2		
31	04/12/93	Tottenham Hotspur	Away	League	2–1		
32	11/12/93	Manchester United	Home	League	1–1	1 Goal	(35)
33	18/12/93	Everton	Away	League	2–0	1 Goal	(36)
34	22/12/93	Leeds United	Home	League	1–1	1 Goal	(37)
35	28/12/93	Chelsea	Away	League	0–1		
36	01/01/94	Manchester City	Home	League	2–0	2 Goals	(39)
37	04/01/94	Norwich City	Away	League	2–1	1 Goal	(40)
38	08/01/94	Coventry City	Home	FA Cup	2–0	1 Goal	(41)
39	16/01/94	Queens Park Rangers	Away	League	2–1		
40	22/01/94	Southampton	Home	League	1–2	1 Goal	(42)
41	29/01/94	Luton Town	Home	FA Cup	1–1		
42	09/02/94	Luton Town	Away	FA Cup	0–2		
43	23/02/94	Coventry City	Home	League	4–0	3 Goals	(45)
44	05/03/94	Sheffield Wednesday	Away	League	1–0	1 Goal	(46)
45	12/03/94	Swindon Town	Home	League	7–1		
46	19/03/94	West Ham United	Away	League	4–2	1 Goal	(47)
47	23/03/94	Ipswich Town	Home	League	2–0	1 Goal	(48)
48	29/03/94	Norwich City	Home	League	3–0	1 Goal	(49)
49	01/04/94	Leeds United	Away	League	1–1	1 Goal	(50)
50	04/04/94	Chelsea	Home	League	0–0		
51	09/04/94	Manchester City	Away	League	1–2		
52	16/04/94	Liverpool	Away	League	2–0	1 Goal	(51)
53	23/04/94	Oldham Athletic	Home	League	3–2		
54	27/04/94	Aston Villa	Home	League	5–1	1 Goal	(52)
55	30/04/94	Sheffield United	Away	League	0–2		
56	07/05/94	Arsenal	Home	League	2–0	1 Goal	(53)

SEASON 1994–95

Premier League

57	21/08/94	Leicester City	Away	League	3–1	1 Goal	(54)
58	24/08/94	Coventry City	Home	League	4–0	1 Goal	(55)
59	27/08/94	Southampton	Home	League	5–1	2 Goals	(57)
60	31/08/94	West Ham United	Away	League	3–1		
61	10/09/94	Chelsea	Home	League	4–2	2 Goals	(59)
62	13/09/94	Royal Antwerp FC	Away	UEFA Cup	5–0		
63	18/09/94	Arsenal	Away	League	3–2		
64	21/09/94	Barnsley	Home	Lge Cup	2–1	1 Goal	(60)
65	24/09/94	Liverpool	Home	League	1–1		
66	27/09/94	Royal Antwerp FC	Home	UEFA Cup	5–2	3 Goals	(63)
67	01/10/94	Aston Villa	Away	League	2–0	1 Goal	(64)
68	05/10/94	Barnsley	Away	Lge Cup	1–0	1 Goal	(65)
69	09/10/94	Blackburn Rovers	Home	League	1–1		
70	15/10/94	Crystal Palace	Away	League	1–0		
71	18/10/94	Athletic Bilbao	Home	UEFA Cup	3–2	1 Goal	(66)
72	22/10/94	Sheffield Wednesday	Home	League	2–1	1 Goal	(67)
73	26/10/94	Manchester United	Home	Lge Cup	2–0		
74	26/11/94	Ipswich Town	Home	League	1–1	1 Goal	(68)
75	30/11/94	Manchester City	Away	Lge Cup	1–1		
76	03/12/94	Tottenham Hotspur	Away	League	2–4		
77	10/12/94	Leicester City	Home	League	3–1		
78	17/12/94	Coventry City	Away	League	0–0		
79	21/12/94	Manchester City	Home	Lge Cup	0–2		
80	26/12/94	Leeds United	Away	League	0–0		
81	31/12/94	Norwich City	Away	League	1–2		
82	02/01/95	Manchester City	Home	League	0–0		
83	08/01/95	Blackburn Rovers	Home	FA Cup	1–1		

Manchester United – Premier League

1	22/01/95	Blackburn Rovers	Home	League	1–0		
2	25/01/95	Crystal Palace	Away	League	1–1		
3	04/02/95	Aston Villa	Home	League	1–0	1 Goal	(1)
4	11/02/95	Manchester City	Away	League	3–0	1 Goal	(2)
5	22/02/95	Norwich City	Away	League	2–0		
6	25/02/95	Everton	Away	League	0–1		
7	04/03/95	Ipswich Town	Home	League	9–0	5 Goals	(7)
8	07/03/95	Wimbledon	Away	League	1–0		
9	15/03/95	Tottenham Hotspur	Home	League	0–0		
Sub+1	19/03/95	Liverpool	Away	League	0–2		
10	22/03/95	Arsenal	Home	League	3–0		
11	02/04/95	Leeds United	Home	League	0–0		
12	15/04/95	Leicester City	Away	League	4–0	2 Goals	(9)

13	17/04/95	Chelsea	Home	League	0–0		
14	01/05/95	Coventry City	Away	League	3–2	2 Goals	(11)
15	07/05/95	Sheffield Wednesday	Home	League	1–0		
16	10/05/95	Southampton	Home	League	2–1	1 Goal	(12)
17	14/05/95	West Ham United	Away	League	1–1		

SEASON 1995–96

Premier League

Sub+2	23/08/95	West Ham United	Home	League	2–1		
18	26/08/95	Wimbledon	Home	League	3–1	1 Goal	(13)
19	28/08/95	Blackburn Rovers	Away	League	2–1		
20	09/09/95	Everton	Away	League	3–2		
21	26/09/95	Rotor Volgograd	Home	UEFA Cup	2–2		
22	01/10/95	Liverpool	Home	League	2–2		
23	03/10/95	York City	Away	Lge Cup	3–1		
24	14/10/95	Manchester City	Home	League	1–0		
25	21/10/95	Chelsea	Away	League	4–1		
26	28/10/95	Middlesbrough	Home	League	2–0	1 Goal	(14)
27	04/11/95	Arsenal	Away	League	0–1		
28	18/11/95	Southampton	Home	League	4–1	1 Goal	(15)
29	22/11/95	Coventry City	Away	League	4–0		
30	27/11/95	Nottingham Forest	Away	League	1–1		
31	02/12/95	Chelsea	Home	League	1–1		
32	09/12/95	Sheffield Wednesday	Home	League	2–2		
33	17/12/95	Liverpool	Away	League	0–2		
34	24/12/95	Leeds United	Away	League	1–3	1 Goal	(16)
35	27/12/95	Newcastle United	Home	League	2–0	1 Goal	(17)
36	30/12/95	Queens Park Rangers	Home	League	2–1	1 Goal	(18)
37	01/01/96	Tottenham Hotspur	Away	League	1–4	1 Goal	(19)
38	06/01/96	Sunderland	Home	FA Cup	2–2		
39	13/01/96	Aston Villa	Home	League	0–0		
40	16/01/96	Sunderland	Away	FA Cup	2–1	1 Goal	(20)
41	22/01/96	West Ham United	Away	League	1–0		
42	27/01/96	Reading	Away	FA Cup	3–0		
43	03/02/96	Wimbledon	Away	League	4–2	1 Goal	(21)
44	10/02/96	Blackburn Rovers	Home	League	1–0		
45	18/02/96	Manchester City	Home	FA Cup	2–1		
46	21/02/96	Everton	Home	League	2–0		
47	25/02/96	Bolton Wanderers	Away	League	6–0	1 Goal	(22)
48	04/03/96	Newcastle United	Away	League	1–0		
49	11/03/96	Southampton	Home	FA Cup	2–0		
50	16/03/96	Queens Park Rangers	Away	League	1–1		
51	20/03/96	Arsenal	Home	League	1–0		
52	24/03/96	Tottenham Hotspur	Home	League	1–0		
53	31/03/96	Chelsea	Neutral	FA Cup	2–1	1 Goal	(23)
54	06/04/96	Manchester City	Away	League	3–2	1 Goal	(24)
55	08/04/96	Coventry City	Home	League	1–0		
56	13/04/96	Southampton	Away	League	1–3		
57	17/04/96	Leeds United	Home	League	1–0		
Sub+3	05/05/96	Middlesbrough	Away	League	3–0	1 Goal	(25)
58	11/05/96	Liverpool	Wembley	FA Cup	1–0		

SEASON 1996–97

Premier League

Sub+4	07/09/96	Leeds United	Away	League	4–0		
Sub+5	11/09/96	Juventus FC	Away	Eur Cup	0–1		
Sub+6	14/09/96	Nottingham Forest	Home	League	4–1		
Sub+7	21/09/96	Aston Villa	Away	League	0–0		
Sub+8	25/09/96	SK Rapid Wien	Home	Eur Cup	2–0		
Sub+9	26/12/96	Nottingham Forest	Away	League	4–0	1 Goal	(26)
Sub+10	28/12/96	Leeds United	Home	League	1–0		
Sub+11	01/01/97	Aston Villa	Home	League	0–0		
Sub+12	12/01/97	Tottenham Hotspur	Away	League	2–1		
Sub+13	25/01/97	Wimbledon	Home	FA Cup	1–1		
Sub+14	29/01/97	Wimbledon	Home	League	2–1	1 Goal	(27)
Sub+15	01/02/97	Southampton	Home	League	2–1		
59	05/01/97	Tottenham Hotspur	Home	FA Cup	2–0		
60	04/02/97	Wimbledon	Away	FA Cup	0–1		
61	19/02/97	Arsenal	Away	League	2–1	1 Goal	(28)
62	22/02/97	Chelsea	Away	League	1–1		
63	01/03/97	Coventry City	Home	League	3–1		
64	05/03/97	FC Porto	Home	Eur Cup	4–0	1 Goal	(29)

Sub+16	08/03/97	Sunderland	Away	League	1–2		
65	15/03/97	Sheffield Wednesday	Home	League	2–0	1 Goal	(30)
66	05/04/97	Derby County	Home	League	2–3		
Sub+17	09/04/97	Borussia Dortmund	Away	Eur Cup	0–1		
67	12/04/97	Blackburn Rovers	Away	League	3–2	1 Goal	(31)
68	19/04/97	Liverpool	Away	League	3–1	1 Goal	(32)
69	23/04/97	Borussia Dortmund	Home	Eur Cup	0–1		
70	03/05/97	Leicester City	Away	League	2–2		
71	05/05/97	Middlesbrough	Home	League	3–3		
72	08/05/97	Newcastle United	Home	League	0–0		

INTERNATIONAL APPEARANCES – ENGLAND

Sub 1	29/03/95	Uruguay	Wembley	0–0	F
Sub 2	04/06/97	Italy	Nantes	2–0	LTDF

APPEARANCES AND GOALS PER SEASON

SEASON 90–91	GAMES	GOALS
League	0+1	0
TOTAL	**0+1**	**0**

SEASON 91–92	GAMES	GOALS
League	25	11
Autoglass Trophy	2	1
FA Charity Shield	0+1	0
TOTAL	**27+1**	**12**

SEASON 92–93	GAMES	GOALS
League	40+1	24
FA Cup	1	0
League Cup	3	4
Anglo–Italian Cup	4	1
TOTAL	**48+1**	**29**

SEASON 93–94	GAMES	GOALS
League	40	34
FA Cup	3	1
League Cup	2	6
TOTAL	**45**	**41**

SEASON 94–95	GAMES	GOALS
League	35+1	21
FA Cup	1	0
League Cup	5	2
UEFA Cup	3	4
TOTAL	**44+1**	**27**

SEASON 95–96	GAMES	GOALS
League	32+2	11
FA Cup	7	2
League Cup	1	0
UEFA Cup	1	0
TOTAL	**41+2**	**13**

SEASON 96–97	GAMES	GOALS
League	10+10	6
FA Cup	2+1	0
European Cup	2+3	1
TOTAL	**14+14**	**7**

CAREER APPEARANCES AND GOALS

COMPETITION	GAMES	TOTAL	GOALS
League	182+15	197	107
FA Cup	14+1	15	3
League Cup	11	11	12
Autoglass Trophy	2	2	1
Anglo–Italian Cup	4	4	1
FA Charity Shield	0+1	1	0
European Cup	2+3	5	1
UEFA Cup	4	4	4
Internationals	0+2	2	0
TOTAL	**219+22**	**241**	**129**

HAT-TRICKS

Bristol City

1	3	Cardiff City	25/08/92	Home	Lge Cup	5–1

Newcastle United

1	3	Barnsley	07/04/93	Home	League	6–0
2	3	Leicester City	09/05/93	Home	League	7–1
3	3	Notts County	22/09/93	Home	Lge Cup	4–0
4	3	Notts County	05/10/93	Away	Lge Cup	7–1
5	3	Liverpool	21/11/93	Home	League	3–0
6	3	Coventry City	23/02/94	Home	League	4–0
7	3	Royal Antwerp FC	27/09/94	Home	UEFA Cup	5–2

Manchester United

1	5	Ipswich Town	04/03/95	Home	League	9–0

League: 5
Lge Cup: 3
UEFA Cup: 1
TOTAL: 9

HONOURS

Winners medals
Premier League Championship: 95/96, 96/97
FA Cup: 95/96
Football League Division One Championship: 92/93

Runner-up medals
Premier League Championship: 94/95
FA Charity Shield: 91/92

STAN COLLYMORE

Born: 22/01/71 – Stone
Height: 6.3
Weight: 14.10 (96–97)

Clubs
Crystal Palace: **1991–92** – Matches: **6+19** – Goals: **2**
Southend United: **1992–93** – Matches: **33** – Goals: **18**
Nottingham Forest: **1993–95** – Matches: **77+1** – Goals: **50**
Liverpool: **1995–97** – Matches: **71+10** – Goals: **35**

Country
England: **1995** – Matches: **1+1** – Goals: **0**

SEASON 1990–91

Crystal Palace – League Division One

Sub+1	16/02/91	Queens Park Rangers	Home	League	0–0		
Sub+2	13/04/91	Aston Villa	Home	League	0–0		
Sub+3	17/04/91	Tottenham Hotspur	Home	League	1–0		
Sub+4	20/04/91	Everton	Home	League	0–0		
Sub+5	23/04/91	Liverpool	Away	League	0–3		
Sub+6	04/05/91	Wimbledon	Away	League	3–0		

SEASON 1991–92

League Division One

Sub+7	17/09/91	West Ham United	Home	League	2–3		
Sub+8	28/09/91	Queens Park Rangers	Home	League	2–2	1 Goal	(1)
Sub+9	01/10/91	Leeds United	Home	League	1–0		
Sub+10	05/10/91	Sheffield Wednesday	Away	League	1–4		
1	08/10/91	Hartlepool United	Home	Lge Cup	6–1	1 Goal	(2)
Sub+11	16/11/91	Southampton	Home	League	1–0		
Sub+12	19/11/91	Birmingham City	Home	Lge Cup	1–1*		

Sub+13	30/11/91	Manchester United	Home	League	1–3		
Sub+14	03/12/91	Birmingham City	Home	Lge Cup	2–1		
Sub+15	11/03/92	Southampton	Away	League	0–1		
2	21/03/92	Aston Villa	Home	League	0–0		
3	28/03/92	Notts County	Away	League	3–2		
4	04/04/92	Everton	Home	League	2–0		
5	11/04/92	Arsenal	Away	League	1–4		
Sub+16	18/04/92	Oldham Athletic	Home	League	0–0		

SEASON 1992–93

Premier League

6	22/09/92	Lincoln City	Home	Lge Cup	3–1		
Sub+17	26/09/92	Southampton	Home	League	1–2		
Sub+18	06/10/92	Lincoln City	Away	Lge Cup	1–1		
Sub+19	17/10/92	Manchester City	Home	League	0–0		

Southend United – Football League Division One

1	21/11/92	Notts County	Home	League	3–1	2 Goals	(2)
2	28/11/92	Sunderland	Home	League	0–1		
3	05/12/92	Millwall	Away	League	1–1		
4	12/12/92	West Ham United	Away	League	0–2		
5	19/12/92	Barnsley	Home	League	3–0	2 Goals	(4)
6	26/12/92	Watford	Home	League	1–2		
7	28/12/92	Bristol Rovers	Away	League	2–0	1 Goal	(5)
8	09/01/93	Portsmouth	Away	League	0–2		
9	13/01/93	Millwall	Home	FA Cup	1–0	1 Goal	(6)
10	16/01/93	Derby County	Home	League	0–0		
11	20/01/93	Newcastle United	Home	League	1–1		
12	23/01/93	Huddersfield Town	Away	FA Cup	2–1	2 Goals	(8)
13	27/01/93	Birmingham City	Home	League	4–0	1 Goal	(9)
14	30/01/93	Peterborough United	Away	League	0–1		
15	10/02/93	Bristol City	Home	League	1–1	1 Goal	(10)
16	13/02/93	Sheffield Wednesday	Away	FA Cup	0–2		
17	21/02/93	Brentford	Home	League	3–0	1 Goal	(11)
18	27/02/93	Wolverhampton Wanderers	Away	League	1–1		
19	06/03/93	Charlton Athletic	Home	League	0–2		
20	10/03/93	Swindon Town	Home	League	1–1		
21	13/03/93	Oxford United	Away	League	1–0	1 Goal	(12)
22	21/03/93	Millwall	Home	League	3–3	1 Goal	(13)
23	23/03/93	Notts County	Away	League	0–4		
24	26/03/93	Tranmere Rovers	Home	League	1–2		
25	03/04/93	Sunderland	Away	League	4–2	1 Goal	(14)
26	07/04/93	West Ham United	Home	League	1–0		
27	10/04/93	Watford	Away	League	0–0		
28	14/04/93	Bristol Rovers	Home	League	3–0	2 Goals	(16)
29	17/04/93	Barnsley	Away	League	1–3	1 Goal	(17)
30	20/04/93	Leicester City	Away	League	1–4		
31	23/04/93	Grimsby Town	Home	League	1–0	1 Goal	(18)
32	01/05/93	Cambridge United	Away	League	1–3		
33	08/05/93	Luton Town	Home	League	2–1		

SEASON 1993–94

Nottingham Forest – Football League Division One

1	24/08/93	Crystal Palace	Away	League	0–2		
2	08/09/93	Derby County	Away	AI Cup	2–3		
3	11/09/93	Barnsley	Away	League	0–1		
4	15/09/93	Notts County	Home	AI Cup	1–1	1 Goal	(1)
5	19/09/93	Stoke City	Home	League	2–3		
6	21/09/93	Wrexham	Away	Lge Cup	3–3	3 Goals	(4)
7	26/09/93	Bolton Wanderers	Away	League	3–4	2 Goals	(6)
8	02/10/93	Portsmouth	Home	League	1–1		
9	06/10/93	Wrexham	Home	Lge Cup	3–1	1 Goal	(7)
10	16/10/93	Tranmere Rovers	Home	League	2–1	1 Goal	(8)
11	24/10/93	Leicester City	Away	League	0–1		
12	27/10/93	West Ham United	Home	Lge Cup	2–1	1 Goal	(9)
13	30/10/93	Notts County	Home	League	1–0	1 Goal	(10)
14	03/11/93	Millwall	Home	League	1–3		
15	06/11/93	Birmingham City	Away	League	3–0	1 Goal	(11)
16	10/11/93	Wolverhampton Wanderers	Away	League	1–1	1 Goal	(12)
17	21/11/93	West Bromwich Albion	Away	League	2–0	2 Goals	(14)
18	27/11/93	Sunderland	Away	League	3–2	2 Goals	(16)
19	04/12/93	Birmingham City	Home	League	1–0		
20	15/12/93	Manchester City	Away	Lge Cup	2–1		

21	19/12/93	Southend United	Home	League	2–0		
22	27/12/93	Middlesbrough	Home	League	1–1	1 Goal	(17)
23	28/12/93	Bristol City	Away	League	4–1	2 Goals	(19)
24	01/01/94	Charlton Athletic	Home	League	1–1		
25	03/01/94	Watford	Away	League	2–1		
26	29/01/94	Tranmere Rovers	Away	Lge Cup	0–2		
Sub+1	19/03/94	Bolton Wanderers	Home	League	3–2	1 Goal	(20)
27	26/03/94	Portsmouth	Away	League	1–2	1 Goal	(21)
28	30/03/94	Watford	Home	League	2–1		
29	17/04/94	Millwall	Away	League	2–2	1 Goal	(22)
30	24/04/94	West Bromwich Albion	Home	League	2–1		
31	27/04/94	Derby County	Away	League	2–0		
32	30/04/94	Peterborough United	Away	League	3–2	2 Goals	(24)
33	03/05/94	Grimsby Town	Away	League	0–0		
34	08/05/94	Sunderland	Home	League	2–2	1 Goal	(25)

SEASON 1994–95

Premier League

35	22/08/94	Manchester United	Home	League	1–1	1 Goal	(26)
36	27/08/94	Leicester City	Home	League	1–0	1 Goal	(27)
37	30/08/94	Everton	Away	League	2–1		
38	10/09/94	Sheffield Wednesday	Home	League	4–1		
39	17/09/94	Southampton	Away	League	1–1	1 Goal	(28)
40	21/09/94	Hereford United	Home	Lge Cup	2–1	2 Goals	(30)
41	24/09/94	Tottenham Hotspur	Away	League	4–1		
42	02/10/94	Queens Park Rangers	Home	League	3–2	1 Goal	(31)
43	04/10/94	Hereford United	Away	Lge Cup	0–0		
44	08/10/94	Manchester City	Away	League	3–3	1 Goal	(32)
45	17/10/94	Wimbledon	Home	League	3–1	1 Goal	(33)
46	22/10/94	Aston Villa	Away	League	2–0		
47	26/10/94	Wolverhampton Wanderers	Away	Lge Cup	3–2		
48	07/11/94	Newcastle United	Home	League	0–0		
49	19/11/94	Chelsea	Home	League	0–1		
50	26/11/94	Leeds United	Away	League	0–1		
51	30/11/94	Millwall	Home	Lge Cup	0–2		
52	03/12/94	Arsenal	Home	League	2–2		
53	10/12/94	Ipswich Town	Home	League	4–1	1 Goal	(34)
54	17/12/94	Manchester United	Away	League	2–1	1 Goal	(35)
55	26/12/94	Coventry City	Away	League	0–0		
56	27/12/94	Norwich City	Home	League	1–0		
57	31/12/94	West Ham United	Away	League	1–3		
58	07/01/95	Plymouth Argyle	Home	FA Cup	2–0	1 Goal	(36)
59	14/01/95	Blackburn Rovers	Away	League	0–3		
60	21/01/95	Aston Villa	Home	League	1–2	1 Goal	(37)
61	25/01/95	Chelsea	Away	League	2–0	2 Goals	(39)
62	28/01/95	Crystal Palace	Home	FA Cup	1–2		
63	04/02/95	Liverpool	Home	League	1–1	1 Goal	(40)
64	11/02/95	Newcastle United	Away	League	1–2		
65	26/02/95	Queens Park Rangers	Away	League	1–1		
66	04/03/95	Tottenham Hotspur	Home	League	2–2		
67	08/03/95	Everton	Home	League	2–1	1 Goal	(41)
68	11/03/95	Leicester City	Away	League	4–2	1 Goal	(42)
69	18/03/95	Southampton	Home	League	3–0	1 Goal	(43)
70	22/03/95	Leeds United	Home	League	3–0	1 Goal	(44)
71	01/04/95	Sheffield Wednesday	Away	League	7–1	2 Goals	(46)
72	08/04/95	West Ham United	Home	League	1–1	1 Goal	(47)
73	12/04/95	Norwich City	Away	League	1–0		
74	17/04/95	Coventry City	Home	League	2–0	1 Goal	(48)
75	29/04/95	Crystal Palace	Away	League	2–1	1 Goal	(49)
76	06/05/95	Manchester City	Home	League	1–0	1 Goal	(50)
77	13/05/95	Wimbledon	Away	League	2–2		

SEASON 1995–96

Liverpool – Premier League

1	19/08/95	Sheffield Wednesday	Home	League	1–0	1 Goal	(1)
2	21/08/95	Leeds United	Away	League	0–1		
3	09/09/95	Wimbledon	Away	League	0–1		
4	12/09/95	Spartak–Alania Vladikavkaz	Away	UEFA Cup	2–1		
5	16/09/95	Blackburn Rovers	Home	League	3–0	1 Goal	(2)
6	20/09/95	Sunderland	Home	Lge Cup	2–0		
7	23/09/95	Bolton Wanderers	Home	League	5–2		

Sub+1	04/10/95	Sunderland	Away	Lge Cup	1–0		
8	14/10/95	Coventry City	Home	League	0–0		
Sub+2	25/10/95	Manchester City	Home	Lge Cup	4–0		
Sub+3	31/10/95	Brondby IF	Home	UEFA Cup	0–1		
Sub+4	04/11/95	Newcastle United	Away	League	1–2		
9	22/11/95	West Ham United	Away	League	0–0		
10	25/11/95	Middlesbrough	Away	League	1–2		
11	29/11/95	Newcastle United	Home	Lge Cup	0–1		
12	02/12/95	Southampton	Home	League	1–1	1 Goal	(3)
13	09/12/95	Bolton Wanderers	Away	League	1–0	1 Goal	(4)
14	17/12/95	Manchester United	Home	League	2–0		
15	23/12/95	Arsenal	Home	League	3–1		
16	30/12/95	Chelsea	Away	League	2–2		
17	01/01/96	Nottingham Forest	Home	League	4–2	1 Goal	(5)
18	06/01/96	Rochdale	Home	FA Cup	7–0	3 Goals	(8)
19	13/01/96	Sheffield Wednesday	Away	League	1–1		
20	20/01/96	Leeds United	Home	League	5–0	1 Goal	(9)
21	31/01/96	Aston Villa	Away	League	2–0	1 Goal	(10)
22	03/02/96	Tottenham Hotspur	Home	League	0–0		
23	11/02/96	Queens Park Rangers	Away	League	2–1		
24	18/02/96	Shrewsbury Town	Away	FA Cup	4–0	1 Goal	(11)
25	24/02/96	Blackburn Rovers	Away	League	3–2	2 Goals	(13)
26	28/02/96	Charlton Athletic	Home	FA Cup	2–1	1 Goal	(14)
27	03/03/96	Aston Villa	Home	League	3–0		
28	10/03/96	Leeds United	Away	FA Cup	0–0		
29	13/03/96	Wimbledon	Home	League	2–2	1 Goal	(15)
30	16/03/96	Chelsea	Home	League	2–0		
31	20/03/96	Leeds United	Home	FA Cup	3–0		
32	23/03/96	Nottingham Forest	Away	League	0–1		
33	31/03/96	Aston Villa	Neutral	FA Cup	3–0		
34	03/04/96	Newcastle United	Home	League	4–3	2 Goals	(17)
35	06/04/96	Coventry City	Away	League	0–1		
36	08/04/96	West Ham United	Home	League	2–0	1 Goal	(18)
37	16/04/96	Everton	Away	League	1–1		
38	27/04/96	Middlesbrough	Home	League	1–0	1 Goal	(19)
39	01/05/96	Arsenal	Away	League	0–0		
40	11/05/96	Manchester United	Wembley	FA Cup	0–1		

SEASON 1996–97

Premier League

41	17/08/96	Middlesbrough	Away	League	3–3		
42	19/08/96	Arsenal	Home	League	2–0		
43	24/08/96	Sunderland	Home	League	0–0		
44	04/09/96	Coventry City	Away	League	1–0		
45	07/09/96	Southampton	Home	League	2–1	1 Goal	(20)
46	12/09/96	MYPA–47	Away	ECW Cup	1–0		
47	15/09/96	Leicester City	Away	League	3–0		
48	26/09/96	MYPA–47	Home	ECW Cup	3–1	1 Goal	(21)
49	29/09/96	West Ham United	Away	League	2–1	1 Goal	(22)
50	12/10/96	Manchester United	Away	League	0–1		
Sub+5	03/11/96	Blackburn Rovers	Away	League	0–3		
Sub+6	20/11/96	Everton	Home	League	1–1		
51	23/11/96	Wimbledon	Home	League	1–1	1 Goal	(23)
52	14/12/96	Middlesbrough	Home	League	5–1		
53	17/12/96	Nottingham Forest	Home	League	4–2	2 Goals	(25)
54	23/12/96	Newcastle United	Away	League	1–1		
55	26/12/96	Leicester City	Home	League	1–1	1 Goal	(26)
56	29/12/96	Southampton	Away	League	1–0		
57	01/01/97	Chelsea	Away	League	0–1		
58	04/01/97	Burnley	Home	FA Cup	1–0	1 Goal	(27)
Sub+7	11/01/97	West Ham United	Home	League	0–0		
59	18/01/97	Aston Villa	Home	League	3–0	1 Goal	(28)
60	26/01/97	Chelsea	Away	FA Cup	2–4	1 Goal	(29)
61	01/02/97	Derby County	Away	League	1–0	1 Goal	(30)
62	19/02/97	Leeds United	Home	League	4–0	2 Goals	(32)
63	22/02/97	Blackburn Rovers	Home	League	0–0		
64	02/03/97	Aston Villa	Away	League	0–1		
Sub+8	15/03/97	Nottingham Forest	Away	League	1–1		
Sub+9	20/03/97	SK Brann	Home	ECW Cup	3–0	1 Goal	(33)
65	24/03/97	Arsenal	Away	League	2–1	1 Goal	(34)
66	06/04/97	Coventry City	Home	League	1–2		
67	10/04/97	Paris Saint–Germain	Away	ECW Cup	0–3		
Sub+10	19/04/97	Manchester United	Home	League	1–3		
68	24/04/97	Paris Saint–Germain	Home	ECW Cup	2–0		

69	03/05/97	Tottenham Hotspur	Home	League	2–1	1 Goal	(35)
70	06/05/97	Wimbledon	Away	League	1–2		
71	11/05/97	Sheffield Wednesday	Away	League	1–1		

INTERNATIONAL APPEARANCES – ENGLAND

1	03/06/95	Japan	Wembley	2–1	UC
Sub 2	11/06/95	Brazil	Wembley	1–3	UC

APPEARANCES AND GOALS PER SEASON

SEASON 90–91	GAMES	GOALS
League	0+6	0
TOTAL	**0+6**	**0**

SEASON 91–92	GAMES	GOALS
League	4+8	1
League Cup	1+2	1
TOTAL	**5+10**	**2**

SEASON 92–93	GAMES	GOALS
League	30+2	15
FA Cup	3	3
League Cup	1+1	0
TOTAL	**34+3**	**18**

SEASON 93–94	GAMES	GOALS
League	27+1	19
League Cup	5	5
Anglo–Italian Cup	2	1
TOTAL	**34+1**	**25**

SEASON 94–95	GAMES	GOALS
League	37	22
FA Cup	2	1
League Cup	4	2
TOTAL	**43**	**25**

SEASON 95–96	GAMES	GOALS
League	30+1	14
FA Cup	7	5
League Cup	2+2	0
UEFA Cup	1+1	0
TOTAL	**40+4**	**19**

SEASON 96–97	GAMES	GOALS
League	25+5	12
FA Cup	2	2
European Cup Winners Cup	4+1	2
TOTAL	**31+6**	**16**

CAREER APPEARANCES AND GOALS

COMPETITION	GAMES	TOTAL	GOALS
League	153+23	176	83
FA Cup	14	14	11
League Cup	13+5	18	8
Anglo–Italian Cup	2	2	1
UEFA Cup	1+1	2	0
European Cup Winners Cup	4+1	5	2
International Appearances	1+1	2	0
TOTAL	**188+31**	**219**	**105**

HAT–TRICKS

Nottingham Forest

1	3	Wrexham	21/09/93	Away	Lge Cup	3–3

Liverpool

1	3	Rochdale	06/01/96	Home	FA Cup	7–0

FA Cup: 1
League Cup: 1
TOTAL: 2

HONOURS

Winners medals
None

Runner–up medals
FA Cup: 95/96
Football League Division One Championship: 93/94

TONY COTTEE

Born: 11/07/65 – West Ham
Height: 5.8
Weight: 11.05 (96–97)

Clubs
West Ham United: **1983–88** – Matches: **247+9** – Goals: **118**
Everton: **1988–94** – Matches: **206+35** – Goals: **99**
West Ham United: **1994–96** – Matches: **76+4** – Goals: **28**

Country
England: **1986–89** – Matches: **1+6** – Goals: **0**

SEASON 1982–83

West Ham United – League Division One

1	01/01/83	Tottenham Hotspur	Home	League	3–0	1 Goal	(1)
2	04/01/83	Luton Town	Home	League	2–3	1 Goal	(2)
3	08/01/83	Manchester United	Away	FA Cup	0–2		
Sub+1	26/02/83	Southampton	Home	League	1–1		
4	05/03/83	Brighton & Hove Albion	Home	League	2–1	1 Goal	(3)
Sub+2	02/04/83	Watford	Home	League	2–1		
Sub+3	09/04/83	Sunderland	Home	League	2–1		
Sub+4	16/04/83	Manchester City	Away	League	0–2		
Sub+5	14/05/83	Coventry City	Away	League	4–2	2 Goals	(5)

SEASON 1983–84

League Division One

5	27/08/83	Birmingham City	Home	League	4–0	2 Goals	(7)
6	29/08/83	Everton	Away	League	1–0		
7	03/09/83	Tottenham Hotspur	Away	League	2–0		
8	06/09/83	Leicester City	Home	League	3–1	1 Goal	(8)
9	10/09/83	Coventry City	Home	League	5–2		
10	17/09/83	West Bromwich Albion	Away	League	0–1		
11	24/09/83	Notts County	Home	League	3–0		
Sub+6	15/10/83	Liverpool	Home	League	1–3		
12	22/10/83	Norwich City	Home	League	0–0		
13	25/10/83	Bury	Home	Lge Cup	10–0	4 Goals	(12)
14	28/10/83	Watford	Away	League	0–0		
15	05/11/83	Ipswich Town	Home	League	2–1		
16	08/11/83	Brighton & Hove Albion	Home	Lge Cup	1–0		
17	12/11/83	Wolverhampton Wanderers	Away	League	3–0	1 Goal	(13)
18	19/11/83	Sunderland	Away	League	1–0		
19	27/11/83	Manchester United	Home	League	1–1		
20	30/11/83	Everton	Home	Lge Cup	2–2		
Sub+7	03/12/83	Aston Villa	Away	League	0–1		
21	06/12/83	Everton	Away	Lge Cup	0–2*		
22	26/12/83	Southampton	Home	League	0–1		
23	27/12/83	Luton Town	Away	League	1–0	1 Goal	(14)
24	31/12/83	Tottenham Hotspur	Home	League	4–1	1 Goal	(15)
25	02/01/84	Notts County	Away	League	2–2		
26	07/01/84	Wigan Athletic	Home	FA Cup	1–0		
27	14/01/84	Birmingham City	Away	League	0–3		
28	21/01/84	West Bromwich Albion	Home	League	1–0	1 Goal	(16)
29	28/01/84	Crystal Palace	Away	FA Cup	1–1		

30	31/01/84	Crystal Palace	Home	FA Cup	2–0*		
31	04/02/84	Stoke City	Home	League	3–0	1 Goal	(17)
32	07/02/84	Queens Park Rangers	Away	League	1–1	1 Goal	(18)
33	11/02/84	Coventry City	Away	League	2–1	1 Goal	(19)
34	18/02/84	Birmingham City	Away	FA Cup	0–3		
35	21/02/84	Watford	Home	League	2–4		
36	25/02/84	Norwich City	Away	League	0–1		
37	03/03/84	Ipswich Town	Away	League	3–0	1 Goal	(20)
38	10/03/84	Wolverhampton Wanderers	Home	League	1–1	1 Goal	(21)
39	17/03/84	Leicester City	Away	League	1–4		
40	31/03/84	Queens Park Rangers	Home	League	2–2	1 Goal	(22)
41	07/04/84	Liverpool	Away	League	0–6		
42	14/04/84	Sunderland	Home	League	0–1		
43	17/04/84	Luton Town	Home	League	3–1	2 Goals	(24)
44	21/04/84	Southampton	Away	League	0–2		
45	28/04/84	Manchester United	Away	League	0–0		
46	05/05/84	Aston Villa	Home	League	0–1		
47	07/05/84	Arsenal	Away	League	3–3		
48	12/05/84	Nottingham Forest	Home	League	1–2		
49	14/05/84	Everton	Home	League	0–1		

SEASON 1984–85

League Division One

50	25/08/84	Ipswich Town	Home	League	0–0		
Sub+8	27/08/84	Liverpool	Away	League	0–3		
51	01/09/84	Southampton	Away	League	3–2		
52	04/09/84	Coventry City	Home	League	3–1	1 Goal	(25)
53	08/09/84	Watford	Home	League	2–0		
54	15/09/84	Chelsea	Away	League	0–3		
55	22/09/84	Nottingham Forest	Home	League	0–0		
56	25/09/84	Bristol City	Away	Lge Cup	2–2	1 Goal	(26)
57	29/09/84	Newcastle United	Away	League	1–1		
58	06/10/84	Leicester City	Home	League	3–1	1 Goal	(27)
59	09/10/84	Bristol City	Home	Lge Cup	6–1	2 Goals	(29)
60	13/10/84	Manchester United	Away	League	1–5		
61	20/10/84	Stoke City	Away	League	4–2	1 Goal	(30)
62	27/10/84	Arsenal	Home	League	3–1	1 Goal	(31)
63	31/10/84	Manchester City	Away	Lge Cup	0–0		
64	03/11/84	Aston Villa	Away	League	0–0		
65	06/11/84	Manchester City	Home	Lge Cup	1–2		
66	10/11/84	Everton	Home	League	0–1		
67	17/11/84	Sunderland	Home	League	1–0	1 Goal	(32)
68	24/11/84	Luton Town	Away	League	2–2		
69	01/12/84	West Bromwich Albion	Home	League	0–2		
70	08/12/84	Norwich City	Away	League	0–1		
71	15/12/84	Sheffield Wednesday	Home	League	0–0		
72	22/12/84	Southampton	Home	League	2–3	2 Goals	(34)
73	26/12/84	Tottenham Hotspur	Away	League	2–2	1 Goal	(35)
74	29/12/84	Coventry City	Away	League	2–1	2 Goals	(37)
75	01/01/85	Queens Park Rangers	Home	League	1–3		
76	05/01/85	Port Vale	Home	FA Cup	4–1		
77	02/02/85	Newcastle United	Home	League	1–1		
78	04/02/85	Norwich City	Home	FA Cup	2–1		
79	23/02/85	Aston Villa	Home	League	1–2		
80	02/03/85	Arsenal	Away	League	1–2	1 Goal	(38)
81	04/03/85	Wimbledon	Away	FA Cup	1–1	1 Goal	(39)
82	06/03/85	Wimbledon	Home	FA Cup	5–1	3 Goals	(42)
83	09/03/85	Manchester United	Away	FA Cup	2–4		
84	15/03/85	Manchester United	Home	League	2–2		
85	23/03/85	Leicester City	Away	League	0–1		
86	30/03/85	Nottingham Forest	Away	League	2–1	1 Goal	(43)
87	02/04/85	Watford	Away	League	0–5		
88	06/04/85	Tottenham Hotspur	Home	League	1–1		
89	08/04/85	Queens Park Rangers	Away	League	2–4	2 Goals	(45)
90	13/04/85	Chelsea	Home	League	1–1	1 Goal	(46)
91	20/04/85	Sunderland	Away	League	1–0		
92	27/04/85	Luton Town	Home	League	0–0		
93	04/05/85	West Bromwich Albion	Away	League	1–5		
94	06/05/85	Norwich City	Home	League	1–0		
95	08/05/85	Everton	Away	League	0–3		
96	11/05/85	Sheffield Wednesday	Away	League	1–2	1 Goal	(47)
97	14/05/85	Stoke City	Home	League	5–1		
98	17/05/85	Ipswich Town	Away	League	1–0	1 Goal	(48)

SEASON 1985–86

League Division One

99	17/08/85	Birmingham City	Away	League	0–1			
100	20/08/85	Queens Park Rangers	Home	League	3–1			
101	24/08/85	Luton Town	Home	League	0–1			
102	26/08/85	Manchester United	Away	League	0–2			
103	31/08/85	Liverpool	Home	League	2–2			
Sub+9	03/09/85	Southampton	Away	League	1–1			
104	07/09/85	Sheffield Wednesday	Away	League	2–2	1 Goal	(49)	
105	14/09/85	Leicester City	Home	League	3–0	1 Goal	(50)	
106	21/09/85	Manchester City	Away	League	2–2	1 Goal	(51)	
107	24/09/85	Swansea City	Home	Lge Cup	3–0	1 Goal	(52)	
108	28/09/85	Nottingham Forest	Home	League	4–2	1 Goal	(53)	
109	05/10/85	Newcastle United	Away	League	2–1	1 Goal	(54)	
110	08/10/85	Swansea City	Away	Lge Cup	3–2	1 Goal	(55)	
111	12/10/85	Arsenal	Home	League	0–0			
112	19/10/85	Aston Villa	Home	League	4–1	2 Goals	(57)	
113	26/10/85	Ipswich Town	Away	League	1–0	1 Goal	(58)	
114	29/10/85	Manchester United	Away	Lge Cup	0–1			
115	02/11/85	Everton	Home	League	2–1			
116	09/11/85	Oxford United	Away	League	2–1	1 Goal	(59)	
117	16/11/85	Watford	Home	League	2–1			
118	23/11/85	Coventry City	Away	League	1–0			
119	30/11/85	West Bromwich Albion	Home	League	4–0	1 Goal	(60)	
120	07/12/85	Queens Park Rangers	Away	League	1–0			
121	14/12/85	Birmingham City	Home	League	2–0			
122	21/12/85	Luton Town	Away	League	0–0			
123	26/12/85	Tottenham Hotspur	Away	League	0–1			
124	05/01/86	Charlton Athletic	Away	FA Cup	1–0	1 Goal	(61)	
125	11/01/86	Leicester City	Away	League	1–0			
126	18/01/86	Liverpool	Away	League	1–3			
127	25/01/86	Ipswich Town	Home	FA Cup	0–0			
128	02/02/86	Manchester United	Home	League	2–1	1 Goal	(62)	
129	04/02/86	Ipswich Town	Away	FA Cup	1–1*	1 Goal	(63)	
130	06/02/86	Ipswich Town	Away	FA Cup	1–0*	1 Goal	(64)	
131	05/03/86	Manchester United	Home	FA Cup	1–1			
132	09/03/86	Manchester United	Away	FA Cup	2–0			
133	12/03/86	Sheffield Wednesday	Away	FA Cup	1–2	1 Goal	(65)	
134	15/03/86	Arsenal	Away	League	0–1			
135	19/03/86	Aston Villa	Away	League	1–2			
136	22/03/86	Sheffield Wednesday	Home	League	1–0			
137	29/03/86	Chelsea	Away	League	4–0	2 Goals	(67)	
138	31/03/86	Tottenham Hotspur	Home	League	2–1	1 Goal	(68)	
139	02/04/86	Nottingham Forest	Away	League	1–2	1 Goal	(69)	
140	08/04/86	Southampton	Home	League	1–0			
141	12/04/86	Oxford United	Home	League	3–1			
142	15/04/86	Chelsea	Home	League	1–2	1 Goal	(70)	
143	19/04/86	Watford	Away	League	2–0	1 Goal	(71)	
144	21/04/86	Newcastle United	Home	League	8–1			
145	26/04/86	Coventry City	Home	League	1–0	1 Goal	(72)	
146	28/04/86	Manchester City	Home	League	1–0			
147	30/04/86	Ipswich Town	Home	League	2–1			
148	03/05/86	West Bromwich Albion	Away	League	3–2	1 Goal	(73)	
149	05/05/86	Everton	Away	League	1–3	1 Goal	(74)	

SEASON 1986–87

League Division One

150	23/08/86	Coventry City	Home	League	1–0			
151	25/08/86	Manchester United	Away	League	3–2			
152	30/08/86	Oxford United	Away	League	0–0			
153	02/09/86	Nottingham Forest	Home	League	1–2			
154	06/09/86	Liverpool	Home	League	2–5	1 Goal	(75)	
155	13/09/86	Queens Park Rangers	Away	League	3–2	3 Goals	(78)	
156	20/09/86	Luton Town	Home	League	2–0			
157	23/09/86	Preston North End	Away	Lge Cup	1–1			
158	27/09/86	Sheffield Wednesday	Away	League	2–2			
159	04/10/86	Watford	Away	League	2–2			
160	07/10/86	Preston North End	Home	Lge Cup	4–1	3 Goals	(81)	
161	11/10/86	Chelsea	Home	League	5–3	2 Goals	(83)	
162	18/10/86	Norwich City	Away	League	1–1			
163	25/10/86	Charlton Athletic	Home	League	1–3	1 Goal	(84)	
164	29/10/86	Watford	Away	Lge Cup	3–2			
165	02/11/86	Everton	Home	League	1–0			

166	08/11/86	Arsenal	Away	League	0-0		
167	15/11/86	Wimbledon	Away	League	1-0	1 Goal	(85)
168	18/11/86	Oxford United	Home	Lge Cup	1-0	1 Goal	(86)
169	22/11/86	Aston Villa	Home	League	1-1	1 Goal	(87)
170	25/11/86	Chelsea	Home	FM Cup	1-2	1 Goal	(88)
171	30/11/86	Newcastle United	Away	League	0-4		
172	06/12/86	Southampton	Home	League	3-1	1 Goal	(89)
173	13/12/86	Manchester City	Away	League	1-3		
174	20/12/86	Queens Park Rangers	Home	League	1-1	1 Goal	(90)
175	26/12/86	Tottenham Hotspur	Away	League	0-4		
176	27/12/86	Wimbledon	Home	League	2-3	1 Goal	(91)
177	01/01/87	Leicester City	Home	League	4-1	2 Goals	(93)
178	03/01/87	Liverpool	Away	League	0-1		
179	10/01/87	Orient	Away	FA Cup	1-1		
180	24/01/87	Coventry City	Away	League	3-1	3 Goals	(96)
181	27/01/87	Tottenham Hotspur	Home	Lge Cup	1-1	1 Goal	(97)
182	31/01/87	Orient	Home	FA Cup	4-1	1 Goal	(98)
183	02/02/87	Tottenham Hotspur	Away	Lge Cup	0-5		
184	07/02/87	Oxford United	Home	League	0-1		
185	09/02/87	Sheffield United	Home	FA Cup	4-0		
186	14/02/87	Nottingham Forest	Away	League	1-1		
187	21/02/87	Sheffield Wednesday	Away	FA Cup	1-1		
188	25/02/87	Sheffield Wednesday	Home	FA Cup	0-2		
189	28/02/87	Luton Town	Away	League	1-2	1 Goal	(99)
190	07/03/87	Charlton Athletic	Away	League	1-2		
191	14/03/87	Norwich City	Home	League	0-2		
192	21/03/87	Chelsea	Away	League	0-1		
193	24/03/87	Sheffield Wednesday	Home	League	0-2		
194	28/03/87	Watford	Home	League	1-0		
195	08/04/87	Arsenal	Home	League	3-1	2 Goals	(101)
196	11/04/87	Everton	Away	League	0-4		
197	14/04/87	Manchester United	Home	League	0-0		
198	18/04/87	Leicester City	Away	League	0-2		
199	20/04/87	Tottenham Hotspur	Home	League	2-1	1 Goal	(102)
200	25/04/87	Aston Villa	Away	League	0-4		
201	02/05/87	Newcastle United	Home	League	1-1		
202	04/05/87	Southampton	Away	League	0-1		
203	09/05/87	Manchester City	Home	League	2-0	1 Goal	(103)

SEASON 1987–88

League Division One

204	15/08/87	Queens Park Rangers	Home	League	0-3		
205	22/08/87	Luton Town	Away	League	2-2		
206	29/08/87	Norwich City	Home	League	2-0	2 Goals	(105)
207	31/08/87	Portsmouth	Away	League	1-2		
208	05/09/87	Liverpool	Home	League	1-1	1 Goal	(106)
209	12/09/87	Wimbledon	Away	League	1-1	1 Goal	(107)
210	19/09/87	Tottenham Hotspur	Home	League	0-1		
211	22/09/87	Barnsley	Away	Lge Cup	0-0		
212	26/09/87	Arsenal	Away	League	0-1		
213	03/10/87	Derby County	Home	League	1-1		
214	06/10/87	Barnsley	Home	Lge Cup	2-5		
215	10/10/87	Charlton Athletic	Home	League	1-1		
216	17/10/87	Oxford United	Away	League	2-1	1 Goal	(108)
217	25/10/87	Manchester United	Home	League	1-1		
218	31/10/87	Watford	Away	League	2-1	1 Goal	(109)
219	07/11/87	Sheffield Wednesday	Home	League	0-1		
220	14/11/87	Everton	Away	League	1-3		
221	21/11/87	Nottingham Forest	Home	League	3-2	2 Goals	(111)
222	28/11/87	Coventry City	Away	League	0-0		
223	05/12/87	Southampton	Home	League	2-1		
224	12/12/87	Chelsea	Away	League	1-1		
225	19/12/87	Newcastle United	Home	League	2-1		
226	26/12/87	Wimbledon	Home	League	1-2		
227	28/12/87	Tottenham Hotspur	Away	League	1-2		
228	01/01/88	Norwich City	Away	League	1-4	1 Goal	(112)
229	02/01/88	Luton Town	Home	League	1-1		
230	09/01/88	Charlton Athletic	Home	FA Cup	2-0	1 Goal	(113)
231	16/01/88	Queens Park Rangers	Away	League	1-0		
232	30/01/88	Queens Park Rangers	Away	FA Cup	1-3	1 Goal	(114)
233	06/02/88	Liverpool	Away	League	0-0		
234	13/02/88	Portsmouth	Home	League	1-1	1 Goal	(115)
235	27/02/88	Derby County	Away	League	0-1		
236	05/03/88	Oxford United	Home	League	1-1		

237	12/03/88	Charlton Athletic	Away	League	0–3		
238	19/03/88	Watford	Home	League	1–0		
239	26/03/88	Manchester United	Away	League	1–3		
240	02/04/88	Sheffield Wednesday	Away	League	1–2		
241	04/04/88	Everton	Home	League	0–0		
242	12/04/88	Arsenal	Home	League	0–1		
243	20/04/88	Nottingham Forest	Away	League	0–0		
244	23/04/88	Coventry City	Home	League	1–1	1 Goal	(116)
245	30/04/88	Southampton	Away	League	1–2	1 Goal	(117)
246	02/05/88	Chelsea	Home	League	4–1	1 Goal	(118)
247	07/05/88	Newcastle United	Away	League	1–2		

SEASON 1988–89

Everton – League Division One

1	27/08/88	Newcastle United	Home	League	4–0	3 Goals	(3)
2	29/08/88	Manchester United	Away	MCC Trophy	0–1		
3	03/09/88	Coventry City	Away	League	1–0	1 Goal	(4)
4	10/09/88	Nottingham Forest	Home	League	1–1		
5	17/09/88	Millwall	Away	League	1–2		
6	24/09/88	Luton Town	Home	League	0–2		
7	27/09/88	Bury	Home	Lge Cup	3–0		
8	01/10/88	Wimbledon	Away	League	1–2		
9	08/10/88	Southampton	Home	League	4–1	2 Goals	(6)
10	11/10/88	Bury	Away	Lge Cup	2–2		
11	22/10/88	Aston Villa	Away	League	0–2		
12	30/10/88	Manchester United	Home	League	1–1	1 Goal	(7)
13	05/11/88	Sheffield Wednesday	Away	League	1–1		
14	08/11/88	Oldham Athletic	Home	Lge Cup	1–1		
15	12/11/88	Charlton Athletic	Away	League	2–1		
16	19/11/88	Norwich City	Home	League	1–1		
17	26/11/88	West Ham United	Away	League	1–0		
18	29/11/88	Oldham Athletic	Away	Lge Cup	2–0	2 Goals	(9)
19	03/12/88	Tottenham Hotspur	Home	League	1–0	1 Goal	(10)
20	11/12/88	Liverpool	Away	League	1–1		
21	14/12/88	Bradford City	Away	Lge Cup	1–3		
22	17/12/88	Queens Park Rangers	Away	League	0–0		
23	20/12/88	Millwall	Home	Simod Cup	2–0	1 Goal	(11)
24	26/12/88	Middlesbrough	Home	League	2–1	1 Goal	(12)
25	31/12/88	Coventry City	Home	League	3–1		
26	02/01/89	Nottingham Forest	Away	League	0–2		
27	07/01/89	West Bromwich Albion	Away	FA Cup	1–1		
28	11/01/89	West Bromwich Albion	Home	FA Cup	1–0		
29	14/01/89	Arsenal	Home	League	1–3		
30	18/01/89	Wimbledon	Away	Simod Cup	2–1		
31	21/01/89	Luton Town	Away	League	0–1		
32	28/01/89	Plymouth Argyle	Away	FA Cup	1–1		
33	31/01/89	Plymouth Argyle	Home	FA Cup	4–0		
34	04/02/89	Wimbledon	Home	League	1–1		
35	11/02/89	Southampton	Away	League	1–1		
36	14/02/89	Aston Villa	Home	League	1–1	1 Goal	(13)
37	18/02/89	Barnsley	Away	FA Cup	1–0		
38	28/02/89	Queens Park Rangers	Home	Simod Cup	1–0		
39	11/03/89	Sheffield Wednesday	Home	League	1–0	1 Goal	(14)
40	19/03/89	Wimbledon	Home	FA Cup	1–0		
41	22/03/89	Newcastle United	Away	League	0–2		
Sub+1	25/03/89	Millwall	Home	League	1–1		
42	27/03/89	Middlesbrough	Away	League	3–3	1 Goal	(15)
43	01/04/89	Queens Park Rangers	Home	League	4–1	1 Goal	(16)
44	08/04/89	Arsenal	Away	League	0–2		
45	15/04/89	Norwich City	Neutral	FA Cup	1–0		
46	22/04/89	Tottenham Hotspur	Away	League	1–2		
47	30/04/89	Nottingham Forest	Wembley	Simod Cup	3–4*	2 Goals	(18)
48	03/05/89	Liverpool	Home	League	0–0		
49	06/05/89	Norwich City	Away	League	0–1		
50	10/05/89	Manchester United	Away	League	2–1		
51	13/05/89	West Ham United	Home	League	3–1		
52	15/05/89	Derby County	Home	League	1–0		
53	20/05/89	Liverpool	Wembley	FA Cup	2–3*		

SEASON 1989–90

League Division One

| Sub+2 | 19/08/89 | Coventry City | Away | League | 0–2 | | |
| 54 | 30/08/89 | Sheffield Wednesday | Away | League | 1–1 | | |

Sub+3	03/10/89	Leyton Orient	Home	Lge Cup	2–2		
55	14/10/89	Millwall	Home	League	2–1		
56	21/10/89	Arsenal	Home	League	3–0		
57	24/10/89	Luton Town	Home	Lge Cup	3–0		
58	28/10/89	Norwich City	Away	League	1–1	1 Goal	(19)
59	05/11/89	Aston Villa	Away	League	2–6	1 Goal	(20)
60	11/11/89	Chelsea	Home	League	0–1		
Sub+4	22/11/89	Nottingham Forest	Away	Lge Cup	0–1		
Sub+5	25/11/89	Nottingham Forest	Away	League	0–1		
61	02/12/89	Coventry City	Home	League	2–0		
62	09/12/89	Tottenham Hotspur	Away	League	1–2	1 Goal	(21)
63	17/12/89	Manchester City	Home	League	0–0		
64	26/12/89	Derby County	Away	League	1–0		
65	30/12/89	Queens Park Rangers	Away	League	0–1		
Sub+6	10/01/90	Middlesbrough	Home	FA Cup	1–1*		
Sub+7	17/01/90	Middlesbrough	Home	FA Cup	1–0		
66	10/02/90	Charlton Athletic	Home	League	2–1	1 Goal	(22)
67	17/02/90	Oldham Athletic	Away	FA Cup	2–2	1 Goal	(23)
68	21/02/90	Oldham Athletic	Home	FA Cup	1–1*		
69	03/03/90	Wimbledon	Away	League	1–3		
70	10/03/90	Oldham Athletic	Away	FA Cup	1–2*	1 Goal	(24)
71	14/03/90	Manchester United	Away	League	0–0		
72	17/03/90	Crystal Palace	Home	League	4–0	2 Goals	(26)
73	21/03/90	Millwall	Away	League	2–1	1 Goal	(27)
74	24/03/90	Norwich City	Home	League	3–1	2 Goals	(29)
75	31/03/90	Arsenal	Away	League	0–1		
76	04/04/90	Nottingham Forest	Home	League	4–0	2 Goals	(31)
77	07/04/90	Queens Park Rangers	Home	League	1–0	1 Goal	(32)
78	14/04/90	Luton Town	Away	League	2–2	1 Goal	(33)
79	16/04/90	Derby County	Home	League	2–1		
80	21/04/90	Manchester City	Away	League	0–1		
81	28/04/90	Chelsea	Away	League	1–2		
82	05/05/90	Aston Villa	Home	League	3–3		

SEASON 1990–91

League Division One

Sub+8	08/09/90	Arsenal	Home	League	1–1		
Sub+9	22/09/90	Liverpool	Home	League	2–3		
83	25/09/90	Wrexham	Away	Lge Cup	5–0	3 Goals	(36)
84	29/09/90	Southampton	Home	League	3–0	2 Goals	(38)
85	07/10/90	Nottingham Forest	Away	League	1–3		
86	09/10/90	Wrexham	Home	Lge Cup	6–0	1 Goal	(39)
87	20/10/90	Crystal Palace	Home	League	0–0		
88	27/10/90	Luton Town	Away	League	1–1		
89	30/10/90	Sheffield United	Away	Lge Cup	1–2		
90	18/11/90	Tottenham Hotspur	Home	League	1–1		
Sub+10	24/11/90	Wimbledon	Away	League	1–2		
91	01/12/90	Manchester City	Home	League	0–1		
92	08/12/90	Coventry City	Home	League	1–0		
Sub+11	16/12/90	Leeds United	Away	League	0–2		
93	18/12/90	Blackburn Rovers	Away	ZDS Cup	4–1	1 Goal	(40)
94	22/12/90	Norwich City	Away	League	0–1		
Sub+12	13/01/91	Manchester City	Home	League	2–0		
Sub+13	19/01/91	Arsenal	Away	League	0–1		
95	22/01/91	Sunderland	Home	ZDS Cup	4–1	4 Goals	(44)
96	27/01/91	Woking	Away	FA Cup	1–0		
Sub+14	02/02/91	Sunderland	Home	League	2–0		
Sub+15	09/02/91	Liverpool	Away	League	1–3		
Sub+16	17/02/91	Liverpool	Away	FA Cup	0–0		
Sub+17	20/02/91	Liverpool	Home	FA Cup	4–4	2 Goals	(46)
97	23/02/91	Sheffield United	Home	League	1–2	1 Goal	(47)
Sub+18	02/03/91	Manchester United	Away	League	2–0		
Sub+19	11/03/91	West Ham United	Away	FA Cup	1–2		
98	13/03/91	Barnsley	Away	ZDS Cup	1–0	1 Goal	(48)
99	16/03/91	Southampton	Away	League	4–3	1 Goal	(49)
Sub+20	19/03/91	Leeds United	Away	ZDS Cup	3–3		
Sub+21	21/03/91	Leeds United	Home	ZDS Cup	3–1	2 Goals	(51)
100	23/03/91	Nottingham Forest	Home	League	0–0		
101	30/03/91	Aston Villa	Away	League	2–2		
102	01/04/91	Norwich City	Home	League	1–0		
103	07/04/91	Crystal Palace	Wembley	ZDS Cup	1–4*		
104	10/04/91	Wimbledon	Home	League	1–2	1 Goal	(52)
105	13/04/91	Chelsea	Home	League	2–2	1 Goal	(53)

106	20/04/91	Crystal Palace	Away	League	0–0		
107	24/04/91	Tottenham Hotspur	Away	League	3–3	1 Goal	(54)
108	04/05/91	Luton Town	Home	League	1–0	1 Goal	(55)
109	08/05/91	Derby County	Away	League	3–2	2 Goals	(57)
110	11/05/91	Queens Park Rangers	Away	League	1–1		

SEASON 1991–92

League Division One

111	17/08/91	Nottingham Forest	Away	League	1–2		
112	20/08/91	Arsenal	Home	League	3–1	1 Goal	(58)
113	24/08/91	Manchester United	Home	League	0–0		
114	28/08/91	Sheffield Wednesday	Away	League	1–2		
115	31/08/91	Liverpool	Away	League	1–3		
Sub+22	14/09/91	Sheffield United	Away	League	1–2		
Sub+23	24/09/91	Watford	Home	Lge Cup	1–0		
Sub+24	28/09/91	Chelsea	Away	League	2–2		
116	01/10/91	Oldham Athletic	Home	ZDS Cup	3–2	1 Goal	(59)
117	05/10/91	Tottenham Hotspur	Home	League	3–1	3 Goals	(62)
118	08/10/91	Watford	Away	Lge Cup	2–1		
119	19/10/91	Aston Villa	Home	League	0–2		
120	26/10/91	Queens Park Rangers	Away	League	1–3	1 Goal	(63)
121	30/10/91	Wolverhampton Wanderers	Home	Lge Cup	4–1	1 Goal	(64)
Sub+25	02/11/91	Luton Town	Away	League	1–0		
122	16/11/91	Wimbledon	Home	League	2–0	1 Goal	(65)
123	23/11/91	Notts County	Home	League	1–0	1 Goal	(66)
124	27/11/91	Leicester City	Away	ZDS Cup	1–2		
125	30/11/91	Leeds United	Away	League	0–1		
126	04/12/91	Leeds United	Home	Lge Cup	1–4		
127	07/12/91	West Ham United	Home	League	4–0	1 Goal	(67)
Sub+26	21/12/91	Arsenal	Away	League	2–4		
128	26/12/91	Sheffield Wednesday	Home	League	0–1		
Sub+27	04/01/92	Southend United	Home	FA Cup	1–0		
Sub+28	11/01/92	Manchester United	Away	League	0–1		
Sub+29	19/01/92	Nottingham Forest	Home	League	1–1		
129	26/01/92	Chelsea	Away	FA Cup	0–1		
130	02/02/92	Aston Villa	Away	League	0–0		
131	23/02/92	Leeds United	Home	League	1–1		
132	29/02/92	West Ham United	Away	League	2–0		
Sub+30	01/04/92	Southampton	Home	League	0–1		
133	11/04/92	Sheffield United	Home	League	0–2		

SEASON 1992–93

Premier League

134	15/09/92	Blackburn Rovers	Away	League	3–2	2 Goals	(69)
135	19/09/92	Crystal Palace	Home	League	0–2		
136	23/09/92	Rotherham United	Away	Lge Cup	0–1		
137	26/09/92	Leeds United	Away	League	0–2		
Sub+31	04/10/92	Oldham Athletic	Away	League	0–1		
138	07/10/92	Rotherham United	Home	Lge Cup	3–0	1 Goal	(70)
139	17/10/92	Coventry City	Home	League	1–1		
140	24/10/92	Arsenal	Away	League	0–2		
141	28/11/92	Ipswich Town	Away	League	0–1		
Sub+32	02/12/92	Chelsea	Home	Lge Cup	2–2		
142	16/01/93	Leeds United	Home	League	2–0	2 Goals	(72)
143	26/01/93	Wimbledon	Away	League	3–1	2 Goals	(74)
144	30/01/93	Norwich City	Home	League	0–1		
145	06/02/93	Sheffield Wednesday	Away	League	1–3	1 Goal	(75)
146	10/02/93	Tottenham Hotspur	Home	League	1–2		
147	20/02/93	Aston Villa	Away	League	1–2		
148	27/02/93	Oldham Athletic	Home	League	2–2		
149	03/03/93	Blackburn Rovers	Home	League	2–1	1 Goal	(76)
150	07/03/93	Coventry City	Away	League	1–0		
151	10/03/93	Chelsea	Away	League	1–2		
152	13/03/93	Nottingham Forest	Home	League	3–0	2 Goals	(78)
153	20/03/93	Liverpool	Away	League	0–1		
154	24/03/93	Ipswich Town	Home	League	3–0	1 Goal	(79)
155	10/04/93	Middlesbrough	Away	League	2–1		
156	12/04/93	Queens Park Rangers	Home	League	3–5	1 Goal	(80)
157	17/04/93	Southampton	Away	League	0–0		
158	01/05/93	Arsenal	Home	League	0–1		
159	04/05/93	Sheffield United	Home	League	0–2		
160	08/05/93	Manchester City	Away	League	5–2		

SEASON 1993–94

Premier League

161	14/08/93	Southampton	Away	League	2–0		
162	17/08/93	Manchester City	Home	League	1–0		
163	21/08/93	Sheffield United	Home	League	4–2	3 Goals	(83)
164	25/08/93	Newcastle United	Away	League	0–1		
165	28/08/93	Arsenal	Away	League	0–2		
166	31/08/93	Aston Villa	Home	League	0–1		
167	11/09/93	Oldham Athletic	Away	League	1–0	1 Goal	(84)
168	18/09/93	Liverpool	Home	League	2–0	1 Goal	(85)
169	21/09/93	Lincoln City	Away	Lge Cup	4–3	1 Goal	(86)
170	25/09/93	Norwich City	Home	League	1–5		
171	03/10/93	Tottenham Hotspur	Away	League	2–3	1 Goal	(87)
172	06/10/93	Lincoln City	Home	Lge Cup	4–2	2 Goals	(89)
173	16/10/93	Swindon Town	Away	League	1–1		
174	23/10/93	Manchester United	Home	League	0–1		
175	26/10/93	Crystal palace	Home	Lge Cup	2–2		
176	30/10/93	Ipswich Town	Away	League	2–0		
177	06/11/93	Coventry City	Away	League	1–2		
178	10/11/93	Crystal Palace	Away	Lge Cup	4–1		
179	20/11/93	Queens Park Rangers	Home	League	0–3		
180	23/11/93	Leeds United	Home	League	1–1	1 Goal	(90)
181	27/11/93	Wimbledon	Away	League	1–1		
182	30/11/93	Manchester United	Home	Lge Cup	0–2		
183	04/12/93	Southampton	Home	League	1–0	1 Goal	(91)
184	08/12/93	Manchester City	Away	League	0–1		
185	11/12/93	Sheffield United	Away	League	0–0		
186	18/12/93	Newcastle United	Home	League	0–2		
187	29/12/93	Blackburn Rovers	Away	League	0–2		
188	01/01/94	West Ham United	Home	League	0–1		
189	03/01/94	Chelsea	Away	League	2–4	1 Goal	(92)
190	08/01/94	Bolton Wanderers	Away	FA Cup	1–1		
191	15/01/94	Swindon Town	Home	League	6–2	3 Goals	(95)
192	19/01/94	Bolton Wanderers	Home	FA Cup	2–3*		
193	22/01/94	Manchester United	Away	League	0–1		
Sub+33	12/02/94	Ipswich Town	Home	League	0–0		
Sub+34	19/02/94	Arsenal	Home	League	1–1	1 Goal	(96)
194	05/03/94	Oldham Athletic	Home	League	2–1		
195	13/03/94	Liverpool	Away	League	1–2		
196	21/03/94	Norwich City	Away	League	0–3		
197	26/03/94	Tottenham Hotspur	Home	League	0–1		
Sub+35	02/04/94	Sheffield Wednesday	Away	League	1–5	1 Goal	(97)
198	04/04/94	Blackburn Rovers	Home	League	0–3		
199	09/04/94	West Ham United	Away	League	1–0	1 Goal	(98)
200	16/04/94	Queens Park Rangers	Away	League	1–2	1 Goal	(99)
201	23/04/94	Coventry City	Home	League	0–0		
202	30/04/94	Leeds United	Away	League	0–3		
203	07/05/94	Wimbledon	Home	League	3–2		

SEASON 1994–95

Premier League

204	20/08/94	Aston Villa	Home	League	2–2		
205	24/08/94	Tottenham Hotspur	Away	League	1–2		
206	27/08/94	Manchester City	Away	League	0–4		

West Ham United – Premier League

1	10/09/94	Liverpool	Away	League	0–0		
2	17/09/94	Aston Villa	Home	League	1–0	1 Goal	(1)
3	20/09/94	Walsall	Away	Lge Cup	1–2		
4	08/10/94	Crystal Palace	Home	League	1–0		
5	15/10/94	Manchester United	Away	League	0–1		
6	22/10/94	Southampton	Home	League	2–0		
7	26/10/94	Chelsea	Home	Lge Cup	1–0		
8	29/10/94	Tottenham Hotspur	Away	League	1–3		
9	01/11/94	Everton	Away	League	0–1		
10	05/11/94	Leicester City	Home	League	1–0		
11	19/11/94	Sheffield Wednesday	Away	League	0–1		
12	26/11/94	Coventry City	Home	League	0–1		
13	30/11/94	Bolton Wanderers	Home	Lge Cup	1–3	1 Goal	(2)
14	04/12/94	Queens Park Rangers	Away	League	1–2		
15	10/12/94	Leeds United	Away	League	2–2		
16	17/12/94	Manchester City	Home	League	3–0	3 Goals	(5)
17	26/12/94	Ipswich Town	Home	League	1–1	1 Goal	(6)

18	28/12/94	Wimbledon	Away	League	0–1		
19	31/12/94	Nottingham Forest	Home	League	3–1	1 Goal	(7)
20	02/01/95	Blackburn Rovers	Away	League	2–4	1 Goal	(8)
21	07/01/95	Wycombe Wanderers	Away	FA Cup	2–0	1 Goal	(9)
22	14/01/95	Tottenham Hotspur	Home	League	1–2		
23	23/01/95	Sheffield Wednesday	Home	League	0–2		
24	28/01/95	Queens Park Rangers	Away	FA Cup	0–1		
25	04/02/95	Leicester City	Away	League	2–1	1 Goal	(10)
26	13/02/95	Everton	Home	League	2–2	2 Goals	(12)
27	18/02/95	Coventry City	Away	League	0–2		
28	25/02/95	Chelsea	Home	League	1–2		
29	05/03/95	Arsenal	Away	League	1–0		
30	08/03/95	Newcastle United	Away	League	0–2		
31	11/03/95	Norwich City	Home	League	2–2	2 Goals	(14)
32	15/03/95	Southampton	Away	League	1–1		
33	18/03/95	Aston Villa	Away	League	2–0		
34	08/04/95	Nottingham Forest	Away	League	1–1		
35	13/04/95	Wimbledon	Home	League	3–0	1 Goal	(15)
36	17/04/95	Ipswich Town	Away	League	1–1		

SEASON 1995–96

Premier League

37	19/08/95	Leeds United	Home	League	1–2		
38	23/08/95	Manchester United	Away	League	1–2		
39	26/08/95	Nottingham Forest	Away	League	1–1		
40	30/08/95	Tottenham Hotspur	Home	League	1–1		
41	11/09/95	Chelsea	Home	League	1–3		
42	16/09/95	Arsenal	Away	League	0–1		
43	20/09/95	Bristol Rovers	Away	Lge Cup	1–0		
44	23/09/95	Everton	Home	League	2–1		
Sub+1	02/10/95	Southampton	Away	League	0–0		
45	04/10/95	Bristol Rovers	Home	Lge Cup	3–0	1 Goal	(16)
46	16/10/96	Wimbledon	Away	League	1–0	1 Goal	(17)
47	21/10/95	Blackburn Rovers	Home	League	1–1		
48	25/10/95	Southampton	Away	Lge Cup	1–2	1 Goal	(18)
49	28/10/95	Sheffield Wednesday	Away	League	1–0		
50	04/11/95	Aston Villa	Home	League	1–4		
51	18/11/95	Bolton Wanderers	Away	League	3–0	1 Goal	(19)
52	22/11/95	Liverpool	Home	League	0–0		
53	25/11/95	Queens Park Rangers	Home	League	1–0	1 Goal	(20)
54	02/12/95	Blackburn Rovers	Away	League	2–4		
55	11/12/95	Everton	Away	League	0–3		
56	16/12/95	Southampton	Home	League	2–1	1 Goal	(21)
57	23/12/95	Middlesbrough	Away	League	2–4	1 Goal	(22)
58	06/01/96	Southend United	Home	FA Cup	2–0		
59	13/01/96	Leeds United	Away	League	0–2		
60	22/01/96	Manchester United	Home	League	0–1		
61	31/01/96	Coventry City	Home	League	3–2	1 Goal	(23)
62	03/02/96	Nottingham Forest	Home	League	1–0		
63	07/02/96	Grimsby Town	Home	FA Cup	1–1		
Sub+2	12/02/96	Tottenham Hotspur	Away	League	1–0		
64	14/02/96	Grimsby Town	Away	FA Cup	0–3		
Sub+3	17/02/96	Chelsea	Away	League	2–1		
65	21/02/96	Newcastle United	Home	League	2–0	1 Goal	(24)
66	24/02/96	Arsenal	Home	League	0–1		
67	02/03/96	Coventry City	Away	League	2–2	1 Goal	(25)
68	09/03/96	Middlesbrough	Home	League	2–0		
69	13/04/96	Bolton Wanderers	Home	League	1–0	1 Goal	(26)
70	17/04/96	Aston Villa	Away	League	1–1	1 Goal	(27)
71	27/04/96	Queens Park Rangers	Away	League	0–3		
72	05/05/96	Sheffield Wednesday	Home	League	1–1		

SEASON 1996–97

Premier League

Sub+4	14/09/96	Wimbledon	Home	League	0–2		
73	18/09/96	Barnet	Away	Lge Cup	1–1	1 Goal	(28)
74	21/09/96	Nottingham Forest	Away	League	2–0		
75	25/09/96	Barnet	Home	Lge Cup	1–0		
76	29/09/96	Liverpool	Home	League	1–2		

Selangor – Malaysian League
The Malaysian season commences in April and concludes in November, match details therefore fall within the 1997–98 season.

INTERNATIONAL APPEARANCES – ENGLAND

Sub 1	10/09/86	Sweden	Stockholm	0–1	F
Sub 2	15/10/86	Northern Ireland	Wembley	3–0	ECQ
Sub 3	27/04/88	Hungary	Budapest	0–0	F
Sub 4	14/09/88	Denmark	Wembley	1–0	F
Sub 5	19/10/88	Sweden	Wembley	0–0	WCQ
Sub 6	23/05/89	Chile	Wembley	0–0	RC
7	27/05/89	Scotland	Hampden Park	2–0	RC

APPEARANCES AND GOALS PER SEASON

SEASON 82–83	GAMES	GOALS
League	3+5	5
FA Cup	1	0
TOTAL	**4+5**	**5**

SEASON 83–84	GAMES	GOALS
League	37+2	15
FA Cup	4	0
League Cup	4	4
TOTAL	**45+2**	**19**

SEASON 84–85	GAMES	GOALS
League	40+1	17
FA Cup	5	4
League Cup	4	3
TOTAL	**49+1**	**24**

SEASON 85–86	GAMES	GOALS
League	41+1	20
FA Cup	7	4
League Cup	3	2
TOTAL	**51+1**	**26**

SEASON 86–87	GAMES	GOALS
League	42	22
FA Cup	5	1
League Cup	6	5
Full Members Cup	1	1
TOTAL	**54**	**29**

SEASON 87–88	GAMES	GOALS
League	40	13
FA Cup	2	2
League Cup	2	0
TOTAL	**44**	**15**

SEASON 88–89	GAMES	GOALS
League	35+1	13
FA Cup	8	0
League Cup	5	2
Simod Cup	4	3
Mercantile Centenary Credit Trophy	1	0
TOTAL	**53+1**	**18**

SEASON 89–90	GAMES	GOALS
League	25+2	13
FA Cup	3+2	2
League Cup	1+2	0
TOTAL	**29+6**	**15**

SEASON 90–91	GAMES	GOALS
League	20+9	10
FA Cup	1+3	2
League Cup	3	4
Zenith Data Systems Cup	4+2	8
TOTAL	**28+14**	**24**

SEASON 91–92	GAMES	GOALS
League	17+7	8
FA Cup	1+1	0
League Cup	3+1	1
Zenith Data Systems Cup	2	1
TOTAL	**23+9**	**10**

SEASON 92–93	GAMES	GOALS
League	25+1	12
League Cup	2+1	1
TOTAL	**27+2**	**13**

SEASON 93–94	GAMES	GOALS
League	36+3	16
FA Cup	2	0
League Cup	5	3
TOTAL	**43+3**	**19**

SEASON 94–95	GAMES	GOALS
League	34	13
FA Cup	2	1
League Cup	3	1
TOTAL	**39**	**15**

SEASON 95–96	GAMES	GOALS
League	30+3	10
FA Cup	3	0
League Cup	3	2
TOTAL	**36+3**	**12**

SEASON 96–97	GAMES	GOALS
League	2+1	0
League Cup	2	1
TOTAL	**4+1**	**1**

CAREER APPEARANCES AND GOALS

COMPETITION	GAMES	TOTAL	GOALS
League	427+36	463	187
FA Cup	44+6	50	16
League Cup	46+4	50	29
Full Members Cup	1	1	1
Simod Cup	4	4	3
Mercantile Centenary Credit Trophy	1	1	0
Zenith Data Systems Cup	6+2	8	9
Internationals	1+6	7	0
TOTAL	**530+54**	**584**	**245**

HAT-TRICKS

West Ham United

1	4	Bury	25/10/83	Home	Lge Cup	10–0
2	3	Wimbledon	06/03/85	Home	FA Cup	5–1
3	3	Queens Park Rangers	13/09/86	Away	League	3–2
4	3	Preston North End	07/10/86	Home	Lge Cup	4–1
5	3	Coventry City	24/01/87	Away	League	3–1

Everton

1	3	Newcastle United	27/08/88	Home	League	4–0
2	3	Wrexham	25/09/90	Away	Lge Cup	5–0
3	4	Sunderland	22/01/91	Home	ZDS Cup	4–1
4	3	Tottenham Hotspur	05/10/91	Home	League	3–1
5	3	Sheffield United	21/08/93	Home	League	4–2
6	3	Swindon Town	15/01/94	Home	League	6–2

West Ham United

1	3	Manchester City	17/12/94	Home	League	3–0

League: 7
FA Cup: 1
League Cup: 3
Zenith Data Systems Cup: 1
TOTAL: 12

HONOURS

Winners medals
None

Runner-up medals
FA Cup: 88/89
Simod Cup: 88/89
Zenith Data Systems Cup: 90/91

TOMMY COYNE

Born: 14/11/62 – Glasgow
Height: 5.11
Weight: 12.00 (96–97)

Clubs
Clydebank: **1981–83** – Matches: **93+2** – Goals: **41**
Dundee United: **1983–86** – Matches: **51+25** – Goals: **14**
Dundee: **1986–89** – Matches: **109+1** – Goals: **61**
Celtic: **1989–93** – Matches: **104+28** – Goals: **52**
Tranmere Rovers: **1993** – Matches: **9+5** – Goals: **1**
Motherwell: **1993–97** – Matches: **104+9** – Goals: **46**

Country
Republic of Ireland: **1992–96** – Matches: **10+11** – Goals: **6**

SEASON 1981–82

Clydebank – Scottish League Division One

1	10/10/81	Raith Rovers	Away	League	2–0	1 Goal	(1)
2	17/10/81	Motherwell	Home	League	1–7	1 Goal	(2)
3	20/10/81	Hamilton Academical	Home	League	2–1	1 Goal	(3)
4	24/10/81	East Stirling	Away	League	0–0		
5	31/10/81	Ayr United	Home	League	2–1		
6	07/11/81	St Johnstone	Away	League	3–1	1 Goal	(4)
7	14/11/81	Queen's Park	Home	League	2–1		
8	21/11/81	Dunfermline Athletic	Away	League	6–3		
9	28/11/81	Falkirk	Away	League	0–3		
10	05/12/81	Queen of the South	Home	League	2–1	1 Goal	(5)
11	12/12/81	Hamilton Academical	Away	League	2–0	1 Goal	(6)
12	19/01/82	Motherwell	Away	League	1–3		
13	23/01/82	Dunfermline Athletic	Away	S Cup	2–1		
14	30/01/82	East Stirling	Home	League	2–1	1 Goal	(7)
15	03/02/82	Raith Rovers	Home	League	0–1		
16	06/02/82	Ayr United	Away	League	1–2		
17	13/02/82	St Mirren	Home	S Cup	0–2		
18	17/02/82	Dumbarton	Home	League	3–0		
19	20/02/82	Hamilton Academical	Away	League	1–3		
20	27/02/82	Falkirk	Home	League	0–2		
21	10/03/82	Queen's Park	Home	League	1–0		
22	13/03/82	Dumbarton	Away	League	2–0		
23	20/03/82	Queen of the South	Home	League	5–1	1 Goal	(8)
24	27/03/82	Heart of Midlothian	Home	League	2–1		
25	03/04/82	Kilmarnock	Away	League	0–0		
26	10/04/82	East Stirling	Away	League	1–0		
Sub+1	14/04/82	Heart of Midlothian	Home	League	1–5		
27	17/04/82	Raith Rovers	Home	League	0–0		
28	21/04/82	Kilmarnock	Away	League	0–2		
Sub+2	24/04/82	Motherwell	Away	League	0–0		
29	01/05/82	Dunfermline Athletic	Home	League	1–0		
30	08/05/82	St Johnstone	Away	League	3–3		
31	15/05/82	Ayr United	Home	League	2–0	1 Goal	(9)

SEASON 1982–83

Scottish League Division One

32	14/08/82	Airdrieonians	Away	S Lge Cup	3–1	2 Goals	(11)
33	18/08/82	Hibernian	Home	S Lge Cup	0–2		
34	21/08/82	Rangers	Home	S Lge Cup	1–4		
35	25/08/82	Hibernian	Away	S Lge Cup	1–1		
36	28/08/82	Airdrieonians	Home	S Lge Cup	1–2		
37	01/09/82	Rangers	Away	S Lge Cup	2–3		
38	11/09/82	Alloa	Away	League	0–2		
39	15/09/82	Dumbarton	Home	League	5–1	2 Goals	(13)
40	18/09/82	Clyde	Away	League	5–3	1 Goal	(14)
41	22/09/82	Airdrieonians	Home	League	0–4		
42	25/09/82	Queen's Park	Home	League	2–0		
43	29/09/82	Heart of Midlothian	Away	League	1 4		

44	02/10/82	Ayr United	Away	League	3–1	2 Goals	(16)
45	09/10/82	Partick Thistle	Away	League	1–0		
46	16/10/82	Dunfermline Athletic	Home	League	1–1		
47	23/10/82	Falkirk	Away	League	2–0		
48	30/10/82	St Johnstone	Home	League	1–0		
49	06/11/82	Hamilton Academical	Away	League	2–0	1 Goal	(17)
50	13/11/82	Heart of Midlothian	Home	League	0–3		
51	20/11/82	Clyde	Home	League	2–2	1 Goal	(18)
52	27/11/82	Airdrieonians	Away	League	2–2		
53	04/12/82	Ayr United	Home	League	0–1		
54	11/12/82	Queen's Park	Away	League	2–2	1 Goal	(19)
55	18/12/82	Raith Rovers	Away	League	3–0	1 Goal	(20)
56	27/12/82	Alloa	Home	League	2–2	1 Goal	(21)
57	01/01/83	Dumbarton	Away	League	4–0	1 Goal	(22)
58	03/01/83	Hamilton Academical	Home	League	2–1		
59	15/01/83	Partick Thistle	Home	League	1–3	1 Goal	(23)
60	22/01/83	St Johnstone	Away	League	1–0		
61	28/01/83	Celtic	Home	S Cup	0–3		
62	05/02/83	Falkirk	Home	League	0–2		
63	12/02/83	Alloa	Away	League	2–1	1 Goal	(24)
64	23/02/83	Dunfermline Athletic	Away	League	1–1		
65	26/02/83	Dumbarton	Home	League	3–1	1 Goal	(25)
66	05/03/83	Ayr United	Away	League	0–1		
67	12/03/83	St Johnstone	Home	League	6–1	2 Goals	(27)
68	19/03/83	Dunfermline Athletic	Away	League	1–1		
69	26/03/83	Raith Rovers	Away	League	3–1	2 Goals	(29)
70	02/04/83	Clyde	Home	League	2–1		
71	09/04/83	Falkirk	Away	League	2–0		
72	16/04/83	Heart of Midlothian	Away	League	2–2		
73	23/04/83	Airdrieonians	Home	League	2–0		
74	30/04/83	Hamilton Academical	Home	League	1–1		
75	07/05/83	Queen's Park	Away	League	3–1		
76	14/05/83	Partick Thistle	Home	League	1–2		

SEASON 1983–84

Scottish League Division One

77	20/08/83	Dumbarton	Away	League	0–2		
78	24/08/83	Ayr United	Away	S Lge Cup	2–1		
79	27/08/83	Ayr United	Home	S Lge Cup	1–0		
80	31/08/83	Rangers	Away	S Lge Cup	0–4		
81	03/09/83	Clyde	Home	League	1–0	1 Goal	(30)
82	07/09/83	St Mirren	Home	S Lge Cup	2–0	1 Goal	(31)
83	10/09/83	Raith Rovers	Away	League	0–0		
84	14/09/83	Airdrieonians	Away	League	0–1		
85	17/09/83	Alloa	Home	League	2–7		
86	24/09/83	Partick Thistle *	Away	League	0–1		
87	28/09/83	Kilmarnock	Home	League	4–0		
88	01/10/83	Meadowbank Thistle	Away	League	3–1	3 Goals	(34)
89	05/10/83	Heart of Midlothian	Away	S Lge Cup	1–1		
90	08/10/83	Ayr United	Home	League	4–1	3 Goals	(37)
91	15/10/83	Morton	Home	League	3–3	2 Goals	(39)
92	22/10/83	Falkirk	Away	League	1–1	1 Goal	(40)
93	26/10/83	St Mirren	Away	S Lge Cup	3–3	1 Goal	(41)

Dundee United – Scottish League Premier Division

Sub+1	29/10/83	Motherwell	Away	League	2–2		
Sub+2	05/11/83	Dundee	Home	League	0–1		
1	12/11/83	St Johnstone	Home	League	7–0		
2	19/11/83	Rangers	Away	League	0–0		
3	22/11/83	St Mirren	Away	League	0–4		
Sub+3	26/11/83	Aberdeen	Home	League	0–2		
Sub+4	27/12/83	Celtic	Away	League	1–1		
4	25/02/84	St Mirren	Away	League	2–2		
5	03/03/84	Celtic	Home	League	3–1		
6	11/03/84	Heart of Midlothian	Home	League	3–1	2 Goals	(2)
7	17/03/84	Aberdeen	Away	S Cup	0–0		
8	21/03/84	SK Rapid Wien	Home	Eur Cup	1–0		
Sub+5	11/04/84	AS Roma	Home	Eur Cup	2–0		
9	14/04/84	St Johnstone	Home	League	3–0	1 Goal	(3)
10	18/04/84	Aberdeen	Away	League	1–5		
11	28/04/84	Motherwell	Away	League	3–1		
12	30/04/84	St Mirren	Home	League	2–0		
Sub+6	05/05/84	St Mirren	Home	League	2–2		
13	07/05/84	Aberdeen	Home	League	0–0		

| 14 | 12/05/84 | Celtic | Away | League | 1–1 | | |
| 15 | 14/05/84 | Rangers | Home | League | 1–2 | | |

SEASON 1984–85

Scottish League Premier Division

16	11/08/84	Heart of Midlothian	Home	League	2–0		
Sub+7	21/08/84	Forfar Athletic	Home	S Lge Cup	5–0		
Sub+8	25/08/84	Aberdeen	Home	League	0–2		
Sub+9	06/10/84	Dumbarton	Home	League	1–0	1 Goal	(4)
Sub+10	13/10/84	Heart of Midlothian	Away	League	0–2		
17	20/10/84	Celtic	Home	League	1–3		
18	03/11/84	St Mirren	Home	League	3–2		
19	07/11/84	Linzer ASK	Home	UEFA Cup	5–1	2 Goals	(6)
20	10/11/84	Dundee	Away	League	2–0	1 Goal	(7)
21	17/11/84	Morton	Home	League	7–0		
22	24/11/84	Hibernian	Away	League	0–0		
23	01/12/84	Rangers	Home	League	1–1		
24	08/12/84	Dumbarton	Away	League	2–2		
25	15/12/84	Heart of Midlothian	Home	League	5–2		
26	22/12/84	Aberdeen	Away	League	1–0		
27	29/12/84	Celtic	Away	League	2–1		
28	09/02/85	Rangers	Away	League	0–0		
29	02/03/85	Celtic	Home	League	0–0		
30	13/03/85	Morton	Away	League	3–0		
31	20/04/85	Hibernian	Away	League	1–1		
32	27/04/85	Dumbarton	Away	League	2–0	1 Goal	(8)
33	04/05/85	Rangers	Home	League	2–1		
Sub+11	11/05/85	Dundee	Away	League	0–1		

SEASON 1985–86

Scottish League Premier Division

34	10/08/85	Rangers	Away	League	0–1		
35	21/08/85	Alloa	Away	S Lge Cup	2–0		
Sub+12	31/08/85	Motherwell	Away	League	1–0		
36	05/10/85	Hibernian	Home	League	2–2		
Sub+13	23/10/85	FK Vardar Skoplje	Home	UEFA Cup	2–0		
Sub+14	26/10/85	Celtic	Away	League	3–0		
Sub+15	09/11/85	Motherwell	Home	League	3–0		
37	16/11/85	Dundee	Away	League	3–0		
38	23/11/85	Clydebank	Away	League	2–1		
39	11/12/85	FC Neuchatel Xamax	Away	UEFA Cup	1–3		
Sub+16	11/01/86	Heart of Midlothian	Away	League	1–1		
40	18/01/86	Clydebank	Home	League	4–0		
41	25/01/86	Morton	Home	S Cup	4–0	2 Goals	(10)
42	01/02/86	St Mirren	Away	League	1–1		
43	08/02/86	Hibernian	Home	League	4–0	2 Goals	(12)
44	15/02/86	Kilmarnock	Home	S Cup	1–1		
Sub+17	08/03/86	Motherwell	Away	S Cup	1–0		
45	12/03/86	Motherwell	Away	League	0–2		
46	26/04/86	St Mirren	Home	League	1–2		

SEASON 1986–87

Scottish League Premier Division

Sub+18	13/08/86	Clydebank	Away	League	0–0		
47	06/09/86	Dundee	Away	League	2–0		
48	01/10/86	RC Lens	Home	UEFA Cup	2–0	1 Goal	(13)
Sub+19	04/10/86	Falkirk	Home	League	2–0		
Sub+20	08/10/86	Motherwell	Home	League	4–0	1 Goal	(14)
49	11/10/86	Aberdeen	Away	League	0–2		
Sub+21	22/10/86	Universitatea Craiova	Home	UEFA Cup	3–0		
Sub+22	05/11/86	Universitatea Craiova	Away	UEFA Cup	0–1		
50	08/11/86	Dundee	Home	League	0–3		
Sub+23	15/11/86	Celtic	Away	League	0–1		
Sub+24	19/11/86	Hamilton Academical	Home	League	3–0		
51	29/11/86	Falkirk	Away	League	1–2		
Sub+25	06/12/86	Aberdeen	Home	League	0–0		

Dundee – Scottish League Premier Division

1	13/12/86	St Mirren	Home	League	6–3		
2	27/12/86	Hibernian	Home	League	2–0		
3	01/01/87	Aberdeen	Away	League	1–2		
4	24/01/87	Heart of Midlothian	Home	League	0–1		

5	27/01/87	Motherwell	Away	League	0–2		
6	03/02/87	East Fife	Home	S Cup	2–2	1 Goal	(1)
7	07/02/87	Clydebank	Away	League	1–1	1 Goal	(2)
8	09/02/87	East Fife	Away	S Cup	4–1	1 Goal	(3)
9	14/02/87	Hamilton Academical	Away	League	1–1	1 Goal	(4)
10	21/02/87	Meadowbank Thistle	Home	S Cup	1–1		
11	25/02/87	Meadowbank Thistle	Away	S Cup	1–1*		
12	28/02/87	Celtic	Home	League	4–1		
13	02/03/87	Meadowbank Thistle	Home	S Cup	2–0	2 Goals	(6)
14	07/03/87	St Mirren	Away	League	1–0		
15	10/03/87	Dundee United	Home	League	1–1		
16	14/03/87	Clydebank	Away	S Cup	4–0	1 Goal	(7)
17	17/03/87	Rangers	Home	League	0–4		
18	21/03/87	Hibernian	Away	League	2–2	1 Goal	(8)
19	28/03/87	Dundee United	Away	League	1–1		
20	04/04/87	Aberdeen	Home	League	1–1		
21	11/04/87	Dundee United	Neutral	S Cup	2–3	1 Goal	(9)
22	14/04/87	Rangers	Away	League	0–2		
23	18/04/87	Motherwell	Home	League	4–1	2 Goals	(11)
24	21/04/87	Falkirk	Away	League	0–0		
25	25/04/87	Clydebank	Home	League	4–1	3 Goals	(14)
26	02/05/87	Heart of Midlothian	Away	League	3–1		
27	09/05/87	Hamilton Academical	Home	League	7–3	1 Goal	(15)

SEASON 1987–88

Scottish League Premier Division

28	08/08/87	Aberdeen	Home	League	1–1		
29	12/08/87	Falkirk	Away	League	3–0		
30	15/08/87	Hibernian	Away	League	4–0	2 Goals	(17)
31	18/08/87	Queen's Park	Away	S Lge Cup	3–0	1 Goal	(18)
32	22/08/87	St Mirren	Home	League	0–2		
33	26/08/87	Meadowbank Thistle	Away	S Lge Cup	3–0	2 Goals	(20)
34	29/08/87	Dunfermline Athletic	Home	League	5–0	4 Goals	(24)
35	02/09/87	Dundee United	Home	S Lge Cup	2–1*	1 Goal	(25)
36	05/09/87	Rangers	Away	League	1–2		
37	12/09/87	Morton	Away	League	3–4	2 Goals	(27)
38	19/09/87	Heart of Midlothian	Home	League	1–3		
39	23/09/87	Aberdeen	Neutral	S Lge Cup	0–2		
40	26/09/87	Motherwell	Away	League	2–0	1 Goal	(28)
41	03/10/87	Dundee United	Home	League	1–1	1 Goal	(29)
42	07/10/87	Celtic	Home	League	1–1		
43	10/10/87	Aberdeen	Away	League	0–0		
44	17/10/87	Dunfermline Athletic	Away	League	1–0		
45	28/10/87	Morton	Home	League	1–0		
46	31/10/87	Heart of Midlothian	Away	League	2–4	1 Goal	(30)
47	07/11/87	Falkirk	Home	League	3–1	2 Goals	(32)
48	14/11/87	Celtic	Away	League	0–5		
49	17/11/87	St Mirren	Away	League	2–1	1 Goal	(33)
50	21/11/87	Hibernian	Home	League	2–1	2 Goals	(35)
51	24/11/87	Motherwell	Home	League	2–0	1 Goal	(36)
52	28/11/87	Dundee United	Away	League	3–1	2 Goals	(38)
53	05/12/87	Aberdeen	Home	League	1–2		
54	12/12/87	Falkirk	Away	League	6–0	2 Goals	(40)
55	16/12/87	Morton	Away	League	7–1	3 Goals	(43)
56	19/12/87	Heart of Midlothian	Home	League	0–0		
57	26/12/87	Rangers	Away	League	0–2		
58	01/01/88	Dunfermline Athletic	Home	League	2–0	2 Goals	(45)
59	06/01/88	Rangers	Home	League	0–1		
60	09/01/88	Motherwell	Away	League	3–3	2 Goals	(47)
61	16/01/88	Dundee United	Home	League	0–2		
62	30/01/88	Brechin City	Home	S Cup	0–0		
63	03/02/88	Brechin City	Away	S Cup	3–0		
64	06/02/88	Hibernian	Away	League	1–2		
65	13/02/88	Celtic	Home	League	1–2		
66	20/02/88	Motherwell	Home	S Cup	2–0		
67	27/02/88	Aberdeen	Away	League	0–1		
68	01/03/88	St Mirren	Home	League	2–1	2 Goals	(49)
69	05/03/88	Morton	Home	League	1–0	1 Goal	(50)
70	12/03/88	Dundee United	Home	S Cup	0–0		
71	15/03/88	Dundee United	Away	S Cup	2–2*		
72	26/03/88	Rangers	Home	League	2–3	1 Goal	(51)
73	28/03/88	Dundee United	Neutral	S Cup	0–3		
74	30/03/88	Heart of Midlothian	Away	League	0–2		
75	02/04/88	Dundee United	Away	League	0–1		

76	06/04/88	Motherwell	Home	League	1–2		
77	16/04/88	Falkirk	Home	League	4–2	1 Goal	(52)
78	23/04/88	Celtic	Away	League	0–3		
79	30/04/88	Hibernian	Home	League	0–0		
80	07/05/88	St Mirren	Away	League	0–1		

SEASON 1988–89

Scottish League Premier Division

Sub+1	17/08/88	Queen of the South	Home	S Lge Cup	5–1		
81	20/08/88	Motherwell	Away	League	1–1		
82	23/08/88	Falkirk	Home	S Lge Cup	2–1		
83	27/08/88	St Mirren	Away	League	0–0		
84	31/08/88	Rangers	Away	S Lge Cup	1–4		
85	03/09/88	Dundee United	Home	League	0–3		
86	17/09/88	Hamilton Academical	Away	League	0–1		
87	24/09/88	Celtic	Home	League	1–0	1 Goal	(53)
88	28/09/88	Heart of Midlothian	Away	League	1–1		
89	01/10/88	Rangers	Away	League	0–2		
90	08/10/88	Hibernian	Home	League	2–1	1 Goal	(54)
91	12/10/88	Motherwell	Home	League	1–1		
92	29/10/88	Celtic	Away	League	3–2		
93	02/11/88	Hamilton Academical	Home	League	5–2	3 Goals	(57)
94	05/11/88	Dundee United	Away	League	0–2		
95	12/11/88	St Mirren	Home	League	0–1		
96	16/11/88	Aberdeen	Away	League	0–1		
97	19/11/88	Rangers	Home	League	0–0		
98	26/11/88	Hibernian	Away	League	1–1	1 Goal	(58)
99	03/12/88	Heart of Midlothian	Home	League	1–1		
100	10/12/88	Hamilton Academical	Away	League	0–1		
101	17/12/88	Motherwell	Away	League	0–1		
102	31/12/88	Aberdeen	Home	League	2–0	2 Goals	(60)
103	03/01/89	St Mirren	Away	League	1–1		
104	07/01/89	Dundee United	Home	League	0–1		
105	14/01/89	Hibernian	Home	League	1–2		
106	21/01/89	Rangers	Away	League	1–3		
107	28/01/89	Dundee United	Home	S Cup	1–2		
108	11/02/89	Heart of Midlothian	Away	League	1–3	1 Goal	(61)
109	25/02/89	Celtic	Home	League	0–3		

Celtic – Scottish League Premier Division

1	11/03/89	Heart of Midlothian	Away	League	1–0		
Sub+1	25/03/89	Dundee United	Home	League	1–0		
Sub+2	01/04/89	Rangers	Home	League	1–2		
2	08/04/89	Hamilton Academical	Away	League	0–2		
3	12/04/89	Motherwell	Away	League	2–2		
4	22/04/89	Dundee	Home	League	2–1		
Sub+3	13/05/89	St Mirren	Away	League	1–0		

SEASON 1989–90

Scottish League Premier Division

5	12/08/89	Heart of Midlothian	Away	League	3–1	3 Goals	(3)
6	15/08/89	Dumbarton	Away	S Lge Cup	3–0		
7	19/08/89	Dunfermline Athletic	Home	League	1–0		
8	26/08/89	Rangers	Home	League	1–1		
9	30/08/89	Heart of Midlothian	Away	S Lge Cup	2–2+		
10	09/09/89	St Mirren	Away	League	0–1		
11	12/09/89	FK Partizan Beograd	Away	ECW Cup	1–2		
12	16/09/89	Dundee United	Away	League	2–2	1 Goal	(4)
13	20/09/89	Aberdeen	Hampden	S Lge Cup	0–1		
14	23/09/89	Motherwell	Home	League	1–1		
Sub+4	30/09/89	Aberdeen	Away	League	1–1		
Sub+5	14/10/89	Dundee	Away	League	3–1	1 Goal	(5)
Sub+6	21/10/89	Heart of Midlothian	Home	League	2–1	1 Goal	(6)
15	28/10/89	Dunfermline Athletic	Away	League	0–2		
16	04/11/89	Rangers	Away	League	0–1		
Sub+7	26/12/89	Heart of Midlothian	Away	League	0–0		
Sub+8	30/12/89	Dunfermline Athletic	Home	League	0–2		
17	02/01/90	Rangers	Home	League	0–1		
Sub+9	27/01/90	Motherwell	Home	League	0–1		
18	03/02/90	Dundee	Away	League	0–0		
19	10/02/90	Hibernian	Home	League	1–1		
20	17/02/90	Aberdeen	Away	League	1–1		
21	25/02/90	Rangers	Home	S Cup	1–0	1 Goal	(7)

22	03/03/90	Dundee United	Home	League	3–0		
23	10/03/90	Heart of Midlothian	Home	League	1–1	1 Goal	(8)
24	17/03/90	Dunfermline Athletic	Away	S Cup	0–0		
25	21/03/90	Dunfermline Athletic	Home	S Cup	3–0	1 Goal	(9)
26	24/03/90	Dunfermline Athletic	Away	League	0–0		
27	01/04/90	Rangers	Away	League	0–3		
28	07/04/90	St Mirren	Home	League	0–3		
Sub+10	12/05/90	Aberdeen	Hampden	S Cup	0–0#		

+ AET Celtic won 3–1 on penalties
# AET Aberdeen won 9–8 on penalties

SEASON 1990–91

Scottish League Premier Division

29	06/11/90	Motherwell	Home	League	2–1	2 Goals	(11)
30	10/11/90	Heart of Midlothian	Away	League	0–1		
Sub+11	17/11/90	St Mirren	Home	League	4–1	1 Goal	(12)
Sub+12	25/11/90	Rangers	Home	League	1–2		
31	01/12/90	Hibernian	Away	League	3–0	2 Goals	(14)
32	08/12/90	Dundee United	Away	League	1–3	1 Goal	(15)
33	15/12/90	Dunfermline Athletic	Home	League	1–2		
34	22/12/90	St Johnstone	Away	League	2–3	1 Goal	(16)
35	29/12/90	Heart of Midlothian	Home	League	1–1	1 Goal	(17)
36	02/01/91	Rangers	Away	League	0–2		
37	05/01/91	Hibernian	Home	League	1–1	1 Goal	(18)
38	19/01/91	Aberdeen	Home	League	1–0	1 Goal	(19)
39	26/01/91	Forfar Athletic	Away	S Cup	2–0	1 Goal	(20)
40	30/01/91	Motherwell	Away	League	1–1		
41	02/02/91	Dundee United	Home	League	1–0	1 Goal	(21)
42	26/02/91	St Mirren	Home	S Cup	3–0		
43	02/03/91	St Johnstone	Home	League	3–0	1 Goal	(22)
44	06/03/91	Dunfermline Athletic	Away	League	1–0		
45	09/03/91	Hibernian	Away	League	2–0		
46	12/03/91	St Mirren	Away	League	2–0		
47	17/03/91	Rangers	Home	S Cup	2–0		
48	24/03/91	Rangers	Home	League	3–0	1 Goal	(23)
49	30/03/91	Motherwell	Home	League	1–2	1 Goal	(24)
50	03/04/91	Motherwell	Hampden	S Cup	0–0		
51	06/04/91	Aberdeen	Away	League	0–1		
52	09/04/91	Motherwell	Hampden	S Cup	2–4		
53	13/04/91	Dundee United	Away	League	1–2		
54	20/04/91	Dunfermline Athletic	Home	League	5–1	2 Goals	(26)
55	27/04/91	Heart of Midlothian	Away	League	1–0		
56	05/05/91	St Mirren	Home	League	1–0	1 Goal	(27)
57	11/05/91	St Johnstone	Away	League	3–2	1 Goal	(28)

SEASON 1991–92

Scottish League Premier Division

58	10/08/91	Dundee United	Away	League	4–3	1 Goal	(29)
59	13/08/91	Dunfermline Athletic	Away	League	3–1	1 Goal	(30)
60	17/08/91	Falkirk	Home	League	4–1	2 Goals	(32)
61	21/08/91	Morton	Away	S Lge Cup	4–2		
62	24/08/91	Aberdeen	Away	League	0–1		
63	27/08/91	Raith Rovers	Home	S Lge Cup	3–1		
64	31/08/91	Rangers	Home	League	0–2		
Sub+13	18/09/91	KFC Germinal Ekeren	Home	UEFA Cup	2–0		
65	21/09/91	Airdrieonians	Home	League	3–1		
66	28/09/91	Hibernian	Away	League	1–1		
67	01/10/91	KFC Germinal Ekeren	Away	UEFA Cup	1–1		
68	05/10/91	Heart of Midlothian	Home	League	3–1		
69	08/10/91	Motherwell	Away	League	2–0	1 Goal	(33)
70	12/10/91	Dundee United	Home	League	4–1	1 Goal	(34)
71	19/10/91	Falkirk	Away	League	3–4		
72	22/10/91	FC Neuchatel Xamax	Away	UEFA Cup	1–5		
73	26/10/91	St Mirren	Away	League	5–0	2 Goals	(36)
74	30/10/91	St Johnstone	Home	League	4–0	1 Goal	(37)
75	02/11/91	Rangers	Away	League	1–1		
76	06/11/91	FC Neuchatel Xamax	Home	UEFA Cup	1–0		
77	09/11/91	Aberdeen	Home	League	2–1		
78	16/11/91	Heart of Midlothian	Away	League	1–3	1 Goal	(38)
79	20/11/91	Motherwell	Home	League	2–2		
80	23/11/91	Airdrieonians	Away	League	3–0	1 Goal	(39)
81	30/11/91	Dunfermline Athletic	Home	League	1–0	1 Goal	(40)

82	04/12/91	Hibernian	Home	League	0–0		
83	07/12/91	Dundee United	Away	League	1–1		
84	14/12/91	St Mirren	Home	League	4–0		
85	28/12/91	Aberdeen	Away	League	2–2		
86	01/01/92	Rangers	Home	League	1–3		
87	04/01/92	Heart of Midlothian	Home	League	1–2		
88	08/01/92	St Johnstone	Away	League	4–2	1 Goal	(41)
89	11/01/92	Motherwell	Away	League	0–0		
90	18/01/92	Dunfermline Athletic	Away	League	1–0	1 Goal	(42)
91	25/01/92	Montrose	Home	S Cup	6–0	3 Goals	(45)
92	01/02/92	Falkirk	Home	League	2–0	1 Goal	(46)
93	08/02/92	Airdrieonians	Home	League	2–0		
94	11/02/92	Dundee United	Home	S Cup	2–1	1 Goal	(47)
95	29/02/92	Heart of Midlothian	Away	League	2–1		
96	07/03/92	Morton	Home	S Cup	3–0		
97	14/03/92	Aberdeen	Home	League	1–0		
Sub+14	17/03/92	Motherwell	Home	League	4–1		
Sub+15	21/03/92	Rangers	Away	League	2–0		
Sub+16	28/03/92	Dundee United	Home	League	3–1		
Sub+17	31/03/92	Rangers	Hampden	S Cup	0–1		
Sub+18	04/04/92	Falkirk	Away	League	3–0		
Sub+19	08/04/92	St Mirren	Away	League	1–1		
Sub+20	25/04/92	Dunfermline Athletic	Home	League	2–0		
Sub+21	02/05/92	Hibernian	Home	League	1–2		

SEASON 1992–93

Scottish League Premier Division

Sub+22	01/08/92	Heart of Midlothian	Away	League	1–0		
Sub+23	05/08/92	Aberdeen	Away	League	1–1		
Sub+24	08/08/92	Motherwell	Home	League	1–1		
Sub+25	12/08/92	Stirling Albion	Hampden	S Lge Cup	3–0	1 Goal	(48)
Sub+26	15/08/92	Dundee United	Home	League	2–0		
Sub+27	09/01/93	Clyde	Away	S Cup	0–0		
98	20/01/93	Clyde	Home	S Cup	1–0	1 Goal	(49)
99	23/01/93	Airdrieonians	Away	League	1–0	1 Goal	(50)
100	30/01/93	Motherwell	Home	League	1–1		
101	03/02/93	St Johnstone	Home	League	5–1	2 Goals	(52)
102	06/02/93	Falkirk	Away	S Cup	0–2		
103	13/02/93	Aberdeen	Away	League	1–1		
104	20/02/93	Partick Thistle	Home	League	0–0		
Sub+28	23/02/93	Dundee	Away	League	1–0		

Tranmere Rovers – Football League Division One

1	13/03/93	Leicester City	Home	League	2–3		
2	16/03/93	Grimsby Town	Away	League	0–0		
3	20/03/93	West Ham United	Away	League	0–2		
4	23/03/93	Portsmouth	Home	League	0–2		
5	26/03/93	Southend United	Away	League	2–1	1 Goal	(1)
6	02/04/93	Derby County	Home	League	2–1		
7	06/04/93	Swindon Town	Home	League	3–1		
Sub+1	12/04/93	Barnsley	Home	League	2–1		
8	17/04/93	Wolverhampton Wanderers	Away	League	2–0		
9	24/04/93	Birmingham City	Away	League	0–0		
Sub+2	01/05/93	Watford	Home	League	2–1		
Sub+3	04/05/93	Sunderland	Home	League	2–1		
Sub+4	16/05/93	Swindon Town	Away	Lge P/O	1–3		
Sub+5	19/05/93	Swindon Town	Home	Lge P/O	3–2		

SEASON 1993–94

Motherwell – Scottish League Premier Division

1	30/11/93	Partick Thistle	Home	League	1–0		
2	04/12/93	Rangers	Home	League	0–2		
3	11/12/93	Hibernian	Away	League	2–3	2 Goals	(2)
4	15/12/93	Heart of Midlothian	Away	League	3–2	2 Goals	(4)
5	18/12/93	Dundee	Away	League	3–1	1 Goal	(5)
6	01/01/94	Kilmarnock	Away	League	0–0		
7	11/01/94	Celtic	Home	League	2–1		
8	22/01/94	Partick Thistle	Away	League	0–0		
9	25/01/94	Raith Rovers	Home	League	3–1	1 Goal	(6)
10	29/01/94	Celtic	Home	S Cup	1–0	1 Goal	(7)
11	05/02/94	Heart of Midlothian	Home	League	1–1		
12	08/02/94	St Johnstone	Away	League	1–2	1 Goal	(8)
13	12/02/94	Dundee United	Away	League	2–1		

14	19/02/94	Dundee United	Away	S Cup	2–2		
15	01/03/94	Dundee United	Home	S Cup	0–1		
16	05/03/94	Rangers	Away	League	1–2		
17	08/03/94	Aberdeen	Home	League	1–1		
18	12/03/94	Hibernian	Home	League	0–0		
19	19/03/94	Dundee	Home	League	3–1	1 Goal	(9)
20	26/03/94	Celtic	Away	League	1–0		
21	30/03/94	Heart of Midlothian	Away	League	0–0		
22	02/04/94	Partick Thistle	Home	League	2–2	1 Goal	(10)
23	16/04/94	Aberdeen	Away	League	0–0		
24	23/04/94	Hibernian	Away	League	2–0	1 Goal	(11)
25	26/04/94	Rangers	Home	League	2–1	1 Goal	(12)
26	30/04/94	Kilmarnock	Home	League	1–0	1 Goal	(13)
27	03/05/94	Dundee United	Home	League	1–2		
28	07/05/94	Raith Rovers	Away	League	3–3		
29	14/05/94	St Johnstone	Home	League	0–1		

SEASON 1994–95

Scottish League Premier Division

30	09/08/94	Havnar Boltfelag	Home	UEFA Cup	3–0	1 Goal	(14)
31	13/08/94	Rangers	Away	League	1–2	1 Goal	(15)
32	16/08/94	Clydebank	Home	S Lge Cup	3–1	1 Goal	(16)
33	20/08/94	Heart of Midlothian	Home	League	1–1	1 Goal	(17)
34	27/08/94	Kilmarnock	Away	League	1–0	1 Goal	(18)
35	31/08/94	Airdrieonians	Home	S Lge Cup	1–2		
36	10/09/94	Dundee United	Away	League	1–1		
37	13/09/94	BV 09 Borussia Dortmund	Away	UEFA Cup	0–1		
38	17/09/94	Hibernian	Home	League	1–1		
39	24/09/94	Partick Thistle	Away	League	2–2	1 Goal	(19)
40	27/09/94	BV 09 Borussia Dortmund	Home	UEFA Cup	0–2		
41	01/10/94	Celtic	Home	League	1–1		
42	08/10/94	Falkirk	Home	League	5–3	2 Goals	(21)
43	15/10/94	Aberdeen	Away	League	3–1	1 Goal	(22)
44	22/10/94	Rangers	Home	League	2–1		
45	29/10/94	Kilmarnock	Home	League	3–2	2 Goals	(24)
46	05/11/94	Heart of Midlothian	Away	League	2–1	1 Goal	(25)
47	08/11/94	Dundee United	Home	League	1–1		
48	19/11/94	Hibernian	Away	League	2–2	1 Goal	(26)
49	26/11/94	Partick Thistle	Home	League	3–1	1 Goal	(27)
50	03/12/94	Celtic	Away	League	2–2	2 Goals	(29)
51	10/12/94	Aberdeen	Home	League	0–1		
52	26/12/94	Falkirk	Away	League	1–0		
53	31/12/94	Rangers	Away	League	1–3		
54	08/01/95	Heart of Midlothian	Home	League	1–2		
55	13/01/95	Hibernian	Home	League	0–0		
56	17/01/95	Kilmarnock	Away	League	0–2		
57	21/01/95	Dundee United	Away	League	1–6	1 Goal	(30)
58	04/02/95	Celtic	Home	League	1–0		
Sub+1	22/03/95	Hibernian	Away	League	0–2		
59	01/04/95	Celtic	Away	League	1–1	1 Goal	(31)
60	08/04/95	Partick Thistle	Home	League	1–2		
61	15/04/95	Falkirk	Away	League	0–3		
62	18/04/95	Aberdeen	Home	League	2–1		
63	29/04/95	Rangers	Away	League	2–0		
64	06/05/95	Kilmarnock	Home	League	2–0		

SEASON 1995–96

Scottish League Premier Division

65	08/08/95	MyPa 47	Home	UEFA Cup	1–3		
66	19/08/95	Clydebank	Away	S Lge Cup	1–1+		
67	16/09/95	Celtic	Away	League	1–1		
68	20/09/95	Aberdeen	Home	S Lge Cup	1–2*		
69	23/09/95	Falkirk	Away	League	0–0		
70	30/09/95	Kilmarnock	Home	League	3–0	2 Goals	(33)
71	03/10/95	Rangers	Away	League	1–2		
72	07/10/95	Raith Rovers	Home	League	0–2		
73	14/10/95	Aberdeen	Home	League	2–1	1 Goal	(34)
74	21/10/95	Hibernian	Away	League	2–4		
75	28/10/95	Partick Thistle	Away	League	0–1		
Sub+2	24/02/96	Raith Rovers	Home	League	1–0		
Sub+3	02/03/96	Falkirk	Home	League	1–0		
Sub+4	16/03/96	Kilmarnock	Away	League	1–0		
Sub+5	23/03/96	Celtic	Home	League	0–0		

| Sub+6 | 30/03/96 | Partick Thistle | Away | League | 2–0 | | |
| 76 | 06/04/96 | Hibernian | Home | League | 3–0 | 1 Goal | (35) |

+ AET Motherwell won 4–1 on penalties

SEASON 1996–97

Scottish League Premier Division

77	10/08/96	Dundee United	Away	League	1–1		
Sub+7	02/11/96	Dundee United	Home	League	1–3		
78	11/11/96	Heart of Midlothian	Home	League	0–2		
79	16/11/96	Kilmarnock	Away	League	4–2	3 Goals	(38)
80	30/11/96	Hibernian	Away	League	0–2		
81	07/12/96	Celtic	Home	League	2–1		
82	11/12/96	Raith Rovers	Home	League	0–1		
83	14/12/96	Aberdeen	Away	League	0–0		
84	21/12/96	Dunfermline Athletic	Home	League	2–3	1 Goal	(39)
85	26/12/96	Dundee United	Away	League	0–2		
86	28/12/96	Heart of Midlothian	Away	League	1–4	1 Goal	(40)
87	04/01/97	Celtic	Away	League	0–5		
88	11/01/97	Hibernian	Home	League	2–1		
89	18/01/97	Rangers	Home	League	1–3		
90	21/01/97	Kilmarnock	Home	League	2–0		
91	25/01/97	Partick Thistle	Away	S Cup	2–0		
92	01/02/97	Dunfermline Athletic	Away	League	1–3		
93	08/02/97	Aberdeen	Home	League	2–2		
94	15/02/97	Hamilton Academical	Home	S Cup	1–1		
95	18/02/97	Raith Rovers	Away	League	5–1	2 Goals	(42)
96	22/02/97	Celtic	Home	League	0–1		
97	26/02/97	Hamilton Academical	Away	S Cup	2–0		
98	01/03/97	Hibernian	Away	League	1–1	1 Goal	(43)
99	08/03/97	Dundee United	Away	League	1–4		
100	16/03/97	Kilmarnock	Away	League	0–1		
Sub+8	22/03/97	Heart of Midlothian	Home	League	0–1		
Sub+9	05/04/97	Aberdeen	Away	League	0–0		
101	12/04/97	Raith Rovers	Home	League	5–0	2 Goals	(45)
102	19/04/97	Dundee United	Home	League	1–1	1 Goal	(46)
103	05/05/97	Rangers	Away	League	2–0		
104	10/05/97	Dunfermline Athletic	Home	League	2–2		

INTERNATIONAL APPEARANCES – REPUBLIC OF IRELAND

1	25/03/92	Switzerland	Lansdowne Road	2–1	F	1 Goal	(1)
2	29/04/92	USA	Lansdowne Road	4–1	F		
Sub 3	26/05/92	Albania	Lansdowne Road	2–0	WCQ		
Sub 4	30/05/92	USA	Washington	1–3	USC		
Sub 5	04/06/92	Italy	Boston	0–2	USC		
Sub 6	07/06/92	Portugal	Boston	2–0	USC	1 Goal	(2)
Sub 7	09/09/92	Latvia	Lansdowne Road	4–0	WCQ		
Sub 8	17/02/93	Wales	Tolka Park	2–1	F	1 Goal	(3)
9	31/03/93	Northern Ireland	Lansdowne Road	3–0	WCQ		
Sub 10	23/03/94	Russia	Lansdowne Road	0–0	F		
11	20/04/94	Holland	Tilburg	1–0	F	1 Goal	(4)
12	24/05/94	Bolivia	Lansdowne Road	1–0	F		
Sub 13	29/05/94	Germany	Hannover	2–0	F		
Sub 14	05/06/94	Czech Republic	Lansdowne Road	1–3	F		
15	18/06/94	Italy	New York	1–0	WC		
16	24/06/94	Mexico	Florida	1–2	WC		
17	04/07/94	Holland	Orlando	0–2	WC		
18	12/10/95	Liechtenstein	Lansdowne Road	4–0	ECQ	2 Goals	(6)
Sub 19	16/11/95	Northern Ireland	Windsor Park	4–0	ECQ		
20	11/06/95	Austria	Lansdowne Road	1–3	ECQ		
Sub 21	27/03/96	Russia	Lansdowne Road	0–2	F		

APPEARANCES AND GOALS PER SEASON

SEASON 81–82	GAMES	GOALS
Scottish League	29+2	9
Scottish Cup	2	0
TOTAL	**31+2**	**9**

SEASON 82–83	GAMES	GOALS
Scottish League	38	18
Scottish Cup	1	0
Scottish League Cup	6	2
TOTAL	**45**	**20**

SEASON 83–84	GAMES	GOALS
Scottish League	24+5	13
Scottish Cup	1	0
Scottish League Cup	6	2
European Cup	1+1	0
TOTAL	**32+6**	**15**

SEASON 84–85	GAMES	GOALS
Scottish League	17+4	3
Scottish League Cup	0+1	0
UEFA Cup	1	2
TOTAL	**18+5**	**5**

SEASON 85–86	GAMES	GOALS
Scottish League	9+4	2
Scottish Cup	2+1	2
Scottish League Cup	1	0
UEFA Cup	1+1	0
TOTAL	**13+6**	**4**

SEASON 86–87	GAMES	GOALS
Scottish League	24+6	10
Scottish Cup	7	6
UEFA Cup	1+2	1
TOTAL	**32+8**	**17**

SEASON 87–88	GAMES	GOALS
Scottish League	43	33
Scottish Cup	6	0
Scottish League Cup	4	4
TOTAL	**53**	**37**

SEASON 88–89	GAMES	GOALS
Scottish League	30+3	9
Scottish Cup	1	0
Scottish League Cup	2+1	0
TOTAL	**33+4**	**9**

SEASON 89–90	GAMES	GOALS
Scottish League	17+6	7
Scottish Cup	3+1	2
Scottish League Cup	3	0
European Cup Winners Cup	1	0
TOTAL	**24+7**	**9**

SEASON 90–91	GAMES	GOALS
Scottish League	24+2	18
Scottish Cup	5	1
TOTAL	**29+2**	**19**

SEASON 91–92	GAMES	GOALS
Scottish League	32+7	15
Scottish Cup	3+1	4
Scottish League Cup	2	0
UEFA Cup	3+1	0
TOTAL	**40+9**	**19**

SEASON 92–93	GAMES	GOALS
League	9+3	1
League Play–offs	0+2	0
Scottish League	5+5	3
Scottish Cup	2+1	1
Scottish League Cup	0+1	1
TOTAL	**16+12**	**6**

SEASON 93–94	GAMES	GOALS
Scottish League	26	12
Scottish Cup	3	1
TOTAL	**29**	**13**

SEASON 94–95	GAMES	GOALS
Scottish League	30+1	16
Scottish League Cup	2	1
UEFA Cup	3	1
TOTAL	**35+1**	**18**

SEASON 95–96	GAMES	GOALS
Scottish League	9+5	4
Scottish League Cup	2	0
UEFA Cup	1	0
TOTAL	**12+5**	**4**

SEASON 96–97	GAMES	GOALS
Scottish League	25+3	11
Scottish Cup	3	0
TOTAL	**28+3**	**11**

CAREER APPEARANCES AND GOALS

COMPETITION	GAMES	TOTAL	GOALS
League	9+3	12	1
League Play–offs	0+2	2	0
European Cup	1+1	2	0
European Cup Winners Cup	1	1	0
UEFA Cup	10+4	14	4
Scottish League	382+53	435	183
Scottish Cup	39+4	43	17
Scottish League Cup	28+3	31	10
Internationals	10+11	21	6
TOTAL	**480+81**	**561**	**221**

HAT-TRICKS

Clydebank

1	3	Meadowbank Thistle	01/10/83	Away	League	3–1
2	3	Ayr United	08/10/83	Home	League	4–1

Dundee

1	3	Clydebank	25/04/87	Home	League	4–1
2	4	Dunfermline Athletic	29/08/87	Home	League	5–0
3	3	Morton	16/12/87	Away	League	7–1
4	3	Hamilton Academical	02/11/88	Home	League	5–2

Celtic

1	3	Heart of Midlothian	12/08/89	Away	League	3–1
2	3	Montrose	25/01/92	Home	S Cup	6–0

Motherwell

1	3	Kilmarnock	16/11/96	Away	League	4–2

Scottish League: 8
Scottish Cup: 1
TOTAL: 9

HONOURS

Winners medals
None

Runner-up medals
Scottish Premier Division Championship: 94/95
Scottish Cup: 89/90

DAVID CROWN

Born: 16/02/58 – Enfield
Height: 5.10
Weight: 11.04 (92–93)

Clubs
Brentford: **1980–81** – Matches: **51+2** – Goals: **10**
Portsmouth: **1981–82** – Matches: **27+3** – Goals: **2**
Exeter City (loan): **1983** – Matches: **6+1** – Goals: **3**
Reading: **1983–85** – Matches: **99+2** – Goals: **17**
Cambridge United: **1985–87** – Matches: **125** – Goals: **55**
Southend United: **1987–90** – Matches: **132** – Goals: **69**
Gillingham: **1990–93** – Matches: **97+3** – Goals: **47**

SEASON 1980–81

Brentford – League Division Three

1	09/08/80	Charlton Athletic	Home	Lge Cup	3–1	1 Goal	(1)
2	12/08/80	Charlton Athletic	Away	Lge Cup	0–5		
3	16/08/80	Charlton Athletic	Away	League	1–3		
4	18/08/80	Millwall	Home	League	1–0		
5	23/08/80	Reading	Home	League	1–2		
6	30/08/80	Walsall	Away	League	3–2		
7	06/09/80	Portsmouth	Away	League	2–0		
8	13/09/80	Fulham	Home	League	1–3		
9	15/09/80	Barnsley	Home	League	1–1		
10	20/09/80	Blackpool	Away	League	3–0	2 Goals	(3)
11	27/09/80	Hull City	Home	League	2–2		
12	30/09/80	Barnsley	Away	League	1–0		
13	04/10/80	Newport County	Home	League	0–1		
14	08/10/80	Exeter City	Away	League	0–0		
15	11/10/80	Carlisle United	Away	League	2–1		
16	18/10/80	Chester	Home	League	0–1		
17	20/10/80	Gillingham	Home	League	3–3	1 Goal	(4)
18	25/10/80	Burnley	Away	League	0–2		
19	28/10/80	Plymouth Argyle	Away	League	1–0		
20	01/11/80	Oxford United	Home	League	3–0	2 Goals	(6)
21	03/11/80	Exeter City	Home	League	0–1		
22	08/11/80	Chesterfield	Away	League	1–2		
23	11/11/80	Millwall	Away	League	2–2		
24	15/11/80	Charlton Athletic	Home	League	0–1		
25	22/11/80	Addlestone & Weybridge Town	Away	FA Cup	2–2		
26	25/11/80	Addlestone & Weybridge Town	Home	FA Cup	2–0	1 Goal	(7)
27	29/11/80	Huddersfield Town	Away	League	0–3		
28	06/12/80	Swindon Town	Home	League	1–1		
29	13/12/80	Fulham	Away	FA Cup	0–1		
30	20/12/80	Rotherham United	Away	League	1–4		
31	26/12/80	Colchester United	Home	League	2–1		
32	27/12/80	Sheffield United	Away	League	0–0		
33	03/01/81	Burnley	Home	League	0–0		
34	10/01/81	Chester	Away	League	0–0		
35	17/01/81	Huddersfield Town	Home	League	0–0		
36	24/01/81	Walsall	Home	League	4–0		
37	31/01/81	Reading	Away	League	0–0		
38	07/02/81	Fulham	Away	League	1–1		
39	07/03/81	Newport County	Away	League	1–1	1 Goal	(8)
40	14/03/81	Carlisle United	Home	League	1–1		
41	21/03/81	Gillingham	Away	League	0–2		
42	28/03/81	Plymouth Argyle	Home	League	0–1		
Sub+1	11/04/81	Chesterfield	Home	League	3–2		

SEASON 1981–82

League Division Three

43	29/08/81	Fulham	Away	League	2–1		
44	02/09/81	Oxford United	Away	Lge Cup	0–1		
45	05/09/81	Walsall	Home	League	0–0		
46	12/09/81	Portsmouth	Away	League	2–2	1 Goal	(9)
47	15/09/81	Oxford United	Home	Lge Cup	0–2		
48	26/09/81	Doncaster Rovers	Away	League	0–1		
49	29/09/81	Newport County	Away	League	1–0		
50	03/10/81	Carlisle United	Home	League	1–2		
51	10/10/81	Exeter City	Away	League	1–3	1 Goal	(10)
Sub+2	19/10/81	Southend United	Home	League	0–1		

Portsmouth – League Division Three

1	31/10/81	Fulham	Away	League	1–1	
2	03/11/81	Wimbledon	Home	League	1–0	
3	07/11/81	Plymouth Argyle	Away	League	0–0	
4	21/11/81	Millwall	Home	FA Cup	1–1	
5	25/11/81	Millwall	Away	FA Cup	2–3*	
6	28/11/81	Huddersfield Town	Home	League	2–1	
7	05/12/81	Doncaster Rovers	Away	League	0–0	
8	26/12/81	Bristol Rovers	Home	League	0–0	
9	06/01/82	Reading	Away	League	1–2	
10	19/01/82	Chester	Away	League	2–3	
11	23/01/82	Lincoln City	Away	League	1–1	
12	30/01/82	Southend United	Home	League	0–0	
13	06/02/82	Brentford	Away	League	2–2	

14	09/02/82	Oxford United	Home	League	1–1		
15	13/02/82	Chesterfield	Home	League	5–1	1 Goal	(1)
16	20/02/82	Bristol City	Away	League	1–0		
17	23/02/82	Swindon Town	Away	League	0–2		
Sub+1	27/02/82	Burnley	Away	League	0–3		
18	06/03/82	Walsall	Home	League	1–0		
19	09/03/82	Gillingham	Home	League	1–0		
20	13/03/82	Newport County	Away	League	1–1	1 Goal	(2)
21	20/03/82	Fulham	Home	League	1–1		
22	27/03/82	Plymouth Argyle	Home	League	1–0		
23	03/04/82	Carlisle United	Away	League	0–2		
24	06/04/82	Preston North End	Home	League	1–1		
25	12/04/82	Reading	Home	League	3–0		
Sub+2	17/04/82	Doncaster Rovers	Home	League	0–0		
26	18/05/82	Wimbledon	Away	League	2–3		
27	21/05/82	Millwall	Home	League	2–2		

SEASON 1982–83

League Division Three

| Sub+3 | 28/12/82 | Reading | Away | League | 2–1 | | |

Exeter City (loan) – League Division Three

1	26/03/83	Bradford City	Home	League	2–1	1 Goal	(1)
2	01/04/83	Plymouth Argyle	Away	League	0–1		
3	02/04/83	Bristol Rovers	Home	League	0–1		
4	16/04/83	Chesterfield	Away	League	3–1	1 Goal	(2)
5	23/04/83	Brentford	Home	League	1–7		
6	30/04/83	Orient	Away	League	1–5		
Sub+1	02/05/83	Southend United	Home	League	4–3	1 Goal	(3)

SEASON 1983–84

Reading – League Division Four

1	27/08/83	Blackpool	Away	League	0–1		
2	30/08/83	Colchester United	Away	Lge Cup	2–3		
3	03/09/83	Stockport County	Home	League	6–2		
4	07/09/83	Doncaster Rovers	Home	League	3–2		
5	10/09/83	Rochdale	Away	League	1–4	1 Goal	(1)
6	14/09/83	Colchester United	Home	Lge Cup	4–3*		
7	17/09/83	Chesterfield	Home	League	1–1		
8	24/09/83	Chester City	Away	League	1–2		
9	27/09/83	Bristol City	Away	League	1–3		
10	01/10/83	Darlington	Home	League	1–0		
11	09/10/83	Northampton Town	Away	League	2–2		
12	14/10/83	Crewe Alexandra	Home	League	5–0	1 Goal	(2)
13	19/10/83	Mansfield Town	Home	League	4–0		
14	22/10/83	York City	Away	League	2–2	1 Goal	(3)
15	29/10/83	Swindon Town	Home	League	2–2		
16	02/11/83	Peterborough United	Away	League	3–3		
17	05/11/83	Colchester United	Away	League	0–3		
18	12/11/83	Wrexham	Home	League	4–1		
19	19/11/83	Hereford United	Home	FA Cup	2–0		
20	26/11/83	Bury	Away	League	3–2		
21	02/12/83	Halifax Town	Home	League	1–0	1 Goal	(4)
22	10/12/83	Oxford United	Home	FA Cup	1–1		
23	14/12/83	Oxford United	Away	FA Cup	0–2		
24	17/12/83	Hartlepool United	Home	League	5–1		
25	26/12/83	Aldershot	Away	League	0–0		
26	27/12/83	Torquay United	Home	League	2–2		
27	30/12/83	Tranmere Rovers	Away	League	3–2	1 Goal	(5)
28	02/01/84	Hereford United	Home	League	3–1	1 Goal	(6)
29	06/01/84	Stockport County	Away	League	0–3		
30	14/01/84	Blackpool	Home	League	2–0		
31	21/01/84	Chesterfield	Away	League	1–2		
32	28/01/84	Rochdale	Home	League	0–0		
33	04/02/84	Darlington	Away	League	1–1		
34	11/02/84	Chester City	Home	League	1–0		
35	15/02/84	Peterborough United	Home	League	1–1		
36	18/02/84	Swindon Town	Away	League	1–1		
37	20/02/84	Southend United	Away	AM Cup	0–5		
38	25/02/84	York City	Home	League	2–0		
39	03/03/84	Mansfield Town	Away	League	0–2		
40	07/03/84	Colchester United	Home	League	1–0		
41	10/03/84	Wrexham	Away	League	3–0		

42	17/03/84	Northampton Town	Home	League	3–0		
43	23/03/84	Crewe Alexandra	Away	League	1–1	1 Goal	(7)
44	07/04/84	Bristol City	Home	League	2–0		
45	13/04/84	Halifax Town	Away	League	1–0		
46	21/04/84	Aldershot	Home	League	1–0		
47	28/04/84	Bury	Home	League	1–1		
48	01/05/84	Doncaster Rovers	Away	League	3–2		
49	05/05/84	Hereford United	Away	League	1–1		
50	07/05/84	Tranmere Rovers	Home	League	1–0		
51	12/05/84	Hartlepool United	Away	League	3–3		

SEASON 1984–85

League Division Three

52	25/08/84	Rotherham United	Home	League	1–0		
53	29/08/84	Millwall	Home	Lge Cup	1–1		
54	01/09/84	Plymouth Argyle	Away	League	2–1		
55	04/09/84	Millwall	Away	Lge Cup	3–4	2 Goals	(9)
56	08/09/84	Doncaster Rovers	Home	League	1–4		
57	15/09/84	Bristol Rovers	Away	League	0–1		
58	18/09/84	Walsall	Away	League	1–3		
59	22/09/84	Derby County	Home	League	0–0		
60	29/09/84	Hull City	Away	League	0–0		
61	03/10/84	Wigan Athletic	Home	League	0–1		
62	06/10/84	Bolton Wanderers	Home	League	3–1		
63	13/10/84	Preston North End	Away	League	2–0		
64	20/10/84	Burnley	Home	League	5–1	2 Goals	(11)
65	23/10/84	Gillingham	Away	League	1–4	1 Goal	(12)
66	27/10/84	Lincoln City	Away	League	1–5		
67	03/11/84	AFC Bournemouth	Home	League	0–2		
68	07/11/84	Orient	Home	League	1–1		
69	10/11/84	Swansea City	Away	League	2–1		
70	17/11/84	Barry Town	Away	FA Cup	2–1		
71	24/11/84	Cambridge United	Home	League	3–1		
72	01/12/84	York City	Away	League	2–2		
73	08/12/84	Bognor Regis Town	Home	FA Cup	6–2		
74	15/12/84	Bradford City	Home	League	0–3		
75	22/12/84	Bristol City	Home	League	1–0		
76	26/12/84	Newport County	Away	League	2–1		
77	29/12/84	Brentford	Away	League	1–2		
78	01/01/85	Millwall	Home	League	2–2		
79	05/01/85	Barnsley	Away	FA Cup	3–4	1 Goal	(13)
80	19/01/85	Doncaster Rovers	Away	League	4–0	1 Goal	(14)
81	26/01/85	Bristol Rovers	Home	League	3–2		
82	02/02/85	Hull City	Home	League	4–2		
Sub+1	06/02/85	Brentford	Home	FR Trophy	1–3		
83	23/02/85	AFC Bournemouth	Away	League	3–0		
84	26/02/85	Brentford	Away	FR Trophy	0–2		
85	02/03/85	Lincoln City	Home	League	1–1		
86	16/03/85	Preston North End	Home	League	3–0		
87	23/03/85	Bolton Wanderers	Away	League	2–1		
88	26/03/85	Rotherham United	Away	League	0–3		
Sub+2	02/04/85	Newport County	Home	League	0–1		
89	09/04/85	Millwall	Away	League	0–0		
90	13/04/85	Swansea City	Home	League	0–1		
91	17/04/85	Derby County	Away	League	1–4		
92	20/04/85	Cambridge United	Away	League	2–0	2 Goals	(16)
93	24/04/85	Plymouth Argyle	Home	League	1–1		
94	27/04/85	York City	Home	League	1–2		
95	01/05/85	Walsall	Home	League	1–1		
96	04/05/85	Bradford City	Away	League	5–2	1 Goal	(17)
97	06/05/85	Brentford	Home	League	0–0		
98	13/05/85	Wigan Athletic	Away	League	1–1		
99	14/05/85	Gillingham	Home	League	0–2		

SEASON 1985–86

Cambridge United – League Division Four

1	17/08/85	Hartlepool United	Home	League	4–2	
2	20/08/85	Brentford	Home	Lge Cup	1–1	
3	23/08/85	Tranmere Rovers	Away	League	2–6	
4	27/08/85	Southend United	Home	League	1–2	
5	31/08/85	Hereford United	Away	League	0–1	
6	03/09/85	Brentford	Away	Lge Cup	0–2	
7	07/09/85	Aldershot	Home	League	0–2	

8	14/09/85	Port Vale	Away	League	1–4		
9	17/09/85	Colchester United	Away	League	1–4	1 Goal	(1)
10	20/09/85	Exeter City	Home	League	1–1	1 Goal	(2)
11	27/09/85	Halifax Town	Away	League	1–1	1 Goal	(3)
12	02/10/85	Preston North End	Home	League	2–0		
13	05/10/85	Mansfield Town	Home	League	4–2	1 Goal	(4)
14	11/10/85	Scunthorpe United	Away	League	0–0		
15	15/10/85	Wrexham	Away	League	2–6	1 Goal	(5)
16	19/10/85	Orient	Home	League	1–2	1 Goal	(6)
17	26/10/85	Peterborough United	Home	League	3–1	2 Goals	(8)
18	01/11/85	Stockport County	Away	League	1–3		
19	06/11/85	Swindon Town	Away	League	0–1		
20	09/11/85	Burnley	Home	League	0–4		
21	16/11/85	Dagenham	Away	FA Cup	1–2	1 Goal	(9)
22	23/11/85	Crewe Alexandra	Away	League	1–0	1 Goal	(10)
23	30/11/85	Northampton Town	Home	League	2–5	1 Goal	(11)
24	06/12/85	Stockport County	Home	League	1–2		
25	14/12/85	Torquay United	Away	League	1–1		
26	20/12/85	Tranmere Rovers	Home	League	3–2	1 Goal	(12)
27	26/12/85	Chester City	Home	League	3–2		
28	11/01/86	Hereford United	Home	League	4–0	1 Goal	(13)
29	14/01/86	Aldershot	Away	FR Trophy	1–0		
30	21/01/86	Peterborough United	Home	FR Trophy	4–1	2 Goals	(15)
31	25/01/86	Port Vale	Home	League	1–3		
32	01/02/86	Aldershot	Away	League	1–2		
33	04/02/86	Wrexham	Home	League	4–3	2 Goals	(17)
34	08/02/86	Orient	Away	League	1–3		
35	21/02/86	Exeter City	Away	League	0–0		
36	24/02/86	Gillingham	Away	FR Trophy	0–2		
37	08/03/86	Mansfield Town	Away	League	0–2		
38	15/03/86	Scunthorpe United	Home	League	0–1		
39	18/03/86	Preston North End	Away	League	2–1	1 Goal	(18)
40	22/03/86	Peterborough United	Away	League	0–0		
41	28/03/86	Rochdale	Home	League	1–0		
42	31/03/86	Chester City	Away	League	1–1		
43	05/04/86	Swindon Town	Home	League	1–1	1 Goal	(19)
44	08/04/86	Halifax Town	Home	League	4–0	3 Goals	(22)
45	12/04/86	Burnley	Away	League	1–1	1 Goal	(23)
46	19/04/86	Crewe Alexandra	Home	League	1–0	1 Goal	(24)
47	26/04/86	Northampton Town	Away	League	2–0	1 Goal	(25)
48	29/04/86	Colchester United	Home	League	1–3	1 Goal	(26)
49	03/05/86	Torquay United	Home	League	3–0	1 Goal	(27)

SEASON 1986–87

League Division Four

50	23/08/86	Wolverhampton Wanderers	Away	League	2–1		
51	26/08/86	Leyton Orient	Away	Lge Cup	2–2	1 Goal	(28)
52	30/08/86	Halifax Town	Home	League	1–0		
53	02/09/86	Orient	Home	Lge Cup	1–0	1 Goal	(29)
54	06/09/86	Hartlepool United	Away	Lge Cup	2–2		
55	13/09/86	Exeter City	Home	League	2–2	1 Goal	(30)
56	16/09/86	Torquay United	Home	League	3–3		
57	20/09/86	Tranmere Rovers	Away	League	1–1	1 Goal	(31)
58	23/09/86	Wimbledon	Home	Lge Cup	1–1		
59	27/09/86	Lincoln City	Home	League	1–1		
60	30/09/86	Scunthorpe United	Away	League	1–1		
61	03/10/86	Stockport County	Home	League	5–0	1 Goal	(32)
62	07/10/86	Wimbledon	Away	Lge Cup	2–2*		
63	11/10/86	Preston North End	Away	League	0–1		
64	17/10/86	Northampton Town	Home	League	3–4	1 Goal	(33)
65	21/10/86	Aldershot	Away	League	1–4	1 Goal	(34)
66	28/10/86	Ipswich Town	Home	Lge Cup	1–0	1 Goal	(35)
67	31/10/86	Crewe Alexandra	Home	League	0–3		
68	04/11/86	Swansea City	Away	League	0–2		
69	08/11/86	Burnley	Home	League	3–1		
70	15/11/86	Exeter City	Away	FA Cup	1–1	1 Goal	(36)
71	22/11/86	Peterborough United	Home	League	1–1		
72	26/11/86	Tottenham Hotspur	Home	Lge Cup	1–3		
73	29/11/86	Cardiff City	Away	League	0–3		
74	02/12/86	Fulham	Home	FR Trophy	0–4		
75	07/12/86	Maidstone	Away	FA Cup	0–1		
76	10/12/86	Wrexham	Away	League	1–2		
77	13/12/86	Hereford United	Away	League	3–2	1 Goal	(37)
78	20/12/86	Rochdale	Home	League	3–0		

79	26/12/86	Colchester United	Away	League	2–1	1 Goal	(38)
80	28/12/86	Southend United	Home	League	1–2		
81	04/01/87	Peterborough United	Away	League	1–2		
82	10/01/87	Wolverhampton Wanderers	Home	League	0–0		
83	24/01/87	Hartlepool United	Home	League	3–0	1 Goal	(39)
84	31/01/87	Exeter City	Away	League	1–1		
85	07/02/87	Torquay United	Away	League	0–1		
86	14/02/87	Tranmere Rovers	Home	League	1–1	1 Goal	(40)
87	22/02/87	Lincoln City	Away	League	3–0	1 Goal	(41)
88	28/02/87	Scunthorpe United	Home	League	1–0	1 Goal	(42)
89	03/03/87	Crewe Alexandra	Away	League	0–0		
90	07/03/87	Wrexham	Home	League	1–0		
91	10/03/87	Leyton Orient	Home	League	2–0		
92	14/03/87	Northampton Town	Away	League	0–3		
93	17/03/87	Aldershot	Home	League	0–3		
94	21/03/87	Preston North End	Home	League	2–0		
95	27/03/87	Stockport County	Away	League	2–3		
96	04/04/87	Burnley	Away	League	2–0		
97	11/04/87	Swansea City	Home	League	1–0		
98	14/04/87	Halifax Town	Away	League	0–1		
99	18/04/87	Leyton Orient	Away	League	0–3		
100	21/04/87	Colchester United	Home	League	0–1		
101	25/04/87	Rochdale	Away	League	0–2		
102	01/05/87	Cardiff City	Home	League	2–1	1 Goal	(43)
103	05/05/87	Southend United	Away	League	1–3		
104	09/05/87	Hereford United	Home	League	2–1		

SEASON 1987–88

League Division Four

105	15/08/87	Exeter City	Away	League	0–3		
106	18/08/87	Aldershot	Home	Lge Cup	1–1		
107	22/08/87	Crewe Alexandra	Home	League	4–1	3 Goals	(46)
108	25/08/87	Aldershot	Away	Lge Cup	4–1	2 Goals	(48)
109	29/08/87	Peterborough United	Away	League	0–1		
110	01/09/87	Cardiff City	Home	League	0–0		
111	05/09/87	Torquay United	Away	League	1–0	1 Goal	(49)
112	12/09/87	Scunthorpe United	Home	League	3–3		
113	16/09/87	Hartlepool United	Away	League	1–2	1 Goal	(50)
114	19/09/87	Burnley	Away	League	2–0	1 Goal	(51)
115	22/09/87	Coventry City	Home	Lge Cup	0–1		
116	26/09/87	Halifax Town	Home	League	2–1	2 Goals	(53)
117	29/09/87	Wrexham	Home	League	0–1		
118	03/10/87	Swansea City	Away	League	1–1		
119	06/10/87	Coventry City	Away	Lge Cup	1–2	1 Goal	(54)
120	10/10/87	Newport County	Home	League	4–0	1 Goal	(55)
121	17/10/87	Leyton Orient	Away	League	2–0		
122	20/10/87	Wolverhampton Wanderers	Away	League	0–3		
123	24/10/87	Colchester United	Home	League	0–1		
124	30/10/87	Tranmere Rovers	Away	League	1–0		
125	03/11/87	Hereford United	Home	League	0–1		

Southend United – League Division Three

1	14/11/87	Walsall	Home	FA Cup	0–0		
2	17/11/87	Walsall	Away	FA Cup	1–2		
3	21/11/87	Aldershot	Home	League	0–1		
4	25/11/87	Brighton & Hove Albion	Away	SV Trophy	2–3		
5	28/11/87	York City	Away	League	3–0	1 Goal	(1)
6	11/12/87	Doncaster Rovers	Home	League	4–1	1 Goal	(2)
7	19/12/87	Blackpool	Away	League	1–1	1 Goal	(3)
8	26/12/87	Brighton & Hove Albion	Away	League	0–0		
9	28/12/87	Bristol Rovers	Home	League	4–2	1 Goal	(4)
10	01/01/88	Gillingham	Home	League	1–3	1 Goal	(5)
11	02/01/88	Brentford	Away	League	0–1		
12	09/01/88	Chester City	Away	League	1–1	1 Goal	(6)
13	15/01/88	Mansfield Town	Home	League	2–1	1 Goal	(7)
14	20/01/88	Brighton & Hove Albion	Away	SV Trophy	2–4		
15	22/01/88	Port Vale	Home	League	3–3	2 Goals	(9)
16	30/01/88	Preston North End	Away	League	1–1		
17	05/02/88	Notts County	Home	League	1–2		
18	13/02/88	Bristol Rovers	Away	League	0–0		
19	20/02/88	Bury	Home	League	1–0	1 Goal	(10)
20	26/02/88	Grimsby Town	Home	League	0–0		
21	02/03/88	Northampton Town	Away	League	0–4		
22	05/03/88	Rotherham United	Away	League	1–1		

23	11/03/88	Bristol City	Home	League	2–0	1 Goal	(11)
24	19/03/88	Walsall	Away	League	1–2	1 Goal	(12)
25	25/03/88	Chesterfield	Home	League	3–0		
26	01/04/88	Wigan Athletic	Home	League	3–2	1 Goal	(13)
27	04/04/88	Aldershot	Away	League	1–0	1 Goal	(14)
28	09/04/88	Sunderland	Home	League	1–4	1 Goal	(15)
29	23/04/88	Fulham	Away	League	1–3		
30	29/04/88	York City	Home	League	3–1	1 Goal	(16)
31	02/05/88	Doncaster Rovers	Away	League	1–0		
32	07/05/88	Blackpool	Home	League	4–0	1 Goal	(17)

SEASON 1988–89

League Division Three

33	27/08/88	Bolton Wanderers	Home	League	2–0	1 Goal	(18)
34	30/08/88	Brighton & Hove Albion	Home	Lge Cup	2–0	1 Goal	(19)
35	03/09/88	Fulham	Away	League	0–1		
36	07/09/88	Brighton & Hove Albion	Away	Lge Cup	1–0		
37	09/09/88	Swansea City	Home	League	0–2		
38	17/09/88	Aldershot	Away	League	2–2	1 Goal	(20)
39	21/09/88	Reading	Away	League	0–4		
40	23/09/88	Cardiff City	Home	League	0–0		
41	28/09/88	Derby County	Away	Lge Cup	0–1		
42	01/10/88	Preston North End	Away	League	2–3	1 Goal	(21)
43	04/10/88	Mansfield Town	Home	League	1–1		
44	09/10/88	Brentford	Away	League	0–4		
45	11/10/88	Derby County	Home	Lge Cup	1–2		
46	15/10/88	Gillingham	Home	League	2–1	1 Goal	(22)
47	22/10/88	Chesterfield	Home	League	3–1	2 Goals	(24)
48	25/10/88	Bury	Away	League	1–3	1 Goal	(25)
49	28/10/88	Wigan Athletic	Home	League	1–2		
50	05/11/88	Wolverhampton Wanderers	Away	League	0–3		
51	08/11/88	Bristol Rovers	Home	League	2–2	2 Goals	(27)
52	12/11/88	Notts County	Away	League	1–1	1 Goal	(28)
53	19/11/88	Bristol City	Away	FA Cup	1–3		
54	22/11/88	Lincoln City	Home	SV Trophy	2–1	2 Goals	(30)
55	26/11/88	Chester City	Away	League	4–2	1 Goal	(31)
56	02/12/88	Port Vale	Home	League	1–1		
57	10/12/88	Wigan Athletic	Away	League	0–3		
58	17/12/88	Sheffield United	Away	League	2–1		
59	31/12/88	Bristol City	Home	League	1–2		
60	02/01/89	Huddersfield Town	Away	League	2–3	1 Goal	(32)
61	13/01/89	Fulham	Home	League	0–0		
62	17/01/89	Northampton Town	Away	SV Trophy	1–2*	1 Goal	(33)
63	21/01/89	Swansea City	Away	League	0–2		
64	28/01/89	Aldershot	Home	League	1–1	1 Goal	(34)
65	03/02/89	Preston North End	Home	League	2–1	1 Goal	(35)
66	11/02/89	Mansfield Town	Away	League	0–4		
67	25/02/89	Gillingham	Away	League	1–1	1 Goal	(36)
68	28/02/89	Bury	Home	League	1–1	1 Goal	(37)
69	04/03/89	Chesterfield	Away	League	1–2		
70	10/03/89	Wolverhampton Wanderers	Home	League	3–1	2 Goals	(39)
71	18/03/89	Bolton Wanderers	Away	League	0–0		
72	25/03/89	Huddersfield Town	Home	League	2–4	2 Goals	(41)
73	27/03/89	Northampton Town	Away	League	2–2	1 Goal	(42)
74	31/03/89	Sheffield United	Home	League	2–1		
75	04/04/89	Blackpool	Home	League	2–1		
76	08/04/89	Bristol City	Away	League	2–0		
77	14/04/89	Reading	Home	League	2–1	2 Goals	(44)
78	18/04/89	Brentford	Home	League	1–1		
79	28/04/89	Notts County	Home	League	1–1	1 Goal	(45)
80	01/05/89	Bristol Rovers	Away	League	1–1		
81	06/05/89	Port Vale	Away	League	0–2		
82	09/05/89	Blackpool	Away	League	2–3	1 Goal	(46)
83	13/05/89	Chester City	Home	League	1–0		

SEASON 1989–90

League Division Four

84	19/08/89	York City	Home	League	2–0	1 Goal	(47)
85	22/08/89	Colchester United	Away	Lge Cup	4–3	2 Goals	(49)
86	26/08/89	Wrexham	Away	League	3–3	1 Goal	(50)
87	29/08/89	Colchester United	Home	Lge Cup	2–1	1 Goal	(51)
88	01/09/89	Hartlepool United	Home	League	3–0		
89	09/09/89	Aldershot	Away	League	5–0	2 Goals	(53)

90	15/09/89	Torquay United	Home	League	1–0		
91	20/09/89	Tottenham Hotspur	Away	Lge Cup	0–1		
92	22/09/89	Doncaster Rovers	Away	League	1–0	1 Goal	(54)
93	26/09/89	Gillingham	Away	League	0–5		
94	30/09/89	Lincoln City	Home	League	2–0		
95	04/10/89	Tottenham Hotspur	Home	Lge Cup	3–2*		
96	07/10/89	Scarborough	Home	League	1–0	1 Goal	(55)
97	14/10/89	Hereford United	Away	League	3–0	2 Goals	(57)
98	16/10/89	Stockport County	Away	League	0–1		
99	21/10/89	Maidstone United	Home	League	0–1		
100	28/10/89	Chesterfield	Away	League	1–1	1 Goal	(58)
101	31/10/89	Burnley	Home	League	3–2	1 Goal	(59)
102	04/11/89	Peterborough United	Home	League	0–0		
103	07/11/89	Gillingham	Home	LD Cup	1–0		
104	10/11/89	Halifax Town	Away	League	2–1		
105	18/11/89	Aylesbury United	Away	FA Cup	0–1		
106	24/11/89	Cambridge United	Home	League	0–0		
107	02/12/89	Scunthorpe United	Away	League	1–1		
108	30/12/89	Exeter City	Home	League	1–2		
109	01/01/90	Rochdale	Away	League	1–0		
110	06/01/90	Carlisle United	Away	League	0–3		
111	12/01/90	Wrexham	Home	League	2–1	1 Goal	(60)
112	17/01/90	Northampton Town	Home	LD Cup	2–1	1 Goal	(61)
113	20/01/90	York City	Away	League	1–2	1 Goal	(62)
114	27/01/90	Aldershot	Home	League	5–0	3 Goals	(65)
115	30/01/90	Walsall	Away	LD Cup	1–4		
116	02/02/90	Doncaster Rovers	Home	League	2–0		
117	06/02/90	Torquay United	Away	League	0–3		
118	13/02/90	Hartlepool United	Away	League	1–1		
119	16/02/90	Scunthorpe United	Home	League	0–0		
120	25/02/90	Cambridge United	Away	League	1–2	1 Goal	(66)
121	03/03/90	Carlisle United	Home	League	2–0		
122	09/03/90	Gillingham	Home	League	2–0		
123	17/03/90	Scarborough	Away	League	1–1		
124	20/03/90	Hereford United	Home	League	2–0		
125	23/03/90	Stockport County	Home	League	2–0		
126	31/03/90	Maidstone United	Away	League	0–3		
127	14/04/90	Rochdale	Home	League	3–2		
128	16/04/90	Colchester United	Away	League	2–0		
129	20/04/90	Grimsby Town	Home	League	0–2		
130	25/04/90	Exeter City	Away	League	1–2	1 Goal	(67)
131	27/04/90	Halifax Town	Home	League	2–0		
132	05/05/90	Peterborough United	Away	League	2–1	2 Goals	(69)

SEASON 1990–91

Gillingham – League Division Four

Sub+1	22/09/90	Maidstone United	Home	League	0–2		
1	20/10/90	Blackpool	Away	League	0–2		
2	23/10/90	Aldershot	Home	League	1–1		
3	27/10/90	Wrexham	Home	League	2–3		
4	03/11/90	Doncaster Rovers	Away	League	1–1		
5	06/11/90	AFC Bournemouth	Away	LD Cup	0–0		
6	09/11/90	Halifax Town	Away	League	2–1	1 Goal	(1)
7	17/11/90	AFC Bournemouth	Away	FA Cup	1–2	1 Goal	(2)
8	24/11/90	Cardiff City	Home	League	4–0	1 Goal	(3)
9	27/11/90	Maidstone United	Home	LD Cup	4–1	1 Goal	(4)
10	01/12/90	Chesterfield	Away	League	1–1		
11	15/12/90	Burnley	Home	League	3–2	3 Goals	(7)
12	22/12/90	Lincoln City	Away	League	1–1		
13	26/12/90	Walsall	Home	League	1–0		
14	29/12/90	Northampton Town	Home	League	0–0		
15	01/01/91	Stockport County	Away	League	1–1		
16	08/01/91	Hereford United	Home	LD Cup	0–1		
17	11/01/91	Torquay United	Home	League	2–2	1 Goal	(8)
18	25/01/91	Scarborough	Home	League	1–1		
19	29/01/91	Darlington	Away	League	1–1	1 Goal	(9)
20	02/02/91	Hereford United	Home	League	2–1		
21	15/02/91	Cardiff City	Away	League	0–2		
22	22/02/91	Halifax Town	Home	League	1–0	1 Goal	(10)
23	26/02/91	Peterborough United	Home	League	2–3		
24	02/03/91	Chesterfield	Home	League	0–1		
25	09/03/91	Burnley	Away	League	2–2	1 Goal	(11)
26	12/03/91	Carlisle United	Away	League	4–0	1 Goal	(12)
27	16/03/91	York City	Home	League	0–0		

28	19/03/91	Scunthorpe United	Home	League	1–1		
29	23/03/91	Rochdale	Away	League	3–1	1 Goal	(13)
30	30/03/91	Walsall	Away	League	0–0		
31	01/04/91	Lincoln City	Home	League	2–2	1 Goal	(14)
32	04/05/91	Wrexham	Away	League	0–3		
33	11/05/91	Doncaster Rovers	Home	League	2–0		

SEASON 1991–92

League Division Four

34	17/08/91	Scunthorpe United	Home	League	4–0	1 Goal	(15)
35	20/08/91	Portsmouth	Away	Lge Cup	1–2		
36	24/08/91	York City	Away	League	1–1	1 Goal	(16)
37	27/08/91	Portsmouth	Home	Lge Cup	3–4	1 Goal	(17)
38	04/09/91	Hereford United	Away	League	0–2		
Sub+2	17/09/91	Blackpool	Away	League	0–2		
39	21/09/91	Barnet	Home	League	3–3	2 Goals	(19)
40	28/09/91	Crewe Alexandra	Away	League	1–2		
41	05/10/91	Chesterfield	Home	League	0–1		
42	12/10/91	Halifax Town	Away	League	3–0	2 Goals	(21)
43	19/10/91	Doncaster Rovers	Away	League	1–1		
44	26/10/91	Northampton Town	Home	League	3–1	3 Goals	(24)
45	02/11/91	Carlisle United	Away	League	0–0		
46	05/11/91	Cardiff City	Home	League	0–0		
47	09/11/91	Maidstone United	Home	League	1–1		
48	18/11/91	Brentford	Away	FA Cup	3–3		
49	23/11/91	Mansfield Town	Away	League	3–4	1 Goal	(25)
50	26/11/91	Brentford	Home	FA Cup	1–3		
51	10/12/91	Maidstone United	Home	A Trophy	4–2	1 Goal	(26)
52	14/12/91	Rotherham United	Away	League	1–1	1 Goal	(27)
53	21/12/91	York City	Home	League	1–1	1 Goal	(28)
54	26/12/91	Scunthorpe United	Away	League	0–2		
55	01/01/92	Hereford United	Home	League	2–1		
56	04/01/92	Lincoln City	Away	League	0–1		
57	11/01/92	Walsall	Home	League	4–0	3 Goals	(31)
58	14/01/92	Fulham	Away	A Trophy	0–2		
59	18/01/92	Burnley	Away	League	1–4		
60	15/02/92	Rotherham United	Home	League	5–1	1 Goal	(32)
61	22/02/92	Walsall	Away	League	1–0		
62	29/02/92	Lincoln City	Home	League	1–3		
63	03/03/92	Burnley	Home	League	3–0	1 Goal	(33)
64	07/03/92	Rochdale	Away	League	1–2	1 Goal	(34)
65	10/03/92	Cardiff City	Away	League	3–2	1 Goal	(35)
66	14/03/92	Carlisle United	Home	League	1–2	1 Goal	(36)
67	17/03/92	Rochdale	Home	League	0–0		
68	21/03/92	Maidstone United	Away	League	1–1		
69	28/03/92	Mansfield Town	Home	League	2–0		
70	31/03/92	Wrexham	Home	League	2–1		
71	04/04/92	Scarborough	Away	League	1–2	1 Goal	(37)
72	11/04/92	Blackpool	Home	League	3–2	1 Goal	(38)
73	18/04/92	Barnet	Away	League	0–2		
74	20/04/92	Crewe Alexandra	Home	League	0–1		

SEASON 1992–93

Football League Division Three

75	18/08/92	Northampton Town	Home	Lge Cup	2–1	1 Goal	(39)
76	22/08/92	Bury	Away	League	0–1		
77	29/08/92	Barnet	Home	League	1–1	1 Goal	(40)
78	01/09/92	Wrexham	Home	League	4–1		
79	05/09/92	Scarborough	Away	League	1–1		
80	09/09/92	Northampton Town	Away	Lge Cup	2–0	1 Goal	(41)
81	24/10/92	Halifax Town	Away	League	0–2		
82	31/10/92	Torquay United	Home	League	0–2		
83	14/11/92	Kettering Town	Home	FA Cup	3–2	1 Goal	(42)
84	21/11/92	Darlington	Home	League	3–1	1 Goal	(43)
85	28/11/92	Lincoln City	Away	League	1–1		
86	05/12/92	Colchester United	Home	FA Cup	1–1	1 Goal	(44)
87	12/12/92	Shrewsbury Town	Away	League	1–2		
Sub+3	27/02/93	Doncaster Rovers	Home	League	1–1	1 Goal	(45)
88	02/03/93	Barnet	Away	League	0–2		
89	06/03/93	Crewe Alexandra	Away	League	1–3		
90	09/03/93	York City	Away	League	1–1		
91	13/03/93	Carlisle United	Home	League	1–0		
92	20/03/93	Hereford United	Away	League	1–3	1 Goal	(46)

93	23/03/93	Lincoln City	Home	League	3–1		
94	06/04/93	Shrewsbury Town	Home	League	1–0	1 Goal	(47)
95	12/04/93	Scunthorpe United	Home	League	1–1		
96	16/04/93	Colchester United	Away	League	0–3		
97	01/05/93	Halifax Town	Home	League	2–0		

APPEARANCES AND GOALS PER SEASON

SEASON 80–81	GAMES	GOALS
League	37+1	6
FA Cup	3	1
League Cup	2	1
TOTAL	**42+1**	**8**

SEASON 81–82	GAMES	GOALS
League	32+3	4
FA Cup	2	0
League Cup	2	0
TOTAL	**36+3**	**4**

SEASON 82–83	GAMES	GOALS
League	6+2	3
TOTAL	**6+2**	**3**

SEASON 83–84	GAMES	GOALS
League	45	7
FA Cup	3	0
League Cup	2	0
Associate Members Cup	1	0
TOTAL	**51**	**7**

SEASON 84–85	GAMES	GOALS
League	42+1	7
FA Cup	3	1
League Cup	2	2
Freight Rover Trophy	1+1	0
TOTAL	**48+2**	**10**

SEASON 85–86	GAMES	GOALS
League	43	24
FA Cup	1	1
League Cup	2	0
Freight Rover Trophy	3	2
TOTAL	**49**	**27**

SEASON 86–87	GAMES	GOALS
League	46	12
FA Cup	2	1
League Cup	6	3
Freight Rover Trophy	1	0
TOTAL	**55**	**16**

SEASON 87–88	GAMES	GOALS
League	45	26
FA Cup	2	0
League Cup	4	3
Sherpa Van Trophy	2	0
TOTAL	**53**	**29**

SEASON 88–89	GAMES	GOALS
League	44	25
FA Cup	1	0
League Cup	4	1
Sherpa Van Trophy	2	3
TOTAL	**51**	**29**

SEASON 89–90	GAMES	GOALS
League	41	19
FA Cup	1	0
League Cup	4	3
Leyland Daf Cup	3	1
TOTAL	**49**	**23**

SEASON 90–91	GAMES	GOALS
League	29+1	12
FA Cup	1	1
Leyland Daf Cup	3	1
TOTAL	**33+1**	**14**

SEASON 91–92	GAMES	GOALS
League	35+1	22
FA Cup	2	0
League Cup	2	1
Autoglass Trophy	2	1
TOTAL	**41+1**	**24**

SEASON 92–93	GAMES	GOALS
League	19+1	5
FA Cup	2	2
League Cup	2	2
TOTAL	**23+1**	**9**

CAREER APPEARANCES AND GOALS

COMPETITION	GAMES	TOTAL	GOALS
League	464+10	474	172
FA Cup	23	23	7
League Cup	32	32	16
Associate Members Cup	1	1	0
Freight Rover Trophy	5+1	6	2
Sherpa Van Trophy	4	4	3
Leyland Daf Cup	6	6	2
Autoglass Trophy	2	2	1
TOTAL	**537+11**	**548**	**203**

HAT-TRICKS

Cambridge United

1	3	Halifax Town	08/04/86	Home	League	4–0
2	3	Crewe Alexandra	22/08/87	Home	League	4–1

Southend United

1	3	Aldershot	27/01/90	Home	League	5–0

Gillingham

1	3	Burnley	15/12/90	Home	League	3–2
2	3	Northampton Town	26/10/91	Home	League	3–1
3	3	Walsall	11/01/92	Home	League	4–0

League: 6
TOTAL: 6

HONOURS

Winners medals
None

Runner-up medals
Promoted to League Division Two: 82/83*
Promoted to League Division Three: 83/84, 89/90

* Played one (0+1/0) League game in the Portsmouth team that won the League Division Three Championship.

GORDON DAVIES

Born: 03/08/55 – Merthyr Tydfil
Height: 5.7
Weight: 10.06 (91–92)

Clubs
Fulham: **1978–84** – Matches: **293+3** – Goals: **128**
Chelsea: **1984–85** – Matches: **13+2** – Goals: **6**
Manchester City: **1985–86** – Matches: **42** – Goals: **15**
Fulham: **1986–91** – Matches: **138+30** – Goals: **52**

Wrexham: **1991–92** – Matches: **26+3** – Goals: **5**
Tornado FK: **1992** – Matches: **12** – Goals: **1**

Country
Wales: **1979–86** – Matches: **14+4** – Goals: **2**

SEASON 1977–78

Fulham – League Division Two

Sub+1	27/03/78	Mansfield Town	Home	League	0–2		
1	18/04/78	Blackpool	Home	League	2–1	1 Goal	(1)
2	22/04/78	Millwall	Home	League	0–1		
3	25/04/78	Burnley	Home	League	0–2		
4	29/04/78	Bolton Wanderers	Home	League	0–0		

SEASON 1978–79

League Division Two

5	05/08/78	Cardiff City	Away	AS Cup	0–1		
6	08/08/78	Bristol Rovers	Home	AS Cup	2–1		
7	12/08/78	Bristol City	Home	AS Cup	0–3		
8	19/08/78	Bristol Rovers	Away	League	1–3		
9	22/08/78	Wrexham	Home	League	0–1		
10	26/08/78	Burnley	Home	League	0–0		
11	29/08/78	Darlington	Home	Lge Cup	2–2	1 Goal	(2)
12	02/09/78	West Ham United	Away	League	1–0		
13	05/09/78	Darlington	Away	Lge Cup	0–1		
14	09/09/78	Sheffield United	Home	League	2–0		
15	16/09/78	Sunderland	Away	League	1–1		
16	23/09/78	Millwall	Home	League	1–0		
17	30/09/78	Oldham Athletic	Away	League	2–0	1 Goal	(3)
18	07/10/78	Stoke City	Home	League	2–0		
19	14/10/78	Brighton & Hove Albion	Away	League	0–3		
20	21/10/78	Preston North End	Home	League	5–3	1 Goal	(4)
21	28/10/78	Crystal Palace	Away	League	1–0		
22	25/11/78	Charlton Athletic	Away	League	0–0		
23	02/12/78	Notts County	Home	League	1–1		
24	16/12/78	Newcastle United	Home	League	1–3		
25	23/12/78	Cardiff City	Away	League	0–2		
26	26/12/78	Cambridge United	Home	League	5–1	1 Goal	(5)
27	30/12/78	Luton Town	Home	League	1–0		
28	06/01/79	Queens Park Rangers	Home	FA Cup	2–0	1 Goal	(6)
29	20/01/79	Sunderland	Home	League	2–2	1 Goal	(7)
30	27/01/79	Manchester United	Away	FA Cup	1–1		
31	06/02/79	Sheffield United	Away	League	1–1		
32	10/02/79	Oldham Athletic	Home	League	1–0	1 Goal	(8)
33	12/02/79	Manchester United	Away	FA Cup	0–1		
34	31/03/79	Charlton Athletic	Home	League	3–1	1 Goal	(9)
35	04/04/79	Stoke City	Away	League	0–2		
36	07/04/79	Notts County	Away	League	1–1		
37	11/04/79	Cardiff City	Home	League	2–2		
38	14/04/79	Cambridge United	Away	League	0–1		
39	16/04/79	Orient	Home	League	2–2	1 Goal	(10)
40	21/04/79	Newcastle United	Away	League	0–0		
41	24/04/79	Millwall	Away	League	0–0		
42	28/04/79	Leicester City	Home	League	3–0	2 Goals	(12)
43	05/05/79	Luton Town	Away	League	0–2		
44	09/05/79	Blackburn Rovers	Away	League	1–2		

SEASON 1979–80

League Division Two

45	11/08/79	Bristol City	Away	AS Cup	0–1		
46	18/08/79	Birmingham City	Away	League	4–3	3 Goals	(15)
47	22/08/79	Orient	Home	League	0–0		
48	25/08/79	Sunderland	Away	League	1–2		
49	29/08/79	West Bromwich Albion	Away	Lge Cup	1–1	1 Goal	(16)
50	01/09/79	Preston North End	Home	League	1–0		
51	05/09/79	West Bromwich Albion	Home	Lge Cup	0–1		
52	08/09/79	Queens Park Rangers	Away	League	0–3		
53	15/09/79	Burnley	Home	League	3–1	2 Goals	(18)
54	22/09/79	Leicester City	Away	League	3–3	3 Goals	(21)
55	29/09/79	Luton Town	Home	League	1–3		
56	06/10/79	Wrexham	Home	League	0–2		
57	09/10/79	Orient	Away	League	0–1		

58	13/10/79	Swansea City	Away	League	1–4		
59	20/10/79	Notts County	Home	League	1–3	1 Goal	(22)
60	27/10/79	Chelsea	Away	League	2–0	1 Goal	(23)
61	03/11/79	Birmingham City	Home	League	2–4	1 Goal	(24)
62	10/11/79	West Ham United	Home	League	1–2	1 Goal	(25)
63	17/11/79	Oldham Athletic	Away	League	1–0		
64	24/11/79	Watford	Home	League	0–0		
65	01/12/79	Newcastle United	Away	League	0–2		
66	08/12/79	Shrewsbury Town	Home	League	2–1		
67	15/12/79	Cambridge United	Away	League	0–4		
68	26/12/79	Cardiff City	Away	League	0–1		
69	29/12/79	Sunderland	Home	League	0–1		
70	05/01/80	Blackburn Rovers	Away	FA Cup	1–1		
71	12/01/80	Preston North End	Away	League	2–3	1 Goal	(26)
72	15/01/80	Blackburn Rovers	Home	FA Cup	0–1		
73	19/01/80	Queens Park Rangers	Home	League	0–2		
74	02/02/80	Burnley	Away	League	1–2		
75	23/02/80	Swansea City	Home	League	1–2		
76	26/02/80	Bristol Rovers	Home	League	1–1		
77	01/03/80	Notts County	Away	League	1–1		
78	08/03/80	Chelsea	Home	League	1–2		
79	15/03/80	Wrexham	Away	League	1–1	1 Goal	(27)
80	22/03/80	West Ham United	Away	League	3–2		
81	28/03/80	Oldham Athletic	Home	League	0–1		
82	04/04/80	Bristol Rovers	Away	League	0–1		
83	08/04/80	Charlton Athletic	Away	League	1–0		
84	12/04/80	Newcastle United	Home	League	1–0	1 Goal	(28)
85	15/04/80	Cardiff City	Home	League	2–1		
86	19/04/80	Watford	Away	League	0–4		
87	22/04/80	Charlton Athletic	Home	League	1–0		
88	26/04/80	Cambridge United	Home	League	1–2		

SEASON 1980–81

League Division Three

89	02/08/80	Bristol City	Away	AS Cup	0–2		
90	04/08/80	Notts County	Home	AS Cup	0–1		
91	05/08/80	Orient	Away	AS Cup	2–1	1 Goal	(29)
92	09/08/80	Peterborough United	Away	Lge Cup	2–3		
93	12/08/80	Peterborough United	Home	Lge Cup	1–2	1 Goal	(30)
94	16/08/80	Rotherham United	Away	League	2–2		
95	20/08/80	Colchester United	Home	League	1–0		
96	23/08/80	Swindon Town	Away	League	4–3	2 Goals	(32)
97	29/08/80	Hull City	Home	League	0–0		
98	06/09/80	Blackpool	Home	League	1–2	1 Goal	(33)
99	13/09/80	Brentford	Away	League	3–1	1 Goal	(34)
100	17/09/80	Exeter City	Away	League	0–1		
101	20/09/80	Walsall	Home	League	2–1	1 Goal	(35)
102	27/09/80	Portsmouth	Away	League	0–1		
103	01/10/80	Exeter City	Home	League	0–1		
104	04/10/80	Burnley	Home	League	0–2		
105	07/10/80	Plymouth Argyle	Away	League	1–2		
106	11/10/80	Gillingham	Away	League	0–1		
107	18/10/80	Oxford United	Home	League	0–4		
108	22/10/80	Millwall	Home	League	1–1	1 Goal	(36)
109	25/10/80	Chester	Away	League	1–0	1 Goal	(37)
110	28/10/80	Newport County	Away	League	1–2		
111	01/11/80	Chesterfield	Home	League	1–1		
112	04/11/80	Plymouth Argyle	Home	League	0–0		
113	08/11/80	Carlisle United	Away	League	2–2		
114	11/11/80	Colchester United	Away	League	2–3	1 Goal	(38)
115	15/11/80	Rotherham United	Home	League	1–1		
116	22/11/80	Reading	Away	FA Cup	2–1	1 Goal	(39)
117	06/12/80	Huddersfield Town	Home	League	2–2	2 Goals	(41)
118	13/12/80	Brentford	Home	FA Cup	1–0		
119	20/12/80	Reading	Away	League	0–0		
120	26/12/80	Sheffield United	Home	League	2–1	1 Goal	(42)
121	27/12/80	Charlton Athletic	Away	League	1–1		
122	03/01/81	Bury	Away	FA Cup	0–0		
123	06/01/81	Bury	Home	FA Cup	0–0		
124	10/01/81	Millwall	Away	League	1–3	1 Goal	(43)
125	12/01/81	Bury	Neutral	FA Cup	1–0	1 Goal	(44)
126	16/01/81	Barnsley	Home	League	2–3		
127	24/01/81	Charlton Athletic	Home	FA Cup	1–2	1 Goal	(45)
128	31/01/81	Swindon Town	Home	League	2–0	1 Goal	(46)

129	07/02/81	Brentford	Home	League	1–1		
130	14/02/81	Blackpool	Away	League	2–0		
131	21/02/81	Portsmouth	Home	League	3–0	1 Goal	(47)
132	01/03/81	Walsall	Away	League	2–1		
133	07/03/81	Burnley	Away	League	0–3		
134	14/03/81	Gillingham	Home	League	3–2	2 Goals	(49)
135	17/03/81	Chester	Home	League	0–1		
136	21/03/81	Oxford United	Away	League	0–2		
137	28/03/81	Newport County	Home	League	2–1	1 Goal	(50)
138	04/04/81	Chesterfield	Away	League	0–0		
139	07/04/81	Hull City	Away	League	1–0		
140	11/04/81	Carlisle United	Home	League	2–3		
141	18/04/81	Charlton Athletic	Home	League	1–0		
142	21/04/81	Sheffield United	Away	League	2–1		
143	25/04/81	Reading	Home	League	1–2		
144	02/05/81	Huddersfield Town	Away	League	2–4	1 Goal	(51)

SEASON 1981–82

League Division Three

145	29/08/81	Brentford	Home	League	1–2	1 Goal	(52)
146	01/09/81	AFC Bournemouth	Away	Lge Cup	1–0	1 Goal	(53)
147	05/09/81	Lincoln City	Away	League	1–1		
148	12/09/81	Bristol City	Home	League	2–1	1 Goal	(54)
149	15/09/81	AFC Bournemouth	Home	Lge Cup	2–0		
150	19/09/81	Chesterfield	Away	League	0–3		
151	22/09/81	Wimbledon	Away	League	3–1	1 Goal	(55)
152	26/09/81	Chester	Home	League	2–0		
153	29/09/81	Southend United	Home	League	2–1	1 Goal	(56)
154	03/10/81	Oxford United	Away	League	0–2		
155	07/10/81	Newcastle United	Away	Lge Cup	2–1		
156	10/10/81	Huddersfield Town	Away	League	0–1		
157	17/10/81	Newport County	Home	League	3–1	2 Goals	(58)
158	20/10/81	Exeter City	Home	League	4–1	2 Goals	(60)
159	24/10/81	Burnley	Away	League	2–2	2 Goals	(62)
160	27/10/81	Newcastle United	Home	Lge Cup	2–0		
161	31/10/81	Portsmouth	Home	League	1–1		
162	03/11/81	Plymouth Argyle	Away	League	1–3	1 Goal	(63)
163	07/11/81	Carlisle United	Away	League	2–1	1 Goal	(64)
164	10/11/81	Oldham Athletic	Away	Lge Cup	1–1		
165	14/11/81	Walsall	Home	League	1–1		
166	17/11/81	Oldham Athletic	Home	Lge Cup	3–0		
167	21/11/81	Bristol Rovers	Away	FA Cup	2–1		
168	28/11/81	Millwall	Home	League	0–0		
169	02/12/81	Tottenham Hotspur	Away	Lge Cup	0–1		
170	05/12/81	Bristol Rovers	Away	League	2–1	1 Goal	(65)
171	30/12/81	Swindon Town	Away	League	4–1	2 Goals	(67)
172	02/01/82	Hereford United	Away	FA Cup	0–1		
173	20/01/82	Reading	Away	League	3–0		
174	30/01/82	Chesterfield	Home	League	1–0	1 Goal	(68)
175	09/02/82	Wimbledon	Home	League	4–1		
176	19/02/82	Southend United	Away	League	0–0		
177	23/02/82	Oxford United	Home	League	0–0		
178	27/02/82	Huddersfield Town	Home	League	2–2		
179	07/03/82	Newport County	Away	League	3–1		
180	10/03/82	Exeter City	Away	League	0–1		
181	13/03/82	Burnley	Home	League	1–1	1 Goal	(69)
182	16/03/82	Plymouth Argyle	Home	League	1–3		
183	20/03/82	Portsmouth	Away	League	1–1		
184	27/03/82	Carlisle United	Home	League	4–1	1 Goal	(70)
185	03/04/82	Walsall	Away	League	1–1		
186	06/04/82	Doncaster Rovers	Home	League	3–1	1 Goal	(71)
187	10/04/82	Gillingham	Away	League	0–2		
188	13/04/82	Swindon Town	Home	League	2–0		
189	17/04/82	Bristol Rovers	Home	League	4–2	1 Goal	(72)
190	20/04/82	Preston North End	Away	League	3–1	2 Goals	(74)
191	25/04/82	Millwall	Away	League	3–4		
192	01/05/82	Reading	Home	League	2–2		
193	15/05/82	Preston North End	Home	League	3–0	2 Goals	(76)
194	18/05/82	Lincoln City	Home	League	1–1		

SEASON 1982–83

League Division Two

| 195 | 28/08/82 | Rotherham United | Home | League | 1–1 | 1 Goal | (77) |
| 196 | 01/09/82 | Southend United | Away | Lge Cup | 0–1 | | |

197	04/09/82	Shrewsbury Town	Away	League	1–0		
198	07/09/82	Queens Park Rangers	Home	League	1–1		
199	11/09/82	Bolton Wanderers	Home	League	4–0		
200	14/09/82	Southend United	Home	Lge Cup	4–2	1 Goal	(78)
201	18/09/82	Middlesbrough	Away	League	4–1	2 Goals	(80)
202	25/09/82	Leeds United	Home	League	3–2	2 Goals	(82)
203	28/09/82	Charlton Athletic	Away	League	0–3		
204	02/10/82	Barnsley	Away	League	3–4	1 Goal	(83)
205	05/10/82	Coventry City	Home	Lge Cup	2–2		
206	09/10/82	Blackburn Rovers	Home	League	3–1	1 Goal	(84)
207	16/10/82	Newcastle United	Away	League	4–1	2 Goals	(86)
208	23/10/82	Burnley	Home	League	3–1		
209	13/11/82	Grimsby Town	Away	League	4–0	2 Goals	(88)
210	20/11/82	Wolverhampton Wanderers	Away	League	4–2	2 Goals	(90)
211	27/11/82	Sheffield Wednesday	Home	League	1–0	1 Goal	(91)
212	18/12/82	Carlisle United	Away	League	2–3		
213	27/12/82	Cambridge United	Home	League	1–1		
214	28/12/82	Chelsea	Away	League	0–0		
215	01/01/83	Wolverhampton Wanderers	Home	League	1–3		
216	03/01/83	Shrewsbury Town	Home	League	2–1	1 Goal	(92)
217	08/01/83	Oldham Athletic	Away	FA Cup	2–0		
218	15/01/83	Rotherham United	Away	League	1–0		
219	22/01/83	Middlesbrough	Home	League	1–0		
220	29/01/83	Watford	Away	FA Cup	1–1		
221	01/02/83	Watford	Home	FA Cup	1–2		
222	05/02/83	Bolton Wanderers	Away	League	1–0		
223	19/02/83	Blackburn Rovers	Away	League	0–0		
224	26/02/83	Newcastle United	Home	League	2–2	1 Goal	(93)
225	05/03/83	Burnley	Away	League	0–1		
226	12/03/83	Crystal Palace	Home	League	1–0		
227	19/03/83	Oldham Athletic	Away	League	0–1		
228	26/03/83	Grimsby Town	Home	League	4–0	1 Goal	(94)
229	02/04/83	Chelsea	Home	League	1–1		
230	05/04/83	Cambridge United	Away	League	0–1		
231	09/04/83	Charlton Athletic	Home	League	2–1	1 Goal	(95)
232	16/04/83	Leeds United	Away	League	1–1		
233	19/04/83	Barnsley	Home	League	1–0		
234	23/04/83	Leicester City	Home	League	0–1		
235	30/04/83	Sheffield Wednesday	Away	League	1–2		
236	02/05/83	Queens Park Rangers	Away	League	1–3	1 Goal	(96)
237	07/05/83	Carlisle United	Home	League	2–0		
238	14/05/83	Derby County	Away	League	0–1		

SEASON 1983–84

League Division Two

239	03/09/83	Portsmouth	Home	League	0–2		
240	07/09/83	Manchester City	Away	League	0–0		
241	11/09/83	Crystal Palace	Away	League	1–1		
242	17/09/83	Leeds United	Home	League	2–1		
243	24/09/83	Grimsby Town	Away	League	1–2	1 Goal	(97)
244	27/09/83	Middlesbrough	Home	League	2–1		
245	01/10/83	Swansea City	Home	League	5–0	2 Goals	(99)
246	05/10/83	Doncaster Rovers	Away	Lge Cup	3–1	1 Goal	(100)
247	08/10/83	Chelsea	Home	League	3–5	3 Goals	(103)
248	15/10/83	Carlisle United	Away	League	0–2		
249	22/10/83	Shrewsbury Town	Away	League	0–0		
250	26/10/83	Doncaster Rovers	Home	Lge Cup	3–1	2 Goals	(105)
251	31/10/83	Cardiff City	Home	League	0–2		
252	05/11/83	Newcastle United	Away	League	2–3		
253	08/11/83	Liverpool	Home	Lge Cup	1–1		
254	11/11/83	Sheffield Wednesday	Home	League	1–1	1 Goal	(106)
255	22/11/83	Liverpool	Away	Lge Cup	1–1		
256	26/11/83	Blackburn Rovers	Home	League	0–1		
257	29/11/83	Liverpool	Home	Lge Cup	0–1		
258	03/12/83	Cambridge United	Away	League	1–1		
259	10/12/83	Charlton Athletic	Home	League	0–1		
Sub+2	27/12/83	Brighton & Hove Albion	Away	League	1–1		
260	31/12/83	Portsmouth	Away	League	4–1	2 Goals	(108)
261	02/01/84	Grimsby Town	Home	League	1–1		
262	07/01/84	Tottenham Hotspur	Home	FA Cup	0–0		
263	11/01/84	Tottenham Hotspur	Away	FA Cup	0–2		
264	05/02/84	Swansea City	Away	League	3–0	2 Goals	(110)
265	11/02/84	Crystal Palace	Home	League	1–1	1 Goal	(111)
266	19/02/84	Cardiff City	Away	League	4–0		

267	25/02/84	Shrewsbury Town	Home	League	3–0	1 Goal	(112)
268	03/03/84	Newcastle United	Home	League	2–2	1 Goal	(113)
269	07/03/84	Sheffield Wednesday	Away	League	1–1		
270	17/03/84	Manchester City	Home	League	5–1	4 Goals	(117)
271	24/03/84	Middlesbrough	Away	League	2–0	1 Goal	(118)
272	31/03/84	Carlisle United	Home	League	0–0		
273	07/04/84	Chelsea	Away	League	0–4		
274	14/04/84	Huddersfield Town	Home	League	0–2		
275	21/04/84	Derby County	Away	League	0–1		
276	23/04/84	Brighton & Hove Albion	Home	League	3–1	1 Goal	(119)
277	29/04/84	Blackburn Rovers	Away	League	1–0	1 Goal	(120)
278	05/05/84	Cambridge United	Home	League	1–0		
279	07/05/84	Charlton Athletic	Away	League	4–3	1 Goal	(121)
280	12/05/84	Oldham Athletic	Home	League	3–0	1 Goal	(122)

SEASON 1984–85

League Division Two

281	25/08/84	Shrewsbury Town	Home	League	1–2		
282	27/08/84	Leeds United	Away	League	0–2		
283	01/09/84	Manchester City	Away	League	3–2		
284	04/09/84	Birmingham City	Home	League	0–1		
Sub+3	22/09/84	Middlesbrough	Home	League	2–1		
285	25/09/84	Carlisle United	Home	Lge Cup	2–0		
286	29/09/84	Brighton & Hove Albion	Away	League	0–2		
287	06/10/84	Huddersfield Town	Home	League	2–1	1 Goal	(123)
288	09/10/84	Carlisle United	Away	Lge Cup	2–1	1 Goal	(124)
289	13/10/84	Charlton Athletic	Away	League	2–1	1 Goal	(125)
290	20/10/84	Cardiff City	Home	League	3–2	1 Goal	(126)
291	27/10/84	Crystal Palace	Away	League	2–2	1 Goal	(127)
292	30/10/84	Sheffield Wednesday	Away	Lge Cup	2–3		
293	12/11/84	Wimbledon	Home	League	3–1	1 Goal	(128)

Chelsea – League Division One

1	08/12/84	Sheffield Wednesday	Away	League	1–1	1 Goal	(1)
2	15/12/84	Stoke City	Home	League	1–1		
3	22/12/84	Everton	Away	League	4–3	3 Goals	(4)
4	26/12/84	Queens Park Rangers	Away	League	2–2		
5	29/12/84	Manchester United	Home	League	1–3	1 Goal	(5)
6	01/01/85	Nottingham Forest	Home	League	1–0		
7	05/01/85	Wigan Athletic	Home	FA Cup	2–2		
8	04/02/85	Millwall	Home	FA Cup	2–3		
9	16/02/85	Newcastle United	Home	League	1–0		
10	30/03/85	Sunderland	Away	League	2–0		
Sub+1	10/04/85	Nottingham Forest	Away	League	0–2		
Sub+2	16/04/85	Aston Villa	Home	League	3–1		
11	27/04/85	Tottenham Hotspur	Home	League	1–1		
12	04/05/85	Liverpool	Away	League	3–4	1 Goal	(6)

SEASON 1985–86

League Division One

| 13 | 14/09/85 | Southampton | Home | League | 2–0 | | |

Manchester City – League Division One

1	12/10/85	Watford	Away	League	2–3		
2	14/10/85	Leeds United	Home	FM Cup	6–1	3 Goals	(3)
3	19/10/85	Queens Park Rangers	Away	League	0–0		
4	22/10/85	Sheffield United	Away	FM Cup	2–1		
5	26/10/85	Everton	Home	League	1–1		
6	30/10/85	Arsenal	Home	Lge Cup	1–2	1 Goal	(4)
7	02/11/85	Arsenal	Away	League	0–1		
8	04/11/85	Sunderland	Home	FM Cup	0–0		
9	09/11/85	Ipswich Town	Home	League	1–1		
10	16/11/85	Nottingham Forest	Away	League	2–0		
11	23/11/85	Newcastle United	Home	League	1–0		
12	26/11/85	Hull City	Away	FM Cup	1–2		
13	30/11/85	Luton Town	Away	League	0–2		
14	07/12/85	Leicester City	Away	League	1–1	1 Goal	(5)
15	11/12/85	Hull City	Home	FM Cup	2–0		
16	14/12/85	Coventry City	Home	League	5–1	2 Goals	(7)
17	21/12/85	Sheffield Wednesday	Away	League	2–3		
18	26/12/85	Liverpool	Home	League	1–0		
19	28/12/85	Birmingham City	Home	League	1–1		
20	04/01/86	Walsall	Away	FA Cup	3–1	1 Goal	(8)

21	11/01/86	Southampton	Home	League	1–0		
22	18/01/86	Tottenham Hotspur	Away	League	2–0	1 Goal	(9)
23	25/01/86	Watford	Home	FA Cup	1–1	1 Goal	(10)
24	01/02/86	West Bromwich Albion	Home	League	2–1	1 Goal	(11)
25	03/02/86	Watford	Away	FA Cup	0–0		
26	06/02/86	Watford	Home	FA Cup	1–3		
27	08/02/86	Queens Park Rangers	Home	League	2–0	1 Goal	(12)
28	12/02/86	Everton	Away	League	0–4		
29	01/03/86	Oxford United	Home	League	0–3		
30	08/03/86	Chelsea	Away	League	0–1		
31	15/03/86	Watford	Home	League	0–1		
32	05/04/86	Arsenal	Home	League	0–1		
33	19/04/86	Nottingham Forest	Home	League	1–2	1 Goal	(13)
34	26/04/86	Newcastle United	Away	League	1–3	1 Goal	(14)
35	28/04/86	West Ham United	Away	League	0–1		
36	03/05/86	Luton Town	Home	League	1–1	1 Goal	(15)

SEASON 1986–87

League Division One

37	23/08/86	Wimbledon	Home	League	3–1		
38	25/08/86	Liverpool	Away	League	0–0		
39	30/08/86	Tottenham Hotspur	Away	League	0–1		
40	03/09/86	Norwich City	Home	League	2–2		
41	06/09/86	Coventry City	Home	League	0–1		
42	06/10/86	Southend United	Home	Lge Cup	2–1		

Fulham – League Division Three

1	01/11/86	Doncaster Rovers	Away	League	1–2		
2	04/11/86	Chesterfield	Away	League	1–3	1 Goal	(1)
3	08/11/86	Bristol City	Home	League	0–3		
4	15/11/86	Hereford United	Away	FA Cup	3–3		
5	22/11/86	Carlisle United	Away	League	3–1	1 Goal	(2)
6	24/11/86	Hereford United	Home	FA Cup	4–0	2 Goals	(4)
7	29/11/86	Darlington	Home	League	3–1	1 Goal	(5)
8	06/12/86	Newport County	Home	FA Cup	2–0	1 Goal	(6)
9	13/12/86	Mansfield Town	Home	League	1–1	1 Goal	(7)
10	20/12/86	York City	Away	League	1–1		
11	26/12/86	Gillingham	Home	League	2–2	1 Goal	(8)
12	27/12/86	AFC Bournemouth	Away	League	2–3		
13	01/01/87	Newport County	Home	League	0–0		
Sub+1	10/02/87	Aldershot	Away	FR Trophy	1–1+		
14	17/02/87	Rotherham United	Home	League	1–1		
15	21/02/87	Middlesbrough	Away	League	0–3		
16	28/02/87	Walsall	Home	League	2–2		
17	03/03/87	Doncaster Rovers	Home	League	0–0		
18	07/03/87	Bury	Away	League	1–2		
19	18/03/87	Bristol Rovers	Away	League	0–0		
Sub+2	25/04/87	York City	Home	League	1–0		
Sub+3	28/04/87	Wigan Athletic	Home	League	2–2		
Sub+4	02/05/87	Darlington	Away	League	1–0		
20	04/05/87	AFC Bournemouth	Home	League	1–3		
21	09/05/87	Mansfield Town	Away	League	1–1	1 Goal	(9)

+ AET Aldershot won 11–10 on penalties

SEASON 1987–88

League Division Three

22	15/08/87	Walsall	Away	League	1–0		
23	18/08/87	Colchester United	Home	Lge Cup	3–1	1 Goal	(10)
24	22/08/87	Doncaster Rovers	Home	League	4–0	2 Goals	(12)
25	25/08/87	Colchester United	Away	Lge Cup	2–0	1 Goal	(13)
26	29/08/87	Brighton & Hove Albion	Away	League	0–2		
27	01/09/87	Notts County	Home	League	0–0		
28	04/09/87	Mansfield Town	Away	League	2–0	1 Goal	(14)
29	12/09/87	Gillingham	Home	League	0–2		
30	16/09/87	Chester City	Away	League	2–1		
31	19/09/87	Port Vale	Away	League	1–1		
32	26/09/87	Bristol Rovers	Home	League	3–1	1 Goal	(15)
33	29/09/87	Sunderland	Home	League	0–2		
34	03/10/87	Blackpool	Away	League	1–2		
35	07/10/87	Bradford City	Away	Lge Cup	1–2		

36	10/10/87	York City	Home	League	3–1	1 Goal	(16)
37	17/10/87	Wigan Athletic	Away	League	3–1		
38	20/10/87	Southend United	Away	League	2–0	1 Goal	(17)
39	24/10/87	Aldershot	Home	League	1–2	1 Goal	(18)
40	27/10/87	Brighton & Hove Albion	Home	SV Trophy	1–6	1 Goal	(19)
41	03/11/87	Grimsby Town	Home	League	5–0	1 Goal	(20)
42	07/11/87	Northampton Town	Home	League	0–0		
43	14/11/87	Gillingham	Away	FA Cup	1–2		
44	21/11/87	Rotherham United	Away	League	2–0	1 Goal	(21)
45	28/11/87	Preston North End	Home	League	0–1		
46	12/12/87	Bury	Away	League	1–1		
47	15/12/87	Bristol City	Away	League	0–4		
48	26/12/87	Bristol Rovers	Away	League	1–3		
49	28/12/87	Brentford	Home	League	2–2		
50	01/01/88	Brighton & Hove Albion	Home	League	1–2	1 Goal	(22)
51	09/01/88	Doncaster Rovers	Away	League	2–2	1 Goal	(23)
52	16/01/88	Port Vale	Home	League	1–2		
53	30/01/88	Notts County	Away	League	1–5		
54	06/02/88	Mansfield Town	Home	League	0–0		
Sub+5	14/02/88	Brentford	Away	League	1–3		
55	20/02/88	Walsall	Home	League	2–0	1 Goal	(24)
56	27/02/88	Blackpool	Home	League	3–1		
57	01/03/88	Sunderland	Away	League	0–2		
58	05/03/88	Wigan Athletic	Home	League	3–2		
59	12/03/88	York City	Away	League	3–1	1 Goal	(25)
Sub+6	02/04/88	Northampton Town	Away	League	2–3		
Sub+7	23/04/88	Southend United	Home	League	3–1		
Sub+8	30/04/88	Preston North End	Away	League	1–2		
60	02/05/88	Bury	Home	League	0–1		
61	07/05/88	Chesterfield	Away	League	0–1		

SEASON 1988–89

League Division Three

Sub+9	03/09/88	Southend United	Home	League	1–0	1 Goal	(26)
Sub+10	06/09/88	Brentford	Away	Lge Cup	0–1		
Sub+11	20/09/88	Bolton Wanderers	Away	League	2–3		
Sub+12	24/09/88	Wigan Athletic	Home	League	1–1		
Sub+13	01/10/88	Huddersfield Town	Away	League	0–2		
62	05/10/88	Wolverhampton Wanderers	Home	League	2–2		
Sub+14	05/11/88	Blackpool	Home	League	1–1		
Sub+15	19/11/88	Colchester United	Home	FA Cup	0–1		
63	22/11/88	Brentford	Home	SV Trophy	0–2		
64	10/12/88	Gillingham	Away	SV Trophy	1–2		
65	17/12/88	Preston North End	Home	League	2–1		
66	26/12/88	Gillingham	Away	League	1–0	1 Goal	(27)
67	31/12/88	Chesterfield	Away	League	1–4		
68	02/01/89	Brentford	Home	League	3–3	2 Goals	(29)
69	07/01/89	Chester City	Home	League	4–1	1 Goal	(30)
70	13/01/89	Southend United	Away	League	0–0		
71	21/01/89	Mansfield Town	Home	League	1–1	1 Goal	(31)
72	28/01/89	Bury	Away	League	1–3		
73	04/02/89	Huddersfield Town	Home	League	1–2		
74	11/02/89	Wolverhampton Wanderers	Away	League	2–5	1 Goal	(32)
75	18/02/89	Bristol City	Home	League	3–1	1 Goal	(33)
76	28/02/89	Northampton Town	Away	League	1–2		
77	04/03/89	Swansea City	Home	League	1–0		
78	11/03/89	Blackpool	Away	League	1–0		
79	14/03/89	Notts County	Home	League	2–1	2 Goals	(35)
80	18/03/89	Cardiff City	Home	League	2–0		
81	24/03/89	Brentford	Away	League	1–0		
82	27/03/89	Gillingham	Home	League	1–2		
83	01/04/89	Preston North End	Away	League	4–1	2 Goals	(37)
84	05/04/89	Chester City	Away	League	0–7		
85	08/04/89	Chesterfield	Home	League	2–1		
86	15/04/89	Bolton Wanderers	Home	League	1–1		
87	22/04/89	Wigan Athletic	Away	League	1–0		
88	25/04/89	Aldershot	Away	League	2–1	1 Goal	(38)
89	29/04/89	Sheffield United	Home	League	2–2	1 Goal	(39)
90	01/05/89	Reading	Away	League	1–0		
91	06/05/89	Bristol Rovers	Away	League	0–0		
92	13/05/89	Port Vale	Home	League	1–2		
93	21/05/89	Bristol Rovers	Away	Lge P/O	0–1		
94	25/05/89	Bristol Rovers	Home	Lge P/O	0–4		

SEASON 1989–90

League Division Three

95	19/08/89	Tranmere Rovers	Home	League	1–2		
96	23/08/89	Oxford United	Away	Lge Cup	0–1		
Sub+16	17/10/89	Reading	Away	League	2–3		
97	28/10/89	Brentford	Away	League	0–2		
98	31/10/89	Northampton Town	Home	League	1–1		
Sub+17	13/02/90	Mansfield Town	Away	League	0–3		
99	17/02/90	Notts County	Home	League	5–2	1 Goal	(40)
100	24/02/90	Wigan Athletic	Away	League	1–2	1 Goal	(41)
101	03/03/90	Preston North End	Home	League	3–1	1 Goal	(42)
102	06/03/90	Chester City	Home	League	1–0		
103	10/03/90	Huddersfield Town	Away	League	1–0		
104	17/03/90	Bristol Rovers	Home	League	1–2		
105	20/03/90	Rotherham United	Away	League	1–2		
106	24/03/90	Reading	Home	League	1–2	1 Goal	(43)
107	31/03/90	Bury	Away	League	0–0		
108	04/04/90	Walsall	Home	League	0–0		
109	07/04/90	Northampton Town	Away	League	2–2	1 Goal	(44)
110	10/04/90	Brentford	Home	League	1–0		
111	14/04/90	Birmingham City	Home	League	1–2		
Sub+18	16/04/90	Bristol City	Away	League	1–5		
112	21/04/90	Blackpool	Home	League	0–0		
Sub+19	24/04/90	Shrewsbury Town	Away	League	0–2		
113	28/04/90	Cardiff City	Away	League	3–3	1 Goal	(45)
114	05/05/90	Leyton Orient	Home	League	1–2		

SEASON 1990–91

League Division Three

Sub+20	15/09/90	Huddersfield Town	Home	League	0–0		
Sub+21	18/09/90	Wigan Athletic	Home	League	1–2		
115	22/09/90	Preston North End	Away	League	0–1		
Sub+22	29/09/90	AFC Bournemouth	Away	League	0–3		
Sub+23	02/10/90	Birmingham City	Home	League	2–2		
116	06/10/90	Rotherham United	Home	League	2–0	1 Goal	(46)
117	13/10/90	Stoke City	Away	League	1–2		
118	20/10/90	Swansea City	Away	League	2–2	1 Goal	(47)
119	23/10/90	Bury	Home	League	2–0		
120	27/10/90	Exeter City	Home	League	3–2	2 Goals	(49)
121	04/11/90	Leyton Orient	Away	League	0–1		
122	10/11/90	Southend United	Away	League	1–1		
123	12/11/90	Leyton Orient	Away	LD Cup	2–0		
124	24/11/90	Tranmere Rovers	Home	League	1–2	1 Goal	(50)
125	27/11/90	Brentford	Home	LD Cup	1–1		
126	07/12/90	Cambridge United	Home	FA Cup	0–0		
127	11/12/90	Cambridge United	Away	FA Cup	1–2	1 Goal	(51)
128	15/12/90	Bolton Wanderers	Home	League	0–1		
Sub+24	22/12/90	Mansfield Town	Away	League	1–1		
Sub+25	26/12/90	Bradford City	Home	League	0–0		
129	29/12/90	Chester City	Home	League	4–1		
130	01/01/91	Grimsby Town	Away	League	0–3		
131	19/01/91	Crewe Alexandra	Home	League	2–1	1 Goal	(52)
132	26/01/91	Huddersfield Town	Away	League	0–1		
133	02/02/91	Wigan Athletic	Away	League	0–2		
134	05/02/91	Preston North End	Home	League	1–0		
135	16/02/91	Tranmere Rovers	Away	League	1–1		
136	19/02/91	Mansfield Town	Away	LD Cup	1–2		
137	23/02/91	Southend United	Home	League	0–3		
Sub+26	02/03/91	Reading	Home	League	1–1		
Sub+27	09/03/91	Bolton Wanderers	Away	League	0–3		
Sub+28	12/03/91	Birmingham City	Away	League	0–2		
Sub+29	16/03/91	AFC Bournemouth	Home	League	1–1		
Sub+30	19/03/91	Stoke City	Home	League	0–1		
138	23/03/91	Rotherham United	Away	League	1–3		

SEASON 1991–92

Wrexham – League Division Four

1	17/08/91	Hereford United	Home	League	0–1	
2	20/08/91	Scunthorpe United	Home	Lge Cup	1–0	
3	24/08/91	Walsall	Away	League	0–0	
4	27/08/91	Scunthorpe United	Away	Lge Cup	0–3	
5	30/08/91	Northampton Town	Home	League	2–2	

6	03/09/91	Mansfield Town	Away	League	0–3		
7	07/09/91	Doncaster Rovers	Away	League	1–3		
8	14/09/91	Gillingham	Home	League	2–1		
9	21/09/91	York City	Away	League	2–2		
10	28/09/91	Scunthorpe United	Home	League	4–0	1 Goal	(1)
11	05/10/91	Cardiff City	Away	League	0–5		
12	12/10/91	Burnley	Home	League	2–6	1 Goal	(2)
Sub+1	22/10/91	Peterborough United	Away	A Trophy	0–2		
Sub+2	03/10/91	Bangor City	Home	Welsh Cup	3–2	1 Goal	(3)
13	02/11/91	Barnet	Home	League	1–0		
14	05/11/91	Scarborough	Away	League	1–4		
15	09/11/91	Crewe Alexandra	Away	League	1–2		
Sub+3	19/11/91	Blackpool	Away	League	0–4		
16	23/11/91	Chesterfield	Home	League	0–1		
17	13/12/91	Halifax Town	Away	League	3–4	1 Goal	(4)
18	20/12/91	Walsall	Home	League	2–1		
19	26/12/91	Hereford United	Away	League	1–3	1 Goal	(5)
20	28/12/91	Northampton Town	Away	League	1–1		
21	01/01/92	Mansfield Town	Home	League	3–2		
22	04/01/92	Arsenal	Home	FA Cup	2–1		
23	11/01/92	Maidstone United	Home	League	0–0		
24	18/01/92	Lincoln City	Away	League	0–0		
25	25/01/92	West Ham United	Away	FA Cup	2–2		
26	04/02/92	West Ham United	Home	FA Cup	0–1		

Tornado FK – Norwegian League Division Two

1	26/04/92	Skarbovik	Away	League	1–1		
2	02/05/92	Ullern	Home	League	1–2		
3	06/05/92	Stryn	Away	Nor Cup	2–3		
4	09/05/92	Stranda	Away	League	0–0		
5	16/05/92	Skeid	Home	League	0–4		
6	23/05/92	Grei	Away	League	0–2		
7	30/05/92	Hareid	Home	League	1–3		
8	06/06/92	Stabaek	Away	League	0–7		
9	13/06/92	Andalsnes	Home	League	0–4		
10	27/06/92	Frigg	Away	League	1–1	1 Goal	(1)
11	01/07/92	Volda	Home	League	2–2		
12	04/07/92	Kjelsas	Home	League	2–2		

INTERNATIONAL APPEARANCES – WALES

1	21/11/79	Turkey	Izmir	ECQ	0–1		
2	02/06/80	Iceland	Reykjavik	WCQ	4–0		
Sub 3	24/03/82	Spain	Valencia	F	1–1		
Sub 4	02/06/82	France	Toulouse	F	1–0		
5	23/02/83	England	Wembley	HC	1–2		
6	27/04/83	Bulgaria	Racecourse	ECQ	1–0		
7	28/05/83	Scotland	Ninian Park	HC	0–2		
8	31/05/83	Northern Ireland	Windsor Park	HC	1–0	1 Goal	(1)
9	12/06/83	Brazil	Ninian Park	F	1–1		
Sub 10	12/10/83	Romania	Racecourse	F	5–0		
Sub 11	28/02/84	Scotland	Hampden Park	HC	1–2		
12	02/05/84	England	Racecourse	HC	1–0		
13	22/05/84	Northern Ireland	Vetch Field	HC	1–1		
14	12/09/84	Iceland	Reykjavik	WCQ	0–1		
15	14/11/84	Iceland	Ninian Park	WCQ	2–1		
16	26/02/85	Norway	Racecourse	F	1–1		
17	25/02/86	Saudi Arabia	Dhahran	F	2–1	1 Goal	(2)
18	26/03/86	Republic of Ireland	Lansdowne Road	F	1–0		

APPEARANCES AND GOALS PER SEASON

SEASON 77–78	**GAMES**	**GOALS**
League	4+1	1
TOTAL	**4+1**	**1**

SEASON 78–79	**GAMES**	**GOALS**
League	32	9
FA Cup	3	1
League Cup	2	1
Anglo–Scottish Cup	3	0
TOTAL	**40**	**11**

SEASON 79–80	GAMES	GOALS
League	39	15
FA Cup	2	0
League Cup	2	1
Anglo–Scottish Cup	1	0
TOTAL	**44**	**16**

SEASON 80–81	GAMES	GOALS
League	45	18
FA Cup	6	3
League Cup	2	1
Anglo–Scottish Cup	3	1
TOTAL	**56**	**23**

SEASON 81–82	GAMES	GOALS
League	41	24
FA Cup	2	0
League Cup	7	1
TOTAL	**50**	**25**

SEASON 82–83	GAMES	GOALS
League	38	19
FA Cup	3	0
League Cup	3	1
TOTAL	**44**	**20**

SEASON 83–84	GAMES	GOALS
League	35+1	23
FA Cup	2	0
League Cup	5	3
TOTAL	**42+1**	**26**

SEASON 84–85	GAMES	GOALS
League	20+3	11
FA Cup	2	0
League Cup	3	1
TOTAL	**25+3**	**12**

SEASON 85–86	GAMES	GOALS
League	27	9
FA Cup	4	2
League Cup	1	1
Full Members Cup	5	3
TOTAL	**37**	**15**

SEASON 86–87	GAMES	GOALS
League	23+3	6
FA Cup	3	3
League Cup	1	0
Freight Rover Trophy	0+1	0
TOTAL	**27+4**	**9**

SEASON 87–88	GAMES	GOALS
League	35+4	13
FA Cup	1	0
League Cup	3	2
Sherpa Van Trophy	1	1
TOTAL	**40+4**	**16**

SEASON 88–89	GAMES	GOALS
League	29+5	14
League Play–offs	2	0
FA Cup	0+1	0
League Cup	0+1	0
Sherpa Van Trophy	2	0
TOTAL	**33+7**	**14**

SEASON 89–90	GAMES	GOALS
League	19+4	6
League Cup	1	0
TOTAL	**20+4**	**6**

SEASON 90–91	GAMES	GOALS
League	19+11	6
FA Cup	2	1
Leyland Daf Cup	3	0
TOTAL	**24+11**	**7**

SEASON 91–92	GAMES	GOALS
League	21+1	4
FA Cup	3	0
League Cup	2	0
Autoglass Trophy	0+1	0
Welsh Cup	0+1	1
Norwegian League	11	1
Norwegian Cup	1	0
TOTAL	**38+3**	**6**

CAREER APPEARANCES AND GOALS

COMPETITION	GAMES	TOTAL	GOALS
League	427+33	460	178
League Play–offs	2	2	0
FA Cup	33+1	34	10
League Cup	32+1	33	12
Anglo–Scottish Cup	7	7	1
Full Members Cup	5	5	3
Freight Rover Trophy	0+1	1	0
Sherpa Van Trophy	3	3	1
Leyland Daf Cup	3	3	0
Autoglass Trophy	0+1	1	0
Welsh Cup	0+1	1	1
Norwegian League	11	11	1
Norwegian Cup	1	1	0
Internationals	14+4	18	2
TOTAL	**538+42**	**580**	**209**

HAT-TRICKS

Fulham

1	3	Birmingham City	18/08/79	Away	League	4–3
2	3	Leicester City	22/09/79	Away	League	3–3
3	3	Chelsea	08/10/83	Home	League	3–5
4	4	Manchester City	17/03/84	Home	League	5–1

Chelsea

1	3	Everton	22/12/84	Away	League	4–3

Manchester City

1	3	Leeds United	14/10/85	Home	FM Cup	6–1

League: 5
Full Members Cup: 1
TOTAL: 6

HONOURS

Winners medals
None

Runner-up medals
Promoted to League Division Two: 81/82

KERRY DIXON

Born: 24/07/61 – Luton
Height: 6.0
Weight: 13.10 (96–97)

Clubs
Reading: **1980–83** – Matches: **124+9** – Goals: **57**
Chelsea: **1983–92** – Matches: **414+7** – Goals: **192**
Southampton: **1992–93** – Matches: **11+1** – Goals: **2**
Luton Town: **1993–95** – Matches: **77+11** – Goals: **20**
Millwall: **1995–96** – Matches: **26+9** – Goals: **9**
Watford: **1996** – Matches: **8+3** – Goals: **0**
Doncaster Rovers: **1996–97** – Matches: **17+3** – Goals: **3**

Country
England: **1985–86** – Matches: **5+3** – Goals: **4**

SEASON 1980–81

Reading – League Division Three

1	08/08/80	Northampton Town	Away	Lge Cup	2–0		
2	13/08/80	Northampton Town	Home	Lge Cup	2–3		
3	16/08/80	Walsall	Home	League	2–0		
4	19/08/80	Gillingham	Away	League	0–2		
5	23/08/80	Brentford	Away	League	2–1	1 Goal	(1)
6	27/08/80	Luton Town	Home	Lge Cup	0–2		
7	30/08/80	Swindon Town	Home	League	4–1	1 Goal	(2)
8	02/09/80	Luton Town	Away	Lge Cup	1–1		
9	06/09/80	Huddersfield Town	Away	League	1–4		
10	13/09/80	Sheffield United	Home	League	1–0		
11	17/09/80	Plymouth Argyle	Home	League	1–1		
12	20/09/80	Rotherham United	Away	League	0–2		
13	27/09/80	Barnsley	Home	League	3–2		
14	30/09/80	Plymouth Argyle	Away	League	1–2		
15	04/10/80	Millwall	Home	League	4–1		
16	07/10/80	Newport County	Away	League	0–0		
17	11/10/80	Chester	Away	League	0–1		
18	18/10/80	Chesterfield	Home	League	2–3	1 Goal	(3)
19	22/10/80	Colchester United	Home	League	1–0		
20	28/10/80	Charlton Athletic	Away	League	2–4		
21	01/11/80	Exeter City	Home	League	2–1		
22	08/11/80	Burnley	Away	League	2–1	1 Goal	(4)
23	12/11/80	Gillingham	Home	League	0–1		
24	15/11/80	Walsall	Away	League	2–2		
25	22/11/80	Fulham	Home	FA Cup	1–2		
Sub+1	02/01/81	Chester	Home	League	3–0	1 Goal	(5)
26	10/01/81	Carlisle United	Home	League	3–1	1 Goal	(6)
27	17/01/81	Blackpool	Away	League	0–0		
28	24/01/81	Swindon Town	Away	League	1–3		
29	31/01/81	Brentford	Home	League	0–0		
30	07/02/81	Sheffield United	Away	League	0–2		
31	10/02/81	Carlisle United	Away	League	0–0		
32	14/02/81	Huddersfield Town	Home	League	2–1		
33	18/02/81	Newport County	Home	League	1–1		
34	21/02/81	Barnsley	Away	League	3–2	2 Goals	(8)
35	28/02/81	Rotherham United	Home	League	1–1		
36	08/03/81	Millwall	Away	League	1–2		
37	28/03/81	Charlton Athletic	Home	League	1–3		
Sub+2	04/04/81	Exeter City	Away	League	1–3		
38	18/04/81	Oxford United	Away	League	1–2		
39	20/04/81	Portsmouth	Home	League	2–1	1 Goal	(9)
40	25/04/81	Fulham	Away	League	2–1	2 Goals	(11)
41	02/05/81	Hull City	Home	League	2–0	2 Goals	(13)
42	05/05/81	Chesterfield	Away	League	2–3		

SEASON 1981–82

League Division Three

43	15/08/81	Watford	Away	FLG Cup	1–4		
44	19/08/81	Aldershot	Home	FLG Cup	4–0		
Sub+3	22/08/81	Oxford United	Home	FLG Cup	2–0		
Sub+4	02/09/81	Charlton Athletic	Home	Lge Cup	2–2		
Sub+5	05/09/81	Gillingham	Home	League	3–2		
45	13/09/81	Millwall	Away	League	1–0		
Sub+6	19/09/81	Bristol Rovers	Home	League	0–3		
46	23/09/81	Newport County	Home	League	2–1	1 Goal	(14)
47	26/09/81	Swindon Town	Away	League	2–0		
48	17/10/81	Preston North End	Away	League	0–0		
49	20/10/81	Bristol City	Away	League	0–2		
50	24/10/81	Wimbledon	Home	League	2–1		
51	31/10/81	Chester	Away	League	3–2	1 Goal	(15)
52	04/11/81	Walsall	Home	League	0–0		
Sub+7	07/11/81	Exeter City	Away	League	3–4		
Sub+8	14/11/81	Burnley	Home	League	1–1		
Sub+9	21/11/81	AFC Bournemouth	Away	FA Cup	0–1		
53	27/11/81	Southend United	Away	League	0–2		
54	05/12/81	Lincoln City	Home	League	3–2		
55	02/01/82	Newport County	Away	League	1–3		
56	06/01/82	Portsmouth	Home	League	2–1	1 Goal	(16)
57	20/01/82	Fulham	Home	League	0–3		
58	23/01/82	Plymouth Argyle	Home	League	2–2	1 Goal	(17)
59	27/01/82	Brentford	Home	League	4–1	2 Goals	(19)

60	30/01/82	Bristol Rovers	Away	League	1–1		
61	03/02/82	Oxford United	Away	League	0–1		
62	06/02/82	Millwall	Home	League	4–0		
63	13/02/82	Huddersfield Town	Away	League	1–6		
64	17/02/82	Doncaster Rovers	Home	League	3–3		
65	20/02/82	Swindon Town	Home	League	1–1		
66	27/02/82	Chesterfield	Away	League	1–2		
67	06/03/82	Preston North End	Home	League	2–1		
68	10/03/82	Bristol City	Home	League	3–1	2 Goals	(21)
69	13/03/82	Wimbledon	Away	League	0–0		
70	16/03/82	Walsall	Away	League	2–1		
71	20/03/82	Chester	Home	League	4–1	1 Goal	(22)
72	23/03/82	Carlisle United	Away	League	1–2		
73	27/03/82	Exeter City	Home	League	4–0	2 Goals	(24)
74	03/04/82	Burnley	Away	League	0–3		
75	10/04/82	Oxford United	Home	League	0–3		
76	12/04/82	Portsmouth	Away	League	0–3		
77	17/04/82	Lincoln City	Away	League	1–2		
78	24/04/82	Southend United	Home	League	0–2		
79	01/05/82	Fulham	Away	League	2–2		
80	08/05/82	Carlisle United	Home	League	2–2	1 Goal	(25)
81	15/05/82	Brentford	Away	League	2–1		
82	18/05/82	Gillingham	Away	League	1–2		

SEASON 1982–83

League Division Three

83	14/08/82	Oxford United	Home	FL Trophy	2–1		
84	18/08/82	AFC Bournemouth	Home	FL Trophy	4–2	2 Goals	(27)
85	21/08/82	Aldershot	Away	FL Trophy	3–3	3 Goals	(30)
86	28/08/82	Bradford City	Away	League	2–3	1 Goal	(31)
87	31/08/82	Oxford United	Home	Lge Cup	0–2		
88	04/09/82	Plymouth Argyle	Home	League	3–2	2 Goals	(33)
89	08/09/82	Brentford	Home	League	1–1	1 Goal	(34)
90	11/09/82	Lincoln City	Away	League	0–4		
91	15/09/82	Oxford United	Away	Lge Cup	0–2		
92	18/09/82	Chesterfield	Home	League	0–0		
93	25/09/82	Doncaster Rovers	Away	League	5–7	4 Goals	(38)
94	28/09/82	Gillingham	Away	League	0–1		
95	02/10/82	Preston North End	Home	League	2–3	2 Goals	(40)
96	09/10/82	Orient	Home	League	3–0		
97	15/10/82	Southend United	Away	League	2–4	1 Goal	(41)
98	19/10/82	Sheffield United	Away	League	1–1		
99	23/10/82	Wigan Athletic	Home	League	2–1	1 Goal	(42)
100	30/10/82	Bristol Rovers	Away	League	0–3		
101	03/11/82	Cardiff City	Home	League	1–2		
102	06/11/82	Newport County	Home	League	4–2	3 Goals	(45)
103	13/11/82	Walsall	Away	League	1–2		
104	20/11/82	Bishop's Stortford	Home	FA Cup	1–2		
105	28/11/82	Millwall	Away	League	1–1		
106	04/12/82	Exeter City	Home	League	3–1	2 Goals	(47)
107	08/12/82	Watford	Home	FL Trophy	5–3	1 Goal	(48)
108	11/12/82	Exeter City	Away	League	2–2	2 Goals	(50)
109	18/12/82	Huddersfield Town	Home	League	1–1	1 Goal	(51)
110	27/12/82	AFC Bournemouth	Away	League	1–1		
111	28/12/82	Portsmouth	Home	League	1–2	1 Goal	(52)
112	01/03/83	Cardiff City	Away	League	0–0		
113	05/03/83	Wigan Athletic	Away	League	2–2		
114	12/03/83	Bristol Rovers	Home	League	1–2	1 Goal	(53)
115	19/03/83	Newport County	Away	League	0–1		
116	25/03/83	Walsall	Home	League	1–1	1 Goal	(54)
117	02/04/83	Portsmouth	Away	League	2–2		
118	04/04/83	AFC Bournemouth	Home	League	2–1		
119	16/04/83	Gillingham	Home	League	0–0		
120	23/04/83	Huddersfield Town	Away	League	1–3		
121	30/04/83	Millwall	Home	League	3–3	1 Goal	(55)
122	02/05/83	Oxford United	Away	League	2–1	1 Goal	(56)
123	07/05/83	Preston North End	Away	League	0–2		
124	14/05/83	Wrexham	Home	League	1–0	1 Goal	(57)

SEASON 1983–84

Chelsea – League Division Two

| 1 | 27/08/83 | Derby County | Home | League | 5–0 | 2 Goals | (2) |
| 2 | 30/08/83 | Gillingham | Away | Lge Cup | 2–1 | 1 Goal | (3) |

3	03/09/83	Brighton & Hove Albion	Away	League	2–1	2 Goals	(5)
4	07/09/83	Blackburn Rovers	Away	League	0–0		
5	10/09/83	Cambridge United	Home	League	2–1		
6	13/09/83	Gillingham	Home	Lge Cup	4–0	4 Goals	(9)
7	17/09/83	Sheffield Wednesday	Away	League	1–2		
8	24/09/83	Middlesbrough	Home	League	0–0		
9	01/10/83	Huddersfield Town	Away	League	3–2	2 Goals	(11)
10	05/10/83	Leicester City	Away	Lge Cup	2–0	1 Goal	(12)
11	08/10/83	Fulham	Away	League	5–3	2 Goals	(14)
12	15/10/83	Cardiff City	Home	League	2–0		
13	22/10/83	Carlisle United	Away	League	0–0		
14	25/10/83	Leicester City	Home	Lge Cup	0–2+		
15	29/10/83	Charlton Athletic	Home	League	3–2	1 Goal	(15)
16	05/11/83	Oldham Athletic	Away	League	1–1		
17	09/11/83	West Bromwich Albion	Home	Lge Cup	0–1		
18	12/11/83	Newcastle United	Home	League	4–0		
19	15/11/83	Charlton Athletic	Away	League	1–1		
20	19/11/83	Crystal Palace	Home	League	2–2		
21	22/11/83	Swansea City	Away	League	3–1	1 Goal	(16)
22	26/11/83	Leeds United	Away	League	1–1	1 Goal	(17)
23	03/12/83	Manchester City	Home	League	0–1		
24	06/12/83	Swansea City	Home	League	6–1	1 Goal	(18)
25	10/12/83	Barnsley	Away	League	0–0		
26	17/12/83	Grimsby Town	Home	League	2–3	1 Goal	(19)
27	26/12/83	Shrewsbury Town	Away	League	4–2	1 Goal	(20)
28	27/12/83	Portsmouth	Home	League	2–2	1 Goal	(21)
29	31/12/83	Brighton & Hove Albion	Home	League	1–0		
30	02/01/84	Middlesbrough	Away	League	1–2		
31	07/01/84	Blackburn Rovers	Away	FA Cup	0–1		
32	14/01/84	Derby County	Away	League	2–1		
33	21/01/84	Sheffield Wednesday	Home	League	3–2		
34	04/02/84	Huddersfield Town	Home	League	3–1	2 Goals	(23)
35	11/02/84	Cambridge United	Away	League	1–0		
36	25/02/84	Carlisle United	Home	League	0–0		
37	03/03/84	Oldham Athletic	Home	League	3–0	1 Goal	(24)
38	10/03/84	Newcastle United	Away	League	1–1		
39	16/03/84	Blackburn Rovers	Home	League	2–1		
40	31/03/84	Cardiff City	Away	League	3–3	1 Goal	(25)
41	07/04/84	Fulham	Home	League	4–0	2 Goals	(27)
42	14/04/84	Crystal Palace	Away	League	1–0		
43	21/04/84	Shrewsbury Town	Home	League	3–0	2 Goals	(29)
44	24/04/84	Portsmouth	Away	League	2–2		
45	28/04/84	Leeds United	Home	League	5–0	3 Goals	(32)
46	04/05/84	Manchester City	Away	League	2–0	1 Goal	(33)
47	07/05/84	Barnsley	Home	League	3–1		
48	12/05/84	Grimsby Town	Away	League	1–0	1 Goal	(34)

+ AET Chelsea won 4–3 on penalties

SEASON 1984–85

League Division One

49	25/08/84	Arsenal	Away	League	1–1	1 Goal	(35)
50	27/08/84	Sunderland	Home	League	1–0		
51	31/08/84	Everton	Home	League	0–1		
52	05/09/84	Manchester United	Away	League	1–1		
53	08/09/84	Aston Villa	Away	League	2–4		
54	15/09/84	West Ham United	Home	League	3–0		
55	22/09/84	Luton Town	Away	League	0–0		
56	26/09/84	Millwall	Home	Lge Cup	3–1	2 Goals	(37)
57	29/09/84	Leicester City	Home	League	3–0	2 Goals	(39)
58	06/10/84	Norwich City	Away	League	0–0		
59	09/10/84	Millwall	Away	Lge Cup	1–1		
60	13/10/84	Watford	Home	League	2–3	2 Goals	(41)
61	20/10/84	Southampton	Away	League	0–1		
62	27/10/84	Ipswich Town	Home	League	2–0	2 Goals	(43)
63	30/10/84	Walsall	Away	Lge Cup	2–2		
64	03/11/84	Coventry City	Home	League	6–2	3 Goals	(46)
65	06/11/84	Walsall	Home	Lge Cup	3–0	1 Goal	(47)
66	10/11/84	Newcastle United	Away	League	1–2	1 Goal	(48)
67	17/11/84	West Bromwich Albion	Home	League	3–1		
68	21/11/84	Manchester City	Home	Lge Cup	4–1	3 Goals	(51)
69	24/11/84	Tottenham Hotspur	Away	League	1–1	1 Goal	(52)
70	01/12/84	Liverpool	Home	League	3–1	1 Goal	(53)
71	15/12/84	Stoke City	Home	League	1–1		

72	22/12/84	Everton	Away	League	4–3	1 Goal	(54)
73	26/12/84	Queens Park Rangers	Away	League	2–2	2 Goals	(56)
74	29/12/84	Manchester United	Home	League	1–3		
75	01/01/85	Nottingham Forest	Home	League	1–1		
76	05/01/85	Wigan Athletic	Home	FA Cup	2–2		
77	19/01/85	Arsenal	Home	League	1–1		
78	26/01/85	Wigan Athletic	Away	FA Cup	5–0	4 Goals	(60)
79	28/01/85	Sheffield Wednesday	Home	Lge Cup	1–1		
80	30/01/85	Sheffield Wednesday	Away	Lge Cup	4–4*	1 Goal	(61)
81	02/02/85	Leicester City	Away	League	1–1		
82	06/02/85	Sheffield Wednesday	Home	Lge Cup	2–1		
83	13/02/85	Sunderland	Away	Lge Cup	0–2		
84	16/02/85	Newcastle United	Home	League	1–0		
85	23/02/85	Coventry City	Away	League	0–1		
86	02/03/85	Ipswich Town	Away	League	0–2		
87	04/03/85	Sunderland	Home	Lge Cup	2–3		
88	09/03/85	Southampton	Home	League	0–2		
89	16/03/85	Watford	Away	League	3–1	1 Goal	(62)
90	30/03/85	Sunderland	Away	League	2–0	1 Goal	(63)
91	06/04/85	Queens Park Rangers	Home	League	1–0	1 Goal	(64)
92	10/04/85	Nottingham Forest	Away	League	0–2		
93	13/04/85	West Ham United	Away	League	1–1		
94	16/04/85	Aston Villa	Home	League	3–1		
95	20/04/85	West Bromwich Albion	Away	League	1–0	1 Goal	(65)
96	27/04/85	Tottenham Hotspur	Home	League	1–1		
97	04/05/85	Liverpool	Away	League	3–4	1 Goal	(66)
98	06/05/85	Sheffield Wednesday	Home	League	2–1	2 Goals	(68)
99	08/05/85	Luton Town	Home	League	2–0	1 Goal	(69)
100	11/05/85	Stoke City	Away	League	1–0		
101	14/05/85	Norwich City	Home	League	1–2		

SEASON 1985–86

League Division One

102	17/08/85	Sheffield Wednesday	Away	League	1–1		
103	20/08/85	Coventry City	Home	League	1–0		
104	24/08/85	Birmingham City	Home	League	2–0		
105	28/08/85	Leicester City	Away	League	0–0		
106	31/08/85	West Bromwich Albion	Home	League	3–0		
107	04/09/85	Tottenham Hotspur	Away	League	1–4	1 Goal	(70)
108	07/09/85	Luton Town	Away	League	1–1	1 Goal	(71)
109	14/09/85	Southampton	Home	League	2–0	1 Goal	(72)
110	21/09/85	Arsenal	Home	League	2–1		
111	25/09/85	Mansfield Town	Away	Lge Cup	2–2		
112	28/09/85	Watford	Away	League	1–3		
113	02/10/85	Portsmouth	Home	FM Cup	3–0	1 Goal	(73)
114	05/10/85	Manchester City	Away	League	1–0	1 Goal	(74)
115	08/10/85	Mansfield Town	Home	Lge Cup	2–0	2 Goals	(76)
116	12/10/85	Everton	Home	League	2–1	1 Goal	(77)
117	19/10/85	Oxford United	Away	League	1–2	1 Goal	(78)
118	23/10/85	Charlton Athletic	Away	FM Cup	3–1		
119	26/10/85	Manchester United	Home	League	1–2		
120	29/10/85	Fulham	Home	Lge Cup	1–1		
121	02/11/85	Ipswich Town	Away	League	2–0	1 Goal	(79)
122	06/11/85	Fulham	Away	Lge Cup	1–0	1 Goal	(80)
123	09/11/85	Nottingham Forest	Home	League	4–2	2 Goals	(82)
124	16/11/85	Newcastle United	Away	League	3–1	1 Goal	(83)
125	23/11/85	Aston Villa	Home	League	2–1	1 Goal	(84)
126	26/11/85	Everton	Home	Lge Cup	2–2	1 Goal	(85)
127	30/11/85	Liverpool	Away	League	1–1		
128	04/12/85	Oxford United	Away	FM Cup	4–1	3 Goals	(88)
129	07/12/85	Coventry City	Away	League	1–1		
130	10/12/85	Everton	Away	Lge Cup	2–1	1 Goal	(89)
131	14/12/85	Sheffield Wednesday	Home	League	2–1		
132	17/12/85	Oxford United	Home	FM Cup	0–1		
133	21/12/85	Birmingham City	Away	League	2–1		
134	28/12/85	Tottenham Hotspur	Home	League	2–0	1 Goal	(90)
135	04/01/86	Shrewsbury Town	Away	FA Cup	1–0		
136	11/01/86	Luton Town	Home	League	1–0		
137	18/01/86	West Bromwich Albion	Away	League	3–0		
138	22/01/86	Queens Park Rangers	Away	Lge Cup	1–1		
139	26/01/86	Liverpool	Home	FA Cup	1–2		
140	08/03/86	Manchester City	Home	League	1–0		
141	16/03/86	Everton	Away	League	1–1		
142	19/03/86	Queens Park Rangers	Home	League	1–1		

143	22/03/86	Southampton	Away	League	1–0	
144	31/03/86	Queens Park Rangers	Away	League	0–6	
145	05/04/86	Ipswich Town	Home	League	1–1	
146	09/04/86	Manchester United	Away	League	2–1	2 Goals (92)
147	12/04/86	Nottingham Forest	Away	League	0–0	
148	15/04/86	West Ham United	Away	League	2–1	
149	19/04/86	Newcastle United	Home	League	1–1	
150	26/04/86	Aston Villa	Away	League	1–3	
151	29/04/86	Arsenal	Away	League	0–2	
152	03/05/86	Liverpool	Home	League	0–1	

SEASON 1986–87

League Division One

153	23/08/86	Norwich City	Home	League	0–0	
154	25/08/86	Oxford United	Away	League	1–1	
155	30/08/86	Sheffield Wednesday	Away	League	0–2	
156	02/09/86	Coventry City	Home	League	0–0	
157	06/09/86	Luton Town	Home	League	1–3	1 Goal (93)
158	13/09/86	Tottenham Hotspur	Away	League	3–1	1 Goal (94)
159	20/09/86	Nottingham Forest	Home	League	2–6	
160	23/09/86	York City	Away	Lge Cup	0–1	
161	28/09/86	Manchester United	Away	League	1–0	1 Goal (95)
162	04/10/86	Charlton Athletic	Home	League	0–1	
163	08/10/86	York City	Home	Lge Cup	3–0	1 Goal (96)
164	11/10/86	West Ham United	Away	League	3–5	1 Goal (97)
165	18/10/86	Manchester City	Home	League	2–1	
166	25/10/86	Arsenal	Away	League	1–3	
167	28/10/86	Cardiff City	Away	Lge Cup	1–2	
168	01/11/86	Watford	Home	League	0–0	
169	08/11/86	Everton	Away	League	2–2	
170	15/11/86	Aston Villa	Away	League	0–0	
171	22/11/86	Newcastle United	Home	League	1–3	
172	25/11/86	West Ham United	Away	FM Cup	2–1	1 Goal (98)
173	29/11/86	Leicester City	Away	League	2–2	
174	06/12/86	Wimbledon	Home	League	0–4	
175	20/12/86	Tottenham Hotspur	Home	League	0–2	
176	26/12/86	Southampton	Away	League	2–1	
177	27/12/86	Aston Villa	Home	League	4–1	2 Goals (100)
178	01/01/87	Queens Park Rangers	Home	League	3–1	
179	03/01/87	Luton Town	Away	League	0–1	
180	10/01/87	Aston Villa	Away	FA Cup	2–2	
181	21/01/87	Aston Villa	Home	FA Cup	2–1*	
Sub+1	01/02/87	Watford	Away	FA Cup	0–1	
182	10/02/87	Oxford United	Home	League	4–0	1 Goal (101)
183	14/02/87	Coventry City	Away	League	0–3	
184	21/02/87	Manchester United	Home	League	1–1	
Sub+2	21/03/87	West Ham United	Home	League	1–0	
185	04/04/87	Everton	Home	League	1–2	1 Goal (102)
186	07/04/87	Charlton Athletic	Away	League	0–0	
187	14/04/87	Watford	Away	League	1–3	
188	18/04/87	Queens Park Rangers	Away	League	1–1	
189	20/04/87	Southampton	Home	League	1–1	
190	25/04/87	Newcastle United	Away	League	0–1	
191	02/05/87	Leicester City	Home	League	3–1	2 Goals (104)
192	05/05/87	Wimbledon	Away	League	1–2	
193	09/05/87	Liverpool	Home	League	3–3	

SEASON 1987–88

League Division One

194	15/08/87	Sheffield Wednesday	Home	League	2–1	1 Goal (105)
195	18/08/87	Portsmouth	Away	League	3–0	1 Goal (106)
196	22/08/87	Tottenham Hotspur	Away	League	0–1	
197	29/08/87	Luton Town	Home	League	3–0	1 Goal (107)
198	31/08/87	Manchester United	Away	League	1–3	
199	05/09/87	Nottingham Forest	Home	League	4–3	
200	19/09/87	Norwich City	Home	League	1–0	1 Goal (108)
201	23/09/87	Reading	Away	Lge Cup	1–3	
202	26/09/87	Watford	Away	League	3–0	1 Goal (109)
203	03/10/87	Newcastle United	Home	League	2–2	1 Goal (110)
204	07/10/87	Reading	Home	Lge Cup	3–2	
205	10/10/87	Everton	Away	League	1–4	1 Goal (111)
206	17/10/87	Coventry City	Home	League	1–0	1 Goal (112)
207	18/11/87	Barnsley	Home	Simod Cup	2–1	

208	28/11/87	Wimbledon	Home	League	1–1		
209	06/12/87	Liverpool	Away	League	1–2		
210	12/12/87	West Ham United	Home	League	1–1		
211	16/12/87	Manchester City	Away	Simod Cup	2–0	1 Goal	(113)
212	20/12/87	Charlton Athletic	Away	League	2–2		
213	26/12/87	Queens Park Rangers	Home	League	1–1		
214	01/01/88	Luton Town	Away	League	0–3		
215	02/01/88	Tottenham Hotspur	Home	League	0–0		
216	13/01/88	Swindon Town	Away	Simod Cup	0–4		
217	09/01/88	Derby County	Away	FA Cup	3–1	1 Goal	(114)
218	16/01/88	Sheffield Wednesday	Away	League	0–3		
219	23/01/88	Portsmouth	Home	League	0–0		
220	30/01/88	Manchester United	Away	FA Cup	0–2		
221	06/02/88	Nottingham Forest	Away	League	2–3	1 Goal	(115)
222	13/02/88	Manchester United	Home	League	1–2		
223	27/02/88	Newcastle United	Away	League	1–3		
224	05/03/88	Coventry City	Away	League	3–3		
225	12/03/88	Everton	Home	League	0–0		
226	19/03/88	Oxford United	Away	League	4–4	2 Goals	(117)
227	26/03/88	Southampton	Home	League	0–1		
228	29/03/88	Watford	Home	League	1–1		
229	02/04/88	Arsenal	Home	League	1–1		
230	23/04/88	Wimbledon	Away	League	2–2		
231	30/04/88	Liverpool	Home	League	1–1		
232	02/05/88	West Ham United	Away	League	1–4		
233	07/05/88	Charlton Athletic	Home	League	1–1		
234	15/05/88	Blackburn Rovers	Away	Lge P/O	2–0		
235	18/05/88	Blackburn Rovers	Home	Lge P/O	4–1	1 Goal	(118)
236	25/05/88	Middlesbrough	Away	Lge P/O	0–2		
237	28/05/88	Middlesbrough	Home	Lge P/O	1–0		

SEASON 1988–89

League Division Two

238	20/09/88	Manchester City	Home	League	1–3		
239	24/09/88	Leeds United	Away	League	2–0		
240	27/09/88	Scunthorpe United	Away	Lge Cup	1–4		
241	01/10/88	Leicester City	Home	League	2–1		
242	04/10/88	Walsall	Home	League	2–0	1 Goal	(119)
243	09/10/88	Swindon Town	Away	League	1–1	1 Goal	(120)
244	12/10/88	Scunthorpe United	Home	Lge Cup	2–2	1 Goal	(121)
245	15/10/88	Oldham Athletic	Away	League	4–1		
246	22/10/88	Plymouth Argyle	Home	League	5–0	1 Goal	(122)
247	25/10/88	Hull City	Away	League	0–3		
248	29/10/88	Brighton & Hove Albion	Home	League	2–0	1 Goal	(123)
249	05/11/88	Watford	Away	League	2–1	1 Goal	(124)
250	12/11/88	Sunderland	Home	League	1–1		
251	19/11/88	Bradford City	Away	League	2–2		
252	26/11/88	Shrewsbury Town	Home	League	2–0	1 Goal	(125)
253	30/11/88	Bradford City	Away	Simod Cup	3–2	1 Goal	(126)
254	03/12/88	Stoke City	Away	League	3–0		
255	10/12/88	Portsmouth	Home	League	3–3	1 Goal	(127)
256	16/12/88	Birmingham City	Away	League	4–1	2 Goals	(129)
257	26/12/88	Ipswich Town	Home	League	3–0	1 Goal	(130)
258	31/12/88	West Bromwich Albion	Home	League	1–1		
259	02/01/89	Oxford United	Away	League	3–2	2 Goals	(132)
260	07/01/89	Barnsley	Away	FA Cup	0–4		
261	10/01/89	Nottingham Forest	Home	Simod Cup	1–4	1 Goal	(133)
262	14/01/89	Crystal Palace	Home	League	1–0		
263	21/01/89	Blackburn Rovers	Away	League	1–1	1 Goal	(134)
264	18/02/89	Plymouth Argyle	Away	League	1–0	1 Goal	(135)
265	25/02/89	Oldham Athletic	Home	League	2–2		
266	28/02/89	Hull City	Home	League	2–1	1 Goal	(136)
267	11/03/89	Watford	Home	League	2–2		
268	15/03/89	Brighton & Hove Albion	Away	League	1–0		
269	18/03/89	Manchester City	Away	League	3–2	1 Goal	(137)
270	21/03/89	Sunderland	Away	League	2–1		
271	25/03/89	AFC Bournemouth	Home	League	2–0		
272	28/03/89	Ipswich Town	Away	League	1–0		
273	01/04/89	Barnsley	Home	League	5–3	4 Goals	(141)
274	04/04/89	Birmingham City	Home	League	3–1	1 Goal	(142)
275	08/04/89	West Bromwich Albion	Away	League	3–2		
276	15/04/89	Leicester City	Away	League	0–2		
277	22/04/89	Leeds United	Home	League	1–0		
278	29/04/89	Shrewsbury Town	Away	League	1–1	1 Goal	(143)

279	01/05/89	Stoke City	Home	League	2–1	1 Goal	(144)
280	06/05/89	Bradford City	Home	League	3–1	2 Goals	(146)
281	13/05/89	Portsmouth	Away	League	3–2		

SEASON 1989–90

League Division One

282	19/08/89	Wimbledon	Away	League	1–0		
283	22/08/89	Queens Park Rangers	Home	League	1–1		
284	26/08/89	Sheffield Wednesday	Home	League	4–0	1 Goal	(147)
285	29/08/89	Charlton Athletic	Away	League	0–3		
286	09/09/89	Nottingham Forest	Home	League	2–2	1 Goal	(148)
287	16/09/89	Tottenham Hotspur	Away	League	4–1	1 Goal	(149)
288	19/09/89	Scarborough	Home	Lge Cup	1–1		
289	23/09/89	Coventry City	Home	League	1–0		
290	30/09/89	Arsenal	Home	League	0–0		
291	04/10/89	Scarborough	Away	Lge Cup	2–3		
292	14/10/89	Norwich City	Away	League	0–2		
293	21/10/89	Derby County	Away	League	1–0	1 Goal	(150)
294	28/10/89	Manchester City	Home	League	1–1	1 Goal	(151)
295	04/11/89	Millwall	Home	League	4–0	2 Goals	(153)
296	11/11/89	Everton	Away	League	1–0		
297	18/11/89	Southampton	Home	League	2–2		
298	25/11/89	Manchester United	Away	League	0–0		
299	28/11/89	Bournemouth	Away	ZDS Cup	3–2*		
300	02/12/89	Wimbledon	Home	League	2–5	1 Goal	(154)
301	09/12/89	Queens Park Rangers	Away	League	2–4		
302	16/12/89	Liverpool	Home	League	2–5	1 Goal	(155)
303	22/12/89	West Ham United	Home	ZDS Cup	4–3	1 Goal	(156)
304	26/12/89	Crystal Palace	Away	League	2–2	1 Goal	(157)
305	30/12/89	Luton Town	Away	League	3–0	1 Goal	(158)
306	01/01/90	Aston Villa	Home	League	0–3		
307	06/01/90	Crewe Alexandra	Home	FA Cup	1–1		
308	10/01/90	Crewe Alexandra	Away	FA Cup	2–0	2 Goals	(160)
309	14/01/90	Sheffield Wednesday	Away	League	1–1		
310	20/01/90	Charlton Athletic	Home	League	3–1	1 Goal	(161)
311	23/01/90	Ipswich Town	Away	ZDS Cup	3–2	1 Goal	(162)
312	27/01/90	Bristol City	Away	FA Cup	1–3		
313	03/02/90	Coventry City	Away	League	2–3	1 Goal	(163)
314	10/02/90	Tottenham Hotspur	Home	League	1–2		
315	17/02/90	Nottingham Forest	Away	League	1–1		
316	21/02/90	Crystal Palace	Away	ZDS Cup	2–0	1 Goal	(164)
317	24/02/90	Manchester United	Home	League	1–0		
318	03/03/90	Southampton	Away	League	3–2		
319	10/03/90	Norwich City	Home	League	0–0		
320	12/03/90	Crystal Palace	Home	ZDS Cup	2–0		
321	17/03/90	Arsenal	Away	League	1–0		
322	21/03/90	Manchester City	Away	League	1–1		
323	25/03/90	Middlesbrough	Wembley	ZDS Cup	1–0		
324	31/03/90	Derby County	Home	League	1–1		
325	07/04/90	Luton Town	Home	League	1–0		
326	14/04/90	Aston Villa	Away	League	0–1		
327	16/04/90	Crystal Palace	Home	League	3–0	1 Goal	(165)
328	21/04/90	Liverpool	Away	League	1–4	1 Goal	(166)
329	28/04/90	Everton	Home	League	2–1	2 Goals	(168)
330	05/05/90	Millwall	Away	League	3–1	3 Goals	(171)

SEASON 1990–91

League Division One

331	25/08/90	Derby County	Home	League	2–1		
332	28/08/90	Crystal Palace	Away	League	1–2		
333	01/09/90	Queens Park Rangers	Away	League	0–1		
334	08/09/90	Sunderland	Home	League	3–2	1 Goal	(172)
335	15/09/90	Arsenal	Away	League	1–4		
336	22/09/90	Manchester City	Home	League	1–1		
337	26/09/90	Walsall	Away	Lge Cup	5–0	1 Goal	(173)
338	29/09/90	Sheffield United	Home	League	2–2		
339	06/10/90	Southampton	Away	League	3–3		
340	10/10/90	Walsall	Home	Lge Cup	4–1	2 Goals	(175)
341	20/10/90	Nottingham Forest	Home	League	0–0		
Sub+3	06/11/90	Portsmouth	Away	Lge Cup	3–2		
342	10/11/90	Norwich City	Home	League	1–1		
343	17/11/90	Wimbledon	Away	League	1–2		
344	25/11/90	Manchester United	Away	League	3–2		

345	28/11/90	Oxford United	Away	Lge Cup	2–1		
346	01/12/90	Tottenham Hotspur	Home	League	3–2	1 Goal	(176)
347	08/12/90	Crystal Palace	Home	League	2–1		
348	12/12/90	Swindon Town	Home	ZDS Cup	1–0		
349	15/12/90	Derby County	Away	League	6–4	2 Goals	(178)
350	22/12/90	Coventry City	Home	League	2–1		
351	26/12/90	Leeds United	Away	League	1–4	1 Goal	(179)
352	29/12/90	Luton Town	Away	League	0–2		
353	01/01/91	Everton	Home	League	1–2		
354	05/01/91	Oxford United	Home	FA Cup	1–3	1 Goal	(180)
355	12/01/91	Queens Park Rangers	Home	League	2–0		
356	16/01/91	Tottenham Hotspur	Home	Lge Cup	0–0		
357	19/01/91	Sunderland	Away	League	0–1		
358	23/01/91	Tottenham Hotspur	Away	Lge Cup	3–0	1 Goal	(181)
359	02/02/91	Arsenal	Home	League	2–1	1 Goal	(182)
360	16/02/91	Wimbledon	Home	League	0–0		
361	18/02/91	Luton Town	Home	ZDS Cup	1–1+		
362	24/02/91	Sheffield Wednesday	Home	Lge Cup	0–2		
363	27/02/91	Sheffield Wednesday	Away	Lge Cup	1–3		
364	02/03/91	Tottenham Hotspur	Away	League	1–1		
365	09/03/91	Manchester United	Home	League	3–2		
366	16/03/91	Sheffield United	Away	League	0–1		
367	30/03/91	Leeds United	Home	League	1–2		
368	01/04/91	Coventry City	Away	League	0–1		
369	13/04/91	Everton	Away	League	2–2	2 Goals	(184)
370	17/04/91	Norwich City	Away	League	3–1		
371	20/04/91	Nottingham Forest	Away	League	0–7		
372	04/05/91	Liverpool	Home	League	4–2	2 Goals	(186)
373	11/05/91	Aston Villa	Away	League	2–2		

+ AET Luton Town won 4–1 on penalties

SEASON 1991–92

League Division One

374	17/08/91	Wimbledon	Home	League	2–2		
375	21/08/91	Oldham Athletic	Away	League	0–3		
376	24/08/91	Tottenham Hotspur	Away	League	3–1	1 Goal	(187)
377	28/08/91	Notts County	Home	League	2–2		
378	31/08/91	Luton Town	Home	League	4–1	1 Goal	(188)
379	03/09/91	Sheffield United	Away	League	1–0		
380	07/09/91	West Ham United	Away	League	1–1	1 Goal	(189)
381	14/09/91	Leeds United	Home	League	0–1		
382	18/09/91	Aston Villa	Home	League	2–0		
383	21/09/91	Queens Park Rangers	Away	League	2–2		
384	25/09/91	Tranmere Rovers	Home	Lge Cup	1–1		
385	28/09/91	Everton	Home	League	2–2		
386	05/10/91	Arsenal	Away	League	2–3		
387	08/10/91	Tranmere Rovers	Away	Lge Cup	1–3		
388	26/10/91	Crystal Palace	Away	League	0–0		
389	02/11/91	Coventry City	Away	League	1–0		
390	16/11/91	Norwich City	Home	League	0–3		
391	23/11/91	Southampton	Away	League	0–1		
392	26/11/91	Ipswich Town	Home	ZDS Cup	2–2+		
393	30/11/91	Nottingham Forest	Home	League	1–0	1 Goal	(190)
394	07/12/91	Sheffield Wednesday	Away	League	0–3		
395	10/12/91	Crystal Palace	Away	ZDS Cup	1–0	1 Goal	(191)
396	15/12/91	Manchester United	Home	League	1–3		
397	21/12/91	Oldham Athletic	Home	League	4–2		
398	26/12/91	Notts County	Away	League	0–2		
399	28/12/91	Luton Town	Away	League	0–2		
400	01/01/92	Manchester City	Home	League	1–1		
401	04/01/92	Hull City	Away	FA Cup	2–0		
402	11/01/92	Tottenham Hotspur	Home	League	2–0		
403	18/01/92	Wimbledon	Away	League	2–1		
404	21/01/92	Southampton	Away	ZDS Cup	0–2		
405	26/01/92	Everton	Home	FA Cup	1–0		
Sub+4	15/02/92	Sheffield United	Home	FA Cup	1–0		
Sub+5	22/02/92	Nottingham Forest	Away	League	1–1		
Sub+6	29/02/92	Sheffield Wednesday	Home	League	0–3		
406	09/03/92	Sunderland	Home	FA Cup	1–1		
407	11/03/92	Norwich City	Away	League	1–0	1 Goal	(192)
408	14/03/92	Coventry City	Home	League	0–1		
409	18/03/92	Sunderland	Away	FA Cup	1–2		
410	21/03/92	Sheffield United	Home	League	1–2		

Sub+7	11/04/92	Leeds United	Away	League	0–3		
411	18/04/92	Queens Park Rangers	Home	League	2–1		
412	20/04/92	Aston Villa	Away	League	1–3		
413	25/04/92	Arsenal	Home	League	1–1		
414	02/05/92	Everton	Away	League	1–2		

+ AET Chelsea won 4–3 on penalties

SEASON 1992–93

Southampton – Premier League

1	15/08/92	Tottenham Hotspur	Home	League	0–0		
2	19/08/92	Queens Park Rangers	Away	League	1–3		
3	22/08/92	Aston Villa	Away	League	1–1		
4	24/08/92	Manchester United	Home	League	0–1		
5	29/08/92	Middlesbrough	Home	League	2–1		
6	01/09/92	Liverpool	Away	League	1–1	1 Goal	(1)
7	19/09/92	Leeds United	Home	League	1–1		
8	23/09/92	Gillingham	Away	Lge Cup	0–0		
9	07/10/92	Gillingham	Home	Lge Cup	3–0		
Sub+1	19/12/92	Everton	Away	League	1–2		
10	03/01/93	Nottingham Forest	Away	FA Cup	1–2		
11	09/01/93	Leeds United	Away	League	1–2	1 Goal	(2)

Luton Town (loan) Football League Division One

1	20/02/93	Charlton Athletic	Home	League	1–0		
2	27/02/93	Barnsley	Home	League	2–2	1 Goal	(1)
3	06/03/93	Portsmouth	Away	League	1–2		
4	09/03/93	Oxford United	Home	League	3–1		
5	13/03/93	Grimsby Town	Away	League	1–3		
6	17/03/93	Swindon Town	Home	League	0–0		
7	20/03/93	Bristol Rovers	Home	League	1–1		
Sub+1	24/03/93	Millwall	Away	League	0–1		
8	27/03/93	Cambridge United	Home	League	2–0	1 Goal	(2)
9	03/04/93	Watford	Away	League	0–0		
10	07/04/93	Wolverhampton Wanderers	Home	League	1–1		
11	10/04/93	Swindon Town	Away	League	0–1		
12	13/04/93	West Ham United	Home	League	2–0		
13	17/04/93	Sunderland	Away	League	2–2		
14	24/04/93	Derby County	Away	League	1–1		
15	01/05/93	Peterborough United	Home	League	0–0		
16	08/05/93	Southend United	Away	League	1–2	1 Goal	(3)

SEASON 1993–94

Luton Town – Football League Division One

17	14/08/93	Watford	Home	League	2–1	1 Goal	(4)
18	21/08/93	Portsmouth	Away	League	0–1		
19	28/08/93	Nottingham Forest	Home	League	1–2		
20	31/08/93	Watford	Away	AI Cup	1–2		
21	07/09/93	Southend United	Home	AI Cup	1–1	1 Goal	(5)
22	11/09/93	Bolton Wanderers	Home	League	0–2		
23	23/10/93	Oxford United	Away	League	1–0		
Sub+2	30/10/93	Leicester City	Home	League	0–2		
24	02/11/93	Crystal Palace	Away	League	2–3		
25	07/11/93	Charlton Athletic	Home	League	1–0		
26	13/11/93	Southend United	Away	League	1–2	1 Goal	(6)
27	27/11/93	Stoke City	Home	League	6–2	3 Goals	(9)
28	04/12/93	Charlton Athletic	Away	League	0–1		
29	11/12/93	Tranmere Rovers	Home	League	0–1		
30	19/12/93	Watford	Away	League	2–2		
31	27/12/93	Peterborough United	Away	League	0–0		
32	29/12/93	Grimsby Town	Home	League	2–1		
33	01/01/94	West Bromwich Albion	Away	League	1–1		
34	15/01/94	Notts County	Away	League	2–1	2 Goals	(11)
35	18/01/94	Southend United	Home	FA Cup	1–0		
36	22/01/94	Derby County	Home	League	2–1		
37	29/01/94	Newcastle United	Away	FA Cup	1–1		
Sub+3	20/02/94	Cardiff City	Away	FA Cup	2–1		
38	22/02/94	Portsmouth	Home	League	4–1		
39	25/02/94	Sunderland	Home	League	2–1		
40	05/03/94	Nottingham Forest	Away	League	0–2		
41	08/03/94	Middlesbrough	Home	League	1–1		
42	14/03/94	West Ham United	Away	FA Cup	0–0		
43	23/03/94	West Ham United	Home	FA Cup	3–2		

44	26/03/94	Barnsley	Away	League	0–1		
45	02/04/94	Peterborough United	Home	League	2–0	2 Goals	(13)
46	09/04/94	Chelsea	Wembley	FA Cup	0–2		
47	12/04/94	Wolverhampton Wanderers	Home	League	0–2		
Sub+4	16/04/94	Crystal Palace	Home	League	0–1		
48	19/04/94	Bristol City	Away	League	0–1		
49	23/04/94	Wolverhampton Wanderers	Away	League	0–1		
50	26/04/94	Millwall	Home	League	1–1		

SEASON 1994–95

Football League Division One

51	13/08/94	West Bromwich Albion	Home	League	1–1		
52	16/08/94	Fulham	Home	Lge Cup	1–1		
53	20/08/94	Derby County	Away	League	0–0		
54	24/08/94	Fulham	Away	Lge Cup	1–1+		
Sub+5	27/08/94	Southend United	Home	League	2–2		
55	03/09/94	Port Vale	Away	League	1–0		
Sub+6	10/09/94	Barnsley	Home	League	0–1		
56	13/09/94	Bolton Wanderers	Home	League	0–3		
57	17/09/94	Watford	Away	League	4–2	1 Goal	(14)
58	24/09/94	Millwall	Away	League	0–0		
59	01/10/94	Bristol City	Home	League	0–1		
60	22/10/94	Sheffield United	Away	League	3–1	1 Goal	(15)
Sub+7	29/10/94	Barnsley	Home	League	0–1		
61	05/11/94	Wolverhampton Wanderers	Away	League	3–2	1 Goal	(16)
62	12/11/94	Oldham Athletic	Away	League	0–0		
63	19/11/94	Portsmouth	Home	League	2–0	1 Goal	(17)
64	26/11/94	Swindon Town	Away	League	2–1	1 Goal	(18)
65	03/12/94	Sheffield United	Home	League	3–6		
66	11/12/94	Derby County	Home	League	0–0		
67	18/12/94	West Bromwich Albion	Away	League	0–1		
68	26/12/94	Reading	Away	League	0–0		
69	14/01/95	Barnsley	Away	League	1–3	1 Goal	(19)
70	18/01/95	Bristol Rovers	Away	FA Cup	1–0		
71	28/01/95	Southampton	Home	FA Cup	1–1		
72	04/02/95	Oldham Athletic	Home	League	2–1		
Sub+8	08/02/95	Southampton	Away	FA Cup	0–6		
73	11/02/95	Grimsby Town	Away	League	0–5		
Sub+9	18/02/95	Swindon Town	Home	League	3–0		
74	21/02/95	Portsmouth	Away	League	2–3		
75	25/02/95	Bristol City	Away	League	2–2		
Sub+10	04/03/95	Millwall	Home	League	1–1		
Sub+11	07/03/95	Port Vale	Home	League	2–1	1 Goal	(20)
76	11/03/95	Southend United	Away	League	0–3		
77	21/03/95	Burnley	Away	League	1–2		

+ AET Fulham won 4–3 on penalties

Millwall – Football League Division One

1	25/03/95	Tranmere Rovers	Home	League	2–1	1 Goal	(1)
2	01/04/95	Burnley	Away	League	2–1		
3	05/04/95	Port Vale	Home	League	1–3		
4	08/04/95	Charlton Athletic	Home	League	3–1	1 Goal	(2)
5	14/04/95	Watford	Away	League	0–1		
6	19/04/95	Notts County	Home	League	0–0		
7	22/04/95	Oldham Athletic	Away	League	1–0		
8	29/04/95	Stoke City	Away	League	3–4	1 Goal	(3)
9	07/05/95	Bristol City	Home	League	1–1	1 Goal	(4)

SEASON 1995–96

Football League Division One

10	12/08/95	Grimsby Town	Home	League	2–1		
11	19/08/95	Millwall	Away	League	1–0	1 Goal	(5)
12	26/08/95	Southend United	Home	League	0–0		
13	29/08/95	Reading	Away	League	2–1	1 Goal	(6)
14	02/09/95	Portsmouth	Away	League	1–0	1 Goal	(7)
15	09/09/95	Barnsley	Home	League	0–1		
16	13/09/95	Luton Town	Home	League	1–0		
17	16/09/95	Norwich City	Away	League	0–0		
18	20/09/95	Everton	Home	Lge Cup	0–0		
19	23/09/95	Sunderland	Home	League	1–2		

Sub+1	01/10/95	Derby County	Away	League	2–2		
Sub+2	04/10/95	Everton	Away	Lge Cup	4–2*		
Sub+3	07/10/95	Watford	Away	League	1–0		
Sub+4	14/10/95	Tranmere Rovers	Home	League	2–2	1 Goal	(8)
Sub+5	22/10/95	Crystal Palace	Away	League	2–1		
Sub+6	25/10/95	Sheffield Wednesday	Home	Lge Cup	0–2		
Sub+7	04/11/95	Birmingham City	Away	League	2–2	1 Goal	(9)
20	11/11/95	Ipswich Town	Home	League	2–1		
21	18/11/95	Huddersfield Town	Home	League	0–0		
22	21/11/95	Oldham Athletic	Away	League	2–2		
23	25/11/95	Stoke City	Away	League	0–1		
Sub+8	02/12/95	Watford	Home	League	1–2		
Sub+9	16/12/95	Derby County	Home	League	0–1		
24	26/12/95	Wolverhampton Wanderers	Away	League	1–1		
25	01/01/96	Leicester City	Home	League	1–1		
26	06/01/96	Oxford United	Home	FA Cup	3–3		

Watford – Football League Division One

1	13/01/96	Huddersfield Town	Home	League	0–1		
2	20/01/96	Sheffield United	Away	League	1–1		
3	03/02/96	Barnsley	Away	League	1–2		
Sub+1	09/03/96	Oldham Athletic	Home	League	2–1		
Sub+2	12/03/96	West Bromwich Albion	Away	League	4–4		
Sub+3	23/03/96	West Bromwich Albion	Home	League	1–1		
4	30/03/96	Wolverhampton Wanderers	Away	League	0–3		
5	02/04/96	Sunderland	Home	League	3–3		
6	06/04/96	Portsmouth	Home	League	1–2		
7	08/04/96	Southend United	Away	League	1–1		
8	13/04/96	Port Vale	Home	League	5–2		

SEASON 1996–97

Doncaster Rovers – Football League Division Three

1	20/08/96	York City	Home	Lge Cup	1–1		
2	24/08/96	Hereford United	Away	League	0–1		
3	27/08/96	Exeter City	Away	League	1–1		
4	31/08/96	Darlington	Home	League	3–2	1 Goal	(1)
5	03/09/96	York City	Away	Lge Cup	0–2		
6	07/09/96	Mansfield Town	Home	League	0–0		
7	10/09/96	Scarborough	Away	League	1–2	1 Goal	(2)
8	14/09/96	Rochdale	Away	League	1–2		
9	21/09/96	Swansea City	Home	League	0–1		
Sub+1	29/10/96	Lincoln City	Home	League	1–3		
Sub+2	02/11/96	Chester City	Home	League	0–1		
10	09/11/96	Scunthorpe United	Away	League	2–1		
11	16/11/96	Stockport County	Away	FA Cup	1–2		
12	19/11/96	Northampton Town	Home	League	1–2		
13	23/11/96	Barnet	Away	League	0–3		
14	03/12/96	Wigan Athletic	Away	League	1–4		
15	10/12/96	Stockport County	Home	AW Shield	1–2		
16	26/12/96	Scarborough	Home	League	1–2	1 Goal	(3)
Sub+3	12/04/97	Leyton Orient	Away	League	1–2		
17	03/05/97	Torquay United	Home	League	2–1		

INTERNATIONAL APPEARANCES – ENGLAND

Sub 1	09/06/85	Mexico	Mexico City	0–1	F		
2	12/06/85	West Germany	Mexico City	3–0	F	2 Goals	(2)
3	16/06/85	USA	Los Angeles	5–0	F	2 Goals	(4)
4	13/11/85	Northern Ireland	Wembley	0–0	WCQ		
5	26/02/86	Israel	Tel Aviv	2–1	F		
Sub 6	17/05/86	Mexico	Los Angeles	3–0	F		
Sub 7	11/06/86	Poland	Monterrey	3–0	WC		
8	10/09/86	Sweden	Stockholm	0–1	F		

APPEARANCES AND GOALS PER SEASON

SEASON 80–81	GAMES	GOALS
League	37+2	13
FA Cup	1	0
League Cup	4	0
TOTAL	**42+2**	**13**

SEASON 81–82	GAMES	GOALS
League	38+4	12
FA Cup	0+1	0
League Cup	0+1	0
Football League Group Cup	2+1	0
TOTAL	**40+7**	**12**

SEASON 82–83	GAMES	GOALS
League	35	26
FA Cup	1	0
League Cup	2	0
Football League Trophy	4	6
TOTAL	**42**	**32**

SEASON 83–84	GAMES	GOALS
League	42	28
FA Cup	1	0
League Cup	5	6
TOTAL	**48**	**34**

SEASON 84–85	GAMES	GOALS
League	41	24
FA Cup	2	4
League Cup	10	7
TOTAL	**53**	**35**

SEASON 85–86	GAMES	GOALS
League	38	14
FA Cup	2	0
League Cup	7	5
Full Members Cup	4	4
TOTAL	**51**	**23**

SEASON 86–87	GAMES	GOALS
League	35+1	10
FA Cup	2+1	0
League Cup	3	1
Full Members Cup	1	1
TOTAL	**41+2**	**12**

SEASON 87–88	GAMES	GOALS
League	33	11
League Play–offs	4	1
FA Cup	2	1
League Cup	2	0
Simod Cup	3	1
TOTAL	**44**	**14**

SEASON 88–89	GAMES	GOALS
League	39	25
FA Cup	1	0
League Cup	2	1
Simod Cup	2	2
TOTAL	**44**	**28**

SEASON 89–90	GAMES	GOALS
League	38	20
FA Cup	3	2
League Cup	2	0
Zenith Data Systems Cup	6	3
TOTAL	**49**	**25**

SEASON 90–91	GAMES	GOALS
League	33	10
FA Cup	1	1
League Cup	7+1	4
Zenith Data Systems Cup	2	0
TOTAL	**43+1**	**15**

SEASON 91–92	GAMES	GOALS
League	32+3	5
FA Cup	4+1	0
League Cup	2	0
Zenith Data Systems Cup	3	1
TOTAL	**41+4**	**6**

Striker

SEASON 92–93	GAMES	GOALS
League	24+2	5
FA Cup	1	0
League Cup	2	0
TOTAL	**27+2**	**5**

SEASON 93–94	GAMES	GOALS
League	27+2	9
FA Cup	5+1	0
Anglo–Italian Cup	2	1
TOTAL	**34+3**	**10**

SEASON 94–95	GAMES	GOALS
League	32+6	11
FA Cup	2+1	0
League Cup	2	0
TOTAL	**36+7**	**11**

SEASON 95–96	GAMES	GOALS
League	23+10	5
FA Cup	1	0
League Cup	1+2	0
TOTAL	**25+12**	**5**

SEASON 96–97	GAMES	GOALS
League	13+3	3
FA Cup	1	0
League Cup	2	0
Auto Windscreens Shield	1	0
TOTAL	**17+3**	**3**

CAREER APPEARANCES AND GOALS

COMPETITION	GAMES	TOTAL	GOALS
League	560+33	593	231
League Play–offs	4	4	1
FA Cup	30+5	35	8
League Cup	53+4	57	24
Football League Group Cup	2+1	3	0
Football League Trophy	4	4	6
Full Members Cup	5	5	5
Simod Cup	5	5	3
Zenith Data Systems Cup	11	11	4
Auto Windscreens Shield	1	1	0
Anglo–Italian Cup	2	2	1
Internationals	5+3	8	4
TOTAL	**682+46**	**728**	**287**

HAT–TRICKS

Reading

1	3	Aldershot	21/08/82	Away	FL Trophy	3–3
2	4	Doncaster Rovers	25/09/82	Away	League	5–7
3	3	Newport County	06/11/82	Home	League	4–2

Chelsea

1	4	Gillingham	13/09/83	Home	Lge Cup	4–0
2	3	Leeds United	28/04/84	Home	League	5–0
3	3	Coventry City	03/11/84	Home	League	6–2
4	3	Manchester City	21/11/84	Home	Lge Cup	4–1
5	4	Wigan Athletic	26/01/85	Away	FA Cup	5–0
6	3	Oxford United	04/12/85	Away	FM Cup	4–1
7	4	Barnsley	01/04/89	Home	League	5–3
8	3	Millwall	05/05/90	Away	League	3–1

Luton Town

1	3	Stoke City	27/11/93	Home	League	6–2

League: 7
FA Cup: 1
League Cup: 2
Full Members Cup: 1
Football League Trophy: 1
TOTAL: 12

HONOURS

Winners medals
League Division Two Championship: 83/84, 88/89
Zenith Data Systems Cup: 89/90

Runner-up medals
None

DION DUBLIN

Born: 22/04/69 – Leicester
Height: 6.1
Weight: 12.04 (96–97)

Clubs
Norwich City: **1988** – No Competitive Matches
Cambridge United: **1988–92** – Matches: **176+26** – Goals: **73**
Manchester United: **1992–94** – Matches: **6+11** – Goals: **3**
Coventry City: **1994–97** – Matches: **113+3** – Goals: **45**

SEASON 1988–89

Norwich City – League Division One
No Competitive Matches

Cambridge United – League Division Four

Sub+1	29/11/88	Peterborough United	Home	SV Trophy	2–2	1 Goal	(1)
Sub+2	16/12/88	Wrexham	Away	League	1–3		
Sub+3	26/12/88	Doncaster Rovers	Home	League	0–0		
1	30/12/88	Rochdale	Home	League	2–0		
2	03/01/89	Peterborough United	Away	League	5–1	3 Goals	(4)
3	07/01/89	Plymouth Argyle	Away	FA Cup	0–2		
4	14/01/89	Hereford United	Home	League	2–1	1 Goal	(5)
5	17/01/89	Chesterfield	Away	SV Trophy	2–4		
6	21/01/89	Grimsby Town	Away	League	0–4		
7	28/01/89	Tranmere Rovers	Home	League	1–1		
Sub+4	04/02/89	Lincoln City	Away	League	0–3		
Sub+5	11/03/89	Exeter City	Away	League	3–0		
Sub+6	14/03/89	Burnley	Home	League	2–1		
Sub+7	17/03/89	Stockport County	Away	League	0–0		
Sub+8	25/03/89	Peterborough United	Home	League	2–1		
Sub+9	31/03/89	Wrexham	Home	League	2–0		
Sub+10	04/04/89	York City	Home	League	1–1		
8	15/04/89	Carlisle United	Away	League	1–1		
9	22/04/89	Crewe Alexandra	Home	League	1–1		
10	29/04/89	Leyton Orient	Away	League	1–1		
11	02/05/89	Darlington	Home	League	1–3		
12	06/05/89	Torquay United	Home	League	3–0	1 Goal	(6)
13	09/05/89	York City	Away	League	2–1	1 Goal	(7)
14	13/05/89	Rotherham United	Away	League	0–0		

SEASON 1989–90

League Division Four

15	19/08/89	Grimsby Town	Away	League	0–0		
16	22/08/89	Maidstone United	Home	Lge Cup	3–1	2 Goals	(9)
17	26/08/89	Hereford United	Home	League	0–1		
18	30/08/89	Maidstone United	Away	Lge Cup	1–0		
19	02/09/89	Scarborough	Away	League	1–1		
20	09/09/89	Chesterfield	Home	League	0–1		
Sub+11	16/09/89	Exeter City	Away	League	2–3		
Sub+12	19/09/89	Derby County	Home	Lge Cup	2–1		
Sub+13	22/09/89	Halifax Town	Home	League	1–0		
Sub+14	26/09/89	Carlisle United	Home	League	1–2		
Sub+15	30/09/89	Maidstone United	Away	League	2–2		
Sub+16	04/10/89	Derby County	Away	Lge Cup	0–5		
Sub+17	07/10/89	York City	Away	League	2–4		
Sub+18	13/10/89	Torquay United	Home	League	5–2		
21	17/10/89	Doncaster Rovers	Home	League	1–0		

22	21/10/89	Wrexham	Away	League	3–2		
23	28/10/89	Scunthorpe United	Home	League	5–3	2 Goals	(11)
24	31/10/89	Hartlepool United	Away	League	2–1	1 Goal	(12)
25	04/11/89	Aldershot	Home	League	2–2	1 Goal	(13)
26	10/11/89	Colchester United	Away	League	2–1	1 Goal	(14)
27	17/11/89	Aldershot	Away	FA Cup	1–0		
28	24/11/89	Southend United	Away	League	0–0		
29	28/11/89	Gillingham	Away	LD Cup	0–2		
30	02/12/89	Rochdale	Home	League	0–3		
31	09/12/89	Woking	Home	FA Cup	3–1		
32	12/12/89	Southend United	Home	LD Cup	3–3		
33	17/12/89	Peterborough United	Home	League	3–2		
34	26/12/89	Lincoln City	Away	League	3–4		
35	29/12/89	Stockport County	Away	League	1–3		
Sub+19	01/01/90	Burnley	Home	League	0–1		
36	06/01/90	Darlington	Home	FA Cup	0–0		
37	09/01/90	Darlington	Away	FA Cup	3–1	1 Goal	(15)
38	13/01/90	Hereford United	Away	League	2–0	1 Goal	(16)
39	20/01/90	Grimsby Town	Home	League	2–0	1 Goal	(17)
40	27/01/90	Millwall	Away	FA Cup	1–1		
41	30/01/90	Millwall	Home	FA Cup	1–0*		
42	02/02/90	Halifax Town	Away	League	0–0		
43	10/02/90	Exeter City	Home	League	3–2		
44	17/02/90	Bristol City	Away	FA Cup	0–0		
45	21/02/90	Bristol City	Home	FA Cup	1–1*	1 Goal	(18)
Sub+20	25/02/90	Southend United	Home	League	2–1		
46	27/02/90	Bristol City	Home	FA Cup	5–1	2 Goals	(20)
47	03/03/90	Gillingham	Away	League	0–1		
48	06/03/90	Maidstone United	Home	League	2–0	2 Goals	(22)
49	10/03/90	Crystal Palace	Home	FA Cup	0–1		
50	16/03/90	York City	Home	League	2–2		
51	20/03/90	Torquay United	Away	League	0–3		
Sub+21	25/03/90	Doncaster Rovers	Away	League	1–2	1 Goal	(23)
52	27/03/90	Rochdale	Away	League	0–2		
53	30/03/90	Wrexham	Home	League	1–1	1 Goal	(24)
54	02/04/90	Scarborough	Home	League	5–2		
55	04/04/90	Carlisle United	Away	League	1–3		
56	07/04/90	Scunthorpe United	Away	League	1–1		
57	10/04/90	Hartlepool United	Home	League	2–1	1 Goal	(25)
58	14/04/90	Burnley	Away	League	3–1	1 Goal	(26)
59	17/04/90	Lincoln City	Home	League	2–1		
60	21/04/90	Peterborough United	Away	League	2–1	1 Goal	(27)
61	23/04/90	Stockport County	Home	League	0–2		
62	25/04/90	Chesterfield	Away	League	1–1		
63	29/04/90	Colchester United	Home	League	4–0		
64	01/05/90	Gillingham	Home	League	2–1	1 Goal	(28)
65	05/05/90	Aldershot	Away	League	2–0		
66	13/05/90	Maidstone United	Home	Lge P/O	1–1		
67	16/05/90	Maidstone United	Away	Lge P/O	2–0*	1 Goal	(29)
68	26/05/90	Chesterfield	Wembley	Lge P/O	1–0	1 Goal	(30)

SEASON 1990–91

League Division Three

69	25/08/90	Birmingham City	Home	League	0–1		
70	28/08/90	Walsall	Away	Lge Cup	2–4	1 Goal	(31)
71	01/09/90	Fulham	Away	League	2–0		
72	04/09/90	Walsall	Home	Lge Cup	2–1		
73	09/09/90	Southend United	Home	League	1–4		
74	15/09/90	Reading	Away	League	2–2		
75	18/09/90	Mansfield Town	Away	League	2–2		
76	21/09/90	Chester City	Home	League	1–1	1 Goal	(32)
77	29/09/90	Exeter City	Away	League	1–0	1 Goal	(33)
78	02/10/90	Leyton Orient	Home	League	1–0		
79	06/10/90	Bury	Home	League	2–2		
80	14/10/90	Brentford	Away	League	3–0		
81	20/10/90	Stoke City	Away	League	1–1	1 Goal	(34)
82	23/10/90	Wigan Athletic	Home	League	2–3		
83	27/10/90	Rotherham United	Home	League	4–1	1 Goal	(35)
84	03/11/90	Swansea City	Away	League	0–0		
85	06/11/90	Peterborough United	Away	LD Cup	2–0		
86	10/11/90	Huddersfield Town	Away	League	1–3		
87	17/11/90	Exeter City	Away	FA Cup	2–1	1 Goal	(36)
88	24/11/90	Shrewsbury Town	Home	League	3–1	1 Goal	(37)
89	30/11/90	Crewe Alexandra	Home	League	3–4	1 Goal	(38)

90	07/12/90	Fulham	Away	FA Cup	0–0		
91	11/12/90	Fulham	Home	FA Cup	2–1	1 Goal	(39)
92	15/12/90	Bradford City	Away	League	1–0		
93	22/12/90	Bolton Wanderers	Away	League	2–2	1 Goal	(40)
94	26/12/90	Tranmere Rovers	Home	League	3–1	1 Goal	(41)
95	29/12/90	Grimsby Town	Home	League	1–0	1 Goal	(42)
96	01/01/91	Preston North End	Away	League	2–0	1 Goal	(43)
97	05/01/91	Wolverhampton Wanderers	Away	FA Cup	1–0		
98	12/01/91	Fulham	Home	League	1–0		
99	19/01/91	Birmingham City	Away	League	3–0	1 Goal	(44)
100	26/01/91	Middlesbrough	Home	FA Cup	2–0		
101	29/01/91	Walsall	Away	LD Cup	1–0		
102	01/02/91	Mansfield Town	Home	League	2–1	1 Goal	(45)
103	16/02/91	Sheffield Wednesday	Home	FA Cup	4–0	2 Goals	(47)
104	20/02/91	Exeter City	Away	LD Cup	1–0	1 Goal	(48)
105	23/02/91	Huddersfield Town	Home	League	0–0		
106	01/03/91	Crewe Alexandra	Away	League	1–3		
107	05/03/91	Birmingham City	Away	LD Cup	1–3	1 Goal	(49)
108	09/03/91	Arsenal	Away	FA Cup	1–2	1 Goal	(50)
109	12/03/91	Leyton Orient	Away	League	3–0		
110	16/03/91	Exeter City	Home	League	1–0		
111	19/03/91	Brentford	Home	League	0–0		
112	23/03/91	Bury	Away	League	1–3	1 Goal	(51)
113	25/03/91	Chester City	Away	League	2–0		
114	29/03/91	Tranmere Rovers	Away	League	0–2		
115	02/04/91	Bolton Wanderers	Home	League	2–1		
116	06/04/91	Grimsby Town	Away	League	0–1		
117	09/04/91	Reading	Home	League	3–0	1 Goal	(52)
118	13/04/91	Preston North End	Home	League	1–1	1 Goal	(53)
119	16/04/91	AFC Bournemouth	Away	League	1–0		
Sub+22	18/04/91	Shrewsbury Town	Away	League	2–1		
Sub+23	20/04/91	Stoke City	Home	League	3–0	1 Goal	(54)
120	24/04/91	AFC Bournemouth	Home	League	4–0		
121	27/04/91	Wigan Athletic	Home	League	1–0	1 Goal	(55)
122	30/04/91	Southend United	Away	League	0–0		
123	04/05/91	Rotherham United	Away	League	2–3		
124	07/05/91	Bradford City	Home	League	2–1		
125	11/05/91	Swansea City	Home	League	2–0		

SEASON 1991–92

League Division Two

126	17/08/91	Grimsby Town	Away	League	4–3	1 Goal	(56)
127	21/08/91	Reading	Home	Lge Cup	1–0		
128	24/08/91	Swindon Town	Home	League	3–2		
129	28/08/91	Reading	Away	Lge Cup	3–0	1 Goal	(57)
130	31/08/91	Watford	Away	League	3–1		
131	03/09/91	Southend United	Home	League	0–1		
Sub+24	21/09/91	Portsmouth	Away	League	0–3		
132	25/09/91	Manchester United	Away	Lge Cup	0–3		
133	29/09/91	Leicester City	Home	League	5–1	2 Goals	(59)
134	02/10/91	Charlton Athletic	Home	ZDS Cup	1–1+		
135	05/10/91	Port Vale	Away	League	0–1		
136	09/10/91	Manchester United	Home	Lge Cup	1–0	1 Goal	(60)
137	12/10/91	Sunderland	Home	League	3–0	1 Goal	(61)
138	18/10/91	Tranmere Rovers	Away	League	2–1	1 Goal	(62)
139	22/10/91	West Ham United	Away	ZDS Cup	1–2		
140	26/10/91	Barnsley	Home	League	2–1	1 Goal	(63)
141	02/11/91	Bristol City	Home	League	0–0		
142	06/11/91	Newcastle United	Away	League	1–1		
143	09/11/91	Ipswich Town	Away	League	2–1		
144	16/11/91	Brighton & Hove Albion	Home	League	0–0		
145	23/11/91	Charlton Athletic	Away	League	2–1	1 Goal	(64)
146	30/11/91	Oxford United	Home	League	1–1	1 Goal	(65)
147	07/12/91	Bristol Rovers	Away	League	2–2	1 Goal	(66)
148	22/12/91	Southend United	Away	League	1–1		
149	26/12/91	Plymouth Argyle	Home	League	1–1	1 Goal	(67)
150	29/12/91	Watford	Home	League	0–1		
151	01/01/92	Blackburn Rovers	Away	League	1–2		
152	04/01/92	Coventry City	Away	FA Cup	1–1	1 Goal	(68)
153	11/01/92	Swindon Town	Away	League	2–0	1 Goal	(69)
154	14/01/92	Coventry City	Home	FA Cup	1–0		
155	18/01/92	Grimsby Town	Home	League	0–1		
156	25/01/92	Swindon Town	Home	FA Cup	0–3		
157	31/01/92	Tranmere Rovers	Home	League	0–0		

158	08/02/92	Barnsley	Away	League	0–0		
159	11/02/92	Plymouth Argyle	Away	League	1–0		
160	15/02/92	Charlton Athletic	Home	League	1–0		
161	22/02/92	Oxford United	Away	League	0–1		
162	25/02/92	Blackburn Rovers	Home	League	2–1		
163	28/02/92	Bristol Rovers	Home	League	6–1	2 Goals	(71)
164	07/03/92	Middlesbrough	Away	League	1–1	1 Goal	(72)
165	10/03/92	Newcastle United	Home	League	0–2		
166	14/03/92	Bristol City	Away	League	2–1		
167	17/03/92	Middlesbrough	Home	League	0–0		
168	21/03/92	Ipswich Town	Home	League	1–1		
169	28/03/92	Brighton & Hove Albion	Away	League	1–1		
170	01/04/92	Derby County	Away	League	0–0		
Sub+25	04/04/92	Millwall	Home	League	1–0	1 Goal	(73)
171	11/04/92	Wolverhampton Wanderers	Away	League	1–2		
172	17/04/92	Portsmouth	Home	League	2–2		
173	21/04/92	Leicester City	Away	League	1–2		
174	25/04/92	Port Vale	Home	League	4–2		
Sub+26	02/05/92	Sunderland	Away	League	2–2		
175	10/05/92	Leicester City	Home	Lge P/O	1–1		
176	13/05/92	Leicester City	Away	Lge P/O	0–5		

+ AET Cambridge United won 4–2 on penalties

SEASON 1992–93

Manchester United – Premier League

Sub+1	15/08/92	Sheffield United	Away	League	1–2		
Sub+2	19/08/92	Everton	Home	League	0–3		
Sub+3	22/08/92	Ipswich Town	Home	League	1–1		
1	24/08/92	Southampton	Away	League	1–0	1 Goal	(1)
2	29/08/92	Nottingham Forest	Away	League	2–0		
3	02/09/92	Crystal Palace	Home	League	1–0		
Sub+4	09/03/93	Oldham Athletic	Away	League	0–1		

SEASON 1993–94

Premier League

4	22/09/93	Stoke City	Away	Lge Cup	1–2	1 Goal	(2)
Sub+5	03/11/93	Galatasaray SK	Away	Eur Cup	0–0		
Sub+6	12/01/94	Portsmouth	Home	Lge Cup	2–2		
Sub+7	20/02/94	Wimbledon	Away	FA Cup	3–0		
Sub+8	26/02/94	West Ham United	Away	League	2–2		
Sub+9	05/03/94	Chelsea	Home	League	0–1		
Sub+10	04/04/94	Oldham Athletic	Home	League	3–2	1 Goal	(3)
5	10/04/94	Oldham Athletic	Wembley	FA Cup	1–1*		
Sub+11	16/04/94	Wimbledon	Away	League	0–1		
6	08/05/94	Coventry City	Home	League	0–0		

SEASON 1994–95

Coventry City – Premier League

1	10/09/94	Queens Park Rangers	Away	League	2–2	1 Goal	(1)
2	17/09/94	Leeds United	Home	League	2–1	1 Goal	(2)
3	20/09/94	Wrexham	Away	Lge Cup	2–1		
4	24/09/94	Southampton	Home	League	1–3	1 Goal	(3)
5	03/10/94	Leicester City	Away	League	2–2	1 Goal	(4)
6	05/10/94	Wrexham	Home	Lge Cup	3–2	2 Goals	(6)
7	10/10/94	Ipswich Town	Home	League	2–0		
8	15/10/94	Everton	Away	League	2–0	1 Goal	(7)
9	23/10/94	Arsenal	Away	League	1–2		
10	26/10/94	Blackburn Rovers	Away	Lge Cup	0–2		
11	29/10/94	Manchester City	Home	League	1–0	1 Goal	(8)
12	02/11/94	Crystal Palace	Home	League	1–4	1 Goal	(9)
13	06/11/94	Chelsea	Away	League	2–2	1 Goal	(10)
14	19/11/94	Norwich City	Home	League	1–0		
15	26/11/94	West Ham United	Away	League	1–0		
16	03/01/95	Manchester United	Away	League	0–2		
17	07/01/95	West Bromwich Albion	Home	FA Cup	1–1		
18	14/01/95	Manchester City	Away	League	0–0		
19	18/01/95	West Bromwich Albion	Away	FA Cup	2–1	1 Goal	(11)
20	21/01/95	Arsenal	Home	League	0–1		
21	25/01/95	Norwich City	Away	League	2–2	1 Goal	(12)
22	28/01/95	Norwich City	Home	FA Cup	0–0		
23	04/02/95	Chelsea	Home	League	2–2		

24	08/02/95	Norwich City	Away	FA Cup	1–3*		
25	11/02/95	Crystal Palace	Away	League	2–0	1 Goal	(13)
26	18/02/95	West Ham United	Home	League	2–0		
27	25/02/95	Leicester City	Home	League	4–2		
28	04/03/95	Southampton	Away	League	0–0		
29	06/03/95	Aston Villa	Away	League	0–0		
30	11/03/95	Blackburn Rovers	Home	League	1–1	1 Goal	(14)
31	14/03/95	Liverpool	Away	League	3–2		
32	01/04/95	Queens Park Rangers	Home	League	0–1		
33	15/04/95	Sheffield Wednesday	Home	League	2–0	1 Goal	(15)
34	17/04/95	Nottingham Forest	Away	League	0–2		
35	01/05/95	Manchester United	Home	League	2–3		
36	06/05/95	Ipswich Town	Away	League	0–2		
37	09/05/95	Tottenham Hotspur	Away	League	3–1	1 Goal	(16)
38	14/05/95	Everton	Home	League	0–0		

SEASON 1995–96

Premier League

39	19/08/95	Newcastle United	Away	League	0–3		
40	23/08/95	Manchester City	Home	League	2–1	1 Goal	(17)
41	26/08/95	Arsenal	Home	League	0–0		
42	30/08/95	Chelsea	Away	League	2–2		
43	09/09/95	Nottingham Forest	Home	League	1–1	1 Goal	(18)
44	16/09/95	Middlesbrough	Away	League	1–2		
Sub+1	25/10/95	Tottenham Hotspur	Home	Lge Cup	3–2		
45	28/10/95	Leeds United	Away	League	1–3	1 Goal	(19)
46	04/11/95	Tottenham Hotspur	Home	League	2–3	1 Goal	(20)
47	19/11/95	Queens Park Rangers	Away	League	1–1	1 Goal	(21)
48	22/11/95	Manchester United	Home	League	0–4		
49	25/11/95	Wimbledon	Home	League	3–3	1 Goal	(22)
50	29/11/95	Wolverhampton Wanderers	Away	Lge Cup	1–2		
51	04/12/95	Sheffield Wednesday	Away	League	3–4	3 Goals	(25)
52	09/12/95	Blackburn Rovers	Home	League	5–0	1 Goal	(26)
53	16/12/95	Aston Villa	Away	League	1–4	1 Goal	(27)
54	23/12/95	Everton	Home	League	2–1		
55	30/12/95	Bolton Wanderers	Away	League	2–1		
56	01/01/96	Southampton	Home	League	1–1		
57	06/01/96	Plymouth Argyle	Away	FA Cup	3–1		
58	14/01/96	Newcastle United	Home	League	0–1		
59	20/01/96	Manchester City	Away	League	1–1	1 Goal	(28)
60	31/01/96	West Ham United	Away	League	2–3	1 Goal	(29)
61	03/02/96	Arsenal	Away	League	1–1		
62	07/02/96	Manchester City	Home	FA Cup	2–2	1 Goal	(30)
63	10/02/96	Chelsea	Home	League	1–0		
64	14/02/96	Manchester City	Away	FA Cup	1–2	1 Goal	(31)
65	24/02/96	Middlesbrough	Home	League	0–0		
66	02/03/96	West Ham United	Home	League	2–2		
67	09/03/96	Everton	Away	League	2–2		
68	16/03/96	Bolton Wanderers	Home	League	0–2		
69	25/03/96	Southampton	Away	League	0–1		
70	30/03/96	Tottenham Hotspur	Away	League	1–3	1 Goal	(32)
71	06/04/96	Liverpool	Home	League	1–0		
72	08/04/96	Manchester United	Away	League	0–1		
73	13/04/96	Queens Park Rangers	Home	League	1–0		
74	17/04/96	Nottingham Forest	Away	League	0–0		
75	27/04/96	Wimbledon	Away	League	2–0		
76	05/05/96	Leeds United	Home	League	0–0		

SEASON 1996–97

Premier League

77	17/08/96	Nottingham Forest	Home	League	0–3		
78	21/08/96	West Ham United	Away	League	1–1		
79	24/08/96	Chelsea	Away	League	0–2		
80	04/09/96	Liverpool	Home	League	0–1		
81	07/09/96	Middlesbrough	Away	League	0–4		
82	14/09/96	Leeds United	Home	League	2–1		
83	18/09/96	Birmingham City	Home	Lge Cup	1–1		
84	21/09/96	Sunderland	Away	League	0–1		
85	24/09/96	Birmingham City	Away	Lge Cup	1–0		
86	28/09/96	Blackburn Rovers	Home	League	0–0		
Sub+2	13/10/96	Southampton	Home	League	1–1	1 Goal	(33)
87	19/10/96	Arsenal	Away	League	0–0		
88	22/10/96	Gillingham	Away	Lge Cup	2–2		

89	26/10/96	Sheffield Wednesday	Home	League	0–0		
90	04/11/96	Everton	Away	League	1–1		
Sub+3	13/11/96	Gillingham	Home	Lge Cup	0–1		
91	16/11/96	Wimbledon	Away	League	2–2	1 Goal	(34)
92	23/11/96	Aston Villa	Home	League	1–2	1 Goal	(35)
93	30/11/96	Derby County	Away	League	1–2	1 Goal	(36)
94	07/12/96	Tottenham Hotspur	Home	League	1–2		
95	17/12/96	Newcastle United	Home	League	2–1		
96	21/12/96	Leicester City	Away	League	2–0	2 Goals	(38)
97	26/12/96	Leeds United	Away	League	3–1	1 Goal	(39)
98	28/12/96	Middlesbrough	Home	League	3–0		
99	01/01/97	Sunderland	Home	League	2–2	1 Goal	(40)
100	11/01/97	Blackburn Rovers	Away	League	0–4		
101	22/02/97	Everton	Home	League	0–0		
102	26/02/97	Derby County	Away	FA Cup	2–3		
103	01/03/97	Manchester United	Away	League	1–3		
104	03/03/97	Wimbledon	Home	League	1–1	1 Goal	(41)
105	08/03/97	Leicester City	Home	League	0–0		
106	15/03/97	Newcastle United	Away	League	0–2		
107	22/03/97	West Ham United	Home	League	1–3		
108	06/04/97	Liverpool	Away	League	2–1	1 Goal	(42)
109	09/04/97	Chelsea	Home	League	3–1	1 Goal	(43)
110	19/04/97	Southampton	Away	League	2–2		
111	21/04/97	Arsenal	Home	League	1–1	1 Goal	(44)
112	03/05/97	Derby County	Home	League	1–3		
113	11/05/97	Tottenham Hotspur	Away	League	2–1	1 Goal	(45)

APPEARANCES AND GOALS PER SEASON

SEASON 88–89	GAMES	GOALS
League	12+9	6
FA Cup	1	0
Sherpa Van Trophy	1+1	1
TOTAL	**14+10**	**7**

SEASON 89–90	GAMES	GOALS
League	37+9	15
League Play–offs	3	2
FA Cup	10	4
League Cup	2+2	2
Leyland Daf Cup	2	0
TOTAL	**54+11**	**23**

SEASON 90–91	GAMES	GOALS
League	44+2	17
FA Cup	7	5
League Cup	2	1
Leyland Daf Cup	4	2
TOTAL	**57+2**	**25**

SEASON 91–92	GAMES	GOALS
League	40+3	15
League Play–offs	2	0
FA Cup	3	1
League Cup	4	2
Zenith Data Systems Cup	2	0
TOTAL	**51+3**	**18**

SEASON 92–93	GAMES	GOALS
League	3+4	1
TOTAL	**3+4**	**1**

SEASON 93–94	GAMES	GOALS
League	1+4	1
FA Cup	1+1	0
League Cup	1+1	1
European Cup	0+1	0
TOTAL	**3+7**	**2**

SEASON 94–95	GAMES	GOALS
League	31	13
FA Cup	4	1
League Cup	3	2
TOTAL	**38**	**16**

SEASON 95–96	GAMES	GOALS
League	34	14
FA Cup	3	2
League Cup	1+1	0
TOTAL	**38+1**	**16**

SEASON 96–97	GAMES	GOALS
League	33+1	13
FA Cup	1	0
League Cup	3+1	0
TOTAL	**37+2**	**13**

CAREER APPEARANCES AND GOALS

COMPETITION	GAMES	TOTAL	GOALS
League	235+32	267	95
League Play–offs	5	5	2
FA Cup	30+1	31	13
League Cup	16+5	21	8
Sherpa Van Trophy	1+1	2	1
Leyland Daf Cup	6	6	2
Zenith Data Systems Cup	2	2	0
European Cup	0+1	1	0
TOTAL	**295+40**	**335**	**121**

HAT-TRICKS

Cambridge United

1	3	Peterborough United	03/01/89	Away	League	5–1

Coventry City

1	3	Sheffield Wednesday	04/12/95	Away	League	3–4

League: 2
TOTAL: 2

HONOURS

Winners medals
FA Charity Shield: 94/95*

Runner-up medals
League Division Three Championship: 90/91
Promoted to League Division Three: 89/90

Played seven (3+4/1) League matches in the Manchester United team that won the 1992/93 Premier League Championship.
Played five (1+4/1) League matches in the Manchester United team that won the 1993/94 Premier League Championship.

* Non–playing substitute

GORDON DURIE

Born: 06/12/65 – Paisley
Height: 5.10
Weight: 13.00 (96–97)

Clubs
East Fife: **1982–84** – Matches: **79+18** – Goals: **27**
Hibernian: **1984–86** – Matches: **56+2** – Goals: **22**
Chelsea: **1986–91** – Matches: **144+8** – Goals: **62**
Tottenham Hotspur: **1991–93** – Matches: **78** – Goals: **17**
Rangers: **1993–97** – Matches: **98+18** – Goals: **48**

Country
Scotland: **1987–97** – Matches: **26+9** – Goals: **5**

SEASON 1981–82

East Fife – Scottish League Division Two

1	20/02/82	Stranraer	Away	League	2–1		
2	27/02/82	Forfar Athletic	Home	League	1–0	1 Goal	(1)
3	06/03/82	Cowdenbeath	Away	League	2–1		
4	13/03/82	Meadowbank Thistle	Home	League	1–0		
5	17/03/82	Albion Rovers	Away	League	0–1		
6	20/03/82	Stirling Albion	Home	League	1–2		
Sub+1	27/03/82	Berwick Rangers	Away	League	0–3		
7	03/04/82	Alloa	Home	League	0–2		
8	07/04/82	Stirling Albion	Away	League	2–0		
Sub+2	10/04/82	Brechin City	Away	League	1–1		
Sub+3	01/05/82	Arbroath	Away	League	1–1		
Sub+4	08/05/82	Albion Rovers	Home	League	1–1		
Sub+5	15/05/82	Montrose	Away	League	2–1		

SEASON 1982–83

Scottish League Division Two

9	14/08/82	Brechin City	Home	S Lge Cup	0–0		
Sub+6	18/08/82	Partick Thistle	Away	S Lge Cup	0–0		
10	25/08/82	Partick Thistle	Home	S Lge Cup	0–3		
11	01/09/82	East Stirling	Away	S Lge Cup	0–0		
12	04/09/82	East Stirling	Home	League	3–1		
13	08/09/82	Brechin City	Away	League	0–0		
14	11/09/82	Albion Rovers	Away	League	0–1		
15	15/09/82	Cowdenbeath	Home	League	1–1		
16	18/09/82	Queen of the South	Away	League	5–1		
Sub+7	16/10/82	Stirling Albion	Away	League	0–1		
17	23/10/82	Forfar Athletic	Away	League	1–4		
18	30/10/82	Stranraer	Home	League	2–2	1 Goal	(2)
19	06/11/82	Berwick Rangers	Away	League	0–1		
Sub+8	13/11/82	Brechin City	Home	League	1–2		
Sub+9	11/12/82	Queen of the South	Away	League	2–1		
20	18/12/82	Arbroath	Away	League	1–3		
Sub+10	03/01/83	Berwick Rangers	Home	League	0–1		
21	08/01/83	Brechin City	Home	S Cup	1–0		
Sub+11	22/01/83	Stranraer	Away	League	2–2		
Sub+12	28/01/83	Raith Rovers	Home	S Cup	1–0		
Sub+13	09/02/83	Stenhousemuir	Away	League	2–3		
22	12/02/83	Stirling Albion	Home	League	1–0		
Sub+14	23/02/83	Stranraer	Home	League	3–0		
Sub+15	26/02/83	Forfar Athletic	Away	League	0–0		
Sub+16	03/03/83	Cowdenbeath	Home	League	0–2		
23	09/03/83	Forfar Athletic	Home	League	0–2		
24	19/03/83	Montrose	Home	League	4–0		
25	26/03/83	Albion Rovers	Away	League	1–1		
26	02/04/83	Berwick Rangers	Home	League	3–0		
27	09/04/83	Stenhousemuir	Away	League	2–0		
28	07/05/83	East Stirling	Away	League	1–1	1 Goal	(3)
29	14/05/83	Arbroath	Home	League	4–0		

SEASON 1983–84

Scottish League Division Two

30	13/08/83	Arbroath	Away	S Lge Cup	1–0		
31	17/08/83	Arbroath	Home	S Lge Cup	1–1		
32	20/08/83	Montrose	Home	League	1–0		
33	24/08/83	St Johnstone	Home	S Lge Cup	1–2		
34	27/08/83	St Johnstone	Away	S Lge Cup	3–6		
Sub+17	03/09/83	Dunfermline Athletic	Away	League	1–1		
Sub+18	10/09/83	Stranraer	Home	League	1–0	1 Goal	(4)
35	14/09/83	East Stirling	Away	League	4–1		
36	17/09/83	Arbroath	Home	League	0–1		
37	24/09/83	Queen's Park	Away	League	2–5		
38	28/09/83	Berwick Rangers	Home	League	1–2		
39	01/10/83	Cowdenbeath	Home	League	2–1	2 Goals	(6)
40	29/10/83	Queen of the South	Home	League	1–2		
41	05/11/83	Stenhousemuir	Away	League	1–3		
42	12/11/83	East Stirling	Home	League	2–1		
43	19/11/83	Arbroath	Away	League	2–0		
44	26/11/83	Forfar Athletic	Home	League	2–3		
45	03/12/83	Cowdenbeath	Away	League	0–0		
46	26/12/83	Queen's Park	Home	League	3–1	1 Goal	(7)

47	31/12/83	Dunfermline Athletic	Home	League	3–1	2 Goals	(9)
48	02/01/84	Montrose	Away	League	1–0		
49	07/01/84	Queen of the South	Away	S Cup	5–0	1 Goal	(10)
50	14/01/84	Albion Rovers	Home	League	1–0		
51	28/01/84	Hibernian	Away	S Cup	0–0		
52	31/01/84	Hibernian	Home	S Cup	2–0		
53	04/02/84	Stenhousemuir	Home	League	0–1		
54	11/02/84	Stranraer	Away	League	0–1		
55	18/02/84	Celtic	Home	S Cup	0–6		
56	21/02/84	Albion Rovers	Home	League	1–4		
57	25/02/84	Forfar Athletic	Home	League	0–0		
58	03/03/84	Montrose	Away	League	1–1		
59	06/03/84	Stirling Albion	Away	League	1–0	1 Goal	(11)
60	10/03/84	Queen of the South	Home	League	0–0		
61	17/03/84	Cowdenbeath	Away	League	5–1		
62	24/03/84	Stirling Albion	Home	League	4–2	1 Goal	(12)
63	31/03/84	Berwick Rangers	Away	League	1–2	1 Goal	(13)
64	07/04/84	Stenhousemuir	Home	League	3–1	1 Goal	(14)
65	14/04/84	East Stirling	Home	League	2–0	1 Goal	(15)
66	21/04/84	Dunfermline Athletic	Away	League	1–0	1 Goal	(16)
67	28/04/84	Arbroath	Away	League	1–0	1 Goal	(17)
68	05/05/84	Queen's Park	Home	League	3–0	2 Goals	(19)
69	12/05/84	Stranraer	Away	League	2–1	1 Goal	(20)

SEASON 1984–85

Scottish League Division One

70	18/08/84	St Johnstone	Away	League	4–3		
71	22/08/84	Hibernian	Away	S Lge Cup	0–1		
72	25/08/84	Hamilton Academical	Away	League	4–2	4 Goals	(24)
73	01/09/84	Ayr United	Home	League	1–1	1 Goal	(25)
74	08/09/84	Brechin City	Away	League	2–2		
75	15/09/84	Meadowbank Thistle	Home	League	1–1		
76	22/09/84	Clyde	Away	League	1–1		
77	29/09/84	Clydebank	Home	League	4–4	2 Goals	(27)
78	06/10/84	Forfar Athletic	Away	League	0–1		
79	13/10/84	Partick Thistle	Away	League	0–0		

Hibernian – Scottish League Premier Division

1	20/10/84	Dundee	Home	League	2–0		
2	27/10/84	Heart of Midlothian	Away	League	0–0		
3	06/11/84	Aberdeen	Home	League	0–3		
4	10/11/84	Rangers	Home	League	2–2		
5	17/11/84	Dumbarton	Away	League	2–2	2 Goals	(2)
6	24/11/84	Dundee United	Home	League	0–0		
7	01/12/84	Morton	Away	League	0–4		
8	08/12/84	St Mirren	Home	League	2–3	1 Goal	(3)
9	15/12/84	Celtic	Home	League	0–1		
10	29/12/84	Dundee	Away	League	0–2		
11	01/01/85	Heart of Midlothian	Home	League	1–2		
12	12/01/85	Rangers	Away	League	2–1		
13	19/01/85	Dumbarton	Home	League	3–1	1 Goal	(4)
14	02/02/85	Dundee United	Away	League	0–2		
15	04/02/85	Dundee United	Away	S Cup	0–3		
16	09/02/85	Morton	Home	League	5–1	3 Goals	(7)
17	23/02/85	St Mirren	Away	League	1–2		
18	02/03/85	Dundee	Home	League	0–1		
19	06/04/85	Dumbarton	Away	League	2–0		
20	20/04/85	Dundee United	Home	League	1–1	1 Goal	(8)
21	27/04/85	St Mirren	Home	League	0–4		
22	04/05/85	Morton	Away	League	2–1		
23	11/05/85	Rangers	Home	League	1–0		

SEASON 1985–86

Scottish League Premier Division

Sub+1	10/08/85	Aberdeen	Away	League	0–3		
Sub+2	17/08/85	Rangers	Home	League	1–3	1 Goal	(9)
24	21/08/85	Cowdenbeath	Home	S Lge Cup	6–0	2 Goals	(11)
25	24/08/85	St Mirren	Home	League	2–3		
26	28/08/85	Motherwell	Home	S Lge Cup	6–1	3 Goals	(14)
27	31/08/85	Heart of Midlothian	Away	League	1–2	1 Goal	(15)
28	04/09/85	Celtic	Home	S Lge Cup	4–4+	2 Goals	(17)
29	07/09/85	Celtic	Home	League	0–5		
30	14/09/85	Dundee	Away	League	0–1		

31	25/09/85	Rangers	Home	S Lge Cup	2–0	1 Goal	(18)
32	28/09/85	Motherwell	Home	League	1–0		
33	01/10/85	Clydebank	Home	League	5–0	2 Goals	(20)
34	05/10/85	Dundee United	Away	League	2–2		
35	09/10/85	Rangers	Away	S Lge Cup	0–1		
36	12/10/85	Aberdeen	Home	League	1–1		
37	19/10/85	Rangers	Away	League	2–1		
38	27/10/85	Aberdeen	Hampden	S Lge Cup	0–3		
39	30/10/85	Clydebank	Away	League	4–2		
40	02/11/85	Dundee	Home	League	2–1	1 Goal	(21)
41	09/11/85	Heart of Midlothian	Home	League	0–0		
42	16/11/85	St Mirren	Away	League	3–1		
43	23/11/85	Celtic	Away	League	1–1		
44	14/12/85	Aberdeen	Away	League	0–4		
45	18/01/86	Celtic	Home	League	2–2	1 Goal	(22)
46	26/01/86	Dunfermline Athletic	Home	S Cup	2–0		
47	01/02/86	Motherwell	Home	League	4–0		
48	16/02/86	Ayr United	Home	S Cup	1–0		
49	22/02/86	Aberdeen	Home	League	0–1		
50	26/02/86	Dundee United	Home	League	0–1		
51	01/03/86	Rangers	Away	League	1–3		
52	08/03/86	Celtic	Home	S Cup	4–3		
53	12/03/86	St Mirren	Home	League	3–0		
54	15/03/86	Clydebank	Away	League	3–1		
55	22/03/86	Heart of Midlothian	Home	League	1–2		
56	05/04/86	Aberdeen	Home	S Cup	0–3		

+ AET Hibernian won 4–3 on penalties

Chelsea – League Division One

1	05/05/86	Watford	Home	League	1–5		

SEASON 1986–87

League Division One

2	23/08/86	Norwich City	Home	League	0–0		
3	25/08/86	Oxford United	Away	League	1–1		
4	30/08/86	Sheffield Wednesday	Away	League	0–2		
Sub+1	06/09/86	Luton Town	Home	League	1–3		
Sub+2	13/09/86	Tottenham Hotspur	Away	League	3–1		
Sub+3	20/09/86	Nottingham Forest	Home	League	2–6		
Sub+4	15/11/86	Aston Villa	Away	League	0–0		
5	22/11/86	Newcastle United	Home	League	1–3	1 Goal	(1)
6	14/12/86	Liverpool	Away	League	0–3		
Sub+5	27/12/86	Aston Villa	Home	League	4–1		
Sub+6	01/01/87	Queens Park Rangers	Home	League	3–1		
Sub+7	03/01/87	Luton Town	Away	League	0–1		
7	10/01/87	Aston Villa	Away	FA Cup	2–2		
8	21/01/87	Aston Villa	Home	FA Cup	2–1*	1 Goal	(2)
9	24/01/87	Norwich City	Away	League	2–2		
10	01/02/87	Watford	Away	FA Cup	0–1		
11	07/02/87	Sheffield Wednesday	Home	League	2–0		
12	10/02/87	Oxford United	Home	League	4–0	1 Goal	(3)
13	14/02/87	Coventry City	Away	League	0–3		
14	21/02/87	Manchester United	Home	League	1–1		
15	28/02/87	Nottingham Forest	Away	League	1–0		
16	14/03/87	Manchester City	Away	League	2–1	1 Goal	(4)
17	21/03/87	West Ham United	Home	League	1–0		
18	04/04/87	Everton	Home	League	1–2		
19	20/04/87	Southampton	Home	League	1–1		
20	25/04/87	Newcastle United	Away	League	0–1		
21	02/05/87	Leicester City	Home	League	3–1	1 Goal	(5)
22	09/05/87	Liverpool	Home	League	3–3	1 Goal	(6)

SEASON 1987–88

League Division One

23	15/08/87	Sheffield Wednesday	Home	League	2–1	1 Goal	(7)
24	18/08/87	Portsmouth	Away	League	3–0		
25	22/08/87	Tottenham Hotspur	Away	League	0–1		
26	29/08/87	Luton Town	Home	League	3–0		
27	31/08/87	Manchester United	Away	League	1–3		
28	05/09/87	Nottingham Forest	Home	League	4–3	2 Goals	(9)
29	12/09/87	Queens Park Rangers	Away	League	1–3	1 Goal	(10)
30	23/09/87	Reading	Away	Lge Cup	1–3	1 Goal	(11)

31	26/09/87	Watford	Away	League	3–0	2 Goals	(13)
32	03/10/87	Newcastle United	Home	League	2–2		
33	07/10/87	Reading	Home	Lge Cup	3–2	3 Goals	(16)
34	10/10/87	Everton	Away	League	1–4		
35	24/10/87	Southampton	Away	League	0–3		
36	31/10/87	Oxford United	Home	League	2–1		
37	03/11/87	Arsenal	Away	League	1–3		
38	22/11/87	Derby County	Away	League	0–2		
39	28/11/87	Wimbledon	Home	League	1–1	1 Goal	(17)
40	06/12/87	Liverpool	Away	League	1–2	1 Goal	(18)
41	26/12/87	Queens Park Rangers	Home	League	1–1		
42	28/12/87	Norwich City	Away	League	0–3		
43	01/01/88	Luton Town	Away	League	0–3		
44	02/01/88	Tottenham Hotspur	Home	League	0–0		
45	09/01/88	Derby County	Away	FA Cup	3–1		
46	02/04/88	Arsenal	Home	League	1–1		
47	09/04/88	Derby County	Home	League	1–0		
48	23/04/88	Wimbledon	Away	League	2–2	2 Goals	(20)
49	30/04/88	Liverpool	Home	League	1–1	1 Goal	(21)
50	02/05/88	West Ham United	Away	League	1–4		
51	07/05/88	Charlton Athletic	Home	League	1–1	1 Goal	(22)
52	15/05/88	Blackburn Rovers	Away	Lge P/O	2–0	1 Goal	(23)
53	18/05/88	Blackburn Rovers	Home	Lge P/O	4–1	1 Goal	(24)
54	25/05/88	Middlesbrough	Away	Lge P/O	0–2		
55	28/05/88	Middlesbrough	Home	Lge P/O	1–0	1 Goal	(25)

SEASON 1988–89

League Division Two

56	27/08/88	Blackburn Rovers	Home	League	1–2		
57	30/08/88	Crystal Palace	Away	League	1–1		
58	03/09/88	AFC Bournemouth	Away	League	0–1		
59	10/09/88	Oxford United	Home	League	1–1		
60	17/09/88	Barnsley	Away	League	1–1		
61	20/09/88	Manchester City	Home	League	1–3		
62	24/09/88	Leeds United	Away	League	2–0	1 Goal	(26)
63	12/10/88	Scunthorpe United	Home	Lge Cup	2–2		
64	22/10/88	Plymouth Argyle	Home	League	5–0	2 Goals	(28)
65	25/10/88	Hull City	Away	League	0–3		
66	29/10/88	Brighton & Hove Albion	Home	League	2–0		
67	05/11/88	Watford	Away	League	2–1	1 Goal	(29)
68	09/11/88	Plymouth Argyle	Home	Simod Cup	6–2		
69	12/11/88	Sunderland	Home	League	1–1		
70	19/11/88	Bradford City	Away	League	2–2		
71	26/11/88	Shrewsbury Town	Home	League	2–0		
72	30/11/88	Bradford City	Away	Simod Cup	3–2		
73	10/12/88	Portsmouth	Home	League	3–3	1 Goal	(30)
74	16/12/88	Birmingham City	Away	League	4–1	2 Goals	(32)
75	26/12/88	Ipswich Town	Home	League	3–0	1 Goal	(33)
76	31/12/88	West Bromwich Albion	Home	League	1–1		
77	02/01/89	Oxford United	Away	League	3–2		
78	07/01/89	Barnsley	Away	FA Cup	0–4		
79	10/01/89	Nottingham Forest	Home	Simod Cup	1–4		
80	04/02/89	Walsall	Away	League	7–0	5 Goals	(38)
81	11/02/89	Swindon Town	Home	League	3–2	1 Goal	(39)
82	18/02/89	Plymouth Argyle	Away	League	1–0		
83	18/03/89	Manchester City	Away	League	3–2		
84	21/03/89	Sunderland	Away	League	2–1		
85	25/03/89	AFC Bournemouth	Home	League	2–0	1 Goal	(40)
86	28/03/89	Ipswich Town	Away	League	1–0	1 Goal	(41)
87	01/04/89	Barnsley	Home	League	5–3	1 Goal	(42)
88	04/04/89	Birmingham City	Home	League	3–1		
89	08/04/89	West Bromwich Albion	Away	League	3–2		
90	15/04/89	Leicester City	Away	League	0–2		
91	22/04/89	Leeds United	Home	League	1–0		
92	29/04/89	Shrewsbury Town	Away	League	1–1		

SEASON 1989–90

League Division One

93	19/08/89	Wimbledon	Away	League	1–0		
94	22/08/89	Queens Park Rangers	Home	League	1–1		
95	29/08/89	Charlton Athletic	Away	League	0–3		
96	09/09/89	Nottingham Forest	Home	League	2–2	1 Goal	(43)
97	16/12/89	Liverpool	Home	League	2–5	1 Goal	(44)

98	22/12/89	West Ham United	Home	ZDS Cup	4–3		
99	10/01/90	Crewe Alexandra	Away	FA Cup	2–0		
Sub+8	03/03/90	Southampton	Away	League	3–2	1 Goal	(45)
100	10/03/90	Norwich City	Home	League	0–0		
101	12/03/90	Crystal Palace	Home	ZDS Cup	2–0		
102	17/03/90	Arsenal	Away	League	1–0		
103	21/03/90	Manchester City	Away	League	1–1	1 Goal	(46)
104	25/03/90	Middlesbrough	Wembley	ZDS Cup	1–0		
105	31/03/90	Derby County	Home	League	1–1		
106	07/04/90	Luton Town	Home	League	1–0	1 Goal	(47)
107	14/04/90	Aston Villa	Away	League	0–1		
108	16/04/90	Crystal Palace	Home	League	3–0		
109	21/04/90	Liverpool	Away	League	1–4		
110	28/04/90	Everton	Home	League	2–1		

SEASON 1990–91

League Division One

111	06/10/90	Southampton	Away	League	3–3		
112	10/10/90	Walsall	Home	Lge Cup	4–1	1 Goal	(48)
113	20/10/90	Nottingham Forest	Home	League	0–0		
114	27/10/90	Liverpool	Away	League	0–2		
115	31/10/90	Portsmouth	Home	Lge Cup	0–0		
116	03/11/90	Aston Villa	Home	League	1–0		
117	06/11/90	Portsmouth	Away	Lge Cup	3–2		
118	10/11/90	Norwich City	Home	League	1–1		
119	17/11/90	Wimbledon	Away	League	1–2	1 Goal	(49)
120	25/11/90	Manchester United	Away	League	3–2		
121	28/11/90	Oxford United	Away	Lge Cup	2–1	2 Goals	(51)
122	01/12/90	Tottenham Hotspur	Home	League	3–2	1 Goal	(52)
123	08/12/90	Crystal Palace	Home	League	2–1	1 Goal	(53)
124	12/12/90	Swindon Town	Home	ZDS Cup	1–0		
125	15/12/90	Derby County	Away	League	6–4	2 Goals	(55)
126	22/12/90	Coventry City	Home	League	2–1		
127	26/12/90	Leeds United	Away	League	1–4		
128	12/01/91	Queens Park Rangers	Home	League	2–0	2 Goals	(57)
129	16/01/91	Tottenham Hotspur	Home	Lge Cup	0–0		
130	19/01/91	Sunderland	Away	League	0–1		
131	23/01/91	Tottenham Hotspur	Away	Lge Cup	3–0		
132	18/02/91	Luton Town	Home	ZDS Cup	1–1+		
133	24/02/91	Sheffield Wednesday	Home	Lge Cup	0–2		
134	27/02/91	Sheffield Wednesday	Away	Lge Cup	1–3		
135	02/03/91	Tottenham Hotspur	Away	League	1–1	1 Goal	(58)
136	09/03/91	Manchester United	Home	League	3–2	1 Goal	(59)
137	16/03/91	Sheffield United	Away	League	0–1		
138	23/03/91	Southampton	Home	League	0–2		
139	30/03/91	Leeds United	Home	League	1–2		
140	01/04/91	Coventry City	Away	League	0–1		
141	17/04/91	Norwich City	Away	League	3–1	2 Goals	(61)
142	20/04/91	Nottingham Forest	Away	League	0–7		
143	04/05/91	Liverpool	Home	League	4–2	1 Goal	(62)
144	11/05/91	Aston Villa	Away	League	2–2		

+ AET Luton Town won 4–1 on penalties

SEASON 1991–92

Tottenham Hotspur – League Division One

1	17/08/91	Southampton	Away	League	3–2	1 Goal	(1)
2	21/08/91	SV Stockerau	Away	ECW Cup	1–0	1 Goal	(2)
3	24/08/91	Chelsea	Home	League	1–3		
4	28/08/91	Nottingham Forest	Away	League	3–1	1 Goal	(3)
5	31/08/91	Norwich City	Away	League	1–0		
6	04/09/91	SV Stockerau	Home	ECW Cup	1–0		
7	07/09/91	Aston Villa	Away	League	0–0		
8	14/09/91	Queens Park Rangers	Home	League	2–0		
9	17/09/91	NK Hajduk Split	Away	ECW Cup	0–1		
10	21/09/91	Wimbledon	Away	League	5–3		
11	25/09/91	Swansea City	Away	Lge Cup	0–1		
12	28/09/91	Manchester United	Home	League	1–2	1 Goal	(4)
13	02/10/91	NK Hajduk Split	Home	ECW Cup	2–0	1 Goal	(5)
14	05/10/91	Everton	Away	League	1–3		
15	09/10/91	Swansea City	Home	Lge Cup	5–1		
16	19/10/91	Manchester City	Home	League	0–1		
17	23/10/91	FC Porto	Home	ECW Cup	3–1	1 Goal	(6)

18	26/10/91	West Ham United	Away	League	1–2		
19	29/10/91	Grimsby Town	Away	Lge Cup	3–0	1 Goal	(7)
20	02/11/91	Sheffield Wednesday	Away	League	0–0		
21	07/11/91	FC Porto	Away	ECW Cup	0–0		
22	23/11/91	Sheffield United	Home	League	0–1		
23	01/12/91	Arsenal	Away	League	0–2		
24	04/12/91	Coventry City	Away	Lge Cup	2–1	1 Goal	(8)
25	07/12/91	Notts County	Home	League	2–1		
26	14/12/91	Leeds United	Away	League	1–1		
27	14/01/92	Aston Villa	Home	FA Cup	0–1		
28	18/01/92	Southampton	Home	League	1–2		
29	25/01/92	Oldham Athletic	Home	League	0–0		
30	01/02/92	Manchester City	Away	League	0–1		
31	09/02/92	Nottingham Forest	Away	Lge Cup	1–1		
32	16/02/92	Crystal Palace	Home	League	0–1		
33	22/02/92	Arsenal	Home	League	1–1		
34	01/03/92	Nottingham Forest	Home	Lge Cup	1–2		
35	04/03/92	SC Feyenoord	Away	ECW Cup	0–1		
36	07/03/92	Leeds United	Home	League	1–3		
37	11/03/92	Luton Town	Away	League	0–0		
38	14/03/92	Sheffield Wednesday	Home	League	0–2		
39	18/03/92	SC Feyenoord	Home	ECW Cup	0–0		
40	21/03/92	Liverpool	Away	League	1–2		
41	28/03/92	Coventry City	Home	League	4–3	3 Goals	(11)
42	01/04/92	West Ham United	Home	League	3–0		
43	04/04/92	Aston Villa	Home	League	2–5		
44	11/04/92	Queens Park Rangers	Away	League	2–1	1 Goal	(12)
45	25/04/92	Everton	Home	League	3–3		
46	02/05/92	Manchester United	Away	League	1–3		

SEASON 1992–93

Premier League

47	15/08/92	Southampton	Away	League	0–0		
48	19/08/92	Coventry City	Home	League	0–2		
49	22/08/92	Crystal Palace	Home	League	2–2	1 Goal	(13)
50	25/08/92	Leeds United	Away	League	0–5		
51	30/08/92	Ipswich Town	Away	League	1–1		
52	02/09/92	Sheffield United	Home	League	2–0	1 Goal	(14)
53	05/09/92	Everton	Home	League	2–1		
54	14/09/92	Coventry City	Away	League	0–1		
55	19/09/92	Manchester United	Home	League	1–1	1 Goal	(15)
56	21/09/92	Brentford	Home	Lge Cup	3–1	1 Goal	(16)
57	17/10/92	Middlesbrough	Home	League	2–2		
58	25/10/92	Wimbledon	Away	League	1–1		
59	31/10/92	Liverpool	Home	League	2–0		
60	07/11/92	Blackburn Rovers	Away	League	2–0		
61	21/11/92	Aston Villa	Home	League	0–0		
62	02/12/92	Nottingham Forest	Away	Lge Cup	0–2		
63	12/12/92	Arsenal	Home	League	1–0		
64	19/12/92	Oldham Athletic	Away	League	1–2		
65	24/01/93	Norwich City	Away	FA Cup	2–0		
66	27/01/93	Ipswich Town	Home	League	0–2		

SEASON 1993–94

Premier League

67	14/08/93	Newcastle United	Away	League	1–0		
68	16/08/93	Arsenal	Home	League	0–1		
69	21/08/93	Manchester City	Home	League	1–0		
70	25/08/93	Liverpool	Away	League	2–1		
71	28/08/93	Aston Villa	Away	League	0–1		
72	01/09/93	Chelsea	Home	League	1–1		
73	11/09/93	Sheffield United	Away	League	2–2		
74	18/09/93	Oldham Athletic	Home	League	5–0	1 Goal	(17)
75	22/09/93	Burnley	Away	Lge Cup	0–0		
76	26/09/93	Ipswich Town	Away	League	2–2		
77	06/10/93	Burnley	Home	Lge Cup	3–1		
78	20/11/93	Leeds United	Home	League	1–1		

Rangers – Scottish League Premier Division

1	27/11/93	Partick Thistle	Away	League	1–1		
2	01/12/93	Aberdeen	Home	League	2–0		
3	04/12/93	Motherwell	Away	League	2–0	2 Goals	(2)
4	11/12/93	Dundee United	Home	League	0–3		

5	18/12/93	St Johnstone	Away	League	4–0	1 Goal	(3)
6	27/12/93	Heart of Midlothian	Home	League	2–2		
7	01/01/94	Celtic	Away	League	4–2		
8	08/01/94	Kilmarnock	Home	League	3–0		
9	15/01/94	Dundee	Away	League	1–1	1 Goal	(4)
10	22/01/94	Aberdeen	Away	League	0–0		
11	29/01/94	Dumbarton	Home	S Cup	4–1	1 Goal	(5)
12	05/02/94	Partick Thistle	Home	League	5–1	2 Goals	(7)
13	12/02/94	Hibernian	Home	League	2–0	1 Goal	(8)
14	26/02/94	Raith Rovers	Away	League	2–1	1 Goal	(9)
15	05/03/94	Motherwell	Home	League	2–1	1 Goal	(10)
16	12/03/94	Heart of Midlothian	Home	S Cup	2–0		
17	19/03/94	St Johnstone	Home	League	4–0	1 Goal	(11)
18	26/03/94	Heart of Midlothian	Away	League	2–1		
Sub+1	29/03/94	Partick Thistle	Away	League	2–1		
19	02/04/94	Aberdeen	Home	League	1–1		
20	05/04/94	Dundee United	Away	League	0–0		
21	10/04/94	Kilmarnock	Hampden	S Cup	0–0		
22	13/04/94	Kilmarnock	Hampden	S Cup	2–1		
23	16/04/94	Raith Rovers	Home	League	4–0		
24	23/04/94	Dundee United	Home	League	2–1	2 Goals	(13)
25	26/04/94	Motherwell	Away	League	1–2		
26	30/04/94	Celtic	Home	League	1–1		
27	14/05/94	Dundee	Home	League	0–0		
28	21/05/94	Dundee United	Hampden	S Cup	0–1		

SEASON 1994–95

Scottish League Premier Division

29	10/08/94	AEK Athina	Away	Eur Cup	0–2		
30	24/08/94	AEK Athina	Home	Eur Cup	0–1		
31	27/08/94	Celtic	Home	League	0–2		
32	31/08/94	Falkirk	Home	S Lge Cup	1–2		
Sub+2	11/09/94	Heart of Midlothian	Home	League	3–0	1 Goal	(14)
33	17/09/94	Falkirk	Away	League	2–0		
34	24/09/94	Aberdeen	Away	League	2–2		
Sub+3	19/11/94	Falkirk	Home	League	1–1		
Sub+4	25/11/94	Aberdeen	Home	League	1–0		
35	04/12/94	Dundee United	Away	League	3–0		
36	10/12/94	Kilmarnock	Away	League	2–1		
37	26/12/94	Hibernian	Home	League	2–0		
38	31/12/94	Motherwell	Away	League	3–1	1 Goal	(15)
39	04/01/95	Celtic	Home	League	1–1		
40	04/02/95	Dundee United	Home	League	1–1		
41	06/02/95	Hamilton Academical	Away	S Cup	3–1		
Sub+5	12/02/95	Aberdeen	Away	League	0–2		
42	20/02/95	Heart of Midlothian	Away	S Cup	2–4	1 Goal	(16)
43	25/02/95	Kilmarnock	Home	League	3–0	1 Goal	(17)
44	04/03/95	Hibernian	Away	League	1–1		
45	11/03/95	Falkirk	Home	League	2–2		
46	18/03/95	Heart of Midlothian	Away	League	1–2		
47	01/04/95	Dundee United	Away	League	2–0	1 Goal	(18)
48	16/04/95	Hibernian	Home	League	3–1	1 Goal	(19)
49	13/05/95	Partick Thistle	Home	League	1–1		

SEASON 1995–96

Scottish League Premier Division

Sub+6	09/08/95	Anorthosis Famagusta	Home	Eur Cup	1–0	1 Goal	(20)
50	23/08/95	Anorthosis Famagusta	Away	Eur Cup	0–0		
51	26/08/95	Kilmarnock	Home	League	1–0		
Sub+7	13/09/95	Steaua Bucuresti	Away	Eur Cup	0–1		
52	16/09/95	Falkirk	Away	League	2–0		
Sub+8	20/09/95	Celtic	Away	S Lge Cup	1–0		
Sub+9	23/09/95	Hibernian	Home	League	0–1		
53	27/09/95	BV 09 Borussia Dortmund	Home	Eur Cup	2–2		
54	03/10/95	Motherwell	Home	League	2–1		
55	07/10/95	Aberdeen	Away	League	1–0		
56	14/10/95	Partick Thistle	Away	League	4–0	3 Goals	(23)
57	18/10/95	FC Juventus	Away	Eur Cup	0–4		
58	21/10/95	Heart of Midlothian	Home	League	4–1	1 Goal	(24)
59	24/10/95	Aberdeen	Hampden	S Lge Cup	1–2		
60	28/10/95	Raith Rovers	Away	League	2–2		
61	04/11/95	Falkirk	Home	League	2–0		
Sub+10	25/11/95	Hibernian	Away	League	4–1	1 Goal	(25)

Sub+11	02/12/95	Heart of Midlothian	Away	League	2–0		
62	06/12/95	BV 09 Borussia Dortmund	Away	Eur Cup	2–2	1 Goal	(26)
63	09/12/95	Partick Thistle	Home	League	1–0	1 Goal	(27)
64	19/12/95	Motherwell	Away	League	0–0		
65	26/12/95	Kilmarnock	Home	League	3–0	1 Goal	(28)
66	30/12/95	Hibernian	Home	League	7–0	4 Goals	(32)
67	03/01/96	Celtic	Away	League	0–0		
68	06/01/96	Falkirk	Away	League	4–0	1 Goal	(33)
69	13/01/96	Raith Rovers	Home	League	4–0	2 Goals	(35)
70	20/01/96	Heart of Midlothian	Home	League	0–3		
71	27/01/96	Keith	Away	S Cup	10–1	1 Goal	(36)
Sub+12	17/03/96	Celtic	Home	League	1–1		
Sub+13	23/03/96	Falkirk	Home	League	3–2		
72	30/03/96	Raith Rovers	Away	League	4–2	1 Goal	(37)
73	07/04/96	Celtic	Hampden	S Cup	2–1		
Sub+14	10/04/96	Heart of Midlothian	Away	League	0–2		
74	13/04/96	Partick Thistle	Home	League	5–0		
75	20/04/96	Motherwell	Away	League	3–1		
76	28/04/96	Aberdeen	Home	League	3–1		
77	04/05/96	Kilmarnock	Away	League	3–0	2 Goals	(39)
78	18/05/96	Heart of Midlothian	Hampden	S Cup	5–1	3 Goals	(42)

SEASON 1996–97

Scottish League Premier Division

79	07/08/96	Spartak–Alania Vladikavkaz	Home	Eur Cup	3–1		
80	10/08/96	Raith Rovers	Home	League	1–0		
Sub+15	21/08/96	Spartak–Alania Vladikavkaz	Away	Eur Cup	7–2		
Sub+16	24/08/96	Dundee United	Home	League	1–0		
81	04/09/96	Ayr United	Home	S Lge Cup	3–1		
82	07/09/96	Motherwell	Away	League	1–0		
83	11/09/96	Grasshoper–Club Zurich	Away	Eur Cup	0–3		
84	14/09/96	Heart of Midlothian	Home	League	3–0	1 Goal	(43)
85	18/09/96	Hibernian	Home	S Lge Cup	4–0	1 Goal	(44)
86	21/09/96	Kilmarnock	Away	League	4–1		
87	25/09/96	AJ Auxerre	Home	Eur Cup	1–2		
Sub+17	25/01/97	St Johnstone	Home	S Cup	2–0		
88	01/02/97	Heart of Midlothian	Home	League	0–0		
89	08/02/97	Dunfermline Athletic	Away	League	3–0	1 Goal	(45)
90	15/02/97	East Fife	Home	S Cup	3–0		
91	23/02/97	Hibernian	Home	League	3–1		
92	01/03/97	Aberdeen	Away	League	2–2		
93	12/03/97	Dundee United	Home	League	0–2		
94	22/03/97	Kilmarnock	Home	League	1–2	1 Goal	(46)
95	05/04/97	Dunfermline Athletic	Home	League	4–0		
96	15/04/97	Raith Rovers	Away	League	6–0	2 Goals	(48)
97	05/05/97	Motherwell	Home	League	0–2		
98	07/05/97	Dundee United	Away	League	1–0		
Sub+18	10/05/97	Heart of Midlothian	Away	League	1–3		

INTERNATIONAL APPEARANCES – SCOTLAND

Sub 1	11/11/87	Bulgaria	Sofia	1–0	ECQ		
Sub 2	22/12/88	Italy	Perugia	0–2	F		
3	26/04/89	Cyprus	Hampden Park	2–1	WCQ		
4	06/09/89	Yugoslavia	Zagreb	1–3	WCQ	1 Goal	(1)
5	25/04/90	East Germany	Hampden Park	0–1	F		
6	16/05/90	Egypt	Hampden Park	1–3	F		
7	16/06/90	Sweden	Genoa	2–1	WC		
Sub 8	17/10/90	Switzerland	Hampden Park	2–1	ECQ		
9	14/11/90	Bulgaria	Sofia	1–1	ECQ		
Sub 10	06/02/91	USSR	Ibrox Park	0–1	F		
11	27/03/91	Bulgaria	Hampden Park	1–1	ECQ		
12	01/05/91	San Marino	Serravalle	2–0	ECQ	1 Goal	(2)
13	11/09/91	Switzerland	Berne	2–2	ECQ	1 Goal	(3)
14	16/10/91	Romania	Bucharest	0–1	ECQ		
15	13/11/91	San Marino	Hampden Park	4–0	ECQ	1 Goal	(4)
Sub 16	19/02/92	Northern Ireland	Hampden Park	1–0	F		
17	25/03/92	Finland	Hampden Park	1–1	F		
18	21/05/92	Canada	Toronto	3–1	F		
Sub 19	03/06/92	Norway	Oslo	0–0	F		
20	12/06/92	Holland	Gothenburg	0–1	EC		
21	15/06/92	Germany	Norrkoping	0–2	EC		
22	09/09/92	Switzerland	Berne	1–3	WCQ		

23	18/11/92	Italy	Ibrox Park	0–0	WCQ		
24	08/09/93	Switzerland	Pittodrie	1–1	WCQ		
25	13/10/93	Italy	Rome	1–3	WCQ		
26	23/03/94	Holland	Hampden Park	0–1	F		
27	27/05/94	Holland	Utrecht	1–3	F		
28	26/05/96	USA	New Britain	1–2	F	1 Goal	(5)
29	10/06/96	Holland	Villa Park	0–0	EC		
30	15/06/96	England	Wembley	0–2	EC		
31	18/06/96	Switzerland	Villa Park	1–0	EC		
Sub 32	31/08/96	Austria	Vienna	0–0	WCQ		
Sub 33	30/04/97	Sweden	Gothenburg	1–2	WCQ		
Sub 34	01/06/97	Malta	Ta'Qali	3–2	F		
35	08/06/97	Belarus	Minsk	1–0	WCQ		

APPEARANCES AND GOALS PER SEASON

SEASON 81–82	GAMES	GOALS
Scottish League	8+5	1
TOTAL	**8+5**	**1**

SEASON 82–83	GAMES	GOALS
Scottish League	17+9	2
Scottish Cup	1+1	0
Scottish League Cup	3+1	0
TOTAL	**21+11**	**2**

SEASON 83–84	GAMES	GOALS
Scottish League	32+2	16
Scottish Cup	4	1
Scottish League Cup	4	0
TOTAL	**40+2**	**17**

SEASON 84–85	GAMES	GOALS
Scottish League	31	15
Scottish Cup	1	0
Scottish League Cup	1	0
TOTAL	**33**	**15**

SEASON 85–86	GAMES	GOALS
League	1	0
Scottish League	23+2	6
Scottish Cup	4	0
Scottish League Cup	6	8
TOTAL	**34+2**	**14**

SEASON 86–87	GAMES	GOALS
League	18+7	5
FA Cup	3	1
TOTAL	**21+7**	**6**

SEASON 87–88	GAMES	GOALS
League	26	12
League Play–offs	4	3
FA Cup	1	0
League Cup	2	4
TOTAL	**33**	**19**

SEASON 88–89	GAMES	GOALS
League	32	17
FA Cup	1	0
League Cup	1	0
Simod Cup	3	0
TOTAL	**37**	**17**

SEASON 89–90	GAMES	GOALS
League	14+1	5
FA Cup	1	0
Zenith Data Systems Cup	3	0
TOTAL	**18+1**	**5**

SEASON 90–91	GAMES	GOALS
League	24	12
League Cup	8	3
Zenith Data Systems Cup	2	0
TOTAL	**34**	**15**

SEASON 91–92	GAMES	GOALS
League	31	7
FA Cup	1	0
League Cup	6	2
European Cup Winners Cup	8	3
TOTAL	**46**	**12**

SEASON 92–93	GAMES	GOALS
League	17	3
FA Cup	1	0
League Cup	2	1
TOTAL	**20**	**4**

SEASON 93–94	GAMES	GOALS
League	10	1
League Cup	2	0
Scottish League	23+1	12
Scottish Cup	5	1
TOTAL	**40+1**	**14**

SEASON 94–95	GAMES	GOALS
Scottish League	16+4	5
Scottish Cup	2	1
Scottish League Cup	1	0
European Cup	2	0
TOTAL	**21+4**	**6**

SEASON 95–96	GAMES	GOALS
Scottish League	21+6	17
Scottish Cup	3	4
Scottish League Cup	1+1	0
European Cup	4+2	2
TOTAL	**29+9**	**23**

SEASON 96–97	GAMES	GOALS
Scottish League	14+2	5
Scottish Cup	1+1	0
Scottish League Cup	2	1
European Cup	3+1	0
TOTAL	**20+4**	**6**

CAREER APPEARANCES AND GOALS

COMPETITION	GAMES	TOTAL	GOALS
League	173+8	181	62
League Play–offs	4	4	3
FA Cup	8	8	1
League Cup	21	21	10
Simod Cup	3	3	0
Zenith Data Systems Cup	5	5	0
European Cup	9+3	12	2
European Cup Winners Cup	8	8	3
Scottish League	185+31	216	79
Scottish Cup	21+2	23	7
Scottish League Cup	18+2	20	9
Internationals	26+9	35	5
TOTAL	**481+55**	**536**	**181**

HAT-TRICKS

East Fife

1	4	Hamilton Academical	25/08/84	Away	League	4–2

Hibernian

1	3	Morton	09/02/85	Home	League	5–1
2	3	Motherwell	28/08/85	Home	S Lge Cup	6–1

Chelsea

1	3	Reading	07/10/87	Home	Lge Cup	3–2
2	5	Walsall	04/02/89	Away	League	7–0

Tottenham Hotspur

1	3	Coventry City	28/03/92	Home	League	4–3

Rangers

1	3	Partick Thistle	14/10/95	Away	League	4–0	
2	4	Hibernian	30/12/95	Home	League	7–0	
3	3	Heart of Midlothian	18/05/96	Hampden	S Cup	5–1	

League: 2
League Cup: 1
Scottish League: 4
Scottish Cup: 1
Scottish League Cup: 1
TOTAL: 9

HONOURS

Winners medals
League Division Two Championship: 88/89
Zenith Data Systems Cup: 89/90
Scottish Premier Division Championship: 93/94, 94/95, 95/96, 96/97
Scottish Cup: 95/96

Runner-up medals
Scottish Cup: 93/94
Scottish League Cup: 85/86
Scottish League Division Two Championship: 83/84

KEITH EDWARDS

Born: 16/07/57 – Stockton
Height: 5.8
Weight: 10.03 (90–91)

Clubs
Sheffield United: **1976–78** – Matches: **73+6** – Goals: **33**
Hull City: **1978–81** – Matches: **153+4** – Goals: **64**
Sheffield United: **1981–86** – Matches: **219+11** – Goals: **138**
Leeds United: **1986–87** – Matches: **34+17** – Goals: **9**
Aberdeen: **1987–88** – Matches: **6+4** – Goals: **3**
Hull City: **1988–89** – Matches: **62+1** – Goals: **33**
Stockport County: **1989–90** – Matches: **31+1** – Goals: **12**
Huddersfield Town: **1990–91** – Matches: **18+14** – Goals: **8**
Plymouth Argyle (loan): **1990** – Matches: **3** – Goals: **1**

SEASON 1975–76

Sheffield United – League Division One

1	03/01/76	Leicester City	Away	FA Cup	0–3	
Sub+1	28/02/76	Queens Park Rangers	Home	League	0–0	
2	13/03/76	Wolverhampton Wanderers	Home	League	1–4	
3	20/03/76	Ipswich Town	Home	League	1–2	

SEASON 1976–77

League Division Two

4	24/08/76	Wolverhampton Wanderers	Home	League	2–2	1 Goal	(1)
5	28/08/76	Hereford United	Home	League	1–1		
6	01/09/76	Chelsea	Away	Lge Cup	1–3		
7	11/09/76	Carlisle United	Home	League	3–0		
8	17/09/76	Hull City	Away	League	1–1	1 Goal	(2)
9	25/09/76	Blackburn Rovers	Home	League	1–1		
10	02/10/76	Burnley	Home	League	1–0		
11	09/10/76	Nottingham Forest	Away	League	1–6		
12	13/11/76	Blackpool	Away	League	0–1		
13	20/11/76	Orient	Home	League	1–1	1 Goal	(3)
14	27/11/76	Millwall	Away	League	1–0		
15	03/12/76	Chelsea	Home	League	1–0		
16	27/12/76	Oldham Athletic	Away	League	2–1		
17	28/12/76	Bolton Wanderers	Home	League	2–3		
18	08/01/77	Newcastle United	Home	FA Cup	0–0		

19	12/02/77	Southampton	Home	League	2–2	1 Goal	(4)
20	19/02/77	Carlisle United	Away	League	1–4		
Sub+2	26/02/77	Hull City	Home	League	1–1		
21	08/03/77	Cardiff City	Home	League	3–0	1 Goal	(5)
22	12/03/77	Burnley	Away	League	0–1		
23	19/03/77	Nottingham Forest	Home	League	2–0	2 Goals	(7)
24	23/03/77	Hereford United	Away	League	2–2	2 Goals	(9)
25	26/03/77	Fulham	Away	League	2–3	1 Goal	(10)
26	28/03/77	Notts County	Away	League	1–2	1 Goal	(11)
27	02/04/77	Charlton Athletic	Home	League	3–0	2 Goals	(13)
28	05/04/77	Oldham Athletic	Home	League	2–1	1 Goal	(14)
29	09/04/77	Bolton Wanderers	Away	League	2–1	1 Goal	(15)
30	12/04/77	Blackpool	Home	League	1–5	1 Goal	(16)
31	16/04/77	Orient	Away	League	2–0		
32	30/04/77	Chelsea	Away	League	0–4		
33	03/05/77	Millwall	Home	League	1–1	1 Goal	(17)
34	07/05/77	Plymouth Argyle	Home	League	1–0	1 Goal	(18)
35	14/05/77	Bristol Rovers	Away	League	1–3		

SEASON 1977–78

League Division Two

36	06/08/77	Oldham Athletic	Away	AS Cup	3–2	3 Goals	(21)
37	09/08/77	Hull City	Away	AS Cup	2–0		
38	13/08/77	Notts County	Home	AS Cup	4–5	1 Goal	(22)
39	20/08/77	Tottenham Hotspur	Away	League	2–4	1 Goal	(23)
40	23/08/77	Hull City	Home	League	2–0	1 Goal	(24)
41	27/08/77	Bolton Wanderers	Away	League	1–2		
42	30/08/77	Everton	Home	Lge Cup	0–3		
43	03/09/77	Sunderland	Home	League	1–1	1 Goal	(25)
44	06/09/77	Notts County	Away	AS Cup	0–3		
45	10/09/77	Stoke City	Away	League	0–4		
46	17/09/77	Crystal Palace	Home	League	0–2		
47	24/09/77	Brighton & Hove Albion	Away	League	1–2		
48	01/10/77	Southampton	Home	League	3–2	1 Goal	(26)
49	04/10/77	Notts County	Home	League	4–1	2 Goals	(28)
50	08/10/77	Mansfield Town	Away	League	1–1		
51	15/10/77	Burnley	Home	League	2–1		
52	22/10/77	Millwall	Away	League	1–1		
53	29/10/77	Fulham	Home	League	2–1		
54	05/11/77	Blackpool	Away	League	1–1		
55	12/11/77	Oldham Athletic	Home	League	1–0		
56	19/11/77	Charlton Athletic	Away	League	0–3		
57	26/11/77	Bristol Rovers	Home	League	1–1		
Sub+3	26/12/77	Orient	Home	League	2–0		
58	31/12/77	Hull City	Away	League	3–2	1 Goal	(29)
59	02/01/78	Tottenham Hotspur	Home	League	2–2	1 Goal	(30)
60	07/01/78	Arsenal	Home	FA Cup	0–5		
61	14/01/78	Bolton Wanderers	Home	League	1–5		
62	11/02/78	Crystal Palace	Away	League	0–1		
63	25/02/78	Southampton	Away	League	1–2		
64	04/03/78	Mansfield Town	Home	League	2–0	1 Goal	(31)
65	11/03/78	Burnley	Away	League	1–4		
66	14/03/78	Stoke City	Home	League	1–2		
Sub+4	18/03/78	Millwall	Home	League	5–2		
Sub+5	24/03/78	Fulham	Away	League	0–2		
Sub+6	27/03/78	Orient	Away	League	1–3		
67	01/04/78	Blackpool	Home	League	0–0		
68	04/04/78	Brighton & Hove Albion	Home	League	2–0		
69	08/04/78	Bristol Rovers	Away	League	1–4		
70	15/04/78	Charlton Athletic	Home	League	1–0	1 Goal	(32)
71	22/04/78	Blackburn Rovers	Away	League	1–1		
72	25/04/78	Notts County	Away	League	2–1	1 Goal	(33)
73	29/04/78	Cardiff City	Home	League	0–1		

SEASON 1978–79

Hull City – League Division Three

1	12/08/78	Peterborough United	Home	Lge Cup	0–1		
2	15/08/78	Peterborough United	Away	Lge Cup	2–1		
3	19/08/78	Carlisle United	Home	League	1–1		
4	22/08/78	Peterborough United	Home	Lge Cup	0–1		
5	26/08/78	Tranmere Rovers	Away	League	3–1	1 Goal	(1)

6	02/09/78	Chester	Home	League	3–0	3 Goals	(4)
7	05/09/78	Rotherham United	Away	League	2–0		
8	09/09/78	Brentford	Away	League	0–1		
9	12/09/78	Walsall	Home	League	4–1	2 Goals	(6)
10	16/09/78	Chesterfield	Home	League	1–1		
11	23/09/78	Exeter City	Away	League	1–3	1 Goal	(7)
12	26/09/78	Shrewsbury Town	Away	League	0–1		
13	30/09/78	Oxford United	Home	League	0–1		
14	07/10/78	Peterborough United	Home	League	1–1		
15	14/10/78	Gillingham	Away	League	0–2		
16	21/10/78	Swansea City	Home	League	2–2		
17	23/10/78	Southend United	Away	League	0–3		
18	28/10/78	Bury	Away	League	1–1		
19	04/11/78	Watford	Home	League	4–0	1 Goal	(8)
20	11/11/78	Chester	Away	League	1–2	1 Goal	(9)
21	18/11/78	Tranmere Rovers	Home	League	2–1	1 Goal	(10)
22	25/11/78	Stafford Rangers	Home	FA Cup	2–1	1 Goal	(11)
23	09/12/78	Swindon Town	Away	League	0–2		
24	16/12/78	Carlisle United	Away	FA Cup	0–3		
25	26/12/78	Mansfield Town	Home	League	3–0	2 Goals	(13)
26	06/01/79	Walsall	Away	League	2–1		
27	03/02/79	Shrewsbury Town	Home	League	1–1		
28	10/02/79	Oxford United	Away	League	0–1		
29	20/02/79	Blackpool	Away	League	1–3		
30	24/02/79	Gillingham	Home	League	0–1		
31	02/03/79	Swansea City	Away	League	3–5		
32	06/03/79	Brentford	Home	League	1–0	1 Goal	(14)
33	10/03/79	Bury	Home	League	4–1	1 Goal	(15)
34	13/03/79	Colchester United	Home	League	1–0		
35	24/03/79	Rotherham United	Home	League	1–0		
36	27/03/79	Carlisle United	Away	League	2–2	1 Goal	(16)
37	31/03/79	Lincoln City	Home	League	0–0		
38	04/04/79	Chesterfield	Away	League	2–1	1 Goal	(17)
39	07/04/79	Plymouth Argyle	Away	League	4–3	2 Goals	(19)
40	13/04/79	Sheffield Wednesday	Home	League	1–1		
41	14/04/79	Mansfield Town	Away	League	2–0	1 Goal	(20)
42	16/04/79	Blackpool	Home	League	0–0		
43	21/04/79	Colchester United	Away	League	1–2	1 Goal	(21)
44	24/04/79	Southend United	Home	League	2–0	1 Goal	(22)
45	28/04/79	Swindon Town	Home	League	1–1		
46	01/05/79	Plymouth Argyle	Home	League	2–1	1 Goal	(23)
47	05/05/79	Lincoln City	Away	League	2–4		
48	07/05/79	Exeter City	Home	League	1–0	1 Goal	(24)
49	11/05/79	Peterborough United	Away	League	0–3		
50	14/05/79	Watford	Away	League	0–4		
51	19/05/79	Sheffield Wednesday	Away	League	3–2	1 Goal	(25)

SEASON 1979–80

League Division Three

52	11/08/79	Sheffield Wednesday	Away	Lge Cup	1–1	1 Goal	(26)
53	14/08/79	Sheffield Wednesday	Home	Lge Cup	1–2		
54	18/08/79	Colchester United	Home	League	0–2		
55	01/09/79	Mansfield Town	Away	League	1–1		
56	08/09/79	Sheffield United	Home	League	3–1	1 Goal	(27)
57	15/09/79	Bury	Away	League	1–0	1 Goal	(28)
58	18/09/79	Chesterfield	Away	League	1–1	1 Goal	(29)
59	22/09/79	Gillingham	Home	League	0–0		
60	29/09/79	Millwall	Away	League	2–3		
61	02/10/79	Chesterfield	Home	League	2–1		
62	06/10/79	Swindon Town	Away	League	0–0		
63	09/10/79	Sheffield Wednesday	Home	League	1–1		
64	23/10/79	Rotherham United	Away	League	1–2	1 Goal	(30)
65	27/10/79	Exeter City	Home	League	2–2		
66	02/11/79	Colchester United	Away	League	1–1		
67	06/11/79	Rotherham United	Home	League	1–1	1 Goal	(31)
68	10/11/79	Reading	Away	League	0–3		
69	17/11/79	Barnsley	Home	League	0–2		
70	24/11/79	Carlisle United	Away	FA Cup	3–3		
71	28/11/79	Carlisle United	Home	FA Cup	0–2		
72	01/12/79	Wimbledon	Home	League	1–1		
73	08/12/79	Brentford	Away	League	2–7		
74	21/12/79	Blackburn Rovers	Home	League	0–1		
75	26/12/79	Blackpool	Away	League	2–2	2 Goals	(33)
76	29/12/79	Oxford United	Away	League	0–3		

77	05/01/80	Plymouth Argyle	Away	League	1–5		
78	12/01/80	Mansfield Town	Home	League	3–1	2 Goals	(35)
79	19/01/80	Sheffield United	Away	League	1–1		
80	25/01/80	Southend United	Away	League	0–3		
81	16/02/80	Millwall	Home	League	1–0	1 Goal	(36)
82	23/02/80	Carlisle United	Away	League	2–3	1 Goal	(37)
83	01/03/80	Chester	Home	League	1–0		
84	04/03/80	Gillingham	Away	League	0–1		
85	08/03/80	Exeter City	Away	League	2–2	2 Goals	(39)
86	14/03/80	Swindon Town	Home	League	1–0		
87	22/03/80	Reading	Home	League	0–1		
88	25/03/80	Grimsby Town	Home	League	2–2	2 Goals	(41)
89	04/04/80	Blackburn Rovers	Away	League	0–1		
90	05/04/80	Blackpool	Home	League	3–1	2 Goals	(43)
91	07/04/80	Grimsby Town	Away	League	1–1		
92	12/04/80	Plymouth Argyle	Home	League	1–0		
93	19/04/80	Wimbledon	Away	League	2–3		
94	26/04/80	Brentford	Home	League	2–1	1 Goal	(44)
95	03/05/80	Southend United	Home	League	1–0	1 Goal	(45)
96	05/05/80	Bury	Home	League	0–1		

SEASON 1980–81

League Division Three

97	28/07/80	Grimsby Town	Home	AS Cup	1–0		
98	02/08/80	Sheffield United	Away	AS Cup	1–2		
99	05/08/80	Chesterfield	Away	AS Cup	1–1		
100	09/08/80	Lincoln City	Away	Lge Cup	0–5		
101	12/08/80	Lincoln City	Home	Lge Cup	0–2		
102	16/08/80	Millwall	Away	League	1–1	1 Goal	(46)
103	19/08/80	Barnsley	Home	League	1–2		
104	23/08/80	Exeter City	Home	League	3–3	1 Goal	(47)
105	29/08/80	Fulham	Away	League	0–0		
106	06/09/80	Walsall	Home	League	0–1		
107	13/09/80	Blackpool	Away	League	2–2		
108	16/09/80	Burnley	Away	League	0–2		
109	20/09/80	Portsmouth	Home	League	2–1	1 Goal	(48)
110	27/09/80	Brentford	Away	League	2–2	1 Goal	(49)
111	30/09/80	Burnley	Home	League	0–0		
112	04/10/80	Oxford United	Home	League	0–1		
113	08/10/80	Chester	Away	League	1–4	1 Goal	(50)
114	11/10/80	Chesterfield	Away	League	0–1		
115	21/10/80	Carlisle United	Home	League	0–1		
116	28/10/80	Colchester United	Away	League	0–2		
117	01/11/80	Plymouth Argyle	Home	League	1–0		
118	04/11/80	Chester	Home	League	0–0		
Sub+1	08/11/80	Newport County	Away	League	0–4		
119	11/11/80	Barnsley	Away	League	0–5		
120	15/11/80	Millwall	Home	League	3–1	1 Goal	(51)
121	22/11/80	Halifax Town	Home	FA Cup	2–1	2 Goals	(53)
122	29/11/80	Swindon Town	Away	League	1–3		
123	06/12/80	Reading	Home	League	2–0	1 Goal	(54)
124	13/12/80	Blyth Spartans	Home	FA Cup	1–1	1 Goal	(55)
125	16/12/80	Blyth Spartans	Away	FA Cup	2–2*	1 Goal	(56)
126	20/12/80	Sheffield United	Away	League	1–3	1 Goal	(57)
127	22/12/80	Blyth Spartans	Home	FA Cup	2–1*		
128	26/12/80	Rotherham United	Home	League	1–2	1 Goal	(58)
129	27/12/80	Huddersfield Town	Away	League	0–5		
130	03/01/81	Doncaster Rovers	Home	FA Cup	1–0		
131	10/01/81	Charlton Athletic	Away	League	2–3	1 Goal	(59)
132	24/01/81	Tottenham Hotspur	Away	FA Cup	0–2		
133	31/01/81	Exeter City	Away	League	3–1		
134	07/02/81	Blackpool	Home	League	2–1	1 Goal	(60)
135	14/02/81	Walsall	Away	League	1–1		
136	21/02/81	Brentford	Home	League	0–0		
137	28/02/81	Portsmouth	Away	League	1–2		
138	07/03/81	Oxford United	Away	League	1–1		
139	14/03/81	Chesterfield	Home	League	0–0		
140	17/03/81	Colchester United	Home	League	0–1		
141	28/03/81	Gillingham	Home	League	2–2		
Sub+2	18/04/81	Huddersfield Town	Home	League	2–1		
142	20/04/81	Rotherham United	Away	League	1–1	1 Goal	(61)
143	25/04/81	Sheffield United	Home	League	1–1		
144	02/05/81	Reading	Away	League	0–2		
145	07/05/81	Newport County	Home	League	3–1	1 Goal	(62)

SEASON 1981–82

League Division Four

Sub+3	15/08/81	Bradford City	Away	FLG Cup	1–3		
Sub+4	18/08/81	Rotherham United	Home	FLG Cup	0–1		
146	22/08/81	Hartlepool United	Home	FLG Cup	1–0	1 Goal	(63)
147	29/08/81	Torquay United	Away	League	1–2		
148	02/09/81	Lincoln City	Away	Lge Cup	0–3		
149	05/09/81	Bradford City	Home	League	2–1		
150	12/09/81	Northampton Town	Away	League	1–1		
151	15/09/81	Lincoln City	Home	Lge Cup	1–1		
152	19/09/81	Sheffield United	Home	League	2–1	1 Goal	(64)
153	22/09/81	Peterborough United	Home	League	1–1		

Sheffield United – League Division Four

1	26/09/81	Scunthorpe United	Home	League	1–0		
2	29/09/81	Crewe Alexandra	Home	League	4–0	2 Goals	(2)
3	03/10/81	York City	Away	League	4–3		
4	10/10/81	Port Vale	Away	League	2–0	1 Goal	(3)
5	17/10/81	Hartlepool United	Home	League	1–1	1 Goal	(4)
6	20/10/81	Mansfield Town	Home	League	4–1	2 Goals	(6)
7	24/10/81	Bradford City	Away	League	2–0	1 Goal	(7)
8	31/10/81	Blackpool	Home	League	3–1		
9	03/11/81	Northampton Town	Away	League	2–1		
10	07/11/81	Tranmere Rovers	Home	League	2–0	1 Goal	(8)
11	14/11/81	Torquay United	Away	League	1–1	1 Goal	(9)
12	21/11/81	Altrincham	Home	FA Cup	2–2	1 Goal	(10)
13	23/11/81	Altrincham	Away	FA Cup	0–3		
14	28/11/81	AFC Bournemouth	Away	League	0–0		
15	05/12/81	Aldershot	Home	League	2–0		
16	02/01/82	Halifax Town	Home	League	2–2		
17	16/01/82	Rochdale	Away	League	1–0	1 Goal	(11)
18	26/01/82	Darlington	Home	League	0–0		
19	30/01/82	Hull City	Home	League	0–0		
20	06/02/82	Colchester United	Away	League	2–5	1 Goal	(12)
21	09/02/82	Stockport County	Home	League	4–0	2 Goals	(14)
22	13/02/82	York City	Home	League	4–0	2 Goals	(16)
23	17/02/82	Hereford United	Away	League	1–1		
24	20/02/82	Scunthorpe United	Away	League	1–2		
25	27/02/82	Port Vale	Home	League	2–1	1 Goal	(17)
26	06/03/82	Hartlepool United	Away	League	3–2	1 Goal	(18)
27	08/03/82	Mansfield Town	Away	League	1–1		
28	16/03/82	Northampton Town	Home	League	7–3	3 Goals	(21)
29	20/03/82	Blackpool	Away	League	1–0	1 Goal	(22)
30	23/03/82	Wigan Athletic	Home	League	1–0	1 Goal	(23)
31	27/03/82	Tranmere Rovers	Away	League	2–2		
32	30/03/82	Bradford City	Home	League	1–1		
33	03/04/82	Torquay United	Home	League	4–1	1 Goal	(24)
34	10/04/82	Bury	Home	League	1–1	1 Goal	(25)
35	12/04/82	Halifax Town	Away	League	5–1	2 Goals	(27)
36	17/04/82	Aldershot	Away	League	1–1		
37	21/04/82	Peterborough United	Away	League	4–0	2 Goals	(29)
38	24/04/82	AFC Bournemouth	Home	League	0–0		
39	27/04/82	Bury	Away	League	1–1	1 Goal	(30)
40	01/05/82	Crewe Alexandra	Away	League	3–2	1 Goal	(31)
41	04/05/82	Rochdale	Home	League	3–1	2 Goals	(33)
42	08/05/82	Peterborough United	Home	League	4–0	2 Goals	(35)
43	15/05/82	Darlington	Away	League	2–0	1 Goal	(36)

SEASON 1982–83

League Division Three

44	14/08/82	Grimsby Town	Home	FL Trophy	1–3		
45	17/08/82	Scunthorpe United	Away	FL Trophy	0–0		
46	21/08/82	Lincoln City	Away	FL Trophy	1–3	1 Goal	(37)
47	28/08/82	Portsmouth	Away	League	1–4	1 Goal	(38)
48	30/08/82	Hull City	Home	Lge Cup	3–1	1 Goal	(39)
49	04/09/82	Preston North End	Home	League	2–1	1 Goal	(40)
50	07/09/82	Huddersfield Town	Home	League	2–0		
51	11/09/82	AFC Bournemouth	Away	League	0–0		
Sub+1	14/09/82	Hull City	Away	Lge Cup	0–1		
52	18/09/82	Plymouth Argyle	Home	League	3–1		
53	25/09/82	Cardiff City	Away	League	0–2		
54	29/09/82	Lincoln City	Away	League	0–3		
55	02/10/82	Gillingham	Home	League	0–2		

Sub+2	16/10/82	Wrexham	Home	League	2–0	1 Goal	(41)
Sub+3	19/10/82	Reading	Home	League	1–1		
Sub+4	26/10/82	Grimsby Town	Home	Lge Cup	5–1	3 Goals	(44)
56	30/10/82	Millwall	Home	League	1–1		
57	02/11/82	Newport County	Away	League	1–3		
58	06/11/82	Oxford United	Away	League	0–0		
59	09/11/82	Barnsley	Home	Lge Cup	1–3	1 Goal	(45)
60	13/11/82	Southend United	Home	League	0–1		
61	20/11/82	Hull City	Away	FA Cup	1–1	1 Goal	(46)
62	23/11/82	Hull City	Home	FA Cup	2–0	1 Goal	(47)
63	27/11/82	Brentford	Home	League	1–2	1 Goal	(48)
64	04/12/82	Wigan Athletic	Away	League	2–3		
65	11/12/82	Boston United	Away	FA Cup	1–1	1 Goal	(49)
66	14/12/82	Boston United	Home	FA Cup	5–1	1 Goal	(50)
67	27/12/82	Doncaster Rovers	Home	League	3–1	1 Goal	(51)
68	28/12/82	Chesterfield	Away	League	1–3		
69	01/01/83	Orient	Home	League	3–0		
70	08/01/83	Stoke City	Home	FA Cup	0–0		
71	12/01/83	Stoke City	Away	FA Cup	2–3	1 Goal	(52)
72	15/01/83	Portsmouth	Home	League	2–1		
73	22/01/83	Huddersfield Town	Away	League	0–0		
74	29/01/83	AFC Bournemouth	Home	League	2–2		
75	05/02/83	Cardiff City	Home	League	2–0		
76	19/02/83	Walsall	Home	League	3–1		
77	23/02/83	Reading	Away	League	0–2		
78	26/02/83	Wrexham	Away	League	1–4		
79	01/03/83	Newport County	Home	League	2–0	1 Goal	(53)
80	05/03/83	Exeter City	Home	League	3–0	2 Goals	(55)
81	12/03/83	Millwall	Away	League	2–1		
82	15/03/83	Gillingham	Away	League	2–0	1 Goal	(56)
83	19/03/83	Oxford United	Home	League	3–2	1 Goal	(57)
Sub+5	26/03/83	Southend United	Away	League	1–3		
84	02/04/83	Chesterfield	Home	League	3–1	1 Goal	(58)
85	05/04/83	Doncaster Rovers	Away	League	0–2		
Sub+6	12/04/83	Preston North End	Away	League	0–1		
Sub+7	16/04/83	Plymouth Argyle	Away	League	1–3		
86	23/04/83	Bradford City	Home	League	2–1	1 Goal	(59)
87	30/04/83	Brentford	Away	League	1–2		
88	02/05/83	Bristol Rovers	Home	League	2–1	1 Goal	(60)
89	07/05/83	Lincoln City	Home	League	0–1		
90	08/05/83	Bradford City	Away	League	0–2		
91	14/05/83	Orient	Away	League	1–4		

SEASON 1983–84

League Division Three

92	27/08/83	Gillingham	Home	League	4–0	4 Goals	(64)
93	29/08/83	Bradford City	Away	Lge Cup	1–0		
94	03/09/83	Lincoln City	Away	League	2–0	1 Goal	(65)
95	06/09/83	Walsall	Away	League	2–1		
96	10/09/83	Preston North End	Home	League	1–1	1 Goal	(66)
97	13/09/83	Bradford City	Home	Lge Cup	1–1	1 Goal	(67)
98	24/09/83	Wigan Athletic	Home	League	2–2	1 Goal	(68)
99	27/09/83	Bradford City	Home	League	2–0		
100	01/10/83	Millwall	Away	League	2–1	1 Goal	(69)
101	04/10/83	Shrewsbury Town	Away	Lge Cup	1–2		
102	08/10/83	Hull City	Away	League	1–4		
103	15/10/83	AFC Bournemouth	Home	League	2–0		
104	18/10/83	Orient	Away	League	0–2		
105	22/10/83	Brentford	Home	League	0–0		
106	25/10/83	Shrewsbury Town	Home	Lge Cup	2–2	1 Goal	(70)
107	29/10/83	Plymouth Argyle	Away	League	1–0		
108	01/11/83	Scunthorpe United	Home	League	5–3	1 Goal	(71)
109	05/11/83	Oxford United	Away	League	2–2	1 Goal	(72)
110	08/11/83	Burnley	Away	League	1–2		
111	12/11/83	Exeter City	Home	League	2–2		
112	19/11/83	Wrexham	Away	FA Cup	5–1	4 Goals	(76)
113	26/11/83	Southend United	Home	League	5–0	3 Goals	(79)
114	03/12/83	Bristol Rovers	Away	League	1–1		
115	10/12/83	Lincoln City	Away	FA Cup	0–0		
116	17/12/83	Newport County	Away	League	2–0	2 Goals	(81)
117	19/12/83	Lincoln City	Home	FA Cup	1–0		
118	26/12/83	Rotherham United	Home	League	3–0	1 Goal	(82)
119	27/12/83	Port Vale	Away	League	0–2		
120	31/12/83	Bolton Wanderers	Home	League	5–0	1 Goal	(83)

121	02/01/84	Wimbledon	Away	League	1–3	1 Goal	(84)
122	07/01/84	Birmingham City	Home	FA Cup	1–1		
123	10/01/84	Birmingham City	Away	FA Cup	0–2		
124	14/01/84	Gillingham	Away	League	2–4	1 Goal	(85)
125	21/01/84	Burnley	Home	League	0–0		
126	31/01/84	Preston North End	Away	League	2–2	1 Goal	(86)
127	11/02/84	Wigan Athletic	Away	League	0–3		
128	21/02/84	Rotherham United	Away	AM Cup	1–0		
129	25/02/84	Brentford	Away	League	3–1	1 Goal	(87)
130	28/02/84	Plymouth Argyle	Home	League	2–0		
131	03/03/84	Orient	Home	League	6–3	3 Goals	(90)
132	06/03/84	Oxford United	Home	League	1–2		
133	10/03/84	Exeter City	Away	League	2–1	1 Goal	(91)
134	13/03/84	Bradford City	Home	AM Cup	2–1		
135	17/03/84	Hull City	Home	League	2–2	1 Goal	(92)
136	20/03/84	Scunthorpe United	Away	AM Cup	3–1	2 Goals	(94)
137	24/03/84	AFC Bournemouth	Away	League	1–0	1 Goal	(95)
138	27/03/84	Scunthorpe United	Away	League	1–1	1 Goal	(96)
139	31/03/84	Walsall	Home	League	2–0	1 Goal	(97)
140	07/04/84	Bradford City	Away	League	1–2	1 Goal	(98)
141	14/04/84	Bristol Rovers	Home	League	4–0	2 Goals	(100)
142	21/04/84	Rotherham United	Away	League	1–0		
143	24/04/84	Port Vale	Home	League	3–1		
144	28/04/84	Southend United	Away	League	1–0		
145	05/05/84	Wimbledon	Home	League	1–2		
146	07/05/84	Bolton Wanderers	Away	League	1–3	1 Goal	(101)
147	12/05/84	Newport County	Home	League	2–0	1 Goal	(102)

SEASON 1984–85

League Division Two

148	25/08/84	Wolverhampton Wanderers	Away	League	2–2	1 Goal	(103)
149	28/08/84	Peterborough United	Home	Lge Cup	1–0		
150	01/09/84	Cardiff City	Home	League	2–1	1 Goal	(104)
151	05/09/84	Peterborough United	Away	Lge Cup	2–2*	1 Goal	(105)
152	08/09/84	Oldham Athletic	Away	League	2–2		
153	15/09/84	Notts County	Home	League	3–0	1 Goal	(106)
154	18/09/84	Crystal Palace	Home	League	1–2	1 Goal	(107)
155	22/09/84	Carlisle United	Away	League	1–1		
156	26/09/84	Everton	Home	Lge Cup	2–2	1 Goal	(108)
157	29/09/84	Grimsby Town	Home	League	2–3		
158	02/10/84	Portsmouth	Away	League	1–2		
159	06/10/84	Leeds United	Away	League	1–1	1 Goal	(109)
160	10/10/84	Everton	Away	Lge Cup	0–4		
161	13/10/84	Middlesbrough	Home	League	0–3		
162	20/10/84	Oxford United	Away	League	1–5		
163	27/10/84	Wimbledon	Home	League	3–0	1 Goal	(110)
164	10/11/84	Charlton Athletic	Home	League	1–1		
165	13/11/84	Barnsley	Away	League	0–1		
166	17/11/84	Manchester City	Home	League	0–0		
167	08/12/84	Blackburn Rovers	Away	League	1–3	1 Goal	(111)
168	15/12/84	Brighton & Hove Albion	Home	League	1–1		
169	22/12/84	Cardiff City	Away	League	3–1	2 Goals	(113)
170	26/12/84	Fulham	Away	League	0–1		
171	29/12/84	Portsmouth	Home	League	4–1	1 Goal	(114)
172	01/01/85	Birmingham City	Home	League	3–4	1 Goal	(115)
173	05/01/85	Watford	Away	FA Cup	0–5		
174	12/01/85	Notts County	Away	League	0–0		
175	26/01/85	Wolverhampton Wanderers	Home	League	2–2		
176	02/02/85	Grimsby Town	Away	League	2–0	1 Goal	(116)
177	12/02/85	Oldham Athletic	Home	League	2–0	1 Goal	(117)
178	23/02/85	Barnsley	Home	League	3–1		
179	02/03/85	Wimbledon	Away	League	0–5		
180	09/03/85	Oxford United	Home	League	1–1		
181	27/04/85	Shrewsbury Town	Home	League	0–1		

SEASON 1985–86

League Division Two

Sub+8	20/08/85	Rotherham United	Away	Lge Cup	3–1		
Sub+9	07/09/85	Norwich City	Away	League	0–4		
Sub+10	21/09/85	Middlesbrough	Home	League	0–1		
182	24/09/85	Luton Town	Home	Lge Cup	1–2		
183	28/09/85	Leeds United	Away	League	1–1		
184	01/10/85	Charlton Athletic	Home	League	1–1		

185	07/10/85	Luton Town	Away	Lge Cup	1–3	1 Goal	(118)
186	12/10/85	Grimsby Town	Away	League	1–0		
187	16/10/85	Leeds United	Away	FM Cup	1–1		
188	19/10/85	Barnsley	Home	League	3–1	2 Goals	(120)
189	22/10/85	Manchester City	Home	FM Cup	1–2		
190	26/10/85	Bradford City	Away	League	4–1	2 Goals	(122)
191	02/11/85	Hull City	Home	League	3–1	3 Goals	(125)
192	09/11/85	Oldham Athletic	Away	League	5–1	2 Goals	(127)
193	16/11/85	Blackburn Rovers	Home	League	3–3		
194	23/11/85	Portsmouth	Away	League	3–0		
195	30/11/85	Crystal Palace	Home	League	0–0		
196	07/12/85	Charlton Athletic	Away	League	0–2		
197	14/12/85	Stoke City	Home	League	1–2	1 Goal	(128)
198	21/12/85	Wimbledon	Away	League	0–5		
199	26/12/85	Sunderland	Away	League	1–2	1 Goal	(129)
200	28/12/85	Fulham	Home	League	2–1		
201	01/01/86	Carlisle United	Home	League	1–0	1 Goal	(130)
202	09/01/86	Fulham	Home	FA Cup	2–0		
203	11/01/86	Huddersfield Town	Away	League	1–3		
Sub+11	18/01/86	Shrewsbury Town	Away	League	1–3		
204	25/01/86	Derby County	Home	FA Cup	0–1		
205	01/02/86	Brighton & Hove Albion	Home	League	3–0	1 Goal	(131)
206	08/03/86	Millwall	Away	League	0–3		
207	11/03/86	Bradford City	Home	League	3–1	2 Goals	(133)
208	15/03/86	Grimsby Town	Home	League	1–1		
209	18/03/86	Middlesbrough	Away	League	2–1	1 Goal	(134)
210	22/03/86	Norwich City	Home	League	2–5	2 Goals	(136)
211	29/03/86	Carlisle United	Away	League	0–1		
212	31/03/86	Sunderland	Home	League	1–0		
213	05/04/86	Hull City	Away	League	0–0		
214	08/04/86	Barnsley	Away	League	1–2		
215	12/04/86	Oldham Athletic	Home	League	2–0		
216	19/04/86	Blackburn Rovers	Away	League	1–6	1 Goal	(137)
217	22/04/86	Leeds United	Home	League	3–2		
218	26/04/86	Portsmouth	Home	League	0–0		
219	03/05/86	Crystal Palace	Away	League	1–1	1 Goal	(138)

SEASON 1986–87

Leeds United – League Division Two

1	23/08/86	Blackburn Rovers	Away	League	1–2		
2	25/08/86	Stoke City	Home	League	2–1		
3	30/08/86	Sheffield United	Home	League	0–1		
4	02/09/86	Barnsley	Away	League	1–0		
5	06/09/86	Huddersfield Town	Away	League	1–1		
6	13/09/86	Reading	Home	League	3–2	1 Goal	(1)
7	20/09/86	Bradford City	Away	League	0–2		
8	23/09/86	Oldham Athletic	Away	Lge Cup	2–3		
9	27/09/86	Hull City	Home	League	3–0		
10	01/10/86	Bradford City	Home	FM Cup	0–1		
11	04/10/86	Plymouth Argyle	Away	League	1–1		
12	08/10/86	Oldham Athletic	Home	Lge Cup	0–1		
13	11/10/86	Crystal Palace	Home	League	3–0	1 Goal	(2)
14	18/10/86	Portsmouth	Home	League	3–1		
15	25/10/86	Grimsby Town	Away	League	0–0		
16	01/11/86	Shrewsbury Town	Home	League	1–0		
17	08/11/86	Millwall	Away	League	0–1		
18	21/11/86	Birmingham City	Away	League	1–2		
19	29/11/86	Derby County	Home	League	2–0	1 Goal	(3)
20	06/12/86	West Bromwich Albion	Away	League	0–3		
21	13/12/86	Brighton & Hove Albion	Home	League	3–1		
22	21/12/86	Stoke City	Away	League	2–7		
23	26/12/86	Sunderland	Home	League	1–1		
Sub+1	01/01/87	Ipswich Town	Away	League	0–2		
24	03/01/87	Huddersfield Town	Home	League	1–1		
25	11/01/87	Telford United	Away	FA Cup	2–1+		
Sub+2	03/02/87	Swindon Town	Away	FA Cup	2–1		
Sub+3	14/02/87	Barnsley	Home	League	2–2		
Sub+4	21/02/87	Queens Park Rangers	Home	FA Cup	2–1		
Sub+5	28/02/87	Bradford City	Home	League	1–0	1 Goal	(4)
26	07/03/87	Grimsby Town	Home	League	2–0		
27	15/03/87	Wigan Athletic	Away	FA Cup	2–0		
Sub+6	28/03/87	Plymouth Argyle	Home	League	4–0		
Sub+7	12/04/87	Coventry City	Neutral	FA Cup	2–3*	1 Goal	(5)
28	22/04/87	Reading	Away	League	1–2		

29	25/04/87	Birmingham City	Home	League	4–0	1 Goal	(6)
Sub+8	02/05/87	Derby County	Away	League	1–2		
Sub+9	09/05/87	Brighton & Hove Albion	Away	League	1–0	1 Goal	(7)
Sub+10	14/05/87	Oldham Athletic	Home	Lge P/O	1–0	1 Goal	(8)
Sub+11	17/05/87	Oldham Athletic	Away	Lge P/O	1–2	1 Goal	(9)
30	23/05/87	Charlton Athletic	Away	Lge P/O	0–1		
Sub+12	25/05/87	Charlton Athletic	Home	Lge P/O	1–0		
Sub+13	29/05/87	Charlton Athletic	Away	Lge P/O	1–2*		

+ Played at The Hawthorns, West Bromwich Albion

SEASON 1987–88

League Division Two

Sub+14	16/08/87	Barnsley	Away	League	1–1		
Sub+15	19/08/87	Leicester City	Home	League	1–0		
31	22/08/87	Reading	Home	League	0–0		
32	31/08/87	West Bromwich Albion	Home	League	1–0		
33	05/09/87	Ipswich Town	Away	League	0–1		
34	12/09/87	Hull City	Home	League	0–2		
Sub+16	15/09/87	Huddersfield Town	Away	League	0–0		
Sub+17	19/09/87	Middlesbrough	Away	League	0–2		

Aberdeen – Scottish League Premier Division

Sub+1	03/10/87	Dunfermline Athletic	Home	League	3–0	1 Goal	(1)
Sub+2	07/10/87	Heart of Midlothian	Away	League	1–2		
1	10/10/87	Dundee	Home	League	0–0		
2	17/10/87	Dundee United	Away	League	0–0		
Sub+3	31/10/87	Celtic	Home	League	0–1		
3	07/11/87	Morton	Away	League	0–0		
4	21/11/87	Motherwell	Home	League	1–0		
5	24/11/87	Hibernian	Home	League	1–1	1 Goal	(2)
6	05/03/88	St Mirren	Away	League	0–0		
Sub+4	12/03/88	Clyde	Home	S Cup	5–0	1 Goal	(3)

Hull City – League Division Two

1	26/03/88	Leicester City	Away	League	1–2	1 Goal	(1)
2	02/04/88	Birmingham City	Away	League	1–1		
3	04/04/88	Middlesbrough	Home	League	0–0		
4	09/04/88	Bradford City	Away	League	0–2		
5	12/04/88	Swindon Town	Home	League	1–4		
6	23/04/88	Huddersfield Town	Home	League	4–0	2 Goals	(3)
7	30/04/88	West Bromwich Albion	Away	League	1–1		
8	02/05/88	Millwall	Home	League	0–1		
9	07/05/88	Reading	Away	League	0–0		

SEASON 1988–89

League Division Two

10	27/08/88	Manchester City	Home	League	1–0	1 Goal	(4)
11	29/08/88	Oxford United	Away	League	0–1		
12	03/09/88	Plymouth Argyle	Away	League	0–2		
13	10/09/88	Barnsley	Home	League	0–0		
14	17/09/88	Portsmouth	Away	League	3–1	2 Goals	(6)
15	20/09/88	Blackburn Rovers	Home	League	1–3	1 Goal	(7)
16	24/09/88	Oldham Athletic	Away	League	2–2		
17	28/09/88	Arsenal	Home	Lge Cup	1–2	1 Goal	(8)
18	01/10/88	Walsall	Home	League	0–0		
19	04/10/88	Leicester City	Home	League	2–2	1 Goal	(9)
20	08/10/88	Shrewsbury Town	Away	League	3–1	2 Goals	(11)
21	12/10/88	Arsenal	Away	Lge Cup	0–3		
22	15/10/88	Sunderland	Home	League	0–0		
23	22/10/88	Crystal Palace	Away	League	1–3		
24	25/10/88	Chelsea	Home	League	3–0	2 Goals	(13)
25	29/10/88	Leeds United	Away	League	1–2		
26	05/11/88	Swindon Town	Home	League	1–0		
27	08/11/88	Portsmouth	Away	Simod Cup	1–2		
28	13/11/88	Stoke City	Away	League	0–4		
29	19/11/88	Birmingham City	Home	League	1–1	1 Goal	(14)
30	26/11/88	Watford	Away	League	0–2		
31	29/11/88	AFC Bournemouth	Away	League	1–5		
32	03/12/88	Brighton & Hove Albion	Home	League	5–2		
33	10/12/88	West Bromwich Albion	Away	League	0–2		

34	02/01/89	Barnsley	Away	League	2–0	2 Goals	(16)
35	07/01/89	Cardiff City	Away	FA Cup	2–1	1 Goal	(17)
36	14/01/89	AFC Bournemouth	Home	League	4–0	3 Goals	(20)
37	21/01/89	Manchester City	Away	League	1–4	1 Goal	(21)
38	28/01/89	Bradford City	Away	FA Cup	2–1	1 Goal	(22)
39	04/02/89	Leicester City	Away	League	2–0	2 Goals	(24)
40	11/02/89	Shrewsbury Town	Home	League	3–0	2 Goals	(26)
41	18/02/89	Liverpool	Home	FA Cup	2–3	1 Goal	(27)
42	25/02/89	Sunderland	Away	League	0–2		
43	28/02/89	Chelsea	Away	League	1–2		
44	04/03/89	Stoke City	Home	League	1–4		
45	11/03/89	Swindon Town	Away	League	0–1		
46	14/03/89	Leeds United	Home	League	1–2		
47	18/03/89	Blackburn Rovers	Away	League	0–4		
48	25/03/89	Plymouth Argyle	Home	League	3–0	2 Goals	(29)
49	27/03/89	Bradford City	Away	League	1–1	1 Goal	(30)
50	01/04/89	Portsmouth	Home	League	1–1	1 Goal	(31)
51	04/04/89	Oxford United	Home	League	1–2		
52	08/04/89	Ipswich Town	Away	League	1–1		
53	11/04/89	Crystal Palace	Home	League	0–1		
54	15/04/89	Walsall	Away	League	1–1	1 Goal	(32)
55	22/04/89	Oldham Athletic	Home	League	1–1		
56	29/04/89	Watford	Home	League	0–3		
57	01/05/89	Brighton & Hove Albion	Away	League	1–1	1 Goal	(33)
58	06/05/89	Birmingham City	Away	League	0–1		
59	13/05/89	West Bromwich Albion	Home	League	0–1		

SEASON 1989–90

League Division Two

60	19/08/89	Leicester City	Home	League	1–1		
61	22/08/89	Grimsby Town	Home	Lge Cup	1–0		
Sub+1	29/08/89	Grimsby Town	Away	Lge Cup	0–2*		
62	09/09/89	Portsmouth	Away	League	2–2		

Stockport County – League Division Four

1	30/09/89	Scarborough	Home	League	3–2	1 Goal	(1)
2	07/10/89	Hereford United	Home	League	2–1	1 Goal	(2)
3	14/10/89	Gillingham	Away	League	3–0	1 Goal	(3)
4	16/10/89	Southend United	Home	League	1–0		
5	21/10/89	Peterborough United	Away	League	0–2		
6	28/10/89	Exeter City	Home	League	2–1	1 Goal	(4)
7	01/11/89	Lincoln City	Away	League	0–0		
8	03/11/89	Halifax Town	Home	League	0–1		
9	11/11/89	Chesterfield	Away	League	1–1		
10	18/11/89	Burnley	Away	FA Cup	1–1		
11	22/11/89	Burnley	Home	FA Cup	1–2	1 Goal	(5)
12	25/11/89	Scunthorpe United	Home	League	4–2		
13	28/11/89	Burnley	Away	LD Cup	2–0		
14	02/12/89	Doncaster Rovers	Away	League	1–2		
15	09/12/89	Scarborough	Away	League	0–2		
16	13/12/89	Preston North End	Home	LD Cup	2–4		
17	26/12/89	Rochdale	Home	League	2–1		
18	29/12/89	Cambridge United	Home	League	3–1	2 Goals	(7)
19	01/01/90	Grimsby Town	Away	League	2–4	1 Goal	(8)
20	05/01/90	Colchester United	Away	League	1–0		
21	09/01/90	Carlisle United	Away	LD Cup	2–1*	1 Goal	(9)
22	13/01/90	Burnley	Home	League	3–1		
23	20/01/90	Torquay United	Away	League	0–3		
24	27/01/90	Maidstone United	Home	League	1–2		
25	03/02/90	Aldershot	Home	League	1–1		
Sub+1	10/02/90	Hartlepool United	Away	League	0–5		
26	13/02/90	York City	Away	League	3–0		
27	16/02/90	Doncaster Rovers	Home	League	3–1	2 Goals	(11)
28	24/02/90	Scunthorpe United	Away	League	0–5		
29	02/03/90	Colchester United	Home	League	1–1		
30	09/03/90	Wrexham	Home	League	0–2		
31	19/03/90	Gillingham	Home	League	1–0	1 Goal	(12)

Huddersfield Town (loan) – League Division Three

Sub+1	31/03/90	Birmingham City	Home	League	1–2		
1	03/04/90	Preston North End	Home	League	0–2		
Sub+2	10/04/90	Bristol Rovers	Home	League	1–1		
Sub+3	14/04/90	Blackpool	Home	League	2–2		

Sub+4	16/04/90	Bury	Away	League	0–6		
2	21/04/90	Rotherham United	Home	League	2–1	2 Goals	(2)
3	24/04/90	Bristol City	Away	League	1–1		
4	28/04/90	Northampton Town	Away	League	0–1		
5	01/05/90	Bolton Wanderers	Away	League	2–2	1 Goal	(3)
6	05/05/90	Chester City	Home	League	4–1	1 Goal	(4)

SEASON 1990–91

Huddersfield Town – League Division Three

Sub+5	25/08/90	Southend United	Home	League	1–2		
Sub+6	29/08/90	Bolton Wanderers	Home	Lge Cup	0–3		
Sub+7	01/09/90	Swansea City	Away	League	0–1		
7	04/09/90	Bolton Wanderers	Away	Lge Cup	1–2		
8	08/09/90	Bolton Wanderers	Home	League	4–0	3 Goals	(7)
9	15/09/90	Fulham	Away	League	0–0		
10	18/09/90	Grimsby Town	Away	League	0–4		
11	22/09/90	Reading	Home	League	0–2		
Sub+8	29/09/90	Chester City	Away	League	2–1		
12	02/10/90	Exeter City	Home	League	1–0		
13	06/10/90	Leyton Orient	Home	League	1–0		
14	13/10/90	Rotherham United	Away	League	3–1		
Sub+9	20/10/90	Brentford	Away	League	0–1		
15	23/10/90	AFC Bournemouth	Home	League	1–3		
Sub+10	07/11/90	Bradford City	Away	LD Cup	1–1		
16	10/12/90	Blackpool	Home	FA Cup	0–2		

Plymouth Argyle (loan) – League Division Two

1	21/12/90	Oldham Athletic	Away	League	3–5	1 Goal	(1)
2	26/12/90	Barnsley	Home	League	1–1		
3	29/12/90	Bristol Rovers	Home	League	2–2		

Huddersfield Town – League Division Three

17	26/03/91	Reading	Away	League	2–1	1 Goal	(8)
18	30/03/91	Shrewsbury Town	Home	League	2–1		
Sub+11	01/04/91	Bury	Away	League	1–2		
Sub+12	06/04/91	Stoke City	Home	League	3–0		
Sub+13	13/04/91	Wigan Athletic	Away	League	1–1		
Sub+14	11/05/91	Birmingham City	Home	League	0–1		

APPEARANCES AND GOALS PER SEASON

SEASON 75–76	GAMES	GOALS
League	2+1	0
FA Cup	1	0
TOTAL	**3+1**	**0**

SEASON 76–77	GAMES	GOALS
League	30+1	18
FA Cup	1	0
League Cup	1	0
TOTAL	**32+1**	**18**

SEASON 77–88	GAMES	GOALS
League	32+4	11
FA Cup	1	0
League Cup	1	0
Anglo–Scottish Cup	4	4
TOTAL	**38+4**	**15**

SEASON 78–79	GAMES	GOALS
League	46	24
FA Cup	2	1
League Cup	3	0
TOTAL	**51**	**25**

SEASON 79–80	GAMES	GOALS
League	41	19
FA Cup	2	0
League Cup	2	1
TOTAL	**45**	**20**

SEASON 80–81	**GAMES**	**GOALS**
League	38+2	13
FA Cup	6	4
League Cup	2	0
Anglo–Scottish Cup	3	0
TOTAL	**49+2**	**17**

SEASON 81–82	**GAMES**	**GOALS**
League	46	36
FA Cup	2	1
League Cup	2	0
Football League Group Cup	1+2	1
TOTAL	**51+2**	**38**

SEASON 82–83	**GAMES**	**GOALS**
League	37+5	13
FA Cup	6	5
League Cup	2+2	5
Football League Trophy	3	1
TOTAL	**48+7**	**24**

SEASON 83–84	**GAMES**	**GOALS**
League	44	34
FA Cup	5	4
League Cup	4	2
Associate Members Cup	3	2
TOTAL	**56**	**42**

SEASON 84–85	**GAMES**	**GOALS**
League	29	13
FA Cup	1	0
League Cup	4	2
TOTAL	**34**	**15**

SEASON 85–86	**GAMES**	**GOALS**
League	32+3	20
FA Cup	2	0
League Cup	2+1	1
Full Members Cup	2	0
TOTAL	**38+4**	**21**

SEASON 86–87	**GAMES**	**GOALS**
League	24+6	6
League Play–offs	1+4	2
FA Cup	2+3	1
League Cup	2	0
Full Members Cup	1	0
TOTAL	**30+13**	**9**

SEASON 87–88	**GAMES**	**GOALS**
League	13+4	3
Scottish League	6+3	2
Scottish Cup	0+1	1
TOTAL	**19+8**	**6**

SEASON 88–89	**GAMES**	**GOALS**
League	44	26
FA Cup	3	3
League Cup	2	1
Simod Cup	1	0
TOTAL	**50**	**30**

SEASON 89–90	**GAMES**	**GOALS**
League	34+5	14
FA Cup	2	1
League Cup	1+1	0
Leyland Daf Cup	3	1
TOTAL	**40+6**	**16**

SEASON 90–91	**GAMES**	**GOALS**
League	13+8	5
FA Cup	1	0
League Cup	1+1	0
Leyland Daf Cup	0+1	0
TOTAL	**15+10**	**5**

CAREER APPEARANCES AND GOALS

COMPETITION	GAMES	TOTAL	GOALS
League	505+39	544	255
League Play-offs	1+4	5	2
FA Cup	37+3	40	20
League Cup	29+5	34	12
Anglo-Scottish Cup	7	7	4
Football League Group Cup	1+2	3	1
Football League Trophy	3	3	1
Associate Members Cup	3	3	2
Full Members Cup	3	3	0
Simod Cup	1	1	0
Leyland Daf Cup	3+1	4	1
Scottish League	6+3	9	2
Scottish Cup	0+1	1	1
TOTAL	**599+58**	**657**	**301**

HAT-TRICKS

Sheffield United

1	3	Oldham Athletic	06/08/77	Away	AS Cup	3-2

Hull City

1	3	Chester	02/09/78	Home	League	3-0

Sheffield United

1	3	Northampton Town	16/03/82	Home	League	7-3
2	3	Grimsby Town (sub)	26/10/82	Home	Lge Cup	5-1
3	4	Gillingham	27/08/83	Home	League	4-0
4	4	Wrexham	19/11/83	Away	FA Cup	5-1
5	3	Southend United	26/11/83	Home	League	5-0
6	3	Orient	03/03/84	Home	League	6-3
7	3	Hull City	02/11/85	Home	League	3-1

Hull City

1	3	AFC Bournemouth	14/01/89	Home	League	4-0

Huddersfield Town

1	3	Bolton Wanderers	08/09/90	Home	League	4-0

League: 8
FA Cup: 1
League Cup: 1
Anglo-Scottish Cup: 1
TOTAL: 11

HONOURS

Winners medals
League Division Four Championship: 81/82

Runner-up medals
Promoted to League Division Two: 83/84

JOHN FASHANU

Born: 18/09/62 – Kensington
Height: 6.1
Weight: 11.02 (95–96)

Clubs
Norwich City: **1981–82** – Matches: **8+1** – Goals: **2**
Crystal Palace (loan): **1983** – Matches: **2** – Goals: **0**
Lincoln City: **1983–84** – Matches: **36+6** – Goals: **11**
Millwall: **1984–86** – Matches: **65** – Goals: **19**
Wimbledon: **1986–94** – Matches: **324+7** – Goals: **129**
Aston Villa: **1994–95** – Matches: **14+2** – Goals: **3**

Country
England: **1989** – Matches: **2** – Goals: **0**

SEASON 1981–82

Norwich City – League Division Two

1	15/08/81	Peterborough United	Home	FLG Cup	2–2		
Sub+1	17/10/81	Shrewsbury Town	Home	League	2–1		
2	24/10/81	Watford	Away	League	0–3		
3	21/11/81	Derby County	Home	League	4–1	1 Goal	(1)
4	24/11/81	Crystal Palace	Away	League	1–2		
5	28/11/81	Blackburn Rovers	Away	League	0–3		

SEASON 1982–83

League Division One

6	18/09/82	Everton	Away	League	1–1		
7	25/09/82	West Bromwich Albion	Home	League	1–3		
8	08/12/82	Lincoln City	Away	FL Trophy	1–3	1 Goal	(2)

SEASON 1983–84

Crystal Palace (loan) – League Division Two

1	11/09/83	Fulham	Home	League	1–1	
2	14/09/83	Peterborough United	Away	Lge Cup	0–3+	

Lincoln City – League Division Three

1	24/09/83	Hull City	Away	League	0–2		
2	28/09/83	Exeter City	Away	League	3–0		
3	01/10/83	AFC Bournemouth	Home	League	3–0		
4	08/10/83	Wigan Athletic	Away	League	0–2		
5	22/10/83	Burnley	Home	League	3–1	1 Goal	(1)
6	29/10/83	Preston North End	Away	League	2–1		
7	02/11/83	Bolton Wanderers	Home	League	0–0		
8	05/11/83	Gillingham	Away	League	0–2		
9	12/11/83	Scunthorpe United	Home	League	2–1		
10	19/11/83	Port Vale	Away	FA Cup	2–1		
11	26/11/83	Bristol Rovers	Home	League	4–0	3 Goals	(4)
12	03/12/83	Wimbledon	Away	League	1–3		
Sub+1	10/12/83	Sheffield United	Home	FA Cup	0–0		
13	17/12/83	Port Vale	Away	League	1–0		
14	19/12/83	Sheffield United	Away	FA Cup	0–1		
Sub+2	04/02/84	AFC Bournemouth	Away	League	0–3		
15	07/02/84	Sheffield United	Away	League	0–0		
Sub+3	11/02/84	Hull City	Home	League	1–3		
16	14/02/84	Bolton Wanderers	Away	League	2–0		
17	18/02/84	Preston North End	Home	League	2–1	1 Goal	(5)
18	22/02/84	Doncaster Rovers	Home	AM Cup	0–2		
19	25/02/84	Burnley	Away	League	0–4		
20	03/03/84	Newport County	Home	League	2–3		
Sub+4	17/03/84	Wigan Athletic	Home	League	0–1		
21	31/03/84	Exeter City	Home	League	1–1		
Sub+5	14/04/84	Wimbledon	Home	League	1–2		
22	21/04/84	Walsall	Away	League	1–0	1 Goal	(6)
23	23/04/84	Southend United	Home	League	1–2		
24	28/04/84	Bristol Rovers	Away	League	1–3		
25	01/05/84	Millwall	Away	League	2–0	1 Goal	(7)

+ AET Peterborough United won 4–2 on penalties

SEASON 1984–85

League Division Three

26	25/08/84	Hull City	Home	League	0–0		
27	29/08/84	Hull City	Home	Lge Cup	0–0		
28	01/09/84	Rotherham United	Away	League	0–0		
29	04/09/84	Hull City	Away	Lge Cup	1–4		
Sub+6	18/09/84	Wigan Athletic	Away	League	0–1		
30	06/10/84	Preston North End	Home	League	4–0	1 Goal	(8)
31	13/10/84	Burnley	Away	League	2–1	1 Goal	(9)
32	20/10/84	AFC Bournemouth	Home	League	0–0		
33	23/10/84	Millwall	Away	League	0–2		
34	27/10/84	Reading	Home	League	5–1	1 Goal	(10)
35	03/11/84	Bolton Wanderers	Away	League	0–1		
36	07/11/84	Newport County	Home	League	2–2	1 Goal	(11)

Millwall – League Division Three

1	15/12/84	Bolton Wanderers	Away	League	0–2

2	18/12/84	Hull City	Home	League	2–2	1 Goal	(1)
3	22/12/84	Plymouth Argyle	Away	League	1–3		
4	29/12/84	AFC Bournemouth	Home	League	2–1		
5	01/01/85	Reading	Away	League	2–2		
6	05/01/85	Crystal Palace	Home	FA Cup	1–1		
7	29/01/85	Orient	Away	League	0–1		
8	02/02/85	Newport County	Home	League	2–0		
9	04/02/85	Chelsea	Away	FA Cup	3–2	1 Goal	(2)
10	09/02/85	Wigan Athletic	Away	League	1–0		
11	19/02/85	Leicester City	Home	FA Cup	2–0	1 Goal	(3)
12	23/02/85	Bradford City	Home	League	4–0	2 Goals	(5)
13	02/03/85	Bristol City	Away	League	1–0		
14	06/03/85	Lincoln City	Away	League	1–0		
15	09/03/85	York City	Home	League	1–0		
16	13/03/85	Luton Town	Away	FA Cup	0–1		
17	16/03/85	Rotherham United	Away	League	0–0		
18	23/03/85	Gillingham	Home	League	2–1		
19	26/03/85	Swansea City	Away	League	2–1	1 Goal	(6)
20	29/03/85	Rotherham United	Home	League	0–0		
21	03/04/85	Derby County	Away	League	2–1		
22	13/04/85	Preston North End	Away	League	1–2		
23	16/04/85	Cambridge United	Home	League	2–1		
24	20/04/85	Bristol Rovers	Home	League	1–0		
25	27/04/85	Burnley	Away	League	1–1		
26	30/04/85	Doncaster Rovers	Home	League	2–1		
27	04/05/85	Bolton Wanderers	Home	League	5–2		
28	08/05/85	AFC Bournemouth	Away	League	2–1		
29	11/05/85	Plymouth Argyle	Home	League	2–0		

SEASON 1985–86

League Division Two

30	17/08/85	Huddersfield Town	Away	League	3–4	1 Goal	(7)
31	21/08/85	Colchester United	Away	Lge Cup	3–2	1 Goal	(8)
32	24/08/85	Norwich City	Home	League	4–2		
33	27/08/85	Shrewsbury Town	Away	League	1–1		
34	31/08/85	Sunderland	Home	League	1–0	1 Goal	(9)
35	02/09/85	Colchester United	Home	Lge Cup	4–1	1 Goal	(10)
36	07/09/85	Stoke City	Away	League	0–0		
37	14/09/85	Brighton & Hove Albion	Home	League	0–1		
38	17/09/85	Hull City	Away	League	0–3		
39	21/09/85	Crystal Palace	Away	League	1–2		
40	25/09/85	Southampton	Home	Lge Cup	0–0		
41	28/09/85	Oldham Athletic	Home	League	0–1		
42	02/10/85	Stoke City	Home	FM Cup	2–2	1 Goal	(11)
43	05/10/85	Sheffield United	Away	League	3–1	2 Goals	(13)
44	08/10/85	Southampton	Away	Lge Cup	0–0+		
45	12/10/85	Blackburn Rovers	Home	League	0–1		
46	15/10/85	Coventry City	Away	FM Cup	1–1		
47	19/10/85	Wimbledon	Away	League	1–1		
48	02/11/85	Grimsby Town	Away	League	1–5		
49	09/11/85	Leeds United	Home	League	3–1		
50	28/12/85	Hull City	Home	League	5–0	1 Goal	(14)
51	04/01/86	Wimbledon	Home	FA Cup	3–1	1 Goal	(15)
52	11/01/86	Stoke City	Home	League	2–3		
53	18/01/86	Sunderland	Away	League	2–1	1 Goal	(16)
54	25/01/86	Aston Villa	Away	FA Cup	1–1		
55	29/01/86	Aston Villa	Home	FA Cup	1–0	1 Goal	(17)
56	01/02/86	Shrewsbury Town	Home	League	2–0		
57	15/02/86	Southampton	Away	FA Cup	0–0		
58	01/03/86	Oldham Athletic	Away	League	0–0		
59	05/03/86	Southampton	Home	FA Cup	0–1		
60	08/03/86	Sheffield United	Home	League	3–0		
61	11/03/86	Wimbledon	Home	League	0–1		
62	15/03/86	Blackburn Rovers	Away	League	2–1	1 Goal	(18)
63	18/03/86	Fulham	Home	League	1–1	1 Goal	(19)
64	22/03/86	Brighton & Hove Albion	Away	League	0–1		
65	25/03/86	Portsmouth	Away	League	1–2		

Wimbledon – League Division Two

Sub+1	29/03/86	Portsmouth	Away	League	1–1		
1	01/04/86	Crystal Palace	Home	League	1–1	1 Goal	(1)
2	06/04/86	Carlisle United	Away	League	3–2	1 Goal	(2)
3	12/04/86	Sunderland	Home	League	3–0		

4	19/04/86	Shrewsbury Town	Away	League	1–1		
5	26/04/86	Hull City	Home	League	3–1	2 Goals	(4)
6	29/04/86	Stoke City	Home	League	1–0		
7	03/05/86	Huddersfield Town	Away	League	1–0		
8	06/05/86	Charlton Athletic	Away	League	0–0		

+ AET Southampton won 5–4 on penalties

SEASON 1986–87

League Division One

9	23/08/86	Manchester City	Away	League	1–3		
10	26/08/86	Aston Villa	Home	League	3–2	1 Goal	(5)
11	30/08/86	Leicester City	Home	League	1–0		
12	02/09/86	Charlton Athletic	Away	League	1–0		
13	06/09/86	Watford	Away	League	0–1		
14	13/09/86	Everton	Home	League	1–2		
15	20/09/86	Newcastle United	Away	League	0–1		
Sub+2	23/09/86	Cambridge United	Away	Lge Cup	1–1		
16	27/09/86	Southampton	Home	League	2–2	2 Goals	(7)
17	04/10/86	Liverpool	Home	League	1–3		
18	19/10/86	Coventry City	Away	League	0–1		
19	25/10/86	Norwich City	Home	League	2–0	1 Goal	(8)
20	01/11/86	Tottenham Hotspur	Away	League	2–1	1 Goal	(9)
21	08/11/86	Luton Town	Home	League	0–1		
22	15/11/86	West Ham United	Home	League	0–1		
23	22/11/86	Nottingham Forest	Away	League	2–3		
24	29/11/86	Manchester United	Home	League	1–0		
25	06/12/86	Chelsea	Away	League	4–0	1 Goal	(10)
26	13/12/86	Sheffield Wednesday	Home	League	3–0	1 Goal	(11)
27	20/12/86	Everton	Away	League	0–3		
28	26/12/86	Oxford United	Home	League	1–1		
29	27/12/86	West Ham United	Away	League	3–2	1 Goal	(12)
30	01/01/87	Arsenal	Away	League	1–3		
31	03/01/87	Watford	Home	League	2–1		
32	10/01/87	Sunderland	Home	FA Cup	2–1		
33	24/01/87	Manchester City	Home	League	0–0		
34	31/01/87	Portsmouth	Home	FA Cup	4–0	2 Goals	(14)
35	15/02/87	Charlton Athletic	Home	League	2–0		
36	22/02/87	Everton	Home	FA Cup	3–1	1 Goal	(15)
37	04/03/87	Aston Villa	Away	League	0–0		
38	07/03/87	Norwich City	Away	League	0–0		
39	15/03/87	Tottenham Hotspur	Home	FA Cup	0–2		
40	21/03/87	Queens Park Rangers	Home	League	1–1		
41	24/03/87	Coventry City	Home	League	2–1	1 Goal	(16)
42	28/03/87	Liverpool	Away	League	2–1		
43	18/04/87	Arsenal	Home	League	1–2		
44	20/04/87	Oxford United	Away	League	1–3		
45	22/04/87	Tottenham Hotspur	Home	League	2–2		
46	25/04/87	Nottingham Forest	Home	League	2–1	1 Goal	(17)
47	02/05/87	Manchester United	Away	League	1–0		
48	05/05/87	Chelsea	Home	League	2–1	1 Goal	(18)
49	09/05/87	Sheffield Wednesday	Away	League	2–0		

SEASON 1987–88

League Division One

50	15/08/87	Watford	Away	League	0–1		
51	18/08/87	Everton	Home	League	1–1		
52	22/08/87	Oxford United	Home	League	1–1		
53	29/08/87	Derby County	Away	League	1–0	1 Goal	(19)
54	01/09/87	Charlton Athletic	Home	League	4–1	2 Goals	(21)
55	05/09/87	Newcastle United	Away	League	2–1	1 Goal	(22)
56	12/09/87	West Ham United	Home	League	1–1		
57	19/09/87	Arsenal	Away	League	0–3		
58	22/09/87	Rochdale	Away	Lge Cup	1–1	1 Goal	(23)
59	26/09/87	Portsmouth	Away	League	1–2		
60	03/10/87	Queens Park Rangers	Home	League	1–2	1 Goal	(24)
61	06/10/87	Rochdale	Home	Lge Cup	2–1	1 Goal	(25)
62	17/10/87	Luton Town	Away	League	0–2		
63	27/10/87	Newcastle United	Home	Lge Cup	2–1	1 Goal	(26)
64	31/10/87	Tottenham Hotspur	Away	League	3–0	1 Goal	(27)
65	04/11/87	Liverpool	Home	League	1–1		

66	07/11/87	Southampton	Home	League	2–0		
67	14/11/87	Coventry City	Away	League	3–3	2 Goals	(29)
68	18/11/87	Oxford United	Away	Lge Cup	1–2		
69	21/11/87	Manchester United	Home	League	2–1		
70	28/11/87	Chelsea	Away	League	1–1		
71	05/12/87	Nottingham Forest	Home	League	1–1		
72	12/12/87	Sheffield Wednesday	Away	League	0–1		
73	18/12/87	Norwich City	Home	League	1–0	1 Goal	(30)
74	26/12/87	West Ham United	Away	League	2–1	1 Goal	(31)
75	28/12/87	Arsenal	Home	League	3–1		
76	01/01/88	Derby County	Home	League	2–1	1 Goal	(32)
77	02/01/88	Oxford United	Away	League	5–2	1 Goal	(33)
78	09/01/88	West Bromwich Albion	Home	FA Cup	4–1	1 Goal	(34)
79	13/01/88	Coventry City	Away	Simod Cup	1–2		
80	16/01/88	Watford	Home	League	1–2		
81	30/01/88	Mansfield Town	Away	FA Cup	2–1		
82	06/02/88	Newcastle United	Home	League	0–0		
83	13/02/88	Charlton Athletic	Away	League	1–1		
84	20/02/88	Newcastle United	Away	FA Cup	3–1	1 Goal	(35)
85	27/02/88	Queens Park Rangers	Away	League	0–1		
86	05/03/88	Luton Town	Home	League	2–0	1 Goal	(36)
87	12/03/88	Watford	Home	FA Cup	2–1	1 Goal	(37)
88	19/03/88	Tottenham Hotspur	Home	League	3–0	1 Goal	(38)
89	26/03/88	Liverpool	Away	League	1–2		
90	29/03/88	Everton	Away	League	2–2		
91	02/04/88	Southampton	Away	League	2–2		
92	05/04/88	Coventry City	Home	League	1–2		
93	09/04/88	Luton Town	Neutral	FA Cup	2–1	1 Goal	(39)
94	19/04/88	Portsmouth	Home	League	2–2		
95	03/05/88	Sheffield Wednesday	Home	League	1–1		
96	07/05/88	Norwich City	Away	League	1–0		
97	09/05/88	Manchester United	Away	League	1–2		
98	14/05/88	Liverpool	Wembley	FA Cup	1–0		

SEASON 1988–89

League Division One

99	20/08/88	Liverpool	Wembley	FA C/S	1–2	1 Goal	(40)
100	27/08/88	Arsenal	Home	League	1–5	1 Goal	(41)
101	29/08/88	Newcastle United	Away	MCC Trophy	0–1		
102	03/09/88	Luton Town	Away	League	2–2	1 Goal	(42)
103	10/09/88	West Ham United	Home	League	0–1		
104	17/09/88	Middlesbrough	Away	League	0–1		
105	24/09/88	Coventry City	Home	League	0–1		
106	27/09/88	Barnsley	Away	Lge Cup	2–0	2 Goals	(44)
107	01/10/88	Everton	Home	League	2–1	1 Goal	(45)
108	08/10/88	Aston Villa	Away	League	1–0		
109	29/10/88	Derby County	Away	League	1–4		
110	02/11/88	Manchester United	Home	Lge Cup	2–1		
111	05/11/88	Norwich City	Home	League	0–2		
112	12/11/88	Tottenham Hotspur	Away	League	2–3		
113	19/11/88	Charlton Athletic	Home	League	1–1	1 Goal	(46)
114	26/11/88	Liverpool	Away	League	1–1		
115	30/11/88	Queens Park Rangers	Away	Lge Cup	0–0		
116	14/12/88	Queens Park Rangers	Home	Lge Cup	0–1		
117	18/12/88	Nottingham Forest	Away	League	1–0		
118	26/12/88	Millwall	Home	League	1–0		
119	31/12/88	Luton Town	Home	League	4–0	1 Goal	(47)
120	02/01/89	West Ham United	Away	League	2–1		
121	07/01/89	Birmingham City	Away	FA Cup	1–0		
122	28/01/89	Aston Villa	Away	FA Cup	1–0		
123	04/02/89	Everton	Away	League	1–1		
124	11/02/89	Aston Villa	Home	League	1–0	1 Goal	(48)
125	18/02/89	Grimsby Town	Home	FA Cup	3–1	1 Goal	(49)
126	25/02/89	Sheffield Wednesday	Home	League	1–0	1 Goal	(50)
127	01/03/89	Derby County	Home	League	4–0	1 Goal	(51)
128	11/03/89	Norwich City	Away	League	0–1		
129	19/03/89	Everton	Away	FA Cup	0–1		
130	25/03/89	Middlesbrough	Home	League	1–1		
131	27/03/89	Millwall	Away	League	1–0	1 Goal	(52)
132	01/04/89	Nottingham Forest	Home	League	4–1	1 Goal	(53)
133	05/04/89	Sheffield Wednesday	Away	League	1–1	1 Goal	(54)
134	08/04/89	Queens Park Rangers	Away	League	3–4	1 Goal	(55)
135	15/04/89	Tottenham Hotspur	Home	League	1–2		

136	22/04/89	Southampton	Away	League	0–0		
137	13/05/89	Liverpool	Home	League	1–2		
138	17/05/89	Arsenal	Away	League	2–2		

SEASON 1989–90

League Division One

139	23/08/89	Derby County	Away	League	1–0		
140	26/08/89	Arsenal	Away	League	0–0		
141	29/08/89	Millwall	Home	League	2–2		
142	09/09/89	Crystal Palace	Away	League	0–2		
143	16/09/89	Manchester City	Home	League	1–0	1 Goal	(56)
144	18/09/89	Port Vale	Away	Lge Cup	2–1	1 Goal	(57)
145	23/09/89	Luton Town	Away	League	1–1		
146	30/09/89	Southampton	Away	League	2–2		
147	04/10/89	Port Vale	Home	Lge Cup	3–0	1 Goal	(58)
148	14/10/89	Liverpool	Home	League	1–2		
149	21/10/89	Nottingham Forest	Home	League	1–3		
150	25/11/89	Aston Villa	Home	League	0–2		
151	21/12/89	Ipswich Town	Away	ZDS Cup	1–3	1 Goal	(59)
152	30/12/89	Manchester United	Home	League	2–2		
153	01/01/90	Norwich City	Away	League	1–0		
154	06/01/90	West Bromwich Albion	Away	FA Cup	0–2		
155	24/02/90	Aston Villa	Away	League	3–0	2 Goals	(61)
156	03/03/90	Everton	Home	League	3–1	2 Goals	(63)
157	17/03/90	Southampton	Home	League	3–3	1 Goal	(64)
158	24/03/90	Sheffield Wednesday	Home	League	1–1	1 Goal	(65)
159	31/03/90	Nottingham Forest	Away	League	1–0		
160	03/04/90	Liverpool	Away	League	1–2		
161	14/04/90	Norwich City	Home	League	1–1	1 Goal	(66)
162	17/04/90	Charlton Athletic	Away	League	2–1	1 Goal	(67)
163	21/04/90	Coventry City	Home	League	0–0		
164	28/04/90	Tottenham Hotspur	Home	League	1–0	1 Goal	(68)
165	02/05/90	Crystal Palace	Home	League	0–1		
166	05/05/90	Queens Park Rangers	Away	League	3–2	1 Goal	(69)

SEASON 1990–91

League Division One

167	25/08/90	Arsenal	Home	League	0–3		
168	29/08/90	Queens Park Rangers	Away	League	1–0	1 Goal	(70)
169	01/09/90	Derby County	Away	League	1–1		
170	08/09/90	Liverpool	Home	League	1–2		
171	15/09/90	Coventry City	Away	League	0–0		
172	22/09/90	Sunderland	Home	League	2–2		
Sub+3	06/10/90	Sheffield United	Away	League	2–1	1 Goal	(71)
173	10/10/90	Plymouth Argyle	Home	Lge Cup	0–2		
174	20/10/90	Aston Villa	Home	League	0–0		
175	27/10/90	Crystal Palace	Away	League	3–4	1 Goal	(72)
176	03/11/90	Southampton	Home	League	1–1		
177	24/11/90	Everton	Home	League	2–1		
178	01/12/90	Norwich City	Away	League	4–0	2 Goals	(74)
179	08/12/90	Queens Park Rangers	Home	League	3–0	2 Goals	(76)
180	15/12/90	Arsenal	Away	League	2–2	1 Goal	(77)
181	22/12/90	Manchester United	Home	League	1–3	1 Goal	(78)
182	26/12/90	Nottingham Forest	Away	League	1–2	1 Goal	(79)
183	29/12/90	Leeds United	Away	League	0–3		
184	01/01/91	Luton Town	Home	League	2–0	1 Goal	(80)
185	05/01/91	Aston Villa	Away	FA Cup	1–1		
186	08/01/91	Aston Villa	Home	FA Cup	1–0*		
187	12/01/91	Derby County	Home	League	3–1	2 Goals	(82)
188	19/01/91	Liverpool	Away	League	1–1		
189	02/02/91	Coventry City	Home	League	1–0		
190	16/02/91	Chelsea	Away	League	0–0		
191	23/02/91	Tottenham Hotspur	Home	League	5–1	1 Goal	(83)
192	02/03/91	Norwich City	Home	League	0–0		
193	16/03/91	Manchester City	Away	League	1–1	1 Goal	(84)
194	23/03/91	Sheffield United	Home	League	1–1		
195	30/03/91	Nottingham Forest	Home	League	3–1	1 Goal	(85)
196	02/04/91	Manchester United	Away	League	1–2		
197	06/04/91	Leeds United	Home	League	0–1		
198	10/04/91	Everton	Away	League	2–1	1 Goal	(86)
199	13/04/91	Luton Town	Away	League	1–0	1 Goal	(87)
200	20/04/91	Aston Villa	Away	League	2–1	1 Goal	(88)
201	23/04/91	Sunderland	Away	League	0–0		

| 202 | 04/05/91 | Crystal Palace | Home | League | 0–3 | | |
| 203 | 11/05/91 | Southampton | Away | League | 1–1 | 1 Goal | (89) |

SEASON 1991–92

League Division One

204	17/08/91	Chelsea	Away	League	2–2	1 Goal	(90)
205	24/08/91	West Ham United	Home	League	2–0	1 Goal	(91)
206	27/08/91	Crystal Palace	Away	League	2–3	1 Goal	(92)
207	31/08/91	Coventry City	Away	League	1–0		
208	03/09/91	Manchester United	Home	League	1–2	1 Goal	(93)
209	14/09/91	Nottingham Forest	Away	League	2–4	1 Goal	(94)
210	18/09/91	Southampton	Away	League	0–1		
211	21/09/91	Tottenham Hotspur	Home	League	3–5	1 Goal	(95)
212	24/09/91	Peterborough United	Home	Lge Cup	1–2		
213	28/09/91	Sheffield United	Away	League	0–0		
214	05/10/91	Norwich City	Home	League	3–1	1 Goal	(96)
215	08/10/91	Peterborough United	Away	Lge Cup	2–2	1 Goal	(97)
216	19/10/91	Queens Park Rangers	Home	League	0–1		
217	23/10/91	Brighton & Hove Albion	Away	ZDS Cup	2–3		
218	26/10/91	Aston Villa	Away	League	1–2	1 Goal	(98)
219	02/11/91	Leeds United	Home	League	0–0		
220	16/11/91	Everton	Away	League	0–2		
221	30/11/91	Manchester City	Away	League	0–0		
222	07/12/91	Oldham Athletic	Home	League	2–1		
223	21/12/91	Sheffield Wednesday	Away	League	0–2		
224	26/12/91	Crystal Palace	Home	League	1–1		
225	28/12/91	Coventry City	Home	League	1–1		
226	01/01/92	Arsenal	Away	League	1–1		
227	04/01/92	Bristol City	Away	FA Cup	1–1	1 Goal	(99)
228	11/01/92	West Ham United	Away	League	1–1		
229	14/01/92	Bristol City	Home	FA Cup	0–1		
230	18/01/92	Chelsea	Home	League	1–2		
231	01/02/92	Queens Park Rangers	Away	League	1–1	1 Goal	(100)
232	08/02/92	Aston Villa	Home	League	2–0	1 Goal	(101)
233	22/02/92	Manchester City	Home	League	2–1	1 Goal	(102)
234	25/02/92	Notts County	Away	League	1–1	1 Goal	(103)
235	29/02/92	Oldham Athletic	Away	League	1–0		
236	07/03/92	Notts County	Home	League	2–0	1 Goal	(104)
237	10/03/92	Everton	Home	League	0–0		
238	14/03/92	Leeds United	Away	League	1–5		
239	28/03/92	Arsenal	Home	League	1–3		
240	02/04/92	Nottingham Forest	Home	League	3–0	2 Goals	(106)
241	04/04/92	Luton Town	Away	League	1–2	1 Goal	(107)
242	08/04/92	Liverpool	Away	League	3–2	1 Goal	(108)
243	18/04/92	Tottenham Hotspur	Away	League	2–3		
244	20/04/92	Southampton	Home	League	0–1		
245	25/04/92	Norwich City	Away	League	1–1		
246	02/05/92	Sheffield United	Home	League	3–0	1 Goal	(109)

SEASON 1992–93

Premier League

247	01/09/92	Manchester City	Home	League	0–1		
248	05/09/92	Arsenal	Home	League	3–2	1 Goal	(110)
249	12/09/92	Ipswich Town	Away	League	1–2		
250	19/09/92	Blackburn Rovers	Home	League	1–1		
251	22/09/92	Bolton Wanderers	Away	Lge Cup	3–1	1 Goal	(111)
252	26/09/92	Liverpool	Away	League	3–2	1 Goal	(112)
253	03/10/92	Aston Villa	Home	League	2–3		
254	17/10/92	Southampton	Away	League	2–2		
255	25/10/92	Tottenham Hotspur	Home	League	1–1		
256	28/10/92	Everton	Away	Lgc Cup	0–0		
Sub+4	10/11/92	Everton	Home	Lge Cup	0–1		
Sub+5	05/12/92	Norwich City	Away	League	1–2		
Sub+6	20/12/92	Nottingham Forest	Away	League	1–1		
257	26/12/92	Crystal Palace	Away	League	0–2		
258	28/12/92	Chelsea	Home	League	0–0		
259	02/01/92	Everton	Home	FA Cup	0–0		
260	09/01/93	Blackburn Rovers	Away	League	0–0		
261	12/01/93	Everton	Away	FA Cup	2–1	1 Goal	(113)
262	14/01/93	Tottenham Hotspur	Away	FA Cup	2–3		
263	16/01/93	Liverpool	Home	League	2–0	1 Goal	(114)
264	23/01/93	Aston Villa	Away	FA Cup	1–1		
265	26/01/93	Everton	Home	League	1–3	1 Goal	(115)

266	30/01/93	Coventry City	Away	League	2–0		
267	03/02/93	Aston Villa	Home	FA Cup	0–0+		
268	06/02/93	Leeds United	Home	League	1–0		
269	10/02/93	Arsenal	Away	League	1–0		
270	20/02/93	Sheffield United	Home	League	2–0	1 Goal	(116)
271	27/02/93	Aston Villa	Away	League	0–1		
272	06/03/93	Southampton	Home	League	1–2		
273	09/03/93	Middlesbrough	Home	League	2–0		
274	13/03/93	Queens Park Rangers	Away	League	2–1	1 Goal	(117)
275	20/03/93	Norwich City	Home	League	3–0		
276	24/03/93	Sheffield Wednesday	Away	League	1–1		
277	03/04/93	Oldham Athletic	Away	League	2–6		
278	21/04/93	Manchester City	Away	League	1–1		
279	01/05/93	Tottenham Hotspur	Away	League	1–1		
280	09/05/93	Manchester United	Home	League	1–2		

+ AET Wimbledon won 6–5 on penalties

SEASON 1993–94

Premier League

281	14/08/93	West Ham United	Away	League	2–0	1 Goal	(118)
282	17/08/93	Chelsea	Home	League	1–1	1 Goal	(119)
283	21/08/93	Aston Villa	Home	League	2–2	1 Goal	(120)
284	24/08/93	Sheffield United	Away	League	1–2		
285	28/08/93	Oldham Athletic	Away	League	1–1		
286	31/08/93	Southampton	Home	League	1–0		
287	11/09/93	Norwich City	Away	League	1–0		
288	20/09/93	Manchester City	Home	League	1–0		
289	22/09/93	Hereford United	Away	Lge Cup	1–0		
290	27/09/93	Queens Park Rangers	Home	League	1–1		
291	02/10/93	Leeds United	Away	League	0–4		
292	05/10/93	Hereford United	Home	Lge Cup	4–1		
Sub+7	25/10/93	Ipswich Town	Home	League	0–2		
293	27/10/93	Newcastle United	Home	Lge Cup	2–1		
294	30/10/93	Newcastle United	Away	League	0–4		
295	06/11/93	Swindon Town	Home	League	3–0	1 Goal	(121)
296	20/11/93	Manchester United	Away	League	1–3	1 Goal	(122)
297	24/11/93	Tottenham Hotspur	Away	League	1–1		
298	27/11/93	Everton	Home	League	1–1		
299	01/12/93	Liverpool	Away	Lge Cup	1–1		
300	11/12/93	Aston Villa	Away	League	1–0		
301	14/12/93	Liverpool	Home	Lge Cup	2–2+		
302	18/12/93	Sheffield United	Home	League	2–0		
303	26/12/93	Coventry City	Home	League	1–2		
304	28/12/93	Liverpool	Away	League	1–1	1 Goal	(123)
305	01/01/94	Arsenal	Home	League	0–3		
306	08/01/94	Scunthorpe United	Home	FA Cup	3–0		
307	11/01/94	Sheffield Wednesday	Home	Lge Cup	1–2		
308	15/01/94	Sheffield Wednesday	Home	League	2–1	1 Goal	(124)
309	22/01/94	Ipswich Town	Away	League	0–0		
310	29/01/94	Sunderland	Home	FA Cup	2–1	1 Goal	(125)
311	05/02/94	Blackburn Rovers	Away	League	0–3		
312	12/02/94	Newcastle United	Home	League	4–2	1 Goal	(126)
313	20/02/94	Manchester United	Home	FA Cup	0–3		
314	05/03/94	Norwich City	Home	League	3–1		
315	12/03/94	Manchester City	Away	League	1–0		
316	16/03/94	Chelsea	Away	League	0–2		
317	26/03/94	Leeds United	Home	League	1–0		
318	29/03/94	Blackburn Rovers	Home	League	4–1	1 Goal	(127)
319	02/04/94	Coventry City	Away	League	2–1		
320	04/04/94	Liverpool	Home	League	1–1		
321	16/04/94	Manchester United	Home	League	1–0	1 Goal	(128)
322	19/04/94	Arsenal	Away	League	1–1		
323	23/04/94	Swindon Town	Away	League	4–2	1 Goal	(129)
324	26/04/94	Oldham Athletic	Home	League	3–0		

+ AET Wimbledon won 4–3 on penalties

SEASON 1994–95

Aston Villa – Premier League

1	20/08/94	Everton	Away	League	2–2	1 Goal	(1)
2	24/08/94	Southampton	Home	League	1–1		
3	27/08/94	Crystal Palace	Home	League	1–1		

4	29/08/94	Coventry City	Away	League	1–0		
5	10/09/94	Ipswich Town	Home	League	2–0		
6	15/09/94	Internazionale Milano	Away	UEFA Cup	0–1		
7	17/09/94	West Ham United	Away	League	0–1		
8	19/12/94	Southampton	Away	League	1–2		
9	26/12/94	Arsenal	Away	League	0–0		
Sub+1	31/12/94	Manchester City	Away	League	2–2		
Sub+2	02/01/95	Leeds United	Home	League	0–0		
10	07/01/95	Barnsley	Away	FA Cup	2–0		
11	14/01/95	Queens Park Rangers	Home	League	2–1	1 Goal	(2)
12	21/01/95	Nottingham Forest	Away	League	2–1	1 Goal	(3)
13	28/01/95	Manchester City	Away	FA Cup	0–1		
14	04/02/95	Manchester United	Away	League	0–1		

INTERNATIONAL APPEARANCES – ENGLAND

1	23/05/89	Chile	Wembley	0–0	RC
2	27/05/89	Scotland	Hampden Park	2–0	RC

APPEARANCES AND GOALS PER SEASON

SEASON 81–82	GAMES	GOALS
League	4+1	1
Football League Group Cup	1	0
TOTAL	**5+1**	**1**

SEASON 82–83	GAMES	GOALS
League	2	0
Football League Trophy	1	1
TOTAL	**3**	**1**

SEASON 83–84	GAMES	GOALS
League	23+4	7
FA Cup	2+1	0
League Cup	1	0
Associate Members Cup	1	0
TOTAL	**27+5**	**7**

SEASON 84–85	GAMES	GOALS
League	34+1	8
FA Cup	4	2
League Cup	2	0
TOTAL	**40+1**	**10**

SEASON 85–86	GAMES	GOALS
League	33+1	12
FA Cup	5	2
League Cup	4	2
Full Members Cup	2	1
TOTAL	**44+1**	**17**

SEASON 86–87	GAMES	GOALS
League	37	11
FA Cup	4	3
League Cup	0+1	0
TOTAL	**41+1**	**14**

SEASON 87–88	GAMES	GOALS
League	38	14
FA Cup	6	4
League Cup	4	3
Simod Cup	1	0
TOTAL	**49**	**21**

SEASON 88–89	GAMES	GOALS
League	30	12
FA Cup	4	1
League Cup	4	2
Mercantile Centenary Credit Trophy	1	0
FA Charity Shield	1	1
TOTAL	**40**	**16**

SEASON 89–90	GAMES	GOALS
League	24	11
FA Cup	1	0
League Cup	2	2
Zenith Data Systems Cup	1	1
TOTAL	**28**	**14**

SEASON 90–91	GAMES	GOALS
League	34+1	20
FA Cup	2	0
League Cup	1	0
TOTAL	**37+1**	**20**

SEASON 91–92	GAMES	GOALS
League	38	18
FA Cup	2	1
League Cup	2	1
Zenith Data Systems Cup	1	0
TOTAL	**43**	**20**

SEASON 92–93	GAMES	GOALS
League	27+2	6
FA Cup	5	1
League Cup	2+1	1
TOTAL	**34+3**	**8**

SEASON 93–94	GAMES	GOALS
League	35+1	11
FA Cup	3	1
League Cup	6	0
TOTAL	**44+1**	**12**

SEASON 94–95	GAMES	GOALS
League	11+2	3
FA Cup	2	0
UEFA Cup	1	0
TOTAL	**14+2**	**3**

CAREER APPEARANCES AND GOALS

COMPETITION	GAMES	TOTAL	GOALS
League	370+13	383	134
FA Cup	40+1	41	15
League Cup	28+2	30	11
Football League Group Cup	1	1	0
Football League Trophy	1	1	1
Associate Members Cup	1	1	0
Full Members Cup	2	2	1
Simod Cup	1	1	0
Mercantile Centenary Credit Trophy	1	1	0
Zenith Data Systems Cup	2	2	1
FA Charity Shield	1	1	1
UEFA Cup	1	1	0
Internationals	2	2	0
TOTAL	**451+16**	**467**	**164**

HAT-TRICKS

Lincoln City

1	3	Bristol Rovers	26/11/83	Home	League	4–0

League: 1
TOTAL: 1

HONOURS

Winners medals
FA Cup: 87/88

Runner-up medals
League Division Three Championship: 84/85
FA Charity Shield: 88/89
Promoted to League Division One: 81/82, 85/86

LES FERDINAND

Born: 18/12/66 – Acton
Height: 5.11
Weight: 13.05 (96–97)

Clubs
Queens Park Rangers: **1987–95** – Matches: **170+14** – Goals: **90**
Brentford (loan): **1988** – Matches: **3** – Goals: **0**
Besiktas JK (loan): **1988–89** – Matches: **32** – Goals: **21**
Newcastle United: **1995–97** – Matches: **82+2** – Goals: **50**

Country
England: **1993–97** – Matches: **11+2** – Goals: **5**

SEASON 1986–87

Queens Park Rangers – League Division One

Sub+1	20/04/87	Coventry City	Away	League	0–4		
Sub+2	02/05/87	Sheffield Wednesday	Away	League	1–7		

SEASON 1987–88

League Division One

Sub+3	27/10/87	Bury	Away	Lge Cup	0–1		
1	13/02/88	Everton	Away	League	0–2		

Brentford (loan) – League Division Three

1	26/03/88	Brighton & Hove Albion	Home	League	1–1		
2	02/04/88	Notts County	Home	League	1–0		
3	04/04/88	Wigan Athletic	Away	League	1–1		

SEASON 1988–89

Besiktas JK (loan) – Turkish League Division One
Turkish League and Cup matches: 32
Turkish League and Cup goals: 21
Individual match details not available

SEASON 1989–90

Queens Park Rangers – League Division One

Sub+4	04/11/89	Wimbledon	Away	League	0–0		
2	25/11/89	Millwall	Home	League	0–0		
3	02/12/89	Crystal Palace	Away	League	3–0		
4	09/12/89	Chelsea	Home	League	4–2	2 Goals	(2)
5	16/12/89	Sheffield Wednesday	Away	League	0–2		
6	14/04/90	Manchester United	Home	League	1–2		
7	16/04/90	Coventry City	Away	League	1–1		
Sub+5	28/04/90	Liverpool	Away	League	1–2		
Sub+6	05/05/90	Wimbledon	Home	League	2–3		

SEASON 1990–91

League Division One

Sub+7	25/08/90	Nottingham Forest	Away	League	1–1		
Sub+8	29/08/90	Wimbledon	Home	League	0–1		
Sub+9	15/09/90	Luton Town	Home	League	6–1		
8	22/09/90	Aston Villa	Away	League	2–2		
9	26/09/90	Peterborough United	Home	Lge Cup	3–1	1 Goal	(3)
10	29/09/90	Coventry City	Away	League	1–3	1 Goal	(4)
11	06/10/90	Tottenham Hotspur	Home	League	0–0		
12	09/10/90	Peterborough United	Away	Lge Cup	1–1	1 Goal	(5)
13	20/10/90	Leeds United	Away	League	3–2		
14	27/10/90	Norwich City	Home	League	1–3		
Sub+10	07/01/91	Manchester United	Away	FA Cup	1–2		
15	19/01/91	Manchester United	Home	League	1–1		
16	02/02/91	Luton Town	Away	League	2–1	2 Goals	(7)
17	16/02/91	Crystal Palace	Away	League	0–0		
18	23/02/91	Southampton	Home	League	2–1	2 Goals	(9)
19	02/03/91	Manchester City	Home	League	1–0	1 Goal	(10)
20	16/03/91	Coventry City	Home	League	1–0	1 Goal	(11)

21	23/03/91	Tottenham Hotspur	Away	League	0–0		
22	30/03/91	Liverpool	Away	League	3–1	1 Goal	(12)
23	06/04/91	Sunderland	Away	League	1–0		
24	10/04/91	Aston Villa	Home	League	2–2		

SEASON 1991–92

League Division One

25	17/08/91	Arsenal	Away	League	1–1		
26	21/08/91	Norwich City	Home	League	0–2		
27	24/08/91	Coventry City	Home	League	1–1		
28	27/08/91	Liverpool	Away	League	0–1		
29	31/08/91	Sheffield Wednesday	Away	League	1–4		
Sub+11	04/09/91	West Ham United	Home	League	0–0		
Sub+12	24/09/91	Hull City	Away	Lge Cup	3–0		
30	05/10/91	Nottingham Forest	Home	League	0–2		
Sub+13	16/11/91	Leeds United	Away	League	0–2		
31	20/11/91	Manchester City	Home	Lge Cup	1–3		
32	23/11/91	Oldham Athletic	Home	League	1–3	1 Goal	(13)
33	26/11/91	Crystal Palace	Home	ZDS Cup	2–3		
34	30/11/91	Notts County	Away	League	1–0	1 Goal	(14)
35	22/02/92	Notts County	Home	League	1–1	1 Goal	(15)
36	29/02/92	Sheffield United	Away	League	0–0		
37	07/03/92	Manchester City	Home	League	4–0	2 Goals	(17)
38	11/03/92	Leeds United	Home	League	4–1	1 Goal	(18)
39	14/03/92	Aston Villa	Away	League	1–0	1 Goal	(19)
40	21/03/92	West Ham United	Away	League	2–2		
41	28/03/92	Manchester United	Home	League	0–0		
42	04/04/92	Southampton	Away	League	1–2	1 Goal	(20)
43	11/04/92	Tottenham Hotspur	Home	League	1–2		
44	18/04/92	Chelsea	Away	League	1–2		
45	20/04/92	Luton Town	Home	League	2–1	2 Goals	(22)
46	25/04/92	Nottingham Forest	Away	League	1–1		
47	02/05/92	Crystal Palace	Home	League	1–0		

SEASON 1992–93

Premier League

48	17/08/92	Manchester City	Away	League	1–1		
49	19/08/92	Southampton	Home	League	3–1	2 Goals	(24)
50	22/08/92	Sheffield United	Home	League	3–2	1 Goal	(25)
51	26/08/92	Coventry City	Away	League	1–0		
52	29/08/92	Chelsea	Away	League	0–1		
53	02/09/92	Arsenal	Home	League	0–0		
54	05/09/92	Ipswich Town	Home	League	0–0		
55	12/09/92	Southampton	Away	League	2–1		
56	19/09/92	Middlesbrough	Home	League	3–3	1 Goal	(26)
57	23/09/92	Grimsby Town	Home	Lge Cup	2–1	2 Goals	(28)
58	26/09/92	Manchester United	Away	League	0–0		
59	24/10/92	Leeds United	Home	League	2–1	1 Goal	(29)
60	27/10/92	Bury	Away	Lge Cup	2–0		
61	01/11/92	Aston Villa	Away	League	0–2		
62	07/11/92	Wimbledon	Away	League	2–0		
63	23/11/92	Liverpool	Home	League	0–1		
64	28/11/92	Blackburn Rovers	Away	League	0–1		
65	02/12/92	Sheffield Wednesday	Away	Lge Cup	0–4		
66	05/12/92	Oldham Athletic	Home	League	3–2	2 Goals	(31)
67	12/12/92	Crystal Palace	Home	League	1–3		
68	19/12/92	Sheffield Wednesday	Away	League	0–1		
69	28/12/92	Everton	Home	League	4–2		
70	04/01/93	Swindon Town	Home	FA Cup	3–0	2 Goals	(33)
71	09/01/93	Middlesbrough	Away	League	1–0	1 Goal	(34)
72	23/01/93	Manchester City	Home	FA Cup	1–2		
73	27/01/93	Chelsea	Home	League	1–1		
74	30/01/93	Sheffield United	Away	League	2–1		
75	06/02/93	Manchester City	Home	League	1–1		
76	09/02/93	Ipswich Town	Away	League	1–1		
77	20/02/93	Coventry City	Home	League	2–0		
78	24/02/93	Nottingham Forest	Away	League	0–1		
79	27/02/93	Tottenham Hotspur	Away	League	2–3		
80	06/03/93	Norwich City	Home	League	3–1	2 Goals	(36)
81	10/03/93	Liverpool	Away	League	0–1		
82	13/03/93	Wimbledon	Home	League	1–2	1 Goal	(37)
83	20/03/93	Oldham Athletic	Away	League	2–2		
84	10/04/93	Nottingham Forest	Home	League	4–3	3 Goals	(40)

85	12/04/93	Everton	Away	League	5–3	3 Goals	(43)
86	01/05/93	Leeds United	Away	League	1–1	1 Goal	(44)
87	04/05/93	Arsenal	Away	League	0–0		
88	09/05/93	Aston Villa	Home	League	2–1	1 Goal	(45)
89	11/05/93	Sheffield Wednesday	Home	League	3–1	1 Goal	(46)

SEASON 1993–94

Premier League

90	14/08/93	Aston Villa	Away	League	1–4	1 Goal	(47)
91	18/08/93	Liverpool	Home	League	1–3		
92	21/08/93	Southampton	Home	League	2–1		
93	25/08/93	Chelsea	Away	League	0–2		
94	28/08/93	West Ham United	Away	League	4–0	2 Goals	(49)
95	01/09/93	Sheffield United	Home	League	2–1		
96	11/09/93	Manchester City	Away	League	0–3		
97	18/09/93	Norwich City	Home	League	2–2	1 Goal	(50)
98	21/09/93	Barnet	Away	Lge Cup	2–1	1 Goal	(51)
99	27/09/93	Wimbledon	Away	League	1–1		
100	16/10/93	Newcastle United	Away	League	2–1	1 Goal	(52)
101	23/10/93	Coventry City	Home	League	5–1	1 Goal	(53)
102	27/10/93	Millwall	Home	Lge Cup	3–0	1 Goal	(54)
103	30/10/93	Manchester United	Away	League	1–2		
104	06/11/93	Blackburn Rovers	Home	League	1–0		
105	20/11/93	Everton	Away	League	3–0		
106	24/11/93	Swindon Town	Away	League	0–1		
107	27/11/93	Tottenham Hotspur	Home	League	1–1	1 Goal	(55)
108	01/12/93	Sheffield Wednesday	Home	Lge Cup	1–2		
109	08/12/93	Liverpool	Away	League	2–3	1 Goal	(56)
110	11/12/93	Southampton	Away	League	1–0	1 Goal	(57)
111	29/12/93	Leeds United	Away	League	1–1		
112	01/01/94	Sheffield Wednesday	Home	League	1–2	1 Goal	(58)
113	03/01/94	Arsenal	Away	League	0–0		
114	08/01/94	Stockport County	Away	FA Cup	1–2		
115	16/01/94	Newcastle United	Home	League	1–2		
116	05/02/94	Manchester United	Home	League	2–3	1 Goal	(59)
117	05/03/94	Manchester City	Home	League	1–1		
Sub+14	16/03/94	Sheffield United	Away	League	1–1		
118	19/03/94	Wimbledon	Home	League	1–0		
119	26/03/94	Ipswich Town	Away	League	3–1	1 Goal	(60)
120	02/04/94	Oldham Athletic	Away	League	1–4	1 Goal	(61)
121	04/04/94	Leeds United	Home	League	0–4		
122	09/04/94	Sheffield Wednesday	Away	League	1–3		
123	13/04/94	Chelsea	Home	League	1–1	1 Goal	(62)
124	16/04/94	Everton	Home	League	2–1	1 Goal	(63)
125	24/04/94	Blackburn Rovers	Away	League	1–1		
126	30/04/94	Swindon Town	Home	League	1–3	1 Goal	(64)
127	03/05/94	West Ham United	Home	League	0–0		
128	07/05/94	Tottenham Hotspur	Away	League	2–1		

SEASON 1994–95

Premier League

129	20/08/94	Manchester United	Away	League	0–2		
130	24/08/94	Sheffield Wednesday	Home	League	3–2	1 Goal	(65)
131	27/08/94	Ipswich Town	Home	League	1–2	1 Goal	(66)
132	31/08/94	Leicester City	Away	League	1–1		
133	10/09/94	Coventry City	Home	League	2–2		
134	17/09/94	Everton	Away	League	2–2	2 Goals	(68)
135	20/09/94	Carlisle United	Away	Lge Cup	1–0	1 Goal	(69)
136	24/09/94	Wimbledon	Home	League	0–1		
137	02/10/94	Nottingham Forest	Away	League	2–3	1 Goal	(70)
138	05/10/94	Carlisle United	Home	Lge Cup	2–0		
139	08/10/94	Tottenham Hotspur	Away	League	1–1		
140	15/10/94	Manchester City	Home	League	1–2		
141	31/10/94	Liverpool	Home	League	2–1	1 Goal	(71)
142	05/11/94	Newcastle United	Away	League	1–2		
143	19/11/94	Leeds United	Home	League	3–2	2 Goals	(73)
144	26/11/94	Blackburn Rovers	Away	League	0–4		
145	04/12/94	West Ham United	Home	League	2–1	1 Goal	(74)
146	10/12/94	Manchester United	Home	League	2–3	2 Goals	(76)
147	17/12/94	Sheffield Wednesday	Away	League	2–0	1 Goal	(77)
148	26/12/94	Crystal Palace	Away	League	0–0		
149	28/12/94	Southampton	Home	League	2–2		
150	31/12/94	Arsenal	Away	League	3–1		

151	07/01/95	Aylesbury United	Away	FA Cup	4–0	1 Goal	(78)
152	14/01/95	Aston Villa	Away	League	1–2		
153	24/01/95	Leeds United	Away	League	0–4		
154	04/02/95	Newcastle United	Home	League	3–0	2 Goals	(80)
155	11/02/95	Liverpool	Away	League	1–1		
156	18/02/95	Millwall	Home	FA Cup	1–0		
157	26/02/95	Nottingham Forest	Home	League	1–1		
158	04/03/95	Wimbledon	Away	League	3–1	2 Goals	(82)
159	12/03/95	Manchester United	Away	FA Cup	0–2		
160	15/03/95	Norwich City	Home	League	2–0	1 Goal	(83)
161	18/03/95	Everton	Home	League	2–3	1 Goal	(84)
162	04/04/95	Blackburn Rovers	Home	League	0–1		
163	08/04/95	Arsenal	Home	League	3–1		
164	11/04/95	Ipswich Town	Away	League	1–0	1 Goal	(85)
165	15/04/95	Southampton	Away	League	1–2	1 Goal	(86)
166	17/04/95	Crystal Palace	Home	League	0–1		
167	29/04/95	Chelsea	Away	League	0–1		
168	03/05/95	West Ham United	Away	League	0–0		
169	06/05/95	Tottenham Hotspur	Home	League	2–1	2 Goals	(88)
170	14/05/95	Manchester City	Away	League	3–2	2 Goals	(90)

SEASON 1995–96

Newcastle United – Premier League

1	19/08/95	Coventry City	Home	League	3–0	1 Goal	(1)
2	22/08/95	Bolton Wanderers	Away	League	3–1	2 Goals	(3)
3	27/08/95	Sheffield Wednesday	Away	League	2–0		
4	30/08/95	Middlesbrough	Home	League	1–0	1 Goal	(4)
5	09/09/95	Southampton	Away	League	0–1		
6	16/09/95	Manchester City	Home	League	3–1	2 Goals	(6)
7	19/09/95	Bristol City	Away	Lge Cup	5–0	1 Goal	(7)
8	24/09/95	Chelsea	Home	League	2–0	2 Goals	(9)
9	01/10/95	Everton	Away	League	3–1	1 Goal	(10)
10	04/10/95	Bristol City	Home	Lge Cup	3–1	1 Goal	(11)
11	14/10/95	Queens Park Rangers	Away	League	3–2	1 Goal	(12)
12	21/10/95	Wimbledon	Home	League	6–1	3 Goals	(15)
13	25/10/95	Stoke City	Away	Lge Cup	4–0	1 Goal	(16)
14	29/10/95	Tottenham Hotspur	Away	League	1–1		
15	04/11/95	Liverpool	Home	League	2–1	1 Goal	(17)
16	08/11/95	Blackburn Rovers	Home	League	1–0		
17	18/11/95	Aston Villa	Away	League	1–1	1 Goal	(18)
18	25/11/95	Leeds United	Home	League	2–1		
19	29/11/95	Liverpool	Away	Lge Cup	1–0		
20	03/12/95	Wimbledon	Away	League	3–3	2 Goals	(20)
21	09/12/95	Chelsea	Away	League	0–1		
22	16/12/95	Everton	Home	League	1–0	1 Goal	(21)
23	23/12/95	Nottingham Forest	Home	League	3–1		
24	27/12/95	Manchester United	Away	League	0–2		
25	02/01/96	Arsenal	Home	League	2–0	1 Goal	(22)
26	07/01/96	Chelsea	Away	FA Cup	1–1	1 Goal	(23)
27	10/01/96	Arsenal	Away	Lge Cup	0–2		
28	14/01/96	Coventry City	Away	League	1–0		
29	17/01/96	Chelsea	Home	FA Cup	2–2+		
30	03/02/96	Sheffield Wednesday	Home	League	2–0	1 Goal	(24)
31	10/02/96	Middlesbrough	Away	League	2–1	1 Goal	(25)
32	21/02/96	West Ham United	Away	League	0–2		
33	24/02/96	Manchester City	Away	League	3–3		
34	04/03/96	Manchester United	Home	League	0–1		
35	18/03/96	West Ham United	Home	League	3–0	1 Goal	(26)
36	23/03/96	Arsenal	Away	League	0–2		
37	03/04/96	Liverpool	Away	League	3–4	1 Goal	(27)
38	06/04/96	Queens Park Rangers	Home	League	2–1		
39	08/04/96	Blackburn Rovers	Away	League	1–2		
40	14/04/96	Aston Villa	Home	League	1–0	1 Goal	(28)
41	17/04/96	Southampton	Home	League	1–0		
42	29/04/96	Leeds United	Away	League	1–0		
43	02/05/96	Nottingham Forest	Away	League	1–1		
44	05/05/96	Tottenham Hotspur	Home	League	1–1	1 Goal	(29)

+ AET Chelsea won 4–2 on penalties

SEASON 1996–97

Premier League

| 45 | 11/08/96 | Manchester United | Wembley | FA C/S | 0–4 | | |
| 46 | 17/08/96 | Everton | Away | League | 0–2 | | |

47	21/08/96	Wimbledon	Home	League	2–0		
48	24/08/96	Sheffield Wednesday	Home	League	1–2		
49	04/09/96	Sunderland	Away	League	2–1	1 Goal	(30)
50	07/09/96	Tottenham Hotspur	Away	League	2–1	2 Goals	(32)
51	10/09/96	Halmstads BK	Home	UEFA Cup	4–0	1 Goal	(33)
52	14/09/96	Blackburn Rovers	Home	League	2–1	1 Goal	(34)
53	24/09/96	Halmstads BK	Away	UEFA Cup	1–2	1 Goal	(35)
54	30/09/96	Aston Villa	Home	League	4–3	2 Goals	(37)
55	12/10/96	Derby County	Away	League	1–0		
56	15/10/96	Ferencvarosi TC	Away	UEFA Cup	2–3	1 Goal	(38)
57	20/10/96	Manchester United	Home	League	5–0	1 Goal	(39)
58	23/10/96	Oldham Athletic	Home	Lge Cup	1–0		
59	26/10/96	Leicester City	Away	League	0–2		
60	29/10/96	Ferencvarosi TC	Home	UEFA Cup	4–0	1 Goal	(40)
61	03/11/96	Middlesbrough	Home	League	3–1		
62	16/11/96	West Ham United	Home	League	1–1		
63	09/12/96	Nottingham Forest	Away	League	0–0		
64	17/12/96	Coventry City	Away	League	1–2		
65	23/12/96	Liverpool	Home	League	1–1		
66	26/12/96	Blackburn Rovers	Away	League	0–1		
67	28/12/96	Tottenham Hotspur	Home	League	7–1	2 Goals	(42)
68	01/01/97	Leeds United	Home	League	3–0	1 Goal	(43)
69	05/01/97	Charlton Athletic	Away	FA Cup	1–1		
Sub+1	15/01/97	Charlton Athletic	Home	FA Cup	2–1*		
70	18/01/97	Southampton	Away	League	2–2	1 Goal	(44)
71	26/01/97	Nottingham Forest	Home	FA Cup	1–2	1 Goal	(45)
72	29/01/97	Everton	Home	League	4–1	1 Goal	(46)
73	02/02/97	Leicester City	Home	League	4–3		
74	22/02/97	Middlesbrough	Away	League	1–0	1 Goal	(47)
75	01/03/97	Southampton	Home	League	0–1		
Sub+2	10/03/97	Liverpool	Away	League	3–4		
76	05/04/97	Sunderland	Home	League	1–1		
77	13/04/97	Sheffield Wednesday	Away	League	1–1		
78	16/04/97	Chelsea	Home	League	3–1		
79	19/04/97	Derby County	Home	League	3–1	1 Goal	(48)
80	03/05/97	Arsenal	Away	League	1–0		
81	08/05/97	Manchester United	Away	League	0–0		
82	11/05/97	Nottingham Forest	Home	League	5–0	2 Goals	(50)

INTERNATIONAL APPEARANCES – ENGLAND

1	17/02/93	San Marino	Wembley	6–0	WCQ	1 Goal	(1)
2	28/04/93	Holland	Wembley	2–2	WCQ		
3	02/06/93	Norway	Oslo	0–2	WCQ		
4	09/06/93	USA	Boston	0–2	F		
5	08/09/93	Poland	Wembley	3–0	WCQ	1 Goal	(2)
6	17/11/93	San Marino	Bologna	7–1	WCQ	1 Goal	(3)
Sub 7	07/09/94	USA	Wembley	2–0	F		
8	12/12/95	Portugal	Wembley	1–1	F		
9	27/03/96	Bulgaria	Wembley	1–0	F	1 Goal	(4)
10	18/05/96	Hungary	Wembley	3–0	F		
11	09/10/96	Poland	Wembley	2–1	WCQ		
12	09/11/96	Georgia	Tblisi	2–0	WCQ	1 Goal	(5)
Sub 13	12/02/97	Italy	Wembley	0–1	WCQ		

APPEARANCES AND GOALS PER SEASON

SEASON 86–87

	GAMES	GOALS
League	0+2	0
TOTAL	**0+2**	**0**

SEASON 87–88

	GAMES	GOALS
League	4	0
League Cup	0+1	0
TOTAL	**4+1**	**0**

SEASON 88–89

	GAMES	GOALS
Turkish League and Cup	32	21
TOTAL	**32**	**21**

SEASON 89–90

	GAMES	GOALS
League	6+3	2
TOTAL	**6+3**	**2**

SEASON 90–91	GAMES	GOALS
League	15+3	8
FA Cup	0+1	0
League Cup	2	2
TOTAL	**17+4**	**10**

SEASON 91–92	GAMES	GOALS
League	21+2	10
League Cup	1+1	0
Zenith Data Systems Cup	1	0
TOTAL	**23+3**	**10**

SEASON 92–93	GAMES	GOALS
League	37	20
FA Cup	2	2
League Cup	3	2
TOTAL	**42**	**24**

SEASON 93–94	GAMES	GOALS
League	35+1	16
FA Cup	1	0
League Cup	3	2
TOTAL	**39+1**	**18**

SEASON 94–95	GAMES	GOALS
League	37	24
FA Cup	3	1
League Cup	2	1
TOTAL	**42**	**26**

SEASON 95–96	GAMES	GOALS
League	37	25
FA Cup	2	1
League Cup	5	3
TOTAL	**44**	**29**

SEASON 96–97	GAMES	GOALS
League	30+1	16
FA Cup	2+1	1
League Cup	1	0
UEFA Cup	4	4
FA Charity Shield	1	0
TOTAL	**38+2**	**21**

CAREER APPEARANCES AND GOALS

COMPETITION	GAMES	TOTAL	GOALS
League	222+12	234	121
FA Cup	10+2	12	5
League Cup	17+2	19	10
Zenith Data Systems Cup	1	1	0
FA Charity Shield	1	1	0
UEFA Cup	4	4	4
Turkish League and Cup	32	32	21
Internationals	11+2	13	5
TOTAL	**298+18**	**316**	**166**

HAT-TRICKS

Queens Park Rangers

1	3	Nottingham Forest	10/04/93	Home	League	4–3
2	3	Everton	12/04/93	Away	League	5–3

Newcastle United

1	3	Wimbledon	21/10/95	Home	League	6–1

League: 3
TOTAL: 3

HONOURS

Winners medals
Turkish Cup: 88/89

Runner-up medals
Premier League Championship: 95/96, 96/97
Turkish League Division One Championship: 88/89
FA Charity Shield: 96/97

ANDY FLOUNDERS

Born: 13/12/63 – Hull
Height: 5.9
Weight: 11.03 (94–95)

Clubs
Hull City: **1980–87** – Matches: **148+43** – Goals: **63**
Scunthorpe United: **1987–91** – Matches: **230+12** – Goals: **100**
Rochdale: **1991–94** – Matches: **100+4** – Goals: **33**
Rotherham United (loan): **1993** – Matches: **6** – Goals: **2**
Carlisle United (loan): **1993** – Matches: **6** – Goals: **2**
Carlisle United (loan): **1994** – Matches: **2+2** – Goals: **0**
Northampton Town: **1994** – Matches: **2** – Goals: **0**

SEASON 1980–81

Hull City – League Division Three

Sub+1	04/10/80	Oxford United	Home	League	0–1		
Sub+2	08/10/80	Chester	Away	League	1–4		
1	11/10/80	Chesterfield	Away	League	0–1		
2	18/10/80	Charlton Athletic	Home	League	0–2		
3	21/10/80	Carlisle United	Home	League	0–1		
Sub+3	22/11/80	Halifax Town	Home	FA Cup	2–1		

SEASON 1981–82

League Division Four

Sub+4	21/01/82	Chelsea	Home	FA Cup	0–2		
4	23/01/82	Torquay United	Home	League	1–0	1 Goal	(1)
Sub+5	30/01/82	Sheffield United	Away	League	0–0		
5	06/02/82	Northampton Town	Home	League	0–1		
6	27/02/82	Mansfield Town	Home	League	2–0	1 Goal	(2)
7	02/03/82	Halifax Town	Home	League	2–0		
8	23/03/82	Darlington	Away	League	1–2	1 Goal	(3)
9	26/03/82	Colchester United	Away	League	0–2		
10	03/04/82	Hereford United	Home	League	2–1	2 Goals	(5)
11	06/04/82	Rochdale	Away	League	1–0		
12	10/04/82	Darlington	Home	League	1–3		
13	12/04/82	Stockport County	Away	League	2–1		
14	01/05/82	AFC Bournemouth	Away	League	0–1		
15	04/05/82	Blackpool	Home	League	1–0		

SEASON 1982–83

League Division Four

Sub+6	14/08/82	Hartlepool United	Away	FL Trophy	2–1		
Sub+7	21/08/82	Bradford City	Home	FL Trophy	0–0		
Sub+8	28/08/82	Bristol City	Away	League	1–2	1 Goal	(6)
Sub+9	31/08/82	Sheffield United	Away	Lge Cup	1–3		
16	04/09/82	Wimbledon	Home	League	1–1	1 Goal	(7)
Sub+10	07/09/82	York City	Home	League	4–0	1 Goal	(8)
17	14/09/82	Sheffield United	Home	Lge Cup	1–0	1 Goal	(9)
18	18/09/82	Hartlepool United	Home	League	1–1		
19	25/09/82	Aldershot	Away	League	2–1		
20	28/09/82	Colchester United	Away	League	0–0		
Sub+11	20/10/82	Hereford United	Away	League	0–2		
21	23/10/82	Northampton Town	Home	League	4–0	1 Goal	(10)
22	11/12/82	Colchester United	Home	League	3–0	2 Goals	(12)
23	17/12/82	Crewe Alexandra	Away	League	3–0		
24	27/12/82	Halifax Town	Home	League	1–1		
Sub+12	03/01/83	Mansfield Town	Away	League	1–3		
25	22/01/83	Hartlepool United	Away	League	0–0		
26	29/01/83	Stockport County	Home	League	7–0	3 Goals	(15)
27	05/02/83	Aldershot	Home	League	2–2	1 Goal	(16)
Sub+13	15/02/83	Hereford United	Home	League	2–0		
28	01/03/83	Bury	Away	League	3–2	1 Goal	(17)
29	05/03/83	Northampton Town	Away	League	2–1	1 Goal	(18)
30	12/03/83	Tranmere Rovers	Home	League	0–1		
31	19/03/83	Peterborough United	Away	League	1–1		

Sub+14	16/04/83	Swindon Town	Away	League	1–0		
32	23/04/83	Crewe Alexandra	Home	League	1–0		
33	02/05/83	Mansfield Town	Home	League	2–2	1 Goal	(19)

SEASON 1983–84

League Division Three

Sub+15	17/09/83	Preston North End	Away	League	0–0		
34	01/10/83	Wigan Athletic	Away	League	1–1	1 Goal	(20)
Sub+16	15/10/83	Brentford	Away	League	1–1		
35	18/10/83	Bolton Wanderers	Away	League	0–0		
Sub+17	22/10/83	Plymouth Argyle	Home	League	1–2		
36	29/10/83	Oxford United	Away	League	1–1		
37	01/11/83	Walsall	Home	League	2–2		
38	05/11/83	AFC Bournemouth	Away	League	3–2		
39	19/11/83	Penrith	Away	FA Cup	2–0		
40	10/12/83	Rotherham United	Away	FA Cup	1–2	1 Goal	(21)
41	17/12/83	Bristol Rovers	Away	League	3–1		
42	26/12/83	Scunthorpe United	Home	League	1–0		
43	27/12/83	Rotherham United	Away	League	1–0		
44	31/12/83	Port Vale	Home	League	1–0		
45	02/01/84	Southend United	Away	League	2–2	2 Goals	(23)
46	28/01/84	Millwall	Away	League	0–1		
Sub+18	21/02/84	York City	Away	AM Cup	2–1		
Sub+19	28/02/84	Oxford United	Home	League	0–1		
47	03/03/84	Bolton Wanderers	Home	League	1–1		
48	06/03/84	AFC Bournemouth	Home	League	3–1	1 Goal	(24)
49	10/03/84	Newport County	Away	League	1–1		
50	13/03/84	Bury	Home	AM Cup	1–0		
51	27/03/84	Walsall	Away	League	1–2	1 Goal	(25)
52	31/03/84	Bradford City	Home	League	1–0		
53	07/04/84	Wimbledon	Away	League	4–1	1 Goal	(26)
54	10/04/84	Preston North End	Home	League	3–0	1 Goal	(27)
55	14/04/84	Exeter City	Home	League	1–0		
Sub+20	17/04/84	Gillingham	Home	League	0–0		
56	21/04/84	Scunthorpe United	Away	League	0–2		
57	23/04/84	Rotherham United	Home	League	5–0	2 Goals	(29)
58	28/04/84	Orient	Away	League	1–3		
Sub+21	07/05/84	Port Vale	Away	League	0–1		
Sub+22	12/05/84	Bristol Rovers	Home	League	0–0		
Sub+23	15/05/84	Burnley	Away	League	2–0		
Sub+24	24/05/84	AFC Bournemouth	Home	AM Cup	1–2		

SEASON 1984–85

League Division Three

Sub+25	15/09/84	Preston North End	Home	League	1–2		
Sub+26	22/09/84	Burnley	Away	League	1–1		
Sub+27	29/09/84	Reading	Home	League	0–0		
59	03/10/84	Bradford City	Away	League	0–2		
60	06/10/84	Plymouth Argyle	Away	League	1–0	1 Goal	(30)
61	09/10/84	Southampton	Home	Lge Cup	2–2	1 Goal	(31)
62	13/10/84	Doncaster Rovers	Home	League	3–2	1 Goal	(32)
63	20/10/84	Derby County	Away	League	1–3		
64	23/10/84	Swansea City	Home	League	4–1		
65	27/10/84	Bristol Rovers	Away	League	1–1		
66	03/11/84	Rotherham United	Home	League	0–0		
67	06/11/84	Cambridge United	Home	League	2–1	1 Goal	(33)
68	10/11/84	Orient	Away	League	5–4	2 Goals	(35)
69	17/11/84	Bolton Wanderers	Home	FA Cup	2–1	1 Goal	(36)
70	24/11/84	Newport County	Home	League	2–0		
71	01/12/84	Wigan Athletic	Away	League	1–1		
72	08/12/84	Tranmere Rovers	Away	FA Cup	3–0		
73	18/12/84	Millwall	Away	League	2–2		
74	22/12/84	Brentford	Home	League	4–0		
75	29/12/84	York City	Away	League	2–1	1 Goal	(37)
76	01/01/85	Bristol City	Home	League	2–1		
77	05/01/85	Brighton & Hove Albion	Away	FA Cup	0–1		
78	12/01/85	AFC Bournemouth	Away	League	1–1	1 Goal	(38)
79	22/01/85	Mansfield Town	Home	FR Trophy	2–2		
80	02/02/85	Reading	Away	League	2–4		
81	06/02/85	Mansfield Town	Away	FR Trophy	1–2		
82	09/02/85	Burnley	Home	League	2–0		
83	16/02/85	Bradford City	Home	League	0–2		
Sub+28	26/02/85	Gillingham	Away	League	0–1		

84	02/03/85	Bristol Rovers	Home	League	2–0	1 Goal	(39)
85	05/03/85	Swansea City	Away	League	2–0		
86	09/03/85	Derby County	Home	League	3–2	1 Goal	(40)
87	16/03/85	Doncaster Rovers	Away	League	2–1	1 Goal	(41)
88	19/03/85	Lincoln City	Home	League	1–0		
89	23/03/85	Plymouth Argyle	Home	League	2–2	1 Goal	(42)
Sub+29	02/04/85	Bolton Wanderers	Home	League	2–2		
90	06/04/85	Millwall	Home	League	2–1	1 Goal	(43)
91	08/04/85	Bristol City	Away	League	0–2		
92	13/04/85	Orient	Home	League	5–1	1 Goal	(44)
93	20/04/85	Newport County	Away	League	1–0		
94	23/04/85	Preston North End	Away	League	4–1	1 Goal	(45)
95	27/04/85	Wigan Athletic	Home	League	3–1		
96	04/05/85	Walsall	Away	League	1–0		
97	06/05/85	York City	Home	League	0–2		
98	11/05/85	Brentford	Away	League	1–2		

SEASON 1985–86

League Division Two

99	20/08/85	Halifax Town	Away	Lge Cup	1–1	1 Goal	(46)
Sub+30	31/08/85	Oldham Athletic	Away	League	1–3		
Sub+31	24/09/85	Queens Park Rangers	Away	Lge Cup	0–3		
100	01/10/85	Crystal Palace	Away	League	2–0		
Sub+32	05/10/85	Stoke City	Home	League	0–2		
101	23/10/85	Bradford City	Home	FM Cup	4–1		
Sub+33	02/11/85	Sheffield United	Away	League	1–3		
Sub+34	05/11/85	Middlesbrough	Home	FM Cup	3–1*		
102	30/11/85	Brighton & Hove Albion	Away	League	1–3		
Sub+35	14/12/85	Portsmouth	Away	League	1–1		
Sub+36	28/12/85	Millwall	Away	League	0–5		
103	01/01/86	Barnsley	Away	League	4–1		
104	04/01/86	Plymouth Argyle	Home	FA Cup	2–2	2 Goals	(48)
105	07/01/86	Plymouth Argyle	Away	FA Cup	1–0		
106	11/01/86	Bradford City	Home	League	1–0		
107	18/01/86	Oldham Athletic	Home	League	4–2	2 Goals	(50)
108	25/01/86	Brighton & Hove Albion	Home	FA Cup	2–3		
109	01/02/86	Blackburn Rovers	Away	League	2–2		
110	25/02/86	Huddersfield Town	Away	League	1–2		
111	04/03/86	Shrewsbury Town	Home	League	4–3	3 Goals	(53)
112	08/03/86	Stoke City	Away	League	1–0		
113	11/03/86	Carlisle United	Away	League	1–2	1 Goal	(54)
114	15/03/86	Sunderland	Home	League	1–1		
115	22/03/86	Middlesbrough	Away	League	2–1	1 Goal	(55)
116	29/03/86	Barnsley	Home	League	0–1		
117	01/04/86	Grimsby Town	Away	League	1–0	1 Goal	(56)
118	05/04/86	Sheffield United	Home	League	0–0		
119	12/04/86	Fulham	Away	League	1–1		
120	19/04/86	Charlton Athletic	Home	League	1–1		
121	26/04/86	Wimbledon	Away	League	1–3	1 Goal	(57)
122	29/04/86	Norwich City	Home	League	1–0		
123	02/05/86	Brighton & Hove Albion	Home	League	2–0	1 Goal	(58)

SEASON 1986–87

League Division Two

124	23/08/86	West Bromwich Albion	Home	League	2–0	1 Goal	(59)
125	26/08/86	Millwall	Away	League	1–0		
126	30/08/86	Oldham Athletic	Away	League	0–0		
127	02/09/86	Portsmouth	Home	League	0–2		
128	06/09/86	Plymouth Argyle	Home	League	0–3		
129	23/09/86	Grimsby Town	Home	Lge Cup	1–0		
130	27/09/86	Leeds United	Away	League	0–3		
131	04/10/86	Ipswich Town	Home	League	2–1		
132	08/10/86	Grimsby Town	Away	Lge Cup	1–1		
Sub+37	11/10/86	Derby County	Away	League	1–1		
133	18/10/86	Reading	Home	League	0–2		
134	21/10/86	Grimsby Town	Away	FM Cup	3–1	2 Goals	(61)
135	25/10/86	Huddersfield Town	Away	League	3–1	1 Goal	(62)
136	28/10/86	Shrewsbury Town	Away	Lge Cup	0–1		
137	01/11/86	Brighton & Hove Albion	Away	League	1–2		
Sub+38	08/11/86	Stoke City	Home	League	0–4		
138	15/11/86	Blackburn Rovers	Away	League	2–0		
139	22/11/86	Bradford City	Home	League	2–1		
140	25/11/86	Southampton	Away	FM Cup	1–2		

141	29/11/86	Shrewsbury Town	Away	League	0–3		
142	06/12/86	Grimsby Town	Home	League	1–1		
143	13/12/86	Crystal Palace	Away	League	1–5		
Sub+39	26/12/86	Sheffield United	Away	League	2–4	1 Goal	(63)
144	27/12/86	Blackburn Rovers	Home	League	0–0		
145	01/01/87	Barnsley	Home	League	3–4		
146	03/01/87	Plymouth Argyle	Away	League	0–4		
Sub+40	24/01/87	West Bromwich Albion	Away	League	1–1		
147	31/01/87	Shrewsbury Town	Away	FA Cup	2–1		
148	03/02/87	Swansea City	Away	FA Cup	1–0		
Sub+41	07/02/87	Oldham Athletic	Home	League	1–0		
Sub+42	14/02/87	Portsmouth	Away	League	0–1		
Sub+43	21/02/87	Wigan Athletic	Away	FA Cup	0–3		

Scunthorpe United – League Division Four

1	07/03/87	Cardiff City	Home	League	1–3		
2	11/03/87	Northampton Town	Away	League	0–1		
3	14/03/87	Torquay United	Away	League	2–2	1 Goal	(1)
4	21/03/87	Swansea City	Home	League	3–2	1 Goal	(2)
5	28/03/87	Wolverhampton Wanderers	Away	League	0–1		
6	03/04/87	Halifax Town	Away	League	1–1		
7	11/04/87	Southend United	Home	League	3–0		
8	13/04/87	Stockport County	Away	League	0–1		
9	17/04/87	Hartlepool United	Away	League	2–0	1 Goal	(3)
10	20/04/87	Peterborough United	Home	League	2–0		
11	25/04/87	Exeter City	Away	League	0–0		
12	28/04/87	Burnley	Home	League	2–1		
13	01/05/87	Hereford United	Home	League	3–1		
14	04/05/87	Lincoln City	Away	League	2–1	2 Goals	(5)
15	09/05/87	Rochdale	Home	League	2–0	1 Goal	(6)

SEASON 1987–88

League Division Four

16	15/08/87	Tranmere Rovers	Home	League	3–0	2 Goals	(8)
17	18/08/87	Hartlepool United	Home	Lge Cup	3–1		
18	22/08/87	Carlisle United	Away	League	1–3		
19	26/08/87	Hartlepool United	Away	Lge Cup	1–0		
20	29/08/87	Colchester United	Home	League	2–2	1 Goal	(9)
21	31/08/87	Wolverhampton Wanderers	Away	League	1–4	1 Goal	(10)
22	05/09/87	Rochdale	Home	League	1–0		
23	12/09/87	Cambridge United	Away	League	3–3	2 Goals	(12)
24	15/09/87	Bolton Wanderers	Home	League	1–1		
25	19/09/87	Newport County	Home	League	3–1	2 Goals	(14)
26	23/09/87	Leicester City	Away	Lge Cup	1–2	1 Goal	(15)
27	26/09/87	Darlington	Away	League	4–1	1 Goal	(16)
28	29/09/87	Stockport County	Home	League	0–0		
29	03/10/87	Peterborough United	Away	League	1–1		
30	06/10/87	Leicester City	Home	Lge Cup	1–2		
31	10/10/87	Halifax Town	Home	League	1–0		
32	13/10/87	Grimsby Town	Home	SV Trophy	2–0		
33	17/10/87	Hereford United	Away	League	3–2		
34	20/10/87	Burnley	Away	League	1–1	1 Goal	(17)
35	24/10/87	Cardiff City	Home	League	2–1		
36	31/10/87	Hartlepool United	Away	League	0–1		
37	03/11/87	Wrexham	Home	League	3–1	2 Goals	(19)
38	07/11/87	Scarborough	Home	League	0–1		
39	14/11/87	Bury	Home	FA Cup	3–1		
40	21/11/87	Crewe Alexandra	Away	League	2–2	1 Goal	(20)
41	24/11/87	Halifax Town	Away	SV Trophy	0–3		
42	28/11/87	Swansea City	Home	League	1–2	1 Goal	(21)
43	05/12/87	Sunderland	Home	FA Cup	2–1		
44	12/12/87	Exeter City	Away	League	1–1		
45	15/12/87	Grimsby Town	Away	SV Trophy	2–1	1 Goal	(22)
46	18/12/87	Torquay United	Home	League	2–3		
47	26/12/87	Darlington	Home	League	1–0	1 Goal	(23)
48	28/12/87	Leyton Orient	Away	League	1–1		
49	01/01/88	Colchester United	Away	League	3–0		
50	02/01/88	Cambridge United	Home	League	3–2		
51	09/01/88	Blackpool	Home	FA Cup	0–0		
52	12/01/88	Blackpool	Away	FA Cup	0–1		
53	16/01/88	Newport County	Away	League	1–1		
54	19/01/88	Mansfield Town	Away	SV Trophy	0–1		
55	30/01/88	Wolverhampton Wanderers	Home	League	0–1		
56	06/02/88	Rochdale	Away	League	1–2	1 Goal	(24)

57	13/02/88	Leyton Orient	Home	League	3–2		
58	20/02/88	Tranmere Rovers	Away	League	3–1	2 Goals	(26)
59	27/02/88	Peterborough United	Home	League	5–0	3 Goals	(29)
60	01/03/88	Stockport County	Away	League	1–1		
61	05/03/88	Hereford United	Home	League	3–0		
62	12/03/88	Halifax Town	Away	League	2–2		
63	19/03/88	Hartlepool United	Home	League	3–0	1 Goal	(30)
64	26/03/88	Cardiff City	Away	League	1–0		
65	02/04/88	Scarborough	Away	League	0–0		
66	04/04/88	Crewe Alexandra	Home	League	2–1	1 Goal	(31)
67	12/04/88	Carlisle United	Home	League	1–0		
68	19/04/88	Bolton Wanderers	Away	League	0–0		
69	23/04/88	Burnley	Home	League	1–1		
70	30/04/88	Swansea City	Away	League	1–1		
71	02/05/88	Exeter City	Home	League	1–1		
72	07/05/88	Torquay United	Away	League	2–1	1 Goal	(32)
73	15/05/88	Torquay United	Away	Lge P/O	1–2	1 Goal	(33)
74	18/05/88	Torquay United	Home	Lge P/O	1–1		

SEASON 1988–89

League Division Four

75	27/08/88	Hereford United	Home	League	3–1		
76	30/08/88	Huddersfield Town	Home	Lge Cup	3–2	1 Goal	(34)
77	03/09/88	Crewe Alexandra	Away	League	2–3	1 Goal	(35)
78	06/09/88	Huddersfield Town	Away	Lge Cup	2–2*	2 Goals	(37)
79	10/09/88	Grimsby Town	Home	League	1–1		
80	17/09/88	York City	Away	League	2–1		
81	20/09/88	Carlisle United	Home	League	1–1	1 Goal	(38)
82	24/09/88	Exeter City	Away	League	2–2		
83	27/09/88	Chelsea	Home	Lge Cup	4–1		
84	01/10/88	Scarborough	Home	League	0–3		
85	05/10/88	Lincoln City	Away	League	0–1		
86	08/10/88	Colchester United	Away	League	2–1	1 Goal	(39)
87	12/10/88	Chelsea	Away	Lge Cup	2–2	1 Goal	(40)
88	15/10/88	Cambridge United	Home	League	1–0		
89	22/10/88	Rochdale	Away	League	0–1		
90	25/10/88	Wrexham	Home	League	3–1	1 Goal	(41)
91	29/10/88	Peterborough United	Away	League	2–1		
92	02/11/88	Bradford City	Away	Lge Cup	1–1		
93	05/11/88	Burnley	Home	League	2–1	1 Goal	(42)
94	08/11/88	Rotherham United	Away	League	3–3	1 Goal	(43)
95	12/11/88	Leyton Orient	Home	League	2–2		
96	19/11/88	Blackpool	Away	FA Cup	1–2		
97	22/11/88	Bradford City	Home	Lge Cup	0–1		
98	26/11/88	Torquay United	Home	League	1–0		
99	03/12/88	Darlington	Away	League	3–3		
100	06/12/88	Halifax Town	Home	SV Trophy	1–2		
101	13/12/88	Huddersfield Town	Away	SV Trophy	0–1		
102	17/12/88	Doncaster Rovers	Away	League	2–2	1 Goal	(44)
103	26/12/88	Hartlepool United	Home	League	1–1		
104	31/12/88	Tranmere Rovers	Home	League	0–1		
Sub+1	02/01/89	Halifax Town	Away	League	1–5		
105	07/01/89	Stockport County	Away	League	2–1	1 Goal	(45)
106	14/01/89	Crewe Alexandra	Home	League	2–2		
107	21/01/89	Hereford United	Away	League	2–1		
108	28/01/89	York City	Home	League	4–2		
109	04/02/89	Carlisle United	Away	League	3–0	1 Goal	(46)
110	11/02/89	Exeter City	Home	League	2–0		
111	18/02/89	Colchester United	Home	League	2–3		
112	25/02/89	Cambridge United	Away	League	3–0	1 Goal	(47)
113	28/02/89	Wrexham	Away	League	0–2		
114	04/03/89	Rochdale	Home	League	4–0		
115	11/03/89	Burnley	Away	League	1–0		
116	14/03/89	Peterborough United	Home	League	3–0	3 Goals	(50)
117	18/03/89	Grimsby Town	Away	League	1–1	1 Goal	(51)
118	25/03/89	Halifax Town	Home	League	0–0		
119	27/03/89	Hartlepool United	Away	League	2–0	1 Goal	(52)
120	01/04/89	Doncaster Rovers	Home	League	2–1		
121	04/04/89	Stockport County	Home	League	1–1		
122	07/04/89	Tranmere Rovers	Away	League	1–2		
123	15/04/89	Scarborough	Away	League	0–1		
124	22/04/89	Lincoln City	Home	League	0–0		
125	28/04/89	Torquay United	Away	League	2–0		
126	01/05/89	Rotherham United	Home	League	0–0		

127	06/05/89	Darlington	Home	League	5–1	1 Goal	(53)
128	13/05/89	Leyton Orient	Away	League	1–4		
129	21/05/89	Wrexham	Away	Lge P/O	1–3		
130	24/05/89	Wrexham	Home	Lge P/O	0–2		

SEASON 1989–90

League Division Four

131	19/08/89	Lincoln City	Away	League	0–1		
132	23/08/89	Scarborough	Away	Lge Cup	0–2		
133	26/08/89	Rochdale	Home	League	0–1		
134	29/08/89	Scarborough	Home	Lge Cup	1–1	1 Goal	(54)
135	02/09/89	Gillingham	Away	League	3–0	2 Goals	(56)
136	09/09/89	Scarborough	Home	League	0–1		
137	16/09/89	Peterborough United	Away	League	1–1		
138	23/09/89	Exeter City	Home	League	5–4		
139	26/09/89	Torquay United	Home	League	2–0	1 Goal	(57)
140	30/09/89	Aldershot	Away	League	2–4		
Sub+2	07/10/89	Hartlepool United	Away	League	2–3		
Sub+3	14/10/89	Maidstone United	Home	League	1–0		
Sub+4	17/10/89	Carlisle United	Away	League	1–0		
Sub+5	28/10/89	Cambridge United	Away	League	3–5		
141	31/10/89	York City	Home	League	1–1	1 Goal	(58)
142	04/11/89	Doncaster Rovers	Away	League	2–1	1 Goal	(59)
143	07/11/89	Scarborough	Home	LD Cup	1–0	1 Goal	(60)
144	11/11/89	Burnley	Home	League	3–0		
145	18/11/89	Matlock Town	Home	FA Cup	4–1		
146	25/11/89	Stockport County	Away	League	2–4	1 Goal	(61)
147	02/12/89	Southend United	Home	League	1–1		
148	09/12/89	Burnley	Home	FA Cup	2–2		
Sub+6	12/12/89	Burnley	Away	FA Cup	1–1		
Sub+7	16/12/89	Hereford United	Away	League	2–1		
Sub+8	18/12/89	Burnley	Away	FA Cup	0–5		
149	22/12/89	Carlisle United	Away	LD Cup	1–1		
Sub+9	26/12/89	Grimsby Town	Home	League	2–2		
150	30/12/89	Chesterfield	Home	League	0–1		
151	01/01/90	Wrexham	Away	League	0–0		
152	06/01/90	Halifax Town	Home	League	1–1		
153	09/01/90	Tranmere Rovers	Away	LD Cup	1–2		
154	13/01/90	Rochdale	Away	League	0–3		
155	20/01/90	Lincoln City	Home	League	1–1		
Sub+10	10/02/90	Peterborough United	Home	League	0–0		
156	13/02/90	Gillingham	Home	League	0–0		
157	16/02/90	Southend United	Away	League	0–0		
158	24/02/90	Stockport County	Home	League	5–0		
159	03/03/90	Halifax Town	Away	League	1–0		
160	06/03/90	Aldershot	Home	League	3–2	1 Goal	(62)
161	10/03/90	Torquay United	Away	League	3–0	1 Goal	(63)
162	17/03/90	Hartlepool United	Home	League	0–1		
163	21/03/90	Maidstone United	Away	League	1–1	1 Goal	(64)
164	24/03/90	Carlisle United	Home	League	2–3	1 Goal	(65)
165	28/03/90	Exeter City	Away	League	0–1		
166	31/03/90	Colchester United	Away	League	0–1		
167	07/04/90	Cambridge United	Home	League	1–1		
168	10/04/90	York City	Away	League	1–0		
169	14/04/90	Wrexham	Home	League	3–1	2 Goals	(67)
170	17/04/90	Grimsby Town	Away	League	1–2	1 Goal	(68)
171	21/04/90	Hereford United	Home	League	3–3	2 Goals	(70)
172	28/04/90	Burnley	Away	League	1–0		
173	01/05/90	Chesterfield	Away	League	1–1		
174	05/05/90	Doncaster Rovers	Home	League	4–1	3 Goals	(73)

SEASON 1990–91

League Division Four

175	25/08/90	Blackpool	Home	League	2–0	1 Goal	(74)
176	28/08/90	Carlisle United	Away	Lge Cup	0–1		
177	01/09/90	Aldershot	Away	League	2–3	1 Goal	(75)
178	04/09/90	Carlisle United	Home	Lge Cup	1–1		
179	08/09/90	Peterborough United	Home	League	1–1	1 Goal	(76)
180	15/09/90	Maidstone United	Away	League	1–6		
181	18/09/90	Torquay United	Away	League	1–1		
182	22/09/90	Lincoln City	Home	League	2–1		
183	29/09/90	Cardiff City	Home	League	0–2		
184	02/10/90	Walsall	Away	League	0–3		

Sub+11	06/10/90	Halifax Town	Away	League	0–0		
185	13/10/90	Gillingham	Home	League	1–0		
186	20/10/90	Scarborough	Home	League	3–0		
187	23/10/90	Chesterfield	Away	League	0–1		
188	27/10/90	Darlington	Away	League	0–0		
189	03/11/90	Stockport County	Home	League	3–0	1 Goal	(77)
190	10/11/90	Rochdale	Home	League	2–1	1 Goal	(78)
191	17/11/90	Rochdale	Away	FA Cup	1–1		
192	20/11/90	Rochdale	Home	FA Cup	2–1*	1 Goal	(79)
193	24/11/90	Wrexham	Away	League	0–1		
194	27/11/90	Doncaster Rovers	Away	LD Cup	0–1		
Sub+12	01/12/90	York City	Away	League	2–2		
195	08/12/90	Tranmere Rovers	Home	FA Cup	3–1	1 Goal	(80)
196	15/12/90	Doncaster Rovers	Home	League	1–1	1 Goal	(81)
197	18/12/90	Chesterfield	Home	LD Cup	3–1		
198	22/12/90	Hereford United	Away	League	0–2		
199	29/12/90	Carlisle United	Home	League	2–0	1 Goal	(82)
200	01/01/91	Burnley	Away	League	1–1		
201	05/01/91	Brighton & Hove Albion	Away	FA Cup	2–3	1 Goal	(83)
202	12/01/91	Aldershot	Home	League	6–2	3 Goals	(86)
203	15/01/91	Doncaster Rovers	Away	LD Cup	0–0+		
204	19/01/91	Blackpool	Away	League	1–3		
205	26/01/91	Maidstone United	Home	League	2–2		
206	29/01/91	Preston North End	Home	LD Cup	1–4		
207	02/02/91	Torquay United	Home	League	3–0	1 Goal	(87)
208	23/02/91	Rochdale	Away	League	1–2	1 Goal	(88)
209	26/02/91	Hartlepool United	Home	League	2–1		
210	02/03/91	York City	Home	League	2–1		
211	05/03/91	Northampton Town	Home	League	3–0		
212	08/03/91	Doncaster Rovers	Away	League	3–2	2 Goals	(90)
213	12/03/91	Walsall	Home	League	1–0		
214	16/03/91	Cardiff City	Away	League	0–1		
215	19/03/91	Gillingham	Away	League	1–1	1 Goal	(91)
216	23/03/91	Halifax Town	Home	League	4–4	1 Goal	(92)
217	30/03/91	Northampton Town	Away	League	1–2		
218	01/04/91	Hereford United	Home	League	3–0	2 Goals	(94)
219	06/04/91	Carlisle United	Away	League	3–0		
220	09/04/91	Hartlepool United	Away	League	0–2		
221	13/04/91	Burnley	Home	League	1–3		
222	17/04/91	Lincoln City	Away	League	2–1	2 Goals	(96)
223	20/04/91	Scarborough	Away	League	1–3	1 Goal	(97)
224	23/04/91	Peterborough United	Away	League	0–0		
225	27/04/91	Chesterfield	Home	League	3–0	2 Goals	(99)
226	04/05/91	Darlington	Home	League	2–1	1 Goal	(100)
227	07/05/91	Wrexham	Home	League	2–0		
228	11/05/91	Stockport County	Away	League	0–5		
229	19/05/91	Blackpool	Home	Lge P/O	1–1		
230	22/05/91	Blackpool	Away	Lge P/O	1–2		

+ AET Scunthorpe United won 4–3 on penalties

SEASON 1991–92

Rochdale – League Division Four

1	17/08/91	York City	Home	League	1–1		
2	20/08/91	Carlisle United	Home	Lge Cup	5–1		
3	27/08/91	Carlisle United	Away	Lge Cup	1–1		
4	31/08/91	Lincoln City	Home	League	1–0	1 Goal	(1)
5	03/09/91	Walsall	Away	League	3–1	2 Goals	(3)
6	07/09/91	Cardiff City	Away	League	2–1		
7	14/09/91	Northampton Town	Home	League	1–0		
8	17/09/91	Rotherham United	Home	League	1–1		
9	21/09/91	Burnley	Away	League	1–0		
10	25/09/91	Coventry City	Away	Lge Cup	0–4		
11	28/09/91	Doncaster Rovers	Home	League	1–1		
12	08/10/91	Coventry City	Home	Lge Cup	1–0		
13	12/10/91	Mansfield Town	Home	League	0–2		
14	19/10/91	Maidstone United	Away	League	1–1		
15	22/10/91	Preston North End	Home	A Trophy	1–1		
16	26/10/91	Halifax Town	Home	League	1–0	1 Goal	(4)
17	02/11/91	Chesterfield	Home	League	3–3	1 Goal	(5)
18	05/11/91	Scunthorpe United	Away	League	2–6		
19	09/11/91	Hereford United	Away	League	1–1		
20	16/11/91	Gretna	Away	FA Cup	0–0		
21	23/11/91	Barnet	Home	League	1–0		

22	27/11/91	Gretna	Home	FA Cup	3–1	1 Goal	(6)
23	30/11/91	Scarborough	Away	League	2–3	1 Goal	(7)
24	07/12/91	Huddersfield Town	Home	FA Cup	1–2		
25	10/12/91	Bolton Wanderers	Away	A Trophy	1–4		
26	14/12/91	Blackpool	Home	League	4–2	1 Goal	(8)
27	26/12/91	York City	Away	League	1–0	1 Goal	(9)
28	28/12/91	Lincoln City	Away	League	3–0	1 Goal	(10)
29	01/01/92	Walsall	Home	League	1–1	1 Goal	(11)
30	11/01/92	Carlisle United	Away	League	0–0		
31	18/01/92	Crewe Alexandra	Home	League	1–0	1 Goal	(12)
32	08/02/92	Halifax Town	Away	League	1–1	1 Goal	(13)
33	11/02/92	Scarborough	Home	League	2–2	1 Goal	(14)
34	15/02/92	Blackpool	Away	League	0–3		
35	22/02/92	Carlisle United	Home	League	3–1		
36	29/02/92	Wrexham	Away	League	1–2		
37	03/03/92	Crewe Alexandra	Away	League	1–1	1 Goal	(15)
38	07/03/92	Gillingham	Home	League	2–1	1 Goal	(16)
39	10/03/92	Scunthorpe United	Home	League	2–0		
40	14/03/92	Chesterfield	Away	League	1–0		
41	17/03/92	Gillingham	Away	League	0–0		
42	21/03/92	Hereford United	Home	League	3–1	1 Goal	(17)
43	28/03/92	Barnet	Away	League	0–3		
44	31/03/92	Northampton Town	Away	League	2–2		
45	04/04/92	Cardiff City	Home	League	2–0		
46	07/04/92	Maidstone United	Home	League	1–2	1 Goal	(18)
47	11/04/92	Rotherham United	Away	League	0–2		
48	20/04/92	Doncaster Rovers	Away	League	0–2		
49	22/04/92	Wrexham	Home	League	2–1		
50	02/05/92	Mansfield Town	Away	League	1–2		
51	05/05/92	Burnley	Home	League	1–3		

SEASON 1992–93

Football League Division Three

52	15/08/92	Halifax Town	Home	League	2–3	1 Goal	(19)
53	18/08/92	Crewe Alexandra	Away	Lge Cup	1–4		
54	22/08/92	Wrexham	Away	League	1–3		
55	25/08/92	Crewe Alexandra	Home	Lge Cup	1–2		
56	29/08/92	Scarborough	Home	League	3–0		
Sub+1	19/09/92	Darlington	Home	League	3–1		
57	26/09/92	Hereford United	Away	League	1–1		
58	10/10/92	Carlisle United	Home	League	2–2		
59	17/10/92	York City	Away	League	0–3		
60	24/10/92	Walsall	Home	League	4–3	1 Goal	(20)
61	31/10/92	Chesterfield	Away	League	3–2		
62	03/11/92	Torquay United	Away	League	2–0		
63	07/11/92	Crewe Alexandra	Home	League	0–1		
64	14/11/92	Blackpool	Away	FA Cup	1–1		
65	21/11/92	Colchester United	Away	League	4–4	2 Goals	(22)
66	25/11/92	Blackpool	Home	FA Cup	1–0*		
67	28/11/92	Doncaster Rovers	Home	League	1–1	1 Goal	(23)
68	01/12/92	Bolton Wanderers	Home	A Trophy	0–0		
69	05/12/92	Bolton Wanderers	Away	FA Cup	0–4		
70	12/12/92	Barnet	Away	League	0–2		
71	19/12/92	Lincoln City	Home	League	5–1	3 Goals	(26)
72	26/12/92	Scunthorpe United	Home	League	2–0	1 Goal	(27)
73	02/01/93	Doncaster Rovers	Away	League	1–1		
74	08/01/93	Gillingham	Away	League	2–4		
75	16/01/93	Hereford United	Home	League	1–3		
76	20/01/93	Scunthorpe United	Home	A Trophy	1–2		
77	23/01/93	Darlington	Away	League	4–0	2 Goals	(29)
78	30/01/93	Wrexham	Home	League	1–2		
79	13/02/93	Shrewsbury Town	Home	League	2–0		

Rotherham United (loan) – Football League Division Two

1	20/02/93	Port Vale	Home	League	4–1	2 Goals	(2)
2	26/02/93	AFC Bournemouth	Home	League	1–2		
3	02/03/93	Stockport County	Home	League	0–2		
4	06/03/93	Huddersfield Town	Away	League	1–1		
5	09/03/93	Leyton Orient	Away	League	1–1		
6	13/03/93	Plymouth Argyle	Home	League	2–2		

Rochdale – Football League Division Three

| 80 | 20/03/93 | Torquay United | Home | League | 1–0 | | |
| 81 | 27/03/93 | Colchester United | Home | League | 5–2 | | |

82	02/04/93	Northampton Town	Away	League	0–1		
83	06/04/93	Barnet	Home	League	0–1		
84	10/04/93	Scunthorpe United	Away	League	1–5		
85	13/04/93	Bury	Home	League	1–2	1 Goal	(30)
86	17/04/93	Lincoln City	Away	League	2–1		
87	24/04/93	York City	Home	League	1–0		
88	01/05/93	Walsall	Away	League	1–3	1 Goal	(31)
89	08/05/93	Chesterfield	Home	League	2–1	1 Goal	(32)

SEASON 1993–94

Football League Division Three

90	14/08/93	Darlington	Away	League	1–1		
91	17/08/93	York City	Home	Lge Cup	2–0	1 Goal	(33)
92	21/08/93	Gillingham	Home	League	3–0		
93	24/08/93	York City	Away	Lge Cup	0–0		
94	28/08/93	Carlisle United	Away	League	1–0		
95	31/08/93	Wigan Athletic	Home	League	1–2		
96	04/09/93	Chester City	Home	League	2–0		
97	11/09/93	Colchester United	Away	League	5–2		
Sub+2	25/09/93	Chesterfield	Home	League	5–1		
Sub+3	02/10/93	Doncaster Rovers	Away	League	1–2		
Sub+4	06/10/93	Leicester City	Away	Lge Cup	1–2		

Carlisle United (loan) – Football League Division Three

1	30/10/93	Walsall	Home	League	2–1		
2	02/11/93	Lincoln City	Home	League	3–3		
3	06/11/93	Wigan Athletic	Away	League	2–0	1 Goal	(1)
4	09/11/93	Burnley	Away	A Trophy	2–1	1 Goal	(2)
5	20/11/93	Preston North End	Home	League	0–1		
6	27/11/93	Colchester United	Away	League	1–2		

Rochdale – Football League Division Three

| 98 | 11/12/93 | Gillingham | Away | League | 2–1 | | |
| 99 | 18/12/93 | Darlington | Home | League | 0–0 | | |

Carlisle United (loan) – Football League Division Three

1	08/02/94	Lincoln City	Home	A Trophy	2–1*		
2	12/02/94	Bury	Away	League	1–2		
Sub+1	25/02/94	Scarborough	Home	League	2–0		
Sub+2	05/03/94	Chesterfield	Away	League	0–3		

Rochdale – Football League Division Three

| 100 | 12/03/94 | Hereford United | Away | League | 1–5 | | |

SEASON 1994–95

Northampton Town – Football League Division Three

| 1 | 26/12/94 | Colchester United | Away | League | 1–0 | | |
| 2 | 27/12/94 | Chesterfield | Home | League | 2–3 | | |

APPEARANCES AND GOALS PER SEASON

SEASON 80–81	GAMES	GOALS
League	3+2	0
FA Cup	0+1	0
TOTAL	**3+3**	**0**

SEASON 81–82	GAMES	GOALS
League	12+1	5
FA Cup	0+1	0
TOTAL	**12+2**	**5**

SEASON 82–83	GAMES	GOALS
League	17+6	13
League Cup	1+1	1
Football League Trophy	0+2	0
TOTAL	**18+9**	**14**

SEASON 83–84	GAMES	GOALS
League	22+8	9
FA Cup	2	1
Associate Members Cup	1+2	0
TOTAL	**25+10**	**10**

SEASON 84–85	GAMES	GOALS
League	34+5	14
FA Cup	3	1
League Cup	1	1
Freight Rover Trophy	2	0
TOTAL	**40+5**	**16**

SEASON 85–86	GAMES	GOALS
League	20+5	10
FA Cup	3	2
League Cup	1+1	1
Full Members Cup	1+1	0
TOTAL	**25+7**	**13**

SEASON 86–87	GAMES	GOALS
League	33+6	9
FA Cup	2+1	0
League Cup	3	0
Full Members Cup	2	2
TOTAL	**40+7**	**11**

SEASON 87–88	GAMES	GOALS
League	45	24
League Play–offs	2	1
FA Cup	4	0
League Cup	4	1
Sherpa Van Trophy	4	1
TOTAL	**59**	**27**

SEASON 88–89	GAMES	GOALS
League	45+1	16
League Play–offs	2	0
FA Cup	1	0
League Cup	6	4
Sherpa Van Trophy	2	0
TOTAL	**56+1**	**20**

SEASON 89–90	GAMES	GOALS
League	37+7	18
FA Cup	2+2	0
League Cup	2	1
Leyland Daf Cup	3	1
TOTAL	**44+9**	**20**

SEASON 90–91	GAMES	GOALS
League	44+2	23
League Play–offs	2	0
FA Cup	4	3
League Cup	2	0
Leyland Daf Cup	4	1
TOTAL	**56+2**	**27**

SEASON 91–92	GAMES	GOALS
League	42	17
FA Cup	3	1
League Cup	4	0
Autoglass Trophy	2	0
TOTAL	**51**	**18**

SEASON 92–93	GAMES	GOALS
League	37+1	16
FA Cup	3	0
League Cup	2	0
Autoglass Trophy	2	0
TOTAL	**44+1**	**16**

SEASON 93–94	GAMES	GOALS
League	15+4	1
League Cup	2+1	1
Autoglass Trophy	2	1
TOTAL	**19+5**	**3**

SEASON 94–95	GAMES	GOALS
League	2	0
TOTAL	**2**	**0**

CAREER APPEARANCES AND GOALS

COMPETITION	GAMES	TOTAL	GOALS
League	408+48	456	175
League Play–offs	6	6	1
FA Cup	27+5	32	8
League Cup	28+3	31	10
Football League Trophy	0+2	2	0
Associate Members Cup	1+2	3	0
Freight Rover Trophy	2	2	0
Full Members Cup	3+1	4	2
Sherpa Van Trophy	6	6	1
Leyland Daf Cup	7	7	2
Autoglass Trophy	6	6	1
TOTAL	494+61	555	200

HAT-TRICKS

Hull City

1	3	Stockport County	29/01/83	Home	League	7–0
2	3	Shrewsbury Town	04/03/86	Home	League	4–3

Scunthorpe United

1	3	Peterborough United	27/02/88	Home	League	5–0
2	3	Peterborough United	14/03/89	Home	League	3–0
3	3	Doncaster Rovers	05/05/90	Home	League	4–1
4	3	Aldershot	12/01/91	Home	League	6–2

Rochdale

1	3	Lincoln City	19/12/92	Home	League	5–1

League: 7
TOTAL: 7

HONOURS

Winners medals
None

Runner-up medals
League Division Four Championship: 82/83
Promoted to League Division Two: 84/85
Associate Members Cup: 83/84

ROBBIE FOWLER

Born: 09/04/75 – Liverpool
Height: 5.11
Weight: 11.10 (96–97)

Club
Liverpool: **1993–97** – Matches: **184+4** – Goals: **116**

Country
England: **1996–97** – Matches: **2+4** – Goals: **1**

SEASON 1993–94

Liverpool – Premier League

1	22/09/93	Fulham	Away	Lge Cup	3–1	1 Goal	(1)
2	25/09/93	Chelsea	Away	League	0–1		
3	02/10/93	Arsenal	Home	League	0–0		
4	05/10/93	Fulham	Home	Lge Cup	5–0	5 Goals	(6)
5	16/10/93	Oldham Athletic	Home	League	2–1	1 Goal	(7)
6	23/10/93	Manchester City	Away	League	1–1		
7	27/10/93	Ipswich Town	Home	Lge Cup	3–2		
8	30/10/93	Southampton	Home	League	4–2	3 Goals	(10)
9	06/11/93	West Ham United	Home	League	2–0		
10	21/11/93	Newcastle United	Away	League	0–3		
11	28/11/93	Aston Villa	Home	League	2–1	1 Goal	(11)

12	01/12/93	Wimbledon	Home	Lge Cup	1–1		
13	04/12/93	Sheffield Wednesday	Away	League	1–3	1 Goal	(12)
14	08/12/93	Queens Park Rangers	Home	League	3–2		
15	11/12/93	Swindon Town	Home	League	2–2		
16	14/12/93	Wimbledon	Away	Lge Cup	2–2+		
17	18/12/93	Tottenham Hotspur	Away	League	3–3	2 Goals	(14)
18	26/12/93	Sheffield United	Away	League	0–0		
19	28/12/93	Wimbledon	Home	League	1–1		
20	01/01/94	Ipswich Town	Away	League	2–1		
21	04/01/94	Manchester United	Home	League	3–3		
22	15/01/94	Oldham Athletic	Away	League	3–0	1 Goal	(15)
23	19/01/94	Bristol City	Away	FA Cup	1–1		
24	13/03/94	Everton	Home	League	2–1	1 Goal	(16)
25	19/03/94	Chelsea	Home	League	2–1		
26	26/03/94	Arsenal	Away	League	0–1		
Sub+1	29/03/94	Manchester United	Away	League	0–1		
27	02/04/94	Sheffield United	Home	League	1–2		
28	04/04/94	Wimbledon	Away	League	1–1		
29	09/04/94	Ipswich Town	Home	League	1–0		
30	16/04/94	Newcastle United	Home	League	0–2		
31	23/04/94	West Ham United	Away	League	2–1	1 Goal	(17)
32	30/04/94	Norwich City	Home	League	0–1		
33	07/05/94	Aston Villa	Away	League	1–2	1 Goal	(18)

+ AET Wimbledon won 4–3 on penalties

SEASON 1994–95

Premier League

34	20/08/94	Crystal Palace	Away	League	6–1	1 Goal	(19)
35	28/08/94	Arsenal	Home	League	3–0	3 Goals	(22)
36	31/08/94	Southampton	Away	League	2–0	1 Goal	(23)
37	10/09/94	West Ham United	Home	League	0–0		
38	17/09/94	Manchester United	Away	League	0–2		
39	21/09/94	Burnley	Home	Lge Cup	2–0	1 Goal	(24)
40	24/09/94	Newcastle United	Away	League	1–1		
41	01/10/94	Sheffield Wednesday	Home	League	4–1		
42	05/10/94	Burnley	Away	Lge Cup	4–1	1 Goal	(25)
43	08/10/94	Aston Villa	Home	League	3–2	2 Goals	(27)
44	15/10/94	Blackburn Rovers	Away	League	2–3	1 Goal	(28)
45	22/10/94	Wimbledon	Home	League	3–0	1 Goal	(29)
46	25/10/94	Stoke City	Home	Lge Cup	2–1		
47	29/10/94	Ipswich Town	Away	League	3–1	2 Goals	(31)
48	31/10/94	Queens Park Rangers	Away	League	1–2		
49	05/11/94	Nottingham Forest	Home	League	1–0	1 Goal	(32)
50	09/11/94	Chelsea	Home	League	3–1	2 Goals	(34)
51	21/11/94	Everton	Away	League	0–2		
52	26/11/94	Tottenham Hotspur	Home	League	1–1	1 Goal	(35)
53	30/11/94	Blackburn Rovers	Away	Lge Cup	3–1		
54	03/12/94	Coventry City	Away	League	1–1		
55	11/12/94	Crystal Palace	Home	League	0–0		
56	18/12/94	Chelsea	Away	League	0–0		
57	26/12/94	Leicester City	Away	League	2–1	1 Goal	(36)
58	28/12/94	Manchester City	Home	League	2–0	1 Goal	(37)
59	31/12/94	Leeds United	Away	League	2–0	1 Goal	(38)
60	02/01/95	Norwich City	Home	League	4–0	2 Goals	(40)
61	07/01/95	Birmingham City	Away	FA Cup	0–0		
62	11/01/95	Arsenal	Home	Lge Cup	1–0		
63	14/01/95	Ipswich Town	Home	League	0–1		
64	18/01/95	Birmingham City	Home	FA Cup	1–1+		
65	24/01/95	Everton	Home	League	0–0		
66	28/01/95	Burnley	Away	FA Cup	0–0		
67	04/02/95	Nottingham Forest	Away	League	1–1	1 Goal	(41)
68	07/02/95	Burnley	Home	FA Cup	1–0		
69	11/02/95	Queens Park Rangers	Home	League	1–1		
70	15/02/95	Crystal Palace	Home	Lge Cup	1–0	1 Goal	(42)
71	19/02/95	Wimbledon	Home	FA Cup	1–1	1 Goal	(43)
72	25/02/95	Sheffield Wednesday	Away	League	2–1		
73	28/02/95	Wimbledon	Away	FA Cup	2–0		
74	04/03/95	Newcastle United	Home	League	2–0	1 Goal	(44)
75	08/03/95	Crystal Palace	Away	Lge Cup	1–0	1 Goal	(45)
76	11/03/95	Tottenham Hotspur	Home	FA Cup	1–2	1 Goal	(46)
77	14/03/95	Coventry City	Home	League	2–3		
78	19/03/95	Manchester United	Home	League	2–0		
79	22/03/95	Tottenham Hotspur	Away	League	0–0		

80	02/04/95	Bolton Wanderers	Wembley	Lge Cup	2–1		
81	05/04/95	Southampton	Home	League	3–1	1 Goal	(47)
82	09/04/95	Leeds United	Home	League	0–1		
83	12/04/95	Arsenal	Away	League	1–0	1 Goal	(48)
84	14/04/95	Manchester City	Away	League	1–2		
85	17/04/95	Leicester City	Home	League	2–0	1 Goal	(49)
86	29/04/95	Norwich City	Away	League	2–1		
87	02/05/95	Wimbledon	Away	League	0–0		
88	06/05/95	Aston Villa	Away	League	0–2		
89	10/05/95	West Ham United	Away	League	0–3		
90	14/05/95	Blackburn Rovers	Home	League	2–1		

+ AET Liverpool won 2–0 on penalties

SEASON 1995–96

Premier League

Sub+2	19/08/95	Sheffield Wednesday	Home	League	1–0		
Sub+3	21/08/95	Leeds United	Away	League	0–1		
91	26/08/95	Tottenham Hotspur	Away	League	3–1	1 Goal	(50)
92	30/08/95	Queens Park Rangers	Home	League	1–0		
93	09/09/95	Wimbledon	Away	League	0–1		
Sub+4	12/09/95	Spartak–Alania Vladikavkaz	Away	UEFA Cup	2–1		
94	16/09/95	Blackburn Rovers	Home	League	3–0	1 Goal	(51)
95	20/09/95	Sunderland	Home	Lge Cup	2–0		
96	23/09/95	Bolton Wanderers	Home	League	5–2	4 Goals	(55)
97	26/09/95	Spartak–Alania Vladikavkaz	Home	UEFA Cup	0–0		
98	01/10/95	Manchester United	Away	League	2–2	2 Goals	(57)
99	04/10/95	Sunderland	Away	Lge Cup	1–0	1 Goal	(58)
100	14/10/95	Coventry City	Home	League	0–0		
101	17/10/95	Brondby IF	Away	UEFA Cup	0–0		
102	22/10/95	Southampton	Away	League	3–1		
103	25/10/95	Manchester City	Home	Lge Cup	4–0	1 Goal	(59)
104	28/10/95	Manchester City	Home	League	6–0	2 Goals	(61)
105	31/10/95	Brondby IF	Home	UEFA Cup	0–1		
106	04/11/95	Newcastle United	Away	League	1–2		
107	18/11/95	Everton	Home	League	1–2	1 Goal	(62)
108	22/11/95	West Ham United	Away	League	0–0		
109	25/11/95	Middlesbrough	Away	League	1–2		
110	29/11/95	Newcastle United	Home	Lge Cup	0–1		
111	02/12/95	Southampton	Home	League	1–1		
112	09/12/95	Bolton Wanderers	Away	League	1–0		
113	17/12/95	Manchester United	Home	League	2–0	2 Goals	(64)
114	23/12/95	Arsenal	Home	League	3–1	3 Goals	(67)
115	30/12/95	Chelsea	Away	League	2–2		
116	01/01/96	Nottingham Forest	Home	League	4–2	2 Goals	(69)
117	06/01/96	Rochdale	Home	FA Cup	7–0	1 Goal	(70)
118	13/01/96	Sheffield Wednesday	Away	League	1–1		
119	20/01/96	Leeds United	Home	League	5–0	2 Goals	(72)
120	31/01/96	Aston Villa	Away	League	2–0	1 Goal	(73)
121	03/02/96	Tottenham Hotspur	Home	League	0–0		
122	11/02/96	Queens Park Rangers	Away	League	2–1	1 Goal	(74)
123	18/02/96	Shrewsbury Town	Away	FA Cup	4–0	1 Goal	(75)
124	24/02/96	Blackburn Rovers	Away	League	3–2		
125	28/02/96	Charlton Athletic	Home	FA Cup	2–1	1 Goal	(76)
126	03/03/96	Aston Villa	Home	League	3–0	2 Goals	(78)
127	10/03/96	Leeds United	Away	FA Cup	0–0		
128	13/03/96	Wimbledon	Home	League	2–2		
129	16/03/96	Chelsea	Home	League	2–0	1 Goal	(79)
130	20/03/96	Leeds United	Home	FA Cup	3–0	1 Goal	(80)
131	23/03/96	Nottingham Forest	Away	League	0–1		
132	31/03/96	Aston Villa	Neutral	FA Cup	3–0	2 Goals	(82)
133	03/04/96	Newcastle United	Home	League	4–3	2 Goals	(84)
134	06/04/96	Coventry City	Away	League	0–1		
135	08/04/96	West Ham United	Home	League	2–0		
136	16/04/96	Everton	Away	League	1–1	1 Goal	(85)
137	27/04/96	Middlesbrough	Home	League	1–0		
138	01/05/96	Arsenal	Away	League	0–0		
139	05/05/96	Manchester City	Away	League	2–2		
140	11/05/96	Manchester United	Wembley	FA Cup	0–1		

SEASON 1996–97

Premier League

141	17/08/96	Middlesbrough	Away	League	3–3	1 Goal	(86)

142	19/08/96	Arsenal	Home	League	2–0		
143	24/08/96	Sunderland	Home	League	0–0		
144	04/09/96	Coventry City	Away	League	1–0		
145	07/09/96	Southampton	Home	League	2–1		
146	12/09/96	MYPA–47	Away	ECW Cup	1–0		
147	15/09/96	Leicester City	Away	League	3–0		
148	21/09/96	Chelsea	Home	League	5–1	1 Goal	(87)
149	17/10/96	FC Sion	Away	ECW Cup	2–1	1 Goal	(88)
150	23/10/96	Charlton Athletic	Away	Lge Cup	1–1	1 Goal	(89)
151	27/10/96	Derby County	Home	League	2–1	2 Goals	(91)
152	31/10/96	FC Sion	Home	ECW Cup	6–3	2 Goals	(93)
153	03/11/96	Blackburn Rovers	Away	League	0–3		
154	13/11/96	Charlton Athletic	Home	Lge Cup	4–1	2 Goals	(95)
155	16/11/96	Leeds United	Away	League	2–0		
156	20/11/96	Everton	Home	League	1–1	1 Goal	(96)
157	23/11/96	Wimbledon	Home	League	1–1		
158	27/11/96	Arsenal	Home	Lge Cup	4–2	2 Goals	(98)
159	02/12/96	Tottenham Hotspur	Away	League	2–0		
160	07/12/96	Sheffield Wednesday	Home	League	0–1		
161	14/12/96	Middlesbrough	Home	League	5–1	4 Goals	(102)
162	17/12/96	Nottingham Forest	Home	League	4–2	1 Goal	(103)
163	23/12/96	Newcastle United	Away	League	1–1	1 Goal	(104)
164	29/12/96	Southampton	Away	League	1–0		
165	01/01/97	Chelsea	Away	League	0–1		
166	08/01/97	Middlesbrough	Away	Lge Cup	1–2		
167	11/01/97	West Ham United	Home	League	0–0		
168	18/01/97	Aston Villa	Home	League	3–0	1 Goal	(105)
169	26/01/97	Chelsea	Away	FA Cup	2–4	1 Goal	(106)
170	01/02/97	Derby County	Away	League	1–0		
171	19/02/97	Leeds United	Home	League	4–0	1 Goal	(107)
172	22/02/97	Blackburn Rovers	Home	League	0–0		
173	02/03/97	Aston Villa	Away	League	0–1		
174	06/03/97	SK Brann	Away	ECW Cup	1–1	1 Goal	(108)
175	10/03/97	Newcastle United	Home	League	4–3	2 Goals	(110)
176	15/03/97	Nottingham Forest	Away	League	1–1	1 Goal	(111)
177	20/03/97	SK Brann	Home	ECW Cup	3–0	2 Goals	(113)
178	24/03/97	Arsenal	Away	League	2–1		
179	06/04/97	Coventry City	Home	League	1–2	1 Goal	(114)
180	10/04/97	Paris Saint–Germain	Away	ECW Cup	0–3		
181	13/04/97	Sunderland	Away	League	2–1	1 Goal	(115)
182	16/04/97	Everton	Away	League	1–1		
183	19/04/97	Manchester United	Home	League	1–3		
184	24/04/97	Paris Saint–Germain	Home	ECW Cup	2–0	1 Goal	(116)

INTERNATIONAL APPEARANCES – ENGLAND

Sub 1	27/03/96	Bulgaria	Wembley	1–0	F		
2	24/04/96	Croatia	Wembley	0–0	F		
Sub 3	23/05/96	China	Beijing	3–0	F		
Sub 4	18/06/96	Holland	Wembley	4–1	EC		
Sub 5	22/06/96	Spain	Wembley	0–0+	EC		
6	29/03/97	Mexico	Wembley	2–0	F	1 Goal	(1)

+ AET England won 4–2 on penalties

APPEARANCES AND GOALS PER SEASON

SEASON 93–94	GAMES	GOALS
League	27+1	12
FA Cup	1	0
League Cup	5	6
TOTAL	**33+1**	**18**

SEASON 94–95	GAMES	GOALS
League	42	25
FA Cup	7	2
League Cup	8	4
TOTAL	**57**	**31**

SEASON 95–96	GAMES	GOALS
League	36+2	28
FA Cup	7	6
League Cup	4	2
UEFA Cup	3+1	0
TOTAL	**50+3**	**36**

SEASON 96–97	GAMES	GOALS
League	32	18
FA Cup	1	1
League Cup	4	5
European Cup Winners Cup	7	7
TOTAL	**44**	**31**

CAREER APPEARANCES AND GOALS

COMPETITION	GAMES	TOTAL	GOALS
League	137+3	140	83
FA Cup	16	16	9
League Cup	21	21	17
European Cup Winners Cup	7	7	7
UEFA Cup	3+1	4	0
Internationals	2+4	6	1
TOTAL	**186+8**	**194**	**117**

HAT-TRICKS

Liverpool

1	5	Fulham	05/10/93	Home	Lge Cup	5–0
2	3	Southampton	30/10/93	Home	League	4–2
3	3	Arsenal	28/08/94	Home	League	3–0
4	4	Bolton Wanderers	23/09/95	Home	League	5–2
5	3	Arsenal	23/12/95	Home	League	3–1
6	4	Middlesbrough	14/12/96	Home	League	5–1

League: 5
League Cup: 1
TOTAL: 6

HONOURS

Winners medals
League Cup: 94/95

Runner-up medals
FA Cup: 95/96

KEVIN FRANCIS

Born: 06/12/67 – Birmingham
Height: 6.7
Weight: 15.08 (96–97)

Clubs
Derby County: **1989–91** – Matches: **2+15** – Goals: **1**
Stockport County: **1991–94** – Matches: **192+5** – Goals: **117**
Birmingham City: **1995–97** – Matches: **43+24** – Goals: **19**

SEASON 1989–90

Derby County – League Division One

Sub+1	29/11/89	West Bromwich Albion	Away	ZDS Cup	5–0		
Sub+2	07/01/90	Port Vale	Away	FA Cup	1–1		
Sub+3	10/01/90	Port Vale	Home	FA Cup	2–3	1 Goal	(1)
Sub+4	17/01/90	West Ham United	Away	Lge Cup	1–1		
Sub+5	20/01/90	Nottingham Forest	Home	League	0–2		
Sub+6	24/01/90	West Ham United	Home	Lge Cup	0–0*		
1	31/01/90	West Ham United	Away	Lge Cup	1–2		
Sub+7	10/03/90	Southampton	Away	League	1–2		
Sub+8	17/03/90	Aston Villa	Home	League	0–1		
Sub+9	31/03/90	Chelsea	Away	League	1–1		
Sub+10	07/04/90	Coventry City	Away	League	0–1		
Sub+11	16/04/90	Everton	Away	League	1–2		
Sub+12	21/04/90	Norwich City	Home	League	0–2		
Sub+13	01/05/90	Liverpool	Away	League	0–1		

SEASON 1990–91

League Division One

Sub+14	01/09/90	Wimbledon	Home	League	1–1		
Sub+15	22/09/90	Norwich City	Away	League	1–2		
2	05/01/91	Newcastle United	Away	FA Cup	0–2		

Stockport County – League Division Four

Sub+1	23/02/91	Lincoln City	Away	League	3–0		
1	26/02/91	Cardiff City	Home	League	1–1		
Sub+2	26/03/91	Rochdale	Home	League	3–0		
2	29/03/91	Hartlepool United	Home	League	1–3		
3	01/04/91	Doncaster Rovers	Away	League	0–1		
4	06/04/91	Chesterfield	Home	League	3–1		
5	09/04/91	Northampton Town	Home	League	2–0	1 Goal	(1)
6	13/04/91	Gillingham	Away	League	3–1		
7	16/04/91	Wrexham	Away	League	3–1	1 Goal	(2)
8	19/04/91	Aldershot	Home	League	3–2	1 Goal	(3)
9	23/04/91	Torquay United	Home	League	2–1		
10	04/05/91	York City	Away	League	2–0		
11	11/05/91	Scunthorpe United	Home	League	5–0	2 Goals	(5)

SEASON 1991–92

League Division Three

12	17/08/91	Swansea City	Home	League	5–0	1 Goal	(6)
13	20/08/91	Bradford City	Home	Lge Cup	1–1		
14	24/08/91	Leyton Orient	Away	League	3–3		
15	28/08/91	Bradford City	Away	Lge Cup	1–3*	1 Goal	(7)
16	30/08/91	Preston North End	Home	League	2–0		
17	03/09/91	Wigan Athletic	Away	League	3–1	1 Goal	(8)
18	14/09/91	West Bromwich Albion	Away	League	0–1		
19	17/09/91	Exeter City	Away	League	1–2	1 Goal	(9)
20	21/09/91	Bury	Home	League	2–0	1 Goal	(10)
21	28/09/91	Stoke City	Away	League	2–2	1 Goal	(11)
22	05/10/91	Bradford City	Home	League	4–1	1 Goal	(12)
23	12/10/91	Birmingham City	Away	League	0–3		
24	15/11/91	Lincoln City	Home	FA Cup	3–1	1 Goal	(13)
25	19/11/91	Carlisle United	Away	A Trophy	0–4		
26	23/11/91	Fulham	Away	League	2–1	1 Goal	(14)
27	26/11/91	Shrewsbury Town	Home	League	1–4		
28	30/11/91	Reading	Away	League	1–1		
29	07/12/91	Wigan Athletic	Away	FA Cup	0–2		
30	14/12/91	Peterborough United	Home	League	3–0	1 Goal	(15)
31	20/12/91	Leyton Orient	Home	League	1–0	1 Goal	(16)
32	26/12/91	Preston North End	Away	League	2–3		
33	28/12/91	Swansea City	Away	League	1–2		
34	01/01/92	Wigan Athletic	Home	League	3–3	1 Goal	(17)
35	04/01/92	Brentford	Home	League	2–1	1 Goal	(18)
36	07/01/92	York City	Home	A Trophy	3–0		
37	11/01/92	Hull City	Away	League	2–0	1 Goal	(19)
38	14/01/92	Carlisle United	Away	A Trophy	3–1	3 Goals	(22)
39	18/01/92	Darlington	Home	League	2–0		
40	04/02/92	Hartlepool United	Home	A Trophy	3–0	3 Goals	(25)
41	07/02/92	Huddersfield Town	Home	League	0–0		
42	11/02/92	Reading	Home	League	1–0		
43	15/02/92	Peterborough United	Away	League	2–3		
44	18/02/92	Hartlepool United	Away	League	1–0	1 Goal	(26)
45	22/02/92	Hull City	Home	League	1–1		
46	03/03/92	Darlington	Away	League	3–1		
47	06/03/92	Hartlepool United	Home	League	0–1		
Sub+3	10/03/92	Bolton Wanderers	Away	League	0–0		
48	13/03/92	AFC Bournemouth	Home	League	5–0	1 Goal	(27)
49	17/03/92	Crewe Alexandra	Away	A Trophy	2–1		
50	31/03/92	West Bromwich Albion	Home	League	3–0		
51	07/04/92	Burnley	Away	A Trophy	1–0	1 Goal	(28)
52	10/04/92	Exeter City	Home	League	4–1		
53	15/04/92	Burnley	Home	A Trophy	2–1	1 Goal	(29)
54	18/04/92	Bury	Away	League	0–0		
55	20/04/92	Stoke City	Home	League	0–0		
56	02/05/92	Birmingham City	Home	League	2–0	1 Goal	(30)
57	10/05/92	Stoke City	Home	Lge P/O	1–0		
58	13/05/92	Stoke City	Away	Lge P/O	1–1		
59	16/05/92	Stoke City	Wembley	A Trophy	0–1		
60	24/05/92	Peterborough United	Wembley	Lge P/O	1–2	1 Goal	(31)

SEASON 1992–93

Football League Division Two

61	15/08/92	Wigan Athletic	Away	League	2–1		
62	18/08/92	Chester City	Home	Lge Cup	1–1		
63	22/08/92	Burnley	Home	League	2–1	1 Goal	(32)
64	25/08/92	Chester City	Away	Lge Cup	2–1		
65	29/08/92	Port Vale	Away	League	0–0		
66	02/09/92	West Bromwich Albion	Away	League	0–3		
67	05/09/92	Exeter City	Home	League	2–2		
68	12/09/92	Hull City	Home	League	5–3	2 Goals	(34)
69	15/09/92	Bradford City	Away	League	3–2	1 Goal	(35)
70	19/09/92	Chester City	Away	League	3–0	1 Goal	(36)
71	23/09/92	Nottingham Forest	Home	Lge Cup	2–3	2 Goals	(38)
72	25/09/92	Fulham	Home	League	0–0		
73	03/10/92	Swansea City	Home	League	1–1		
74	07/10/92	Nottingham Forest	Away	Lge Cup	1–2		
75	10/10/92	Mansfield Town	Away	League	0–2		
76	16/10/92	Blackpool	Home	League	0–0		
Sub+4	24/10/92	AFC Bournemouth	Away	League	0–1		
77	30/10/92	Huddersfield Town	Home	League	5–0	2 Goals	(40)
78	03/11/92	Preston North End	Home	League	3–0	1 Goal	(41)
79	07/11/92	Brighton & Hove Albion	Away	League	0–2		
80	14/11/92	York City	Away	FA Cup	3–1	2 Goals	(43)
81	20/11/92	Plymouth Argyle	Home	League	3–0	2 Goals	(45)
82	28/11/92	Hartlepool United	Away	League	2–3	1 Goal	(46)
83	05/12/92	Macclesfield Town	Away	FA Cup	2–0		
84	08/12/92	Chesterfield	Away	A Trophy	3–0	2 Goals	(48)
85	15/12/92	Chester City	Home	A Trophy	2–0		
86	19/12/92	Reading	Away	League	4–2	1 Goal	(49)
87	28/12/92	Leyton Orient	Home	League	1–1		
88	02/01/93	Derby County	Away	FA Cup	1–2		
89	09/01/93	Bradford City	Home	League	2–2	1 Goal	(50)
90	22/01/93	Chester City	Home	League	2–0	1 Goal	(51)
91	30/01/93	Burnley	Away	League	1–1		
92	02/02/93	Bradford City	Away	A Trophy	4–3	2 Goals	(53)
93	05/02/93	Wigan Athletic	Home	League	3–0	2 Goals	(55)
94	09/02/93	Bolton Wanderers	Home	League	2–0	1 Goal	(56)
95	20/02/93	West Bromwich Albion	Home	League	5–1	1 Goal	(57)
96	23/02/93	Chesterfield	Home	A Trophy	2–1	1 Goal	(58)
97	28/02/93	Mansfield Town	Home	League	0–1		
98	02/03/93	Rotherham United	Away	League	2–0	1 Goal	(59)
99	05/03/93	Swansea City	Away	League	2–2	1 Goal	(60)
100	09/03/93	Stoke City	Away	League	1–2	1 Goal	(61)
101	13/03/93	Brighton & Hove Albion	Home	League	0–0		
102	16/03/93	Wigan Athletic	Away	A Trophy	1–2		
103	20/03/93	Preston North End	Away	League	3–2		
104	23/03/93	Hartlepool United	Home	League	4–1	1 Goal	(62)
105	27/03/93	Plymouth Argyle	Away	League	4–3	3 Goals	(65)
106	03/04/93	Stoke City	Home	League	1–1		
107	06/04/93	Bolton Wanderers	Away	League	1–2	1 Goal	(66)
108	09/04/93	Rotherham United	Home	League	2–2	2 Goals	(68)
109	12/04/93	Leyton Orient	Away	League	0–3		
110	16/04/93	Reading	Home	League	2–2		
111	20/04/93	Wigan Athletic	Home	A Trophy	2–0	1 Goal	(69)
112	24/04/93	Blackpool	Away	League	0–2		
113	27/04/93	Hull City	Away	League	2–0		
114	01/05/93	AFC Bournemouth	Home	League	0–0		
115	22/05/93	Port Vale	Wembley	A Trophy	1–2	1 Goal	(70)

SEASON 1993–94

Football League Division Two

116	14/08/93	Plymouth Argyle	Away	League	3–2	2 Goals	(72)
117	17/08/93	Hartlepool United	Home	Lge Cup	1–1		
118	21/08/93	Cambridge United	Home	League	3–1	1 Goal	(73)
119	24/08/93	Hartlepool United	Away	Lge Cup	1–2	1 Goal	(74)
120	28/08/93	Huddersfield Town	Away	League	1–1		
121	31/08/93	Bradford City	Home	League	4–1	1 Goal	(75)
122	04/09/93	Wrexham	Home	League	1–0		
123	11/09/93	Hartlepool United	Away	League	0–1		
124	14/09/93	York City	Away	League	2–1		
125	18/09/93	Burnley	Home	League	2–1		
126	25/09/93	Rotherham United	Home	League	2–0		
127	28/09/93	Wigan Athletic	Home	A Trophy	2–0		

128	02/10/93	AFC Bournemouth	Away	League	1–1	1 Goal	(76)
129	09/10/93	Brighton & Hove Albion	Away	League	1–1		
130	16/10/93	Exeter City	Home	League	4–0	1 Goal	(77)
131	23/10/93	Fulham	Away	League	1–0		
132	30/10/93	Swansea City	Home	League	4–0	1 Goal	(78)
133	02/11/93	Leyton Orient	Home	League	3–0	1 Goal	(79)
134	06/11/93	Cardiff City	Away	League	1–3		
135	11/11/93	Bury	Away	A Trophy	3–1	1 Goal	(80)
136	13/11/93	Rotherham United	Away	FA Cup	2–1		
137	20/11/93	Bristol Rovers	Home	League	0–2		
138	27/11/93	Hull City	Away	League	1–0	1 Goal	(81)
139	04/12/93	Halifax Town	Home	FA Cup	5–1	2 Goals	(83)
140	11/12/93	Cambridge United	Away	League	0–0		
141	17/12/93	Plymouth Argyle	Home	League	2–3		
142	28/12/93	Reading	Away	League	0–2		
143	01/01/94	Barnet	Home	League	2–1	2 Goals	(85)
144	03/01/94	Brentford	Away	League	1–1	1 Goal	(86)
145	08/01/94	Queens Park Rangers	Home	FA Cup	2–1	1 Goal	(87)
146	11/01/94	Scunthorpe United	Home	A Trophy	2–0	1 Goal	(88)
147	22/01/94	Brighton & Hove Albion	Home	League	3–0		
148	01/02/94	Blackpool	Home	League	1–0	1 Goal	(89)
149	05/02/94	Fulham	Home	League	2–4	1 Goal	(90)
150	09/02/94	Bristol City	Home	FA Cup	0–4		
151	12/02/94	Port Vale	Away	League	1–1	1 Goal	(91)
152	19/02/94	Huddersfield Town	Home	League	3–0	2 Goals	(93)
153	01/03/94	Huddersfield Town	Home	A Trophy	0–1		
154	05/03/94	Hartlepool United	Home	League	5–0	3 Goals	(96)
155	08/03/94	Wrexham	Away	League	1–0		
156	12/03/94	Burnley	Away	League	1–1		
157	15/03/94	York City	Home	League	1–2		
158	19/03/94	Rotherham United	Away	League	2–1	1 Goal	(97)
159	26/03/94	AFC Bournemouth	Home	League	0–2		
160	29/03/94	Brentford	Home	League	3–1	2 Goals	(99)
161	09/04/94	Barnet	Away	League	0–0		
162	12/04/94	Swansea City	Away	League	2–1		
163	16/04/94	Leyton Orient	Away	League	0–0		
164	19/04/94	Port Vale	Home	League	2–1	2 Goals	(101)
165	23/04/94	Cardiff City	Home	League	2–2		
166	26/04/94	Bradford City	Away	League	2–1		
167	28/04/94	Reading	Home	League	1–1	1 Goal	(102)
168	30/04/94	Bristol Rovers	Away	League	1–1		
169	02/05/94	Exeter City	Away	League	2–1	2 Goals	(104)
170	07/05/94	Hull City	Home	League	0–0		
171	15/05/94	York City	Away	Lge P/O	0–0		
172	18/05/94	York City	Home	Lge P/O	1–0		
173	29/05/94	Burnley	Wembley	Lge P/O	1–2		

SEASON 1994–95

Football League Division Two

174	13/08/94	Cardiff City	Home	League	4–1	2 Goals	(106)
175	17/08/94	Preston North End	Away	Lge Cup	1–1+		
176	20/08/94	Cambridge United	Away	League	4–3	2 Goals	(108)
177	27/08/94	Brentford	Home	League	0–1		
178	30/08/94	Crewe Alexandra	Away	League	1–2		
179	03/09/94	Bristol Rovers	Away	League	2–2		
180	10/09/94	AFC Bournemouth	Home	League	1–0	1 Goal	(109)
181	13/09/94	Shrewsbury Town	Home	League	2–1		
182	17/09/94	Huddersfield Town	Away	League	1–2		
183	20/09/94	Sheffield United	Home	Lge Cup	1–5	1 Goal	(110)
184	24/09/94	Wycombe Wanderers	Home	League	4–1	2 Goals	(112)
185	27/09/94	Sheffield United	Away	Lge Cup	0–1		
186	01/10/94	York City	Away	League	4–2	1 Goal	(113)
187	08/10/94	Rotherham United	Home	League	1–0	1 Goal	(114)
188	15/10/94	Peterborough United	Away	League	1–0		
189	22/10/94	Plymouth Argyle	Home	League	2–4	1 Goal	(115)
190	29/10/94	Leyton Orient	Away	League	1–0	1 Goal	(116)
191	02/11/94	Chester City	Away	League	0–1		
192	26/11/94	Birmingham City	Home	League	0–1		
Sub+5	31/12/94	Bradford City	Home	League	1–2	1 Goal	(117)

+ Played at Gigg Lane, Bury

Birmingham City – Football League Division Two

| 1 | 31/01/95 | Swansea City | Home | AW Shield | 3–2 | 1 Goal | (1) |
| 2 | 04/02/95 | Stockport County | Home | League | 1–0 | | |

3	11/02/95	Crewe Alexandra	Away	League	1–2		
4	18/02/95	York City	Home	League	4–2	2 Goals	(3)
5	21/02/95	AFC Bournemouth	Away	League	1–2	1 Goal	(4)
6	25/02/95	Wrexham	Home	League	5–2	2 Goals	(6)
7	28/02/95	Leyton Orient	Home	AW Shield	1–0		
8	04/03/95	Hull City	Away	League	0–0		
9	18/03/95	Wycombe Wanderers	Away	League	3–0		
10	21/03/95	Oxford United	Home	League	3–0	1 Goal	(7)
11	25/03/95	Peterborough United	Away	League	1–1		
12	29/03/95	Bristol Rovers	Away	League	1–1		
13	01/04/95	Rotherham United	Home	League	2–1	1 Goal	(8)
14	04/04/95	Blackpool	Away	League	1–1		
15	11/04/95	Shrewsbury Town	Home	League	2–0		
16	19/04/95	Plymouth Argyle	Away	League	3–1		
17	23/04/95	Carlisle United	Wembley	AW Shield	1–0		
18	26/04/95	Brentford	Home	League	2–0	1 Goal	(9)

SEASON 1995–96

Football League Division One

19	26/11/95	Leicester City	Home	League	2–2		
20	29/11/95	Middlesbrough	Away	Lge Cup	0–0		
21	02/12/95	Southend United	Away	League	1–3		
22	09/12/95	Watford	Home	League	1–0	1 Goal	(10)
23	13/12/95	AC Cesena	Home	AI Cup	3–1		
24	16/12/95	Oldham Athletic	Away	League	0–4		
25	20/12/95	Middlesbrough	Home	Lge Cup	2–0	2 Goals	(12)
26	23/12/95	Tranmere Rovers	Home	League	1–0		
27	26/12/95	Sheffield United	Away	League	1–1	1 Goal	(13)
28	06/01/96	Wolverhampton Wanderers	Home	FA Cup	1–1		
29	10/01/96	Norwich City	Away	Lge Cup	1–1	1 Goal	(14)
Sub+1	14/01/96	Charlton Athletic	Home	League	3–4		
30	17/01/96	Wolverhampton Wanderers	Away	FA Cup	1–2		
31	20/01/96	Ipswich Town	Away	League	0–2		
32	24/01/96	Norwich City	Home	Lge Cup	2–1		
33	04/02/96	Norwich City	Away	League	1–1		
34	11/02/96	Leeds United	Home	Lge Cup	1–2	1 Goal	(15)
35	17/02/96	Stoke City	Away	League	0–1		
36	25/02/96	Leeds United	Away	Lge Cup	0–3		
37	27/02/96	Crystal Palace	Away	League	2–3		
Sub+2	20/03/96	West Bromwich Albion	Home	League	1–1		
38	23/03/96	Wolverhampton Wanderers	Away	League	2–3		
Sub+3	30/03/96	Grimsby Town	Away	League	1–2		
Sub+4	02/04/96	Portsmouth	Home	League	2–0		
Sub+5	10/04/96	Millwall	Away	League	0–2		
Sub+6	13/04/96	Luton Town	Home	League	4–0	1 Goal	(16)
Sub+7	16/04/96	Sunderland	Away	League	0–3		
Sub+8	20/04/96	Derby County	Away	League	1–1		

SEASON 1996–97

Football League Division One

Sub+9	07/12/96	Grimsby Town	Home	League	0–0		
39	04/01/97	Stevenage Borough	Away	FA Cup	2–0	1 Goal	(17)
Sub+10	18/01/97	Reading	Home	League	4–1		
Sub+11	25/01/97	Stockport County	Home	FA Cup	3–1	1 Goal	(18)
Sub+12	29/01/97	Queens Park Rangers	Away	League	1–1		
Sub+13	01/02/97	Bolton Wanderers	Away	League	1–2		
Sub+14	04/02/97	West Bromwich Albion	Home	League	2–3		
Sub+15	04/03/97	Wolverhampton Wanderers	Home	League	1–2		
40	08/03/97	Southend United	Home	League	2–1		
41	11/03/97	Manchester City	Home	League	2–0	1 Goal	(19)
42	16/03/97	West Bromwich Albion	Away	League	0–2		
Sub+16	22/03/97	Sheffield United	Home	League	1–1		
Sub+17	29/03/97	Crystal Palace	Away	League	1–0		
Sub+18	31/03/97	Charlton Athletic	Home	League	0–0		
Sub+19	05/04/97	Barnsley	Away	League	1–0		
Sub+20	08/04/97	Oldham Athletic	Away	League	2–2		
Sub+21	12/04/97	Huddersfield Town	Home	League	1–0		
Sub+22	15/04/97	Tranmere Rovers	Home	League	0–0		
Sub+23	19/04/97	Bradford City	Away	League	2–0		
43	26/04/97	Oxford United	Home	League	2–0		
Sub+24	04/05/97	Ipswich Town	Away	League	1–1		

APPEARANCES AND GOALS PER SEASON

SEASON 89–90	GAMES	GOALS
League	0+8	0
FA Cup	0+2	1
League Cup	1+2	0
Zenith Data Systems Cup	0+1	0
TOTAL	**1+13**	**1**

SEASON 90–91	GAMES	GOALS
League	11+4	5
FA Cup	1	0
TOTAL	**12+4**	**5**

SEASON 91–92	GAMES	GOALS
League	34+1	15
League Play–offs	3	1
FA Cup	2	1
League Cup	2	1
Autoglass Trophy	8	8
TOTAL	**49+1**	**26**

SEASON 92–93	GAMES	GOALS
League	41+1	28
FA Cup	3	2
League Cup	4	2
Autoglass Trophy	7	7
TOTAL	**55+1**	**39**

SEASON 93–94	GAMES	GOALS
League	45	28
League Play–offs	3	0
FA Cup	4	3
League Cup	2	1
Autoglass Trophy	4	2
TOTAL	**58**	**34**

SEASON 94–95	GAMES	GOALS
League	31+1	20
League Cup	3	1
Auto Windscreens Shield	3	1
TOTAL	**37+1**	**22**

SEASON 95–96	GAMES	GOALS
League	11+8	3
FA Cup	2	0
League Cup	6	4
Anglo–Italian Cup	1	0
TOTAL	**20+8**	**7**

SEASON 96–97	GAMES	GOALS
League	4+15	1
FA Cup	1+1	2
TOTAL	**5+16**	**3**

CAREER APPEARANCES AND GOALS

COMPETITION	GAMES	TOTAL	GOALS
League	177+38	215	100
League Play–offs	6	6	1
FA Cup	13+3	16	9
League Cup	18+2	20	9
Zenith Data Systems Cup	0+1	1	0
Autoglass Trophy	19	19	17
Auto Windscreens Shield	3	3	1
Anglo–Italian Cup	1	1	0
TOTAL	**237+44**	**281**	**137**

HAT–TRICKS

Stockport County

1	3	Carlisle United	14/01/92	Away	A Trophy	3–1
2	3	Hartlepool United	04/02/92	Home	A Trophy	3–0

| 3 | 3 | Plymouth Argyle | 27/03/93 | Away | League | 4–3 |
| 4 | 3 | Hartlepool United | 05/03/94 | Home | League | 5–0 |

League: 2
Autoglass Trophy: 2
TOTAL: 4

HONOURS

Winners medals
Football League Division One Championship: 94/95
Auto Windscreens Shield: 94/95

Runner–up medals
League Division Four Championship: 90/91
Autoglass Trophy: 91/92, 92/93

MARCO GABBIADINI

Born: 20/01/68 – Nottingham
Height: 5.10
Weight: 13.04 (96–97)

Clubs
York City: **1985–87** – Matches: **50+21** – Goals: **18**
Sunderland: **1987–91** – Matches: **183+2** – Goals: **87**
Crystal Palace: **1991–92** – Matches: **25** – Goals: **7**
Derby County: **1992–97** – Matches: **200+27** – Goals: **68**
Birmingham City (loan): **1996** – Matches: **0+2** – Goals: **0**
Oxford United (loan): **1997** – Matches: **5** – Goals: **1**

Country
England: Under 21, England B

SEASON 1984–85

York City – League Division Three

| Sub+1 | 29/03/85 | Bolton Wanderers | | Home | League | 0–3 | |

SEASON 1985–86

League Division Three

1	17/08/85	Plymouth Argyle	Home	League	3–1	1 Goal	(1)
Sub+2	20/08/85	Lincoln City	Home	Lge Cup	2–1		
Sub+3	26/08/85	Wigan Athletic	Home	League	4–1		
Sub+4	21/09/85	Bristol City	Home	League	1–1		
Sub+5	22/10/85	AFC Bournemouth	Home	League	2–1		
Sub+6	20/12/85	Bury	Home	League	0–0		
Sub+7	26/12/85	Doncaster Rovers	Home	League	0–1		
Sub+8	01/01/86	Walsall	Away	League	1–3		
2	14/01/86	Rotherham United	Home	FR Trophy	0–0		
3	28/01/86	Hartlepool United	Away	FR Trophy	2–3		
Sub+9	01/03/86	Gillingham	Home	League	2–0		
Sub+10	04/03/86	Bolton Wanderers	Away	League	1–1		
Sub+11	09/03/86	Darlington	Away	League	0–1		
4	12/03/86	Bristol Rovers	Home	League	4–0	1 Goal	(2)
5	15/03/86	Chesterfield	Home	League	2–0	1 Goal	(3)
6	18/03/86	Wigan Athletic	Away	League	0–1		
7	22/03/86	Rotherham United	Away	League	1–4	1 Goal	(4)
8	29/03/86	Walsall	Home	League	1–0		
9	31/03/86	Doncaster Rovers	Away	League	1–1		
10	05/04/86	Newport County	Home	League	3–1		
11	12/04/86	Reading	Away	League	0–0		
Sub+12	19/04/86	Lincoln City	Home	League	2–1		
Sub+13	22/04/86	Notts County	Home	League	2–2		
Sub+14	03/05/86	Swansea City	Home	League	3–1		
12	06/05/86	Blackpool	Home	League	3–0		

SEASON 1986-87

League Division Three

Sub+15	26/08/86	Sunderland	Away	Lge Cup	4–2		
Sub+16	02/09/86	Sunderland	Home	Lge Cup	1–3*		
13	06/09/86	Bristol Rovers	Home	League	1–0		
14	13/09/86	Port Vale	Away	League	3–2	1 Goal	(5)
15	16/09/86	Gillingham	Away	League	0–2		
16	20/09/86	Bury	Home	League	1–0		
17	23/09/86	Chelsea	Home	Lge Cup	1–0		
18	27/09/86	Doncaster Rovers	Away	League	1–3	1 Goal	(6)
19	30/09/86	AFC Bournemouth	Home	League	2–0		
20	04/10/86	Mansfield Town	Home	League	1–3		
21	08/10/86	Chelsea	Away	Lge Cup	0–3		
22	11/10/86	Bristol City	Away	League	0–3		
23	18/10/86	Brentford	Away	League	1–3		
Sub+17	21/10/86	Chester City	Home	League	1–1		
Sub+18	04/11/86	Newport County	Away	League	1–1		
Sub+19	08/11/86	Chesterfield	Home	League	1–1	1 Goal	(7)
Sub+20	22/11/86	Walsall	Home	League	1–5		
24	25/11/86	Darlington	Home	FR Trophy	4–1	3 Goals	(10)
25	29/11/86	Bolton Wanderers	Away	League	1–3	1 Goal	(11)
26	13/12/86	Notts County	Away	League	1–5		
27	20/12/86	Fulham	Home	League	1–1	1 Goal	(12)
28	26/12/86	Blackpool	Away	League	1–2	1 Goal	(13)
29	27/12/86	Wigan Athletic	Home	League	1–1		
30	23/01/87	Bristol Rovers	Away	League	0–1		
31	27/01/87	Mansfield Town	Home	FR Trophy	0–1		
32	07/02/87	Gillingham	Home	League	2–1	1 Goal	(14)
33	14/02/87	Bury	Away	League	0–1		
34	21/02/87	Doncaster Rovers	Home	League	1–1		
35	24/02/87	Darlington	Away	League	2–2	1 Goal	(15)
36	28/02/87	AFC Bournemouth	Away	League	0–3		
37	07/03/87	Rotherham United	Away	League	0–0		
38	14/03/87	Brentford	Home	League	2–1	1 Goal	(16)
39	18/03/87	Chester City	Away	League	1–2		
40	21/03/87	Bristol City	Home	League	1–1		
Sub+21	04/05/87	Wigan Athletic	Away	League	2–3		

SEASON 1987-88

League Division Three

41	15/08/87	Brighton & Hove Albion	Away	League	0–1		
42	18/08/87	Halifax Town	Away	Lge Cup	1–1	1 Goal	(17)
43	22/08/87	Notts County	Home	League	3–5		
44	25/08/87	Halifax Town	Home	Lge Cup	1–0		
45	29/08/87	Chester City	Away	League	0–1		
46	31/08/87	Walsall	Home	League	1–3		
47	05/09/87	Port Vale	Away	League	1–2		
48	12/09/87	Preston North End	Home	League	1–1		
49	16/09/87	Bristol Rovers	Away	League	1–2		
50	19/09/87	Gillingham	Away	League	1–3	1 Goal	(18)

Sunderland – League Division Three

1	26/09/87	Chester City	Home	League	0–2		
2	29/09/87	Fulham	Away	League	2–0	2 Goals	(2)
3	03/10/87	Aldershot	Home	League	3–1	2 Goals	(4)
4	10/10/87	Wigan Athletic	Home	League	4–1	2 Goals	(6)
5	17/10/87	Blackpool	Away	League	2–0		
6	20/10/87	Bristol City	Away	League	1–0		
7	24/10/87	York City	Home	League	4–2	1 Goal	(7)
8	31/10/87	Notts county	Away	League	1–2		
9	03/11/87	Southend United	Home	League	7–0	1 Goal	(8)
10	07/11/87	Grimsby Town	Home	League	1–1		
11	14/11/87	Darlington	Home	FA Cup	2–0		
12	28/11/87	Port Vale	Home	League	2–1		
13	05/12/87	Scunthorpe United	Away	FA Cup	1–2		
14	12/12/87	Northampton Town	Away	League	2–0	1 Goal	(9)
15	20/12/87	Rotherham United	Home	League	3–0		
16	26/12/87	Chester City	Away	League	2–1		
17	28/12/87	Preston North End	Home	League	1–1		
18	01/01/88	Doncaster Rovers	Home	League	3–1	1 Goal	(10)
19	02/01/88	Bury	Away	League	3–2		
20	16/01/88	Brighton & Hove Albion	Home	League	1–0		
21	19/01/88	Crewe Alexandra	Home	SV Trophy	1–0	1 Goal	(11)

22	30/01/88	Gillingham	Home	League	2–1	1 Goal	(12)
23	06/02/88	Walsall	Home	League	1–1		
24	09/02/88	Hartlepool United	Home	SV Trophy	0–1		
25	13/02/88	Preston North End	Away	League	2–2		
26	27/02/88	Aldershot	Away	League	2–3	1 Goal	(13)
27	01/03/88	Fulham	Home	League	2–0	1 Goal	(14)
28	05/03/88	Blackpool	Home	League	2–2		
29	12/03/88	Wigan Athletic	Away	League	2–2	1 Goal	(15)
30	19/03/88	Notts County	Home	League	1–1	1 Goal	(16)
31	26/03/88	York City	Away	League	1–2		
32	02/04/88	Grimsby Town	Away	League	1–0	1 Goal	(17)
33	04/04/88	Chesterfield	Home	League	3–2	1 Goal	(18)
34	09/04/88	Southend United	Away	League	4–1	1 Goal	(19)
35	23/04/88	Bristol City	Home	League	0–1		
36	26/04/88	Mansfield Town	Away	League	4–0	1 Goal	(20)
37	30/04/88	Port Vale	Away	League	1–0		
38	02/05/88	Northampton Town	Home	League	3–1		
39	07/05/88	Rotherham United	Away	League	4–1	2 Goals	(22)

SEASON 1988–89

League Division Two

40	27/08/88	AFC Bournemouth	Home	League	1–1		
41	30/08/88	York City	Away	Lge Cup	0–0		
42	03/09/88	Ipswich Town	Away	League	0–2		
43	06/09/88	York City	Home	Lge Cup	4–0	2 Goals	(24)
44	10/09/88	Bradford City	Home	League	0–0		
Sub+1	20/09/88	Crystal Palace	Home	League	1–1		
45	27/09/88	West Ham United	Home	Lge Cup	0–3		
46	01/10/88	Oldham Athletic	Home	League	3–2	1 Goal	(25)
47	04/10/88	Leeds United	Home	League	2–1	1 Goal	(26)
48	08/10/88	Walsall	Away	League	0–2		
49	12/10/88	West Ham United	Away	Lge Cup	1–2	1 Goal	(27)
50	15/10/88	Hull City	Away	League	0–0		
51	22/10/88	Swindon Town	Home	League	4–0	2 Goals	(29)
52	25/10/88	Blackburn Rovers	Home	League	2–0	1 Goal	(30)
53	29/10/88	Manchester City	Away	League	1–1		
54	02/11/88	Oxford United	Away	League	4–2	1 Goal	(31)
55	05/11/88	Stoke City	Home	League	1–1		
56	08/11/88	Charlton Athletic	Away	Simod Cup	1–0	1 Goal	(32)
57	12/11/88	Chelsea	Away	League	1–1	1 Goal	(33)
58	19/11/88	West Bromwich Albion	Home	League	1–1		
59	26/11/88	Brighton & Hove Albion	Away	League	0–3		
60	03/12/88	Watford	Home	League	1–1		
61	10/12/88	Leicester City	Away	League	1–3		
62	18/12/88	Plymouth Argyle	Away	League	4–1	1 Goal	(34)
63	22/12/88	Blackburn Rovers	Away	Simod Cup	1–2	1 Goal	(35)
64	26/12/88	Barnsley	Home	League	1–0		
65	31/12/88	Portsmouth	Home	League	4–0		
66	02/01/89	Bradford City	Away	League	0–1		
67	07/01/89	Oxford United	Home	FA Cup	1–1		
68	11/01/89	Oxford united	Away	FA Cup	0–2		
69	21/01/89	AFC Bournemouth	Away	League	1–0		
70	25/02/89	Hull City	Home	League	2–0	1 Goal	(36)
71	28/02/89	Blackburn Rovers	Away	League	2–2	2 Goals	(38)
72	11/03/89	Stoke City	Away	League	0–2		
73	14/03/89	Manchester City	Home	League	2–4	1 Goal	(39)
74	18/03/89	Crystal Palace	Away	League	0–1		
75	21/03/89	Chelsea	Home	League	1–2	1 Goal	(40)
76	25/03/89	Ipswich Town	Home	League	4–0	3 Goals	(43)
77	27/03/89	Barnsley	Away	League	0–3		
78	01/04/89	Birmingham City	Home	League	2–2	1 Goal	(44)
79	04/04/89	Plymouth Argyle	Home	League	2–1		
80	01/05/89	Watford	Away	League	1–0	1 Goal	(45)
81	06/05/89	West Bromwich Albion	Away	League	0–0		
82	13/05/89	Leicester City	Home	League	2–2		

SEASON 1989–90

League Division Two

83	19/08/89	Swindon Town	Away	League	2–0		
84	22/08/89	Ipswich Town	Home	League	2–4	1 Goal	(46)
85	27/08/89	Middlesbrough	Home	League	2–1		
86	02/09/89	West Bromwich Albion	Away	League	1–1	1 Goal	(47)
87	09/09/89	Watford	Home	League	4–0	3 Goals	(50)

88	16/09/89	Blackburn Rovers	Away	League	1–1		
89	24/09/89	Newcastle United	Home	League	0–0		
90	27/09/89	Leicester City	Away	League	3–2		
91	30/09/89	Sheffield United	Home	League	1–1		
92	03/10/89	Fulham	Away	Lge Cup	3–0	2 Goals	(52)
93	07/10/89	AFC Bournemouth	Home	League	3–2	1 Goal	(53)
94	14/10/89	Leeds United	Away	League	0–2		
95	18/10/89	West Ham United	Away	League	0–5		
96	21/10/89	Bradford City	Home	League	1–0		
97	24/10/89	AFC Bournemouth	Home	Lge Cup	1–1	1 Goal	(54)
98	28/10/89	Stoke City	Away	League	2–0	1 Goal	(55)
99	31/10/89	Barnsley	Home	League	4–2		
100	01/11/89	AFC Bournemouth	Away	Lge Cup	1–0	1 Goal	(56)
101	04/11/89	Oldham Athletic	Away	League	1–2		
102	11/11/89	Wolverhampton Wanderers	Home	League	1–1		
103	14/11/89	Port Vale	Home	ZDS Cup	1–2		
104	18/11/89	Plymouth Argyle	Home	League	3–1	1 Goal	(57)
105	25/11/89	Brighton & Hove Albion	Away	League	2–1	1 Goal	(58)
106	29/11/89	Exeter City	Away	Lge Cup	2–2		
107	02/12/89	Swindon Town	Home	League	2–2		
108	05/12/89	Exeter City	Home	Lge Cup	5–2		
109	09/12/89	Ipswich Town	Away	League	1–1		
110	16/12/89	Portsmouth	Away	League	3–3	1 Goal	(59)
111	26/12/89	Oxford United	Home	League	1–0	1 Goal	(60)
112	30/12/89	Port Vale	Home	League	2–2	1 Goal	(61)
113	01/01/90	Hull City	Away	League	2–3		
114	06/01/90	Reading	Away	FA Cup	1–2		
115	14/01/90	Middlesbrough	Away	League	0–3		
116	17/01/90	Coventry City	Home	Lge Cup	0–0		
117	20/01/90	West Bromwich Albion	Home	League	1–1	1 Goal	(62)
118	24/01/90	Coventry City	Away	Lge Cup	0–5		
119	04/02/90	Newcastle United	Away	League	1–1	1 Goal	(63)
120	10/02/90	Blackburn Rovers	Home	League	0–1		
121	17/02/90	Watford	Away	League	1–1		
122	24/02/90	Brighton & Hove Albion	Home	League	2–1		
123	03/03/90	Plymouth Argyle	Away	League	0–3		
124	10/03/90	Leicester City	Home	League	2–2	1 Goal	(64)
125	17/03/90	AFC Bournemouth	Away	League	1–0	1 Goal	(65)
126	20/03/90	Leeds United	Home	League	0–1		
127	24/03/90	West Ham United	Home	League	4–3	1 Goal	(66)
128	31/03/90	Bradford City	Away	League	1–0		
129	03/04/90	Sheffield United	Away	League	3–1	2 Goals	(68)
130	07/04/90	Stoke City	Home	League	2–1	1 Goal	(69)
131	10/04/90	Barnsley	Away	League	0–1		
132	14/04/90	Hull City	Home	League	0–1		
133	16/04/90	Oxford United	Away	League	1–0	1 Goal	(70)
134	21/04/90	Portsmouth	Home	League	2–2		
135	28/04/90	Wolverhampton Wanderers	Away	League	1–0		
136	01/05/90	Port Vale	Away	League	2–1		
137	05/05/90	Oldham Athletic	Home	League	2–3		
138	13/05/90	Newcastle United	Home	Lge P/O	0–0		
139	16/05/90	Newcastle United	Away	Lge P/O	2–0	1 Goal	(71)
140	28/05/90	Swindon Town	Wembley	Lge P/O	0–1		

SEASON 1990–91

League Division One

141	25/08/90	Norwich City	Away	League	2–3	1 Goal	(72)
142	28/08/90	Tottenham Hotspur	Home	League	0–0		
143	01/09/90	Manchester United	Home	League	2–1		
144	08/09/90	Chelsea	Away	League	2–3	1 Goal	(73)
145	15/09/90	Everton	Home	League	2–2	1 Goal	(74)
146	22/09/90	Wimbledon	Away	League	2–2		
147	25/09/90	Bristol City	Home	Lge Cup	0–1		
148	29/09/90	Liverpool	Home	League	0–1		
149	06/10/90	Aston Villa	Away	League	0–3		
150	09/10/90	Bristol City	Away	Lge Cup	6–1	2 Goals	(76)
151	20/10/90	Luton Town	Home	League	2–0	1 Goal	(77)
152	27/10/90	Arsenal	Away	League	0–1		
153	31/10/90	Derby County	Away	Lge Cup	0–6		
154	03/11/90	Manchester City	Home	League	1–1		
155	10/11/90	Coventry City	Home	League	0–0		
156	17/11/90	Nottingham Forest	Away	League	0–2		
157	24/11/90	Sheffield United	Away	League	2–0	2 Goals	(79)

158	01/12/90	Derby County	Home	League	1–2		
159	08/12/90	Tottenham Hotspur	Away	League	3–3		
160	15/12/90	Norwich City	Home	League	1–2		
161	23/12/90	Leeds United	Home	League	0–1		
162	26/12/90	Crystal Palace	Away	League	1–2		
163	12/01/91	Manchester United	Away	League	0–3		
164	19/01/91	Chelsea	Home	League	1–0		
165	22/01/91	Everton	Away	ZDS Cup	1–4		
166	02/02/91	Everton	Away	League	0–2		
167	16/02/91	Nottingham Forest	Home	League	1–0	1 Goal	(80)
168	23/02/91	Coventry City	Away	League	0–0		
169	02/03/91	Derby County	Away	League	3–3	1 Goal	(81)
170	09/03/91	Sheffield United	Home	League	0–1		
171	16/03/91	Liverpool	Away	League	1–2		
Sub+2	20/04/91	Luton Town	Away	League	2–1		
172	23/04/91	Wimbledon	Home	League	0–0		
173	04/05/91	Arsenal	Home	League	0–0		
174	11/05/91	Manchester City	Away	League	2–3	1 Goal	(82)

SEASON 1991–92

League Division Two

175	17/08/91	Derby County	Home	League	1–1		
176	20/08/91	Barnsley	Away	League	3–0		
177	24/08/91	Millwall	Away	League	1–4		
178	31/08/91	Oxford United	Home	League	2–0	1 Goal	(83)
179	03/09/91	Portsmouth	Away	League	0–1		
180	07/09/91	Blackburn Rovers	Home	League	1–1		
181	14/09/91	Swindon Town	Away	League	3–5	1 Goal	(84)
182	17/09/91	Charlton Athletic	Away	League	4–1	3 Goals	(87)
183	21/09/91	Grimsby Town	Home	League	1–2		

Crystal Palace – League Division One

1	01/10/91	Leeds United	Home	League	1–0		
2	05/10/91	Sheffield Wednesday	Away	League	1–4		
3	08/10/91	Hartlepool United	Home	Lge Cup	6–1	1 Goal	(1)
4	19/10/91	Coventry City	Away	League	2–1	1 Goal	(2)
5	22/10/91	Southend United	Home	ZDS Cup	4–0		
6	26/10/91	Chelsea	Home	League	0–0		
7	29/10/91	Birmingham City	Away	Lge Cup	1–1		
8	02/11/91	Liverpool	Away	League	2–1	1 Goal	(3)
9	16/11/91	Southampton	Home	League	1–0		
10	19/11/91	Birmingham City	Home	Lge Cup	1–1*		
11	23/11/91	Nottingham Forest	Away	League	1–5		
12	26/11/91	Queens Park Rangers	Away	ZDS Cup	3–2	1 Goal	(4)
13	30/11/91	Manchester United	Home	League	1–3		
14	03/12/91	Birmingham City	Home	Lge Cup	2–1		
15	07/12/91	Norwich City	Away	League	3–3		
16	10/12/91	Chelsea	Home	ZDS Cup	0–1		
17	17/12/91	Swindon Town	Away	Lge Cup	1–0		
18	22/12/91	Tottenham Hotspur	Home	League	1–2		
19	26/12/91	Wimbledon	Away	League	1–1	1 Goal	(5)
20	28/12/91	Sheffield United	Away	League	1–1	1 Goal	(6)
21	01/01/92	Notts County	Home	League	1–0	1 Goal	(7)
22	04/01/92	Leicester City	Away	FA Cup	0–1		
23	08/01/92	Nottingham Forest	Home	Lge Cup	1–1		
24	11/01/92	Manchester City	Home	League	1–1		
25	18/01/92	Leeds United	Away	League	1–1		

Derby County – League Division Two

1	01/02/92	Portsmouth	Away	League	1–0	1 Goal	(1)
2	08/02/92	Millwall	Home	League	0–2		
3	11/02/92	Blackburn Rovers	Away	League	0–2		
4	15/02/92	Bristol Rovers	Home	League	1–0		
5	22/02/92	Leicester City	Away	League	2–1		
6	29/02/92	Watford	Home	League	3–1		
7	07/03/92	Plymouth Argyle	Away	League	1–1		
8	11/03/92	Port Vale	Home	League	3–1	1 Goal	(2)
9	14/03/92	Tranmere Rovers	Away	League	3–4		
10	21/03/92	Wolverhampton Wanderers	Home	League	1–2		
11	24/03/92	Plymouth Argyle	Home	League	2–0		
12	28/03/92	Ipswich Town	Away	League	1–2		
13	01/04/92	Cambridge United	Home	League	0–0		
14	04/04/92	Barnsley	Away	League	3–0		

15	07/04/92	Grimsby Town	Away	League	1–0	1 Goal	(3)
16	11/04/92	Oxford United	Home	League	2–2		
17	15/04/92	Brighton & Hove Albion	Away	League	2–1	2 Goals	(5)
18	20/04/92	Newcastle United	Home	League	4–1		
19	25/04/92	Bristol City	Away	League	2–1	1 Goal	(6)
20	02/05/92	Swindon Town	Home	League	2–1		
21	10/05/92	Blackburn Rovers	Away	Lge P/O	2–4	1 Goal	(7)
22	13/05/92	Blackburn Rovers	Home	Lge P/O	2–1		

SEASON 1992–93

Football League Division One

23	15/08/92	Peterborough United	Away	League	0–1		
24	22/08/92	Newcastle United	Home	League	1–2		
Sub+1	29/08/92	Watford	Away	League	0–0		
Sub+2	02/09/92	Notts County	Home	AI Cup	4–2	1 Goal	(8)
25	06/09/92	Bristol City	Home	League	3–4		
26	12/09/92	Barnsley	Away	League	1–1		
27	20/09/92	West Ham United	Away	League	1–1		
28	23/09/92	Southend United	Away	Lge Cup	0–1		
29	26/09/92	Southend United	Home	League	2–0	1 Goal	(9)
30	29/09/92	Barnsley	Away	AI Cup	2–1		
31	03/10/92	Cambridge United	Away	League	3–1	1 Goal	(10)
32	07/10/92	Southend United	Home	Lge Cup	7–0	2 Goals	(12)
33	11/10/92	Oxford United	Home	League	0–1		
34	17/10/92	Luton Town	Away	League	3–1		
35	24/10/92	Charlton Athletic	Home	League	4–3	1 Goal	(13)
36	28/10/92	Arsenal	Home	Lge Cup	1–1		
37	31/10/92	Wolverhampton Wanderers	Away	League	2–0		
38	03/11/92	Notts County	Away	League	2–0		
39	07/11/92	Millwall	Home	League	1–2		
40	11/11/92	SC Pisa	Home	AI Cup	3–0		
41	14/11/92	Bristol Rovers	Away	League	2–1		
42	21/11/92	Sunderland	Home	League	0–1		
43	24/11/92	Cosenza Calcio	Away	AI Cup	3–0	1 Goal	(14)
44	28/11/92	Tranmere Rovers	Home	League	1–2		
45	01/12/92	Arsenal	Away	Lge Cup	1–2		
46	06/12/92	Swindon Town	Away	League	4–2		
47	08/12/92	US Cremonese	Home	AI Cup	1–3		
48	12/12/92	Birmingham City	Home	League	3–1		
49	16/12/92	AC Reggiana	Away	AI Cup	3–0	1 Goal	(15)
50	20/12/92	Grimsby Town	Away	League	2–0		
51	26/12/92	Brentford	Away	League	1–2		
52	28/12/92	Portsmouth	Home	League	2–4		
53	02/01/93	Stockport County	Home	FA Cup	2–1		
Sub+3	10/01/93	West Ham United	Home	League	0–2		
54	16/01/93	Southend United	Away	League	0–0		
55	23/01/93	Luton Town	Away	FA Cup	5–1	1 Goal	(16)
56	27/01/93	Brentford	Away	AI Cup	4–3	1 Goal	(17)
57	31/01/93	Newcastle United	Away	League	1–1		
58	03/02/93	Brentford	Home	AI Cup	1–2	1 Goal	(18)
59	06/02/93	Peterborough United	Home	League	2–3		
60	10/02/93	Barnsley	Home	League	3–0	1 Goal	(19)
61	13/02/93	Bolton Wanderers	Home	FA Cup	3–1		
62	20/02/93	Watford	Home	League	1–2		
63	24/02/93	Leicester City	Home	League	2–0	1 Goal	(20)
64	27/02/93	Oxford United	Away	League	1–0		
65	03/03/93	Cambridge United	Home	League	0–0		
66	08/03/93	Sheffield Wednesday	Home	FA Cup	3–3	1 Goal	(21)
67	10/03/93	Bristol Rovers	Home	League	3–1	1 Goal	(22)
68	13/03/93	Millwall	Away	League	0–1		
69	17/03/93	Sheffield Wednesday	Away	FA Cup	0–1		
70	21/03/93	Swindon Town	Home	League	2–1		
71	24/03/93	Sunderland	Away	League	0–1		
72	27/03/93	US Cremonese	Wembley	AI Cup	1–3	1 Goal	(23)
73	02/04/93	Tranmere Rovers	Away	League	1–2		
74	10/04/93	Brentford	Home	League	3–2	1 Goal	(24)
75	12/04/93	Portsmouth	Away	League	0–3		
76	17/04/93	Grimsby Town	Home	League	2–1		
77	20/04/93	Bristol City	Away	League	0–0		
78	24/04/93	Luton Town	Home	League	1–1		
79	01/05/93	Charlton Athletic	Away	League	1–2	1 Goal	(25)
80	05/05/93	Notts County	Home	League	2–0		
81	08/05/93	Wolverhampton Wanderers	Home	League	2–0	1 Goal	(26)

SEASON 1993–94

Football League Division One

82	14/08/93	Sunderland	Home	League	5–0	1 Goal	(27)
83	18/08/93	Nottingham Forest	Away	League	1–1		
84	21/08/93	Middlesbrough	Away	League	0–3		
85	28/08/93	Bristol City	Home	League	1–0	1 Goal	(28)
86	04/09/93	Birmingham City	Away	League	0–3		
87	08/09/93	Nottingham Forest	Home	AI Cup	3–2		
88	11/09/93	Peterborough United	Home	League	2–0	1 Goal	(29)
89	18/09/93	Millwall	Away	League	0–0		
90	22/09/93	Exeter City	Away	Lge Cup	3–1	1 Goal	(30)
91	25/09/93	Notts County	Away	League	1–4	1 Goal	(31)
92	03/10/93	West Bromwich Albion	Home	League	5–3		
93	06/10/93	Exeter City	Home	Lge Cup	2–0	1 Goal	(32)
94	09/10/93	Luton Town	Home	League	2–1		
95	16/10/93	Portsmouth	Away	League	2–3		
96	20/11/93	Grimsby Town	Home	League	2–1		
97	27/11/93	Southend United	Home	League	1–3		
98	05/12/93	Wolverhampton Wanderers	Away	League	2–2	2 Goals	(34)
99	18/12/93	Sunderland	Away	League	0–1		
100	27/12/93	Barnsley	Away	League	1–0		
101	28/12/93	Leicester City	Home	League	3–2	1 Goal	(35)
102	01/01/94	Stoke City	Away	League	1–2	1 Goal	(36)
103	03/01/94	Tranmere Rovers	Home	League	4–0	3 Goals	(39)
104	08/01/94	Oldham Athletic	Away	FA Cup	1–2		
105	15/01/94	Portsmouth	Home	League	1–0		
106	22/01/94	Luton Town	Away	League	1–2		
107	29/01/94	Watford	Home	League	1–2		
108	05/02/94	Crystal Palace	Away	League	1–1		
109	12/02/94	Bolton Wanderers	Home	League	2–0	1 Goal	(40)
110	19/02/94	Watford	Away	League	4–3	1 Goal	(41)
111	22/02/94	Middlesbrough	Home	League	0–1		
112	25/02/94	Birmingham City	Home	League	1–1		
113	05/03/94	Bristol City	Away	League	0–0		
114	12/03/94	Millwall	Home	League	0–0		
115	16/03/94	Peterborough United	Away	League	2–2		
116	26/03/94	West Bromwich Albion	Away	League	2–1		
117	29/03/94	Tranmere Rovers	Away	League	0–4		
Sub+4	05/04/94	Leicester City	Away	League	3–3		
Sub+5	16/04/94	Charlton Athletic	Home	League	2–0		
Sub+6	20/04/94	Notts County	Home	League	1–1		
Sub+7	23/04/94	Grimsby Town	Away	League	1–1		
118	27/04/94	Nottingham Forest	Home	League	0–2		
Sub+8	30/04/94	Oxford United	Home	League	2–1		
Sub+9	08/05/94	Southend United	Away	League	3–4		
119	15/05/94	Millwall	Home	Lge P/O	2–0		
120	19/05/94	Millwall	Away	Lge P/O	3–1	1 Goal	(42)
121	30/05/94	Leicester City	Wembley	Lge P/O	1–2		

SEASON 1994–95

Football League Division One

122	13/08/94	Barnsley	Away	League	1–2		
Sub+10	20/08/94	Luton Town	Home	League	0–0		
123	24/08/94	Ancona Calcio	Away	AI Cup	1–2		
124	06/09/94	AC Cesena	Home	AI Cup	6–1		
125	11/09/94	Swindon Town	Away	League	1–1		
126	13/09/94	Bristol City	Away	League	2–0		
127	17/09/94	Oldham Athletic	Home	League	2–1		
128	20/09/94	Reading	Away	Lge Cup	1–3	1 Goal	(43)
129	25/09/94	Stoke City	Home	League	3–0	1 Goal	(44)
130	28/09/94	Reading	Home	Lge Cup	2–0	1 Goal	(45)
131	26/10/94	Portsmouth	Away	Lge Cup	1–0		
132	29/10/94	Charlton Athletic	Home	League	2–2		
133	02/11/94	Reading	Home	League	1–2	1 Goal	(46)
134	06/11/94	Portsmouth	Away	League	1–0	1 Goal	(47)
135	12/11/94	Sheffield United	Away	League	1–2		
Sub+11	26/12/94	Tranmere Rovers	Away	League	1–3		
136	07/01/95	Everton	Away	FA Cup	0–1		
137	14/01/95	Charlton Athletic	Away	League	4–3	2 Goals	(49)
138	22/01/95	Portsmouth	Home	League	3–0		
139	04/02/95	Sheffield United	Home	League	2–3		
140	11/02/95	Reading	Away	League	0–1		
141	21/02/95	Port Vale	Away	League	0–1		

142	26/02/95	Bolton Wanderers	Home	League	2–1		
143	04/03/95	Stoke City	Away	League	0–0		
144	07/03/95	Grimsby Town	Away	League	1–0		
145	11/03/95	Millwall	Home	League	3–2	1 Goal	(50)
146	15/03/95	Burnley	Home	League	4–0	1 Goal	(51)
147	18/03/95	Middlesbrough	Away	League	4–2	1 Goal	(52)
148	22/03/95	Swindon Town	Home	League	3–1		
149	25/03/95	Oldham Athletic	Away	League	0–1		
150	01/04/95	Bristol City	Home	League	3–1	1 Goal	(53)
151	08/04/95	Sunderland	Home	League	0–1		
152	12/04/95	Wolverhampton Wanderers	Home	League	3–3	1 Goal	(54)
153	15/04/95	Burnley	Away	League	1–3		
154	17/04/95	Tranmere Rovers	Home	League	5–0	1 Goal	(55)
155	22/04/95	West Bromwich Albion	Away	League	0–0		
156	29/04/95	Southend United	Home	League	1–2		
157	07/05/95	Watford	Away	League	1–2		

SEASON 1995–96

Football League Division One

158	13/08/95	Port Vale	Home	League	0–0		
159	10/09/95	Leicester City	Home	League	0–1		
160	13/09/95	Southend United	Home	League	1–0		
161	16/09/95	Portsmouth	Away	League	2–2		
162	19/09/95	Shrewsbury Town	Away	Lge Cup	3–1	1 Goal	(56)
163	23/09/95	Barnsley	Away	League	0–2		
164	04/10/95	Shrewsbury Town	Home	Lge Cup	1–1		
165	07/10/95	Sheffield United	Away	League	2–0	1 Goal	(57)
166	14/10/95	Ipswich Town	Home	League	1–1	1 Goal	(58)
167	22/10/95	Stoke City	Away	League	1–1		
168	25/10/95	Leeds United	Home	Lge Cup	0–1		
169	28/10/95	Oldham Athletic	Home	League	2–1		
170	04/11/95	Tranmere Rovers	Away	League	1–5		
171	08/11/95	West Bromwich Albion	Home	League	3–0	2 Goals	(60)
172	18/11/95	Charlton Athletic	Home	League	2–0	1 Goal	(61)
173	21/11/95	Birmingham City	Away	League	4–1	1 Goal	(62)
174	25/11/95	Crystal Palace	Away	League	0–0		
175	02/12/95	Sheffield United	Home	League	4–2	1 Goal	(63)
176	09/12/95	Barnsley	Home	League	4–1	1 Goal	(64)
177	16/12/95	Millwall	Away	League	1–0		
178	23/12/95	Sunderland	Home	League	3–1	1 Goal	(65)
179	26/12/95	Huddersfield Town	Away	League	1–0		
180	01/01/96	Norwich City	Home	League	2–1	1 Goal	(66)
181	07/01/96	Leeds United	Home	FA Cup	2–4	1 Goal	(67)
182	20/01/96	Port Vale	Away	League	1–1		
183	03/02/96	Grimsby Town	Away	League	1–1		
184	10/02/96	Wolverhampton Wanderers	Home	League	0–0		
Sub+12	17/02/96	Southend United	Away	League	2–1		
Sub+13	21/02/96	Luton Town	Home	League	1–1		
Sub+14	24/02/96	Portsmouth	Home	League	3–2	1 Goal	(68)
Sub+15	28/02/96	Leicester City	Away	League	0–0		
Sub+16	02/03/96	Huddersfield Town	Home	League	3–2		
185	05/03/96	Watford	Away	League	0–0		
186	09/03/96	Sunderland	Away	League	0–3		
187	16/03/96	Watford	Home	League	1–1		
188	23/03/96	Norwich City	Away	League	0–1		
189	30/03/96	Stoke City	Home	League	3–1		
190	02/04/96	Ipswich Town	Away	League	0–1		
191	06/04/96	Oldham Athletic	Away	League	1–0		
192	08/04/96	Tranmere Rovers	Home	League	6–2		
193	14/04/96	Charlton Athletic	Away	League	0–0		
Sub+17	20/04/96	Birmingham City	Home	League	1–1		
194	28/04/96	Crystal Palace	Home	League	2–1		

SEASON 1996–97

Premier League

195	17/08/96	Leeds United	Home	League	3–3		
196	21/08/96	Tottenham Hotspur	Away	League	1–1		
Sub+18	24/08/96	Aston Villa	Away	League	0–2		
Sub+19	04/09/96	Manchester United	Home	League	1–1		
Sub+20	09/09/96	Blackburn Rovers	Away	League	2–1		
197	14/09/96	Sunderland	Home	League	1–0		
198	21/09/96	Sheffield Wednesday	Away	League	0–0		
199	25/09/96	Luton Town	Home	Lge Cup	2–2		

| Sub+21 | 28/09/96 | Wimbledon | Home | League | 0–2 |
| Sub+22 | 12/10/96 | Newcastle United | Home | League | 0–1 |

Birmingham City (loan) – Football League Division One

| Sub+1 | 15/10/96 | Ipswich Town | Home | League | 1–0 |
| Sub+2 | 18/10/96 | Oxford United | Away | League | 0–0 |

Derby County – Premier League

Sub+23	16/12/96	Everton	Home	League	0–1
Sub+24	21/12/96	Southampton	Away	League	1–3
Sub+25	26/12/96	Sunderland	Away	League	0–2
Sub+26	28/12/96	Blackburn Rovers	Home	League	0–0
200	29/01/97	Leeds United	Away	League	0–0

Oxford United (loan) – Football League Division One

1	02/02/97	Manchester City	Home	League	1–4		
2	07/02/97	Stoke City	Away	League	1–2		
3	15/02/97	Oldham Athletic	Home	League	3–1		
4	22/02/97	Ipswich Town	Away	League	1–2	1 Goal	(1)
5	01/03/97	Crystal Palace	Home	League	1–4		

Derby County – Premier League

| Sub+27 | 08/03/97 | Middlesbrough | Home | FA Cup | 0–2 |

APPEARANCES AND GOALS PER SEASON

SEASON 84–85	GAMES	GOALS
League	0+1	0
TOTAL	**0+1**	**0**

SEASON 85–86	GAMES	GOALS
League	10+12	4
League Cup	0+1	0
Freight Rover Trophy	2	0
TOTAL	**12+13**	**4**

SEASON 86–87	GAMES	GOALS
League	24+5	9
League Cup	2+2	0
Freight Rover Trophy	2	3
TOTAL	**28+7**	**12**

SEASON 87–88	GAMES	GOALS
League	43	22
FA Cup	2	0
League Cup	2	1
Sherpa Van Trophy	2	1
TOTAL	**49**	**24**

SEASON 88–89	GAMES	GOALS
League	35+1	18
FA Cup	2	0
League Cup	4	3
Simod Cup	2	2
TOTAL	**43+1**	**23**

SEASON 89–90	GAMES	GOALS
League	46	21
League Play–offs	3	1
FA Cup	1	0
League Cup	7	4
Zenith Data Systems Cup	1	0
TOTAL	**58**	**26**

SEASON 90–91	GAMES	GOALS
League	30+1	9
League Cup	3	2
Zenith Data Systems Cup	1	0
TOTAL	**34+1**	**11**

SEASON 91–92	GAMES	GOALS
League	44	16
League Play–offs	2	1
FA Cup	1	0
League Cup	6	1
Zenith Data Systems Cup	3	1
TOTAL	**56**	**19**

SEASON 92–93	GAMES	GOALS
League	42+2	9
FA Cup	5	2
League Cup	4	2
Anglo–Italian Cup	8+1	6
TOTAL	**59+3**	**19**

SEASON 93–94	GAMES	GOALS
League	33+6	13
League Play–offs	3	1
FA Cup	1	0
League Cup	2	2
Anglo–Italian Cup	1	0
TOTAL	**40+6**	**16**

SEASON 94–95	GAMES	GOALS
League	30+2	11
FA Cup	1	0
League Cup	3	2
Anglo–Italian Cup	2	0
TOTAL	**36+2**	**13**

SEASON 95–96	GAMES	GOALS
League	33+6	11
FA Cup	1	1
League Cup	3	1
TOTAL	**37+6**	**13**

SEASON 96–97	GAMES	GOALS
League	10+11	1
FA Cup	0+1	0
League Cup	1	0
TOTAL	**11+12**	**1**

CAREER APPEARANCES AND GOALS

COMPETITION	GAMES	TOTAL	GOALS
League	380+47	427	144
League Play–offs	8	8	3
FA Cup	14+1	15	3
League Cup	37+3	40	18
Freight Rover Trophy	4	4	3
Sherpa Van Trophy	2	2	1
Simod Cup	2	2	2
Zenith Data Systems Cup	5	5	1
Anglo–Italian Cup	11+1	12	6
TOTAL	**463+52**	**515**	**181**

HAT-TRICKS

York City

1	3	Darlington	25/11/86	Home	FR Trophy	4–1

Sunderland

1	3	Ipswich Town	25/03/89	Home	League	4–0
2	3	Watford	09/09/89	Home	League	4–0
3	3	Charlton Athletic	17/09/91	Away	League	4–1

Derby County

1	3	Tranmere Rovers	03/01/94	Home	League	4–0

League: 4
Freight Rover Trophy: 1
TOTAL: 5

HONOURS

Winners medals
League Division Three Championship: 87/88

Runner-up medals
Football League Division One Championship: 95/96
Anglo–Italian Cup: 92/93
Promoted to League Division One: 89/90*

* Promoted after Swindon Town were relegated due to financial irregularities.

SIMON GARNER

Born: 23/11/59 – Boston
Height: 5.9
Weight: 12.11 (95–96)

Clubs
Blackburn Rovers: **1978–92** – Matches: **528+37** – Goals: **192**
West Bromwich Albion: **1992–94** – Matches: **35+10** – Goals: **9**
Wycombe Wanderers: **1994–95** – Matches: **65+16** – Goals: **23**
Torquay United (loan): **1996** – Matches: **10+1** – Goals: **1**

SEASON 1978–79

Blackburn Rovers – League Division Two

1	29/08/78	Exeter City	Away	Lge Cup	1–2		
Sub+1	09/09/78	Newcastle United	Away	League	1–3		
2	16/09/78	Leicester City	Home	League	1–1		
3	23/09/78	Cardiff City	Away	League	0–2		
Sub+2	28/10/78	Wrexham	Home	League	1–1		
4	03/11/78	Fulham	Away	League	2–1	2 Goals	(2)
5	11/11/78	Crystal Palace	Away	League	0–3		
6	25/11/78	Stoke City	Home	League	2–2	1 Goal	(3)
7	09/12/78	Brighton & Hove Albion	Home	League	1–1		
8	30/12/78	West Ham United	Away	League	0–4		
9	10/01/79	Millwall	Away	FA Cup	2–1		
10	17/01/79	Sunderland	Home	League	1–1	1 Goal	(4)
11	20/01/79	Leicester City	Away	League	1–1	1 Goal	(5)
12	30/01/79	Liverpool	Away	FA Cup	0–1		
13	10/02/79	Charlton Athletic	Away	League	0–2		
14	24/02/79	Luton Town	Away	League	1–2	1 Goal	(6)
15	28/02/79	Cardiff City	Home	League	1–4	1 Goal	(7)
Sub+3	10/03/79	Wrexham	Away	League	1–2		
16	14/03/79	Oldham Athletic	Home	League	0–2		
Sub+4	04/04/79	Bristol Rovers	Home	League	0–2		
17	07/04/79	Sheffield United	Home	League	2–0		
18	14/04/79	Burnley	Home	League	1–2	1 Goal	(8)
19	16/04/79	Sunderland	Away	League	1–0		
Sub+5	21/04/79	Millwall	Home	League	1–1		
20	25/04/79	Newcastle United	Home	League	1–3		
21	28/04/79	Brighton & Hove Albion	Away	League	1–2		
22	05/05/79	West Ham United	Home	League	1–0		
23	09/05/79	Fulham	Home	League	2–1		

SEASON 1979–80

League Division Three

Sub+6	14/08/79	Bury	Home	Lge Cup	3–2		
Sub+7	29/08/79	Nottingham Forest	Home	Lge Cup	1–1		
24	05/09/79	Nottingham Forest	Away	Lge Cup	1–6		
25	08/09/79	Wimbledon	Away	League	0–1		
Sub+8	15/09/79	Southend United	Home	League	1–1		
26	02/10/79	Barnsley	Away	League	1–1		
Sub+9	27/10/79	Colchester United	Home	League	3–0		
Sub+10	03/11/79	Millwall	Away	League	0–1		
27	26/12/79	Mansfield Town	Home	League	0–0		
28	01/01/80	Sheffield United	Away	League	1–2		
29	08/01/80	Fulham	Home	FA Cup	1–1		
30	12/01/80	Grimsby Town	Away	League	2–1		
31	15/01/80	Fulham	Away	FA Cup	1–0		
32	19/01/80	Wimbledon	Home	League	3–0		
33	26/01/80	Coventry City	Home	FA Cup	1–0		
34	02/02/80	Southend United	Away	League	1–0		
35	05/02/80	Rotherham United	Away	League	3–1	2 Goals	(10)
36	09/02/80	Blackpool	Home	League	2–0		
37	16/02/80	Aston Villa	Home	FA Cup	1–1		
38	20/02/80	Aston Villa	Away	FA Cup	0–1		
39	23/02/80	Plymouth Argyle	Away	League	1–0	1 Goal	(11)
40	27/02/80	Exeter City	Home	League	1–1		

41	01/03/80	Brentford	Home	League	3–0		
42	08/03/80	Colchester United	Away	League	1–0		
43	14/03/80	Gillingham	Home	League	3–1		
44	22/03/80	Chesterfield	Away	League	1–0	1 Goal	(12)
45	29/03/80	Swindon Town	Home	League	2–0		
46	04/04/80	Hull City	Home	League	1–0		
47	05/04/80	Mansfield Town	Away	League	1–0		
48	07/04/80	Sheffield United	Home	League	1–0		
49	12/04/80	Exeter City	Away	League	0–2		
50	19/04/80	Reading	Home	League	4–2		
51	22/04/80	Sheffield Wednesday	Home	League	1–2		
52	26/04/80	Oxford United	Away	League	1–0	1 Goal	(13)
53	29/04/80	Bury	Away	League	2–1		
54	03/05/80	Bury	Home	League	1–2	1 Goal	(14)

SEASON 1980–81

League Division Two

55	09/08/80	Huddersfield Town	Home	Lge Cup	0–0		
56	12/08/80	Huddersfield Town	Away	Lge Cup	1–1	1 Goal	(15)
57	16/08/80	Cardiff City	Away	League	2–1		
58	20/08/80	Oldham Athletic	Home	League	1–0		
59	23/08/80	Orient	Away	League	1–1		
60	27/08/80	Gillingham	Home	Lge Cup	0–0		
61	30/08/80	Shrewsbury Town	Home	League	2–0	1 Goal	(16)
62	02/09/80	Gillingham	Away	Lge Cup	2–1*		
63	06/09/80	Derby County	Away	League	2–2	1 Goal	(17)
64	13/09/80	Luton Town	Home	League	3–0	2 Goals	(19)
65	20/09/80	Grimsby Town	Home	League	2–0	1 Goal	(20)
66	23/09/80	Birmingham City	Away	Lge Cup	0–1		
67	27/09/80	Wrexham	Away	League	1–0		
68	04/10/80	Queens Park Rangers	Home	League	2–1		
69	07/10/80	Sheffield Wednesday	Away	League	1–2		
70	11/10/80	West Ham United	Away	League	0–2		
71	18/10/80	Chelsea	Home	League	1–1		
72	22/10/80	Cambridge United	Home	League	2–0	1 Goal	(21)
73	25/10/80	Notts County	Away	League	0–2		
74	01/11/80	Swansea City	Home	League	0–0		
75	08/11/80	Bristol City	Away	League	0–2		
76	11/11/80	Oldham Athletic	Away	League	0–1		
77	15/11/80	Cardiff City	Home	League	2–3		
78	22/11/80	Watford	Away	League	1–1		
Sub+11	03/01/81	Notts County	Away	FA Cup	1–2		
79	10/01/81	Watford	Home	League	0–0		
80	17/01/81	Shrewsbury Town	Away	League	1–1		
81	31/01/81	Orient	Home	League	2–0		
82	07/02/81	Luton Town	Away	League	1–3		
Sub+12	14/02/81	Derby County	Home	League	1–0		
Sub+13	21/02/81	Wrexham	Home	League	1–1	1 Goal	(22)
83	28/02/81	Grimsby Town	Away	League	0–0		
84	21/03/81	Chelsea	Away	League	0–0		
85	28/03/81	Notts County	Home	League	0–0		
86	04/04/81	Swansea City	Away	League	0–2		
87	11/04/81	Bristol City	Home	League	1–0		
88	15/04/81	Newcastle United	Away	League	0–0		
89	18/04/81	Bolton Wanderers	Home	League	0–0		
90	21/04/81	Preston North End	Away	League	0–0		

SEASON 1981–82

League Division Two

91	23/09/81	Cambridge United	Home	League	1–0		
Sub+14	26/09/81	Leicester City	Home	League	0–2		
92	07/10/81	Sheffield Wednesday	Home	Lge Cup	1–1	1 Goal	(23)
93	10/10/81	Barnsley	Home	League	2–1	2 Goals	(25)
94	17/10/81	Derby County	Away	League	1–1		
95	24/10/81	Grimsby Town	Away	League	1–1	1 Goal	(26)
96	27/10/81	Sheffield Wednesday	Away	Lge Cup	2–1	1 Goal	(27)
97	31/10/81	Wrexham	Home	League	0–0		
98	07/11/81	Crystal Palace	Away	League	2–1	2 Goals	(29)
99	11/11/81	Nottingham Forest	Home	Lge Cup	0–1		
100	14/11/81	Luton Town	Home	League	0–1		
101	21/11/81	Watford	Away	League	2–3		
102	25/11/81	Shrewsbury Town	Home	League	0–0		
103	28/11/81	Norwich City	Home	League	3–0	2 Goals	(31)

104	05/12/81	Newcastle United	Away	League	0–0		
105	19/12/81	Chelsea	Away	League	1–1		
106	26/12/81	Oldham Athletic	Away	League	3–0	1 Goal	(32)
107	28/12/81	Bolton Wanderers	Away	League	2–2		
108	02/01/82	West Bromwich Albion	Away	FA Cup	2–3	2 Goals	(34)
109	13/01/82	Charlton Athletic	Home	League	0–2		
110	16/01/82	Sheffield Wednesday	Away	League	2–2		
111	23/01/82	Rotherham United	Home	League	2–0		
112	30/01/82	Cardiff City	Home	League	1–0	1 Goal	(35)
113	06/02/82	Orient	Away	League	0–0		
114	16/02/82	Queens Park Rangers	Home	League	2–1		
115	20/02/82	Leicester City	Away	League	0–1		
116	27/02/82	Barnsley	Away	League	1–0	1 Goal	(36)
117	06/03/82	Derby County	Home	League	4–1	1 Goal	(37)
118	13/03/82	Grimsby Town	Home	League	2–0	1 Goal	(38)
119	20/03/82	Wrexham	Away	League	0–1		
120	27/03/82	Crystal Palace	Home	League	1–0		
121	03/04/82	Luton Town	Away	League	0–2		
122	09/04/82	Oldham Athletic	Home	League	0–0		
123	12/04/82	Bolton Wanderers	Home	League	0–2		
124	17/04/82	Watford	Home	League	1–2		
125	24/04/82	Norwich City	Away	League	0–2		
126	01/05/82	Newcastle United	Home	League	4–1	1 Goal	(39)
127	04/05/82	Cambridge United	Away	League	0–1		
128	08/05/82	Rotherham United	Away	League	1–4		
129	15/05/82	Chelsea	Home	League	1–1	1 Goal	(40)

SEASON 1982–83

League Division Two

130	28/08/82	Wolverhampton Wanderers	Away	League	1–2	1 Goal	(41)
131	01/09/82	Newcastle United	Home	League	1–2		
132	04/09/82	Cambridge United	Home	League	3–1	2 Goals	(43)
133	07/09/82	Grimsby Town	Away	League	0–5		
134	11/09/82	Crystal Palace	Away	League	0–2		
135	18/09/82	Leicester City	Home	League	3–1	1 Goal	(44)
136	25/09/82	Derby County	Away	League	2–1	1 Goal	(45)
137	02/10/82	Sheffield Wednesday	Home	League	2–3	1 Goal	(46)
138	05/10/82	Brentford	Away	Lge Cup	2–3		
139	09/10/82	Fulham	Away	League	1–3		
140	16/10/82	Chelsea	Home	League	3–0	2 Goals	(48)
141	23/10/82	Leeds United	Home	League	0–0		
142	27/10/82	Brentford	Home	Lge Cup	0–0		
143	30/10/82	Charlton Athletic	Away	League	0–3		
144	06/11/82	Carlisle United	Home	League	3–2	2 Goals	(50)
145	13/11/82	Queens Park Rangers	Away	League	2–2		
146	20/11/82	Bolton Wanderers	Home	League	1–1		
Sub+15	04/12/82	Barnsley	Home	League	1–1		
147	11/12/82	Shrewsbury Town	Away	League	0–0		
148	18/12/82	Rotherham United	Home	League	3–0	1 Goal	(51)
149	27/12/82	Burnley	Away	League	1–0	1 Goal	(52)
150	29/12/82	Oldham Athletic	Home	League	2–2	2 Goals	(54)
151	01/01/83	Bolton Wanderers	Home	League	0–1		
152	03/01/83	Cambridge United	Away	League	0–2		
153	08/01/83	Liverpool	Home	FA Cup	1–2	1 Goal	(55)
154	15/01/83	Wolverhampton Wanderers	Home	League	2–2		
155	22/01/83	Leicester City	Away	League	1–0		
156	05/02/83	Grimsby Town	Home	League	2–1		
157	15/02/83	Sheffield Wednesday	Away	League	0–0		
158	19/02/83	Fulham	Home	League	0–0		
159	26/02/83	Chelsea	Away	League	0–2		
160	05/03/83	Leeds United	Away	League	1–2		
161	13/03/83	Charlton Athletic	Home	League	2–0		
162	19/03/83	Carlisle United	Away	League	1–3		
163	26/03/83	Queens Park Rangers	Home	League	1–3	1 Goal	(56)
164	01/04/83	Oldham Athletic	Away	League	0–0		
165	04/04/83	Burnley	Home	League	2–1	2 Goals	(58)
166	09/04/83	Newcastle United	Away	League	2–3		
167	16/04/83	Crystal Palace	Home	League	3–0	2 Goals	(60)
168	23/04/83	Barnsley	Away	League	2–2	1 Goal	(61)
169	30/04/83	Middlesbrough	Home	League	1–1		
170	02/05/83	Derby County	Home	League	2–0	1 Goal	(62)
171	07/05/83	Rotherham United	Away	League	1–3		
172	14/05/83	Shrewsbury Town	Home	League	1–0	1 Goal	(63)

SEASON 1983–84

League Division Two

173	27/08/83	Huddersfield Town	Home	League	2–2		
174	29/08/83	Cardiff City	Away	League	1–0		
175	03/09/83	Cambridge United	Away	League	0–2		
176	07/09/83	Chelsea	Home	League	0–0		
177	10/09/83	Derby County	Home	League	5–1	5 Goals	(68)
178	17/09/83	Manchester City	Away	League	0–6		
179	24/09/83	Brighton & Hove Albion	Home	League	2–2	1 Goal	(69)
180	01/10/83	Sheffield Wednesday	Away	League	2–4		
181	05/10/83	Ipswich Town	Away	Lge Cup	3–4	2 Goals	(71)
182	08/10/83	Middlesbrough	Away	League	2–1	1 Goal	(72)
183	16/10/83	Shrewsbury Town	Home	League	1–1	1 Goal	(73)
184	22/10/83	Oldham Athletic	Home	League	3–1		
185	26/10/83	Ipswich Town	Home	Lge Cup	1–2	1 Goal	(74)
186	29/10/83	Swansea City	Away	League	1–0	1 Goal	(75)
187	05/11/83	Charlton Athletic	Away	League	0–2		
188	12/11/83	Leeds United	Home	League	1–1		
189	19/11/83	Portsmouth	Home	League	2–1	1 Goal	(76)
190	26/11/83	Fulham	Away	League	1–0		
191	04/12/83	Grimsby Town	Home	League	1–1		
192	10/12/83	Cardiff City	Away	League	1–0		
193	17/12/83	Crystal Palace	Home	League	2–1	1 Goal	(77)
194	26/12/83	Newcastle United	Away	League	1–1		
195	28/12/83	Barnsley	Home	League	1–1	1 Goal	(78)
196	31/12/83	Cambridge United	Home	League	1–0		
197	02/01/84	Brighton & Hove Albion	Away	League	1–1	1 Goal	(79)
198	07/01/84	Chelsea	Home	FA Cup	1–0		
199	14/01/84	Huddersfield Town	Away	League	2–0		
200	21/01/84	Manchester City	Home	League	2–1		
201	28/01/84	Swindon Town	Away	FA Cup	2–1	1 Goal	(80)
202	04/02/84	Sheffield Wednesday	Home	League	0–0		
203	11/02/84	Derby County	Away	League	1–1		
204	17/02/84	Southampton	Away	FA Cup	0–1		
205	25/02/84	Oldham Athletic	Away	League	0–0		
206	07/03/84	Swansea City	Home	League	4–1		
207	10/03/84	Leeds United	Away	League	0–1		
208	16/03/84	Chelsea	Away	League	1–2	1 Goal	(81)
209	21/03/84	Charlton Athletic	Home	League	1–1		
210	24/03/84	Carlisle United	Home	League	4–1	1 Goal	(82)
211	30/03/84	Shrewsbury Town	Away	League	0–1		
212	07/04/84	Middlesbrough	Home	League	1–0		
213	14/04/84	Portsmouth	Away	League	4–2	3 Goals	(85)
214	20/04/84	Newcastle United	Home	League	1–1		
215	23/04/84	Barnsley	Away	League	0–0		
216	29/04/84	Fulham	Home	League	0–1		
217	05/05/84	Grimsby Town	Away	League	2–3	1 Goal	(86)
218	07/05/84	Cardiff City	Home	League	1–1		
219	12/05/84	Crystal Palace	Away	League	2–0		

SEASON 1984–85

League Division Two

220	25/08/84	Crystal Palace	Away	League	1–1		
221	01/09/84	Carlisle United	Home	League	4–0	1 Goal	(87)
222	04/09/84	Huddersfield Town	Away	League	1–1		
223	08/09/84	Fulham	Away	League	2–3		
224	15/09/84	Grimsby Town	Home	League	3–1	2 Goals	(89)
225	18/09/84	Cardiff City	Home	League	2–1		
226	22/09/84	Notts County	Away	League	3–0	1 Goal	(90)
227	25/09/84	Oxford United	Home	Lge Cup	1–1	1 Goal	(91)
228	29/09/84	Wimbledon	Home	League	2–0	1 Goal	(92)
229	06/10/84	Shrewsbury Town	Home	League	3–1	1 Goal	(93)
230	10/10/84	Oxford United	Away	Lge Cup	1–3*	1 Goal	(94)
231	13/10/84	Birmingham City	Away	League	2–0		
232	20/10/84	Oldham Athletic	Home	League	1–1		
233	27/10/84	Manchester City	Away	League	1–2		
234	03/11/84	Oxford United	Away	League	1–2	1 Goal	(95)
235	10/11/84	Brighton & Hove Albion	Home	League	2–0	1 Goal	(96)
236	17/11/84	Middlesbrough	Away	League	2–1		
237	24/11/84	Charlton Athletic	Home	League	3–0	1 Goal	(97)
238	01/12/84	Portsmouth	Away	League	2–2		
239	08/12/84	Sheffield United	Home	League	3–1		
240	26/12/84	Leeds United	Home	League	2–1		

241	29/12/84	Huddersfield Town	Home	League	1–3		
242	01/01/85	Barnsley	Away	League	1–1		
Sub+16	30/01/85	Oxford United	Away	FA Cup	1–0		
Sub+17	15/02/85	Manchester United	Home	FA Cup	0–2		
243	23/02/85	Oxford United	Home	League	1–1		
244	02/03/85	Manchester City	Home	League	0–1		
245	06/03/85	Brighton & Hove Albion	Away	League	1–3		
246	09/03/85	Oldham Athletic	Away	League	0–2		
247	16/03/85	Birmingham City	Home	League	2–1		
248	23/03/85	Shrewsbury Town	Away	League	0–3		
249	30/03/85	Notts County	Home	League	1–0	1 Goal	(98)
250	06/04/85	Leeds United	Away	League	0–0		
251	08/04/85	Barnsley	Home	League	0–0		
252	13/04/85	Cardiff City	Away	League	2–1	1 Goal	(99)
253	20/04/85	Middlesbrough	Home	League	3–0	1 Goal	(100)
254	23/04/85	Crystal Palace	Home	League	0–1		
255	27/04/85	Charlton Athletic	Away	League	0–1		
256	04/05/85	Portsmouth	Home	League	0–1		
257	06/05/85	Sheffield United	Away	League	3–1		
258	11/05/85	Wolverhampton Wanderers	Home	League	3–0		

SEASON 1985–86

League Division Two

259	17/08/85	Sunderland	Away	League	2–0		
260	20/08/85	Norwich City	Home	League	2–1	1 Goal	(101)
261	24/08/85	Shrewsbury Town	Home	League	1–1	1 Goal	(102)
262	26/08/85	Hull City	Away	League	2–2		
263	31/08/85	Carlisle United	Home	League	2–0	1 Goal	(103)
264	03/09/85	Huddersfield Town	Away	League	0–0		
265	07/09/85	Brighton & Hove Albion	Away	League	1–3		
266	14/09/85	Wimbledon	Home	League	2–0		
267	21/09/85	Fulham	Home	League	1–0		
268	24/09/85	Wimbledon	Away	Lge Cup	0–5		
269	28/09/85	Portsmouth	Away	League	0–3		
270	05/10/85	Bradford City	Home	League	3–0	1 Goal	(104)
271	08/10/85	Wimbledon	Home	Lge Cup	2–1		
272	12/10/85	Millwall	Away	League	1–0	1 Goal	(105)
273	19/10/85	Oldham Athletic	Home	League	0–0		
274	26/10/85	Crystal Palace	Away	League	0–2		
275	02/11/85	Middlesbrough	Away	League	0–0		
276	09/11/85	Barnsley	Home	League	0–3		
Sub+18	23/11/85	Charlton Athletic	Home	League	0–0		
277	30/11/85	Grimsby Town	Away	League	2–5		
278	14/12/85	Sunderland	Home	League	2–0	1 Goal	(106)
279	20/12/85	Shrewsbury Town	Away	League	0–2		
280	26/12/85	Leeds United	Home	League	2–0		
281	01/01/86	Stoke City	Away	League	2–2	1 Goal	(107)
282	04/01/86	Nottingham Forest	Home	FA Cup	1–1		
283	13/01/86	Nottingham Forest	Home	FA Cup	3–2		
284	18/01/86	Carlisle United	Away	League	1–2	1 Goal	(108)
285	25/01/86	Everton	Away	FA Cup	1–3		
286	01/02/86	Hull City	Home	League	2–2		
287	15/02/86	Crystal Palace	Home	League	1–2		
288	01/03/86	Portsmouth	Home	League	1–0	1 Goal	(109)
289	08/03/86	Bradford City	Away	League	2–3		
290	11/03/86	Fulham	Away	League	3–3	1 Goal	(110)
291	15/03/86	Millwall	Home	League	1–2		
292	18/03/86	Brighton & Hove Albion	Home	League	1–4		
Sub+19	29/03/86	Stoke City	Home	League	0–1		
293	31/03/86	Leeds United	Away	League	1–1		
294	05/04/86	Middlesbrough	Home	League	0–1		
295	12/04/86	Barnsley	Away	League	1–1		
296	15/04/86	Huddersfield Town	Home	League	0–1		
297	19/04/86	Sheffield United	Home	League	6–1	1 Goal	(111)
298	26/04/86	Charlton Athletic	Away	League	0–3		
299	05/05/86	Grimsby Town	Home	League	3–1	1 Goal	(112)

SEASON 1986–87

League Division Two

300	23/08/86	Leeds United	Home	League	2–1		
301	26/08/86	Wigan Athletic	Away	Lge Cup	3–1		
302	30/08/86	Shrewsbury Town	Away	League	1–0		
303	02/09/86	Wigan Athletic	Home	Lge Cup	2–0		

304	06/09/86	Sunderland	Home	League	6–1	4 Goals	(116)
305	13/09/86	Portsmouth	Away	League	0–1		
306	16/09/86	Huddersfield Town	Away	FM Cup	2–1*		
307	20/09/86	Crystal Palace	Home	League	0–2		
308	27/09/86	Millwall	Away	League	2–2		
309	23/09/86	Queens Park Rangers	Away	Lge Cup	1–2	1 Goal	(117)
310	30/09/86	Plymouth Argyle	Home	League	1–2		
311	04/10/86	Reading	Away	League	0–4		
312	07/10/86	Queens Park Rangers	Home	Lge Cup	2–2		
313	11/10/86	West Bromwich Albion	Home	League	0–1		
314	18/10/86	Stoke City	Away	League	0–1		
315	01/11/86	Barnsley	Away	League	1–1		
316	04/11/86	Sheffield United	Home	FM Cup	1–0	1 Goal	(118)
317	08/11/86	Sheffield United	Home	League	0–2		
318	15/11/86	York City	Home	League	0–2		
319	22/11/86	Brighton & Hove Albion	Away	League	2–0		
320	29/11/86	Ipswich Town	Home	League	0–0		
Sub+20	02/12/86	Grimsby Town	Away	League	0–1		
321	06/12/86	Birmingham City	Away	League	1–1		
322	21/12/86	Sunderland	Away	League	0–3		
323	26/12/86	Huddersfield Town	Home	League	1–2	1 Goal	(119)
324	27/12/86	Hull City	Away	League	0–0		
325	03/01/87	Portsmouth	Home	League	1–0		
326	10/01/87	Portsmouth	Away	FA Cup	0–2		
327	17/01/87	Grimsby Town	Home	League	2–2		
328	20/01/87	Oxford United	Home	FM Cup	4–3	1 Goal	(120)
329	24/01/87	Leeds United	Away	League	0–0		
330	31/01/87	Oldham Athletic	Home	League	1–0		
331	07/02/87	Shrewsbury Town	Home	League	2–1		
332	14/02/87	Plymouth Argyle	Away	League	1–1		
333	21/02/87	Millwall	Home	League	1–0		
334	28/02/87	Crystal Palace	Away	League	0–2		
335	03/03/87	Chelsea	Home	FM Cup	1–0	1 Goal	(121)
336	07/03/87	Bradford City	Away	League	0–2		
337	11/03/87	Ipswich Town	Home	FM Cup	3–0	1 Goal	(122)
338	18/03/87	Derby County	Away	League	2–3		
339	24/03/87	Bradford City	Home	League	2–1		
340	29/03/87	Charlton Athletic	Wembley	FM Cup	1–0		
341	04/04/87	Sheffield United	Away	League	1–4		
342	11/04/87	Barnsley	Home	League	4–2		
343	14/04/87	Reading	Home	League	0–0		
344	17/04/87	Derby County	Home	League	3–1	2 Goals	(124)
345	20/04/87	Huddersfield Town	Away	League	2–1	2 Goals	(126)
346	25/04/87	Brighton & Hove Albion	Home	League	1–1		
347	02/05/87	Ipswich Town	Away	League	1–3		
348	05/05/87	Birmingham City	Home	League	1–0	1 Goal	(127)
349	09/05/87	Oldham Athletic	Away	League	0–3		

SEASON 1987–88

League Division Two

350	15/08/87	Hull City	Away	League	2–2	1 Goal	(128)
351	18/08/87	Barnsley	Home	League	0–1		
352	22/08/87	West Bromwich Albion	Home	League	3–1	1 Goal	(129)
353	29/08/87	Sheffield United	Away	League	1–3	1 Goal	(130)
354	01/09/87	Ipswich Town	Home	League	1–0		
355	15/09/87	Birmingham City	Away	League	0–1		
356	19/09/87	Bradford City	Away	League	1–2		
357	23/09/87	Liverpool	Home	Lge Cup	1–1		
358	26/09/87	Middlesbrough	Home	League	0–2		
359	30/09/87	Aston Villa	Away	League	1–1		
360	03/10/87	Leeds United	Home	League	1–1	1 Goal	(131)
361	06/10/87	Liverpool	Away	Lge Cup	0–1		
362	10/10/87	AFC Bournemouth	Away	League	1–1		
363	17/10/87	Stoke City	Home	League	2–0	1 Goal	(132)
364	24/10/87	Plymouth Argyle	Home	League	1–1		
365	31/10/87	Leicester City	Away	League	2–1	1 Goal	(133)
366	07/11/87	Oldham Athletic	Home	League	1–0		
367	21/11/87	Crystal Palace	Home	League	2–0		
368	28/11/87	Reading	Away	League	0–0		
369	05/12/87	Millwall	Home	League	2–1		
370	12/12/87	West Bromwich Albion	Away	League	1–0		
371	19/12/87	Birmingham City	Home	League	2–0		
372	26/12/87	Middlesbrough	Away	League	1–1	1 Goal	(134)
373	28/12/87	Bradford City	Home	League	1–1		

374	01/01/88	Sheffield United	Home	League	4–1	1 Goal	(135)
375	02/01/88	Huddersfield Town	Away	League	2–1	1 Goal	(136)
376	09/01/88	Portsmouth	Home	FA Cup	1–2	1 Goal	(137)
377	30/01/88	Ipswich Town	Away	League	2–0		
378	06/02/88	Manchester City	Home	League	2–1	1 Goal	(138)
379	13/02/88	Barnsley	Away	League	1–0		
380	20/02/88	Aston Villa	Home	League	3–2	1 Goal	(139)
381	27/02/88	Leeds United	Away	League	2–2	1 Goal	(140)
382	05/03/88	Stoke City	Away	League	1–2		
383	12/03/88	AFC Bournemouth	Home	League	3–1		
384	19/03/88	Leicester City	Home	League	3–3		
385	26/03/88	Plymouth Argyle	Away	League	0–3		
386	01/04/88	Oldham Athletic	Away	League	2–4		
387	04/04/88	Shrewsbury Town	Home	League	2–2		
388	09/04/88	Swindon Town	Away	League	2–1		
389	25/04/88	Swindon Town	Home	League	0–0		
390	30/04/88	Crystal Palace	Away	League	0–2		
391	02/05/88	Reading	Home	League	1–1		
392	07/05/88	Millwall	Away	League	4–1	2 Goals	(142)
393	15/05/88	Chelsea	Home	Lge P/O	0–2		
394	18/05/88	Chelsea	Away	Lge P/O	1–4		

SEASON 1988–89

League Division Two

395	27/08/88	Chelsea	Away	League	2–1		
396	03/09/88	Oldham Athletic	Home	League	3–1	3 Goals	(145)
397	10/09/88	Stoke City	Away	League	1–0		
398	17/09/88	Swindon Town	Home	League	0–0		
399	20/09/88	Hull City	Away	League	3–1	2 Goals	(147)
400	24/09/88	Birmingham City	Home	League	3–0	2 Goals	(149)
401	27/09/88	Brentford	Home	Lge Cup	3–1	1 Goal	(150)
402	01/10/88	Manchester City	Away	League	0–1		
403	05/10/88	Bradford City	Away	League	1–1		
404	08/10/88	Crystal Palace	Home	League	5–4	2 Goals	(152)
405	12/10/88	Brentford	Away	Lge Cup	3–4	1 Goal	(153)
406	15/10/88	Barnsley	Home	League	2–1		
407	22/10/88	Oxford United	Away	League	1–1	1 Goal	(154)
408	25/10/88	Sunderland	Away	League	0–2		
409	29/10/88	West Bromwich Albion	Home	League	1–2		
410	01/11/88	Tottenham Hotspur	Away	Lge Cup	0–0		
411	05/11/88	Plymouth Argyle	Away	League	3–4	1 Goal	(155)
412	09/11/88	Tottenham Hotspur	Home	Lge Cup	1–2		
413	12/11/88	Brighton & Hove Albion	Home	League	2–1		
414	19/11/88	Walsall	Away	League	2–1		
415	22/11/88	Shrewsbury Town	Home	League	0–1		
416	26/11/88	Portsmouth	Home	League	3–1		
417	03/12/88	AFC Bournemouth	Away	League	1–2	1 Goal	(156)
418	10/12/88	Ipswich Town	Home	League	1–0		
419	13/12/88	Manchester City	Home	Simod Cup	3–2*		
420	17/12/88	Watford	Home	League	2–1		
421	26/12/88	Leeds United	Away	League	0–2		
422	31/12/88	Leicester City	Away	League	0–4		
423	02/01/89	Stoke City	Home	League	4–3		
424	07/01/89	Welling United	Away	FA Cup	1–0		
425	10/01/89	Ipswich Town	Away	Simod Cup	0–1		
426	14/01/89	Shrewsbury Town	Away	League	1–1		
427	21/01/89	Chelsea	Home	League	1–1		
428	28/01/89	Sheffield Wednesday	Home	FA Cup	2–1	1 Goal	(157)
429	04/02/89	Bradford City	Home	League	2–1		
430	11/02/89	Crystal Palace	Away	League	2–2		
431	18/02/89	Brentford	Home	FA Cup	0–2		
432	21/02/89	Oxford United	Home	League	3–1		
433	25/02/89	Barnsley	Away	League	1–0	1 Goal	(158)
434	28/02/89	Sunderland	Home	League	2–2		
435	04/03/89	Brighton & Hove Albion	Away	League	0–3		
Sub+21	11/03/89	Plymouth Argyle	Home	League	1–2		
436	15/03/89	West Bromwich Albion	Away	League	0–2		
437	18/03/89	Hull City	Home	League	4–0	1 Goal	(159)
438	24/03/89	Oldham Athletic	Away	League	1–1	1 Goal	(160)
439	04/04/89	Watford	Away	League	2–2		
440	08/04/89	Leicester City	Home	League	0–0		
441	15/04/89	Manchester City	Home	League	4–0	3 Goals	(163)
442	22/04/89	Birmingham City	Away	League	0–2		
443	29/04/89	Portsmouth	Away	League	2–1		

444	01/05/89	AFC Bournemouth	Home	League	2–0	1 Goal	(164)
445	06/05/89	Walsall	Home	League	3–0	1 Goal	(165)
446	13/05/89	Ipswich Town	Away	League	0–2		
447	21/05/89	Watford	Home	Lge P/O	0–0		
448	24/05/89	Watford	Away	Lge P/O	1–1*	1 Goal	(166)
449	31/05/89	Crystal Palace	Home	Lge P/O	3–1	1 Goal	(167)
450	03/06/89	Crystal Palace	Away	Lge P/O	0–3*		

SEASON 1989–90

League Division Two

451	19/08/89	Oldham Athletic	Home	League	1–0	1 Goal	(168)
452	23/08/89	Leicester City	Away	League	1–0		
453	26/08/89	Leeds United	Away	League	1–1		
454	02/09/89	Oxford United	Home	League	2–2		
455	09/09/89	Port Vale	Away	League	0–0		
456	23/09/89	AFC Bournemouth	Away	League	4–2		
457	27/09/89	West Bromwich Albion	Away	League	2–2	1 Goal	(169)
458	30/09/89	Barnsley	Home	League	5–0	3 Goals	(172)
459	03/10/89	Exeter City	Home	Lge Cup	2–1		
460	14/10/89	Portsmouth	Away	League	1–1		
461	18/10/89	Newcastle United	Away	League	1–2		
462	21/10/89	Watford	Home	League	2–2	1 Goal	(173)
463	28/10/89	Plymouth Argyle	Away	League	2–2		
464	31/10/89	Hull City	Home	League	0–0		
465	04/11/89	Brighton & Hove Albion	Away	League	2–1	1 Goal	(174)
466	07/11/89	Leeds United	Away	ZDS Cup	0–1		
467	11/11/89	Ipswich Town	Home	League	2–2		
468	18/11/89	Wolverhampton Wanderers	Away	League	2–1	1 Goal	(175)
469	25/11/89	West Ham United	Home	League	5–4	1 Goal	(176)
470	01/12/89	Oldham Athletic	Away	League	0–2		
471	09/12/89	Leicester City	Home	League	2–4	1 Goal	(177)
472	26/12/89	Swindon Town	Away	League	3–4	1 Goal	(178)
473	30/12/89	Sheffield United	Away	League	2–1	1 Goal	(179)
474	01/01/90	Bradford City	Home	League	2–2		
475	06/01/90	Aston Villa	Home	FA Cup	2–2		
476	10/01/90	Aston Villa	Away	FA Cup	1–3		
477	13/01/90	Leeds United	Home	League	1–2	1 Goal	(180)
478	20/01/90	Oxford United	Away	League	1–1		
Sub+22	03/02/90	AFC Bournemouth	Home	League	1–1		
479	10/02/90	Sunderland	Away	League	1–0		
480	17/02/90	Port Vale	Home	League	1–0	1 Goal	(181)
481	24/02/90	West Ham United	Away	League	1–1		
482	03/03/90	Wolverhampton Wanderers	Home	League	2–3	1 Goal	(182)
483	10/03/90	West Bromwich Albion	Home	League	2–1		
484	17/03/90	Middlesbrough	Away	League	3–0	1 Goal	(183)
485	20/03/90	Portsmouth	Home	League	2–0	1 Goal	(184)
486	24/03/90	Newcastle United	Home	League	2–0		
487	31/03/90	Watford	Away	League	1–3		
488	03/04/90	Barnsley	Away	League	0–0		
489	07/04/90	Plymouth Argyle	Home	League	2–0		
490	10/04/90	Hull City	Away	League	0–2		
491	14/04/90	Bradford City	Away	League	1–0		
492	16/04/90	Swindon Town	Home	League	2–1	1 Goal	(185)
493	21/04/90	Stoke City	Away	League	1–0		
494	28/04/90	Ipswich Town	Away	League	1–3		
495	01/05/90	Sheffield United	Home	League	0–0		
496	05/05/90	Brighton & Hove Albion	Home	League	1–1		
497	13/05/90	Swindon Town	Home	Lge P/O	1–2		
Sub+23	16/05/90	Swindon Town	Away	Lge P/O	1–2		

SEASON 1990–91

League Division Two

498	20/10/90	Plymouth Argyle	Home	League	0–0		
499	24/10/90	West Ham United	Away	League	0–1		
500	27/10/90	Wolverhampton Wanderers	Away	League	3–2		
501	31/10/90	Queens Park Rangers	Away	Lge Cup	1–2		
502	03/11/90	Millwall	Home	League	1–0		
Sub+24	01/12/90	Swindon Town	Away	League	1–1		
503	08/12/90	Hull City	Away	League	1–3		
504	05/01/91	Liverpool	Home	FA Cup	1–1	1 Goal	(186)
505	08/01/91	Liverpool	Away	FA Cup	0–3		
506	12/01/91	Newcastle United	Away	League	0–1		
507	19/01/91	Ipswich Town	Home	League	0–1		

508	26/01/91	Leicester City	Away	League	3–1	
509	09/02/91	Portsmouth	Home	League	1–1	
510	16/02/91	West Bromwich Albion	Home	League	0–3	
511	02/03/91	Swindon Town	Home	League	2–1	1 Goal (187)

SEASON 1991–92

League Division Two

Sub+25	17/08/91	Portsmouth	Home	League	1–1	
512	20/08/91	Hull City	Home	Lge Cup	1–1	
513	24/08/91	Bristol City	Away	League	0–1	
514	27/08/91	Hull City	Away	Lge Cup	0–1	
Sub+26	04/09/91	Derby County	Away	League	2–0	
Sub+27	14/09/91	Port Vale	Home	League	1–0	
Sub+28	17/09/91	Watford	Home	League	1–0	
Sub+29	21/09/91	Leicester City	Away	League	0–3	
515	28/09/91	Tranmere Rovers	Home	League	0–0	
516	01/10/91	Port Vale	Away	ZDS Cup	0–1	
517	05/10/91	Millwall	Away	League	3–1	1 Goal (188)
518	12/10/91	Plymouth Argyle	Home	League	5–2	2 Goals (190)
Sub+30	19/10/91	Swindon Town	Away	League	1–2	
519	26/10/91	Grimsby Town	Home	League	2–1	1 Goal (191)
520	02/11/91	Brighton & Hove Albion	Home	League	1–0	
Sub+31	05/11/91	Southend United	Away	League	0–3	
521	09/11/91	Charlton Athletic	Away	League	2–0	
Sub+32	16/11/91	Barnsley	Home	League	3–0	
522	30/11/91	Middlesbrough	Home	League	2–1	
523	07/12/91	Oxford United	Away	League	3–1	1 Goal (192)
524	14/12/91	Bristol Rovers	Home	League	3–0	
525	26/12/91	Wolverhampton Wanderers	Away	League	0–0	
Sub+33	04/01/92	Kettering Town	Home	FA Cup	4–1	
Sub+34	01/02/92	Swindon Town	Home	League	2–1	
Sub+35	04/02/92	Notts County	Away	FA Cup	1–2	
Sub+36	11/02/92	Derby County	Home	League	2–0	
526	22/02/92	Middlesbrough	Away	League	0–0	
527	25/02/92	Cambridge United	Away	League	1–2	
528	29/02/92	Oxford United	Home	League	1–1	
Sub+37	21/03/92	Charlton Athletic	Home	League	0–2	

SEASON 1992–93

West Bromwich Albion – Football League Division Two

1	15/08/92	Blackpool	Home	League	3–1	
2	19/08/92	Plymouth Argyle	Home	Lge Cup	1–0	
3	22/08/92	Huddersfield Town	Away	League	1–0	1 Goal (1)
4	25/08/92	Plymouth Argyle	Away	Lge Cup	0–2	
5	29/08/92	AFC Bournemouth	Home	League	2–1	
6	02/09/92	Stockport County	Home	League	3–0	2 Goals (3)
7	05/09/92	Fulham	Away	League	1–1	
8	09/09/92	Reading	Home	League	3–0	1 Goal (4)
9	15/09/92	Bolton Wanderers	Away	League	2–0	
10	19/09/92	Stoke City	Away	League	3–4	1 Goal (5)
11	26/09/92	Exeter City	Home	League	2–0	
12	03/10/92	Burnley	Away	League	1–2	1 Goal (6)
13	10/10/92	Port Vale	Home	League	0–1	
14	31/10/92	Hull City	Away	League	2–1	1 Goal (7)
15	14/11/92	Aylesbury United	Home	FA Cup	8–0	
16	21/11/92	Bradford City	Home	League	1–1	
17	28/11/92	Preston North End	Away	League	1–1	
18	06/12/92	Wycombe Wanderers	Away	FA Cup	2–2	
19	12/12/92	Swansea City	Away	League	0–0	
Sub+1	26/12/92	Chester City	Home	League	2–0	
Sub+2	28/12/92	Plymouth Argyle	Away	League	0–0	
20	02/01/93	West Ham United	Home	FA Cup	0–2	
21	06/03/93	Burnley	Home	League	2–0	1 Goal (8)
22	10/03/93	Brighton & Hove Albion	Away	League	1–3	
23	13/03/93	Leyton Orient	Home	League	2–0	
24	20/03/93	Hartlepool United	Away	League	2–2	
25	24/03/93	Preston North End	Home	League	3–2	
26	28/03/93	Bradford City	Away	League	2–2	
Sub+3	03/04/93	Brighton & Hove Albion	Home	League	3–1	
Sub+4	07/04/93	Swansea City	Home	League	3–0	
Sub+5	31/05/93	Port Vale	Wembley	Lge P/O	3–0	

SEASON 1993–94

Football League Division One

Sub+6	14/08/93	Barnsley	Away	League	1–1		
Sub+7	21/08/93	Oxford United	Home	League	3–1		
27	25/08/93	Bristol Rovers	Home	Lge Cup	0–0		
28	05/09/93	Wolverhampton Wanderers	Home	League	3–2		
29	08/09/93	Leicester City	Away	AI Cup	0–0		
30	11/09/93	Notts County	Away	League	0–1		
31	15/09/93	Peterborough United	Home	AI Cup	3–1		
32	12/10/93	Pescara Calcio	Home	AI Cup	1–2		
Sub+8	02/11/93	Tranmere Rovers	Away	League	0–3		
33	09/11/93	AC Padova	Home	AI Cup	3–4	1 Goal	(9)
Sub+9	21/11/93	Nottingham Forest	Home	League	0–2		
Sub+10	22/12/93	Cosenza Calcio	Away	AI Cup	1–2		
34	28/12/93	Birmingham City	Away	League	0–2		
35	01/01/94	Luton Town	Home	League	1–1		

Wycombe Wanderers – Football League Division Three

1	08/02/94	Fulham	Away	A Trophy	2–2+		
2	12/02/94	Mansfield Town	Away	League	0–3		
3	19/02/94	Wigan Athletic	Home	League	0–1		
Sub+1	25/02/94	Gillingham	Away	League	1–0		
4	01/03/94	Swansea City	Away	A Trophy	1–3	1 Goal	(1)
5	05/03/94	Bury	Home	League	2–1	1 Goal	(2)
6	12/03/94	Colchester United	Away	League	2–0		
Sub+2	04/04/94	Rochdale	Away	League	2–2	1 Goal	(3)
7	09/04/94	Walsall	Home	League	3–0	1 Goal	(4)
8	16/04/94	Scarborough	Away	League	1–3		
9	19/04/94	Rochdale	Home	League	1–1	1 Goal	(5)
10	23/04/94	Scunthorpe United	Home	League	2–2		
11	30/04/94	Crewe Alexandra	Away	League	1–2		
12	07/05/94	Preston North End	Home	League	1–1		
13	15/05/94	Carlisle United	Away	Lge P/O	2–0	1 Goal	(6)
14	18/05/94	Carlisle United	Home	Lge P/O	2–1	1 Goal	(7)
15	28/05/94	Preston North End	Wembley	Lge P/O	4–2	1 Goal	(8)

+ AET Wycombe Wanderers won 4–2 on penalties

SEASON 1994–95

Football League Division Two

16	13/08/94	Cambridge United	Home	League	3–0	1 Goal	(9)
17	17/08/94	Brighton & Hove Albion	Away	Lge Cup	1–2		
18	20/08/94	Huddersfield Town	Away	League	1–0	1 Goal	(10)
19	23/08/94	Brighton & Hove Albion	Home	Lge Cup	1–3		
20	27/08/94	Bristol Rovers	Home	League	0–0		
21	30/08/94	Birmingham City	Away	League	1–0		
22	03/09/94	Bradford City	Away	League	1–2		
23	10/09/94	Brentford	Home	League	4–3	2 Goals	(12)
24	13/09/94	Hull City	Home	League	1–2		
25	17/09/94	Crewe Alexandra	Away	League	2–1		
26	24/09/94	Stockport County	Away	League	1–4		
27	01/10/94	Swansea City	Home	League	1–0		
28	15/10/94	Plymouth Argyle	Away	League	2–2		
29	22/10/94	Peterborough United	Away	League	3–1	1 Goal	(13)
30	29/10/94	York City	Home	League	0–0		
31	01/11/94	Shrewsbury Town	Home	League	1–0		
32	05/11/94	Wrexham	Away	League	1–4		
33	12/11/94	Chelmsford City	Home	FA Cup	4–0		
34	19/11/94	Cardiff City	Home	League	3–1		
35	03/12/94	Hitchin Town	Away	FA Cup	5–0	3 Goals	(16)
36	10/12/94	Huddersfield Town	Home	League	2–1	1 Goal	(17)
37	16/12/94	Cambridge United	Away	League	2–2		
38	26/12/94	Brighton & Hove Albion	Home	League	0–0		
39	27/12/94	Oxford United	Away	League	2–0	1 Goal	(18)
40	31/12/94	AFC Bournemouth	Home	League	1–1		
41	07/01/95	West Ham United	Home	FA Cup	0–2		
42	14/01/95	Rotherham United	Away	League	0–2		
43	31/01/95	Chester City	Away	League	2–0		
44	04/02/95	Blackpool	Home	League	1–1		
45	11/02/95	Shrewsbury Town	Away	League	2–2		
46	18/02/95	Rotherham United	Home	League	2–0		
47	21/02/95	Cardiff City	Away	League	0–2		
48	25/02/95	Swansea City	Away	League	1–1		

49	11/03/95	Bristol Rovers	Away	League	0–1	
50	14/03/95	York City	Away	League	0–0	
51	18/03/95	Birmingham City	Home	League	0–3	
52	21/03/95	Brentford	Away	League	0–0	
53	25/03/95	Crewe Alexandra	Home	League	0–0	
54	28/03/95	Peterborough United	Home	League	3–1	2 Goals (20)
55	01/04/95	Hull City	Away	League	0–0	
Sub+3	04/04/95	Bradford City	Home	League	3–1	
Sub+4	08/04/95	AFC Bournemouth	Away	League	0–2	
Sub+5	15/04/95	Oxford United	Home	League	1–0	
Sub+6	19/04/95	Brighton & Hove Albion	Away	League	1–1	
Sub+7	22/04/95	Chester City	Home	League	3–2	
Sub+8	29/04/95	Plymouth Argyle	Home	League	1–2	

SEASON 1995–96

Football League Division Two

Sub+9	12/08/95	Crewe Alexandra	Home	League	1–1	
Sub+10	15/08/95	Leyton Orient	Home	Lge Cup	3–0	
Sub+11	22/08/95	Leyton Orient	Away	Lge Cup	0–2	
Sub+12	26/08/95	AFC Bournemouth	Home	League	1–2	
56	29/08/95	Brighton & Hove Albion	Away	League	2–1	
57	02/09/95	Bradford City	Away	League	4–0	
58	09/09/95	Peterborough United	Home	League	1–1	1 Goal (21)
Sub+13	28/10/95	Hull City	Home	League	2–2	
59	31/10/95	York City	Home	League	2–1	1 Goal (22)
60	04/11/95	Swansea City	Away	League	2–0	1 Goal (23)
61	07/11/95	Walsall	Away	AW Shield	0–5	
62	13/11/95	Gillingham	Home	FA Cup	1–1	
63	18/11/95	Bristol Rovers	Home	League	1–1	
Sub+14	21/11/95	Gillingham	Away	FA Cup	0–1	
64	26/11/95	Carlisle United	Away	League	2–4	
Sub+15	09/12/95	Wrexham	Away	League	0–1	
65	16/12/95	Bristol City	Home	League	1–1	
Sub+16	23/12/95	Shrewsbury Town	Home	League	2–0	

Torquay United (loan) – Football League Division Three

1	20/01/96	Leyton Orient	Home	League	2–1	
2	03/02/96	Fulham	Home	League	2–1	1 Goal (1)
3	06/02/96	Barnet	Home	League	1–1	
4	10/02/96	Gillingham	Away	League	0–2	
5	17/02/96	Hartlepool United	Home	League	0–0	
6	24/02/96	Wigan Athletic	Away	League	0–3	
7	27/02/96	Cardiff City	Home	League	0–0	
8	02/03/96	Exeter City	Home	League	0–2	
Sub+1	09/03/96	Darlington	Away	League	2–1	
9	12/03/96	Gillingham	Home	League	0–0	
10	16/03/96	Barnet	Away	League	0–4	

APPEARANCES AND GOALS PER SEASON

SEASON 78–79	GAMES	GOALS
League	20+5	8
FA Cup	2	0
League Cup	1	0
TOTAL	**23+5**	**8**

SEASON 79–80	GAMES	GOALS
League	25+3	6
FA Cup	5	0
League Cup	1+2	0
TOTAL	**31+5**	**6**

SEASON 80–81	GAMES	GOALS
League	31+2	7
FA Cup	0+1	0
League Cup	5	1
TOTAL	**36+3**	**8**

SEASON 81–82	GAMES	GOALS
League	35+1	14
FA Cup	1	2
League Cup	3	2
TOTAL	**39+1**	**18**

SEASON 82–83	**GAMES**	**GOALS**
League	40+1	22
FA Cup	1	1
League Cup	2	0
TOTAL	**43+1**	**23**

SEASON 83–84	**GAMES**	**GOALS**
League	42	19
FA Cup	3	1
League Cup	2	3
TOTAL	**47**	**23**

SEASON 84–85	**GAMES**	**GOALS**
League	37	12
FA Cup	0+2	0
League Cup	2	2
TOTAL	**39+2**	**14**

SEASON 85–86	**GAMES**	**GOALS**
League	36+2	12
FA Cup	3	0
League Cup	2	0
TOTAL	**41+2**	**12**

SEASON 86–87	**GAMES**	**GOALS**
League	39+1	10
FA Cup	1	0
League Cup	4	1
Full Members Cup	6	4
TOTAL	**50+1**	**15**

SEASON 87–88	**GAMES**	**GOALS**
League	40	14
League Play–offs	2	0
FA Cup	1	1
League Cup	2	0
TOTAL	**45**	**15**

SEASON 88–89	**GAMES**	**GOALS**
League	43+1	20
League Play–offs	4	2
FA Cup	3	1
League Cup	4	2
Simod Cup	2	0
TOTAL	**56+1**	**25**

SEASON 89–90	**GAMES**	**GOALS**
League	42+1	18
League Play–offs	1+1	0
FA Cup	2	0
League Cup	1	0
Zenith Data Systems Cup	1	0
TOTAL	**47+2**	**18**

SEASON 90–91	**GAMES**	**GOALS**
League	11+1	1
FA Cup	2	1
League Cup	1	0
TOTAL	**14+1**	**2**

SEASON 91–92	**GAMES**	**GOALS**
League	14+11	5
FA Cup	0+2	0
League Cup	2	0
Zenith Data Systems Cup	1	0
TOTAL	**17+13**	**5**

SEASON 92–93	**GAMES**	**GOALS**
League	21+4	8
League Play–offs	0+1	0
FA Cup	3	0
League Cup	2	0
TOTAL	**26+5**	**8**

SEASON 93–94	GAMES	GOALS
League	14+6	4
League Play–offs	3	3
League Cup	1	0
Autoglass Trophy	2	1
Anglo–Italian Cup	4+1	1
TOTAL	**24+7**	**9**

SEASON 94–95	GAMES	GOALS
League	35+6	9
FA Cup	3	3
League Cup	2	0
TOTAL	**40+6**	**12**

SEASON 95–96	GAMES	GOALS
League	18+6	4
FA Cup	1+1	0
League Cup	0+2	0
Auto Windscreens Shield	1	0
TOTAL	**20+9**	**4**

CAREER APPEARANCES AND GOALS

COMPETITION	GAMES	TOTAL	GOALS
League	543+51	594	193
League Play–offs	10+2	12	5
FA Cup	31+6	37	10
League Cup	37+4	41	11
Full Members Cup	6	6	4
Simod Cup	2	2	0
Zenith Data Systems Cup	2	2	0
Autoglass Trophy	2	2	1
Anglo–Italian Cup	4+1	5	1
Auto Windscreens Shield	1	1	0
TOTAL	**638+64**	**702**	**225**

HAT-TRICKS

Blackburn Rovers

1	5	Derby County	10/09/83	Home	League	5–1
2	3	Portsmouth	14/04/84	Away	League	4–2
3	4	Sunderland	06/09/86	Home	League	6–1
4	3	Oldham Athletic	03/09/88	Home	League	3–1
5	3	Manchester City	15/04/89	Home	League	4–0
6	3	Barnsley	30/09/89	Home	League	5–0

Wycombe Wanderers

1	3	Hitchin Town	03/12/94	Away	FA Cup	5–0

League: 6
FA Cup: 1
TOTAL: 7

HONOURS

Winners medals
Full Members Cup: 86/87

Runner-up medals
League Division Three Championship: 79/80
Promoted to the Premier League: 91/92
Promoted to Football League Division One: 92/93
Promoted to Football League Division Two: 93/94

MICK HARFORD

Born: 12/02/59 – Sunderland
Height: 6.2
Weight: 14.05 (96–97)

Clubs
Lincoln City: **1977–80** – Matches: **120+6** – Goals: **46**
Newcastle United: **1980–81** – Matches: **18+1** – Goals: **4**
Bristol City: **1981–82** – Matches: **40** – Goals: **14**
Birmingham City: **1982–84** – Matches: **109** – Goals: **33**
Luton Town: **1984–90** – Matches: **182+4** – Goals: **80**
Derby County: **1990–91** – Matches: **68** – Goals: **18**
Luton Town: **1991–92** – Matches: **31** – Goals: **12**
Chelsea: **1992–93** – Matches: **33+1** – Goals: **11**
Sunderland: **1993** – Matches: **10+1** – Goals: **2**
Coventry City: **1993** – Matches: **0+1** – Goals: **1**
Wimbledon: **1994–97** – Matches: **48+35** – Goals: **11**

Country
England: **1988** – Matches: **1+1** – Goals: **0**

SEASON 1977–78

Lincoln City – League Division Three

Sub+1	10/12/77	Gillingham	Home	League	0–2		
1	26/12/77	Colchester United	Away	League	1–1		
2	27/12/77	Tranmere Rovers	Home	League	1–1		
3	31/12/77	Chester	Away	League	2–2	1 Goal	(1)
4	02/01/78	Plymouth Argyle	Home	League	2–2		
5	14/01/78	Bury	Home	League	0–0		
6	21/01/78	Shrewsbury Town	Away	League	1–0		
7	28/01/78	Port Vale	Home	League	3–0	2 Goals	(3)
8	04/02/78	Peterborough United	Away	League	1–0		
9	07/02/78	Walsall	Away	League	1–3		
10	11/02/78	Portsmouth	Home	League	1–0		
11	24/02/78	Wrexham	Home	League	0–1		
12	01/03/78	Chesterfield	Away	League	0–0		
13	04/03/78	Swindon Town	Away	League	0–1		
14	08/03/78	Oxford United	Home	League	1–0		
Sub+2	11/03/78	Exeter City	Away	League	0–3		
15	13/03/78	Plymouth Argyle	Away	League	2–1		
16	18/03/78	Sheffield Wednesday	Home	League	3–1	1 Goal	(4)
17	24/03/78	Rotherham United	Home	League	3–3	2 Goals	(6)
18	25/03/78	Tranmere Rovers	Away	League	1–3		
19	27/03/78	Colchester United	Home	League	0–0		
20	05/04/78	Hereford United	Away	League	1–1		
21	08/04/78	Cambridge United	Home	League	4–1	2 Goals	(8)
22	15/04/78	Preston North End	Away	League	0–4		
23	22/04/78	Bradford City	Home	League	3–2		
24	26/04/78	Carlisle United	Home	League	2–1	1 Goal	(9)
25	29/04/78	Gillingham	Away	League	0–0		

SEASON 1978–79

League Division Three

26	12/08/78	Bradford City	Away	Lge Cup	0–2	
27	16/08/78	Bradford City	Home	Lge Cup	1–1	
28	19/08/78	Tranmere Rovers	Home	League	2–1	
29	22/08/78	Swansea City	Away	League	0–3	
30	26/08/78	Plymouth Argyle	Away	League	1–2	
31	02/09/78	Sheffield Wednesday	Home	League	1–2	
32	09/09/78	Rotherham United	Away	League	0–2	
33	16/09/78	Carlisle United	Home	League	1–1	
34	25/11/78	Blackpool	Away	FA Cup	1–2	
Sub+3	09/12/78	Oxford United	Home	League	2–2	
35	23/12/78	Chesterfield	Home	League	0–1	
36	26/12/78	Peterborough United	Away	League	1–0	
37	30/12/78	Exeter City	Away	League	2–3	
38	06/01/79	Watford	Away	League	0–2	

39	20/01/79	Carlisle United	Away	League	0–2		
40	23/01/79	Colchester United	Away	League	0–2		
41	03/03/79	Swindon Town	Away	League	0–6		
42	07/03/79	Chester	Away	League	1–5		
Sub+4	10/03/79	Southend United	Home	League	1–1		
Sub+5	13/03/79	Walsall	Away	League	1–4	1 Goal	(10)
43	21/03/79	Brentford	Home	League	1–0		
44	24/03/79	Swansea City	Home	League	2–1	1 Goal	(11)
45	26/03/79	Tranmere Rovers	Away	League	0–0		
46	31/03/79	Hull City	Away	League	0–0		
47	04/04/79	Rotherham United	Home	League	3–0		
48	07/04/79	Chester	Home	League	0–0		
49	14/04/79	Peterborough United	Home	League	0–1		
50	16/04/79	Bury	Away	League	2–2		
51	28/04/79	Oxford United	Away	League	1–2	1 Goal	(12)
52	02/05/79	Shrewsbury Town	Home	League	1–2	1 Goal	(13)
53	05/05/79	Hull City	Home	League	4–2	1 Goal	(14)
54	07/05/79	Blackpool	Home	League	1–2	1 Goal	(15)
55	09/05/79	Bury	Home	League	1–4		
56	11/05/79	Mansfield Town	Away	League	0–2		

SEASON 1979–80

League Division Four

57	11/08/79	Barnsley	Home	Lge Cup	2–1		
58	14/08/79	Barnsley	Away	Lge Cup	1–2*		
59	18/08/79	Peterborough United	Home	League	0–1		
60	22/08/79	Crewe Alexandra	Away	League	2–0	1 Goal	(16)
61	25/08/79	York City	Away	League	2–0		
62	01/09/79	Huddersfield Town	Home	League	2–0	2 Goals	(18)
63	08/09/79	Bradford City	Away	League	1–1		
64	15/09/79	Doncaster Rovers	Home	League	1–1		
65	18/09/79	Walsall	Away	League	0–3		
66	22/09/79	Tranmere Rovers	Home	League	3–0		
67	29/09/79	Newport County	Away	League	1–1	1 Goal	(19)
68	03/10/79	Walsall	Home	League	2–2		
69	06/10/79	Port Vale	Away	League	2–1	1 Goal	(20)
70	10/10/79	Crewe Alexandra	Home	League	3–0	1 Goal	(21)
71	13/10/79	Scunthorpe United	Home	League	4–0	1 Goal	(22)
72	20/10/79	Wigan Athletic	Away	League	1–2		
73	23/10/79	Aldershot	Away	League	0–2		
74	27/10/79	Stockport County	Home	League	1–0	1 Goal	(23)
75	03/11/79	Peterborough United	Away	League	1–3		
76	10/11/79	AFC Bournemouth	Home	League	1–1		
77	17/11/79	Portsmouth	Away	League	0–4		
78	24/11/79	Sheffield Wednesday	Away	FA Cup	0–3		
79	30/11/79	Hartlepool United	Home	League	3–3	1 Goal	(24)
80	08/12/79	Halifax Town	Away	League	0–1		
81	29/12/79	York City	Home	League	1–1		
82	12/01/80	Huddersfield Town	Away	League	2–3	1 Goal	(25)
83	26/01/80	Torquay United	Home	League	2–0		
84	30/01/80	Bradford City	Home	League	1–0		
85	02/02/80	Doncaster Rovers	Away	League	1–1	1 Goal	(26)
86	06/02/80	Hereford United	Home	League	2–0		
87	09/02/80	Tranmere Rovers	Away	League	0–1		
88	13/02/80	Northampton Town	Home	League	0–0		
89	16/02/80	Newport County	Home	League	2–1		
90	23/02/80	Scunthorpe United	Away	League	0–1		
91	29/02/80	Wigan Athletic	Home	League	4–0	3 Goals	(29)
92	04/03/80	Darlington	Away	League	1–1		
Sub+6	19/04/80	Hartlepool United	Away	League	0–0		
93	25/04/80	Halifax Town	Home	League	4–0	1 Goal	(30)
94	03/05/80	Torquay United	Away	League	5–2	1 Goal	(31)

SEASON 1980–81

League Division Four

95	09/08/80	Hull City	Home	Lge Cup	5–0	3 Goals	(34)
96	12/08/80	Hull City	Away	Lge Cup	2–0	2 Goals	(36)
97	16/08/80	Peterborough United	Home	League	1–1	1 Goal	(37)
98	20/08/80	Torquay United	Away	League	2–1	2 Goals	(39)
99	23/08/80	Wigan Athletic	Home	League	2–0		
100	27/08/80	Swindon Town	Home	Lge Cup	1–1		
101	30/08/80	Crewe Alexandra	Away	League	3–0		
102	02/09/80	Swindon Town	Away	Lge Cup	0–2		

103	06/09/80	Halifax town	Home	League	3–0		
104	13/09/80	Stockport County	Away	League	0–0		
105	17/09/80	Aldershot	Home	League	0–1		
106	20/09/80	Wimbledon	Away	League	1–0		
107	27/09/80	Scunthorpe United	Home	League	2–2	1 Goal	(40)
108	30/09/80	Aldershot	Away	League	0–0		
109	04/10/80	Doncaster Rovers	Away	League	1–0		
110	08/10/80	Rochdale	Home	League	3–0		
111	11/10/80	York City	Home	League	1–1		
112	22/10/80	Bradford City	Away	League	2–1	1 Goal	(41)
113	25/10/80	Northampton Town	Home	League	8–0	2 Goals	(43)
114	29/10/80	Tranmere Rovers	Home	League	2–0		
115	01/11/80	Hereford United	Away	League	2–0		
116	04/11/80	Rochdale	Away	League	0–1		
117	08/11/80	Southend United	Home	League	2–1		
118	12/11/80	Torquay United	Home	League	5–0	3 Goals	(46)
119	13/12/80	Bury	Away	FA Cup	0–2		
120	20/12/80	AFC Bournemouth	Home	League	2–0		

Newcastle United – League Division Two

1	26/12/80	Grimsby Town	Away	League	0–0		
2	27/12/80	Derby County	Home	League	0–2		
3	10/01/81	Wrexham	Away	League	0–0		
4	17/01/81	Luton Town	Away	League	1–0	1 Goal	(1)
Sub+1	07/02/81	Queens Park Rangers	Home	League	1–0		
5	21/02/81	Bristol Rovers	Home	League	0–0		
6	25/02/81	Cardiff City	Away	League	0–1		
7	28/02/81	Oldham Athletic	Away	League	0–0		
8	07/03/81	West Ham United	Away	League	0–1		
9	14/03/81	Preston North End	Home	League	2–0	2 Goals	(3)
10	21/03/81	Shrewsbury Town	Away	League	0–1		
11	28/03/81	Chelsea	Home	League	1–0		
12	04/04/81	Watford	Away	League	0–0		
13	11/04/81	Cambridge United	Home	League	2–1		
14	15/04/81	Blackburn Rovers	Home	League	0–0		
15	18/04/81	Derby County	Away	League	0–2		
16	20/04/81	Grimsby Town	Home	League	1–1		
17	25/04/81	Blackburn Rovers	Away	League	0–3		
18	02/05/81	Orient	Home	League	3–1	1 Goal	(4)

SEASON 1981–82

Bristol City – League Division Three

1	29/08/81	Carlisle United	Away	League	2–2	1 Goal	(1)
2	01/09/81	Walsall	Home	Lge Cup	2–0	1 Goal	(2)
3	05/09/81	Doncaster Rovers	Home	League	2–2	1 Goal	(3)
4	12/09/81	Fulham	Away	League	1–2		
5	15/09/81	Walsall	Away	Lge Cup	0–1		
6	19/09/81	Newport County	Home	League	2–1		
7	22/09/81	Plymouth Argyle	Home	League	3–2	1 Goal	(4)
8	26/09/81	Portsmouth	Away	League	0–2		
9	29/09/81	Gillingham	Away	League	1–1	1 Goal	(5)
10	03/10/81	Walsall	Home	League	0–1		
11	06/10/81	Carlisle United	Away	Lge Cup	0–0		
12	10/10/81	Preston North End	Home	League	0–0		
13	17/10/81	Oxford United	Away	League	0–1		
14	20/10/81	Reading	Home	League	2–0		
15	24/10/81	Lincoln City	Away	League	2–1	2 Goals	(7)
16	27/10/81	Carlisle United	Home	Lge Cup	2–1		
17	31/10/81	Chesterfield	Home	League	0–0		
18	03/11/81	Millwall	Away	League	0–2		
19	07/11/81	Brentford	Away	League	1–0	1 Goal	(8)
20	10/11/81	Queens Park Rangers	Away	Lge Cup	0–3		
21	14/11/81	Southend United	Home	League	0–2		
22	20/11/81	Torquay United	Home	FA Cup	0–0		
23	25/11/81	Torquay United	Away	FA Cup	2–1		
24	28/11/81	Burnley	Home	League	2–3		
25	05/12/81	Swindon Town	Away	League	0–0		
26	15/12/81	Northampton Town	Home	FA Cup	3–0	2 Goals	(10)
27	29/12/81	Bristol Rovers	Away	League	0–1		
28	02/01/82	Wimbledon	Home	League	1–3		
29	06/01/82	Peterborough United	Away	FA Cup	1–0		
30	16/01/82	Huddersfield Town	Home	League	0–0		
31	23/01/82	Aston Villa	Home	FA Cup	0–1		
32	30/01/82	Newport County	Away	League	1–1	1 Goal	(11)

33	06/02/82	Fulham	Home	League	0–0		
34	09/02/82	Plymouth Argyle	Away	League	1–2		
35	13/02/82	Walsall	Away	League	1–0		
36	20/02/82	Portsmouth	Home	League	0–1		
37	23/02/82	Exeter City	Home	League	3–2	2 Goals	(13)
38	27/02/82	Preston North End	Away	League	3–1	1 Goal	(14)
39	06/03/82	Oxford United	Home	League	0–2		
40	20/03/82	Chesterfield	Away	League	0–1		

Birmingham City – League Division One

1	27/03/82	Brighton & Hove Albion	Home	League	1–0	1 Goal	(1)
2	30/03/82	Liverpool	Away	League	1–3	1 Goal	(2)
3	06/04/82	Everton	Home	League	0–2		
4	10/04/82	Leeds United	Home	League	0–1		
5	17/04/82	Wolverhampton Wanderers	Away	League	1–1	1 Goal	(3)
6	24/04/82	Swansea City	Home	League	2–1	1 Goal	(4)
7	28/04/82	Tottenham Hotspur	Away	League	1–1	1 Goal	(5)
8	01/05/82	Notts County	Away	League	4–1	1 Goal	(6)
9	04/05/82	Arsenal	Home	League	0–1		
10	08/05/82	Liverpool	Home	League	0–1		
11	12/05/82	Leeds United	Away	League	3–3	2 Goals	(8)
12	15/05/82	Coventry City	Away	League	1–0	1 Goal	(9)

SEASON 1982–83

League Division One

13	28/08/82	Manchester United	Away	League	0–3		
14	31/08/82	Liverpool	Home	League	0–0		
15	04/09/82	Stoke City	Home	League	1–4		
16	08/09/82	Norwich City	Away	League	1–5		
17	11/09/82	West Ham United	Away	League	0–5		
18	18/12/82	Tottenham Hotspur	Away	League	1–2		
19	27/12/82	Aston Villa	Home	League	3–0		
20	29/12/82	Swansea City	Away	League	0–0		
21	01/01/83	Manchester City	Home	League	2–2		
22	03/01/83	Stoke City	Away	League	1–1		
23	08/01/83	Walsall	Away	FA Cup	0–0		
24	15/01/83	Manchester United	Home	League	1–2		
25	22/01/83	Liverpool	Away	League	0–1		
26	29/01/83	Crystal Palace	Away	FA Cup	0–1		
27	05/02/83	West Ham United	Home	League	3–0	1 Goal	(10)
28	26/02/83	Nottingham Forest	Home	League	1–1	1 Goal	(11)
29	05/03/83	Ipswich Town	Away	League	1–3		
30	15/03/83	Arsenal	Home	League	2–1		
31	19/03/83	West Bromwich Albion	Away	League	0–2		
32	22/03/83	Watford	Away	League	1–2		
33	26/03/83	Notts County	Home	League	3–0	1 Goal	(12)
34	02/04/83	Swansea City	Home	League	1–1		
35	04/04/83	Aston Villa	Away	League	0–1		
36	09/04/83	Norwich City	Home	League	0–4		
37	12/04/83	Luton Town	Away	League	1–3		
38	16/04/83	Coventry	Away	League	1–0		
39	23/04/83	Everton	Home	League	1–0		
40	30/04/83	Sunderland	Away	League	2–1	1 Goal	(13)
41	02/05/83	Brighton & Hove Albion	Home	League	1–1		
42	07/05/83	Tottenham Hotspur	Home	League	2–0	1 Goal	(14)
43	14/05/83	Southampton	Away	League	1–0	1 Goal	(15)

SEASON 1983–84

League Division One

44	27/08/83	West Ham United	Away	League	0–4		
45	30/08/83	Notts County	Away	League	1–2	1 Goal	(16)
46	03/09/83	Watford	Home	League	2–0		
47	06/09/83	Stoke City	Home	League	1–0		
48	10/09/83	Wolverhampton Wanderers	Away	League	1–1		
49	17/09/83	Ipswich Town	Home	League	1–0		
50	24/09/83	Everton	Away	League	1–1		
51	01/10/83	Leicester City	Home	League	2–1	1 Goal	(17)
52	05/10/83	Derby County	Away	Lge Cup	3–0		
53	15/10/83	Aston Villa	Away	League	0–1		
54	22/10/83	Tottenham Hotspur	Home	League	0–1		
55	25/10/83	Derby County	Home	Lge Cup	4–0	3 Goals	(20)
56	29/10/83	West Bromwich Albion	Away	League	2–1	1 Goal	(21)
57	05/11/83	Coventry City	Home	League	1–2		

58	19/11/83	Queens Park Rangers	Away	League	1–2	1 Goal	(22)
59	22/11/83	Notts County	Away	Lge Cup	0–0*		
60	26/11/83	Sunderland	Home	League	0–1		
61	29/11/83	Notts County	Home	Lge Cup	0–0*		
62	03/12/83	Liverpool	Away	League	0–1		
63	05/12/83	Notts County	Away	Lge Cup	3–1	1 Goal	(23)
64	10/12/83	Norwich City	Home	League	0–1		
65	17/12/83	Southampton	Away	League	1–2		
66	20/12/83	Liverpool	Home	Lge Cup	1–1	1 Goal	(24)
67	22/12/83	Liverpool	Away	Lge Cup	0–3		
68	26/12/83	Nottingham Forest	Home	League	1–2		
69	27/12/83	Arsenal	Away	League	1–1		
70	31/12/83	Watford	Away	League	0–1		
71	02/01/84	Everton	Home	League	0–2		
72	07/01/84	Sheffield United	Away	FA Cup	1–1		
73	10/01/84	Sheffield United	Home	FA Cup	2–0	1 Goal	(25)
74	14/01/84	West Ham United	Home	League	3–0	1 Goal	(26)
75	21/01/84	Ipswich Town	Away	League	2–1	1 Goal	(27)
76	28/01/84	Sunderland	Away	FA Cup	2–1	1 Goal	(28)
77	04/02/84	Leicester City	Away	League	3–2		
78	07/02/84	Manchester United	Home	League	2–2		
79	11/02/84	Wolverhampton Wanderers	Home	League	0–0		
80	18/02/84	West Ham United	Home	FA Cup	3–0		
81	25/02/84	Tottenham Hotspur	Away	League	1–0	1 Goal	(29)
82	28/02/84	West Bromwich Albion	Home	League	2–1		
83	03/03/84	Coventry City	Away	League	1–0		
84	10/03/84	Watford	Home	FA Cup	1–3		
85	17/03/84	Stoke City	Away	League	1–2		
86	20/03/84	Luton Town	Home	League	1–1		
87	24/03/84	Notts County	Home	League	0–0		
88	07/04/84	Manchester United	Away	League	0–1		
89	14/04/84	Queens Park Rangers	Home	League	0–2		
90	21/04/84	Nottingham Forest	Away	League	1–5	1 Goal	(30)
91	23/04/84	Arsenal	Home	League	1–1		
92	28/04/84	Sunderland	Away	League	1–2		
93	05/05/84	Liverpool	Home	League	0–0		
94	07/05/84	Norwich City	Away	League	1–1		

SEASON 1984–85

League Division Two

95	04/09/84	Fulham	Away	League	1–0		
96	08/09/84	Crystal Palace	Away	League	2–0		
97	15/09/84	Carlisle United	Home	League	2–0	1 Goal	(31)
98	18/09/84	Portsmouth	Home	League	0–1		
99	22/09/84	Wolverhampton Wanderers	Away	League	2–0		
100	25/09/84	Plymouth Argyle	Home	Lge Cup	4–1	1 Goal	(32)
101	29/09/84	Huddersfield Town	Home	League	1–0		
102	06/10/84	Brighton & Hove Albion	Away	League	0–2		
103	09/10/84	Plymouth Argyle	Away	Lge Cup	1–0		
104	13/10/84	Blackburn Rovers	Home	League	0–2		
105	20/10/84	Notts County	Away	League	3–1	1 Goal	(33)
106	27/10/84	Oxford United	Home	League	0–0		
107	30/10/84	West Bromwich Albion	Home	Lge Cup	0–0		
108	03/11/84	Shrewsbury Town	Home	League	0–0		
109	10/11/84	Manchester City	Away	League	0–1		

Luton Town – League Division One

1	15/12/84	Leicester City	Away	League	2–2	1 Goal	(1)
2	18/12/84	West Bromwich Albion	Home	League	1–2		
3	26/12/84	Coventry City	Home	League	2–0		
4	29/12/84	Liverpool	Away	League	0–1		
5	01/01/85	Everton	Away	League	1–2	1 Goal	(2)
6	05/01/85	Stoke City	Home	FA Cup	1–1		
7	09/01/85	Stoke City	Away	FA Cup	3–2	1 Goal	(3)
8	26/01/85	Huddersfield Town	Home	FA Cup	2–0		
9	02/02/85	Tottenham Hotspur	Home	League	2–2		
10	23/02/85	Newcastle United	Away	League	0–1		
11	02/03/85	Sunderland	Home	League	2–1	1 Goal	(4)
12	04/03/85	Watford	Home	FA Cup	0–0		
13	06/03/85	Watford	Away	FA Cup	2–2*		
14	09/03/85	Watford	Home	FA Cup	1–0		
15	13/03/85	Millwall	Home	FA Cup	1–0		
16	16/03/85	Sheffield Wednesday	Away	League	1–1	1 Goal	(5)
17	19/03/85	Watford	Away	League	0–3		

18	23/03/85	Queens Park Rangers	Home	League	2–0	2 Goals	(7)
19	30/03/85	Ipswich Town	Home	League	3–1	2 Goals	(9)
20	02/04/85	Southampton	Away	League	0–1		
21	08/04/85	Stoke City	Away	League	4–0	2 Goals	(11)
22	13/04/85	Everton	Neutral	FA Cup	1–2*		
23	21/04/85	Manchester United	Home	League	2–1	2 Goals	(13)
24	24/04/85	Nottingham Forest	Home	League	1–2		
25	04/05/85	Arsenal	Home	League	3–1	2 Goals	(15)
26	06/05/85	Aston Villa	Away	League	1–0		
27	08/05/85	Chelsea	Away	League	0–2		
28	11/05/85	Leicester City	Home	League	4–0	1 Goal	(16)
29	23/05/85	Coventry City	Away	League	0–1		
30	28/05/85	Everton	Home	League	2–0		

SEASON 1985–86

League Division One

31	17/08/85	Nottingham Forest	Home	League	1–1		
32	21/08/85	Newcastle United	Away	League	2–2	1 Goal	(17)
33	24/08/85	West Ham United	Away	League	1–0	1 Goal	(18)
34	27/08/85	Arsenal	Home	League	2–2		
35	31/08/85	Aston Villa	Away	League	1–3		
36	07/09/85	Chelsea	Home	League	1–1	1 Goal	(19)
37	14/09/85	Everton	Away	League	0–2		
38	21/09/85	Queens Park Rangers	Home	League	2–0	1 Goal	(20)
39	24/09/85	Sheffield United	Away	Lge Cup	2–0		
40	28/09/85	Sheffield Wednesday	Away	League	2–3	2 Goals	(22)
41	01/10/85	Ipswich Town	Home	League	1–0		
42	12/10/85	Oxford United	Away	League	1–1		
43	19/10/85	Southampton	Home	League	7–0		
44	26/10/85	Liverpool	Away	League	2–3	1 Goal	(23)
45	29/10/85	Norwich City	Home	Lge Cup	0–2		
46	02/11/85	Birmingham City	Home	League	2–0	1 Goal	(24)
47	09/11/85	Tottenham Hotspur	Away	League	3–1	1 Goal	(25)
48	16/11/85	Coventry City	Home	League	0–1		
49	23/11/85	Watford	Away	League	2–1		
50	30/11/85	Manchester City	Home	League	2–1		
51	07/12/85	Newcastle United	Home	League	2–0	1 Goal	(26)
52	14/12/85	Nottingham Forest	Away	League	0–2		
53	21/12/85	West Ham United	Home	League	0–0		
54	26/12/85	West Bromwich Albion	Away	League	2–1	1 Goal	(27)
55	28/12/85	Ipswich Town	Away	League	1–1		
56	01/01/86	Leicester City	Home	League	3–1	3 Goals	(30)
57	06/01/86	Crystal Palace	Away	FA Cup	2–1		
58	25/01/86	Bristol Rovers	Home	FA Cup	4–0	1 Goal	(31)
59	01/02/86	Arsenal	Away	League	1–2	1 Goal	(32)
60	08/02/86	Southampton	Away	League	2–1		
61	15/02/86	Arsenal	Home	FA Cup	2–2	1 Goal	(33)
62	22/02/86	Queens Park Rangers	Away	League	1–1		
63	01/03/86	Sheffield Wednesday	Home	League	1–0	1 Goal	(34)
64	03/03/86	Arsenal	Away	FA Cup	0–0		
65	05/03/86	Arsenal	Home	FA Cup	3–0		
66	08/03/86	Everton	Home	FA Cup	2–2	1 Goal	(35)
67	12/03/86	Everton	Away	FA Cup	0–1		
68	15/03/86	Oxford United	Home	League	1–2		
69	22/03/86	Everton	Home	League	2–1		
70	29/03/86	Leicester City	Away	League	0–0		
71	01/04/86	West Bromwich Albion	Home	League	3–0	1 Goal	(36)
72	06/04/86	Birmingham City	Away	League	2–0	2 Goals	(38)
73	12/04/86	Tottenham Hotspur	Home	League	1–1		
74	16/04/86	Liverpool	Home	League	0–1		
75	19/04/86	Coventry City	Away	League	0–1		
76	26/04/86	Watford	Home	League	3–2	3 Goals	(41)

SEASON 1986–87

League Division One

77	28/12/86	Nottingham Forest	Away	League	2–2		
78	01/01/87	Coventry City	Away	League	1–0		
79	03/01/87	Chelsea	Home	League	1–0		
80	11/01/87	Liverpool	Home	FA Cup	0–0		
81	24/01/87	Leicester City	Home	League	1–0		
82	26/01/87	Liverpool	Away	FA Cup	0–0*		
83	28/01/87	Liverpool	Home	FA Cup	3–0	1 Goal	(42)
84	31/01/87	Queens Park Rangers	Home	FA Cup	1–1	1 Goal	(43)

85	04/02/87	Queens Park Rangers	Away	FA Cup	1–2	1 Goal	(44)
86	07/02/87	Newcastle United	Away	League	2–2		
87	14/02/87	Aston Villa	Home	League	2–1	1 Goal	(45)
88	21/02/87	Manchester City	Away	League	1–1		
89	28/02/87	West Ham United	Home	League	2–1		
90	07/03/87	Liverpool	Away	League	0–2		
91	14/03/87	Manchester United	Home	League	2–1	1 Goal	(46)
92	21/03/87	Norwich City	Away	League	0–0		
93	24/03/87	Southampton	Away	League	0–3		
94	28/03/87	Tottenham Hotspur	Home	League	3–1	1 Goal	(47)
95	04/04/87	Wimbledon	Home	League	0–0		
96	18/04/87	Coventry City	Home	League	2–0		
97	21/04/87	Watford	Away	League	0–2		
98	25/04/87	Sheffield Wednesday	Home	League	0–0		
99	02/05/87	Charlton Athletic	Away	League	1–0	1 Goal	(48)

SEASON 1987–88

League Division One

100	15/08/87	Derby County	Away	League	0–1		
101	18/08/87	Coventry City	Home	League	0–1		
102	22/08/87	West Ham United	Home	League	2–2	2 Goals	(50)
103	05/09/87	Oxford United	Away	League	5–2	1 Goal	(51)
104	12/09/87	Everton	Home	League	2–1		
105	19/09/87	Charlton Athletic	Away	League	0–1		
106	22/09/87	Wigan Athletic	Away	Lge Cup	1–0		
107	26/09/87	Queens Park Rangers	Away	League	0–2		
108	03/10/87	Manchester United	Home	League	1–1	1 Goal	(52)
109	06/10/87	Wigan Athletic	Home	Lge Cup	4–2	3 Goals	(55)
110	10/10/87	Portsmouth	Away	League	1–3	1 Goal	(56)
111	17/10/87	Wimbledon	Home	League	2–0		
112	24/10/87	Liverpool	Home	League	0–1		
113	27/10/87	Coventry City	Home	Lge Cup	3–1+	2 Goals	(58)
Sub+1	18/12/87	Southampton	Home	League	2–2	1 Goal	(59)
114	26/12/87	Everton	Away	League	0–2		
115	28/12/87	Charlton Athletic	Home	League	1–0		
116	01/01/88	Chelsea	Home	League	3–0	1 Goal	(60)
117	02/01/88	West Ham United	Away	League	1–1		
118	19/01/88	Bradford City	Home	Lge Cup	2–0	1 Goal	(61)
119	30/01/88	Southampton	Home	FA Cup	2–1		
120	06/02/88	Oxford United	Home	League	7–4	2 Goals	(63)
121	10/02/88	Oxford United	Away	Lge Cup	1–1		
122	13/02/88	Arsenal	Away	League	1–2		
123	20/02/88	Queens Park Rangers	Away	FA Cup	1–1	1 Goal	(64)
124	24/02/88	Queens Park Rangers	Home	FA Cup	1–0		
125	28/02/88	Oxford United	Home	Lge Cup	2–0		
126	01/03/88	Stoke City	Away	Simod Cup	4–1	2 Goals	(66)
127	05/03/88	Wimbledon	Away	League	0–2		
128	08/03/88	Swindon Town	Home	Simod Cup	2–1		
129	12/03/88	Portsmouth	Home	FA Cup	3–1	1 Goal	(67)
130	15/03/88	Coventry City	Away	League	0–4		
131	27/03/88	Reading	Wembley	Simod Cup	1–4	1 Goal	(68)
132	02/04/88	Newcastle United	Away	League	0–4		
133	05/04/88	Sheffield Wednesday	Home	League	2–2		
134	09/04/88	Wimbledon	Neutral	FA Cup	1–2	1 Goal	(69)
135	12/04/88	Manchester United	Away	League	0–1		
136	19/04/88	Queens Park Rangers	Home	League	2–1		
137	24/04/88	Arsenal	Wembley	Lge Cup	3–2		
138	13/05/88	Nottingham Forest	Home	League	1–1		

+ Match played at Filbert Street, Leicester City

SEASON 1988–89

League Division One

139	27/08/88	Sheffield Wednesday	Away	League	0–1		
140	03/09/88	Wimbledon	Home	League	2–2		
141	10/09/88	Southampton	Away	League	1–2		
142	17/09/88	Manchester United	Home	League	0–2		
143	24/09/88	Everton	Away	League	2–0		
144	27/09/88	Burnley	Home	Lge Cup	1–1		
145	01/10/88	Nottingham Forest	Away	League	0–0		
146	08/10/88	Liverpool	Home	League	1–0	1 Goal	(70)
147	11/10/88	Burnley	Away	Lge Cup	1–0		
148	22/10/88	Middlesbrough	Away	League	1–2		

149	25/10/88	Arsenal	Home	League	1–1		
150	12/11/88	Coventry City	Away	League	0–1		
151	19/11/88	West Ham United	Home	League	4–1		
152	26/11/88	Norwich City	Away	League	2–2		
153	29/11/88	Manchester City	Home	Lge Cup	3–1		
154	10/12/88	Derby County	Away	League	1–0	1 Goal	(71)
155	17/12/88	Aston Villa	Home	League	1–1		
156	26/12/88	Tottenham Hotspur	Away	League	0–0		
157	31/12/88	Wimbledon	Away	League	0–4		
158	02/01/89	Southampton	Home	League	6–1	2 Goals	(73)
159	07/01/89	Millwall	Away	FA Cup	2–3		
160	10/01/89	Crystal Palace	Away	Simod Cup	1–4		
161	21/01/89	Everton	Home	League	1–0		
162	25/01/89	Southampton	Away	Lge Cup	2–1*	1 Goal	(74)
163	04/02/89	Nottingham Forest	Home	League	2–3	1 Goal	(75)
164	12/02/89	West Ham United	Away	Lge Cup	3–0	1 Goal	(76)
165	18/02/89	Middlesbrough	Home	League	1–0		
166	25/02/89	Arsenal	Away	League	0–2		
167	01/03/89	West Ham United	Home	Lge Cup	2–0	1 Goal	(77)
168	11/03/89	Millwall	Home	League	1–2		
169	14/03/89	Liverpool	Away	League	0–5		
170	18/03/89	Sheffield Wednesday	Home	League	0–1		
171	21/03/89	Queens Park Rangers	Away	League	1–1		
172	25/03/89	Manchester United	Away	League	0–2		
173	28/03/89	Tottenham Hotspur	Home	League	1–3		
174	01/04/89	Aston Villa	Away	League	1–2		
175	09/04/89	Nottingham Forest	Wembley	Lge Cup	1–3	1 Goal	(78)
176	22/04/89	Newcastle United	Away	League	0–0		
177	29/04/89	Derby County	Home	League	3–0	1 Goal	(79)
178	02/05/89	Charlton Athletic	Home	League	5–2	1 Goal	(80)
179	06/05/89	West Ham United	Away	League	0–1		
180	13/05/89	Norwich City	Home	League	1–0		

SEASON 1989–90

League Division One

Sub+2	26/12/89	Nottingham Forest	Home	League	1–1		
Sub+3	30/12/89	Chelsea	Home	League	0–3		
Sub+4	01/01/90	Everton	Away	League	1–2		
181	06/01/90	Brighton & Hove Albion	Away	FA Cup	1–4		
182	13/01/90	Liverpool	Away	League	2–2		

Derby County – League Division One

1	20/01/90	Nottingham Forest	Home	League	0–2		
2	24/01/90	West Ham United	Home	Lge Cup	0–0		
3	31/01/90	West Ham United	Away	Lge Cup	1–2		
4	10/02/90	Queens Park Rangers	Home	League	2–0		
5	24/02/90	Tottenham Hotspur	Home	League	2–1	1 Goal	(1)
6	03/03/90	Sheffield Wednesday	Away	League	0–1		
7	10/03/90	Southampton	Away	League	1–2		
8	17/03/90	Aston Villa	Home	League	0–1		
9	20/03/90	Crystal Palace	Away	League	1–1		
10	24/03/90	Arsenal	Home	League	1–3		
11	31/03/90	Chelsea	Away	League	1–1	1 Goal	(2)
12	07/04/90	Coventry City	Away	League	0–1		
13	14/04/90	Millwall	Home	League	2–0	2 Goals	(4)
14	16/04/90	Everton	Away	League	1–2		
15	21/04/90	Norwich City	Home	League	0–2		
16	28/04/90	Manchester City	Away	League	1–0		
17	01/05/90	Liverpool	Away	League	0–1		
18	05/05/90	Luton Town	Home	League	2–3		

SEASON 1990–91

League Division One

19	25/08/90	Chelsea	Away	League	1–2	
20	29/08/90	Sheffield United	Home	League	1–1	
21	01/09/90	Wimbledon	Home	League	1–1	
22	08/09/90	Tottenham Hotspur	Away	League	0–3	
23	15/09/90	Aston Villa	Home	League	0–2	
24	22/09/90	Norwich City	Away	League	1–2	
25	25/09/90	Carlisle United	Away	Lge Cup	1–1	
26	29/09/90	Crystal Palace	Home	League	0–2	
27	06/10/90	Liverpool	Away	League	0–2	
28	10/10/90	Carlisle United	Home	Lge Cup	1–0	

29	20/10/90	Manchester City	Home	League	1–1		
30	27/10/90	Southampton	Away	League	1–0	1 Goal	(5)
31	31/10/90	Sunderland	Home	Lge Cup	6–0	3 Goals	(8)
32	10/11/90	Manchester United	Home	League	0–0		
33	17/11/90	Leeds United	Away	League	0–3		
34	24/11/90	Nottingham Forest	Home	League	2–1		
35	28/11/90	Sheffield Wednesday	Home	Lge Cup	1–1		
36	01/12/90	Sunderland	Away	League	2–1	1 Goal	(9)
37	12/12/90	Sheffield Wednesday	Away	Lge Cup	1–2		
38	15/12/90	Chelsea	Home	League	4–6		
39	19/12/90	Coventry City	Home	ZDS Cup	1–0		
40	23/12/90	Queens Park Rangers	Home	League	1–1		
41	26/12/90	Arsenal	Away	League	0–3		
42	29/12/90	Everton	Away	League	0–2		
43	01/01/91	Coventry City	Home	League	1–1	1 Goal	(10)
44	05/01/91	Newcastle United	Away	FA Cup	0–2		
45	12/01/91	Wimbledon	Away	League	1–3	1 Goal	(11)
46	20/01/91	Tottenham Hotspur	Home	League	0–1		
47	22/01/91	Leeds United	Away	ZDS Cup	1–2		
48	26/01/91	Sheffield United	Away	League	0–1		
49	02/02/91	Aston Villa	Away	League	2–3	1 Goal	(12)
50	23/02/91	Norwich City	Home	League	0–0		
51	02/03/91	Sunderland	Home	League	3–3		
52	23/03/91	Liverpool	Home	League	1–7		
53	30/03/91	Arsenal	Home	League	0–2		
54	01/04/91	Queens Park Rangers	Away	League	1–1	1 Goal	(13)
55	10/04/91	Nottingham Forest	Away	League	0–1		
56	13/04/91	Coventry City	Away	League	0–3		
57	16/04/91	Manchester United	Away	League	1–3		
58	20/04/91	Manchester City	Away	League	1–2	1 Goal	(14)
59	23/04/91	Leeds United	Home	League	0–1		
60	04/05/91	Southampton	Home	League	6–2		
61	08/05/91	Everton	Home	League	2–3	1 Goal	(15)
62	11/05/91	Luton Town	Away	League	0–2		

SEASON 1991–92

League Division Two

63	17/08/91	Sunderland	Away	League	1–1	1 Goal	(16)
64	21/08/91	Middlesbrough	Home	League	2–0	1 Goal	(17)
65	24/08/91	Southend United	Home	League	1–2		
66	01/09/91	Charlton Athletic	Away	League	2–0	1 Goal	(18)
67	04/09/91	Blackburn Rovers	Home	League	0–2		
68	07/09/91	Barnsley	Home	League	1–1		

Luton Town – League Division One

1	14/09/91	Oldham Athletic	Home	League	2–1	2 Goals	(2)
2	17/09/91	Queens Park Rangers	Home	League	0–1		
3	21/09/91	Manchester United	Away	League	0–5		
4	28/09/91	Notts County	Home	League	1–1		
5	08/10/91	Birmingham City	Away	Lge Cup	2–3		
6	19/10/91	Sheffield Wednesday	Home	League	2–2	1 Goal	(3)
7	22/10/91	Ipswich Town	Away	ZDS Cup	1–1+		
8	02/11/91	Everton	Home	League	0–1		
9	16/11/91	Tottenham Hotspur	Away	League	1–4	1 Goal	(4)
10	23/11/91	Manchester City	Home	League	2–2	1 Goal	(5)
11	30/11/91	Sheffield United	Away	League	1–1		
12	07/12/91	Leeds United	Home	League	0–2		
13	20/12/91	Coventry City	Home	League	1–0	1 Goal	(6)
14	26/12/91	Arsenal	Home	League	1–0	1 Goal	(7)
15	28/12/91	Chelsea	Home	League	2–0		
16	01/01/92	Nottingham Forest	Away	League	1–1		
17	01/02/92	Sheffield Wednesday	Away	League	2–3		
18	08/02/92	Norwich City	Home	League	2–0	1 Goal	(8)
19	15/02/92	Manchester City	Away	League	0–4		
20	22/02/92	Sheffield United	Home	League	2–1	1 Goal	(9)
21	25/02/92	Crystal Palace	Away	League	1–1		
22	29/02/92	Leeds United	Away	League	0–2		
23	14/03/92	Everton	Away	League	1–1		
24	21/03/92	Southampton	Away	League	1–2		
25	04/04/92	Wimbledon	Home	League	2–1		
26	11/04/92	Oldham Athletic	Away	League	1–5	1 Goal	(10)
27	14/04/92	Nottingham Forest	Home	League	2–1	1 Goal	(11)
28	18/04/92	Manchester United	Home	League	1–1	1 Goal	(12)
29	20/04/92	Queens Park Rangers	Away	League	1–2		

| 30 | 25/04/92 | Aston Villa | Home | League | 2–0 | | |
| 31 | 02/05/92 | Notts County | Away | League | 1–2 | | |

+ AET Ipswich Town won 2–1 on penalties

SEASON 1992–93

Chelsea – Premier League

1	15/08/92	Oldham Athletic	Home	League	1–1	1 Goal	(1)
2	19/08/92	Norwich City	Away	League	1–2		
3	22/08/92	Sheffield Wednesday	Away	League	3–3		
4	26/08/92	Blackburn Rovers	Home	League	0–0		
5	29/08/92	Queens Park Rangers	Home	League	1–0	1 Goal	(2)
6	02/09/92	Aston Villa	Away	League	3–1		
7	05/09/92	Liverpool	Away	League	1–2	1 Goal	(3)
8	12/09/92	Norwich City	Home	League	2–3	1 Goal	(4)
9	20/09/92	Manchester City	Away	League	1–0	1 Goal	(5)
10	23/09/92	Walsall	Away	Lge Cup	3–0		
11	26/09/92	Nottingham Forest	Home	League	0–0		
12	03/10/92	Arsenal	Away	League	1–2		
13	07/10/92	Walsall	Home	Lge Cup	1–0		
14	17/10/92	Ipswich Town	Home	League	2–1	1 Goal	(6)
15	24/10/92	Coventry City	Away	League	2–1	1 Goal	(7)
16	28/10/92	Newcastle United	Home	Lge Cup	2–0	1 Goal	(8)
17	31/10/92	Sheffield United	Home	League	1–2		
18	07/11/92	Crystal Palace	Home	League	3–1	1 Goal	(9)
19	21/11/92	Everton	Away	League	1–0		
20	29/11/92	Leeds United	Home	League	1–0		
21	02/12/92	Everton	Away	Lge Cup	2–2	1 Goal	(10)
Sub+1	19/12/92	Manchester United	Home	League	1–1		
22	06/01/93	Crystal Palace	Away	Lge Cup	1–3		
23	09/01/93	Manchester City	Home	League	2–4		
24	13/01/93	Middlesbrough	Away	FA Cup	1–2		
25	16/01/93	Nottingham Forest	Away	League	0–3		
26	27/01/93	Queens Park Rangers	Away	League	1–1		
27	30/01/93	Sheffield Wednesday	Home	League	0–2		
28	06/02/93	Oldham Athletic	Away	League	1–3	1 Goal	(11)
29	10/02/93	Liverpool	Home	League	0–0		
30	13/02/93	Aston Villa	Home	League	0–1		
31	21/02/93	Blackburn Rovers	Away	League	0–2		
32	01/03/93	Arsenal	Home	League	1–0		
33	10/03/93	Everton	Home	League	2–1		

Sunderland – Football League Division One

1	21/03/93	Barnsley	Away	League	0–2		
2	24/03/93	Derby County	Home	League	1–0		
3	27/03/93	Wolverhampton Wanderers	Away	League	1–2	1 Goal	(1)
4	03/04/93	Southend United	Home	League	2–4	1 Goal	(2)
5	06/04/93	Brentford	Away	League	1–1		
6	10/04/93	Birmingham City	Home	League	1–2		
7	12/04/93	Grimsby Town	Away	League	0–1		
8	17/04/93	Luton Town	Home	League	2–2		
9	25/04/93	Newcastle United	Away	League	0–1		
Sub+1	04/05/93	Tranmere Rovers	Away	League	1–2		
10	08/05/93	Notts County	Away	League	1–3		

SEASON 1993–94

Coventry City – Premier League

| Sub+1 | 18/08/93 | Newcastle United | Home | League | 2–1 | 1 Goal | (1) |

SEASON 1994–95

Wimbledon – Premier League

1	20/08/94	Coventry City	Away	League	1–1		
2	27/08/94	Sheffield Wednesday	Home	League	0–1		
3	31/08/94	Manchester United	Away	League	0–3		
4	10/09/94	Leicester City	Home	League	2–1	1 Goal	(1)
5	17/09/94	Crystal Palace	Away	League	0–0		
6	20/09/94	Torquay United	Home	Lge Cup	2–0	1 Goal	(2)
7	24/09/94	Queens Park Rangers	Away	League	1–0		
8	01/10/94	Tottenham Hotspur	Home	League	1–2		
9	05/10/94	Torquay United	Away	Lge Cup	1–0		
10	08/10/94	Arsenal	Home	League	1–3		
Sub+1	25/10/94	Crystal Palace	Home	Lge Cup	0–1		
Sub+2	09/11/94	Aston Villa	Home	League	4–3		

Sub+3	19/11/94	Newcastle United	Home	League	3–2	1 Goal	(3)
Sub+4	03/12/94	Blackburn Rovers	Home	League	0–3		
11	10/12/94	Coventry City	Home	League	2–0	1 Goal	(4)
Sub+5	16/12/94	Ipswich Town	Away	League	2–2		
12	26/12/94	Southampton	Away	League	3–2	1 Goal	(5)
13	28/12/94	West Ham United	Home	League	1–0		
14	31/12/94	Chelsea	Away	League	1–1		
15	02/01/95	Everton	Home	League	2–1	2 Goals	(7)
16	07/01/95	Colchester United	Home	FA Cup	1–0	1 Goal	(8)
17	29/01/95	Tranmere Rovers	Away	FA Cup	2–0		
18	04/02/95	Leeds United	Home	League	0–0		
19	11/02/95	Aston Villa	Away	League	1–7		
Sub+6	19/02/95	Liverpool	Away	FA Cup	1–1		
Sub+7	21/02/95	Blackburn Rovers	Away	League	1–2		
Sub+8	28/02/95	Liverpool	Home	FA Cup	0–2		
20	04/03/95	Queens Park Rangers	Home	League	1–3		
Sub+9	11/03/95	Sheffield Wednesday	Away	League	1–0		
Sub+10	18/03/95	Crystal Palace	Home	League	2–0		
Sub+11	21/03/95	Manchester City	Home	League	2–0		
Sub+12	01/04/95	Leicester City	Away	League	4–3		
Sub+13	10/04/95	Chelsea	Home	League	1–1		
21	13/04/95	West Ham United	Away	League	0–3		

SEASON 1995–96

Premier League

22	09/09/95	Liverpool	Home	League	1–0	1 Goal	(9)
23	16/09/95	Aston Villa	Away	League	0–2		
Sub+14	03/10/95	Charlton Athletic	Away	Lge Cup	3–3		
24	21/10/95	Newcastle United	Away	League	1–6		
Sub+15	06/11/95	Nottingham Forest	Away	League	1–4		
Sub+16	22/11/95	Manchester City	Away	League	0–1		
25	25/11/95	Coventry City	Away	League	3–3		
26	03/12/95	Newcastle United	Home	League	3–3		
27	09/12/95	Leeds United	Away	League	1–1		
28	16/12/95	Tottenham Hotspur	Home	League	0–1		
29	23/12/95	Blackburn Rovers	Home	League	1–1		
30	26/12/95	Chelsea	Away	League	2–1		
31	30/12/95	Arsenal	Away	League	3–1		
32	01/01/96	Everton	Home	League	2–3		
33	06/01/96	Watford	Away	FA Cup	1–1		
34	13/01/96	Bolton Wanderers	Away	League	0–1		
35	17/01/96	Watford	Home	FA Cup	1–0		
36	20/01/96	Queens Park Rangers	Home	League	2–1		
37	07/02/96	Middlesbrough	Away	FA Cup	0–0		
38	10/02/96	Sheffield Wednesday	Away	League	1–2		
39	13/02/96	Middlesbrough	Home	FA Cup	1–0		
40	17/02/96	Huddersfield Town	Away	FA Cup	2–2		
41	24/02/96	Aston Villa	Home	League	3–3	1 Goal	(10)
42	09/03/96	Chelsea	Away	FA Cup	2–2		
43	13/03/96	Liverpool	Away	League	2–2		
44	16/03/96	Arsenal	Home	League	0–3		
45	20/03/96	Chelsea	Home	FA Cup	1–3		
Sub+17	27/04/96	Coventry City	Home	League	0–2		
Sub+18	05/05/96	Southampton	Away	League	0–0		

SEASON 1996–97

Premier League

Sub+19	17/08/96	Manchester United	Home	League	0–3	
Sub+20	04/09/96	Tottenham Hotspur	Home	League	1–0	
Sub+21	07/09/96	Everton	Home	League	4–0	
Sub+22	18/09/96	Portsmouth	Home	Lge Cup	1–0	
Sub+23	28/09/96	Derby County	Away	League	2–0	
Sub+24	12/11/96	Luton Town	Away	Lge Cup	2–1*	
Sub+25	26/11/96	Aston Villa	Home	Lge Cup	1–0	
Sub+26	30/11/96	Nottingham Forest	Home	League	1–0	
Sub+27	07/12/96	Sunderland	Away	League	3–1	
Sub+28	08/01/97	Bolton Wanderers	Away	Lge Cup	2–0	
Sub+29	18/01/97	Leicester City	Away	League	0–1	
Sub+30	21/01/97	Crewe Alexandra	Home	FA Cup	2–0	
Sub+31	04/02/97	Manchester United	Home	FA Cup	1–0	
Sub+32	01/03/97	Leicester City	Home	League	1–3	
Sub+33	03/03/97	Coventry City	Away	League	1–1	
Sub+34	11/03/97	Leicester City	Home	Lge Cup	1–1*	

Sub+35	15/03/97	Blackburn Rovers	Away	League	1–3		
46	18/03/97	West Ham United	Home	League	1–1	1 Goal	(11)
47	23/03/97	Newcastle United	Home	League	1–1		
48	09/04/97	Aston Villa	Home	League	0–2		

INTERNATIONAL APPEARANCES – ENGLAND

Sub 1	17/02/88	Israel	Tel Aviv	0–0	F
2	14/09/88	Denmark	Wembley	1–0	F

APPEARANCES AND GOALS PER SEASON

SEASON 77–88	GAMES	GOALS
League	25+2	9
TOTAL	**25+2**	**9**

SEASON 78–79	GAMES	GOALS
League	28+3	6
FA Cup	1	0
League Cup	2	0
TOTAL	**31+3**	**6**

SEASON 79–80	GAMES	GOALS
League	35+1	16
FA Cup	1	0
League Cup	2	0
TOTAL	**38+1**	**16**

SEASON 80–81	GAMES	GOALS
League	39+1	14
FA Cup	1	0
League Cup	4	5
TOTAL	**44+1**	**19**

SEASON 81–82	GAMES	GOALS
League	42	20
FA Cup	5	2
League Cup	5	1
TOTAL	**52**	**23**

SEASON 82–83	GAMES	GOALS
League	29	6
FA Cup	2	0
TOTAL	**31**	**6**

SEASON 83–84	GAMES	GOALS
League	39	8
FA Cup	5	2
League Cup	7	5
TOTAL	**51**	**15**

SEASON 84–85	GAMES	GOALS
League	34	17
FA Cup	8	1
League Cup	3	1
TOTAL	**45**	**19**

SEASON 85–86	GAMES	GOALS
League	37	22
FA Cup	7	3
League Cup	2	0
TOTAL	**46**	**25**

SEASON 86–87	GAMES	GOALS
League	18	4
FA Cup	5	3
TOTAL	**23**	**7**

SEASON 87–88	GAMES	GOALS
League	24+1	9
FA Cup	5	3
League Cup	7	6
Simod Cup	3	3
TOTAL	**39+1**	**21**

SEASON 88–89	GAMES	GOALS
League	33	7
FA Cup	1	0
League Cup	7	4
Simod Cup	1	0
TOTAL	**42**	**11**

SEASON 89–90	GAMES	GOALS
League	17+3	4
FA Cup	1	0
League Cup	2	0
TOTAL	**20+3**	**4**

SEASON 90–91	GAMES	GOALS
League	36	8
FA Cup	1	0
League Cup	5	3
Zenith Data Systems Cup	2	0
TOTAL	**44**	**11**

SEASON 91–92	GAMES	GOALS
League	35	15
League Cup	1	0
Zenith Data Systems Cup	1	0
TOTAL	**37**	**15**

SEASON 92–93	GAMES	GOALS
League	37+2	11
FA Cup	1	0
League Cup	5	2
TOTAL	**43+2**	**13**

SEASON 93–94	GAMES	GOALS
League	0+1	1
TOTAL	**0+1**	**1**

SEASON 94–95	GAMES	GOALS
League	17+10	6
FA Cup	2+2	1
League Cup	2+1	1
TOTAL	**21+13**	**8**

SEASON 95–96	GAMES	GOALS
League	17+4	2
FA Cup	7	0
League Cup	0+1	0
TOTAL	**24+5**	**2**

SEASON 96–97	GAMES	GOALS
League	3+10	1
FA Cup	0+2	0
League Cup	0+5	0
TOTAL	**3+17**	**1**

CAREER APPEARANCES AND GOALS

COMPETITION	GAMES	TOTAL	GOALS
League	545+38	583	186
FA Cup	53+4	57	15
League Cup	54+7	61	28
Simod Cup	4	4	3
Zenith Data Systems Cup	3	3	0
Internationals	1+1	2	0
TOTAL	**660+50**	**710**	**232**

HAT-TRICKS

Lincoln City

1	3	Wigan Athletic	29/02/80	Home	League	4–0
2	3	Hull City	09/08/80	Home	Lge Cup	5–0
3	3	Torquay United	12/11/80	Home	League	5–0

Birmingham City

1	3	Derby County	25/10/83	Home	Lge Cup	4–0

Luton Town

1	3	Leicester City	01/01/86	Home	League	3–1
2	3	Watford	26/04/86	Home	League	3–2
3	3	Wigan Athletic	06/10/87	Home	Lge Cup	4–2

Derby County

1	3	Sunderland	31/10/90	Home	Lge Cup	6–0

League: 4
League Cup: 4
TOTAL: 8

HONOURS

Winners medals
League Cup: 87/88

Runner-up medals
League Division Two Championship: 84/85
League Division Four Championship: 80/81
League Cup: 88/89
Simod Cup: 87/88

MARK HATELY

Born: 07/11/61 – Liverpool
Height: 6.2
Weight: 13.00 (96–97)

Clubs
Coventry City: **1979–83** – Matches: **104+8** – Goals: **34**
Detroit Express: **1980** – Matches: **12+7** – Goals: **2**
Portsmouth: **1983–84** – Matches: **44** – Goals: **25**
Milan AC: **1984–87** – Matches: **81+5** – Goals: **21**
AS Monaco: **1987–90** – Matches: **65+2** – Goals: **23**
Rangers: **1990–95** – Matches: **210+8** – Goals: **114**
Queens Park Rangers: **1995–97** – Matches: **21+12** – Goals: **5**
Leeds United (loan): **1996** – Matches: **5+1** – Goals: **0**
Rangers: **1997** – Matches: **4** – Goals: **1**

Country
England: **1984–92** – Matches: **20+12** – Goals: **9**

SEASON 1978–79

Coventry City – League Division One

1	05/05/79	Wolverhampton Wanderers	Home	League	3–0

SEASON 1979–80

League Division One

Sub+1	21/08/79	Bristol City	Home	League	3–1
Sub+2	01/09/79	Norwich City	Home	League	2–0
2	12/01/80	Norwich City	Away	League	0–1
3	19/01/80	Liverpool	Home	League	1–0
4	26/01/80	Blackburn Rovers	Away	FA Cup	0–1

Detroit Express – North American Soccer League – Season 1980

1	31/05/80	Vancouver Whitecaps	Home	League	0–1		
2	05/06/80	Toronto Blizzard	Away	League	2–1	1 Goal	(1)
3	08/06/80	Tulsa Roughnecks	Away	League	1–0		
4	11/06/80	San Jose Earthquakes	Home	League	0–1+		
5	14/06/80	Atlanta Chiefs	Away	League	1–3		
6	24/06/80	Philadelphia Fury	Home	League	1–2		
Sub+1	28/06/80	San Diego Sockers	Home	League	1–0+		
Sub+2	04/07/80	Houston Hurricane	Home	League	2–0		
7	06/07/80	Houston Hurricane	Away	League	3–4+		
8	09/07/80	Fort Lauderdale Strikers	Away	League	1–3		
Sub+3	12/07/80	New York Cosmos	Home	League	1–0+		
Sub+4	19/07/80	Rochester Lancers	Home	League	2–1	1 Goal	(2)

9	23/07/80	Chicago Sting	Home	League	1–2+
Sub+5	02/08/80	San Jose Earthquakes	Away	League	1–3
10	06/08/80	San Diego Sockers	Away	League	0–1
11	09/08/80	California Surf	Home	League	1–2
Sub+6	13/08/80	Tampa Bay Rowdies	Away	League	2–3
Sub+7	16/08/80	Philadelphia Fury	Away	League	3–2*
12	24/08/80	Fort Lauderdale Strikers	Home	League	3–2

* Sudden–death overtime
+ Decided on penalties

SEASON 1980–81

Coventry City – League Division One

5	30/08/80	Aston Villa	Away	League	0–1		
Sub+3	06/09/80	Crystal Palace	Home	League	3–1		
6	13/09/80	Wolverhampton Wanderers	Away	League	1–0		
7	20/09/80	Ipswich Town	Away	League	0–2		
8	23/09/80	Brighton & Hove Albion	Away	Lge Cup	2–1		
9	27/09/80	Everton	Home	League	0–5		
10	04/10/80	Brighton & Hove Albion	Home	League	3–3		
11	01/11/80	Leeds United	Home	League	2–1		
12	04/11/80	Cambridge United	Away	Lge Cup	1–0		
13	08/11/80	Manchester United	Away	League	0–0		
14	11/11/80	Liverpool	Away	League	1–2		
15	15/11/80	Birmingham City	Home	League	2–1		
16	22/11/80	Manchester City	Away	League	0–3		
17	02/12/80	Watford	Away	Lge Cup	2–2		
18	06/12/80	Southampton	Away	League	0–1		
19	09/12/80	Watford	Home	Lge Cup	5–0	2 Goals	(2)
20	13/12/80	West Bromwich Albion	Home	League	3–0		
21	20/12/80	Norwich City	Away	League	0–2		
22	26/12/80	Middlesbrough	Home	League	1–0		
23	27/12/80	Stoke City	Away	League	2–2	1 Goal	(3)
24	03/01/81	Leeds United	Away	FA Cup	1–1		
25	06/01/81	Leeds United	Home	FA Cup	1–0		
Sub+4	17/01/81	Aston Villa	Home	League	1–2	1 Goal	(4)
26	27/01/81	West Ham United	Home	Lge Cup	3–2		
27	31/01/81	Arsenal	Away	League	2–2		
28	07/02/81	Wolverhampton Wanderers	Home	League	2–2	1 Goal	(5)
29	10/02/81	West Ham United	Away	Lge Cup	0–2		
Sub+5	14/02/81	Tottenham Hotspur	Away	FA Cup	1–3		

SEASON 1981–82

League Division One

Sub+6	22/09/81	Liverpool	Home	League	1–2		
Sub+7	26/09/81	Southampton	Home	League	4–2		
Sub+8	03/10/81	Sunderland	Away	League	0–0		
30	06/10/81	Everton	Away	Lge Cup	1–1	1 Goal	(6)
31	10/10/81	Aston Villa	Home	League	1–1	1 Goal	(7)
32	17/10/81	Nottingham Forest	Away	League	1–2		
33	24/10/81	Swansea City	Home	League	3–1	2 Goals	(9)
34	27/10/81	Everton	Home	Lge Cup	0–1		
35	31/10/81	Arsenal	Away	League	0–1		
36	21/11/81	West Ham United	Away	League	2–5		
37	24/11/81	Stoke City	Home	League	3–0		
38	28/11/81	Middlesbrough	Home	League	1–1	1 Goal	(10)
39	05/12/81	Tottenham Hotspur	Away	League	2–1		
40	12/12/81	Manchester City	Home	League	0–1		
41	26/12/81	West Bromwich Albion	Home	League	0–2		
42	02/01/82	Sheffield Wednesday	Home	FA Cup	3–1	1 Goal	(11)
43	16/01/82	Ipswich Town	Home	League	2–4		
44	23/01/82	Manchester City	Away	FA Cup	3–1	1 Goal	(12)
45	26/01/82	Birmingham City	Away	League	3–3	1 Goal	(13)
46	30/01/82	Brighton & Hove Albion	Home	League	0–1		
47	06/02/82	Leeds United	Away	League	0–0		
48	13/02/82	Oxford United	Home	FA Cup	4–0	2 Goals	(15)
49	16/02/82	Notts County	Home	League	1–5	1 Goal	(16)
50	20/02/82	Liverpool	Away	League	0–4		
51	27/02/82	Aston Villa	Away	League	1–2		
52	06/03/82	West Bromwich Albion	Away	FA Cup	0–2		
53	09/03/82	Nottingham Forest	Home	League	0–1		
54	13/03/82	Swansea City	Away	League	0–0		
55	17/03/82	Manchester United	Away	League	1–0		

56	20/03/82	Arsenal	Home	League	1–0	1 Goal	(17)
57	27/03/82	Wolverhampton Wanderers	Home	League	0–0		
58	03/04/82	Ipswich Town	Away	League	0–1		
59	10/04/82	West Bromwich Albion	Away	League	2–1		
60	13/04/82	Everton	Home	League	1–0		
61	17/04/82	West Ham United	Home	League	1–0	1 Goal	(18)
62	24/04/82	Middlesbrough	Away	League	0–0		
63	27/04/82	Sunderland	Home	League	6–1	2 Goals	(20)
64	01/05/82	Tottenham Hotspur	Home	League	0–0		
65	04/05/82	Southampton	Away	League	5–5	3 Goals	(23)
66	08/05/82	Manchester City	Away	League	3–1		

SEASON 1982–83

League Division One

67	28/08/82	Southampton	Home	League	1–0		
68	31/08/82	Swansea City	Away	League	1–2		
69	04/09/82	Ipswich Town	Away	League	1–1		
70	07/09/82	Sunderland	Home	League	1–0		
71	30/10/82	Norwich City	Home	League	2–0	1 Goal	(24)
72	06/11/82	Aston Villa	Home	League	0–0		
73	13/11/82	Liverpool	Away	League	0–4		
74	20/11/82	Luton Town	Home	League	4–2		
75	23/11/82	Ipswich Town	Home	League	1–1		
76	27/11/82	West Bromwich Albion	Away	League	0–2		
77	04/12/82	Brighton & Hove Albion	Home	League	2–0		
78	11/12/82	West Ham United	Away	League	3–0	1 Goal	(25)
79	18/12/82	Stoke City	Home	League	2–0	2 Goals	(27)
80	27/12/82	Nottingham Forest	Away	League	2–4		
81	28/12/82	Manchester United	Home	League	3–0	1 Goal	(28)
82	01/01/83	Luton Town	Away	League	2–1		
83	08/01/83	Worcester City	Home	FA Cup	3–1	1 Goal	(29)
84	15/01/83	Southampton	Away	League	1–1	1 Goal	(30)
85	22/01/83	Swansea City	Home	League	0–0		
86	29/01/83	Norwich City	Home	FA Cup	2–2		
87	02/02/83	Norwich City	Away	FA Cup	1–2	1 Goal	(31)
88	05/02/83	Sunderland	Away	League	1–2		
89	12/02/83	Manchester City	Home	League	4–0	1 Goal	(32)
90	26/02/83	Notts County	Away	League	1–5		
91	05/03/83	Watford	Home	League	0–1		
92	12/03/83	Tottenham Hotspur	Home	League	1–1		
93	19/03/83	Aston Villa	Away	League	0–4		
94	23/03/83	Norwich City	Away	League	1–1		
95	02/04/83	Manchester United	Away	League	0–3		
96	05/04/83	Nottingham Forest	Home	League	1–2		
97	09/04/83	Arsenal	Away	League	1–2	1 Goal	(33)
98	12/04/83	Liverpool	Home	League	0–0		
99	16/04/83	Birmingham City	Home	League	0–1		
100	23/04/83	Brighton & Hove Albion	Away	League	0–1		
101	30/04/83	West Bromwich Albion	Home	League	0–1		
102	02/05/83	Everton	Away	League	0–1		
103	07/05/83	Stoke City	Away	League	3–0	1 Goal	(34)
104	14/05/83	West Ham United	Home	League	2–4		

SEASON 1983–84

Portsmouth – League Division Two

1	27/08/83	Middlesbrough	Home	League	0–1		
2	31/08/83	Hereford United	Away	Lge Cup	2–3	1 Goal	(1)
3	03/09/83	Fulham	Away	League	2–0	1 Goal	(2)
4	06/09/83	Barnsley	Home	League	2–1	1 Goal	(3)
5	13/09/83	Hereford United	Home	Lge Cup	3–1		
6	24/09/83	Shrewsbury Town	Home	League	4–1	1 Goal	(4)
7	27/09/83	Crystal Palace	Away	League	1–2		
8	01/10/83	Newcastle United	Away	League	2–4		
9	04/10/83	Aston Villa	Home	Lge Cup	2–2	1 Goal	(5)
10	08/10/83	Brighton & Hove Albion	Away	League	1–0		
11	15/10/83	Sheffield Wednesday	Home	League	0–1		
12	26/10/83	Aston Villa	Away	Lge Cup	2–3*		
13	29/10/83	Leeds United	Away	League	1–2		
14	01/11/83	Cambridge United	Home	League	5–0	3 Goals	(8)
15	05/11/83	Grimsby Town	Home	League	4–0	3 Goals	(11)
16	12/11/83	Carlisle United	Away	League	0–0		
17	19/11/83	Blackburn Rovers	Away	League	1–2		
18	26/11/83	Oldham Athletic	Home	League	3–4		

19	03/12/83	Huddersfield Town	Away	League	1–2	1 Goal	(12)
20	10/12/83	Derby County	Home	League	3–0		
21	17/12/83	Swansea City	Away	League	2–1	1 Goal	(13)
22	26/12/83	Charlton Athletic	Home	League	4–0	1 Goal	(14)
23	27/12/83	Chelsea	Away	League	2–2	1 Goal	(15)
24	31/12/83	Fulham	Home	League	1–4		
25	02/01/84	Shrewsbury Town	Away	League	0–2		
26	07/01/84	Grimsby Town	Home	FA Cup	2–1	1 Goal	(16)
27	21/01/84	Cardiff City	Home	League	1–1		
28	28/01/84	Southampton	Away	FA Cup	0–1		
29	04/02/84	Newcastle United	Home	League	1–4		
30	11/02/84	Manchester City	Away	League	1–2		
31	18/02/84	Leeds United	Home	League	2–3	1 Goal	(17)
32	25/02/84	Cambridge United	Away	League	3–1	2 Goals	(19)
33	03/03/84	Grimsby Town	Away	League	4–3	1 Goal	(20)
34	10/03/84	Carlisle United	Home	League	0–1		
35	17/03/84	Barnsley	Away	League	3–0	1 Goal	(21)
36	24/03/84	Crystal Palace	Home	League	0–1		
37	31/03/84	Brighton & Hove Albion	Home	League	5–1	1 Goal	(22)
38	07/04/84	Sheffield Wednesday	Away	League	0–2		
39	14/04/84	Blackburn Rovers	Home	League	2–4		
40	24/04/84	Chelsea	Home	League	2–2		
41	28/04/84	Oldham Athletic	Away	League	2–3	1 Goal	(23)
42	05/05/84	Huddersfield Town	Home	League	1–1	1 Goal	(24)
43	09/05/84	Derby County	Away	League	0–2		
44	12/05/84	Swansea City	Home	League	5–0	1 Goal	(25)

SEASON 1984–85

Milan AC – Italian League Division One

1	22/08/84	Parma AC	Away	It Cup	2–1	1 Goal	(1)
2	26/08/84	Brescia Calcio	Home	It Cup	1–1		
3	29/08/84	Carrarese Calcio	Away	It Cup	2–0		
4	16/09/84	Udinese Calcio	Home	League	2–2	1 Goal	(2)
5	23/09/84	AC Fiorentina	Away	League	0–0		
6	30/09/84	US Cremonese	Home	League	2–1	2 Goals	(4)
7	07/10/84	Juventus FC	Away	League	1–1		
8	14/10/84	AS Roma	Home	League	2–1	1 Goal	(5)
9	21/10/84	SSC Napoli	Away	League	0–0		
10	28/10/84	Internazionale Milano	Home	League	2–1	1 Goal	(6)
11	11/11/84	Torino Calcio	Away	League	0–2		
12	16/12/84	Atalanta BC	Home	League	2–2		
13	13/01/85	Como Calcio	Home	League	0–2		
14	20/01/85	Udinese Calcio	Away	League	1–1	1 Goal	(7)
15	27/01/85	AC Fiorentina	Home	League	1–1	1 Goal	(8)
16	10/02/85	US Cremonese	Away	League	1–0		
17	17/02/85	Juventus FC	Home	League	3–2		
18	24/02/85	AS Roma	Away	League	1–0		
19	03/03/85	SSC Napoli	Home	League	2–1		
20	17/03/85	Internazionale Milano	Away	League	2–2		
21	24/03/85	Torino Calcio	Home	League	0–1		
22	21/04/85	Hellas–Verona AC	Home	League	0–0		
23	12/05/85	SS Lazio	Home	League	2–0		
24	19/05/85	Como Calcio	Away	League	0–0		
25	19/06/85	Juventus FC	Away	It Cup	1–0		
26	26/06/85	Internazionale Milano	Home	It Cup	1–1		
27	30/06/85	Sampdoria UC	Home	It Cup	0–1		
28	03/07/85	Sampdoria UC	Away	It Cup	1–2		

SEASON 1985–86

Italian League Division One

29	21/08/85	Genoa 1893	Away	It Cup	2–2		
30	25/08/85	Cagliari Calcio	Away	It Cup	1–0	1 Goal	(9)
31	28/08/85	AC Reggiana	Home	It Cup	1–0		
32	04/09/85	Udinese Calcio	Away	It Cup	0–1		
33	08/09/85	AS Bari	Away	League	1–0		
34	15/09/85	US Lecce	Home	League	1–0		
35	18/09/85	AJ Auxerre	Home	UEFA Cup	1–3		
36	22/09/85	AC Fiorentina	Away	League	0–2		
37	29/09/85	US Avellino	Home	League	3–0	2 Goals	(11)
38	02/10/85	AJ Auxerre	Away	UEFA Cup	3–0	1 Goal	(12)
39	06/10/85	Sampdoria UC	Away	League	1–1	1 Goal	(13)
40	13/10/85	Como Calcio	Home	League	1–0		
41	23/10/85	1.FC Lokomotive Leipzig	Home	UEFA Cup	2–0	1 Goal	(14)

42	27/10/85	Hellas–Verona AC	Away	League	0–1		
43	03/11/85	SC Pisa	Home	League	1–0		
44	06/11/85	1.FC Lokomotive Leipzig	Away	UEFA Cup	1–3		
45	01/12/85	Internazionale Milano	Home	League	2–2		
46	08/12/85	SSC Napoli	Away	League	0–2		
47	05/01/86	AS Bari	Home	League	0–0		
48	12/01/86	US Lecce	Away	League	2–0	1 Goal	(15)
49	19/01/86	AC Fiorentina	Home	League	1–0		
50	26/01/86	US Avellino	Away	League	1–1		
51	09/02/86	Sampdoria UC	Home	League	2–2		
52	09/03/86	SC Pisa	Away	League	1–0	1 Goal	(16)
53	16/03/86	Udinese Calcio	Home	League	2–0	2 Goals	(18)
54	23/03/86	AS Roma	Home	League	0–1		
55	06/04/86	Internazionale Milano	Away	League	0–1		
56	13/04/86	SSC Napoli	Home	League	1–2		
57	20/04/86	Juventus FC	Away	League	0–1		
58	27/04/86	Atalanta BC	Home	League	1–1	1 Goal	(19)

SEASON 1986–87

Italian League Division One

59	24/08/86	Sambenedettese	Home	It Cup	1–0		
60	27/08/86	US Triestina	Away	It Cup	1–0		
61	31/08/86	Barletta CS	Away	It Cup	3–0		
62	14/09/86	Ascoli Calcio	Home	League	0–1		
63	21/09/86	Hellas–Verona AC	Away	League	0–1		
Sub+1	28/09/86	Atalanta BC	Home	League	2–1		
64	05/10/86	Juventus FC	Away	League	0–0		
65	12/10/86	Internazionale Milano	Home	League	0–0		
Sub+2	26/10/86	Brescia Calcio	Home	League	2–0		
66	20/11/86	Sampdoria UC	Away	League	0–3		
Sub+3	23/11/86	US Avellino	Home	League	2–0	1 Goal	(20)
67	30/11/86	Torino Calcio	Away	League	0–0		
68	14/12/86	SSC Napoli	Home	League	0–0		
Sub+4	01/02/87	Hellas–Verona AC	Home	League	1–0		
69	08/02/87	Atalanta BC	Away	League	2–1		
Sub+5	22/02/87	Juventus FC	Home	League	1–1		
70	25/02/87	Parma AC	Home	It Cup	0–1		
71	01/03/87	Internazionale Milano	Away	League	1–3		
72	08/03/87	Empoli FC	Home	League	1–0		
73	15/03/87	Brescia Calcio	Away	League	0–1		
74	29/03/87	Sampdoria UC	Home	League	0–2		
75	05/04/87	US Avellino	Away	League	1–2		
76	08/04/87	Parma AC	Home	It Cup	0–0		
77	12/04/87	Torino Calcio	Home	League	1–0	1 Goal	(21)
78	26/04/87	SSC Napoli	Away	League	1–2		
79	03/05/87	AS Roma	Home	League	4–1		
80	10/05/87	Como Calcio	Home	League	0–0		
81	17/05/87	Udinese Calcio	Away	League	0–0		

SEASON 1987–88

AS Monaco – French League Division One

1	18/07/87	Olympique de Marseille	Home	League	3–1	1 Goal	(1)
2	25/07/87	RC Lens	Away	League	3–1	1 Goal	(2)
3	01/08/87	Le Havre AC	Home	League	2–0		
4	08/08/87	Montpellier HSC	Away	League	1–2		
5	15/08/87	Toulouse FC	Home	League	5–1	2 Goals	(4)
6	19/08/87	Paris Saint–Germain FC	Away	League	1–0	1 Goal	(5)
7	22/08/87	Chamois Niortais de Niort	Home	League	1–3		
8	29/08/87	Stade Lavallois de Laval	Home	League	2–0	2 Goals	(7)
9	02/09/87	AS Cannes	Away	League	1–1		
10	12/09/87	Girondins de Bordeaux	Home	League	1–0	1 Goal	(8)
11	19/09/87	SC Toulon	Away	League	0–0		
12	31/09/87	OGC Nice	Away	League	0–0		
13	07/11/87	FC Metz	Home	League	2–1		
14	22/11/87	RC Lens	Home	League	3–0	2 Goals	(10)
15	28/11/87	Le Havre AC	Away	League	0–0		
16	05/12/87	Montpellier HSC	Home	League	0–0		
17	20/02/88	Chamois Niortais de Niort	Away	League	0–0		
18	26/02/88	Stade Lavallois de Laval	Away	League	0–0		
19	05/03/88	AS Cannes	Home	League	4–1	2 Goals	(12)
20	12/03/88	Saint–Dizier	Neutral	FR Cup	2–1		
21	19/03/88	Girondins de Bordeaux	Away	League	1–3	1 Goal	(13)
22	26/03/88	SC Toulon	Home	League	0–0		

23	02/04/88	Lille OSC	Away	League	1–0		
24	05/04/88	OGC Nice	Away	FR Cup	0–2		
25	09/04/88	Brest–Armorique	Home	League	2–0		
26	16/04/88	AS Saint–Etienne	Away	League	0–3		
27	30/04/88	Racing Matra	Home	League	3–0		
28	14/05/88	OGC Nice	Home	League	1–0		
29	21/05/88	FC Metz	Away	League	2–2		
30	27/05/88	AJ Auxerre	Home	League	3–2	1 Goal	(14)

SEASON 1988–89

French League Division One

31	15/07/88	FC Nantes	Away	League	1–1	1 Goal	(15)
32	23/07/88	AS Cannes	Home	League	2–0		
33	27/07/88	Lille OSC	Home	League	1–1		
34	30/07/88	SM Caen	Away	League	3–0		
35	06/08/88	Paris Saint–Germain FC	Home	League	1–0		
36	13/08/88	SC Toulon	Away	League	0–1		
37	20/08/88	AS Saint–Etienne	Away	League	0–0		
38	27/08/88	Toulouse FC	Home	League	1–0		
39	09/11/88	Club Brugge KV	Home	Eur Cup	6–1		
40	12/11/88	FC Metz	Home	League	1–1		
41	25/11/88	AS Cannes	Away	League	2–3	1 Goal	(16)
42	03/12/88	Lille OSC	Away	League	4–2	1 Goal	(17)
43	10/12/88	SM Caen	Home	League	3–1	1 Goal	(18)
44	14/12/88	Paris Saint–Germain FC	Away	League	2–0	1 Goal	(19)
45	17/12/88	SC Toulon	Home	League	2–2		
46	04/02/89	AJ Auxerre	Away	League	0–0		
47	11/02/89	AS Saint–Etienne	Home	League	2–2	1 Goal	(20)
48	18/02/89	Toulouse FC	Away	League	0–2		
49	22/02/89	Matra Racing Paris	Home	League	1–0		
50	01/03/89	Galatasary SK	Home	Eur Cup	0–1		
51	26/04/89	Pont–Saint–Esprit	Neutral	FR Cup	6–1	1 Goal	(21)

SEASON 1989–90

French League Division One

Sub+1	17/10/89	BFC Dynamo Berlin	Home	ECW Cup	0–0		
52	21/10/89	FC Mulhouse	Home	League	0–0		
53	28/10/89	Toulouse FC	Away	League	1–0		
54	01/11/89	BFC Dynamo Berlin	Away	ECW Cup	1–1		
55	04/11/89	OGC Nice	Home	League	1–0		
56	08/11/89	FC Metz	Away	League	0–1		
57	11/11/89	Montpellier HSC	Home	League	1–0		
58	22/11/89	Olympique de Marseille	Home	League	1–3		
Sub+2	03/12/89	Lille OSC	Home	League	1–1		
59	09/12/89	AS Saint–Etienne	Away	League	2–0	1 Goal	(22)
60	17/12/89	SM Caen	Home	League	2–1		
61	04/02/90	Brest–Armorique	Away	League	1–1		
62	11/02/90	SC Toulon	Home	League	2–1		
63	16/02/90	Olympique Avignon	Away	FR Cup	2–3*		
64	21/02/90	AS Cannes	Home	League	0–0		
65	25/02/90	Olympique de Marseille	Away	League	2–2	1 Goal	(23)

SEASON 1990–91

Rangers – Scottish League Premier Division

1	21/08/90	East Stirling	Home	S Lge Cup	5–0	2 Goals	(2)
2	25/08/90	Dunfermline Athletic	Home	League	3–1	1 Goal	(3)
Sub+1	28/08/90	Kilmarnock	Away	S Lge Cup	1–0		
3	01/09/90	Hibernian	Away	League	0–0		
4	04/09/90	Raith Rovers	Home	S Lge Cup	6–2		
5	08/09/90	Heart of Midlothian	Away	League	3–1		
6	15/09/90	Celtic	Home	League	1–1		
7	19/09/90	Valletta FC	Away	Eur Cup	4–0	1 Goal	(4)
8	22/09/90	Dundee United	Away	League	1–2		
Sub+2	29/09/90	Motherwell	Home	League	1–0		
Sub+3	06/10/90	Aberdeen	Away	League	0–0		
Sub+4	20/10/90	St Johnstone	Away	League	0–0		
9	28/10/90	Celtic	Hampden	S Lge Cup	2–1*		
10	03/11/90	Hibernian	Home	League	4–0	2 Goals	(6)
11	07/11/90	Crvena Zvezda Beograd	Home	Eur Cup	1–1		
12	10/11/90	Dundee United	Home	League	1–2		
13	17/11/90	Motherwell	Away	League	4–2		
14	20/11/90	Dunfermline Athletic	Away	League	1–0	1 Goal	(7)

15	25/11/90	Celtic	Away	League	2–1		
16	01/12/90	Heart of Midlothian	Home	League	4–0		
17	08/12/90	St Johnstone	Home	League	4–1		
18	15/12/90	St Mirren	Away	League	3–0	1 Goal	(8)
19	22/12/90	Aberdeen	Home	League	2–2		
20	29/12/90	Dundee United	Away	League	2–1		
21	02/01/91	Celtic	Home	League	2–0	1 Goal	(9)
22	05/01/91	Heart of Midlothian	Away	League	1–0	1 Goal	(10)
23	12/01/91	Dunfermline Athletic	Home	League	2–0		
24	19/01/91	Hibernian	Away	League	2–0		
25	29/01/91	Dunfermline Athletic	Home	S Cup	2–0		
26	16/02/91	Motherwell	Home	League	2–0	1 Goal	(11)
27	23/02/91	Cowdenbeath	Home	S Cup	5–0	2 Goals	(13)
28	26/02/91	St Johnstone	Away	League	1–1		
29	02/03/91	Aberdeen	Away	League	0–1		
30	09/03/91	Heart of Midlothian	Home	League	2–1		
31	17/03/91	Celtic	Away	S Cup	0–2		
32	30/03/91	Dunfermline Athletic	Away	League	1–0		
33	06/04/91	Hibernian	Home	League	0–0		
34	13/04/91	St Johnstone	Home	League	3–0		
35	20/04/91	St Mirren	Away	League	1–0		
36	24/04/91	Dundee United	Home	League	1–0		
37	04/05/91	Motherwell	Away	League	0–3		
38	11/05/91	Aberdeen	Home	League	2–0	2 Goals	(15)

SEASON 1991–92

Scottish League Premier Division

39	10/08/91	St Johnstone	Home	League	6–0	3 Goals	(18)
40	13/08/91	Motherwell	Home	League	2–0		
41	17/08/91	Heart of Midlothian	Away	League	0–1		
42	31/08/91	Celtic	Away	League	2–0	2 Goals	(20)
43	04/09/91	Heart of Midlothian	Away	S Lge Cup	1–0		
44	07/09/91	Falkirk	Away	League	2–0		
45	14/09/91	Dundee United	Home	League	1–1		
46	18/09/91	AC Sparta Praha	Away	Eur Cup	0–1		
47	21/09/91	St Mirren	Away	League	2–1		
48	25/09/91	Hibernian	Hampden	S Lge Cup	0–1		
49	28/09/91	Aberdeen	Home	League	0–2		
50	19/10/91	Heart of Midlothian	Home	League	2–0		
Sub+5	26/10/91	Falkirk	Home	League	1–1		
51	29/10/91	Dundee United	Away	League	2–3		
52	02/11/91	Celtic	Home	League	1–1		
53	09/11/91	Dunfermline Athletic	Away	League	5–0	1 Goal	(21)
54	16/11/91	Airdrieonians	Home	League	4–0	2 Goals	(23)
55	19/11/91	Hibernian	Away	League	3–0	1 Goal	(24)
56	23/11/91	St Mirren	Home	League	0–1		
57	30/11/91	Motherwell	Away	League	2–0		
58	04/12/91	Aberdeen	Away	League	3–2	2 Goals	(26)
59	07/12/91	St Johnstone	Home	League	3–1	1 Goal	(27)
60	14/12/91	Falkirk	Away	League	3–1	1 Goal	(28)
61	21/12/91	Dundee United	Home	League	2–0		
62	01/01/92	Celtic	Away	League	3–1	1 Goal	(29)
63	25/02/92	Aberdeen	Home	League	0–0		
64	29/02/92	Airdrieonians	Home	League	5–0	3 Goals	(32)
65	03/03/92	St Johnstone	Away	S Cup	3–0	1 Goal	(33)
66	10/03/92	Hibernian	Away	League	3–1	2 Goals	(35)
67	14/03/92	Dunfermline Athletic	Away	League	3–1		
68	21/03/92	Celtic	Home	League	0–2		
69	28/03/92	St Johnstone	Away	League	2–1	2 Goals	(37)
70	28/04/92	Heart of Midlothian	Home	League	1–1		
71	02/05/92	Aberdeen	Away	League	2–0		
72	09/05/92	Airdrieonians	Hampden	S Cup	2–1	1 Goal	(38)

SEASON 1992–93

Scottish League Premier Division

73	01/08/92	St Johnstone	Home	League	1–0		
74	04/08/92	Airdrieonians	Home	League	2–0	1 Goal	(39)
75	08/08/92	Hibernian	Away	League	0–0		
76	11/08/92	Dumbarton	Away	S Lge Cup	5–0+	1 Goal	(40)
77	15/08/92	Dundee	Away	League	3–4		
78	19/08/92	Stranraer	Away	S Lge Cup	5–0	2 Goals	(42)
79	22/08/92	Celtic	Home	League	1–1		
Sub+6	12/09/92	Partick Thistle	Away	League	4–1	1 Goal	(43)

80	16/09/92	Lyngby BK Kobenhavn	Home	Eur Cup	2–0	1 Goal	(44)
81	22/09/92	St Johnstone	Hampden	S Lge Cup	3–1		
82	26/09/92	Dundee United	Away	League	4–0		
83	30/09/92	Lyngby BK Kobenhavn	Away	Eur Cup	1–0		
84	03/10/92	Falkirk	Home	League	4–0		
85	07/10/92	St Johnstone	Away	League	5–1	2 Goals	(46)
86	17/10/92	Hibernian	Home	League	1–0		
87	21/10/92	Leeds United	Home	Eur Cup	2–1		
88	25/10/92	Aberdeen	Hampden	S Lge Cup	2–1		
89	04/11/92	Leeds United	Away	Eur Cup	2–1	1 Goal	(47)
90	07/11/92	Celtic	Away	League	1–0		
91	11/11/92	Dundee	Home	League	3–1	1 Goal	(48)
92	21/11/92	Heart of Midlothian	Away	League	1–1		
93	25/11/92	Olympique de Marseille	Home	Eur Cup	2–2	1 Goal	(49)
94	01/12/92	Airdrieonians	Away	League	1–1		
95	09/12/92	CSKA Moskva	Away	Eur Cup	1–0		
96	12/12/92	Falkirk	Away	League	2–1	1 Goal	(50)
97	19/12/92	St Johnstone	Home	League	2–0		
98	26/12/92	Dundee	Away	League	3–1	2 Goals	(52)
99	02/01/93	Celtic	Home	League	1–0		
100	05/01/93	Dundee United	Home	League	3–2	1 Goal	(53)
101	09/01/93	Motherwell	Away	S Cup	2–0		
102	30/01/93	Hibernian	Away	League	4–3	2 Goals	(55)
103	02/02/93	Aberdeen	Away	League	1–0	1 Goal	(56)
104	06/02/93	Ayr United	Away	S Cup	2–0		
105	09/02/93	Falkirk	Home	League	5–0	2 Goals	(58)
106	13/02/93	Airdrieonians	Home	League	2–2		
107	20/02/93	Dundee United	Away	League	0–0		
108	23/02/93	Motherwell	Away	League	4–0	2 Goals	(60)
109	27/02/93	Heart of Midlothian	Home	League	2–1		
110	03/03/93	Club Brugge KV	Away	Eur Cup	1–1		
111	06/03/93	Arbroath	Away	S Cup	3–0	1 Goal	(61)
112	10/03/93	St Johnstone	Away	League	1–1		
113	13/03/93	Hibernian	Home	League	3–0	1 Goal	(62)
114	17/03/93	Club Brugge KV	Home	Eur Cup	2–1		
115	20/03/93	Celtic	Away	League	1–2	1 Goal	(63)
116	27/03/93	Dundee	Home	League	3–0		
117	30/03/93	Aberdeen	Home	League	2–0		
118	03/04/93	Heart of Midlothian	Hampden	S Cup	2–1		
119	10/04/93	Motherwell	Home	League	1–0		
120	14/04/93	Heart of Midlothian	Away	League	3–2	2 Goals	(65)
121	17/04/93	Partick Thistle	Home	League	3–1		
122	01/05/93	Airdrieonians	Away	League	1–0		
123	04/05/93	Partick Thistle	Away	League	0–3		
124	15/05/93	Falkirk	Away	League	2–1	1 Goal	(66)
125	29/05/93	Aberdeen	Hampden	S Cup	2–1	1 Goal	(67)

+ Played at Hampden Park

SEASON 1993–94

Scottish League Premier Division

126	07/08/93	Heart of Midlothian	Home	League	2–1	1 Goal	(68)
127	10/08/93	Dumbarton	Home	S Lge Cup	1–0		
128	21/08/93	Celtic	Away	League	0–0		
129	24/08/93	Dunfermline Athletic	Away	S Lge Cup	2–0		
130	28/08/93	Kilmarnock	Home	League	1–2		
131	01/09/93	Aberdeen	Home	S Lge Cup	2–1*	1 Goal	(69)
132	04/09/93	Dundee	Away	League	1–1	1 Goal	(70)
133	11/09/93	Partick Thistle	Home	League	1–1	1 Goal	(71)
134	15/09/93	FK Levski Sofija	Home	Eur Cup	3–2	2 Goals	(73)
135	18/09/93	Aberdeen	Away	League	0–2		
136	22/09/93	Celtic	Home	S Lge Cup	1–0	1 Goal	(74)
137	25/09/93	Hibernian	Home	League	2–1	1 Goal	(75)
138	29/09/93	FK Levski Sofija	Away	Eur Cup	1–2		
139	02/10/93	Raith Rovers	Away	League	1–1		
140	06/10/93	Motherwell	Home	League	1–2		
141	09/10/93	Dundee United	Away	League	3–1	1 Goal	(76)
142	16/10/93	St Johnstone	Home	League	2–0	1 Goal	(77)
143	24/10/93	Hibernian	Neutral	S Lge Cup	2–1		
144	30/10/93	Celtic	Home	League	1–2		
145	03/11/93	Heart of Midlothian	Away	League	2–2	2 Goals	(79)
146	06/11/93	Kilmarnock	Away	League	2–0		
147	10/11/93	Dundee	Home	League	3–1		
148	13/11/93	Raith Rovers	Home	League	2–2	2 Goals	(81)

149	20/11/93	Hibernian	Away	League	1–0	
150	27/11/93	Partick Thistle	Away	League	1–1	
151	01/12/93	Aberdeen	Home	League	2–0	2 Goals (83)
152	04/12/93	Motherwell	Away	League	2–0	
153	11/12/93	Dundee United	Home	League	0–3	
154	18/12/93	St Johnstone	Away	League	4–0	2 Goals (85)
155	27/12/93	Heart of Midlothian	Home	League	2–2	2 Goals (87)
156	01/01/94	Celtic	Away	League	4–2	1 Goal (88)
157	08/01/94	Kilmarnock	Home	League	3–0	2 Goals (90)
158	15/01/94	Dundee	Away	League	1–1	
159	22/01/94	Aberdeen	Away	League	0–0	
160	29/01/94	Dumbarton	Home	S Cup	4–1	1 Goal (91)
161	05/02/94	Partick Thistle	Home	League	5–1	
162	12/02/94	Hibernian	Home	League	2–0	
163	19/02/94	Alloa	Home	S Cup	6–0	
164	26/02/94	Raith Rovers	Away	League	2–1	
165	05/03/94	Motherwell	Home	League	2–1	1 Goal (92)
166	12/03/94	Heart of Midlothian	Home	S Cup	2–0	1 Goal (93)
167	19/03/94	St Johnstone	Home	League	4–0	1 Goal (94)
168	26/03/94	Heart of Midlothian	Away	League	2–1	1 Goal (95)
169	29/03/94	Partick Thistle	Away	League	2–1	
170	02/04/94	Aberdeen	Home	League	1–1	
Sub+7	05/04/94	Dundee United	Away	League	0–0	
171	10/04/94	Kilmarnock	Hampden	S Cup	0–0	
172	13/04/94	Kilmarnock	Hampden	S Cup	2–1	2 Goals (97)
Sub+8	16/04/94	Raith Rovers	Home	League	4–0	
173	23/04/94	Dundee United	Home	League	2–1	
174	30/04/94	Celtic	Home	League	1–1	
175	03/05/94	Hibernian	Away	League	0–1	
176	07/05/94	Kilmarnock	Away	League	0–1	
177	14/05/94	Dundee	Home	League	0–0	
178	21/05/94	Dundee United	Hampden	S Cup	0–1	

SEASON 1994–95

Scottish League Premier Division

179	10/08/94	AEK Athina	Away	Eur Cup	0–2	
180	13/08/94	Motherwell	Home	League	2–1	1 Goal (98)
181	17/08/94	Arbroath	Away	S Lge Cup	6–1	2 Goals (100)
182	20/08/94	Partick Thistle	Away	League	2–0	1 Goal (101)
183	24/08/94	AEK Athina	Home	Eur Cup	0–1	
184	27/08/94	Celtic	Home	League	0–2	
185	31/08/94	Falkirk	Home	S Lge Cup	1–2	
186	11/09/94	Heart of Midlothian	Home	League	3–0	2 Goals (103)
187	17/09/94	Falkirk	Away	League	2–0	
188	24/09/94	Aberdeen	Away	League	2–2	1 Goal (104)
189	01/10/94	Dundee United	Home	League	2–0	1 Goal (105)
190	08/10/94	Hibernian	Away	League	1–2	
191	15/10/94	Kilmarnock	Home	League	2–0	
192	22/10/94	Motherwell	Away	League	1–2	
193	30/10/94	Celtic	Away	League	3–1	2 Goals (107)
194	05/11/94	Partick Thistle	Home	League	3–0	1 Goal (108)
195	09/11/94	Heart of Midlothian	Away	League	1–1	1 Goal (109)
196	19/11/94	Falkirk	Home	League	1–1	1 Goal (110)
197	25/11/94	Aberdeen	Home	League	1–0	
198	26/12/94	Hibernian	Home	League	2–0	1 Goal (111)
199	04/02/95	Dundee United	Home	League	1–1	
200	06/02/95	Hamilton Academical	Away	S Cup	3–1	
201	12/02/95	Aberdeen	Away	League	0–2	
202	08/04/95	Aberdeen	Home	League	3–2	1 Goal (112)
203	16/04/95	Hibernian	Home	League	3–1	
204	29/04/95	Motherwell	Home	League	0–2	
205	07/05/95	Celtic	Away	League	0–3	
206	13/05/95	Partick Thistle	Home	League	1–1	

SEASON 1995–96

Scottish League Premier Division

207	09/08/95	Anorthosis Famagusta	Home	Eur Cup	1–0	
208	19/08/95	Morton	Home	S Lge Cup	3–0	1 Goal (113)
209	23/08/95	Anorthosis Famagusta	Away	Eur Cup	0–0	
210	30/08/95	Stirling Albion	Home	S Lge Cup	3–2	1 Goal (114)

Queens Park Rangers – Premier League

Sub+1	29/11/95	Aston Villa	Away	Lge Cup	0–1	

1	02/12/95	Middlesbrough	Home	League	1–1			
2	09/12/95	Tottenham Hotspur	Away	League	0–1			
3	16/12/95	Bolton Wanderers	Home	League	2–1			
4	23/12/95	Aston Villa	Home	League	1–0			
5	26/12/95	Arsenal	Away	League	0–3			
Sub+2	13/01/96	Blackburn Rovers	Home	League	0–1			
6	20/01/96	Wimbledon	Away	League	1–2	1 Goal	(1)	
7	29/01/96	Chelsea	Home	FA Cup	1–2			
8	03/02/96	Manchester City	Away	League	0–2			
Sub+3	16/03/96	Manchester United	Home	League	1–1			
Sub+4	23/03/96	Chelsea	Away	League	1–1			
Sub+5	06/04/96	Newcastle United	Away	League	1–2			
9	08/04/96	Everton	Home	League	3–1	1 Goal	(2)	
10	13/04/96	Coventry City	Away	League	0–1			
11	27/04/96	West Ham United	Home	League	3–0			

SEASON 1996–97

Football League Division One

12	17/08/96	Oxford United	Home	League	2–1	

Leeds United (loan) – Premier League

1	20/08/96	Sheffield Wednesday	Home	League	0–2	
2	24/08/96	Wimbledon	Home	League	1–0	
Sub+1	07/09/96	Manchester United	Home	League	0–4	
3	14/09/96	Coventry City	Away	League	1–2	
4	12/10/96	Nottingham Forest	Home	League	2–0	
5	19/10/96	Aston Villa	Away	League	0–2	

Queens Park Rangers – Football League Division One

Sub+6	26/10/96	Sheffield United	Away	League	1–1		
13	30/10/96	Ipswich Town	Home	League	0–1		
Sub+7	14/12/96	Southend United	Home	League	4–0		
Sub+8	04/01/97	Huddersfield Town	Home	FA Cup	1–1	1 Goal	(3)
14	11/01/97	Barnsley	Home	League	3–1		
15	14/01/97	Huddersfield Town	Away	FA Cup	2–1		
16	19/01/97	Port Vale	Away	League	4–4		
Sub+9	25/01/97	Barnsley	Home	FA Cup	3–2		
Sub+10	01/02/97	Crystal Palace	Home	League	0–1		
17	05/02/97	Swindon Town	Away	League	1–1	1 Goal	(4)
18	08/02/97	Ipswich Town	Away	League	0–2		
19	15/02/97	Wimbledon	Away	FA Cup	1–2	1 Goal	(5)
20	22/02/97	Stoke City	Away	League	0–0		
21	01/03/97	Oldham Athletic	Home	League	0–1		
Sub+11	04/03/97	Charlton Athletic	Away	League	1–2		
Sub+12	12/03/97	Reading	Home	League	0–2		

Rangers – Scottish League Premier Division

1	16/03/97	Celtic	Away	League	1–0		
2	05/04/97	Dunfermline Athletic	Home	League	4–0	1 Goal	(1)
3	15/04/97	Raith Rovers	Away	League	6–0		
4	05/05/97	Motherwell	Home	League	0–2		

INTERNATIONAL APPEARANCES – ENGLAND

Sub 1	02/06/84	USSR	Wembley	0–2	F			
2	10/06/84	Brazil	Rio de Janeiro	2–0	F	1 Goal	(1)	
3	13/06/84	Uruguay	Montevideo	0–2	F			
4	17/06/84	Chile	Santiago	0–0	F			
Sub 5	12/09/84	East Germany	Wembley	1–0	F			
6	17/10/84	Finland	Wembley	5–0	WCQ	2 Goals	(3)	
7	27/02/85	Northern Ireland	Windsor Park	1–0	WCQ	1 Goal	(4)	
8	26/03/85	Republic of Ireland	Wembley	2–1	F			
9	22/05/85	Finland	Helsinki	1–1	WCQ	1 Goal	(5)	
10	25/05/85	Scotland	Hampden Park	0–1	RC			
11	06/06/85	Italy	Mexico City	1–2	F	1 Goal	(6)	
12	09/06/85	Mexico	Mexico City	0–1	F			
13	11/09/85	Romania	Wembley	1–1	WCQ			
14	16/10/85	Turkey	Wembley	5–0	WCQ			
15	29/01/86	Egypt	Cairo	4–0	F			
16	23/04/86	Scotland	Wembley	2–1	RC			
17	17/05/86	Mexico	Los Angeles	3–0	F	2 Goals	(8)	
18	24/05/86	Canada	Vancouver	1–0	F	1 Goal	(9)	
19	03/06/86	Portugal	Monterrey	0–1	WC			

20	06/06/86	Morocco	Monterrey	0–0	WC
Sub 21	18/06/86	Paraguay	Mexico City	3–0	WC
Sub 22	29/04/87	Turkey	Izmir	0–0	ECQ
Sub 23	19/05/87	Brazil	Wembley	1–1	RC
24	23/05/87	Scotland	Hampden Park	0–0	RC
Sub 25	09/09/87	West Germany	Dusseldorf	1–3	F
Sub 26	23/03/88	Holland	Wembley	2–2	F
Sub 27	27/04/88	Hungary	Budapest	0–0	F
Sub 28	24/05/88	Colombia	Wembley	1–1	RC
Sub 29	12/06/88	Republic of Ireland	Stuttgart	0–1	EC
Sub 30	15/06/88	Holland	Dusseldorf	1–3	EC
Sub 31	18/06/88	USSR	Frankfurt	1–3	EC
32	25/03/92	Czechoslovakia	Prague	2–2	F

APPEARANCES AND GOALS PER SEASON

SEASON 78–79	GAMES	GOALS
League	1	0
TOTAL	**1**	**0**

SEASON 79–80	GAMES	GOALS
League	2+2	0
FA Cup	1	0
North American Soccer League	12+7	2
TOTAL	**15+9**	**2**

SEASON 80–81	GAMES	GOALS
League	17+2	3
FA Cup	2+1	0
League Cup	6	2
TOTAL	**25+3**	**5**

SEASON 81–82	GAMES	GOALS
League	31+3	13
FA Cup	4	4
League Cup	2	1
TOTAL	**37+3**	**18**

SEASON 82–83	GAMES	GOALS
League	35	9
FA Cup	3	2
TOTAL	**38**	**11**

SEASON 83–84	GAMES	GOALS
League	38	22
FA Cup	2	1
League Cup	4	2
TOTAL	**44**	**25**

SEASON 84–85	GAMES	GOALS
Italian League	21	7
Italian Cup	7	1
TOTAL	**28**	**8**

SEASON 85–86	GAMES	GOALS
Italian League	22	8
Italian Cup	4	1
UEFA Cup	4	2
TOTAL	**30**	**11**

SEASON 86–87	GAMES	GOALS
Italian League	18+5	2
Italian Cup	5	0
TOTAL	**23+5**	**2**

SEASON 87–88	GAMES	GOALS
French League	28	14
French Cup	2	0
TOTAL	**30**	**14**

SEASON 88–89	GAMES	GOALS
French League	18	6
French Cup	1	1
European Cup	2	0
TOTAL	**21**	**7**

SEASON 89–90	GAMES	GOALS
French League	12+1	2
French Cup	1	0
European Cup Winners Cup	1+1	0
TOTAL	**14+2**	**2**

SEASON 90–91	GAMES	GOALS
Scottish League	30+3	10
Scottish Cup	3	2
Scottish League Cup	3+1	2
European Cup	2	1
TOTAL	**38+4**	**15**

SEASON 91–92	GAMES	GOALS
Scottish League	29+1	21
Scottish Cup	2	2
Scottish League Cup	2	0
European Cup	1	0
TOTAL	**34+1**	**23**

SEASON 92–93	GAMES	GOALS
Scottish League	36+1	21
Scottish Cup	5	2
Scottish League Cup	4	3
European Cup	8	3
TOTAL	**53+1**	**29**

SEASON 93–94	GAMES	GOALS
Scottish League	40+2	22
Scottish Cup	6	4
Scottish League Cup	5	2
European Cup	2	2
TOTAL	**53+2**	**30**

SEASON 94–95	GAMES	GOALS
Scottish League	23	13
Scottish Cup	1	0
Scottish League Cup	2	2
European Cup	2	0
TOTAL	**28**	**15**

SEASON 95–96	GAMES	GOALS
League	10+4	2
FA Cup	1	0
League Cup	0+1	0
Scottish League Cup	2	2
European Cup	2	0
TOTAL	**15+5**	**4**

SEASON 96–97	GAMES	GOALS
League	13+6	1
FA Cup	2+2	2
Scottish League	4	1
TOTAL	**19+8**	**4**

CAREER APPEARANCES AND GOALS

COMPETITION	GAMES	TOTAL	GOALS
League	147+17	164	50
FA Cup	15+3	18	9
League Cup	12+1	13	5
European Cup	19	19	6
European Cup Winners Cup	1+1	2	0
UEFA Cup	4	4	2
Italian League	61+5	66	17
Italian Cup	16	16	2
French League	58+1	59	22
French Cup	4	4	1
Scottish League	162+7	169	88
Scottish Cup	17	17	10
Scottish League Cup	18+1	19	11
North American Soccer League	12+7	19	2
Internationals	20+12	32	9
TOTAL	**566+55**	**621**	**234**

HAT-TRICKS

Coventry City

1	3	Southampton	04/05/82	Away	League	5–5

Portsmouth

1	3	Cambridge United	01/11/83	Home	League	5–0
2	3	Grimsby Town	05/11/83	Home	League	4–0

Rangers

1	3	St Johnstone	10/08/91	Home	League	6–0
2	3	Airdrieonians	29/02/92	Home	League	5–0

League: 3
Scottish League: 2
TOTAL: 5

HONOURS

Winners medals
Scottish Premier Division Championship: 90/91, 91/92, 92/93, 93/94, 94/95
Scottish Cup: 91/92, 92/93
Scottish League Cup: 90/91, 92/93, 93/94
French League Division One Championship: 87/88

Runner-up medals
Scottish Cup: 93/94
Italian Cup: 84/85

Played four (4+0/1) League matches in the Rangers team that won the 1996/97 Scottish Premier Division Championship.

DAVID HIRST

Born: 07/12/67 – Cudworth
Height: 5.11
Weight: 13.10 (96–97)

Clubs
Barnsley: **1985–86** – Matches: **27+2** – Goals: **9**
Sheffield Wednesday: **1986–97** – Matches: **306+46** – Goals: **128**

Country
England: **1991–92** – Matches: **2+1** – Goals: **1**

SEASON 1985–86

Barnsley – League Division Two

1	17/08/85	Charlton Athletic	Away	League	1–2			
2	20/08/85	Brighton & Hove Albion	Home	League	3–2			
3	24/08/85	Stoke City	Home	League	0–0			
Sub+1	31/08/85	Fulham	Home	League	2–0			
4	05/10/85	Portsmouth	Home	League	0–1			
5	08/10/85	Newcastle United	Home	Lge Cup	1–1*			
6	12/10/85	Bradford City	Away	League	0–2			
7	27/10/85	Leeds United	Home	League	3–0	1 Goal	(1)	
8	02/11/85	Oldham Athletic	Home	League	1–0			
9	09/11/85	Blackburn Rovers	Away	League	3–0	2 Goals	(3)	
10	16/11/85	Sunderland	Home	League	1–1	1 Goal	(4)	
11	23/11/85	Crystal Palace	Away	League	0–1			
12	30/11/85	Millwall	Home	League	2–1			
13	07/12/85	Brighton & Hove Albion	Away	League	1–0	1 Goal	(5)	
14	14/12/85	Charlton Athletic	Home	League	2–1	2 Goals	(7)	
15	21/12/85	Stoke City	Away	League	0–0			
16	26/12/85	Huddersfield Town	Away	League	1–1	1 Goal	(8)	
17	28/12/85	Wimbledon	Home	League	0–1			
18	01/01/86	Hull City	Home	League	1–4			
19	11/01/86	Shrewsbury Town	Away	League	0–3			
20	01/02/86	Norwich City	Home	League	2–2	1 Goal	(9)	

21	15/02/86	Leeds United	Away	League	2–0		
22	25/03/86	Middlesbrough	Home	League	0–0		
23	29/03/86	Hull City	Away	League	1–0		
24	31/03/86	Huddersfield Town	Home	League	1–3		
25	06/04/86	Oldham Athletic	Away	League	1–1		
26	19/04/86	Sunderland	Away	League	0–2		
Sub+2	22/04/86	Grimsby Town	Away	League	2–1		
27	26/04/86	Crystal Palace	Home	League	2–4		

SEASON 1986–87

Sheffield Wednesday – League Division One

Sub+1	23/08/86	Charlton Athletic	Away	League	1–1		
Sub+2	25/08/86	Everton	Home	League	2–2	1 Goal	(1)
Sub+3	23/09/86	Stockport County	Home	Lge Cup	3–0		
1	06/10/86	Stockport County	Away	Lge Cup	7–0		
2	28/10/86	Everton	Away	Lge Cup	0–4		
3	01/11/86	Nottingham Forest	Away	League	2–3		
4	08/11/86	Southampton	Home	League	3–1		
5	16/11/86	Liverpool	Away	League	1–1		
6	22/11/86	Luton Town	Home	League	1–0		
7	25/11/86	Portsmouth	Away	FM Cup	0–1		
Sub+4	26/12/86	Manchester City	Away	League	0–1		
8	27/12/86	Liverpool	Home	League	0–1		
Sub+5	14/02/87	Arsenal	Home	League	1–1		
9	21/02/87	West Ham United	Home	FA Cup	1–1		
Sub+6	07/03/87	Coventry City	Away	League	0–1		
Sub+7	14/03/87	Coventry City	Home	FA Cup	0–3		
Sub+8	21/03/87	Manchester United	Home	League	1–0	1 Goal	(2)
Sub+9	24/03/87	West Ham United	Away	League	2–0		
Sub+10	28/03/87	Oxford United	Away	League	1–2		
10	07/04/87	Tottenham Hotspur	Home	League	0–1		
11	14/04/87	Nottingham Forest	Home	League	2–3	1 Goal	(3)
12	18/04/87	Norwich City	Away	League	0–1		
13	20/04/87	Manchester City	Home	League	2–1		
14	25/04/87	Luton Town	Away	League	0–0		
15	02/05/87	Queens Park Rangers	Home	League	7–1	2 Goals	(5)
16	04/05/87	Aston Villa	Away	League	2–1	1 Goal	(6)
17	09/05/87	Wimbledon	Home	League	0–2		

SEASON 1987–88

League Division One

18	15/08/87	Chelsea	Away	League	1–2		
19	18/08/87	Oxford United	Home	League	1–1		
20	22/08/87	Newcastle United	Home	League	0–1		
21	29/08/87	Everton	Away	League	0–4		
22	31/08/87	Coventry City	Home	League	0–3		
Sub+11	05/09/87	Southampton	Away	League	1–1		
Sub+12	12/09/87	Watford	Home	League	2–3		
Sub+13	06/10/87	Shrewsbury Town	Home	Lge Cup	2–1		
Sub+14	10/10/87	Manchester United	Home	League	2–4		
23	17/10/87	Nottingham Forest	Away	League	0–3		
Sub+15	27/10/87	Barnsley	Away	Lge Cup	2–1	1 Goal	(7)
24	31/10/87	Portsmouth	Away	League	2–1		
Sub+16	05/12/87	Arsenal	Away	League	1–3		
Sub+17	06/02/88	Southampton	Home	League	2–1		
25	27/02/88	Tottenham Hotspur	Home	League	0–3		
26	05/03/88	Nottingham Forest	Home	League	0–1		
27	12/03/88	Manchester United	Away	League	1–4		
28	19/03/88	Portsmouth	Home	League	1–0		
29	26/03/88	Norwich City	Away	League	3–0		
30	02/04/88	West Ham United	Home	League	2–1	1 Goal	(8)
31	05/04/88	Luton Town	Away	League	2–2		
32	13/04/88	Oxford United	Away	League	3–0		
33	23/04/88	Queens Park Rangers	Away	League	1–1		
34	30/04/88	Arsenal	Home	League	3–3	1 Goal	(9)
35	03/05/88	Wimbledon	Away	League	1–1		
36	07/05/88	Liverpool	Home	League	1–5	1 Goal	(10)

SEASON 1988–89

League Division One

| Sub+18 | 27/08/88 | Luton Town | Home | League | 1–0 | | |
| Sub+19 | 03/09/88 | Nottingham Forest | Away | League | 1–1 | | |

37	10/09/88	Coventry City	Home	League	1–2	1 Goal	(11)
38	17/09/88	Queens Park Rangers	Away	League	0–2		
39	24/09/88	Arsenal	Home	League	2–1		
40	27/09/88	Blackpool	Away	Lge Cup	0–2		
41	01/10/88	Aston Villa	Home	League	1–0	1 Goal	(12)
42	12/10/88	Blackpool	Home	Lge Cup	3–1*	1 Goal	(13)
Sub+20	12/11/88	Norwich City	Away	League	1–1		
Sub+21	20/11/88	Tottenham Hotspur	Home	League	0–2		
43	23/11/88	Manchester United	Away	League	1–1		
44	26/11/88	Middlesbrough	Away	League	1–0		
45	03/12/88	Derby County	Home	League	1–1		
46	10/12/88	West Ham United	Away	League	0–0		
47	17/12/88	Millwall	Away	League	0–1		
48	26/12/88	Newcastle United	Home	League	1–2	1 Goal	(14)
49	31/12/88	Nottingham Forest	Home	League	0–3		
Sub+22	28/01/89	Blackburn Rovers	Away	FA Cup	1–2	1 Goal	(15)
50	01/02/89	Queens Park Rangers	Home	Simod Cup	0–1*		
51	04/02/89	Aston Villa	Away	League	0–2		
52	11/02/89	Manchester United	Home	League	0–2		
53	18/02/89	Southampton	Home	League	1–1		
54	25/02/89	Wimbledon	Away	League	0–1		
55	04/03/89	Charlton Athletic	Home	League	3–1	1 Goal	(16)
56	11/03/89	Everton	Away	League	0–1		
57	18/03/89	Luton Town	Away	League	1–0	1 Goal	(17)
58	25/03/89	Queens Park Rangers	Home	League	0–2		
59	27/03/89	Newcastle United	Away	League	3–1	1 Goal	(18)
60	01/04/89	Millwall	Home	League	3–0		
61	05/04/89	Wimbledon	Home	League	1–1	1 Goal	(19)
62	08/04/89	Liverpool	Away	League	1–5		
63	12/04/89	Tottenham Hotspur	Away	League	0–0		
64	22/04/89	Derby County	Away	League	0–1		
65	09/05/89	West Ham United	Home	League	0–2		
66	13/05/89	Middlesbrough	Home	League	1–0		
67	17/05/89	Norwich City	Home	League	2–2		

SEASON 1989–90

League Division One

Sub+23	19/08/89	Norwich City	Home	League	0–2		
68	22/08/89	Luton Town	Away	League	0–2		
69	26/08/89	Chelsea	Away	League	0–4		
70	30/08/89	Everton	Home	League	1–1		
71	09/09/89	Arsenal	Away	League	0–5		
72	16/09/89	Aston Villa	Home	League	1–0		
73	20/09/89	Aldershot	Home	Lge Cup	0–0		
74	23/09/89	Millwall	Away	League	0–2		
75	30/09/89	Coventry City	Home	League	0–0		
Sub+24	03/10/89	Aldershot	Away	Lge Cup	8–0		
Sub+25	14/10/89	Manchester United	Away	League	0–0		
76	21/10/89	Tottenham Hotspur	Away	League	0–3		
Sub+26	25/10/89	Derby County	Away	Lge Cup	1–2	1 Goal	(20)
77	28/10/89	Wimbledon	Home	League	0–1		
78	04/11/89	Nottingham Forest	Away	League	1–0		
79	11/11/89	Charlton Athletic	Home	League	3–0	2 Goals	(22)
80	18/11/89	Derby County	Away	League	0–2		
81	21/11/89	Sheffield United	Home	ZDS Cup	3–2		
82	25/11/89	Crystal Palace	Home	League	2–2	1 Goal	(23)
83	29/11/89	Liverpool	Home	League	2–0	1 Goal	(24)
84	02/12/89	Norwich City	Away	League	1–2	1 Goal	(25)
85	09/12/89	Luton Town	Home	League	1–1		
86	16/12/89	Queens Park Rangers	Home	League	2–0	1 Goal	(26)
87	20/12/89	Middlesbrough	Away	ZDS Cup	1–4		
88	26/12/89	Liverpool	Away	League	1–2		
89	30/12/89	Southampton	Away	League	2–2		
90	01/01/90	Manchester City	Home	League	2–0	1 Goal	(27)
91	06/01/90	Wolverhampton Wanderers	Away	FA Cup	2–1		
92	14/01/90	Chelsea	Home	League	1–1		
93	20/01/90	Everton	Away	League	0–2		
94	28/01/90	Everton	Home	FA Cup	1–2	1 Goal	(28)
95	03/02/90	Millwall	Home	League	1–1	1 Goal	(29)
96	10/02/90	Aston Villa	Away	League	0–1		
97	17/02/90	Arsenal	Home	League	1–0		
98	24/02/90	Crystal Palace	Away	League	1–1		
99	03/03/90	Derby County	Home	League	1–0		
100	17/03/90	Coventry City	Away	League	4–1	1 Goal	(30)

101	21/03/90	Manchester United	Home	League	1–0	1 Goal	(31)
102	24/03/90	Wimbledon	Away	League	1–1		
103	31/03/90	Tottenham Hotspur	Home	League	2–4	1 Goal	(32)
104	07/04/90	Southampton	Home	League	0–1		
105	14/04/90	Manchester City	Away	League	1–2	1 Goal	(33)
106	21/04/90	Queens Park Rangers	Away	League	0–1		
107	28/04/90	Charlton Athletic	Away	League	2–1	2 Goals	(35)
108	05/05/90	Nottingham Forest	Home	League	0–3		

SEASON 1990–91

League Division Two

109	25/08/90	Ipswich Town	Away	League	2–0		
110	01/09/90	Hull City	Home	League	5–1	4 Goals	(39)
111	08/09/90	Charlton Athletic	Away	League	1–0		
112	15/09/90	Watford	Home	League	2–0		
113	18/09/90	Newcastle United	Home	League	2–2	1 Goal	(40)
114	22/09/90	Leicester City	Away	League	4–2	2 Goals	(42)
115	26/09/90	Brentford	Home	Lge Cup	2–1	1 Goal	(43)
116	29/09/90	West Ham United	Home	League	1–1	1 Goal	(44)
Sub+27	20/10/90	Port Vale	Home	League	1–1		
117	23/10/90	Barnsley	Away	League	1–1		
118	27/10/90	Millwall	Away	League	2–4	2 Goals	(46)
119	31/10/90	Swindon Town	Home	Lge Cup	0–0		
120	03/11/90	Oldham Athletic	Home	League	2–2		
121	06/11/90	Swindon Town	Away	Lge Cup	1–0		
122	10/11/90	Blackburn Rovers	Away	League	0–1		
123	17/11/90	Swindon Town	Home	League	2–1		
124	24/11/90	West Bromwich Albion	Away	League	2–1		
125	27/11/90	Derby County	Home	Lge Cup	1–1	1 Goal	(47)
126	01/12/90	Notts County	Home	League	2–2	1 Goal	(48)
127	08/12/90	Bristol City	Away	League	1–1		
128	12/12/90	Derby County	Away	Lge Cup	2–1		
129	15/12/90	Ipswich Town	Home	League	2–2		
130	18/12/90	Barnsley	Home	ZDS Cup	3–3+	3 Goals	(51)
131	22/12/90	Oxford United	Away	League	2–2	1 Goal	(52)
132	26/12/90	Wolverhampton Wanderers	Home	League	2–2		
133	29/12/90	Portsmouth	Home	League	2–1	2 Goals	(54)
134	01/01/91	Middlesbrough	Away	League	2–0	1 Goal	(55)
135	05/01/91	Mansfield Town	Away	FA Cup	2–0		
136	12/01/91	Hull City	Away	League	1–0		
137	19/01/91	Charlton Athletic	Home	League	0–0		
138	23/01/91	Coventry City	Away	Lge Cup	1–0		
139	26/01/91	Millwall	Away	FA Cup	4–4	1 Goal	(56)
140	30/01/91	Millwall	Home	FA Cup	2–0	1 Goal	(57)
141	02/02/91	Watford	Away	League	2–2		
142	16/02/91	Cambridge United	Away	FA Cup	0–4		
143	19/02/91	Swindon Town	Away	League	1–2	1 Goal	(58)
144	24/02/91	Chelsea	Away	Lge Cup	2–0	1 Goal	(59)
145	27/02/91	Chelsea	Home	Lge Cup	3–1		
Sub+28	13/03/91	Brighton & Hove Albion	Home	League	1–1		
146	16/03/91	West Ham United	Away	League	3–1	1 Goal	(60)
147	19/03/91	Plymouth Argyle	Away	League	1–1		
148	23/03/91	Bristol Rovers	Home	League	2–1		
149	30/03/91	Wolverhampton Wanderers	Away	League	2–3		
150	01/04/91	Oxford United	Home	League	0–2		
151	06/04/91	Portsmouth	Away	League	0–2		
152	10/04/91	Blackburn Rovers	Home	League	3–1		
153	13/04/91	Middlesbrough	Home	League	2–0		
154	17/04/91	Newcastle United	Away	League	0–1		
155	21/04/91	Manchester United	Wembley	Lge Cup	1–0		
156	24/04/91	Leicester City	Home	League	0–0		
157	27/04/91	Barnsley	Home	League	3–1	1 Goal	(61)
158	04/05/91	Millwall	Home	League	2–1	2 Goals	(63)
159	06/05/91	Port Vale	Away	League	1–1	1 Goal	(64)
160	08/05/91	Bristol City	Home	League	3–1	2 Goals	(66)
161	11/05/91	Oldham Athletic	Away	League	2–3	1 Goal	(67)

+ AET Barnsley won 4–2 on penalties

SEASON 1991–92

League Division One

| 162 | 17/08/91 | Aston Villa | Home | League | 2–3 | 1 Goal | (68) |
| 163 | 24/08/91 | Leeds United | Away | League | 1–1 | 1 Goal | (69) |

164	28/08/91	Everton	Home	League	2–1		
165	31/08/91	Queens Park Rangers	Home	League	4–1		
166	03/09/91	Notts County	Away	League	1–2		
167	05/10/91	Crystal Palace	Home	League	4–1	2 Goals	(71)
168	09/10/91	Leyton Orient	Home	Lge Cup	4–1		
169	19/10/91	Luton Town	Away	League	2–2	1 Goal	(72)
170	23/10/91	Manchester City	Home	ZDS Cup	3–2	1 Goal	(73)
171	26/10/91	Manchester United	Home	League	3–2	1 Goal	(74)
172	30/10/91	Southampton	Home	Lge Cup	1–1	1 Goal	(75)
173	02/11/91	Tottenham Hotspur	Home	League	0–0		
174	17/11/91	Sheffield United	Away	League	0–2		
175	20/11/91	Southampton	Away	Lge Cup	0–1		
176	23/11/91	Arsenal	Home	League	1–1	1 Goal	(76)
177	26/11/91	Notts County	Away	ZDS Cup	0–1		
178	30/11/91	West Ham United	Away	League	2–1		
179	07/12/91	Chelsea	Home	League	3–0	2 Goals	(78)
180	21/12/91	Wimbledon	Home	League	2–0		
181	26/12/91	Everton	Away	League	1–0	1 Goal	(79)
182	28/12/91	Queens Park Rangers	Away	League	1–1	1 Goal	(80)
183	01/01/92	Oldham Athletic	Home	League	1–1		
184	27/01/92	Middlesbrough	Home	FA Cup	1–2	1 Goal	(81)
185	01/02/92	Luton Town	Home	League	3–2	1 Goal	(82)
186	08/02/92	Manchester United	Away	League	1–1	1 Goal	(83)
187	15/02/92	Arsenal	Away	League	1–7		
188	22/02/92	West Ham United	Home	League	2–1		
189	29/02/92	Chelsea	Away	League	3–0		
190	07/03/92	Coventry City	Home	League	1–1		
191	11/03/92	Sheffield United	Home	League	1–3		
192	14/03/92	Tottenham Hotspur	Away	League	2–0	1 Goal	(84)
193	21/03/92	Notts County	Home	League	1–0	1 Goal	(85)
194	28/03/92	Oldham Athletic	Away	League	0–3		
195	04/04/92	Nottingham Forest	Away	League	2–0	1 Goal	(86)
196	08/04/92	Coventry City	Away	League	0–0		
197	11/04/92	Manchester City	Home	League	2–0	1 Goal	(87)
198	18/04/92	Southampton	Away	League	1–0	1 Goal	(88)
199	25/04/92	Crystal Palace	Away	League	1–1		
200	02/05/92	Liverpool	Home	League	0–0		

SEASON 1992–93

Premier League

201	15/08/92	Everton	Away	League	1–1		
202	19/08/92	Nottingham Forest	Home	League	2–0	2 Goals	(90)
203	22/08/92	Chelsea	Home	League	3–3	2 Goals	(92)
204	25/08/92	Crystal Palace	Away	League	1–1		
205	29/08/92	Arsenal	Away	League	1–2	1 Goal	(93)
206	17/10/92	Oldham Athletic	Home	League	2–1		
207	20/10/92	1.FC Kaiserslautern	Away	UEFA Cup	1–3	1 Goal	(94)
208	27/10/92	Leicester City	Home	Lge Cup	7–1	1 Goal	(95)
209	31/10/92	Blackburn Rovers	Home	League	0–0		
210	08/11/92	Sheffield United	Away	League	1–1	1 Goal	(96)
211	21/11/92	Ipswich Town	Home	League	1–1		
212	28/11/92	Wimbledon	Away	League	1–1		
213	02/12/92	Queens Park Rangers	Home	Lge Cup	4–0	1 Goal	(97)
214	05/12/92	Aston Villa	Home	League	1–2		
215	12/12/92	Leeds United	Away	League	1–3		
216	19/12/92	Queens Park Rangers	Home	League	1–0		
217	26/12/92	Manchester United	Home	League	3–3	1 Goal	(98)
218	28/12/92	Southampton	Away	League	2–1	1 Goal	(99)
219	10/01/93	Norwich City	Home	League	1–0		
220	13/01/93	Cambridge United	Away	FA Cup	2–1		
221	16/01/93	Tottenham Hotspur	Away	League	2–0	1 Goal	(100)
222	19/01/93	Ipswich Town	Away	Lge Cup	1–1		
223	10/03/93	Ipswich Town	Away	League	1–0	1 Goal	(101)
Sub+29	14/03/93	Blackburn Rovers	Home	Lge Cup	2–1	1 Goal	(102)
Sub+30	17/03/93	Derby County	Home	FA Cup	1–0		
Sub+31	03/04/93	Sheffield United	Wembley	FA Cup	2–1		
Sub+32	18/04/93	Arsenal	Wembley	Lge Cup	1–2		
224	21/04/93	Sheffield United	Home	League	1–1		
225	01/05/93	Middlesbrough	Home	League	2–3		
226	04/05/93	Leeds United	Home	League	1–1	1 Goal	(103)
227	08/05/93	Blackburn Rovers	Away	League	0–1		
228	15/05/93	Arsenal	Wembley	FA Cup	1–1*	1 Goal	(104)
229	20/05/93	Arsenal	Wembley	FA Cup	1–2*		

SEASON 1993–94

Premier League

230	14/08/93	Liverpool	Away	League	0–2		
231	18/08/93	Aston Villa	Home	League	0–0		
232	21/08/93	Arsenal	Home	League	0–1		
233	25/08/93	West Ham United	Away	League	0–2		
234	18/09/93	Southampton	Home	League	2–0	1 Goal	(105)
Sub+33	29/01/94	Chelsea	Away	FA Cup	1–1		
Sub+34	05/02/94	Tottenham Hotspur	Away	League	3–1		
235	13/02/94	Manchester United	Away	Lge Cup	0–1		
236	25/02/94	Norwich City	Away	League	1–1		
237	02/03/94	Manchester United	Home	Lge Cup	1–4		

SEASON 1994–95

Premier League

238	20/08/94	Tottenham Hotspur	Home	League	3–4	1 Goal	(106)
239	24/08/94	Queens Park Ranger	Away	League	2–3		
240	27/08/94	Wimbledon	Away	League	1–0		
241	31/08/94	Norwich City	Home	League	0–0		
242	10/09/94	Nottingham Forest	Away	League	1–4		
243	17/09/94	Manchester City	Home	League	1–1		
244	21/09/94	Bradford City	Home	Lge Cup	2–1		
Sub+35	26/09/94	Leeds United	Home	League	1–1		
Sub+36	01/10/94	Liverpool	Away	League	1–4		
Sub+37	04/10/94	Bradford City	Away	Lge Cup	1–1		
245	08/10/94	Manchester United	Home	League	1–0	1 Goal	(107)
246	16/10/94	Ipswich Town	Away	League	2–1	1 Goal	(108)
247	22/10/94	Newcastle United	Away	League	1–2		
248	08/04/95	Leicester City	Home	League	1–0		
249	15/04/95	Coventry City	Away	League	0–2		
250	17/04/95	Everton	Home	League	0–0		
251	14/05/95	Ipswich Town	Home	League	4–1		

SEASON 1995–96

Premier League

252	15/07/95	Karlsruhe	Away	IT Cup	1–1		
253	22/07/95	AGF Aarhus	Home	IT Cup	3–1+		
Sub+38	19/08/95	Liverpool	Away	League	0–1		
254	23/08/95	Blackburn Rovers	Home	League	2–1		
255	27/08/95	Newcastle United	Home	League	0–2		
256	30/08/95	Wimbledon	Away	League	2–2	1 Goal	(109)
257	16/09/95	Tottenham Hotspur	Home	League	1–3	1 Goal	(110)
258	23/09/95	Manchester United	Home	League	0–0		
259	30/09/95	Leeds United	Away	League	0–2		
260	04/10/95	Crewe Alexandra	Home	Lge Cup	5–2	1 Goal	(111)
261	25/10/95	Millwall	Away	Lge Cup	2–0		
262	28/10/95	West Ham United	Home	League	0–1		
263	04/11/95	Chelsea	Away	League	0–0		
264	18/11/95	Manchester City	Home	League	1–1	1 Goal	(112)
265	21/11/95	Arsenal	Away	League	2–4	1 Goal	(113)
Sub+39	29/11/95	Arsenal	Away	Lge Cup	1–2		
266	04/12/95	Coventry City	Home	League	4–3	1 Goal	(114)
267	09/12/95	Manchester United	Away	League	2–2		
268	16/12/95	Leeds United	Home	League	6–2	2 Goals	(116)
269	23/12/95	Southampton	Home	League	2–2	2 Goals	(118)
270	26/12/95	Nottingham Forest	Away	League	0–1		
271	01/01/96	Bolton Wanderers	Home	League	4–2	2 Goals	(120)
272	06/01/96	Charlton Athletic	Away	FA Cup	0–2		
273	13/01/96	Liverpool	Home	League	1–1		
274	20/01/96	Blackburn Rovers	Away	League	0–3		
275	03/02/96	Newcastle United	Away	League	0–2		
276	24/02/96	Tottenham Hotspur	Away	League	0–1		
277	16/03/96	Aston Villa	Home	League	2–0	1 Goal	(121)
278	20/03/96	Southampton	Away	League	1–0		
279	23/03/96	Bolton Wanderers	Away	League	1–2		
280	05/04/96	Middlesbrough	Away	League	1–3		
281	08/04/96	Arsenal	Home	League	1–0		
282	13/04/96	Manchester City	Away	League	0–1		
283	17/04/96	Chelsea	Home	League	0–0		
284	27/04/96	Everton	Home	League	2–5	1 Goal	(122)
285	05/05/96	West Ham United	Away	League	1–1		

+ Played at Millmoor Ground, Rotherham United

SEASON 1996–97

Premier League

286	02/09/96	Leicester City	Home	League	2–1			
287	04/09/96	Chelsea	Home	League	0–2			
288	16/09/96	Arsenal	Away	League	1–4			
289	18/09/96	Oxford United	Home	Lge Cup	1–1			
290	21/09/96	Derby County	Home	League	0–0			
291	28/09/96	Everton	Away	League	0–2			
292	12/10/96	Wimbledon	Away	League	2–4			
293	19/10/96	Blackburn Rovers	Home	League	1–1			
Sub+40	18/12/96	Manchester United	Home	League	1–1			
Sub+41	21/12/96	Tottenham Hotspur	Away	League	1–1			
294	26/12/96	Arsenal	Home	League	0–0			
Sub+42	11/01/97	Everton	Home	League	2–1	1 Goal	(123)	
Sub+43	18/01/97	Middlesbrough	Away	League	2–4			
295	29/01/97	Aston Villa	Away	League	1–0			
296	01/02/97	Coventry City	Home	League	0–0			
Sub+44	16/02/97	Bradford City	Away	FA Cup	1–0			
Sub+45	19/02/97	Derby County	Away	League	2–2	1 Goal	(124)	
297	22/02/97	Southampton	Away	League	3–2	2 Goals	(126)	
298	01/03/97	Middlesbrough	Home	League	3–1			
299	05/03/97	Nottingham Forest	Away	League	3–0			
Sub+46	09/03/97	Wimbledon	Home	FA Cup	0–2			
300	12/03/97	Sunderland	Home	League	2–1	1 Goal	(127)	
301	15/03/97	Manchester United	Away	League	0–2			
302	22/03/97	Leeds United	Home	League	2–2	1 Goal	(128)	
303	09/04/97	Tottenham Hotspur	Home	League	2–1			
304	03/05/97	West Ham United	Away	League	1–5			
305	07/05/97	Leicester City	Away	League	0–1			
306	11/05/97	Liverpool	Home	League	1–1			

INTERNATIONAL APPEARANCES – ENGLAND

1	01/06/91	Australia	Sydney	1–0	F		
Sub 2	08/06/91	New Zealand	Wellington	2–0	F	1 Goal	(1)
3	19/02/92	France	Wembley	2–0	F		

APPEARANCES AND GOALS PER SEASON

SEASON 85–86	GAMES	GOALS
League	26+2	9
League Cup	1	0
TOTAL	**27+2**	**9**

SEASON 86–87	GAMES	GOALS
League	13+8	6
FA Cup	1+1	0
League Cup	2+1	0
Full Members Cup	1	0
TOTAL	**17+10**	**6**

SEASON 87–88	GAMES	GOALS
League	19+5	3
League Cup	0+2	1
TOTAL	**19+7**	**4**

SEASON 88–89	GAMES	GOALS
League	28+4	7
FA Cup	0+1	1
League Cup	2	1
Simod Cup	1	0
TOTAL	**31+5**	**9**

SEASON 89–90	GAMES	GOALS
League	36+2	14
FA Cup	2	1
League Cup	1+2	1
Zenith Data Systems Cup	2	0
TOTAL	**41+4**	**16**

SEASON 90–91	GAMES	GOALS
League	39+2	24
FA Cup	4	2
League Cup	9	3
Zenith Data Systems Cup	1	3
TOTAL	**53+2**	**32**

SEASON 91–92	GAMES	GOALS
League	33	18
FA Cup	1	1
League Cup	3	1
Zenith Data Systems Cup	2	1
TOTAL	**39**	**21**

SEASON 92–93	GAMES	GOALS
League	22	11
FA Cup	3+2	1
League Cup	3+2	3
UEFA Cup	1	1
TOTAL	**29+4**	**16**

SEASON 93–94	GAMES	GOALS
League	6+1	1
FA Cup	0+1	0
League Cup	2	0
TOTAL	**8+2**	**1**

SEASON 94–95	GAMES	GOALS
League	13+2	3
League Cup	1+1	0
TOTAL	**14+3**	**3**

SEASON 95–96	GAMES	GOALS
League	29+1	13
FA Cup	1	0
League Cup	2+1	1
Inter–Toto Cup	2	0
TOTAL	**34+2**	**14**

SEASON 96–97	GAMES	GOALS
League	20+5	6
FA Cup	0+2	0
League Cup	1	0
TOTAL	**21+7**	**6**

CAREER APPEARANCES AND GOALS

COMPETITION	GAMES	TOTAL	GOALS
League	284+32	316	115
FA Cup	12+7	19	6
League Cup	27+9	36	11
Full Members Cup	1	1	0
Simod Cup	1	1	0
Zenith Data Systems Cup	5	5	4
UEFA Cup	1	1	1
Inter–Toto Cup	2	2	0
Internationals	2+1	3	1
TOTAL	**335+49**	**384**	**138**

HAT-TRICKS

Sheffield Wednesday

1	4	Hull City	01/09/90	Home	League	5–1
2	3	Barnsley	18/12/90	Home	ZDS Cup	3–3

League: 1
Zenith Data Systems Cup: 1
TOTAL: 2

HONOURS

Winners medals
League Cup: 90/91

Runner-up medals
FA Cup: 92/93
League Cup: 92/93
Promoted to League Division One: 90/91

DEAN HOLDSWORTH

Born 08/11/68 – Walthamstow
Height: 5.11
Weight: 11.13 (96–97)

Clubs
Watford: **1987–89** – Matches: **2+18** – Goals: **3**
Carlisle United (loan): **1988** – Matches: **4** – Goals: **1**
Port Vale (loan): **1988** – Matches: **6** – Goals: **2**
Swansea City (loan): **1988** – Matches: **4+1** – Goals: **1**
Brentford (loan): **1988** – Matches: **2+5** – Goals: **1**
Brentford: **1989–92** – Matches: **131+7** – Goals: **75**
Wimbledon: **1992–97** – Matches: **173+29** – Goals: **76**

Country
England: England B

SEASON 1987–88

Watford – League Division One

Sub+1	12/12/87	Luton Town	Home	League	0–1
Sub+2	25/01/88	Ipswich Town	Away	Simod Cup	2–5

Carlisle United (loan) – League Division Four

1	20/02/88	Peterborough United	Home	League	0–2		
2	27/02/88	Rochdale	Home	League	2–0	1 Goal	(1)
3	05/03/88	Bolton Wanderers	Home	League	0–2		
4	12/03/88	Wolverhampton Wanderers	Away	League	1–3		

Port Vale (loan) – League Division Three

1	19/03/88	Gillingham	Away	League	0–0		
2	26/03/88	Walsall	Home	League	2–1	1 Goal	(1)
3	02/04/88	Doncaster Rovers	Home	League	5–0		
4	04/04/88	Blackpool	Away	League	2–1		
5	09/04/88	Chester City	Home	League	1–1	1 Goal	(2)
6	12/04/88	Wigan Athletic	Away	League	0–2		

Watford – League Division One

Sub+3	30/04/88	Derby County	Home	League	1–1

SEASON 1988–89

Swansea City (loan) – League Division Four

Sub+1	27/08/88	Gillingham	Away	League	3–2		
1	03/09/88	Bury	Home	League	1–1		
2	10/09/88	Southend United	Away	League	2–0		
3	17/09/88	Brentford	Home	League	1–1		
4	24/09/88	Wolverhampton Wanderers	Home	League	2–5	1 Goal	(1)

Brentford (loan) – League Division Three

Sub+1	15/10/88	Bury	Away	League	1–3		
1	22/10/88	Preston North End	Home	League	0–2		
2	25/10/88	Chesterfield	Away	League	2–2		
Sub+2	29/10/88	Port Vale	Home	League	2–1	1 Goal	(1)
Sub+3	05/11/88	Reading	Away	League	2–2		
Sub+4	08/11/88	Notts County	Home	League	2–1		
Sub+5	12/11/88	Mansfield Town	Away	League	0–1		

Watford – League Division Two

Sub+4	17/12/88	Blackburn Rovers	Away	League	1–2	1 Goal	(1)
Sub+5	14/02/89	Queens Park Rangers	Home	Simod Cup	1–1+		
Sub+6	27/03/89	Portsmouth	Away	League	2–2		
1	01/04/89	Ipswich Town	Home	League	3–2		
2	04/04/89	Blackburn Rovers	Home	League	2–2		
Sub+7	08/04/89	AFC Bournemouth	Away	League	1–0		
Sub+8	11/04/89	Stoke City	Home	League	3–2		
Sub+9	15/04/89	Swindon Town	Away	League	1–1		

Sub+10	18/04/89	Walsall	Home	League	5–0		
Sub+11	22/04/89	Leicester City	Home	League	2–1	1 Goal	(2)
Sub+12	06/05/89	Shrewsbury Town	Home	League	0–0		
Sub+13	21/05/89	Blackburn Rovers	Away	Lge P/O	0–0		
Sub+14	24/05/89	Blackburn Rovers	Home	Lge P/O	1–1*		

+ AET Queens Park Rangers won 2–1 on penalties

SEASON 1989–90

League Division Two

Sub+15	19/08/89	Portsmouth	Home	League	1–0		
Sub+16	22/08/89	Oldham Athletic	Away	League	1–1	1 Goal	(3)
Sub+17	26/08/89	Oxford United	Away	League	1–1		
Sub+18	09/09/89	Sunderland	Away	League	0–4		

Brentford – League Division Three

1	30/09/89	Wigan Athletic	Home	League	3–1	1 Goal	(1)
2	04/10/89	Manchester City	Away	Lge Cup	1–4		
3	07/10/89	Bristol City	Home	League	0–2		
4	14/10/89	Preston North End	Away	League	2–4	1 Goal	(2)
5	17/10/89	Bolton Wanderers	Home	League	1–2	1 Goal	(3)
6	21/10/89	Shrewsbury Town	Away	League	0–1		
7	28/10/89	Fulham	Home	League	2–0		
8	31/10/89	Notts County	Away	League	1–3		
9	04/11/89	Tranmere Rovers	Home	League	2–4		
10	07/11/89	Leyton Orient	Home	LD Cup	3–0	2 Goals	(5)
11	11/11/89	Blackpool	Away	League	0–4		
12	18/11/89	Colchester United	Home	FA Cup	0–1		
13	25/11/89	Northampton Town	Away	League	2–0	1 Goal	(6)
14	03/12/89	Leyton Orient	Home	League	4–3	1 Goal	(7)
15	09/12/89	Mansfield Town	Away	LD Cup	1–2	1 Goal	(8)
16	17/12/89	Mansfield Town	Home	League	2–1	2 Goals	(10)
17	26/12/89	Reading	Away	League	0–1		
18	30/12/89	Swansea City	Away	League	1–2		
19	01/01/90	Walsall	Home	League	4–0	1 Goal	(11)
20	06/01/90	Rotherham United	Home	League	4–2	3 Goals	(14)
21	12/01/90	Chester City	Away	League	1–1		
22	20/01/90	Bristol City	Home	League	2–1		
23	23/01/90	Reading	Home	LD Cup	2–1		
24	27/01/90	Bury	Away	League	2–0	1 Goal	(15)
25	06/02/90	Bristol Rovers	Home	LD Cup	2–2+	1 Goal	(16)
26	10/02/90	Huddersfield Town	Home	League	2–1	2 Goals	(18)
27	18/02/90	Leyton Orient	Away	League	1–0	1 Goal	(19)
28	21/02/90	Cardiff City	Home	League	0–1		
29	25/02/90	Northampton Town	Home	League	3–2	1 Goal	(20)
30	03/03/90	Rotherham United	Away	League	1–2		
31	06/03/90	Wigan Athletic	Away	League	1–2		
32	10/03/90	Crewe Alexandra	Home	League	0–2		
33	13/03/90	Birmingham City	Away	League	1–0	1 Goal	(21)
34	17/03/90	Bristol City	Away	League	0–2		
35	20/03/90	Preston North End	Home	League	2–2	1 Goal	(22)
36	24/03/90	Bolton Wanderers	Away	League	1–0	1 Goal	(23)
37	31/03/90	Shrewsbury Town	Home	League	1–1		
38	07/04/90	Notts County	Home	League	0–1		
39	10/04/90	Fulham	Away	League	0–1		
40	14/04/90	Walsall	Away	League	1–2		
41	16/04/90	Reading	Home	League	1–1		
42	21/04/90	Mansfield Town	Away	League	3–2	2 Goals	(25)
43	28/04/90	Blackpool	Home	League	5–0	1 Goal	(26)
44	02/05/90	Swansea City	Home	League	2–1	2 Goals	(28)
45	05/05/90	Tranmere Rovers	Away	League	2–2		

+ AET Bristol Rovers won 4–3 on penalties

SEASON 1990–91

League Division Three

46	25/08/90	AFC Bournemouth	Home	League	0–0		
47	28/08/90	Hereford United	Home	Lge Cup	2–0		
48	15/09/90	Swansea City	Away	League	2–2		
49	18/09/90	Rotherham United	Away	League	2–2	1 Goal	(29)
50	22/09/90	Bolton Wanderers	Home	League	4–2	1 Goal	(30)
51	26/09/90	Sheffield Wednesday	Away	Lge Cup	1–2		
52	23/10/90	Reading	Away	League	2–1	1 Goal	(31)

53	26/10/90	Tranmere Rovers	Away	League	1–2	1 Goal	(32)
54	10/11/90	Bury	Home	League	2–2		
55	17/11/90	Yeovil Town	Home	FA Cup	5–0	2 Goals	(34)
56	24/11/90	Exeter City	Away	League	1–1		
57	02/12/90	Leyton Orient	Home	League	1–0		
58	01/01/91	Shrewsbury Town	Home	League	3–0		
59	05/01/91	Oldham Athletic	Away	FA Cup	1–3	1 Goal	(35)
60	12/01/91	Mansfield Town	Home	League	0–0		
Sub+1	02/02/91	Rotherham United	Home	League	1–2		
Sub+2	05/02/91	Bolton Wanderers	Away	League	0–1		
61	16/02/91	Exeter City	Home	League	1–0		
62	21/02/91	Wrexham	Home	LD Cup	0–0+		
Sub+3	28/02/91	Hereford United	Away	LD Cup	2–0	1 Goal	(36)
63	03/03/91	Leyton Orient	Away	League	2–1	1 Goal	(37)
64	05/03/91	Southend United	Away	LD Cup	3–0		
65	09/03/91	Stoke City	Home	League	0–4		
66	12/03/91	Preston North End	Home	League	2–0		
Sub+4	16/03/91	Grimsby Town	Away	League	0–2		
67	19/03/91	Cambridge United	Away	League	0–0		
68	23/03/91	Bradford City	Home	League	6–1		
69	26/03/91	Birmingham City	Away	LD Cup	1–2		
70	30/03/91	Birmingham City	Home	League	2–2		
71	01/04/91	Wigan Athletic	Away	League	0–1		
72	06/04/91	Crewe Alexandra	Home	League	1–0		
73	09/04/91	Birmingham City	Home	LD Cup	0–1		
74	13/04/91	Shrewsbury Town	Away	League	1–1		
75	16/04/91	Fulham	Home	League	1–2		
76	20/04/91	Huddersfield Town	Away	League	2–1		
77	23/04/91	Fulham	Away	League	1–0		
78	27/04/91	Reading	Home	League	1–0		
79	30/04/91	Chester City	Away	League	2–1		
80	04/05/91	Tranmere Rovers	Home	League	0–2		
81	19/05/91	Tranmere Rovers	Home	Lge P/O	2–2		
82	22/05/91	Tranmere Rovers	Away	Lge P/O	0–1		

+ AET Brentford won 3–0 on penalties

SEASON 1991–92

League Division Three

83	17/08/91	Leyton Orient	Home	League	4–3	3 Goals	(40)
84	20/08/91	Barnet	Away	Lge Cup	5–5	2 Goals	(42)
85	24/08/91	Exeter City	Away	League	2–1		
86	27/08/91	Barnet	Home	Lge Cup	3–1	1 Goal	(43)
87	03/09/91	Hartlepool United	Away	League	0–1		
88	07/09/91	Shrewsbury Town	Away	League	0–1		
89	14/09/91	Reading	Home	League	1–0		
90	17/09/91	Hull City	Home	League	4–1	1 Goal	(44)
91	21/09/91	Darlington	Away	League	2–1	1 Goal	(45)
92	24/09/91	Brighton & Hove Albion	Home	Lge Cup	4–1	2 Goals	(47)
93	28/09/91	Bolton Wanderers	Home	League	3–2	2 Goals	(49)
Sub+5	09/10/91	Brighton & Hove Albion	Away	Lge Cup	2–4*	1 Goal	(50)
94	12/10/91	Peterborough United	Home	League	2–1		
Sub+6	22/10/91	Aldershot	Away	A Trophy	2–0		
95	26/10/91	Bury	Away	League	3–0	2 Goals	(52)
96	30/10/91	Norwich City	Away	Lge Cup	1–4		
97	02/11/91	Bradford City	Away	League	1–0		
98	06/11/91	Birmingham City	Home	League	2–2		
99	09/11/91	Wigan Athletic	Home	League	4–0	2 Goals	(54)
100	18/11/91	Gillingham	Home	FA Cup	3–3	2 Goals	(56)
101	22/11/91	AFC Bournemouth	Away	League	0–0		
102	26/11/91	Gillingham	Away	FA Cup	3–1	2 Goals	(58)
103	30/11/91	Swansea City	Home	League	3–2	1 Goal	(59)
104	07/12/91	AFC Bournemouth	Away	FA Cup	1–2		
105	14/12/91	Torquay United	Away	League	1–1		
106	17/12/91	Barnet	Home	A Trophy	3–6	2 Goals	(61)
Sub+7	28/12/91	Leyton Orient	Away	League	2–4		
107	01/01/92	Hartlepool United	Home	League	1–0	1 Goal	(62)
108	04/01/92	Stockport County	Away	League	1–2		
109	11/01/92	Stoke City	Home	League	2–0	1 Goal	(63)
110	18/01/92	Chester City	Away	League	1–1		
111	21/01/92	Leyton Orient	Away	A Trophy	2–3	2 Goals	(65)
112	25/01/92	Preston North End	Home	League	1–0		
113	01/02/92	West Bromwich Albion	Away	League	0–2		
114	08/02/92	Bury	Home	League	0–3		

115	11/02/92	Swansea City	Away	League	1–1		
116	15/02/92	Torquay United	Home	League	3–2		
117	22/02/92	Stoke City	Away	League	1–2		
118	29/02/92	Stockport County	Home	League	2–1	1 Goal	(66)
119	03/03/92	Chester City	Home	League	2–0	1 Goal	(67)
120	07/03/92	Preston North End	Away	League	2–3		
121	10/03/92	Birmingham City	Away	League	0–1		
122	14/03/92	Bradford City	Home	League	3–4	1 Goal	(68)
123	20/03/92	Wigan Athletic	Away	League	1–2	1 Goal	(69)
124	29/03/92	AFC Bournemouth	Home	League	2–2		
125	01/04/92	Reading	Away	League	0–0		
126	04/04/92	Shrewsbury Town	Home	League	2–0	1 Goal	(70)
127	11/04/92	Hull City	Away	League	3–0	2 Goals	(72)
128	17/04/92	Darlington	Home	League	4–1	2 Goals	(74)
129	20/04/92	Bolton Wanderers	Away	League	2–1		
130	26/04/92	Fulham	Home	League	4–0	1 Goal	(75)
131	02/05/92	Peterborough United	Away	League	1–0		

SEASON 1992–93

Wimbledon – Premier League

1	15/08/92	Leeds United	Away	League	1–2		
2	18/08/92	Ipswich Town	Home	League	0–1		
3	22/08/92	Coventry City	Home	League	1–2	1 Goal	(1)
4	25/08/92	Sheffield United	Away	League	2–2	1 Goal	(2)
5	29/08/92	Everton	Away	League	0–0		
6	01/09/92	Manchester City	Home	League	0–1		
7	05/09/92	Arsenal	Home	League	3–2		
8	12/09/92	Ipswich Town	Away	League	1–2	1 Goal	(3)
9	19/09/92	Blackburn Rovers	Home	League	1–1		
10	22/09/92	Bolton Wanderers	Away	Lge Cup	3–1		
11	26/09/92	Liverpool	Away	League	3–2		
Sub+1	25/10/92	Tottenham Hotspur	Home	League	1–1		
Sub+2	28/10/92	Everton	Away	Lge Cup	0–0		
12	31/10/92	Manchester United	Away	League	1–0		
13	07/11/92	Queens Park Rangers	Home	League	0–2		
14	10/11/92	Everton	Home	Lge Cup	0–1		
15	21/11/92	Middlesbrough	Away	League	0–2		
16	28/11/92	Sheffield Wednesday	Home	League	1–1		
17	05/12/92	Norwich City	Away	League	1–2		
18	12/12/92	Oldham Athletic	Home	League	5–2	2 Goals	(5)
19	20/12/92	Nottingham Forest	Away	League	1–1		
20	26/12/92	Crystal Palace	Away	League	0–2		
Sub+3	16/01/93	Liverpool	Home	League	2–0		
Sub+4	23/01/93	Aston Villa	Away	FA Cup	1–1		
21	26/01/93	Everton	Home	League	1–3		
22	30/01/93	Coventry City	Away	League	2–0	1 Goal	(6)
23	03/02/93	Aston Villa	Home	FA Cup	0–0+		
24	06/02/93	Leeds United	Home	League	1–0	1 Goal	(7)
25	10/02/93	Arsenal	Away	League	1–0	1 Goal	(8)
26	13/02/93	Tottenham Hotspur	Away	FA Cup	2–3		
27	20/02/93	Sheffield United	Home	League	2–0		
28	06/03/93	Southampton	Home	League	1–2	1 Goal	(9)
29	09/03/93	Middlesbrough	Home	League	2–0	1 Goal	(10)
30	13/03/93	Queens Park Rangers	Away	League	2–1		
31	20/03/93	Norwich City	Home	League	3–0	2 Goals	(12)
32	24/03/93	Sheffield Wednesday	Away	League	1–1	1 Goal	(13)
33	03/04/93	Oldham Athletic	Away	League	2–6	2 Goals	(15)
34	09/04/93	Crystal Palace	Home	League	4–0	2 Goals	(17)
35	12/04/93	Chelsea	Away	League	2–4	1 Goal	(18)
36	17/04/93	Nottingham Forest	Home	League	1–0		
37	01/05/93	Tottenham Hotspur	Away	League	1–1		
38	09/05/93	Manchester United	Home	League	1–2	1 Goal	(19)

+ AET Wimbledon won 6–5 on penalties

SEASON 1993–94

Premier League

39	14/08/93	West Ham United	Away	League	2–0		
40	17/08/93	Chelsea	Home	League	1–1		
41	21/08/93	Aston Villa	Home	League	2–2	1 Goal	(20)
42	24/08/93	Sheffield United	Away	League	1–2		
43	28/08/93	Oldham Athletic	Away	League	1–1		
44	31/08/93	Southampton	Home	League	1–0		

45	11/09/93	Norwich City	Away	League	1–0		
46	20/09/93	Manchester City	Home	League	1–0		
47	22/09/93	Hereford United	Away	Lge Cup	1–0		
48	27/09/93	Queens Park Rangers	Home	League	1–1		
49	02/10/93	Leeds United	Away	League	0–4		
50	05/10/93	Hereford United	Home	Lge Cup	4–1	1 Goal	(21)
51	16/10/93	Sheffield Wednesday	Away	League	2–2		
52	25/10/93	Ipswich Town	Home	League	0–2		
53	27/10/93	Newcastle United	Home	Lge Cup	2–1	1 Goal	(22)
54	30/10/93	Newcastle United	Away	League	0–4		
55	06/11/93	Swindon Town	Home	League	3–0	1 Goal	(23)
56	20/11/93	Manchester United	Away	League	1–3		
57	24/11/93	Tottenham Hotspur	Away	League	1–1	1 Goal	(24)
58	27/11/93	Everton	Home	League	1–1		
59	01/12/93	Liverpool	Away	Lge Cup	1–1		
60	04/12/93	West Ham United	Home	League	1–2	1 Goal	(25)
61	11/12/93	Aston Villa	Away	League	1–0	1 Goal	(26)
62	14/12/93	Liverpool	Home	Lge Cup	2–2+	1 Goal	(27)
63	18/12/93	Sheffield United	Home	League	2–0	1 Goal	(28)
64	26/12/93	Coventry City	Home	League	1–2	1 Goal	(29)
65	28/12/93	Liverpool	Away	League	1–1		
66	01/01/94	Arsenal	Home	League	0–3		
67	08/01/94	Scunthorpe United	Home	FA Cup	3–0	3 Goals	(32)
68	11/01/94	Sheffield Wednesday	Home	Lge Cup	1–2	1 Goal	(33)
69	15/01/94	Sheffield Wednesday	Home	League	2–1		
70	22/01/94	Ipswich Town	Away	League	0–0		
71	29/01/94	Sunderland	Home	FA Cup	2–1		
72	05/02/94	Blackburn Rovers	Away	League	0–3		
73	12/02/94	Newcastle United	Home	League	4–2	1 Goal	(34)
74	20/02/94	Manchester United	Home	FA Cup	0–3		
75	25/02/94	Southampton	Away	League	0–1		
76	05/03/94	Norwich City	Home	League	3–1	1 Goal	(35)
77	12/03/94	Manchester City	Away	League	1–0		
78	16/03/94	Chelsea	Away	League	0–2		
79	19/03/94	Queens Park Rangers	Away	League	0–1		
80	26/03/94	Leeds United	Home	League	1–0		
81	29/03/94	Blackburn Rovers	Home	League	4–1	1 Goal	(36)
82	02/04/94	Coventry City	Away	League	2–1	1 Goal	(37)
83	04/04/94	Liverpool	Home	League	1–1		
84	16/04/94	Manchester United	Home	League	1–0		
85	19/04/94	Arsenal	Away	League	1–1		
86	23/04/94	Swindon Town	Away	League	4–2	1 Goal	(38)
87	26/04/94	Oldham Athletic	Home	League	3–0	3 Goals	(41)
88	30/04/94	Tottenham Hotspur	Home	League	2–1	1 Goal	(42)
89	07/05/94	Everton	Away	League	2–3	1 Goal	(43)

+ AET Wimbledon won 4–3 on penalties

SEASON 1994–95

Premier League

90	20/08/94	Coventry City	Away	League	1–1		
91	23/08/94	Ipswich Town	Home	League	1–1		
92	10/09/94	Leicester City	Home	League	2–1	1 Goal	(44)
93	17/09/94	Crystal Palace	Away	League	0–0		
94	20/09/94	Torquay United	Home	Lge Cup	2–0		
95	01/10/94	Tottenham Hotspur	Home	League	1–2		
96	05/10/94	Torquay United	Away	Lge Cup	1–0	1 Goal	(45)
97	08/10/94	Arsenal	Home	League	1–3		
98	26/11/94	Manchester City	Away	League	0–2		
99	03/12/94	Blackburn Rovers	Home	League	0–3		
100	10/12/94	Coventry City	Home	League	2–0		
101	16/12/94	Ipswich Town	Away	League	2–2	1 Goal	(46)
102	26/12/94	Southampton	Away	League	3–2	2 Goals	(48)
103	28/12/94	West Ham United	Home	League	1–0		
104	31/12/94	Chelsea	Away	League	1–1		
105	07/01/95	Colchester United	Home	FA Cup	1–0		
106	14/01/95	Norwich City	Away	League	2–1		
107	11/02/95	Aston Villa	Away	League	1–7		
Sub+5	19/02/95	Liverpool	Away	FA Cup	1–1		
Sub+6	21/02/95	Blackburn Rovers	Away	League	1–2		
Sub+7	28/02/95	Liverpool	Home	FA Cup	0–2		
108	04/03/95	Queens Park Rangers	Home	League	1–3	1 Goal	(49)
109	07/03/95	Manchester United	Home	League	0–1		
110	11/03/95	Sheffield Wednesday	Away	League	1–0		

111	18/03/95	Crystal Palace	Home	League	2–0		
112	21/03/95	Manchester City	Home	League	2–0		
113	01/04/95	Leicester City	Away	League	4–3		
114	10/04/95	Chelsea	Home	League	1–1		
115	13/04/95	West Ham United	Away	League	0–3		
116	17/04/95	Southampton	Home	League	0–2		
117	29/04/95	Everton	Away	League	0–0		
118	04/05/95	Arsenal	Away	League	0–0		
119	13/05/95	Nottingham Forest	Home	League	2–2	2 Goals	(51)

SEASON 1995–96

Premier League

120	19/08/95	Bolton Wanderers	Home	League	3–2	1 Goal	(52)
121	23/08/95	Queens Park Rangers	Away	League	3–0	1 Goal	(53)
122	26/08/95	Manchester United	Away	League	1–3		
123	30/08/95	Sheffield Wednesday	Home	League	2–2	1 Goal	(54)
Sub+8	16/09/95	Aston Villa	Away	League	0–2		
124	19/09/95	Charlton Athletic	Home	Lge Cup	4–5	2 Goals	(56)
125	23/09/95	Leeds United	Home	League	2–4	1 Goal	(57)
126	30/09/95	Tottenham Hotspur	Away	League	1–3		
127	03/10/95	Charlton Athletic	Away	Lge Cup	3–3	2 Goals	(59)
128	16/10/95	West Ham United	Home	League	0–1		
129	21/10/95	Newcastle United	Away	League	1–6		
130	28/10/95	Southampton	Home	League	1–2		
131	06/11/95	Nottingham Forest	Away	League	1–4		
132	18/11/95	Middlesbrough	Home	League	0–0		
133	22/11/95	Manchester City	Away	League	0–1		
134	03/12/95	Newcastle United	Home	League	3–3	2 Goals	(61)
135	09/12/95	Leeds United	Away	League	1–1		
136	16/12/95	Tottenham Hotspur	Home	League	0–1		
137	23/12/95	Blackburn Rovers	Home	League	1–1		
138	26/12/95	Chelsea	Away	League	2–1		
139	30/12/95	Arsenal	Away	League	3–1	1 Goal	(62)
140	01/01/96	Everton	Home	League	2–3	1 Goal	(63)
141	06/01/96	Watford	Away	FA Cup	1–1		
142	13/01/96	Bolton Wanderers	Away	League	0–1		
143	20/01/96	Queens Park Rangers	Home	League	2–1		
144	03/02/96	Manchester United	Home	League	2–4		
145	07/02/96	Middlesbrough	Away	FA Cup	0–0		
146	10/02/96	Sheffield Wednesday	Away	League	1–2		
147	13/02/96	Middlesbrough	Home	FA Cup	1–0	1 Goal	(64)
148	17/02/96	Huddersfield Town	Away	FA Cup	2–2		
Sub+9	09/03/96	Chelsea	Away	FA Cup	2–2	1 Goal	(65)
149	13/03/96	Liverpool	Away	League	2–2	1 Goal	(66)
150	16/03/96	Arsenal	Home	League	0–3		
Sub+10	30/03/96	Nottingham Forest	Home	League	1–0	1 Goal	(67)
151	06/04/96	West Ham United	Away	League	1–1		
152	08/04/96	Manchester City	Home	League	3–0		
153	13/04/96	Middlesbrough	Away	League	2–1		
154	17/04/96	Blackburn Rovers	Away	League	2–3		
155	27/04/96	Coventry City	Home	League	0–2		
156	05/05/96	Southampton	Away	League	0–0		

SEASON 1996–97

Premier League

157	17/08/96	Manchester United	Home	League	0–3		
158	21/08/96	Newcastle United	Away	League	0–2		
159	18/09/96	Portsmouth	Home	Lge Cup	1–0	1 Goal	(68)
160	23/09/96	Southampton	Home	League	3–1		
161	25/09/96	Portsmouth	Away	Lge Cup	1–1		
Sub+11	12/10/96	Sheffield Wednesday	Home	League	4–2		
Sub+12	19/10/96	Chelsea	Away	League	4–2		
162	22/10/96	Luton Town	Home	Lge Cup	1–1	1 Goal	(69)
Sub+13	26/10/96	Middlesbrough	Away	League	0–0		
163	12/11/96	Luton Town	Away	Lge Cup	2–1*		
Sub+14	16/11/96	Coventry City	Home	League	2–2		
Sub+15	30/11/96	Nottingham Forest	Home	League	1–0		
Sub+16	07/12/96	Sunderland	Away	League	3–1	1 Goal	(70)
Sub+17	14/12/96	Blackburn Rovers	Home	League	1–0	1 Goal	(71)
Sub+18	22/12/96	Aston Villa	Away	League	0–5		
164	21/01/97	Crewe Alexandra	Home	FA Cup	2–0	1 Goal	(72)

Sub+19	25/01/97	Manchester United	Away	FA Cup	1–1		
Sub+20	29/01/97	Manchester United	Away	League	1–2		
Sub+21	01/02/97	Middlesbrough	Home	League	1–1		
165	04/02/97	Manchester United	Home	FA Cup	1–0		
166	15/02/97	Queens Park Rangers	Home	FA Cup	2–1		
Sub+22	18/02/97	Leicester City	Away	Lge Cup	0–0		
Sub+23	23/02/97	Arsenal	Away	League	1–0		
Sub+24	26/02/97	Southampton	Away	League	0–0		
167	01/03/97	Leicester City	Home	League	1–3	1 Goal	(73)
Sub+25	03/03/97	Coventry City	Away	League	1–1		
Sub+26	09/03/97	Sheffield Wednesday	Away	FA Cup	2–0	1 Goal	(74)
Sub+27	18/03/97	West Ham United	Home	League	1–1		
Sub+28	23/03/97	Newcastle United	Home	League	1–1		
168	05/04/97	Tottenham Hotspur	Away	League	0–1		
Sub+29	13/04/97	Chelsea	Neutral	FA Cup	0–3		
169	16/04/97	Leeds United	Home	League	2–0	1 Goal	(75)
170	19/04/97	Sheffield Wednesday	Away	League	1–3		
171	22/04/97	Chelsea	Home	League	0–1		
172	06/05/97	Liverpool	Home	League	2–1	1 Goal	(76)
173	11/05/97	Sunderland	Home	League	1–0		

APPEARANCES AND GOALS PER SEASON

SEASON 87–88	**GAMES**	**GOALS**
League	10+2	3
Simod Cup	0+1	0
TOTAL	**10+3**	**3**

SEASON 88–89	**GAMES**	**GOALS**
League	8+14	4
League Play–offs	0+2	0
Simod Cup	0+1	0
TOTAL	**8+17**	**4**

SEASON 89–90	**GAMES**	**GOALS**
League	39+4	25
FA Cup	1	0
League Cup	1	0
Leyland Daf Cup	4	4
TOTAL	**45+4**	**29**

SEASON 90–91	**GAMES**	**GOALS**
League	27+3	5
League Play–offs	2	0
FA Cup	2	3
League Cup	2	0
Leyland Daf Cup	4+1	1
TOTAL	**37+4**	**9**

SEASON 91–92	**GAMES**	**GOALS**
League	40+1	24
FA Cup	3	4
League Cup	4+1	6
Autoglass Trophy	2+1	4
TOTAL	**49+3**	**38**

SEASON 92–93	**GAMES**	**GOALS**
League	34+2	19
FA Cup	2+1	0
League Cup	2+1	0
TOTAL	**38+4**	**19**

SEASON 93–94	**GAMES**	**GOALS**
League	42	17
FA Cup	3	3
League Cup	6	4
TOTAL	**51**	**24**

SEASON 94–95	**GAMES**	**GOALS**
League	27+1	7
FA Cup	1+2	0
League Cup	2	1
TOTAL	**30+3**	**8**

SEASON 95–96	GAMES	GOALS
League	31+2	10
FA Cup	4+1	2
League Cup	2	4
TOTAL	**37+3**	**16**

SEASON 96–97	GAMES	GOALS
League	10+15	5
FA Cup	3+3	2
League Cup	4+1	2
TOTAL	**17+19**	**9**

CAREER APPEARANCES AND GOALS

COMPETITION	GAMES	TOTAL	GOALS
League	268+44	312	119
League Play–offs	2+2	4	0
FA Cup	19+7	26	14
League Cup	23+3	26	17
Simod Cup	0+2	2	0
Leyland Daf Cup	8+1	9	5
Autoglass Trophy	2+1	3	4
TOTAL	**322+60**	**382**	**159**

HAT-TRICKS

Brentford

1	3	Rotherham United	06/01/90	Home	League	4–2
2	3	Leyton Orient	17/08/91	Home	League	4–3

Wimbledon

1	3	Scunthorpe United	08/01/94	Home	FA Cup	3–0
2	3	Oldham Athletic	26/04/94	Home	League	3–0

League: 3
FA Cup: 1
TOTAL: 4

HONOURS

Winners medals
League Division Three Championship: 91/92

Runner-up medals
None

MARK HUGHES

Born: 01/11/63 – Wrexham
Height: 5.10
Weight: 13.00 (96–97)

Clubs
Manchester United: **1983–86** – Matches: **114+7** – Goals: **47**
FC Barcelona: **1986–87** – Matches: **39** – Goals: **7**
FC Bayern Munchen (loan): **1987–88** – Matches: **23** – Goals: **7**
Manchester United: **1988–95** – Matches: **345+7** – Goals: **115**
Chelsea: **1995–97** – Matches: **79+4** – Goals: **26**

Country
Wales: **1984–97** – Matches: **65** – Goals: **16**

SEASON 1983–84

Manchester United – League Division One

Sub+1	26/10/83	Port Vale	Home	Lge Cup	2–0		
Sub+2	02/11/83	Spartak Varna	Home	ECW Cup	2–0		
1	30/11/83	Oxford United	Away	Lge Cup	1–1	1 Goal	(1)

Sub+3	21/01/84	Southampton	Home	League	3–2		
2	07/03/84	FC Barcelona	Away	ECW Cup	0–2		
3	10/03/84	Leicester City	Home	League	2–0	1 Goal	(2)
Sub+4	17/03/84	Arsenal	Home	League	4–0		
Sub+5	21/03/84	FC Barcelona	Home	ECW Cup	3–0		
Sub+6	07/04/84	Birmingham City	Home	League	1–0		
Sub+7	14/04/84	Notts County	Away	League	0–1		
4	21/04/84	Coventry City	Home	League	4–1	2 Goals	(4)
5	25/04/84	Juventus FC	Away	ECW Cup	0–2		
6	28/04/84	West Ham United	Home	League	0–0		
7	05/05/84	Everton	Away	League	1–1		
8	07/05/84	Ipswich Town	Home	League	1–2	1 Goal	(5)
9	12/05/84	Tottenham Hotspur	Away	League	1–1		
10	16/05/84	Nottingham Forest	Away	League	0–2		

SEASON 1984–85

League Division One

11	25/08/84	Watford	Home	League	1–1		
12	28/08/84	Southampton	Away	League	0–0		
13	01/09/84	Ipswich Town	Away	League	1–1	1 Goal	(6)
14	05/09/84	Chelsea	Home	League	1–1		
15	08/09/84	Newcastle United	Home	League	5–0	1 Goal	(7)
16	15/09/84	Coventry City	Away	League	3–0		
17	19/09/84	Raba ETO Gyor	Home	UEFA Cup	3–0	1 Goal	(8)
18	22/09/84	Liverpool	Home	League	1–1		
19	26/09/84	Burnley	Home	Lge Cup	4–0	3 Goals	(11)
20	29/09/84	West Bromwich Albion	Away	League	2–1		
21	03/10/84	Raba ETO Gyor	Away	UEFA Cup	2–2		
22	06/10/84	Aston Villa	Away	League	0–3		
23	13/10/84	West Ham United	Home	League	5–1	1 Goal	(12)
24	20/10/84	Tottenham Hotspur	Home	League	1–0	1 Goal	(13)
25	24/10/84	PSV Eindhoven	Away	UEFA Cup	0–0		
26	27/10/84	Everton	Away	League	0–5		
27	30/10/84	Everton	Home	Lge Cup	1–2		
28	02/11/84	Arsenal	Home	League	4–2	1 Goal	(14)
29	07/11/84	PSV Eindhoven	Home	UEFA Cup	1–0		
30	10/11/84	Leicester City	Away	League	3–2	1 Goal	(15)
31	17/11/84	Luton Town	Home	League	2–0		
32	24/11/84	Sunderland	Away	League	2–3	1 Goal	(16)
33	28/11/84	Dundee United	Home	UEFA Cup	2–2		
34	01/12/84	Norwich City	Home	League	2–0	1 Goal	(17)
35	12/12/84	Dundee United	Away	UEFA Cup	3–2	1 Goal	(18)
36	22/12/84	Ipswich Town	Home	League	3–0		
37	26/12/84	Stoke City	Away	League	1–2		
38	29/12/84	Chelsea	Away	League	3–1	1 Goal	(19)
39	01/01/85	Sheffield Wednesday	Home	League	1–2	1 Goal	(20)
40	05/01/85	AFC Bournemouth	Home	FA Cup	3–0		
41	12/01/85	Coventry City	Home	League	0–1		
42	26/01/85	Coventry City	Home	FA Cup	2–1	1 Goal	(21)
43	02/02/85	West Bromwich Albion	Home	League	2–0		
44	09/02/85	Newcastle United	Away	League	1–1		
45	15/02/85	Blackburn Rovers	Away	FA Cup	2–0		
46	23/02/85	Arsenal	Away	League	1–0		
47	02/03/85	Everton	Home	League	1–1		
48	06/03/85	Videoton Szekesfehervar	Home	UEFA Cup	1–0		
49	09/03/85	West Ham United	Home	FA Cup	4–2	1 Goal	(22)
50	12/03/85	Tottenham Hotspur	Away	League	2–1	1 Goal	(23)
51	15/03/85	West Ham United	Away	League	2–2		
52	20/03/85	Videoton Szekesfehervar	Away	UEFA Cup	0–1+		
53	23/03/85	Aston Villa	Home	League	4–0	3 Goals	(26)
54	31/03/85	Liverpool	Away	League	1–0		
55	03/04/85	Leicester City	Home	League	2–1		
56	06/04/85	Stoke City	Home	League	5–0	2 Goals	(28)
57	09/04/85	Sheffield Wednesday	Away	League	0–1		
58	13/04/85	Liverpool	Neutral	FA Cup	2–2*		
59	17/04/85	Liverpool	Neutral	FA Cup	2–1	1 Goal	(29)
60	21/04/85	Luton Town	Away	League	1–2		
61	24/04/85	Southampton	Home	League	0–0		
62	27/04/85	Sunderland	Home	League	2–2		
63	04/05/85	Norwich City	Away	League	1–0		
64	13/05/85	Watford	Away	League	1–5		
65	18/05/85	Everton	Wembley	FA Cup	1–0		

+ AET Videoton Szekesfehervar won 5–4 on penalties

SEASON 1985–86

League Division One

66	10/08/85	Everton	Wembley	FA C/S	0–2		
67	17/08/85	Aston Villa	Home	League	4–0	2 Goals	(31)
68	20/08/85	Ipswich Town	Away	League	1–0		
69	24/08/85	Arsenal	Away	League	2–1	1 Goal	(32)
70	26/08/85	West Ham United	Home	League	2–0	1 Goal	(33)
71	31/08/85	Nottingham Forest	Away	League	3–1	1 Goal	(34)
72	04/09/85	Newcastle United	Home	League	3–0	1 Goal	(35)
73	07/09/85	Oxford United	Home	League	3–0		
74	14/09/85	Manchester City	Away	League	3–0		
75	18/09/85	Everton	Home	SSS Cup	2–4		
76	28/09/85	Southampton	Home	League	1–0	1 Goal	(36)
77	05/10/85	Luton Town	Away	League	1–1	1 Goal	(37)
78	09/10/85	Crystal Palace	Home	Lge Cup	1–0		
79	12/10/85	Queens Park Rangers	Home	League	2–0	1 Goal	(38)
80	19/10/85	Liverpool	Home	League	1–1		
81	26/10/85	Chelsea	Away	League	2–1	1 Goal	(39)
82	29/10/85	West Ham United	Home	Lge Cup	1–0		
83	02/11/85	Coventry City	Home	League	2–0		
84	06/11/85	Norwich City	Home	SSS Cup	1–0		
85	09/11/85	Sheffield Wednesday	Away	League	0–1		
86	16/11/85	Tottenham Hotspur	Home	League	0–0		
87	23/11/85	Leicester City	Away	League	0–3		
88	30/11/85	Watford	Home	League	1–1		
89	04/12/85	Everton	Away	SSS Cup	0–1		
90	07/12/85	Ipswich Town	Home	League	1–0		
91	14/12/85	Aston Villa	Away	League	3–1	1 Goal	(40)
92	21/12/85	Arsenal	Home	League	0–1		
93	26/12/85	Everton	Away	League	1–3		
94	01/01/86	Birmingham City	Home	League	1–0		
95	09/01/86	Rochdale	Home	FA Cup	2–0	1 Goal	(41)
96	11/01/86	Oxford United	Away	League	3–1	1 Goal	(42)
97	18/01/86	Nottingham Forest	Home	League	2–3		
98	02/02/86	West Ham United	Away	League	1–2		
99	09/02/86	Liverpool	Away	League	1–1		
100	22/02/86	West Bromwich Albion	Home	League	3–0		
101	01/03/86	Southampton	Away	League	0–1		
102	05/03/86	West Ham United	Away	FA Cup	1–1		
103	09/03/86	West Ham United	Home	FA Cup	0–2		
104	19/03/86	Luton Town	Home	League	2–0	1 Goal	(43)
105	22/03/86	Manchester City	Home	League	2–2		
106	29/03/86	Birmingham City	Away	League	1–1		
107	31/03/86	Everton	Home	League	0–0		
108	05/04/86	Coventry City	Away	League	3–1		
109	09/04/86	Chelsea	Home	League	1–2		
110	13/04/86	Sheffield Wednesday	Home	League	0–2		
111	16/04/86	Newcastle United	Away	League	4–2	2 Goals	(45)
112	19/04/86	Tottenham Hotspur	Away	League	0–0		
113	26/04/86	Leicester City	Home	League	4–0	1 Goal	(46)
114	03/05/86	Watford	Away	League	1–1	1 Goal	(47)

SEASON 1986–87

FC Barcelona – Spanish League Division One

1	30/08/86	Racing Santander	Home	League	2–0		
2	06/09/86	RCD Mallorca	Away	League	1–1		
3	10/09/86	Cadiz CF	Home	League	2–0	1 Goal	(1)
4	13/09/86	CE Sabadell FC	Away	League	1–1		
5	17/09/86	KS Flamurtari Vlore	Away	UEFA Cup	1–1		
6	21/09/86	Sevilla FC	Home	League	1–0		
7	27/09/86	Athletic Bilbao	Away	League	2–2		
8	01/10/86	KS Flamurtari Vlore	Home	UEFA Cup	0–0		
9	04/10/86	Real Valladolid	Home	League	3–0		
10	08/10/86	Real Madrid CF	Away	League	1–1		
11	12/10/86	RCD Espanol	Home	League	1–0		
12	19/10/86	CR Murcia	Away	League	0–1		
13	22/10/86	Sporting CP Lisboa	Home	UEFA Cup	1–0		
14	26/10/86	UD Las Palmas	Home	League	4–0	1 Goal	(2)
15	02/11/86	Sporting Gijon	Away	League	0–0		
16	16/11/86	Real Betis	Away	League	1–0		
17	22/11/86	Real Sociedad	Home	League	1–0		
18	26/11/86	FC Bayer 05 Uerdingen	Away	UEFA Cup	2–0	1 Goal	(3)
19	06/12/86	CA Osasuna	Away	League	2–0		

20	10/12/86	FC Bayer 05 Uerdingen	Home	UEFA Cup	2–0		
21	14/12/86	Atletico Madrid	Home	League	1–1		
22	17/12/86	Racing Santander	Away	League	0–0		
23	21/12/86	RCD Mallorca	Home	League	3–1		
24	28/12/86	Cadiz CF	Away	League	1–0	1 Goal	(4)
25	04/01/87	CE Sabadell FC	Home	League	3–1		
26	11/01/87	Sevilla FC	Away	League	0–0		
27	17/01/87	Athletic Bilbao	Home	League	4–1	1 Goal	(5)
28	25/01/87	Real Valladolid	Away	League	0–0		
29	28/01/87	CA Osasuna	Home	Sp Cup	0–1		
30	08/02/87	RCD Espanol	Away	League	1–1		
31	11/02/87	CA Osasuna	Away	Sp Cup	1–0+		
32	15/02/87	CR Murcia	Home	League	2–0		
33	22/02/87	UD Las Palmas	Away	League	0–0		
34	28/02/87	Sporting Gijon	Home	League	0–4		
35	04/03/87	Dundee United	Away	UEFA Cup	0–1		
36	08/03/87	Real Zaragoza	Away	League	0–2		
37	18/03/87	Dundee United	Home	UEFA Cup	1–2		
38	23/06/87	Internazionale Milano	Away	Stars Cup	1–3	1 Goal	(6)
39	25/06/87	Paris Saint–Germain FC	Neutral	Stars Cup	3–1	1 Goal	(7)

+ AET CA Osasuna won 5–3 on penalties

SEASON 1987–88

FC Bayern Munchen (loan) – German League Division One

1	07/11/87	Bayer 05 Uerdingen	Home	League	3–0	1 Goal	(1)
2	11/11/87	Borussia Monchengladbach	Home	Ger Cup	3–2*		
3	14/11/87	VFB Stuttgart	Away	League	0–3		
4	21/11/87	Bayer 04 Leverkusen	Home	League	3–2		
5	28/11/87	BV 09 Borussia Dortmund	Home	League	1–3		
6	05/12/87	Hamburger SV	Away	League	2–2		
7	13/02/88	1.FC Nurnberg	Home	Ger Cup	3–1	1 Goal	(2)
8	20/02/88	SV Waldhof 07 Mannheim	Away	League	2–1		
9	27/02/88	FC 08 Homburg/Saar	Home	League	6–0		
10	02/03/88	Real Madrid CF	Home	Eur Cup	3–2		
11	05/03/88	1.FC Nurnberg	Away	League	3–0	1 Goal	(3)
12	08/03/88	Hamburger SV	Home	Ger Cup	1–2		
13	12/03/88	Borussia Monchengladbach	Home	League	1–0		
14	16/03/88	Real Madrid CF	Away	Eur Cup	0–2		
15	19/03/88	SG Eintracht Frankfurt	Away	League	1–1		
16	23/03/88	1.FC Koln	Home	League	2–2	1 Goal	(4)
17	26/03/88	SV Werder Bremen	Away	League	1–3		
18	16/04/88	Hannoverscher SV 96	Away	League	1–2		
19	23/04/88	Karlsruher SC	Home	League	2–1		
20	30/04/88	1.FC Kaiserlautern	Away	League	1–3		
21	03/05/88	VFL Bochum 1848	Home	League	5–0	3 Goals	(7)
22	07/05/88	Bayer 05 Uerdingen	Away	League	0–0		
23	14/05/88	VFB Stuttgart	Home	League	2–1		

SEASON 1988–89

Manchester United – League Division One

1	27/08/88	Queens Park Rangers	Home	League	0–0		
2	29/08/88	Everton	Home	MCC Trophy	1–0		
3	03/09/88	Liverpool	Away	League	0–1		
4	10/09/88	Middlesbrough	Home	League	1–0		
5	17/09/88	Luton Town	Away	League	2–0		
6	21/09/88	Newcastle United	Home	MCC Trophy	2–0*		
7	24/09/88	West Ham United	Home	League	2–0	1 Goal	(1)
8	28/09/88	Rotherham United	Away	Lge Cup	1–0		
9	01/10/88	Tottenham Hotspur	Away	League	2–2	1 Goal	(2)
10	09/10/88	Arsenal	Neutral	MCC Trophy	1–2		
11	12/10/88	Rotherham United	Home	Lge Cup	5–0		
12	22/10/88	Wimbledon	Away	League	1–1	1 Goal	(3)
13	26/10/88	Norwich City	Home	League	1–2	1 Goal	(4)
14	30/10/88	Everton	Away	League	1–1	1 Goal	(5)
15	02/11/88	Wimbledon	Away	Lge Cup	1–2		
16	05/11/88	Aston Villa	Home	League	1–1		
17	12/11/88	Derby County	Away	League	2–2	1 Goal	(6)
18	19/11/88	Southampton	Home	League	2–2	1 Goal	(7)
19	23/11/88	Sheffield Wednesday	Home	League	1–1	1 Goal	(8)
20	27/11/88	Newcastle United	Away	League	0–0		
21	03/12/88	Charlton Athletic	Home	League	3–0	1 Goal	(9)
22	10/12/88	Coventry City	Away	League	0–1		

23	17/12/88	Arsenal	Away	League	1–2	1 Goal	(10)
24	26/12/88	Nottingham Forest	Home	League	2–0	1 Goal	(11)
25	01/01/89	Liverpool	Home	League	3–1	1 Goal	(12)
26	02/01/89	Middlesbrough	Away	League	0–1		
27	07/01/89	Queens Park Rangers	Home	FA Cup	0–0		
28	11/01/89	Queens Park Rangers	Away	FA Cup	2–2*		
29	14/01/89	Millwall	Home	League	3–0	1 Goal	(13)
30	21/01/89	West Ham United	Away	League	3–1		
31	23/01/89	Queens Park Rangers	Home	FA Cup	3–0		
32	28/01/89	Oxford United	Home	FA Cup	4–0	1 Goal	(14)
33	05/02/89	Tottenham Hotspur	Home	League	1–0		
34	11/02/89	Sheffield Wednesday	Away	League	2–0		
35	18/02/89	AFC Bournemouth	Away	FA Cup	1–1	1 Goal	(15)
36	22/02/89	AFC Bournemouth	Home	FA Cup	1–0		
37	25/02/89	Norwich City	Away	League	1–2		
38	12/03/89	Aston Villa	Away	League	0–0		
39	18/03/89	Nottingham Forest	Home	FA Cup	0–1		
40	25/03/89	Luton Town	Home	League	2–0		
41	27/03/89	Nottingham Forest	Away	League	0–2		
42	02/04/89	Arsenal	Home	League	1–1		
43	08/04/89	Millwall	Away	League	0–0		
44	15/04/89	Derby County	Home	League	0–2		
45	22/04/89	Charlton Athletic	Away	League	0–1		
46	29/04/89	Coventry City	Home	League	0–1		
47	02/05/89	Wimbledon	Home	League	1–0		
48	06/05/89	Southampton	Away	League	1–2		
49	08/05/89	Queens Park Rangers	Away	League	2–3		
50	10/05/89	Everton	Home	League	1–2	1 Goal	(16)
51	13/05/89	Newcastle United	Home	League	2–0		

SEASON 1989–90

League Division One

52	19/08/89	Arsenal	Home	League	4–1	1 Goal	(17)
53	22/08/89	Crystal Palace	Away	League	1–1		
54	26/08/89	Derby County	Away	League	0–2		
55	30/08/89	Norwich City	Home	League	0–2		
56	09/09/89	Everton	Away	League	2–3		
57	16/09/89	Millwall	Home	League	5–1	3 Goals	(20)
58	20/09/89	Portsmouth	Away	Lge Cup	3–2		
59	23/09/89	Manchester City	Away	League	1–5	1 Goal	(21)
60	03/10/89	Portsmouth	Home	Lge Cup	0–0		
61	14/10/89	Sheffield Wednesday	Home	League	0–0		
62	21/10/89	Coventry City	Away	League	4–1	2 Goals	(23)
63	25/10/89	Tottenham Hotspur	Home	Lge Cup	0–3		
64	28/10/89	Southampton	Home	League	2–1		
65	04/11/89	Charlton Athletic	Away	League	0–2		
66	12/11/89	Nottingham Forest	Home	League	1–0		
67	18/11/89	Luton Town	Away	League	3–1	1 Goal	(24)
68	25/11/89	Chelsea	Home	League	0–0		
69	03/12/89	Arsenal	Away	League	0–1		
Sub+1	09/12/89	Crystal Palace	Home	League	1–2		
70	16/12/89	Tottenham Hotspur	Home	League	0–1		
71	23/12/89	Liverpool	Away	League	0–0		
72	26/12/89	Aston Villa	Away	League	0–3		
73	30/12/89	Wimbledon	Away	League	2–2	1 Goal	(25)
74	01/01/90	Queens Park Rangers	Home	League	0–0		
75	07/01/90	Nottingham Forest	Away	FA Cup	1–0		
76	13/01/90	Derby County	Home	League	1–2		
77	21/01/90	Norwich City	Away	League	0–2		
78	28/01/90	Hereford United	Away	FA Cup	1–0		
79	03/02/90	Manchester City	Home	League	1–1		
80	10/02/90	Millwall	Away	League	2–1	1 Goal	(26)
81	18/02/90	Newcastle United	Away	FA Cup	3–2		
82	24/02/90	Chelsea	Away	League	0–1		
83	03/03/90	Luton Town	Home	League	4–1	1 Goal	(27)
84	11/03/90	Sheffield United	Away	FA Cup	1–0		
85	14/03/90	Everton	Home	League	0–0		
86	18/03/90	Liverpool	Home	League	1–2		
87	21/03/90	Sheffield Wednesday	Away	League	0–1		
88	24/03/90	Southampton	Away	League	2–0		
89	31/03/90	Coventry City	Home	League	3–0	2 Goals	(29)
90	08/04/90	Oldham Athletic	Neutral	FA Cup	3–3*		
91	11/04/90	Oldham Athletic	Neutral	FA Cup	2–1*		
92	14/04/90	Queens Park Rangers	Away	League	2–1		

93	17/04/90	Aston Villa	Home	League	2–0		
94	21/04/90	Tottenham Hotspur	Away	League	1–2		
95	30/04/90	Wimbledon	Home	League	0–0		
96	05/05/90	Charlton Athletic	Home	League	1–0		
97	12/05/90	Crystal Palace	Wembley	FA Cup	3–3*	2 Goals	(31)
98	17/05/90	Crystal Palace	Wembley	FA Cup	1–0		

SEASON 1990–91

League Division One

99	18/08/90	Liverpool	Wembley	FA C/S	1–1		
100	25/08/90	Coventry City	Home	League	2–0		
101	28/08/90	Leeds United	Away	League	0–0		
102	01/09/90	Sunderland	Away	League	1–2		
Sub+2	04/09/90	Luton Town	Away	League	1–0		
103	16/09/90	Liverpool	Away	League	0–4		
Sub+3	19/09/90	Pecsi MSC	Home	ECW Cup	2–0		
104	22/09/90	Southampton	Home	League	3–2	1 Goal	(32)
105	26/09/90	Halifax Town	Away	Lge Cup	3–1		
Sub+4	29/09/90	Nottingham Forest	Home	League	0–1		
106	03/10/90	Pecsi MSC	Away	ECW Cup	1–0		
107	10/10/90	Halifax Town	Home	Lge Cup	2–1		
108	20/10/90	Arsenal	Home	League	0–1		
109	23/10/90	Wrexham	Home	ECW Cup	3–0		
110	27/10/90	Manchester City	Away	League	3–3	1 Goal	(33)
111	31/10/90	Liverpool	Home	Lge Cup	3–1	1 Goal	(34)
112	10/11/90	Derby County	Away	League	0–0		
113	17/11/90	Sheffield United	Home	League	2–0	1 Goal	(35)
114	25/11/90	Chelsea	Home	League	2–3	1 Goal	(36)
115	27/11/90	Arsenal	Away	Lge Cup	6–2	1 Goal	(37)
116	01/12/90	Everton	Away	League	1–0		
117	08/12/90	Leeds United	Home	League	1–1		
118	15/12/90	Coventry City	Away	League	2–2	1 Goal	(38)
119	22/12/90	Wimbledon	Away	League	3–1	1 Goal	(39)
120	26/12/90	Norwich City	Home	League	3–0	1 Goal	(40)
121	29/12/90	Aston Villa	Home	League	1–1		
122	01/01/91	Tottenham Hotspur	Away	League	2–1		
123	07/01/91	Queens Park Rangers	Home	FA Cup	2–1	1 Goal	(41)
124	12/01/91	Sunderland	Home	League	3–0	2 Goals	(43)
125	16/01/91	Southampton	Away	Lge Cup	1–1	1 Goal	(44)
126	19/01/91	Queens Park Rangers	Away	League	1–1		
127	23/01/91	Southampton	Home	Lge Cup	3–2	3 Goals	(47)
128	26/01/91	Bolton Wanderers	Home	FA Cup	1–0	1 Goal	(48)
129	03/02/91	Liverpool	Home	League	1–1		
130	10/02/91	Leeds United	Home	Lge Cup	2–1		
131	18/02/91	Norwich City	Away	FA Cup	1–2		
132	24/02/91	Leeds United	Away	Lge Cup	1–0		
133	06/03/91	Montpellier–Herault SC	Home	ECW Cup	1–1		
134	09/03/91	Chelsea	Away	League	2–3	1 Goal	(49)
135	16/03/91	Nottingham Forest	Away	League	1–1		
136	19/03/91	Montpellier–Herault SC	Away	ECW Cup	2–0		
137	23/03/91	Luton Town	Home	League	4–1		
138	30/03/91	Norwich City	Away	League	3–0		
139	06/04/91	Aston Villa	Away	League	1–1		
140	10/04/91	CWKS Legia Warszawa	Away	ECW Cup	3–1	1 Goal	(50)
141	16/04/91	Derby County	Home	League	3–1		
142	21/04/91	Sheffield Wednesday	Wembley	Lge Cup	0–1		
143	24/04/91	CWKS Legia Warszawa	Home	ECW Cup	1–1		
144	04/05/91	Manchester City	Home	League	1–0		
145	06/05/91	Arsenal	Away	League	1–3		
146	15/05/91	FC Barcelona	Neutral	ECW Cup	2–1	2 Goals	(52)
147	20/05/91	Tottenham Hotspur	Home	League	1–1		

SEASON 1991–92

League Division One

148	17/08/91	Notts County	Home	League	2–0	1 Goal	(53)
149	21/08/91	Aston Villa	Away	League	1–0		
150	24/08/91	Everton	Away	League	0–0		
151	28/08/91	Oldham Athletic	Home	League	1–0		
152	31/08/91	Leeds United	Home	League	1–1		
153	03/09/91	Wimbledon	Away	League	2–1		
154	07/09/91	Norwich City	Home	League	3–0		
155	14/09/91	Southampton	Away	League	1–0	1 Goal	(54)
156	18/09/91	AS Athinaikos	Away	ECW Cup	0–0		

157	21/09/91	Luton Town	Home	League	5–0	1 Goal	(55)
158	25/09/91	Cambridge United	Home	Lge Cup	3–0		
159	28/09/91	Tottenham Hotspur	Away	League	2–1	1 Goal	(56)
160	01/10/91	AS Athinaikos	Home	ECW Cup	2–0	1 Goal	(57)
161	06/10/91	Liverpool	Home	League	0–0		
162	09/10/91	Cambridge United	Away	Lge Cup	1–1		
163	19/10/91	Arsenal	Home	League	1–1		
164	23/10/91	Atletico Madrid	Away	ECW Cup	0–3		
165	06/11/91	Atletico Madrid	Home	ECW Cup	1–1	1 Goal	(58)
166	16/11/91	Manchester City	Away	League	0–0		
167	19/11/91	Crvena Zvezda Beograd	Home	ES Cup	1–0		
168	23/11/91	West Ham United	Home	League	2–1		
169	30/11/91	Crystal Palace	Away	League	3–1		
170	04/12/91	Oldham Athletic	Home	Lge Cup	2–0		
171	07/12/91	Coventry City	Home	League	4–0	1 Goal	(59)
172	15/12/91	Chelsea	Away	League	3–1		
173	26/12/91	Oldham Athletic	Away	League	6–3		
174	29/12/91	Leeds United	Away	League	1–1		
175	01/01/92	Queens Park Rangers	Home	League	1–4		
176	08/01/92	Leeds United	Away	Lge Cup	3–1		
177	11/01/92	Everton	Home	League	1–0		
178	15/01/92	Leeds United	Away	FA Cup	1–0	1 Goal	(60)
179	18/01/92	Notts County	Away	League	1–1		
180	22/01/92	Aston Villa	Home	League	1–0	1 Goal	(61)
181	27/01/92	Southampton	Away	FA CUP	0–0		
182	01/02/92	Arsenal	Away	League	1–1		
Sub+5	05/02/92	Southampton	Home	FA Cup	2–2+		
183	08/02/92	Sheffield Wednesday	Home	League	1–1		
184	22/02/92	Crystal Palace	Home	League	2–0	2 Goals	(63)
185	26/02/92	Chelsea	Home	League	1–1	1 Goal	(64)
186	29/02/92	Coventry City	Away	League	0–0		
187	04/03/92	Middlesbrough	Away	Lge Cup	0–0		
188	18/03/92	Nottingham Forest	Away	League	0–1		
189	21/03/92	Wimbledon	Home	League	0–0		
190	28/03/92	Queens Park Rangers	Away	League	0–0		
191	31/03/92	Norwich City	Away	League	3–1		
192	07/04/92	Manchester City	Home	League	1–1		
193	12/04/92	Nottingham Forest	Wembley	Lge Cup	1–0		
194	16/04/92	Southampton	Home	League	1–0		
195	18/04/92	Luton Town	Away	League	1–1		
Sub+6	20/04/92	Nottingham Forest	Home	League	1–2		
196	22/04/92	West Ham United	Away	League	0–1		
197	26/04/92	Liverpool	Away	League	0–2		
198	02/05/92	Tottenham Hotspur	Home	League	3–1	2 Goals	(66)

+ AET Southampton won 4–2 on penalties

SEASON 1992–93

Premier League

199	15/08/92	Sheffield United	Away	League	1–2	1 Goal	(67)
200	19/08/92	Everton	Home	League	0–3		
201	22/08/92	Ipswich Town	Home	League	1–1		
202	24/08/92	Southampton	Away	League	1–0		
203	29/08/92	Nottingham Forest	Away	League	2–0	1 Goal	(68)
204	02/09/92	Crystal Palace	Home	League	1–0	1 Goal	(69)
205	06/09/92	Leeds United	Home	League	2–0		
206	12/09/92	Everton	Away	League	2–0		
207	16/09/92	Torpedo Moskva	Home	UEFA Cup	0–0		
208	19/09/92	Tottenham Hotspur	Away	League	1–1		
209	23/09/92	Brighton & Hove Albion	Away	Lge Cup	1–1		
210	26/09/92	Queens Park Rangers	Home	League	0–0		
211	29/09/92	Torpedo Moskva	Away	UEFA Cup	0–0+		
212	03/10/92	Middlesbrough	Away	League	1–1		
213	07/10/92	Brighton & Hove Albion	Home	Lge Cup	1–0	1 Goal	(70)
214	18/10/92	Liverpool	Home	League	2–2	2 Goals	(72)
215	24/10/92	Blackburn Rovers	Away	League	0–0		
216	28/10/92	Aston Villa	Away	Lge Cup	0–1		
217	31/10/92	Wimbledon	Home	League	0–1		
218	07/11/92	Aston Villa	Away	League	0–1		
219	21/11/92	Oldham Athletic	Home	League	3–0	1 Goal	(73)
220	28/11/92	Arsenal	Away	League	1–0	1 Goal	(74)
221	06/12/92	Manchester City	Home	League	2–1	1 Goal	(75)
222	12/12/92	Norwich City	Home	League	1–0	1 Goal	(76)
223	19/12/92	Chelsea	Away	League	1–1		

224	26/12/92	Sheffield Wednesday	Away	League	3–3		
225	28/12/92	Coventry City	Home	League	5–0	1 Goal	(77)
226	05/01/93	Bury	Home	FA Cup	2–0		
227	09/01/93	Tottenham Hotspur	Home	League	4–1		
228	18/01/93	Queens Park Rangers	Away	League	3–1		
229	27/01/93	Nottingham Forest	Home	League	2–0	1 Goal	(78)
230	30/01/93	Ipswich Town	Away	League	1–2		
231	06/02/93	Sheffield United	Home	League	2–1		
232	08/02/93	Leeds United	Away	League	0–0		
233	14/02/93	Sheffield United	Away	FA Cup	1–2		
234	20/02/93	Southampton	Home	League	2–1		
235	27/02/93	Middlesbrough	Home	League	3–0		
236	06/03/93	Liverpool	Away	League	2–1	1 Goal	(79)
237	09/03/93	Oldham Athletic	Away	League	0–1		
238	14/03/93	Aston Villa	Home	League	1–1	1 Goal	(80)
239	20/03/93	Manchester City	Away	League	1–1		
240	24/03/93	Arsenal	Home	League	0–0		
241	10/04/93	Sheffield Wednesday	Home	League	2–1		
242	12/04/93	Coventry City	Away	League	1–0		
243	17/04/93	Chelsea	Home	League	3–0	1 Goal	(81)
244	21/04/93	Crystal Palace	Away	League	2–0	1 Goal	(82)
245	03/05/93	Blackburn Rovers	Home	League	3–1		
246	09/05/93	Wimbledon	Away	League	2–1		

+ AET Torpedo Moskva won 4–3 on penalties

SEASON 1993–94

Premier League

247	07/08/93	Arsenal	Wembley	FA C/S	1–1+	1 Goal	(83)
248	15/08/93	Norwich City	Away	League	2–0		
249	18/08/93	Sheffield United	Home	League	3–0	1 Goal	(84)
250	21/08/93	Newcastle United	Home	League	1–1		
251	23/08/93	Aston Villa	Away	League	2–1		
252	28/08/93	Southampton	Away	League	3–1		
253	19/09/93	Arsenal	Home	League	1–0		
254	22/09/93	Stoke City	Away	Lge Cup	1–2		
255	25/09/93	Swindon Town	Home	League	4–2	2 Goals	(86)
256	29/09/93	Kispest Honved	Home	Eur Cup	2–1		
257	02/10/93	Sheffield Wednesday	Away	League	3–2	2 Goals	(88)
258	06/10/93	Stoke City	Home	Lge Cup	2–0		
259	16/10/93	Tottenham Hotspur	Home	League	2–1		
260	20/10/93	Galatasaray SK	Home	Eur Cup	3–3		
261	23/10/93	Everton	Away	League	1–0		
262	27/10/93	Leicester City	Home	Lge Cup	5–1	1 Goal	(89)
263	30/10/93	Queens Park Rangers	Home	League	2–1	1 Goal	(90)
264	07/11/93	Manchester City	Away	League	3–2		
265	20/11/93	Wimbledon	Home	League	3–1	1 Goal	(91)
266	24/11/93	Ipswich Town	Home	League	0–0		
267	27/11/93	Coventry City	Away	League	1–0		
268	30/11/93	Everton	Home	Lge Cup	2–0	1 Goal	(92)
269	04/12/93	Norwich City	Home	League	2–2		
270	07/12/93	Sheffield United	Away	League	3–0	1 Goal	(93)
271	11/12/93	Newcastle United	Away	League	1–1		
272	19/12/93	Aston Villa	Home	League	3–1		
273	26/12/93	Blackburn Rovers	Home	League	1–1		
274	09/01/94	Sheffield United	Away	FA Cup	1–0	1 Goal	(94)
275	12/01/94	Portsmouth	Home	Lge Cup	2–2		
276	15/01/94	Tottenham Hotspur	Away	League	1–0		
277	22/01/94	Everton	Home	League	1–0		
278	30/01/94	Norwich City	Away	FA Cup	2–0		
279	05/02/94	Queens Park Rangers	Away	League	3–2		
280	13/02/94	Sheffield Wednesday	Home	Lge Cup	1–0		
281	20/02/94	Wimbledon	Away	FA Cup	3–0		
282	26/02/94	West Ham United	Away	League	2–2	1 Goal	(95)
283	02/03/94	Sheffield Wednesday	Away	Lge Cup	4–1	2 Goals	(97)
284	05/03/94	Chelsea	Home	League	0–1		
285	12/03/94	Charlton Athletic	Home	FA Cup	3–1	1 Goal	(98)
286	16/03/94	Sheffield Wednesday	Home	League	5–0	1 Goal	(99)
287	19/03/94	Swindon Town	Away	League	2–2		
288	22/03/94	Arsenal	Away	League	2–2		
289	27/03/94	Aston Villa	Wembley	Lge Cup	1–3	1 Goal	(100)
290	30/03/94	Liverpool	Home	League	1–0		
291	02/04/94	Blackburn Rovers	Away	League	0–2		
292	04/04/94	Oldham Athletic	Home	League	3–2		

293	10/04/94	Oldham Athletic	Wembley	FA Cup	1–1*	1 Goal	(101)
294	13/04/94	Oldham Athletic	Neutral	FA Cup	4–1		
295	16/04/94	Wimbledon	Away	League	0–1		
296	23/04/94	Manchester City	Home	League	2–0		
297	27/04/94	Leeds United	Away	League	2–0		
298	01/05/94	Ipswich Town	Away	League	2–1		
299	04/05/94	Southampton	Home	League	2–0	1 Goal	(102)
300	14/05/94	Chelsea	Wembley	FA Cup	4–0	1 Goal	(103)

+ Manchester United won 5–4 on penalties

SEASON 1994–95

Premier League

301	14/08/94	Blackburn Rovers	Wembley	FA C/S	2–0		
302	20/08/94	Queens Park Rangers	Home	League	2–0	1 Goal	(104)
303	22/08/94	Nottingham Forest	Away	League	1–1		
304	27/08/94	Tottenham Hotspur	Away	League	1–0		
305	31/08/94	Wimbledon	Home	League	3–0		
306	11/09/94	Leeds United	Away	League	1–2		
307	14/09/94	IFK Goteborg	Home	Eur Cup	4–2		
308	17/09/94	Liverpool	Home	League	2–0		
309	28/09/94	Galatasaray SK	Away	Eur Cup	0–0		
310	01/10/94	Everton	Home	League	2–0		
311	08/10/94	Sheffield Wednesday	Away	League	0–1		
312	15/10/94	West Ham United	Home	League	1–0		
313	19/10/94	FC Barcelona	Home	Eur Cup	2–2	1 Goal	(105)
314	23/10/94	Blackburn Rovers	Away	League	4–2	1 Goal	(106)
315	29/10/94	Newcastle United	Home	League	2–0		
316	02/11/94	FC Barcelona	Away	Eur Cup	0–4		
317	10/11/94	Manchester City	Home	League	5–0	1 Goal	(107)
318	19/11/94	Crystal Palace	Home	League	3–0		
319	23/11/94	IFK Goteborg	Away	Eur Cup	1–3	1 Goal	(108)
320	26/11/94	Arsenal	Away	League	0–0		
321	03/12/94	Norwich City	Home	League	1–0		
322	17/12/94	Nottingham Forest	Home	League	1–2		
323	26/12/94	Chelsea	Away	League	3–2	1 Goal	(109)
324	28/12/94	Leicester City	Home	League	1–1		
325	31/12/94	Southampton	Away	League	2–2		
326	09/01/95	Sheffield United	Away	FA Cup	2–0	1 Goal	(110)
327	15/01/95	Newcastle United	Away	League	1–1	1 Goal	(111)
328	19/02/95	Leeds United	Home	FA Cup	3–1	1 Goal	(112)
329	22/02/95	Norwich City	Away	League	2–0		
330	25/02/95	Everton	Away	League	1–0		
331	04/03/95	Ipswich Town	Home	League	9–0	2 Goals	(114)
332	07/03/95	Wimbledon	Away	League	1–0		
333	12/03/95	Queens Park Rangers	Home	FA Cup	2–0		
334	15/03/95	Tottenham Hotspur	Home	League	0–0		
335	19/03/95	Liverpool	Away	League	0–2		
336	22/03/95	Arsenal	Home	League	3–0	1 Goal	(115)
337	02/04/95	Leeds United	Home	League	0–0		
338	09/04/95	Crystal Palace	Neutral	FA Cup	2–2*		
339	12/04/95	Crystal Palace	Neutral	FA Cup	2–0		
340	15/04/95	Leicester City	Away	League	4–0		
341	17/04/95	Chelsea	Home	League	0–0		
342	01/05/95	Coventry City	Away	League	3–2		
343	07/05/95	Sheffield Wednesday	Home	League	1–0		
344	10/05/95	Southampton	Home	League	2–1		
Sub+7	14/05/95	West Ham United	Away	League	1–1		
345	20/05/95	Everton	Wembley	FA Cup	0–1		

SEASON 1995–96

Chelsea – Premier League

1	19/08/95	Everton	Home	League	0–0		
2	23/08/95	Nottingham Forest	Away	League	0–0		
3	26/08/95	Middlesbrough	Away	League	0–2		
4	30/08/95	Coventry City	Home	League	2–2	1 Goal	(1)
5	10/09/95	West Ham United	Away	League	3–1		
6	16/09/95	Southampton	Home	League	3–0	1 Goal	(2)
7	20/09/95	Stoke City	Away	Lge Cup	0–0		
8	24/09/95	Newcastle United	Away	League	0–2		
9	30/09/95	Arsenal	Home	League	1–0	1 Goal	(3)

10	04/10/95	Stoke City	Home	Lge Cup	0–1		
11	14/10/95	Aston Villa	Away	League	1–0		
12	21/10/95	Manchester United	Home	League	1–4	1 Goal	(4)
13	28/10/95	Blackburn Rovers	Away	League	0–3		
14	04/11/95	Sheffield Wednesday	Home	League	0–0		
15	18/11/95	Leeds United	Away	League	0–1		
16	22/11/95	Bolton Wanderers	Home	League	3–2		
17	25/11/95	Tottenham Hotspur	Home	League	0–0		
18	02/12/95	Manchester United	Away	League	1–1		
19	09/12/95	Newcastle United	Home	League	1–0		
20	16/12/95	Arsenal	Away	League	1–1		
21	23/12/95	Manchester City	Away	League	1–0		
22	26/12/95	Wimbledon	Home	League	1–2		
23	07/01/96	Newcastle United	Home	FA Cup	1–1	1 Goal	(5)
24	13/01/96	Everton	Away	League	1–1		
25	17/01/96	Newcastle United	Away	FA Cup	2–2+		
26	20/01/96	Nottingham Forest	Home	League	1–0		
27	24/02/96	Southampton	Away	League	3–2		
28	28/02/96	Grimsby Town	Home	FA Cup	4–1	1 Goal	(6)
29	02/03/96	Wimbledon	Away	League	1–1		
30	09/03/96	Wimbledon	Home	FA Cup	2–2	1 Goal	(7)
31	12/03/96	Manchester City	Home	League	1–1		
32	16/03/96	Liverpool	Away	League	0–2		
33	20/03/96	Wimbledon	Away	FA Cup	3–1	1 Goal	(8)
34	23/03/96	Queens Park Rangers	Home	League	1–1		
35	31/03/96	Manchester United	Neutral	FA Cup	1–2		
36	13/04/96	Leeds United	Home	League	4–1	3 Goals	(11)
37	17/04/96	Sheffield Wednesday	Away	League	0–0		
38	27/04/96	Tottenham Hotspur	Away	League	1–1	1 Goal	(12)
39	05/05/96	Blackburn Rovers	Home	League	2–3		

+ AET Chelsea won 4–2 on penalties

SEASON 1996–97

Premier League

40	18/08/96	Southampton	Away	League	0–0		
41	21/08/96	Middlesbrough	Home	League	1–0		
42	24/08/96	Coventry City	Home	League	2–0		
43	04/09/96	Arsenal	Away	League	3–3		
44	07/09/96	Sheffield Wednesday	Away	League	2–0		
45	15/09/96	Aston Villa	Home	League	1–1		
46	18/09/96	Blackpool	Away	Lge Cup	4–1	1 Goal	(13)
47	21/09/96	Liverpool	Away	League	1–5		
48	28/09/96	Nottingham Forest	Home	League	1–1		
49	12/10/96	Leicester City	Away	League	3–1	1 Goal	(14)
50	19/10/96	Wimbledon	Home	League	2–4		
51	22/10/96	Bolton Wanderers	Away	Lge Cup	1–2		
52	26/10/96	Tottenham Hotspur	Home	League	3–1		
53	02/11/96	Manchester United	Away	League	2–1		
54	16/11/96	Blackburn Rovers	Away	League	1–1		
55	23/11/96	Newcastle United	Home	League	1–1		
56	01/12/96	Leeds United	Away	League	0–2		
Sub+1	15/12/96	Sunderland	Away	League	0–3		
57	21/12/96	West Ham United	Home	League	3–1	2 Goals	(16)
58	26/12/96	Aston Villa	Away	League	2–0		
59	28/12/96	Sheffield Wednesday	Home	League	2–2	1 Goal	(17)
60	01/01/97	Liverpool	Home	League	1–0		
61	04/01/97	West Bromwich Albion	Home	FA Cup	3–0		
62	11/01/97	Nottingham Forest	Away	League	0–2		
63	18/01/97	Derby County	Home	League	3–1		
Sub+2	26/01/97	Liverpool	Home	FA Cup	4–2	1 Goal	(18)
64	01/02/97	Tottenham Hotspur	Away	League	2–1		
65	16/02/97	Leicester City	Away	FA Cup	2–2	1 Goal	(19)
66	22/02/97	Manchester United	Home	League	1–1		
67	26/02/97	Leicester City	Home	FA Cup	1–0		
68	01/03/97	Derby County	Away	League	2–3		
69	05/03/97	Blackburn Rovers	Home	League	1–1		
70	09/03/97	Portsmouth	Away	FA Cup	4–1	1 Goal	(20)
Sub+3	12/03/97	West Ham United	Away	League	2–3	1 Goal	(21)
71	16/03/97	Sunderland	Home	League	6–2	2 Goals	(23)
72	19/03/97	Southampton	Home	League	1–0		
Sub+4	22/03/97	Middlesbrough	Away	League	0–1		
73	09/04/97	Coventry City	Away	League	1–3		

74	13/04/97	Wimbledon	Neutral	FA Cup	3–0	2 Goals	(25)
75	16/04/97	Newcastle United	Away	League	1–3		
76	19/04/97	Leicester City	Home	League	2–1	1 Goal	(26)
77	03/05/97	Leeds United	Home	League	0–0		
78	11/05/97	Everton	Away	League	2–1		
79	17/05/97	Middlesbrough	Wembley	FA Cup	2–0		

INTERNATIONAL APPEARANCES – WALES

1	02/05/84	England	Racecourse	1–0	HC	1 Goal	(1)
2	22/05/84	Northern Ireland	Vetch Field	1–1	HC	1 Goal	(2)
3	12/09/84	Iceland	Reykjavik	0–1	WCQ		
4	17/10/84	Spain	Seville	0–3	WCQ		
5	14/11/84	Iceland	Ninian Park	2–1	WCQ	1 Goal	(3)
6	26/02/85	Norway	Racecourse	1–1	F		
7	27/03/85	Scotland	Hampden Park	1–0	WCQ		
8	30/04/85	Spain	Racecourse	3–0	WCQ	1 Goal	(4)
9	05/06/85	Norway	Bergen	2–4	F	1 Goal	(5)
10	10/09/85	Scotland	Ninian Park	1–1	WCQ	1 Goal	(6)
11	16/10/85	Hungary	Ninian Park	0–3	F		
12	21/04/86	Uruguay	Racecourse	0–0	F		
13	18/02/87	USSR	Vetch Field	0–0	F		
14	29/04/87	Czechoslovakia	Racecourse	1–1	WCQ		
15	09/09/87	Denmark	Ninian Park	1–0	WCQ	1 Goal	(7)
16	14/10/87	Denmark	Copenhagen	0–1	WCQ		
17	11/11/87	Czechoslovakia	Prague	0–2	WCQ		
18	27/04/88	Sweden	Stockholm	1–4	F		
19	01/06/88	Malta	Valletta	3–2	F	1 Goal	(8)
20	04/06/88	Italy	Brescia	1–0	F		
21	14/09/88	Holland	Amsterdam	0–1	WCQ		
22	19/10/88	Finland	Vetch Field	2–2	WCQ		
23	08/02/89	Israel	Tel Aviv	3–3	F		
24	26/04/89	Sweden	Racecourse	0–2	F		
25	31/05/89	West Germany	Cardiff Arms Park	0–0	WCQ		
26	06/09/89	Finland	Helsinki	0–1	WCQ		
27	15/11/89	West Germany	Cologne	1–2	WCQ		
28	20/05/90	Costa Rica	Ninian Park	1–0	F		
29	11/09/90	Denmark	Copenhagen	0–1	F		
30	17/10/90	Belgium	Cardiff Arms Park	3–1	ECQ	1 Goal	(9)
31	14/11/90	Luxembourg	Luxembourg	1–0	ECQ		
32	27/03/91	Belgium	Brussels	1–1	ECQ		
33	01/05/91	Iceland	Ninian Park	1–0	F		
34	29/05/91	Poland	Radom	0–0	F		
35	05/06/91	West Germany	Cardiff Arms Park	1–0	ECQ		
36	11/09/91	Brazil	Cardiff Arms Park	1–0	F		
37	16/10/91	West Germany	Nuremberg	1–4	ECQ		
38	13/11/91	Luxembourg	Cardiff Arms Park	1–0	ECQ		
39	19/02/92	Republic of Ireland	RS Showground	1–0	F		
40	20/05/92	Romania	Bucharest	1–5	WCQ		
41	30/05/92	Holland	Utrecht	0–4	F		
42	03/06/92	Argentina	Tokyo	0–1	F		
43	07/06/92	Japan	Matsuyama	1–0	F		
44	09/09/92	Faroe Islands	Cardiff Arms Park	6–0	WCQ		
45	14/10/92	Cyprus	Nicosia	1–0	WCQ	1 Goal	(10)
46	18/11/92	Belgium	Brussels	0–2	WCQ		
47	17/02/93	Republic of Ireland	Tolka Park	1–2	F	1 Goal	(11)
48	31/03/93	Belgium	Cardiff Arms Park	2–0	WCQ		
49	28/04/93	Czechoslovakia	Ostrava	1–1	WCQ	1 Goal	(12)
50	06/06/93	Faroe Islands	Toftir	3–0	WCQ		
51	08/09/93	Czechoslovakia	Cardiff Arms Park	2–2	WCQ		
52	13/10/93	Cyprus	Cardiff Arms Park	2–0	WCQ		
53	09/03/94	Norway	Ninian Park	1–3	F		
54	16/11/94	Georgia	Tbilisi	0–5	ECQ		
55	14/12/94	Bulgaria	Cardiff Arms Park	0–3	ECQ		
56	26/04/95	Germany	Dusseldorf	1–1	ECQ		
57	07/06/95	Georgia	Cardiff Arms Park	0–1	ECQ		
58	06/09/95	Moldova	Cardiff Arms Park	1–0	ECQ		
59	24/01/96	Italy	Terni	0–3	ECQ		
60	02/06/96	San Marino	Serravalle	5–0	WCQ	2 Goals	(14)
61	31/08/96	San Marino	Cardiff Arms Park	6–0	WCQ	2 Goals	(16)
62	05/10/96	Holland	Cardiff Arms Park	1–3	WCQ		
63	14/12/96	Turkey	Cardiff Arms Park	0–0	WCQ		
64	11/02/97	Republic of Ireland	Cardiff Arms Park	0–0	F		
65	29/03/97	Belgium	Cardiff Arms Park	1–2	WCQ		

APPEARANCES AND GOALS PER SEASON

SEASON 83–84	GAMES	GOALS
League	7+4	4
League Cup	1+1	1
European Cup Winners Cup	2+2	0
TOTAL	**10+7**	**5**

SEASON 84–85	GAMES	GOALS
League	38	16
FA Cup	7	3
League Cup	2	3
UEFA Cup	8	2
TOTAL	**55**	**24**

SEASON 85–86	GAMES	GOALS
League	40	17
FA Cup	3	1
League Cup	2	0
Screen Sport Super Cup	3	0
FA Charity Shield	1	0
TOTAL	**49**	**18**

SEASON 86–87	GAMES	GOALS
Spanish League	28	4
Spanish Cup	2	0
UEFA Cup	7	1
Stars Cup	2	2
TOTAL	**39**	**7**

SEASON 87–88	GAMES	GOALS
German League	18	6
German Cup	3	1
European Cup	2	0
TOTAL	**23**	**7**

SEASON 88–89	GAMES	GOALS
League	38	14
FA Cup	7	2
League Cup	3	0
Mercantile Credit Centenary Trophy	3	0
TOTAL	**51**	**16**

SEASON 89–90	GAMES	GOALS
League	36+1	13
FA Cup	8	2
League Cup	3	0
TOTAL	**47+1**	**15**

SEASON 90–91	GAMES	GOALS
League	29+2	10
FA Cup	3	2
League Cup	9	6
European Cup Winners Cup	7+1	3
FA Charity Shield	1	0
TOTAL	**49+3**	**21**

SEASON 91–92	GAMES	GOALS
League	38+1	11
FA Cup	2+1	1
League Cup	6	0
European Cup Winners Cup	4	2
European Super Cup	1	0
TOTAL	**51+2**	**14**

SEASON 92–93	GAMES	GOALS
League	41	15
FA Cup	2	0
League Cup	3	1
UEFA Cup	2	0
TOTAL	**48**	**16**

SEASON 93–94	GAMES	GOALS
League	36	11
FA Cup	7	4
League Cup	8	5
European Cup	2	0
FA Charity Shield	1	1
TOTAL	**54**	**21**

SEASON 94–95	GAMES	GOALS
League	33+1	8
FA Cup	6	2
European Cup	5	2
FA Charity Shield	1	0
TOTAL	**45+1**	**12**

SEASON 95–96	GAMES	GOALS
League	31	8
FA Cup	6	4
League Cup	2	0
TOTAL	**39**	**12**

SEASON 96–97	GAMES	GOALS
League	32+3	8
FA Cup	6+1	5
League Cup	2	1
TOTAL	**40+4**	**14**

CAREER APPEARANCES AND GOALS

COMPETITION	GAMES	TOTAL	GOALS
League	399+12	411	135
FA Cup	57+2	59	26
League Cup	41+1	42	17
Screen Sport Super Cup	3	3	0
Mercantile Credit Centenary Trophy	3	3	0
FA Charity Shield	4	4	1
European Cup	9	9	2
European Cup Winners Cup	13+3	16	5
UEFA Cup	17	17	3
European Super Cup	1	1	0
Spanish League	28	28	4
Spanish Cup	2	2	0
Stars Cup	2	2	2
German League	18	18	6
German Cup	3	3	1
Internationals	65	65	16
TOTAL	**665+18**	**683**	**218**

HAT-TRICKS

Manchester United

1	3	Burnley	26/09/84	Home	Lge Cup	4–0
2	3	Aston Villa	23/03/85	Home	League	4–0

FC Bayern Munchen (loan)

1	3	VFL Bochum 1848	03/05/88	Home	League	5–0

Manchester United

1	3	Millwall	16/09/89	Home	League	5–1
2	3	Southampton	23/01/91	Home	Lge Cup	3–2

Chelsea

1	3	Leeds United	13/04/96	Home	League	4–1

League: 3
League Cup: 2
German League: 1
TOTAL: 6

HONOURS

Winners medals
Premier League Championship: 92/93, 93/94
FA Cup: 84/85, 89/90, 93/94, 96/97
League Cup: 91/92
European Cup Winners Cup: 90/91
European Super Cup: 91/92
FA Charity Shield: 90/91, 93/94, 94/95

Runner-up medals
Premier League Championship: 94/95
League Division One Championship: 91/92
FA Cup: 94/95
League Cup: 90/91, 93/94
Mercantile Credit Centenary Trophy: 88/89
FA Charity Shield: 85/86

MO JOHNSTON

Born: 30/04/63 – Glasgow
Height: 5.9
Weight: 10.06 (95–96)

Clubs
Partick Thistle: **1981–83** – Matches: **101+3** – Goals: **55**
Watford: **1983–84** – Matches: **45+1** – Goals: **27**
Celtic: **1984–87** – Matches: **125+2** – Goals: **71**
FC Nantes: **1987–89** – Matches: **69** – Goals: **21**
Rangers: **1989–91** – Matches: **99+2** – Goals: **47**
Everton: **1991–93** – Matches: **32+7** – Goals: **10**
Heart of Midlothian: **1993–94** – Matches: **38+1** – Goals: **6**
Falkirk: **1995–96** – Matches: **44** – Goals: **8**
Kansas City Wiz: **1996** – Matches: **35** – Goals: **7**

Country
Scotland: **1984–91** – Matches: **34+4** – Goals: **14**

SEASON 1981–82

Partick Thistle – Scottish League Premier Division

Sub+1	19/08/81	Dundee United	Home	S Lge Cup	1–2	1 Goal	(1)
1	22/08/81	Motherwell	Away	S Lge Cup	1–0		
Sub+2	29/08/81	Rangers	Home	League	0–1		
2	03/10/81	St Mirren	Home	League	1–1		
3	10/10/81	Dundee United	Away	League	0–0		
4	17/10/81	Hibernian	Home	League	1–0		
5	24/10/81	Airdrieonians	Away	League	1–1		
6	31/10/81	Rangers	Away	League	2–0	1 Goal	(2)
7	07/11/81	Dundee	Home	League	1–2	1 Goal	(3)
8	14/11/81	Aberdeen	Away	League	1–2		
9	21/11/81	Morton	Home	League	2–2	1 Goal	(4)
10	28/11/81	Celtic	Home	League	0–2		
11	05/12/81	St Mirren	Away	League	1–2		
12	19/12/81	Hibernian	Away	League	0–3		
13	24/01/82	Dumbarton	Home	S Cup	1–2	1 Goal	(5)
14	30/01/82	Morton	Away	League	0–0		
Sub+3	03/02/82	Aberdeen	Home	League	0–0		
15	06/02/82	St Mirren	Home	League	0–0		
16	17/02/82	Rangers	Home	League	2–0	1 Goal	(6)
17	20/02/82	Celtic	Away	League	2–2		
18	27/02/82	Airdrieonians	Away	League	1–3		
19	06/03/82	Hibernian	Home	League	1–2	1 Goal	(7)
20	13/03/82	Dundee United	Away	League	1–5		
21	20/03/82	Rangers	Away	League	1–4	1 Goal	(8)
22	27/03/82	Dundee	Home	League	0–2		
23	07/04/82	Airdrieonians	Home	League	4–1	2 Goals	(10)
24	10/04/82	Morton	Home	League	4–0	1 Goal	(11)
25	14/04/82	Dundee United	Home	League	2–3		

26	17/04/82	St Mirren	Away	League	0–2		
27	21/04/82	Dundee	Away	League	2–1		
28	24/04/82	Celtic	Home	League	0–3		
29	01/05/82	Airdrieonians	Home	League	0–0		
30	03/05/82	Aberdeen	Away	League	1–3		
31	08/05/82	Hibernian	Away	League	1–1		
32	15/05/82	Dundee United	Home	League	1–2		

SEASON 1982–83

Scottish League Division One

33	14/08/82	East Stirling	Away	S Lge Cup	4–0	2 Goals	(13)
34	18/08/82	East Fife	Home	S Lge Cup	0–0		
35	21/08/82	Brechin City	Home	S Lge Cup	0–0		
36	25/08/82	East Fife	Away	S Lge Cup	3–0	1 Goal	(14)
37	28/08/82	East Stirling	Home	S Lge Cup	4–2	2 Goals	(16)
38	01/09/82	Brechin City	Away	S Lge Cup	1–1		
39	04/09/82	Dunfermline Athletic	Home	League	1–1		
40	08/09/82	Celtic	Away	S Lge Cup	0–4		
41	11/09/82	Queen's Park	Home	League	2–3		
42	15/09/82	Ayr United	Away	League	1–2		
43	18/09/82	Airdrieonians	Away	League	3–1	1 Goal	(17)
44	25/09/82	Raith Rovers	Home	League	2–1		
45	29/09/82	Falkirk	Away	League	1–2	1 Goal	(18)
46	02/10/82	Hamilton Academical	Away	League	2–1	2 Goals	(20)
47	05/10/82	Clyde	Home	League	2–1	1 Goal	(21)
48	09/10/82	Clydebank	Home	League	0–1		
49	16/10/82	Alloa	Away	League	1–2		
50	23/10/82	Dumbarton	Away	League	1–1		
51	30/10/82	Heart of Midlothian	Home	League	1–1		
52	06/11/82	St Johnstone	Home	League	3–1	1 Goal	(22)
53	13/11/82	Dunfermline Athletic	Away	League	4–0	2 Goals	(24)
54	20/11/82	Airdrieonians	Home	League	1–0		
55	27/11/82	Clyde	Away	League	3–1		
56	04/12/82	Hamilton Academical	Home	League	1–1		
57	11/12/82	Raith Rovers	Away	League	2–2	1 Goal	(25)
58	27/12/82	Queen's Park	Away	League	4–1	1 Goal	(26)
59	01/01/83	Ayr United	Home	League	2–2	1 Goal	(27)
60	03/01/83	St Johnstone	Away	League	0–1		
61	08/01/83	Alloa	Home	League	1–1	1 Goal	(28)
62	15/01/83	Clydebank	Away	League	3–1	1 Goal	(29)
63	22/01/83	Heart of Midlothian	Away	League	1–0		
64	28/01/83	Kilmarnock	Home	S Cup	1–1	1 Goal	(30)
65	02/02/83	Kilmarnock	Away	S Cup	0–0*		
66	05/02/83	Dumbarton	Home	League	3–2		
67	07/02/83	Kilmarnock	Home	S Cup	2–2*	1 Goal	(31)
68	09/02/83	Kilmarnock	Away	S Cup	1–0	1 Goal	(32)
69	19/02/83	Clyde	Home	S Cup	2–2	1 Goal	(33)
70	26/02/83	Clyde	Away	League	2–0	1 Goal	(34)
71	28/02/83	Clyde	Away	S Cup	6–0	3 Goals	(37)
72	05/03/83	Dunfermline Athletic	Away	League	3–0		
73	12/03/83	Aberdeen	Home	S Cup	1–2		
74	15/03/83	Alloa	Home	League	1–2		
75	19/03/83	Heart of Midlothian	Away	League	0–4		
76	22/03/83	Raith Rovers	Home	League	1–0		
77	26/03/83	Ayr United	Home	League	3–1	1 Goal	(38)
78	02/04/83	St Johnstone	Home	League	2–1		
79	06/04/83	Falkirk	Home	League	1–1	1 Goal	(39)
80	09/04/83	Hamilton Academical	Away	League	0–0		
81	16/04/83	Falkirk	Home	League	4–2	3 Goals	(42)
82	23/04/83	Queen's Park	Away	League	1–0	1 Goal	(43)
83	30/04/83	Dumbarton	Away	League	1–2	1 Goal	(44)
84	07/05/83	Airdrieonians	Home	League	0–1		
85	14/05/83	Clydebank	Away	League	2–1	1 Goal	(45)

SEASON 1983–84

Scottish League Division One

86	20/08/83	Clyde	Away	League	2–1		
87	23/08/83	Meadowbank Thistle	Away	S Lge Cup	1–2		
88	27/08/83	Meadowbank Thistle	Home	S Lge Cup	1–2		
89	03/09/83	Kilmarnock	Home	League	2–0	1 Goal	(46)
90	10/09/83	Dumbarton	Away	League	1–0		
91	14/09/83	Alloa	Away	League	4–3	2 Goals	(48)
92	17/09/83	Raith Rovers	Home	League	2–0	1 Goal	(49)

93	24/09/83	Clydebank	Home	League	1–0	1 Goal	(50)
94	28/09/83	Morton	Away	League	2–1		
95	01/10/83	Brechin City	Away	League	0–2		
96	08/10/83	Hamilton Academical	Home	League	0–0		
97	15/10/83	Meadowbank Thistle	Away	League	1–2		
98	22/10/83	Ayr United	Home	League	4–3	2 Goals	(52)
99	29/10/83	Airdrieonians	Home	League	2–1	1 Goal	(53)
100	05/11/83	Falkirk	Away	League	2–2		
101	12/11/83	Alloa	Home	League	5–0	2 Goals	(55)

Watford – League Division One

1	19/11/83	Manchester United	Away	League	1–4		
2	26/11/83	Luton Town	Home	League	3–2		
3	03/12/83	Wolverhampton Wanderers	Away	League	5–0	3 Goals	(3)
4	10/12/83	Nottingham Forest	Home	League	3–2	1 Goal	(4)
5	17/12/83	Arsenal	Away	League	1–3	1 Goal	(5)
6	26/12/83	Aston Villa	Home	League	3–2		
7	27/12/83	Southampton	Away	League	0–1		
8	31/12/83	Birmingham City	Home	League	1–0	1 Goal	(6)
9	02/01/84	Tottenham Hotspur	Away	League	3–2	2 Goals	(8)
10	07/01/84	Luton Town	Away	FA Cup	2–2	1 Goal	(9)
11	10/01/84	Luton Town	Home	FA Cup	4–3*	1 Goal	(10)
12	14/01/84	Coventry City	Away	League	2–1		
13	21/01/84	Stoke City	Home	League	2–0	1 Goal	(11)
14	28/01/84	Charlton Athletic	Away	FA Cup	2–0	1 Goal	(12)
15	01/02/84	Liverpool	Away	League	0–3		
16	04/02/84	West Bromwich Albion	Home	League	3–1	1 Goal	(13)
17	11/02/84	Notts County	Away	League	5–3	1 Goal	(14)
18	18/02/84	Brighton & Hove Albion	Home	FA Cup	3–1	1 Goal	(15)
19	21/02/84	West Ham United	Away	League	4–2	1 Goal	(16)
20	25/02/84	Everton	Home	League	4–4	1 Goal	(17)
21	03/03/84	Leicester City	Away	League	1–4		
22	10/03/84	Birmingham City	Away	FA Cup	3–1		
Sub+1	17/03/84	Queens Park Rangers	Home	League	1–0		
23	20/03/84	Sunderland	Home	League	2–1	2 Goals	(19)
24	24/03/84	Ipswich Town	Away	League	0–0		
25	31/03/84	Liverpool	Home	League	0–2		
26	07/04/84	Norwich City	Away	League	1–6	1 Goal	(20)
27	14/04/84	Plymouth Argyle	Neutral	FA Cup	1–0		
28	17/04/84	Manchester United	Home	League	0–0		
29	21/04/84	Aston Villa	Away	League	1–2		
30	24/04/84	Southampton	Home	League	1–1	1 Goal	(21)
31	28/04/84	Luton Town	Away	League	2–1	1 Goal	(22)
32	05/05/84	Wolverhampton Wanderers	Home	League	0–0		
33	07/05/84	Nottingham Forest	Away	League	1–5	1 Goal	(23)
34	12/05/84	Arsenal	Home	League	2–1	1 Goal	(24)
35	19/05/84	Everton	Wembley	FA Cup	0–2		

SEASON 1984–85

League Division One

36	25/08/84	Manchester United	Away	League	1–1		
37	28/08/84	Queens Park Rangers	Home	League	1–1		
38	01/09/84	Arsenal	Home	League	3–4	1 Goal	(25)
39	05/09/84	Leicester City	Away	League	1–1		
40	08/09/84	West Ham United	Away	League	0–2		
41	15/09/84	Aston Villa	Home	League	3–3	1 Goal	(26)
42	22/09/84	Norwich City	Away	League	2–3	1 Goal	(27)
43	25/09/84	Cardiff City	Home	Lge Cup	3–1		
44	29/09/84	Everton	Home	League	4–5		
45	06/10/84	Coventry City	Home	League	0–1		

Celtic – Scottish League Premier Division

1	13/10/84	Hibernian	Home	League	3–0		
2	20/10/84	Dundee United	Away	League	3–1	1 Goal	(1)
3	03/11/84	Morton	Away	League	1–2	1 Goal	(2)
4	10/11/84	Dumbarton	Home	League	2–0	1 Goal	(3)
5	17/11/84	Heart of Midlothian	Away	League	5–1	1 Goal	(4)
6	24/11/84	St Mirren	Home	League	7–1		
7	01/12/84	Dundee	Home	League	5–1	3 Goals	(7)
8	08/12/84	Aberdeen	Away	League	2–4	1 Goal	(8)
9	15/12/84	Hibernian	Away	League	1–0	1 Goal	(9)
10	22/12/84	Rangers	Home	League	1–1		
11	29/12/84	Dundee United	Home	League	1–2		
12	01/01/85	Rangers	Away	League	2–1	1 Goal	(10)

13	30/01/85	Hamilton Academical	Away	S Cup	2–1		
14	02/02/85	St Mirren	Away	League	2–0	1 Goal	(11)
15	09/02/85	Dundee	Away	League	0–2		
16	16/02/85	Inverness Thistle	Home	S Cup	6–0	1 Goal	(12)
17	19/02/85	Morton	Home	League	4–0		
18	23/02/85	Aberdeen	Home	League	2–0	1 Goal	(13)
19	02/03/85	Dundee United	Away	League	0–0		
20	09/03/85	Dundee	Away	S Cup	1–1	1 Goal	(14)
21	13/03/85	Dundee	Home	S Cup	2–1	1 Goal	(15)
22	16/03/85	Hibernian	Home	League	0–1		
23	20/03/85	Heart of Midlothian	Home	League	3–2	1 Goal	(16)
24	23/03/85	Morton	Away	League	7–2		
25	03/04/85	Dumbarton	Away	League	2–0	1 Goal	(17)
26	06/04/85	Heart of Midlothian	Away	League	2–0		
27	13/04/85	Motherwell	Hampden	S Cup	1–1		
28	17/04/85	Motherwell	Hampden	S Cup	3–0	2 Goals	(19)
29	20/04/85	St Mirren	Home	League	3–0		
30	27/04/85	Aberdeen	Away	League	1–1		
31	01/05/85	Rangers	Home	League	1–1		
32	04/05/85	Dundee	Home	League	0–1		
33	11/05/85	Dumbarton	Home	League	2–0		
34	18/05/85	Dundee United	Hampden	S Cup	2–1		

SEASON 1985–86

Scottish League Premier Division

35	10/08/85	Heart of Midlothian	Away	League	1–1		
36	17/08/85	Motherwell	Home	League	2–1		
37	21/08/85	Queen of the South	Away	S Lge Cup	4–1	2 Goals	(21)
38	24/08/85	Clydebank	Away	League	2–0	2 Goals	(23)
39	28/08/85	Brechin City	Home	S Lge Cup	7–0	2 Goals	(25)
40	31/08/85	Rangers	Home	League	1–1		
41	04/09/85	Hibernian	Away	S Lge Cup	4–4+	2 Goals	(27)
42	07/09/85	Hibernian	Away	League	5–0	1 Goal	(28)
43	14/09/85	Aberdeen	Home	League	2–1		
44	18/09/85	Atletico Madrid	Away	ECW Cup	1–1	1 Goal	(29)
45	28/09/85	Dundee	Away	League	2–0	1 Goal	(30)
46	02/10/85	Atletico Madrid	Home	ECW Cup	1–2#		
47	05/10/85	St Mirren	Home	League	2–0		
48	12/10/85	Heart of Midlothian	Home	League	0–1		
49	19/10/85	Motherwell	Away	League	2–1		
50	26/10/85	Dundee United	Home	League	0–3		
Sub+1	09/11/85	Rangers	Away	League	0–3		
51	16/11/85	Clydebank	Home	League	2–0		
52	23/11/85	Hibernian	Home	League	1–1	1 Goal	(31)
53	14/12/85	Heart of Midlothian	Away	League	1–1		
54	23/12/85	Dundee United	Away	League	0–1		
55	28/12/85	Clydebank	Home	League	2–0	1 Goal	(32)
56	11/01/86	Aberdeen	Home	League	1–1		
57	15/01/86	Motherwell	Home	League	3–2	1 Goal	(33)
58	18/01/86	Hibernian	Away	League	2–2		
59	25/01/86	St Johnstone	Home	S Cup	2–0	1 Goal	(34)
60	01/02/86	Dundee	Away	League	3–1	1 Goal	(35)
61	08/02/86	St Mirren	Home	League	1–1		
62	15/02/86	Queen's Park	Home	S Cup	2–1		
63	22/02/86	Heart of Midlothian	Home	League	1–1	1 Goal	(36)
64	08/03/86	Hibernian	Away	S Cup	3–4		
65	15/03/86	Dundee United	Home	League	1–1		
66	22/03/86	Rangers	Away	League	4–4	1 Goal	(37)
67	29/03/86	Clydebank	Away	League	5–0		
68	02/04/86	Dundee	Home	League	2–1	1 Goal	(38)
69	12/04/86	Aberdeen	Away	League	1–0	1 Goal	(39)
70	19/04/86	Hibernian	Home	League	2–0		
71	26/04/86	Dundee	Home	League	2–0	1 Goal	(40)
72	30/04/86	Motherwell	Away	League	2–0		
73	03/05/86	St Mirren	Away	League	5–0	2 Goals	(42)

+ AET Hibernian won 4–3 on penalties
# Played behind closed doors

SEASON 1986–87

Scottish League Premier Division

| 74 | 09/08/86 | Dundee | Home | League | 1–0 | 1 Goal | (43) |
| 75 | 13/08/86 | Motherwell | Away | League | 4–0 | 2 Goals | (45) |

76	16/08/86	Clydebank	Away	League	1–0	1 Goal	(46)
77	20/08/86	Airdrieonians	Home	S Lge Cup	2–0		
78	23/08/86	Aberdeen	Home	League	1–1		
79	27/08/86	Dumbarton	Home	S Lge Cup	3–0	2 Goals	(48)
80	31/08/86	Rangers	Away	League	0–1		
81	03/09/86	Aberdeen	Away	S Lge Cup	1–1+	1 Goal	(49)
82	06/09/86	Hamilton Academical	Home	League	4–1	1 Goal	(50)
83	13/09/86	Dundee United	Away	League	2–2		
84	17/09/86	Shamrock Rovers	Away	Eur Cup	1–0		
85	20/09/86	Hibernian	Home	League	5–1	1 Goal	(51)
86	23/09/86	Motherwell	Hampden	S Lge Cup	2–2#		
87	27/09/86	Falkirk	Away	League	1–0	1 Goal	(52)
88	01/10/86	Shamrock Rovers	Home	Eur Cup	2–0	2 Goals	(54)
89	04/10/86	St Mirren	Home	League	2–0	1 Goal	(55)
90	08/10/86	Heart of Midlothian	Home	League	2–0	1 Goal	(56)
91	11/10/86	Dundee	Away	League	3–0	2 Goals	(58)
92	18/10/86	Motherwell	Home	League	3–1		
93	22/10/86	Dinamo Kijev	Home	Eur Cup	1–1	1 Goal	(59)
94	26/10/86	Rangers	Hampden	S Lge Cup	1–2		
95	01/11/86	Rangers	Home	League	1–1		
96	05/11/86	Dinamo Kijev	Away	Eur Cup	1–3		
97	08/11/86	Hamilton Academical	Away	League	2–1	1 Goal	(60)
98	15/11/86	Dundee United	Home	League	1–0	1 Goal	(61)
99	19/11/86	Hibernian	Away	League	1–0		
100	22/11/86	Falkirk	Home	League	4–2	2 Goals	(63)
101	26/11/86	Aberdeen	Away	League	1–1		
102	29/11/86	St Mirren	Away	League	1–0		
103	03/12/86	Heart of Midlothian	Away	League	0–1		
104	06/12/86	Dundee	Home	League	2–0	2 Goals	(65)
105	13/12/86	Motherwell	Away	League	1–1		
106	20/12/86	Aberdeen	Home	League	1–1		
107	27/12/86	Clydebank	Away	League	1–1		
108	01/01/87	Rangers	Away	League	0–2		
109	21/01/87	Hibernian	Home	League	1–0		
110	24/01/87	Falkirk	Away	League	2–1	2 Goals	(67)
111	01/02/87	Aberdeen	Away	S Cup	2–2		
112	04/02/87	Aberdeen	Home	S Cup	0–0*		
113	07/02/87	St Mirren	Home	League	3–0	2 Goals	(69)
114	09/02/87	Aberdeen	Neutral	S Cup	1–0		
115	14/02/87	Heart of Midlothian	Home	League	1–1		
116	21/02/87	Heart of Midlothian	Away	S Cup	0–1		
117	28/02/87	Dundee	Away	League	1–4		
118	07/03/87	Motherwell	Home	League	3–1		
119	14/03/87	Aberdeen	Away	League	0–1		
Sub+2	28/03/87	Hamilton Academical	Away	League	3–2		
120	04/04/87	Rangers	Home	League	3–1		
121	11/04/87	Hibernian	Away	League	4–1	1 Goal	(70)
122	18/04/87	Dundee United	Home	League	1–1		
123	25/04/87	St Mirren	Away	League	3–1	1 Goal	(71)
124	02/05/87	Falkirk	Home	League	1–2		
125	09/05/87	Heart of Midlothian	Away	League	0–1		

+ AET Celtic won 4–2 on penalties
# AET Celtic won 5–4 on penalties

SEASON 1987–88

FC Nantes – French League Division One

1	18/07/87	Lille OSC	Away	League	0–3		
2	25/07/87	Brest–Armorique FC	Home	League	1–0	1 Goal	(1)
3	01/08/87	AS Saint-Etienne	Away	League	1–1		
4	08/08/87	Matra–Racing de Paris	Home	League	1–1	1 Goal	(2)
5	15/08/87	Stade Lavallois de Laval	Away	League	1–1	1 Goal	(3)
6	19/08/87	OGC Nice	Away	League	1–3		
7	22/08/87	FC Metz	Home	League	0–0		
8	29/08/87	AJ Auxerre	Away	League	0–1		
9	01/09/87	Olympique de Marseille	Home	League	5–0	2 Goals	(5)
10	12/09/87	RC Lens	Away	League	2–1	1 Goal	(6)
11	19/09/87	Le Havre AC	Home	League	2–0		
12	23/09/87	Montpellier HSC	Away	League	0–0		
13	03/10/87	Toulouse FC	Home	League	3–1	1 Goal	(7)
14	07/10/87	Paris Saint–Germain FC	Away	League	2–0		
15	17/10/87	Chamois Niortais de Niort	Home	League	2–1		
16	24/10/87	AS Monaco	Away	League	1–2	1 Goal	(8)
17	31/10/87	AS Cannes	Home	League	2–1	1 Goal	(9)

18	07/11/87	Girondins de Bordeaux	Away	League	1–2	1 Goal	(10)
19	11/11/87	SC Toulon	Home	League	1–1		
20	21/11/87	Brest–Armorique FC	Away	League	0–0		
21	28/11/87	AS Saint–Etienne	Home	League	2–3	1 Goal	(11)
22	05/12/87	Matra Racing de Paris	Away	League	2–2		
23	12/12/87	Stade Lavallois de Laval	Home	League	1–2		
24	19/12/87	OGC Nice	Home	League	0–1		
25	20/02/88	FC Metz	Away	League	0–1		
26	27/02/88	AJ Auxerre	Home	League	0–0		
27	02/04/88	Montpellier HSC	Home	League	0–0		
28	05/04/88	AJ Auxerre	Home	FR Cup	0–0		
29	09/04/88	Toulouse FC	Away	League	1–0		
30	16/04/88	Paris Saint–Germain FC	Home	League	0–0		
31	15/05/88	AS Cannes	Away	League	4–1	1 Goal	(12)
32	27/05/88	SC Toulon	Away	League	2–5	1 Goal	(13)
33	04/06/88	Lille OSC	Home	League	1–1		

SEASON 1988–89

French League Division One

34	15/07/88	AS Monaco	Home	League	1–1		
35	23/07/88	SM Caen	Away	League	3–2	1 Goal	(14)
36	27/07/88	SC Toulon	Home	League	0–0		
37	30/07/88	Paris Saint–Germain	Away	League	0–1		
38	06/08/88	AJ Auxerre	Home	League	3–2	1 Goal	(15)
39	13/08/88	Lille OSC	Away	League	1–0		
40	17/08/88	Toulouse FC	Home	League	1–2		
41	20/08/88	Montpellier HSC	Away	League	4–1	2 Goals	(17)
42	27/08/88	AS Saint–Etienne	Home	League	1–1		
43	03/09/88	FC Sochaux	Away	League	1–0		
44	10/09/88	RC Strasbourg	Home	League	2–2		
45	17/09/88	Matra Racing de Paris	Away	League	0–2		
46	21/09/88	Olympique de Marseille	Home	League	1–1		
47	01/10/88	Stade Lavallois de Laval	Away	League	2–0	2 Goals	(19)
48	08/10/88	RC Lens	Home	League	3–1		
49	14/10/88	Girondins de Bordeaux	Away	League	0–5		
50	29/10/88	FC Metz	Home	League	1–0		
51	05/11/88	OGC Nice	Away	League	0–1		
52	12/11/88	AS Cannes	Away	League	2–1	1 Goal	(20)
53	26/11/88	SM Caen	Home	League	3–1		
54	03/12/88	SC Toulon	Away	League	0–1		
55	10/12/88	Paris Saint–Germain FC	Home	League	1–1		
56	14/12/88	AJ Auxerre	Away	League	0–1		
57	17/12/88	Lille OSC	Home	League	1–0		
58	04/02/89	Toulouse FC	Away	League	2–1	1 Goal	(21)
59	18/02/89	AS Saint–Etienne	Away	League	1–1		
60	25/02/89	FC Sochaux	Home	League	0–0		
61	11/03/89	RC Strasbourg	Away	League	0–2		
62	18/03/89	Matra Racing Paris	Home	League	1–0		
63	01/04/89	Stade Lavallois de Laval	Home	League	1–0		
64	04/04/89	Olympique de Marseille	Away	League	0–1		
65	08/04/89	AS Monaco	Home	FR Cup	0–0		
66	12/04/89	RC Lens	Away	League	0–0		
67	15/04/89	AS Monaco	Away	FR Cup	1–2		
68	21/04/89	Girondins de Bordeaux	Home	League	1–0		
69	06/05/89	FC Metz	Away	League	0–0		

SEASON 1989–90

Rangers – Scottish League Premier Division

1	12/08/89	St Mirren	Home	League	0–1		
2	15/08/89	Arbroath	Home	S Lge Cup	4–0		
3	19/08/89	Hibernian	Away	League	0–2		
4	23/08/89	Morton	Away	S Lge Cup	2–1		
5	26/08/89	Celtic	Away	League	1–1		
6	30/08/89	Hamilton Academical	Away	S Lge Cup	3–0		
7	09/09/89	Aberdeen	Home	League	1–0	1 Goal	(1)
8	13/09/89	FC Bayern Munchen	Home	Eur Cup	1–3		
9	16/09/89	Dundee	Home	League	2–2		
10	19/09/89	Dunfermline Athletic	Hampden	S Lge Cup	5–0	1 Goal	(2)
11	23/09/89	Dunfermline Athletic	Away	League	1–1		
12	27/09/89	FC Bayern Munchen	Away	Eur Cup	0–0		
13	30/09/89	Heart of Midlothian	Home	League	1–0	1 Goal	(3)
14	03/10/89	Motherwell	Away	League	0–1		
15	14/10/89	Dundee United	Home	League	2–1	1 Goal	(4)

16	22/10/89	Aberdeen	Hampden	S Lge Cup	1–2*		
17	25/10/89	St Mirren	Away	League	2–0	1 Goal	(5)
18	28/10/89	Hibernian	Home	League	3–0	1 Goal	(6)
19	04/11/89	Celtic	Home	League	1–0	1 Goal	(7)
20	18/11/89	Dundee	Away	League	2–0	1 Goal	(8)
21	22/11/89	Aberdeen	Away	League	0–1		
22	25/11/89	Dunfermline Athletic	Home	League	3–0	1 Goal	(9)
23	02/12/89	Heart of Midlothian	Away	League	2–1		
24	09/12/89	Motherwell	Home	League	3–0		
25	16/12/89	Dundee United	Away	League	1–1	1 Goal	(10)
26	19/12/89	Arsenal	Home	ZDSC Cup	1–2	1 Goal	(11)
27	23/12/89	St Mirren	Home	League	1–0		
28	30/12/89	Hibernian	Away	League	0–0		
29	02/01/90	Celtic	Away	League	1–0		
30	06/01/90	Aberdeen	Home	League	2–0		
31	13/01/90	Dundee	Home	League	3–0	1 Goal	(12)
32	20/01/90	St Johnstone	Home	S Cup	3–0	1 Goal	(13)
33	27/01/90	Dunfermline Athletic	Away	League	1–0		
34	03/02/90	Dundee United	Home	League	3–1	1 Goal	(14)
35	10/02/90	Motherwell	Away	League	1–1	1 Goal	(15)
36	17/02/90	Heart of Midlothian	Home	League	0–0		
37	25/02/90	Celtic	Away	S Cup	0–1		
38	03/03/90	Dundee	Away	League	2–2	1 Goal	(16)
39	17/03/90	St Mirren	Away	League	0–0		
40	24/03/90	Hibernian	Home	League	0–1		
41	01/04/90	Celtic	Home	League	3–0	1 Goal	(17)
42	08/04/90	Aberdeen	Away	League	0–0		
43	14/04/90	Motherwell	Home	League	2–1	1 Goal	(18)
44	21/04/90	Dundee United	Away	League	1–0		
45	28/04/90	Dunfermline Athletic	Home	League	2–0		
46	05/05/90	Heart of Midlothian	Away	League	1–1		

SEASON 1990–91

Scottish League Premier Division

47	21/08/90	East Stirling	Home	S Lge Cup	5–0	1 Goal	(19)
48	25/08/90	Dunfermline Athletic	Home	League	3–1	1 Goal	(20)
49	28/08/90	Kilmarnock	Away	S Lge Cup	1–0	1 Goal	(21)
50	01/09/90	Hibernian	Away	League	0–0		
51	04/09/90	Raith Rovers	Home	S Lge Cup	6–2	1 Goal	(22)
52	08/09/90	Heart of Midlothian	Away	League	3–1		
53	15/09/90	Celtic	Home	League	1–1		
54	19/09/90	Valletta FC	Away	Eur Cup	4–0	2 Goals	(24)
55	22/09/90	Dundee United	Away	League	1–2	1 Goal	(25)
56	26/09/90	Aberdeen	Hampden	S Lge Cup	1–0		
57	29/09/90	Motherwell	Home	League	1–0		
58	02/10/90	Valletta FC	Home	Eur Cup	6–0	3 Goals	(28)
59	06/10/90	Aberdeen	Away	League	0–0		
60	13/10/90	St Mirren	Home	League	5–0	1 Goal	(29)
61	20/10/90	St Johnstone	Away	League	0–0		
62	24/10/90	Crvena Zvezda Beograd	Away	Eur Cup	0–3		
63	17/11/90	Motherwell	Away	League	4–2	1 Goal	(30)
64	20/11/90	Dunfermline Athletic	Away	League	1–0		
65	25/11/90	Celtic	Away	League	2–1	1 Goal	(31)
66	01/12/90	Heart of Midlothian	Home	League	4–0	1 Goal	(32)
67	08/12/90	St Johnstone	Home	League	4–1	1 Goal	(33)
68	15/12/90	St Mirren	Away	League	3–0	1 Goal	(34)
69	22/12/90	Aberdeen	Home	League	2–2		
70	29/12/90	Dundee United	Away	League	2–1	1 Goal	(35)
71	02/01/91	Celtic	Home	League	2–0		
72	05/01/91	Heart of Midlothian	Away	League	1–0		
73	12/01/91	Dunfermline Athletic	Home	League	2–0	1 Goal	(36)
74	19/01/91	Hibernian	Away	League	2–0	1 Goal	(37)
75	29/01/91	Dunfermline Athletic	Home	S Cup	2–0		
Sub+1	23/02/91	Cowdenbeath	Home	S Cup	5–0		
76	26/02/91	St Johnstone	Away	League	1–1		
77	02/03/91	Aberdeen	Away	League	0–1		
78	17/03/91	Celtic	Away	S Cup	0–2		
79	24/03/91	Celtic	Away	League	0–3		
80	30/03/91	Dunfermline Athletic	Away	League	1–0		
81	06/04/91	Hibernian	Home	League	0–0		
82	24/04/91	Dundee United	Home	League	1–0		
83	04/05/91	Motherwell	Away	League	0–3		
84	11/05/91	Aberdeen	Home	League	2–0		

SEASON 1991–92

Scottish League Premier Division

85	10/08/91	St Johnstone	Home	League	6–0	2 Goals	(39)
86	13/08/91	Motherwell	Home	League	2–0		
87	17/08/91	Heart of Midlothian	Away	League	0–1		
88	20/08/91	Queens Park	Home	S Lge Cup	6–0	4 Goals	(43)
89	24/08/91	Dunfermline Athletic	Home	League	4–0	1 Goal	(44)
90	28/08/91	Partick Thistle	Away	S Lge Cup	2–0	1 Goal	(45)
91	31/08/91	Celtic	Away	League	2–0		
92	04/09/91	Heart of Midlothian	Away	S Lge Cup	1–0		
93	21/09/91	St Mirren	Away	League	2–1		
94	25/09/91	Hibernian	Hampden	S Lge Cup	0–1		
95	28/09/91	Aberdeen	Home	League	0–2		
96	02/10/91	AC Sparta Praha	Home	Eur Cup	2–1*		
97	05/10/91	Airdrieonians	Away	League	4–0	1 Goal	(46)
98	08/10/91	Hibernian	Home	League	4–2		
99	26/10/91	Falkirk	Home	League	1–1	1 Goal	(47)
Sub+2	29/10/91	Dundee United	Away	League	2–3		

Everton – League Division One

1	23/11/91	Notts County	Home	League	1–0		
2	27/11/91	Leicester City	Away	ZDS Cup	1–2		
3	04/12/91	Leeds United	Home	Lge Cup	1–4		
4	07/12/91	West Ham United	Home	League	4–0	1 Goal	(1)
5	14/12/91	Oldham Athletic	Away	League	2–2		
6	21/12/91	Arsenal	Away	League	2–4	1 Goal	(2)
7	26/12/91	Sheffield Wednesday	Home	League	0–1		
8	28/12/91	Liverpool	Home	League	1–1	1 Goal	(3)
9	01/01/92	Southampton	Away	League	2–1		
10	04/01/92	Southend United	Home	FA Cup	1–0		
11	11/01/92	Manchester United	Away	League	0–1		
12	19/01/92	Nottingham Forest	Home	League	1–1		
13	08/02/92	Queens Park Rangers	Home	League	0–0		
14	23/02/92	Leeds United	Home	League	1–1		
15	29/02/92	West Ham United	Away	League	2–0	1 Goal	(4)
16	07/03/92	Oldham Athletic	Home	League	2–1		
17	10/03/92	Wimbledon	Away	League	0–0		
18	14/03/92	Luton Town	Home	League	1–1	1 Goal	(5)
19	17/03/92	Notts County	Away	League	0–0		
20	21/03/92	Norwich City	Away	League	3–4	2 Goals	(7)
21	01/04/92	Southampton	Home	League	0–1		
22	04/04/92	Crystal Palace	Away	League	0–2		
23	11/04/92	Sheffield United	Home	League	0–2		
24	18/04/92	Coventry City	Away	League	1–0		

SEASON 1992–93

Premier League

Sub+1	19/08/92	Manchester United	Away	League	3–0	1 Goal	(8)
Sub+2	22/08/92	Norwich City	Away	League	1–1		
25	25/08/92	Aston Villa	Home	League	1–0	1 Goal	(9)
Sub+3	29/08/92	Wimbledon	Home	League	0–0		
26	05/09/92	Tottenham Hotspur	Away	League	1–2		
27	12/09/92	Manchester United	Home	League	0–2		
Sub+4	19/09/92	Crystal Palace	Home	League	0–2		
Sub+5	26/09/92	Leeds United	Away	League	0–2		
28	04/10/92	Oldham Athletic	Away	League	0–1		
Sub+6	07/10/92	Rotherham United	Home	Lge Cup	3–0		
29	02/12/92	Chelsea	Home	Lge Cup	2–2		
30	07/12/92	Liverpool	Home	League	2–1	1 Goal	(10)
31	12/12/92	Sheffield United	Away	League	0–1		
Sub+7	10/02/93	Tottenham Hotspur	Home	League	1–2		
32	20/02/93	Aston Villa	Away	League	1–2		

SEASON 1993–94

Heart of Midlothian – Scottish League Premier Division

1	23/10/93	Partick Thistle	Away	League	0–0		
2	30/10/93	Hibernian	Away	League	2–0		
3	03/11/93	Rangers	Home	League	2–2		
4	06/11/93	Dundee United	Home	League	1–1	1 Goal	(1)
5	13/11/93	Dundee	Home	League	1–2		
6	20/11/93	Celtic	Away	League	0–0		
7	30/11/93	Kilmarnock	Away	League	0–0		

8	04/12/93	Aberdeen	Home	League	1–1		
9	11/12/93	St Johnstone	Away	League	0–2		
10	15/12/93	Motherwell	Home	League	2–3	1 Goal	(2)
11	18/12/93	Raith Rovers	Home	League	0–1		
12	27/12/93	Rangers	Away	League	2–2		
13	12/01/94	Hibernian	Home	League	1–1		
14	15/01/94	Partick Thistle	Home	League	1–0		
15	22/01/94	Kilmarnock	Home	League	1–1		
16	29/01/94	Partick Thistle	Away	S Cup	1–0	1 Goal	(3)
17	05/02/94	Motherwell	Away	League	1–1		
18	12/02/94	Celtic	Home	League	0–2		
19	20/02/94	Hibernian	Away	S Cup	2–1		
20	01/03/94	Dundee	Away	League	2–0	2 Goals	(5)
21	05/03/94	Aberdeen	Away	League	1–0		
22	12/03/94	Rangers	Away	S Cup	0–2		
23	19/03/94	Raith Rovers	Away	League	2–2		
24	26/03/94	Rangers	Home	League	1–2		
25	30/03/94	Motherwell	Home	League	0–0		
26	02/04/94	Kilmarnock	Away	League	1–0		
27	06/04/94	St Johnstone	Home	League	2–2		
28	09/04/94	Celtic	Away	League	2–2		
29	16/04/94	Dundee	Home	League	0–2		
30	23/04/94	St Johnstone	Away	League	0–0		
31	27/04/94	Aberdeen	Home	League	1–1		
32	30/04/94	Hibernian	Away	League	0–0		
33	07/05/94	Dundee United	Home	League	2–0		
34	14/05/94	Partick Thistle	Away	League	1–0		

SEASON 1994–95

Scottish League Premier Division

35	16/08/94	Dumbarton	Away	S Lge Cup	4–0		
36	20/08/94	Motherwell	Away	League	1–1	1 Goal	(6)
37	27/08/94	Hibernian	Home	League	0–1		
38	11/09/94	Rangers	Away	League	0–3		
Sub+1	17/09/94	Dundee United	Home	League	2–1		

Falkirk – Scottish League Premier Division

1	04/03/95	Motherwell	Away	League	2–2		
2	11/03/95	Rangers	Away	League	2–2		
3	18/03/95	Kilmarnock	Home	League	2–0		
4	01/04/95	Heart of Midlothian	Away	League	1–0		
5	08/04/95	Dundee United	Home	League	2–1	1 Goal	(1)
6	15/04/95	Motherwell	Home	League	3–0		
7	19/04/95	Hibernian	Away	League	2–0		
8	29/04/95	Celtic	Home	League	1–2		
9	06/05/95	Partick Thistle	Away	League	0–0		
10	13/05/95	Aberdeen	Home	League	0–2		

SEASON 1995–96

Scottish League Premier Division

11	19/08/95	Queen of the South	Away	S Lge Cup	2–0	1 Goal	(2)
12	26/08/95	Aberdeen	Home	League	2–3		
13	30/08/95	Aberdeen	Home	S Lge Cup	1–4	1 Goal	(3)
14	09/09/95	Heart of Midlothian	Away	League	1–4		
15	16/09/95	Rangers	Home	League	0–2		
16	23/09/95	Motherwell	Home	League	0–0		
17	30/09/95	Partick Thistle	Away	League	1–1	1 Goal	(4)
18	04/10/95	Celtic	Home	League	0–1		
19	07/10/95	Hibernian	Away	League	1–2		
20	14/10/95	Kilmarnock	Home	League	0–2		
21	21/10/95	Raith Rovers	Away	League	1–0		
22	28/10/95	Heart of Midlothian	Home	League	2–0	1 Goal	(5)
23	04/11/95	Rangers	Away	League	0–2		
24	08/11/95	Aberdeen	Away	League	1–3		
25	11/11/95	Hibernian	Home	League	2–0	2 Goals	(7)
26	18/11/95	Partick Thistle	Home	League	0–1		
27	25/11/95	Motherwell	Away	League	1–1		
28	02/12/95	Raith Rovers	Home	League	2–1		
29	09/12/95	Kilmarnock	Away	League	0–4		
30	16/12/95	Celtic	Away	League	0–1		
31	06/01/96	Rangers	Home	League	0–4		

32	09/01/96	Partick Thistle	Away	League	3–0		
33	23/01/96	Motherwell	Home	League	0–1		
34	30/01/96	Stenhousemuir	Home	S Cup	0–2		
35	03/02/96	Kilmarnock	Home	League	4–2		
36	10/02/96	Celtic	Home	League	0–0		
37	02/03/96	Motherwell	Away	League	0–1		
38	16/03/96	Partick Thistle	Home	League	1–2		
39	23/03/96	Rangers	Away	League	2–3	1 Goal	(8)
40	30/03/96	Heart of Midlothian	Home	League	0–2		
41	06/04/96	Raith Rovers	Home	League	2–3		
42	13/04/96	Kilmarnock	Away	League	0–1		
43	20/04/96	Celtic	Away	League	0–4		
44	27/04/96	Hibernian	Home	League	1–1		

Kansas City Wiz – Major League Soccer

1	02/05/96	Columbus Crew	Home	League	6–4	2 Goals	(2)
2	05/05/96	Colorado Rapids	Away	League	0–4		
3	08/05/96	Tampa Bay Mutiny	Away	League	1–2		
4	11/05/96	Dallas Burn	Home	League	2–3		
5	19/05/96	Los Angeles Galaxy	Away	League	0–2		
6	22/05/96	NY/NJ MetroStars	Home	League	2–1		
7	29/05/96	San Jose Clash	Away	League	1–2		
8	01/06/96	New England Revolution	Home	League	2–1	1 Goal	(3)
9	05/06/96	Tampa Bay Mutiny	Home	League	1–3		
10	08/06/96	Columbus Crew	Away	League	4–3+		
11	15/06/96	New England Revolution	Away	League	1–2		
12	20/06/96	Washington D.C.United	Home	League	5–1		
13	25/06/96	NY/NJ MetroStars	Away	League	0–2		
14	29/06/96	Dallas Burn	Away	League	1–0		
15	06/07/96	Los Angeles Galaxy	Home	League	3–1		
16	10/07/96	Colorado Rapids	Home	League	2–0		
17	18/07/96	Tampa Bay Mutiny	Away	League	2–3	1 Goal	(4)
18	20/07/96	Dallas Burn	Home	League	1–2		
19	27/07/96	New England Revolution	Home	League	4–2		
20	31/07/96	Washington D.C.United	Away	League	3–2		
21	04/08/96	Washington D.C.United	Away	League	4–2		
22	07/08/96	Colorado Rapids	Away	League	2–4		
23	11/08/96	Los Angeles Galaxy	Home	League	3–2+		
24	15/08/96	San Jose Clash	Home	League	4–1	1 Goal	(5)
25	21/08/96	Los Angeles Galaxy	Away	League	2–1+		
26	24/08/96	Columbus Crew	Away	League	1–2	1 Goal	(6)
27	01/09/96	NY/NJ MetroStars	Home	League	3–2+		
28	07/09/96	Columbus Crew	Home	League	1–5		
29	15/09/96	Colorado Rapids	Home	US Open Cup	2–3		
30	21/09/96	San Jose Clash	Home	League	0–1+		
31	26/09/96	Dallas Burn	Home	Lge P/O	3–2	1 Goal	(7)
32	29/09/96	Dallas Burn	Away	Lge P/O	1–2		
33	02/10/96	Dallas Burn	Away	Lge P/O	3–2+		
34	10/10/96	Los Angeles Galaxy	Away	Lge P/O	1–2		
35	13/10/96	Los Angeles Galaxy	Home	Lge P/O	1–2+		

+ Decided by a shoot–out

INTERNATIONAL APPEARANCES – SCOTLAND

Sub 1	28/02/84	Wales	Hampden Park	2–1	HC	1 Goal	(1)
Sub 2	26/05/84	England	Hampden Park	1–1	HC		
3	01/06/84	France	Marseille	0–2	F		
4	12/09/84	Yugoslavia	Hampden Park	6–1	F	1 Goal	(2)
5	17/10/84	Iceland	Hampden Park	3–0	WCQ		
6	14/11/84	Spain	Hampden Park	3–1	WCQ	2 Goals	(4)
7	27/02/85	Spain	Seville	0–1	WCQ		
8	27/03/85	Wales	Hampden Park	0–1	WCQ		
9	16/10/85	East Germany	Hampden Park	0–0	F		
10	10/09/86	Bulgaria	Hampden Park	0–0	ECQ		
11	15/10/86	Republic of Ireland	Lansdowne Road	0–0	ECQ		
12	12/11/86	Luxembourg	Hampden Park	3–0	ECQ	1 Goal	(5)
13	18/02/87	Republic of Ireland	Hampden Park	0–1	ECQ		
14	09/09/87	Hungary	Hampden Park	2–0	F		
15	14/10/87	Belgium	Hampden Park	2–0	ECQ		
16	02/12/87	Luxembourg	Esch sur Alzette	0–0	ECQ		
17	17/02/88	Saudi Arabia	Riyadh	2–2	F	1 Goal	(6)
18	27/04/88	Spain	Madrid	0–0	F		

19	17/05/88	Colombia	Hampden Park	0–0	RC		
20	21/05/88	England	Wembley	0–1	RC		
21	14/09/88	Norway	Oslo	2–1	WCQ	1 Goal	(7)
22	19/10/88	Yugoslavia	Hampden Park	1–1	WCQ	1 Goal	(8)
23	22/12/88	Italy	Perugia	0–2	F		
24	08/02/89	Cyprus	Limassol	3–2	WCQ	1 Goal	(9)
25	08/03/89	France	Hampden Park	2–0	WCQ	2 Goals	(11)
26	26/04/89	Cyprus	Hampden Park	2–1	WCQ	1 Goal	(12)
27	27/05/89	England	Hampden Park	0–2	RC		
Sub 28	30/05/89	Chile	Hampden Park	2–0	RC		
29	11/10/89	France	Paris	0–3	WCQ		
30	15/11/89	Norway	Hampden Park	1–1	WCQ		
31	25/04/90	East Germany	Hampden Park	0–1	F		
32	19/05/90	Poland	Hampden Park	1–1	F	1 Goal	(13)
33	28/05/90	Malta	Valetta	2–1	F		
34	11/06/90	Costa Rica	Genoa	0–1	WC		
35	16/06/90	Sweden	Genoa	2–1	WC	1 Goal	(14)
36	20/06/90	Brazil	Turin	0–1	WC		
37	11/09/91	Switzerland	Bern	2–2	ECQ		
Sub 38	13/11/91	San Marino	Hampden Park	4–0	ECQ		

APPEARANCES AND GOALS PER SEASON

SEASON 81–82	GAMES	GOALS
Scottish League	30+2	9
Scottish Cup	1	1
Scottish League Cup	1+1	1
TOTAL	**32+3**	**11**

SEASON 82–83	GAMES	GOALS
Scottish League	39	22
Scottish Cup	7	7
Scottish League Cup	7	5
TOTAL	**53**	**34**

SEASON 83–84	GAMES	GOALS
League	28+1	20
FA Cup	7	4
Scottish League	14	10
Scottish League Cup	2	0
TOTAL	**51+1**	**34**

SEASON 84–85	GAMES	GOALS
League	9	3
League Cup	1	0
Scottish League	27	14
Scottish Cup	7	5
TOTAL	**44**	**22**

SEASON 85–86	GAMES	GOALS
Scottish League	31+1	15
Scottish Cup	3	1
Scottish League Cup	3	6
European Cup Winners Cup	2	1
TOTAL	**39+1**	**23**

SEASON 86–87	GAMES	GOALS
Scottish League	39+1	23
Scottish Cup	4	0
Scottish League Cup	5	3
European Cup	4	3
TOTAL	**52+1**	**29**

SEASON 87–88	GAMES	GOALS
French League	32	13
French Cup	1	0
TOTAL	**33**	**13**

SEASON 88–89	GAMES	GOALS
French League	34	8
French Cup	2	0
TOTAL	**36**	**8**

SEASON 89–90	GAMES	GOALS
Scottish League	36	15
Scottish Cup	2	1
Scottish League Cup	5	1
European Cup	2	0
Zenith Data Systems Challenge Cup	1	1
TOTAL	**46**	**18**

SEASON 90–91	GAMES	GOALS
Scottish League	29	11
Scottish Cup	2+1	0
Scottish League Cup	4	3
European Cup	3	5
TOTAL	**38+1**	**19**

SEASON 91–92	GAMES	GOALS
League	21	7
FA Cup	1	0
League Cup	1	0
Zenith Data Systems Cup	1	0
Scottish League	10+1	5
Scottish League Cup	4	5
European Cup	1	0
TOTAL	**39+1**	**17**

SEASON 92–93	GAMES	GOALS
League	7+6	3
League Cup	1+1	0
TOTAL	**8+7**	**3**

SEASON 93–94	GAMES	GOALS
Scottish League	31	4
Scottish Cup	3	1
TOTAL	**34**	**5**

SEASON 94–95	GAMES	GOALS
Scottish League	13+1	2
Scottish League Cup	1	0
TOTAL	**14+1**	**2**

SEASON 95–96	GAMES	GOALS
Scottish League	31	5
Scottish Cup	1	0
Scottish League Cup	2	2
Major League Soccer	29	6
Major League Soccer Play–offs	5	1
US Open Cup	1	0
TOTAL	**69**	**14**

CAREER APPEARANCES AND GOALS

COMPETITION	GAMES	TOTAL	GOALS
League	65+7	72	33
FA Cup	8	8	4
League Cup	3+1	4	0
Zenith Data Systems Cup	1	1	0
European Cup	10	10	8
European Cup Winners Cup	2	2	1
Scottish League	330+6	336	135
Scottish Cup	30+1	31	16
Scottish League Cup	34+1	35	26
Zenith Data Systems Challenge Cup	1	1	1
French League	66	66	21
French Cup	3	3	0
Major League Soccer	29	29	6
Major League Soccer Play–offs	5	5	1
US Open Cup	1	1	0
Internationals	34+4	38	14
TOTAL	**622+20**	**642**	**266**

HAT-TRICKS

Partick Thistle

1	3	Clyde	28/02/83	Away	S Cup	6–0
2	3	Falkirk	16/04/83	Home	League	4–2

Watford

1	3	Wolverhampton Wanderers	03/12/83	Away	League	5–0

Celtic

1	3	Dundee	01/12/84	Home	League	5–1

Rangers

1	3	Valletta FC	02/10/90	Home	Eur Cup	6–0
2	4	Queens Park	20/08/91	Home	S Lge Cup	6–0

League: 1
European Cup: 1
Scottish League: 2
Scottish Cup: 1
Scottish League Cup: 1
TOTAL: 6

HONOURS

Winners medals
Scottish Premier Division Championship: 85/86, 89/90, 90/91, 91/92
Scottish Cup: 84/85
Scottish League Cup: 90/91

Runner-up medals
FA Cup: 83/84
Scottish Premier Division Championship: 84/85, 86/87
Scottish League Cup: 86/87, 89/90
Zenith Data Systems Challenge Cup: 89/90

DAVID KELLY

Born: 25/11/65 – Birmingham
Height: 5.11
Weight: 11.03 (96–97)

Clubs
Walsall: **1984–88** – Matches: **152+38** – Goals: **80**
West Ham United: **1988–90** – Matches: **48+16** – Goals: **14**
Leicester City: **1990–91** – Matches: **72+3** – Goals: **25**
Newcastle United: **1991–93** – Matches: **83** – Goals: **39**
Wolverhampton Wanderers: **1993–95** – Matches: **96+7** – Goals: **36**
Sunderland: **1995–97** – Matches: **37+3** – Goals: **2**

Country
Republic of Ireland: **1987–97** – Matches: **15+8** – Goals: **9**

SEASON 1983–84

Walsall – League Division Three

Sub+1	21/02/84	Northampton Town	Home	AM Cup	3–1		
Sub+2	14/04/84	Millwall	Away	League	0–2		
1	23/04/84	Burnley	Away	League	2–0	1 Goal	(1)
2	28/04/84	Wigan Athletic	Home	League	3–0	1 Goal	(2)
3	05/05/84	Plymouth Argyle	Away	League	1–3	1 Goal	(3)
4	07/05/84	Preston North End	Home	League	2–1		
5	12/05/84	Brentford	Away	League	1–1		

SEASON 1984–85

League Division Three

Sub+3	15/09/84	Millwall	Home	League	3–3		
6	29/09/84	Bristol City	Home	League	4–1	2 Goals	(5)

7	02/10/84	Bolton Wanderers	Away	League	1–3		
8	06/10/84	Cambridge United	Away	League	1–0		
9	09/10/84	Coventry City	Away	Lge Cup	3–0	2 Goals	(7)
10	13/10/84	Wigan Athletic	Home	League	0–0		
11	20/10/84	Swansea City	Away	League	2–1		
12	23/10/84	Derby County	Home	League	0–0		
13	27/10/84	Newport County	Home	League	1–1	1 Goal	(8)
14	30/10/84	Chelsea	Home	Lge Cup	2–2		
15	03/11/84	Orient	Away	League	3–0		
16	06/11/84	Chelsea	Away	Lge Cup	0–3		
17	10/11/84	AFC Bournemouth	Home	League	0–0		
18	17/11/84	Stockport County	Away	FA Cup	2–1	1 Goal	(9)
19	24/11/84	Plymouth Argyle	Away	League	3–1		
20	01/12/84	Rotherham United	Home	League	0–2		
21	08/12/84	Chesterfield	Home	FA Cup	1–0		
22	15/12/84	Hull City	Away	League	0–1		
23	22/12/84	Burnley	Away	League	2–1	1 Goal	(10)
24	26/12/84	Preston North End	Home	League	2–1	1 Goal	(11)
25	29/12/84	Lincoln City	Home	League	0–0		
26	01/01/85	Doncaster Rovers	Away	League	1–4		
27	05/01/85	York City	Away	FA Cup	0–3		
28	26/01/85	Millwall	Away	League	0–0		
29	02/02/85	Bristol City	Away	League	2–1	1 Goal	(12)
30	06/02/85	Derby County	Away	FR Trophy	0–1		
Sub+4	26/02/85	York City	Home	League	3–0		
Sub+5	02/03/85	Newport County	Away	League	2–1		
31	06/03/85	Derby County	Away	League	0–2		
Sub+6	09/03/85	Swansea City	Home	League	3–0		
Sub+7	12/03/85	Colchester United	Home	FR Trophy	1–0		
Sub+8	17/03/85	Wigan Athletic	Away	League	2–1		
Sub+9	19/03/85	Bolton Wanderers	Home	League	1–0		
32	23/03/85	Cambridge United	Home	League	5–0	1 Goal	(13)
33	27/03/85	Brentford	Away	League	1–3		
Sub+10	30/03/85	Bristol Rovers	Home	League	1–2		
Sub+11	02/04/85	Bradford City	Home	League	0–0		
34	18/04/85	AFC Bournemouth	Away	FR Trophy	1–2	1 Goal	(14)
35	20/04/85	Plymouth Argyle	Home	League	0–3		
Sub+12	01/05/85	Reading	Away	League	1–1		
Sub+13	04/05/85	Hull City	Home	League	0–1		

SEASON 1985–86

League Division Three

Sub+14	26/08/85	Lincoln City	Away	League	2–3	1 Goal	(15)
Sub+15	31/08/85	Chesterfield	Home	League	3–0	1 Goal	(16)
Sub+16	07/09/85	Reading	Away	League	1–2		
Sub+17	14/09/85	Bolton Wanderers	Home	League	2–0		
Sub+18	17/09/85	Rotherham United	Home	League	3–1		
Sub+19	21/09/85	Bristol Rovers	Away	League	1–0		
36	28/09/85	Newport County	Home	League	2–0	1 Goal	(17)
37	01/10/85	Wigan Athletic	Away	League	0–2		
Sub+20	05/10/85	Doncaster Rovers	Away	League	0–1		
Sub+21	08/10/85	Leeds United	Home	Lge Cup	0–3		
Sub+22	10/12/85	Port Vale	Home	FA Cup	2–1		
Sub+23	14/12/85	AFC Bournemouth	Home	League	4–2		
Sub+24	28/12/85	Lincoln City	Home	League	2–1	1 Goal	(18)
Sub+25	01/01/86	York City	Home	League	3–1		
Sub+26	04/01/86	Manchester City	Home	FA Cup	1–3		
Sub+27	07/01/86	Swansea City	Away	League	1–2	1 Goal	(19)
Sub+28	18/01/86	Bristol City	Home	League	2–1		
38	21/01/86	Plymouth Argyle	Away	FR Trophy	1–0		
Sub+29	28/01/86	Bristol City	Home	FR Trophy	1–2		
39	15/02/86	Rotherham United	Away	League	0–3		
40	28/02/86	Newport County	Away	League	5–1	1 Goal	(20)
41	08/03/86	Doncaster Rovers	Home	League	1–0		
Sub+30	12/03/86	Derby County	Away	League	1–3		
Sub+31	18/03/86	Bristol Rovers	Home	League	6–0	1 Goal	(21)
Sub+32	22/03/86	Darlington	Home	League	0–0		
42	25/03/86	Chesterfield	Away	League	3–2		
Sub+33	05/04/86	Cardiff City	Away	League	1–1		
43	08/04/86	Notts County	Away	League	1–3		
Sub+34	12/04/86	Gillingham	Home	League	4–1		
Sub+35	15/04/86	Wigan Athletic	Home	League	3–3	1 Goal	(22)
Sub+36	19/04/86	Blackpool	Away	League	1–2	1 Goal	(23)

Sub+37	26/04/86	Bury	Home	League	3–2	1 Goal	(24)
Sub+38	03/05/86	AFC Bournemouth	Away	League	1–0		

SEASON 1986–87

League Division Three

44	23/08/86	Bristol Rovers	Home	League	0–3		
45	26/08/86	Mansfield Town	Home	Lge Cup	1–0		
46	30/08/86	Chesterfield	Away	League	2–3		
47	02/09/86	Mansfield Town	Away	Lge Cup	4–2	1 Goal	(25)
48	06/09/86	Doncaster Rovers	Home	League	1–3		
49	13/09/86	Carlisle United	Away	League	3–0	1 Goal	(26)
50	16/09/86	Wigan Athletic	Away	League	1–5	1 Goal	(27)
51	27/09/86	Port Vale	Away	League	1–4	1 Goal	(28)
52	30/09/86	Fulham	Home	League	1–1	1 Goal	(29)
53	04/10/86	Blackpool	Away	League	1–1	1 Goal	(30)
54	07/10/86	Millwall	Home	Lge Cup	0–1		
55	11/10/86	Bolton Wanderers	Home	League	3–3	1 Goal	(31)
56	14/10/86	Millwall	Away	Lge Cup	2–3	1 Goal	(32)
57	18/10/86	Middlesbrough	Away	League	1–3		
58	21/10/86	Rotherham United	Home	League	4–1	1 Goal	(33)
59	25/10/86	Brentford	Home	League	5–2	2 Goals	(35)
60	01/11/86	Chester City	Away	League	0–0		
61	04/11/86	AFC Bournemouth	Home	League	2–0		
62	08/11/86	Notts County	Away	League	1–2	1 Goal	(36)
63	15/11/86	Chesterfield	Home	FA Cup	2–0		
64	22/11/86	York City	Away	League	5–1	2 Goals	(38)
65	25/11/86	Swindon Town	Home	League	1–0	1 Goal	(39)
66	09/12/86	Swansea City	Away	FR Trophy	0–3		
67	13/12/86	Darlington	Home	League	4–2		
68	16/12/86	Torquay United	Home	FR Trophy	1–0		
69	20/12/86	Bury	Away	League	0–4		
70	26/12/86	Newport County	Home	League	2–0		
71	27/12/86	Bristol City	Away	League	1–2	1 Goal	(40)
72	01/01/87	Gillingham	Away	League	0–4		
73	10/01/87	Charlton Athletic	Away	FA Cup	2–1	1 Goal	(41)
74	24/01/87	Doncaster Rovers	Away	League	1–1		
75	26/01/87	Brentford	Away	FR Trophy	2–4		
76	31/01/87	Birmingham City	Home	FA Cup	1–0		
77	07/02/87	Wigan Athletic	Home	League	2–3		
78	21/02/87	Watford	Home	FA Cup	1–1		
79	24/02/87	Watford	Away	FA Cup	4–4*		
80	28/02/87	Fulham	Away	League	2–2		
81	02/03/87	Watford	Home	FA Cup	0–1		
82	11/03/87	Bristol Rovers	Away	League	3–0	1 Goal	(42)
83	21/03/87	Bolton Wanderers	Away	League	0–1		
84	24/03/87	York City	Home	League	3–2		
85	28/03/87	Blackpool	Home	League	2–1		
86	04/04/87	Notts County	Home	League	1–1	1 Goal	(43)
87	07/04/87	Carlisle United	Home	League	3–0	1 Goal	(44)
88	11/04/87	AFC Bournemouth	Away	League	0–1		
89	14/04/87	Chesterfield	Home	League	2–1	1 Goal	(45)
90	18/04/87	Gillingham	Home	League	1–0		
91	20/04/87	Newport County	Away	League	4–2		
92	22/04/87	Chester City	Home	League	1–0	1 Goal	(46)
93	25/04/87	Bury	Home	League	3–1		
94	28/04/87	Port Vale	Home	League	5–2	1 Goal	(47)
95	02/05/87	Mansfield Town	Away	League	0–2		
96	04/05/87	Bristol City	Home	League	1–1	1 Goal	(48)
97	06/05/87	Swindon Town	Away	League	0–0		
98	09/05/87	Darlington	Away	League	3–1	2 Goals	(50)

SEASON 1987–88

League Division Three

99	15/08/87	Fulham	Home	League	0–1		
100	19/08/87	West Bromwich Albion	Away	Lge Cup	3–2		
101	22/08/87	Blackpool	Away	League	2–1		
102	25/08/87	West Bromwich Albion	Home	Lge Cup	0–0		
103	29/08/87	Northampton Town	Home	League	1–0		
104	05/09/87	Sunderland	Home	League	2–2	1 Goal	(51)
105	12/09/87	Rotherham United	Away	League	1–0		
106	15/09/87	Bristol City	Home	League	1–1	1 Goal	(52)
107	19/09/87	Wigan Athletic	Home	League	1–2	1 Goal	(53)
108	23/09/87	Charlton Athletic	Away	Lge Cup	0–3		

109	06/10/87	Charlton Athletic	Home	Lge Cup	2–0		
110	10/10/87	Brighton & Hove Albion	Home	League	1–1		
111	17/10/87	Brentford	Away	League	0–0		
112	20/10/87	Doncaster Rovers	Away	League	4–0	1 Goal	(54)
113	24/10/87	Port Vale	Home	League	2–1	2 Goals	(56)
114	27/10/87	Wrexham	Away	SV Trophy	2–2	1 Goal	(57)
115	30/10/87	Southend United	Away	League	1–1		
116	03/11/87	Aldershot	Home	League	2–0	2 Goals	(59)
117	07/11/87	Chester City	Away	League	1–1		
118	14/11/87	Southend United	Away	FA Cup	0–0		
119	17/11/87	Southend United	Home	FA Cup	2–1		
120	21/11/87	Notts County	Away	League	1–3		
121	24/11/87	Cardiff City	Home	SV Trophy	3–1	1 Goal	(60)
122	28/11/87	Mansfield Town	Home	League	2–1		
123	05/12/87	Gillingham	Away	FA Cup	1–2	1 Goal	(61)
124	12/12/87	Bristol Rovers	Home	League	0–0		
125	18/12/87	Gillingham	Away	League	1–0		
126	26/12/87	Grimsby Town	Home	League	3–2	2 Goals	(63)
127	01/01/88	Northampton Town	Away	League	2–2		
128	02/01/88	Rotherham United	Home	League	5–2	1 Goal	(64)
129	09/01/88	Aldershot	Away	League	1–0		
130	16/01/88	Wigan Athletic	Away	League	1–3	1 Goal	(65)
131	19/01/88	Peterborough United	Home	SV Trophy	1–2		
132	30/01/88	York City	Home	League	2–1	1 Goal	(66)
133	06/02/88	Sunderland	Away	League	1–1		
134	09/02/88	Bristol City	Away	League	0–0		
135	13/02/88	Chesterfield	Home	League	0–0		
136	20/02/88	Fulham	Away	League	0–2		
137	23/02/88	Blackpool	Home	League	3–2		
138	27/02/88	Preston North End	Away	League	0–1		
139	05/03/88	Brentford	Home	League	4–2		
140	12/03/88	Brighton & Hove Albion	Home	League	1–2		
141	19/03/88	Southend United	Home	League	2–1	2 Goals	(68)
142	02/04/88	Chester City	Home	League	1–0		
143	05/04/88	Mansfield Town	Away	League	3–1	3 Goals	(71)
144	09/04/88	Doncaster Rovers	Home	League	2–1	1 Goal	(72)
145	30/04/88	Notts County	Home	League	2–1	1 Goal	(73)
146	02/05/88	Bristol Rovers	Away	League	0–3		
147	07/05/88	Gillingham	Home	League	0–0		
148	15/05/88	Notts County	Away	Lge P/O	3–1	2 Goals	(75)
149	18/05/88	Notts County	Home	Lge P/O	1–1		
150	25/05/88	Bristol City	Away	Lge P/O	3–1	2 Goals	(77)
151	28/05/88	Bristol City	Home	Lge P/O	0–2		
152	30/05/88	Bristol City	Home	Lge P/O	4–0	3 Goals	(80)

SEASON 1988–89

West Ham United – League Division One

1	27/08/88	Southampton	Away	League	0–4		
2	03/09/88	Charlton Athletic	Home	League	1–3		
3	10/09/88	Wimbledon	Away	League	1–0		
4	17/09/88	Aston Villa	Home	League	2–2	1 Goal	(1)
5	24/09/88	Manchester United	Away	League	0–2		
6	27/09/88	Sunderland	Away	Lge Cup	3–0	2 Goals	(3)
7	01/10/88	Arsenal	Home	League	1–4		
8	08/10/88	Middlesbrough	Away	League	0–1		
9	12/10/88	Sunderland	Home	Lge Cup	2–1	1 Goal	(4)
10	15/10/88	Queens Park Rangers	Away	League	1–2	1 Goal	(5)
11	22/10/88	Newcastle United	Home	League	2–0		
12	29/10/88	Liverpool	Home	League	0–2		
13	01/11/88	Derby County	Home	Lge Cup	5–0		
14	05/11/88	Coventry City	Away	League	1–1	1 Goal	(6)
15	09/11/88	West Bromwich Albion	Home	Simod Cup	5–2	1 Goal	(7)
16	12/11/88	Nottingham Forest	Home	League	3–3	2 Goals	(9)
17	30/11/88	Liverpool	Home	Lge Cup	4–1		
18	03/12/88	Millwall	Away	League	1–0		
19	10/12/88	Sheffield Wednesday	Home	League	0–0		
20	17/12/88	Tottenham Hotspur	Home	League	0–2		
21	27/12/88	Norwich City	Away	League	1–2		
22	31/12/88	Charlton Athletic	Away	League	0–0		
23	02/01/89	Wimbledon	Home	League	1–2		
24	08/01/89	Arsenal	Home	FA Cup	2–2		
25	11/01/89	Arsenal	Away	FA Cup	1–0		
26	14/01/89	Derby County	Away	League	2–1	1 Goal	(10)
27	18/01/89	Aston Villa	Home	Lge Cup	2–1	1 Goal	(11)

28	21/01/89	Manchester United	Home	League	1–3		
29	28/01/89	Swindon Town	Away	FA Cup	0–0		
30	01/02/89	Swindon Town	Home	FA Cup	1–0		
Sub+1	04/02/89	Arsenal	Away	League	1–2		
Sub+2	12/02/89	Luton Town	Home	Lge Cup	0–3		
31	01/03/89	Luton Town	Away	Lge Cup	0–2		
32	11/03/89	Coventry City	Home	League	1–1		
33	18/03/89	Norwich City	Home	FA Cup	0–0		
34	22/03/89	Norwich City	Away	FA Cup	1–3		
Sub+3	03/05/89	Newcastle United	Away	League	2–1		
Sub+4	06/05/89	Luton Town	Home	League	1–0		
Sub+5	13/05/89	Everton	Away	League	1–3		

SEASON 1989–90

League Division Two

Sub+6	19/08/89	Stoke City	Away	League	1–1		
35	23/08/89	Bradford City	Home	League	2–0		
36	26/08/89	Plymouth Argyle	Home	League	3–2	1 Goal	(12)
37	02/09/89	Hull City	Away	League	1–1		
38	09/09/89	Swindon Town	Home	League	1–1		
39	30/09/89	West Bromwich Albion	Home	League	2–3		
Sub+7	04/10/89	Birmingham City	Home	Lge Cup	1–1		
Sub+8	25/10/89	Aston Villa	Away	Lge Cup	0–0		
Sub+9	11/11/89	Newcastle United	Home	League	0–0		
40	29/11/89	Plymouth Argyle	Home	ZDS Cup	5–0		
Sub+10	02/12/89	Stoke City	Home	League	0–0		
Sub+11	22/12/89	Chelsea	Away	ZDS Cup	3–4	1 Goal	(13)
Sub+12	26/12/89	Ipswich Town	Away	League	0–1		
41	30/12/89	Leicester City	Away	League	0–1		
Sub+13	01/01/90	Barnsley	Home	League	4–2		
42	17/01/90	Derby County	Home	Lge Cup	1–1		
Sub+14	20/01/90	Hull City	Home	League	1–2		
43	24/01/90	Derby County	Away	Lge Cup	0–0*		
44	31/01/90	Derby County	Home	Lge Cup	2–1		
45	10/02/90	Brighton & Hove Albion	Home	League	3–1		
46	14/02/90	Oldham Athletic	Away	Lge Cup	0–6		
Sub+15	18/02/90	Swindon Town	Away	League	2–2		
Sub+16	24/02/90	Blackburn Rovers	Home	League	1–1		
47	07/03/90	Oldham Athletic	Home	Lge Cup	3–0	1 Goal	(14)
48	10/03/90	Portsmouth	Home	League	2–1		

Leicester City – League Division Two

1	24/03/90	Plymouth Argyle	Home	League	1–1		
2	31/03/90	Swindon Town	Away	League	1–1	1 Goal	(1)
3	03/04/90	Oldham Athletic	Home	League	3–0	2 Goals	(3)
4	07/04/90	Barnsley	Home	League	2–2	2 Goals	(5)
5	10/04/90	Wolverhampton Wanderers	Away	League	0–5		
6	14/04/90	Portsmouth	Home	League	1–1		
7	21/04/90	Middlesbrough	Home	League	2–1	2 Goals	(7)
8	28/04/90	Leeds United	Away	League	1–2		
9	02/05/90	West Ham United	Away	League	1–3		
10	05/05/90	Sheffield United	Home	League	2–5		

SEASON 1990–91

League Division Two

11	25/08/90	Bristol Rovers	Home	League	3–2	1 Goal	(8)
12	28/08/90	Oldham Athletic	Away	League	0–2		
13	01/09/90	Port Vale	Away	League	0–2		
14	08/09/90	West Ham United	Home	League	1–2		
15	15/09/90	Plymouth Argyle	Away	League	0–2		
16	18/09/90	Blackburn Rovers	Away	League	1–4		
17	22/09/90	Sheffield Wednesday	Home	League	2–4	1 Goal	(9)
18	26/09/90	Leeds United	Home	Lge Cup	1–0	1 Goal	(10)
19	29/09/90	Middlesbrough	Away	League	0–6		
20	03/10/90	Bristol City	Home	League	3–0	2 Goals	(12)
21	06/10/90	Notts County	Home	League	2–1	1 Goal	(13)
22	10/10/90	Leeds United	Away	Lge Cup	0–3		
23	13/10/90	Charlton Athletic	Away	League	2–1		
24	20/10/90	Portsmouth	Away	League	1–3		
25	24/10/90	Swindon Town	Home	League	2–2		
26	27/10/90	Ipswich Town	Home	League	1–2	1 Goal	(14)
27	03/11/90	Oxford United	Away	League	2–2	1 Goal	(15)
28	10/11/90	Barnsley	Away	League	1–1		

29	17/11/90	Wolverhampton Wanderers	Home	League	1–0	1 Goal	(16)
30	23/11/90	Hull City	Away	League	2–5		
31	27/11/90	Wolverhampton Wanderers	Home	ZDS Cup	0–1		
32	01/12/90	Newcastle United	Home	League	5–4	3 Goals	(19)
33	15/12/90	Bristol Rovers	Away	League	0–0		
34	23/12/90	Watford	Home	League	0–0		
35	26/12/90	Millwall	Away	League	1–2		
36	01/01/91	West Bromwich Albion	Home	League	2–1		
37	05/01/91	Millwall	Away	FA Cup	1–2		
38	12/01/91	Port Vale	Home	League	1–1		
39	19/01/91	West Ham United	Away	League	0–1		
40	26/01/91	Blackburn Rovers	Home	League	1–3	1 Goal	(20)
41	02/02/91	Plymouth Argyle	Home	League	3–1	1 Goal	(21)
42	20/02/91	Brighton & Hove Albion	Away	League	0–3		
43	23/02/91	Barnsley	Home	League	2–1		
44	02/03/91	Newcastle United	Away	League	1–2		
45	05/03/91	Wolverhampton Wanderers	Away	League	1–2		
46	09/03/91	Hull City	Home	League	0–1		
47	12/03/91	Bristol City	Home	League	0–2		
Sub+1	23/03/91	Notts County	Away	League	2–0		
Sub+2	30/03/91	Millwall	Home	League	1–2	1 Goal	(22)
Sub+3	01/04/91	Watford	Away	League	0–1		
48	06/04/91	Brighton & Hove Albion	Home	League	3–0		
49	10/04/91	Oldham Athletic	Home	League	0–0		
50	13/04/91	West Bromwich Albion	Away	League	1–2		
51	20/04/91	Portsmouth	Home	League	2–1		
52	24/04/91	Sheffield Wednesday	Away	League	0–0		
53	27/04/91	Swindon Town	Away	League	2–5		
54	04/05/91	Ipswich Town	Away	League	2–3		
55	11/05/91	Oxford United	Home	League	1–0		

SEASON 1991–92

League Division Two

56	17/08/91	Swindon Town	Away	League	0–0		
57	21/08/91	Maidstone United	Home	Lge Cup	3–0	1 Goal	(23)
58	24/08/91	Plymouth Argyle	Home	League	2–0		
59	28/08/91	Maidstone United	Away	Lge Cup	1–0		
60	31/08/91	Southend United	Away	League	2–1		
61	04/09/91	Grimsby Town	Home	League	2–0		
62	07/09/91	Bristol City	Home	League	2–1		
63	14/09/91	Middlesbrough	Away	League	0–3		
64	17/09/91	Barnsley	Away	League	1–3	1 Goal	(24)
65	21/09/91	Blackburn Rovers	Home	League	3–0		
66	25/09/91	Arsenal	Home	Lge Cup	1–1		
67	29/09/91	Cambridge United	Away	League	1–5		
68	02/10/91	Barnsley	Home	ZDS Cup	4–3	1 Goal	(25)
69	05/10/91	Charlton Athletic	Home	League	0–2		
70	08/10/91	Arsenal	Away	Lge Cup	0–2		
71	12/10/91	Newcastle United	Away	League	0–2		
72	23/11/91	Port Vale	Home	League	0–1		

Newcastle United – League Division Two

1	07/12/91	Port Vale	Home	League	2–2		
2	14/12/91	Brighton & Hove Albion	Away	League	2–2	1 Goal	(1)
3	20/12/91	Plymouth Argyle	Away	League	0–2		
4	26/12/91	Middlesbrough	Home	League	0–1		
5	28/12/91	Bristol Rovers	Home	League	2–1	1 Goal	(2)
6	01/01/92	Southend United	Away	League	0–4		
7	04/01/92	AFC Bournemouth	Away	FA Cup	0–0		
8	11/01/92	Watford	Away	League	2–2	1 Goal	(3)
9	18/01/92	Charlton Athletic	Home	League	3–4		
10	01/02/92	Oxford United	Away	League	2–5		
11	08/02/92	Bristol City	Home	League	3–0	2 Goals	(5)
12	15/02/92	Blackburn Rovers	Away	League	1–3	1 Goal	(6)
13	22/02/92	Barnsley	Home	League	1–1	1 Goal	(7)
14	29/02/92	Port Vale	Away	League	1–0		
15	07/03/92	Brighton & Hove Albion	Home	League	0–1		
16	10/03/92	Cambridge United	Away	League	2–0	1 Goal	(8)
17	14/03/92	Swindon Town	Home	League	3–1	1 Goal	(9)
18	21/03/92	Grimsby Town	Away	League	1–1		
19	29/03/92	Sunderland	Home	League	1–0	1 Goal	(10)
20	31/03/92	Wolverhampton Wanderers	Away	League	2–6		
21	04/04/92	Tranmere Rovers	Home	League	2–3		
22	11/04/92	Ipswich Town	Away	League	2–3		

23	18/04/92	Millwall	Home	League	0–1		
24	20/04/92	Derby County	Away	League	1–4		
25	25/04/92	Portsmouth	Home	League	1–0	1 Goal	(11)
26	02/05/92	Leicester City	Away	League	2–1		

SEASON 1992–93

Football League Division One

27	15/08/92	Southend United	Home	League	3–2		
28	19/08/92	Mansfield Town	Home	Lge Cup	2–1		
29	22/08/92	Derby County	Away	League	2–1		
30	25/08/92	Mansfield Town	Away	Lge Cup	0–0		
31	29/08/92	West Ham United	Home	League	2–0	1 Goal	(12)
32	02/09/92	Luton Town	Home	League	2–0	1 Goal	(13)
33	05/09/92	Bristol Rovers	Away	League	2–1		
34	12/09/92	Portsmouth	Home	League	3–1	1 Goal	(14)
35	16/09/92	Grimsby Town	Away	AI Cup	2–2	1 Goal	(15)
36	19/09/92	Bristol City	Home	League	5–0		
37	23/09/92	Middlesbrough	Home	Lge Cup	0–0		
38	26/09/92	Peterborough United	Away	League	1–0		
39	30/09/92	Leicester City	Home	AI Cup	4–0		
40	04/10/92	Brentford	Away	League	2–1	1 Goal	(16)
41	07/10/92	Middlesbrough	Away	Lge Cup	3–1	2 Goals	(18)
42	10/10/92	Tranmere Rovers	Home	League	1–0	1 Goal	(19)
43	18/10/92	Sunderland	Away	League	2–1		
44	31/10/92	Leicester City	Away	League	1–2		
45	04/11/92	Birmingham City	Away	League	3–2		
46	08/11/92	Swindon Town	Home	League	0–0		
47	14/11/92	Charlton Athletic	Away	League	3–1		
48	21/11/92	Watford	Home	League	2–0		
49	24/11/92	Ascoli Calcio 1898	Home	AI Cup	0–1		
50	28/11/92	Cambridge United	Home	League	4–1	3 Goals	(22)
51	05/12/92	Notts County	Away	League	2–0		
52	13/12/92	Barnsley	Away	League	0–1		
53	16/12/92	AC Cesena	Home	AI Cup	2–2		
54	20/12/92	Millwall	Home	League	1–1	1 Goal	(23)
55	26/12/92	Wolverhampton Wanderers	Home	League	2–1	2 Goals	(25)
56	28/12/92	Oxford United	Away	League	2–4		
57	02/01/93	Port Vale	Home	FA Cup	4–0		
58	09/01/93	Bristol City	Away	League	2–1	1 Goal	(26)
59	16/01/93	Peterborough United	Home	League	3–0	1 Goal	(27)
60	20/01/93	Southend United	Away	League	1–1		
61	23/01/93	Rotherham United	Away	FA Cup	1–1		
62	27/01/93	Luton Town	Away	League	0–0		
63	31/01/93	Derby County	Home	League	1–1		
64	03/02/93	Rotherham United	Home	FA Cup	2–0	1 Goal	(28)
65	09/02/93	Portsmouth	Away	League	0–2		
66	13/02/93	Blackburn Rovers	Away	FA Cup	0–1		
67	21/02/93	West Ham United	Away	League	0–0		
68	24/02/93	Bristol Rovers	Home	League	0–0		
69	28/02/93	Tranmere Rovers	Away	League	3–0	1 Goal	(29)
70	06/03/93	Brentford	Home	League	5–1	1 Goal	(30)
71	10/03/93	Charlton Athletic	Home	League	2–2	1 Goal	(31)
72	13/03/93	Swindon Town	Away	League	1–2	1 Goal	(32)
73	20/03/93	Notts County	Home	League	4–0	2 Goals	(34)
74	23/03/93	Watford	Away	League	0–1		
75	28/03/93	Birmingham City	Home	League	2–2		
76	03/04/93	Cambridge United	Away	League	3–0	1 Goal	(35)
77	07/04/93	Barnsley	Home	League	6–0		
78	10/04/93	Wolverhampton Wanderers	Away	League	0–1		
79	17/04/93	Millwall	Away	League	2–1		
80	25/04/93	Sunderland	Home	League	1–0		
81	04/05/93	Grimsby Town	Away	League	2–0	1 Goal	(36)
82	06/05/93	Oxford United	Home	League	2–1		
83	09/05/93	Leicester City	Home	League	7–1	3 Goals	(39)

SEASON 1993–94

Wolverhampton Wanderers – Football League Division One

1	14/08/93	Bristol City	Home	League	3–1		
2	22/08/93	Birmingham City	Away	League	2–2		
3	25/08/93	Millwall	Home	League	2–0	1 Goal	(1)
4	28/08/93	Middlesbrough	Home	League	2–3	1 Goal	(2)
5	31/08/93	Stoke City	Home	AI Cup	3–3	1 Goal	(3)
6	05/09/93	West Bromwich Albion	Away	League	2–3		

7	11/09/93	Portsmouth	Home	League	1–1	1 Goal	(4)
8	18/09/93	Sunderland	Away	League	2–0		
9	22/09/93	Swindon Town	Away	Lge Cup	0–2		
10	25/09/93	Grimsby Town	Away	League	0–2		
11	02/10/93	Charlton Athletic	Home	League	1–1		
12	05/10/93	Swindon Town	Home	Lge Cup	2–1		
13	17/10/93	Crystal Palace	Away	League	1–1	1 Goal	(5)
14	23/10/93	Stoke City	Home	League	1–1	1 Goal	(6)
15	30/10/93	Southend United	Away	League	1–1		
16	02/11/93	Notts County	Home	League	3–0		
17	07/11/93	Derby County	Away	League	4–0		
18	10/11/93	Nottingham Forest	Home	League	1–1	1 Goal	(7)
19	13/11/93	Barnsley	Home	League	1–1	1 Goal	(8)
20	27/11/93	Leicester City	Away	League	2–2		
21	05/12/93	Derby County	Home	League	2–2	1 Goal	(9)
22	11/12/93	Watford	Home	League	2–0		
23	18/12/93	Bristol City	Away	League	1–2	1 Goal	(10)
24	27/12/93	Tranmere Rovers	Away	League	1–1		
25	28/12/93	Oxford United	Home	League	2–1		
26	01/01/94	Peterborough United	Away	League	1–0		
27	03/01/94	Bolton Wanderers	Home	League	1–0		
28	08/01/94	Crystal Palace	Home	FA Cup	1–0	1 Goal	(11)
29	15/01/94	Crystal Palace	Home	League	2–0		
30	23/01/94	Nottingham Forest	Away	League	0–0		
31	29/01/94	Port Vale	Away	FA Cup	2–0		
32	05/02/94	Stoke City	Away	League	1–1		
33	12/02/94	Southend United	Home	League	0–1		
34	19/02/94	Ipswich Town	Home	FA Cup	1–1	1 Goal	(12)
35	22/02/94	Birmingham City	Home	League	3–0	1 Goal	(13)
36	25/02/94	West Bromwich Albion	Home	League	1–2		
37	02/03/94	Ipswich Town	Away	FA Cup	2–1		
38	05/03/94	Middlesbrough	Away	League	0–1		
39	13/03/94	Chelsea	Away	FA Cup	0–1		
40	15/03/94	Portsmouth	Away	League	0–3		
41	19/03/94	Grimsby Town	Home	League	0–0		
42	26/03/94	Charlton Athletic	Away	League	1–0		
Sub+1	03/05/94	Sunderland	Home	League	1–1		
43	08/05/94	Leicester City	Home	League	1–1	1 Goal	(14)

SEASON 1994–95

Football League Division One

44	13/08/94	Reading	Home	League	1–0		
45	21/08/94	Notts County	Away	League	1–1		
46	24/08/94	US Lecce	Away	AI Cup	1–0	1 Goal	(15)
47	28/08/94	West Bromwich Albion	Home	League	2–0	1 Goal	(16)
48	30/08/94	Watford	Away	League	1–2		
49	03/09/94	Sunderland	Home	League	1–1		
Sub+2	10/09/94	Tranmere Rovers	Home	League	2–0		
50	13/09/94	Southend United	Home	League	5–0	1 Goal	(17)
51	17/09/94	Burnley	Away	League	1–0		
52	20/09/94	Chesterfield	Away	Lge Cup	3–1	1 Goal	(18)
53	24/09/94	Portsmouth	Away	League	2–1	1 Goal	(19)
54	27/09/94	Chesterfield	Home	Lge Cup	1–1		
55	08/10/94	Swindon Town	Away	League	2–3	2 Goals	(21)
56	15/10/94	Grimsby Town	Home	League	2–1		
57	22/10/94	Millwall	Home	League	3–3		
58	26/10/94	Nottingham Forest	Home	Lge Cup	2–3	1 Goal	(22)
59	30/10/94	Stoke City	Away	League	1–1		
60	01/11/94	Bristol City	Away	League	5–1	3 Goals	(25)
61	05/11/94	Luton Town	Home	League	2–3		
62	20/11/94	Middlesbrough	Away	League	0–1		
63	23/11/94	Bolton Wanderers	Home	League	3–1		
64	27/11/94	Derby County	Home	League	0–2		
65	04/12/94	Millwall	Away	League	0–1		
Sub+3	10/12/94	Notts County	Home	League	1–0		
Sub+4	31/12/94	Barnsley	Away	League	3–1		
66	02/01/95	Sheffield United	Home	League	2–2		
67	07/01/95	Mansfield Town	Away	FA Cup	3–2	1 Goal	(26)
68	14/01/95	Stoke City	Home	League	2–0	1 Goal	(27)
69	30/01/95	Sheffield Wednesday	Away	FA Cup	0–0		
70	04/02/95	Bolton Wanderers	Away	League	1–5		
71	08/02/95	Sheffield Wednesday	Home	FA Cup	1–1+	1 Goal	(28)
72	11/02/95	Bristol City	Home	League	2–0	1 Goal	(29)
73	18/02/95	Leicester City	Home	FA Cup	1–0	1 Goal	(30)

74	21/02/95	Middlesbrough	Home	League	0–2		
75	25/02/95	Port Vale	Away	League	4–2		
76	05/03/95	Portsmouth	Home	League	1–0		
77	08/03/95	Sunderland	Home	League	1–0		
78	11/03/95	Crystal Palace	Away	FA Cup	1–1		
79	15/03/95	West Bromwich Albion	Away	League	0–2		
80	18/03/95	Watford	Home	League	1–1		
81	22/03/95	Crystal Palace	Home	FA Cup	1–4	1 Goal	(31)
82	24/03/95	Burnley	Home	League	2–0		
83	01/04/95	Southend United	Away	League	1–0		
Sub+5	04/04/95	Luton Town	Away	League	3–3	2 Goals	(33)
84	08/04/95	Barnsley	Home	League	0–0		
85	12/04/95	Derby County	Away	League	3–3		
86	15/04/95	Charlton Athletic	Away	League	2–3		
87	17/04/95	Oldham Athletic	Home	League	2–1	2 Goals	(35)
88	22/04/95	Sheffield United	Away	League	3–3	1 Goal	(36)
89	29/04/95	Grimsby Town	Away	League	0–0		
90	03/05/95	Tranmere Rovers	Away	League	1–1		
91	07/05/95	Swindon Town	Home	League	1–1		
92	14/05/95	Bolton Wanderers	Home	Lge P/O	2–1		
93	17/05/95	Bolton Wanderers	Away	Lge P/O	0–2		

+ AET Wolverhampton Wanderers won 4–3 on penalties

SEASON 1995–96

Football League Division One

94	12/08/95	Tranmere Rovers	Away	League	2–2		
95	20/08/95	West Bromwich Albion	Home	League	1–1		
96	26/08/95	Sunderland	Away	League	0–2		
Sub+6	02/09/95	Leicester City	Away	League	0–1		
Sub+7	13/09/95	Norwich City	Home	League	0–2		

Sunderland – Football League Division One

1	23/09/95	Millwall	Away	League	2–1		
2	30/09/95	Reading	Home	League	2–2	1 Goal	(1)
3	04/10/95	Liverpool	Home	Lge Cup	0–1		
4	07/10/95	Crystal Palace	Away	League	1–0	1 Goal	(2)
5	21/10/95	Huddersfield Town	Away	League	1–1		
6	05/11/95	Charlton Athletic	Away	League	1–1		
7	18/11/95	Sheffield United	Home	League	2–0		
8	22/11/95	Stoke City	Away	League	0–1		
9	03/12/95	Crystal Palace	Home	League	1–0		
Sub+1	23/12/95	Derby County	Away	League	1–3		
10	06/01/96	Manchester United	Away	FA Cup	2–2		
11	14/01/96	Norwich City	Home	League	0–1		

SEASON 1996–97

Premier League

12	17/08/96	Leicester City	Home	League	0–0		
Sub+2	24/09/96	Watford	Home	Lge Cup	1–0		
13	19/10/96	Southampton	Away	League	0–3		
14	23/10/96	Tottenham Hotspur	Away	Lge Cup	1–2		
15	26/10/96	Aston Villa	Home	League	1–0		
16	02/11/96	Leeds United	Away	League	0–3		
17	16/11/96	Tottenham Hotspur	Away	League	0–2		
18	23/11/96	Sheffield Wednesday	Home	League	1–1		
19	30/11/96	Everton	Away	League	3–1		
20	07/12/96	Wimbledon	Home	League	1–3		
21	15/12/96	Chelsea	Home	League	3–0		
22	21/12/96	Manchester United	Away	League	0–5		
23	26/12/96	Derby County	Home	League	2–0		
24	28/12/96	West Ham United	Away	League	0–2		
25	01/01/97	Coventry City	Away	League	2–2		
26	04/01/97	Arsenal	Away	FA Cup	1–1		
27	11/01/97	Arsenal	Home	League	1–0		
28	15/01/97	Arsenal	Home	FA Cup	0–2		
29	18/01/97	Blackburn Rovers	Home	League	0–0		
30	29/01/97	Leicester City	Away	League	1–1		
31	31/01/97	Aston Villa	Away	League	0–1		
32	22/02/97	Leeds United	Home	League	0–1		
33	01/03/97	Blackburn Rovers	Away	League	0–1		
34	04/03/97	Tottenham Hotspur	Home	League	0–4		

35	08/03/97	Manchester United	Home	League	2–1
36	12/03/97	Sheffield Wednesday	Away	League	1–2
37	16/03/97	Chelsea	Away	League	2–6
Sub+3	05/04/97	Newcastle United	Away	League	1–1

INTERNATIONAL APPEARANCES – REPUBLIC OF IRELAND

1	10/11/87	Israel	Dalymount Park	5–0	F	3 Goals	(3)
2	23/03/88	Romania	Lansdowne Road	2–0	F	1 Goal	(4)
3	27/04/88	Yugoslavia	Lansdowne Road	2–0	F		
Sub 4	19/10/88	Tunisia	Lansdowne Road	4–0	F		
5	25/04/90	USSR	Lansdowne Road	1–0	F		
6	02/06/90	Malta	Valletta	3–0	F		
7	12/09/90	Morocco	Lansdowne Road	1–0	F	1 Goal	(5)
Sub 8	06/02/91	Wales	Racecourse	3–0	F		
9	22/05/91	Chile	Lansdowne Road	1–1	F	1 Goal	(6)
10	02/06/91	USA	Massachusetts	1–1	F		
11	11/09/91	Hungary	Gyor	2–1	F	1 Goal	(7)
Sub 12	04/06/92	Italy	Boston	0–2	USC		
13	07/06/92	Portugal	Boston	2–0	USC		
Sub 14	14/10/92	Denmark	Copenhagen	0–0	WCQ		
15	17/02/93	Wales	Tolka Park	2–1	F		
16	23/03/94	Russia	Lansdowne Road	0–0	F		
Sub 17	28/06/94	Norway	New York	0–0	WC		
18	15/02/95	England	Lansdowne Road	Aba	F	1 Goal	(8)
19	29/03/95	Northern Ireland	Lansdowne Road	1–1	ECQ		
Sub 20	11/10/95	Latvia	Lansdowne Road	2–1	ECQ		
21	10/11/96	Iceland	Lansdowne Road	0–0	WCQ		
Sub 22	11/02/97	Wales	Cardiff Arms Park	0–0	Fr		
Sub 23	02/04/97	Macedonia	Skopje	2–3	WCQ	1 Goal	(9)

APPEARANCES AND GOALS PER SEASON

SEASON 83–84	GAMES	GOALS
League	5+1	3
Associate Members Cup	0+1	0
TOTAL	**5+2**	**3**

SEASON 84–85	GAMES	GOALS
League	22+10	7
FA Cup	3	1
League Cup	3	2
Freight Rover Trophy	2+1	1
TOTAL	**30+11**	**11**

SEASON 85–86	GAMES	GOALS
League	7+21	10
FA Cup	0+2	0
League Cup	0+1	0
Freight Rover Trophy	1+1	0
TOTAL	**8+25**	**10**

SEASON 86–87	GAMES	GOALS
League	42	23
FA Cup	6	1
League Cup	4	2
Freight Rover Trophy	3	0
TOTAL	**55**	**26**

SEASON 87–88	GAMES	GOALS
League	39	20
League Play-offs	5	7
FA Cup	3	1
League Cup	4	0
Sherpa Van Trophy	3	2
TOTAL	**54**	**30**

SEASON 88–89	GAMES	GOALS
League	21+4	6
FA Cup	6	0
League Cup	6+1	4
Simod Cup	1	1
TOTAL	**34+5**	**11**

SEASON 89–90	GAMES	GOALS
League	18+8	8
League Cup	5+2	1
Zenith Data Systems Cup	1+1	1
TOTAL	**24+11**	**10**

SEASON 90–91	GAMES	GOALS
League	41+3	14
FA Cup	1	0
League Cup	2	1
Zenith Data Systems Cup	1	0
TOTAL	**45+3**	**15**

SEASON 91–92	GAMES	GOALS
League	37	12
FA Cup	1	0
League Cup	4	1
Zenith Data Systems Cup	1	1
TOTAL	**43**	**14**

SEASON 92–93	GAMES	GOALS
League	45	24
FA Cup	4	1
League Cup	4	2
Anglo–Italian Cup	4	1
TOTAL	**57**	**28**

SEASON 93–94	GAMES	GOALS
League	35+1	11
FA Cup	5	2
League Cup	2	0
Anglo–Italian Cup	1	1
TOTAL	**43+1**	**14**

SEASON 94–95	GAMES	GOALS
League	38+4	15
League Play–offs	2	0
FA Cup	6	4
League Cup	3	2
Anglo–Italian Cup	1	1
TOTAL	**50+4**	**22**

SEASON 95–96	GAMES	GOALS
League	12+3	2
FA Cup	1	0
League Cup	1	0
TOTAL	**14+3**	**2**

SEASON 96–97	GAMES	GOALS
League	23+1	0
FA Cup	2	0
League Cup	1+1	0
TOTAL	**26+2**	**0**

CAREER APPEARANCES AND GOALS

COMPETITION	GAMES	TOTAL	GOALS
League	385+56	441	155
League Play–offs	7	7	7
FA Cup	38+2	40	10
League Cup	39+5	44	15
Associate Members Cup	0+1	1	0
Freight Rover Trophy	6+2	8	1
Sherpa Van Trophy	3	3	2
Simod Cup	1	1	1
Zenith Data Systems Cup	3+1	4	2
Anglo–Italian Cup	6	6	3
Internationals	15+8	23	9
TOTAL	**503+75**	**578**	**205**

HAT-TRICKS

Walsall

1	3	Mansfield Town	05/04/88	Away	League	3–1
2	3	Bristol City	30/05/88	Home	Lge P/O	4–0

Leicester City

1	3	Newcastle United	01/12/90	Home		League	5–4

Newcastle United

1	3	Cambridge United	28/11/92	Home		League	4–1
2	3	Leicester City	09/05/93	Home		League	7–1

Wolverhampton Wanderers

1	3	Bristol City	01/11/94	Away		League	5–1

Republic of Ireland

1	3	Israel	10/11/87	Dalymount Park	F		5–0

League: 5
League Play–offs: 1
International: 1
TOTAL: 7

HONOURS

Winners medals
Football League Division One Championship: 92/93, 95/96

Runner-up medals
Promoted to League Division Two: 87/88

MATTHEW LE TISSIER

Born: 14/10/68 – Guernsey
Height: 6.1
Weight: 13.08 (96–97)

Club
Southampton: **1986–97** – Matches: **397+44** – Goals: **184**

Country
England: **1994–97** – Matches: **3+5** – Goals: **0**

SEASON 1986–87

Southampton – League Division One

Sub+1	30/08/86	Norwich City	Away	League	3–4		
1	02/09/86	Tottenham Hotspur	Home	League	2–0		
2	06/09/86	Nottingham Forest	Home	League	1–3		
Sub+2	13/09/86	Manchester United	Away	League	1–5		
Sub+3	04/10/86	Newcastle United	Home	League	4–1		
Sub+4	08/10/86	Swindon Town	Away	Lge Cup	0–0		
Sub+5	18/10/86	Everton	Home	League	0–2		
Sub+6	01/11/86	Manchester City	Home	League	1–1		
Sub+7	04/11/86	Manchester United	Home	Lge Cup	4–1	2 Goals	(2)
Sub+8	08/11/86	Sheffield Wednesday	Away	League	1–3	1 Goal	(3)
Sub+9	15/11/86	Arsenal	Home	League	0–4		
3	25/11/86	Hull City	Home	FM Cup	2–1	2 Goals	(5)
Sub+10	29/11/86	Watford	Home	League	3–1		
Sub+11	09/12/86	Norwich City	Home	FM Cup	1–2		
Sub+12	26/12/86	Chelsea	Home	League	1–2		
Sub+13	03/01/87	Oxford United	Away	League	1–1		
Sub+14	10/01/87	Everton	Away	FA Cup	1–2		
4	24/01/87	Queens Park Rangers	Away	League	1–2		
Sub+15	27/01/87	Shrewsbury Town	Home	Lge Cup	1–0		
Sub+16	25/02/87	Liverpool	Away	Lge Cup	0–3		
5	28/02/87	Liverpool	Away	League	0–1		
6	07/03/87	Leicester City	Home	League	4–0	3 Goals	(8)
7	14/03/87	Everton	Away	League	0–3		
8	21/03/87	Aston Villa	Home	League	5–0		

9	24/03/87	Luton Town	Home	League	3–0		
10	28/03/87	Newcastle United	Away	League	0–2		
11	07/04/87	Wimbledon	Home	League	2–2		
Sub+17	22/04/87	Sheffield Wednesday	Home	League	1–1	1 Goal	(9)
Sub+18	25/04/87	Charlton Athletic	Home	League	2–2		
12	02/05/87	Watford	Away	League	1–1	1 Goal	(10)
13	04/05/87	West Ham United	Home	League	1–0		

SEASON 1987–88

League Division One

Sub+19	29/08/87	Queens Park Rangers	Home	League	0–1		
Sub+20	05/09/87	Sheffield Wednesday	Home	League	1–1		
Sub+21	03/10/87	Everton	Home	League	0–4		
14	06/10/87	AFC Bournemouth	Home	Lge Cup	2–2	1 Goal	(11)
15	17/10/87	Watford	Home	League	1–0		
16	20/10/87	Coventry City	Away	League	3–2		
17	24/10/87	Chelsea	Home	League	3–0		
18	31/10/87	Charlton Athletic	Away	League	1–1		
Sub+22	12/12/87	Liverpool	Home	League	2–2		
Sub+23	18/12/87	Luton Town	Away	League	2–2		
Sub+24	01/01/88	Queens Park Rangers	Away	League	0–3		
Sub+25	03/01/88	Portsmouth	Home	League	0–2		
19	09/01/88	Reading	Away	FA Cup	1–0	1 Goal	(12)
20	16/01/88	Manchester United	Away	League	2–0		
21	23/01/88	Norwich City	Home	League	0–0		
22	25/01/88	Bradford City	Away	Simod Cup	0–1		
23	01/03/88	Newcastle United	Home	League	1–1		
24	05/03/88	Watford	Away	League	1–0		
25	12/03/88	Coventry City	Home	League	1–2		
26	19/03/88	Charlton Athletic	Home	League	0–1		
Sub+26	30/04/88	West Ham United	Home	League	2–1		
Sub+27	07/05/88	Luton Town	Home	League	1–1		

SEASON 1988–89

League Division One

Sub+28	27/08/88	West Ham United	Home	League	4–0	1 Goal	(13)
27	03/09/88	Queens Park Rangers	Away	League	1–0	1 Goal	(14)
28	10/09/88	Luton Town	Home	League	2–1		
29	17/09/88	Arsenal	Away	League	2–2	1 Goal	(15)
Sub+29	01/10/88	Derby County	Home	League	0–0		
Sub+30	08/10/88	Everton	Away	League	1–4		
Sub+31	22/10/88	Sheffield Wednesday	Home	League	1–2		
Sub+32	25/10/88	Tottenham Hotspur	Away	League	2–1		
30	29/10/88	Norwich City	Away	League	1–1		
31	02/11/88	Scarborough	Away	Lge Cup	2–2	1 Goal	(16)
32	05/11/88	Charlton Athletic	Home	League	2–0		
33	08/11/88	Stoke City	Home	Simod Cup	3–0		
34	12/11/88	Aston Villa	Home	League	3–1	2 Goals	(18)
35	19/11/88	Manchester United	Away	League	2–2	1 Goal	(19)
36	22/11/88	Scarborough	Home	Lge Cup	1–0	1 Goal	(20)
37	26/11/88	Millwall	Home	League	2–2		
38	29/11/88	Tottenham Hotspur	Home	Lge Cup	2–1		
39	03/12/88	Wimbledon	Away	League	1–2		
40	10/12/88	Nottingham Forest	Home	League	1–1		
41	13/12/88	Crystal Palace	Home	Simod Cup	1–2		
42	17/12/88	Newcastle United	Away	League	3–3	2 Goals	(22)
43	26/12/88	Coventry City	Home	League	2–2		
44	31/12/88	Queens Park Rangers	Home	League	1–4	1 Goal	(23)
45	02/01/89	Luton Town	Away	League	1–6		
46	07/01/89	Derby County	Away	FA Cup	1–1		
47	10/01/89	Derby County	Home	FA Cup	1–2*		
48	14/01/89	Middlesbrough	Home	League	1–3		
Sub+33	25/01/89	Luton Town	Home	Lge Cup	1–2*		
49	04/02/89	Derby County	Away	League	1–3		
Sub+34	08/04/89	Middlesbrough	Away	League	3–3		
Sub+35	12/04/89	Nottingham Forest	Away	League	0–3		
50	19/04/89	Norwich City	Home	League	0–0		
51	22/04/89	Wimbledon	Home	League	0–0		
52	02/05/89	Aston Villa	Away	League	2–1		
53	06/05/89	Manchester United	Home	League	2–1		
54	13/05/89	Millwall	Away	League	1–1		

SEASON 1989–90

League Division One

55	19/08/89	Millwall	Home	League	1–2			
56	23/08/89	Manchester City	Away	League	2–1			
57	26/08/89	Everton	Away	League	0–3			
58	16/09/89	Crystal Palace	Home	League	1–1			
Sub+36	20/09/89	York City	Away	Lge Cup	1–0			
59	23/09/89	Derby County	Away	League	1–0			
60	30/09/89	Wimbledon	Home	League	2–2	2 Goals	(25)
61	03/10/89	York City	Home	Lge Cup	2–0			
62	14/10/89	Queens Park Rangers	Away	League	4–1	1 Goal	(26)
63	21/10/89	Liverpool	Home	League	4–1	1 Goal	(27)
64	24/10/89	Charlton Athletic	Home	Lge Cup	1–0			
65	28/10/89	Manchester United	Away	League	1–2	1 Goal	(28)
66	04/11/89	Tottenham Hotspur	Home	League	1–1			
67	11/11/89	Coventry City	Away	League	0–1			
68	18/11/89	Chelsea	Away	League	2–2	2 Goals	(30)
69	25/11/89	Luton Town	Home	League	6–3	1 Goal	(31)
70	29/11/89	Swindon Town	Away	Lge Cup	0–0			
71	02/12/89	Millwall	Away	League	2–2	1 Goal	(32)
72	09/12/89	Manchester City	Home	League	2–1			
73	17/12/89	Nottingham Forest	Away	League	0–2			
74	26/12/89	Arsenal	Home	League	1–0			
75	30/12/89	Sheffield Wednesday	Home	League	2–2	2 Goals	(34)
76	01/01/90	Charlton Athletic	Away	League	4–2	1 Goal	(35)
77	06/01/90	Tottenham Hotspur	Away	FA Cup	3–1	1 Goal	(36)
78	13/01/90	Everton	Home	League	2–2			
79	16/01/90	Swindon Town	Home	Lge Cup	4–2*	1 Goal	(37)
80	20/01/90	Aston Villa	Away	League	1–2			
81	24/01/90	Oldham Athletic	Home	Lge Cup	2–2	2 Goals	(39)
82	27/01/90	Oxford United	Home	FA Cup	1–0			
83	31/01/90	Oldham Athletic	Away	Lge Cup	0–2			
84	10/02/90	Crystal Palace	Away	League	1–3			
85	27/02/90	Norwich City	Home	League	4–1	3 Goals	(42)
86	03/03/90	Chelsea	Home	League	2–3			
87	10/03/90	Derby County	Home	League	2–1	1 Goal	(43)
88	17/03/90	Wimbledon	Away	League	3–3	3 Goals	(46)
89	24/03/90	Manchester United	Home	League	0–2			
90	31/03/90	Liverpool	Away	League	2–3			
91	03/04/90	Queens Park Rangers	Home	League	0–2			
92	07/04/90	Sheffield Wednesday	Away	League	1–0			
93	14/04/90	Charlton Athletic	Home	League	3–2			
94	21/04/90	Nottingham Forest	Home	League	2–0			
95	28/04/90	Coventry City	Home	League	3–0	1 Goal	(47)
96	02/05/90	Arsenal	Away	League	1–2			
97	05/05/90	Tottenham Hotspur	Away	League	1–2			

SEASON 1990–91

League Division One

98	25/08/90	Aston Villa	Away	League	1–1	1 Goal	(48)
99	28/08/90	Norwich City	Home	League	1–0			
100	01/09/90	Luton Town	Home	League	1–2			
101	08/09/90	Nottingham Forest	Away	League	1–3			
102	15/09/90	Sheffield United	Home	League	2–0	1 Goal	(49)
103	22/09/90	Manchester United	Away	League	2–3			
104	25/09/90	Rochdale	Away	Lge Cup	5–0			
105	29/09/90	Everton	Away	League	0–3			
106	06/10/90	Chelsea	Home	League	3–3			
107	20/10/90	Coventry City	Away	League	2–1	1 Goal	(50)
108	27/10/90	Derby County	Home	League	0–1			
109	30/10/90	Ipswich Town	Away	Lge Cup	2–0	1 Goal	(51)
110	03/11/90	Wimbledon	Away	League	1–1	1 Goal	(52)
111	10/11/90	Queens Park Rangers	Home	League	3–1	1 Goal	(53)
112	17/11/90	Arsenal	Away	League	0–4			
113	20/11/90	Queens Park Rangers	Home	ZDS Cup	4–0			
114	24/11/90	Crystal Palace	Home	League	2–3			
115	27/11/90	Crystal Palace	Home	Lge Cup	2–0	1 Goal	(54)
116	01/12/90	Leeds United	Away	League	1–2			
117	08/12/90	Norwich City	Away	League	1–3	1 Goal	(55)
118	15/12/90	Aston Villa	Home	League	1–1	1 Goal	(56)
119	22/12/90	Liverpool	Away	League	2–3			
120	26/12/90	Manchester City	Home	League	2–1	1 Goal	(57)
121	29/12/90	Tottenham Hotspur	Home	League	3–0	2 Goals	(59)
122	01/01/91	Sunderland	Away	League	0–1			

123	05/01/91	Ipswich Town	Home	FA Cup	3–2	2 Goals	(61)
124	12/01/91	Luton Town	Away	League	4–3	2 Goals	(63)
125	16/01/91	Manchester United	Home	Lge Cup	1–1		
126	19/01/91	Nottingham Forest	Home	League	1–1		
127	23/02/91	Queens Park Rangers	Away	League	1–2	1 Goal	(64)
128	25/02/91	Nottingham Forest	Home	FA Cup	1–1		
Sub+37	02/03/91	Leeds United	Home	League	2–0		
129	04/03/91	Nottingham Forest	Away	FA Cup	1–3		
130	13/03/91	Manchester United	Home	League	1–1		
131	23/03/91	Chelsea	Away	League	2–0	1 Goal	(65)
132	30/03/91	Manchester City	Away	League	3–3	1 Goal	(66)
133	01/04/91	Liverpool	Home	League	1–0	1 Goal	(67)
134	06/04/91	Tottenham Hotspur	Away	League	0–2		
135	09/04/91	Arsenal	Home	League	1–1	1 Goal	(68)
136	13/04/91	Sunderland	Home	League	3–1	1 Goal	(69)
137	20/04/91	Coventry City	Home	League	2–1		
138	04/05/91	Derby County	Away	League	2–6	1 Goal	(70)
139	11/05/91	Wimbledon	Home	League	1–1		

SEASON 1991–92

League Division One

140	17/08/91	Tottenham Hotspur	Home	League	2–3		
141	20/08/91	Notts County	Away	League	0–1		
142	24/08/91	Sheffield United	Away	League	2–0	1 Goal	(71)
143	28/08/91	Leeds United	Home	League	0–4		
144	31/08/91	Aston Villa	Home	League	1–1		
145	04/09/91	Luton Town	Away	League	1–2	1 Goal	(72)
146	07/09/91	Queens Park Rangers	Away	League	2–2		
147	14/09/91	Manchester United	Home	League	0–1		
148	18/09/91	Wimbledon	Home	League	1–0		
Sub+38	21/09/91	Sheffield Wednesday	Away	League	0–2		
149	24/09/91	Scarborough	Away	Lge Cup	3–1		
150	28/09/91	Arsenal	Home	League	0–4		
151	09/10/91	Scarborough	Home	Lge Cup	2–0	1 Goal	(73)
152	19/10/91	Norwich City	Home	League	0–0		
153	22/10/91	Bristol City	Away	ZDS Cup	2–1	1 Goal	(74)
154	26/10/91	Nottingham Forest	Away	League	3–1	2 Goals	(76)
155	30/10/91	Sheffield Wednesday	Away	Lge Cup	1–1		
156	02/11/91	Manchester City	Home	League	0–3		
157	16/11/91	Crystal Palace	Away	League	0–1		
158	20/11/91	Sheffield Wednesday	Home	Lge Cup	1–0		
159	23/11/91	Chelsea	Home	League	1–0		
160	26/11/91	Plymouth Argyle	Away	ZDS Cup	1–0	1 Goal	(77)
161	30/11/91	Coventry City	Away	League	0–2		
162	04/12/91	Nottingham Forest	Away	Lge Cup	0–0		
163	17/12/91	Nottingham Forest	Home	Lge Cup	0–1		
164	20/12/91	Notts County	Home	League	1–1		
165	04/01/92	Queens Park Rangers	Home	FA Cup	2–0	1 Goal	(78)
166	07/01/92	West Ham United	Home	ZDS Cup	2–1	1 Goal	(79)
167	11/01/92	Sheffield United	Home	League	2–4	1 Goal	(80)
168	18/01/92	Tottenham Hotspur	Away	League	2–1		
169	21/01/92	Chelsea	Home	ZDS Cup	2–0		
170	27/01/92	Manchester United	Home	FA Cup	0–0		
171	29/01/92	Chelsea	Away	ZDS Cup	3–0	3 Goals	(83)
172	01/02/92	Norwich City	Away	League	1–2		
173	05/02/92	Manchester United	Away	FA Cup	2–2+		
174	12/02/92	Chelsea	Away	League	1–1		
175	16/02/92	Bolton Wanderers	Away	FA Cup	2–2		
176	22/02/92	Coventry City	Home	League	0–0		
177	26/02/92	Bolton Wanderers	Home	FA Cup	3–2*		
178	29/02/92	Liverpool	Away	League	0–0		
179	03/03/92	West Ham United	Home	League	1–0		
180	07/03/92	Norwich City	Home	FA Cup	0–0		
181	11/03/92	Crystal Palace	Home	League	1–0	1 Goal	(84)
182	18/03/92	Norwich City	Away	FA Cup	1–2*		
183	29/03/92	Nottingham Forest	Wembley	ZDS Cup	2–3*	1 Goal	(85)
184	14/04/92	West Ham United	Away	League	1–0		
185	16/04/92	Manchester United	Away	League	0–1		
186	18/04/92	Sheffield Wednesday	Home	League	0–1		
187	20/04/92	Wimbledon	Away	League	1–0		
188	25/04/92	Oldham Athletic	Home	League	1–0		
189	02/05/92	Arsenal	Away	League	1–5		

+ AET Southampton won 4–2 on penalties

SEASON 1992–93

Premier League

190	15/08/92	Tottenham Hotspur	Home	League	0–0		
191	19/08/92	Queens Park Rangers	Away	League	1–3	1 Goal	(86)
192	22/08/92	Aston Villa	Away	League	1–1		
193	29/08/92	Middlesbrough	Home	League	2–1	1 Goal	(87)
194	01/09/92	Liverpool	Away	League	1–1		
195	05/09/92	Norwich City	Away	League	0–1		
196	12/09/92	Queens Park Rangers	Home	League	1–2	1 Goal	(88)
197	19/09/92	Leeds United	Home	League	1–1		
198	23/09/92	Gillingham	Away	Lge Cup	0–0		
199	26/09/92	Crystal Palace	Away	League	2–1		
200	03/10/92	Sheffield United	Away	League	0–2		
201	07/10/92	Gillingham	Home	Lge Cup	3–0	2 Goals	(90)
202	24/10/92	Manchester City	Away	League	0–1		
203	28/10/92	Crystal Palace	Home	Lge Cup	0–2		
204	31/10/92	Oldham Athletic	Home	League	1–0		
205	07/11/92	Ipswich Town	Away	League	0–0		
206	22/11/92	Blackburn Rovers	Home	League	1–1	1 Goal	(91)
207	28/11/92	Nottingham Forest	Away	League	2–1	1 Goal	(92)
208	05/12/92	Arsenal	Home	League	2–0		
209	12/12/92	Coventry City	Home	League	2–2		
210	19/12/92	Everton	Away	League	1–2	1 Goal	(93)
211	26/12/92	Chelsea	Away	League	1–1		
212	28/12/92	Sheffield Wednesday	Home	League	1–2		
213	03/01/93	Nottingham Forest	Away	FA Cup	1–2	1 Goal	(94)
214	09/01/93	Leeds United	Away	League	1–2		
215	16/01/93	Crystal Palace	Home	League	1–0		
216	26/01/93	Middlesbrough	Away	League	1–2	1 Goal	(95)
217	30/01/93	Aston Villa	Home	League	2–0		
218	07/02/93	Tottenham Hotspur	Away	League	2–4		
219	10/02/93	Norwich City	Home	League	3–0		
220	13/02/93	Liverpool	Home	League	2–1		
221	20/02/93	Manchester United	Away	League	1–2		
222	27/02/93	Sheffield United	Home	League	3–2		
223	06/03/93	Wimbledon	Away	League	2–1	1 Goal	(96)
224	09/03/93	Blackburn Rovers	Away	League	0–0		
225	13/03/93	Ipswich Town	Home	League	4–3	2 Goals	(98)
226	20/03/93	Arsenal	Away	League	3–4	1 Goal	(99)
227	24/03/93	Nottingham Forest	Home	League	1–2	1 Goal	(100)
228	03/04/93	Coventry City	Away	League	0–2		
229	10/04/93	Chelsea	Home	League	1–0		
230	12/04/93	Sheffield Wednesday	Away	League	2–5		
231	17/04/93	Everton	Home	League	0–0		
232	01/05/93	Manchester City	Home	League	0–1		
233	08/05/93	Oldham Athletic	Away	League	3–4	3 Goals	(103)

SEASON 1993–94

Premier League

234	14/08/93	Everton	Home	League	0–2		
235	17/08/93	Ipswich Town	Away	League	0–1		
236	21/08/93	Queens Park Rangers	Away	League	1–2		
237	25/08/93	Swindon Town	Home	League	5–1	2 Goals	(105)
238	28/08/93	Manchester United	Home	League	1–3		
239	31/08/93	Wimbledon	Away	League	0–1		
240	11/09/93	Leeds United	Home	League	0–2		
241	18/09/93	Sheffield Wednesday	Away	League	0–2		
242	24/10/93	Newcastle United	Home	League	2–1	2 Goals	(107)
243	30/10/93	Liverpool	Away	League	2–4	2 Goals	(109)
244	06/11/93	Tottenham Hotspur	Home	League	1–0		
245	20/11/93	Blackburn Rovers	Away	League	0–2		
246	24/11/93	Aston Villa	Away	League	2–0	2 Goals	(111)
247	29/11/93	West Ham United	Home	League	0–2		
248	04/12/93	Everton	Away	League	0–1		
249	08/12/93	Ipswich Town	Home	League	0–1		
250	11/12/93	Queens Park Rangers	Home	League	0–1		
251	18/12/93	Swindon Town	Away	League	1–2	1 Goal	(112)
252	27/12/93	Chelsea	Home	League	3–1		
253	28/12/93	Manchester City	Away	League	1–1		
254	01/01/94	Norwich City	Home	League	0–1		
255	08/01/94	Port Vale	Home	FA Cup	1–1		
256	15/01/94	Coventry City	Home	League	1–0	1 Goal	(113)
257	18/01/94	Port Vale	Away	FA Cup	0–1		

258	22/01/94	Newcastle United	Away	League	2–1	1 Goal	(114)
259	05/02/94	Oldham Athletic	Away	League	1–2	1 Goal	(115)
260	14/02/94	Liverpool	Home	League	4–2	3 Goals	(118)
261	25/02/94	Wimbledon	Home	League	1–0	1 Goal	(119)
262	05/03/94	Leeds United	Away	League	0–0		
263	12/03/94	Sheffield Wednesday	Home	League	1–1		
264	19/03/94	Arsenal	Home	League	0–4		
265	26/03/94	Sheffield United	Away	League	0–0		
266	30/03/94	Oldham Athletic	Home	League	1–3	1 Goal	(120)
267	02/04/94	Chelsea	Away	League	0–2		
268	04/04/94	Manchester City	Home	League	0–1		
269	09/04/94	Norwich City	Away	League	5–4	3 Goals	(123)
270	16/04/94	Blackburn Rovers	Home	League	3–1	1 Goal	(124)
271	30/04/94	Aston Villa	Home	League	4–1	2 Goals	(126)
272	04/05/94	Manchester United	Away	League	0–2		
273	07/05/94	West Ham United	Away	League	3–3	2 Goals	(128)

SEASON 1994–95

Premier League

274	20/08/94	Blackburn Rovers	Home	League	1–1		
275	24/08/94	Aston Villa	Away	League	1–1	1 Goal	(129)
276	27/08/94	Newcastle United	Away	League	1–5		
277	31/08/94	Liverpool	Home	League	0–2		
278	12/09/94	Tottenham Hotspur	Away	League	2–1	2 Goals	(131)
279	17/09/94	Nottingham Forest	Home	League	1–1	1 Goal	(132)
280	20/09/94	Huddersfield Town	Away	Lge Cup	1–0	1 Goal	(133)
281	24/09/94	Coventry City	Away	League	3–1		
282	01/10/94	Ipswich Town	Home	League	3–1		
283	05/10/94	Huddersfield Town	Home	Lge Cup	4–0	4 Goals	(137)
284	08/10/94	Everton	Home	League	2–0	1 Goal	(138)
285	15/10/94	Leicester City	Away	League	3–4	1 Goal	(139)
286	22/10/94	West Ham United	Away	League	0–2		
287	26/10/94	Sheffield Wednesday	Away	Lge Cup	0–1		
288	29/10/94	Leeds United	Home	League	1–3		
289	02/11/94	Norwich City	Home	League	1–1	1 Goal	(140)
290	05/11/94	Manchester City	Away	League	3–3		
291	19/11/94	Arsenal	Home	League	1–0		
292	26/11/94	Crystal Palace	Away	League	0–0		
293	03/12/94	Chelsea	Home	League	0–1		
294	10/12/94	Blackburn Rovers	Away	League	2–3	2 Goals	(142)
295	19/12/94	Aston Villa	Home	League	2–1	1 Goal	(143)
296	26/12/94	Wimbledon	Home	League	2–3	1 Goal	(144)
297	28/12/94	Queens Park Rangers	Away	League	2–2		
298	31/12/94	Manchester United	Home	League	2–2		
299	02/01/95	Sheffield Wednesday	Away	League	1–1	1 Goal	(145)
300	07/01/95	Southend United	Home	FA Cup	2–0	1 Goal	(146)
301	14/01/95	Leeds United	Away	League	0–0		
302	24/01/95	Arsenal	Away	League	1–1		
303	28/01/95	Luton Town	Away	FA Cup	1–1		
304	04/02/95	Manchester City	Home	League	2–2	1 Goal	(147)
305	08/02/95	Luton Town	Home	FA Cup	6–0	2 Goals	(149)
306	11/02/95	Norwich City	Away	League	2–2		
307	18/02/95	Tottenham Hotspur	Away	FA Cup	1–1	1 Goal	(150)
308	25/02/95	Ipswich Town	Away	League	1–2		
309	01/03/95	Tottenham Hotspur	Home	FA Cup	2–6	1 Goal	(151)
310	04/03/95	Coventry City	Home	League	0–0		
311	15/03/95	West Ham United	Home	League	1–1		
312	18/03/95	Nottingham Forest	Away	League	0–3		
313	22/03/95	Newcastle United	Home	League	3–1		
314	02/04/95	Tottenham Hotspur	Home	League	4–3	2 Goals	(153)
315	05/04/95	Liverpool	Away	League	1–3		
316	12/04/95	Chelsea	Away	League	2–0	1 Goal	(154)
317	15/04/95	Queens Park Rangers	Home	League	2–1		
318	17/04/95	Wimbledon	Away	League	2–0	1 Goal	(155)
319	29/04/95	Sheffield Wednesday	Home	League	0–0		
320	03/05/95	Crystal Palace	Home	League	3–1	2 Goals	(157)
321	10/05/95	Manchester United	Away	League	1–2		
322	14/05/95	Leicester City	Home	League	2–2	1 Goal	(158)

SEASON 1995–96

Premier League

323	19/08/95	Nottingham Forest	Home	League	3–4	3 Goals	(161)
324	26/08/95	Everton	Away	League	0–2		

325	30/08/95	Leeds United	Home	League	1–1		
326	09/09/95	Newcastle United	Home	League	1–0		
327	12/09/95	Middlesbrough	Away	League	0–0		
328	16/09/95	Chelsea	Away	League	0–3		
329	18/09/95	Cardiff City	Away	Lge Cup	3–0	2 Goals	(163)
330	23/09/95	Arsenal	Away	League	2–4		
331	02/10/95	West Ham United	Home	League	0–0		
332	04/10/95	Cardiff City	Home	Lge Cup	2–1		
333	14/10/95	Blackburn Rovers	Away	League	1–2		
334	22/10/95	Liverpool	Home	League	1–3		
335	25/10/95	West Ham United	Home	Lge Cup	2–1		
336	28/10/95	Wimbledon	Away	League	2–1		
337	04/11/95	Queens Park Rangers	Home	League	2–0	1 Goal	(164)
338	20/11/95	Aston Villa	Home	League	0–1		
339	25/11/95	Bolton Wanderers	Home	League	1–0		
340	28/11/95	Reading	Away	Lge Cup	1–2		
341	02/12/95	Liverpool	Away	League	1–1		
342	09/12/95	Arsenal	Home	League	0–0		
343	16/12/95	West Ham United	Away	League	1–2		
344	26/12/95	Tottenham Hotspur	Home	League	0–0		
345	07/01/96	Portsmouth	Home	FA Cup	3–0		
346	13/01/96	Nottingham Forest	Away	League	0–1		
347	20/01/96	Middlesbrough	Home	League	2–1		
348	31/01/96	Manchester City	Home	League	1–1		
349	03/02/96	Everton	Home	League	2–2		
350	07/02/96	Crewe Alexandra	Home	FA Cup	1–1	1 Goal	(165)
351	13/02/96	Crewe Alexandra	Away	FA Cup	3–2		
352	17/02/96	Swindon Town	Away	FA Cup	1–1		
353	24/02/96	Chelsea	Home	League	2–3		
354	02/03/96	Tottenham Hotspur	Away	League	0–1		
355	11/03/96	Manchester United	Away	FA Cup	0–2		
356	16/03/96	Manchester City	Away	League	1–2		
357	20/03/96	Sheffield Wednesday	Home	League	0–1		
358	25/03/96	Coventry City	Home	League	1–0		
359	03/04/96	Leeds United	Away	League	0–1		
360	06/04/96	Blackburn Rovers	Home	League	1–0	1 Goal	(166)
361	08/04/96	Aston Villa	Away	League	0–3		
362	13/04/96	Manchester United	Home	League	3–1	1 Goal	(167)
363	17/04/96	Newcastle United	Away	League	0–1		
364	27/04/96	Bolton Wanderers	Away	League	1–0	1 Goal	(168)
365	05/05/96	Wimbledon	Home	League	0–0		

SEASON 1996–97

Premier League

366	18/08/96	Chelsea	Home	League	0–0		
367	21/08/96	Leicester City	Away	League	1–2	1 Goal	(169)
368	24/08/96	West Ham United	Away	League	1–2		
369	04/09/96	Nottingham Forest	Home	League	2–2	1 Goal	(170)
370	07/09/96	Liverpool	Away	League	1–2		
371	14/09/96	Tottenham Hotspur	Home	League	0–1		
372	18/09/96	Peterborough United	Home	Lge Cup	2–0	1 Goal	(171)
373	23/09/96	Wimbledon	Away	League	1–3		
374	25/09/96	Peterborough United	Away	Lge Cup	4–1		
375	28/09/96	Middlesbrough	Home	League	4–0	2 Goals	(173)
376	13/10/96	Coventry City	Away	League	1–1	1 Goal	(174)
377	19/10/96	Sunderland	Home	League	3–0	1 Goal	(175)
378	23/10/96	Lincoln City	Home	Lge Cup	2–2	1 Goal	(176)
379	26/10/96	Manchester United	Home	League	6–3	1 Goal	(177)
380	02/11/96	Sheffield Wednesday	Away	League	1–1	1 Goal	(178)
381	12/11/96	Lincoln City	Away	Lge Cup	3–1		
382	16/11/96	Everton	Away	League	1–7		
383	23/11/96	Leeds United	Home	League	0–2		
Sub+39	26/12/96	Tottenham Hotspur	Away	League	1–3	1 Goal	(179)
Sub+40	29/12/96	Liverpool	Home	League	0–1		
384	04/01/97	Reading	Away	FA Cup	1–3		
Sub+41	11/01/97	Middlesbrough	Away	League	1–0		
385	18/01/97	Newcastle United	Home	League	2–2	1 Goal	(180)
386	22/01/97	Stockport County	Away	Lge Cup	2–2		
387	29/01/97	Stockport County	Home	Lge Cup	1–2	1 Goal	(181)
388	01/02/97	Manchester United	Away	League	1–2		
389	22/02/97	Sheffield Wednesday	Home	League	2–3	1 Goal	(182)
390	26/02/97	Wimbledon	Home	League	0–0		
391	01/03/97	Newcastle United	Away	League	1–0	1 Goal	(183)
392	05/03/97	Everton	Home	League	2–2		

393	12/03/97	Leeds United	Away	League	0–0	
394	15/03/97	Arsenal	Home	League	0–2	
Sub+42	19/03/97	Chelsea	Away	League	0–1	
395	22/03/97	Leicester City	Home	League	2–2	
396	05/04/97	Nottingham Forest	Away	League	3–1	
397	09/04/97	Derby County	Away	League	1–1	
Sub+43	03/05/97	Blackburn Rovers	Home	League	2–0	1 Goal (184)
Sub+44	11/05/97	Aston Villa	Away	League	0–1	

INTERNATIONAL APPEARANCES – ENGLAND

Sub 1	09/03/94	Denmark	Wembley	1–0	F
Sub 2	17/05/94	Greece	Wembley	5–0	F
Sub 3	22/05/94	Norway	Wembley	0–0	F
4	12/10/94	Romania	Wembley	1–1	F
Sub 5	16/11/94	Nigeria	Wembley	1–0	F
6	15/02/95	Republic of Ireland	Lansdowne Road	Aba	F
Sub 7	01/09/96	Moldova	Kishinev	3–0	WCQ
8	12/02/97	Italy	Wembley	0–1	WCQ

APPEARANCES AND GOALS PER SEASON

SEASON 86–87

	GAMES	GOALS
League	12+12	6
FA Cup	0+1	0
League Cup	0+4	2
Full Members Cup	1+1	2
TOTAL	**13+18**	**10**

SEASON 87–88

	GAMES	GOALS
League	10+9	0
FA Cup	1	1
League Cup	1	1
Simod Cup	1	0
TOTAL	**13+9**	**2**

SEASON 88–89

	GAMES	GOALS
League	21+7	9
FA Cup	2	0
League Cup	3+1	2
Simod Cup	2	0
TOTAL	**28+8**	**11**

SEASON 89–90

	GAMES	GOALS
League	35	20
FA Cup	2	1
League Cup	6+1	3
TOTAL	**43+1**	**24**

SEASON 90–91

	GAMES	GOALS
League	34+1	19
FA Cup	3	2
League Cup	4	2
Zenith Data Systems Cup	1	0
TOTAL	**42+1**	**23**

SEASON 91–92

	GAMES	GOALS
League	31+1	6
FA Cup	7	1
League Cup	6	1
Zenith Data Systems Cup	6	7
TOTAL	**50+1**	**15**

SEASON 92–93

	GAMES	GOALS
League	40	15
FA Cup	1	1
League Cup	3	2
TOTAL	**44**	**18**

SEASON 93–94

	GAMES	GOALS
League	38	25
FA Cup	2	0
TOTAL	**40**	**25**

SEASON 94–95	GAMES	GOALS
League	41	20
FA Cup	5	5
League Cup	3	5
TOTAL	**49**	**30**

SEASON 95–96	GAMES	GOALS
League	34	7
FA Cup	5	1
League Cup	4	2
TOTAL	**43**	**10**

SEASON 96–97	GAMES	GOALS
League	25+6	13
FA Cup	1	0
League Cup	6	3
TOTAL	**32+6**	**16**

CAREER APPEARANCES AND GOALS

COMPETITION	GAMES	TOTAL	GOALS
League	321+36	357	140
FA Cup	29+1	30	12
League Cup	36+6	42	23
Full Members Cup	1+1	2	2
Simod Cup	3	3	0
Zenith Data Systems Cup	7	7	7
Internationals	3+5	8	0
TOTAL	**400+49**	**449**	**184**

HAT–TRICKS

Southampton

1	3	Leicester City	07/03/87	Home	League	4–0
2	3	Norwich City	27/02/90	Home	League	4–1
3	3	Wimbledon	17/03/90	Away	League	3–3
4	3	Chelsea	29/01/92	Away	ZDS Cup	3–0
5	3	Oldham Athletic	08/05/93	Away	League	3–4
6	3	Liverpool	14/02/94	Home	League	4–2
7	3	Norwich City	09/04/94	Away	League	5–4
8	4	Huddersfield Town	05/10/94	Home	Lge Cup	4–0
9	3	Nottingham Forest	19/08/95	Home	League	3–4

League: 7
League Cup: 1
Zenith Data Systems Cup: 1
TOTAL: 9

HONOURS

Winners medals
None

Runner–up medals
Zenith Data Systems Cup: 91/92

GARY LINEKER

Born: 30/11/60 – Leicester
Height: 5.10
Weight: 11.11 (93–94)

Clubs
Leicester City: **1979–85** – Matches: **209+7** – Goals: **103**
Everton: **1985–86** – Matches: **57** – Goals: **40**
FC Barcelona: **1986–89** – Matches: **137+4** – Goals: **55**
Tottenham Hotspur: **1989–92** – Matches: **139** – Goals: **80**
Nagoya Grampus Eight: **1993–94** – Matches: **22+2** – Goals: **8**

Country
England: **1984–92** – Matches: **74+6** – Goals: **48**

SEASON 1978–79

Leicester City – League Division Two

1	01/01/79	Oldham Athletic	Home	League	2–0		
2	17/04/79	Preston North End	Away	League	0–4		
3	20/04/79	Crystal Palace	Home	League	1–1		
4	24/04/79	Notts County	Away	League	1–0	1 Goal	(1)
5	28/04/79	Fulham	Away	League	0–3		
6	05/05/79	Millwall	Home	League	0–0		
7	08/05/79	Sheffield United	Away	League	2–2		

SEASON 1979–80

League Division Two

Sub+1	13/10/79	West Ham United	Home	League	1–2		
Sub+2	20/10/79	Oldham Athletic	Away	League	1–1		
8	27/10/79	Sunderland	Home	League	2–1	2 Goals	(3)
9	03/11/79	Watford	Away	League	3–1		
10	10/11/79	Burnley	Home	League	1–1		
11	17/11/79	Preston North End	Away	League	1–1	1 Goal	(4)
12	24/11/79	Wrexham	Home	League	2–0		
13	01/12/79	Birmingham City	Away	League	2–1		
14	08/12/79	Orient	Home	League	2–2		
15	15/12/79	Charlton Athletic	Away	League	0–2		
16	21/12/79	Cardiff City	Home	League	0–0		
17	08/01/80	Harlow	Away	FA Cup	0–1		
18	19/01/80	Notts County	Away	League	1–0		
19	02/02/80	Newcastle United	Home	League	1–0		
20	09/02/80	Fulham	Away	League	0–0		
21	08/03/80	Sunderland	Away	League	0–0		
Sub+3	15/03/80	Shrewsbury Town	Home	League	2–0		
22	05/04/80	Chelsea	Home	League	1–0		
23	08/04/80	Cardiff City	Away	League	1–0		
24	26/04/80	Charlton Athletic	Home	League	2–1		

SEASON 1980–81

League Division One

25	08/10/80	Stoke City	Home	League	1–1		
26	11/10/80	Coventry City	Home	League	1–3	1 Goal	(5)
27	08/11/80	Manchester City	Home	League	1–1		
28	12/11/80	Everton	Home	League	0–1		
29	15/11/80	Ipswich Town	Away	League	1–3		
30	22/11/80	West Bromwich Albion	Away	League	1–3	1 Goal	(6)
31	13/12/80	Middlesbrough	Home	League	1–0		
32	03/01/81	Cardiff City	Home	FA Cup	3–0	1 Goal	(7)
33	10/01/81	West Bromwich Albion	Home	League	0–2		
34	25/04/81	Birmingham City	Home	League	1–0		

SEASON 1981–82

League Division Two

35	29/08/81	Grimsby Town	Away	League	2–2	1 Goal	(8)
36	05/09/81	Wrexham	Home	League	1–0		
37	08/09/81	Barnsley	Home	League	1–0		
Sub+4	12/09/81	Derby County	Away	League	1–3		
38	19/09/81	Luton Town	Home	League	1–2		
Sub+5	03/10/81	Crystal Palace	Home	League	1–1	1 Goal	(9)
39	10/10/81	Bolton Wanderers	Away	League	3–0		
40	16/10/81	Chelsea	Home	League	1–1		
41	24/10/81	Queens Park Rangers	Away	League	0–2		
42	28/10/81	Preston North End	Home	Lge Cup	4–0		
43	31/10/81	Sheffield Wednesday	Home	League	0–0		
44	07/11/81	Charlton Athletic	Away	League	4–1	2 Goals	(11)
45	11/11/81	Aston Villa	Home	Lge Cup	0–0		
46	14/11/81	Orient	Home	League	0–1		
47	21/11/81	Cardiff City	Away	League	1–3		
48	25/11/81	Aston Villa	Away	Lge Cup	0–2		
49	28/11/81	Cambridge United	Home	League	4–1	1 Goal	(12)
50	05/12/81	Norwich City	Away	League	0–0		
51	12/12/81	Watford	Home	League	1–1	1 Goal	(13)
52	28/12/81	Oldham Athletic	Away	League	1–1		

53	02/01/82	Southampton	Home	FA Cup	3–1	1 Goal	(14)
54	23/01/82	Hereford United	Away	FA Cup	1–0		
55	30/01/82	Luton Town	Away	League	1–2	1 Goal	(15)
56	06/02/82	Derby County	Home	League	2–1	1 Goal	(16)
57	13/02/82	Watford	Home	FA Cup	2–0		
58	20/02/82	Blackburn Rovers	Home	League	1–0		
59	27/02/82	Bolton Wanderers	Home	League	1–0		
60	02/03/82	Newcastle United	Home	League	3–0	2 Goals	(18)
61	06/03/82	Shrewsbury Town	Home	FA Cup	5–2	1 Goal	(19)
62	09/03/82	Chelsea	Away	League	1–4		
63	13/03/82	Queens Park Rangers	Home	League	3–2		
64	17/03/82	Rotherham United	Home	League	1–0		
65	20/03/82	Sheffield Wednesday	Away	League	0–2		
66	23/03/82	Crystal Palace	Away	League	2–0	1 Goal	(20)
67	27/03/82	Charlton Athletic	Home	League	3–1		
68	30/03/82	Shrewsbury Town	Away	League	1–1	1 Goal	(21)
69	03/04/82	Tottenham Hotspur	Neutral	FA Cup	0–2		
70	10/04/82	Newcastle United	Away	League	0–0		
71	13/04/82	Oldham Athletic	Home	League	2–1	1 Goal	(22)
72	17/04/82	Cardiff City	Home	League	3–1	2 Goals	(24)
73	20/04/82	Wrexham	Away	League	0–0		
74	24/04/82	Cambridge United	Away	League	2–1	1 Goal	(25)
75	01/05/82	Norwich City	Home	League	1–4		
76	04/05/82	Barnsley	Away	League	2–0	1 Goal	(26)
77	08/05/82	Watford	Away	League	1–3		
78	12/05/82	Grimsby Town	Home	League	1–2		
79	15/05/82	Shrewsbury Town	Home	League	0–0		

SEASON 1982–83

League Division Two

80	27/08/82	Charlton Athletic	Home	League	1–2		
Sub+6	31/08/82	Rotherham United	Away	League	3–1	1 Goal	(27)
81	04/09/82	Chelsea	Away	League	1–1	1 Goal	(28)
82	08/09/82	Leeds United	Home	League	0–1		
83	11/09/82	Carlisle United	Home	League	6–0	3 Goals	(31)
84	18/09/82	Blackburn Rovers	Away	League	1–3		
85	25/09/82	Queens Park Rangers	Home	League	0–1		
86	02/10/82	Shrewsbury Town	Away	League	2–0		
87	06/10/82	Lincoln City	Away	Lge Cup	0–2		
88	09/10/82	Grimsby Town	Home	League	2–0	1 Goal	(32)
89	16/10/82	Wolverhampton Wanderers	Away	League	3–0	1 Goal	(33)
90	23/10/82	Derby County	Away	League	4–0	3 Goals	(36)
91	27/10/82	Lincoln City	Home	Lge Cup	0–1		
92	30/10/82	Sheffield Wednesday	Home	League	0–2		
93	06/11/82	Cambridge United	Away	League	1–3	1 Goal	(37)
94	13/11/82	Newcastle United	Home	League	2–2	1 Goal	(38)
95	20/11/82	Crystal Palace	Home	League	0–1		
96	27/11/82	Bolton Wanderers	Away	League	1–3		
97	04/12/82	Fulham	Home	League	2–0	1 Goal	(39)
98	11/12/82	Burnley	Away	League	4–2	1 Goal	(40)
99	18/12/82	Oldham Athletic	Home	League	2–1		
100	27/12/82	Middlesbrough	Away	League	1–1	1 Goal	(41)
101	28/12/82	Barnsley	Home	League	1–0		
102	01/01/83	Crystal Palace	Away	League	0–1		
103	03/01/83	Chelsea	Home	League	3–0	2 Goals	(43)
104	08/01/83	Notts County	Home	FA Cup	2–3		
105	15/01/83	Charlton Athletic	Away	League	1–2		
106	22/01/83	Blackburn Rovers	Home	League	0–1		
107	05/02/83	Carlisle United	Away	League	1–0		
108	19/02/83	Grimsby Town	Away	League	0–2		
109	22/02/83	Shrewsbury Town	Home	League	3–2	2 Goals	(45)
110	26/02/83	Wolverhampton Wanderers	Home	League	5–0	1 Goal	(46)
111	05/03/83	Derby County	Home	League	1–1		
112	19/03/83	Cambridge United	Home	League	4–0		
113	22/03/83	Sheffield Wednesday	Away	League	2–2		
114	26/03/83	Newcastle United	Away	League	2–2	2 Goals	(48)
115	02/04/83	Barnsley	Away	League	2–1		
116	05/04/83	Middlesbrough	Home	League	1–0		
117	09/04/83	Queens Park Rangers	Away	League	2–2	2 Goals	(50)
118	16/04/83	Rotherham United	Home	League	3–1	2 Goals	(52)
119	23/04/83	Fulham	Away	League	1–0		
120	30/04/83	Bolton Wanderers	Home	League	0–0		
121	02/05/83	Leeds United	Away	League	2–2		

SEASON 1983–84

League Division One

122	27/08/83	Notts County	Home	League	0–4		
123	31/08/83	Luton Town	Home	League	0–3		
124	03/09/83	West Bromwich Albion	Away	League	0–1		
125	06/09/83	West Ham United	Away	League	1–3	1 Goal	(53)
126	10/09/83	Tottenham Hotspur	Home	League	0–3		
127	17/09/83	Coventry City	Away	League	1–2	1 Goal	(54)
128	24/09/83	Stoke City	Home	League	2–2	1 Goal	(55)
129	01/10/83	Birmingham City	Away	League	1–2	1 Goal	(56)
130	05/10/83	Chelsea	Home	Lge Cup	0–2		
131	19/10/83	Norwich City	Away	League	1–3		
132	22/10/83	Ipswich Town	Away	League	0–0		
Sub+7	12/11/83	Manchester United	Home	League	1–1		
133	19/11/83	Aston Villa	Away	League	1–3		
134	26/11/83	Arsenal	Home	League	3–0	1 Goal	(57)
135	30/11/83	Southampton	Home	League	2–1	1 Goal	(58)
136	10/12/83	Wolverhampton Wanderers	Home	League	5–1	1 Goal	(59)
137	18/12/83	Sunderland	Away	League	1–1		
138	26/12/83	Queens Park Rangers	Home	League	2–1	1 Goal	(60)
139	27/12/83	Liverpool	Away	League	2–2		
140	31/12/83	West Bromwich Albion	Home	League	1–1		
141	02/01/84	Stoke City	Away	League	1–0		
142	07/01/84	Crystal Palace	Away	FA Cup	0–1		
143	14/01/84	Notts County	Away	League	5–2	3 Goals	(63)
144	21/01/84	Coventry City	Home	League	1–1	1 Goal	(64)
145	04/02/84	Birmingham City	Home	League	2–3		
146	11/02/84	Tottenham Hotspur	Away	League	2–3	2 Goals	(66)
147	25/02/84	Ipswich Town	Home	League	2–0		
148	03/03/84	Watford	Home	League	4–1	1 Goal	(67)
149	10/03/84	Manchester United	Away	League	0–2		
150	17/03/84	West Ham United	Home	League	4–1	1 Goal	(68)
151	20/03/84	Everton	Away	League	1–1	1 Goal	(69)
152	24/03/84	Luton Town	Away	League	0–0		
153	31/03/84	Norwich City	Home	League	2–1		
154	07/04/84	Southampton	Away	League	2–2	2 Goals	(71)
155	14/04/84	Aston Villa	Home	League	2–0		
156	18/04/84	Liverpool	Home	League	3–3	1 Goal	(72)
157	21/04/84	Queens Park Rangers	Away	League	0–2		
158	28/04/84	Arsenal	Away	League	1–2	1 Goal	(73)
159	05/05/84	Nottingham Forest	Home	League	2–1	1 Goal	(74)
160	07/05/84	Wolverhampton Wanderers	Away	League	0–1		
161	12/05/84	Sunderland	Home	League	0–2		

SEASON 1984–85

League Division One

162	25/08/84	Newcastle United	Home	League	2–3	2 Goals	(76)
163	27/08/84	Tottenham Hotspur	Away	League	2–2		
164	01/09/84	Coventry City	Away	League	0–2		
165	05/09/84	Watford	Home	League	1–1	1 Goal	(77)
166	08/09/84	Ipswich Town	Home	League	2–1	1 Goal	(78)
167	15/09/84	Stoke City	Away	League	2–2	1 Goal	(79)
168	22/09/84	West Bromwich Albion	Home	League	2–1		
169	26/09/84	Brentford	Home	Lge Cup	4–2	1 Goal	(80)
170	29/09/84	Chelsea	Away	League	0–3		
171	06/10/84	West Ham United	Away	League	1–3		
172	09/10/84	Brentford	Away	Lge Cup	2–0		
173	13/10/84	Arsenal	Home	League	1–4		
174	20/10/84	Sheffield Wednesday	Away	League	0–5		
175	27/10/84	Aston Villa	Home	League	5–0	3 Goals	(83)
176	30/10/84	Luton Town	Away	Lge Cup	1–3	1 Goal	(84)
177	03/11/84	Everton	Away	League	0–3		
178	10/11/84	Manchester United	Home	League	2–3	1 Goal	(85)
179	17/11/84	Norwich City	Home	League	2–0		
180	25/11/84	Nottingham Forest	Away	League	1–2		
181	01/12/84	Queens Park Rangers	Home	League	4–0	1 Goal	(86)
182	08/12/84	Sunderland	Away	League	4–0	1 Goal	(87)
183	23/12/84	Coventry City	Home	League	5–1	2 Goals	(89)
184	26/12/84	Liverpool	Away	League	2–1	1 Goal	(90)
185	29/12/84	Watford	Away	League	1–4		
186	01/01/85	Southampton	Home	League	1–2		
187	05/01/85	Burton Albion	Away	FA Cup	6–1+	3 Goals	(93)
188	12/01/85	Stoke City	Home	League	0–0		

189	16/01/85	Burton Albion	Neutral	FA Cup	1–0#		
190	26/01/85	Carlisle United	Home	FA Cup	1–0		
191	02/02/85	Chelsea	Home	League	1–1	1 Goal	(94)
192	16/02/85	Millwall	Away	FA Cup	0–2		
193	23/02/85	Everton	Home	League	1–2		
194	02/03/85	Aston Villa	Away	League	1–0		
195	09/03/85	Sheffield Wednesday	Home	League	3–1	1 Goal	(95)
196	16/03/85	Arsenal	Away	League	0–2		
197	20/03/85	Newcastle United	Away	League	4–1	1 Goal	(96)
198	23/03/85	West Ham United	Home	League	1–0	1 Goal	(97)
199	30/03/85	West Bromwich Albion	Away	League	0–2		
200	03/04/85	Manchester United	Away	League	1–2	1 Goal	(98)
201	06/04/85	Liverpool	Home	League	0–1		
202	09/04/85	Southampton	Away	League	1–3		
203	13/04/85	Tottenham Hotspur	Home	League	1–2		
204	20/04/85	Norwich City	Away	League	3–1		
205	23/04/85	Ipswich Town	Away	League	0–2		
206	27/04/85	Nottingham Forest	Home	League	1–0	1 Goal	(99)
207	04/05/85	Queens Park Rangers	Away	League	3–4	2 Goals	(101)
208	06/05/85	Sunderland	Home	League	2–0	2 Goals	(103)
209	11/05/85	Luton Town	Away	League	0–4		

+ The FA ordered the match to be replayed after the Burton Albion keeper Evans was struck by a missile
# Played behind closed doors at Highfield Road, Coventry City

SEASON 1985–86

Everton – League Division One

1	10/08/85	Manchester United	Wembley	FA C/S	2–0		
2	17/08/85	Leicester City	Away	League	1–3		
3	20/08/85	West Bromwich Albion	Home	League	2–0		
4	24/08/85	Coventry City	Home	League	1–1		
5	26/08/85	Tottenham Hotspur	Away	League	1–0	1 Goal	(1)
6	31/08/85	Birmingham City	Home	League	4–1	3 Goals	(4)
7	03/09/85	Sheffield Wednesday	Away	League	5–1	2 Goals	(6)
8	07/09/85	Queens Park Rangers	Away	League	0–3		
9	14/09/85	Luton Town	Home	League	2–0		
10	18/09/85	Manchester United	Away	SSS Cup	4–2	1 Goal	(7)
11	21/09/85	Liverpool	Home	League	2–3	1 Goal	(8)
12	25/09/85	AFC Bournemouth	Home	Lge Cup	3–2	1 Goal	(9)
13	28/09/85	Aston Villa	Away	League	0–0		
14	02/10/85	Norwich City	Home	SSS Cup	1–0	1 Goal	(10)
15	05/10/85	Oxford United	Home	League	2–0		
16	08/10/85	AFC Bournemouth	Away	Lge Cup	2–0	1 Goal	(11)
17	12/10/85	Chelsea	Away	League	1–2		
18	19/10/85	Watford	Home	League	4–1		
19	23/10/85	Norwich City	Away	SSS Cup	0–1		
20	26/10/85	Manchester City	Away	League	1–1		
21	29/10/85	Shrewsbury Town	Away	Lge Cup	4–1		
22	02/11/85	West Ham United	Away	League	1–2		
23	09/11/85	Arsenal	Home	League	6–1	2 Goals	(13)
24	16/11/85	Ipswich Town	Away	League	4–3		
25	23/11/85	Nottingham Forest	Home	League	1–1		
26	26/11/85	Chelsea	Away	Lge Cup	2–2		
27	30/11/85	Southampton	Away	League	3–2	1 Goal	(14)
28	04/12/85	Manchester United	Home	SSS Cup	1–0		
29	07/12/85	West Bromwich Albion	Away	League	3–0	1 Goal	(15)
30	10/12/85	Chelsea	Home	Lge Cup	1–2	1 Goal	(16)
31	14/12/85	Leicester City	Home	League	1–2		
32	21/12/85	Coventry City	Away	League	3–1	2 Goals	(18)
33	26/12/85	Manchester United	Home	League	3–1	1 Goal	(19)
34	28/12/85	Sheffield Wednesday	Home	League	3–1	2 Goals	(21)
35	01/01/86	Newcastle United	Away	League	2–2		
36	05/01/86	Exeter City	Home	FA Cup	1–0		
37	11/01/86	Queens Park Rangers	Home	League	4–3	1 Goal	(22)
38	18/01/86	Birmingham City	Away	League	2–0	2 Goals	(24)
39	25/01/86	Blackburn Rovers	Home	FA Cup	3–1	2 Goals	(26)
40	01/02/86	Tottenham Hotspur	Home	League	1–0		
41	11/02/86	Manchester City	Home	League	4–0	3 Goals	(29)
42	22/02/86	Liverpool	Away	League	2–0	1 Goal	(30)
43	01/03/86	Aston Villa	Home	League	2–0	1 Goal	(31)
44	04/03/86	Tottenham Hotspur	Away	FA Cup	2–1	1 Goal	(32)
45	08/03/86	Luton Town	Away	FA Cup	2–2		
46	12/03/86	Luton Town	Home	FA Cup	1–0	1 Goal	(33)

47	16/03/86	Chelsea	Home	League	1–1		
48	22/03/86	Luton Town	Away	League	1–2		
49	29/03/86	Newcastle United	Home	League	1–0		
50	31/03/86	Manchester United	Away	League	0–0		
51	12/04/86	Arsenal	Away	League	1–0		
52	15/04/86	Watford	Away	League	2–0	1 Goal	(34)
53	26/04/86	Nottingham Forest	Away	League	0–0		
54	30/04/86	Oxford United	Away	League	0–1		
55	03/05/86	Southampton	Home	League	6–1	3 Goals	(37)
56	05/05/86	West Ham United	Home	League	3–1	2 Goals	(39)
57	10/05/86	Liverpool	Wembley	FA Cup	1–3	1 Goal	(40)

SEASON 1986–87

FC Barcelona – Spanish League Division One

1	30/08/86	Racing Santander	Home	League	2–0	2 Goals	(2)
2	06/09/86	RCD Mallorca	Away	League	1–1		
3	10/09/86	Cadiz CF	Home	League	2–0	1 Goal	(3)
4	13/09/86	CE Sabadell FC	Away	League	1–1		
5	17/09/86	KS Flamurtari Vlore	Away	UEFA Cup	1–1		
6	21/09/86	Sevilla FC	Home	League	1–0		
7	27/09/86	Athletic Bilbao	Away	League	2–2	1 Goal	(4)
8	01/10/86	KS Flamurtari Vlore	Home	UEFA Cup	0–0		
9	04/10/86	Real Valladolid	Home	League	3–0	1 Goal	(5)
10	08/10/86	Real Madrid CF	Away	League	1–1		
11	12/10/86	RCD Espanol	Home	League	1–0		
12	19/10/86	CR Murcia	Away	League	0–1		
13	22/10/86	Sporting CP Lisboa	Home	UEFA Cup	1–0		
14	26/10/86	UD Las Palmas	Home	League	4–0	2 Goals	(7)
15	02/11/86	Sporting Gijon	Away	League	0–0		
16	05/11/86	Sporting CP Lisboa	Away	UEFA Cup	1–2		
17	08/11/86	Real Zaragoza	Home	League	0–0		
18	26/11/86	FC Bayer 05 Uerdingen	Away	UEFA Cup	2–0		
19	06/12/86	CA Osasuna	Away	League	2–0		
20	10/12/86	FC Bayer 05 Uerdingen	Home	UEFA Cup	2–0		
21	14/12/86	Atletico Madrid	Home	League	1–1		
22	17/12/86	Racing Santander	Away	League	0–0		
23	21/12/86	RCD Mallorca	Home	League	3–1		
24	28/12/86	Cadiz CF	Away	League	1–0		
25	04/01/87	CE Sabadell FC	Home	League	3–1	2 Goals	(9)
26	11/01/87	Sevilla FC	Away	League	0–0		
27	17/01/87	Athletic Bilbao	Home	League	4–1	1 Goal	(10)
28	31/01/87	Real Madrid CF	Home	League	3–2	3 Goals	(13)
29	08/02/87	RCD Espanol	Away	League	1–1		
30	11/02/87	CA Osasuna	Away	Sp Cup	1–0+	1 Goal	(14)
31	15/02/87	CR Murcia	Home	League	2–0	1 Goal	(15)
32	22/02/87	UD Las Palmas	Away	League	0–0		
33	28/02/87	Sporting Gijon	Home	League	0–4		
34	04/03/87	Dundee United	Away	UEFA Cup	0–1		
35	08/03/87	Real Zaragoza	Away	League	0–2		
36	14/03/87	Real Betis	Home	League	2–0		
37	18/03/87	Dundee United	Home	UEFA Cup	1–2		
38	22/03/87	Real Sociedad	Away	League	1–1		
39	25/03/87	CA Osasuna	Home	League	4–2	2 Goals	(17)
40	05/04/87	Atletico Madrid	Away	League	4–0	1 Goal	(18)
41	12/04/87	Real Madrid	Away	Lge P/O	0–0		
42	19/04/87	RCD Mallorca	Home	Lge P/O	1–0		
43	03/05/87	RCD Espanol	Away	Lge P/O	0–0		
44	09/05/87	Sporting Gijon	Home	Lge P/O	2–0		
45	17/05/87	Real Zaragoza	Away	Lge P/O	1–2	1 Goal	(19)
46	23/05/87	Real Madrid	Home	Lge P/O	2–1	1 Goal	(20)
47	31/05/87	RCD Mallorca	Away	Lge P/O	1–0	1 Goal	(21)
48	07/06/87	RCD Espanol	Home	Lge P/O	2–1		
49	14/06/87	Sporting Gijon	Away	Lge P/O	0–1		
50	21/06/87	Real Zaragoza	Home	Lge P/O	3–2	1 Goal	(22)
51	25/06/87	Paris Saint–Germain	Neutral	Stars Cup	3–1	2 Goals	(24)
52	29/06/87	AC Milan	Away	Stars Cup	0–1		

+ AET CA Osasuna won 5–3 on penalties

SEASON 1987–88

Spanish League Division One

| 53 | 30/08/87 | UD Las Palmas | Away | League | 2–1 | | |
| 54 | 06/09/87 | Sevilla FC | Home | League | 1–2 | | |

55	12/09/87	RCD Espanol	Away	League	0–2		
56	16/09/87	CF OS Belenenses Lisboa	Home	UEFA Cup	2–0		
57	20/09/87	Valencia CF	Home	League	0–1		
58	26/09/87	Athletic Bilbao	Away	League	0–1		
59	30/09/87	CF OS Belenenses Lisboa	Away	UEFA Cup	0–1		
60	03/10/87	Atletico Madrid	Home	League	1–2		
61	18/10/87	CE Sabadell FC	Away	League	1–0		
62	21/10/87	Dinamo Moskva	Home	UEFA Cup	2–0		
63	25/10/87	RCD Mallorca	Home	League	2–2	1 Goal	(25)
64	01/11/87	CD Logrones	Away	League	1–0		
65	04/11/87	Dinamo Moskva	Away	UEFA Cup	0–0		
Sub+1	08/11/87	RC Celta Vigo	Home	League	2–0		
66	21/11/87	Real Betis	Away	League	2–1	1 Goal	(26)
67	25/11/87	KS Flamurtari Vlore	Home	UEFA Cup	4–1	2 Goals	(28)
68	29/11/87	Cadiz CF	Home	League	1–3		
69	02/12/87	CR Murcia	Away	Sp Cup	3–0		
70	06/12/87	CR Murcia	Home	League	4–1	2 Goals	(30)
71	09/12/87	KS Flamurtari Vlore	Away	UEFA Cup	0–1		
72	12/12/87	Real Sociaded	Away	League	1–4		
73	16/12/87	RCD Espanol	Away	Sp Cup	3–1		
74	20/12/87	Real Valladolid	Home	League	2–4	1 Goal	(31)
75	02/01/88	Real Madrid CF	Away	League	1–2		
Sub+2	09/01/88	Sporting Gijon	Home	League	1–0		
76	13/01/88	CD Castellon	Away	Sp Cup	1–1		
77	17/01/88	Real Zaragoza	Away	League	1–1		
78	20/01/88	CD Castellon	Home	Sp Cup	2–0		
79	24/01/88	CA Osasuna	Home	League	0–1		
80	31/01/88	UD Las Palmas	Home	League	1–1		
81	07/02/88	Sevilla FC	Away	League	1–1		
82	10/02/88	RCD Espanol	Home	League	3–2	1 Goal	(32)
83	14/02/88	Valencia CF	Away	League	1–1		
84	17/02/88	CA Osasuna	Home	Sp Cup	3–0	2 Goals	(34)
85	20/02/88	Athletic Bilbao	Home	League	1–2		
86	27/02/88	Atletico Madrid	Away	League	2–0	2 Goals	(36)
87	02/03/88	SV Bayer 04 Leverkusen	Away	UEFA Cup	0–0		
88	06/03/88	CE Sabadell FC	Home	League	0–0		
89	09/03/88	RCD Mallorca	Away	League	0–1		
90	12/03/88	CD Logrones	Home	League	2–1	1 Goal	(37)
91	16/03/88	SV Bayer 04 Leverkusen	Home	UEFA Cup	0–1		
92	20/03/88	RC Celta Vigo	Away	League	1–0	1 Goal	(38)
93	30/03/88	Real Sociedad	Neutral	Sp Cup	1–0		
94	03/04/88	Cadiz FC	Away	League	2–0	1 Goal	(39)
95	10/04/88	CR Murcia	Away	League	0–0		
96	17/04/88	Real Sociedad	Home	League	2–0	1 Goal	(40)
97	24/04/88	Real Valladolid	Away	League	1–1	1 Goal	(41)
98	30/04/88	Real Madrid CF	Home	League	2–0	1 Goal	(42)
99	08/05/88	Sporting Gijon	Away	League	0–1		
100	14/05/88	Real Zaragoza	Home	League	4–2	2 Goals	(44)

SEASON 1988–89

Spanish League Division One

Sub+3	24/09/88	CA Osasuna	Away	League	1–1		
Sub+4	29/09/88	Real Madrid	Home	Sp S Cup	2–1		
101	02/10/88	Sporting Gijon	Home	League	4–0		
102	05/10/88	Fram Reykjavik	Home	ECW Cup	5–0	1 Goal	(45)
103	22/10/88	Real Madrid CF	Away	League	2–3		
104	26/10/88	KKS Lech Poznan	Home	ECW Cup	1–1		
105	06/11/88	Real Valladolid	Away	League	0–0		
106	09/11/88	KKS Lech Poznan	Away	ECW Cup	1–1+		
107	20/11/88	Real Oviedo	Away	League	2–1	1 Goal	(46)
108	27/11/88	CR Murcia	Home	League	3–1	2 Goals	(48)
109	01/12/88	RC Celta Vigo	Away	League	3–0		
110	04/12/88	CD Logrones	Home	League	2–1		
111	01/01/89	Atletico Madrid	Away	League	3–1	1 Goal	(49)
112	08/01/89	Cadiz CF	Home	League	3–0		
113	11/01/89	Sevilla FC	Home	League	4–0	1 Goal	(50)
114	15/01/89	CD Malaga	Away	League	2–2		
115	25/01/89	Cartagena FC	Away	Sp Cup	3–0		
116	29/01/89	RCD Espanol	Away	League	2–2		
117	12/02/89	Elche CF	Home	League	2–0		
118	15/02/89	Racing Santander	Away	Sp Cup	1–0	1 Goal	(51)
119	18/02/89	Valencia CF	Away	League	1–1		
120	26/02/89	CA Osasuna	Home	League	1–2		
121	01/03/89	Arhus GF	Away	ECW Cup	1–0	1 Goal	(52)

122	04/03/89	Sporting Gijon	Away	League	2–0		
123	11/03/89	Real Sociedad	Home	League	4–1	1 Goal	(53)
124	15/03/89	Arhus GF	Home	ECW Cup	0–0		
125	25/03/89	Real Betis	Away	League	2–0		
126	29/03/89	Atletico Madrid	Home	Sp Cup	3–3		
127	04/04/89	CFKA Sredets Sofija	Home	ECW Cup	4–2	1 Goal	(54)
128	09/04/89	Real Zaragoza	Away	League	0–0		
129	12/04/89	Atletico Madrid	Away	Sp Cup	0–4		
130	15/04/89	Real Valladolid	Home	League	0–0		
131	19/04/89	CFKA Sredets Sofija	Away	ECW Cup	2–1	1 Goal	(55)
132	30/04/89	Real Oviedo	Home	League	7–1		
133	10/05/89	Sampdoria UC	Neutral	ECW Cup	2–0		
134	14/05/89	RC Celta Vigo	Home	League	3–1		
135	21/05/89	CD Logrones	Away	League	2–0		
136	25/05/89	CR Murcia	Away	League	0–2		
137	27/05/89	Athletic Bilbao	Home	League	3–0		

+ AET FC Barcelona won 5–4 on penalties

SEASON 1989–90

Tottenham Hotspur – League Division One

1	19/08/89	Luton Town	Home	League	2–1		
2	22/08/89	Everton	Away	League	1–2		
3	26/08/89	Manchester City	Away	League	1–1		
4	09/09/89	Aston Villa	Away	League	0–2		
5	16/09/89	Chelsea	Home	League	1–4		
6	23/09/89	Norwich City	Away	League	2–2	1 Goal	(1)
7	30/09/89	Queens Park Rangers	Home	League	3–2	3 Goals	(4)
8	04/10/89	Southend United	Away	Lge Cup	2–3*		
9	14/10/89	Charlton Athletic	Away	League	3–1	1 Goal	(5)
10	18/10/89	Arsenal	Home	League	2–1		
11	21/10/89	Sheffield Wednesday	Home	League	3–0	2 Goals	(7)
12	25/10/89	Manchester United	Away	Lge Cup	3–0	1 Goal	(8)
13	29/10/89	Liverpool	Away	League	0–1		
14	04/11/89	Southampton	Away	League	1–1		
15	11/11/89	Wimbledon	Home	League	0–1		
16	18/11/89	Crystal Palace	Away	League	3–2	1 Goal	(9)
17	22/11/89	Tranmere Rovers	Away	Lge Cup	2–2		
18	25/11/89	Derby County	Home	League	1–2		
19	29/11/89	Tranmere Rovers	Home	Lge Cup	4–0		
20	02/12/89	Luton Town	Away	League	0–0		
21	09/12/89	Everton	Home	League	2–1	1 Goal	(10)
22	16/12/89	Manchester United	Away	League	1–0	1 Goal	(11)
23	26/12/89	Millwall	Home	League	3–1	1 Goal	(12)
24	30/12/89	Nottingham Forest	Home	League	2–3	2 Goals	(14)
25	01/01/90	Coventry City	Away	League	0–0		
26	06/01/90	Southampton	Home	FA Cup	1–3		
27	13/01/90	Manchester City	Home	League	1–1		
28	17/01/90	Nottingham Forest	Away	Lge Cup	2–2	1 Goal	(15)
29	20/01/90	Arsenal	Away	League	0–1		
30	24/01/90	Nottingham Forest	Home	Lge Cup	2–3		
31	04/02/90	Norwich City	Home	League	4–0	3 Goals	(18)
32	10/02/90	Chelsea	Away	League	2–1	1 Goal	(19)
33	21/02/90	Aston Villa	Home	League	0–2		
34	24/02/90	Derby County	Away	League	1–2		
35	03/03/90	Crystal Palace	Home	League	0–1		
36	10/03/90	Charlton Athletic	Home	League	3–0	1 Goal	(20)
37	17/03/90	Queens Park Rangers	Away	League	1–3		
38	21/03/90	Liverpool	Home	League	1–0		
39	31/03/90	Sheffield Wednesday	Away	League	4–2	2 Goals	(22)
40	07/04/90	Nottingham Forest	Away	League	3–1		
41	14/04/90	Coventry City	Home	League	3–2	2 Goals	(24)
42	16/04/90	Millwall	Away	League	1–0	1 Goal	(25)
43	21/04/90	Manchester United	Home	League	2–1	1 Goal	(26)
44	28/04/90	Wimbledon	Away	League	0–1		
45	05/05/90	Southampton	Home	League	2–1		

SEASON 1990–91

League Division One

46	25/08/90	Manchester City	Home	League	3–1	2 Goals	(28)
47	28/08/90	Sunderland	Away	League	0–0		
48	01/09/90	Arsenal	Home	League	0–0		
49	08/09/90	Derby County	Home	League	3–0		

50	15/09/90	Leeds United	Away	League	2–0	1 Goal	(29)
51	22/09/90	Crystal Palace	Home	League	1–1		
52	26/09/90	Hartlepool United	Home	Lge Cup	5–0	1 Goal	(30)
53	29/09/90	Aston Villa	Home	League	2–1	1 Goal	(31)
54	06/10/90	Queens Park Rangers	Away	League	0–0		
55	27/10/90	Nottingham Forest	Away	League	2–1		
56	30/10/90	Bradford City	Home	Lge Cup	2–1		
57	04/11/90	Liverpool	Home	League	1–3	1 Goal	(32)
58	10/11/90	Wimbledon	Home	League	4–2	1 Goal	(33)
59	18/11/90	Everton	Away	League	1–1		
60	24/11/90	Norwich City	Home	League	2–1	2 Goals	(35)
61	27/11/90	Sheffield United	Away	Lge Cup	2–0		
62	01/12/90	Chelsea	Away	League	2–3	1 Goal	(36)
63	08/12/90	Sunderland	Home	League	3–3	1 Goal	(37)
64	15/12/90	Manchester City	Away	League	1–2		
65	22/12/90	Luton Town	Home	League	2–1		
66	26/12/90	Coventry City	Away	League	0–2		
67	29/12/90	Southampton	Away	League	0–3		
68	01/01/91	Manchester United	Home	League	1–2	1 Goal	(38)
69	05/01/91	Blackpool	Away	FA Cup	1–0		
70	12/01/91	Arsenal	Home	League	0–0		
71	16/01/91	Chelsea	Away	Lge Cup	0–0		
72	20/01/91	Derby County	Away	League	1–0	1 Goal	(39)
73	23/01/91	Chelsea	Home	Lge Cup	0–3		
74	26/01/91	Oxford United	Home	FA Cup	4–2	1 Goal	(40)
75	02/02/91	Leeds United	Home	League	0–0		
76	16/02/91	Portsmouth	Away	FA Cup	2–1		
77	23/02/91	Wimbledon	Away	League	1–5		
78	02/03/91	Chelsea	Home	League	1–1	1 Goal	(41)
79	10/03/91	Notts County	Home	FA Cup	2–1		
80	16/03/91	Aston Villa	Away	League	2–3		
81	23/03/91	Queens Park Rangers	Home	League	0–0		
82	06/04/91	Southampton	Home	League	2–0	2 Goals	(43)
83	14/04/91	Arsenal	Wembley	FA Cup	3–1	2 Goals	(45)
84	24/04/91	Everton	Home	League	3–3		
85	04/05/91	Nottingham Forest	Home	League	1–1		
86	11/05/91	Liverpool	Away	League	0–2		
87	18/05/91	Nottingham Forest	Wembley	FA Cup	2–1*		
88	20/05/91	Manchester United	Away	League	1–1		

SEASON 1991–92

League Division One

89	10/08/91	Arsenal	Wembley	FA C/S	0–0		
90	17/08/91	Southampton	Away	League	3–2	2 Goals	(47)
91	21/08/91	SV Stockerau	Away	ECW Cup	1–0		
92	24/08/91	Chelsea	Home	League	1–3	1 Goal	(48)
93	28/08/91	Nottingham Forest	Away	League	3–1	1 Goal	(49)
94	31/08/91	Norwich City	Away	League	1–0	1 Goal	(50)
95	04/09/91	SV Stockerau	Home	ECW Cup	1–0		
96	07/09/91	Aston Villa	Away	League	0–0		
97	14/09/91	Queens Park Rangers	Home	League	2–0	2 Goals	(52)
98	17/09/91	NK Hajduk Split	Away	ECW Cup	0–1		
99	21/09/91	Wimbledon	Away	League	5–3	4 Goals	(56)
100	28/09/91	Manchester United	Home	League	1–2		
101	02/10/91	NK Hajduk Split	Home	ECW Cup	2–0		
102	05/10/91	Everton	Away	League	1–3	1 Goal	(57)
103	09/10/91	Swansea City	Home	Lge Cup	5–1	1 Goal	(58)
104	19/10/91	Manchester City	Home	League	0–1		
105	23/10/91	FC Porto	Home	ECW Cup	3–1	2 Goals	(60)
106	26/10/91	West Ham United	Away	League	1–2	1 Goal	(61)
107	29/10/91	Grimsby Town	Away	Lge Cup	3–0	1 Goal	(62)
108	02/11/91	Sheffield Wednesday	Away	League	0–0		
109	07/11/91	FC Porto	Away	ECW Cup	0–0		
110	16/11/91	Luton Town	Home	League	4–1	2 Goals	(64)
111	23/11/91	Sheffield United	Home	League	0–1		
112	18/12/91	Liverpool	Home	League	1–2		
113	22/12/91	Crystal Palace	Away	League	2–1	1 Goal	(65)
114	26/12/91	Nottingham Forest	Home	League	1–2		
115	28/12/91	Norwich City	Home	League	3–0	1 Goal	(66)
116	01/01/92	Coventry City	Away	League	2–1	1 Goal	(67)
117	05/01/92	Aston Villa	Away	FA Cup	0–0		
118	08/01/92	Norwich City	Home	Lge Cup	2–1	1 Goal	(68)
119	14/01/92	Aston Villa	Home	FA Cup	0–1		
120	18/01/92	Southampton	Home	League	1–2		

121	25/01/92	Oldham Athletic	Home	League	0–0		
122	01/02/92	Manchester City	Away	League	0–1		
123	09/02/92	Nottingham Forest	Away	Lge Cup	1–1	1 Goal	(69)
124	16/02/92	Crystal Palace	Home	League	0–1		
125	22/02/92	Arsenal	Home	League	1–1		
126	01/03/92	Nottingham Forest	Home	Lge Cup	1–2*	1 Goal	(70)
127	04/03/92	SC Feyenoord	Away	ECW Cup	0–1		
128	07/03/92	Leeds United	Home	League	1–3		
129	18/03/92	SC Feyenoord	Home	ECW Cup	0–0		
130	28/03/92	Coventry City	Home	League	4–3	1 Goal	(71)
131	01/04/92	West Ham United	Home	League	3–0	3 Goals	(74)
132	04/04/92	Aston Villa	Home	League	2–5	1 Goal	(75)
133	07/04/92	Notts County	Away	League	2–0	2 Goals	(77)
134	11/04/92	Queens Park Rangers	Away	League	2–1		
135	14/04/92	Sheffield United	Away	League	0–2		
136	18/04/92	Wimbledon	Home	League	3–2	2 Goals	(79)
137	20/04/92	Oldham Athletic	Away	League	0–1		
138	25/04/92	Everton	Home	League	3–3		
139	02/05/92	Manchester United	Away	League	1–3	1 Goal	(80)

SEASON 1992–93

Nagoya Grampus Eight – Japanese J League – Season 1993

1	16/05/93	Kashima Antlers	Away	League	0–5		
2	19/05/93	Urawa Red Diamonds	Away	League	3–0		
3	22/05/93	Yokohama Marinos	Home	League	1–1+		
4	26/05/93	Yokohama Flugels	Home	League	1–2	1 Goal	(1)
5	29/05/93	Shimizu S–Pulse	Away	League	0–0#		
6	05/06/93	Gamba Osaka	Away	League	1–3		
7	03/09/93	Sanfrecce Hirosima	Home	League	1–0		
8	10/09/93	Shimizu S–Pulse	Away	J Cup	1–2	1 Goal	(2)
9	18/09/93	Jubiro Iwata	Home	J Cup	1–3		
10	25/09/93	Yokohama Marinos	Home	J Cup	4–1	2 Goals	(4)
11	02/10/93	Urawa Red Diamons	Away	J Cup	2–3	1 Goal	(5)
12	16/10/93	Yokohama Flugels	Home	J Cup	1–0		

+ Nagoya Grampus Eight won shoot–out 4–3
# Nagoya Grampus Eight won shoot–out 6–5

SEASON 1993–94

Japanese J League – Season 1994

Sub+1	15/06/94	Yokohama Marinos	Home	League	1–0		
13	27/07/94	Jef United Ichihara	Home	J Cup	1–3		
14	10/08/94	Sanfrecce Hirosima	Away	League	0–4		
15	13/08/94	Jubiro Iwata	Away	League	3–2	1 Goal	(6)
16	17/08/94	Gamba Osaka	Home	League	2–3		
Sub+2	31/08/94	Bellmare Hiratsuka	Away	League	0–2		
17	03/09/94	Kashima Antlers	Home	League	2–4	1 Goal	(7)
18	07/09/94	Verdy Kawasaki	Home	League	1–2	1 Goal	(8)
19	14/09/94	Shimizu S–Pulse	Away	League	1–2		
20	26/10/94	Urawa Red Diamonds	Away	League	1–1+		
21	29/10/94	Bellmare Hiratsuka	Home	League	0–4		
22	19/11/94	Sanfrecce Hirosima	Home	League	1–0		

+ Urawa Red Diamonds won shoot–out 4–3

INTERNATIONAL APPEARANCES – ENGLAND

Sub 1	26/05/84	Scotland	Hampden Park	1–1	HC		
2	26/03/85	Republic of Ireland	Wembley	2–1	F	1 Goal	(1)
Sub 3	01/05/85	Romania	Bucharest	0–0	WCQ		
Sub 4	25/05/85	Scotland	Hampden Park	0–1	RC		
Sub 5	06/06/85	Italy	Mexico City	1–2	F		
6	12/06/85	West Germany	Mexico City	3–0	F		
7	16/06/85	USA	Los Angeles	5–0	F	2 Goals	(3)
8	11/09/85	Romania	Wembley	1–1	WCQ		
9	16/10/85	Turkey	Wembley	5–0	WCQ	3 Goals	(6)
10	13/11/85	Northern Ireland	Wembley	0–0	WCQ		
11	29/01/86	Egypt	Cairo	4–0	F		
12	26/03/86	USSR	Tbilisi	1–0	F		
13	24/05/86	Canada	Vancouver	1–0	F		
14	03/06/86	Portugal	Monterrey	0–1	WC		

15	06/06/86	Morocco	Monterrey	0–0	WC		
16	11/06/86	Poland	Monterrey	3–0	WC	3 Goals	(9)
17	18/06/86	Paraguay	Mexico City	3–0	WC	2 Goals	(11)
18	22/06/86	Argentina	Mexico City	1–2	WC	1 Goal	(12)
19	15/10/86	Northern Ireland	Wembley	3–0	ECQ	2 Goals	(14)
20	12/11/86	Yugoslavia	Wembley	2–0	ECQ		
21	18/02/87	Spain	Madrid	4–2	F	4 Goals	(18)
22	01/04/87	Northern Ireland	Windsor Park	2–0	ECQ		
23	29/04/87	Turkey	Izmir	0–0	ECQ		
24	19/05/87	Brazil	Wembley	1–1	RC	1 Goal	(19)
25	09/09/87	West Germany	Dusseldorf	1–3	F	1 Goal	(20)
26	14/10/87	Turkey	Wembley	8–0	ECQ	3 Goals	(23)
27	11/11/87	Yugoslavia	Belgrade	4–1	ECQ		
28	23/03/88	Holland	Wembley	2–2	F	1 Goal	(24)
29	27/04/88	Hungary	Budapest	0–0	F		
30	21/05/88	Scotland	Wembley	1–0	RC		
31	24/05/88	Colombia	Wembley	1–1	RC	1 Goal	(25)
32	28/05/88	Switzerland	Lausanne	1–0	F	1 Goal	(26)
33	12/06/88	Republic of Ireland	Stuttgart	0–1	EC		
34	15/06/88	Holland	Dusseldorf	1–3	EC		
35	18/06/88	USSR	Frankfurt	1–3	EC		
36	19/10/88	Sweden	Wembley	0–0	WCQ		
37	16/11/88	Saudi Arabia	Riyadh	1–1	F		
38	08/02/89	Greece	Athens	2–1	F		
39	08/03/89	Albania	Tirana	2–0	WCQ		
40	26/04/89	Albania	Wembley	5–0	WCQ	1 Goal	(27)
41	03/06/89	Poland	Wembley	3–0	WCQ	1 Goal	(28)
42	07/06/89	Denmark	Copenhagen	1–1	F	1 Goal	(29)
43	06/09/89	Sweden	Solna	0–0	WCQ		
44	11/10/89	Poland	Katowice	0–0	WCQ		
45	15/11/89	Italy	Wembley	0–0	F		
46	13/12/89	Yugoslavia	Wembley	2–1	F		
47	28/03/90	Brazil	Wembley	1–0	F	1 Goal	(30)
48	25/04/90	Czechoslovakia	Wembley	4–2	F		
49	15/05/90	Denmark	Wembley	1–0	F	1 Goal	(31)
50	22/05/90	Uruguay	Wembley	1–2	F		
51	02/06/90	Tunisia	Tunis	1–1	F		
52	11/06/90	Republic of Ireland	Cagliari	1–1	WC	1 Goal	(32)
53	16/06/90	Holland	Cagliari	0–0	WC		
54	21/06/90	Egypt	Cagliari	1–0	WC		
55	26/06/90	Belgium	Bologna	1–0*	WC		
56	01/07/90	Cameroon	Naples	3–2*	WC	2 Goals	(34)
57	04/07/90	West Germany	Turin	1–1+	WC	1 Goal	(35)
58	07/07/90	Italy	Bari	1–2	WC		
59	12/09/90	Hungary	Wembley	1–0	F	1 Goal	(36)
60	17/10/90	Poland	Wembley	2–0	ECQ	1 Goal	(37)
61	14/11/90	Republic of Ireland	Lansdowne Road	1–1	ECQ		
62	06/02/91	Cameroon	Wembley	2–0	F	2 Goals	(39)
63	27/03/91	Republic of Ireland	Wembley	1–1	ECQ		
64	01/05/91	Turkey	Izmir	1–0	ECQ		
65	25/05/91	Argentina	Wembley	2–2	F	1 Goal	(40)
66	01/06/91	Australia	Sydney	1–0	F		
67	03/06/91	New Zealand	Auckland	1–0	F	1 Goal	(41)
68	12/06/91	Malaysia	Kuala Lumpur	4–2	F	4 Goals	(45)
69	11/09/91	Germany	Wembley	0–1	F		
70	16/10/91	Turkey	Wembley	1–0	ECQ		
71	13/11/91	Poland	Poznan	1–1	ECQ	1 Goal	(46)
Sub 72	19/02/92	France	Wembley	2–0	F	1 Goal	(47)
Sub 73	25/03/92	Czechoslovakia	Prague	2–2	F		
74	29/04/92	CIS	Moscow	2–2	F	1 Goal	(48)
75	12/05/92	Hungary	Budapest	1–0	F		
76	17/05/92	Brazil	Wembley	1–1	F		
77	03/06/92	Finland	Helsinki	2–1	F		
78	11/06/92	Denmark	Malmo	0–0	EC		
79	14/06/92	France	Malmo	0–0	EC		
80	17/06/92	Sweden	Solna	1–2	EC		

+ AET West Germany won 4–3 on penalties

APPEARANCES AND GOALS PER SEASON

SEASON 78–79	GAMES	GOALS
League	7	1
TOTAL	7	1

SEASON 79–80	GAMES	GOALS
League	16+3	3
FA Cup	1	0
TOTAL	**17+3**	**3**

SEASON 80–81	GAMES	GOALS
League	9	2
FA Cup	1	1
TOTAL	**10**	**3**

SEASON 81–82	GAMES	GOALS
League	37+2	17
FA Cup	5	2
League Cup	3	0
TOTAL	**45+2**	**19**

SEASON 82–83	GAMES	GOALS
League	39+1	26
FA Cup	1	0
League Cup	2	0
TOTAL	**42+1**	**26**

SEASON 83–84	GAMES	GOALS
League	38+1	22
FA Cup	1	0
League Cup	1	0
TOTAL	**40+1**	**22**

SEASON 84–85	GAMES	GOALS
League	41	24
FA Cup	4	3
League Cup	3	2
TOTAL	**48**	**29**

SEASON 85–86	GAMES	GOALS
League	41	30
FA Cup	6	5
League Cup	5	3
Screen Sport Super Cup	4	2
FA Charity Shield	1	0
TOTAL	**57**	**40**

SEASON 86–87	GAMES	GOALS
Spanish League	31	17
Spanish League Play–offs	10	4
Spanish Cup	1	1
UEFA Cup	8	0
Stars Cup	2	2
TOTAL	**52**	**24**

SEASON 87–88	GAMES	GOALS
Spanish League	34+2	16
Spanish Cup	6	2
UEFA Cup	8	2
TOTAL	**48+2**	**20**

SEASON 88–89	GAMES	GOALS
Spanish League	25+1	6
Spanish Cup	4	1
European Cup Winners Cup	8	4
Spanish Super Cup	0+1	0
TOTAL	**37+2**	**11**

SEASON 89–90	GAMES	GOALS
League	38	24
FA Cup	1	0
League Cup	6	2
TOTAL	**45**	**26**

SEASON 90–91	GAMES	GOALS
League	32	15
FA Cup	6	3
League Cup	5	1
TOTAL	**43**	**19**

SEASON 91–92	GAMES	GOALS
League	35	28
FA Cup	2	0
League Cup	5	5
European Cup Winners Cup	8	2
FA Charity Shield	1	0
TOTAL	**51**	**35**

SEASON 92–93	GAMES	GOALS
Japanese League	7	1
Japanese Cup	5	4
TOTAL	**12**	**5**

SEASON 93–94	GAMES	GOALS
Japanese League	9+2	3
Japanese Cup	1	0
TOTAL	**10+2**	**3**

CAREER APPEARANCES AND GOALS

COMPETITION	GAMES	TOTAL	GOALS
League	333+7	340	192
FA Cup	28	28	14
League Cup	30	30	13
Screen Sport Super Cup	4	4	2
FA Charity Shield	2	2	0
European Cup Winners Cup	16	16	6
UEFA Cup	16	16	2
Spanish League	90+3	93	39
Spanish League Play–offs	10	10	4
Spanish Cup	11	11	4
Spanish Super Cup	0+1	1	0
Spanish Stars Cup	2	2	2
Japanese League	16+2	18	4
Japanese Cup	6	6	4
Internationals	74+6	80	48
TOTAL	**638+19**	**657**	**334**

HAT-TRICKS

Leicester City

1	3	Carlisle United	11/09/82	Home	League	6–0
2	3	Derby County	23/10/82	Away	League	4–0
3	3	Notts County	14/01/84	Away	League	5–2
4	3	Aston Villa	27/10/84	Home	League	5–0
5	3	Burton Albion	05/01/85	Away	FA Cup	6–1

Everton

1	3	Birmingham City	31/08/85	Home	League	4–1
2	3	Manchester City	11/02/86	Home	League	4–0
3	3	Southampton	03/05/86	Home	League	6–1

FC Barcelona

1	3	Real Madrid CF	31/01/87	Home	Sp League	3–2

Tottenham Hotspur

1	3	Queens Park Rangers	30/09/89	Home	League	3–2
2	3	Norwich City	04/02/90	Home	League	4–0
3	4	Wimbledon	21/09/91	Away	League	5–3
4	3	West Ham United	01/04/92	Home	League	3–0

England

1	3	Turkey	16/10/85	Wembley	WCQ	5–0
2	3	Poland	11/06/86	Monterrey	WC	3–0
3	4	Spain	18/02/87	Madrid	F	4–2
4	3	Turkey	14/10/87	Wembley	ECQ	8–0
5	4	Malaysia	12/06/91	Kuala Lumpur	F	4–2

League: 11
Spanish League: 1
FA Cup: 1
International: 5
TOTAL: 18

HONOURS

Winners medals
FA Cup: 90/91
League Division Two Championship: 79/80
FA Charity Shield: 85/86, 91/92
European Cup Winners Cup: 88/89
Spanish Cup: 87/88
Spanish Super Cup: 88/89

Runner-up medals
League Division One Championship: 85/86
FA Cup: 85/86
Promoted to League Division One: 82/83
Spanish League Championship: 86/87, 88/89

BRIAN MCCLAIR

Born: 08/12/63 – Bellshill
Height: 5.10
Weight: 12.13 (96–97)

Clubs
Aston Villa: **1981** – No Competitive Matches
Motherwell: **1981–83** – Matches: **44+8** – Goals: **20**
Celtic: **1983–87** – Matches: **175+23** – Goals: **122**
Manchester United: **1987–97** – Matches: **395+59** – Goals: **128**

Country
Scotland: **1986–93** – Matches: **20+10** – Goals: **2**

SEASON 1981–82

Aston Villa – League Division One
No Competitive Matches

Motherwell – Scottish League Division One

1	12/08/81	Ayr United	Home	S Lge Cup	2–3		
2	19/08/81	Ayr United	Away	S Lge Cup	0–1		
3	22/08/81	Partick Thistle	Home	S Lge Cup	0–1		
4	26/08/81	Dundee United	Away	S Lge Cup	1–1		
5	29/08/81	Kilmarnock	Away	League	0–2		
Sub+1	07/11/81	Queen's Park	Away	League	1–0		
Sub+2	06/02/82	Queen of the South	Home	League	2–1		
Sub+3	03/04/82	East Stirling	Away	League	2–1		
Sub+4	14/04/82	Ayr United	Away	League	3–4		
6	17/04/82	Falkirk	Away	League	3–1	1 Goal	(1)
7	21/04/82	Raith Rovers	Away	League	1–0		
8	24/04/82	Clydebank	Home	League	0–0		
9	01/05/82	Queen of the South	Away	League	5–2	2 Goals	(3)
10	08/05/82	Dunfermline Athletic	Home	League	2–2	1 Goal	(4)
11	15/05/82	Heart of Midlothian	Away	League	1–0		

SEASON 1982–83

Scottish League Premier Division

12	14/08/82	Heart of Midlothian	Home	S Lge Cup	2–1		
13	18/08/82	Clyde	Away	S Lge Cup	3–3	1 Goal	(5)
14	21/08/82	Forfar Athletic	Home	S Lge Cup	1–1		
Sub+5	25/08/82	Clyde	Home	S Lge Cup	3–1	3 Goals	(8)
15	28/08/82	Heart of Midlothian	Away	S Lge Cup	0–1		
16	01/09/82	Forfar Athletic	Away	S Lge Cup	1–0		
17	11/09/82	Dundee	Away	League	1–3		
18	18/09/82	Celtic	Home	League	0–7		
19	25/09/82	Morton	Away	League	1–3		
Sub+6	30/10/82	Kilmarnock	Home	League	4–1	1 Goal	(9)
20	06/11/82	Rangers	Away	League	0–4		
21	13/11/82	Dundee	Home	League	1–0		

22	20/11/82	Celtic	Away	League	1–3		
Sub+7	11/12/82	St Mirren	Away	League	0–3		
Sub+8	18/12/82	Hibernian	Home	League	0–1		
23	27/12/82	Dundee United	Away	League	0–5		
24	01/01/83	Kilmarnock	Away	League	2–0		
25	03/01/83	Rangers	Home	League	3–0	3 Goals	(12)
26	08/01/83	Dundee	Away	League	1–3		
27	15/01/83	Celtic	Home	League	2–1	2 Goals	(14)
28	22/01/83	Morton	Away	League	1–0	1 Goal	(15)
29	28/01/83	Clyde	Away	S Cup	0–0		
30	02/02/83	Clyde	Home	S Cup	3–4	1 Goal	(16)
31	05/02/83	Aberdeen	Away	League	1–5		
32	26/02/83	Hibernian	Away	League	1–1		
33	01/03/83	St Mirren	Home	League	0–0		
34	05/03/83	Dundee United	Home	League	1–4		
35	12/03/83	Kilmarnock	Home	League	3–1	1 Goal	(17)
36	19/03/83	Rangers	Away	League	0–1		
37	26/03/83	Dundee	Home	League	1–1		
38	02/04/83	Celtic	Away	League	0–3		
39	09/04/83	Morton	Home	League	4–1	1 Goal	(18)
40	23/04/83	St Mirren	Away	League	0–4		
41	27/04/83	Aberdeen	Home	League	0–3		
42	30/04/83	Hibernian	Home	League	2–0	1 Goal	(19)
43	07/05/83	Dundee United	Away	League	0–4		
44	14/05/83	Kilmarnock	Away	League	1–1	1 Goal	(20)

SEASON 1983–84

Celtic – Scottish League Premier Division

1	24/08/83	Brechin City	Away	S Lge Cup	1–0		
Sub+1	31/08/83	Airdrieonians	Away	S Lge Cup	6–1		
Sub+2	03/09/83	Rangers	Home	League	2–1		
Sub+3	10/09/83	St Johnstone	Home	League	5–2		
Sub+4	14/09/83	Arhus GF	Home	UEFA Cup	1–0		
2	17/09/83	Motherwell	Away	League	3–0		
3	24/09/83	Dundee	Away	League	6–2	4 Goals	(4)
Sub+5	01/10/83	St Mirren	Home	League	1–1		
4	05/10/83	Kilmarnock	Home	S Lge Cup	1–1		
Sub+6	08/10/83	Dundee United	Away	League	1–2		
Sub+7	15/10/83	Heart of Midlothian	Home	League	1–1		
Sub+8	19/10/83	Sporting CP Lisboa	Away	UEFA Cup	0–2		
5	22/10/83	Aberdeen	Away	League	1–3		
6	26/10/83	Hibernian	Away	S Lge Cup	0–0		
7	29/10/83	Hibernian	Home	League	5–1	2 Goals	(6)
8	02/11/83	Sporting CP Lisboa	Home	UEFA Cup	5–0	1 Goal	(7)
9	05/11/83	Rangers	Away	League	2–1		
10	09/11/83	Airdrieonians	Home	S Lge Cup	0–0		
11	12/11/83	Motherwell	Home	League	4–0	2 Goals	(9)
12	19/11/83	St Mirren	Away	League	2–4		
13	23/11/83	Nottingham Forest	Away	UEFA Cup	0–0		
14	26/11/83	Dundee	Home	League	1–0		
15	30/11/83	Kilmarnock	Away	S Lge Cup	1–0		
16	03/12/83	St Johnstone	Away	League	3–0		
17	07/12/83	Nottingham Forest	Home	UEFA Cup	1–2		
18	10/12/83	Aberdeen	Home	League	0–0		
19	17/12/83	Heart of Midlothian	Away	League	3–1	2 Goals	(11)
20	27/12/83	Dundee United	Home	League	1–1	1 Goal	(12)
21	31/12/83	Hibernian	Away	League	1–0		
22	07/01/84	Motherwell	Away	League	2–2		
23	28/01/84	Berwick Rangers	Away	S Cup	4–0	2 Goals	(14)
24	04/02/84	Aberdeen	Away	League	0–1		
25	11/02/84	St Johnstone	Home	League	5–2	2 Goals	(16)
26	14/02/84	St Mirren	Home	League	2–0		
27	18/02/84	East Fife	Away	S Cup	6–0	1 Goal	(17)
28	22/02/84	Aberdeen	Away	S Lge Cup	0–0		
29	25/02/84	Heart of Midlothian	Home	League	4–1	3 Goals	(20)
30	03/03/84	Dundee United	Away	League	1–3		
31	10/03/84	Aberdeen	Home	S Lge Cup	1–0		
32	17/03/84	Motherwell	Away	S Cup	6–0	2 Goals	(22)
33	20/03/84	Dundee	Away	League	2–3		
34	25/03/84	Rangers	Hampden	S Lge Cup	2–3*	1 Goal	(23)
35	31/03/84	Aberdeen	Home	League	1–0		
36	02/04/84	Rangers	Home	League	3–0		
Sub+9	07/04/84	St Johnstone	Away	League	0–0		
37	10/04/84	Motherwell	Home	League	4–2	2 Goals	(25)

38	14/04/84	St Mirren	Hampden	S Cup	2–1	1 Goal	(26)
Sub+10	18/04/84	St Mirren	Away	League	4–2	2 Goals	(28)
39	21/04/84	Rangers	Away	League	0–1		
40	24/04/84	Dundee	Home	League	3–0	1 Goal	(29)
41	28/04/84	Hibernian	Home	League	3–2	2 Goals	(31)
42	05/05/84	Heart of Midlothian	Away	League	1–1		
43	12/05/84	Dundee United	Home	League	1–1		
44	19/05/84	Aberdeen	Hampden	S Cup	1–2*		

SEASON 1984–85

Scottish League Premier Division

45	11/08/84	Hibernian	Away	League	0–0		
46	18/08/84	Dundee United	Home	League	1–1	1 Goal	(32)
47	22/08/84	Dunfermline Athletic	Away	S Lge Cup	3–2	2 Goals	(34)
48	25/08/84	Rangers	Away	League	0–0		
49	29/08/84	Airdrieonians	Away	S Lge Cup	4–0	1 Goal	(35)
50	01/09/84	Morton	Home	League	5–0	2 Goals	(37)
51	05/09/84	Dundee United	Away	S Lge Cup	1–2*		
52	08/09/84	Dumbarton	Away	League	1–1		
53	15/09/84	Heart of Midlothian	Home	League	1–1		
54	19/09/84	KAA Gent	Away	ECW Cup	0–1		
Sub+11	22/09/84	St Mirren	Away	League	2–1	1 Goal	(38)
55	27/09/84	Dundee	Away	League	3–2		
56	03/10/84	KAA Gent	Home	ECW Cup	3–0		
57	06/10/84	Aberdeen	Home	League	2–1		
Sub+12	13/10/84	Hibernian	Home	League	3–0	1 Goal	(39)
Sub+13	20/10/84	Dundee United	Away	League	3–1		
58	24/10/84	SK Rapid Wien	Away	ECW Cup	1–3	1 Goal	(40)
Sub+14	03/11/84	Morton	Away	League	1–2		
59	07/11/84	SK Rapid Wien	Home	ECW Cup	3–0+	1 Goal	(41)
60	10/11/84	Dumbarton	Home	League	2–0		
61	17/11/84	Heart of Midlothian	Away	League	5–1	3 Goals	(44)
62	24/11/84	St Mirren	Home	League	7–1	1 Goal	(45)
63	01/12/84	Dundee	Home	League	5–1		
64	08/12/84	Aberdeen	Away	League	2–4		
65	12/12/84	SK Rapid Wien	Neutral	ECW Cup	0–1		
66	15/12/84	Hibernian	Away	League	1–0		
67	22/12/84	Rangers	Home	League	1–1	1 Goal	(46)
68	29/12/84	Dundee United	Home	League	1–2		
69	01/01/85	Rangers	Away	League	2–1	1 Goal	(47)
70	30/01/85	Hamilton Athletic	Away	S Cup	2–1		
Sub+15	02/03/85	Dundee United	Away	League	0–0		
Sub+16	09/03/85	Dundee	Away	S Cup	1–1		
Sub+17	13/03/85	Dundee	Home	S Cup	2–1		
71	16/03/85	Hibernian	Home	League	0–1		
Sub+18	20/03/85	Heart of Midlothian	Home	League	3–2	1 Goal	(48)
72	23/03/85	Morton	Away	League	7–2	4 Goals	(52)
73	03/04/85	Dumbarton	Away	League	2–0	1 Goal	(53)
74	06/04/85	Heart of Midlothian	Away	League	2–0	1 Goal	(54)
75	13/04/85	Motherwell	Hampden	S Cup	1–1		
76	17/04/85	Motherwell	Hampden	S Cup	3–0		
77	20/04/85	St Mirren	Home	League	3–0		
Sub+19	27/04/85	Aberdeen	Away	League	1–1		
78	01/05/85	Rangers	Home	League	1–1		
79	04/05/85	Dundee	Home	League	0–1		
80	11/05/85	Dumbarton	Home	League	2–0	1 Goal	(55)
Sub+20	18/05/85	Dundee United	Hampden	S Cup	2–1		

+ Match replayed after crowd trouble

SEASON 1985–86

Scottish League Premier Division

81	10/08/85	Heart of Midlothian	Away	League	1–1		
82	17/08/85	Motherwell	Home	League	2–1	1 Goal	(56)
83	21/08/85	Queen of the South	Away	S Lge Cup	4–1	1 Goal	(57)
84	24/08/85	Clydebank	Away	League	2–0		
85	28/08/85	Brechin City	Home	S Lge Cup	7–0		
86	31/08/85	Rangers	Home	League	1–1		
87	04/09/85	Hibernian	Away	S Lge Cup	4–4+		
88	07/09/85	Hibernian	Away	League	5–0	2 Goals	(59)
89	18/09/85	Atletico Madrid	Away	ECW Cup	1–1		
90	14/09/85	Aberdeen	Home	League	2–1	2 Goals	(61)
91	28/09/85	Dundee	Away	League	2–0	1 Goal	(62)

92	05/10/85	St Mirren	Home	League	2–0	1 Goal	(63)
93	12/10/85	Heart of Midlothian	Home	League	0–1		
94	19/10/85	Motherwell	Away	League	2–1		
95	26/10/85	Dundee United	Home	League	0–3		
96	02/11/85	Aberdeen	Away	League	1–4		
97	09/11/85	Rangers	Away	League	0–3		
Sub+21	23/11/85	Hibernian	Home	League	1–1		
98	14/12/85	Heart of Midlothian	Away	League	1–1		
99	23/12/85	Dundee United	Away	League	0–1		
100	01/01/86	Rangers	Home	League	2–0	1 Goal	(64)
101	04/01/86	Dundee United	Away	League	2–4	2 Goals	(66)
102	11/01/86	Aberdeen	Home	League	1–1		
103	15/01/86	Motherwell	Home	League	3–2	1 Goal	(67)
104	18/01/86	Hibernian	Away	League	2–2		
Sub+22	25/01/86	St Johnstone	Home	S Cup	2–0		
105	01/02/86	Dundee	Away	League	3–1	1 Goal	(68)
106	08/02/86	St Mirren	Home	League	1–1		
107	15/02/86	Queen's Park	Home	S Cup	2–1	1 Goal	(69)
108	22/02/86	Heart of Midlothian	Home	League	1–1		
109	08/03/86	Hibernian	Away	S Cup	3–4	2 Goals	(71)
110	15/03/86	Dundee United	Home	League	1–1		
111	22/03/86	Rangers	Away	League	4–4	1 Goal	(72)
112	29/03/86	Clydebank	Away	League	5–0	3 Goals	(75)
113	02/04/86	Dundee	Home	League	2–1		
114	05/04/86	St Mirren	Away	League	2–1		
115	12/04/86	Aberdeen	Away	League	1–0		
116	19/04/86	Hibernian	Home	League	2–0	1 Goal	(76)
117	26/04/86	Dundee	Home	League	2–0	1 Goal	(77)
118	30/04/86	Motherwell	Away	League	2–0	2 Goals	(79)
119	03/05/86	St Mirren	Away	League	5–0	2 Goals	(81)

+ AET Hibernian won 4–3 on penalties

SEASON 1986–87

Scottish League Premier Division

120	09/08/86	Dundee	Home	League	1–0		
121	13/08/86	Motherwell	Away	League	4–0	2 Goals	(83)
122	16/08/86	Clydebank	Away	League	1–0		
123	20/08/86	Airdrieonians	Home	S Lge Cup	2–0	2 Goals	(85)
124	23/08/86	Aberdeen	Home	League	1–1		
125	27/08/86	Dumbarton	Home	S Lge Cup	3–0		
126	31/08/86	Rangers	Away	League	0–1		
127	03/09/86	Aberdeen	Away	S Lge Cup	1–1+		
Sub+23	06/09/86	Hamilton Academical	Home	League	4–1		
128	13/09/86	Dundee United	Away	League	2–2	1 Goal	(86)
129	17/09/86	Shamrock Rovers	Away	Eur Cup	1–0		
130	20/09/86	Hibernian	Home	League	5–1	2 Goals	(88)
131	23/09/86	Motherwell	Hampden	S Lge Cup	2–2#	1 Goal	(89)
132	27/09/86	Falkirk	Away	League	1–0		
133	01/10/86	Shamrock Rovers	Home	Eur Cup	2–0		
134	04/10/86	St Mirren	Home	League	2–0	1 Goal	(90)
135	08/10/86	Heart of Midlothian	Home	League	2–0	1 Goal	(91)
136	11/10/86	Dundee	Away	League	3–0	1 Goal	(92)
137	18/10/86	Motherwell	Home	League	3–1		
138	22/10/86	Dinamo Kijev	Home	Eur Cup	1–1		
139	26/10/86	Rangers	Hampden	S Lge Cup	1–2	1 Goal	(93)
140	29/10/86	Clydebank	Home	League	6–0	2 Goals	(95)
141	01/11/86	Rangers	Home	League	1–1	1 Goal	(96)
142	05/11/86	Dinamo Kijev	Away	Eur Cup	1–3		
143	08/11/86	Hamilton Academical	Away	League	2–1	1 Goal	(97)
144	15/11/86	Dundee United	Home	League	1–0		
145	19/11/86	Hibernian	Away	League	1–0	1 Goal	(98)
146	22/11/86	Falkirk	Home	League	4–2		
147	26/11/86	Aberdeen	Away	League	1–1	1 Goal	(99)
148	29/11/86	St Mirren	Away	League	1–0		
149	03/12/86	Heart of Midlothian	Away	League	0–1		
150	06/12/86	Dundee	Home	League	2–0		
151	13/12/86	Motherwell	Away	League	1–1	1 Goal	(100)
152	20/12/86	Aberdeen	Home	League	1–1		
153	27/12/86	Clydebank	Away	League	1–1	1 Goal	(101)
154	01/01/87	Rangers	Away	League	0–2		
155	03/01/87	Hamilton Academical	Home	League	8–3	4 Goals	(105)
156	10/01/87	Dundee United	Away	League	2–3	2 Goals	(107)
157	21/01/87	Hibernian	Home	League	1–0		

158	24/01/87	Falkirk	Away	League	2–1		
159	01/02/87	Aberdeen	Away	S Cup	2–2	1 Goal	(108)
160	04/02/87	Aberdeen	Home	S Cup	0–0*		
161	07/02/87	St Mirren	Home	League	3–0	1 Goal	(109)
162	09/02/87	Aberdeen	Neutral	S Cup	1–0	1 Goal	(110)
163	14/02/87	Heart of Midlothian	Home	League	1–1	1 Goal	(111)
164	21/02/87	Heart of Midlothian	Away	S Cup	0–1		
165	28/02/87	Dundee	Away	League	1–4	1 Goal	(112)
166	07/03/87	Motherwell	Home	League	3–1		
167	14/03/87	Aberdeen	Away	League	0–1		
168	21/03/87	Clydebank	Home	League	3–0	2 Goals	(114)
169	28/03/87	Hamilton Academical	Away	League	3–2	1 Goal	(115)
170	04/04/87	Rangers	Home	League	3–1	2 Goals	(117)
171	11/04/87	Hibernian	Away	League	4–1	1 Goal	(118)
172	18/04/87	Dundee United	Home	League	1–1	1 Goal	(119)
173	25/04/87	St Mirren	Away	League	3–1	2 Goals	(121)
174	02/05/87	Falkirk	Home	League	1–2	1 Goal	(122)
175	09/05/87	Heart of Midlothian	Away	League	0–1		

+ AET Celtic won 4–2 on penalties
# AET Celtic won 5–4 on penalties

SEASON 1987–88

Manchester United – League Division One

1	15/08/87	Southampton	Away	League	2–2		
2	19/08/87	Arsenal	Home	League	0–0		
3	22/08/87	Watford	Home	League	2–0	1 Goal	(1)
4	29/08/87	Charlton Athletic	Away	League	3–1	1 Goal	(2)
5	31/08/87	Chelsea	Home	League	3–1	1 Goal	(3)
6	05/09/87	Coventry City	Away	League	0–0		
7	12/09/87	Newcastle United	Home	League	2–2	1 Goal	(4)
8	19/09/87	Everton	Away	League	1–2		
9	23/09/87	Hull City	Home	Lge Cup	5–0	1 Goal	(5)
10	26/09/87	Tottenham Hotspur	Home	League	1–0	1 Goal	(6)
11	03/10/87	Luton Town	Away	League	1–1	1 Goal	(7)
12	07/10/87	Hull City	Away	Lge Cup	1–0	1 Goal	(8)
13	10/10/87	Sheffield Wednesday	Away	League	4–2	2 Goals	(10)
14	17/10/87	Norwich City	Home	League	2–1		
15	25/10/87	West Ham United	Away	League	1–1		
16	28/10/87	Crystal Palace	Home	Lge Cup	2–1	2 Goals	(12)
17	31/10/87	Nottingham Forest	Home	League	2–2		
18	15/11/87	Liverpool	Home	League	1–1		
19	18/11/87	Bury	Away	Lge Cup	2–1	1 Goal	(13)
20	21/11/87	Wimbledon	Away	League	1–2		
21	05/12/87	Queens Park Rangers	Away	League	2–0		
22	12/12/87	Oxford United	Home	League	3–1		
23	19/12/87	Portsmouth	Away	League	2–1	1 Goal	(14)
24	26/12/87	Newcastle United	Away	League	0–1		
25	28/12/87	Everton	Home	League	2–1	2 Goals	(16)
26	01/01/88	Charlton Athletic	Home	League	0–0		
27	02/01/88	Watford	Away	League	1–0	1 Goal	(17)
28	10/01/88	Ipswich Town	Away	FA Cup	2–1		
29	16/01/88	Southampton	Home	League	0–2		
30	20/01/88	Oxford United	Away	Lge Cup	0–2		
31	24/01/88	Arsenal	Away	League	1–1	1 Goal	(18)
32	30/01/88	Chelsea	Home	FA Cup	2–0	1 Goal	(19)
33	06/02/88	Coventry City	Home	League	1–0		
34	10/02/88	Derby County	Away	League	2–1		
35	13/02/88	Chelsea	Away	League	2–1		
36	20/02/88	Arsenal	Away	FA Cup	1–2	1 Goal	(20)
37	23/02/88	Tottenham Hotspur	Away	League	1–1	1 Goal	(21)
38	05/03/88	Norwich City	Away	League	0–1		
39	12/03/88	Sheffield Wednesday	Neutral	League	4–1	2 Goals	(23)
40	19/03/88	Nottingham Forest	Away	League	0–0		
41	26/03/88	West Ham United	Home	League	3–1		
42	02/04/88	Derby County	Home	League	4–1	3 Goals	(26)
43	04/04/88	Liverpool	Away	League	3–3		
44	12/04/88	Luton Town	Home	League	3–0	1 Goal	(27)
45	30/04/88	Queens Park Rangers	Home	League	2–1		
46	02/05/88	Oxford United	Away	League	2–0		
47	07/05/88	Portsmouth	Home	League	4–1	2 Goals	(29)
48	09/05/88	Wimbledon	Home	League	2–1	2 Goals	(31)

SEASON 1988–89

League Division One

49	27/08/88	Queens Park Rangers	Home	League	0–0			
50	29/08/88	Everton	Home	MCC Trophy	1–0			
51	03/09/88	Liverpool	Away	League	0–1			
52	10/09/88	Middlesbrough	Home	League	1–0			
53	17/09/88	Luton Town	Away	League	2–0			
54	21/09/88	Newcastle United	Home	MCC Trophy	2–0*	1 Goal	(32)	
55	24/09/88	West Ham United	Home	League	2–0			
56	28/09/88	Rotherham United	Away	Lge Cup	1–0			
57	01/10/88	Tottenham Hotspur	Away	League	2–2	1 Goal	(33)	
58	09/10/88	Arsenal	Neutral	MCC Trophy	1–2			
59	12/10/88	Rotherham United	Home	Lge Cup	5–0	3 Goals	(36)	
60	22/10/88	Wimbledon	Away	League	1–1			
61	26/10/88	Norwich City	Home	League	1–2			
62	30/10/88	Everton	Away	League	1–1			
63	02/11/88	Wimbledon	Away	Lge Cup	1–2			
64	05/11/88	Aston Villa	Home	League	1–1			
65	12/11/88	Derby County	Away	League	2–2	1 Goal	(37)	
66	19/11/88	Southampton	Home	League	2–2			
67	23/11/88	Sheffield Wednesday	Home	League	1–1			
68	27/11/88	Newcastle United	Away	League	0–0			
69	03/12/88	Charlton Athletic	Home	League	3–0	1 Goal	(38)	
70	10/12/88	Coventry City	Away	League	0–1			
71	17/12/88	Arsenal	Away	League	1–2			
72	26/12/88	Nottingham Forest	Home	League	2–0			
73	01/01/89	Liverpool	Home	League	3–1	1 Goal	(39)	
74	02/01/89	Middlesbrough	Away	League	0–1			
75	07/01/89	Queens Park Rangers	Home	FA Cup	0–0			
76	11/01/89	Queens Park Rangers	Away	FA Cup	2–2*			
77	14/01/89	Millwall	Home	League	3–0			
78	21/01/89	West Ham United	Away	League	3–1	1 Goal	(40)	
79	23/01/89	Queens Park Rangers	Home	FA Cup	3–0	2 Goals	(42)	
80	28/01/89	Oxford United	Home	FA Cup	4–0			
81	05/02/89	Tottenham Hotspur	Home	League	1–0	1 Goal	(43)	
82	11/02/89	Sheffield Wednesday	Away	League	2–0	2 Goals	(45)	
83	18/02/89	AFC Bournemouth	Away	FA Cup	1–1			
84	22/02/89	AFC Bournemouth	Home	FA Cup	1–0	1 Goal	(46)	
85	25/02/89	Norwich City	Away	League	1–2			
86	12/03/89	Aston Villa	Away	League	0–0			
87	18/03/89	Nottingham Forest	Home	FA Cup	0–1			
88	25/03/89	Luton Town	Home	League	2–0			
89	27/03/89	Nottingham Forest	Away	League	0–2			
90	02/04/89	Arsenal	Home	League	1–1			
91	08/04/89	Millwall	Away	League	0–0			
92	15/04/89	Derby County	Home	League	0–2			
93	22/04/89	Charlton Athletic	Away	League	0–1			
94	29/04/89	Coventry City	Home	League	0–1			
95	02/05/89	Wimbledon	Home	League	1–0	1 Goal	(47)	
96	06/05/89	Southampton	Away	League	1–2			
97	08/05/89	Queens Park Rangers	Away	League	2–3			
98	10/05/89	Everton	Away	League	1–2			
99	13/05/89	Newcastle United	Home	League	2–0	1 Goal	(48)	

SEASON 1989–90

League Division One

100	19/08/89	Arsenal	Home	League	4–1	1 Goal	(49)	
101	22/08/89	Crystal Palace	Away	League	1–1			
102	26/08/89	Derby County	Away	League	1–2			
103	30/08/89	Norwich City	Home	League	0–2			
104	09/09/89	Everton	Away	League	2–3	1 Goal	(50)	
105	16/09/89	Millwall	Home	League	5–1			
106	20/09/89	Portsmouth	Away	Lge Cup	3–2			
107	23/09/89	Manchester City	Away	League	1–5			
108	03/10/89	Portsmouth	Home	Lge Cup	0–0			
109	14/10/89	Sheffield Wednesday	Home	League	0–0			
110	21/10/89	Coventry City	Away	League	4–1			
111	25/10/89	Tottenham Hotspur	Home	Lge Cup	0–3			
112	28/10/89	Southampton	Home	League	2–1	2 Goals	(52)	
113	04/11/89	Charlton Athletic	Away	League	0–2			
114	12/11/89	Nottingham Forest	Home	League	1–0			
115	18/11/89	Luton Town	Away	League	3–1			
116	25/11/89	Chelsea	Home	League	0–0			

117	03/12/89	Arsenal	Away	League	0–1		
118	09/12/89	Crystal Palace	Home	League	1–2		
119	16/12/89	Tottenham Hotspur	Home	League	0–1		
120	23/12/89	Liverpool	Away	League	0–0		
121	26/12/89	Aston Villa	Away	League	0–3		
122	30/12/89	Wimbledon	Away	League	2–2		
123	01/01/90	Queens Park Rangers	Home	League	0–0		
124	07/01/90	Nottingham Forest	Away	FA Cup	1–0		
125	13/01/90	Derby County	Home	League	1–2		
126	21/01/90	Norwich City	Away	League	0–2		
127	28/01/90	Hereford United	Away	FA Cup	1–0		
128	03/02/90	Manchester City	Home	League	1–1		
129	10/02/90	Millwall	Away	League	2–1		
130	18/02/90	Newcastle United	Away	FA Cup	3–2	1 Goal	(53)
131	24/02/90	Chelsea	Away	League	0–1		
132	03/03/90	Luton Town	Home	League	4–1	1 Goal	(54)
133	11/03/90	Sheffield United	Away	FA Cup	1–0	1 Goal	(55)
134	14/03/90	Everton	Home	League	0–0		
135	18/03/90	Liverpool	Home	League	1–2		
136	21/03/90	Sheffield Wednesday	Away	League	0–1		
137	24/03/90	Southampton	Away	League	2–0		
138	31/03/90	Coventry City	Home	League	3–0		
139	08/04/90	Oldham Athletic	Neutral	FA Cup	3–3*		
140	11/04/90	Oldham Athletic	Neutral	FA Cup	2–1*	1 Goal	(56)
141	14/04/90	Queens Park Rangers	Away	League	2–1		
142	17/04/90	Aston Villa	Home	League	2–0		
143	21/04/90	Tottenham Hotspur	Away	League	1–2		
144	02/05/90	Nottingham Forest	Away	League	0–4		
145	05/05/90	Charlton Athletic	Home	League	1–0		
146	12/05/90	Crystal Palace	Wembley	FA Cup	3–3*		
147	17/05/90	Crystal Palace	Wembley	FA Cup	1–0		

SEASON 1990–91

League Division One

148	18/08/90	Liverpool	Wembley	FA C/S	1–1		
149	25/08/90	Coventry City	Home	League	2–0		
150	28/08/90	Leeds United	Away	League	0–0		
151	01/09/90	Sunderland	Away	League	1–2	1 Goal	(57)
152	04/09/90	Luton Town	Away	League	1–0		
153	08/09/90	Queens Park Rangers	Home	League	3–1	1 Goal	(58)
154	16/09/90	Liverpool	Away	League	0–4		
155	19/09/90	Pecsi MSC	Home	ECW Cup	2–0		
156	22/09/90	Southampton	Home	League	3–2	1 Goal	(59)
157	26/09/90	Halifax Town	Away	Lge Cup	3–1	1 Goal	(60)
158	29/09/90	Nottingham Forest	Home	League	0–1		
159	03/10/90	Pecsi MSC	Away	ECW Cup	1–0	1 Goal	(61)
160	10/10/90	Halifax Town	Home	Lge Cup	2–1		
161	20/10/90	Arsenal	Home	League	0–1		
162	23/10/90	Wrexham	Home	ECW Cup	3–0	1 Goal	(62)
163	27/10/90	Manchester City	Away	League	3–3	2 Goals	(64)
164	31/10/90	Liverpool	Home	Lge Cup	3–1		
165	03/11/90	Crystal Palace	Home	League	2–0		
166	07/11/90	Wrexham	Away	ECW Cup	0–0		
167	10/11/90	Derby County	Away	League	0–0		
168	17/11/90	Sheffield United	Home	League	2–0		
169	25/11/90	Chelsea	Home	League	2–3		
170	27/11/90	Arsenal	Away	Lge Cup	6–2		
171	01/12/90	Everton	Away	League	1–0		
172	08/12/90	Leeds United	Home	League	1–1		
173	15/12/90	Coventry City	Away	League	2–2		
174	22/12/90	Wimbledon	Away	League	3–1		
175	26/12/90	Norwich City	Home	League	3–0	2 Goals	(66)
176	29/12/90	Aston Villa	Home	League	1–1		
177	01/01/91	Tottenham Hotspur	Away	League	2–1	1 Goal	(67)
178	07/01/91	Queens Park Rangers	Home	FA Cup	2–1	1 Goal	(68)
179	12/01/91	Sunderland	Home	League	3–0	1 Goal	(69)
180	16/01/91	Southampton	Away	Lge Cup	1–1		
181	19/01/91	Queens Park Rangers	Away	League	1–1		
182	23/01/91	Southampton	Home	Lge Cup	3–2		
183	26/01/91	Bolton Wanderers	Home	FA Cup	1–0		
184	03/02/91	Liverpool	Home	League	1–1		
185	10/02/91	Leeds United	Home	Lge Cup	2–1	1 Goal	(70)
186	18/02/91	Norwich City	Away	FA Cup	1–2	1 Goal	(71)
187	24/02/91	Leeds United	Away	Lge Cup	1–0		

188	26/02/91	Sheffield United	Away	League	1–2		
189	02/03/91	Everton	Home	League	0–2		
190	06/03/91	Montpellier HSC	Home	ECW Cup	1–1	1 Goal	(72)
191	09/03/91	Chelsea	Away	League	2–3	1 Goal	(73)
192	13/03/91	Southampton	Away	League	1–1		
193	19/03/91	Montpellier HSC	Away	ECW Cup	2–0		
194	23/03/91	Luton Town	Home	League	4–1	1 Goal	(74)
Sub+1	30/03/91	Norwich City	Away	League	3–0		
195	02/04/91	Wimbledon	Home	League	2–1	1 Goal	(75)
196	06/04/91	Aston Villa	Away	League	1–1		
197	10/04/91	CWKS Legia Warszawa	Away	ECW Cup	3–1	1 Goal	(76)
Sub+2	16/04/91	Derby County	Home	League	3–1	1 Goal	(77)
198	21/04/91	Sheffield Wednesday	Wembley	Lge Cup	0–1		
199	24/04/91	CWKS Legia Warszawa	Home	ECW Cup	1–1		
200	04/05/91	Manchester City	Home	League	1–0		
201	06/05/91	Arsenal	Away	League	1–3		
202	15/05/91	FC Barcelona	Neutral	ECW Cup	2–1		
203	20/05/91	Tottenham Hotspur	Home	League	1–1		

SEASON 1991–92

League Division One

204	17/08/91	Notts County	Home	League	2–0		
205	21/08/91	Aston Villa	Away	League	1–0		
206	24/08/91	Everton	Away	League	0–0		
207	28/08/91	Oldham Athletic	Home	League	1–0	1 Goal	(78)
208	31/08/91	Leeds United	Home	League	1–1		
209	03/09/91	Wimbledon	Away	League	2–1		
210	07/09/91	Norwich City	Home	League	3–0	1 Goal	(79)
211	14/09/91	Southampton	Away	League	1–0		
212	18/09/91	AS Athinaikos	Away	ECW Cup	0–0		
Sub+3	21/09/91	Luton Town	Home	League	5–0	2 Goals	(81)
213	25/09/91	Cambridge United	Home	Lge Cup	3–0	1 Goal	(82)
214	28/09/91	Tottenham Hotspur	Away	League	2–1		
215	01/10/91	AS Athinaikos	Home	ECW Cup	2–0	1 Goal	(83)
216	06/10/91	Liverpool	Home	League	0–0		
217	09/10/91	Cambridge United	Away	Lge Cup	1–1	1 Goal	(84)
218	19/10/91	Arsenal	Home	League	1–1		
219	23/10/91	Atletico Madrid	Away	ECW Cup	0–3		
220	26/10/91	Sheffield Wednesday	Away	League	2–3	2 Goals	(86)
221	30/10/91	Portsmouth	Home	Lge Cup	3–1		
222	02/11/91	Sheffield United	Home	League	2–0		
223	06/11/91	Atletico Madrid	Home	ECW Cup	1–1		
224	16/11/91	Manchester City	Away	League	0–0		
225	19/11/91	Crvena Zvezda Beograd	Home	ES Cup	1–0	1 Goal	(87)
226	23/11/91	West Ham United	Home	League	2–1		
227	30/11/91	Crystal Palace	Away	League	3–1	1 Goal	(88)
228	04/12/91	Oldham Athletic	Home	Lge Cup	2–0	1 Goal	(89)
229	07/12/91	Coventry City	Home	League	4–0	1 Goal	(90)
230	15/12/91	Chelsea	Away	League	3–1	1 Goal	(91)
231	26/12/91	Oldham Athletic	Away	League	6–3	2 Goals	(93)
232	29/12/91	Leeds United	Away	League	1–1		
233	01/01/92	Queens Park Rangers	Home	League	1–4	1 Goal	(94)
234	08/01/92	Leeds United	Away	Lge Cup	3–1		
235	11/01/92	Everton	Home	League	1–0		
236	15/01/92	Leeds United	Away	FA Cup	1–0		
237	18/01/92	Notts County	Away	League	1–1		
238	22/01/92	Aston Villa	Home	League	1–0		
239	27/01/92	Southampton	Away	FA Cup	0–0		
240	01/02/92	Arsenal	Away	League	1–1	1 Goal	(95)
241	05/02/92	Southampton	Home	FA Cup	2–2+	1 Goal	(96)
242	08/02/92	Sheffield Wednesday	Home	League	1–1	1 Goal	(97)
243	22/02/92	Crystal Palace	Home	League	2–0		
244	26/02/92	Chelsea	Home	League	1–1		
245	29/02/92	Coventry City	Away	League	0–0		
246	04/03/92	Middlesbrough	Away	Lge Cup	0–0		
247	11/03/92	Middlesbrough	Home	Lge Cup	2–1		
248	14/03/92	Sheffield United	Away	League	2–1	1 Goal	(98)
249	18/03/92	Nottingham Forest	Away	League	0–1		
250	21/03/92	Wimbledon	Home	League	0–0		
251	28/03/92	Queens Park Rangers	Away	League	0–0		
252	31/03/92	Norwich City	Away	League	3–1	1 Goal	(99)
253	07/04/92	Manchester City	Home	League	1–1		
254	12/04/92	Nottingham Forest	Wembley	Lge Cup	1–0	1 Goal	(100)
255	16/04/92	Southampton	Home	League	1–0		

256	18/04/92	Luton Town	Away	League	1–1		
257	20/04/92	Nottingham Forest	Home	League	1–2	1 Goal	(101)
258	22/04/92	West Ham United	Away	League	0–1		
259	26/04/92	Liverpool	Away	League	0–2		
260	02/05/92	Tottenham Hotspur	Home	League	3–1	1 Goal	(102)

+ AET Southampton won 4–2 on penalties

SEASON 1992–93

Premier League

261	15/08/92	Sheffield United	Away	League	1–2		
262	19/08/92	Everton	Home	League	0–3		
263	22/08/92	Ipswich Town	Home	League	1–1		
264	24/08/92	Southampton	Away	League	1–0		
265	29/08/92	Nottingham Forest	Away	League	2–0		
266	02/09/92	Crystal Palace	Home	League	1–0		
267	06/09/92	Leeds United	Home	League	2–0		
268	12/09/92	Everton	Away	League	2–0	1 Goal	(103)
269	16/09/92	Torpedo Moskva	Home	UEFA Cup	0–0		
270	19/09/92	Tottenham Hotspur	Away	League	1–1		
271	23/09/92	Brighton & Hove Albion	Away	Lge Cup	1–1		
272	26/09/92	Queens Park Rangers	Home	League	0–0		
273	29/09/92	Torpedo Moskva	Away	UEFA Cup	0–0+		
274	03/10/92	Middlesbrough	Away	League	1–1		
275	07/10/92	Brighton & Hove Albion	Home	Lge Cup	1–0		
276	18/10/92	Liverpool	Home	League	2–2		
277	24/10/92	Blackburn Rovers	Away	League	0–0		
278	28/10/92	Aston Villa	Away	Lge Cup	0–1		
279	31/10/92	Wimbledon	Home	League	0–1		
Sub+4	07/11/92	Aston Villa	Away	League	0–1		
280	21/11/92	Oldham Athletic	Home	League	3–0	2 Goals	(105)
281	28/11/92	Arsenal	Away	League	1–0		
282	06/12/92	Manchester City	Home	League	2–1		
283	12/12/92	Norwich City	Home	League	1–0		
284	19/12/92	Chelsea	Away	League	1–1		
285	26/12/92	Sheffield Wednesday	Away	League	3–3	2 Goals	(107)
286	28/12/92	Coventry City	Home	League	5–0		
287	05/01/93	Bury	Home	FA Cup	2–0		
288	09/01/93	Tottenham Hotspur	Home	League	4–1	1 Goal	(108)
289	18/01/93	Queens Park Rangers	Away	League	3–1		
290	23/01/93	Brighton & Hove Albion	Home	FA Cup	1–0		
291	27/01/93	Nottingham Forest	Home	League	2–0		
292	30/01/93	Ipswich Town	Away	League	1–2	1 Goal	(109)
293	06/02/93	Sheffield United	Home	League	2–1	1 Goal	(110)
294	08/02/93	Leeds United	Away	League	0–0		
295	14/02/93	Sheffield United	Away	FA Cup	1–2		
296	20/02/93	Southampton	Home	League	2–1		
297	27/02/93	Middlesbrough	Home	League	3–0		
298	06/03/93	Liverpool	Away	League	2–1	1 Goal	(111)
299	09/03/93	Oldham Athletic	Away	League	0–1		
300	14/03/93	Aston Villa	Home	League	1–1		
301	20/03/93	Manchester City	Away	League	1–1		
302	24/03/93	Arsenal	Home	League	0–0		
303	05/04/93	Norwich City	Away	League	3–1		
304	10/04/93	Sheffield Wednesday	Home	League	2–1		
305	12/04/93	Coventry City	Away	League	1–0		
306	17/04/93	Chelsea	Home	League	3–0		
307	21/04/93	Crystal Palace	Away	League	2–0		
308	03/05/93	Blackburn Rovers	Home	League	3–1		
309	09/05/93	Wimbledon	Away	League	2–1		

+ AET Torpedo Moskva won 4–3 on penalties

SEASON 1993–94

Premier League

Sub+5	18/08/93	Sheffield United	Home	League	3–0		
Sub+6	21/08/93	Newcastle United	Home	League	1–1		
Sub+7	28/08/93	Southampton	Away	League	3–1		
Sub+8	01/09/93	West Ham United	Home	League	3–0		
Sub+9	11/09/93	Chelsea	Away	League	0–1		

Sub+10	19/09/93	Arsenal	Home	League	1–0		
310	22/09/93	Stoke City	Away	Lge Cup	1–2		
Sub+11	25/09/93	Swindon Town	Home	League	4–2		
311	06/10/93	Stoke City	Home	Lge Cup	2–0	1 Goal	(112)
Sub+12	16/10/93	Tottenham Hotspur	Home	League	2–1		
312	23/10/93	Everton	Away	League	1–0		
313	27/10/93	Leicester City	Home	Lge Cup	5–1	1 Goal	(113)
314	04/12/93	Norwich City	Home	League	2–2	1 Goal	(114)
315	07/12/93	Sheffield United	Away	League	3–0		
316	11/12/93	Newcastle United	Away	League	1–1		
Sub+13	26/12/93	Blackburn Rovers	Home	League	1–1		
Sub+14	29/12/93	Oldham Athletic	Away	League	5–2		
317	01/01/94	Leeds United	Home	League	0–0		
318	04/01/94	Liverpool	Away	League	3–3		
319	12/01/94	Portsmouth	Home	Lge Cup	2–2	1 Goal	(115)
Sub+15	15/01/94	Tottenham Hotspur	Away	League	1–0		
320	26/01/94	Portsmouth	Away	Lge Cup	1–0		
Sub+16	30/01/94	Norwich City	Away	FA Cup	2–0		
Sub+17	20/02/94	Wimbledon	Away	FA Cup	3–0		
321	25/02/94	West Ham United	Away	League	2–2		
322	02/03/94	Sheffield Wednesday	Away	Lge Cup	4–1	1 Goal	(116)
323	05/03/94	Chelsea	Home	League	0–1		
Sub+18	16/03/94	Sheffield Wednesday	Home	League	5–0		
324	19/03/94	Swindon Town	Away	League	2–2		
Sub+19	22/03/94	Arsenal	Away	League	2–2		
Sub+20	27/03/94 ·	Aston Villa	Wembley	Lge Cup	1–3		
Sub+21	02/04/94	Blackburn Rovers	Away	League	0–2		
325	04/04/94	Oldham Athletic	Home	League	3–2		
326	10/04/94	Oldham Athletic	Wembley	FA Cup	1–1*		
Sub+22	13/04/94	Oldham Athletic	Neutral	FA Cup	4–1		
327	16/04/94	Wimbledon	Away	League	0–1		
328	08/05/94	Coventry City	Home	League	0–0		
Sub+23	14/05/94	Chelsea	Wembley	FA Cup	4–0	1 Goal	(117)

+ Manchester United won 5–4 on penalties

SEASON 1994–95

Premier League

329	14/08/94	Blackburn Rovers	Wembley	FA C/S	2–0		
330	20/08/94	Queens Park Rangers	Home	League	2–0	1 Goal	(118)
331	22/08/94	Nottingham Forest	Away	League	1–1		
332	27/08/94	Tottenham Hotspur	Away	League	1–0		
333	31/08/94	Wimbledon	Home	League	3–0	1 Goal	(119)
334	11/09/94	Leeds United	Away	League	1–2		
Sub+24	17/09/94	Liverpool	Home	League	2–0	1 Goal	(120)
335	21/09/94	Port Vale	Away	Lge Cup	2–1		
336	24/09/94	Ipswich Town	Away	League	2–3		
Sub+25	01/10/94	Everton	Home	League	2–0		
337	05/10/94	Port Vale	Home	Lge Cup	2–0	1 Goal	(121)
338	08/10/94	Sheffield Wednesday	Away	League	0–1		
Sub+26	23/10/94	Blackburn Rovers	Away	League	4–2		
339	26/10/94	Newcastle United	Away	Lge Cup	0–2		
340	29/10/94	Newcastle United	Home	League	2–0		
Sub+27	06/11/94	Aston Villa	Away	League	2–1		
341	10/11/94	Manchester City	Home	League	5–0		
342	19/11/94	Crystal Palace	Home	League	3–0		
343	23/11/94	IFK Goteborg	Away	Eur Cup	1–3		
344	26/11/94	Arsenal	Away	League	0–0		
345	03/12/94	Norwich City	Home	League	1–0		
346	07/12/94	Galatasaray SK	Home	Eur Cup	4–0		
347	10/12/94	Queens Park Rangers	Away	League	3–2		
348	17/12/94	Nottingham Forest	Home	League	1–2		
349	26/12/94	Chelsea	Away	League	3–2	1 Goal	(122)
350	28/12/94	Leicester City	Home	League	1–1		
351	31/12/94	Southampton	Away	League	2–2		
Sub+28	03/01/95	Coventry City	Home	League	2–0		
352	09/01/95	Sheffield United	Away	FA Cup	2–0		
353	15/01/95	Newcastle United	Away	League	1–1		
354	22/01/95	Blackburn Rovers	Home	League	1–0		
355	25/01/95	Crystal Palace	Away	League	1–1		
356	28/01/95	Wrexham	Home	FA Cup	5–2	1 Goal	(123)
357	04/02/95	Aston Villa	Home	League	1–0		
358	11/02/95	Manchester City	Away	League	3–0		

359	19/02/95	Leeds United	Home	FA Cup	3–1	1 Goal	(124)
360	22/02/95	Norwich City	Away	League	2–0		
361	25/02/95	Everton	Away	League	1–0		
362	04/03/95	Ipswich Town	Home	League	9–0		
363	07/03/95	Wimbledon	Away	League	1–0		
364	12/03/95	Queens Park Rangers	Home	FA Cup	2–0		
365	15/03/95	Tottenham Hotspur	Home	League	0–0		
366	19/03/95	Liverpool	Away	League	0–2		
367	02/04/95	Leeds United	Home	League	0–0		
368	09/04/95	Crystal Palace	Neutral	FA Cup	2–2*		
Sub+29	12/04/95	Crystal Palace	Neutral	FA Cup	2–0		
369	15/04/95	Leicester City	Away	League	4–0		
370	17/04/95	Chelsea	Home	League	0–0		
371	01/05/95	Coventry City	Away	League	3–2		
372	07/05/95	Sheffield Wednesday	Home	League	1–0		
373	10/05/95	Southampton	Home	League	2–1		
374	14/05/95	West Ham United	Away	League	1–1	1 Goal	(125)
375	20/05/95	Everton	Wembley	FA Cup	0–1		

SEASON 1995–96

Premier League

376	19/08/95	Aston Villa	Away	League	1–3		
377	23/08/95	West Ham United	Home	League	2–0		
378	20/09/95	York City	Home	Lge Cup	0–3		
379	23/09/95	Sheffield Wednesday	Away	League	0–0		
Sub+30	14/10/95	Manchester City	Home	League	1–0		
Sub+31	21/10/95	Chelsea	Away	League	4–1	1 Goal	(126)
Sub+32	28/10/95	Middlesbrough	Home	League	2–0		
Sub+33	04/11/95	Arsenal	Away	League	0–1		
Sub+34	18/11/95	Southampton	Home	League	4–1		
380	22/11/95	Coventry City	Away	League	4–0	2 Goals	(128)
381	27/11/95	Nottingham Forest	Away	League	1–1		
382	02/12/95	Chelsea	Home	League	1–1		
383	09/12/95	Sheffield Wednesday	Home	League	2–2		
384	17/12/95	Liverpool	Away	League	0–2		
385	24/12/95	Leeds United	Away	League	1–3		
Sub+35	27/12/95	Newcastle United	Home	League	2–0		
Sub+36	30/12/95	Queens Park Rangers	Home	League	2–1		
Sub+37	01/01/96	Tottenham Hotspur	Away	League	1–4		
Sub+38	25/02/96	Bolton Wanderers	Home	League	6–0		
386	16/03/96	Queens Park Rangers	Away	League	1–1		
Sub+39	24/03/96	Tottenham Hotspur	Home	League	1–0		
387	08/04/96	Coventry City	Home	League	1–0		
388	17/04/96	Leeds United	Home	League	1–0		

SEASON 1996–97

Premier League

Sub+40	17/08/96	Wimbledon	Away	League	3–0		
Sub+41	21/08/96	Everton	Home	League	2–2		
389	25/08/96	Blackburn Rovers	Home	League	2–2		
Sub+42	07/09/96	Leeds United	Away	League	4–0		
Sub+43	11/09/96	Juventus FC	Away	Eur Cup	0–1		
Sub+44	14/09/96	Nottingham Forest	Home	League	4–1		
Sub+45	20/10/96	Newcastle United	Away	League	0–5		
390	23/10/96	Swindon Town	Home	Lge Cup	2–1		
Sub+46	26/10/96	Southampton	Away	League	3–6		
Sub+47	20/11/96	Juventus FC	Home	Eur Cup	0–1		
Sub+48	23/11/96	Middlesbrough	Away	League	2–2		
391	27/11/96	Leicester City	Away	Lge Cup	0–2		
Sub+49	04/12/96	SK Rapid Wien	Away	Eur Cup	0–0		
392	08/12/96	West Ham United	Away	League	2–2		
Sub+50	21/12/96	Sunderland	Home	League	5–0		
Sub+51	26/12/96	Nottingham Forest	Away	League	4–0		
Sub+52	05/01/97	Tottenham Hotspur	Home	FA Cup	2–0		
393	25/01/97	Wimbledon	Home	FA Cup	1–1		
Sub+53	04/02/97	Wimbledon	Away	FA Cup	0–1		
Sub+54	19/02/97	Arsenal	Away	League	2–1		
394	22/02/97	Chelsea	Away	League	1–1		
Sub+55	01/03/97	Coventry City	Home	League	3–1		
395	08/03/97	Sunderland	Away	League	1–2		
Sub+56	22/03/97	Everton	Away	League	2–0		

Sub+57	19/04/97	Liverpool	Away	League	3–1	
Sub+58	08/05/97	Newcastle United	Home	League	0–0	
Sub+59	11/05/97	West Ham United	Home	League	2–0	

INTERNATIONAL APPEARANCES – SCOTLAND

1	12/11/86	Luxembourg	Hampden Park	3–0	ECQ		
2	18/02/87	Republic of Ireland	Hampden Park	0–1	ECQ		
3	23/05/87	England	Hampden Park	0–0	RC		
Sub 4	26/05/87	Brazil	Hampden Park	0–2	RC		
5	11/11/87	Bulgaria	Sofia	1–0	ECQ		
Sub 6	22/03/88	Malta	Valletta	1–1	F		
Sub 7	27/04/88	Spain	Madrid	0–0	F		
8	14/09/88	Norway	Oslo	2–1	WCQ		
9	19/10/88	Yugoslavia	Hampden Park	1–1	WCQ		
Sub 10	22/12/88	Italy	Perugia	0–2	F		
11	08/02/89	Cyprus	Limassol	3–2	WCQ		
Sub 12	08/03/89	France	Hampden Park	2–0	WCQ		
Sub 13	15/11/89	Norway	Hampden Park	1–1	WCQ		
Sub 14	28/03/90	Argentina	Hampden Park	1–0	F		
15	14/11/90	Bulgaria	Sofia	1–1	ECQ		
16	27/03/91	Bulgaria	Hampden Park	1–1	ECQ		
17	01/05/91	San Marino	Serravalle	2–0	ECQ		
Sub 18	11/09/91	Switzerland	Berne	2–2	ECQ		
19	16/10/91	Romania	Bucharest	0–1	ECQ		
20	19/02/92	Northern Ireland	Hampden Park	1–0	F		
21	17/05/92	USA	Denver	1–0	F		
Sub 22	21/05/92	Canada	Toronto	3–1	F		
23	03/06/92	Norway	Oslo	0–0	F		
24	12/06/92	Holland	Gothenburg	0–1	EC		
25	15/06/92	Germany	Norrkoping	0–2	EC		
26	18/06/92	CIS	Norrkoping	3–0	EC	1 Goal	(1)
27	09/09/92	Switzerland	Berne	1–3	WCQ		
Sub 28	14/10/92	Portugal	Ibrox Park	0–0	WCQ		
29	19/05/93	Estonia	Tallinn	3–0	WCQ		
30	02/06/93	Estonia	Pittodrie	3–1	WCQ	1 Goal	(2)

APPEARANCES AND GOALS PER SEASON

SEASON 81–82	GAMES	GOALS
Scottish League	7+4	4
Scottish League Cup	4	0
TOTAL	**11+4**	**4**

SEASON 82–83	GAMES	GOALS
Scottish League	26+3	11
Scottish Cup	2	1
Scottish League Cup	5+1	4
TOTAL	**33+4**	**16**

SEASON 83–84	GAMES	GOALS
Scottish League	28+7	23
Scottish Cup	5	6
Scottish League Cup	8+1	1
UEFA Cup	3+2	1
TOTAL	**44+10**	**31**

SEASON 84–85	GAMES	GOALS
Scottish League	25+7	19
Scottish Cup	3+3	0
Scottish League Cup	3	3
European Cup Winners Cup	5	2
TOTAL	**36+10**	**24**

SEASON 85–86	GAMES	GOALS
Scottish League	33+1	22
Scottish Cup	2+1	3
Scottish League Cup	3	1
European Cup Winners Cup	1	0
TOTAL	**39+2**	**26**

SEASON 86–87	GAMES	GOALS
Scottish League	43+1	35
Scottish Cup	4	2
Scottish League Cup	5	4
European Cup	4	0
TOTAL	**56+1**	**41**

SEASON 87–88	GAMES	GOALS
League	40	24
FA Cup	3	2
League Cup	5	5
TOTAL	**48**	**31**

SEASON 88–89	GAMES	GOALS
League	38	10
FA Cup	7	3
League Cup	3	3
Mercantile Credit Centenary Trophy	3	1
TOTAL	**51**	**17**

SEASON 89–90	GAMES	GOALS
League	37	5
FA Cup	8	3
League Cup	3	0
TOTAL	**48**	**8**

SEASON 90–91	GAMES	GOALS
League	34+2	13
FA Cup	3	2
League Cup	9	2
European Cup Winners Cup	9	4
FA Charity Shield	1	0
TOTAL	**56+2**	**21**

SEASON 91–92	GAMES	GOALS
League	41+1	18
FA Cup	3	1
League Cup	8	4
European Cup Winners Cup	4	1
European Super Cup	1	1
TOTAL	**57+1**	**25**

SEASON 92–93	GAMES	GOALS
League	41+1	9
FA Cup	3	0
League Cup	3	0
UEFA Cup	2	0
TOTAL	**49+1**	**9**

SEASON 93–94	GAMES	GOALS
League	12+14	1
FA Cup	1+4	1
League Cup	6+1	4
TOTAL	**19+19**	**6**

SEASON 94–95	GAMES	GOALS
League	35+5	5
FA Cup	6+1	2
League Cup	3	1
European Cup	2	0
FA Charity Shield	1	0
TOTAL	**47+6**	**8**

SEASON 95–96	GAMES	GOALS
League	12+10	3
League Cup	1	0
TOTAL	**13+10**	**3**

SEASON 96–97	GAMES	GOALS
League	4+15	0
FA Cup	1+2	0
League Cup	2	0
European Cup	0+3	0
TOTAL	**7+20**	**0**

CAREER APPEARANCES AND GOALS

COMPETITION	GAMES	TOTAL	GOALS
League	294+48	342	88
FA Cup	35+7	42	14
League Cup	43+1	44	19
Mercantile Credit Centenary Trophy	3	3	1
FA Charity Shield	2	2	0
European Cup	6+3	9	0
European Cup Winners Cup	19	19	7
UEFA Cup	5+2	7	1
European Super Cup	1	1	1
Scottish League	162+23	185	114
Scottish Cup	16+4	20	12
Scottish League Cup	28+2	30	13
Internationals	20+10	30	2
TOTAL	**634+100**	**734**	**272**

HAT-TRICKS

Motherwell

1	3	Clyde (sub)	25/08/82	Home	S Lge Cup	3–1
2	3	Rangers	03/01/83	Home	League	3–0

Celtic

1	4	Dundee	24/09/83	Away	League	6–2
2	3	Heart of Midlothian	25/02/84	Home	League	4–1
3	3	Heart of Midlothian	17/11/84	Away	League	5–1
4	4	Morton	23/03/85	Away	League	7–2
5	3	Clydebank	29/03/86	Away	League	5–0
6	4	Hamilton Academical	03/01/87	Home	League	8–3

Manchester United

1	3	Derby County	02/04/88	Home	League	4–1
2	3	Rotherham United	12/10/88	Home	Lge Cup	5–0

League: 1
League Cup: 1
Scottish League: 7
Scottish League Cup: 1
TOTAL: 10

HONOURS

Winners medals
Premier League Championship: 92/93, 93/94, 95/96, 96/97
FA Cup: 89/90, 93/94
League Cup: 91/92
European Cup Winners Cup: 90/91
European Super Cup: 91/92
FA Charity Shield: 90/91, 93/94, 94/95, 96/97*
Scottish Premier Division Championship: 85/86
Scottish League Division One Championship: 81/82
Scottish Cup: 84/85

Runner-up medals
Premier League Championship: 94/95
League Division One Championship: 87/88, 91/92
FA Cup: 94/95
League Cup: 90/91, 93/94
Mercantile Credit Centenary Trophy: 88/89
Scottish Premier Division Championship: 83/84, 84/85, 86/87
Scottish Cup: 83/84
Scottish League Cup: 83/84, 86/87

* Non-playing substitute

ALLY MCCOIST

Born: 24/09/62 – Bellshill
Height: 5.10
Weight: 12.00 (96–97)

Clubs
St Johnstone: **1979–81** – Matches: **57+6** – Goals: **23**
Sunderland: **1981–83** – Matches: **46+19** – Goals: **9**
Rangers: **1983–97** – Matches: **485+70** – Goals: **339**

Country
Scotland: **1986–97** – Matches: **42+16** – Goals: **19**

SEASON 1978–79

St Johnstone – Scottish League Division One

1	07/04/79	Raith Rovers	Home	League	3–0
2	14/04/79	Ayr United	Away	League	2–4
3	18/04/79	Clydebank	Away	League	0–1
4	21/04/79	Stirling Albion	Home	League	0–2

SEASON 1979–80

Scottish League Division One

Sub+1	11/08/79	Hamilton Academical	Away	League	2–2		
5	25/08/79	Arbroath	Away	League	2–2		
Sub+2	08/09/79	Raith Rovers	Home	League	2–2		
6	15/12/79	Dunfermline Athletic	Home	League	1–3		
Sub+3	12/01/80	Berwick Rangers	Away	League	0–5		
7	30/01/80	Airdrieonians	Away	S Cup	1–3		
Sub+4	09/02/80	Motherwell	Away	League	2–1		
Sub+5	16/02/80	Dumbarton	Away	League	1–0		
Sub+6	23/02/80	Dunfermline Athletic	Away	League	0–1		
8	02/04/80	Clyde	Home	League	1–2		
9	05/04/80	Ayr United	Away	League	2–2		
10	12/04/80	Clydebank	Home	League	3–1		
11	16/04/80	Heart of Midlothian	Home	League	0–1		
12	19/04/80	Dumbarton	Away	League	2–5		
13	23/04/80	Ayr United	Home	League	2–1		
14	26/04/80	Heart of Midlothian	Home	League	0–3		

SEASON 1980–81

Scottish League Division One

15	09/08/80	Stirling Albion	Home	League	0–1		
16	13/08/80	Clydebank	Home	S Lge Cup	0–2		
17	16/08/80	Dumbarton	Away	League	3–0	1 Goal	(1)
18	20/08/80	Clydebank	Away	S Lge Cup	0–0		
19	23/08/80	Dundee	Home	League	1–0	1 Goal	(2)
20	03/09/80	East Stirling	Home	League	0–2		
21	06/09/80	Raith Rovers	Away	League	0–0		
22	09/09/80	Berwick Rangers	Away	League	1–0	1 Goal	(3)
23	13/09/80	Hamilton Academical	Home	League	1–0		
24	17/09/80	Clydebank	Home	League	1–1		
25	20/09/80	Dunfermline Athletic	Away	League	2–0	2 Goals	(5)
26	27/09/80	Falkirk	Home	League	0–0		
27	04/10/80	Motherwell	Away	League	2–2	1 Goal	(6)
28	11/10/80	Ayr United	Away	League	0–0		
29	18/10/80	Hibernian	Home	League	1–2		
30	25/10/80	Hamilton Academical	Away	League	3–0		
31	01/11/80	Raith Rovers	Home	League	0–3		
32	08/11/80	Clydebank	Away	League	2–0	1 Goal	(7)
33	22/11/80	Falkirk	Away	League	3–0		
34	29/11/80	Motherwell	Home	League	2–2	2 Goals	(9)
35	06/12/80	Ayr United	Home	League	1–0	1 Goal	(10)
36	13/12/80	Hibernian	Away	League	0–4		
37	20/12/80	East Stirling	Away	League	1–1		
38	27/12/80	Dumbarton	Home	League	2–0		

39	01/01/81	Dundee	Away	League	2–2		
40	03/01/81	Berwick Rangers	Home	League	1–0	1 Goal	(11)
41	10/01/81	Stirling Albion	Away	League	1–0		
42	17/01/81	Ayr United	Away	League	3–3	2 Goals	(13)
43	24/01/81	Hamilton Academical	Away	S Cup	3–0		
44	31/01/81	Hamilton Academical	Home	League	2–1	1 Goal	(14)
45	14/02/81	Rangers	Home	S Cup	3–3		
46	18/02/81	Rangers	Away	S Cup	1–3	1 Goal	(15)
47	21/02/81	Dunfermline Athletic	Home	League	4–1	1 Goal	(16)
48	28/02/81	Motherwell	Away	League	2–3		
49	07/03/81	Falkirk	Home	League	2–1		
50	18/03/81	Hibernian	Away	League	2–1		
51	21/03/81	Berwick Rangers	Home	League	6–2	4 Goals	(20)
52	24/03/81	Clydebank	Away	League	3–1	1 Goal	(21)
53	28/03/81	Dumbarton	Home	League	2–1		
54	04/04/81	Dundee	Away	League	1–4	1 Goal	(22)
55	11/04/81	Raith Rovers	Home	League	2–0		
56	18/04/81	East Stirling	Away	League	2–2	1 Goal	(23)
57	25/04/81	Stirling Albion	Home	League	1–0		

SEASON 1981–82

Sunderland – League Division One

Sub+1	29/08/81	Ipswich Town	Away	League	3–3		
Sub+2	02/09/81	Aston Villa	Home	League	2–1		
Sub+3	05/09/81	West Ham United	Home	League	0–2		
1	12/09/81	Arsenal	Away	League	1–1		
2	19/09/81	Wolverhampton Wanderers	Home	League	0–0		
Sub+4	23/09/81	Nottingham Forest	Away	League	0–2		
Sub+5	26/09/81	Swansea City	Away	League	0–2		
3	03/10/81	Coventry City	Home	League	0–0		
4	07/10/81	Rotherham United	Home	Lge Cup	2–0		
Sub+6	10/10/81	Notts County	Away	League	0–2		
5	17/10/81	Tottenham Hotspur	Home	League	0–2		
6	24/10/81	Leeds United	Away	League	0–1		
7	31/10/81	Liverpool	Home	League	0–2		
8	14/11/81	Middlesbrough	Away	League	0–0		
9	21/11/81	Everton	Away	League	2–1		
10	25/11/81	Nottingham Forest	Home	League	2–3	1 Goal	(1)
11	28/11/81	West Bromwich Albion	Home	League	1–2		
12	05/12/81	Brighton & Hove Albion	Away	League	1–2		
13	19/12/81	Manchester City	Away	League	3–2		
14	02/01/81	Rotherham United	Away	FA Cup	1–1		
15	18/01/81	Rotherham United	Home	FA Cup	1–0		
16	23/01/81	Liverpool	Home	FA Cup	0–3		
Sub+7	06/02/82	Arsenal	Home	League	0–0		
Sub+8	16/02/82	Birmingham City	Away	League	0–2		
17	20/02/82	Swansea City	Home	League	0–1		
18	27/02/82	Notts County	Home	League	1–1		
19	10/03/82	Southampton	Home	League	2–0	1 Goal	(2)
20	13/03/82	Leeds United	Home	League	0–1		
21	20/03/82	Liverpool	Away	League	0–1		
22	27/03/82	Manchester United	Away	League	0–0		
23	03/04/82	Middlesbrough	Home	League	0–2		
Sub+9	27/04/82	Coventry City	Away	League	1–6		

SEASON 1982–83

League Division One

24	28/08/82	Aston Villa	Away	League	3–1	1 Goal	(3)
25	01/09/82	Notts County	Home	League	1–1		
26	04/09/82	West Ham United	Home	League	1–0		
27	07/09/82	Coventry City	Away	League	0–1		
28	11/09/82	Brighton & Hove Albion	Away	League	2–3	1 Goal	(4)
29	18/09/82	Tottenham Hotspur	Home	League	0–1		
30	25/09/82	Watford	Away	League	0–8		
31	02/10/82	Norwich City	Home	League	4–1	1 Goal	(5)
32	05/10/82	Wolverhampton Wanderers	Away	Lge Cup	1–1		
33	09/10/82	Southampton	Home	League	1–1	1 Goal	(6)
34	16/10/82	Manchester City	Away	League	2–2	1 Goal	(7)
35	23/10/82	Everton	Away	League	1–3	1 Goal	(8)
36	27/10/82	Wolverhampton Wanderers	Home	Lge Cup	5–0	1 Goal	(9)
37	30/10/82	Stoke City	Home	League	2–2		
38	06/11/82	Swansea City	Away	League	0–3		
39	10/11/82	Norwich City	Away	Lge Cup	0–0		

40	13/11/82	Luton Town	Home	League	1–1		
Sub+10	20/11/82	Nottingham Forest	Home	League	0–1		
41	24/11/82	Norwich City	Away	Lge Cup	1–3		
42	27/11/82	Birmingham City	Away	League	1–2		
43	04/12/82	Ipswich Town	Home	League	2–3		
Sub+11	28/12/82	Liverpool	Home	League	0–0		
Sub+12	12/01/82	Manchester City	Away	FA Cup	1–2		
Sub+13	15/01/83	Aston Villa	Home	League	2–0		
Sub+14	22/01/83	Tottenham Hotspur	Away	League	1–1		
Sub+15	19/03/83	Swansea City	Home	League	1–1		
Sub+16	04/04/83	Manchester United	Home	League	0–0		
Sub+17	09/04/83	West Ham United	Away	League	1–2		
44	16/04/83	Norwich City	Away	League	0–2		
Sub+18	23/04/83	Ipswich Town	Away	League	1–4		
Sub+19	02/05/83	Watford	Home	League	2–2		
45	07/05/83	Arsenal	Away	League	1–0		
46	14/05/83	West Bromwich Albion	Home	League	1–1		

SEASON 1983–84

Rangers – Scottish League Premier Division

1	20/08/83	St Mirren	Home	League	1–1		
2	24/08/83	Queen of the South	Home	S Lge Cup	4–0		
3	27/08/83	Queen of the South	Away	S Lge Cup	4–1	1 Goal	(1)
4	31/08/83	Clydebank	Home	S Lge Cup	4–0	2 Goals	(3)
5	03/09/83	Celtic	Away	League	1–2	1 Goal	(4)
6	07/09/83	Heart of Midlothian	Away	S Lge Cup	3–0		
7	14/09/83	Valletta FC	Away	ECW Cup	8–0		
8	10/09/83	Heart of Midlothian	Away	League	1–3		
9	17/09/83	Aberdeen	Home	League	0–2		
10	24/09/83	St Johnstone	Home	League	6–3	2 Goals	(6)
11	01/10/83	Dundee United	Away	League	2–0		
12	05/10/83	St Mirren	Home	S Lge Cup	5–0	2 Goals	(8)
13	08/10/83	Hibernian	Home	League	1–0		
14	15/10/83	Dundee	Away	League	2–3		
15	19/10/83	FC Porto	Home	ECW Cup	2–1		
16	22/10/83	Motherwell	Home	League	1–2	1 Goal	(9)
17	26/10/83	Heart of Midlothian	Home	S Lge Cup	2–0		
18	29/10/83	St Mirren	Away	League	0–3		
Sub+1	02/11/83	FC Porto	Away	ECW Cup	0–1		
19	05/11/83	Celtic	Home	League	1–2		
20	09/11/83	Clydebank	Away	S Lge Cup	3–0	1 Goal	(10)
21	12/11/83	Aberdeen	Away	League	0–3		
22	19/11/83	Dundee United	Home	League	0–0		
23	26/11/83	St Johnstone	Away	League	1–0		
Sub+2	21/01/84	St Johnstone	Home	League	2–0		
Sub+3	28/01/84	Dunfermline Athletic	Home	S Cup	2–1	1 Goal	(11)
24	04/02/84	Motherwell	Home	League	2–1	1 Goal	(12)
25	11/02/84	Heart of Midlothian	Away	League	2–2	1 Goal	(13)
26	15/02/84	Dundee United	Away	S Lge Cup	1–1		
27	18/02/84	Inverness Caledonian	Away	S Cup	6–0	2 Goals	(15)
28	22/02/84	Dundee United	Home	S Lge Cup	2–0		
29	25/02/84	Dundee	Away	League	3–1		
30	03/03/84	Hibernian	Home	League	0–0		
31	06/03/84	St Johnstone	Away	League	4–1	1 Goal	(16)
32	10/03/84	Dundee	Away	S Cup	2–2		
33	17/03/84	Dundee	Home	S Cup	2–3		
34	25/03/84	Celtic	Hampden	S Lge Cup	3–2*	3 Goals	(19)
35	31/03/84	Motherwell	Away	League	3–0		
36	02/04/84	Celtic	Away	League	0–3		
37	07/04/84	Heart of Midlothian	Home	League	0–0		
38	21/04/84	Celtic	Home	League	1–0		
39	28/04/84	St Mirren	Away	League	1–1		
40	02/05/84	Dundee United	Home	League	2–2		
41	05/05/84	Dundee	Home	League	2–2		
42	09/05/84	Aberdeen	Away	League	0–0		
43	12/05/84	Hibernian	Away	League	0–0		
44	14/05/84	Dundee United	Away	League	2–1	1 Goal	(20)

SEASON 1984–85

Scottish League Premier Division

45	11/08/84	St Mirren	Home	League	0–0		
46	18/08/84	Dumbarton	Away	League	2–1	1 Goal	(21)
47	22/08/84	Falkirk	Home	S Lge Cup	1–0		

Sub+4	25/08/84	Celtic	Home	League	0–0		
48	29/08/84	Raith Rovers	Home	S Lge Cup	4–0	2 Goals	(23)
49	01/09/84	Dundee	Away	League	2–0		
50	05/09/84	Cowdenbeath	Away	S Lge Cup	3–1		
51	15/09/84	Aberdeen	Away	League	0–0		
52	18/09/84	Bohemians FC	Away	UEFA Cup	2–3	1 Goal	(24)
53	22/09/84	Morton	Home	League	2–0	1 Goal	(25)
54	26/09/84	Meadowbank Thistle	Home	S Lge Cup	4–0	2 Goals	(27)
55	29/09/84	Dundee United	Home	League	1–0		
56	03/10/84	Bohemians FC	Home	UEFA Cup	2–0		
57	06/10/84	Heart of Midlothian	Away	League	0–1		
58	09/10/84	Meadowbank Thistle	Away	S Lge Cup	1–1	1 Goal	(28)
59	13/10/84	St Mirren	Away	League	2–0		
60	20/10/84	Dumbarton	Home	League	0–0		
61	24/10/84	Internazionale Milano	Away	UEFA Cup	0–3		
62	28/10/84	Dundee United	Hampden	S Lge Cup	1–0		
63	03/11/84	Dundee	Home	League	0–0		
Sub+5	07/11/84	Internazionale Milano	Home	UEFA Cup	3–1		
Sub+6	29/12/84	Dumbarton	Away	League	4–2		
Sub+7	05/01/84	Dundee	Away	League	2–2		
64	19/01/84	Aberdeen	Away	League	1–5		
65	26/01/84	Morton	Away	S Cup	3–3		
66	30/01/84	Morton	Home	S Cup	3–1		
67	02/02/84	Morton	Home	League	2–0		
68	09/02/84	Dundee United	Home	League	0–0		
69	16/02/84	Dundee	Home	S Cup	0–1		
70	02/03/84	Dumbarton	Home	League	3–1	2 Goals	(30)
71	16/03/84	St Mirren	Away	League	1–2	1 Goal	(31)
72	23/03/84	Dundee	Home	League	1–3	1 Goal	(32)
73	06/04/84	Aberdeen	Home	League	1–2		
74	20/04/84	Morton	Away	League	3–0	3 Goals	(35)
75	27/04/84	Heart of Midlothian	Home	League	3–1	1 Goal	(36)
76	01/05/84	Celtic	Away	League	1–1	1 Goal	(37)
77	04/05/84	Dundee United	Away	League	1–2	1 Goal	(38)
78	11/05/84	Hibernian	Away	League	0–1		

SEASON 1985–86

Scottish League Premier Division

79	10/08/85	Dundee United	Home	League	1–0	1 Goal	(39)
80	17/08/85	Hibernian	Away	League	3–1	1 Goal	(40)
81	21/08/85	Clyde	Home	S Lge Cup	5–0	1 Goal	(41)
82	24/08/85	Heart of Midlothian	Home	League	3–1		
83	31/08/85	Celtic	Away	League	1–1	1 Goal	(42)
84	04/09/85	Hamilton Academical	Away	S Lge Cup	2–1		
85	18/09/85	CA Osasuna Pamplona	Home	UEFA Cup	1–0		
86	25/09/85	Hibernian	Away	S Lge Cup	0–2		
87	28/09/85	Aberdeen	Home	League	0–3		
88	02/10/85	CA Osasuna Pamplona	Away	UEFA Cup	0–2		
89	05/10/85	Motherwell	Away	League	3–0	2 Goals	(44)
90	09/10/85	Hibernian	Home	S Lge Cup	1–0		
91	12/10/85	Dundee United	Away	League	1–1	1 Goal	(45)
92	19/10/85	Hibernian	Home	League	1–2		
93	26/10/85	St Mirren	Away	League	1–2	1 Goal	(46)
94	02/11/85	Clydebank	Home	League	0–0		
95	09/11/85	Celtic	Home	League	3–0	1 Goal	(47)
96	16/11/85	Heart of Midlothian	Away	League	0–3		
97	23/11/85	Dundee	Away	League	2–3	2 Goals	(49)
98	07/12/85	Motherwell	Home	League	1–0	1 Goal	(50)
99	14/12/85	Dundee United	Home	League	1–1	1 Goal	(51)
100	21/12/85	Hibernian	Away	League	1–1		
101	28/12/85	Heart of Midlothian	Home	League	0–2		
102	01/01/86	Celtic	Away	League	0–2		
103	04/01/86	Dundee	Home	League	5–0	3 Goals	(54)
104	11/01/86	Clydebank	Home	League	4–2	1 Goal	(55)
105	18/01/86	St Mirren	Home	League	2–0	1 Goal	(56)
106	25/01/86	Heart of Midlothian	Away	S Cup	2–3	1 Goal	(57)
107	01/02/86	Aberdeen	Home	League	1–1		
108	08/02/86	Motherwell	Away	League	0–1		
109	19/02/86	Aberdeen	Away	League	0–1		
110	22/02/86	Dundee United	Away	League	1–1	1 Goal	(58)
111	01/03/86	Hibernian	Home	League	3–1	3 Goals	(61)
112	15/03/86	Dundee	Away	League	1–2	1 Goal	(62)
113	22/03/86	Celtic	Home	League	4–4	1 Goal	(63)
114	29/03/86	Heart of Midlothian	Away	League	1–3	1 Goal	(64)

115	12/04/86	Clydebank	Away	League	1–2		
116	19/04/86	St Mirren	Away	League	1–2		
117	26/04/86	Aberdeen	Away	League	1–1		
118	03/05/86	Motherwell	Home	League	2–0	1 Goal	(65)

SEASON 1986–87

Scottish League Premier Division

119	09/08/86	Hibernian	Away	League	1–2	1 Goal	(66)
120	13/08/86	Falkirk	Home	League	1–0	1 Goal	(67)
121	16/08/86	Dundee United	Home	League	2–3	2 Goals	(69)
122	20/08/86	Stenhousemuir	Away	S Lge Cup	4–1	1 Goal	(70)
123	23/08/86	Hamilton Academical	Away	League	2–1		
124	27/08/86	East Fife	Away	S Lge Cup	0–0+		
125	31/08/86	Celtic	Home	League	1–0		
126	03/09/86	Dundee	Home	S Lge Cup	3–1*		
127	06/09/86	Motherwell	Away	League	2–0		
128	13/09/86	Clydebank	Home	League	4–0		
129	17/09/86	FC Ilves Tampere	Home	UEFA Cup	4–0	1 Goal	(71)
130	20/09/86	Dundee	Away	League	0–1		
131	24/09/86	Dundee United	Hampden	S Lge Cup	2–1	1 Goal	(72)
132	27/09/86	Aberdeen	Home	League	2–0	1 Goal	(73)
133	01/10/86	FC Ilves Tampere	Away	UEFA Cup	0–2		
134	04/10/86	Heart of Midlothian	Away	League	1–1		
135	08/10/86	St Mirren	Away	League	1–0		
136	11/10/86	Hibernian	Home	League	3–0		
137	18/10/86	Falkirk	Away	League	5–1	1 Goal	(74)
138	23/10/86	Boavista FC Porto	Home	UEFA Cup	2–1	1 Goal	(75)
139	26/10/86	Celtic	Hampden	S Lge Cup	2–1		
140	29/10/86	Dundee United	Away	League	0–0		
141	01/11/86	Celtic	Away	League	1–1	1 Goal	(76)
142	04/11/86	Boavista FC Porto	Away	UEFA Cup	1–0		
143	08/11/86	Motherwell	Home	League	0–1		
144	15/11/86	Clydebank	Away	League	4–1	2 Goals	(78)
145	19/11/86	Dundee	Home	League	2–1	1 Goal	(79)
146	22/11/86	Aberdeen	Away	League	0–1		
147	26/11/86	Borussia Monchengladbach	Home	UEFA Cup	1–1		
148	29/11/86	Heart of Midlothian	Home	League	3–0	1 Goal	(80)
149	03/12/86	St Mirren	Home	League	2–0		
150	06/12/86	Hibernian	Away	League	0–0		
151	10/12/86	Borussia Monchengladbach	Away	UEFA Cup	0–0		
152	13/12/86	Falkirk	Home	League	4–0		
153	20/12/86	Hamilton Academical	Away	League	2–0	1 Goal	(81)
154	27/12/86	Dundee United	Home	League	2–0	1 Goal	(82)
155	01/01/87	Celtic	Home	League	2–0	1 Goal	(83)
156	06/01/87	Motherwell	Away	League	1–0		
157	10/01/87	Clydebank	Home	League	5–0	2 Goals	(85)
158	17/01/87	Hamilton Academical	Home	League	2–0	1 Goal	(86)
159	24/01/87	Aberdeen	Home	League	0–0		
160	31/01/87	Hamilton Academical	Home	S Cup	0–1		
161	07/02/87	Heart of Midlothian	Away	League	5–2	1 Goal	(87)
162	14/02/87	St Mirren	Away	League	3–1	3 Goals	(90)
163	28/02/87	Hibernian	Home	League	1–1		
164	07/03/87	Falkirk	Away	League	2–1	2 Goals	(92)
165	14/03/87	Hamilton Academical	Home	League	2–0	1 Goal	(93)
166	17/03/87	Dundee	Away	League	4–0	2 Goals	(95)
167	21/03/87	Dundee United	Away	League	1–0		
168	28/03/87	Motherwell	Home	League	1–0	1 Goal	(96)
169	04/04/87	Celtic	Away	League	1–3	1 Goal	(97)
170	14/04/87	Dundee	Home	League	2–0	1 Goal	(98)
171	18/04/87	Clydebank	Away	League	3–0	2 Goals	(100)
172	25/04/87	Heart of Midlothian	Home	League	3–0	3 Goals	(103)
173	02/05/87	Aberdeen	Away	League	1–1		
174	09/05/87	St Mirren	Home	League	1–0		

+ AET Rangers won 5–4 on penalties

SEASON 1987–88

Scottish League Premier Division

175	08/08/87	Dundee United	Home	League	1–1	1 Goal	(104)
176	12/08/87	Hibernian	Away	League	0–1		
177	15/08/87	Aberdeen	Away	League	0–2		
178	19/08/87	Stirling Albion	Away	S Lge Cup	2–1	1 Goal	(105)
179	22/08/87	Falkirk	Home	League	4–0	3 Goals	(108)

180	26/08/87	Dunfermline Athletic	Away	S Lge Cup	4–1	3 Goals	(111)
181	29/08/87	Celtic	Away	League	0–1		
182	02/09/87	Heart of Midlothian	Home	S Lge Cup	4–1	2 Goals	(113)
183	05/09/87	Dundee	Home	League	2–1	1 Goal	(114)
184	12/09/87	Dunfermline Athletic	Home	League	4–0	3 Goals	(117)
185	16/09/87	Dinamo Kijev	Away	Eur Cup	0–1		
186	19/09/87	Motherwell	Away	League	1–0		
187	23/09/87	Motherwell	Hampden	S Lge Cup	3–1		
188	26/09/87	Morton	Home	League	7–0	3 Goals	(120)
189	30/09/87	Dinamo Kijev	Home	Eur Cup	2–0	1 Goal	(121)
190	03/10/87	Heart of Midlothian	Away	League	0–0		
191	06/10/87	St Mirren	Home	League	3–1		
192	10/10/87	Dundee United	Away	League	0–1		
193	17/10/87	Celtic	Home	League	2–2	1 Goal	(122)
194	21/10/87	KS Gornik Zabrze	Home	Eur Cup	3–1	1 Goal	(123)
195	25/10/87	Aberdeen	Hampden	S Lge Cup	3–3+		
196	28/10/87	Dunfermline Athletic	Away	League	4–0	1 Goal	(124)
197	31/10/87	Motherwell	Home	League	1–0	1 Goal	(125)
198	04/11/87	KS Gornik Zabrze	Away	Eur Cup	1–1	1 Goal	(126)
199	07/11/87	Hibernian	Home	League	1–0		
200	14/11/87	St Mirren	Away	League	2–2	2 Goals	(128)
201	17/11/87	Aberdeen	Home	League	0–1		
202	21/11/87	Falkirk	Away	League	1–0		
203	24/11/87	Morton	Away	League	3–0	1 Goal	(129)
204	28/11/87	Heart of Midlothian	Home	League	3–2		
205	05/12/87	Dundee United	Home	League	1–0	1 Goal	(130)
206	12/12/87	Hibernian	Away	League	2–0		
207	15/12/87	Dunfermline Athletic	Home	League	2–2	1 Goal	(131)
208	19/12/87	Motherwell	Away	League	2–0	1 Goal	(132)
209	26/12/87	Dundee	Home	League	2–0	2 Goals	(134)
210	02/01/88	Celtic	Away	League	0–2		
211	06/01/88	Dundee	Away	League	1–0	1 Goal	(135)
212	09/01/88	Morton	Home	League	5–0	3 Goals	(138)
213	16/01/88	Heart of Midlothian	Away	League	1–1		
214	23/01/88	Falkirk	Home	League	3–1		
215	06/02/88	Aberdeen	Away	League	2–1	1 Goal	(139)
216	08/02/88	Raith Rovers	Away	S Cup	0–0		
217	10/02/88	Raith Rovers	Home	S Cup	4–1	1 Goal	(140)
218	02/03/88	Steaua Bucuresti	Away	Eur Cup	0–2		
219	05/03/88	Dunfermline Athletic	Away	League	3–0	1 Goal	(141)
220	12/03/88	Motherwell	Home	League	1–0		
221	16/03/88	Steaua Bucuresti	Home	Eur Cup	2–1	1 Goal	(142)
222	20/03/88	Celtic	Home	League	1–2		
223	26/03/88	Dundee	Away	League	3–2		
224	09/04/88	Morton	Away	League	2–3		
225	23/04/88	St Mirren	Away	League	3–0	1 Goal	(143)
226	30/04/88	Aberdeen	Home	League	0–1		
227	07/05/88	Falkirk	Away	League	5–0	2 Goals	(145)

+ AET Rangers won 5–3 on penalties

SEASON 1988–89

Scottish League Premier Division

228	13/08/88	Hamilton Academical	Away	League	2–0	1 Goal	(146)
229	17/08/88	Clyde	Away	S Lge Cup	3–0		
230	20/08/88	Hibernian	Home	League	0–0		
231	24/08/88	Clydebank	Home	S Lge Cup	6–0	1 Goal	(147)
232	27/08/88	Celtic	Home	League	5–1	2 Goals	(149)
233	31/08/88	Dundee	Home	S Lge Cup	4–1	1 Goal	(150)
234	27/09/88	Dundee United	Away	League	1–0		
235	01/10/88	Dundee	Home	League	2–0		
236	05/10/88	GKS Katowice	Away	UEFA Cup	4–2		
237	08/10/88	Aberdeen	Away	League	1–2		
238	12/10/88	Hibernian	Away	League	1–0	1 Goal	(151)
239	23/10/88	Aberdeen	Hampden	S Lge Cup	3–2	2 Goals	(153)
240	26/10/88	1.FC Koln	Away	UEFA Cup	0–2		
241	29/10/88	St Mirren	Away	League	1–1		
Sub+8	21/01/89	Dundee	Home	League	3–1	1 Goal	(154)
Sub+9	28/01/89	Raith Rovers	Away	S Cup	1–1		
242	01/02/89	Raith Rovers	Home	S Cup	3–0		
243	18/02/89	Stranraer	Home	S Cup	8–0	2 Goals	(156)
244	25/02/89	St Mirren	Home	League	3–1	1 Goal	(157)
245	11/03/89	Hamilton Academical	Home	League	3–0		
246	21/03/89	Dundee United	Home	S Cup	2–2	1 Goal	(158)

247	25/03/89	Hibernian	Away	League	1–0		
248	27/03/89	Dundee United	Away	S Cup	1–0	1 Goal	(159)
249	01/04/89	Celtic	Away	League	2–1		
250	08/04/89	Motherwell	Home	League	1–0	1 Goal	(160)
251	15/04/89	St Johnstone	Neutral	S Cup	0–0		
252	18/04/89	St Johnstone	Neutral	S Cup	4–0	1 Goal	(161)
253	22/04/89	St Mirren	Away	League	2–0	1 Goal	(162)
254	29/04/89	Heart of Midlothian	Home	League	4–0		
255	02/05/89	Dundee United	Home	League	2–0	1 Goal	(163)
256	06/05/89	Dundee	Away	League	2–1		
257	13/05/89	Aberdeen	Home	League	0–3		
258	20/05/89	Celtic	Hampden	S Cup	0–1		

SEASON 1989–90

Scottish League Premier Division

259	12/08/89	St Mirren	Home	League	0–1		
260	15/08/89	Arbroath	Home	S Lge Cup	4–0	3 Goals	(166)
261	19/08/89	Hibernian	Away	League	0–2		
Sub+10	26/08/89	Celtic	Away	League	1–1		
262	30/08/89	Hamilton Academical	Away	S Lge Cup	3–0		
Sub+11	09/09/89	Aberdeen	Home	League	1–0		
263	16/09/89	Dundee	Home	League	2–2	2 Goals	(168)
264	19/09/89	Dunfermline Athletic	Hampden	S Lge Cup	5–0	1 Goal	(169)
265	23/09/89	Dunfermline Athletic	Away	League	1–1	1 Goal	(170)
266	30/09/89	Heart of Midlothian	Home	League	1–0		
267	03/10/89	Motherwell	Away	League	0–1		
268	14/10/89	Dundee United	Home	League	2–1	1 Goal	(171)
269	22/10/89	Aberdeen	Hampden	S Lge Cup	1–2*		
270	25/10/89	St Mirren	Away	League	2–0	1 Goal	(172)
271	28/10/89	Hibernian	Home	League	3–0	2 Goals	(174)
272	04/11/89	Celtic	Home	League	1–0		
273	18/11/89	Dundee	Away	League	2–0		
274	22/11/89	Aberdeen	Away	League	0–1		
275	25/11/89	Dunfermline Athletic	Home	League	3–0	1 Goal	(175)
276	02/12/89	Heart of Midlothian	Away	League	2–1		
277	09/12/89	Motherwell	Home	League	3–0	1 Goal	(176)
278	16/12/89	Dundee United	Away	League	1–1		
279	23/12/89	St Mirren	Home	League	1–0		
280	30/12/89	Hibernian	Away	League	0–0		
281	02/01/90	Celtic	Away	League	1–0		
282	06/01/90	Aberdeen	Home	League	2–0	1 Goal	(177)
283	13/01/90	Dundee	Home	League	3–0	1 Goal	(178)
284	20/01/90	St Johnstone	Home	S Cup	3–0		
285	27/01/90	Dunfermline Athletic	Away	League	1–0		
286	03/02/90	Dundee United	Home	League	3–1	1 Goal	(179)
287	10/02/90	Motherwell	Away	League	1–1		
288	17/02/90	Heart of Midlothian	Home	League	0–0		
289	25/02/90	Celtic	Away	S Cup	0–1		
290	24/03/90	Hibernian	Home	League	0–1		
291	01/04/90	Celtic	Home	League	3–0	1 Goal	(180)
292	08/04/90	Aberdeen	Away	League	0–0		
293	14/04/90	Motherwell	Home	League	2–1		
294	21/04/90	Dundee United	Away	League	1–0		
295	28/04/90	Dunfermline Athletic	Home	League	2–0	1 Goal	(181)
296	05/05/90	Heart of Midlothian	Away	League	1–1		

SEASON 1990–91

Scottish League Premier Division

Sub+12	25/08/90	Dunfermline Athletic	Home	League	3–1		
297	28/08/90	Kilmarnock	Away	S Lge Cup	1–0		
Sub+13	01/09/90	Hibernian	Away	League	0–0		
298	04/09/90	Raith Rovers	Home	S Lge Cup	6–2	3 Goals	(184)
299	08/09/90	Heart of Midlothian	Away	League	3–1	2 Goals	(186)
300	15/09/90	Celtic	Home	League	1–1		
301	19/09/90	Valletta FC	Away	Eur Cup	4–0	1 Goal	(187)
302	22/09/90	Dundee United	Away	League	1–2		
303	26/09/90	Aberdeen	Hampden	S Lge Cup	1–0		
304	29/09/90	Motherwell	Home	League	1–0		
Sub+14	02/10/90	Valletta FC	Home	Eur Cup	6–0	1 Goal	(188)
305	06/10/90	Aberdeen	Away	League	0–0		
306	13/10/90	St Mirren	Home	League	5–0	2 Goals	(190)
307	20/10/90	St Johnstone	Away	League	0–0		
Sub+15	24/10/90	Crvena Zvezda Beograd	Away	Eur Cup	0–3		

308	28/10/90	Celtic	Hampden	S Lge Cup	2-1*		
309	03/11/90	Hibernian	Home	League	4-0		
310	07/11/90	Crvena Zvezda Beograd	Home	Eur Cup	1-1	1 Goal	(191)
311	10/11/90	Dundee United	Home	League	1-2	1 Goal	(192)
Sub+16	17/11/90	Motherwell	Away	League	4-2		
312	20/11/90	Dunfermline Athletic	Away	League	1-0		
Sub+17	25/11/90	Celtic	Away	League	2-1	1 Goal	(193)
Sub+18	01/12/90	Heart of Midlothian	Home	League	4-0	1 Goal	(194)
Sub+19	08/12/90	St Johnstone	Home	League	4-1		
Sub+20	15/12/90	St Mirren	Away	League	3-0		
Sub+21	22/12/90	Aberdeen	Home	League	2-2	2 Goals	(196)
Sub+22	29/12/90	Dundee United	Away	League	2-1		
Sub+23	19/01/91	Hibernian	Away	League	2-0		
Sub+24	29/01/91	Dunfermline Athletic	Home	S Cup	2-0		
313	09/02/91	St Mirren	Home	League	1-0	1 Goal	(197)
314	16/02/91	Motherwell	Home	League	2-0	1 Goal	(198)
315	23/02/91	Cowdenbeath	Home	S Cup	5-0	1 Goal	(199)
316	26/02/91	St Johnstone	Away	League	1-1		
317	09/03/91	Heart of Midlothian	Home	League	2-1		
318	24/03/91	Celtic	Away	League	0-3		
Sub+25	11/05/91	Aberdeen	Home	League	2-0		

SEASON 1991-92

Scottish League Premier Division

Sub+26	20/08/91	Queen's Park	Home	S Lge Cup	6-0		
Sub+27	24/08/91	Dunfermline Athletic	Home	League	4-0	1 Goal	(200)
Sub+28	27/08/91	Partick Thistle	Away	S Lge Cup	2-0		
319	04/09/91	Heart of Midlothian	Away	S Lge Cup	1-0	1 Goal	(201)
320	07/09/91	Falkirk	Away	League	2-0		
321	14/09/91	Dundee United	Home	League	1-1	1 Goal	(202)
322	18/09/91	AC Sparta Praha	Away	Eur Cup	0-1		
Sub+29	25/09/91	Hibernian	Hampden	S Lge Cup	0-1		
323	02/10/91	AC Sparta Praha	Home	Eur Cup	2-1*		
324	05/10/91	Airdrieonians	Away	League	4-0	2 Goals	(204)
325	08/10/91	Hibernian	Home	League	4-2	2 Goals	(206)
326	12/10/91	St Johnstone	Away	League	3-2	2 Goals	(208)
327	19/10/91	Heart of Midlothian	Home	League	2-0	1 Goal	(209)
328	26/10/91	Falkirk	Home	League	1-1		
329	29/10/91	Dundee United	Away	League	2-3	2 Goals	(211)
330	02/11/91	Celtic	Home	League	1-1	1 Goal	(212)
331	09/11/91	Dunfermline Athletic	Away	League	5-0	1 Goal	(213)
332	16/11/91	Airdrieonians	Home	League	4-0	1 Goal	(214)
333	19/11/91	Hibernian	Away	League	3-0	2 Goals	(216)
334	23/11/91	St Mirren	Home	League	0-1		
335	30/11/91	Motherwell	Away	League	2-0		
336	04/12/91	Aberdeen	Away	League	3-2	1 Goal	(217)
337	07/12/91	St Johnstone	Home	League	3-1		
338	14/12/91	Falkirk	Away	League	3-1	1 Goal	(218)
339	21/12/91	Dundee United	Home	League	2-0	2 Goals	(220)
340	28/12/91	Dunfermline Athletic	Home	League	2-1		
341	01/01/92	Celtic	Away	League	3-1	1 Goal	(221)
342	04/01/92	Airdrieonians	Away	League	0-0		
343	11/01/92	Hibernian	Home	League	2-0	1 Goal	(222)
344	18/01/92	Motherwell	Home	League	2-0	1 Goal	(223)
345	22/01/92	Aberdeen	Away	S Cup	1-0	1 Goal	(224)
346	01/02/92	Heart of Midlothian	Away	League	1-0	1 Goal	(225)
347	08/02/92	St Mirren	Away	League	2-1	1 Goal	(226)
348	15/02/92	Motherwell	Home	S Cup	2-1		
349	25/02/92	Aberdeen	Home	League	0-0		
350	29/02/92	Airdrieonians	Home	League	5-0		
351	03/03/92	St Johnstone	Away	S Cup	3-0	1 Goal	(227)
352	10/03/92	Hibernian	Away	League	3-1	1 Goal	(228)
353	14/03/92	Dunfermline Athletic	Away	League	3-1		
354	21/03/92	Celtic	Home	League	0-2		
355	28/03/92	St Johnstone	Away	League	2-1		
356	31/03/92	Celtic	Hampden	S Cup	1-0	1 Goal	(229)
357	07/04/92	Falkirk	Home	League	4-1	3 Goals	(232)
358	11/04/92	Dundee United	Away	League	2-1		
359	18/04/92	St Mirren	Home	League	4-0	2 Goals	(234)
360	23/04/92	Motherwell	Away	League	2-1		
361	28/04/92	Heart of Midlothian	Home	League	1-1	1 Goal	(235)
362	02/05/92	Aberdeen	Away	League	2-0	2 Goals	(237)
363	09/05/92	Airdrieonians	Hampden	S Cup	2-1	1 Goal	(238)

SEASON 1992–93

Scottish League Premier Division

364	01/08/92	St Johnstone	Home	League	1–0	1 Goal	(239)
365	04/08/92	Airdrieonians	Home	League	2–0		
366	08/08/92	Hibernian	Away	League	0–0		
367	11/08/92	Dumbarton	Away	S Lge Cup	5–0+	1 Goal	(240)
368	15/08/92	Dundee	Away	League	3–4	2 Goals	(242)
369	19/08/92	Stranraer	Away	S Lge Cup	5–0	3 Goals	(245)
370	22/08/92	Celtic	Home	League	1–1		
371	26/08/92	Dundee United	Away	S Lge Cup	3–2*	1 Goal	(246)
372	29/08/92	Aberdeen	Home	League	3–1	1 Goal	(247)
373	02/09/92	Motherwell	Away	League	4–1	3 Goals	(250)
374	12/09/92	Partick Thistle	Away	League	4–1		
375	16/09/92	Lyngby BK Kobenhavn	Home	Eur Cup	2–0		
376	19/09/92	Heart of Midlothian	Home	League	2–0	1 Goal	(251)
377	22/09/92	St Johnstone	Hampden	S Lge Cup	3–1	3 Goals	(254)
378	26/09/92	Dundee United	Away	League	4–0	1 Goal	(255)
379	30/09/92	Lyngby BK Kobenhavn	Away	Eur Cup	1–0		
380	03/10/92	Falkirk	Home	League	4–0	4 Goals	(259)
381	07/10/92	St Johnstone	Away	League	5–1	2 Goals	(261)
Sub+30	17/10/92	Hibernian	Home	League	1–0	1 Goal	(262)
382	21/10/92	Leeds United	Home	Eur Cup	2–1	1 Goal	(263)
383	25/10/92	Aberdeen	Hampden	S Lge Cup	2–1		
384	31/10/92	Motherwell	Home	League	4–2	3 Goals	(266)
385	04/11/92	Leeds United	Away	Eur Cup	2–1	1 Goal	(267)
386	07/11/92	Celtic	Away	League	1–0		
387	11/11/92	Dundee	Home	League	3–1	2 Goals	(269)
388	21/11/92	Heart of Midlothian	Away	League	1–1	1 Goal	(270)
389	09/12/92	CSKA Moskva	Away	Eur Cup	1–0		
390	12/12/92	Falkirk	Away	League	2–1	1 Goal	(271)
391	19/12/92	St Johnstone	Home	League	2–0		
392	26/12/92	Dundee	Away	League	3–1	1 Goal	(272)
393	05/01/93	Dundee United	Home	League	3–2	1 Goal	(273)
394	09/01/93	Motherwell	Away	S Cup	2–0	2 Goals	(275)
395	30/01/93	Hibernian	Away	League	4–3	1 Goal	(276)
396	02/02/93	Aberdeen	Away	League	1–0		
397	06/02/93	Ayr United	Away	S Cup	2–0	1 Goal	(277)
398	09/02/93	Falkirk	Home	League	5–0		
399	13/02/93	Airdrieonians	Home	League	2–2	2 Goals	(279)
400	20/02/93	Dundee United	Away	League	0–0		
401	23/02/93	Motherwell	Away	League	4–0	1 Goal	(280)
402	27/02/93	Heart of Midlothian	Home	League	2–1	1 Goal	(281)
403	03/03/93	Club Brugge KV	Away	Eur Cup	1–1		
404	06/03/93	Arbroath	Away	S Cup	3–0	1 Goal	(282)
405	10/03/93	St Johnstone	Away	League	1–1	1 Goal	(283)
406	13/03/93	Hibernian	Home	League	3–0	1 Goal	(284)
407	17/03/93	Club Brugge KV	Home	Eur Cup	2–1		
Sub+31	20/03/93	Celtic	Away	League	1–2		
408	27/03/93	Dundee	Home	League	3–0	1 Goal	(285)
409	30/03/93	Aberdeen	Home	League	2–0	1 Goal	(286)
410	03/04/93	Heart of Midlothian	Hampden	S Cup	2–1	1 Goal	(287)
411	07/04/93	Olympique de Marseille	Away	Eur Cup	1–1		
412	10/04/93	Motherwell	Home	League	1–0		
413	21/04/93	CSKA Moskva	Home	Eur Cup	0–0		

+ Played at Hampden Park

SEASON 1993–94

Scottish League Premier Division

414	02/10/93	Raith Rovers	Away	League	1–1		
Sub+32	09/10/93	Dundee United	Away	League	3–1		
415	16/10/93	St Johnstone	Home	League	2–0		
Sub+33	24/10/93	Hibernian	Neutral	S Lge Cup	2–1	1 Goal	(288)
416	30/10/93	Celtic	Home	League	1–2	1 Goal	(289)
417	03/11/93	Heart of Midlothian	Away	League	2–2		
418	06/11/93	Kilmarnock	Away	League	2–0		
419	10/11/93	Dundee	Home	League	3–1	2 Goals	(291)
Sub+34	29/01/94	Dumbarton	Home	S Cup	4–1		
Sub+35	12/02/94	Hibernian	Home	League	2–0		
420	19/02/94	Alloa	Home	S Cup	6–0	3 Goals	(294)
421	26/02/94	Raith Rovers	Away	League	2–1		
Sub+36	05/03/94	Motherwell	Home	League	2–1		
422	12/03/94	Heart of Midlothian	Home	S Cup	2–0		

423	19/03/94	St Johnstone	Home	League	4–0			
424	26/03/94	Heart of Midlothian	Away	League	2–1	1 Goal	(295)	
425	29/03/94	Partick Thistle	Away	League	2–1	1 Goal	(296)	
426	02/04/94	Aberdeen	Home	League	1–1			
Sub+37	10/04/94	Kilmarnock	Hampden	S Cup	0–0			
427	13/04/94	Kilmarnock	Hampden	S Cup	2–1			
428	16/04/94	Raith Rovers	Home	League	4–0	1 Goal	(297)	
429	23/04/94	Dundee United	Home	League	2–1			
430	26/04/94	Motherwell	Away	League	1–2	1 Goal	(298)	
431	30/04/94	Celtic	Home	League	1–1			
Sub+38	03/05/94	Hibernian	Away	League	0–1			
432	07/05/94	Kilmarnock	Away	League	0–1			
Sub+39	14/05/94	Dundee	Home	League	0–0			
433	21/05/94	Dundee United	Hampden	S Cup	0–1			

SEASON 1994–95

Scottish League Premier Division

434	13/08/94	Motherwell	Home	League	2–1			
Sub+40	01/10/94	Dundee United	Home	League	2–0			
Sub+41	08/10/94	Hibernian	Away	League	1–2			
Sub+42	30/10/94	Celtic	Away	League	3–1			
Sub+43	09/11/94	Heart of Midlothian	Away	League	1–1			
435	19/11/94	Falkirk	Home	League	1–1			
436	25/11/94	Aberdeen	Home	League	1–0	1 Goal	(299)	
437	04/12/94	Dundee United	Away	League	3–0			
Sub+44	04/02/95	Dundee United	Home	League	1–1			

SEASON 1995–96

Scottish League Premier Division

438	19/08/95	Greenock Morton	Home	S Lge Cup	3–0	1 Goal	(300)	
439	26/08/95	Kilmarnock	Home	League	1–0			
440	30/08/95	Stirling Albion	Home	S Lge Cup	3–2	1 Goal	(301)	
441	09/09/95	Raith Rovers	Home	League	4–0	2 Goals	(303)	
442	13/09/95	Steaua Bucuresti	Away	Eur Cup	0–1			
Sub+45	16/09/95	Falkirk	Away	League	2–0			
443	20/09/95	Celtic	Away	S Lge Cup	1–0	1 Goal	(304)	
444	23/09/95	Hibernian	Home	League	0–1			
445	27/09/95	BV 09 Borussia Dortmund	Home	Eur Cup	2–2			
446	30/09/95	Celtic	Away	League	2–0			
447	03/10/95	Motherwell	Home	League	2–1	1 Goal	(305)	
Sub+46	14/10/95	Partick Thistle	Away	League	4–0			
448	18/10/95	FC Juventus	Away	Eur Cup	1–4			
449	24/10/95	Aberdeen	Hampden	S Lge Cup	1–2			
450	28/10/95	Raith Rovers	Away	League	2–2			
Sub+47	01/11/95	FC Juventus	Home	Eur Cup	0–4			
451	04/11/95	Falkirk	Home	League	2–0	2 Goals	(307)	
452	08/11/95	Kilmarnock	Away	League	2–0			
Sub+48	11/11/95	Aberdeen	Home	League	1–1			
Sub+49	19/11/95	Celtic	Home	League	3–3	1 Goal	(308)	
453	22/11/95	Steaua Bucuresti	Home	Eur Cup	1–1			
454	25/11/95	Hibernian	Away	League	4–1	1 Goal	(309)	
455	02/12/95	Heart of Midlothian	Away	League	2–0	1 Goal	(310)	
Sub+50	06/12/95	BV 09 Borussia Dortmund	Away	Eur Cup	2–2			
456	09/12/95	Partick Thistle	Home	League	1–0			
457	06/01/96	Falkirk	Away	League	4–0	2 Goals	(312)	
458	13/01/96	Raith Rovers	Home	League	4–0	1 Goal	(313)	
Sub+51	10/02/96	Motherwell	Home	League	3–2	1 Goal	(314)	
Sub+52	03/03/96	Hibernian	Away	League	2–0			
459	09/03/96	Caledonian Thistle	Away	S Cup	3–0			
460	17/03/96	Celtic	Home	League	1–1			
461	23/03/96	Falkirk	Home	League	3–2			
462	30/03/96	Raith Rovers	Away	League	4–2	3 Goals	(317)	
463	07/04/96	Celtic	Hampden	S Cup	2–1	1 Goal	(318)	
464	10/04/96	Heart of Midlothian	Away	League	0–2			
Sub+53	28/04/96	Aberdeen	Home	League	3–1			
465	04/05/96	Kilmarnock	Away	League	3–0	1 Goal	(319)	

SEASON 1996–97

Scottish League Premier Division

466	07/08/96	Spartak–Alania Vladikavkaz	Home	Eur Cup	3–1	1 Goal	(320)	
467	10/08/96	Raith Rovers	Home	League	1–0			
Sub+54	14/08/96	Clydebank	Away	S Lge Cup	3–0	1 Goal	(321)	

468	17/08/96	Dunfermline Athletic	Away	League	5–2	3 Goals	(324)
469	21/08/96	Spartak–Alania Vladikavkaz	Away	Eur Cup	7–2	3 Goals	(327)
470	24/08/96	Dundee United	Home	League	1–0		
471	11/09/96	Grasshopper–Club Zurich	Away	Eur Cup	0–3		
Sub+55	14/09/96	Heart of Midlothian	Home	League	3–0	1 Goal	(328)
472	18/09/96	Hibernian	Home	S Lge Cup	4–0		
Sub+56	26/10/96	Motherwell	Home	League	5–0		
Sub+57	30/10/96	Ajax	Home	Eur Cup	0–1		
473	02/11/96	Raith Rovers	Away	League	2–2	1 Goal	(329)
474	20/11/96	Grasshopper–Club Zurich	Home	Eur Cup	2–1	2 Goals	(331)
475	24/11/96	Heart of Midlothian	Neutral	S Lge Cup	4–3	2 Goals	(333)
476	01/12/96	Aberdeen	Away	League	3–0		
Sub+58	04/12/96	AJ Auxerre	Away	Eur Cup	1–2		
477	07/12/96	Hibernian	Home	League	4–3	2 Goals	(335)
478	10/12/96	Dundee United	Away	League	0–1		
479	14/12/96	Dunfermline Athletic	Home	League	3–1	1 Goal	(336)
Sub+59	17/12/96	Kilmarnock	Home	League	4–2		
Sub+60	21/12/96	Heart of Midlothian	Away	League	4–1		
480	26/12/96	Raith Rovers	Home	League	4–0	1 Goal	(337)
481	02/01/97	Celtic	Home	League	3–1		
Sub+61	04/01/97	Hibernian	Away	League	2–1		
482	15/01/97	Kilmarnock	Away	League	1–1		
Sub+62	25/01/97	St Johnstone	Home	S Cup	2–0		
483	01/02/97	Heart of Midlothian	Home	League	0–0		
484	15/02/97	East Fife	Home	S Cup	3–0	1 Goal	(338)
Sub+63	01/03/97	Aberdeen	Away	League	2–2		
Sub+64	06/03/97	Celtic	Away	S Cup	0–2		
Sub+65	12/03/97	Dundee United	Home	League	0–2		
Sub+66	16/03/97	Celtic	Away	League	1–0		
Sub+67	22/03/97	Kilmarnock	Home	League	1–2		
Sub+68	15/04/97	Raith Rovers	Away	League	6–0	1 Goal	(339)
Sub+69	05/05/97	Motherwell	Home	League	0–2		
Sub+70	07/05/97	Dundee United	Away	League	1–0		
485	10/05/97	Heart of Midlothian	Away	League	1–3		

INTERNATIONAL APPEARANCES – SCOTLAND

1	29/04/86	Holland	Eindhoven	0–0	F		
Sub 2	12/11/86	Luxembourg	Hampden Park	3–0	ECQ		
Sub 3	18/02/87	Republic of Ireland	Hampden Park	0–1	ECQ		
4	01/04/87	Belgium	Brussels	1–4	ECQ		
5	23/05/87	England	Hampden Park	0–0	RC		
6	26/05/87	Brazil	Hampden Park	0–2	RC		
7	09/09/87	Hungary	Hampden Park	2–0	F	2 Goals	(2)
8	14/10/87	Belgium	Hampden Park	2–0	ECQ	1 Goal	(3)
9	22/03/88	Malta	Valletta	1–1	F		
10	27/04/88	Spain	Madrid	0–0	F		
11	17/05/88	Colombia	Hampden Park	0–0	RC		
12	21/05/88	England	Wembley	0–1	RC		
Sub 13	19/10/88	Yugoslavia	Hampden Park	1–1	WCQ		
14	08/03/89	France	Hampden Park	2–0	WCQ		
15	26/04/89	Cyprus	Hampden Park	2–1	WCQ	1 Goal	(4)
16	27/05/89	England	Hampden Park	0–2	RC		
17	06/09/89	Yugoslavia	Zagreb	1–3	WCQ		
18	11/10/89	France	Paris	0–3	WCQ		
19	15/11/89	Norway	Hampden Park	1–1	WCQ	1 Goal	(5)
Sub 20	25/04/90	East Germany	Hampden Park	0–1	F		
21	16/05/90	Egypt	Hampden Park	1–3	F	1 Goal	(6)
22	19/05/90	Poland	Hampden Park	1–1	F		
Sub 23	28/05/90	Malta	Valetta	2–1	F		
Sub 24	11/06/90	Costa Rica	Genoa	0–1	WC		
Sub 25	16/06/90	Sweden	Genoa	2–1	WC		
26	20/06/90	Brazil	Turin	0–1	WC		
27	12/09/90	Romania	Hampden Park	2–1	ECQ	1 Goal	(7)
28	17/10/90	Switzerland	Hampden Park	2–1	ECQ		
29	14/11/90	Bulgaria	Sofia	1–1	ECQ	1 Goal	(8)
30	06/02/91	USSR	Ibrox Park	0–1	F		
31	27/03/91	Bulgaria	Hampden Park	1–1	ECQ		
32	11/09/91	Switzerland	Berne	2–2	ECQ	1 Goal	(9)
33	13/11/91	San Marino	Hampden Park	4–0	ECQ	1 Goal	(10)
34	19/02/92	Northern Ireland	Hampden Park	1–0	F	1 Goal	(11)
Sub 35	25/03/92	Finland	Hampden Park	1–1	F		
36	17/05/92	USA	Denver	1–0	F		
37	21/05/92	Canada	Toronto	3–1	F	1 Goal	(12)

38	03/06/92	Norway	Oslo	0–0	F		
39	12/06/92	Holland	Gothenburg	0–1	EC		
40	15/06/92	Germany	Norrkoping	0–2	EC		
41	18/06/92	CIS	Norrkoping	3–0	EC		
42	09/09/92	Switzerland	Berne	1–3	WCQ	1 Goal	(13)
43	14/10/92	Portugal	Ibrox Park	0–0	WCQ		
44	18/11/92	Italy	Ibrox Park	0–0	WCQ		
45	17/02/93	Malta	Ibrox Park	3–0	WCQ	2 Goals	(15)
46	28/04/93	Portugal	Lisbon	0–5	WCQ		
Sub 47	16/08/95	Greece	Hampden Park	1–0	ECQ	1 Goal	(16)
Sub 48	06/09/95	Finland	Hampden Park	1–0	ECQ		
Sub 49	15/11/95	San Marino	Hampden Park	5–0	ECQ	1 Goal	(17)
50	27/03/96	Australia	Hampden Park	1–0	F	1 Goal	(18)
Sub 51	24/04/96	Denmark	Copenhagen	0–2	F		
52	29/05/96	Colombia	Miami	0–1	F		
Sub 53	15/06/96	England	Wembley	0–2	EC		
54	18/06/96	Switzerland	Villa Park	1–0	EC	1 Goal	(19)
55	31/08/96	Austria	Vienna	0–0	WCQ		
Sub 56	10/11/96	Sweden	Ibrox Park	1–0	WCQ		
Sub 57	11/02/97	Estonia	Monte Carlo	0–0	WCQ		
Sub 58	02/04/97	Austria	Celtic Park	2–0	WCQ		

APPEARANCES AND GOALS PER SEASON

SEASON 78–79	**GAMES**	**GOALS**
Scottish League	4	0
TOTAL	**4**	**0**

SEASON 79–80	**GAMES**	**GOALS**
Scottish League	9+6	0
Scottish Cup	1	0
TOTAL	**10+6**	**0**

SEASON 80–81	**GAMES**	**GOALS**
Scottish League	38	22
Scottish Cup	3	1
Scottish League Cup	2	0
TOTAL	**43**	**23**

SEASON 81–82	**GAMES**	**GOALS**
League	19+9	2
FA Cup	3	0
League Cup	1	0
TOTAL	**23+9**	**2**

SEASON 82–83	**GAMES**	**GOALS**
League	19+9	6
FA Cup	0+1	0
League Cup	4	1
TOTAL	**23+10**	**7**

SEASON 83–84	**GAMES**	**GOALS**
Scottish League	29+1	8
Scottish Cup	3+1	3
Scottish League Cup	10	9
European Cup Winners Cup	2+1	0
TOTAL	**44+3**	**20**

SEASON 84–85	**GAMES**	**GOALS**
Scottish League	22+3	12
Scottish Cup	3	0
Scottish League Cup	6	5
UEFA Cup	3+1	1
TOTAL	**34+4**	**18**

SEASON 85–86	**GAMES**	**GOALS**
Scottish League	33	25
Scottish Cup	1	1
Scottish League Cup	4	1
UEFA Cup	2	0
TOTAL	**40**	**27**

SEASON 86–87	GAMES	GOALS
Scottish League	44	34
Scottish Cup	1	0
Scottish League Cup	5	2
UEFA Cup	6	2
TOTAL	**56**	**38**

SEASON 87–88	GAMES	GOALS
Scottish League	40	31
Scottish Cup	2	1
Scottish League Cup	5	6
European Cup	6	4
TOTAL	**53**	**42**

SEASON 88–89	GAMES	GOALS
Scottish League	18+1	9
Scottish Cup	7+1	5
Scottish League Cup	4	4
UEFA Cup	2	0
TOTAL	**31+2**	**18**

SEASON 89–90	GAMES	GOALS
Scottish League	32+2	14
Scottish Cup	2	0
Scottish League Cup	4	4
TOTAL	**38+2**	**18**

SEASON 90–91	GAMES	GOALS
Scottish League	15+11	11
Scottish Cup	1+1	1
Scottish League Cup	4	3
European Cup	2+2	3
TOTAL	**22+14**	**18**

SEASON 91–92	GAMES	GOALS
Scottish League	37+1	34
Scottish Cup	5	4
Scottish League Cup	1+3	1
European Cup	2	0
TOTAL	**45+4**	**39**

SEASON 92–93	GAMES	GOALS
Scottish League	32+2	34
Scottish Cup	4	5
Scottish League Cup	5	8
European Cup	9	2
TOTAL	**50+2**	**49**

SEASON 93–94	GAMES	GOALS
Scottish League	16+5	7
Scottish Cup	4+2	3
Scottish League Cup	0+1	1
TOTAL	**20+8**	**11**

SEASON 94–95	GAMES	GOALS
Scottish League	4+5	1
TOTAL	**4+5**	**1**

SEASON 95–96	GAMES	GOALS
Scottish League	18+7	16
Scottish Cup	2	1
Scottish League Cup	4	3
European Cup	4+2	0
TOTAL	**28+9**	**20**

SEASON 96–97	GAMES	GOALS
Scottish League	13+12	10
Scottish Cup	1+2	1
Scottish League Cup	2+1	3
European Cup	4+2	6
TOTAL	**20+17**	**20**

CAREER APPEARANCES AND GOALS

COMPETITION	GAMES	TOTAL	GOALS
League	38+18	56	8
FA Cup	3+1	4	0
League Cup	5	5	1
European Cup	27+6	33	15
European Cup Winners Cup	2+1	3	0
UEFA Cup	13+1	14	3
Scottish League	404+56	460	268
Scottish Cup	40+7	47	26
Scottish League Cup	56+5	61	50
Internationals	42+16	58	19
TOTAL	**630+111**	**741**	**390**

HAT-TRICKS

St Johnstone

1	4	Berwick Rangers	21/03/81	Home	League	6–2

Rangers

1	3	Celtic	25/03/84	Hampden	S Lge Cup	3–2*
2	3	Morton	20/04/84	Away	League	3–0
3	3	Dundee	04/01/86	Home	League	5–0
4	3	Hibernian	01/03/86	Home	League	3–1
5	3	St Mirren	14/02/87	Away	League	3–1
6	3	Heart of Midlothian	25/04/87	Home	League	3–0
7	3	Falkirk	22/08/87	Home	League	4–0
8	3	Dunfermline Athletic	26/08/87	Away	S Lge Cup	4–1
9	3	Dunfermline Athletic	12/09/87	Home	League	4–0
10	3	Morton	26/09/87	Home	League	7–0
11	3	Morton	09/01/88	Home	League	5–0
12	3	Arbroath	15/08/89	Home	S Lge Cup	4–0
13	3	Raith Rovers	04/09/90	Home	S Lge Cup	6–2
14	3	Falkirk	07/04/92	Home	League	4–1
15	3	Stranraer	19/08/92	Away	S Lge Cup	5–0
16	3	Motherwell	02/09/92	Away	League	4–1
17	3	St Johnstone	22/09/92	Hampden	S Lge Cup	3–1
18	4	Falkirk	03/10/92	Home	League	4–0
19	3	Motherwell	31/10/92	Home	League	4–2
20	3	Alloa	19/02/94	Home	S Cup	6–0
21	3	Raith Rovers	30/03/96	Away	League	4–2
22	3	Dunfermline Athletic	17/08/96	Away	League	5–2
23	3	Spartak–Alania Vladikavkaz	21/08/96	Away	Eur Cup	7–2

Scottish League: 16
Scottish Cup: 1
Scottish League Cup: 6
European Cup: 1
TOTAL: 24

HONOURS

Winners medals
Scottish Premier Division Championship: 86/87, 88/89, 89/90, 90/91, 91/92, 92/93, 93/94, 95/96, 96/97
Scottish Cup: 91/92
Scottish League Cup: 83/84, 84/85, 86/87, 87/88, 88/89, 90/91, 92/93, 93/94, 96/97

Runner-up medals
Scottish Cup: 88/89, 93/94
Scottish League Cup: 89/90

Played nine (4+5/1) League matches in the Rangers team that won the 1994/95 Scottish Premier Division Championship.

JOHN MCGINLAY

Born: 08/04/64 – Inverness
Height: 5.9
Weight: 11.06 (96–97)

Clubs
Shrewsbury Town: **1989–90** – Matches: **66+2** – Goals: **31**
Bury: **1990–91** – Matches: **19+10** – Goals: **9**
Millwall: **1991–92** – Matches: **33+8** – Goals: **11**
Bolton Wanderers: **1992–97** – Matches: **224+11** – Goals: **116**

Country
Scotland: **1994–97** – Matches: **11+2** – Goals: **4**

SEASON 1988–89

Shrewsbury Town – League Division Two

Sub+1	25/02/89	Walsall	Away	League	1–1		
1	28/02/89	Plymouth Argyle	Home	League	2–0	1 Goal	(1)
2	03/03/89	Oldham Athletic	Away	League	0–3		
3	11/03/89	Brighton & Hove Albion	Home	League	1–1		
4	15/03/89	Leicester City	Away	League	1–1		
5	18/03/89	Ipswich Town	Away	League	0–2		
6	27/03/89	Birmingham City	Away	League	2–1		
7	01/04/89	Crystal Palace	Home	League	2–1	1 Goal	(2)
8	04/04/89	Manchester City	Home	League	0–1		
9	08/04/89	Barnsley	Away	League	0–1		
Sub+2	15/04/89	Oxford United	Home	League	2–2	1 Goal	(3)
10	22/04/89	Sunderland	Away	League	1–2	1 Goal	(4)
11	29/04/89	Chelsea	Home	League	1–1	1 Goal	(5)
12	01/05/89	Swindon Town	Away	League	0–1		
13	06/05/89	Watford	Away	League	0–0		
14	13/05/89	Leeds United	Home	League	3–3		

SEASON 1989–90

League Division Three

15	22/08/89	Notts County	Home	Lge Cup	3–0		
16	26/08/89	Leyton Orient	Home	League	3–3		
17	29/08/89	Notts County	Away	Lge Cup	1–3		
18	02/09/89	Blackpool	Away	League	4–2	2 Goals	(7)
19	09/09/89	Birmingham City	Home	League	1–0		
20	16/09/89	Northampton Town	Away	League	2–0	1 Goal	(8)
21	19/09/89	Swindon Town	Home	Lge Cup	0–3		
22	23/09/89	Bury	Home	League	3–1	1 Goal	(9)
23	26/09/89	Bristol City	Away	League	1–2		
24	30/09/89	Crewe Alexandra	Home	League	0–0		
25	03/10/89	Swindon Town	Away	Lge Cup	1–3		
26	07/10/89	Mansfield Town	Home	League	0–1		
27	14/10/89	Wigan Athletic	Away	League	0–0		
28	17/10/89	Walsall	Away	League	2–0		
29	21/10/89	Brentford	Home	League	1–0		
30	28/10/89	Huddersfield Town	Away	League	1–1		
31	31/10/89	Tranmere Rovers	Home	League	3–1	2 Goals	(11)
32	04/11/89	Preston North End	Away	League	1–2		
33	11/11/89	Bristol Rovers	Home	League	2–3	1 Goal	(12)
34	18/11/89	Chesterfield	Home	FA Cup	2–3	2 Goals	(14)
35	25/11/89	Rotherham United	Away	League	2–4		
36	28/11/89	Walsall	Away	LD Cup	1–0		
37	02/12/89	Chester City	Home	League	2–0	1 Goal	(15)
38	16/12/89	Bolton Wanderers	Home	League	3–3	1 Goal	(16)
39	19/12/89	Cardiff City	Home	LD Cup	4–0	2 Goals	(18)
40	26/12/89	Notts County	Away	League	0–4		
41	30/12/89	Fulham	Away	League	1–2	1 Goal	(19)
42	01/01/90	Swansea City	Home	League	1–1	1 Goal	(20)
43	13/01/90	Leyton Orient	Away	League	0–1		
44	20/01/90	Reading	Home	League	1–1	1 Goal	(21)
45	23/01/90	Exeter City	Home	LD Cup	0–1		

46	27/01/90	Birmingham City	Away	League	1–0	1 Goal	(22)
47	03/02/90	Bury	Away	League	0–0		
48	13/02/90	Blackpool	Home	League	1–1		
49	17/02/90	Chester City	Away	League	0–1		
50	24/02/90	Rotherham United	Home	League	1–1		
51	02/03/90	Cardiff City	Away	League	1–0		
52	06/03/90	Crewe Alexandra	Away	League	1–1	1 Goal	(23)
53	10/03/90	Bristol City	Home	League	0–1		
54	13/03/90	Cardiff City	Home	League	0–0		
55	17/03/90	Mansfield Town	Away	League	1–2		
56	20/03/90	Wigan Athletic	Home	League	1–3		
57	24/03/90	Walsall	Home	League	2–0		
58	31/03/90	Brentford	Away	League	1–1		
59	03/04/90	Northampton Town	Home	League	2–0	1 Goal	(24)
60	07/04/90	Huddersfield Town	Home	League	3–3	3 Goals	(27)
61	09/04/90	Tranmere Rovers	Away	League	1–3		
62	14/04/90	Swansea City	Away	League	1–0	1 Goal	(28)
63	17/04/90	Notts County	Home	League	2–2		
64	21/04/90	Bolton Wanderers	Away	League	1–0	1 Goal	(29)
65	24/04/90	Fulham	Home	League	2–0	1 Goal	(30)
66	05/05/90	Preston North End	Home	League	2–0	1 Goal	(31)

SEASON 1990–91

Bury – League Division Three

1	25/08/90	Chester City	Home	League	2–1	1 Goal	(1)
2	29/08/90	Bradford City	Away	Lge Cup	0–2		
Sub+1	15/09/90	Birmingham City	Away	League	0–1		
Sub+2	18/09/90	Swansea City	Away	League	2–1		
Sub+3	22/09/90	Mansfield Town	Home	League	1–0		
3	29/09/90	Crewe Alexandra	Home	League	1–3		
4	02/10/90	Shrewsbury Town	Away	League	1–1	1 Goal	(2)
5	06/10/90	Cambridge United	Away	League	2–2		
6	13/10/90	Bolton Wanderers	Home	League	2–2		
7	20/10/90	Reading	Home	League	2–1		
8	23/10/90	Fulham	Away	League	0–2		
9	27/10/90	Southend United	Away	League	1–2		
10	03/11/90	Tranmere Rovers	Home	League	3–0	2 Goals	(4)
11	10/11/90	Brentford	Away	League	2–2		
12	17/11/90	Chorley	Away	FA Cup	1–2		
13	24/11/90	Stoke City	Home	League	1–1	1 Goal	(5)
14	27/11/90	Chester City	Away	LD Cup	0–2		
15	01/12/90	Wigan Athletic	Away	League	2–1		
Sub+4	11/12/90	Wigan Athletic	Home	LD Cup	2–1		
Sub+5	15/12/90	Exeter City	Home	League	3–1		
Sub+6	22/12/90	Huddersfield Town	Away	League	1–2		
Sub+7	29/12/90	Preston North End	Home	League	3–1		
Sub+8	12/01/91	AFC Bournemouth	Home	League	2–4		
Sub+9	05/03/91	Rotherham United	Away	League	3–0		
Sub+10	09/03/91	Exeter City	Away	League	0–2		
16	12/03/91	Shrewsbury Town	Home	League	2–1		
17	16/03/91	Crewe Alexandra	Away	League	2–2	1 Goal	(6)
18	19/03/91	Bolton Wanderers	Away	League	3–1	3 Goals	(9)
19	23/03/91	Cambridge United	Home	League	3–1		

Millwall – League Division Two

1	16/04/91	Hull City	Away	League	1–1		
2	20/04/91	Notts County	Home	League	1–2		
3	22/05/91	Brighton & Hove Albion	Home	Lge P/O	1–2	1 Goal	(1)

SEASON 1991–92

League Division Two

Sub+1	05/11/91	Tranmere Rovers	Away	League	1–2		
4	16/11/91	Wolverhampton Wanderers	Home	League	2–1	1 Goal	(2)
5	23/11/91	Grimsby Town	Away	League	1–1	1 Goal	(3)
6	30/11/91	Bristol Rovers	Home	League	0–1		
7	07/12/91	Leicester City	Away	League	1–1		
8	21/12/91	Brighton & Hove Albion	Away	League	4–3	2 Goals	(5)
9	26/12/91	Watford	Home	League	0–4		
10	28/12/91	Plymouth Argyle	Home	League	2–1	1 Goal	(6)
11	01/01/92	Swindon Town	Away	League	1–3	1 Goal	(7)
12	04/01/92	Huddersfield Town	Away	FA Cup	4–0		
13	11/01/92	Sunderland	Away	League	2–6		
14	18/01/92	Middlesbrough	Home	League	2–0	1 Goal	(8)

15	01/02/92	Ipswich Town	Home	League	2–3		
16	05/02/92	Norwich City	Away	FA Cup	1–2		
17	08/02/92	Derby County	Away	League	2–0	1 Goal	(9)
18	15/02/92	Grimsby Town	Home	League	1–1		
19	22/02/92	Bristol Rovers	Away	League	2–3		
20	26/02/92	Charlton Athletic	Home	League	1–0		
21	29/02/92	Leicester City	Home	League	2–0		
22	07/03/92	Charlton Athletic	Away	League	0–1		
23	11/03/92	Tranmere Rovers	Home	League	0–3		
24	14/03/92	Portsmouth	Away	League	1–6		
Sub+2	28/03/92	Wolverhampton Wanderers	Away	League	0–0		
Sub+3	04/04/92	Cambridge United	Away	League	0–1		
Sub+4	11/04/92	Bristol City	Home	League	2–3		
Sub+5	18/04/92	Newcastle United	Away	League	1–0		
Sub+6	22/04/92	Barnsley	Home	League	1–1		

SEASON 1992–93

Football League Division One

25	15/08/92	Watford	Away	League	1–3	1 Goal	(10)
26	18/08/92	Leyton Orient	Away	Lge Cup	2–2		
27	22/08/92	Oxford United	Home	League	3–1		
28	26/08/92	Leyton Orient	Home	Lge Cup	3–0		
29	29/08/92	Barnsley	Away	League	0–0		
30	02/09/92	Charlton Athletic	Home	AI Cup	1–2		
31	05/09/92	Swindon Town	Home	League	2–1	1 Goal	(11)
32	12/09/92	Birmingham City	Home	League	0–0		
33	15/09/92	Peterborough United	Away	League	0–0		
Sub+7	19/09/92	Notts County	Home	League	6–0		
Sub+8	22/09/92	Arsenal	Away	Lge Cup	1–1		

Bolton Wanderers – Football League Division Two

1	03/10/92	Leyton Orient	Away	League	0–1		
Sub+1	10/10/92	Hartlepool United	Home	League	1–2		
2	17/10/92	Chester City	Away	League	2–2	1 Goal	(1)
3	24/10/92	Hull City	Home	League	2–0	1 Goal	(2)
4	31/10/92	Preston North End	Away	League	2–2		
Sub+2	07/11/92	Port Vale	Home	League	1–1	1 Goal	(3)
Sub+3	21/11/92	Fulham	Away	League	4–1		
5	28/11/92	Burnley	Home	League	4–0		
6	01/12/92	Rochdale	Away	A Trophy	0–0		
7	05/12/92	Rochdale	Home	FA Cup	4–0	2 Goals	(5)
8	08/12/92	Bury	Home	A Trophy	1–1	1 Goal	(6)
9	19/12/92	Bradford City	Home	League	5–0	2 Goals	(8)
10	26/12/92	Wigan Athletic	Home	League	2–1		
11	28/12/92	Swansea City	Away	League	2–1	1 Goal	(9)
12	03/01/93	Liverpool	Home	FA Cup	2–2	1 Goal	(10)
13	09/01/93	West Bromwich Albion	Away	League	1–3		
14	13/01/93	Liverpool	Away	FA Cup	2–0	1 Goal	(11)
15	16/01/93	Plymouth Argyle	Home	League	3–1		
16	19/01/93	Darlington	Away	A Trophy	4–3*		
17	24/01/93	Wolverhampton Wanderers	Away	FA Cup	2–0	1 Goal	(12)
18	27/01/93	Reading	Away	League	2–1		
19	30/01/93	Brighton & Hove Albion	Home	League	0–1		
20	02/02/93	Huddersfield Town	Away	A Trophy	0–3		
21	09/02/93	Stockport County	Away	League	0–2		
22	13/02/93	Derby County	Away	FA Cup	1–3		
23	20/02/93	Blackpool	Away	League	1–1	1 Goal	(13)
24	27/02/93	Hartlepool United	Away	League	2–0	1 Goal	(14)
25	06/03/93	Leyton Orient	Home	League	1–0		
26	09/03/93	Mansfield Town	Home	League	2–1		
27	20/03/93	Exeter City	Home	League	4–1	2 Goals	(16)
28	23/03/93	Burnley	Away	League	1–0	1 Goal	(17)
29	27/03/93	Fulham	Home	League	1–0		
30	30/03/93	Rotherham United	Home	League	2–0		
31	03/04/93	Mansfield Town	Away	League	1–1		
32	06/04/93	Stockport County	Home	League	2–1	1 Goal	(18)
33	10/04/93	Wigan Athletic	Away	League	2–0		
34	12/04/93	Swansea City	Home	League	3–1		
35	17/04/93	Bradford City	Away	League	1–2	1 Goal	(19)
36	24/04/93	Chester City	Home	League	5–0	1 Goal	(20)
37	27/04/93	AFC Bournemouth	Away	League	2–1		
38	30/04/93	Hull City	Away	League	2–1	1 Goal	(21)
39	04/05/93	Stoke City	Home	League	1–0		
40	08/05/93	Preston North End	Home	League	1–0	1 Goal	(22)

SEASON 1993–94

Football League Division One

41	14/08/93	Grimsby Town	Away	League	0–0		
42	17/08/93	Bury	Home	Lge Cup	0–2		
43	21/08/93	Stoke City	Home	League	1–1		
44	24/08/93	Bury	Away	Lge Cup	2–0+	1 Goal	(23)
45	28/08/93	Charlton Athletic	Away	League	0–3		
46	31/08/93	Oxford United	Home	League	1–0	1 Goal	(24)
47	07/09/93	Tranmere Rovers	Away	AI Cup	2–1	1 Goal	(25)
48	11/09/93	Luton Town	Away	League	2–0	2 Goals	(27)
49	18/09/93	Leicester City	Home	League	1–2	1 Goal	(28)
50	02/10/93	Bristol City	Away	League	0–2		
51	06/10/93	Sheffield Wednesday	Away	Lge Cup	0–1		
52	09/10/93	Tranmere Rovers	Away	League	1–2		
53	12/10/93	Ancona Calcio	Home	AI Cup	5–0	2 Goals	(30)
54	16/10/93	Millwall	Home	League	4–0	2 Goals	(32)
55	19/10/93	Birmingham City	Away	League	1–2		
56	23/10/93	Watford	Away	League	3–4		
57	30/10/93	Derby County	Home	League	0–2		
58	02/11/93	Peterborough United	Home	League	1–1	1 Goal	(33)
59	06/11/93	West Bromwich Albion	Away	League	2–2		
60	09/11/93	Brescia Calcio	Home	AI Cup	3–3	1 Goal	(34)
61	13/11/93	Gretna	Away	FA Cup	3–2	1 Goal	(35)
62	16/11/93	SC Pisa	Away	AI Cup	1–1		
63	21/11/93	Middlesbrough	Away	League	1–0	1 Goal	(36)
64	24/11/93	Crystal Palace	Home	League	1–0	1 Goal	(37)
65	27/11/93	Barnsley	Away	League	1–1		
66	04/12/93	Lincoln City	Away	FA Cup	3–1		
67	07/12/93	West Bromwich Albion	Home	League	1–1		
68	11/12/93	Oxford United	Away	League	2–0		
69	08/01/94	Everton	Home	FA Cup	1–1		
70	12/01/94	Southend United	Away	League	2–0	1 Goal	(38)
71	15/01/94	Millwall	Away	League	0–1		
72	19/01/94	Everton	Away	FA Cup	3–2*	1 Goal	(39)
73	23/01/94	Tranmere Rovers	Home	League	2–1	2 Goals	(41)
74	31/01/94	Arsenal	Home	FA Cup	2–2		
75	05/02/94	Watford	Home	League	3–1	1 Goal	(42)
76	09/02/94	Arsenal	Away	FA Cup	3–1*	1 Goal	(43)
77	12/02/94	Derby County	Away	League	0–2		
78	20/02/94	Aston Villa	Home	FA Cup	1–0		
79	22/02/94	Stoke City	Away	League	0–2		
80	25/02/94	Crystal Palace	Away	League	1–1		
81	05/03/94	Charlton Athletic	Home	League	3–2	3 Goals	(46)
82	12/03/94	Oldham Athletic	Home	FA Cup	0–1		
83	19/03/94	Nottingham Forest	Away	League	2–3		
84	29/03/94	Wolverhampton Wanderers	Home	League	1–3	1 Goal	(47)
85	02/04/94	Sunderland	Away	League	0–2		
86	04/04/94	Portsmouth	Home	League	1–1	1 Goal	(48)
87	09/04/94	Notts County	Away	League	1–2	1 Goal	(49)
88	12/04/94	Southend United	Home	League	0–2		
89	16/04/94	Peterborough United	Away	League	3–2		
90	23/04/94	Middlesbrough	Home	League	4–1	3 Goals	(52)
91	30/04/94	Birmingham City	Home	League	1–1		
92	03/05/94	Leicester City	Away	League	1–1	1 Goal	(53)
93	05/05/94	Luton Town	Home	League	2–1	1 Goal	(54)
94	08/05/94	Barnsley	Home	League	2–3	1 Goal	(55)

+ AET Bolton Wanderers won 3–0 on penalties

SEASON 1994–95

Football League Division One

95	13/08/94	Grimsby Town	Away	League	3–3	1 Goal	(56)
96	20/08/94	Bristol City	Home	League	0–2		
Sub+4	27/08/94	Middlesbrough	Away	League	0–1		
Sub+5	30/08/94	Millwall	Home	League	1–0		
97	03/09/94	Stoke City	Home	League	4–0	1 Goal	(57)
98	10/09/94	Sheffield United	Away	League	1–3	1 Goal	(58)
99	13/09/94	Luton Town	Away	League	3–0	2 Goals	(60)
100	17/09/94	Portsmouth	Home	League	1–1	1 Goal	(61)
101	21/09/94	Ipswich Town	Away	Lge Cup	3–0	1 Goal	(62)
102	24/09/94	Southend United	Away	League	1–2		
103	01/10/94	Derby County	Home	League	1–0	1 Goal	(63)
104	05/10/94	Ipswich Town	Home	Lge Cup	1–0		

105	08/10/94	Burnley	Away	League	2–2	1 Goal	(64)
106	16/10/94	Oldham Athletic	Home	League	2–2		
107	22/10/94	Port Vale	Away	League	1–1		
108	25/10/94	Sheffield United	Home	Lge Cup	2–1		
109	29/10/94	Watford	Home	League	3–0	2 Goals	(66)
110	26/11/94	Barnsley	Away	League	0–3		
111	30/11/94	West Ham United	Away	Lge Cup	3–1	2 Goals	(68)
112	06/12/94	Port Vale	Home	League	1–0		
113	10/12/94	Bristol City	Away	League	1–0		
114	27/12/94	Tranmere Rovers	Home	League	1–0		
115	31/12/94	West Bromwich Albion	Away	League	0–1		
116	02/01/95	Reading	Home	League	1–0		
117	07/01/95	Portsmouth	Away	FA Cup	1–3		
118	11/01/95	Norwich City	Home	Lge Cup	1–0		
119	14/01/95	Watford	Away	League	0–0		
120	21/01/95	Charlton Athletic	Home	League	5–1	2 Goals	(70)
Sub+6	12/02/95	Swindon Town	Away	Lge Cup	2–1		
121	18/02/95	Barnsley	Home	League	2–1		
122	26/02/95	Derby County	Away	League	1–2		
123	04/03/95	Southend United	Home	League	3–0		
124	08/03/95	Swindon Town	Home	Lge Cup	3–1	1 Goal	(71)
125	11/03/95	Middlesbrough	Home	League	1–0		
126	19/03/95	Millwall	Away	League	1–0	1 Goal	(72)
127	22/03/95	Sheffield United	Home	League	1–1		
128	02/04/95	Liverpool	Wembley	Lge Cup	1–2		
129	05/04/95	Swindon Town	Away	League	1–0		
130	08/04/95	West Bromwich Albion	Home	League	1–0		
Sub+7	11/04/95	Luton Town	Home	League	0–0		
131	14/04/95	Tranmere Rovers	Away	League	0–1		
132	17/04/95	Sunderland	Home	League	1–0	1 Goal	(73)
133	21/04/95	Reading	Away	League	1–2		
134	29/04/95	Oldham Athletic	Away	League	1–3	1 Goal	(74)
135	03/05/95	Stoke City	Away	League	1–1	1 Goal	(75)
136	07/05/95	Burnley	Home	League	1–1		
137	14/05/95	Wolverhampton Wanderers	Away	Lge P/O	1–2		
138	17/05/95	Wolverhampton Wanderers	Home	Lge P/O	2–0	2 Goals	(77)
139	29/05/95	Reading	Wembley	Lge P/O	4–3*		

SEASON 1995–96

Premier League

140	30/08/95	Aston Villa	Away	League	0–1		
141	09/09/95	Middlesbrough	Home	League	1–1	1 Goal	(78)
142	16/09/95	Manchester United	Away	League	0–3		
143	19/09/95	Brentford	Home	Lge Cup	1–0		
144	23/09/95	Liverpool	Away	League	2–5		
145	30/09/95	Queens Park Rangers	Home	League	0–1		
146	03/10/95	Brentford	Away	Lge Cup	3–2	1 Goal	(79)
147	14/10/95	Everton	Home	League	1–1		
148	21/10/95	Nottingham Forest	Away	League	2–3		
149	24/10/95	Leicester City	Home	Lge Cup	0–0		
150	30/10/95	Arsenal	Home	League	1–0	1 Goal	(80)
151	04/11/95	Manchester City	Away	League	0–1		
152	08/11/95	Leicester City	Away	Lge Cup	3–2	1 Goal	(81)
153	18/11/95	West Ham United	Home	League	0–3		
154	22/11/95	Chelsea	Away	League	2–3		
155	25/11/95	Southampton	Away	League	0–1		
156	29/11/95	Norwich City	Away	Lge Cup	0–0		
157	02/12/95	Nottingham Forest	Home	League	1–1		
158	09/12/95	Liverpool	Home	League	0–1		
159	16/12/95	Queens Park Rangers	Away	League	1–2		
160	20/12/95	Norwich City	Home	Lge Cup	0–0+		
161	23/12/95	Tottenham Hotspur	Away	League	2–2		
162	27/12/95	Leeds United	Home	League	0–2		
163	30/12/95	Coventry City	Home	League	1–2	1 Goal	(82)
164	01/01/96	Sheffield Wednesday	Away	League	2–4		
165	06/01/96	Bradford City	Away	FA Cup	3–0	1 Goal	(83)
166	13/01/96	Wimbledon	Home	League	1–0	1 Goal	(84)
167	20/01/96	Newcastle United	Away	League	1–2		
168	03/02/96	Blackburn Rovers	Away	League	1–3		
Sub+8	10/02/96	Aston Villa	Home	League	0–2		
Sub+9	14/02/96	Leeds United	Home	FA Cup	0–1		
Sub+10	25/02/96	Manchester United	Home	League	0–6		
Sub+11	20/03/96	Tottenham Hotspur	Home	League	2–3		
169	23/03/96	Sheffield Wednesday	Home	League	2–1		

170	30/03/96	Manchester City	Home	League	1–1	1 Goal	(85)
171	06/04/96	Everton	Away	League	0–3		
172	08/04/96	Chelsea	Home	League	2–1	1 Goal	(86)
173	13/04/96	West Ham United	Away	League	0–1		
174	27/04/96	Southampton	Home	League	0–1		
175	05/05/96	Arsenal	Away	League	1–2		

+ AET Norwich City won 3–2 on penalties

SEASON 1996–97

Football League Division One

176	17/08/96	Port Vale	Away	League	1–1		
177	20/08/96	Manchester City	Home	League	1–0		
178	24/08/96	Norwich City	Home	League	3–1		
179	01/09/96	Queens Park Rangers	Away	League	2–1	1 Goal	(87)
180	07/09/96	Southend United	Away	League	2–5	1 Goal	(88)
181	10/09/96	Grimsby Town	Home	League	6–1		
182	14/09/96	Portsmouth	Home	League	2–0		
183	18/09/96	Bristol City	Away	Lge Cup	0–0		
184	21/09/96	Bradford City	Away	League	4–2		
185	24/09/96	Bristol City	Home	Lge Cup	3–1*	1 Goal	(89)
186	28/09/96	Stoke City	Home	League	1–1		
187	02/10/96	Wolverhampton Wanderers	Away	League	2–1	2 Goals	(91)
188	12/10/96	Oldham Athletic	Home	League	3–1	2 Goals	(93)
189	15/10/96	Tranmere Rovers	Home	League	1–0		
190	19/10/96	Charlton Athletic	Away	League	3–3	2 Goals	(95)
191	22/10/96	Chelsea	Home	Lge Cup	2–1	1 Goal	(96)
192	25/10/96	Barnsley	Away	League	2–2	1 Goal	(97)
193	29/10/96	Reading	Home	League	2–1	1 Goal	(98)
194	02/11/96	Huddersfield Town	Home	League	2–0	1 Goal	(99)
195	13/11/96	Birmingham City	Away	League	1–3		
196	16/11/96	Crystal Palace	Home	League	2–2	1 Goal	(100)
197	19/11/96	Oxford United	Away	League	0–0		
198	22/11/96	Sheffield United	Away	League	1–1		
199	27/11/96	Tottenham Hotspur	Home	Lge Cup	6–1	3 Goals	(103)
200	30/11/96	Barnsley	Home	League	2–2		
201	08/12/96	West Bromwich Albion	Away	League	2–2		
202	14/12/96	Ipswich Town	Home	League	1–2		
203	22/12/96	Swindon Town	Away	League	2–2	1 Goal	(104)
204	26/12/96	Grimsby Town	Away	League	2–1		
205	28/12/96	Southend United	Home	League	3–1	1 Goal	(105)
206	01/01/97	Bradford City	Home	League	2–1		
207	05/01/97	Wimbledon	Home	Lge Cup	0–2		
208	18/01/97	Wolverhampton Wanderers	Home	League	3–0	1 Goal	(106)
209	25/01/97	Luton Town	Home	FA Cup	6–2	1 Goal	(107)
210	29/01/97	Stoke City	Away	League	2–1	1 Goal	(108)
211	01/02/97	Birmingham City	Home	League	2–1	1 Goal	(109)
212	08/02/97	Reading	Away	League	2–3	1 Goal	(110)
213	15/02/97	Sheffield United	Home	League	2–2		
214	22/02/97	Huddersfield Town	Away	League	2–1		
215	02/03/97	West Bromwich Albion	Home	League	1–0		
216	04/03/97	Crystal Palace	Away	League	1–1		
217	08/03/97	Swindon Town	Home	League	7–0	1 Goal	(111)
218	15/03/97	Ipswich Town	Away	League	1–0	1 Goal	(112)
219	18/03/97	Port Vale	Home	League	4–2		
220	22/03/97	Norwich City	Away	League	1–0		
221	05/04/97	Queens Park Rangers	Home	League	2–1	1 Goal	(113)
222	09/04/97	Manchester City	Away	League	2–1		
223	25/04/97	Charlton Athletic	Home	League	4–1	2 Goals	(115)
224	04/05/97	Tranmere Rovers	Away	League	2–2	1 Goal	(116)

INTERNATIONAL APPEARANCES – SCOTLAND

1	20/04/94	Austria	Vienna	2–1	F	1 Goal	(1)
2	27/05/94	Holland	Utrecht	1–3	F		
3	12/10/94	Faroe Islands	Hampden Park	5–1	ECQ	1 Goal	(2)
4	16/11/94	Russia	Hampden Park	1–1	ECQ		
5	18/12/94	Greece	Athens	0–1	ECQ		
6	29/03/95	Russia	Moscow	0–0	ECQ		
7	26/04/95	San Marino	Serravalle	2–0	ECQ		
8	07/06/95	Faroe Islands	Toftir	2–0	ECQ	1 Goal	(3)
9	11/10/95	Sweden	Stockholm	0–2	F		
10	10/11/96	Sweden	Ibrox Park	1–0	WCQ	1 Goal	(4)
11	11/02/97	Estonia	Monte Carlo	0–0	WCQ		

| Sub 12 | 29/03/97 | Estonia | Rugby Park | 2–0 | WCQ |
| Sub 13 | 02/04/97 | Austria | Celtic Park | 2–0 | WCQ |

APPEARANCES AND GOALS PER SEASON

SEASON 88–89	GAMES	GOALS
League	14+2	5
TOTAL	**14+2**	**5**

SEASON 89–90	GAMES	GOALS
League	44	22
FA Cup	1	2
League Cup	4	0
Leyland Daf Cup	3	2
TOTAL	**52**	**26**

SEASON 90–91	GAMES	GOALS
League	18+9	9
League Play–offs	1	1
FA Cup	1	0
League Cup	1	0
Leyland Daf Cup	1+1	0
TOTAL	**22+10**	**10**

SEASON 91–92	GAMES	GOALS
League	19+6	8
FA Cup	2	0
TOTAL	**21+6**	**8**

SEASON 92–93	GAMES	GOALS
League	37+4	18
FA Cup	5	5
League Cup	2+1	0
Anglo–Italian Cup	1	0
Autoglass Trophy	4	1
TOTAL	**49+5**	**24**

SEASON 93–94	GAMES	GOALS
League	39	25
FA Cup	8	3
League Cup	3	1
Anglo–Italian Cup	4	4
TOTAL	**54**	**33**

SEASON 94–95	GAMES	GOALS
League	34+3	16
League Play–offs	3	2
FA Cup	1	0
League Cup	7+1	4
TOTAL	**45+4**	**22**

SEASON 95–96	GAMES	GOALS
League	29+3	6
FA Cup	1+1	1
League Cup	6	2
TOTAL	**36+4**	**9**

SEASON 96–97	GAMES	GOALS
League	43	24
FA Cup	1	1
League Cup	5	5
TOTAL	**49**	**30**

CAREER APPEARANCES AND GOALS

COMPETITION	GAMES	TOTAL	GOALS
League	277+27	304	133
League Play–offs	4	4	3
FA Cup	20+1	21	12
League Cup	28+2	30	12
Leyland Daf Cup	4+1	5	2
Anglo–Italian Cup	5	5	4
Autoglass Trophy	4	4	1
Internationals	11+2	13	4
TOTAL	**353+33**	**386**	**171**

HAT-TRICKS

Shrewsbury Town

1	3	Huddersfield Town	07/04/90	Home	League	3–3

Bury

1	3	Bolton Wanderers	19/03/91	Away	League	3–1

Bolton Wanderers

1	3	Charlton Athletic	05/03/94	Home	League	3–2
2	3	Middlesbrough	23/04/94	Home	League	4–1
3	3	Tottenham Hotspur	27/11/96	Home	Lge Cup	6–1

League: 4
League Cup: 1
TOTAL: 5

HONOURS

Winners medals
Football League Division One Championship: 96/97

Runner-up medals
League Cup: 94/95
Football League Division Two Championship: 92/93
Promoted to the Premier League: 94/95

CHARLIE NICHOLAS

Born: 30/12/61 – Glasgow
Height: 5.10
Weight: 11.00 (95–96)

Clubs
Celtic: **1980–83** – Matches: **100+11** – Goals: **82**
Arsenal: **1983–87** – Matches: **176+8** – Goals: **54**
Aberdeen: **1988–90** – Matches: **103+2** – Goals: **36**
Celtic: **1990–95** – Matches: **108+31** – Goals: **43**
Clyde: **1995–96** – Matches: **36** – Goals: **7**

Country
Scotland: **1983–89** – Matches: **11+9** – Goals: **5**

SEASON 1980–81

Celtic – Scottish League Premier Division

Sub+1	16/08/80	Kilmarnock	Away	League	3–0		
Sub+2	20/08/80	Dyosgyori VTK Miskolc	Home	ECW Cup	6–0		
Sub+3	30/08/80	Stirling Albion	Home	S Lge Cup	6–1*	2 Goals	(2)
1	03/09/80	Dyosgyori VTK Miskolc	Away	ECW Cup	1–2	1 Goal	(3)
2	06/09/80	Partick Thistle	Home	League	4–1	2 Goals	(5)
3	13/09/80	Heart of Midlothian	Away	League	2–0	1 Goal	(6)
4	17/09/80	Politehnica Timisoara	Home	ECW Cup	2–1	2 Goals	(8)
5	20/09/80	Airdrieonians	Home	League	1–1	1 Goal	(9)
6	22/09/80	Hamilton Academical	Away	S Lge Cup	3–1	1 Goal	(10)
7	24/09/80	Hamilton Academical	Home	S Lge Cup	4–1	1 Goal	(11)
8	27/09/80	Aberdeen	Away	League	2–2	1 Goal	(12)
9	01/10/80	Politehnica Timisoara	Away	ECW Cup	0–1		
10	04/10/80	Dundee United	Home	League	2–0	1 Goal	(13)
11	08/10/80	Partick Thistle	Away	S Lge Cup	1–0	1 Goal	(14)
12	11/10/80	St Mirren	Away	League	2–0		
13	18/10/80	Morton	Away	League	3–2	1 Goal	(15)
14	20/10/80	Partick Thistle	Home	S Lge Cup	2–1*		
15	25/10/80	Kilmarnock	Home	League	4–1	2 Goals	(17)
16	01/11/80	Rangers	Away	League	0–3		
17	08/11/80	Aberdeen	Home	League	0–2		
Sub+4	12/11/80	Dundee United	Away	S Lge Cup	1–1	1 Goal	(18)
18	15/11/80	Airdrieonians	Away	League	4–1	1 Goal	(19)

19	19/11/80	Dundee United	Home	S Lge Cup	0–3		
20	22/11/80	St Mirren	Home	League	1–2		
Sub+5	27/12/80	Aberdeen	Away	League	1–4	1 Goal	(20)
21	01/01/81	Kilmarnock	Away	League	2–1		
22	03/01/81	Morton	Home	League	3–0		
23	10/01/81	Dundee United	Home	League	2–1	1 Goal	(21)
24	24/01/81	Berwick Rangers	Away	S Cup	2–0	1 Goal	(22)
25	31/01/81	Heart of Midlothian	Away	League	3–0		
26	14/02/81	Stirling Albion	Home	S Cup	3–0		
27	21/02/81	Rangers	Home	League	3–1	2 Goals	(24)
28	28/02/81	Morton	Away	League	3–0		
29	08/03/81	East Stirling	Home	S Cup	2–0		
30	14/03/81	St Mirren	Home	League	7–0	1 Goal	(25)
31	18/03/81	Partick Thistle	Home	League	4–1		
32	21/03/81	Airdrieonians	Away	League	2–1		
33	28/03/81	Aberdeen	Home	League	1–1		
Sub+6	05/04/81	Partick Thistle	Away	League	1–0		
34	11/04/81	Dundee United	Hampden	S Cup	0–0		
35	15/04/81	Dundee United	Hampden	S Cup	2–3	2 Goals	(27)
36	18/04/81	Rangers	Away	League	1–0	1 Goal	(28)
37	22/04/81	Dundee United	Away	League	3–2		
38	25/04/81	Kilmarnock	Home	League	1–1		
39	02/05/81	St Mirren	Away	League	1–3		

SEASON 1981–82

Scottish League Premier Division

40	08/08/81	St Mirren	Home	S Lge Cup	1–3		
41	15/08/81	Hibernian	Home	S Lge Cup	4–1	2 Goals	(30)
42	19/08/81	St Johnstone	Home	S Lge Cup	4–1	1 Goal	(31)
Sub+7	29/08/81	Airdrieonians	Home	League	5–2	1 Goal	(32)
43	16/09/81	Juventus FC	Home	Eur Cup	1–0		
44	26/09/81	Partick Thistle	Home	League	2–0	1 Goal	(33)
45	03/10/81	Dundee	Away	League	3–1		
46	10/10/81	St Mirren	Away	League	2–1	1 Goal	(34)
47	17/10/81	Dundee United	Home	League	1–1		
48	24/10/81	Hibernian	Away	League	0–1		
49	31/10/81	Airdrieonians	Away	League	3–1		
Sub+8	14/11/81	Morton	Away	League	1–1		
Sub+9	28/11/81	Partick Thistle	Away	League	2–0		
50	09/01/82	Rangers	Away	League	0–1		

SEASON 1982–83

Scottish League Premier Division

Sub+10	14/08/82	Dunfermline Athletic	Home	S Lge Cup	6–0		
Sub+11	21/08/82	Arbroath	Away	S Lge Cup	3–0	1 Goal	(35)
51	25/08/82	Alloa	Home	S Lge Cup	4–1	1 Goal	(36)
52	28/08/82	Dunfermline Athletic	Away	S Lge Cup	7–1	4 Goals	(40)
53	01/09/82	Arbroath	Home	S Lge Cup	4–1	1 Goal	(41)
54	04/09/82	Dundee	Home	League	2–0		
55	08/09/82	Partick Thistle	Home	S Lge Cup	4–0	1 Goal	(42)
56	11/09/82	St Mirren	Away	League	2–1	2 Goals	(44)
57	15/09/82	AFC Ajax	Home	Eur Cup	2–2	1 Goal	(45)
58	18/09/82	Motherwell	Away	League	7–0	3 Goals	(48)
59	22/09/82	Partick Thistle	Away	S Lge Cup	3–0	2 Goals	(50)
60	25/09/82	Hibernian	Home	League	2–0		
61	29/09/82	AFC Ajax	Away	Eur Cup	2–1	1 Goal	(51)
62	02/10/82	Dundee United	Away	League	2–2		
63	09/10/82	Aberdeen	Home	League	1–3	1 Goal	(52)
64	16/10/82	Kilmarnock	Home	League	2–1	2 Goals	(54)
65	20/10/82	Real Sociedad	Away	Eur Cup	0–2		
66	23/10/82	Morton	Away	League	2–1	1 Goal	(55)
67	27/10/82	Dundee United	Home	S Lge Cup	2–0	1 Goal	(56)
68	30/10/82	Rangers	Home	League	3–2		
69	03/11/82	Real Sociedad	Home	Eur Cup	2–1		
70	06/11/82	Dundee	Away	League	3–2	1 Goal	(57)
71	10/11/82	Dundee United	Away	S Lge Cup	1–2	1 Goal	(58)
72	13/11/82	St Mirren	Home	League	5–0	3 Goals	(61)
73	20/11/82	Motherwell	Home	League	3–1	1 Goal	(62)
74	27/11/82	Hibernian	Away	League	3–2		
75	04/12/82	Rangers	Hampden	S Lge Cup	2–1	1 Goal	(63)
76	11/12/82	Aberdeen	Away	League	2–1		

77	18/12/82	Kilmarnock	Away	League	4–0		
78	27/12/82	Morton	Home	League	5–1	1 Goal	(64)
79	01/01/83	Rangers	Away	League	2–1	1 Goal	(65)
80	03/01/83	Dundee	Home	League	2–2	1 Goal	(66)
81	08/01/83	St Mirren	Away	League	1–0		
82	22/01/83	Hibernian	Home	League	4–1	1 Goal	(67)
83	29/01/83	Clydebank	Away	S Cup	3–0	2 Goals	(69)
84	05/02/83	Dundee United	Away	League	1–1	1 Goal	(70)
85	12/02/83	Aberdeen	Home	League	1–3	1 Goal	(71)
86	19/02/83	Dunfermline Athletic	Home	S Cup	3–0		
87	26/02/83	Kilmarnock	Home	League	4–0	1 Goal	(72)
88	05/03/83	Morton	Away	League	3–0		
89	12/03/83	Heart of Midlothian	Home	S Cup	4–1	2 Goals	(74)
90	19/03/83	Dundee	Away	League	1–2		
91	23/03/83	Rangers	Home	League	0–0		
92	26/03/83	St Mirren	Home	League	1–1		
93	02/04/83	Motherwell	Home	League	3–0		
94	06/04/83	Dundee United	Home	League	2–0	1 Goal	(75)
95	09/04/83	Hibernian	Away	League	3–0	2 Goals	(77)
96	20/04/83	Dundee United	Home	League	2–3	1 Goal	(78)
97	23/04/83	Aberdeen	Away	League	0–1		
98	30/04/83	Kilmarnock	Away	League	5–0	1 Goal	(79)
99	07/05/83	Morton	Home	League	2–0	1 Goal	(80)
100	14/05/83	Rangers	Away	League	4–2	2 Goals	(82)

SEASON 1983–84

Arsenal – League Division One

1	27/08/83	Luton Town	Home	League	2–1		
2	29/08/83	Wolverhampton Wanderers	Away	League	2–1	2 Goals	(2)
3	03/09/83	Southampton	Away	League	0–1		
4	06/09/83	Manchester United	Home	League	2–3		
5	10/09/83	Liverpool	Home	League	0–2		
6	17/09/83	Notts County	Away	League	4–0		
7	24/09/83	Norwich City	Home	League	3–0		
8	01/10/83	Queens Park Rangers	Away	League	0–2		
9	04/10/83	Plymouth Argyle	Away	Lge Cup	1–1		
10	15/10/83	Coventry City	Home	League	0–1		
11	22/10/83	Nottingham Forest	Home	League	4–1		
12	25/10/83	Plymouth Argyle	Home	Lge Cup	1–0		
13	29/10/83	Aston Villa	Away	League	6–2		
14	05/11/83	Sunderland	Home	League	1–2		
15	09/11/83	Tottenham Hotspur	Away	Lge Cup	2–1	1 Goal	(3)
16	12/11/83	Ipswich Town	Away	League	0–1		
17	19/11/83	Everton	Home	League	2–1		
18	26/11/83	Leicester City	Away	League	0–3		
19	29/11/83	Walsall	Home	Lge Cup	1–2		
20	03/12/83	West Bromwich Albion	Home	League	0–1		
21	10/12/83	West Ham United	Away	League	1–3		
22	17/12/83	Watford	Home	League	3–1		
23	26/12/83	Tottenham Hotspur	Away	League	4–2	2 Goals	(5)
24	27/12/83	Birmingham City	Home	League	1–1	1 Goal	(6)
25	31/12/83	Southampton	Home	League	2–2	1 Goal	(7)
26	02/01/84	Norwich City	Away	League	1–1		
27	07/01/84	Middlesbrough	Away	FA Cup	2–3	1 Goal	(8)
28	14/01/84	Luton Town	Away	League	2–1		
29	21/01/84	Notts County	Home	League	1–1	1 Goal	(9)
30	28/01/84	Stoke City	Away	League	0–1		
31	04/02/84	Queens Park Rangers	Home	League	0–2		
32	11/02/84	Liverpool	Away	League	1–2		
33	18/02/84	Aston Villa	Home	League	1–1		
34	25/02/84	Nottingham Forest	Away	League	1–0		
35	03/03/84	Sunderland	Away	League	2–2	1 Goal	(10)
36	10/03/84	Ipswich Town	Home	League	4–1		
37	17/03/84	Manchester United	Away	League	0–4		
38	24/03/84	Wolverhampton Wanderers	Home	League	4–1	1 Goal	(11)
39	31/03/84	Coventry City	Away	League	4–1		
40	07/04/84	Stoke City	Home	League	3–1	1 Goal	(12)
41	09/04/84	Everton	Away	League	0–0		
42	21/04/84	Tottenham Hotspur	Home	League	3–2	1 Goal	(13)
43	23/04/84	Birmingham City	Away	League	1–1		
44	28/04/84	Leicester City	Home	League	2–1		
45	05/05/84	West Bromwich Albion	Away	League	3–1		
46	07/05/84	West Ham United	Home	League	3–3		

SEASON 1984–85

League Division One

47	29/08/84	Nottingham Forest	Away	League	0–2		
48	01/09/84	Watford	Away	League	4–3	2 Goals	(15)
49	04/09/84	Newcastle United	Home	League	2–0		
50	08/09/84	Liverpool	Home	League	3–1		
51	15/09/84	Ipswich Town	Away	League	1–2	1 Goal	(16)
52	22/09/84	Stoke City	Home	League	4–0		
53	25/09/84	Bristol Rovers	Home	Lge Cup	4–0	2 Goals	(18)
54	29/09/84	Coventry City	Away	League	2–1		
55	06/10/84	Everton	Home	League	1–0	1 Goal	(19)
56	09/10/84	Bristol Rovers	Away	Lge Cup	1–1		
57	13/10/84	Leicester City	Away	League	4–1		
58	20/10/84	Sunderland	Home	League	3–2		
59	27/10/84	West Ham United	Away	League	1–3		
60	31/10/84	Oxford United	Away	Lge Cup	2–3		
61	02/11/84	Manchester United	Away	League	2–4		
62	10/11/84	Aston Villa	Home	League	1–1		
63	17/11/84	Queens Park Rangers	Home	League	1–0		
64	25/11/84	Sheffield Wednesday	Away	League	1–2		
65	22/12/84	Watford	Home	League	1–1		
Sub+1	26/12/84	Norwich City	Away	League	0–1		
66	29/12/84	Newcastle United	Away	League	3–1	2 Goals	(21)
67	01/01/85	Tottenham Hotspur	Home	League	1–2		
68	05/01/85	Hereford United	Away	FA Cup	1–1		
69	19/01/85	Chelsea	Away	League	1–1		
70	21/01/85	Hereford United	Home	FA Cup	7–2	1 Goal	(22)
71	26/01/85	York City	Away	FA Cup	0–1		
Sub+2	02/02/85	Coventry City	Home	League	2–1		
Sub+3	12/02/85	Liverpool	Away	League	0–3		
72	23/02/85	Manchester United	Home	League	0–1		
73	02/03/85	West Ham United	Home	League	2–1		
74	09/03/85	Sunderland	Away	League	0–0		
75	13/03/85	Aston Villa	Away	League	0–0		
76	16/03/85	Leicester City	Home	League	2–0		
77	19/03/85	Ipswich Town	Home	League	1–1		
78	23/03/85	Everton	Away	League	0–2		
79	30/03/85	Stoke City	Away	League	0–2		
80	06/04/85	Norwich City	Home	League	2–0	1 Goal	(23)
81	13/04/85	Nottingham Forest	Home	League	1–1		
82	17/04/85	Tottenham Hotspur	Away	League	2–0	1 Goal	(24)
83	20/04/85	Queens Park Rangers	Away	League	0–1		
84	27/04/85	Sheffield Wednesday	Home	League	1–0		
85	04/05/85	Luton Town	Away	League	1–3	1 Goal	(25)
86	06/05/85	Southampton	Home	League	1–0		
87	11/05/85	West Bromwich Albion	Away	League	2–2		

SEASON 1985–86

League Division One

88	17/08/85	Liverpool	Away	League	0–2		
89	20/08/85	Southampton	Home	League	3–2		
90	24/08/85	Manchester United	Home	League	1–2		
91	27/08/85	Luton Town	Away	League	2–2		
92	31/08/85	Leicester City	Home	League	1–0		
93	03/09/85	Queens Park Rangers	Away	League	1–0		
94	07/09/85	Coventry City	Away	League	2–0	1 Goal	(26)
95	14/09/85	Sheffield Wednesday	Home	League	1–0		
96	21/09/85	Chelsea	Away	League	1–2	1 Goal	(27)
97	25/09/85	Hereford United	Away	Lge Cup	0–0		
98	28/09/85	Newcastle United	Home	League	0–0		
99	05/10/85	Aston Villa	Home	League	3–2		
100	07/10/85	Hereford United	Home	Lge Cup	2–1	1 Goal	(28)
101	12/10/85	West Ham United	Away	League	0–0		
102	19/10/85	Ipswich Town	Home	League	1–0		
103	26/10/85	Nottingham Forest	Away	League	2–3		
104	30/10/85	Manchester City	Away	Lge Cup	2–1	1 Goal	(29)
105	02/11/85	Manchester City	Home	League	1–0		
106	09/11/85	Everton	Away	League	1–6	1 Goal	(30)
107	16/11/85	Oxford United	Home	League	2–1		
108	19/11/85	Southampton	Home	Lge Cup	0–0		
109	23/11/85	West Bromwich Albion	Away	League	0–0		

110	26/11/85	Southampton	Away	Lge Cup	3–1	1 Goal	(31)
111	30/11/85	Birmingham City	Home	League	0–0		
112	07/12/85	Southampton	Away	League	0–3		
113	14/12/85	Liverpool	Home	League	2–0	1 Goal	(32)
114	21/12/85	Manchester United	Away	League	1–0	1 Goal	(33)
115	28/12/85	Queens Park Rangers	Home	League	3–1	1 Goal	(34)
116	01/01/86	Tottenham Hotspur	Home	League	0–0		
117	04/01/86	Grimsby Town	Away	FA Cup	4–3	3 Goals	(37)
118	18/01/86	Leicester City	Away	League	2–2	1 Goal	(38)
119	22/01/86	Aston Villa	Away	Lge Cup	1–1	1 Goal	(39)
120	25/01/86	Rotherham United	Home	FA Cup	5–1	1 Goal	(40)
121	01/02/86	Luton Town	Home	League	2–1		
122	04/02/86	Aston Villa	Home	Lge Cup	1–2		
123	15/02/86	Luton Town	Away	FA Cup	2–2		
124	01/03/86	Newcastle United	Away	League	0–1		
125	03/03/86	Luton Town	Home	FA Cup	0–0*		
126	05/03/86	Luton Town	Away	FA Cup	0–3		
127	08/03/86	Aston Villa	Away	League	4–1	1 Goal	(41)
128	11/03/86	Ipswich Town	Away	League	2–1	1 Goal	(42)
129	15/03/86	West Ham United	Home	League	1–0		
130	22/03/86	Coventry City	Home	League	3–0		
131	29/03/86	Tottenham Hotspur	Away	League	0–1		
132	31/03/86	Watford	Home	League	0–2		
133	01/04/86	Watford	Away	League	0–3		
134	05/04/86	Manchester City	Away	League	1–0		
135	08/04/86	Nottingham Forest	Home	League	1–1		
136	12/04/86	Everton	Home	League	0–1		
137	16/04/86	Sheffield Wednesday	Away	League	0–2		
138	29/04/86	Chelsea	Home	League	2–0	1 Goal	(43)
139	03/05/86	Birmingham City	Away	League	1–0		
140	05/05/86	Oxford United	Away	League	0–3		

SEASON 1986–87

League Division One

141	23/08/86	Manchester United	Home	League	1–0	1 Goal	(44)
142	26/08/86	Coventry City	Away	League	1–2		
143	30/08/86	Liverpool	Away	League	1–2		
144	02/09/86	Sheffield Wednesday	Home	League	2–0		
145	06/09/86	Tottenham Hotspur	Home	League	0–0		
146	13/09/86	Luton Town	Away	League	0–0		
147	20/09/86	Oxford United	Home	League	0–0		
148	23/09/86	Huddersfield Town	Home	Lge Cup	2–0		
149	27/09/86	Nottingham Forest	Away	League	0–1		
Sub+4	06/12/86	Queens Park Rangers	Home	League	3–1		
Sub+5	20/12/86	Luton Town	Home	League	3–0		
150	27/12/86	Southampton	Home	League	1–0		
151	01/01/87	Wimbledon	Home	League	3–1	2 Goals	(46)
152	04/01/87	Tottenham Hotspur	Away	League	2–1		
153	10/01/87	Reading	Away	FA Cup	3–1	2 Goals	(48)
154	18/01/87	Coventry City	Home	League	0–0		
155	21/01/87	Nottingham Forest	Home	Lge Cup	2–0	1 Goal	(49)
156	24/01/87	Manchester United	Away	League	0–2		
157	31/01/87	Plymouth Argyle	Home	FA Cup	6–1	1 Goal	(50)
158	08/02/87	Tottenham Hotspur	Home	Lge Cup	0–1		
Sub+6	21/02/87	Barnsley	Home	FA Cup	2–0	1 Goal	(51)
Sub+7	25/02/87	Oxford United	Away	League	0–0		
159	01/03/87	Tottenham Hotspur	Away	Lge Cup	2–1*		
160	04/03/87	Tottenham Hotspur	Away	Lge Cup	2–1		
Sub+8	14/03/87	Watford	Home	FA Cup	1–3		
161	17/03/87	Nottingham Forest	Home	League	0–0		
162	21/03/87	Watford	Away	League	0–2		
163	28/03/87	Everton	Home	League	0–1		
164	05/04/87	Liverpool	Wembley	Lge Cup	2–1	2 Goals	(53)
165	08/04/87	West Ham United	Away	League	1–3		
166	11/04/87	Charlton Athletic	Home	League	2–1		
167	14/04/87	Newcastle United	Home	League	0–1		
168	18/04/87	Wimbledon	Away	League	2–1		
169	20/04/87	Leicester City	Home	League	4–1	1 Goal	(54)
170	25/04/87	Manchester City	Away	League	0–3		
171	02/05/87	Aston Villa	Home	League	2–1		
172	04/05/87	Queens Park Rangers	Away	League	4–1		
173	09/05/87	Norwich City	Home	League	1–2		

SEASON 1987–88

League Division One

174	15/08/87	Liverpool	Home	League	1–2		
175	19/08/87	Manchester United	Away	League	0–0		
176	22/08/87	Queens Park Rangers	Away	League	0–2		

Aberdeen – Scottish League Premier Division

1	09/01/88	Hibernian	Away	League	0–0		
2	16/01/88	Dunfermline Athletic	Home	League	1–0		
3	23/01/88	Motherwell	Away	League	1–2	1 Goal	(1)
4	30/01/88	St Johnstone	Away	S Cup	1–0		
5	06/02/88	Rangers	Home	League	1–2		
6	13/02/88	Heart of Midlothian	Away	League	2–2		
7	20/02/88	Hamilton Academical	Away	S Cup	2–0	1 Goal	(2)
8	27/02/88	Dundee	Home	League	1–0		
9	05/03/88	St Mirren	Away	League	0–0		
10	12/03/88	Clyde	Home	S Cup	5–0		
11	19/03/88	Dundee United	Away	League	2–0	1 Goal	(3)
12	26/03/88	Falkirk	Home	League	2–0		
13	30/03/88	Celtic	Home	League	0–1		
14	02/04/88	Dunfermline Athletic	Away	League	1–1		
15	09/04/88	Dundee United	Neutral	S Cup	0–0		
16	13/04/88	Dundee United	Neutral	S Cup	1–1*	1 Goal	(4)
17	16/04/88	Morton	Away	League	2–0	1 Goal	(5)
18	20/04/88	Dundee United	Neutral	S Cup	0–1		
19	23/04/88	Heart of Midlothian	Home	League	0–0		
20	30/04/88	Rangers	Away	League	1–0		
21	04/05/88	Hibernian	Home	League	0–2		
22	07/05/88	Motherwell	Home	League	0–0		

SEASON 1988–89

Scottish League Premier Division

23	13/08/88	Dundee	Away	League	1–1		
24	31/08/88	Hibernian	Away	S Lge Cup	2–1*	1 Goal	(6)
Sub+1	03/09/88	Hibernian	Home	League	0–0		
25	07/09/88	SG Dynamo Dresden	Home	UEFA Cup	0–0		
26	17/09/88	Celtic	Away	League	3–1		
27	20/09/88	Dundee United	Neutral	S Lge Cup	2–0		
28	24/09/88	Heart of Midlothian	Home	League	1–0	1 Goal	(7)
29	27/09/88	Hamilton Academical	Away	League	1–0		
30	01/10/88	Motherwell	Away	League	1–1		
31	08/10/88	Rangers	Home	League	2–1	1 Goal	(8)
32	12/10/88	St Mirren	Away	League	1–1		
33	23/10/88	Rangers	Hampden	S Lge Cup	2–3		
34	29/10/88	Heart of Midlothian	Away	League	1–1		
35	02/11/88	Celtic	Home	League	2–2	1 Goal	(9)
36	05/11/88	Hibernian	Away	League	2–1	2 Goals	(11)
37	12/11/88	Dundee United	Home	League	1–1		
38	19/11/88	Motherwell	Home	League	2–1	1 Goal	(12)
39	26/11/88	Rangers	Away	League	0–1		
40	03/12/88	Hamilton Academical	Home	League	1–1	1 Goal	(13)
41	10/12/88	Celtic	Away	League	0–0		
42	03/01/89	Dundee United	Away	League	1–1	1 Goal	(14)
43	07/01/89	Hibernian	Home	League	2–0	2 Goals	(16)
44	14/01/89	Rangers	Home	League	1–2	1 Goal	(17)
45	21/01/89	Motherwell	Away	League	2–0		
46	28/01/89	Dunfermline Athletic	Away	S Cup	0–0		
47	01/02/89	Dunfermline Athletic	Home	S Cup	3–1	1 Goal	(18)
48	14/02/89	Hamilton Academical	Away	League	2–0		
49	18/02/89	Dundee United	Home	S Cup	1–1		
50	22/02/89	Dundee United	Away	S Cup	1–1*		
51	27/02/89	Dundee United	Away	S Cup	0–1		
52	11/03/89	Dundee	Home	League	2–0	1 Goal	(19)
53	25/03/89	St Mirren	Away	League	3–1	1 Goal	(20)
54	01/04/89	Dundee United	Home	League	1–0	1 Goal	(21)
55	08/04/89	Hibernian	Away	League	2–1		
56	15/04/89	Hamilton Academical	Home	League	3–0	2 Goals	(23)
57	22/04/89	Heart of Midlothian	Away	League	0–1		
58	29/04/89	Celtic	Home	League	0–0		
59	06/05/89	Motherwell	Home	League	0–0		

SEASON 1989–90

Scottish League Premier Division

60	12/08/89	Hibernian	Home	League	1–0		
61	15/08/89	Albion Rovers	Away	S Lge Cup	2–0+		
62	19/08/89	Motherwell	Away	League	0–0		
63	23/08/89	Airdrieonians	Home	S Lge Cup	4–0		
64	26/08/89	Dundee	Home	League	1–0		
65	30/08/89	St Mirren	Home	S Lge Cup	3–1		
66	09/09/89	Rangers	Away	League	0–1		
67	13/09/89	SK Rapid Wien	Home	UEFA Cup	2–1		
68	16/09/89	Dunfermline Athletic	Home	League	2–1		
69	20/09/89	Celtic	Hampden	S Lge Cup	1–0		
70	23/09/89	St Mirren	Away	League	2–0		
71	27/09/89	SK Rapid Wien	Away	UEFA Cup	0–1		
72	30/09/89	Celtic	Home	League	1–1		
73	04/10/89	Dundee United	Away	League	0–2		
74	14/10/89	Heart of Midlothian	Home	League	1–3		
75	22/10/89	Rangers	Hampden	S Lge Cup	2–1*		
Sub+2	25/10/89	Hibernian	Away	League	3–0		
76	28/10/89	Motherwell	Home	League	1–0		
77	18/11/89	Dunfermline Athletic	Away	League	3–0		
78	22/11/89	Rangers	Home	League	1–0		
79	25/11/89	St Mirren	Home	League	5–0	3 Goals	(26)
80	02/12/89	Celtic	Away	League	0–1		
81	09/12/89	Dundee United	Home	League	2–0	1 Goal	(27)
82	20/12/89	Heart of Midlothian	Away	League	1–1		
83	26/12/89	Hibernian	Home	League	1–2		
84	30/12/89	Motherwell	Away	League	2–2		
85	02/01/90	Dundee	Home	League	5–2	1 Goal	(28)
86	06/01/90	Rangers	Away	League	0–2		
87	13/01/90	Dunfermline Athletic	Home	League	4–1	1 Goal	(29)
88	20/01/90	Partick Thistle	Away	S Cup	6–2		
89	27/01/90	St Mirren	Away	League	0–1		
90	03/02/90	Heart of Midlothian	Home	League	2–2	2 Goals	(31)
91	10/02/90	Dundee United	Away	League	1–1		
92	17/02/90	Celtic	Home	League	1–1	1 Goal	(32)
93	24/02/90	Morton	Home	S Cup	2–1	1 Goal	(33)
94	03/03/90	Dunfermline Athletic	Away	League	4–2	1 Goal	(34)
95	10/03/90	Hibernian	Away	League	2–3		
96	17/03/90	Heart of Midlothian	Home	S Cup	4–1	1 Goal	(35)
97	24/03/90	Motherwell	Home	League	2–0		
98	31/03/90	Dundee	Away	League	1–1		
99	08/04/90	Rangers	Home	League	0–0		
100	14/04/90	Dundee United	Neutral	S Cup	4–0		
101	18/04/90	Dundee United	Home	League	1–0		
102	28/04/90	St Mirren	Home	League	2–0	1 Goal	(36)
103	12/05/90	Celtic	Hampden	S Cup	0–0#		

+ Played at Fir Park, Motherwell
# AET Aberdeen won 9–8 on penalties

SEASON 1990–91

Celtic – Scottish League Premier Division

1	01/09/90	Aberdeen	Home	League	0–3		
2	05/09/90	Queen of the South	Home	S Lge Cup	2–1		
3	17/11/90	St Mirren	Home	League	4–1		
4	25/11/90	Rangers	Home	League	1–2		
5	01/12/90	Hibernian	Away	League	3–0	1 Goal	(1)
6	08/12/90	Dundee United	Away	League	1–3		
Sub+1	15/12/90	Dunfermline Athletic	Home	League	1–2	1 Goal	(2)
7	22/12/90	St Johnstone	Away	League	2–3		
8	29/12/90	Heart of Midlothian	Home	League	1–1		
Sub+2	02/01/91	Rangers	Away	League	0–2		
9	13/04/91	Dundee United	Away	League	1–2		
10	20/04/91	Dunfermline Athletic	Home	League	5–1	2 Goals	(4)
11	27/04/91	Heart of Midlothian	Away	League	1–0	1 Goal	(5)
12	05/05/91	St Mirren	Home	League	1–0		
13	11/05/91	St Johnstone	Away	League	3–2	1 Goal	(6)

SEASON 1991–92

Scottish League Premier Division

14	10/08/91	Dundee United	Away	League	4–3	1 Goal	(7)
15	13/08/91	Dunfermline Athletic	Away	League	3–1	2 Goals	(9)

16	17/08/91	Falkirk	Home	League	4–1		
17	21/08/91	Morton	Away	S Lge Cup	4–2	2 Goals	(11)
18	24/08/91	Aberdeen	Away	League	0–1		
19	31/08/91	Rangers	Home	League	0–2		
20	03/09/91	Airdrieonians	Away	S Lge Cup	0–0+		
Sub+3	07/09/91	St Mirren	Home	League	0–0		
Sub+4	14/09/91	St Johnstone	Away	League	0–1		
21	18/09/91	KFC Germinal Ekeren	Home	UEFA Cup	2–0	2 Goals	(13)
22	21/09/91	Airdrieonians	Home	League	3–1	1 Goal	(14)
23	28/09/91	Hibernian	Away	League	1–1	1 Goal	(15)
24	01/10/91	KFC Germinal Ekeren	Away	UEFA Cup	1–1		
25	05/10/91	Heart of Midlothian	Home	League	3–1	1 Goal	(16)
26	08/10/91	Motherwell	Away	League	2–0	1 Goal	(17)
27	12/10/91	Dundee United	Home	League	4–1	2 Goals	(19)
28	19/10/91	Falkirk	Away	League	3–4		
29	22/10/91	FC Neuchatel Xamax	Away	UEFA Cup	1–5		
30	26/10/91	St Mirren	Away	League	5–0		
31	30/10/91	St Johnstone	Home	League	4–0	2 Goals	(21)
32	02/11/91	Rangers	Away	League	1–1		
33	06/11/91	FC Neuchatel Xamax	Home	UEFA Cup	1–0		
34	09/11/91	Aberdeen	Home	League	2–1	1 Goal	(22)
35	16/11/91	Heart of Midlothian	Away	League	1–3		
36	20/11/91	Motherwell	Home	League	2–2	2 Goals	(24)
37	30/11/91	Dunfermline Athletic	Home	League	1–0		
38	04/12/91	Hibernian	Home	League	0–0		
39	07/12/91	Dundee United	Away	League	1–1		
40	14/12/91	St Mirren	Home	League	4–0		
41	28/12/91	Aberdeen	Away	League	2–2		
Sub+5	01/02/92	Falkirk	Home	League	2–0		
Sub+6	08/02/92	Airdrieonians	Home	League	2–0		
Sub+7	11/02/92	Dundee United	Home	S Cup	2–1		
42	22/02/92	Hibernian	Away	League	2–0	1 Goal	(25)
Sub+8	29/02/92	Heart of Midlothian	Away	League	2–1		
Sub+9	07/03/92	Morton	Home	S Cup	3–0		
43	17/03/92	Motherwell	Home	League	4–1	1 Goal	(26)
44	21/03/92	Rangers	Away	League	2–0	1 Goal	(27)
45	28/03/92	Dundee United	Home	League	3–1	1 Goal	(28)
46	31/03/92	Rangers	Hampden	S Cup	0–1		
47	04/04/92	Falkirk	Away	League	3–0	1 Goal	(29)
48	08/04/92	St Mirren	Away	League	1–1		
49	11/04/92	St Johnstone	Home	League	3–2	2 Goals	(31)
50	18/04/92	Airdrieonians	Away	League	0–0		
51	25/04/92	Dunfermline Athletic	Home	League	2–0		
52	02/05/92	Hibernian	Home	League	1–2		

+ AET Airdrieonians won 4–2 on penalties

SEASON 1992–93

Scottish League Premier Division

53	01/08/92	Heart of Midlothian	Away	League	1–0		
54	05/08/92	Aberdeen	Away	League	1–1		
55	08/08/92	Motherwell	Home	League	1–1		
56	12/08/92	Stirling Albion	Hampden	S Lge Cup	3–0		
Sub+10	15/09/92	1.FC Köln	Away	UEFA Cup	0–2		
Sub+11	20/10/92	BV 09 Borussia Dortmund	Away	UEFA Cup	0–1		
Sub+12	24/10/92	Airdrieonians	Home	League	2–0		
57	03/11/92	BV 09 Borussia Dortmund	Home	UEFA Cup	1–2		
Sub+13	07/11/92	Rangers	Home	League	0–1		
Sub+14	11/11/92	Dundee United	Away	League	1–1	1 Goal	(32)
58	21/11/92	Falkirk	Home	League	3–2		
59	28/11/92	Hibernian	Away	League	2–1		
60	05/12/92	Partick Thistle	Away	League	3–2		
Sub+15	03/02/93	St Johnstone	Home	League	5–1		
61	27/03/93	Dundee United	Away	League	3–2		
62	03/04/93	Motherwell	Away	League	0–2		
63	06/04/93	Airdrieonians	Home	League	4–0		
64	10/04/93	St Johnstone	Away	League	1–1		
65	17/04/93	Hibernian	Away	League	1–3	1 Goal	(33)
66	20/04/93	Falkirk	Home	League	1–0		

SEASON 1993–94

Scottish League Premier Division

| Sub+16 | 07/08/93 | Motherwell | Away | League | 2–2 | | |
| 67 | 10/08/93 | Stirling Albion | Away | S Lge Cup | 2–0 | | |

68	14/08/93	Hibernian	Home	League	1–1	1 Goal	(34)
69	21/08/93	Rangers	Home	League	0–0		
70	25/08/93	Arbroath	Away	S Lge Cup	9–1	1 Goal	(35)
71	28/08/93	Partick Thistle	Away	League	1–0		
72	31/08/93	Airdrieonians	Home	S Lge Cup	1–0		
73	04/09/93	Aberdeen	Home	League	0–1		
74	11/09/93	Raith Rovers	Away	League	4–1	2 Goals	(37)
75	14/09/93	Young Boys BSC Bern	Away	UEFA Cup	0–0		
76	18/09/93	Dundee United	Home	League	1–1		
Sub+17	29/09/93	Young Boys BSC Bern	Home	UEFA Cup	1–0*		
Sub+18	02/10/93	Kilmarnock	Home	League	0–0		
77	06/10/93	St Johnstone	Away	League	1–2		
78	09/10/93	Dundee	Home	League	2–1		
79	16/10/93	Hibernian	Away	League	1–1		
80	20/10/93	Sporting CP Lisboa	Home	UEFA Cup	1–0		
81	30/10/93	Rangers	Away	League	2–1		
82	03/11/93	Sporting CP Lisboa	Away	UEFA Cup	0–2		
83	06/11/93	Partick Thistle	Home	League	3–0	1 Goal	(38)
Sub+19	09/11/93	Aberdeen	Away	League	1–1		
84	13/11/93	Kilmarnock	Away	League	2–2	1 Goal	(39)
85	20/11/93	Heart of Midlothian	Home	League	0–0		
86	24/11/93	Motherwell	Home	League	2–0		
87	27/11/93	Raith Rovers	Home	League	2–0		
88	30/11/93	Dundee United	Away	League	0–1		
Sub+20	18/12/93	Hibernian	Home	League	1–0		
89	01/01/94	Rangers	Home	League	2–4	1 Goal	(40)
90	08/01/94	Partick Thistle	Away	League	0–1		
91	11/01/94	Motherwell	Away	League	1–2		
92	19/01/94	Aberdeen	Home	League	2–2		
93	22/01/94	Dundee United	Home	League	0–0		
94	05/02/94	Raith Rovers	Away	League	0–0		
95	12/02/94	Heart of Midlothian	Away	League	2–0	2 Goals	(42)
96	01/03/94	Kilmarnock	Home	League	1–0		
97	05/03/94	St Johnstone	Away	League	1–0		
98	19/03/94	Hibernian	Away	League	0–0		
99	26/03/94	Motherwell	Home	League	0–1		
100	09/04/94	Heart of Midlothian	Home	League	2–2		
Sub+21	16/04/94	Kilmarnock	Away	League	0–2		
101	23/04/94	Dundee	Away	League	2–0		
102	27/04/94	St Johnstone	Home	League	1–1		

SEASON 1994–95

Scottish League Premier Division

103	20/08/94	Dundee United	Home	League	2–1		
Sub+22	27/08/94	Rangers	Away	League	2–0		
Sub+23	31/08/94	Dundee	Away	S Lge Cup	2–1		
Sub+24	10/09/94	Partick Thistle	Away	League	2–1		
Sub+25	17/09/94	Kilmarnock	Home	League	1–1		
Sub+26	21/09/94	Dundee United	Home	S Lge Cup	1–0		
104	24/09/94	Hibernian	Home	League	2–0		
105	01/10/94	Motherwell	Away	League	1–1		
Sub+27	08/10/94	Aberdeen	Home	League	0–0		
Sub+28	15/10/94	Heart of Midlothian	Away	League	0–1		
106	22/10/94	Falkirk	Home	League	0–2		
Sub+29	26/10/94	Aberdeen	Neutral	S Lge Cup	1–0		
Sub+30	30/10/94	Rangers	Home	League	1–3		
107	09/11/94	Partick Thistle	Home	League	0–0		
108	27/11/94	Raith Rovers	Neutral	S Lge Cup	2–2+	1 Goal	(43)
Sub+31	13/05/95	Dundee United	Away	League	1–0		

+ AET Raith Rovers won 6–5 on penalties

SEASON 1995–96

Clyde – Scottish League Division Two

1	12/08/95	Ayr United	Away	League	1–1	1 Goal	(1)
2	22/08/95	St Johnstone	Home	SLC Cup	0–2		
3	26/08/95	Forfar Athletic	Home	League	1–2		
4	02/09/95	Queen of the South	Away	League	3–0	1 Goal	(2)
5	09/09/95	Berwick Rangers	Home	League	3–1	1 Goal	(3)
6	16/09/95	Montrose	Away	League	0–0		
7	23/09/95	Stenhousemuir	Home	League	0–1		
8	30/09/95	Stirling Albion	Away	League	0–1		

9	07/10/95	Stranraer	Home	League	1–1		
10	14/10/95	East Fife	Away	League	0–0		
11	21/10/95	Ayr United	Home	League	1–2		
12	28/10/95	Forfar Athletic	Away	League	0–1		
13	25/11/95	Stenhousemuir	Away	League	1–0		
14	02/12/95	Stranraer	Away	League	0–0		
15	16/12/95	East Fife	Home	League	0–1		
16	06/01/96	Brechin City	Home	S Cup	2–2	1 Goal	(4)
17	09/01/96	Brechin City	Away	S Cup	3–1		
18	13/01/96	Stenhousemuir	Home	League	3–0		
19	20/01/96	Stranraer	Home	League	2–2		
20	24/01/96	Stirling Albion	Away	League	0–3		
21	31/01/96	Dundee	Home	S Cup	3–1	1 Goal	(5)
22	03/02/96	East Fife	Away	League	1–1		
23	15/02/96	Rangers	Home	S Cup	1–4		
24	18/02/96	Berwick Rangers	Home	League	2–1		
25	24/02/96	Forfar Athletic	Home	League	3–1		
26	27/02/96	Ayr United	Away	League	1–2		
27	02/03/96	Queen of the South	Away	League	1–2		
28	05/03/96	Queen of the South	Home	League	2–1		
29	09/03/96	Stenhousemuir	Away	League	0–1		
30	12/03/96	Montrose	Away	League	3–2	1 Goal	(6)
31	16/03/96	Stirling Albion	Home	League	1–3		
32	23/03/96	Montrose	Home	League	1–3		
33	30/03/96	Berwick Rangers	Away	League	3–2		
34	06/04/96	Stranraer	Away	League	2–2		
35	13/04/96	East Fife	Home	League	2–2	1 Goal	(7)
36	20/04/96	Ayr United	Home	League	2–0		

INTERNATIONAL APPEARANCES – SCOTLAND

1	30/03/83	Switzerland	Hampden Park	2–2	ECQ	1 Goal	(1)
2	24/05/83	Northern Ireland	Hampden Park	0–0	HC		
3	01/06/83	England	Wembley	0–2	HC		
4	12/06/83	Canada	Vancouver	2–0	F		
5	16/06/83	Canada	Edmonton	3–0	F	1 Goal	(2)
6	20/06/83	Canada	Toronto	2–0	F		
7	12/10/83	Belgium	Hampden Park	1–1	ECQ	1 Goal	(3)
Sub+8	01/06/84	France	Marseille	0–2	F		
Sub+9	12/09/84	Yugoslavia	Hampden Park	6–1	F	1 Goal	(4)
Sub+10	17/10/84	Iceland	Hampden Park	3–0	WCQ	1 Goal	(5)
Sub+11	27/02/85	Spain	Seville	0–1	WCQ		
Sub+12	27/03/85	Wales	Hampden Park	0–1	WCQ		
13	28/01/86	Israel	Tel Aviv	1–0	F		
Sub+14	26/03/86	Romania	Hampden Park	3–0	F		
15	23/04/86	England	Wembley	1–2	RC		
16	04/06/86	Denmark	Nezahualcoyotl	0–1	WC		
Sub+17	13/06/86	Uruguay	Nezahualcoyotl	0–0	WC		
18	10/09/86	Bulgaria	Hampden Park	0–0	ECQ		
Sub+19	23/05/87	England	Hampden Park	0–0	RC		
Sub+20	26/04/89	Cyprus	Hampden Park	2–1	WCQ		

APPEARANCES AND GOALS PER SEASON

SEASON 80–81	GAMES	GOALS
Scottish League	26+3	16
Scottish Cup	5	3
Scottish League Cup	5+2	6
European Cup Winners Cup	3+1	3
TOTAL	**39+6**	**28**

SEASON 81–82	GAMES	GOALS
Scottish League	7+3	3
Scottish League Cup	3	3
European Cup	1	0
TOTAL	**11+3**	**6**

SEASON 82–83	GAMES	GOALS
Scottish League	35	29
Scottish Cup	3	4
Scottish League Cup	8+2	13
European Cup	4	2
TOTAL	**50+2**	**48**

SEASON 83–84	GAMES	GOALS
League	41	11
FA Cup	1	1
League Cup	4	1
TOTAL	**46**	**13**

SEASON 84–85	GAMES	GOALS
League	35+3	9
FA Cup	3	1
League Cup	3	2
TOTAL	**41+3**	**12**

SEASON 85–86	GAMES	GOALS
League	41	10
FA Cup	5	4
League Cup	7	4
TOTAL	**53**	**18**

SEASON 86–87	GAMES	GOALS
League	25+3	4
FA Cup	2+2	4
League Cup	6	3
TOTAL	**33+5**	**11**

SEASON 87–88	GAMES	GOALS
League	3	0
Scottish League	16	3
Scottish Cup	6	2
TOTAL	**25**	**5**

SEASON 88–89	GAMES	GOALS
Scottish League	28+1	16
Scottish Cup	5	1
Scottish League Cup	3	1
UEFA Cup	1	0
TOTAL	**37+1**	**18**

SEASON 89–90	GAMES	GOALS
Scottish League	32+1	11
Scottish Cup	5	2
Scottish League Cup	5	0
UEFA Cup	2	0
TOTAL	**44+1**	**13**

SEASON 90–91	GAMES	GOALS
Scottish League	12+2	6
Scottish League Cup	1	0
TOTAL	**13+2**	**6**

SEASON 91–92	GAMES	GOALS
Scottish League	32+5	21
Scottish Cup	1+2	0
Scottish League Cup	2	2
UEFA Cup	4	2
TOTAL	**39+7**	**25**

SEASON 92–93	GAMES	GOALS
Scottish League	12+4	2
Scottish League Cup	1	0
UEFA Cup	1+2	0
TOTAL	**14+6**	**2**

SEASON 93–94	GAMES	GOALS
Scottish League	30+5	8
Scottish League Cup	3	1
UEFA Cup	3+1	0
TOTAL	**36+6**	**9**

SEASON 94–95	GAMES	GOALS
Scottish League	5+7	0
Scottish League Cup	1+3	1
TOTAL	**6+10**	**1**

SEASON 95–96	GAMES	GOALS
Scottish League	31	5
Scottish Cup	4	2
Scottish League Challenge Cup	1	0
TOTAL	**36**	**7**

CAREER APPEARANCES AND GOALS

COMPETITION	GAMES	TOTAL	GOALS
League	145+6	151	34
FA Cup	11+2	13	10
League Cup	20	20	10
European Cup	5	5	2
European Cup Winners Cup	3+1	4	3
UEFA Cup	11+3	14	2
Scottish League	266+31	297	120
Scottish Cup	29+2	31	14
Scottish League Cup	32+7	39	27
Scottish League Challenge Cup	1	1	0
Internationals	11+9	20	5
TOTAL	**534+61**	**595**	**227**

HAT-TRICKS

Celtic

1	4	Dunfermline Athletic	28/08/82	Away	S Lge Cup	7–1
2	3	Motherwell	18/09/82	Away	League	7–0
3	3	St Mirren	13/11/82	Home	League	5–0

Arsenal

1	3	Grimsby Town	04/01/86	Away	FA Cup	4–3

Aberdeen

1	3	St Mirren	25/11/89	Home	League	5–0

FA Cup: 1
Scottish League: 3
Scottish League Cup: 1
TOTAL: 5

HONOURS

Winners medals
League Cup: 86/87
Scottish Premier Division Championship: 80/81
Scottish Cup: 89/90
Scottish League Cup: 82/83, 89/90

Runner-up medals
Scottish Premier Division Championship: 82/83, 88/89, 89/90
Scottish League Cup: 88/89, 94/95

Played ten (7+3/3) League matches in the Celtic team that won the 1981/82 Scottish Premier Division Championship.

DAVID PLATT

Born: 10/06/66 – Chadderton
Height: 5.10
Weight: 11.12 (96–97)

Clubs
Manchester United: **1984–85** – No Competitive Matches
Crewe Alexandra: **1985–88** – Matches: **152** – Goals: **60**
Aston Villa: **1988–91** – Matches: **155** – Goals: **68**
AS Bari: **1991–92** – Matches: **35** – Goals: **15**
Juventus FC: **1992–93** – Matches: **28** – Goals: **4**
Sampdoria UC: **1993–95** – Matches: **71** – Goals: **21**
Arsenal: **1995–97** – Matches: **63+4** – Goals: **11**

Country
England: **1989–96** – Matches: **52+10** – Goals: **27**

SEASON 1984–85

Manchester United – League Division One
No Competitive Matches

Crewe Alexandra – League Division Four

1	26/01/85	Mansfield Town	Home	League	1–1		
2	01/02/85	Hartlepool United	Home	League	2–0	1 Goal	(1)
3	05/02/85	Bolton Wanderers	Home	FR Trophy	0–0		
4	16/02/85	Scunthorpe United	Home	League	1–1		
5	23/02/85	Peterborough United	Home	League	2–1		
6	26/02/85	Tranmere Rovers	Home	League	1–3		
7	02/03/85	Rochdale	Away	League	3–1	1 Goal	(2)
8	06/03/85	Chester City	Away	League	2–0	1 Goal	(3)
9	09/03/85	Stockport County	Home	League	2–1		
10	12/03/85	Darlington	Away	League	1–2		
11	16/03/85	Swindon Town	Away	League	1–1		
12	22/03/85	Port Vale	Home	League	0–0		
13	30/03/85	Northampton Town	Away	League	3–1	1 Goal	(4)
14	02/04/85	Wrexham	Away	League	3–1		
15	06/04/85	Aldershot	Home	League	1–1		
16	09/04/85	Blackpool	Away	League	1–6		
17	13/04/85	Bury	Home	League	1–0		
18	19/04/85	Halifax Town	Away	League	1–1		
19	24/04/85	Hereford United	Away	League	2–3	1 Goal	(5)
20	27/04/85	Exeter City	Home	League	0–0		
21	04/05/85	Chesterfield	Away	League	1–3		
22	06/05/85	Darlington	Home	League	2–2		
23	10/05/85	Colchester United	Away	League	1–4		

SEASON 1985–86

League Division Four

24	17/08/85	Southend United	Home	League	1–1		
25	20/08/85	Carlisle United	Home	Lge Cup	3–3		
26	24/08/85	Hartlepool United	Away	League	1–4	1 Goal	(6)
27	27/08/85	Hereford United	Home	League	2–0		
28	31/08/85	Wrexham	Away	League	1–2		
29	03/09/85	Carlisle United	Away	Lge Cup	4–3	2 Goals	(8)
30	06/09/85	Stockport County	Home	League	0–1		
31	14/09/85	Northampton Town	Away	League	1–0		
32	17/09/85	Swindon Town	Home	League	2–0	1 Goal	(9)
33	21/09/85	Chester City	Away	League	0–4		
34	24/09/85	Watford	Home	Lge Cup	1–3		
35	28/09/85	Torquay United	Home	League	1–0		
36	01/10/85	Scunthorpe United	Away	League	1–3		
37	05/10/85	Preston North End	Home	League	3–3	1 Goal	(10)
38	08/10/85	Watford	Away	Lge Cup	2–3		
39	12/10/85	Rochdale	Away	League	0–1		
40	19/10/85	Burnley	Home	League	3–1		
41	23/10/85	Peterborough United	Away	League	0–0		
42	26/10/85	Aldershot	Away	League	2–3	1 Goal	(11)
43	02/11/85	Halifax Town	Home	League	2–2	1 Goal	(12)
44	05/11/85	Orient	Home	League	1–3		
45	09/11/85	Mansfield Town	Away	League	2–2		
46	16/11/85	Derby County	Away	FA Cup	1–5		
47	23/11/85	Cambridge United	Home	League	0–1		
48	13/12/85	Exeter City	Home	League	0–1		
49	20/12/85	Hartlepool United	Home	League	0–0		
50	26/12/85	Port Vale	Away	League	0–3		
51	28/12/85	Hereford United	Away	League	1–4		
52	04/01/86	Halifax Town	Away	League	0–1		
53	11/01/86	Wrexham	Home	League	3–2	1 Goal	(13)
54	14/01/86	Stockport County	Home	FR Trophy	4–1		
55	18/01/86	Southend United	Away	League	1–0	1 Goal	(14)
56	25/01/86	Northampton Town	Home	League	0–1		
57	28/01/86	Bolton Wanderers	Away	FR Trophy	0–1		
58	22/02/86	Chester City	Home	League	2–2	1 Goal	(15)
59	01/03/86	Torquay United	Away	League	0–0		
60	04/03/86	Scunthorpe United	Home	League	4–0		
61	08/03/86	Preston North End	Away	League	2–1		
62	15/03/86	Rochdale	Home	League	4–2		
63	18/03/86	Tranmere Rovers	Home	League	2–1		
64	22/03/86	Aldershot	Home	League	2–0		
65	25/03/86	Colchester United	Away	League	2–1		

66	29/03/86	Tranmere Rovers	Away	League	1–0		
67	31/03/86	Port Vale	Home	League	0–1		
68	11/04/86	Mansfield Town	Home	League	2–1		
69	15/04/86	Burnley	Away	League	1–0		
70	19/04/86	Cambridge United	Away	League	0–1		
71	26/04/86	Colchester United	Home	League	0–2		
72	03/05/86	Exeter City	Away	League	2–1		
73	05/05/86	Swindon Town	Away	League	0–1		

SEASON 1986–87

League Division Four

74	23/08/86	Rochdale	Away	League	1–1		
75	26/08/86	Shrewsbury Town	Away	Lge Cup	0–0		
76	30/08/86	Hereford United	Home	League	1–2		
77	02/09/86	Shrewsbury Town	Home	Lge Cup	0–4		
78	07/09/86	Scunthorpe United	Away	League	1–2	1 Goal	(16)
79	13/09/86	Wolverhampton Wanderers	Home	League	1–1	1 Goal	(17)
80	16/09/86	Exeter City	Home	League	2–2		
81	20/09/86	Peterborough United	Away	League	2–1		
82	27/09/86	Swansea City	Home	League	1–1		
83	01/10/86	Hartlepool United	Away	League	5–0	2 Goals	(19)
84	10/10/86	Orient	Home	League	3–2	2 Goals	(21)
85	18/10/86	Southend United	Away	League	1–3		
86	21/10/86	Colchester United	Home	League	1–1		
87	25/10/86	Halifax Town	Home	League	2–2	1 Goal	(22)
88	31/10/86	Cambridge United	Away	League	3–0		
89	04/11/86	Lincoln City	Away	League	1–2		
90	08/11/86	Wrexham	Home	League	1–1		
91	15/11/86	York City	Away	FA Cup	1–3	1 Goal	(23)
92	22/11/86	Tranmere Rovers	Away	League	2–3		
93	28/11/86	Northampton Town	Home	League	0–5		
94	02/12/86	Chester City	Home	FR Trophy	1–2		
95	13/12/86	Torquay United	Home	League	1–0		
96	20/12/86	Aldershot	Away	League	0–1		
97	26/12/86	Preston North End	Home	League	2–2		
98	27/12/86	Burnley	Away	League	0–4		
99	01/01/87	Stockport County	Away	League	1–2		
100	03/01/87	Tranmere Rovers	Home	League	3–2	2 Goals	(25)
101	05/01/87	Preston North End	Away	FR Trophy	0–1		
102	24/01/87	Scunthorpe United	Home	League	2–2	1 Goal	(26)
103	28/01/87	Hereford United	Away	League	0–2		
104	14/02/87	Peterborough United	Home	League	1–3	1 Goal	(27)
105	21/02/87	Swansea City	Away	League	1–1		
106	28/02/87	Hartlepool United	Home	League	1–0		
107	03/03/87	Cambridge United	Home	League	0–0		
108	07/03/87	Halifax Town	Away	League	3–0	1 Goal	(28)
109	13/03/87	Southend United	Home	League	2–1		
110	17/03/87	Colchester United	Away	League	1–2		
111	21/03/87	Orient	Away	League	1–1	1 Goal	(29)
112	28/03/87	Cardiff City	Home	League	1–2		
113	31/03/87	Rochdale	Home	League	5–1	3 Goals	(32)
114	04/04/87	Wrexham	Away	League	1–2	1 Goal	(33)
115	11/04/87	Lincoln City	Home	League	1–2	1 Goal	(34)
116	17/04/87	Stockport County	Home	League	5–0	2 Goals	(36)
117	20/04/87	Preston North End	Away	League	1–2		
118	25/04/87	Aldershot	Home	League	1–3	1 Goal	(37)
119	29/04/87	Northampton Town	Away	League	1–2		
120	04/05/87	Burnley	Home	League	1–0	1 Goal	(38)
121	09/05/87	Torquay United	Away	League	2–2	1 Goal	(39)

SEASON 1987–88

League Division Four

122	15/08/87	Bolton Wanderers	Away	League	1–1	1 Goal	(40)
123	22/08/87	Cambridge United	Away	League	1–4		
124	25/08/87	Shrewsbury Town	Home	Lge Cup	3–3	1 Goal	(41)
125	29/08/87	Wrexham	Home	League	2–0	1 Goal	(42)
126	31/08/87	Rochdale	Away	League	2–2	2 Goals	(44)
127	04/09/87	Colchester United	Home	League	0–0		
128	08/09/87	Shrewsbury Town	Away	Lge Cup	1–4	1 Goal	(45)
129	12/09/87	Wolverhampton Wanderers	Away	League	2–2	2 Goals	(47)
130	15/09/87	Tranmere Rovers	Home	League	0–0		
131	18/09/87	Leyton Orient	Home	League	3–3		
132	26/09/87	Swansea City	Away	League	4–2	1 Goal	(48)

133	29/09/87	Burnley	Away	League	0–0		
134	03/10/87	Hartlepool United	Home	League	1–1	1 Goal	(49)
135	17/10/87	Scarborough	Home	League	1–0	1 Goal	(50)
136	20/10/87	Stockport County	Home	League	3–1	2 Goals	(52)
137	24/10/87	Exeter City	Away	League	1–3	1 Goal	(53)
138	31/10/87	Carlisle United	Home	League	4–1	1 Goal	(54)
139	03/11/87	Darlington	Away	League	0–1		
140	07/11/87	Hereford United	Away	League	1–1		
141	14/11/87	Lincoln City	Away	FA Cup	1–2		
142	21/11/87	Scunthorpe United	Home	League	2–2	2 Goals	(56)
143	27/11/87	Halifax Town	Away	League	2–1	1 Goal	(57)
144	04/12/87	Bury	Home	SV Trophy	0–0		
145	12/12/87	Cardiff City	Home	League	0–0		
146	18/12/87	Peterborough United	Away	League	4–0	1 Goal	(58)
147	26/12/87	Swansea City	Home	League	2–2	2 Goals	(60)
148	28/12/87	Newport County	Away	League	2–1		
149	01/01/88	Wrexham	Away	League	1–2		
150	02/01/88	Wolverhampton Wanderers	Home	League	0–2		
151	16/01/88	Leyton Orient	Away	League	1–1		
152	19/01/88	Sunderland	Away	SV Trophy	0–1		

Aston Villa – League Division Two

1	20/02/88	Blackburn Rovers	Away	League	2–3	1 Goal	(1)
2	27/02/88	Plymouth Argyle	Home	League	5–2	1 Goal	(2)
3	05/03/88	AFC Bournemouth	Away	League	2–1	1 Goal	(3)
4	12/03/88	Leeds United	Home	League	1–2		
5	19/03/88	Reading	Away	League	2–0		
6	26/03/88	Stoke City	Home	League	0–1		
7	02/04/88	Millwall	Away	League	1–2		
8	04/04/88	Oldham Athletic	Home	League	1–2		
9	09/04/88	Crystal Palace	Away	League	1–1	1 Goal	(4)
10	02/05/88	Bradford City	Home	League	1–0	1 Goal	(5)
11	07/05/88	Swindon Town	Away	League	0–0		

SEASON 1988–89

League Division One

12	27/08/88	Millwall	Home	League	2–2		
13	03/09/88	Arsenal	Away	League	3–2		
14	10/09/88	Liverpool	Home	League	1–1		
15	17/09/88	West Ham United	Away	League	2–2		
16	24/09/88	Nottingham Forest	Home	League	1–1		
17	27/09/88	Birmingham City	Away	Lge Cup	2–0		
18	01/10/88	Sheffield Wednesday	Away	League	0–1		
19	08/10/88	Wimbledon	Home	League	0–1		
20	12/10/88	Birmingham City	Home	Lge Cup	5–0		
21	15/10/88	Charlton Athletic	Away	League	2–2	1 Goal	(6)
22	22/10/88	Everton	Home	League	2–0	1 Goal	(7)
23	29/10/88	Tottenham Hotspur	Home	League	2–1		
24	02/11/88	Millwall	Home	Lge Cup	3–1	1 Goal	(8)
25	05/11/88	Manchester United	Away	League	1–1		
26	09/11/88	Birmingham City	Home	Simod Cup	6–0	1 Goal	(9)
27	12/11/88	Southampton	Away	League	1–3		
28	19/11/88	Derby County	Home	League	1–2		
29	23/11/88	Derby County	Away	Simod Cup	1–2		
30	26/11/88	Coventry City	Away	League	1–2		
31	30/11/88	Ipswich Town	Home	Lge Cup	6–2	4 Goals	(13)
32	03/12/88	Norwich City	Home	League	3–1	1 Goal	(14)
33	10/12/88	Middlesbrough	Away	League	3–3		
34	17/12/88	Luton Town	Away	League	1–1		
35	26/12/88	Queens Park Rangers	Home	League	2–1		
36	31/12/88	Arsenal	Home	League	0–3		
37	03/01/89	Liverpool	Away	League	0–1		
38	07/01/89	Crewe Alexandra	Away	FA Cup	3–2	1 Goal	(15)
39	14/01/89	Newcastle United	Home	League	3–1		
40	18/01/89	West Ham United	Away	Lge Cup	1–2	1 Goal	(16)
41	21/01/89	Nottingham Forest	Away	League	0–4		
42	28/01/89	Wimbledon	Home	FA Cup	0–1		
43	04/02/89	Sheffield Wednesday	Home	League	2–0	1 Goal	(17)
44	11/02/89	Wimbledon	Away	League	0–1		
45	14/02/89	Everton	Away	League	1–1		
46	25/02/89	Charlton Athletic	Home	League	1–2		
47	01/03/89	Tottenham Hotspur	Away	League	0–2		
48	12/03/89	Manchester United	Home	League	0–0		
49	18/03/89	Millwall	Away	League	0–2		

50	25/03/89	West Ham United	Home	League	0–1		
51	27/03/89	Queens Park Rangers	Away	League	0–1		
52	01/04/89	Luton Town	Home	League	2–1		
53	08/04/89	Newcastle United	Away	League	2–1	1 Goal	(18)
54	22/04/89	Norwich City	Away	League	2–2		
55	29/04/89	Middlesbrough	Home	League	1–1		
56	02/05/89	Southampton	Home	League	1–2		
57	06/05/89	Derby County	Away	League	1–2	1 Goal	(19)
58	13/05/89	Coventry City	Home	League	1–1	1 Goal	(20)

SEASON 1989–90

League Division One

59	19/08/89	Nottingham Forest	Away	League	1–1		
60	23/08/89	Liverpool	Home	League	1–1	1 Goal	(21)
61	26/08/89	Charlton Athletic	Home	League	1–1		
62	29/08/89	Southampton	Home	League	1–2	1 Goal	(22)
63	09/09/89	Tottenham Hotspur	Home	League	2–0		
64	16/09/89	Sheffield Wednesday	Away	League	0–1		
65	20/09/89	Wolverhampton Wanderers	Home	Lge Cup	2–1	1 Goal	(23)
66	23/09/89	Queens Park Rangers	Home	League	1–3	1 Goal	(24)
67	30/09/89	Derby County	Home	League	1–0	1 Goal	(25)
68	04/10/89	Wolverhampton Wanderers	Away	Lge Cup	1–1		
69	14/10/89	Luton Town	Away	League	1–0		
70	22/10/89	Manchester City	Away	League	2–0		
71	25/10/89	West Ham United	Home	Lge Cup	0–0		
72	28/10/89	Crystal Palace	Home	League	2–1	2 Goals	(27)
73	05/11/89	Everton	Home	League	6–2	2 Goals	(29)
74	08/11/89	West Ham United	Away	Lge Cup	0–1		
75	11/11/89	Norwich City	Away	League	0–2		
76	18/11/89	Coventry City	Home	League	4–1	1 Goal	(30)
77	25/11/89	Wimbledon	Away	League	2–0	1 Goal	(31)
78	27/11/89	Hull City	Away	ZDS Cup	2–1	1 Goal	(32)
79	02/12/89	Nottingham Forest	Home	League	2–1	1 Goal	(33)
80	09/12/89	Liverpool	Away	League	1–1		
81	16/12/89	Millwall	Away	League	0–2		
82	22/12/89	Nottingham Forest	Home	ZDS Cup	2–1	1 Goal	(34)
83	26/12/89	Manchester United	Home	League	3–0	1 Goal	(35)
84	30/12/89	Arsenal	Home	League	2–1	1 Goal	(36)
85	01/01/90	Chelsea	Away	League	3–0	1 Goal	(37)
86	06/01/90	Blackburn Rovers	Away	FA Cup	2–2		
87	10/01/90	Blackburn Rovers	Home	FA Cup	3–1		
88	13/01/90	Charlton Athletic	Away	League	2–0		
89	17/01/90	Leeds United	Home	ZDS Cup	2–0	1 Goal	(38)
90	20/01/90	Southampton	Home	League	2–1		
91	27/01/90	Port Vale	Home	FA Cup	6–0	1 Goal	(39)
92	30/01/90	Middlesbrough	Home	ZDS Cup	1–2		
93	06/02/90	Middlesbrough	Away	ZDS Cup	1–2*		
94	10/02/90	Sheffield Wednesday	Home	League	1–0	1 Goal	(40)
95	17/02/90	West Bromwich Albion	Away	FA Cup	2–0		
96	21/02/90	Tottenham Hotspur	Away	League	2–0	1 Goal	(41)
97	24/02/90	Wimbledon	Home	League	0–3		
98	04/03/90	Coventry City	Away	League	0–2		
99	10/03/90	Luton Town	Home	League	2–0	1 Goal	(42)
100	14/03/90	Oldham Athletic	Away	FA Cup	0–3		
101	17/03/90	Derby County	Away	League	1–0		
102	20/03/90	Queens Park Rangers	Away	League	1–1		
103	24/03/90	Crystal Palace	Away	League	0–1		
104	01/04/90	Manchester City	Home	League	1–2		
105	11/04/90	Arsenal	Away	League	1–0		
106	14/04/90	Chelsea	Home	League	1–0		
107	17/04/90	Manchester United	Away	League	0–2		
108	21/04/90	Millwall	Home	League	1–0	1 Goal	(43)
109	28/04/90	Norwich City	Home	League	3–3	1 Goal	(44)

SEASON 1990–91

League Division One

110	25/08/90	Southampton	Home	League	1–1		
111	01/09/90	Liverpool	Away	League	1–2	1 Goal	(45)
112	05/09/90	Manchester City	Away	League	1–2	1 Goal	(46)
113	08/09/90	Coventry City	Home	League	2–1	1 Goal	(47)
114	15/09/90	Derby County	Away	League	2–0	1 Goal	(48)
115	19/09/90	FC Banik OKD Ostrava	Home	UEFA Cup	3–1	1 Goal	(49)
116	22/09/90	Queens Park Rangers	Home	League	2–2		

117	26/09/90	Barnsley	Home	Lge Cup	1–0	1 Goal	(50)
118	29/09/90	Tottenham Hotspur	Away	League	1–2	1 Goal	(51)
119	03/10/90	FC Banik OKD Ostrava	Away	UEFA Cup	2–1		
120	06/10/90	Sunderland	Home	League	3–0	1 Goal	(52)
121	09/10/90	Barnsley	Away	Lge Cup	1–0		
122	20/10/90	Wimbledon	Away	League	0–0		
123	24/10/90	Internazionale Milano	Home	UEFA Cup	2–0	1 Goal	(53)
124	27/10/90	Leeds United	Home	League	0–0		
125	31/10/90	Millwall	Home	Lge Cup	2–0	1 Goal	(54)
126	03/11/90	Chelsea	Away	League	0–1		
127	07/11/90	Internazionale Milano	Away	UEFA Cup	0–3		
128	10/11/90	Nottingham Forest	Home	League	1–1		
129	17/11/90	Norwich City	Away	League	0–2		
130	24/11/90	Luton Town	Away	League	0–2		
131	28/11/90	Middlesbrough	Home	Lge Cup	3–2	1 Goal	(55)
132	01/12/90	Sheffield United	Home	League	2–1	1 Goal	(56)
133	15/12/90	Southampton	Away	League	1–1	1 Goal	(57)
134	23/12/90	Arsenal	Home	League	0–0		
135	26/12/90	Everton	Away	League	0–1		
136	29/12/90	Manchester United	Away	League	1–1		
137	01/01/91	Crystal Palace	Home	League	2–0	2 Goals	(59)
138	05/01/91	Wimbledon	Home	FA Cup	1–1		
139	09/01/91	Wimbledon	Away	FA Cup	0–1*		
140	12/01/91	Liverpool	Home	League	0–0		
141	16/01/91	Leeds United	Away	Lge Cup	1–4		
142	19/01/91	Coventry City	Away	League	1–2	1 Goal	(60)
143	09/03/91	Luton Town	Home	League	1–2		
144	16/03/91	Tottenham Hotspur	Home	League	3–2	3 Goals	(63)
145	23/03/91	Sunderland	Away	League	3–1	1 Goal	(64)
146	30/03/91	Everton	Home	League	2–2	1 Goal	(65)
147	03/04/91	Arsenal	Away	League	0–5		
148	06/04/91	Manchester United	Home	League	1–1		
149	10/04/91	Queens Park Rangers	Away	League	1–2	1 Goal	(66)
150	13/04/91	Crystal Palace	Away	League	0–0		
151	20/04/91	Wimbledon	Home	League	1–2		
152	23/04/91	Manchester City	Home	League	1–5	1 Goal	(67)
153	04/05/91	Leeds United	Away	League	2–5		
154	08/05/91	Norwich City	Home	League	2–1		
155	11/05/91	Chelsea	Home	League	2–2	1 Goal	(68)

SEASON 1991–92

AS Bari – Italian League Division One

1	21/08/91	Empoli FC	Home	It Cup	0–0		
2	24/08/91	Empoli FC	Away	It Cup	1–1		
3	28/08/91	Ascoli Calcio 1898	Home	It Cup	2–1	1 Goal	(1)
4	01/09/91	Torino Calcio	Home	League	1–1	1 Goal	(2)
5	04/09/91	Ascoli Calcio 1898	Away	It Cup	3–1	1 Goal	(3)
6	08/09/91	Parma AC	Away	League	0–1		
7	15/09/91	Sampdoria UC	Home	League	1–1	1 Goal	(4)
8	22/09/91	FC Verona	Away	League	1–2		
9	29/09/91	Juventus FC	Away	League	0–2		
10	06/10/91	US Cremonese	Home	League	0–0		
11	20/10/91	AC Fiorentina	Away	League	0–2		
12	27/10/91	Milan AC	Home	League	0–1		
13	30/10/91	Sampdoria UC	Away	It Cup	1–1	1 Goal	(5)
14	03/11/91	Foggia Calcio	Away	League	1–4		
15	17/11/91	SS Lazio	Home	League	1–2	1 Goal	(6)
16	24/11/91	SSC Napoli	Away	League	0–1		
17	01/12/91	Genoa 1893	Home	League	1–2	1 Goal	(7)
18	04/12/91	Sampdoria UC	Home	It Cup	2–2*	1 Goal	(8)
19	08/12/91	Ascoli Calcio 1898	Away	League	2–2	1 Goal	(9)
20	05/01/92	Cagliari Calcio	Home	League	1–0		
21	12/01/92	Internazionale Milano	Away	League	0–1		
22	19/01/92	AS Roma	Home	League	2–1	2 Goals	(11)
23	26/01/92	Torino Calcio	Away	League	0–1		
24	02/02/92	Parma AC	Home	League	1–1		
25	09/02/92	Sampdoria UC	Away	League	1–1		
26	01/03/92	US Cremonese	Away	League	1–3		
27	08/03/92	AC Fiorentina	Home	League	1–0		
28	15/03/92	Milan AC	Away	League	0–2		
29	29/03/92	Foggia Calcio	Home	League	1–3	1 Goal	(12)
30	05/04/92	SS Lazio	Away	League	1–3		
31	12/04/92	SSC Napoli	Home	League	1–3	1 Goal	(13)
32	26/04/92	Ascoli Calcio 1898	Home	League	2–1	1 Goal	(14)

33	03/05/92	Atalanta BC	Away	League	1–2	1 Goal	(15)
34	10/05/92	Cagliari Calcio	Away	League	0–0		
35	24/05/92	AS Roma	Away	League	0–2		

SEASON 1992–93

Juventus FC – Italian League Division One

1	27/08/92	Fidelis Andria	Home	It Cup	4–0		
2	02/09/92	Fidelis Andria	Away	It Cup	1–1		
3	16/09/92	Anorthosi FC Amokhostos	Home	UEFA Cup	6–1		
4	20/09/92	Genoa 1893	Away	League	2–2	1 Goal	(1)
5	27/09/92	AS Roma	Home	League	1–1		
6	29/09/92	Anorthosi FC Amokhostos	Away	UEFA Cup	4–0		
7	07/10/92	Genoa 1893	Home	It Cup	1–0		
8	18/10/92	Brescia Calcio	Home	League	0–0		
9	20/10/92	Panathinaikos AO Athina	Away	UEFA Cup	1–0	1 Goal	(2)
10	25/10/92	Internazionale Milano	Away	League	1–3		
11	28/10/92	Genoa 1893	Away	It Cup	4–3		
12	04/11/92	Panathinaikos AO Athina	Home	UEFA Cup	0–0		
13	08/11/92	Udinese Calcio	Home	League	5–1		
14	07/02/93	Atalanta BC	Away	League	1–2		
15	10/02/93	Parma AC	Away	It Cup	1–1		
16	14/02/93	Genoa 1893	Home	League	1–0		
17	28/02/93	AS Roma	Away	League	1–2		
18	07/03/93	SSC Napoli	Home	League	4–3	1 Goal	(3)
19	09/03/93	Torino Calcio	Away	It Cup	1–1		
20	14/03/93	Brescia Calcio	Away	League	0–2		
21	21/03/93	Internazionale Milano	Home	League	0–2		
22	04/04/93	Udinese Calcio	Away	League	0–0		
23	06/04/93	Paris Saint–Germain	Home	UEFA Cup	2–1		
24	22/04/93	Paris Saint–Germain	Away	UEFA Cup	1–0		
25	09/05/93	Foggia Calcio	Home	League	4–2		
26	15/05/93	Parma AC	Away	League	1–2		
27	23/05/93	Sampdoria UC	Home	League	1–1	1 Goal	(4)
28	06/06/93	SS Lazio	Home	League	4–1		

SEASON 1993–94

Sampdoria UC – Italian League Division One

1	29/08/93	SSC Napoli	Away	League	2–1	1 Goal	(1)
2	12/09/93	US Lecce	Home	League	2–0	1 Goal	(2)
3	19/09/93	Udinese Calcio	Away	League	2–0	1 Goal	(3)
4	26/09/93	Parma AC	Home	League	1–1		
5	03/10/93	Atalanta BC	Away	League	4–1	1 Goal	(4)
6	06/10/93	SC Pisa	Home	It Cup	0–0		
7	17/10/93	AS Roma	Home	League	0–1		
8	24/10/93	Torino Calcio	Away	League	3–2		
9	27/10/93	SC Pisa	Away	It Cup	0–0+		
10	31/10/93	Milan AC	Home	League	3–2		
11	07/11/93	Cagliari Calcio	Home	League	1–2		
12	10/11/93	AS Roma	Home	It Cup	2–1		
13	21/11/93	Foggia Calcio	Away	League	2–1		
14	28/11/93	US Cremonese	Home	League	3–1	1 Goal	(5)
15	05/12/93	Genoa 1893	Away	League	1–1	1 Goal	(6)
16	12/12/93	Internazionale Milano	Away	League	0–3		
17	15/12/93	AS Roma	Away	It Cup	1–2#	1 Goal	(7)
18	19/12/93	AC Reggiana	Home	League	1–0		
19	02/01/94	SS Lazio	Away	League	1–1		
20	06/01/94	Internazionale Milano	Home	It Cup	1–0		
21	09/01/94	SSC Napoli	Home	League	4–1		
22	16/01/94	Piacenza Calcio	Away	League	1–2		
23	23/01/94	Juventus FC	Home	League	1–1		
24	06/02/94	Udinese Calcio	Home	League	6–2	1 Goal	(8)
25	08/02/94	Parma AC	Home	It Cup	2–1	1 Goal	(9)
26	13/02/94	Parma AC	Away	League	1–2		
27	24/02/94	Parma AC	Away	It Cup	1–0		
28	27/02/94	AS Roma	Away	League	1–0		
29	06/03/94	Torino Calcio	Home	League	1–0		
30	13/03/94	Milan AC	Away	League	0–1		
31	27/03/94	Foggia Calcio	Home	League	6–0	2 Goals	(11)
32	02/04/94	US Cremonese	Away	League	0–0		
33	06/04/94	Ancona Calcio	Away	It Cup	0–0		
34	10/04/94	Genoa 1893	Home	League	1–1		
35	17/04/94	Internazionale Milano	Home	League	3–1		
36	20/04/94	Ancona Calcio	Home	It Cup	6–1		

| 37 | 24/04/94 | AC Reggiana | Away | League | 1–1 | | |
| 38 | 01/05/94 | SS Lazio | Home | League | 3–4 | | |

+ AET Sampdoria UC won 3–1 on penalties
\# AET Sampdoria UC won 7–6 on penalties

SEASON 1994–95

Italian League Division One

39	04/09/94	Padova Calcio	Home	League	5–0	1 Goal	(12)
40	11/09/94	AC Reggiana	Away	League	2–0		
41	15/09/94	FK Bodo/Glimt	Away	ECW Cup	2–3	1 Goal	(13)
42	18/09/94	Foggia Calcio	Home	League	1–1		
43	21/09/94	AC Vicenza	Away	It Cup	1–2		
44	25/09/94	Juventus FC	Away	League	0–1		
45	29/09/94	FK Bodo/Glimt	Home	ECW Cup	2–0	1 Goal	(14)
46	26/10/94	AC Fiorentina	Home	It Cup	1–1		
47	30/10/94	SSC Napoli	Home	League	0–0		
48	03/11/94	Grasshopper–Club Zurich	Away	ECW Cup	2–3		
49	06/11/94	US Cremonese	Away	League	0–2		
50	20/11/94	Torino Calcio	Home	League	1–1		
51	27/11/94	AC Fiorentina	Away	League	2–2	1 Goal	(15)
52	04/12/94	Genoa 1893	Home	League	3–2		
53	18/12/94	Cagliari Calcio	Home	League	5–0		
54	08/01/95	SS Lazio	Home	League	3–1	2 Goals	(17)
55	15/01/95	Internazionale Milano	Away	League	0–2		
56	22/01/95	AS Bari	Home	League	1–1		
57	29/01/95	Padova Calcio	Away	League	4–1	1 Goal	(18)
58	19/02/95	Foggia Calcio	Away	League	1–1		
59	02/03/95	FC Porto	Home	ECW Cup	0–1		
60	05/03/95	AS Roma	Home	League	3–0		
61	12/03/95	Parma AC	Away	League	2–3		
62	16/03/95	FC Porto	Away	ECW Cup	1–0+		
63	19/03/95	Milan AC	Home	League	0–3		
64	02/04/95	SSC Napoli	Away	League	0–2		
65	09/04/95	US Cremonese	Home	League	2–1		
66	15/04/95	Torino Calcio	Away	League	0–0		
67	30/04/95	Genoa 1893	Away	League	1–2	1 Goal	(19)
68	07/05/95	Brescia Calcio	Home	League	2–1	2 Goals	(21)
69	14/05/95	Cagliari Calcio	Away	League	2–0		
70	21/05/95	SS Lazio	Away	League	0–1		
71	28/05/95	Internazionale Milano	Home	League	2–2		

+ AET Sampdoria UC won 5–3 on penalties

SEASON 1995–96

Arsenal – Premier League

1	20/08/95	Middlesbrough	Home	League	1–1		
2	23/08/95	Everton	Away	League	2–0	1 Goal	(1)
3	26/08/95	Coventry City	Away	League	0–0		
4	29/08/95	Nottingham Forest	Home	League	1–1	1 Goal	(2)
Sub+1	30/10/95	Bolton Wanderers	Away	League	0–1		
5	04/11/95	Manchester United	Home	League	1–0		
6	18/11/95	Tottenham Hotspur	Away	League	1–2		
7	21/11/95	Sheffield Wednesday	Home	League	4–2		
8	26/11/95	Blackburn Rovers	Home	League	0–0		
9	29/11/95	Sheffield Wednesday	Home	Lge Cup	2–1		
10	02/12/95	Aston Villa	Away	League	1–1	1 Goal	(3)
11	09/12/95	Southampton	Away	League	0–0		
12	16/12/95	Chelsea	Home	League	1–1		
13	23/12/95	Liverpool	Away	League	1–3		
14	26/12/95	Queens Park Rangers	Home	League	3–0		
15	30/12/95	Wimbledon	Home	League	1–3		
16	02/01/96	Newcastle United	Away	League	0–2		
17	10/01/96	Newcastle United	Home	Lge Cup	2–0		
18	13/01/96	Middlesbrough	Away	League	3–2	1 Goal	(4)
19	17/01/96	Sheffield United	Away	FA Cup	0–1		
Sub+2	21/02/96	Aston Villa	Away	Lge Cup	0–0*		
Sub+3	24/02/96	West Ham United	Away	League	1–0		
20	02/03/96	Queens Park Rangers	Away	League	1–1		
21	05/03/96	Manchester City	Home	League	3–1		
22	16/03/96	Wimbledon	Away	League	3–0	1 Goal	(5)
23	20/03/96	Manchester United	Away	League	0–1		
24	23/03/96	Newcastle United	Home	League	2–0		

25	06/04/96	Leeds United	Home	League	2–1		
26	08/04/96	Sheffield Wednesday	Away	League	0–1		
27	15/04/96	Tottenham Hotspur	Home	League	0–0		
28	27/04/96	Blackburn Rovers	Away	League	1–1		
29	01/05/96	Liverpool	Home	League	0–0		
30	05/05/96	Bolton Wanderers	Home	League	2–1	1 Goal	(6)

SEASON 1996–97

Premier League

Sub+4	04/09/96	Chelsea	Home	League	3–3		
31	07/09/96	Aston Villa	Away	League	2–2		
32	10/09/96	Borussia Monchengladbach	Home	UEFA Cup	2–3		
33	16/09/96	Sheffield Wednesday	Home	League	4–1	1 Goal	(7)
34	21/09/96	Middlesbrough	Away	League	2–0		
35	25/09/96	Borussia Monchengladbach	Away	UEFA Cup	2–3		
36	28/09/96	Sunderland	Home	League	2–0		
37	12/10/96	Blackburn Rovers	Away	League	2–0		
38	19/10/96	Coventry City	Home	League	0–0		
39	23/10/96	Stoke City	Away	Lge Cup	1–1		
40	26/10/96	Leeds United	Home	League	3–0		
41	02/11/96	Wimbledon	Away	League	2–2		
42	13/11/96	Stoke City	Home	Lge Cup	5–2	1 Goal	(8)
43	16/11/96	Manchester United	Away	League	0–1		
44	24/11/96	Tottenham Hotspur	Home	League	3–1		
45	27/11/96	Liverpool	Away	Lge Cup	2–4		
46	30/11/96	Newcastle United	Away	League	2–1		
47	04/12/96	Southampton	Home	League	3–1		
48	07/12/96	Derby County	Home	League	2–2		
49	21/12/96	Nottingham Forest	Away	League	1–2		
50	26/12/96	Sheffield Wednesday	Away	League	0–0		
51	11/01/97	Sunderland	Away	League	0–1		
52	15/01/97	Sunderland	Away	FA Cup	2–0		
53	19/01/97	Everton	Home	League	3–1		
54	01/03/97	Everton	Away	League	2–0		
55	08/03/97	Nottingham Forest	Home	League	2–0		
56	15/03/97	Southampton	Away	League	2–0		
57	24/03/97	Liverpool	Home	League	1–2		
58	05/04/97	Chelsea	Away	League	3–0	1 Goal	(9)
59	12/04/97	Leicester City	Home	League	2–0	1 Goal	(10)
60	19/04/97	Blackburn Rovers	Home	League	1–1	1 Goal	(11)
61	21/04/97	Coventry City	Away	League	1–1		
62	03/05/97	Newcastle United	Home	League	0–1		
63	11/05/97	Derby County	Away	League	3–1		

INTERNATIONAL APPEARANCES – ENGLAND

Sub 1	15/11/89	Italy	Wembley	0–0	F		
Sub 2	13/12/89	Yugoslavia	Wembley	2–1	F		
3	28/03/90	Brazil	Wembley	1–0	F		
Sub 4	15/05/90	Denmark	Wembley	1–0	F		
Sub 5	02/06/90	Tunisia	Tunis	1–1	F		
Sub 6	16/06/90	Holland	Cagliari	0–0	WC		
Sub 7	21/06/90	Egypt	Cagliari	1–0	WC		
Sub 8	26/06/90	Belgium	Bologna	1–0*	WC	1 Goal	(1)
9	01/07/90	Cameroon	Naples	3–2*	WC	1 Goal	(2)
10	04/07/90	West Germany	Turin	1–1+	WC		
11	07/07/90	Italy	Bari	1–2	WC	1 Goal	(3)
12	12/09/90	Hungary	Wembley	1–0	F		
13	17/10/90	Poland	Wembley	2–0	ECQ		
14	14/11/90	Republic of Ireland	Lansdowne Road	1–1	ECQ	1 Goal	(4)
15	27/03/91	Republic of Ireland	Wembley	1–1	ECQ		
16	01/05/91	Turkey	Izmir	1–0	ECQ		
17	21/05/91	USSR	Wembley	3–1	F	2 Goals	(6)
18	25/05/91	Argentina	Wembley	2–2	F	1 Goal	(7)
19	01/06/91	Australia	Sydney	1–0	F		
20	03/06/91	New Zealand	Auckland	1–0	F		
21	08/06/91	New Zealand	Wellington	2–0	F		
22	12/06/91	Malaysia	Kuala Lumpur	4–2	F		
23	11/09/91	Germany	Wembley	0–1	F		
24	16/10/91	Turkey	Wembley	1–0	ECQ		
25	13/11/91	Poland	Poznan	1–1	ECQ		
26	25/03/92	Czechoslovakia	Prague	2–2	F		
27	29/04/92	CIS	Moscow	2–2	F		

28	17/05/92	Brazil	Wembley	1–1	F	1 Goal	(8)
29	03/06/92	Finland	Helsinki	2–1	F	2 Goals	(10)
30	11/06/92	Denmark	Malmo	0–0	EC		
31	14/06/92	France	Malmo	0–0	EC		
32	17/06/92	Sweden	Solna	1–2	EC	1 Goal	(11)
33	09/09/92	Spain	Santander	0–1	F		
34	14/10/92	Norway	Wembley	1–1	WCQ	1 Goal	(12)
35	18/11/92	Turkey	Wembley	4–0	WCQ		
36	17/02/93	San Marino	Wembley	6–0	WCQ	4 Goals	(16)
37	31/03/93	Turkey	Izmir	2–0	WCQ	1 Goal	(17)
38	28/04/93	Holland	Wembley	2–2	WCQ	1 Goal	(18)
39	29/05/93	Poland	Katowice	1–1	WCQ		
40	02/06/93	Norway	Oslo	0–2	WCQ		
41	13/06/93	Brazil	Washington	1–1	USC	1 Goal	(19)
42	19/06/93	Germany	Detroit	1–2	USC	1 Goal	(20)
43	08/09/93	Poland	Wembley	3–0	WCQ		
44	13/10/93	Holland	Rotterdam	0–2	WCQ		
45	17/11/93	San Marino	Bologna	7–1	WCQ		
46	09/03/94	Denmark	Wembley	1–0	F	1 Goal	(21)
47	17/05/94	Greece	Wembley	5–0	F	2 Goals	(23)
48	22/05/94	Norway	Wembley	0–0	F		
49	07/09/94	USA	Wembley	2–0	F		
50	16/11/94	Nigeria	Wembley	1–0	F	1 Goal	(24)
51	15/02/95	Republic of Ireland	Lansdowne Road	Aba	F		
52	29/03/95	Uruguay	Wembley	0–0	F		
53	03/06/95	Japan	Wembley	2–1	UC	1 Goal	(25)
54	08/06/95	Sweden	Elland Road	3–3	UC	1 Goal	(26)
55	11/06/95	Brazil	Wembley	1–3	UC		
Sub 56	27/03/96	Bulgaria	Wembley	1–0	F		
57	24/04/96	Croatia	Wembley	0–0	F		
58	18/05/96	Hungary	Wembley	3–0	F	1 Goal	(27)
Sub 59	08/06/96	Switzerland	Wembley	1–1	EC		
Sub 60	18/06/96	Holland	Wembley	4–1	EC		
61	22/06/96	Spain	Wembley	0–0#	EC		
62	26/06/96	Germany	Wembley	1–1++	EC		

+ AET West Germany won 4–3 on penalties
# AET England won 4–2 on penalties
++ AET Germany won 6–5 on penalties

APPEARANCES AND GOALS PER SEASON

SEASON 84–85	GAMES	GOALS
League	22	5
Freight Rover Trophy	1	0
TOTAL	**23**	**5**

SEASON 85–86	GAMES	GOALS
League	43	8
FA Cup	1	0
League Cup	4	2
Freight Rover Trophy	2	0
TOTAL	**50**	**10**

SEASON 86–87	GAMES	GOALS
League	43	23
FA Cup	1	1
League Cup	2	0
Freight Rover Trophy	2	0
TOTAL	**48**	**24**

SEASON 87–88	GAMES	GOALS
League	37	24
FA Cup	1	0
League Cup	2	2
Sherpa Van Trophy	2	0
TOTAL	**42**	**26**

SEASON 88–89	GAMES	GOALS
League	38	7
FA Cup	2	1
League Cup	5	6
Simod Cup	2	1
TOTAL	**47**	**15**

SEASON 89–90	GAMES	GOALS
League	37	19
FA Cup	5	1
League Cup	4	1
Zenith Data Systems Cup	5	3
TOTAL	**51**	**24**

SEASON 90–91	GAMES	GOALS
League	35	19
FA Cup	2	0
League Cup	5	3
UEFA Cup	4	2
TOTAL	**46**	**24**

SEASON 91–92	GAMES	GOALS
Italian League	29	11
Italian Cup	6	4
TOTAL	**35**	**15**

SEASON 92–93	GAMES	GOALS
Italian League	16	3
Italian Cup	6	0
UEFA Cup	6	1
TOTAL	**28**	**4**

SEASON 93–94	GAMES	GOALS
Italian League	29	9
Italian Cup	9	2
TOTAL	**38**	**11**

SEASON 94–95	GAMES	GOALS
Italian League	26	8
Italian Cup	2	0
European Cup Winners Cup	5	2
TOTAL	**33**	**10**

SEASON 95–96	GAMES	GOALS
League	27+2	6
FA Cup	1	0
League Cup	2+1	0
TOTAL	**30+3**	**6**

SEASON 96–97	GAMES	GOALS
League	27+1	4
FA Cup	1	0
League Cup	3	1
UEFA Cup	2	0
TOTAL	**33+1**	**5**

CAREER APPEARANCES AND GOALS

COMPETITION	GAMES	TOTAL	GOALS
League	309+3	312	115
FA Cup	14	14	3
League Cup	27+1	28	15
Freight Rover Trophy	5	5	0
Sherpa Van Trophy	2	2	0
Simod Cup	2	2	1
Zenith Data Systems Cup	5	5	3
European Cup Winners Cup	5	5	2
UEFA Cup	12	12	3
Italian League	100	100	31
Italian Cup	23	23	6
Internationals	52+10	62	27
TOTAL	**556+14**	**570**	**206**

HAT-TRICKS

Crewe Alexandra

1	3	Rochdale	31/03/87	Home	League	5–1

Aston Villa

1	4	Ipswich Town	30/11/88	Home	Lge Cup	6–2
2	3	Tottenham Hotspur	16/03/91	Home	League	3–2

England

| 1 | 4 | San Marino | 17/02/93 | Wembley | WCQ | 6–0 |

League: 2
League Cup: 1
International: 1
TOTAL: 4

HONOURS

Winners medals
Italian Cup: 93/94

Runner-up medals
League Division One Championship: 89/90

JIMMY QUINN

Born: 18/11/59 – Belfast, Northern Ireland
Height: 6.0
Weight: 11.06 (96–97)

Clubs
Swindon Town: **1982–84** – Matches: **41+19** – Goals: **18**
Blackburn Rovers: **1984–86** – Matches: **70+14** – Goals: **23**
Swindon Town: **1986–88** – Matches: **82+4** – Goals: **43**
Leicester City: **1988–89** – Matches: **15+21** – Goals: **6**
Bradford City: **1989** – Matches: **38** – Goals: **14**
West Ham United: **1990–91** – Matches: **42+15** – Goals: **22**
AFC Bournemouth: **1991–92** – Matches: **54** – Goals: **24**
Reading: **1992–97** – Matches: **176+40** – Goals: **94**

Country: Northern Ireland: **1984–95** – Matches: **31+15** – Goals: **12**

SEASON 1981–82

Swindon Town – League Division Three

Sub+1	09/03/82	Walsall	Home	League	2–2
1	07/04/82	Oxford United	Away	League	0–5
2	10/04/82	Plymouth Argyle	Home	League	0–2
Sub+2	17/04/82	Bristol City	Away	League	3–0

SEASON 1982–83

League Division Four

Sub+3	08/09/82	Hereford United	Away	League	2–1	1 Goal	(1)
Sub+4	11/09/82	Halifax Town	Home	League	0–1		
Sub+5	14/09/82	Bristol City	Away	Lge Cup	0–2		
Sub+6	23/10/82	Mansfield Town	Home	League	4–0		
Sub+7	13/11/82	York City	Home	League	3–2		
Sub+8	11/12/82	Brentford	Home	FA Cup	2–2		
3	28/12/82	Wimbledon	Home	League	0–1		
Sub+9	08/01/83	Aldershot	Home	FA Cup	7–0		
Sub+10	29/01/83	Burnley	Away	FA Cup	1–3		
Sub+11	12/02/83	Hereford United	Home	League	3–2		
4	18/02/83	Colchester United	Away	League	0–1		
Sub+12	28/02/83	Tranmere Rovers	Away	League	0–2		
5	05/03/83	Mansfield Town	Away	League	0–1		
Sub+13	30/04/83	Stockport County	Home	League	2–0	1 Goal	(2)
Sub+14	02/05/83	Scunthorpe United	Away	League	0–2		
Sub+15	08/05/83	Northampton Town	Home	League	1–5	1 Goal	(3)
6	14/05/83	Bristol City	Home	League	2–0		

SEASON 1983–84

League Division Four

Sub+16	06/09/83	Halifax Town	Away	League	1–1		
7	13/09/83	Plymouth Argyle	Away	Lge Cup	1–4		
8	17/09/83	Blackpool	Home	League	0–0		
Sub+17	01/10/83	Rochdale	Home	League	2–1	1 Goal	(4)

9	15/10/83	York City	Home	League	3–2		
10	17/10/83	Tranmere Rovers	Away	League	1–2		
Sub+18	12/11/83	Hartlepool United	Home	League	3–2		
11	19/11/83	Kettering Town	Away	FA Cup	7–0	2 Goals	(6)
12	26/11/83	Mansfield Town	Away	League	2–2	2 Goals	(8)
13	03/12/83	Doncaster Rovers	Home	League	2–1	1 Goal	(9)
14	10/12/83	Millwall	Away	FA Cup	3–2	2 Goals	(11)
15	17/12/83	Bury	Home	League	0–0		
16	26/12/83	Torquay United	Away	League	0–1		
17	27/12/83	Wrexham	Home	League	0–1		
18	31/12/83	Peterborough United	Away	League	1–1	1 Goal	(12)
19	07/01/84	Carlisle United	Away	FA Cup	1–1		
20	10/01/84	Carlisle United	Home	FA Cup	3–1	1 Goal	(13)
21	14/01/84	Chesterfield	Home	League	1–2		
22	21/01/84	Blackpool	Away	League	1–1		
23	24/01/84	Bristol City	Home	League	1–1	1 Goal	(14)
24	28/01/84	Blackburn Rovers	Home	FA Cup	1–2	1 Goal	(15)
25	04/02/84	Rochdale	Away	League	3–3		
26	08/02/84	Chester City	Away	League	3–0		
27	11/02/84	Stockport County	Home	League	2–1		
28	15/02/84	Hereford United	Away	League	1–2		
29	18/02/84	Reading	Home	League	1–1		
30	22/02/84	Oxford United	Away	AM Cup	3–1	2 Goals	(17)
31	25/02/84	Colchester United	Away	League	0–0		
32	03/03/84	Tranmere Rovers	Home	League	1–1		
Sub+19	30/03/84	Halifax Town	Away	League	1–2	1 Goal	(18)
33	07/04/84	Aldershot	Home	League	0–2		
34	14/04/84	Doncaster Rovers	Away	League	0–3		
35	17/04/84	Darlington	Home	League	1–0		
36	20/04/84	Wrexham	Away	League	3–0		
37	21/04/84	Torquay United	Home	League	2–3		
38	29/04/84	Mansfield Town	Home	League	1–1		
39	05/05/84	Bristol City	Away	League	0–1		
40	07/05/84	Peterborough United	Home	League	2–0		
41	12/05/84	Bury	Away	League	1–2		

SEASON 1984–85

Blackburn Rovers – League Division Two

Sub+1	25/08/84	Crystal Palace	Away	League	1–1		
Sub+2	08/09/84	Fulham	Away	League	2–3		
Sub+3	29/09/84	Wimbledon	Home	League	2–0		
Sub+4	10/10/84	Oxford United	Away	Lge Cup	1–3*		
Sub+5	20/10/84	Oldham Athletic	Home	League	1–1		
Sub+6	27/10/84	Manchester City	Away	League	1–2		
Sub+7	03/11/84	Oxford United	Away	League	1–2		
Sub+8	10/11/84	Brighton & Hove Albion	Home	League	2–0		
Sub+9	08/12/84	Sheffield United	Home	League	3–1	2 Goals	(2)
1	15/12/84	Wolverhampton Wanderers	Away	League	3–0	2 Goals	(4)
2	23/12/84	Carlisle United	Away	League	1–0		
Sub+10	29/12/84	Huddersfield Town	Home	League	1–3		
3	05/01/85	Portsmouth	Away	FA Cup	0–0		
4	12/01/85	Grimsby Town	Away	League	1–1		
5	26/01/85	Portsmouth	Home	FA Cup	2–1	2 Goals	(6)
6	30/01/85	Oxford United	Away	FA Cup	1–0	1 Goal	(7)
7	02/02/85	Wimbledon	Away	League	1–1	1 Goal	(8)
8	09/02/85	Fulham	Home	League	2–1	1 Goal	(9)
9	15/02/85	Manchester United	Home	FA Cup	0–2		
10	23/02/85	Oxford United	Home	League	1–1	1 Goal	(10)
11	02/03/85	Manchester City	Home	League	0–1		
12	06/03/85	Brighton & Hove Albion	Away	League	1–3		
13	09/03/85	Oldham Athletic	Away	League	0–2		
14	16/03/85	Birmingham City	Home	League	2–1		
15	23/03/85	Shrewsbury Town	Away	League	0–3		
Sub+11	23/04/85	Crystal Palace	Home	League	0–1		
Sub+12	27/04/85	Charlton Athletic	Away	League	0–1		
16	04/05/85	Portsmouth	Home	League	0–1		
17	06/05/85	Sheffield United	Away	League	3–1	3 Goals	(13)
18	11/05/85	Wolverhampton Wanderers	Home	League	3–0		

SEASON 1985–86

League Division Two

| 19 | 17/08/85 | Sunderland | Away | League | 2–0 | 1 Goal | (14) |
| 20 | 20/08/85 | Norwich City | Home | League | 2–1 | | |

21	24/08/85	Shrewsbury Town	Home	League	1–1		
22	26/08/85	Hull City	Away	League	2–2		
23	31/08/85	Carlisle United	Home	League	2–0		
24	03/09/85	Huddersfield Town	Away	League	0–0		
25	07/09/85	Brighton & Hove Albion	Away	League	1–3		
26	14/09/85	Wimbledon	Home	League	2–0		
27	21/09/85	Fulham	Home	League	1–0		
28	24/09/85	Wimbledon	Away	Lge Cup	0–5		
29	28/09/85	Portsmouth	Away	League	0–3		
30	05/10/85	Bradford City	Home	League	3–0	1 Goal	(15)
31	08/10/85	Wimbledon	Home	Lge Cup	2–1	1 Goal	(16)
32	12/10/85	Millwall	Away	League	1–0		
33	19/10/85	Oldham Athletic	Home	League	0–0		
34	26/10/85	Crystal Palace	Away	League	0–2		
35	02/11/85	Middlesbrough	Away	League	0–0		
36	09/11/85	Barnsley	Home	League	0–3		
37	16/11/85	Sheffield United	Away	League	3–3		
38	23/11/85	Charlton Athletic	Home	League	0–0		
39	30/11/85	Grimsby Town	Away	League	2–5		
40	07/12/85	Norwich City	Away	League	0–3		
Sub+13	01/02/86	Hull City	Home	League	2–2		
41	08/02/86	Oldham Athletic	Away	League	1–3		
42	15/02/86	Crystal Palace	Home	League	1–2		
43	01/03/86	Portsmouth	Home	League	1–0		
44	08/03/86	Bradford City	Away	League	2–3	1 Goal	(17)
45	11/03/86	Fulham	Away	League	3–3	1 Goal	(18)
46	15/03/86	Millwall	Home	League	1–2		
47	18/03/86	Brighton & Hove Albion	Home	League	1–4		
48	22/03/86	Wimbledon	Away	League	1–1		
49	29/03/86	Stoke City	Home	League	0–1		
Sub+14	05/04/86	Middlesbrough	Home	League	0–1		

SEASON 1986–87

League Division Two

50	23/08/86	Leeds United	Home	League	2–1	1 Goal	(19)
51	26/08/86	Wigan Athletic	Away	Lge Cup	3–1		
52	30/08/86	Shrewsbury Town	Away	League	1–0		
53	02/09/86	Wigan Athletic	Home	Lge Cup	2–0		
54	06/09/86	Sunderland	Home	League	6–1	1 Goal	(20)
55	13/09/86	Portsmouth	Away	League	0–1		
56	16/09/86	Huddersfield Town	Away	FM Cup	2–1*	1 Goal	(21)
57	20/09/86	Crystal Palace	Home	League	0–2		
58	23/09/86	Queens Park Rangers	Away	Lge Cup	1–2		
59	27/09/86	Millwall	Away	League	2–2		
60	04/10/86	Reading	Away	League	0–4		
61	07/10/86	Queens Park Rangers	Home	Lge Cup	2–2	1 Goal	(22)
62	11/10/86	West Bromwich Albion	Home	League	0–1		
63	18/10/86	Stoke City	Away	League	0–1		
64	04/11/86	Sheffield United	Home	FM Cup	1–0		
65	08/11/86	Sheffield United	Home	League	0–2		
66	15/11/86	York City	Home	League	0–2		
67	22/11/86	Brighton & Hove Albion	Away	League	2–0	1 Goal	(23)
68	29/11/86	Ipswich Town	Home	League	0–0		
69	02/12/86	Grimsby Town	Away	League	0–1		
70	06/12/86	Birmingham City	Away	League	1–1		

Swindon Town – League Division Three

1	21/12/86	Doncaster Rovers	Away	League	2–2		
2	26/12/86	Brentford	Home	League	2–0		
3	27/12/86	Gillingham	Away	League	3–1		
4	01/01/87	AFC Bournemouth	Away	League	0–1		
5	03/01/87	Bury	Home	League	1–0		
6	06/01/87	Brentford	Away	FR Trophy	2–4		
7	10/01/87	Fulham	Away	FA Cup	1–0		
8	25/01/87	Newport County	Home	League	3–0	1 Goal	(1)
Sub+1	28/01/87	AFC Bournemouth	Home	FR Trophy	2–2+		
9	03/02/87	Leeds United	Home	FA Cup	1–2		
10	07/02/87	Blackpool	Away	League	1–1		
11	11/02/87	Hereford United	Home	FR Trophy	4–2	1 Goal	(2)
12	21/02/87	Rotherham United	Away	League	2–1	1 Goal	(3)
13	28/02/87	Middlesbrough	Home	League	1–0		
14	03/03/87	York City	Away	League	3–0	2 Goals	(5)
15	10/03/87	Aldershot	Home	FR Trophy	2–3	1 Goal	(6)
16	14/03/87	Chesterfield	Away	League	3–1	1 Goal	(7)

17	17/03/87	Port Vale	Home	League	1–0	
18	21/03/87	Fulham	Home	League	2–0	2 Goals (9)
19	24/03/87	Bolton Wanderers	Home	League	2–0	
Sub+2	03/04/87	Mansfield Town	Home	League	3–0	
20	11/04/87	Bristol Rovers	Away	League	4–3	2 Goals (11)
21	18/04/87	AFC Bournemouth	Home	League	1–1	
22	20/04/87	Brentford	Away	League	1–1	
23	22/04/87	Darlington	Home	League	1–0	
24	25/04/87	Doncaster Rovers	Home	League	1–1	
25	06/05/87	Walsall	Home	League	0–0	
Sub+3	09/05/87	Bristol City	Away	League	1–1	
26	14/05/87	Wigan Athletic	Away	Lge P/O	3–2	1 Goal (12)
27	17/05/87	Wigan Athletic	Home	Lge P/O	0–0	
28	22/05/87	Gillingham	Away	Lge P/O	0–1	

+ AET Swindon Town won 4–2 on penalties

SEASON 1987–88

League Division Two

29	15/08/87	Bradford City	Away	League	0–2	
30	18/08/87	Bristol City	Home	Lge Cup	3–0	3 Goals (15)
31	22/08/87	Sheffield Wednesday	Home	League	2–0	1 Goal (16)
32	25/08/87	Bristol City	Away	Lge Cup	2–3	
33	29/08/87	West Bromwich Albion	Away	League	2–1	1 Goal (17)
34	31/08/87	Hull City	Home	League	0–0	
35	05/09/87	Middlesbrough	Away	League	3–2	1 Goal (18)
36	12/09/87	Birmingham City	Home	League	0–2	
37	15/09/87	Barnsley	Away	League	1–0	
38	19/09/87	Ipswich Town	Away	League	2–3	1 Goal (19)
39	22/09/87	Portsmouth	Home	Lge Cup	3–1	3 Goals (22)
40	26/09/87	Reading	Home	League	4–0	1 Goal (23)
41	29/09/87	Shrewsbury Town	Home	League	1–1	1 Goal (24)
Sub+4	03/10/87	Millwall	Away	League	2–2	1 Goal (25)
42	07/10/87	Portsmouth	Away	Lge Cup	3–1	
43	10/10/87	Oldham Athletic	Home	League	2–0	
44	20/10/87	Stoke City	Home	League	3–0	1 Goal (26)
45	27/10/87	Watford	Home	Lge Cup	1–1	1 Goal (27)
46	31/10/87	Manchester City	Home	League	3–4	
47	03/11/87	Watford	Away	Lge Cup	2–4	1 Goal (28)
48	07/11/87	Leicester City	Away	League	2–3	1 Goal (29)
49	14/11/87	Plymouth Argyle	Home	League	1–1	
50	21/11/87	Leeds United	Away	League	2–4	
51	28/11/87	AFC Bournemouth	Home	League	4–2	1 Goal (30)
52	01/12/87	Huddersfield Town	Home	League	4–1	1 Goal (31)
53	05/12/87	Aston Villa	Away	League	1–2	1 Goal (32)
54	20/12/87	Sheffield United	Away	League	0–1	
55	23/12/87	Derby County	Home	Simod Cup	2–1	1 Goal (33)
56	26/12/87	Reading	Away	League	1–0	1 Goal (34)
57	28/12/87	Ipswich Town	Home	League	4–2	1 Goal (35)
58	01/01/88	West Bromwich Albion	Home	League	2–0	
59	02/01/88	Birmingham City	Away	League	1–1	
60	09/01/88	Norwich City	Home	FA Cup	0–0	
61	13/01/88	Norwich City	Away	FA Cup	2–0	
62	19/01/88	Chelsea	Home	Simod Cup	4–0	1 Goal (36)
63	30/01/88	Newcastle United	Away	FA Cup	0–5	
64	06/02/88	Middlesbrough	Home	League	1–1	
65	13/02/88	Huddersfield Town	Away	League	3–0	
66	20/02/88	Shrewsbury Town	Away	League	1–2	
67	23/02/88	Norwich City	Home	Simod Cup	2–0	
68	27/02/88	Millwall	Home	League	0–1	
69	08/03/88	Luton Town	Away	Simod Cup	1–2	
70	12/03/88	Oldham Athletic	Away	League	3–4	1 Goal (37)
71	15/03/88	Barnsley	Home	League	3–0	1 Goal (38)
72	19/03/88	Manchester City	Away	League	1–1	
73	27/03/88	Crystal Palace	Home	League	2–2	
74	30/03/88	Bradford City	Home	League	2–2	
75	02/04/88	Leicester City	Home	League	3–2	2 Goals (40)
76	04/04/88	Plymouth Argyle	Away	League	0–1	
77	09/04/88	Blackburn Rovers	Home	League	1–2	
78	12/04/88	Hull City	Away	League	4–1	2 Goals (42)
79	23/04/88	Stoke City	Away	League	0–1	
80	30/04/88	Leeds United	Home	League	1–2	1 Goal (43)
81	02/05/88	AFC Bournemouth	Away	League	0–2	
82	07/05/88	Aston Villa	Home	League	0–0	

SEASON 1988–89

Leicester City – League Division Two

Sub+1	27/08/88	West Bromwich Albion	Home	League	1–1			
Sub+2	29/08/88	Portsmouth	Home	League	0–3			
1	03/09/88	Birmingham City	Away	League	3–2	1 Goal	(1)	
2	10/09/88	Ipswich Town	Home	League	0–1			
3	17/09/88	Oxford United	Away	League	1–1			
4	21/09/88	Plymouth Argyle	Home	League	1–0			
Sub+3	28/09/88	Watford	Home	Lge Cup	4–0			
Sub+4	01/10/88	Chelsea	Away	League	1–2	1 Goal	(2)	
5	04/10/88	Hull City	Away	League	2–2			
Sub+5	08/10/88	Brighton & Hove Albion	Home	League	1–0	1 Goal	(3)	
Sub+6	22/10/88	Leeds United	Away	League	1–1	1 Goal	(4)	
6	26/10/88	Swindon Town	Home	League	3–3			
Sub+7	29/10/88	Shrewsbury Town	Away	League	0–3			
Sub+8	05/11/88	Manchester City	Home	League	0–0			
Sub+9	08/11/88	Watford	Away	Simod Cup	0–2*			
Sub+10	12/11/88	Walsall	Away	League	1–0			
7	19/11/88	Crystal Palace	Away	League	2–4			
8	26/11/88	Bradford City	Home	League	1–0	1 Goal	(5)	
9	30/11/88	Nottingham Forest	Home	Lge Cup	0–0			
10	03/12/88	Oldham Athletic	Away	League	1–1	1 Goal	(6)	
11	10/12/88	Sunderland	Home	League	3–1			
12	14/12/88	Nottingham Forest	Away	Lge Cup	1–2			
Sub+11	17/12/88	Barnsley	Away	League	0–3			
13	26/12/88	AFC Bournemouth	Home	League	0–1			
Sub+12	31/12/88	Blackburn Rovers	Home	League	4–0			
Sub+13	02/01/89	Ipswich Town	Away	League	0–2			
Sub+14	07/01/89	Manchester City	Away	FA Cup	0–1			
14	14/01/89	Portsmouth	Home	League	2–1			
Sub+15	21/01/89	West Bromwich Albion	Away	League	1–1			
15	04/02/89	Hull City	Home	League	0–2			
Sub+16	11/02/89	Brighton & Hove Albion	Away	League	1–1			
Sub+17	18/02/89	Leeds United	Home	League	1–2			
Sub+18	25/02/89	Stoke City	Away	League	2–2			
Sub+19	28/02/89	Swindon Town	Away	League	1–2			
Sub+20	11/03/89	Manchester City	Away	League	2–4			
Sub+21	15/03/89	Shrewsbury Town	Home	League	1–1			

Bradford City – League Division Two

1	18/03/89	Watford	Home	League	2–1			
2	25/03/89	Shrewsbury Town	Away	League	3–1	2 Goals	(2)	
3	27/03/89	Hull City	Home	League	1–1	1 Goal	(3)	
4	01/04/89	Oldham Athletic	Away	League	1–1	1 Goal	(4)	
5	04/04/89	Swindon Town	Away	League	0–1			
6	08/04/89	Walsall	Home	League	3–1	1 Goal	(5)	
7	15/04/89	Ipswich	Home	League	2–2			
8	22/04/89	Portsmouth	Away	League	2–1			
9	29/04/89	Leicester City	Home	League	2–1	1 Goal	(6)	
10	01/05/89	Birmingham City	Away	League	0–1			
11	06/05/89	Chelsea	Away	League	1–3	1 Goal	(7)	
12	13/05/89	Manchester City	Home	League	1–1			

SEASON 1989–90

League Division Two

13	19/08/89	Port Vale	Home	League	2–2			
14	23/08/89	West Ham United	Away	League	0–2			
15	26/08/89	Wolverhampton Wanderers	Away	League	1–1			
16	02/09/89	Portsmouth	Home	League	1–1	1 Goal	(8)	
17	09/09/89	Oxford United	Away	League	1–2			
18	16/09/89	Leicester City	Home	League	2–0	1 Goal	(9)	
19	20/09/89	West Bromwich Albion	Away	Lge Cup	3–1			
20	23/09/89	Barnsley	Away	League	0–2			
21	26/09/89	Stoke City	Away	League	1–1			
22	30/09/89	Swindon Town	Home	League	1–1			
23	04/10/89	West Bromwich Albion	Home	Lge Cup	3–5*	1 Goal	(10)	
24	07/10/89	Brighton & Hove Albion	Home	League	2–0			
25	14/10/89	Newcastle United	Away	League	0–1			
26	18/10/89	Ipswich Town	Home	League	1–0			
27	21/10/89	Sunderland	Away	League	0–1			
28	28/10/89	Leeds United	Home	League	0–1			
29	31/10/89	Oldham Athletic	Away	League	2–2	2 Goals	(12)	
30	04/11/89	Plymouth Argyle	Away	League	1–1			

31	11/11/89	Hull City	Home	League	2–3		
32	18/11/89	Sheffield United	Away	League	1–1		
33	25/11/89	AFC Bournemouth	Home	League	1–0		
34	28/11/89	Stoke City	Away	ZDS Cup	1–2		
35	02/12/89	Port Vale	Away	League	2–3		
36	09/12/89	West Ham United	Home	League	2–1	1 Goal	(13)
37	16/12/89	Watford	Away	League	2–7	1 Goal	(14)
38	26/12/89	Middlesbrough	Home	League	0–1		

West Ham United – League Division Two

1	01/01/90	Barnsley	Home	League	4–2		
2	06/01/90	Torquay United	Away	FA Cup	0–1		
3	13/01/90	Plymouth Argyle	Away	League	1–1	1 Goal	(1)
4	20/01/90	Hull City	Home	League	1–2		
Sub+1	10/02/90	Brighton & Hove Albion	Home	League	3–1	2 Goals	(3)
5	18/02/90	Swindon Town	Away	League	2–2	2 Goals	(5)
6	24/02/90	Blackburn Rovers	Home	League	1–1	1 Goal	(6)
7	03/03/90	Middlesbrough	Away	League	1–0		
Sub+2	10/03/90	Portsmouth	Home	League	2–1		
8	13/03/90	Watford	Away	League	1–0		
9	17/03/90	Leeds United	Away	League	2–3		
10	21/03/90	Sheffield United	Home	League	5–0	3 Goals	(9)
11	24/03/90	Sunderland	Away	League	3–4	2 Goals	(11)
12	31/03/90	Port Vale	Home	League	2–2		
13	04/04/90	West Bromwich Albion	Away	League	3–1	1 Goal	(12)
14	07/04/90	Oxford United	Away	League	2–0	1 Goal	(13)
15	11/04/90	AFC Bournemouth	Home	League	4–1		
16	14/04/90	Barnsley	Away	League	1–1		
17	17/04/90	Ipswich Town	Home	League	2–0		
18	21/04/90	Oldham Athletic	Away	League	0–3		
19	28/04/90	Newcastle United	Away	League	1–2		
Sub+3	05/05/90	Wolverhampton Wanderers	Home	League	4–0		

SEASON 1990–91

League Division Two

Sub+4	01/09/90	Watford	Home	League	1–0		
Sub+5	08/09/90	Leicester City	Away	League	2–1		
Sub+6	19/09/90	Ipswich Town	Home	League	3–1	1 Goal	(14)
20	22/09/90	Newcastle United	Away	League	1–1		
21	26/09/90	Stoke City	Home	Lge Cup	3–0	1 Goal	(15)
22	29/09/90	Sheffield Wednesday	Away	League	1–1		
23	03/10/90	Oxford United	Home	League	2–0	2 Goals	(17)
24	06/10/90	Hull City	Home	League	7–1		
25	10/10/90	Stoke City	Away	Lge Cup	2–1		
26	13/10/90	Bristol City	Away	League	1–1		
27	20/10/90	Swindon Town	Away	League	1–0		
28	24/10/90	Blackburn Rovers	Home	League	1–0		
29	31/10/90	Oxford United	Away	Lge Cup	1–2		
Sub+7	08/12/90	Portsmouth	Away	League	1–0		
Sub+8	15/12/90	Middlesbrough	Home	League	0–0		
30	19/12/90	Luton Town	Away	ZDS Cup	1–5		
Sub+9	22/12/90	Barnsley	Away	League	0–1		
31	26/12/90	Oldham Athletic	Home	League	2–0		
32	29/12/90	Port Vale	Home	League	0–0		
33	01/01/91	Bristol Rovers	Away	League	1–0	1 Goal	(18)
34	05/01/91	Aldershot	Away	FA Cup	0–0+		
35	12/01/91	Watford	Away	League	1–0		
36	16/01/91	Aldershot	Home	FA Cup	6–1	1 Goal	(19)
37	19/01/91	Leicester City	Home	League	1–0		
Sub+10	02/02/91	Wolverhampton Wanderers	Away	League	1–2		
Sub+11	16/02/91	Crewe Alexandra	Home	FA Cup	1–0	1 Goal	(20)
38	05/03/91	Plymouth Argyle	Home	League	2–2		
39	11/03/91	Everton	Home	FA Cup	2–1		
40	13/03/91	Oxford United	Away	League	1–2	1 Goal	(21)
41	16/03/91	Sheffield Wednesday	Home	League	1–3	1 Goal	(22)
42	20/03/91	Bristol City	Home	League	1–0		
Sub+12	10/04/91	Brighton & Hove Albion	Away	League	0–1		
Sub+13	14/04/91	Nottingham Forest	Neutral	FA Cup	0–4		
Sub+14	27/04/91	Blackburn Rovers	Away	League	1–3		
Sub+15	04/05/91	Charlton Athletic	Away	League	1–1		

+ Played at West Ham United

SEASON 1991–92

AFC Bournemouth – League Division Three

1	17/08/91	Darlington	Home	League	1–2			
2	21/08/91	Cardiff City	Away	Lge Cup	2–3			
3	24/08/91	Stoke City	Away	League	1–1	1 Goal	(1)	
4	27/08/91	Cardiff City	Home	Lge Cup	4–1	1 Goal	(2)	
5	31/08/91	Hull City	Home	League	0–0			
6	03/09/91	Preston North End	Away	League	2–2			
7	07/09/91	Chester City	Away	League	1–0			
8	14/09/91	Bolton Wanderers	Home	League	1–2	1 Goal	(3)	
9	17/09/91	Shrewsbury Town	Home	League	1–0			
10	21/09/91	Huddersfield Town	Away	League	0–0			
11	24/09/91	Middlesbrough	Away	Lge Cup	1–1			
12	27/09/91	Fulham	Home	League	0–0			
13	05/10/91	Reading	Away	League	0–0			
14	08/10/91	Middlesbrough	Home	Lge Cup	1–2*	1 Goal	(4)	
15	12/10/91	Hartlepool United	Home	League	2–0	1 Goal	(5)	
16	22/10/91	Swansea City	Home	A Trophy	3–0			
17	19/10/91	Leyton Orient	Away	League	1–1	1 Goal	(6)	
18	26/10/91	Bradford City	Home	League	1–3	1 Goal	(7)	
19	01/11/91	Stockport County	Home	League	1–0			
20	06/11/91	Torquay United	Away	League	0–1			
21	08/11/91	Swansea City	Away	League	1–3	1 Goal	(8)	
22	16/11/91	Bromsgrove Rovers	Home	FA Cup	3–1			
23	22/11/91	Brentford	Home	League	0–0			
24	30/11/91	Bury	Away	League	1–0			
25	07/12/91	Brentford	Home	FA Cup	2–1	2 Goals	(10)	
26	10/12/91	Cardiff City	Away	A Trophy	3–3	1 Goal	(11)	
27	14/12/91	Birmingham City	Home	League	2–1	1 Goal	(12)	
28	21/12/91	Stoke City	Home	League	1–2			
29	26/12/91	Hull City	Away	League	1–0	1 Goal	(13)	
30	28/12/91	Darlington	Away	League	0–0			
31	01/01/92	Preston North End	Home	League	1–0			
32	04/01/92	Newcastle United	Home	FA Cup	0–0			
33	18/01/92	Wigan Athletic	Home	League	3–0	1 Goal	(14)	
34	22/01/92	Newcastle United	Away	FA Cup	2–2+			
35	01/02/92	Leyton Orient	Home	League	0–1			
36	05/02/92	Ipswich Town	Away	FA Cup	0–3			
37	08/02/92	Bradford City	Away	League	1–3	1 Goal	(15)	
38	11/02/92	Bury	Home	League	4–0	1 Goal	(16)	
39	15/02/92	Birmingham City	Away	League	1–0	1 Goal	(17)	
40	29/02/92	Exeter City	Away	League	3–0	2 Goals	(19)	
41	03/03/92	Wigan Athletic	Away	League	0–2			
42	07/03/92	Peterborough United	Home	League	1–2			
43	10/03/92	Torquay United	Home	League	2–1	1 Goal	(20)	
44	13/03/92	Stockport County	Away	League	0–5			
45	20/03/92	Swansea City	Home	League	3–0			
46	24/03/92	Exeter City	Home	League	1–0	1 Goal	(21)	
47	29/03/92	Brentford	Away	League	2–2			
48	31/03/92	Bolton Wanderers	Away	League	2–0			
49	03/04/92	Chester City	Home	League	2–0			
50	08/04/92	Peterborough United	Away	League	0–2			
51	11/04/92	Shrewsbury Town	Away	League	2–1	1 Goal	(22)	
52	20/04/92	Fulham	Away	League	0–2			
53	25/04/92	Reading	Home	League	3–2	2 Goals	(24)	
54	02/05/92	Hartlepool United	Away	League	0–1			

+ AET AFC Bournemouth won 4–3 on penalties

SEASON 1992–93

Reading – Football League Division Two

1	15/08/92	Hartlepool United	Away	League	1–1	1 Goal	(1)	
2	22/08/92	Leyton Orient	Home	League	1–1			
3	29/08/92	Bolton Wanderers	Away	League	1–2			
4	05/09/92	Hull City	Home	League	1–2			
5	09/09/92	West Bromwich Albion	Away	League	0–3			
6	16/09/92	Rotherham United	Home	League	3–1	2 Goals	(3)	
7	19/09/92	Wigan Athletic	Home	League	4–0	2 Goals	(5)	
8	22/09/92	Watford	Away	Lge Cup	2–2	1 Goal	(6)	
9	26/09/92	Brighton & Hove Albion	Away	League	1–0			
10	02/10/92	Fulham	Home	League	3–0	1 Goal	(7)	
11	07/10/92	Watford	Away	Lge Cup	0–2			

12	10/10/92	Huddersfield Town	Away	League	0–0		
13	17/10/92	Bradford City	Home	League	1–1		
14	20/10/92	Preston North End	Away	League	0–2		
15	31/10/92	Plymouth Argyle	Home	League	3–0	1 Goal	(8)
16	03/11/92	Burnley	Away	League	1–1		
17	07/11/92	Blackpool	Home	League	0–0		
18	15/11/92	Birmingham City	Home	FA Cup	1–0	1 Goal	(9)
19	21/11/92	AFC Bournemouth	Away	League	1–1		
20	28/11/92	Exeter City	Home	League	2–3	1 Goal	(10)
21	01/12/92	Brighton & Hove Albion	Home	A Trophy	1–1		
22	05/12/92	Leyton Orient	Home	FA Cup	3–0	2 Goals	(12)
23	28/12/92	Mansfield Town	Away	League	1–1		
24	02/01/93	Manchester City	Away	FA Cup	1–1		
25	05/01/93	AFC Bournemouth	Away	A Trophy	1–1		
26	09/01/93	Rotherham United	Away	League	2–3	2 Goals	(14)
27	13/01/93	Manchester City	Home	FA Cup	0–4		
28	16/01/93	Brighton & Hove Albion	Home	League	3–0		
29	23/01/93	Wigan Athletic	Away	League	1–1		
30	27/01/93	Bolton Wanderers	Home	League	1–2		
31	30/01/93	Leyton Orient	Away	League	2–1		
32	06/02/93	Hartlepool United	Home	League	2–0	1 Goal	(15)
33	09/02/93	Exeter City	Away	A Trophy	2–2+	2 Goals	(17)
34	13/02/93	Hull City	Away	League	1–1		
35	20/02/93	Preston North End	Home	League	4–0	1 Goal	(18)
36	27/02/93	Huddersfield Town	Home	League	2–1		
37	06/03/93	Fulham	Away	League	0–0		
38	10/03/93	Port Vale	Home	League	1–0		
39	13/03/93	Blackpool	Away	League	1–0	1 Goal	(19)
40	20/03/93	Burnley	Home	League	1–0		
41	23/03/93	Exeter City	Away	League	0–0		
42	27/03/93	AFC Bournemouth	Home	League	3–2	1 Goal	(20)
43	03/04/93	Port Vale	Away	League	1–3	1 Goal	(21)
44	07/04/93	Chester City	Home	League	1–0		
45	10/04/93	Stoke City	Away	League	0–2		
46	12/04/93	Mansfield Town	Home	League	3–1		
47	16/04/93	Stockport County	Away	League	2–2	1 Goal	(22)
48	21/04/93	West Bromwich Albion	Home	League	1–1		
49	24/04/93	Bradford City	Away	League	0–3		
50	01/05/93	Swansea City	Home	League	2–0	1 Goal	(23)
51	08/05/93	Plymouth Argyle	Away	League	2–2		

+ AET Exeter City won 4–2 on penalties

SEASON 1993–94

Football League Division Two

52	14/08/93	Huddersfield Town	Away	League	3–0	1 Goal	(24)
53	18/08/93	Northampton Town	Home	Lge Cup	3–0	1 Goal	(25)
54	21/08/93	Burnley	Home	League	2–1	1 Goal	(26)
55	28/08/93	Brentford	Away	League	0–1		
56	01/09/93	Barnet	Home	League	4–1	1 Goal	(27)
57	04/09/93	Cambridge United	Home	League	3–1	2 Goals	(29)
58	11/09/93	Wrexham	Away	League	2–3		
59	15/09/93	Bradford City	Away	League	4–2	2 Goals	(31)
60	18/09/93	Plymouth Argyle	Home	League	3–2	2 Goals	(33)
61	22/09/93	Manchester City	Away	Lge Cup	1–1		
62	25/09/93	Hull City	Home	League	1–1		
63	01/10/93	Swansea City	Away	League	1–1		
64	06/10/93	Manchester City	Home	Lge Cup	1–2	1 Goal	(34)
65	09/10/93	Exeter City	Away	League	6–4	2 Goals	(36)
66	16/10/93	Leyton Orient	Home	League	2–1	2 Goals	(38)
Sub+1	20/10/93	Brighton & Hove Albion	Away	A Trophy	2–2	2 Goals	(40)
67	23/10/93	Port Vale	Away	League	4–0	2 Goals	(42)
68	30/10/93	Fulham	Home	League	1–0	1 Goal	(43)
69	02/11/93	Rotherham United	Away	League	2–2		
70	06/11/93	Blackpool	Home	League	1–1	1 Goal	(44)
71	10/11/93	Fulham	Home	A Trophy	2–0		
72	13/11/93	Cambridge United	Away	FA Cup	0–0		
73	20/11/93	Brighton & Hove Albion	Away	League	1–0		
74	24/11/93	Cambridge United	Home	FA Cup	1–2		
75	27/11/93	AFC Bournemouth	Home	League	3–0	2 Goals	(46)
76	01/12/93	Northampton Town	Home	A Trophy	4–1	1 Goal	(47)
77	11/12/93	Burnley	Away	League	1–0		

78	18/12/93	Huddersfield Town	Home	League	0–0		
79	28/12/93	Stockport County	Home	League	2–0		
80	01/01/94	Cardiff City	Away	League	0–3		
81	03/01/94	York City	Home	League	2–1	2 Goals	(49)
82	08/01/94	Hartlepool United	Home	League	4–0	1 Goal	(50)
83	11/01/94	Fulham	Away	A Trophy	0–1		
84	15/01/94	Leyton Orient	Away	League	1–1		
85	22/01/94	Exeter City	Home	League	1–0		
86	26/01/94	Bristol Rovers	Away	League	1–1	1 Goal	(51)
87	30/01/94	Fulham	Away	League	0–1		
88	05/02/94	Port Vale	Home	League	1–2	1 Goal	(52)
89	12/02/94	Hartlepool United	Away	League	4–1	1 Goal	(53)
90	19/02/94	Brentford	Home	League	2–1	1 Goal	(54)
91	25/02/94	Cambridge United	Away	League	1–0	1 Goal	(55)
92	05/03/94	Wrexham	Home	League	0–1		
93	12/03/94	Plymouth Argyle	Away	League	1–3		
94	15/03/94	Bradford City	Home	League	1–1		
95	19/03/94	Hull City	Away	League	2–1	2 Goals	(57)
96	26/03/94	Swansea City	Home	League	2–1	1 Goal	(58)
97	29/03/94	York City	Away	League	0–1		
98	02/04/94	Bristol Rovers	Home	League	2–0	1 Goal	(59)
99	09/04/94	Cardiff City	Home	League	1–1		
100	12/04/94	Barnet	Away	League	1–0		
101	16/04/94	Rotherham United	Home	League	0–0		
102	23/04/94	Blackpool	Away	League	4–0	1 Goal	(60)
103	28/04/94	Stockport County	Away	League	1–1		
104	30/04/94	Brighton & Hove Albion	Home	League	2–0	2 Goals	(62)
105	05/05/94	AFC Bournemouth	Away	League	1–2	1 Goal	(63)

SEASON 1994–95

Football League Division One

106	13/08/94	Wolverhampton Wanderers	Away	League	0–1		
107	16/08/94	Gillingham	Away	Lge Cup	1–0		
108	20/08/94	Portsmouth	Home	League	0–0		
109	23/08/94	Gillingham	Home	Lge Cup	3–0	2 Goals	(65)
110	27/08/94	Barnsley	Away	League	2–0		
111	30/08/94	Stoke City	Home	League	4–0		
112	03/09/94	Millwall	Home	League	0–0		
113	10/09/94	Oldham Athletic	Away	League	3–1		
114	14/09/94	Swindon Town	Away	League	0–1		
115	17/09/94	Sheffield United	Home	League	1–0	1 Goal	(66)
116	20/09/94	Derby County	Home	Lge Cup	3–1	2 Goals	(68)
117	24/09/94	Watford	Away	League	2–2		
118	28/09/94	Derby County	Away	Lge Cup	0–2		
119	01/10/94	Notts County	Home	League	2–0		
120	08/10/94	Charlton Athletic	Away	League	2–1		
121	15/10/94	Bristol City	Home	League	1–0		
122	22/10/94	Sunderland	Home	League	0–2		
123	19/11/94	Southend United	Away	League	1–4	1 Goal	(69)
124	26/11/94	Tranmere Rovers	Home	League	1–3		
125	03/12/94	Sunderland	Away	League	1–0		
126	06/12/94	Middlesbrough	Home	League	1–1		
127	10/12/94	Portsmouth	Away	League	1–1	1 Goal	(70)
128	18/12/94	Wolverhampton Wanderers	Home	League	4–2	1 Goal	(71)
129	26/12/94	Luton Town	Home	League	0–0		
130	28/12/94	Port Vale	Away	League	2–0	1 Goal	(72)
131	31/12/94	Grimsby Town	Home	League	1–1		
132	02/01/95	Bolton Wanderers	Away	League	0–1		
133	07/01/95	Oldham Athletic	Home	FA Cup	1–3		
134	14/01/95	West Bromwich Albion	Home	League	0–2		
135	21/01/95	Burnley	Away	League	2–1		
136	04/02/95	Middlesbrough	Away	League	1–0		
137	11/02/95	Derby County	Home	League	1–0		
138	18/02/95	Tranmere Rovers	Away	League	0–1		
Sub+2	21/02/95	Southend United	Home	League	2–0		
Sub+3	25/02/95	Notts County	Away	League	0–1		
Sub+4	08/03/95	Millwall	Away	League	0–2		
139	11/03/95	Barnsley	Home	League	0–3		
140	18/03/95	Stoke City	Away	League	1–0		
141	21/03/95	Oldham Athletic	Home	League	2–1		
Sub+5	07/05/95	Charlton Athletic	Home	League	2–1		
Sub+6	17/05/95	Tranmere Rovers	Home	Lge P/O	0–0		
Sub+7	29/05/95	Bolton Wanderers	Wembley	Lge P/O	3–4*	1 Goal	(73)

SEASON 1995–96

Football League Division One

Sub+8	01/09/95	Southend United	Away	League	0–0		
Sub+9	09/09/95	Luton Town	Home	League	3–1		
Sub+10	12/09/95	Grimsby Town	Home	League	0–2		
Sub+11	20/09/95	West Bromwich Albion	Home	Lge Cup	1–1		
142	23/09/95	Port Vale	Home	League	2–2		
Sub+12	30/09/95	Sunderland	Away	League	2–2		
143	03/10/95	West Bromwich Albion	Away	Lge Cup	4–2	2 Goals	(75)
144	07/10/95	West Bromwich Albion	Home	League	0–2		
145	14/10/95	Huddersfield Town	Home	League	3–1	1 Goal	(76)
146	21/10/95	Oldham Athletic	Away	League	1–2		
147	28/10/95	Ipswich Town	Home	League	1–4		
Sub+13	07/11/95	Bury	Home	Lge Cup	2–1	1 Goal	(77)
Sub+14	21/11/95	Charlton Athletic	Away	League	1–2		
Sub+15	25/11/95	Sheffield United	Away	League	0–0		
Sub+16	28/11/95	Southampton	Home	Lge Cup	2–1		
Sub+17	02/12/95	West Bromwich Albion	Home	League	3–1		
Sub+18	09/12/95	Port Vale	Away	League	2–3	1 Goal	(78)
Sub+19	16/12/95	Sunderland	Home	League	1–1	1 Goal	(79)
Sub+20	30/12/95	Norwich City	Away	League	3–3		
148	01/01/96	Tranmere Rovers	Home	League	1–0		
149	06/01/96	Gillingham	Home	FA Cup	3–1	2 Goals	(81)
150	10/01/96	Leeds United	Away	Lge Cup	1–2	1 Goal	(82)
151	13/01/96	Derby County	Away	League	0–3		
152	20/01/96	Stoke City	Home	League	1–0		
153	27/01/96	Manchester United	Home	FA Cup	0–3		
154	04/02/96	Portsmouth	Home	League	0–1		
155	10/02/96	Millwall	Away	League	1–1		
Sub+21	27/02/96	Luton Town	Away	League	2–1		
156	02/03/96	Watford	Home	League	0–0		
Sub+22	16/03/96	Norwich City	Home	League	0–3		
Sub+23	19/03/96	Southend United	Home	League	3–3		
Sub+24	23/03/96	Tranmere Rovers	Away	League	1–2		
Sub+25	30/03/96	Oldham Athletic	Home	League	2–0	2 Goals	(84)
157	02/04/96	Huddersfield Town	Away	League	1–3		
158	06/04/96	Ipswich Town	Away	League	2–1	1 Goal	(85)
159	08/04/96	Crystal Palace	Home	League	0–2		
160	13/04/96	Barnsley	Away	League	1–0	1 Goal	(86)
161	16/04/96	Watford	Away	League	2–4	1 Goal	(87)
162	20/04/96	Charlton Athletic	Home	League	0–0		
163	27/04/96	Sheffield United	Home	League	0–3		
164	30/04/96	Wolverhampton Wanderers	Home	League	3–0	2 Goals	(89)
165	05/05/96	Birmingham City	Away	League	2–1	1 Goal	(90)

SEASON 1996–97

Football League Division One

166	17/08/96	Sheffield United	Home	League	1–0	1 Goal	(91)
167	20/08/96	Wycombe Wanderers	Home	Lge Cup	1–1	1 Goal	(92)
168	24/08/96	Ipswich Town	Away	League	2–5		
169	28/08/96	Barnsley	Away	League	0–3		
Sub+26	03/09/96	Wycombe Wanderers	Away	Lge Cup	0–2		
Sub+27	08/09/96	Oxford United	Home	League	2–0		
Sub+28	10/09/96	West Bromwich Albion	Away	League	2–3		
170	14/09/96	Charlton Athletic	Away	League	0–1		
171	21/09/96	Crystal Palace	Home	League	1–6		
Sub+29	19/10/96	Oldham Athletic	Away	League	1–1	1 Goal	(93)
Sub+30	29/10/96	Bolton Wanderers	Away	League	1–2		
Sub+31	02/11/96	Southend United	Away	League	1–2		
Sub+32	26/11/96	Birmingham City	Home	League	0–0		
Sub+33	30/11/96	Swindon Town	Away	League	1–3		
Sub+34	26/12/96	West Bromwich Albion	Home	League	2–2	1 Goal	(94)
Sub+35	28/12/96	Oxford United	Away	League	1–2		
Sub+36	18/01/97	Birmingham City	Away	League	1–4		
Sub+37	29/01/97	Tranmere Rovers	Away	League	2–2		
Sub+38	08/02/97	Bolton Wanderers	Home	League	3–2		
Sub+39	01/03/97	Port Vale	Away	League	0–1		
172	04/03/97	Norwich City	Home	League	2–1		
173	12/03/97	Queens Park Rangers	Away	League	2–0		
174	15/03/97	Bradford City	Home	League	0–0		
Sub+40	31/03/97	Barnsley	Home	League	1–2		
175	05/04/97	Stoke City	Away	League	1–1		
176	12/04/97	Wolverhampton Wanderers	Home	League	2–1		

INTERNATIONAL APPEARANCES – NORTHERN IRELAND

1	16/10/84	Israel	Windsor Park	3–0	F	1 Goal	(1)
2	14/11/84	Finland	Windsor Park	2–1	WCQ		
3	27/02/85	England	Windsor Park	0–1	WCQ		
4	27/03/85	Spain	Palma	0–0	F		
5	01/05/85	Turkey	Windsor Park	2–0	WCQ		
6	11/09/85	Turkey	Izmir	0–0	WCQ		
7	16/10/85	Romania	Bucharest	1–0	WCQ	1 Goal	(2)
8	13/11/85	England	Wembley	0–0	WCQ		
9	26/02/86	France	Paris	0–0	F		
Sub 10	26/03/86	Denmark	Windsor Park	1–1	F		
Sub 11	23/04/86	Morocco	Windsor Park	2–1	F	1 Goal	(3)
Sub 12	15/10/86	England	Wembley	0–3	ECQ		
13	12/11/86	Turkey	Izmir	0–0	ECQ		
Sub 14	14/10/87	Yugoslavia	Sarajevo	0–3	ECQ		
15	11/11/87	Turkey	Windsor Park	1–0	ECQ	1 Goal	(4)
16	17/02/88	Greece	Athens	2–3	F		
17	23/03/88	Poland	Windsor Park	1–1	F		
Sub 18	27/04/88	France	Windsor Park	0–0	F		
19	21/05/88	Malta	Windsor Park	3–0	WCQ	1 Goal	(5)
20	14/09/88	Republic of Ireland	Windsor Park	0–0	WCQ		
Sub 21	19/10/88	Hungary	Budapest	0–1	WCQ		
Sub 22	21/12/88	Spain	Seville	0–4	WCQ		
23	08/02/89	Spain	Windsor Park	0–2	WCQ		
24	26/04/89	Malta	Valletta	2–0	WCQ		
25	26/05/89	Chile	Windsor Park	0–1	F		
26	06/09/89	Hungary	Windsor Park	1–2	WCQ		
27	27/03/90	Norway	Windsor Park	2–3	F	1 Goal	(6)
Sub 28	27/03/91	Yugoslavia	Belgrade	1–4	ECQ		
29	28/04/92	Lithuania	Windsor Park	2–2	WCQ		
30	14/10/92	Spain	Windsor Park	0–0	WCQ		
31	18/11/92	Denmark	Windsor Park	0–1	WCQ		
Sub 32	17/02/93	Albania	Tirana	2–1	WCQ		
Sub 33	31/03/93	Republic of Ireland	Lansdowne Road	0–3	WCQ		
Sub 34	02/06/93	Latvia	Riga	2–1	WCQ		
35	08/09/93	Latvia	Windsor Park	2–0	WCQ	1 Goal	(7)
Sub 36	13/10/93	Denmark	Copenhagen	0–1	WCQ		
37	17/11/93	Republic of Ireland	Windsor Park	1–1	WCQ	1 Goal	(8)
38	23/03/94	Romania	Windsor Park	2–0	F		
39	20/04/94	Liechtenstein	Windsor Park	4–1	ECQ	2 Goals	(10)
40	04/06/94	Colombia	Boston	0–2	F		
41	11/06/94	Mexico	Miami	0–3	F		
42	07/09/94	Portugal	Windsor Park	1–2	ECQ	1 Goal	(11)
Sub 43	12/10/94	Austria	Vienna	2–1	ECQ		
Sub 44	26/04/95	Latvia	Riga	1–0	ECQ		
45	11/10/95	Liechtenstein	Vaduz	4–0	ECQ	1 Goal	(12)
Sub 46	15/11/95	Austria	Windsor Park	5–3	ECQ		

APPEARANCES AND GOALS PER SEASON

SEASON 81–82	GAMES	GOALS
League	2+2	0
TOTAL	**2+2**	**0**

SEASON 82–83	GAMES	GOALS
League	4+9	3
FA Cup	0+3	0
League Cup	0+1	0
TOTAL	**4+13**	**3**

SEASON 83–84	GAMES	GOALS
League	28+4	7
FA Cup	5	6
League Cup	1	0
Associate Members Cup	1	2
TOTAL	**35+4**	**15**

SEASON 84–85	GAMES	GOALS
League	14+11	10
FA Cup	4	3
League Cup	0+1	0
TOTAL	**18+12**	**13**

SEASON 85–86	GAMES	GOALS
League	29+2	4
League Cup	2	1
TOTAL	**31+2**	**5**

SEASON 86–87	GAMES	GOALS
League	35+2	12
League Play–offs	3	1
FA Cup	2	0
League Cup	4	1
Full Members Cup	2	1
Freight Rover Trophy	3+1	2
TOTAL	**49+3**	**17**

SEASON 87–88	GAMES	GOALS
League	41+1	21
FA Cup	3	0
League Cup	6	8
Simod Cup	4	2
TOTAL	**54+1**	**31**

SEASON 88–89	GAMES	GOALS
League	25+18	13
FA Cup	0+1	0
League Cup	2+1	0
Simod Cup	0+1	0
TOTAL	**27+21**	**13**

SEASON 89–90	GAMES	GOALS
League	41+3	19
FA Cup	1	0
League Cup	2	1
Zenith Data Systems Cup	1	0
TOTAL	**45+3**	**20**

SEASON 90–91	GAMES	GOALS
League	16+10	6
FA Cup	3+2	2
League Cup	3	1
Zenith Data Systems Cup	1	0
TOTAL	**23+12**	**9**

SEASON 91–92	GAMES	GOALS
League	43	19
FA Cup	5	2
League Cup	4	2
Autoglass Trophy	2	1
TOTAL	**54**	**24**

SEASON 92–93	GAMES	GOALS
League	42	17
FA Cup	4	3
League Cup	2	1
Autoglass Trophy	3	2
TOTAL	**51**	**23**

SEASON 93–94	GAMES	GOALS
League	46	35
FA Cup	2	0
League Cup	3	2
Autoglass Trophy	3+1	3
TOTAL	**54+1**	**40**

SEASON 94–95	GAMES	GOALS
League	31+4	5
League Play–offs	0+2	1
FA Cup	1	0
League Cup	4	4
TOTAL	**36+6**	**10**

SEASON 95–96	GAMES	GOALS
League	20+15	11
FA Cup	2	2
League Cup	2+3	4
TOTAL	**24+18**	**17**

SEASON 96–97	GAMES	GOALS
League	10+14	3
League Cup	1+1	1
TOTAL	**11+15**	**4**

CAREER APPEARANCES AND GOALS

COMPETITION	GAMES	TOTAL	GOALS
League	427+95	522	185
League Play–offs	3+2	5	2
FA Cup	32+6	38	18
League Cup	36+7	43	26
Associate Members Cup	1	1	2
Full Members Cup	2	2	1
Freight Rover Trophy	3+1	4	2
Simod Cup	4+1	5	2
Zenith Data Systems Cup	2	2	0
Autoglass Trophy	8+1	9	6
Internationals	31+15	46	12
TOTAL	**549+128**	**677**	**256**

HAT-TRICKS

Blackburn Rovers

1	3	Sheffield United	06/05/85	Away	League	3–1

Swindon Town

1	3	Bristol City	18/08/87	Home	Lge Cup	3–0
2	3	Portsmouth	22/09/87	Home	Lge Cup	3–1

West Ham United

1	3	Sheffield United	21/03/90	Home	League	5–0

League: 2
League Cup: 2
TOTAL: 4

HONOURS

Winners medals
Football League Division Two Championship: 93/94

Runner-up medals
Football League Division One Championship: 94/95
League Division Two Championship: 90/91
Promoted to League Division Two: 86/87

MICK QUINN

Born: 02/05/62 – Liverpool
Height: 5.9
Weight: 13.00 (95–96)

Clubs
Wigan Athletic: **1980–82** – Matches: **64+13** – Goals: **21**
Stockport County: **1982–84** – Matches: **69+1** – Goals: **41**
Oldham Athletic: **1984–86** – Matches: **84+2** – Goals: **37**
Portsmouth: **1986–89** – Matches: **133+6** – Goals: **68**
Newcastle United: **1989–92** – Matches: **132+8** – Goals: **71**
Coventry City: **1992–94** – Matches: **59+9** – Goals: **26**
Plymouth Argyle (loan): **1994** – Matches: **3** – Goals: **0**
Watford (loan): **1995** – Matches: **4+1** – Goals: **0**
PAOK Salonika: **1995** – Matches: **8+6** – Goals: **4**

SEASON 1979–80

Wigan Athletic – League Division Four

1	12/04/80	Halifax Town	Home	League	3–1	1 Goal	(1)
2	19/04/80	Northampton Town	Away	League	1–1		

| 3 | 26/04/80 | Walsall | Home | League | 3–0 | |
| 4 | 30/04/80 | Doncaster Rovers | Home | League | 0–0 | |

SEASON 1980–81

League Division Four

Sub+1	16/08/80	Hartlepool United	Home	League	0–3	
5	23/08/80	Lincoln City	Away	League	0–2	
6	30/08/80	Aldershot	Home	League	1–0	
7	03/09/80	Preston North End	Home	Lge Cup	1–2	
Sub+2	20/09/80	Bury	Home	League	2–1	
8	01/10/80	Halifax Town	Home	League	4–1	2 Goals (3)
9	04/10/80	Rochdale	Away	League	0–3	
10	08/10/80	Doncaster Rovers	Home	League	3–0	3 Goals (6)
11	11/10/80	Peterborough United	Home	League	1–1	
12	18/10/80	Torquay United	Away	League	0–2	
13	20/10/80	Southend United	Away	League	0–1	
14	25/10/80	Tranmere Rovers	Home	League	1–1	1 Goal (7)
15	29/10/80	York City	Home	League	1–0	
16	01/11/80	AFC Bournemouth	Away	League	0–3	
17	04/11/80	Doncaster Rovers	Away	League	1–1	1 Goal (8)
18	08/11/80	Bradford City	Home	League	0–1	
19	12/11/80	Northampton Town	Home	League	3–0	2 Goals (10)
20	15/11/80	Hartlepool United	Away	League	1–3	
21	22/11/80	Chesterfield	Home	FA Cup	2–2	
22	29/11/80	Hereford United	Away	League	1–1	
23	06/12/80	Scunthorpe United	Home	League	1–1	
Sub+3	24/01/81	Aldershot	Away	League	1–0	
Sub+4	31/01/81	Lincoln City	Home	League	0–2	
24	03/02/81	Northampton Town	Away	League	1–1	1 Goal (11)
25	07/02/81	Darlington	Home	League	3–1	1 Goal (12)
26	11/02/81	Hereford United	Home	League	1–0	
27	14/02/81	Port Vale	Away	League	0–3	
28	21/02/81	Mansfield Town	Home	League	2–0	1 Goal (13)
29	28/02/81	Bury	Away	League	0–0	
30	07/03/81	Rochdale	Home	League	0–1	
31	13/03/81	Peterborough United	Away	League	0–0	
32	21/03/81	Torquay United	Home	League	2–0	
33	29/03/81	Tranmere Rovers	Away	League	3–2	
34	31/03/81	Wimbledon	Home	League	0–1	
35	04/04/81	AFC Bournemouth	Home	League	0–1	
36	11/04/81	Bradford City	Away	League	3–3	1 Goal (14)
37	25/04/81	Wimbledon	Home	League	1–0	
38	02/05/81	Scunthorpe United	Away	League	4–4	1 Goal (15)

SEASON 1981–82

League Division Four

39	29/08/81	Bradford City	Away	League	3–3	
40	31/08/81	Stockport County	Home	Lge Cup	3–0	1 Goal (16)
41	05/09/81	Sheffield United	Home	League	0–1	
42	12/09/81	Hartlepool United	Away	League	1–2	
43	14/09/81	Stockport County	Away	Lge Cup	2–1	
44	19/09/81	Northampton Town	Home	League	3–1	1 Goal (17)
45	23/09/81	Port Vale	Home	League	2–0	
46	26/09/81	Tranmere Rovers	Away	League	0–0	
47	29/09/81	AFC Bournemouth	Away	League	0–0	
48	03/10/81	Torquay United	Home	League	1–0	
Sub+5	24/10/81	Scunthorpe United	Home	League	2–1	
49	27/10/81	Aldershot	Home	Lge Cup	1–0	
50	21/11/81	Hartlepool United	Home	FA Cup	2–2	1 Goal (18)
51	25/11/81	Hartlepool United	Away	FA Cup	0–1	
52	28/11/81	Rochdale	Away	League	1–1	
53	01/12/81	Aston Villa	Home	Lge Cup	1–2	
54	05/12/81	Halifax Town	Home	League	2–0	
Sub+6	05/01/82	Tranmere Rovers	Home	League	0–0	
55	19/01/82	Peterborough United	Home	League	5–0	
56	23/01/82	Bradford City	Home	League	4–1	1 Goal (19)
57	26/01/82	Crewe Alexandra	Away	League	1–0	
58	30/01/82	Northampton Town	Away	League	3–2	
59	06/02/82	Hartlepool United	Home	League	1–1	1 Goal (20)
60	08/02/82	Port Vale	Away	League	1–1	
61	13/02/82	Torquay United	Away	League	0–0	
62	17/02/82	Aldershot	Home	League	1–0	
63	26/02/82	Stockport County	Away	League	1–0	1 Goal (21)

64	06/03/82	Hull City	Home	League	2–1		
Sub+7	09/03/82	Bury	Home	League	3–2		
Sub+8	16/03/82	Darlington	Away	League	1–3		
Sub+9	23/03/82	Sheffield United	Away	League	0–1		
Sub+10	27/03/82	Hereford United	Away	League	0–3		
Sub+11	02/04/82	York City	Home	League	4–2		
Sub+12	24/04/82	Rochdale	Home	League	1–1		
Sub+13	15/05/82	Aldershot	Away	League	0–2		

SEASON 1982–83

Stockport County – League Division Four

1	28/08/82	Peterborough United	Home	League	1–1		
2	30/08/82	Wigan Athletic	Home	Lge Cup	1–1		
3	04/09/82	Torquay United	Away	League	0–3		
4	07/09/82	Scunthorpe United	Away	League	0–3		
5	10/09/82	Hull City	Home	League	1–1		
6	14/09/82	Wigan Athletic	Away	Lge Cup	1–1+		
7	18/09/82	Tranmere Rovers	Away	League	1–1	1 Goal	(1)
8	24/09/82	Northampton Town	Home	League	0–1		
Sub+1	02/10/82	Port Vale	Away	League	3–2		
9	19/10/82	Bury	Away	League	2–3	1 Goal	(2)
10	22/10/82	York City	Home	League	2–1	1 Goal	(3)
11	30/10/82	Wimbledon	Away	League	1–2	1 Goal	(4)
12	01/11/82	Hereford United	Home	League	2–1		
13	06/11/82	Bristol City	Away	League	2–2	1 Goal	(5)
14	12/11/82	Darlington	Home	League	2–1	2 Goals	(7)
15	20/11/82	Mansfield Town	Away	FA Cup	2–3		
16	26/11/82	Swindon Town	Home	League	1–2		
17	04/12/82	Mansfield Town	Away	League	0–1		
18	10/12/82	Crewe Alexandra	Home	League	3–2	3 Goals	(10)
19	17/12/82	Colchester United	Away	League	0–3		
20	27/12/82	Blackpool	Home	League	3–0	1 Goal	(11)
21	28/12/82	Chester	Away	League	2–0	1 Goal	(12)
22	01/01/83	Halifax Town	Home	League	4–2	3 Goals	(15)
23	03/01/83	Crewe Alexandra	Away	League	0–3		
24	15/01/83	Peterborough United	Away	League	0–1		
25	12/02/83	Scunthorpe United	Home	League	1–1		
26	14/02/83	Bury	Home	League	2–1	1 Goal	(16)
27	19/02/83	Hartlepool United	Away	League	2–3	2 Goals	(18)
28	26/02/83	Aldershot	Home	League	2–1	2 Goals	(20)
29	02/03/83	Hereford United	Away	League	0–0		
30	05/03/83	York City	Away	League	1–3		
31	11/03/83	Wimbledon	Home	League	1–3		
32	26/03/83	Darlington	Away	League	1–3		
33	01/04/83	Blackpool	Away	League	0–0		
34	02/04/83	Chester	Home	League	3–3	2 Goals	(22)
35	08/04/83	Mansfield Town	Home	League	1–1		
36	16/04/83	Rochdale	Away	League	0–1		
37	17/04/83	Torquay United	Home	League	1–0	1 Goal	(23)
38	22/04/83	Colchester United	Home	League	3–0	1 Goal	(24)
39	30/04/83	Swindon Town	Away	League	0–2		
40	06/05/83	Port Vale	Home	League	0–2		
41	13/05/83	Halifax Town	Away	League	0–1		

+ AET Wigan Athletic won 5–4 on penalties

SEASON 1983–84

League Division Four

42	27/08/83	York City	Home	League	0–2		
43	30/08/83	Rochdale	Away	Lge Cup	3–0	2 Goals	(26)
44	03/09/83	Reading	Away	League	2–6		
45	06/09/83	Mansfield Town	Away	League	2–1	1 Goal	(27)
46	09/09/83	Colchester United	Home	League	0–0		
47	23/09/83	Swindon Town	Home	League	1–3		
48	26/09/83	Wrexham	Home	League	1–1		
49	30/09/83	Crewe Alexandra	Away	League	3–0	3 Goals	(30)
50	03/10/83	Oldham Athletic	Home	Lge Cup	0–2		
51	08/10/83	Chesterfield	Away	League	0–2		
52	15/10/83	Darlington	Home	League	2–0	1 Goal	(31)
53	17/10/83	Aldershot	Home	League	2–2		
54	22/10/83	Chester City	Away	League	4–2	2 Goals	(33)
55	25/10/83	Oldham Athletic	Away	Lge Cup	2–2		
56	29/10/83	Blackpool	Home	League	1–2		

57	01/11/83	Bury	Away	League	1–2	1 Goal	(34)
58	05/11/83	Rochdale	Away	League	2–2	1 Goal	(35)
59	11/11/83	Halifax Town	Home	League	4–0	2 Goals	(37)
60	19/11/83	Telford United	Away	FA Cup	0–3		
61	26/11/83	Peterborough United	Away	League	0–2		
62	02/12/83	Torquay United	Home	League	2–1		
63	10/12/83	Aldershot	Away	League	1–1	1 Goal	(38)
64	16/12/83	Tranmere Rovers	Home	League	2–1	1 Goal	(39)
65	26/12/83	Bristol City	Away	League	1–3		
66	27/12/83	Hereford United	Home	League	1–0		
67	31/12/83	Doncaster Rovers	Away	League	1–2	1 Goal	(40)
68	02/01/84	Hartlepool United	Home	League	1–0		
69	06/01/84	Reading	Home	League	3–0	1 Goal	(41)

Oldham Athletic – League Division Two

1	04/02/84	Cambridge United	Home	League	0–0		
2	11/02/84	Huddersfield Town	Away	League	1–0	1 Goal	(1)
3	18/02/84	Carlisle United	Away	League	0–2		
4	25/02/84	Blackburn Rovers	Home	League	0–0		
5	03/03/84	Chelsea	Away	League	0–3		
6	10/03/84	Crystal Palace	Home	League	3–2	1 Goal	(2)
7	17/03/84	Swansea City	Home	League	3–3		
8	24/03/84	Charlton Athletic	Away	League	1–2		
9	31/03/84	Middlesbrough	Away	League	2–3	1 Goal	(3)
10	07/04/84	Shrewsbury Town	Home	League	0–1		
11	14/04/84	Cardiff City	Away	League	0–2		
12	20/04/84	Manchester City	Home	League	2–2	1 Goal	(4)
13	05/05/84	Barnsley	Away	League	1–0		
14	07/05/84	Grimsby Town	Home	League	2–1	1 Goal	(5)

SEASON 1984–85

League Division Two

15	25/08/84	Birmingham City	Home	League	0–1		
16	28/08/84	Bolton Wanderers	Away	Lge Cup	0–2		
17	01/09/84	Barnsley	Away	League	1–0		
18	04/09/84	Bolton Wanderers	Home	Lge Cup	4–4*	2 Goals	(7)
19	08/09/84	Sheffield United	Home	League	2–2	1 Goal	(8)
20	15/09/84	Charlton Athletic	Away	League	1–2		
21	18/09/84	Shrewsbury Town	Away	League	0–3		
22	22/09/84	Brighton & Hove Albion	Home	League	1–0		
23	29/09/84	Leeds United	Away	League	0–6		
24	02/10/84	Middlesbrough	Home	League	2–0	1 Goal	(9)
25	06/10/84	Grimsby Town	Away	League	1–4		
26	13/10/84	Wolverhampton Wanderers	Home	League	3–2		
27	20/10/84	Blackburn Rovers	Away	League	1–1	1 Goal	(10)
28	27/10/84	Notts County	Home	League	3–2	1 Goal	(11)
29	03/11/84	Portsmouth	Home	League	0–2		
30	10/11/84	Cardiff City	Away	League	2–2		
31	17/11/84	Oxford United	Home	League	0–0		
32	25/11/84	Crystal Palace	Away	League	0–3		
33	01/12/84	Manchester City	Home	League	0–2		
34	07/12/84	Fulham	Away	League	1–3		
35	15/12/84	Carlisle United	Home	League	2–3	2 Goals	(13)
36	23/12/84	Barnsley	Home	League	2–1	1 Goal	(14)
37	26/12/84	Huddersfield Town	Away	League	1–2		
38	01/01/85	Wimbledon	Home	League	0–1		
39	04/01/85	Brentford	Home	FA Cup	2–1	1 Goal	(15)
40	12/01/85	Charlton Athletic	Home	League	2–1	1 Goal	(16)
41	26/01/85	Sheffield Wednesday	Away	FA Cup	1–5		
42	02/02/85	Leeds United	Home	League	1–1		
43	05/02/85	Middlesbrough	Away	League	2–1	2 Goals	(18)
44	12/02/85	Sheffield United	Away	League	0–2		
45	02/03/85	Notts County	Away	League	0–0		
46	05/03/85	Birmingham City	Away	League	1–0		
47	09/03/85	Blackburn Rovers	Home	League	2–0		
48	16/03/85	Wolverhampton Wanderers	Away	League	3–0	1 Goal	(19)
49	23/03/85	Grimsby Town	Home	League	2–0		
50	29/03/85	Brighton & Hove Albion	Away	League	0–2		
51	06/04/85	Huddersfield Town	Home	League	2–2	1 Goal	(20)
52	09/04/85	Wimbledon	Away	League	0–1		
53	13/04/85	Shrewsbury Town	Home	League	0–1		
54	20/04/85	Oxford United	Away	League	2–5	1 Goal	(21)
55	27/04/85	Crystal Palace	Home	League	1–0	1 Goal	(22)
56	04/05/85	Manchester City	Away	League	0–0		

| 57 | 06/05/85 | Fulham | Home | League | 2–1 | 1 Goal | (23) |
| 58 | 11/05/85 | Carlisle United | Away | League | 5–2 | 3 Goals | (26) |

SEASON 1985–86

League Division Two

59	17/08/85	Norwich City	Away	League	0–1		
60	20/08/85	Shrewsbury Town	Home	League	4–3		
61	24/08/85	Huddersfield Town	Home	League	1–1		
62	26/08/85	Sunderland	Away	League	3–0	1 Goal	(27)
63	31/08/85	Hull City	Home	League	3–1	1 Goal	(28)
64	07/09/85	Wimbledon	Away	League	0–0		
65	13/09/85	Charlton Athletic	Home	League	2–1	1 Goal	(29)
66	17/09/85	Carlisle United	Away	League	1–3		
67	21/09/85	Portsmouth	Home	League	2–0		
68	24/09/85	Liverpool	Away	Lge Cup	0–3		
69	28/09/85	Millwall	Away	League	1–0		
70	05/10/85	Grimsby Town	Home	League	2–1	2 Goals	(31)
71	09/10/85	Liverpool	Home	Lge Cup	2–5		
72	12/10/85	Crystal Palace	Away	League	2–3		
73	19/10/85	Blackburn Rovers	Away	League	0–0		
74	26/10/85	Brighton & Hove Albion	Home	League	4–0	2 Goals	(33)
75	02/11/85	Barnsley	Away	League	0–1		
76	09/11/85	Sheffield United	Home	League	1–5		
77	16/11/85	Middlesbrough	Away	League	2–3	1 Goal	(34)
78	23/11/85	Stoke City	Home	League	2–4	2 Goals	(36)
79	30/11/85	Fulham	Away	League	2–2		
Sub+1	07/12/85	Shrewsbury Town	Away	League	0–2		
80	14/12/85	Norwich City	Home	League	1–3		
81	01/02/86	Sunderland	Home	League	2–2		
82	08/02/86	Blackburn Rovers	Home	League	3–1	1 Goal	(37)
Sub+2	22/02/86	Portsmouth	Away	League	2–1		
83	01/03/86	Millwall	Home	League	0–0		
84	04/03/86	Bradford City	Away	League	0–1		

Portsmouth – League Division Two

1	15/03/86	Charlton Athletic	Away	League	2–1		
2	25/03/86	Millwall	Home	League	2–1	1 Goal	(1)
3	29/03/86	Wimbledon	Home	League	1–1		
4	31/03/86	Brighton & Hove Albion	Away	League	3–2	2 Goals	(3)
5	05/04/86	Leeds United	Home	League	2–3		
6	08/04/86	Crystal Palace	Away	League	1–2		
7	12/04/86	Middlesbrough	Away	League	0–1		
8	19/04/86	Grimsby Town	Home	League	3–1	1 Goal	(4)
9	22/04/86	Stoke City	Away	League	0–2		
10	26/04/86	Sheffield United	Away	League	0–0		
11	03/05/86	Bradford City	Home	League	4–0	2 Goals	(6)

SEASON 1986–87

League Division Two

12	23/08/86	Brighton & Hove Albion	Away	League	0–0		
13	30/08/86	Ipswich Town	Home	League	1–1		
14	02/09/86	Hull City	Away	League	2–0	2 Goals	(8)
15	06/09/86	Barnsley	Away	League	2–0	2 Goals	(10)
16	13/09/86	Blackburn Rovers	Home	League	1–0		
17	20/09/86	Stoke City	Away	League	1–1		
18	24/09/86	Wrexham	Away	Lge Cup	2–1	1 Goal	(11)
19	04/10/86	Sunderland	Away	League	0–0		
20	07/10/86	Wrexham	Home	Lge Cup	2–0	2 Goals	(13)
21	11/10/86	Birmingham City	Home	League	2–0	2 Goals	(15)
22	18/10/86	Leeds United	Away	League	1–3	1 Goal	(16)
23	21/10/86	Derby County	Home	League	3–1	3 Goals	(19)
24	25/10/86	West Bromwich Albion	Home	League	2–1		
25	29/10/86	Bradford City	Away	Lge Cup	1–3	1 Goal	(20)
26	01/11/86	Oldham Athletic	Away	League	0–0		
27	04/11/86	Millwall	Home	FM Cup	3–2*		
28	08/11/86	Bradford City	Home	League	2–1	1 Goal	(21)
29	15/11/86	Shrewsbury Town	Away	League	0–1		
30	22/11/86	Grimsby Town	Home	League	2–1		
31	29/11/86	Millwall	Away	League	1–1		
32	06/12/86	Crystal Palace	Home	League	2–0	1 Goal	(22)
33	13/12/86	Sheffield United	Away	League	0–1		
34	20/12/86	Barnsley	Home	League	2–1	1 Goal	(23)
35	26/12/86	Plymouth Argyle	Away	League	3–2	1 Goal	(24)

36	29/12/86	Shrewsbury Town	Home	League	3–0	1 Goal	(25)
37	01/01/87	Reading	Home	League	1–0		
38	03/01/87	Blackburn Rovers	Away	League	0–1		
39	10/01/87	Blackburn Rovers	Home	FA Cup	2–0	2 Goals	(27)
40	07/02/87	Ipswich Town	Away	League	1–0		
41	14/02/87	Hull City	Home	League	1–0	1 Goal	(28)
42	21/02/87	Huddersfield Town	Away	League	0–2		
43	25/02/87	Norwich City	Away	FM Cup	1–3		
44	28/02/87	Stoke City	Home	League	3–0	2 Goals	(30)
45	04/03/87	Derby County	Away	League	0–0		
46	10/03/87	Leeds United	Home	League	1–1		
47	28/03/87	Sunderland	Home	League	3–1		
48	04/04/87	Bradford City	Away	League	0–1		
49	11/04/87	Oldham Athletic	Home	League	3–0	1 Goal	(31)
50	18/04/87	Reading	Away	League	2–2	1 Goal	(32)
51	20/04/87	Plymouth Argyle	Home	League	0–1		
52	25/04/87	Grimsby Town	Away	League	2–0	1 Goal	(33)
53	29/04/87	West Bromwich Albion	Away	League	0–1		
54	02/05/87	Millwall	Home	League	2–0		
55	04/05/87	Crystal Palace	Away	League	0–1		
56	09/05/87	Sheffield United	Home	League	1–2	1 Goal	(34)

SEASON 1987–88

League Division One

57	15/08/87	Oxford United	Away	League	2–4		
58	18/08/87	Chelsea	Home	League	0–3		
59	22/08/87	Southampton	Home	League	2–2		
Sub+1	12/09/87	Charlton Athletic	Home	League	1–1	1 Goal	(35)
60	19/09/87	Watford	Away	League	0–0		
61	22/09/87	Swindon Town	Away	Lge Cup	1–3	1 Goal	(36)
62	26/09/87	Wimbledon	Home	League	2–1	1 Goal	(37)
63	03/10/87	Liverpool	Away	League	0–4		
64	07/10/87	Swindon Town	Home	Lge Cup	1–3		
65	10/10/87	Luton Town	Home	League	3–1		
66	24/10/87	Queens Park Rangers	Away	League	1–2		
67	10/11/87	Stoke City	Home	Simod Cup	0–3		
Sub+2	14/11/87	Nottingham Forest	Away	League	0–5		
68	21/11/87	Everton	Home	League	0–1		
69	28/11/87	Norwich City	Away	League	1–0		
70	05/12/87	Coventry City	Home	League	0–0		
71	12/12/87	Newcastle United	Away	League	1–1		
Sub+3	19/12/87	Manchester United	Home	League	1–2		
72	26/12/87	Charlton Athletic	Away	League	1–2	1 Goal	(38)
73	28/12/87	Watford	Home	League	1–1		
74	01/01/88	Arsenal	Home	League	1–1		
75	03/01/88	Southampton	Away	League	2–0		
76	09/01/88	Blackburn Rovers	Away	FA Cup	2–1	1 Goal	(39)
77	16/01/88	Oxford United	Home	League	2–2	1 Goal	(40)
78	23/01/88	Chelsea	Away	League	0–0		
79	01/02/88	Sheffield United	Home	FA Cup	2–1	1 Goal	(41)
80	06/02/88	Derby County	Home	League	2–1	1 Goal	(42)
81	20/02/88	Bradford City	Home	FA Cup	3–0	1 Goal	(43)
82	27/02/88	Liverpool	Home	League	0–2		
83	12/03/88	Luton Town	Away	FA Cup	1–3	1 Goal	(44)
84	19/03/88	Sheffield Wednesday	Away	League	0–1		
85	02/04/88	Tottenham Hotspur	Away	League	1–0		
86	04/04/88	Nottingham Forest	Home	League	0–1		
87	09/04/88	Everton	Away	League	1–2		
88	19/04/88	Wimbledon	Away	League	2–2		
89	23/04/88	Norwich City	Home	League	2–2	1 Goal	(45)
90	30/04/88	Coventry City	Away	League	0–1		
91	02/05/88	Newcastle United	Home	League	1–2	1 Goal	(46)
92	07/05/88	Manchester United	Away	League	1–4	1 Goal	(47)

SEASON 1988–89

League Division Two

93	27/08/88	Shrewsbury Town	Away	League	2–1		
94	29/08/88	Leicester City	Home	League	3–0	1 Goal	(48)
95	03/09/88	Leeds United	Home	League	4–0	1 Goal	(49)
96	11/09/88	Swindon Town	Away	League	1–1		
97	17/09/88	Hull City	Home	League	1–3		
98	24/09/88	Crystal Palace	Home	League	1–1		
99	27/09/88	Scarborough	Home	Lge Cup	2–2	1 Goal	(50)

Sub+4	01/10/88	Bradford City	Away	League	1–2		
Sub+5	05/10/88	Manchester City	Away	League	1–4		
100	08/10/88	Oxford United	Home	League	2–1	1 Goal	(51)
101	12/10/88	Scarborough	Away	Lge Cup	1–3		
Sub+6	15/10/88	AFC Bournemouth	Home	League	2–1	1 Goal	(52)
102	22/10/88	Walsall	Away	League	1–1	1 Goal	(53)
103	25/10/88	Ipswich Town	Away	League	1–0		
104	29/10/88	Oldham Athletic	Home	League	1–1		
105	05/11/88	Birmingham City	Away	League	0–0		
106	08/11/88	Hull City	Home	Simod Cup	2–1	1 Goal	(54)
107	12/11/88	Plymouth Argyle	Home	League	2–0	1 Goal	(55)
108	19/11/88	Barnsley	Home	League	3–0	1 Goal	(56)
109	26/11/88	Blackburn Rovers	Away	League	1–3		
110	03/12/88	West Bromwich Albion	Home	League	0–0		
111	10/12/88	Chelsea	Away	League	3–3	1 Goal	(57)
112	17/12/88	Brighton & Hove Albion	Home	League	2–0		
113	26/12/88	Watford	Away	League	0–1		
114	31/12/88	Sunderland	Away	League	0–4		
115	02/01/89	Swindon Town	Home	League	0–2		
116	07/01/89	Swindon Town	Home	FA Cup	1–1	1 Goal	(58)
117	10/01/89	Swindon Town	Away	FA Cup	0–2		
118	14/01/89	Leicester City	Away	League	1–2	1 Goal	(59)
119	21/01/89	Shrewsbury Town	Home	League	2–0		
120	04/02/89	Manchester City	Home	League	0–1		
121	11/02/89	Oxford United	Away	League	0–1		
122	18/02/89	Walsall	Home	League	1–1	1 Goal	(60)
123	04/03/89	Plymouth Argyle	Away	League	1–0	1 Goal	(61)
124	11/03/89	Birmingham City	Home	League	1–0		
125	14/03/89	Oldham Athletic	Away	League	3–5	2 Goals	(63)
126	18/03/89	Stoke City	Home	League	0–0		
127	25/03/89	Leeds United	Away	League	0–1		
128	27/03/89	Watford	Home	League	2–2	1 Goal	(64)
129	01/04/89	Hull City	Away	League	1–1	1 Goal	(65)
130	05/04/89	Brighton & Hove Albion	Away	League	1–2		
131	08/04/89	Sunderland	Home	League	2–0	2 Goals	(67)
132	29/04/89	Blackburn Rovers	Home	League	1–2		
133	13/05/89	Chelsea	Home	League	2–3	1 Goal	(68)

SEASON 1989–90

Newcastle United – League Division Two

1	19/08/89	Leeds United	Home	League	5–2	4 Goals	(4)
2	26/08/89	Leicester City	Away	League	2–2	1 Goal	(5)
3	02/09/89	Oldham Athletic	Home	League	2–1	2 Goals	(7)
4	09/09/89	AFC Bournemouth	Away	League	1–2	1 Goal	(8)
5	13/09/89	Oxford United	Away	League	1–2	1 Goal	(9)
6	16/09/89	Portsmouth	Home	League	1–0		
7	19/09/89	Reading	Away	Lge Cup	1–3		
8	24/09/89	Sunderland	Away	League	0–0		
9	27/09/89	Watford	Home	League	2–1	1 Goal	(10)
10	30/09/89	Hull City	Away	League	3–1		
11	07/10/89	Ipswich Town	Away	League	1–2		
12	14/10/89	Bradford City	Home	League	1–0		
13	18/10/89	Blackburn Rovers	Home	League	2–1	1 Goal	(11)
14	21/10/89	Brighton & Hove Albion	Away	League	3–0	3 Goals	(14)
15	25/10/89	West Bromwich Albion	Home	Lge Cup	0–1		
16	28/10/89	Port Vale	Home	League	2–2	1 Goal	(15)
17	01/11/89	West Bromwich Albion	Away	League	5–1		
18	04/11/89	Middlesbrough	Home	League	2–2		
19	11/11/89	West Ham United	Away	League	0–0		
20	18/11/89	Barnsley	Away	League	1–1	1 Goal	(16)
21	25/11/89	Sheffield United	Home	League	2–0	1 Goal	(17)
22	28/11/89	Oldham Athletic	Home	ZDS Cup	2–0	2 Goals	(19)
23	02/12/89	Leeds United	Away	League	0–1		
24	09/12/89	Oxford United	Home	League	2–3	1 Goal	(20)
25	20/12/89	Derby County	Away	ZDS Cup	3–2*		
26	26/12/89	Stoke City	Away	League	1–2		
27	30/12/89	Swindon Town	Away	League	1–1	1 Goal	(21)
28	01/01/90	Wolverhampton Wanderers	Home	League	1–4		
29	06/01/90	Hull City	Away	FA Cup	1–0		
30	13/01/90	Leicester City	Home	League	5–4	2 Goals	(23)
31	27/01/90	Reading	Away	FA Cup	3–3	1 Goal	(24)
32	31/01/90	Reading	Home	FA Cup	4–1	1 Goal	(25)
33	04/02/90	Sunderland	Home	League	1–1		
34	10/02/90	Portsmouth	Away	League	1–1	1 Goal	(26)

35	18/02/90	Manchester United	Home	FA Cup	2–3		
36	24/02/90	Sheffield United	Away	League	1–1		
37	28/02/90	AFC Bournemouth	Home	League	3–0	2 Goals	(28)
38	03/03/90	Barnsley	Home	League	4–1		
39	07/03/90	Hull City	Home	League	2–0		
40	10/03/90	Watford	Away	League	0–0		
41	17/03/90	Ipswich Town	Home	League	2–1	2 Goals	(30)
42	21/03/90	Bradford City	Away	League	2–3		
43	24/03/90	Blackburn Rovers	Away	League	0–2		
44	31/03/90	Brighton & Hove Albion	Home	League	2–0	1 Goal	(31)
45	03/04/90	Plymouth Argyle	Home	League	3–1	1 Goal	(32)
46	07/04/90	Port Vale	Away	League	2–1	1 Goal	(33)
47	11/04/90	West Bromwich Albion	Home	League	2–1	1 Goal	(34)
48	14/04/90	Wolverhampton Wanderers	Away	League	1–0		
49	16/04/90	Stoke City	Home	League	3–0	1 Goal	(35)
50	21/04/90	Plymouth Argyle	Away	League	1–1		
51	25/04/90	Swindon Town	Home	League	0–0		
52	28/04/90	West Ham United	Home	League	2–1	1 Goal	(36)
53	05/05/90	Middlesbrough	Away	League	1–4		
54	13/05/90	Sunderland	Away	Lge P/O	0–0		
55	16/05/90	Sunderland	Home	Lge P/O	0–2		

SEASON 1990–91

League Division Two

56	25/08/90	Plymouth Argyle	Home	League	2–0	1 Goal	(37)
57	01/09/90	Blackburn Rovers	Away	League	1–0		
58	08/09/90	Millwall	Home	League	1–2	1 Goal	(38)
59	15/09/90	Port Vale	Away	League	1–2	1 Goal	(39)
60	18/09/90	Sheffield Wednesday	Away	League	2–2		
61	22/09/90	West Ham United	Home	League	1–1		
62	25/09/90	Middlesbrough	Away	Lge Cup	0–2		
63	29/09/90	Bristol City	Away	League	0–1		
64	03/10/90	Middlesbrough	Home	League	0–0		
65	06/10/90	Portsmouth	Home	League	2–1	2 Goals	(41)
66	10/10/90	Middlesbrough	Home	Lge Cup	1–0		
67	13/10/90	Oxford United	Away	League	0–0		
68	20/10/90	Ipswich Town	Away	League	1–2	1 Goal	(42)
69	10/11/90	Wolverhampton Wanderers	Away	League	1–2		
70	17/11/90	Barnsley	Home	League	0–0		
71	21/11/90	Nottingham Forest	Away	ZDS Cup	1–2		
72	24/11/90	Watford	Home	League	1–0	1 Goal	(43)
73	01/12/90	Leicester City	Away	League	4–5	3 Goals	(46)
74	16/12/90	Plymouth Argyle	Away	League	1–0		
75	22/12/90	Bristol Rovers	Away	League	1–1		
76	26/12/90	Swindon Town	Home	League	1–1	1 Goal	(47)
77	29/12/90	Notts County	Home	League	0–2		
78	01/01/91	Oldham Athletic	Away	League	1–1	1 Goal	(48)
79	05/01/91	Derby County	Home	FA Cup	2–0	1 Goal	(49)
80	12/01/91	Blackburn Rovers	Home	League	1–0		
81	16/01/91	Brighton & Hove Albion	Away	League	2–4	1 Goal	(50)
82	19/01/91	Millwall	Away	League	1–0		
83	02/02/91	Port Vale	Home	League	2–0	1 Goal	(51)
84	13/02/91	Nottingham Forest	Home	FA Cup	2–2	1 Goal	(52)
85	18/02/91	Nottingham Forest	Away	FA Cup	0–3		
86	23/02/91	Wolverhampton Wanderers	Home	League	0–0		
87	27/02/91	Brighton & Hove Albion	Home	League	0–0		
88	02/03/91	Leicester City	Home	League	2–1		
89	09/03/91	Watford	Away	League	2–1	1 Goal	(53)
90	12/03/91	Middlesbrough	Away	League	0–3		
91	16/03/91	Bristol City	Home	League	0–0		
92	23/03/91	Portsmouth	Away	League	1–0		
93	30/03/91	Swindon Town	Away	League	2–3	1 Goal	(54)
94	01/04/91	Bristol Rovers	Home	League	0–2		
95	06/04/91	Notts County	Away	League	0–3		
96	10/04/91	Oxford United	Home	League	2–2		
97	13/04/91	Oldham Athletic	Home	League	3–2		
98	17/04/91	Sheffield Wednesday	Home	League	1–0		
99	20/04/91	Ipswich Town	Home	League	2–2	1 Goal	(55)
100	24/04/91	West Ham United	Away	League	1–1		
101	27/04/91	Charlton Athletic	Away	League	0–1		
102	04/05/91	West Bromwich Albion	Away	League	1–1	1 Goal	(56)
103	07/05/91	Barnsley	Away	League	1–1		
104	11/05/91	Hull City	Home	League	1–2		

SEASON 1991–92

League Division Two

105	18/08/91	Charlton Athletic	Away	League	1–2		
106	24/08/91	Watford	Home	League	2–2		
107	27/08/91	Middlesbrough	Away	League	0–3		
108	31/08/91	Bristol Rovers	Away	League	2–1	1 Goal	(57)
109	04/09/91	Plymouth Argyle	Home	League	2–2	1 Goal	(58)
110	07/09/91	Tranmere Rovers	Away	League	2–3		
111	14/09/91	Wolverhampton Wanderers	Home	League	1–2		
112	17/09/91	Ipswich Town	Home	League	1–1	1 Goal	(59)
113	21/09/91	Millwall	Away	League	1–2		
114	24/09/91	Crewe Alexandra	Away	Lge Cup	4–3		
115	28/09/91	Derby County	Home	League	2–2	1 Goal	(60)
116	01/10/91	Tranmere Rovers	Away	ZDS Cup	6–6+	3 Goals	(63)
117	05/10/91	Portsmouth	Away	League	1–3	1 Goal	(64)
118	29/02/92	Port Vale	Away	League	1–0		
Sub+1	07/03/92	Brighton & Hove Albion	Home	League	0–1		
119	10/03/92	Cambridge United	Away	League	2–0		
120	14/03/92	Swindon Town	Home	League	3–1	1 Goal	(65)
121	21/03/92	Grimsby Town	Away	League	1–1		
122	29/03/92	Sunderland	Home	League	1–0		
123	31/03/92	Wolverhampton Wanderers	Away	League	2–6	1 Goal	(66)
124	04/04/92	Tranmere Rovers	Home	League	2–3		
Sub+2	11/04/92	Ipswich Town	Away	League	2–3		
Sub+3	18/04/92	Millwall	Home	League	0–1		
Sub+4	25/04/92	Portsmouth	Home	League	1–0		

+ AET Tranmere Rovers won 3–2 on penalties

SEASON 1992–93

Football League Division One

Sub+5	19/08/92	Mansfield Town	Home	Lge Cup	2–1		
125	12/09/92	Portsmouth	Home	League	3–1	2 Goals	(68)
126	16/09/92	Grimsby Town	Away	AI Cup	2–2	1 Goal	(69)
Sub+6	19/09/92	Bristol City	Home	League	5–0		
127	23/09/92	Middlesbrough	Home	Lge Cup	0–0		
128	26/09/92	Peterborough United	Away	League	1–0		
129	30/09/92	Leicester City	Home	AI Cup	4–0	2 Goals	(71)
Sub+7	07/10/92	Middlesbrough	Away	Lge Cup	3–1		
130	10/10/92	Tranmere Rovers	Home	League	1–0		
131	24/10/92	Grimsby Town	Home	League	0–1		
132	28/10/92	Chelsea	Away	Lge Cup	1–2		
Sub+8	11/11/92	US Lucchese Libertas	Away	AI Cup	1–1		

Coventry City – Premier League

1	21/11/92	Manchester City	Home	League	2–3	2 Goals	(2)
2	28/11/92	Sheffield United	Away	League	1–1	1 Goal	(3)
3	05/12/92	Ipswich Town	Home	League	2–2	1 Goal	(4)
4	12/12/92	Southampton	Away	League	2–2	2 Goals	(6)
5	19/12/92	Liverpool	Home	League	5–1	2 Goals	(8)
6	26/12/92	Aston Villa	Home	League	3–0	2 Goals	(10)
7	28/12/92	Manchester United	Away	League	0–5		
8	09/01/93	Nottingham Forest	Home	League	0–1		
9	13/01/93	Norwich City	Away	FA Cup	0–1		
10	16/01/93	Norwich City	Away	League	1–1	1 Goal	(11)
11	23/01/93	Oldham Athletic	Home	League	3–0		
12	26/01/93	Blackburn Rovers	Away	League	5–2	2 Goals	(13)
13	30/01/93	Wimbledon	Home	League	0–2		
14	06/02/93	Middlesbrough	Away	League	2–0	1 Goal	(14)
15	20/02/93	Queens Park Rangers	Away	League	0–2		
16	27/02/93	Crystal Palace	Away	League	0–0		
17	03/03/93	Sheffield Wednesday	Home	League	1–0		
18	07/03/93	Everton	Home	League	0–1		
19	10/03/93	Manchester City	Away	League	0–1		
20	20/03/93	Ipswich Town	Away	League	0–0		
21	24/03/93	Sheffield United	Home	League	1–3		
22	03/04/93	Southampton	Home	League	2–0	1 Goal	(15)
23	10/04/93	Aston Villa	Away	League	0–0		
24	12/04/93	Manchester United	Home	League	0–1		
25	17/04/93	Liverpool	Away	League	0–4		
26	01/05/93	Chelsea	Away	League	1–2	1 Goal	(16)
27	08/05/93	Leeds United	Home	League	3–3	1 Goal	(17)

SEASON 1993–94

Premier League

28	14/08/93	Arsenal	Away	League	3–0	3 Goals	(20)
29	18/08/93	Newcastle United	Home	League	2–1		
30	21/08/93	West Ham United	Home	League	1–1		
31	24/08/93	Oldham Athletic	Away	League	3–3		
32	01/09/93	Liverpool	Home	League	1–0		
33	11/09/93	Aston Villa	Away	League	0–0		
34	18/09/93	Chelsea	Home	League	1–1		
35	25/09/93	Leeds United	Home	League	0–2		
36	22/09/93	Wycombe Wanderers	Home	Lge Cup	3–0	1 Goal	(21)
37	02/10/93	Norwich City	Away	League	0–1		
38	16/10/93	Southampton	Home	League	1–1		
39	23/10/93	Queens Park Rangers	Away	League	1–5		
Sub+1	26/10/93	Oldham Athletic	Away	Lge Cup	0–2		
40	31/10/93	Sheffield United	Home	League	0–0		
41	06/11/93	Everton	Home	League	2–1	2 Goals	(23)
42	20/11/93	Sheffield Wednesday	Away	League	0–0		
43	23/11/93	Blackburn Rovers	Away	League	1–2		
44	27/11/93	Manchester United	Home	League	0–1		
45	04/12/93	Arsenal	Home	League	1–0	1 Goal	(24)
46	11/12/93	West Ham United	Away	League	2–3		
47	18/12/93	Oldham Athletic	Home	League	1–1		
Sub+2	01/01/94	Tottenham Hotspur	Away	League	2–1		
Sub+3	03/01/94	Swindon Town	Home	League	1–1		
Sub+4	08/01/94	Newcastle United	Away	FA Cup	0–2		
48	15/01/94	Southampton	Away	League	0–1		
49	22/01/94	Queens Park Rangers	Home	League	0–1		
Sub+5	02/02/94	Ipswich Town	Home	League	1–0		
Sub+6	05/02/94	Swindon Town	Away	League	1–3		
50	12/02/94	Sheffield United	Away	League	0–0		
51	19/02/94	Manchester City	Home	League	4–0	1 Goal	(25)
52	25/02/94	Liverpool	Away	League	0–1		
53	06/03/94	Aston Villa	Home	League	0–1		
54	19/03/94	Leeds United	Away	League	0–1		
55	26/03/94	Norwich City	Home	League	2–1	1 Goal	(26)
56	02/04/94	Wimbledon	Home	League	1–2		

SEASON 1994–95

Premier League

57	20/08/94	Wimbledon	Home	League	1–1		
58	24/08/94	Newcastle United	Away	League	0–4		
59	27/08/94	Blackburn Rovers	Away	League	0–4		

Plymouth Argyle (loan) – Football League Division Two

1	19/11/94	Wrexham	Home	League	4–1	
2	26/11/94	York City	Away	League	0–1	
3	10/12/94	Brighton & Hove Albion	Home	League	0–3	

Coventry City – Premier League

Sub+7	26/12/94	Nottingham Forest	Home	League	0–0	
Sub+8	28/12/94	Sheffield Wednesday	Away	League	1–5	
Sub+9	31/12/94	Tottenham Hotspur	Home	League	0–4	

Watford (loan) – Football League Division One

1	18/03/95	Wolverhampton Wanderers	Away	League	1–1	
2	21/03/95	Barnsley	Home	League	3–2	
3	26/03/95	Luton Town	Away	League	1–1	
4	01/04/95	Oldham Athletic	Home	League	1–2	
Sub+1	14/04/95	Millwall	Home	League	1–0	

SEASON 1995–96

PAOK Salonika – Greek League Division One

Sub+1	27/08/95	Xanthi	Away	League	2–2		
Sub+2	30/08/95	Hania	Away	Gk Cup	2–0	1 Goal	(1)
1	10/09/95	Athinaikos	Home	League	1–0		
Sub+3	17/09/95	Panionios	Away	League	1–2		
Sub+4	24/09/95	Paniliakos	Away	League	1–1		
2	01/10/95	Aris	Home	League	1–0		
3	04/10/95	Pierikos	Home	Gk Cup	5–0		
4	22/10/95	Ethnikos	Home	League	2–0		

5	25/10/95	Korinthos	Away	Gk Cup	2–0	1 Goal	(2)
Sub+5	29/10/95	Iraklis	Away	League	2–2	1 Goal	(3)
Sub+6	06/11/95	AEK	Home	League	1–3+		
6	19/11/95	Ionikos	Away	League	0–0		
7	22/11/95	Kozani	Home	Gk Cup	1–0	1 Goal	(4)
8	26/11/95	Olympiakos	Home	League	0–0#		

+ Match abandoned after 74 minutes, result stands
# Played at a neutral ground

APPEARANCES AND GOALS PER SEASON

SEASON 79–80	GAMES	GOALS
League	4	1
TOTAL	**4**	**1**

SEASON 80–81	GAMES	GOALS
League	32+4	14
FA Cup	1	0
League Cup	1	0
TOTAL	**34+4**	**14**

SEASON 81–82	GAMES	GOALS
League	20+9	4
FA Cup	2	1
League Cup	4	1
TOTAL	**26+9**	**6**

SEASON 82–83	GAMES	GOALS
League	38+1	24
FA Cup	1	0
League Cup	2	0
TOTAL	**41+1**	**24**

SEASON 83–84	GAMES	GOALS
League	38	20
FA Cup	1	0
League Cup	3	2
TOTAL	**42**	**22**

SEASON 84–85	GAMES	GOALS
League	40	18
FA Cup	2	1
League Cup	2	2
TOTAL	**44**	**21**

SEASON 85–86	GAMES	GOALS
League	35+2	17
League Cup	2	0
TOTAL	**37+2**	**17**

SEASON 86–87	GAMES	GOALS
League	39	22
FA Cup	1	2
League Cup	3	4
Full Members Cup	2	0
TOTAL	**45**	**28**

SEASON 87–88	GAMES	GOALS
League	29+3	8
FA Cup	4	4
League Cup	2	1
Simod Cup	1	0
TOTAL	**36+3**	**13**

SEASON 88–89	GAMES	GOALS
League	36+3	18
FA Cup	2	1
League Cup	2	1
Simod Cup	1	1
TOTAL	**41+3**	**21**

SEASON 89–90	GAMES	GOALS
League	45	32
League Play–offs	2	0
FA Cup	4	2
League Cup	2	0
Zenith Data Systems Cup	2	2
TOTAL	**55**	**36**

SEASON 90–91	GAMES	GOALS
League	43	18
FA Cup	3	2
League Cup	2	0
Zenith Data Systems Cup	1	0
TOTAL	**49**	**20**

SEASON 91–92	GAMES	GOALS
League	18+4	7
League Cup	1	0
Zenith Data Systems Cup	1	3
TOTAL	**20+4**	**10**

SEASON 92–93	GAMES	GOALS
League	30+1	19
FA Cup	1	0
League Cup	2+2	0
Anglo–Italian Cup	2+1	3
TOTAL	**35+4**	**22**

SEASON 93–94	GAMES	GOALS
League	28+4	8
FA Cup	0+1	0
League Cup	1+1	1
TOTAL	**29+6**	**9**

SEASON 94–95	GAMES	GOALS
League	10+4	0
TOTAL	**10+4**	**0**

SEASON 95–96	GAMES	GOALS
Greek League	5+5	1
Greek Cup	3+1	3
TOTAL	**8+6**	**4**

CAREER APPEARANCES AND GOALS

COMPETITION	GAMES	TOTAL	GOALS
League	485+35	520	230
League Play–offs	2	2	0
FA Cup	22+1	23	13
League Cup	29+3	32	12
Full Members Cup	2	2	0
Simod Cup	2	2	1
Zenith Data Systems Cup	4	4	5
Anglo–Italian Cup	2+1	3	3
Greek League	5+5	10	1
Greek Cup	3+1	4	3
TOTAL	**556+46**	**602**	**268**

HAT-TRICKS

Wigan Athletic

1	3	Doncaster Rovers	08/10/80	Home	League	3–0

Stockport County

1	3	Crewe Alexandra	10/12/82	Home	League	3–2
2	3	Halifax Town	01/01/83	Home	League	4–2
3	3	Crewe Alexandra	30/09/83	Away	League	3–0

Oldham Athletic

1	3	Carlisle United	11/05/85	Away	League	5–2

Portsmouth

1	3	Derby County	21/10/86	Home	League	3–1

Newcastle United

1	4	Leeds United	19/08/89	Home	League	5–2
2	3	Brighton & Hove Albion	21/10/89	Away	League	3–0
3	3	Leicester City	01/12/90	Away	League	4–5
4	3	Tranmere Rovers	01/10/91	Away	ZDS Cup	6–6

Coventry City

1	3	Arsenal	14/08/93	Away	League	3–0

League: 10
Zenith Data Systems Cup: 1
TOTAL: 11

HONOURS

Winners medals
None

Runner-up medals
League Division Two Championship: 86/87
Promoted to League Division Three: 81/82

CYRILLE REGIS

Born: 09/02/58 – French Guyana
Height: 6.0
Weight: 13.07 (95–96)

Clubs
West Bromwich Albion: **1977–84** – Matches: **295+5** – Goals: **112**
Coventry City: **1984–91** – Matches: **274+8** – Goals: **62**
Aston Villa: **1991–93** – Matches: **54+9** – Goals: **12**
Wolverhampton Wanderers: **1993–94** – Matches: **10+13** – Goals: **2**
Wycombe Wanderers: **1994–95** – Matches: **33+5** – Goals: **10**
Chester City: **1995–96** – Matches: **33** – Goals: **7**

Country
England: **1982–87** – Matches: **2+3** – Goals: **0**

SEASON 1977–78

West Bromwich Albion – League Division One

1	31/08/77	Rotherham United	Home	Lge Cup	4–0	2 Goals	(2)
2	03/09/77	Middlesbrough	Home	League	2–1	1 Goal	(3)
3	10/09/77	Newcastle United	Away	League	3–0	1 Goal	(4)
4	17/09/77	Wolverhampton Wanderers	Home	League	2–2		
5	24/09/77	Birmingham City	Home	League	3–1	1 Goal	(5)
6	01/10/77	Coventry City	Away	League	2–1		
7	04/10/77	Everton	Away	League	1–3		
8	08/10/77	Ipswich Town	Home	League	1–0		
9	15/10/77	Derby County	Away	League	1–1	1 Goal	(6)
Sub+1	29/10/77	Queens Park Rangers	Away	League	1–2		
Sub+2	29/11/77	Bury	Away	Lge Cup	0–1		
10	03/12/77	Norwich City	Home	League	0–0		
11	10/12/77	Aston Villa	Away	League	0–3		
12	17/12/77	West Ham United	Home	League	1–0		
13	26/12/77	Bristol City	Away	League	1–3		
14	27/12/77	Arsenal	Home	League	1–3		
15	31/12/77	Leeds United	Home	League	1–0		
16	02/01/78	Chelsea	Away	League	2–2		
17	07/01/78	Blackpool	Home	FA Cup	4–1	1 Goal	(7)
18	14/01/78	Liverpool	Home	League	0–1		
19	21/01/78	Middlesbrough	Away	League	0–1		
20	28/01/78	Manchester United	Away	FA Cup	1–1		
21	01/02/78	Manchester United	Home	FA Cup	3–2	2 Goals	(9)
22	18/02/78	Derby County	Away	FA Cup	3–2	2 Goals	(11)
23	25/02/78	Coventry City	Home	League	3–3		
24	28/02/78	Birmingham City	Away	League	2–1		
25	04/03/78	Ipswich Town	Away	League	2–2		
26	11/03/78	Nottingham Forest	Home	FA Cup	2–0	1 Goal	(12)

27	14/03/78	Wolverhampton Wanderers	Away	League	1–1		
28	18/03/78	Manchester United	Away	League	1–1		
29	22/03/78	Queens Park Rangers	Home	League	2–0	1 Goal	(13)
30	25/03/78	Arsenal	Away	League	0–4		
31	27/03/78	Bristol City	Home	League	2–1		
32	01/04/78	Leicester City	Away	League	1–0		
33	08/04/78	Ipswich Town	Neutral	FA Cup	1–3		
34	12/04/78	Newcastle United	Home	League	2–0	1 Goal	(14)
35	15/04/78	Manchester City	Away	League	3–1	1 Goal	(15)
36	18/04/78	Derby County	Home	League	1–0		
37	22/04/78	Aston Villa	Home	League	0–3		
38	25/04/78	Everton	Home	League	3–1	2 Goals	(17)
39	29/04/78	Norwich City	Away	League	1–1	1 Goal	(18)
40	02/05/78	Nottingham Forest	Home	League	2–2		

SEASON 1978–79

League Division One

41	19/08/78	Ipswich town	Home	League	2–1		
42	22/08/78	Queens Park Rangers	Away	League	1–0		
43	26/08/78	Bolton Wanderers	Home	League	4–0	1 Goal	(19)
44	29/08/78	Leeds United	Home	Lge Cup	0–0		
45	02/09/78	Nottingham Forest	Away	League	0–0		
46	06/09/78	Leeds United	Away	Lge Cup	0–0*		
47	09/09/78	Norwich City	Home	League	2–2		
48	13/09/78	Galatasaray SK	Away	UEFA Cup	3–1	1 Goal	(20)
49	16/09/78	Derby County	Away	League	2–3	1 Goal	(21)
50	23/09/78	Liverpool	Home	League	1–1		
51	27/09/78	Galatasaray SK	Home	UEFA Cup	3–1		
52	30/09/78	Chelsea	Away	League	3–1	1 Goal	(22)
53	02/10/78	Leeds United	Neutral	Lge Cup	0–1		
54	07/10/78	Tottenham Hotspur	Home	League	0–1		
55	14/10/78	Leeds United	Away	League	3–1	2 Goals	(24)
56	18/10/78	Sporting Clube de Braga	Away	UEFA Cup	2–0	2 Goals	(26)
57	21/10/78	Coventry City	Home	League	7–1	2 Goals	(28)
58	28/10/78	Manchester City	Away	League	2–2	1 Goal	(29)
59	01/11/78	Sporting Clube de Braga	Home	UEFA Cup	1–0		
60	04/11/78	Birmingham City	Home	League	1–0		
61	11/11/78	Ipswich Town	Away	League	1–0		
62	22/11/78	Valencia CF	Away	UEFA Cup	1–1		
63	25/11/78	Aston Villa	Home	League	1–1		
64	06/12/78	Valencia CF	Home	UEFA Cup	2–0		
65	09/12/78	Middlesbrough	Home	League	2–0	1 Goal	(30)
66	16/12/78	Wolverhampton Wanderers	Away	League	3–0		
67	26/12/78	Arsenal	Away	League	2–1		
68	30/12/78	Manchester United	Away	League	5–3	1 Goal	(31)
69	01/01/79	Bristol City	Home	League	3–1		
70	09/01/79	Coventry City	Away	FA Cup	2–2+		
71	13/01/79	Norwich City	Away	League	1–1	1 Goal	(32)
72	15/01/79	Coventry City	Home	FA Cup	4–0		
73	03/02/79	Liverpool	Away	League	1–2		
74	24/02/79	Leeds United	Home	League	1–2		
75	26/02/79	Leeds United	Home	FA Cup	3–3	1 Goal	(33)
76	01/03/79	Leeds United	Home	FA Cup	2–0*		
77	03/03/79	Coventry City	Away	League	3–1		
78	07/03/79	Crvena Zvezda Beograd	Away	UEFA Cup	0–1		
79	10/03/79	Southampton	Home	FA Cup	1–1		
80	12/03/79	Southampton	Away	FA Cup	1–2*		
81	14/03/79	Chelsea	Home	League	2–0		
82	21/03/79	Crvena Zvezda Beograd	Home	UEFA Cup	1–1	1 Goal	(34)
83	04/04/79	Manchester City	Home	League	4–0		
84	07/04/79	Everton	Home	League	1–0		
85	13/04/79	Southampton	Away	League	1–1	1 Goal	(35)
86	14/04/79	Arsenal	Home	League	1–1		
87	17/04/79	Bristol City	Away	League	0–1		
88	21/04/79	Wolverhampton Wanderers	Home	League	1–1		
89	24/04/79	Birmingham City	Away	League	1–1		
Sub+3	28/04/79	Middlesbrough	Away	League	1–1		
90	01/05/79	Everton	Away	League	2–0		
91	05/05/79	Manchester United	Home	League	1–0	1 Goal	(36)
92	08/05/79	Southampton	Home	League	1–0		
93	11/05/79	Aston Villa	Away	League	1–0		
94	14/05/79	Tottenham Hotspur	Away	League	0–1		
95	18/05/79	Nottingham Forest	Home	League	0–1		

+ Played at West Bromwich Albion

SEASON 1979–80

League Division One

96	31/10/79	Norwich City	Home	Lge Cup	0–0		
Sub+4	03/11/79	Derby County	Away	League	1–2		
97	07/11/79	Norwich City	Away	Lge Cup	0–3		
98	24/11/79	Wolverhampton Wanderers	Away	League	0–0		
99	01/12/79	Everton	Home	League	1–1	1 Goal	(37)
100	08/12/79	Stoke City	Away	League	2–3	1 Goal	(38)
101	15/12/79	Arsenal	Home	League	2–2		
102	26/12/79	Bristol City	Home	League	3–0		
103	29/12/79	Liverpool	Home	League	0–2		
Sub+5	01/01/80	Ipswich Town	Away	League	0–4		
104	05/01/80	West Ham United	Home	FA Cup	1–1	1 Goal	(39)
105	08/01/80	West Ham United	Away	FA Cup	1–2		
106	12/01/80	Nottingham Forest	Away	League	1–3	1 Goal	(40)
107	26/01/80	Crystal Palace	Away	League	2–2	1 Goal	(41)
108	02/02/80	Manchester City	Away	League	3–1	1 Goal	(42)
109	09/02/80	Tottenham Hotspur	Home	League	2–1	2 Goals	(44)
110	16/02/80	Brighton & Hove Albion	Away	League	0–0		
111	23/02/80	Aston Villa	Home	League	1–2		
112	01/03/80	Southampton	Away	League	1–1	1 Goal	(45)
113	08/03/80	Coventry City	Away	League	2–0		
114	14/03/80	Middlesbrough	Home	League	0–0		
115	18/03/80	Bolton Wanderers	Home	League	4–4		
116	29/03/80	Leeds United	Home	League	2–1		
117	01/04/80	Crystal Palace	Home	League	3–0		
118	05/04/80	Bristol City	Away	League	0–0		
119	07/04/80	Ipswich Town	Home	League	0–0		
120	19/04/80	Wolverhampton Wanderers	Home	League	0–0		
121	26/04/80	Arsenal	Away	League	1–1		
122	28/04/80	Everton	Away	League	0–0		
123	03/05/80	Stoke City	Home	League	0–1		

SEASON 1980–81

League Division One

124	16/08/80	Arsenal	Home	League	0–1		
125	20/08/80	Stoke City	Away	League	0–0		
126	23/08/80	Wolverhampton Wanderers	Home	League	1–1	1 Goal	(46)
127	26/08/80	Leicester City	Home	Lge Cup	1–0		
128	30/08/80	Brighton & Hove Albion	Away	League	2–1	1 Goal	(47)
129	03/09/80	Leicester City	Away	Lge Cup	1–0	1 Goal	(48)
130	06/09/80	Norwich City	Home	League	3–0		
131	13/09/80	Liverpool	Away	League	0–4		
132	20/09/80	Birmingham City	Away	League	1–1		
133	24/09/80	Everton	Away	Lge Cup	2–1		
134	27/09/80	Southampton	Home	League	2–1		
135	04/10/80	Crystal Palace	Away	League	1–0	1 Goal	(49)
136	11/10/80	Manchester City	Home	League	3–1	1 Goal	(50)
137	18/10/80	Nottingham Forest	Away	League	1–2		
138	21/10/80	Everton	Away	League	1–1		
139	25/10/80	Middlesbrough	Home	League	3–0	2 Goals	(52)
140	29/10/80	Preston North End	Home	Lge Cup	0–0		
141	01/11/80	Ipswich Town	Away	League	0–0		
142	04/11/80	Preston North End	Away	Lge Cup	1–1		
143	08/11/80	Aston Villa	Home	League	0–0		
144	12/11/80	Preston North End	Home	Lge Cup	2–1	2 Goals	(54)
145	15/11/80	Arsenal	Away	League	2–2		
146	22/11/80	Leicester City	Home	League	3–1		
147	25/11/80	Stoke City	Home	League	0–0		
148	29/11/80	Tottenham Hotspur	Away	League	3–2		
149	03/12/80	Manchester City	Away	Lge Cup	1–2		
150	06/12/80	Leeds United	Home	League	1–2		
151	13/12/80	Coventry City	Away	League	0–3		
152	26/12/80	Sunderland	Away	League	0–0		
153	27/12/80	Manchester United	Home	League	3–1	1 Goal	(55)
154	03/01/81	Grimsby Town	Home	FA Cup	3–0		
155	17/01/81	Brighton & Hove Albion	Home	League	2–0	1 Goal	(56)
156	24/01/81	Middlesbrough	Away	FA Cup	0–1		
157	31/01/81	Wolverhampton Wanderers	Away	League	0–2		
158	07/02/81	Liverpool	Home	League	2–0	1 Goal	(57)
159	14/02/81	Norwich City	Away	League	2–0	1 Goal	(58)
160	21/02/81	Southampton	Away	League	2–2	1 Goal	(59)
161	28/02/81	Birmingham City	Home	League	2–2		

162	21/03/81	Nottingham Forest	Home	League	2–1		
163	28/03/81	Middlesbrough	Away	League	1–2		
164	31/03/81	Everton	Home	League	2–0		
165	04/04/81	Ipswich Town	Home	League	3–1		
166	08/04/81	Aston Villa	Away	League	0–1		
167	18/04/81	Manchester United	Away	League	1–2	1 Goal	(60)
168	20/04/81	Sunderland	Home	League	2–1	2 Goals	(62)
169	02/05/81	Tottenham Hotspur	Home	League	4–2		
170	06/05/81	Leeds United	Away	League	0–0		

SEASON 1981–82

League Division One

171	05/09/81	Swansea City	Home	League	4–1	3 Goals	(65)
172	12/09/81	Nottingham Forest	Away	League	0–0		
173	16/09/81	Grasshoppers–Club Zurich	Away	UEFA Cup	0–1		
174	19/09/81	West Ham United	Home	League	0–0		
175	22/09/81	Ipswich Town	Away	League	0–1		
176	26/09/81	Everton	Away	League	0–1		
177	30/09/81	Grasshoppers–Club Zurich	Home	UEFA Cup	1–3		
178	03/10/81	Middlesbrough	Home	League	2–0	1 Goal	(66)
179	06/10/81	Shrewsbury Town	Away	Lge Cup	3–3	1 Goal	(67)
180	10/10/81	Brighton & Hove Albion	Home	League	0–0		
181	17/10/81	Leeds United	Away	League	1–3		
182	24/10/81	Southampton	Home	League	1–1		
183	28/10/81	Shrewsbury Town	Home	Lge Cup	2–1		
184	31/10/81	Birmingham City	Away	League	3–3	3 Goals	(70)
185	07/11/81	Tottenham Hotspur	Away	League	2–1		
186	10/11/81	West Ham United	Away	Lge Cup	2–1	1 Goal	(71)
187	14/11/81	Stoke City	Home	League	1–2		
188	21/11/81	Liverpool	Home	League	1–1	1 Goal	(72)
189	24/11/81	West Ham United	Home	Lge Cup	1–1*	1 Goal	(73)
190	28/11/81	Sunderland	Away	League	2–1	1 Goal	(74)
191	01/12/81	West Ham United	Away	Lge Cup	1–0	1 Goal	(75)
192	05/12/81	Wolverhampton Wanderers	Home	League	3–0	2 Goals	(77)
193	15/12/81	Crystal Palace	Away	Lge Cup	3–1	2 Goals	(79)
194	26/12/81	Coventry City	Away	League	2–0	1 Goal	(80)
195	02/01/82	Blackburn Rovers	Home	FA Cup	3–2		
196	19/01/82	Aston Villa	Away	Lge Cup	1–0		
197	23/01/82	Gillingham	Away	FA Cup	1–0		
198	30/01/82	West Ham United	Away	League	1–3		
199	03/02/82	Tottenham Hotspur	Home	Lge Cup	0–0		
200	06/02/82	Nottingham Forest	Home	League	2–1		
201	13/02/82	Norwich City	Home	FA Cup	1–0	1 Goal	(81)
202	10/02/82	Tottenham Hotspur	Away	Lge Cup	0–1		
203	20/02/82	Everton	Home	League	0–0		
204	27/02/82	Brighton & Hove Albion	Away	League	2–2		
205	06/03/82	Coventry City	Home	FA Cup	2–0	1 Goal	(82)
206	09/03/82	Middlesbrough	Away	League	0–1		
207	13/03/82	Southampton	Away	League	0–0		
208	20/03/82	Birmingham City	Home	League	1–1		
209	24/03/82	Notts County	Home	League	2–4	1 Goal	(83)
210	27/03/82	Tottenham Hotspur	Home	League	1–0	1 Goal	(84)
211	03/04/82	Queens Park Rangers	Neutral	FA Cup	0–1		
212	06/04/82	Swansea City	Away	League	1–3		
213	10/04/82	Coventry City	Home	League	1–2		
214	12/04/82	Manchester United	Away	League	0–1		
215	17/04/82	Liverpool	Away	League	0–1		
216	21/04/82	Manchester City	Home	League	0–1		
217	24/04/82	Sunderland	Home	League	2–3		
218	01/05/82	Wolverhampton Wanderers	Away	League	2–1	1 Goal	(85)
219	05/05/82	Ipswich Town	Home	League	1–2		
220	08/05/82	Aston Villa	Home	League	0–1		
221	12/05/82	Manchester United	Home	League	0–3		
222	15/05/82	Notts County	Away	League	2–1	1 Goal	(86)
223	18/05/82	Leeds United	Home	League	2–0	1 Goal	(87)

SEASON 1982–83

League Division One

224	04/09/82	Manchester United	Home	League	3–1		
225	08/09/82	Stoke City	Away	League	3–0	1 Goal	(88)
226	11/09/82	Watford	Away	League	0–3		
227	18/09/82	West Ham United	Home	League	1–2		
228	25/09/82	Norwich City	Away	League	3–1	3 Goals	(91)

229	06/10/82	Nottingham Forest	Away	Lge Cup	1–6	1 Goal	(92)
230	09/10/82	Nottingham Forest	Home	League	2–1	1 Goal	(93)
231	16/10/82	Arsenal	Away	League	0–2		
232	23/10/82	Luton Town	Home	League	1–0		
233	27/10/82	Nottingham Forest	Home	Lge Cup	3–1	1 Goal	(94)
234	30/10/82	Ipswich Town	Away	League	1–6	1 Goal	(95)
235	06/11/82	Birmingham City	Away	League	1–2		
236	13/11/82	Swansea City	Home	League	3–3		
237	20/11/82	Everton	Away	League	0–0		
238	27/11/82	Coventry City	Home	League	2–0	1 Goal	(96)
239	04/12/82	Tottenham Hotspur	Away	League	1–1		
240	11/12/82	Sunderland	Home	League	3–0		
241	18/12/82	Southampton	Away	League	1–4	1 Goal	(97)
242	27/12/82	Notts County	Home	League	2–2		
243	28/12/82	Manchester City	Away	League	1–2		
244	01/01/83	Everton	Home	League	2–2		
245	03/01/83	Manchester United	Away	League	0–0		
246	08/01/83	Queens Park Rangers	Home	FA Cup	3–2		
247	15/01/83	Liverpool	Home	League	0–1		
248	22/01/83	West Ham United	Away	League	1–0		
249	12/03/83	Ipswich Town	Home	League	4–1		
250	19/03/83	Birmingham City	Home	League	2–0	1 Goal	(98)
251	26/03/83	Swansea City	Away	League	1–2		
252	23/04/83	Tottenham Hotspur	Home	League	0–1		

SEASON 1983–84

League Division One

253	27/08/83	Aston Villa	Away	League	3–4	1 Goal	(99)
254	29/08/83	Stoke City	Away	League	1–3		
255	03/09/83	Leicester City	Home	League	1–0		
256	07/09/83	Tottenham Hotspur	Home	League	1–1	1 Goal	(100)
257	10/09/83	Everton	Away	League	0–0		
258	17/09/83	West Ham United	Home	League	1–0		
259	24/09/83	Ipswich Town	Away	League	4–3	1 Goal	(101)
260	01/10/83	Watford	Home	League	2–0	1 Goal	(102)
261	04/10/83	Millwall	Away	Lge Cup	0–3		
262	15/10/83	Manchester United	Away	League	0–3		
263	22/10/83	Coventry City	Away	League	2–1	1 Goal	(103)
264	25/10/83	Millwall	Home	Lge Cup	5–1	2 Goals	(105)
265	29/10/83	Birmingham City	Home	League	1–2		
266	30/11/83	Aston Villa	Home	Lge Cup	1–2	1 Goal	(106)
267	18/12/83	Luton Town	Away	League	0–2		
268	26/12/83	Liverpool	Home	League	1–2		
269	27/12/83	Sunderland	Away	League	0–3		
270	31/12/83	Leicester City	Away	League	1–1		
271	02/01/84	Ipswich Town	Home	League	2–1		
272	07/01/84	Rotherham United	Away	FA Cup	0–0		
273	11/01/84	Rotherham United	Home	FA Cup	3–0		
274	14/01/84	Aston Villa	Home	League	3–1	1 Goal	(107)
275	21/01/84	West Ham United	Away	League	0–1		
276	01/02/84	Scunthorpe United	Home	FA Cup	1–0		
277	04/02/84	Watford	Away	League	1–3		
278	08/02/84	Nottingham Forest	Home	League	0–5		
279	17/03/84	Tottenham Hotspur	Away	League	1–0	1 Goal	(108)
280	24/03/84	Stoke City	Home	League	3–0		
281	31/03/84	Manchester United	Home	League	2–0	1 Goal	(109)
282	07/04/84	Nottingham Forest	Away	League	1–3		
283	21/04/84	Liverpool	Away	League	0–3		
284	23/04/84	Sunderland	Home	League	3–1	1 Goal	(110)
285	28/04/84	Wolverhampton Wanderers	Away	League	0–0		
286	05/05/84	Arsenal	Home	League	1–3		
287	07/05/84	Queens Park Rangers	Away	League	1–1		
288	12/05/84	Luton Town	Home	League	3–0	1 Goal	(111)

SEASON 1984–85

League Division One

289	25/08/84	Queens Park Rangers	Away	League	1–3		
290	27/08/84	Everton	Home	League	2–1		
291	01/09/84	Luton Town	Home	League	4–0	1 Goal	(112)
292	05/09/84	Norwich City	Away	League	1–2		
293	08/09/84	Sunderland	Away	League	1–1		
294	15/09/84	Sheffield Wednesday	Home	League	2–2		
295	29/09/84	Manchester United	Home	League	1–2		

Coventry City – League Division One

1	13/10/84	Newcastle United	Home	League	1–1		
2	20/10/84	Queens Park Rangers	Away	League	1–2		
3	27/10/84	Sheffield Wednesday	Home	League	1–0		
4	03/11/84	Chelsea	Away	League	2–6		
5	17/11/84	Nottingham Forest	Home	League	1–3		
6	24/11/84	West Bromwich Albion	Away	League	2–5	1 Goal	(1)
7	01/12/84	Tottenham Hotspur	Home	League	1–1	1 Goal	(2)
8	04/12/84	Liverpool	Away	League	1–3		
9	15/12/84	Southampton	Home	League	2–1		
10	23/12/84	Leicester City	Away	League	1–5		
11	26/12/84	Luton Town	Away	League	0–2		
12	29/12/84	West Ham United	Home	League	1–2		
Sub+1	12/01/85	Manchester United	Away	League	1–0		
13	19/01/85	Aston Villa	Home	League	0–3		
14	26/01/85	Manchester United	Away	FA Cup	1–2		
15	02/02/85	Arsenal	Away	League	1–2		
16	23/02/85	Chelsea	Home	League	1–0		
17	02/03/85	Sheffield Wednesday	Away	League	0–1		
18	09/03/85	Queens Park Rangers	Home	League	3–0		
19	23/03/85	Watford	Home	League	3–1		
20	30/03/85	Norwich City	Away	League	1–2		
21	13/04/85	Sunderland	Home	League	0–1		
22	17/04/85	Newcastle United	Away	League	1–0		
23	20/04/85	Nottingham Forest	Away	League	0–2		
24	27/04/85	West Bromwich Albion	Home	League	2–1		
25	04/05/85	Tottenham Hotspur	Away	League	2–4		
26	06/05/85	Liverpool	Home	League	0–2		
27	11/05/85	Southampton	Away	League	1–2	1 Goal	(3)
28	14/05/85	Ipswich Town	Away	League	0–0		
29	17/05/85	Stoke City	Away	League	1–0		
30	23/05/85	Luton Town	Home	League	1–0		
31	26/05/85	Everton	Home	League	4–1	2 Goals	(5)

SEASON 1985–86

League Division One

32	17/08/85	Manchester City	Home	League	1–1		
33	20/08/85	Chelsea	Away	League	0–1		
34	24/08/85	Everton	Away	League	1–1		
35	26/08/85	Newcastle United	Home	League	1–2		
36	31/08/85	Watford	Away	League	0–3		
37	03/09/85	Oxford United	Home	League	5–2		
38	07/09/85	Arsenal	Home	League	0–2		
39	28/09/85	West Bromwich Albion	Home	League	3–0		
40	06/10/85	Leicester City	Home	League	3–0	1 Goal	(6)
41	09/10/85	Chester City	Home	Lge Cup	7–2	5 Goals	(11)
42	12/10/85	Sheffield Wednesday	Away	League	2–2		
43	20/10/85	Tottenham Hotspur	Home	League	2–3		
44	26/10/85	Birmingham City	Away	League	1–0		
45	29/10/85	West Bromwich Albion	Home	Lge Cup	0–0		
46	30/11/85	Queens Park Rangers	Away	League	2–0		
47	07/12/85	Chelsea	Home	League	1–1		
48	14/12/85	Manchester City	Away	League	1–5		
49	21/12/85	Everton	Home	League	1–3		
50	26/12/85	Ipswich Town	Home	League	0–1		
51	01/01/86	Nottingham Forest	Away	League	2–5	1 Goal	(12)
52	04/01/86	Watford	Home	FA Cup	1–3		
53	11/01/86	Aston Villa	Home	League	3–3	1 Goal	(13)
54	18/01/86	Watford	Home	League	0–2		
55	25/01/86	Oxford United	Away	League	1–0		
56	01/02/86	Newcastle United	Away	League	2–3	1 Goal	(14)
57	08/02/86	Tottenham Hotspur	Away	League	1–0	1 Goal	(15)
58	16/02/86	Birmingham City	Home	League	4–4		
59	22/02/86	Southampton	Home	League	3–2		
60	08/03/86	Leicester City	Away	League	1–2		
61	15/03/86	Sheffield Wednesday	Home	League	0–1		
62	19/03/86	West Bromwich Albion	Away	League	0–0		
63	31/03/86	Ipswich Town	Away	League	0–1		
64	05/04/86	Manchester United	Home	League	1–3		
65	12/04/86	Liverpool	Away	League	0–5		
66	19/04/86	Luton Town	Home	League	1–0		
67	26/04/86	West Ham United	Away	League	0–1		
68	03/05/86	Queens Park Rangers	Home	League	2–1		

SEASON 1986–87

League Division One

69	23/08/86	West Ham United	Away	League	0–1		
70	26/08/86	Arsenal	Home	League	2–1	1 Goal	(16)
71	30/08/86	Everton	Home	League	1–1		
72	02/09/86	Chelsea	Away	League	0–0		
73	06/09/86	Manchester City	Away	League	1–0	1 Goal	(17)
74	13/09/86	Newcastle United	Home	League	3–0		
75	20/09/86	Charlton Athletic	Away	League	1–1		
76	23/09/86	Rotherham United	Home	Lge Cup	3–2	1 Goal	(18)
77	27/09/86	Watford	Home	League	1–0		
78	04/10/86	Aston Villa	Home	League	0–1		
79	07/10/86	Rotherham United	Away	Lge Cup	1–0		
80	11/10/86	Oxford United	Away	League	0–2		
81	19/10/86	Wimbledon	Home	League	1–0		
82	25/10/86	Sheffield Wednesday	Away	League	2–2	1 Goal	(19)
83	28/10/86	Oldham Athletic	Home	Lge Cup	2–1	1 Goal	(20)
84	01/11/86	Manchester United	Away	League	1–1		
85	08/11/86	Nottingham Forest	Home	League	1–0		
86	15/11/86	Tottenham Hotspur	Away	League	0–1		
87	19/11/86	Liverpool	Home	Lge Cup	0–0		
88	22/11/86	Norwich City	Home	League	2–1		
89	26/11/86	Liverpool	Away	Lge Cup	1–3		
90	29/11/86	Liverpool	Away	League	0–2		
91	06/12/86	Leicester City	Home	League	1–0	1 Goal	(21)
92	21/12/86	Manchester City	Home	League	2–2		
93	26/12/86	Queens Park Rangers	Away	League	1–3		
94	27/12/86	Tottenham Hotspur	Home	League	4–3	1 Goal	(22)
95	01/01/87	Luton Town	Home	League	0–1		
96	03/01/87	Newcastle United	Away	League	2–1	1 Goal	(23)
97	10/01/87	Bolton Wanderers	Home	FA Cup	3–0	1 Goal	(24)
98	18/01/87	Arsenal	Away	League	0–0		
99	24/01/87	West Ham United	Home	League	1–3		
100	31/01/87	Manchester United	Away	FA Cup	1–0		
101	03/02/87	Southampton	Away	League	0–2		
102	07/02/87	Everton	Away	League	1–3	1 Goal	(25)
103	14/02/87	Chelsea	Home	League	3–0		
104	21/02/87	Stoke City	Away	FA Cup	1–0		
105	28/02/87	Charlton Athletic	Home	League	2–1	1 Goal	(26)
106	07/03/87	Sheffield Wednesday	Home	League	1–0		
107	14/03/87	Sheffield Wednesday	Away	FA Cup	3–0	1 Goal	(27)
108	20/03/87	Oxford United	Home	League	3–0	2 Goals	(29)
109	24/03/87	Wimbledon	Away	League	1–2		
110	28/03/87	Aston Villa	Away	League	0–1		
111	04/04/87	Nottingham Forest	Away	League	0–0		
112	12/04/87	Leeds United	Neutral	FA Cup	3–2*		
113	20/04/87	Queens Park Rangers	Home	League	4–1	2 Goals	(31)
114	25/04/87	Norwich City	Away	League	1–1		
115	30/04/87	Watford	Away	League	3–2		
116	02/05/87	Liverpool	Home	League	1–0		
117	04/05/87	Leicester City	Away	League	1–1		
118	06/05/87	Manchester United	Home	League	1–1		
119	16/05/87	Tottenham Hotspur	Wembley	FA Cup	3–2*		

SEASON 1987–88

League Division One

120	15/08/87	Tottenham Hotspur	Home	League	2–1		
121	22/08/87	Norwich City	Away	League	1–3		
122	29/08/87	Liverpool	Home	League	1–4	1 Goal	(32)
Sub+2	05/09/87	Manchester United	Home	League	0–0		
123	19/09/87	Nottingham Forest	Home	League	0–3		
124	22/09/87	Cambridge United	Away	Lge Cup	1–0		
125	26/09/87	Everton	Away	League	2–1	1 Goal	(33)
126	03/10/87	Watford	Home	League	1–0		
127	06/10/87	Cambridge United	Home	Lge Cup	2–1	1 Goal	(34)
128	17/10/87	Chelsea	Away	League	0–1		
129	24/10/87	Newcastle United	Home	League	1–3	1 Goal	(35)
130	31/10/87	Derby County	Home	League	0–2		
131	07/11/87	Oxford United	Away	League	0–1		
132	14/11/87	Wimbledon	Away	League	3–3		
133	13/12/87	Arsenal	Home	League	0–0		
134	18/12/87	Queens Park Rangers	Away	League	2–1	1 Goal	(36)
135	28/12/87	Nottingham Forest	Away	League	1–4	1 Goal	(37)

136	01/01/88	Liverpool	Away	League	0–4		
137	09/01/88	Torquay United	Home	FA Cup	2–0	1 Goal	(38)
138	13/01/88	Wimbledon	Home	Simod Cup	2–1		
139	16/01/88	Tottenham Hotspur	Away	League	2–2	1 Goal	(39)
140	30/01/88	Watford	Home	FA Cup	0–1		
141	06/02/88	Manchester United	Away	League	0–1		
142	27/02/88	Watford	Away	League	1–0		
143	02/03/88	Reading	Away	Simod Cup	1–1+		
144	05/03/88	Chelsea	Home	League	3–3		
145	12/03/88	Southampton	Away	League	2–1		
146	15/03/88	Luton Town	Home	League	4–0	1 Goal	(40)
147	19/03/88	Derby County	Home	League	0–3		
148	26/03/88	Newcastle United	Away	League	2–2		
149	02/04/88	Oxford United	Home	League	1–0	1 Goal	(41)
150	09/04/88	Charlton Athletic	Home	League	0–0		
151	19/04/88	Everton	Home	League	1–2	1 Goal	(42)
152	23/04/88	West Ham United	Away	League	1–1	1 Goal	(43)
153	30/04/88	Portsmouth	Home	League	1–0		
154	02/05/88	Arsenal	Away	League	1–1		
155	07/05/88	Queens Park Rangers	Home	League	0–0		

+ AET Reading won 4–3 on penalties

SEASON 1988–89

League Division One

156	03/09/88	Everton	Home	League	0–1		
157	10/09/88	Sheffield Wednesday	Away	League	2–1	1 Goal	(44)
158	17/09/88	Charlton Athletic	Home	League	3–0		
159	24/09/88	Wimbledon	Away	League	1–0		
160	27/09/88	AFC Bournemouth	Away	Lge Cup	4–0		
161	01/10/88	Middlesbrough	Home	League	3–4		
162	08/10/88	Newcastle United	Away	League	3–0	1 Goal	(45)
163	11/10/88	AFC Bournemouth	Home	Lge Cup	3–1		
164	15/10/88	Millwall	Home	League	0–0		
165	22/10/88	Liverpool	Away	League	0–0		
166	29/10/88	Arsenal	Away	League	0–2		
167	02/11/88	Nottingham Forest	Away	Lge Cup	2–3		
168	05/11/88	West Ham United	Home	League	1–1		
169	12/11/88	Luton Town	Home	League	1–0		
170	19/11/88	Nottingham Forest	Away	League	0–0		
171	23/11/88	Tottenham Hotspur	Away	League	1–1		
172	26/11/88	Aston Villa	Home	League	2–1	1 Goal	(46)
173	03/12/88	Queens Park Rangers	Away	League	1–2		
174	10/12/88	Manchester United	Home	League	1–0	1 Goal	(47)
175	17/12/88	Derby County	Home	League	0–2		
176	02/01/89	Sheffield Wednesday	Home	League	5–0		
177	07/01/89	Sutton United	Away	FA Cup	1–2		
178	14/01/89	Norwich City	Away	League	2–1		
179	21/01/89	Wimbledon	Home	League	2–1		
180	04/02/89	Middlesbrough	Away	League	1–1	1 Goal	(48)
181	11/02/89	Newcastle United	Home	League	1–2		
182	21/02/89	Arsenal	Home	League	1–0		
183	25/02/89	Millwall	Away	League	0–1		
184	11/03/89	West Ham United	Away	League	1–1		
185	22/03/89	Liverpool	Home	League	1–3		
186	25/03/89	Charlton Athletic	Away	League	0–0		
187	01/04/89	Derby County	Away	League	0–1		
188	08/04/89	Norwich City	Home	League	2–1		
189	15/04/89	Luton Town	Away	League	2–2	1 Goal	(49)
190	22/04/89	Queens Park Rangers	Home	League	0–3		
191	29/04/89	Manchester United	Away	League	1–0		
192	13/05/89	Aston Villa	Away	League	1–1		
193	15/05/89	Nottingham Forest	Home	League	2–2	1 Goal	(50)

SEASON 1989–90

League Division One

194	19/08/89	Everton	Home	League	2–0		
195	22/08/89	Arsenal	Away	League	0–2		
196	26/08/89	Crystal Palace	Away	League	1–0		
197	30/08/89	Manchester City	Home	League	2–1		
198	09/09/89	Millwall	Away	League	1–4		
199	16/09/89	Luton Town	Home	League	1–0		
200	04/10/89	Grimsby Town	Home	Lge Cup	3–0		

201	14/10/89	Nottingham Forest	Home	League	0–2		
202	21/10/89	Manchester United	Home	League	1–4		
203	25/10/89	Queens Park Rangers	Away	Lge Cup	2–1		
204	28/10/89	Charlton Athletic	Away	League	1–1		
205	04/11/89	Liverpool	Away	League	1–0	1 Goal	(51)
206	11/11/89	Southampton	Home	League	1–0		
207	18/11/89	Aston Villa	Away	League	1–4		
208	22/11/89	Manchester United	Away	Lge Cup	1–0	1 Goal	(52)
209	25/11/89	Norwich City	Home	League	1–0	1 Goal	(53)
210	29/11/89	Wimbledon	Home	ZDS Cup	1–3		
211	02/12/89	Everton	Away	League	0–2		
212	09/12/89	Arsenal	Home	League	0–1		
213	16/12/89	Wimbledon	Home	League	2–1		
Sub+3	30/12/89	Derby County	Away	League	1–4		
Sub+4	01/01/90	Tottenham Hotspur	Home	League	0–0		
Sub+5	06/01/90	Northampton Town	Away	FA Cup	0–1		
214	13/01/90	Crystal Palace	Home	League	1–0		
215	17/01/90	Sunderland	Away	Lge Cup	0–0		
216	20/01/90	Manchester City	Away	League	0–1		
217	24/01/90	Sunderland	Home	Lge Cup	5–0		
218	03/02/90	Chelsea	Home	League	3–2	1 Goal	(54)
219	11/02/90	Nottingham Forest	Away	Lge Cup	1–2		
220	17/02/90	Millwall	Home	League	3–1		
221	25/02/90	Nottingham Forest	Home	Lge Cup	0–0		
222	04/03/90	Aston Villa	Home	League	2–0		
223	07/03/90	Luton Town	Away	League	2–3	1 Goal	(55)
224	10/03/90	Nottingham Forest	Away	League	4–2		
225	14/03/90	Norwich City	Away	League	0–0		
226	17/03/90	Sheffield Wednesday	Home	League	1–4		
227	24/03/90	Charlton Athletic	Home	League	1–2		
228	31/03/90	Manchester United	Away	League	0–3		
229	07/04/90	Derby County	Home	League	1–0		
230	14/04/90	Tottenham Hotspur	Away	League	2–3		
231	16/04/90	Queens Park Rangers	Home	League	1–1		
232	21/04/90	Wimbledon	Away	League	0–0		
233	05/05/90	Liverpool	Home	League	1–6		

SEASON 1990–91

League Division One

Sub+6	25/08/90	Manchester United	Away	League	0–2		
Sub+7	01/09/90	Nottingham Forest	Home	League	2–2		
Sub+8	08/09/90	Aston Villa	Away	League	1–2		
234	26/09/90	Bolton Wanderers	Home	Lge Cup	4–2		
235	29/09/90	Queens Park Rangers	Home	League	3–1		
236	06/10/90	Manchester City	Away	League	0–2		
237	09/10/90	Bolton Wanderers	Away	Lge Cup	3–2	2 Goals	(57)
238	20/10/90	Southampton	Home	League	1–2		
239	27/10/90	Sheffield United	Away	League	1–0		
240	31/10/90	Hull City	Home	Lge Cup	3–0	1 Goal	(58)
241	03/11/90	Arsenal	Home	League	0–2		
242	10/11/90	Sunderland	Away	League	0–0		
243	17/11/90	Liverpool	Home	League	0–1		
244	24/11/90	Leeds United	Home	League	1–1		
245	28/11/90	Nottingham Forest	Home	Lge Cup	5–4		
246	01/12/90	Crystal Palace	Away	League	1–2	1 Goal	(59)
247	15/12/90	Manchester United	Home	League	2–2	1 Goal	(60)
248	19/12/90	Derby County	Away	ZDS Cup	0–1		
249	22/12/90	Chelsea	Away	League	1–2		
250	26/12/90	Tottenham Hotspur	Home	League	2–0		
251	29/12/90	Norwich City	Home	League	2–0		
252	01/01/91	Derby County	Away	League	1–1	1 Goal	(61)
253	05/01/91	Wigan Athletic	Home	FA Cup	1–1		
254	09/01/91	Wigan Athletic	Away	FA Cup	1–0		
255	12/01/91	Nottingham Forest	Away	League	0–3		
256	19/01/91	Aston Villa	Home	League	2–1		
257	23/01/91	Sheffield Wednesday	Home	Lge Cup	0–1		
258	26/01/91	Southampton	Home	FA Cup	1–1		
259	29/01/91	Coventry City	Away	FA Cup	0–2		
260	02/02/91	Wimbledon	Away	League	0–1		
261	23/02/91	Sunderland	Home	League	0–0		
262	02/03/91	Crystal Palace	Home	League	3–1		
263	09/03/91	Leeds United	Away	League	0–2		
264	13/03/91	Luton Town	Home	League	2–1		
265	16/03/91	Queens Park Rangers	Away	League	0–1		

266	23/03/91	Manchester City	Home	League	3–1	1 Goal	(62)
267	30/03/91	Tottenham Hotspur	Away	League	2–2		
268	01/04/91	Chelsea	Home	League	1–0		
269	06/04/91	Norwich City	Away	League	2–2		
270	09/04/91	Liverpool	Away	League	1–1		
271	13/04/91	Derby County	Home	League	3–0		
272	20/04/91	Southampton	Away	League	1–2		
273	04/05/91	Sheffield United	Home	League	0–0		
274	11/05/91	Arsenal	Away	League	1–6		

SEASON 1991–92

Aston Villa – League Division One

1	17/08/91	Sheffield Wednesday	Away	League	3–2	1 Goal	(1)
2	21/08/91	Manchester United	Home	League	0–1		
3	24/08/91	Arsenal	Home	League	3–1		
4	28/08/91	West Ham United	Away	League	1–3		
5	31/08/91	Southampton	Away	League	1–1		
6	04/09/91	Crystal Palace	Home	League	0–1		
7	07/09/91	Tottenham Hotspur	Home	League	0–0		
8	14/09/91	Liverpool	Away	League	1–1		
9	18/09/91	Chelsea	Away	League	0–2		
10	21/09/91	Nottingham Forest	Home	League	3–1		
11	25/09/91	Grimsby Town	Away	Lge Cup	0–0		
12	28/09/91	Coventry City	Away	League	0–1		
13	05/10/91	Luton Town	Home	League	4–0	1 Goal	(2)
14	09/10/91	Grimsby Town	Home	Lge Cup	1–1*		
15	19/10/91	Everton	Away	League	2–0	1 Goal	(3)
16	26/10/91	Wimbledon	Home	League	2–1		
17	02/11/91	Queens Park Rangers	Away	League	1–0		
18	16/11/91	Notts County	Home	League	1–0		
19	24/11/91	Leeds United	Home	League	1–4		
20	30/11/91	Oldham Athletic	Away	League	2–3	1 Goal	(4)
21	07/12/91	Manchester City	Home	League	3–1	1 Goal	(5)
22	14/12/91	Sheffield United	Away	League	0–2		
23	26/12/91	West Ham United	Home	League	3–1		
24	28/12/91	Southampton	Home	League	2–1	1 Goal	(6)
25	01/01/92	Norwich City	Away	League	1–2	1 Goal	(7)
26	05/01/92	Tottenham Hotspur	Home	FA Cup	0–0		
27	11/01/92	Arsenal	Away	League	0–0		
28	14/01/92	Tottenham Hotspur	Away	FA Cup	1–0		
29	18/01/92	Sheffield Wednesday	Home	League	0–1		
30	22/01/92	Manchester United	Away	League	0–1		
31	02/02/92	Everton	Home	League	0–0		
32	05/02/92	Derby County	Away	FA Cup	4–3		
33	08/02/92	Wimbledon	Away	League	0–2		
34	16/02/92	Swindon Town	Away	FA Cup	2–1		
35	22/02/92	Oldham Athletic	Home	League	1–0	1 Goal	(8)
36	29/02/92	Manchester City	Away	League	0–2		
37	03/03/92	Leeds United	Away	League	0–0		
38	08/03/92	Liverpool	Away	FA Cup	0–1		
39	14/03/92	Queens Park Rangers	Home	League	0–1		
40	28/03/92	Norwich City	Home	League	1–0		
41	31/03/92	Sheffield United	Home	League	1–1	1 Goal	(9)
42	04/04/92	Tottenham Hotspur	Away	League	5–2	1 Goal	(10)
43	11/04/92	Liverpool	Home	League	1–0		
44	18/04/92	Nottingham Forest	Away	League	0–2		
45	25/04/92	Luton Town	Away	League	0–2		
46	02/05/92	Coventry City	Home	League	2–0	1 Goal	(11)

SEASON 1992–93

Premier League

Sub+1	15/08/92	Ipswich Town	Away	League	1–1		
Sub+2	19/08/92	Leeds United	Home	League	1–1		
Sub+3	25/08/92	Everton	Away	League	0–1		
47	29/08/92	Sheffield United	Away	League	2–0		
48	02/09/92	Chelsea	Home	League	1–3		
Sub+4	21/11/92	Tottenham Hotspur	Away	League	0–0		
Sub+5	28/11/92	Norwich City	Home	League	2–3		
Sub+6	02/12/92	Ipswich Town	Home	Lge Cup	2–2		
49	12/12/92	Nottingham Forest	Home	League	2–1	1 Goal	(12)
50	15/12/92	Ipswich Town	Away	Lge Cup	0–1		
51	26/12/92	Coventry City	Away	League	0–3		
Sub+7	02/01/93	Bristol Rovers	Home	FA Cup	1–1		

Sub+8	20/01/93	Bristol Rovers	Away	FA Cup	3–0		
52	27/02/93	Wimbledon	Home	League	1–0		
Sub+9	10/03/93	Tottenham Hotspur	Home	League	0–0		
53	20/03/93	Sheffield Wednesday	Home	League	2–0		
54	24/03/93	Norwich City	Away	League	0–1		

SEASON 1993–94

Wolverhampton Wanderers – Football League Division One

Sub+1	14/08/93	Bristol City	Home	League	3–1		
Sub+2	22/08/93	Birmingham City	Away	League	2–2		
1	31/08/93	Stoke City	Home	AI Cup	3–3		
Sub+3	05/09/93	West Bromwich Albion	Away	League	2–3		
2	07/09/93	Watford	Away	League	0–1		
3	11/09/93	Portsmouth	Home	League	1–1		
4	17/10/93	Crystal Palace	Away	League	1–1		
5	23/10/93	Stoke City	Home	League	1–1		
Sub+4	30/10/93	Southend United	Away	League	1–1		
Sub+5	05/12/93	Derby County	Home	League	2–2		
Sub+6	28/12/93	Oxford United	Home	League	2–1		
Sub+7	01/01/94	Peterborough United	Away	League	1–0	1 Goal	(1)
Sub+8	03/01/94	Bolton Wanderers	Home	League	1–0		
Sub+9	08/01/94	Crystal Palace	Home	FA Cup	1–0		
Sub+10	29/01/94	Port Vale	Away	FA Cup	2–0		
6	05/02/94	Stoke City	Away	League	1–1		
7	12/02/94	Southend United	Home	League	0–1		
8	19/02/94	Ipswich Town	Away	FA Cup	1–1		
9	22/02/94	Birmingham City	Home	League	3–0	1 Goal	(2)
10	25/02/94	West Bromwich Albion	Home	League	1–2		
Sub+11	02/04/94	Tranmere Rovers	Home	League	2–1		
Sub+12	04/04/94	Oxford United	Away	League	0–4		
Sub+13	09/04/94	Peterborough United	Home	League	1–1		

SEASON 1994–95

Wycombe Wanderers – Football League Division Two

1	13/08/94	Cambridge United	Home	League	3–0		
2	17/08/94	Brighton & Hove Albion	Away	Lge Cup	1–2	1 Goal	(1)
3	20/08/94	Huddersfield Town	Away	League	1–0		
4	23/08/94	Brighton & Hove Albion	Home	Lge Cup	1–3		
5	27/08/94	Bristol Rovers	Home	League	0–0		
6	30/08/94	Birmingham City	Away	League	1–0	1 Goal	(2)
7	03/09/94	Bradford City	Away	League	1–2		
8	10/09/94	Brentford	Home	League	4–3	1 Goal	(3)
9	13/09/94	Hull City	Home	League	1–2		
10	17/09/94	Crewe Alexandra	Away	League	2–1	1 Goal	(4)
11	24/09/94	Stockport County	Away	League	1–4		
12	01/10/94	Swansea City	Home	League	1–0		
13	08/10/94	Leyton Orient	Home	League	2–1	1 Goal	(5)
14	15/10/94	Plymouth Argyle	Away	League	2–2	2 Goals	(7)
15	22/10/94	Peterborough United	Away	League	3–1	1 Goal	(8)
16	29/10/94	York City	Home	League	0–0		
17	01/11/94	Shrewsbury Town	Home	League	1–0	1 Goal	(9)
18	05/11/94	Wrexham	Away	League	1–4		
19	26/12/94	Brighton & Hove Albion	Home	League	0–0		
20	27/12/94	Oxford United	Away	League	2–0		
21	31/12/94	AFC Bournemouth	Home	League	1–1		
22	07/01/95	West Ham United	Home	FA Cup	0–2		
23	14/01/95	Rotherham United	Away	League	0–2		
24	31/01/95	Chester City	Away	League	2–0		
25	04/02/95	Blackpool	Home	League	1–1		
26	11/02/95	Shrewsbury Town	Away	League	2–2		
27	18/02/95	Rotherham United	Home	League	2–0		
28	21/02/95	Cardiff City	Away	League	0–2		
29	25/02/95	Swansea City	Away	League	1–1		
30	04/03/95	Stockport County	Home	League	1–1		
31	11/03/95	Bristol Rovers	Away	League	0–1		
32	14/03/95	York City	Away	League	0–0		
33	18/03/95	Birmingham City	Home	League	0–3		
Sub+1	21/03/95	Brentford	Away	League	0–0		
Sub+2	25/03/95	Crewe Alexandra	Home	League	0–0		
Sub+3	08/04/95	AFC Bournemouth	Away	League	0–2		
Sub+4	19/04/95	Brighton & Hove Albion	Away	League	1–1		
Sub+5	06/05/95	Leyton Orient	Away	League	1–0	1 Goal	(10)

SEASON 1995–96

Chester City – Football League Division Three

1	12/08/95	Hartlepool United	Home	League	2–0		
2	15/08/95	Wigan Athletic	Home	Lge Cup	4–1		
3	19/08/95	Bury	Away	League	1–1		
4	22/08/95	Wigan Athletic	Away	Lge Cup	3–1		
5	26/08/95	Plymouth Argyle	Home	League	3–1	1 Goal	(1)
6	29/08/95	Wigan Athletic	Away	League	1–2		
7	02/09/95	Hereford United	Home	League	2–1	1 Goal	(2)
8	09/09/95	Colchester United	Away	League	2–1	1 Goal	(3)
9	12/09/95	Scunthorpe United	Away	League	2–0		
10	16/09/95	Lincoln City	Home	League	5–1		
11	30/09/95	Preston North End	Away	League	0–2		
12	04/10/95	Tottenham Hotspur	Home	Lge Cup	1–3		
13	07/10/95	Doncaster Rovers	Home	League	0–3		
14	14/10/95	Leyton Orient	Away	League	2–0	1 Goal	(4)
15	21/10/95	Fulham	Home	League	1–1		
16	28/10/95	Scarborough	Away	League	0–0		
17	31/10/95	Rochdale	Away	League	3–1	1 Goal	(5)
18	04/11/95	Torquay United	Home	League	4–1	1 Goal	(6)
19	11/11/95	Blackpool	Away	FA Cup	1–2		
20	18/11/95	Mansfield Town	Away	League	4–3		
21	25/11/95	Darlington	Home	League	4–1		
22	16/12/95	Preston North End	Home	League	1–1		
23	06/01/96	Cambridge United	Away	League	1–1		
24	09/01/96	Gillingham	Away	League	1–3		
25	13/01/96	Bury	Home	League	1–1	1 Goal	(7)
26	20/01/96	Hartlepool United	Away	League	1–2		
27	03/02/96	Plymouth Argyle	Away	League	2–4		
28	17/02/96	Scunthorpe United	Home	League	3–0		
29	20/02/96	Hereford United	Away	League	0–1		
30	16/03/96	Exeter City	Home	League	2–2		
31	19/03/96	Wigan Athletic	Home	League	0–0		
32	26/03/96	Cambridge United	Home	League	1–1		
33	30/03/96	Doncaster Rovers	Away	League	2–1		

INTERNATIONAL APPEARANCES – ENGLAND

Sub 1	23/02/82	Northern Ireland	Wembley	4–0	HC
Sub 2	27/04/82	Wales	Ninian Park	1–0	HC
3	02/06/82	Iceland	Reykjavik	1–1	F
4	13/10/82	West Germany	Wembley	1–2	F
Sub 5	14/10/87	Turkey	Wembley	8–0	ECQ

APPEARANCES AND GOALS PER SEASON

SEASON 77–78	**GAMES**	**GOALS**
League	33+1	10
FA Cup	6	6
League Cup	1+1	2
TOTAL	**40+2**	**18**

SEASON 78–79	**GAMES**	**GOALS**
League	38+1	13
FA Cup	6	1
League Cup	3	0
UEFA Cup	8	4
TOTAL	**55+1**	**18**

SEASON 79–80	**GAMES**	**GOALS**
League	24+2	8
FA Cup	2	1
League Cup	2	0
TOTAL	**28+2**	**9**

SEASON 80–81	**GAMES**	**GOALS**
League	38	14
FA Cup	2	0
League Cup	7	3
TOTAL	**47**	**17**

SEASON 81–82	**GAMES**	**GOALS**
League	37	17
FA Cup	5	2
League Cup	9	6
UEFA Cup	2	0
TOTAL	**53**	**25**

SEASON 82–83	**GAMES**	**GOALS**
League	26	9
FA Cup	1	0
League Cup	2	2
TOTAL	**29**	**11**

SEASON 83–84	**GAMES**	**GOALS**
League	30	10
FA Cup	3	0
League Cup	3	3
TOTAL	**36**	**13**

SEASON 84–85	**GAMES**	**GOALS**
League	37+1	6
FA Cup	1	0
TOTAL	**38+1**	**6**

SEASON 85–86	**GAMES**	**GOALS**
League	34	5
FA Cup	1	0
League Cup	2	5
TOTAL	**37**	**10**

SEASON 86–87	**GAMES**	**GOALS**
League	40	12
FA Cup	6	2
League Cup	5	2
TOTAL	**51**	**16**

SEASON 87–88	**GAMES**	**GOALS**
League	30+1	10
FA Cup	2	1
League Cup	2	1
Simod Cup	2	0
TOTAL	**36+1**	**12**

SEASON 88–89	**GAMES**	**GOALS**
League	34	7
FA Cup	1	0
League Cup	3	0
TOTAL	**38**	**7**

SEASON 89–90	**GAMES**	**GOALS**
League	32+2	4
FA Cup	0+1	0
League Cup	7	1
Zenith Data Systems Cup	1	0
TOTAL	**40+3**	**5**

SEASON 90–91	**GAMES**	**GOALS**
League	31+3	4
FA Cup	4	0
League Cup	5	3
Zenith Data Systems Cup	1	0
TOTAL	**41+3**	**7**

SEASON 91–92	**GAMES**	**GOALS**
League	39	11
FA Cup	5	0
League Cup	2	0
TOTAL	**46**	**11**

SEASON 92–93	**GAMES**	**GOALS**
League	7+6	1
FA Cup	0+2	0
League Cup	1+1	0
TOTAL	**8+9**	**1**

SEASON 93–94	GAMES	GOALS
League	8+11	2
FA Cup	1+2	0
Anglo–Italian Cup	1	0
TOTAL	**10+13**	**2**

SEASON 94–95	GAMES	GOALS
League	30+5	9
FA Cup	1	0
League Cup	2	1
TOTAL	**33+5**	**10**

SEASON 95–96	GAMES	GOALS
League	29	7
FA Cup	1	0
League Cup	3	0
TOTAL	**33**	**7**

CAREER APPEARANCES AND GOALS

COMPETITION	GAMES	TOTAL	GOALS
League	577+33	610	159
FA Cup	48+5	53	13
League Cup	59+2	61	29
Simod Cup	2	2	0
Zenith Data Systems Cup	2	2	0
Anglo–Italian Cup	1	1	0
UEFA Cup	10	10	4
Internationals	2+3	5	0
TOTAL	**701+43**	**744**	**205**

HAT-TRICKS

West Bromwich Albion

1	3	Swansea City	05/09/81	Home	League	4–1
2	3	Birmingham City	31/10/81	Away	League	3–3
3	3	Norwich City	25/09/82	Away	League	3–1

Coventry City

1	5	Chester City	09/10/85	Home	Lge Cup	7–2

League: 3
League Cup: 1
TOTAL: 4

HONOURS

Winners medals
FA Cup: 86/87

Runner-up medals
Premier League Championship: 92/93

ANDY RITCHIE

Born: 28/11/60 – Manchester
Height: 5.10
Weight: 11.10 (96–97)

Clubs
Manchester United: **1977–80** – Matches: **32+10** – Goals: **13**
Brighton & Hove Albion: **1980–83** – Matches: **94+8** – Goals: **26**
Leeds United: **1983–87** – Matches: **149+10** – Goals: **44**
Oldham Athletic: **1987–95** – Matches: **216+34** – Goals: **104**
Scarborough: **1995–97** – Matches: **68+10** – Goals: **20**
Oldham Athletic: **1997** – Matches: **4+6** – Goals: **0**

Country
England: Schools, Youth, Under 21

SEASON 1977–78

Manchester United – League Division One

1	26/12/77	Everton	Away	League	6–2		
2	27/12/77	Leicester City	Home	League	3–1		
3	31/12/77	Coventry City	Away	League	0–3		
4	02/01/78	Birmingham City	Home	League	1–2		

SEASON 1978–79

League Division One

5	09/12/78	Derby County	Away	League	3–1	2 Goals	(2)
6	16/12/78	Tottenham Hotspur	Home	League	2–0	1 Goal	(3)
7	22/12/78	Bolton Wanderers	Away	League	0–3		
8	26/12/78	Liverpool	Home	League	0–3		
9	30/12/78	West Bromwich Albion	Home	League	3–5		
Sub+1	03/02/79	Arsenal	Home	League	0–2		
10	10/02/79	Manchester City	Away	League	3–0	1 Goal	(4)
11	12/02/79	Fulham	Home	FA Cup	1–0		
12	20/02/79	Colchester United	Away	FA Cup	1–0		
13	24/02/79	Aston Villa	Home	League	1–1		
14	28/02/79	Queens Park Rangers	Home	League	2–0		
15	03/03/79	Bristol City	Away	League	2–1	1 Goal	(5)
16	10/03/79	Tottenham Hotspur	Away	FA Cup	1–1		
17	24/03/79	Leeds United	Home	League	4–1	3 Goals	(8)
Sub+2	04/04/79	Liverpool	Neutral	FA Cup	1–0		
18	11/04/79	Bolton Wanderers	Home	League	1–2		
19	14/04/79	Liverpool	Away	League	0–2		
20	16/04/79	Coventry City	Home	League	0–0		
21	28/04/79	Derby County	Home	League	0–0		
22	30/04/79	Southampton	Away	League	1–1	1 Goal	(9)
23	07/05/79	Wolverhampton Wanderers	Home	League	3–2	1 Goal	(10)

SEASON 1979–80

League Division One

Sub+3	22/08/79	West Bromwich Albion	Home	League	2–0		
24	29/08/79	Tottenham Hotspur	Away	Lge Cup	1–2		
Sub+4	05/09/79	Tottenham Hotspur	Home	Lge Cup	3–1		
25	15/09/79	Derby County	Home	League	1–0		
Sub+5	26/09/79	Norwich City	Away	Lge Cup	1–4		
Sub+6	16/02/80	Stoke City	Away	League	1–1		
Sub+7	23/02/80	Bristol City	Home	League	4–0		
Sub+8	07/04/80	Bolton Wanderers	Away	League	3–1		
26	12/04/80	Tottenham Hotspur	Home	League	4–1	3 Goals	(13)
27	19/04/80	Norwich City	Away	League	2–0		
Sub+9	03/05/80	Leeds United	Away	League	0–2		

SEASON 1980–81

League Division One

Sub+10	19/08/80	Wolverhampton Wanderers	Away	League	0–1		
28	23/08/80	Birmingham City	Away	League	0–0		
29	27/08/80	Coventry City	Home	Lge Cup	0–1		
30	30/08/80	Sunderland	Home	League	1–1		
31	02/09/80	Coventry City	Away	Lge Cup	0–1		
32	06/09/80	Tottenham Hotspur	Away	League	0–0		

Brighton & Hove Albion – League Division One

1	22/10/80	Aston Villa	Away	League	1–4		
2	25/10/80	Manchester City	Home	League	1–2		
3	01/11/80	Arsenal	Away	League	0–2		
4	08/11/80	Middlesbrough	Home	League	0–1		
5	11/11/80	Ipswich Town	Home	League	1–0		
6	15/11/80	Wolverhampton Wanderers	Away	League	2–0		
7	22/11/80	Manchester United	Home	League	1–4	1 Goal	(1)
8	29/11/80	Leeds United	Away	League	0–1		
9	06/12/80	Sunderland	Home	League	2–1	1 Goal	(2)
10	13/12/80	Everton	Away	League	3–4	1 Goal	(3)
11	20/12/80	Aston Villa	Home	League	1–0		
12	26/12/80	Leicester City	Away	League	1–0		
13	27/12/80	Crystal Palace	Home	League	3–2		
14	03/01/81	Manchester United	Away	FA Cup	2–2	1 Goal	(4)
15	07/01/81	Manchester United	Home	FA Cup	0–2		
16	10/01/81	Manchester United	Away	League	1–2	1 Goal	(5)

17	17/01/81	West Bromwich Albion	Away	League	0–2		
18	31/01/81	Tottenham Hotspur	Home	League	0–2		
19	07/02/81	Birmingham City	Away	League	1–2		
Sub+1	14/03/81	Nottingham Forest	Away	League	1–4		
20	21/03/81	Stoke City	Home	League	1–1		
Sub+2	28/03/81	Manchester City	Away	League	1–1		
Sub+3	04/04/81	Arsenal	Home	League	0–1		
21	11/04/81	Middlesbrough	Away	League	0–1		
22	18/04/81	Crystal Palace	Away	League	3–0		
23	20/04/81	Leicester City	Home	League	2–1		
24	25/04/81	Sunderland	Away	League	2–1		
25	02/05/81	Leeds United	Home	League	2–0	1 Goal	(6)

SEASON 1981–82

League Division One

26	29/08/81	West Ham United	Away	League	1–1		
27	01/09/81	Swansea City	Home	League	1–2	1 Goal	(7)
28	05/09/81	Middlesbrough	Home	League	2–0		
29	12/09/81	Everton	Away	League	1–1		
30	19/09/81	Coventry City	Home	League	2–2		
31	22/09/81	Wolverhampton Wanderers	Away	League	1–0	1 Goal	(8)
32	26/09/81	Nottingham Forest	Away	League	1–2		
33	03/10/81	Manchester City	Home	League	4–1	2 Goals	(10)
34	10/10/81	West Bromwich Albion	Away	League	0–0		
35	17/10/81	Liverpool	Home	League	3–3	1 Goal	(11)
36	24/10/81	Tottenham Hotspur	Away	League	1–0		
37	27/10/81	Huddersfield Town	Home	Lge Cup	2–0	1 Goal	(12)
38	31/10/81	Stoke City	Home	League	0–0		
39	07/11/81	Birmingham City	Home	League	1–1		
40	10/11/81	Barnsley	Away	Lge Cup	1–4		
Sub+4	05/12/81	Sunderland	Home	League	2–1	1 Goal	(13)
41	08/12/81	Southampton	Away	League	2–0	1 Goal	(14)
42	28/12/81	Aston Villa	Home	League	0–1		
43	02/01/82	Barnet	Away	FA Cup	0–0		
44	05/01/82	Barnet	Home	FA Cup	3–1		
45	16/01/82	West Ham United	Home	League	1–0	1 Goal	(15)
46	23/01/82	Oxford United	Home	FA Cup	0–3		
47	26/01/82	Arsenal	Away	League	0–0		
48	30/01/82	Coventry City	Away	League	1–0	1 Goal	(16)
49	06/02/82	Everton	Home	League	3–1		
50	13/02/82	Manchester City	Away	League	0–4		
51	20/02/82	Nottingham Forest	Home	League	0–1		
52	27/02/82	West Bromwich Albion	Home	League	2–2	1 Goal	(17)
53	02/03/82	Leeds United	Home	League	1–0		
54	06/03/82	Liverpool	Away	League	1–0	1 Goal	(18)
55	09/03/82	Tottenham Hotspur	Home	League	1–3		
56	20/03/82	Stoke City	Away	League	0–0		
57	27/03/82	Birmingham City	Away	League	0–1		
58	30/03/82	Ipswich Town	Away	League	1–3		
59	03/04/82	Southampton	Home	League	1–1		
60	10/04/82	Arsenal	Home	League	2–1	1 Goal	(19)
61	12/04/82	Aston Villa	Away	League	0–3		
62	17/04/82	Notts County	Away	League	1–4		
63	20/04/82	Middlesbrough	Away	League	1–2	1 Goal	(20)
64	24/04/82	Manchester United	Home	League	0–1		
65	01/05/82	Sunderland	Away	League	0–3		
66	04/05/82	Wolverhampton Wanderers	Home	League	2–0		
67	08/05/82	Ipswich Town	Home	League	0–1		
68	15/05/82	Leeds United	Away	League	1–2		

SEASON 1982–83

League Division One

69	28/08/82	Ipswich Town	Home	League	1–1	1 Goal	(21)
70	01/09/82	West Bromwich Albion	Away	League	0–5		
71	04/09/82	Nottingham Forest	Away	League	0–4		
72	07/09/82	Arsenal	Home	League	1–0		
73	11/09/82	Sunderland	Home	League	3–2		
74	18/09/82	Luton Town	Away	League	0–5		
75	25/09/82	Birmingham City	Home	League	1–0		
76	02/10/82	Everton	Away	League	2–2		
77	06/10/82	Tottenham Hotspur	Away	Lge Cup	1–1		
78	09/10/82	Swansea City	Home	League	1–1		
79	16/10/82	Stoke City	Away	League	0–3		

Sub+5	26/10/82	Tottenham Hotspur	Home	Lge Cup	0–1		
Sub+6	27/11/82	Notts County	Home	League	0–2		
80	11/12/82	Norwich City	Home	League	3–0	1 Goal	(22)
81	18/12/82	Manchester City	Away	League	1–1	1 Goal	(23)
82	27/12/82	Southampton	Home	League	0–1		
83	28/12/82	Tottenham Hotspur	Away	League	0–2		
Sub+7	03/01/83	Nottingham Forest	Home	League	1–1		
84	08/01/83	Newcastle United	Home	FA Cup	1–1	1 Goal	(24)
85	12/01/83	Newcastle United	Away	FA Cup	1–0		
86	15/01/83	Ipswich Town	Away	League	0–2		
Sub+8	22/01/83	Luton Town	Home	League	2–4	1 Goal	(25)
87	29/01/83	Manchester City	Home	FA Cup	4–0		
88	05/02/83	Arsenal	Away	League	1–3		
89	12/02/83	West Bromwich Albion	Home	League	0–0		
90	26/02/83	Stoke City	Home	League	1–2	1 Goal	(26)
91	01/03/83	Swansea City	Away	League	2–1		
92	05/03/83	West Ham United	Away	League	1–2		
93	12/03/83	Norwich City	Home	FA Cup	1–0		
94	19/03/83	Manchester United	Away	League	1–1		

Leeds United – League Division Two

1	26/03/83	Crystal Palace	Home	League	2–1	1 Goal	(1)
2	02/04/83	Bolton Wanderers	Away	League	2–1		
3	05/04/83	Oldham Athletic	Home	League	0–0		
4	09/04/83	Burnley	Away	League	2–1	1 Goal	(2)
5	23/04/83	Queens Park Rangers	Away	League	0–1		
6	27/04/83	Sheffield Wednesday	Home	League	1–2	1 Goal	(3)
7	30/04/83	Barnsley	Home	League	0–0		
8	02/05/83	Leicester City	Home	League	2–2		
9	07/05/83	Shrewsbury Town	Away	League	0–0		
10	14/05/83	Rotherham United	Home	League	2–2		

SEASON 1983–84

League Division Two

11	27/08/83	Newcastle United	Home	League	0–1		
12	29/08/83	Brighton & Hove Albion	Home	League	3–2		
13	03/09/83	Middlesbrough	Away	League	2–2		
14	10/09/83	Cardiff City	Home	League	1–0		
15	17/09/83	Fulham	Away	League	1–2	1 Goal	(4)
16	24/09/83	Manchester City	Home	League	1–2	1 Goal	(5)
17	01/10/83	Shrewsbury Town	Away	League	1–5	1 Goal	(6)
18	05/10/83	Chester City	Home	Lge Cup	0–1		
19	08/10/83	Sheffield Wednesday	Away	League	1–3		
20	14/10/83	Cambridge United	Home	League	3–1		
21	22/10/83	Barnsley	Away	League	2–0		
22	26/10/83	Chester City	Away	Lge Cup	4–1	2 Goals	(8)
23	29/10/83	Portsmouth	Home	League	2–1		
24	05/11/83	Crystal Palace	Home	League	1–1		
25	09/11/83	Oxford United	Home	Lge Cup	1–1		
26	12/11/83	Blackburn Rovers	Away	League	1–1		
27	19/11/83	Derby County	Away	League	1–1	1 Goal	(9)
28	23/11/83	Oxford United	Away	Lge Cup	1–4		
29	26/11/83	Chelsea	Home	League	1–1		
30	03/12/83	Carlisle United	Away	League	0–1		
31	15/12/83	Charlton Athletic	Away	League	0–2		
32	26/12/83	Huddersfield Town	Home	League	1–2		
33	27/12/83	Oldham Athletic	Away	League	2–3		
34	31/12/83	Middlesbrough	Home	League	4–1		
35	02/01/84	Manchester City	Away	League	1–1		
36	07/01/84	Scunthorpe United	Home	FA Cup	1–1		
37	10/01/84	Scunthorpe United	Away	FA Cup	1–1*		
38	16/01/84	Scunthorpe United	Away	FA Cup	2–4	1 Goal	(10)
39	21/01/84	Fulham	Home	League	1–0		
40	04/02/84	Shrewsbury Town	Home	League	3–0		
41	11/02/84	Cardiff City	Away	League	1–0		
42	15/02/84	Swansea City	Home	League	1–0		
43	18/02/84	Portsmouth	Away	League	3–2		
44	10/03/84	Blackburn Rovers	Home	League	1–0		
45	17/03/84	Grimsby Town	Home	League	2–1		
46	24/03/84	Brighton & Hove Albion	Away	League	0–3		
47	28/03/84	Newcastle United	Away	League	0–1		
48	31/03/84	Sheffield Wednesday	Home	League	1–1	1 Goal	(11)
49	07/04/84	Cambridge United	Away	League	2–2		
50	14/04/84	Derby County	Home	League	0–0		

51	21/04/84	Huddersfield Town	Away	League	2–2		
52	24/04/84	Oldham Athletic	Home	League	2–0	1 Goal	(12)
53	28/04/84	Chelsea	Away	League	0–5		
54	05/05/84	Carlisle United	Home	League	3–0	1 Goal	(13)
55	07/05/84	Swansea City	Away	League	2–2		

SEASON 1984–85

League Division Two

Sub+1	15/09/84	Portsmouth	Home	League	0–1		
56	22/09/84	Crystal Palace	Away	League	1–3		
57	25/09/84	Gillingham	Away	Lge Cup	2–1	1 Goal	(14)
58	29/09/84	Oldham Athletic	Home	League	6–0	3 Goals	(17)
59	06/10/84	Sheffield United	Home	League	1–1		
60	10/10/84	Gillingham	Home	Lge Cup	3–2		
61	13/10/84	Barnsley	Away	League	0–1		
62	20/10/84	Huddersfield Town	Away	League	0–1		
63	27/10/84	Middlesbrough	Home	League	2–0	1 Goal	(18)
64	31/10/84	Watford	Home	Lge Cup	0–4		
Sub+2	10/11/84	Carlisle United	Home	League	1–1		
65	17/11/84	Brighton & Hove Albion	Home	League	1–0	1 Goal	(19)
66	24/11/84	Oxford United	Away	League	2–5		
67	01/12/84	Wimbledon	Home	League	5–2	3 Goals	(22)
68	08/12/84	Shrewsbury Town	Away	League	3–2	2 Goals	(24)
69	15/12/84	Birmingham City	Home	League	0–1		
70	01/01/85	Manchester City	Home	League	1–1	1 Goal	(25)
71	19/01/85	Notts County	Home	League	5–0		
72	02/02/85	Oldham Athletic	Away	League	1–1		
73	09/02/85	Grimsby Town	Home	League	0–0		
74	23/02/85	Charlton Athletic	Home	League	1–0		
75	26/02/85	Carlisle United	Away	League	2–2		
76	02/03/85	Middlesbrough	Away	League	0–0		
77	09/03/85	Huddersfield Town	Home	League	0–0		
78	12/03/85	Portsmouth	Away	League	1–3		
Sub+3	23/03/85	Sheffield United	Away	League	1–2	1 Goal	(26)
79	30/03/85	Fulham	Away	League	2–0		
80	06/04/85	Blackburn Rovers	Home	League	0–0		
Sub+4	04/05/85	Wimbledon	Away	League	2–2		
Sub+5	06/05/85	Shrewsbury Town	Home	League	1–0		
Sub+6	11/05/85	Birmingham City	Away	League	0–1		

SEASON 1985–86

League Division Two

81	08/10/85	Walsall	Away	Lge Cup	3–0		
82	12/10/85	Middlesbrough	Home	League	1–0		
83	19/10/85	Grimsby Town	Home	League	1–1		
84	27/10/85	Barnsley	Away	League	0–3		
85	30/10/85	Aston Villa	Home	Lge Cup	0–3		
86	02/11/85	Portsmouth	Home	League	2–1		
87	09/11/85	Millwall	Away	League	1–3	1 Goal	(27)
88	16/11/85	Crystal Palace	Home	League	1–3		
89	23/11/85	Carlisle United	Away	League	2–1	1 Goal	(28)
90	30/11/85	Norwich City	Home	League	0–2		
91	07/12/85	Wimbledon	Away	League	3–0		
92	14/12/85	Fulham	Home	League	1–0		
93	22/12/85	Hull City	Away	League	1–2		
94	26/12/85	Blackburn Rovers	Away	League	0–2		
95	28/12/85	Brighton & Hove Albion	Home	League	2–3		
96	01/01/86	Oldham Athletic	Home	League	3–1	1 Goal	(29)
97	04/01/86	Peterborough United	Away	FA Cup	0–1		
98	11/01/86	Sunderland	Away	League	2–4		
99	18/01/86	Charlton Athletic	Away	League	0–4		
100	01/02/86	Stoke City	Home	League	4–0		
101	08/02/86	Grimsby Town	Away	League	0–1		
102	15/02/86	Barnsley	Home	League	0–2		
Sub+7	15/03/86	Middlesbrough	Away	League	2–2		
103	28/03/86	Oldham Athletic	Away	League	1–3	1 Goal	(30)
104	31/03/86	Blackburn Rovers	Home	League	1–1	1 Goal	(31)
105	05/04/86	Portsmouth	Away	League	3–2	2 Goals	(33)
106	09/04/86	Bradford City	Away	League	1–0		
107	12/04/86	Millwall	Home	League	3–1	1 Goal	(34)
108	19/04/86	Crystal Palace	Away	League	0–3		

109	22/04/86	Sheffield United	Away	League	2–3	1 Goal	(35)
110	26/04/86	Carlisle United	Home	League	2–0	2 Goals	(37)
111	03/05/86	Norwich City	Away	League	0–4		

SEASON 1986–87

League Division Two

112	23/08/86	Blackburn Rovers	Away	League	1–2	1 Goal	(38)
113	25/08/86	Stoke City	Home	League	2–1		
114	30/08/86	Sheffield United	Home	League	0–1		
115	02/09/86	Barnsley	Away	League	1–0		
116	06/09/86	Huddersfield Town	Away	League	1–1		
117	13/09/86	Reading	Home	League	3–2	1 Goal	(39)
118	20/09/86	Bradford City	Away	League	0–2		
119	23/09/86	Oldham Athletic	Away	Lge Cup	2–3		
120	27/09/86	Hull City	Home	League	3–0	1 Goal	(40)
121	04/10/86	Plymouth Argyle	Away	League	1–1		
122	08/10/86	Oldham Athletic	Home	Lge Cup	0–1		
123	11/10/86	Crystal Palace	Home	League	3–0		
124	18/10/86	Portsmouth	Home	League	3–1	1 Goal	(41)
125	25/10/86	Grimsby Town	Away	League	0–0		
126	01/11/86	Shrewsbury Town	Home	League	1–0		
127	08/11/86	Millwall	Away	League	0–1		
128	15/11/86	Oldham Athletic	Home	League	0–2		
129	29/11/86	Derby County	Home	League	2–0		
Sub+8	06/12/86	West Bromwich Albion	Away	League	0–3		
Sub+9	21/12/86	Stoke City	Away	League	2–7		
130	26/12/86	Sunderland	Home	League	1–1		
131	27/12/86	Oldham Athletic	Away	League	1–0	1 Goal	(42)
132	01/01/87	Ipswich Town	Away	League	0–2		
133	03/01/87	Huddersfield Town	Home	League	1–1		
134	11/01/87	Telford United	Away	FA Cup	2–1+		
135	24/01/87	Blackburn Rovers	Home	League	0–0		
136	03/02/87	Swindon Town	Away	FA Cup	2–1		
137	21/02/87	Queens Park Rangers	Home	FA Cup	2–1		
138	28/02/87	Bradford City	Home	League	1–0		
139	07/03/87	Grimsby Town	Home	League	2–0	1 Goal	(43)
140	15/03/87	Wigan Athletic	Away	FA Cup	2–0		
141	28/03/87	Plymouth Argyle	Home	League	4–0		
142	04/04/87	Millwall	Home	League	2–0	1 Goal	(44)
143	08/04/87	Hull City	Away	League	0–0		
144	12/04/87	Coventry City	Neutral	FA Cup	2–3*		
145	14/04/87	Shrewsbury Town	Away	League	2–0		
146	18/04/87	Ipswich Town	Home	League	3–2		
147	20/04/87	Sunderland	Away	League	1–1		
148	14/05/87	Oldham Athletic	Home	Lge P/O	1–0		
Sub+10	23/05/87	Charlton Athletic	Away	Lge P/O	0–1		
149	25/05/87	Charlton Athletic	Home	Lge P/O	1–0		

+ Played at The Hawthorns, West Bromwich Albion

SEASON 1987–88

Oldham Athletic – League Division Two

1	15/08/87	West Bromwich Albion	Away	League	0–0		
2	18/08/87	Bradford City	Home	League	0–2		
3	22/08/87	Manchester City	Home	League	1–1		
4	29/08/87	Middlesbrough	Away	League	0–1		
5	31/08/87	Huddersfield Town	Home	League	3–2	2 Goals	(2)
6	05/09/87	Reading	Away	League	0–3		
7	12/09/87	Sheffield United	Home	League	3–2		
8	16/09/87	Leicester City	Away	League	1–4	1 Goal	(3)
9	19/09/87	Hull City	Away	League	0–1		
10	22/09/87	Carlisle United	Away	Lge Cup	3–4	1 Goal	(4)
11	10/10/87	Swindon Town	Away	League	0–2		
12	28/11/87	Plymouth Argyle	Home	League	0–1		
13	05/12/87	AFC Bournemouth	Away	League	2–2		
14	08/12/87	Stoke City	Away	League	2–2		
15	12/12/87	Leicester City	Home	League	2–0		
16	19/12/87	Manchester City	Away	League	2–1		
17	26/12/87	Barnsley	Away	League	1–1		
18	28/12/87	Hull City	Home	League	1–2		
19	01/01/88	Middlesbrough	Home	League	3–1	2 Goals	(6)
20	02/01/88	Sheffield United	Away	League	5–0		
21	09/01/88	Tottenham Hotspur	Home	FA Cup	2–4		

22	16/01/88	West Bromwich Albion	Home	League	2–1	1 Goal	(7)
23	29/01/88	Crystal Palace	Home	League	1–0		
24	06/02/88	Reading	Home	League	4–2	1 Goal	(8)
25	13/02/88	Bradford City	Away	League	3–5	2 Goals	(10)
26	20/02/88	Millwall	Away	League	1–1		
27	05/03/88	Crystal Palace	Away	League	1–3		
28	12/03/88	Swindon Town	Home	League	4–3	2 Goals	(12)
29	19/03/88	Birmingham City	Away	League	3–1	2 Goals	(14)
30	26/03/88	Shrewsbury Town	Home	League	2–2		
31	01/04/88	Blackburn Rovers	Home	League	4–2	2 Goals	(16)
32	04/04/88	Aston Villa	Away	League	2–1		
33	09/04/88	Stoke City	Home	League	5–1	1 Goal	(17)
34	19/04/88	Huddersfield Town	Away	League	2–2	1 Goal	(18)
35	23/04/88	Leeds United	Away	League	1–1		
36	30/04/88	Ipswich Town	Home	League	3–1	1 Goal	(19)
37	02/05/88	Plymouth Argyle	Away	League	0–1		
38	07/05/88	AFC Bournemouth	Home	League	2–0	1 Goal	(20)

SEASON 1988–89

League Division Two

Sub+1	24/09/88	Hull City	Home	League	2–2		
39	26/09/88	Darlington	Away	Lge Cup	0–2		
40	01/10/88	Sunderland	Away	League	2–3		
41	04/10/88	Watford	Away	League	1–3		
42	08/10/88	Stoke City	Home	League	2–2		
43	11/10/88	Darlington	Home	Lge Cup	4–0	1 Goal	(21)
44	15/10/88	Chelsea	Home	League	1–4		
45	05/11/88	Walsall	Home	League	3–0	1 Goal	(22)
46	08/11/88	Everton	Away	Lge Cup	1–1	1 Goal	(23)
47	11/11/88	Shrewsbury Town	Away	League	0–0		
48	19/11/88	Leeds United	Home	League	2–2		
49	26/11/88	Plymouth Argyle	Away	League	0–3		
50	29/11/88	Everton	Home	Lge Cup	0–2		
51	03/12/88	Leicester City	Home	League	1–1	1 Goal	(24)
52	10/12/88	Swindon Town	Away	League	2–2		
53	14/12/88	Middlesbrough	Away	Simod Cup	0–1		
54	16/12/88	Ipswich Town	Away	League	1–2		
55	26/12/88	West Bromwich Albion	Home	League	1–3		
56	30/12/88	Crystal Palace	Home	League	2–3	1 Goal	(25)
57	14/01/89	Manchester City	Home	League	0–1		
58	21/01/89	Barnsley	Away	League	3–4	2 Goals	(27)
59	04/02/89	Watford	Home	League	3–1	2 Goals	(29)
60	11/02/89	Stoke City	Away	League	0–0		
61	18/02/89	Brighton & Hove Albion	Home	League	2–1		
62	25/02/89	Chelsea	Away	League	2–2	1 Goal	(30)
63	28/02/89	AFC Bournemouth	Away	League	2–2		
64	03/03/89	Shrewsbury Town	Home	League	3–0	2 Goals	(32)
65	11/03/89	Walsall	Away	League	2–2		
66	14/03/89	Portsmouth	Home	League	5–3	1 Goal	(33)
67	18/03/89	Oxford United	Away	League	1–1	1 Goal	(34)
68	24/03/89	Blackburn Rovers	Home	League	1–1		
69	27/03/89	West Bromwich Albion	Away	League	1–3	1 Goal	(35)
70	01/04/89	Bradford City	Home	League	1–1		
71	04/04/89	Ipswich Town	Home	League	4–0	1 Goal	(36)
72	08/04/89	Crystal Palace	Away	League	0–2		
73	13/05/89	Swindon Town	Home	League	2–2		

SEASON 1989–90

League Division Two

74	19/08/89	Blackburn Rovers	Away	League	0–1		
75	22/08/89	Watford	Home	League	1–1		
76	26/08/89	Swindon Town	Home	League	2–2		
77	02/09/89	Newcastle United	Away	League	1–2		
78	09/09/89	Plymouth Argyle	Home	League	3–2	1 Goal	(37)
79	16/09/89	Stoke City	Away	League	2–1	1 Goal	(38)
80	19/09/89	Leeds United	Home	Lge Cup	2–1	1 Goal	(39)
81	23/09/89	West Bromwich Albion	Home	League	2–1	2 Goals	(41)
82	26/09/89	Sheffield United	Away	League	1–2		
83	30/09/89	Leicester City	Home	League	1–0		
84	03/10/89	Leeds United	Away	Lge Cup	2–1	1 Goal	(42)
85	07/10/89	Barnsley	Home	League	2–0		
86	14/10/89	AFC Bournemouth	Away	League	0–2		
87	17/10/89	Hull City	Away	League	0–0		

88	21/10/89	Middlesbrough	Home	League	2–0	2 Goals	(44)
89	25/10/89	Scarborough	Home	Lge Cup	7–0	1 Goal	(45)
90	28/10/89	Wolverhampton Wanderers	Away	League	1–1		
91	31/10/89	Bradford City	Home	League	2–2	1 Goal	(46)
92	04/11/89	Sunderland	Home	League	2–1	1 Goal	(47)
93	11/11/89	Oxford United	Away	League	1–0	1 Goal	(48)
94	18/11/89	Brighton & Hove Albion	Home	League	1–1		
95	22/11/89	Arsenal	Home	Lge Cup	3–1	2 Goals	(50)
96	25/11/89	Ipswich Town	Away	League	1–1		
97	28/11/89	Newcastle United	Away	ZDS Cup	0–2		
98	01/12/89	Blackburn Rovers	Home	League	2–0	1 Goal	(51)
99	09/12/89	Watford	Away	League	0–3		
100	16/12/89	West Ham United	Away	League	2–0		
101	26/12/89	Port Vale	Home	League	2–1		
102	30/12/89	Portsmouth	Home	League	3–3		
103	20/01/90	Newcastle United	Home	League	1–1	1 Goal	(52)
104	24/01/90	Southampton	Away	Lge Cup	2–2	2 Goals	(54)
105	27/01/90	Brighton & Hove Albion	Home	FA Cup	2–1	1 Goal	(55)
106	31/01/90	Southampton	Home	Lge Cup	2–1	1 Goal	(56)
107	03/02/90	West Bromwich Albion	Away	League	2–2	1 Goal	(57)
108	10/02/90	Stoke City	Home	League	2–0	1 Goal	(58)
109	14/02/90	West Ham United	Home	Lge Cup	6–0	2 Goals	(60)
110	17/02/90	Everton	Home	FA Cup	2–2	1 Goal	(61)
111	03/03/90	Brighton & Hove Albion	Away	League	1–1		
112	03/04/90	Leicester City	Away	League	0–3		
113	08/04/90	Manchester United	Neutral	FA Cup	3–3*		
114	11/04/90	Manchester United	Neutral	FA Cup	1–2*	1 Goal	(62)
Sub+2	13/04/90	Leeds United	Home	League	3–1		
115	16/04/90	Port Vale	Away	League	0–2		
116	18/04/90	Plymouth Argyle	Away	League	0–2		
117	21/04/90	West Ham United	Home	League	3–0	1 Goal	(63)
118	24/04/90	Portsmouth	Away	League	1–2		
119	29/04/90	Nottingham Forest	Wembley	Lge Cup	0–1		
120	01/05/90	Oxford United	Home	League	4–1		
121	03/05/90	Wolverhampton Wanderers	Home	League	1–1		
122	05/05/90	Sunderland	Away	League	3–2	1 Goal	(64)
123	07/05/90	Bradford City	Away	League	1–1		

SEASON 1990–91

League Division Two

124	25/08/90	Wolverhampton Wanderers	Away	League	3–2		
125	28/08/90	Leicester City	Home	League	2–0	1 Goal	(65)
126	01/09/90	Portsmouth	Home	League	3–1		
127	08/09/90	Barnsley	Away	League	1–0		
128	22/09/90	Middlesbrough	Away	League	1–0		
Sub+3	29/09/90	West Bromwich Albion	Away	League	0–0		
129	02/10/90	Swindon Town	Home	League	3–2		
Sub+4	27/10/90	Notts County	Home	League	2–1	1 Goal	(66)
130	31/10/90	Leeds United	Away	Lge Cup	0–2		
131	03/11/90	Sheffield Wednesday	Away	League	2–2		
132	10/11/90	Watford	Home	League	4–1	2 Goals	(68)
133	17/11/90	Port Vale	Away	League	0–1		
134	24/11/90	Bristol Rovers	Away	League	0–2		
135	01/12/90	Brighton & Hove Albion	Home	League	6–1	1 Goal	(69)
136	15/12/90	Wolverhampton Wanderers	Home	League	4–1	1 Goal	(70)
137	12/01/91	Portsmouth	Away	League	4–1		
138	19/01/91	Barnsley	Home	League	2–0	1 Goal	(71)
139	26/01/91	Notts County	Away	FA Cup	0–2		
140	02/02/91	Oxford United	Away	League	1–5		
141	16/02/91	Port Vale	Home	League	2–0		
142	23/02/91	Watford	Away	League	1–1		
143	02/03/91	Brighton & Hove Albion	Away	League	2–1	2 Goals	(73)
144	09/03/91	Bristol Rovers	Home	League	2–0	1 Goal	(74)
145	12/03/91	Swindon Town	Away	League	2–2	1 Goal	(75)
146	16/03/91	West Bromwich Albion	Home	League	2–1		
147	20/03/91	Hull City	Home	League	1–2	1 Goal	(76)
148	23/03/91	Blackburn Rovers	Away	League	0–2		
149	29/03/91	West Ham United	Home	League	1–1	1 Goal	(77)
150	01/04/91	Plymouth Argyle	Away	League	2–1	1 Goal	(78)
151	06/04/91	Millwall	Home	League	1–1	1 Goal	(79)
152	10/04/91	Leicester City	Away	League	0–0		
153	13/04/91	Newcastle United	Away	League	2–3		
154	16/04/91	Charlton Athletic	Away	League	1–1		

SEASON 1991–92

League Division One

Sub+5	07/09/91	Sheffield United	Home	League	2–1		
Sub+6	14/09/91	Luton Town	Away	League	1–2		
Sub+7	21/09/91	Crystal Palace	Home	League	2–3		
155	24/09/91	Torquay United	Home	Lge Cup	7–1	4 Goals	(83)
156	28/09/91	Manchester City	Away	League	2–1		
157	01/10/91	Everton	Away	ZDS Cup	2–3		
Sub+8	07/12/91	Wimbledon	Away	League	1–2		
158	21/12/91	Chelsea	Away	League	2–4		
159	26/12/91	Manchester United	Home	League	3–6		
Sub+9	18/01/92	Liverpool	Home	League	2–3		
Sub+10	07/03/92	Everton	Away	League	1–2		
Sub+11	10/03/92	Arsenal	Away	League	1–2	1 Goal	(84)
160	14/03/92	Notts County	Home	League	4–3	2 Goals	(86)
161	21/03/92	Coventry City	Away	League	1–1		
162	28/03/92	Sheffield Wednesday	Home	League	3–0		
163	11/04/92	Luton Town	Home	League	5–1		

SEASON 1992–93

Premier League

164	26/01/93	Manchester City	Home	League	0–1		
Sub+12	30/01/93	Nottingham Forest	Away	League	0–2		
165	06/02/93	Chelsea	Home	League	3–1		
166	13/02/93	Leeds United	Away	League	0–2		
167	20/02/93	Arsenal	Home	League	0–1		
168	27/02/93	Everton	Away	League	2–2		
169	22/03/93	Middlesbrough	Away	League	3–2	1 Goal	(87)
170	03/04/93	Wimbledon	Home	League	6–2		
171	13/04/93	Sheffield United	Home	League	1–1	1 Goal	(88)
172	17/04/93	Tottenham Hotspur	Away	League	1–4		
Sub+13	05/05/93	Liverpool	Home	League	3–2		
173	08/05/93	Southampton	Home	League	4–3	1 Goal	(89)

SEASON 1993–94

Premier League

174	14/08/93	Ipswich Town	Home	League	0–3		
Sub+14	21/08/93	Blackburn Rovers	Away	League	0–1		
175	24/08/93	Coventry City	Home	League	3–3	1 Goal	(90)
176	28/08/93	Wimbledon	Home	League	1–1		
Sub+15	30/08/93	Leeds United	Away	League	0–1		
177	11/09/93	Everton	Home	League	0–1		
178	18/09/93	Tottenham Hotspur	Away	League	0–5		
Sub+16	21/09/93	Swansea City	Away	Lge Cup	1–2		
179	25/09/93	Aston Villa	Home	League	1–1		
Sub+17	20/11/93	West Ham United	Away	League	0–2		
180	24/11/93	Sheffield Wednesday	Away	League	0–3		
181	27/11/93	Norwich City	Home	League	2–1		
182	30/11/93	Tranmere Rovers	Away	Lge Cup	0–3		
Sub+18	07/12/93	Swindon Town	Home	League	2–1		
Sub+19	11/12/93	Blackburn Rovers	Home	League	1–2		
Sub+20	18/12/93	Coventry City	Away	League	1–1		
Sub+21	27/12/93	Queens Park Rangers	Away	League	0–2		
183	01/01/94	Sheffield United	Away	League	1–2		
184	08/01/94	Derby County	Home	FA Cup	2–1		
185	15/01/94	Liverpool	Home	League	0–3		
Sub+22	19/02/94	Barnsley	Home	FA Cup	1–0	1 Goal	(91)
186	19/03/94	Aston Villa	Away	League	2–1		
187	26/03/94	Manchester City	Home	League	0–0		
Sub+23	30/03/94	Southampton	Away	League	3–1		
Sub+24	13/04/94	Manchester United	Neutral	FA Cup	1–4		
Sub+25	05/05/94	Tottenham Hotspur	Home	League	0–2		
188	07/05/94	Norwich City	Away	League	1–1		

SEASON 1994–95

Football League Division One

Sub+26	20/08/94	Port Vale	Away	League	1–3		
Sub+27	27/08/94	Burnley	Home	League	3–0	1 Goal	(92)
Sub+28	03/09/94	Southend United	Away	League	0–1		
Sub+29	10/09/94	Reading	Home	League	1–3		

Sub+30	13/09/94	Watford	Home	League	0–2		
189	17/09/94	Derby County	Away	League	1–2		
190	20/09/94	Oxford United	Away	Lge Cup	1–1	1 Goal	(93)
191	24/09/94	Barnsley	Home	League	1–0		
192	01/10/94	Sheffield United	Away	League	0–2		
193	04/10/94	Oxford United	Home	Lge Cup	1–0		
194	01/11/94	Middlesbrough	Away	League	1–2		
Sub+31	09/11/94	Arsenal	Away	Lge Cup	0–2		
195	12/11/94	Luton Town	Home	League	0–0		
196	19/11/94	West Bromwich Albion	Away	League	1–3		
197	26/11/94	Bristol City	Home	League	2–0		
198	04/12/94	Stoke City	Away	League	1–0		
199	10/12/94	Port Vale	Home	League	3–2	3 Goals	(96)
200	17/12/94	Charlton Athletic	Away	League	0–2		
201	26/12/94	Wolverhampton Wanderers	Home	League	4–1	3 Goals	(99)
202	27/12/94	Grimsby Town	Away	League	3–1	1 Goal	(100)
203	31/12/94	Swindon Town	Home	League	1–1		
204	14/01/95	Sunderland	Home	League	0–0		
205	22/01/95	Tranmere Rovers	Away	League	1–3		
206	28/01/95	Leeds United	Away	FA Cup	2–3		
207	04/02/95	Luton Town	Away	League	1–2		
208	18/02/95	Bristol City	Away	League	2–2	1 Goal	(101)
209	21/02/95	West Bromwich Albion	Home	League	1–0		
210	25/02/95	Sheffield United	Home	League	3–3	1 Goal	(102)
211	07/03/95	Southend United	Home	League	0–2		
212	11/03/95	Burnley	Away	League	1–2		
Sub+32	21/03/95	Reading	Away	League	1–2		
Sub+33	25/03/95	Derby County	Home	League	1–0		
Sub+34	05/04/95	Middlesbrough	Home	League	1–0	1 Goal	(103)
213	08/04/95	Swindon Town	Away	League	1–3	1 Goal	(104)
214	15/04/95	Grimsby Town	Home	League	1–0		
215	17/04/95	Wolverhampton Wanderers	Away	League	1–2		
216	22/04/95	Millwall	Home	League	0–1		

SEASON 1995–96

Scarborough – Football League Division Three

1	12/08/95	Doncaster Rovers	Away	League	0–1		
2	15/08/95	Hartlepool United	Home	Lge Cup	1–0		
3	19/08/95	Fulham	Home	League	2–2	1 Goal	(1)
4	22/08/95	Hartlepool United	Away	Lge Cup	0–1+		
5	26/08/95	Exeter City	Away	League	0–2		
6	30/08/95	Leyton Orient	Home	League	2–1		
7	02/09/95	Wigan Athletic	Home	League	0–0		
8	12/09/95	Cardiff City	Away	League	1–2		
9	16/09/95	Hereford United	Home	League	2–2		
10	30/09/95	Torquay United	Home	League	2–1		
11	07/10/95	Preston North End	Away	League	2–3	1 Goal	(2)
12	14/10/95	Lincoln City	Home	League	0–0		
13	21/10/95	Bury	Away	League	2–0		
14	28/10/95	Chester City	Home	League	0–0		
Sub+1	31/10/95	Plymouth Argyle	Home	League	2–2		
15	04/11/95	Cambridge United	Away	League	1–4	1 Goal	(3)
16	11/11/95	Chesterfield	Home	FA Cup	0–2		
17	25/11/95	Scunthorpe United	Away	League	3–3		
18	09/12/95	Darlington	Home	League	1–2		
19	16/12/95	Torquay United	Away	League	0–0		
20	23/12/95	Northampton Town	Home	League	2–1	1 Goal	(4)
21	06/01/96	Hartlepool United	Away	League	1–1		
22	09/01/96	Barnet	Home	League	1–1	1 Goal	(5)
23	13/01/96	Fulham	Away	League	0–1		
24	20/01/96	Doncaster Rovers	Home	League	0–2		
Sub+2	23/01/96	Rochdale	Home	League	1–1		
Sub+3	06/02/96	Colchester United	Away	League	1–1		
Sub+4	20/02/96	Wigan Athletic	Away	League	0–2		
25	24/02/96	Hereford United	Away	League	0–0		
26	27/02/96	Mansfield Town	Home	League	1–1	1 Goal	(6)
27	02/03/96	Hartlepool United	Home	League	1–2		
28	09/03/96	Northampton Town	Away	League	2–0		
29	16/03/96	Colchester United	Home	League	0–0		
30	30/03/96	Preston North End	Home	League	1–2	1 Goal	(7)
31	02/04/96	Lincoln City	Away	League	1–3		
32	06/04/96	Chester City	Away	League	0–5		
33	09/04/96	Bury	Home	League	0–2		

34	13/04/96	Plymouth Argyle	Away	League	1–5	1 Goal	(8)
35	20/04/96	Cambridge United	Home	League	2–0		
36	27/04/96	Scunthorpe United	Home	League	1–4		

+ AET Hartlepool United won 7–6 on penalties

SEASON 1996–97

Football League Division Three

37	17/08/96	Cardiff City	Home	League	0–0		
38	20/08/96	Hull City	Away	Lge Cup	2–2	1 Goal	(9)
39	24/08/96	Exeter City	Away	League	2–2	1 Goal	(10)
40	27/08/96	Scunthorpe United	Away	League	2–0	1 Goal	(11)
41	31/08/96	Northampton Town	Home	League	1–1		
42	03/09/96	Hull City	Home	Lge Cup	3–2		
43	07/09/96	Brighton & Hove Albion	Away	League	2–3	1 Goal	(12)
44	10/09/96	Doncaster Rovers	Home	League	2–1		
Sub+5	25/09/96	Leicester City	Away	Lge Cup	1–2	1 Goal	(13)
45	28/09/96	Wigan Athletic	Home	League	3–1	2 Goals	(15)
46	01/10/96	Barnet	Away	League	3–1	1 Goal	(16)
47	05/10/96	Hereford United	Away	League	2–2	1 Goal	(17)
48	12/10/96	Chester City	Home	League	0–0		
49	15/10/96	Hull City	Home	League	3–2	1 Goal	(18)
50	19/10/96	Lincoln City	Away	League	1–1		
51	26/10/96	Mansfield Town	Home	League	2–1		
52	29/10/96	Leyton Orient	Away	League	1–0		
53	02/11/96	Darlington	Away	League	1–1		
54	09/11/96	Hartlepool United	Home	League	2–4	1 Goal	(19)
55	16/11/96	Shrewsbury Town	Away	FA Cup	1–1	1 Goal	(20)
56	23/11/96	Swansea City	Home	League	0–1		
57	26/11/96	Shrewsbury Town	Home	FA Cup	1–0		
58	30/11/96	Mansfield Town	Away	League	0–2		
59	03/12/96	Colchester United	Home	League	1–1		
60	07/12/96	Chesterfield	Away	FA Cup	0–2		
61	10/12/96	Notts County	Home	AW Shield	0–1		
62	14/12/96	Torquay United	Away	League	0–1		
63	21/12 96	Fulham	Home	League	0–2		
Sub+6	26/12/96	Doncaster Rovers	Away	League	2–1		
64	28/12/96	Brighton & Hove Albion	Home	League	1–1		
65	14/01/97	Cambridge United	Home	League	1–0		
66	18/01/97	Barnet	Home	League	1–1		
67	25/01/97	Leyton Orient	Home	League	2–1		
68	01/02/97	Hartlepool United	Away	League	0–1		
Sub+7	04/02/97	Rochdale	Away	League	3–3		
Sub+8	08/02/97	Darlington	Home	League	4–1		
Sub+9	11/02/97	Carlisle United	Away	League	0–1		
Sub+10	15/02/97	Swansea City	Away	League	2–1		

Oldham Athletic – Football League Division One

Sub+1	22/02/97	Bradford City	Home	League	1–2		
Sub+2	04/03/97	Tranmere Rovers	Home	League	1–2		
Sub+3	15/03/97	Wolverhampton Wanderers	Home	League	3–2		
Sub+4	23/03/97	Crystal Palace	Home	League	0–1		
Sub+5	29/03/97	Stoke City	Away	League	1–2		
1	31/03/97	Swindon Town	Home	League	5–1		
2	05/04/97	Ipswich Town	Away	League	0–4		
3	08/04/97	Birmingham City	Home	League	2–2		
4	26/04/97	Reading	Away	League	0–2		
Sub+6	04/05/97	Norwich City	Home	League	3–0		

APPEARANCES AND GOALS PER SEASON

SEASON 77–88	GAMES	GOALS
League	4	0
TOTAL	**4**	**0**

SEASON 78–79	GAMES	GOALS
League	16+1	10
FA Cup	3+1	0
TOTAL	**19+2**	**10**

SEASON 79–80	GAMES	GOALS
League	3+5	3
League Cup	1+2	0
TOTAL	**4+7**	**3**

SEASON 80–81	GAMES	GOALS
League	26+4	5
FA Cup	2	1
League Cup	2	0
TOTAL	**30+4**	**6**

SEASON 81–82	GAMES	GOALS
League	38+1	13
FA Cup	3	0
League Cup	2	1
TOTAL	**43+1**	**14**

SEASON 82–83	GAMES	GOALS
League	31+3	8
FA Cup	4	1
League Cup	1+1	0
TOTAL	**36+4**	**9**

SEASON 83–84	GAMES	GOALS
League	38	7
FA Cup	3	1
League Cup	4	2
TOTAL	**45**	**10**

SEASON 84–85	GAMES	GOALS
League	22+6	12
League Cup	3	1
TOTAL	**25+6**	**13**

SEASON 85–86	GAMES	GOALS
League	28+1	11
FA Cup	1	0
League Cup	2	0
TOTAL	**31+1**	**11**

SEASON 86–87	GAMES	GOALS
League	29+2	7
League Play–offs	2+1	0
FA Cup	5	0
League Cup	2	0
TOTAL	**38+3**	**7**

SEASON 87–88	GAMES	GOALS
League	36	19
FA Cup	1	0
League Cup	1	1
TOTAL	**38**	**20**

SEASON 88–89	GAMES	GOALS
League	30+1	14
League Cup	4	2
Simod Cup	1	0
TOTAL	**35+1**	**16**

SEASON 89–90	GAMES	GOALS
League	37+1	15
FA Cup	4	3
League Cup	8	10
Zenith Data Systems Cup	1	0
TOTAL	**50+1**	**28**

SEASON 90–91	GAMES	GOALS
League	29+2	15
FA Cup	1	0
League Cup	1	0
TOTAL	**31+2**	**15**

SEASON 91–92	GAMES	GOALS
League	7+7	3
League Cup	1	4
Zenith Data Systems Cup	1	0
TOTAL	**9+7**	**7**

SEASON 92–93	GAMES	GOALS
League	10+2	3
TOTAL	**10+2**	**3**

SEASON 93–94	GAMES	GOALS
League	13+9	1
FA Cup	1+2	1
League Cup	1+1	0
TOTAL	**15+12**	**2**

SEASON 94–95	GAMES	GOALS
League	25+8	12
FA Cup	1	0
League Cup	2+1	1
TOTAL	**28+9**	**13**

SEASON 95–96	GAMES	GOALS
League	33+4	8
FA Cup	1	0
League Cup	2	0
TOTAL	**36+4**	**8**

SEASON 96–97	GAMES	GOALS
League	30+11	9
FA Cup	3	1
League Cup	2+1	2
Auto Windscreens Shield	1	0
TOTAL	**36+12**	**12**

CAREER APPEARANCES AND GOALS

COMPETITION	GAMES	TOTAL	GOALS
League	485+68	553	175
League Play–offs	2+1	3	0
FA Cup	33+3	36	8
League Cup	39+6	45	24
Simod Cup	1	1	0
Zenith Data Systems Cup	2	2	0
Auto Windscreens Shield	1	1	0
TOTAL	**563+78**	**641**	**207**

HAT-TRICKS

Manchester United

1	3	Leeds United	24/03/79	Home	League	4–1
2	3	Tottenham Hotspur	12/04/80	Home	League	4–1

Leeds United

1	3	Oldham Athletic	29/09/84	Home	League	6–0
2	3	Wimbledon	01/12/84	Home	League	5–2

Oldham Athletic

1	4	Torquay United	24/09/91	Home	Lge Cup	7–1
2	3	Port Vale	10/12/94	Home	League	3–2
3	3	Wolverhampton Wanderers	26/12/94	Home	League	4–1

League: 6
League Cup: 1
TOTAL: 7

HONOURS

Winners medals
League Division Two Championship: 90/91

Runner-up medals
League Cup: 89/90

JOHN ROBERTSON

Born: 02/10/64 – Edinburgh
Height: 5.7
Weight: 11.06 (96–97)

Clubs
Heart of Midlothian: **1981–88** – Matches: **235+18** – Goals: **129**
Newcastle United: **1988** – Matches: **9+7** – Goals: **0**
Heart of Midlothian: **1988–97** – Matches: **313+41** – Goals: **136**

Country
Scotland: **1990–95** – Matches: **8+8** – Goals: **3**

SEASON 1981–82

Heart of Midlothian – Scottish League Division One

| Sub+1 | 17/02/82 | Queen of the South | Home | League | 4–1 | | |

SEASON 1982–83

Scottish League Division One

Sub+2	01/09/82	Clyde	Home	S Lge Cup	3–0		
Sub+3	09/10/82	Alloa	Home	League	3–0	1 Goal	(1)
Sub+4	16/10/82	Hamilton Academical	Away	League	3–1		
Sub+5	23/10/82	Dunfermline Athletic	Away	League	4–1		
Sub+6	30/10/82	Partick Thistle	Away	League	1–1	1 Goal	(2)
1	06/11/82	Airdrieonians	Home	League	2–4		
2	10/11/82	Rangers	Home	S Lge Cup	1–2		
3	13/11/82	Clydebank	Away	League	3–0	1 Goal	(3)
4	20/11/82	Falkirk	Home	League	3–1	2 Goals	(5)
5	27/11/82	Dumbarton	Away	League	1–1		
6	04/12/82	Raith Rovers	Home	League	2–0		
7	28/01/83	Queen of the South	Away	S Cup	1–1		
8	09/02/83	Dunfermline Athletic	Away	League	1–2		
9	20/02/83	East Fife	Home	S Cup	2–1		
10	26/02/83	Queen's Park	Away	League	3–0	3 Goals	(8)
11	05/03/83	Falkirk	Home	League	1–2		
12	12/03/83	Celtic	Away	S Cup	1–4		
13	19/03/83	Partick Thistle	Home	League	4–0	3 Goals	(11)
14	26/03/83	Clyde	Home	League	3–1	1 Goal	(12)
15	29/03/83	Raith Rovers	Away	League	2–4		
16	02/04/83	Airdrieonians	Away	League	2–0	1 Goal	(13)
17	06/04/83	Queen's Park	Home	League	2–0	1 Goal	(14)
18	09/04/83	St Johnstone	Away	League	1–2		
19	16/04/83	Clydebank	Home	League	2–2	2 Goals	(16)
20	23/04/83	Alloa	Away	League	1–1		
21	30/04/83	Dunfermline Athletic	Home	League	3–3	3 Goals	(19)
22	07/05/83	Dumbarton	Away	League	4–0	2 Goals	(21)
23	14/05/83	Hamilton Academical	Home	League	2–0		

SEASON 1983–84

Scottish League Premier Division

24	20/08/83	St Johnstone	Away	League	1–0		
25	24/08/83	Cowdenbeath	Away	S Lge Cup	0–0		
26	27/08/83	Cowdenbeath	Home	S Lge Cup	1–1+		
27	31/08/83	St Mirren	Away	S Lge Cup	2–2	1 Goal	(22)
28	03/09/83	Hibernian	Home	League	3–2	2 Goals	(24)
29	10/09/83	Rangers	Home	League	3–1	1 Goal	(25)
30	17/09/83	Dundee	Away	League	2–1	1 Goal	(26)
31	24/09/83	St Mirren	Away	League	1–0		
32	01/10/83	Aberdeen	Home	League	0–2		
33	05/10/83	Clydebank	Home	S Lge Cup	1–1		
34	08/10/83	Motherwell	Home	League	0–0		
35	15/10/83	Celtic	Away	League	1–1		
36	22/10/83	Dundee United	Away	League	0–1		
Sub+7	26/10/83	Rangers	Away	S Lge Cup	0–2		
37	29/10/83	St Johnstone	Home	League	2–0	2 Goals	(28)

38	05/11/83	Hibernian	Away	League	1–1	1 Goal	(29)
Sub+8	09/11/83	St Mirren	Home	S Lge Cup	3–1	1 Goal	(30)
39	13/11/83	Dundee	Home	League	1–3		
40	19/11/83	Aberdeen	Away	League	0–2		
41	26/11/83	St Mirren	Home	League	2–2		
42	30/11/83	Clydebank	Away	S Lge Cup	3–0	2 Goals	(32)
43	03/12/83	Rangers	Away	League	0–3		
44	10/12/83	Dundee United	Home	League	0–0		
45	17/12/83	Celtic	Home	League	1–3	1 Goal	(33)
46	26/12/83	Motherwell	Away	League	1–1		
Sub+9	31/12/83	St Johnstone	Away	League	2–1		
47	02/01/84	Hibernian	Home	League	1–1		
48	07/01/84	Dundee	Away	League	1–4	1 Goal	(34)
49	06/02/84	Partick Thistle	Home	S Cup	2–0		
50	11/02/84	Rangers	Home	League	2–2	1 Goal	(35)
51	18/02/84	Dundee United	Away	S Cup	1–2	1 Goal	(36)
52	25/02/84	Celtic	Away	League	1–4		
53	03/03/84	Motherwell	Home	League	2–1	2 Goals	(38)
54	11/03/84	Dundee United	Away	League	1–3		
55	17/03/84	St Mirren	Away	League	1–1		
56	24/03/84	St Mirren	Home	League	2–1	1 Goal	(39)
57	31/03/84	Dundee United	Home	League	0–0		
58	02/04/84	Aberdeen	Away	League	1–1	1 Goal	(40)
59	07/04/84	Rangers	Away	League	0–0		
60	28/04/84	St Johnstone	Home	League	2–2		
61	02/05/84	Aberdeen	Home	League	0–1		
62	05/05/84	Celtic	Home	League	1–1		
63	09/05/84	Dundee	Home	League	1–1		
64	12/05/84	Motherwell	Away	League	1–0	1 Goal	(41)

+ AET Heart of Midlothian won 4–2 on penalties

SEASON 1984–85

Scottish League Premier Division

65	11/08/84	Dundee United	Away	League	0–2		
66	18/08/84	Morton	Home	League	1–2		
67	22/08/84	East Stirling	Home	S Lge Cup	4–0		
68	25/08/84	Hibernian	Away	League	2–1		
69	29/08/84	Ayr United	Home	S Lge Cup	1–0		
70	01/09/84	Dumbarton	Home	League	1–0		
71	04/09/84	Dundee	Away	S Lge Cup	1–0		
72	08/09/84	St Mirren	Home	League	1–2	1 Goal	(42)
73	15/09/84	Celtic	Away	League	0–1		
74	19/09/84	Paris Saint–Germain FC	Away	UEFA Cup	0–4		
75	26/09/84	Dundee United	Home	S Lge Cup	1–2	1 Goal	(43)
76	29/09/84	Aberdeen	Away	League	0–4		
77	03/10/84	Paris Saint–Germain FC	Home	UEFA Cup	2–2	2 Goals	(45)
78	06/10/84	Rangers	Home	League	1–0	1 Goal	(46)
79	10/10/84	Dundee United	Away	S Lge Cup	1–3		
80	13/10/84	Dundee United	Home	League	2–0	1 Goal	(47)
81	20/10/84	Morton	Away	League	3–2	1 Goal	(48)
82	27/10/84	Hibernian	Home	League	0–0		
83	03/11/84	Dumbarton	Away	League	1–0		
84	24/11/84	Dundee	Away	League	1–2		
85	01/12/84	Aberdeen	Home	League	1–2		
86	08/12/84	Rangers	Away	League	1–1		
87	15/12/84	Dundee United	Away	League	2–5		
88	29/12/84	Morton	Home	League	1–0		
89	01/01/85	Hibernian	Away	League	2–1		
90	05/01/85	Dumbarton	Home	League	5–1		
91	12/01/85	St Mirren	Home	League	0–1		
92	30/01/85	Inverness Caledonian	Home	S Cup	6–0	1 Goal	(49)
93	03/02/85	Dundee	Home	League	3–3	1 Goal	(50)
94	09/02/85	Aberdeen	Away	League	2–2	1 Goal	(51)
95	16/02/85	Brechin City	Away	S Cup	1–1	1 Goal	(52)
96	20/02/85	Brechin City	Home	S Cup	1–0		
97	23/02/85	Rangers	Home	League	2–0		
98	02/03/85	Morton	Away	League	1–0		
99	09/03/85	Aberdeen	Home	S Cup	1–1		
100	13/03/85	Aberdeen	Away	S Cup	0–1		
101	16/03/85	Dundee United	Home	League	0–1		
102	20/03/85	Celtic	Away	League	2–3	1 Goal	(53)
103	23/03/85	Dumbarton	Away	League	3–1		
104	02/04/85	Hibernian	Home	League	2–2	1 Goal	(54)

105	06/04/85	Celtic	Home	League	0–2		
106	20/04/85	Dundee	Away	League	0–3		
107	27/04/85	Rangers	Away	League	1–3		
108	04/05/85	Aberdeen	Home	League	0–3		
109	11/05/85	St Mirren	Away	League	2–5		

SEASON 1985–86

Scottish League Premier Division

110	10/08/85	Celtic	Home	League	1–1		
111	17/08/85	St Mirren	Away	League	2–6	1 Goal	(55)
112	20/08/85	Montrose	Away	S Lge Cup	3–1	1 Goal	(56)
113	24/08/85	Rangers	Away	League	1–3	1 Goal	(57)
114	27/08/85	Stirling Albion	Home	S Lge Cup	2–1*		
115	31/08/85	Hibernian	Home	League	2–1		
116	04/09/85	Aberdeen	Away	S Lge Cup	0–1		
Sub+10	14/09/85	Dundee United	Home	League	2–0	1 Goal	(58)
117	21/09/85	Motherwell	Away	League	1–2		
118	28/09/85	Clydebank	Away	League	0–1		
119	05/10/85	Dundee	Home	League	1–1		
120	12/10/85	Celtic	Away	League	1–0	1 Goal	(59)
121	19/10/85	St Mirren	Home	League	3–0	2 Goals	(61)
122	30/10/85	Aberdeen	Home	League	1–0		
123	02/11/85	Dundee United	Away	League	1–1		
124	09/11/85	Hibernian	Away	League	0–0		
125	16/11/85	Rangers	Home	League	3–0	1 Goal	(62)
126	23/11/85	Motherwell	Home	League	3–0		
127	30/11/85	Clydebank	Home	League	4–1	1 Goal	(63)
128	07/12/85	Dundee	Away	League	1–1		
129	14/12/85	Celtic	Home	League	1–1	1 Goal	(64)
130	21/12/85	St Mirren	Away	League	1–0		
131	28/12/85	Rangers	Away	League	2–0		
132	01/01/86	Hibernian	Home	League	3–1	1 Goal	(65)
133	04/01/86	Motherwell	Away	League	3–1	1 Goal	(66)
134	11/01/86	Dundee United	Home	League	1–1		
135	18/01/86	Aberdeen	Away	League	1–0		
136	25/01/86	Rangers	Home	S Cup	3–2	1 Goal	(67)
137	01/02/86	Clydebank	Away	League	1–1		
138	08/02/86	Dundee	Home	League	3–1	1 Goal	(68)
139	22/02/86	Celtic	Away	League	1–1	1 Goal	(69)
140	03/03/86	Hamilton Academical	Away	S Cup	2–1	1 Goal	(70)
141	09/03/86	St Mirren	Home	S Cup	4–1	2 Goals	(72)
142	15/03/86	Motherwell	Home	League	2–0	1 Goal	(73)
143	22/03/86	Hibernian	Away	League	2–1	1 Goal	(74)
144	25/03/86	St Mirren	Home	League	3–0	1 Goal	(75)
145	29/03/86	Rangers	Home	League	3–1	2 Goals	(77)
146	05/04/86	Dundee United	Hampden	S Cup	1–0		
147	12/04/86	Dundee United	Away	League	3–0	2 Goals	(79)
148	20/04/86	Aberdeen	Home	League	1–1		
149	26/04/86	Clydebank	Home	League	1–0		
150	03/05/86	Dundee	Away	League	0–2		
151	10/05/86	Aberdeen	Hampden	S Cup	0–3		

SEASON 1986–87

Scottish League Premier Division

152	09/08/86	St Mirren	Away	League	0–0		
153	13/08/86	Hamilton Academical	Home	League	1–0	1 Goal	(80)
154	16/08/86	Falkirk	Home	League	1–0		
155	19/08/86	Montrose	Home	S Lge Cup	0–2		
Sub+11	23/08/86	Dundee United	Away	League	0–1		
156	30/08/86	Hibernian	Away	League	3–1	1 Goal	(81)
157	06/09/86	Clydebank	Home	League	2–1		
Sub+12	13/09/86	Aberdeen	Away	League	1–0		
Sub+13	17/09/86	FC Dukla Praha	Home	UEFA Cup	3–2	1 Goal	(82)
Sub+14	20/09/86	Motherwell	Home	League	4–0	1 Goal	(83)
158	27/09/86	Dundee	Away	League	0–0		
Sub+15	01/10/86	FC Dukla Praha	Away	UEFA Cup	0–1		
159	04/10/86	Rangers	Home	League	1–1		
160	08/10/86	Celtic	Away	League	0–2		
Sub+16	11/10/86	St Mirren	Home	League	0–0		
Sub+17	18/10/86	Hamilton Academical	Away	League	3–1		
Sub+18	15/11/86	Aberdeen	Home	League	2–1	1 Goal	(84)
161	19/11/86	Motherwell	Away	League	3–2		
162	22/11/86	Dundee	Home	League	3–1	1 Goal	(85)

163	29/11/86	Rangers	Away	League	0–3		
164	03/12/86	Celtic	Home	League	1–0		
165	06/12/86	St Mirren	Away	League	0–0		
166	13/12/86	Hamilton Academical	Home	League	7–0	2 Goals	(87)
167	20/12/86	Dundee United	Away	League	1–3	1 Goal	(88)
168	27/12/86	Falkirk	Home	League	4–0	2 Goals	(90)
169	03/01/87	Clydebank	Home	League	3–0	1 Goal	(91)
170	06/01/87	Hibernian	Away	League	2–2		
171	21/01/87	Aberdeen	Away	League	1–2		
172	24/01/87	Dundee	Away	League	1–0		
173	31/01/87	Kilmarnock	Home	S Cup	0–0		
174	04/02/87	Kilmarnock	Away	S Cup	1–1*		
175	07/02/87	Rangers	Home	League	2–5	2 Goals	(93)
176	09/02/87	Kilmarnock	Away	S Cup	3–1		
177	14/02/87	Celtic	Away	League	1–1		
178	21/02/87	Celtic	Home	S Cup	1–0	1 Goal	(94)
179	25/02/87	Motherwell	Home	League	1–1	1 Goal	(95)
180	28/02/87	St Mirren	Home	League	1–0		
181	07/03/87	Hamilton Academical	Away	League	1–0		
182	14/03/87	Motherwell	Home	S Cup	1–1	1 Goal	(96)
183	17/03/87	Motherwell	Away	S Cup	1–0		
184	21/03/87	Falkirk	Away	League	0–0		
185	18/04/87	Aberdeen	Home	League	1–1		
186	25/04/87	Rangers	Away	League	0–3		
187	02/05/87	Dundee	Home	League	1–3		
188	09/05/87	Celtic	Home	League	1–0	1 Goal	(97)
189	11/05/87	Dundee United	Home	League	1–1	1 Goal	(98)

SEASON 1987–88

Scottish League Premier Division

190	08/08/87	Falkirk	Home	League	4–2	2 Goals	(100)
191	12/08/87	Celtic	Away	League	0–1		
192	15/08/87	St Mirren	Away	League	1–1	1 Goal	(101)
193	19/08/87	Kilmarnock	Home	S Lge Cup	6–1		
194	22/08/87	Dundee United	Home	League	4–1	1 Goal	(102)
195	25/08/87	Clyde	Home	S Lge Cup	2–0	2 Goals	(104)
196	29/08/87	Hibernian	Home	League	1–0	1 Goal	(105)
197	02/09/87	Rangers	Away	S Lge Cup	1–4	1 Goal	(106)
198	05/09/87	Morton	Away	League	2–1	1 Goal	(107)
199	12/09/87	Motherwell	Home	League	1–0		
200	19/09/87	Dundee	Home	League	3–1	1 Goal	(108)
201	26/09/87	Dunfermline Athletic	Away	League	1–0		
202	03/10/87	Rangers	Home	League	0–0		
203	07/10/87	Aberdeen	Home	League	2–1	1 Goal	(109)
204	10/10/87	Falkirk	Away	League	5–1	1 Goal	(110)
205	17/10/87	Hibernian	Away	League	1–2	1 Goal	(111)
206	24/10/87	Morton	Home	League	3–0		
207	27/10/87	Motherwell	Away	League	3–0	1 Goal	(112)
208	31/10/87	Dundee	Home	League	4–2	2 Goals	(114)
209	07/11/87	Celtic	Home	League	1–1		
210	14/11/87	Aberdeen	Away	League	0–0		
211	18/11/87	Dundee United	Away	League	3–0	2 Goals	(116)
212	21/11/87	St Mirren	Home	League	0–0		
213	24/11/87	Dunfermline Athletic	Home	League	3–2	1 Goal	(117)
214	28/11/87	Rangers	Away	League	2–3	1 Goal	(118)
215	05/12/87	Falkirk	Home	League	1–0	1 Goal	(119)
216	12/12/87	Celtic	Away	League	2–2	1 Goal	(120)
217	16/12/87	Motherwell	Home	League	1–1		
218	19/12/87	Dundee	Away	League	0–0		
219	26/12/87	Morton	Away	League	0–0		
220	02/01/88	Hibernian	Home	League	0–0		
221	09/01/88	Dunfermline Athletic	Away	League	4–0	2 Goals	(122)
222	16/01/88	Rangers	Home	League	1–1		
223	30/01/88	Falkirk	Away	S Cup	3–1	2 Goals	(124)
224	03/02/88	Dundee United	Away	League	1–1		
225	06/02/88	St Mirren	Away	League	6–0	2 Goals	(126)
226	13/02/88	Aberdeen	Home	League	2–2	1 Goal	(127)
227	20/02/88	Morton	Home	S Cup	2–0		
228	27/02/88	Falkirk	Away	League	0–2		
229	08/03/88	Motherwell	Away	League	2–0	1 Goal	(128)
230	12/03/88	Dunfermline Athletic	Home	S Cup	3–0		
231	19/03/88	Hibernian	Away	League	0–0		
232	26/03/88	Morton	Home	League	2–0		
233	30/03/88	Dundee	Home	League	2–0		

234	02/04/88	Rangers	Away	League	2–1	1 Goal	(129)
235	09/04/88	Celtic	Hampden	S Cup	1–2		

SEASON 1988–89

Newcastle United – League Division One

1	27/08/88	Everton	Away	League	0–4		
2	29/08/88	Wimbledon	Home	MCC Trophy	1–0		
3	03/09/88	Tottenham Hotspur	Home	League	2–2		
4	10/09/88	Derby County	Away	League	0–2		
5	17/09/88	Norwich City	Home	League	0–2		
6	21/09/88	Manchester United	Away	MCC Trophy	0–2*		
7	24/09/88	Charlton Athletic	Away	League	2–2		
Sub+1	27/09/88	Sheffield United	Away	Lge Cup	0–3		
Sub+2	01/10/88	Liverpool	Away	League	2–1		
Sub+3	08/10/88	Coventry City	Home	League	0–3		
Sub+4	12/10/88	Sheffield United	Home	Lge Cup	2–0		
Sub+5	22/10/88	West Ham United	Away	League	0–2		
Sub+6	26/10/88	Middlesbrough	Home	League	3–0		
Sub+7	29/10/88	Nottingham Forest	Home	League	0–1		
8	05/11/88	Queens Park Rangers	Away	League	0–3		
9	12/11/88	Arsenal	Home	League	0–1		

Heart of Midlothian – Scottish League Premier Division

1	10/12/88	Rangers	Home	League	2–0		
2	17/12/88	Hamilton Academical	Home	League	2–0		
3	31/12/88	Celtic	Away	League	2–4	2 Goals	(2)
4	04/01/89	Hibernian	Away	League	0–1		
5	07/01/89	St Mirren	Home	League	2–0		
6	21/01/89	Dundee United	Away	League	0–0		
7	28/01/89	Ayr United	Home	S Cup	4–1		
8	11/02/89	Dundee	Home	League	3–1		
9	18/02/89	Partick Thistle	Home	S Cup	2–0		
10	25/02/89	Aberdeen	Away	League	0–3		
Sub+1	11/03/89	Celtic	Home	League	0–1		
Sub+2	15/03/89	FC Bayern Munchen	Away	UEFA Cup	0–2		
Sub+3	18/03/89	Celtic	Away	S Cup	1–2		
Sub+4	25/03/89	Hamilton Academical	Away	League	2–0		
Sub+5	01/04/89	Hibernian	Home	League	2–1	1 Goal	(3)
Sub+6	08/04/89	St Mirren	Away	League	1–1	1 Goal	(4)
Sub+7	15/04/89	Dundee	Away	League	1–2		
Sub+8	22/04/89	Aberdeen	Home	League	1–0		
Sub+9	29/04/89	Rangers	Away	League	0–4		

SEASON 1989–90

Scottish League Premier Division

Sub+10	30/08/89	Celtic	Home	S Lge Cup	2–2+	1 Goal	(5)
Sub+11	09/09/89	Dundee	Away	League	2–2		
11	16/09/89	Motherwell	Away	League	3–1	1 Goal	(6)
12	23/09/89	Dundee United	Home	League	1–1		
13	30/09/89	Rangers	Away	League	0–1		
14	04/10/89	Dunfermline Athletic	Home	League	1–2		
Sub+12	14/10/89	Aberdeen	Away	League	3–1		
Sub+13	21/10/89	Celtic	Away	League	1–2		
Sub+14	28/10/89	St Mirren	Home	League	4–0	2 Goals	(8)
Sub+15	04/11/89	Hibernian	Away	League	1–1		
15	11/11/89	Dundee	Home	League	6–3	1 Goal	(9)
16	25/11/89	Dundee United	Away	League	1–2		
Sub+16	02/12/89	Rangers	Home	League	1–2		
17	09/12/89	Dunfermline Athletic	Away	League	2–0	2 Goals	(11)
18	20/12/89	Aberdeen	Home	League	1–1	1 Goal	(12)
19	26/12/89	Celtic	Home	League	0–0		
20	30/12/89	St Mirren	Away	League	0–2		
21	01/01/90	Hibernian	Home	League	2–0	2 Goals	(14)
22	06/01/90	Dundee	Away	League	1–0		
23	13/01/90	Motherwell	Away	League	3–0	2 Goals	(16)
24	20/01/90	Falkirk	Home	S Cup	2–0	2 Goals	(18)
25	27/01/90	Dundee United	Home	League	3–2	1 Goal	(19)
26	03/02/90	Aberdeen	Away	League	2–2		
27	10/02/90	Dunfermline Athletic	Home	League	0–2		
28	17/02/90	Rangers	Away	League	0–0		
29	24/02/90	Motherwell	Home	S Cup	4–0	2 Goals	(21)
30	03/03/90	Motherwell	Home	League	2–0	1 Goal	(22)
31	10/03/90	Celtic	Away	League	1–1	1 Goal	(23)

32	17/03/90	Aberdeen	Away	S Cup	1–4		
33	24/03/90	St Mirren	Home	League	0–0		
34	31/03/90	Hibernian	Away	League	2–1	2 Goals	(25)
35	04/04/90	Dundee	Home	League	0–0		
36	14/04/90	Dunfermline Athletic	Away	League	1–0		
37	21/04/90	Aberdeen	Home	League	1–0		
Sub+17	28/04/90	Dundee United	Away	League	1–1		
38	05/05/90	Rangers	Home	League	1–1	1 Goal	(26)

+ AET Celtic won 3–1 on penalties

SEASON 1990–91

Scottish League Premier Division

39	22/08/90	Cowdenbeath	Away	S Lge Cup	2–0	1 Goal	(27)
40	25/08/90	St Mirren	Home	League	1–1	1 Goal	(28)
41	29/08/90	St Mirren	Away	S Lge Cup	1–0*		
42	01/09/90	Dunfermline Athletic	Away	League	0–2		
43	05/09/90	Aberdeen	Away	S Lge Cup	0–3		
44	08/09/90	Rangers	Home	League	1–3		
45	15/09/90	Hibernian	Away	League	3–0	2 Goals	(30)
46	18/09/90	Dnepr Dnepropetrovsk	Away	UEFA Cup	1–1	1 Goal	(31)
47	22/09/90	Celtic	Away	League	0–3		
48	03/10/90	Dnepr Dnepropetrovsk	Home	UEFA Cup	3–1	2 Goals	(33)
49	06/10/90	Motherwell	Away	League	1–1		
50	13/10/90	St Johnstone	Home	League	2–3		
51	20/10/90	Aberdeen	Away	League	0–3		
52	07/11/90	FC Bologna	Away	UEFA Cup	0–3		
53	10/11/90	Celtic	Home	League	1–0		
54	17/11/90	Dundee United	Away	League	1–1		
55	24/11/90	Hibernian	Home	League	1–1		
56	08/12/90	Aberdeen	Home	League	1–0		
57	15/12/90	St Johnstone	Away	League	1–2		
58	22/12/90	Motherwell	Home	League	3–2	1 Goal	(34)
59	29/12/90	Celtic	Away	League	1–1		
60	02/01/91	Hibernian	Away	League	4–1		
61	05/01/91	Rangers	Home	League	0–1		
62	22/01/91	St Mirren	Home	League	2–0	2 Goals	(36)
63	26/01/91	Airdrieonians	Away	S Cup	1–2		
64	02/02/91	Aberdeen	Away	League	0–5		
65	16/02/91	Dundee United	Home	League	2–1	1 Goal	(37)
66	23/02/91	Dunfermline Athletic	Away	League	1–3		
67	02/03/91	Motherwell	Away	League	3–1	1 Goal	(38)
68	06/03/91	St Johnstone	Home	League	2–1		
69	09/03/91	Rangers	Away	League	1–2		
70	23/03/91	Hibernian	Home	League	3–1	1 Goal	(39)
71	30/03/91	St Mirren	Away	League	0–0		
72	06/04/91	Dunfermline Athletic	Home	League	4–1	2 Goals	(41)
73	13/04/91	Aberdeen	Home	League	1–4		
74	27/04/91	Celtic	Home	League	0–1		
75	04/05/91	Dundee United	Away	League	1–2		
76	11/05/91	Motherwell	Home	League	2–1	1 Goal	(42)

SEASON 1991–92

Scottish League Premier Division

77	10/08/91	Dunfermline Athletic	Away	League	2–1	1 Goal	(43)
78	13/08/91	Airdrieonians	Away	League	3–2	2 Goals	(45)
79	17/08/91	Rangers	Home	League	1–0		
80	20/08/91	Clydebank	Home	S Lge Cup	3–0	1 Goal	(46)
81	24/08/91	St Johnstone	Away	League	1–0		
82	28/08/91	Hamilton Academical	Away	S Lge Cup	2–0	1 Goal	(47)
83	31/08/91	Hibernian	Home	League	0–0		
84	04/09/91	Rangers	Home	S Lge Cup	0–1		
85	07/09/91	Motherwell	Home	League	2–0		
86	14/09/91	St Mirren	Away	League	3–2		
87	21/09/91	Dundee United	Home	League	1–1		
88	28/09/91	Falkirk	Away	League	2–1		
89	05/10/91	Celtic	Away	League	1–3	1 Goal	(48)
90	09/10/91	Aberdeen	Home	League	1–0		
91	12/10/91	Dunfermline Athletic	Home	League	1–0		
92	19/10/91	Rangers	Away	League	0–2		
93	26/10/91	Motherwell	Away	League	1–0		
94	30/10/91	St Mirren	Home	League	0–0		
95	02/11/91	Hibernian	Away	League	1–1	1 Goal	(49)
96	09/11/91	St Johnstone	Home	League	2–1		

97	16/11/91	Celtic	Home	League	3–1		
98	20/11/91	Aberdeen	Away	League	2–0	1 Goal	(50)
99	23/11/91	Dundee United	Away	League	1–0	1 Goal	(51)
100	30/11/91	Airdrieonians	Home	League	1–0		
101	04/12/91	Falkirk	Home	League	1–1		
102	07/12/91	Dunfermline Athletic	Away	League	2–0		
103	14/12/91	Motherwell	Home	League	3–1		
104	21/12/91	St Mirren	Away	League	1–0		
105	28/12/91	St Johnstone	Away	League	5–0	2 Goals	(53)
106	01/01/92	Hibernian	Home	League	1–1		
107	04/01/92	Celtic	Away	League	2–1		
108	11/01/92	Aberdeen	Home	League	0–4		
109	18/01/92	Airdrieonians	Away	League	1–2	1 Goal	(54)
110	25/01/92	St Mirren	Away	S Cup	0–0		
111	01/02/92	Rangers	Home	League	0–1		
112	05/02/92	St Mirren	Home	S Cup	3–0	3 Goals	(57)
113	08/02/92	Dundee United	Home	League	1–0		
114	15/02/92	Dunfermline Athletic	Away	S Cup	2–1		
115	29/02/92	Celtic	Home	League	1–2	1 Goal	(58)
116	04/03/92	Falkirk	Away	League	2–1		
117	08/03/92	Falkirk	Home	S Cup	3–1	1 Goal	(59)
118	14/03/92	St Johnstone	Home	League	2–0		
119	18/03/92	Aberdeen	Away	League	0–2		
120	21/03/92	Hibernian	Away	League	2–1		
121	28/03/92	Dunfermline Athletic	Home	League	1–0	1 Goal	(60)
122	04/04/92	Airdrieonians	Hampden	S Cup	0–0		
123	07/04/92	Motherwell	Away	League	1–0	1 Goal	(61)
124	11/04/92	St Mirren	Home	League	0–0		
125	14/04/92	Airdrieonians	Hampden	S Cup	1–1+		
126	28/04/92	Rangers	Away	League	1–1	1 Goal	(62)
127	02/05/92	Falkirk	Home	League	2–0		

+ AET Airdrieonians won 4–2 on penalties

SEASON 1992–93

Scottish League Premier Division

Sub+18	01/08/92	Celtic	Home	League	0–1		
128	05/08/92	Falkirk	Home	League	3–0	2 Goals	(64)
129	08/08/92	Dundee United	Away	League	1–1		
130	12/08/92	Clydebank	Home	S Lge Cup	1–0		
131	15/08/92	Partick Thistle	Home	League	2–1		
132	19/08/92	Brechin City	Away	S Lge Cup	2–1*	1 Goal	(65)
133	22/08/92	Hibernian	Away	League	0–0		
134	26/08/92	Celtic	Home	S Lge Cup	1–2		
135	29/08/92	Motherwell	Home	League	1–0		
136	01/09/92	Dundee	Away	League	3–1	1 Goal	(66)
137	12/09/92	Aberdeen	Home	League	1–0	1 Goal	(67)
138	16/09/92	SK Slavia Praha	Away	UEFA Cup	0–1		
139	30/09/92	SK Slavia Praha	Home	UEFA Cup	4–0		
140	03/10/92	St Johnstone	Home	League	1–1	1 Goal	(68)
141	07/10/92	Celtic	Away	League	1–1		
142	17/10/92	Dundee United	Home	League	1–0		
143	21/10/92	Standard Club Liege	Home	UEFA Cup	0–1		
144	24/10/92	Motherwell	Away	League	3–1	1 Goal	(69)
145	31/10/92	Dundee	Home	League	1–0		
146	04/11/92	Standard Club Liege	Away	UEFA Cup	0–1		
147	07/11/92	Hibernian	Home	League	1–0		
148	10/11/92	Partick Thistle	Away	League	1–1		
149	21/11/92	Rangers	Home	League	1–1		
150	28/11/92	Aberdeen	Away	League	2–6		
151	02/12/92	Falkirk	Away	League	1–2	1 Goal	(70)
152	05/12/92	Airdrieonians	Home	League	1–3		
153	12/12/92	St Johnstone	Away	League	1–1		
154	19/12/92	Celtic	Home	League	1 0		
155	26/12/92	Partick Thistle	Home	League	1–1		
156	02/01/93	Hibernian	Away	League	0–0		
157	09/01/93	Huntly	Home	S Cup	6–0	1 Goal	(71)
158	20/01/93	St Johnstone	Home	League	2–0	1 Goal	(72)
159	23/01/93	Motherwell	Home	League	0–0		
160	30/01/93	Dundee United	Away	League	1–0	1 Goal	(73)
161	03/02/93	Dundee	Away	League	0–1		
162	06/02/93	Dundee	Home	S Cup	2–0	1 Goal	(74)
163	13/02/93	Falkirk	Home	League	3–1		
164	20/02/93	Airdrieonians	Away	League	0–0		

165	27/02/93	Rangers	Away	League	1–2		
166	06/03/93	Falkirk	Home	S Cup	2–0	1 Goal	(75)
167	10/03/93	Celtic	Away	League	0–1		
168	13/03/93	Dundee United	Home	League	1–0		
169	20/03/93	Hibernian	Home	League	1–0	1 Goal	(76)
170	27/03/93	Partick Thistle	Away	League	1–1		
171	03/04/93	Rangers	Neutral	S Cup	1–2		
172	10/04/93	Dundee	Home	League	0–0		
173	14/04/93	Rangers	Home	League	2–3	1 Goal	(77)
174	17/04/93	Aberdeen	Away	League	2–3		
175	20/04/93	Motherwell	Away	League	1–2		
176	01/05/93	Falkirk	Away	League	0–6		
177	05/05/93	Aberdeen	Home	League	1–2		
178	08/05/93	Airdrieonians	Home	League	1–1		
179	15/05/93	St Johnstone	Away	League	1–3		

SEASON 1993–94

Scottish League Premier Division

180	07/08/93	Rangers	Away	League	1–2		
181	11/08/93	Stranraer	Home	S Lge Cup	2–0	2 Goals	(79)
182	14/08/93	Raith Rovers	Home	League	1–0	1 Goal	(80)
183	21/08/93	Hibernian	Home	League	1–0		
184	25/08/93	Falkirk	Home	S Lge Cup	0–1		
185	11/09/93	Motherwell	Away	League	0–2		
186	14/09/93	Atletico Madrid	Home	UEFA Cup	2–1	1 Goal	(81)
187	18/09/93	Kilmarnock	Home	League	0–1		
188	25/09/93	Celtic	Home	League	1–0	1 Goal	(82)
189	28/09/93	Atletico Madrid	Away	UEFA Cup	0–3		
190	02/10/93	Dundee	Away	League	0–2		
191	09/10/93	St Johnstone	Home	League	1–1	1 Goal	(83)
192	16/10/93	Raith Rovers	Away	League	0–1		
193	30/10/93	Hibernian	Away	League	2–0		
194	03/11/93	Rangers	Home	League	2–2		
195	06/11/93	Dundee United	Home	League	1–1		
196	13/11/93	Dundee	Home	League	1–2		
197	30/11/93	Kilmarnock	Away	League	0–0		
198	04/12/93	Aberdeen	Home	League	1–1		
199	11/12/93	St Johnstone	Away	League	0–2		
Sub+19	27/12/93	Rangers	Away	League	2–2	1 Goal	(84)
Sub+20	08/01/94	Dundee United	Away	League	0–3		
200	12/01/94	Hibernian	Home	League	1–1		
201	15/01/94	Partick Thistle	Home	League	1–0		
202	22/01/94	Kilmarnock	Home	League	1–1	1 Goal	(85)
203	29/01/94	Partick Thistle	Away	S Cup	1–0		
204	05/02/94	Motherwell	Away	League	1–1	1 Goal	(86)
205	12/02/94	Celtic	Home	League	0–2		
206	20/02/94	Hibernian	Away	S Cup	2–1	1 Goal	(87)
Sub+21	05/03/94	Aberdeen	Away	League	1–0		
Sub+22	12/03/94	Rangers	Away	S Cup	0–2		
Sub+23	19/03/94	Raith Rovers	Away	League	2–2		
207	26/03/94	Rangers	Home	League	1–2		
208	30/03/94	Motherwell	Home	League	0–0		
209	02/04/94	Kilmarnock	Away	League	1–0		
210	06/04/94	St Johnstone	Home	League	2–2	1 Goal	(88)
211	09/04/94	Celtic	Away	League	2–2		
212	16/04/94	Dundee	Home	League	0–2		
213	23/04/94	St Johnstone	Away	League	0–0		
214	27/04/94	Aberdeen	Home	League	1–1	1 Goal	(89)
215	30/04/94	Hibernian	Away	League	0–0		
216	07/05/94	Dundee United	Home	League	2–0		
217	14/05/94	Partick Thistle	Away	League	1–0		

SEASON 1994–95

Scottish League Premier Division

218	13/08/94	Aberdeen	Away	League	1–3		
219	16/08/94	Dumbarton	Away	S Lge Cup	4–0	1 Goal	(90)
220	20/08/94	Motherwell	Away	League	1–1		
221	27/08/94	Hibernian	Home	League	0–1		
222	31/08/94	St Johnstone	Home	S Lge Cup	2–4		
223	11/09/94	Rangers	Away	League	0–3		
224	17/09/94	Dundee United	Home	League	2–1		
225	24/09/94	Kilmarnock	Home	League	3–0		
226	01/10/94	Falkirk	Away	League	1–2	1 Goal	(91)

227	08/10/94	Partick Thistle	Away	League	1–0	1 Goal	(92)
228	15/10/94	Celtic	Home	League	1–0	1 Goal	(93)
229	22/10/94	Aberdeen	Home	League	2–0	1 Goal	(94)
230	29/10/94	Hibernian	Away	League	1–2	1 Goal	(95)
231	05/11/94	Motherwell	Home	League	1–2	1 Goal	(96)
232	09/11/94	Rangers	Home	League	1–1		
233	19/11/94	Dundee United	Away	League	2–5		
234	26/11/94	Kilmarnock	Away	League	1–3	1 Goal	(97)
235	03/12/94	Falkirk	Home	League	1–1		
236	26/12/94	Partick Thistle	Home	League	3–0	1 Goal	(98)
237	31/12/94	Aberdeen	Away	League	1–3		
Sub+24	08/01/95	Motherwell	Away	League	2–1		
Sub+25	11/01/95	Celtic	Away	League	1–1		
238	14/01/95	Dundee United	Home	League	2–0		
239	18/01/95	Hibernian	Home	League	2–0		
Sub+26	21/01/95	Rangers	Away	League	0–1		
240	01/02/95	Clydebank	Away	S Cup	1–1	1 Goal	(99)
241	04/02/95	Falkirk	Away	League	0–2		
242	07/02/95	Clydebank	Home	S Cup	2–1	1 Goal	(100)
243	11/02/95	Kilmarnock	Home	League	2–2		
244	20/02/95	Rangers	Home	S Cup	4–2	1 Goal	(101)
245	12/03/95	Dundee United	Home	S Cup	2–1		
246	18/03/95	Rangers	Home	League	2–1	1 Goal	(102)
247	01/04/95	Falkirk	Home	League	0–1		
248	04/04/95	Partick Thistle	Away	League	1–3		
249	08/04/95	Airdrieonians	Neutral	S Cup	0–1		
Sub+27	29/04/95	Aberdeen	Home	League	1–2		
250	06/05/95	Hibernian	Away	League	1–3		
251	13/05/95	Motherwell	Home	League	2–0	1 Goal	(103)

SEASON 1995–96

Scottish League Premier Division

252	30/08/95	Dunfermline Athletic	Home	S Lge Cup	2–1		
253	09/09/95	Falkirk	Home	League	4–1	1 Goal	(104)
254	16/09/95	Partick Thistle	Away	League	0–2		
255	20/09/95	Dundee	Away	S Lge Cup	4–4+	1 Goal	(105)
256	23/09/95	Celtic	Home	League	0–4		
257	01/10/95	Hibernian	Away	League	2–2	1 Goal	(106)
258	04/10/95	Aberdeen	Home	League	1–2	1 Goal	(107)
259	07/10/95	Kilmarnock	Away	League	1–3		
260	14/10/95	Raith Rovers	Home	League	4–2	1 Goal	(108)
261	21/10/95	Rangers	Away	League	1–4		
262	28/10/95	Falkirk	Away	League	0–2		
263	04/11/95	Partick Thistle	Home	League	3–0		
264	07/11/95	Motherwell	Away	League	0–0		
265	11/11/95	Kilmarnock	Home	League	2–1	1 Goal	(109)
266	19/11/95	Hibernian	Home	League	2–1	1 Goal	(110)
267	02/12/95	Rangers	Home	League	0–2		
268	09/12/95	Raith Rovers	Away	League	1–1	1 Goal	(111)
269	16/12/95	Aberdeen	Away	League	2–1		
270	01/01/96	Hibernian	Away	League	1–2		
Sub+28	06/01/96	Partick Thistle	Away	League	1–0		
271	10/01/96	Motherwell	Home	League	4–0		
272	13/01/96	Falkirk	Home	League	2–1	1 Goal	(112)
273	17/01/96	Celtic	Home	League	1–2	1 Goal	(113)
Sub+29	20/01/96	Rangers	Away	League	3–0		
274	31/01/96	Partick Thistle	Home	S Cup	1–0		
275	03/02/96	Raith Rovers	Home	League	2–0	1 Goal	(114)
276	10/02/96	Aberdeen	Home	League	1–3	1 Goal	(115)
Sub+30	17/02/96	Kilmarnock	Away	S Cup	2–1		
277	24/02/96	Kilmarnock	Away	League	2–0	1 Goal	(116)
Sub+31	02/03/96	Celtic	Away	League	0–4		
278	07/03/96	St Johnstone	Away	S Cup	2–1		
279	16/03/96	Hibernian	Home	League	1–1		
Sub+32	23/03/96	Partick Thistle	Home	League	2–5		
Sub+33	06/04/96	Aberdeen	Hampden	S Cup	2–1	1 Goal	(117)
280	10/04/96	Rangers	Home	League	2–0		
281	13/04/96	Raith Rovers	Away	League	3–1		
282	20/04/96	Aberdeen	Away	League	1–1		
283	27/04/96	Kilmarnock	Home	League	1–0		
Sub+34	04/05/96	Motherwell	Away	League	1–1		
Sub+35	18/05/96	Rangers	Hampden	S Cup	1–5		

+ AET Dundee won 5–4 on penalties

SEASON 1996–97

Scottish League Premier Division

284	14/08/96	Stenhousemuir	Home	S Lge Cup	1–1+			
Sub+36	22/08/96	Crvena Zvezda Beograd	Home	ECW Cup	1–1			
Sub+37	03/09/96	St Johnstone	Away	S Lge Cup	3–1*	1 Goal	(118)
285	07/09/96	Dundee United	Home	League	1–0	1 Goal	(119)
286	10/09/96	Dunfermline Athletic	Away	League	1–2			
287	14/09/96	Rangers	Away	League	0–3			
288	17/09/96	Celtic	Home	S Lge Cup	1–0*	1 Goal	(120)
Sub+38	21/09/96	Motherwell	Home	League	1–1			
289	28/09/96	Hibernian	Away	League	3–1	1 Goal	(121)
290	12/10/96	Raith Rovers	Away	League	1–1	1 Goal	(122)
291	20/10/96	Celtic	Home	League	2–2			
292	23/10/96	Dundee	Neutral	S Lge Cup	3–1			
293	11/11/96	Motherwell	Away	League	2–0	1 Goal	(123)
294	16/11/96	Hibernian	Home	League	0–0			
295	24/11/96	Rangers	Neutral	S Lge Cup	3–4	1 Goal	(124)
296	30/11/96	Celtic	Away	League	2–2			
297	07/12/96	Raith Rovers	Home	League	0–0			
298	11/12/96	Aberdeen	Home	League	1–2			
299	21/12/96	Rangers	Home	League	1–4	1 Goal	(125)
300	26/12/96	Dunfermline Athletic	Away	League	3–2	1 Goal	(126)
301	28/12/96	Motherwell	Home	League	4–1	2 Goals	(128)
302	01/01/97	Hibernian	Away	League	4–0	1 Goal	(129)
303	04/01/97	Raith Rovers	Away	League	2–1	1 Goal	(130)
304	11/01/97	Celtic	Home	League	1–2			
305	18/01/97	Dundee United	Home	League	1–2	1 Goal	(131)
306	25/01/97	Cowdenbeath	Home	S Cup	5–0	2 Goals	(133)
307	01/02/97	Rangers	Away	League	0–0			
Sub+39	16/02/97	Dundee United	Home	S Cup	1–1			
308	22/02/97	Raith Rovers	Home	League	3–2			
Sub+40	25/02/97	Dundee United	Away	S Cup	0–1			
309	01/03/97	Celtic	Away	League	0–2			
310	15/03/97	Hibernian	Home	League	1–0			
Sub+41	12/04/97	Aberdeen	Home	League	0–0			
311	19/04/97	Dunfermline Athletic	Home	League	1–1	1 Goal	(134)
312	03/05/97	Dundee United	Away	League	0–1			
313	10/05/97	Rangers	Home	League	3–1	2 Goals	(136)

+ AET Heart of Midlothian won 5–4 on penalties

INTERNATIONAL APPEARANCES – SCOTLAND

1	12/09/90	Romania	Hampden Park	2–1	ECQ	1 Goal	(1)
2	17/10/90	Switzerland	Hampden Park	2–1	ECQ	1 Goal	(2)
Sub 3	27/03/91	Bulgaria	Hampden Park	1–1	ECQ		
Sub 4	01/05/91	San Marino	Serravalle	2–0	ECQ		
5	13/11/91	San Marino	Hampden Park	4–0	ECQ		
Sub 6	19/02/92	Northern Ireland	Hampden Park	1–0	F		
7	25/03/92	Finland	Hampden Park	1–1	F		
Sub 8	18/11/92	Italy	Ibrox Park	0–0	WCQ		
Sub 9	17/02/93	Malta	Ibrox Park	3–0	WCQ		
10	24/03/93	Germany	Ibrox Park	0–1	F		
11	19/05/93	Estonia	Tallinn	3–0	WCQ		
Sub 12	21/05/95	Japan	Hiroshima	0–0	KC		
13	24/05/95	Ecuador	Toyama	2–1	KC	1 Goal	(3)
Sub 14	07/06/95	Faroe Islands	Toftir	2–0	ECQ		
Sub 15	16/08/95	Greece	Hampden Park	1–0	ECQ		
16	11/10/95	Sweden	Stockholm	0–2	F		

APPEARANCES AND GOALS PER SEASON

SEASON 81–82	**GAMES**	**GOALS**
Scottish League	0+1	0
TOTAL	**0+1**	**0**

SEASON 82–83	**GAMES**	**GOALS**
Scottish League	19+4	21
Scottish Cup	3	0
Scottish League Cup	1+1	0
TOTAL	**23+5**	**21**

SEASON 83–84	GAMES	GOALS
Scottish League	34+1	15
Scottish Cup	2	1
Scottish League Cup	5+2	4
TOTAL	**41+3**	**20**

SEASON 84–85	GAMES	GOALS
Scottish League	33	8
Scottish Cup	5	2
Scottish League Cup	5	1
UEFA Cup	2	2
TOTAL	**45**	**13**

SEASON 85–86	GAMES	GOALS
Scottish League	34+1	20
Scottish Cup	5	4
Scottish League Cup	3	1
TOTAL	**42+1**	**25**

SEASON 86–87	GAMES	GOALS
Scottish League	31+6	16
Scottish Cup	6	2
Scottish League Cup	1	0
UEFA Cup	0+2	1
TOTAL	**38+8**	**19**

SEASON 87–88	GAMES	GOALS
Scottish League	39	26
Scottish Cup	4	2
Scottish League Cup	3	3
TOTAL	**46**	**31**

SEASON 88–89	GAMES	GOALS
League	7+5	0
League Cup	0+2	0
Mercantile Credit Centenary Trophy	2	0
Scottish League	8+7	4
Scottish Cup	2+1	0
UEFA Cup	0+1	0
TOTAL	**19+16**	**4**

SEASON 89–90	GAMES	GOALS
Scottish League	25+7	17
Scottish Cup	3	4
Scottish League Cup	0+1	1
TOTAL	**28+8**	**22**

SEASON 90–91	GAMES	GOALS
Scottish League	31	12
Scottish Cup	1	0
Scottish League Cup	3	1
UEFA Cup	3	3
TOTAL	**38**	**16**

SEASON 91–92	GAMES	GOALS
Scottish League	42	14
Scottish Cup	6	4
Scottish League Cup	3	2
TOTAL	**51**	**20**

SEASON 92–93	GAMES	GOALS
Scottish League	41+1	11
Scottish Cup	4	3
Scottish League Cup	3	1
UEFA Cup	4	0
TOTAL	**52+1**	**15**

SEASON 93–94	GAMES	GOALS
Scottish League	32+4	8
Scottish Cup	2+1	1
Scottish League Cup	2	2
UEFA Cup	2	1
TOTAL	**38+5**	**12**

SEASON 94–95	GAMES	GOALS
Scottish League	27+4	10
Scottish Cup	5	3
Scottish League Cup	2	1
TOTAL	**34+4**	**14**

SEASON 95–96	GAMES	GOALS
Scottish League	28+5	12
Scottish Cup	2+3	1
Scottish League Cup	2	1
TOTAL	**32+8**	**14**

SEASON 96–97	GAMES	GOALS
Scottish League	25+2	14
Scottish Cup	1+2	2
Scottish League Cup	4+1	3
European Cup Winners Cup	0+1	0
TOTAL	**30+6**	**19**

CAREER APPEARANCES AND GOALS

COMPETITION	GAMES	TOTAL	GOALS
League	7+5	12	0
League Cup	0+2	2	0
Mercantile Credit Centenary Trophy	2	2	0
UEFA Cup	11+3	14	7
European Cup Winners Cup	0+1	1	0
Scottish League	449+43	492	208
Scottish Cup	51+7	58	29
Scottish League Cup	37+5	42	21
Internationals	8+8	16	3
TOTAL	**565+74**	**639**	**268**

HAT-TRICKS

Heart of Midlothian

1	3	Queen's Park	26/02/83	Away	League	3–0
2	3	Partick Thistle	19/03/83	Home	League	4–0
3	3	Dunfermline Athletic	30/04/83	Home	League	3–3
4	3	St Mirren	05/02/92	Home	S Cup	3–0

Scottish League: 3
Scottish Cup: 1
TOTAL: 4

HONOURS

Winners medals
None

Runner-up medals
Scottish Premier Division Championship: 85/86, 87/88, 91/92
Scottish Cup: 85/86, 95/96
Scottish League Cup: 96/97
Scottish League Division One Championship: 82/83

IAN RUSH

Born: 20/10/61 – St Asaph
Height: 6.0
Weight: 12.06 (96–97)

Clubs
Chester: **1979–80** – Matches: **40+1** – Goals: **18**
Liverpool: **1980–87** – Matches: **330+1** – Goals: **207**
Juventus FC: **1987–88** – Matches: **39+1** – Goals: **13**
Liverpool: **1988–96** – Matches: **300+29** – Goals: **139**
Leeds United: **1996–97** – Matches: **38+4** – Goals: **3**

Country
Wales: **1980–96** – Matches: **70+3** – Goals: **28**

SEASON 1978–79

Chester – League Division Three

1	28/04/79	Sheffield Wednesday	Home	League	2–2		

SEASON 1979–80

League Division Three

2	15/09/79	Gillingham	Away	League	2–2	1 Goal	(1)
3	22/09/79	Reading	Home	League	0–2		
Sub+1	09/10/79	Grimsby Town	Away	League	2–0		
4	27/10/79	Barnsley	Away	League	1–1		
5	03/11/79	Wimbledon	Home	League	3–1	1 Goal	(2)
6	07/11/79	Blackburn Rovers	Away	League	0–2		
7	10/11/79	Oxford United	Away	League	1–0	1 Goal	(3)
8	17/11/79	Mansfield Town	Home	League	1–0		
9	24/11/79	Workington	Home	FA Cup	5–1	1 Goal	(4)
10	01/12/79	Sheffield Wednesday	Home	League	2–2	1 Goal	(5)
11	07/12/79	Southend United	Away	League	1–4	1 Goal	(6)
12	18/12/79	Barnsley	Home	FA Cup	1–0		
13	21/12/79	Rotherham United	Home	League	3–1	2 Goals	(8)
14	26/12/79	Brentford	Away	League	2–2		
15	29/12/79	Blackpool	Home	League	1–0	1 Goal	(9)
16	05/01/80	Newcastle United	Away	FA Cup	2–0	1 Goal	(10)
17	08/01/80	Colchester United	Away	League	1–1		
18	12/01/80	Bury	Home	League	1–0		
19	19/01/80	Millwall	Away	League	1–3		
20	21/01/80	Bangor City	Home	Welsh Cup	1–1		
21	26/01/80	Millwall	Home	FA Cup	2–0	1 Goal	(11)
22	05/02/80	Bangor City	Away	Welsh Cup	2–0	1 Goal	(12)
23	09/02/80	Reading	Away	League	1–2	1 Goal	(13)
24	16/02/80	Ipswich Town	Away	FA Cup	1–2		
25	20/02/80	Carlisle United	Home	League	1–0	1 Goal	(14)
26	26/02/80	Sheffield United	Away	League	1–1	1 Goal	(15)
27	01/03/80	Hull City	Away	League	0–1		
28	08/03/80	Barnsley	Home	League	0–0		
29	15/03/80	Plymouth Argyle	Away	League	0–1		
30	19/03/80	Swindon Town	Home	League	1–0		
31	22/03/80	Oxford United	Home	League	1–0	1 Goal	(16)
32	26/03/80	Exeter City	Home	League	1–3		
33	29/03/80	Mansfield Town	Away	League	1–2		
34	01/04/80	Rotherham United	Away	League	0–2		
35	05/04/80	Brentford	Home	League	1–1		
36	07/04/80	Chesterfield	Away	League	0–2		
37	12/04/80	Colchester United	Home	League	2–1	2 Goals	(18)
38	19/04/80	Sheffield Wednesday	Away	League	0–3		
39	23/04/80	Chesterfield	Home	League	1–0		
40	26/04/80	Southend United	Home	League	2–1		

SEASON 1980–81

Liverpool – League Division One

1	13/12/80	Ipswich Town	Away	League	1–1		
2	14/03/81	West Ham United	Neutral	Lge Cup	2–1		
3	03/04/81	Stoke City	Home	League	3–0		
4	08/04/81	FC Bayern Munchen	Home	Eur Cup	0–0		
5	11/04/81	Nottingham Forest	Away	League	0–0		
6	14/04/81	Manchester United	Home	League	0–1		
7	25/04/81	Tottenham Hotspur	Away	League	1–1		
8	02/05/81	Sunderland	Home	League	0–1		
9	05/05/81	Middlesbrough	Away	League	2–1		

SEASON 1981–82

League Division One

Sub+1	30/09/81	OPS Oulu	Home	Eur Cup	7–0	1 Goal	(1)
10	07/10/81	Exeter City	Home	Lge Cup	5–0	2 Goals	(3)
11	10/10/81	Leeds United	Home	League	3–0	2 Goals	(5)
12	17/10/81	Brighton & Hove Albion	Away	League	3–3		
13	28/10/81	Exeter City	Away	Lge Cup	6–0	2 Goals	(7)
14	31/10/81	Sunderland	Away	League	2–0		
15	04/11/81	AZ 67 Alkmaar	Home	Eur Cup	3–2	1 Goal	(8)
16	07/11/81	Everton	Home	League	3–1	1 Goal	(9)
17	10/11/81	Middlesbrough	Home	Lge Cup	4–0	1 Goal	(10)
18	28/11/81	Southampton	Home	League	0–1		

19	01/12/81	Arsenal	Away	Lge Cup	0–0		
20	05/12/81	Nottingham Forest	Away	League	2–0		
21	08/12/81	Arsenal	Home	Lge Cup	3–0		
22	26/12/81	Manchester City	Home	League	1–3		
23	02/01/82	Swansea City	Away	FA Cup	4–0	2 Goals	(12)
24	05/01/82	West Ham United	Home	League	3–0		
25	12/01/82	Barnsley	Home	Lge Cup	0–0		
26	16/01/82	Wolverhampton Wanderers	Home	League	2–1		
27	19/01/82	Barnsley	Away	Lge Cup	3–1		
28	23/01/82	Sunderland	Away	FA Cup	3–0	1 Goal	(13)
29	26/01/82	Notts County	Away	League	4–0	3 Goals	(16)
30	30/01/82	Aston Villa	Away	League	3–0	1 Goal	(17)
31	02/02/82	Ipswich Town	Away	Lge Cup	2–0	1 Goal	(18)
32	06/02/82	Ipswich Town	Home	League	4–0	1 Goal	(19)
33	09/02/82	Ipswich Town	Home	Lge Cup	2–2	1 Goal	(20)
34	13/02/82	Chelsea	Away	FA Cup	0–2		
35	16/02/82	Swansea City	Away	League	0–2		
36	20/02/82	Coventry City	Home	League	4–0	1 Goal	(21)
37	27/02/82	Leeds United	Away	League	2–0	1 Goal	(22)
38	03/03/82	CSKA Septemvri Zname	Home	Eur Cup	1–0		
39	06/03/82	Brighton & Hove Albion	Home	League	0–1		
40	09/03/82	Stoke City	Away	League	5–1		
41	13/03/82	Tottenham Hotspur	Wembley	Lge Cup	3–1	1 Goal	(23)
42	17/03/82	CSKA Septemvri Zname	Away	Eur Cup	0–2*		
43	20/03/82	Sunderland	Home	League	1–0	1 Goal	(24)
44	27/03/82	Everton	Away	League	3–1		
45	30/03/82	Birmingham City	Home	League	3–1	2 Goals	(26)
46	02/04/82	Notts County	Home	League	1–0		
47	07/04/82	Manchester United	Away	League	1–0		
48	10/04/82	Manchester City	Away	League	5–0	1 Goal	(27)
49	13/04/82	Stoke City	Home	League	2–0		
50	17/04/82	West Bromwich Albion	Home	League	1–0		
51	24/04/82	Southampton	Away	League	3–2	1 Goal	(28)
52	01/05/82	Nottingham Forest	Home	League	2–0		
53	03/05/82	Tottenham Hotspur	Away	League	2–2		
54	08/05/82	Birmingham City	Away	League	1–0	1 Goal	(29)
55	11/05/82	Arsenal	Away	League	1–1	1 Goal	(30)
56	15/05/82	Tottenham Hotspur	Home	League	3–1		
57	18/05/82	Middlesbrough	Away	League	0–0		

SEASON 1982–83

League Division One

58	21/08/82	Tottenham Hotspur	Wembley	FA C/S	1–0	1 Goal	(31)
59	28/08/82	West Bromwich Albion	Home	League	2–0		
60	31/08/82	Birmingham City	Away	League	0–0		
61	04/09/82	Arsenal	Away	League	2–0		
62	07/09/82	Nottingham Forest	Home	League	4–3	1 Goal	(32)
63	11/09/82	Luton Town	Home	League	3–3	1 Goal	(33)
64	15/09/82	Dundalk	Away	Eur Cup	4–1	1 Goal	(34)
65	18/09/82	Swansea City	Away	League	3–0	2 Goals	(36)
66	25/09/82	Southampton	Home	League	5–0		
67	05/10/82	Ipswich Town	Away	Lge Cup	2–1	2 Goals	(38)
68	09/10/82	West Ham United	Away	League	1–3		
69	12/10/82	Ipswich Town	Home	Lge Cup	2–0		
70	16/10/82	Manchester United	Home	League	0–0		
71	20/10/82	HJK Helsinki	Away	Eur Cup	0–1		
72	23/10/82	Stoke City	Away	League	1–1		
73	30/10/82	Brighton & Hove Albion	Home	League	3–1		
74	03/11/82	HJK Helsinki	Home	Eur Cup	5–0		
75	06/11/82	Everton	Away	League	5–0	4 Goals	(42)
76	10/11/82	Rotherham United	Home	Lge Cup	1–0		
77	13/11/82	Coventry City	Home	League	4–0	3 Goals	(45)
78	20/11/82	Notts County	Away	League	2–1		
79	27/11/82	Tottenham Hotspur	Home	League	3–0		
80	30/11/82	Norwich City	Home	Lge Cup	2–0		
81	04/12/82	Norwich City	Away	League	0–1		
82	11/12/82	Watford	Home	League	3–1	1 Goal	(46)
83	18/12/82	Aston Villa	Away	League	4–2	1 Goal	(47)
84	27/12/82	Manchester City	Home	League	5–2	1 Goal	(48)
85	28/12/82	Sunderland	Away	League	0–0		
86	01/01/83	Notts County	Home	League	5–1	3 Goals	(51)
87	03/01/83	Arsenal	Home	League	3–1	1 Goal	(52)
88	08/01/83	Blackburn Rovers	Away	FA Cup	2–1	1 Goal	(53)
89	15/01/83	West Bromwich Albion	Away	League	1–0	1 Goal	(54)

90	18/01/83	West Ham United	Home	Lge Cup	2–1		
91	29/01/83	Stoke City	Home	FA Cup	2–0	1 Goal	(55)
92	05/02/83	Luton Town	Away	League	3–1	1 Goal	(56)
93	08/02/83	Burnley	Home	Lge Cup	3–0		
94	12/02/83	Ipswich Town	Home	League	1–0		
95	15/02/83	Burnley	Away	Lge Cup	1–0		
96	20/02/83	Brighton & Hove Albion	Away	FA Cup	1–2		
97	26/02/83	Manchester United	Away	League	1–1		
98	02/03/83	RTS Widzew Lodz	Away	Eur Cup	0–2		
99	05/03/83	Stoke City	Home	League	5–1		
100	12/03/83	West Ham United	Home	League	3–0	1 Goal	(57)
101	16/03/83	RTS Widzew Lodz	Home	Eur Cup	3–2	1 Goal	(58)
102	19/03/83	Everton	Home	League	0–0		
103	22/03/83	Brighton & Hove Albion	Away	League	2–2	2 Goals	(60)
104	26/03/83	Manchester United	Wembley	Lge Cup	2–1*		
105	09/04/83	Swansea City	Home	League	3–0	1 Goal	(61)
106	12/04/83	Coventry City	Away	League	0–0		
107	30/04/83	Tottenham Hotspur	Away	League	0–2		
108	02/05/83	Nottingham Forest	Away	League	0–1		

SEASON 1983–84

League Division One

109	20/08/83	Manchester United	Wembley	FA C/S	0–2		
110	27/08/83	Wolverhampton Wanderers	Away	League	1–1	1 Goal	(62)
111	31/08/83	Norwich City	Away	League	1–0		
112	03/09/83	Nottingham Forest	Home	League	1–0	1 Goal	(63)
113	06/09/83	Southampton	Home	League	1–1	1 Goal	(64)
114	10/09/83	Arsenal	Away	League	2–0		
115	14/09/83	Odense BK	Away	Eur Cup	1–0		
116	17/09/83	Aston Villa	Home	League	2–1	1 Goal	(65)
117	24/09/83	Manchester United	Away	League	0–1		
118	28/09/83	Odense BK	Home	Eur Cup	5–0		
119	01/10/83	Sunderland	Home	League	0–1		
120	05/10/83	Brentford	Away	Lge Cup	4–1	2 Goals	(67)
121	15/10/83	West Ham United	Away	League	3–1		
122	19/10/83	Athletic Bilbao	Home	Eur Cup	0–0		
123	22/10/83	Queens Park Rangers	Away	League	1–0		
124	29/10/83	Luton Town	Home	League	6–0	5 Goals	(72)
125	02/11/83	Athletic Bilbao	Away	Eur Cup	1–0	1 Goal	(73)
126	06/11/83	Everton	Home	League	3–0	1 Goal	(74)
127	08/11/83	Fulham	Away	Lge Cup	1–1	1 Goal	(75)
128	12/11/83	Tottenham Hotspur	Away	League	2–2	1 Goal	(76)
129	19/11/83	Stoke City	Home	League	1–0	1 Goal	(77)
130	22/11/83	Fulham	Home	Lge Cup	1–1*		
131	26/11/83	Ipswich Town	Away	League	1–1		
132	29/11/83	Fulham	Away	Lge Cup	1–0*		
133	03/12/83	Birmingham City	Home	League	1–0	1 Goal	(78)
134	10/12/83	Coventry City	Away	League	0–4		
135	17/12/83	Notts County	Home	League	5–0	1 Goal	(79)
136	20/12/83	Birmingham City	Away	Lge Cup	1–1		
137	22/12/83	Birmingham City	Home	Lge Cup	3–0	2 Goals	(81)
138	26/12/83	West Bromwich Albion	Away	League	2–1		
139	27/12/83	Leicester City	Home	League	2–2	1 Goal	(82)
140	31/12/83	Nottingham Forest	Away	League	1–0	1 Goal	(83)
141	02/01/84	Manchester United	Home	League	1–1		
142	06/01/84	Newcastle United	Home	FA Cup	4–0	2 Goals	(85)
143	14/01/84	Wolverhampton Wanderers	Home	League	0–1		
144	17/01/84	Sheffield Wednesday	Away	Lge Cup	2–2		
145	20/01/84	Aston Villa	Away	League	3–1	3 Goals	(88)
146	25/01/84	Sheffield Wednesday	Home	Lge Cup	3–0	2 Goals	(90)
147	29/01/84	Brighton & Hove Albion	Away	FA Cup	0–2		
148	01/02/84	Watford	Home	League	3–0	1 Goal	(91)
149	04/02/84	Sunderland	Away	League	0–0		
150	07/02/84	Walsall	Home	Lge Cup	2–2		
151	11/02/84	Arsenal	Home	League	2–1		
152	14/02/84	Walsall	Away	Lge Cup	2–0	1 Goal	(92)
153	18/02/84	Luton Town	Away	League	0–0		
154	25/02/84	Queens Park Rangers	Home	League	2–0	1 Goal	(93)
155	03/03/84	Everton	Away	League	1–1	1 Goal	(94)
156	07/03/84	Sport Lisboa E Benfica	Home	Eur Cup	1–0	1 Goal	(95)
157	16/03/84	Southampton	Away	League	0–2		
158	21/03/84	Sport Lisboa E Benfica	Away	Eur Cup	4–1	1 Goal	(96)
159	25/03/84	Everton	Wembley	Lge Cup	0–0*		
160	28/03/84	Everton	Neutral	Lge Cup	1–0		

161	31/03/84	Watford	Away	League	2–0	1 Goal	(97)
162	07/04/84	West Ham United	Home	League	6–0	2 Goals	(99)
163	11/04/84	Dinamo Bucuresti	Home	Eur Cup	1–0		
164	14/04/84	Stoke City	Away	League	0–2		
165	18/04/84	Leicester City	Away	League	3–3	1 Goal	(100)
166	21/04/84	West Bromwich Albion	Home	League	3–0		
167	25/04/84	Dinamo Bucuresti	Away	Eur Cup	2–1	2 Goals	(102)
168	28/04/84	Ipswich Town	Home	League	2–2	1 Goal	(103)
169	05/05/84	Birmingham City	Away	League	0–0		
170	07/05/84	Coventry City	Home	League	5–0	4 Goals	(107)
171	12/05/84	Notts County	Away	League	0–0		
172	15/05/84	Norwich City	Home	League	1–1	1 Goal	(108)
173	30/05/84	AS Roma	Neutral	Eur Cup	1–1+		

+ AET Liverpool won 4–2 on penalties

SEASON 1984–85

League Division One

174	18/08/84	Everton	Wembley	FA C/S	0–1		
175	20/10/84	Everton	Home	League	0–1		
176	24/10/84	Sport Lisboa E Benfica	Home	Eur Cup	3–1	3 Goals	(111)
177	28/10/84	Nottingham Forest	Away	League	2–0	1 Goal	(112)
178	31/10/84	Tottenham Hotspur	Away	Lge Cup	0–1		
179	03/11/84	Stoke City	Away	League	1–0		
180	07/11/84	Sport Lisboa E Benfica	Away	Eur Cup	0–1		
181	10/11/84	Southampton	Home	League	1–1	1 Goal	(113)
182	18/11/84	Newcastle United	Away	League	2–0		
183	24/11/84	Ipswich Town	Home	League	2–0		
184	01/12/84	Chelsea	Away	League	1–3		
185	04/12/84	Coventry City	Home	League	3–1	1 Goal	(114)
186	09/12/84	Independiente	Neutral	WCC	0–1		
187	15/12/84	Aston Villa	Away	League	0–0		
188	21/12/84	Queens Park Rangers	Away	League	2–0	1 Goal	(115)
189	01/01/85	Watford	Away	League	1–1	1 Goal	(116)
190	05/01/85	Aston Villa	Home	FA Cup	3–0	2 Goals	(118)
191	16/01/85	Juventus FC	Away	ES Cup	0–2		
192	19/01/85	Norwich City	Home	League	4–0	2 Goals	(120)
193	27/01/85	Tottenham Hotspur	Home	FA Cup	1–0	1 Goal	(121)
194	02/02/85	Sheffield Wednesday	Away	League	1–1		
195	12/02/85	Arsenal	Home	League	3–0	1 Goal	(122)
196	16/02/85	York City	Away	FA Cup	1–1	1 Goal	(123)
197	20/02/85	York City	Home	FA Cup	7–0		
198	23/02/85	Stoke City	Home	League	2–0		
199	02/03/85	Nottingham Forest	Home	League	1–0		
200	06/03/85	FK Austria Wien	Away	Eur Cup	1–1		
201	10/03/85	Barnsley	Away	FA Cup	4–0	3 Goals	(126)
202	16/03/85	Tottenham Hotspur	Home	League	0–1		
203	20/03/85	FK Austria Wien	Home	Eur Cup	4–1		
204	23/03/85	West Bromwich Albion	Away	League	5–0		
205	31/03/85	Manchester United	Home	League	0–1		
206	03/04/85	Sunderland	Away	League	3–0	2 Goals	(128)
207	06/04/85	Leicester City	Away	League	1–0		
208	10/04/85	Panathinaikos AO Athina	Home	Eur Cup	4–0	2 Goals	(130)
209	13/04/85	Manchester United	Neutral	FA Cup	2–2*		
210	04/05/85	Chelsea	Home	League	4–3	1 Goal	(131)
211	06/05/85	Coventry City	Away	League	2–0		
212	11/05/85	Aston Villa	Home	League	2–1	1 Goal	(132)
213	14/05/85	Southampton	Away	League	1–1		
214	17/05/85	Watford	Home	League	4–3	2 Goals	(134)
215	20/05/85	West Ham United	Away	League	3–0		
216	23/05/85	Everton	Away	League	0–1		
217	29/05/85	Juventus FC	Neutral	Eur Cup	0–1		

SEASON 1985–86

League Division One

218	17/08/85	Arsenal	Home	League	2–0		
219	21/08/85	Aston Villa	Away	League	2–2	1 Goal	(135)
220	24/08/85	Newcastle United	Away	League	0–1		
221	26/08/85	Ipswich Town	Home	League	5–0	2 Goals	(137)
222	31/08/85	West Ham United	Away	League	2–2		
223	03/09/85	Nottingham Forest	Home	League	2–0		
224	07/09/85	Watford	Home	League	3–1	1 Goal	(138)
225	14/09/85	Oxford United	Away	League	2–2	1 Goal	(139)

226	21/09/85	Everton	Away	League	3–2	1 Goal	(140)
227	24/09/85	Oldham Athletic	Home	Lge Cup	3–0	1 Goal	(141)
228	28/09/85	Tottenham Hotspur	Home	League	4–1	1 Goal	(142)
229	05/10/85	Queens Park Rangers	Away	League	1–2		
230	09/10/85	Oldham Athletic	Away	Lge Cup	5–2	1 Goal	(143)
231	12/10/85	Southampton	Home	League	1–0		
232	19/10/85	Manchester United	Away	League	1–1		
233	02/11/85	Leicester City	Home	League	1–0	1 Goal	(144)
234	09/11/85	Coventry City	Away	League	3–0	1 Goal	(145)
235	16/11/85	West Bromwich Albion	Home	League	4–1		
236	23/11/85	Birmingham City	Away	League	2–0	1 Goal	(146)
237	26/11/85	Manchester United	Home	Lge Cup	2–1		
238	30/11/85	Chelsea	Home	League	1–1		
239	03/12/85	Tottenham Hotspur	Home	SSS Cup	2–0		
240	07/12/85	Aston Villa	Home	League	3–0		
241	14/12/85	Arsenal	Away	League	0–2		
242	21/12/85	Newcastle United	Home	League	1–1		
243	26/12/85	Manchester City	Away	League	0–1		
244	28/12/85	Nottingham Forest	Away	League	1–1		
245	01/01/86	Sheffield Wednesday	Home	League	2–2	1 Goal	(147)
246	04/01/86	Norwich City	Home	FA Cup	5–0		
247	12/01/86	Watford	Away	League	3–2	1 Goal	(148)
248	14/01/86	Tottenham Hotspur	Away	SSS Cup	3–0	2 Goals	(150)
249	18/01/86	West Ham United	Home	League	3–1	1 Goal	(151)
250	21/01/86	Ipswich Town	Home	Lge Cup	3–0	1 Goal	(152)
251	26/01/86	Chelsea	Away	FA Cup	2–1	1 Goal	(153)
252	09/02/86	Manchester United	Home	League	1–1		
253	12/02/86	Queens Park Rangers	Away	Lge Cup	0–1		
254	15/02/86	York City	Away	FA Cup	1–1		
255	18/02/86	York City	Home	FA Cup	3–1*		
256	22/02/86	Everton	Home	League	0–2		
257	02/03/86	Tottenham Hotspur	Away	League	2–1	1 Goal	(154)
258	05/03/86	Queens Park Rangers	Home	Lge Cup	2–2		
259	08/03/86	Queens Park Rangers	Home	League	4–1	1 Goal	(155)
260	11/03/86	Watford	Home	FA Cup	0–0		
261	15/03/86	Southampton	Away	League	2–1	1 Goal	(156)
262	17/03/86	Watford	Away	FA Cup	2–1*	1 Goal	(157)
263	22/03/86	Oxford United	Home	League	6–0	2 Goals	(159)
264	29/03/86	Sheffield Wednesday	Away	League	0–0		
265	31/03/86	Manchester City	Home	League	2–0		
266	05/04/86	Southampton	Neutral	FA Cup	2–0*	2 Goals	(161)
267	12/04/86	Coventry City	Home	League	5–0	1 Goal	(162)
268	16/04/86	Luton Town	Away	League	1–0		
269	19/04/86	West Bromwich Albion	Away	League	2–1	1 Goal	(163)
270	26/04/86	Birmingham City	Home	League	5–0	1 Goal	(164)
271	30/04/86	Leicester City	Away	League	2–0	1 Goal	(165)
272	03/05/86	Chelsea	Away	League	1–0		
273	10/05/86	Everton	Wembley	FA Cup	3–1	2 Goals	(167)

SEASON 1986–87

League Division One

274	16/08/86	Everton	Wembley	FA C/S	1–1	1 Goal	(168)
275	23/08/86	Newcastle United	Away	League	2–0	2 Goals	(170)
276	25/08/86	Manchester City	Home	League	0–0		
277	30/08/86	Arsenal	Home	League	2–1	1 Goal	(171)
278	03/09/86	Leicester City	Away	League	1–2		
279	06/09/86	West Ham United	Away	League	5–2	1 Goal	(172)
280	13/09/86	Charlton Athletic	Home	League	2–0	1 Goal	(173)
281	16/09/86	Everton	Home	SSS Cup	3–1	2 Goals	(175)
282	20/09/86	Southampton	Away	League	1–2		
283	23/09/86	Fulham	Home	Lge Cup	10–0	2 Goals	(177)
284	27/09/86	Aston Villa	Home	League	3–3		
285	30/09/86	Everton	Away	SSS Cup	4–1	3 Goals	(180)
286	04/10/86	Wimbledon	Away	League	3–1	2 Goals	(182)
287	07/10/86	Fulham	Away	Lge Cup	3–2		
288	11/10/86	Tottenham Hotspur	Home	League	0–1		
289	18/10/86	Oxford United	Home	League	4–0	2 Goals	(184)
290	25/10/86	Luton Town	Away	League	1–4		
291	29/10/86	Leicester City	Home	Lge Cup	4–1		
292	01/11/86	Norwich City	Home	League	6–2	2 Goals	(186)
293	08/11/86	Queens Park Rangers	Away	League	3–1	1 Goal	(187)
294	16/11/86	Sheffield Wednesday	Home	League	1–1	1 Goal	(188)
295	19/11/86	Coventry City	Away	Lge Cup	0–0		
296	23/11/86	Everton	Away	League	0–0		

297	26/11/86	Coventry City	Home	Lge Cup	3–1		
298	29/11/86	Coventry City	Home	League	2–0		
299	06/12/86	Watford	Away	League	0–2		
300	14/12/86	Chelsea	Home	League	3–0	1 Goal	(189)
301	20/12/86	Charlton Athletic	Away	League	0–0		
302	26/12/86	Manchester United	Home	League	0–1		
303	27/12/86	Sheffield Wednesday	Away	League	1–0	1 Goal	(190)
304	01/01/87	Nottingham Forest	Away	League	1–1	1 Goal	(191)
305	03/01/87	West Ham United	Home	League	1–0		
306	11/01/87	Luton Town	Away	FA Cup	0–0		
307	17/01/87	Manchester City	Away	League	1–0	1 Goal	(192)
308	21/01/87	Everton	Away	Lge Cup	1–0	1 Goal	(193)
309	24/01/87	Newcastle United	Home	League	2–0	1 Goal	(194)
310	26/01/87	Luton Town	Home	FA Cup	0–0*		
311	28/01/87	Luton Town	Away	FA Cup	0–3		
312	11/02/87	Southampton	Away	Lge Cup	0–0		
313	14/02/87	Leicester City	Home	League	4–3	3 Goals	(197)
314	21/02/87	Aston Villa	Away	League	2–2		
315	25/02/87	Southampton	Home	Lge Cup	3–0		
316	28/02/87	Southampton	Home	League	1–0		
317	07/03/87	Luton Town	Home	League	2–0		
318	10/03/87	Arsenal	Away	League	1–0	1 Goal	(198)
319	14/03/87	Oxford United	Away	League	3–1	1 Goal	(199)
320	18/03/87	Queens Park Rangers	Home	League	2–1	2 Goals	(201)
321	22/03/87	Tottenham Hotspur	Away	League	0–1		
322	28/03/87	Wimbledon	Home	League	1–2		
323	05/04/87	Arsenal	Wembley	Lge Cup	1–2	1 Goal	(202)
324	11/04/87	Norwich City	Away	League	1–2	1 Goal	(203)
325	18/04/87	Nottingham Forest	Home	League	3–0		
326	20/04/87	Manchester United	Away	League	0–1		
327	25/04/87	Everton	Home	League	3–1	2 Goals	(205)
328	02/05/87	Coventry City	Away	League	0–1		
329	04/05/87	Watford	Home	League	1–0	1 Goal	(206)
330	09/05/87	Chelsea	Away	League	3–3	1 Goal	(207)

SEASON 1987–88

Juventus FC – Italian League Division One

1	23/08/87	US Lecce	Away	It Cup	3–0		
2	20/09/87	Empoli FC	Away	League	0–1		
3	27/09/87	Pescara Calcio	Home	League	3–1	2 Goals	(2)
4	30/09/87	Valletta FC	Home	UEFA Cup	3–0	1 Goal	(3)
5	04/10/87	Hellas–Verona	Away	League	1–2		
6	11/10/87	AS Roma	Home	League	1–0		
7	21/10/87	Panathinaikos AO Athina	Away	UEFA Cup	0–1		
8	25/10/87	Internazionale Milano	Away	League	1–2		
9	01/11/87	US Avellino	Home	League	3–0	1 Goal	(4)
10	04/11/87	Panathinaikos AO Athina	Home	UEFA Cup	3–2		
11	08/11/87	SC Pisa	Away	League	2–1		
12	22/11/87	AC Cesena	Home	League	0–2		
13	29/11/87	Ascoli Calcio	Home	League	1–0		
14	13/12/87	SSC Napoli	Away	League	1–2		
15	20/12/87	Sampdoria UC	Home	League	1–1		
16	03/01/88	Torino Calcio	Away	League	2–2		
17	06/01/88	Pescara Calcio	Home	It Cup	1–0	1 Goal	(5)
18	10/01/88	Milan AC	Home	League	0–1		
19	17/01/88	AC Fiorentina	Away	League	1–1		
20	20/01/88	Pescara Calcio	Away	It Cup	6–2	4 Goals	(9)
21	24/01/88	Como Calcio	Away	League	1–1		
22	31/01/88	Empoli FC	Home	League	4–0	1 Goal	(10)
23	07/02/88	Pescara Calcio	Away	League	0–2		
24	10/02/88	US Avellino	Away	It Cup	1–1		
25	14/02/88	Hellas–Verona	Home	League	0–0		
26	28/02/88	AS Roma	Away	League	0–2		
Sub+1	02/03/88	US Avellino	Home	It Cup	1–0		
27	06/03/88	Internazionale Milano	Home	League	1–0		
28	13/03/88	US Avellino	Away	League	0–1		
29	20/03/88	SC Pisa	Home	League	2–1		
30	27/03/88	AC Cesena	Away	League	0–0		
31	06/04/88	Torino Calcio	Away	It Cup	0–2		
32	10/04/88	Ascoli Calcio	Away	League	1–1	1 Goal	(11)
33	17/04/88	SSC Napoli	Home	League	3–1	1 Goal	(12)
34	20/04/88	Torino Calcio	Home	It Cup	2–1		
35	24/04/88	Sampdoria UC	Away	League	2–2		

36	01/05/88	Torino Calcio	Home	League	2–1	1 Goal	(13)
37	08/05/88	Milan AC	Away	League	0–0		
38	15/05/88	AC Fiorentina	Home	League	1–2		
39	23/05/88	Torino Calcio	Away	Lge P/O	0–0+		

+ AET Juventus FC won 4–2 on penalties

SEASON 1988–89

Liverpool – League Division One

Sub+1	27/08/88	Charlton Athletic	Away	League	3–0		
1	29/08/88	Nottingham Forest	Home	MCC Trophy	4–1		
Sub+2	03/09/88	Manchester United	Home	League	1–0		
2	10/09/88	Aston Villa	Away	League	1–1		
3	17/09/88	Tottenham Hotspur	Home	League	1–1		
4	20/09/88	Arsenal	Away	MCC Trophy	1–2		
5	28/09/88	Walsall	Home	Lge Cup	1–0		
Sub+3	01/10/88	Newcastle United	Home	League	1–2		
6	08/10/88	Luton Town	Away	League	0–1		
7	12/10/88	Walsall	Away	Lge Cup	3–1	1 Goal	(1)
8	22/10/88	Coventry City	Home	League	0–0		
9	26/10/88	Nottingham Forest	Away	League	1–2	1 Goal	(2)
10	29/10/88	West Ham United	Away	League	2–0	1 Goal	(3)
11	02/11/88	Arsenal	Home	Lge Cup	1–1		
12	05/11/88	Middlesbrough	Home	League	3–0	1 Goal	(4)
13	19/11/88	Queens Park Rangers	Away	League	1–0		
14	23/11/88	Arsenal	Away	Lge Cup	2–1		
15	26/11/88	Wimbledon	Home	League	1–1		
Sub+4	11/12/88	Everton	Home	League	1–1		
16	17/12/88	Norwich City	Home	League	0–1		
17	26/12/88	Derby County	Away	League	1–0	1 Goal	(5)
18	14/01/89	Sheffield Wednesday	Away	League	2–2		
19	21/01/89	Southampton	Home	League	2–0	1 Goal	(6)
20	29/01/89	Millwall	Away	FA Cup	2–0	1 Goal	(7)
21	04/02/89	Newcastle United	Away	League	2–2	1 Goal	(8)
Sub+5	03/05/89	Everton	Away	League	0–0		
Sub+6	10/05/89	Nottingham Forest	Home	League	1–0		
Sub+7	13/05/89	Wimbledon	Away	League	2–1		
Sub+8	16/05/89	Queens Park Rangers	Home	League	2–0		
22	23/05/89	West Ham United	Home	League	5–1	1 Goal	(9)
Sub+9	20/05/89	Everton	Wembley	FA Cup	3–2*	2 Goals	(11)
23	26/05/89	Arsenal	Home	League	0–2		

SEASON 1989–90

League Division One

24	12/08/89	Arsenal	Wembley	FA C/S	1–0		
25	19/08/89	Manchester City	Home	League	3–1		
26	23/08/89	Aston Villa	Away	League	1–1		
27	26/08/89	Luton Town	Away	League	0–0		
28	09/09/89	Derby County	Away	League	3–0	1 Goal	(12)
29	12/09/89	Crystal Palace	Home	League	9–0	1 Goal	(13)
30	16/09/89	Norwich City	Home	League	0–0		
31	19/09/89	Wigan Athletic	Home	Lge Cup	5–2	2 Goals	(15)
32	23/09/89	Everton	Away	League	3–1	2 Goals	(17)
33	04/10/89	Wigan Athletic	Away	Lge Cup	3–0+		
34	21/10/89	Southampton	Away	League	1–4		
35	25/10/89	Arsenal	Away	Lge Cup	0–1		
36	29/10/89	Tottenham Hotspur	Home	League	1–0		
37	04/11/89	Coventry City	Home	League	0–1		
38	11/11/89	Queens Park Rangers	Away	League	2–3		
39	19/11/89	Millwall	Away	League	2–1	1 Goal	(18)
40	26/11/89	Arsenal	Home	League	2–1		
41	29/11/89	Sheffield Wednesday	Away	League	0–2		
42	02/12/89	Manchester City	Away	League	4–1	2 Goals	(20)
43	09/12/89	Aston Villa	Home	League	1–1		
44	16/12/89	Chelsea	Away	League	5–2	2 Goals	(22)
45	23/12/89	Manchester United	Home	League	0–0		
46	26/12/89	Sheffield Wednesday	Home	League	2–1	1 Goal	(23)
47	30/12/89	Charlton Athletic	Home	League	1–0		
48	01/01/90	Nottingham Forest	Away	League	2–2	2 Goals	(25)
49	06/01/90	Swansea City	Away	FA Cup	0–0		
50	09/01/90	Swansea City	Home	FA Cup	8–0	3 Goals	(28)
51	13/01/90	Luton Town	Home	League	2–2		

52	20/01/90	Crystal Palace	Away	League	2–0	1 Goal	(29)
53	28/01/90	Norwich City	Away	FA Cup	0–0		
54	31/01/90	Norwich City	Home	FA Cup	3–1		
55	03/02/90	Everton	Home	League	2–1		
56	10/02/90	Norwich City	Away	League	0–0		
57	17/02/90	Southampton	Home	FA Cup	3–0	1 Goal	(30)
58	03/03/90	Millwall	Home	League	1–0		
59	11/03/90	Queens Park Rangers	Away	FA Cup	2–2	1 Goal	(31)
60	14/03/90	Queens Park Rangers	Home	FA Cup	1–0		
61	18/03/90	Manchester United	Away	League	2–1		
62	21/03/90	Tottenham Hotspur	Away	League	0–1		
63	31/03/90	Southampton	Home	League	3–2	1 Goal	(32)
64	03/04/90	Wimbledon	Home	League	2–1	1 Goal	(33)
65	08/04/90	Crystal Palace	Neutral	FA Cup	3–4*	1 Goal	(34)
66	14/04/90	Nottingham Forest	Home	League	2–2		
67	18/04/90	Arsenal	Away	League	1–1		
68	21/04/90	Chelsea	Home	League	4–1	1 Goal	(35)
69	28/04/90	Queens Park Rangers	Home	League	2–1	1 Goal	(36)
70	01/05/90	Derby County	Home	League	1–0		
71	05/05/90	Coventry City	Away	League	6–1	1 Goal	(37)

+ Played at Liverpool

SEASON 1990–91

League Division One

72	18/08/90	Manchester United	Wembley	FA C/S	1–1		
73	25/08/90	Sheffield United	Away	League	3–1	1 Goal	(38)
74	28/08/90	Nottingham Forest	Home	League	2–0	1 Goal	(39)
75	01/09/90	Aston Villa	Home	League	2–1		
76	08/09/90	Wimbledon	Away	League	2–1		
77	16/09/90	Manchester United	Home	League	4–0		
78	22/09/90	Everton	Away	League	3–2		
79	25/09/90	Crewe Alexandra	Home	Lge Cup	5–1	2 Goals	(41)
80	29/09/90	Sunderland	Away	League	1–0		
81	06/10/90	Derby County	Home	League	2–0		
82	09/10/90	Crewe Alexandra	Away	Lge Cup	4–1	3 Goals	(44)
83	20/10/90	Norwich City	Away	League	1–1		
84	27/10/90	Chelsea	Home	League	2–0	1 Goal	(45)
85	31/10/90	Manchester United	Away	Lge Cup	1–3		
86	04/11/90	Tottenham Hotspur	Away	League	3–1	2 Goals	(47)
87	10/11/90	Luton Town	Home	League	4–0	2 Goals	(49)
88	17/11/90	Coventry City	Away	League	1–0		
89	24/11/90	Manchester City	Home	League	2–2	1 Goal	(50)
90	02/12/90	Arsenal	Away	League	0–3		
91	15/12/90	Sheffield United	Home	League	2–0	1 Goal	(51)
92	22/12/90	Southampton	Home	League	3–2		
93	26/12/90	Queens Park Rangers	Away	League	1–1		
94	30/12/90	Crystal Palace	Away	League	0–1		
95	01/01/91	Leeds United	Home	League	3–0	1 Goal	(52)
96	05/01/91	Blackburn Rovers	Away	FA Cup	1–1		
97	08/01/91	Blackburn Rovers	Home	FA Cup	3–0	1 Goal	(53)
98	12/01/91	Aston Villa	Away	League	0–0		
99	19/01/91	Wimbledon	Home	League	1–1		
100	26/01/91	Brighton & Hove Albion	Home	FA Cup	2–2	2 Goals	(55)
101	30/01/91	Brighton & Hove Albion	Away	FA Cup	3–2*	1 Goal	(56)
102	03/02/91	Manchester United	Away	League	1–1		
103	17/02/91	Everton	Home	FA Cup	0–0		
104	20/02/91	Everton	Away	FA Cup	4–4*	1 Goal	(57)
105	23/02/91	Luton Town	Away	League	1–3		
106	27/02/91	Everton	Away	FA Cup	0–1		
107	03/03/91	Arsenal	Home	League	0–1		
108	09/03/91	Manchester City	Away	League	3–0		
109	16/03/91	Sunderland	Home	League	2–1	1 Goal	(58)
110	23/03/91	Derby County	Away	League	7–1	1 Goal	(59)
111	30/03/91	Queens Park Rangers	Home	League	1–3		
112	01/04/91	Southampton	Away	League	0–1		
113	09/04/91	Coventry City	Home	League	1–1	1 Goal	(60)
114	13/04/91	Leeds United	Away	League	5–4		
115	20/04/91	Norwich City	Home	League	3–0	1 Goal	(61)
116	23/04/91	Crystal Palace	Home	League	3–0	1 Goal	(62)
117	04/05/91	Chelsea	Away	League	2–4		
118	06/05/91	Nottingham Forest	Away	League	1–2		
119	11/05/91	Tottenham Hotspur	Home	League	2–0	1 Goal	(63)

SEASON 1991–92

League Division One

Sub+10	14/09/91	Aston Villa	Home	League	1–1		
120	18/09/91	FC Kuusysi Lahti	Home	UEFA Cup	6–2		
121	21/09/91	Leeds United	Away	League	0–1		
122	25/09/91	Stoke City	Home	Lge Cup	2–2	2 Goals	(65)
123	28/09/91	Sheffield Wednesday	Home	League	1–1		
124	01/10/91	FC Kuusysi Lahti	Away	UEFA Cup	0–1		
125	06/10/91	Manchester United	Away	League	0–0		
126	09/10/91	Stoke City	Away	Lge Cup	3–2		
127	19/10/91	Chelsea	Away	League	2–2	1 Goal	(66)
128	23/10/91	AJ Auxerre	Away	UEFA Cup	0–2		
129	26/10/91	Coventry City	Home	League	1–0		
130	29/10/91	Port Vale	Home	Lge Cup	2–2	1 Goal	(67)
131	02/11/91	Crystal Palace	Home	League	1–2		
132	06/11/91	AJ Auxerre	Home	UEFA Cup	3–0		
133	17/11/91	West Ham United	Away	League	0–0		
Sub+11	11/02/92	Bristol Rovers	Home	FA Cup	2–1		
134	16/02/92	Ipswich Town	Away	FA Cup	0–0		
135	22/02/92	Norwich City	Away	League	0–3		
Sub+12	14/03/92	Crystal Palace	Away	League	0–1		
136	18/03/92	Genoa 1893	Home	UEFA Cup	1–2	1 Goal	(68)
137	21/03/92	Tottenham Hotspur	Home	League	2–1		
138	28/03/92	Sheffield United	Away	League	0–2		
139	31/03/92	Notts County	Home	League	4–0	1 Goal	(69)
140	05/04/92	Portsmouth	Neutral	FA Cup	1–1		
141	13/04/92	Portsmouth	Neutral	FA Cup	0–0+		
142	18/04/92	Leeds United	Home	League	0–0		
143	20/04/92	Arsenal	Away	League	0–4		
144	22/04/92	Nottingham Forest	Away	League	1–1	1 Goal	(70)
145	26/04/92	Manchester United	Home	League	2–0	1 Goal	(71)
146	02/05/92	Sheffield Wednesday	Away	League	0–0		
147	09/05/92	Sunderland	Wembley	FA Cup	2–0	1 Goal	(72)

+ AET Liverpool won 3–1 on penalties

SEASON 1992–93

Premier League

148	08/08/92	Leeds United	Wembley	FA C/S	3–4	1 Goal	(73)
149	16/08/92	Nottingham Forest	Away	League	0–2		
150	25/08/92	Ipswich Town	Away	League	2–2		
151	29/08/92	Leeds United	Away	League	2–2		
152	01/09/92	Southampton	Home	League	1–1		
153	05/09/92	Chelsea	Home	League	2–1		
154	12/09/92	Sheffield United	Away	League	0–1		
155	16/09/92	Apollon FC Lemesos	Home	ECW Cup	6–1	4 Goals	(77)
156	29/09/92	Apollon FC Lemesos	Away	ECW Cup	2–1	1 Goal	(78)
157	03/10/92	Sheffield Wednesday	Home	League	1–0		
158	06/10/92	Chesterfield	Away	Lge Cup	4–1	1 Goal	(79)
159	18/10/92	Manchester United	Away	League	2–2	1 Goal	(80)
160	22/10/92	Spartak Moskva	Away	ECW Cup	2–4		
161	28/10/92	Sheffield United	Away	Lge Cup	0–0		
162	31/10/92	Tottenham Hotspur	Away	League	0–2		
163	04/11/92	Spartak Moskva	Home	ECW Cup	0–2		
164	07/11/92	Middlesbrough	Home	League	4–1	1 Goal	(81)
165	11/11/92	Sheffield United	Home	Lge Cup	3–0		
166	23/11/92	Queens Park Rangers	Away	League	1–0		
167	13/12/92	Blackburn Rovers	Home	League	2–1		
168	16/12/92	Crystal Palace	Away	Lge Cup	1–2		
169	19/12/92	Coventry City	Away	League	1–5		
170	28/12/92	Manchester City	Home	League	1–1	1 Goal	(82)
171	03/01/93	Bolton Wanderers	Away	FA Cup	2–2	1 Goal	(83)
172	31/01/93	Arsenal	Away	League	1–0		
173	06/02/93	Nottingham Forest	Home	League	0–0		
174	10/02/93	Chelsea	Away	League	0–0		
175	13/02/93	Southampton	Away	League	1–2		
176	20/02/93	Ipswich Town	Home	League	0–0		
Sub+13	06/03/93	Manchester United	Home	League	1–2	1 Goal	(84)
177	10/03/93	Queens Park Rangers	Home	League	1–0	1 Goal	(85)
178	13/03/93	Middlesbrough	Away	League	2–1	1 Goal	(86)
179	20/03/93	Everton	Home	League	1–0		
180	23/03/93	Crystal Palace	Away	League	1–1	1 Goal	(87)
181	03/04/93	Blackburn Rovers	Away	League	1–4	1 Goal	(88)

182	10/04/93	Oldham Athletic	Home	League	1–0	1 Goal	(89)
183	12/04/93	Manchester City	Away	League	1–1	1 Goal	(90)
184	17/04/93	Coventry City	Home	League	4–0		
185	21/04/93	Leeds United	Home	League	2–0		
186	01/05/93	Norwich City	Away	League	0–1		
187	05/05/93	Oldham Athletic	Away	League	2–3	2 Goals	(92)
188	08/05/93	Tottenham Hotspur	Home	League	6–2	2 Goals	(94)

SEASON 1993–94

Premier League

189	14/08/93	Sheffield Wednesday	Home	League	2–0		
190	18/08/93	Queens Park Rangers	Away	League	3–1	1 Goal	(95)
191	22/08/93	Swindon Town	Away	League	5–0		
192	25/08/93	Tottenham Hotspur	Home	League	1–2		
193	28/08/93	Leeds United	Home	League	2–0	1 Goal	(96)
194	01/09/93	Coventry City	Away	League	0–1		
195	12/09/93	Blackburn Rovers	Home	League	0–1		
196	18/09/93	Everton	Away	League	0–2		
197	22/09/93	Fulham	Away	Lge Cup	3–1	1 Goal	(97)
198	25/09/93	Chelsea	Away	League	0–1		
199	02/10/93	Arsenal	Home	League	0–0		
200	05/10/93	Fulham	Home	Lge Cup	5–0		
201	16/10/93	Oldham Athletic	Home	League	2–1		
202	23/10/93	Manchester City	Away	League	1–1	1 Goal	(98)
203	27/10/93	Ipswich Town	Home	Lge Cup	3–2	3 Goals	(101)
204	30/10/93	Southampton	Home	League	4–2	1 Goal	(102)
205	06/11/93	West Ham United	Home	League	2–0		
206	21/11/93	Newcastle United	Away	League	0–3		
207	28/11/93	Aston Villa	Home	League	2–1		
208	01/12/93	Wimbledon	Home	Lge Cup	1–1		
Sub+14	04/12/93	Sheffield Wednesday	Away	League	1–3		
209	08/12/93	Queens Park Rangers	Home	League	3–2	1 Goal	(103)
210	11/12/93	Swindon Town	Home	League	2–2		
211	14/12/93	Wimbledon	Away	Lge Cup	2–2+		
212	18/12/93	Tottenham Hotspur	Away	League	3–3		
213	26/12/93	Sheffield United	Away	League	0–0		
214	28/12/93	Wimbledon	Home	League	1–1		
215	01/01/94	Ipswich Town	Away	League	2–1	1 Goal	(104)
216	04/01/94	Manchester United	Home	League	3–3		
217	15/01/94	Oldham Athletic	Away	League	3–0		
218	19/01/94	Bristol City	Away	FA Cup	1–1	1 Goal	(105)
219	22/01/94	Manchester City	Home	League	2–1	2 Goals	(107)
220	25/01/94	Bristol City	Home	FA Cup	0–1		
221	05/02/94	Norwich City	Away	League	2–2		
222	14/02/94	Southampton	Away	League	2–4	1 Goal	(108)
223	19/02/94	Leeds United	Away	League	0–2		
224	25/02/94	Coventry City	Home	League	1–0	1 Goal	(109)
225	05/03/94	Blackburn Rovers	Away	League	0–2		
226	13/03/94	Everton	Home	League	2–1	1 Goal	(110)
227	19/03/94	Chelsea	Home	League	2–1	1 Goal	(111)
228	26/03/94	Arsenal	Away	League	0–1		
229	29/03/94	Manchester United	Away	League	0–1		
230	02/04/94	Sheffield United	Home	League	1–2	1 Goal	(112)
231	04/04/94	Wimbledon	Away	League	1–1		
232	09/04/94	Ipswich Town	Home	League	1–0		
233	16/04/94	Newcastle United	Home	League	0–2		
234	23/04/94	West Ham United	Away	League	2–1	1 Goal	(113)
235	30/04/94	Norwich City	Home	League	0–1		
236	07/05/94	Aston Villa	Away	League	1–2		

+ AET Wimbledon won 4–3 on penalties

SEASON 1994–95

Premier League

237	20/08/94	Crystal Palace	Away	League	6–1	2 Goals	(115)
238	28/08/94	Arsenal	Home	League	3–0		
239	31/08/94	Southampton	Away	League	2–0		
240	10/09/94	West Ham United	Home	League	0–0		
241	17/09/94	Manchester United	Away	League	0–2		
242	21/09/94	Burnley	Home	Lge Cup	2–0		
243	24/09/94	Newcastle United	Away	League	1–1	1 Goal	(116)
244	01/10/94	Sheffield Wednesday	Home	League	4–1	1 Goal	(117)
245	08/10/94	Aston Villa	Home	League	3–2		

246	15/10/94	Blackburn Rovers	Away	League	2–3	
247	22/10/94	Wimbledon	Home	League	3–0	
248	25/10/94	Stoke City	Home	Lge Cup	2–1	2 Goals (119)
249	29/10/94	Ipswich Town	Away	League	3–1	
250	31/10/94	Queens Park Rangers	Away	League	1–2	
251	05/11/94	Nottingham Forest	Home	League	1–0	
252	09/11/94	Chelsea	Home	League	3–1	
253	21/11/94	Everton	Away	League	0–2	
254	26/11/94	Tottenham Hotspur	Home	League	1–1	
255	30/11/94	Blackburn Rovers	Away	Lge Cup	3–1	3 Goals (122)
256	03/12/94	Coventry City	Away	League	1–1	1 Goal (123)
257	18/12/94	Chelsea	Away	League	0–0	
258	26/12/94	Leicester City	Away	League	2–1	1 Goal (124)
259	28/12/94	Manchester City	Home	League	2–0	
260	31/12/94	Leeds United	Away	League	2–0	
261	02/01/95	Norwich City	Home	League	4–0	1 Goal (125)
262	07/01/95	Birmingham City	Away	FA Cup	0–0	
263	11/01/95	Arsenal	Home	Lge Cup	1–0	1 Goal (126)
264	14/01/95	Ipswich Town	Home	League	0–1	
265	18/01/95	Birmingham City	Home	FA Cup	1–1+	
266	24/01/95	Everton	Home	League	0–0	
267	28/01/95	Burnley	Away	FA Cup	0–0	
268	04/02/95	Nottingham Forest	Away	League	1–1	
269	07/02/95	Burnley	Home	FA Cup	1–0	
270	11/02/95	Queens Park Rangers	Home	League	1–1	
271	15/02/95	Crystal Palace	Home	Lge Cup	1–0	
272	19/02/95	Wimbledon	Home	FA Cup	1–1	
273	28/02/95	Wimbledon	Away	FA Cup	2–0	1 Goal (127)
274	04/03/95	Newcastle United	Home	League	2–0	1 Goal (128)
275	08/03/95	Crystal Palace	Away	Lge Cup	1–0	
276	11/03/95	Tottenham Hotspur	Home	FA Cup	1–2	
277	14/03/95	Coventry City	Home	League	2–3	
278	19/03/95	Manchester United	Home	League	2–0	
279	02/04/95	Bolton Wanderers	Wembley	Lge Cup	2–1	
280	05/04/95	Southampton	Home	League	3–1	2 Goals (130)
281	09/04/95	Leeds United	Home	League	0–1	
282	14/04/95	Manchester City	Away	League	1–2	
283	17/04/95	Leicester City	Home	League	2–0	1 Goal (131)
284	29/04/95	Norwich City	Away	League	2–1	1 Goal (132)
285	02/05/95	Wimbledon	Away	League	0–0	
286	06/05/95	Aston Villa	Away	League	0–2	

+ AET Liverpool won 2–0 on penalties

SEASON 1995–96

Premier League

287	19/08/95	Sheffield Wednesday	Home	League	1–0	
288	21/08/95	Leeds United	Away	League	0–1	
289	26/08/95	Tottenham Hotspur	Away	League	3–1	
290	30/08/95	Queens Park Rangers	Home	League	1–0	
Sub+15	26/09/95	Spartak–Alania Vladikavkaz	Home	UEFA Cup	0–0	
291	01/10/95	Manchester United	Away	League	2–2	
292	04/10/95	Sunderland	Away	Lge Cup	1–0	
Sub+16	14/10/95	Coventry City	Home	League	0–0	
293	17/10/95	Brøndby IF	Away	UEFA Cup	0–0	
294	22/10/95	Southampton	Away	League	3–1	
295	25/10/95	Manchester City	Home	Lge Cup	4–0	1 Goal (133)
296	28/10/95	Manchester City	Home	League	6–0	2 Goals (135)
297	31/10/95	Brøndby IF	Home	UEFA Cup	0–1	
298	04/11/95	Newcastle United	Away	League	1–2	1 Goal (136)
299	18/11/95	Everton	Home	League	1–2	
Sub+17	06/01/96	Rochdale	Home	FA Cup	7–0	1 Goal (137)
Sub+18	13/01/96	Sheffield Wednesday	Away	League	1–1	1 Goal (138)
Sub+19	03/02/96	Tottenham Hotspur	Home	League	0–0	
Sub+20	28/02/96	Charlton Athletic	Home	FA Cup	2–1	
Sub+21	03/03/96	Aston Villa	Home	League	3–0	
Sub+22	23/03/96	Nottingham Forest	Away	League	0–1	
Sub+23	31/03/96	Aston Villa	Neutral	FA Cup	3–0	
Sub+24	03/04/96	Newcastle United	Home	League	4–3	
Sub+25	06/04/96	Coventry City	Away	League	0–1	
Sub+26	16/04/96	Everton	Away	League	1–1	
Sub+27	27/04/96	Middlesbrough	Home	League	1–0	
Sub+28	01/05/96	Arsenal	Away	League	0–0	
300	05/05/96	Manchester City	Away	League	2–2	1 Goal (139)
Sub+29	11/05/96	Manchester United	Wembley	FA Cup	0–1	

Striker

SEASON 1996–97

Leeds United – Premier League

1	17/08/96	Derby County	Away	League	3–3		
2	20/08/96	Sheffield Wednesday	Home	League	0–2		
3	24/08/96	Wimbledon	Home	League	1–0		
4	04/09/96	Blackburn Rovers	Away	League	1–0		
5	07/09/96	Manchester United	Home	League	0–4		
6	14/09/96	Coventry City	Away	League	1–2		
7	18/09/96	Darlington	Home	Lge Cup	2–2		
8	21/09/96	Newcastle United	Home	League	0–1		
9	12/10/96	Nottingham Forest	Home	League	2–0		
10	19/10/96	Aston Villa	Away	League	0–2		
11	23/10/96	Aston Villa	Home	Lge Cup	1–2		
12	26/10/96	Arsenal	Away	League	0–3		
13	02/11/96	Sunderland	Home	League	3–0		
14	16/11/96	Liverpool	Home	League	0–2		
15	23/11/96	Southampton	Away	League	2–0		
16	01/12/96	Chelsea	Home	League	2–0	1 Goal	(1)
17	07/12/96	Middlesbrough	Away	League	0–0		
18	14/12/96	Tottenham Hotspur	Home	League	0–0		
19	21/12/96	Everton	Away	League	0–0		
20	26/12/96	Coventry City	Home	League	1–3		
21	28/12/96	Manchester United	Away	League	0–1		
22	01/01/97	Newcastle United	Away	League	0–3		
23	11/01/97	Leicester City	Home	League	3–0	2 Goals	(3)
24	14/01/97	Crystal Palace	Away	FA Cup	2–2		
25	20/01/97	West Ham United	Away	League	2–0		
26	25/01/97	Crystal Palace	Home	FA Cup	1–0		
Sub+1	29/01/97	Derby County	Home	League	0–0		
27	01/02/97	Arsenal	Home	League	0–0		
Sub+2	04/02/97	Arsenal	Away	FA Cup	1–0		
Sub+3	15/02/97	Portsmouth	Home	FA Cup	2–3		
Sub+4	19/02/97	Liverpool	Away	League	0–4		
28	22/02/97	Sunderland	Away	League	1–0		
29	01/03/97	West Ham United	Home	League	1–0		
30	08/03/97	Everton	Home	League	1–0		
31	12/03/97	Southampton	Home	League	0–0		
32	15/03/97	Tottenham Hotspur	Away	League	0–1		
33	22/03/97	Sheffield Wednesday	Away	League	2–2		
34	07/04/97	Blackburn Rovers	Home	League	0–0		
35	16/04/97	Wimbledon	Away	League	0–2		
36	22/04/97	Aston Villa	Home	League	0–0		
37	03/05/97	Chelsea	Away	League	0–0		
38	11/05/97	Middlesbrough	Home	League	1–1		

INTERNATIONAL APPEARANCES – WALES

Sub 1	21/05/80	Scotland	Hampden Park	0–1	HC		
2	23/05/80	Northern Ireland	Ninian Park	0–1	HC		
Sub 3	20/05/81	England	Wembley	0–0	HC		
Sub 4	14/10/81	Iceland	Vetch Field	2–2	WCQ		
5	18/11/81	USSR	Tbilisi	0–3	WCQ		
6	27/04/82	England	Ninian Park	0–1	HC		
7	24/05/82	Scotland	Hampden Park	0–1	HC		
8	27/05/82	Northern Ireland	Racecourse	3–0	HC	1 Goal	(1)
9	02/06/82	France	Toulouse	1–0	F	1 Goal	(2)
10	22/09/82	Norway	Vetch Field	1–0	ECQ	1 Goal	(3)
11	15/12/82	Yugoslavia	Titograd	4–4	ECQ	1 Goal	(4)
12	23/02/83	England	Wembley	1–2	HC	1 Goal	(5)
13	27/04/83	Bulgaria	Racecourse	1–0	ECQ		
14	21/09/83	Norway	Oslo	0–0	ECQ		
15	12/10/83	Romania	Racecourse	5–0	F	2 Goals	(7)
16	16/11/83	Bulgaria	Sofia	0–1	ECQ		
17	14/12/83	Yugoslavia	Ninian Park	1–1	ECQ		
18	28/02/84	Scotland	Hampden Park	1–2	HC		
19	02/05/84	England	Racecourse	1–0	HC		
20	22/05/84	Northern Ireland	Vetch Field	1–1	HC		
21	14/11/84	Iceland	Ninian Park	2–1	WCQ		
22	26/02/85	Norway	Racecourse	1–1	F	1 Goal	(8)
23	27/03/85	Scotland	Hampden Park	1–0	WCQ	1 Goal	(9)
24	30/04/85	Spain	Racecourse	3–0	WCQ	2 Goals	(11)
25	10/09/85	Scotland	Ninian Park	1–1	WCQ		
26	25/02/86	Saudi Arabia	Dhahran	2–1	F		

27	26/03/86	Republic of Ireland	Lansdowne Road	1–0	F	1 Goal	(12)
28	21/04/86	Uruguay	Ninian Park	0–0	F		
29	10/09/86	Finland	Helsinki	1–1	WCQ		
30	18/02/87	USSR	Vetch Field	0–0	F		
31	01/04/87	Finland	Racecourse	4–0	WCQ	1 Goal	(13)
32	29/04/87	Czechoslovakia	Racecourse	1–1	WCQ	1 Goal	(14)
33	14/10/87	Denmark	Copenhagen	0–1	WCQ		
34	11/11/87	Czechoslovakia	Prague	0–2	WCQ		
35	23/03/88	Yugoslavia	Vetch Field	1–2	F		
36	27/04/88	Sweden	Stockholm	1–4	F		
37	01/06/88	Malta	Valletta	3–2	F	1 Goal	(15)
38	04/06/88	Italy	Brescia	1–0	F	1 Goal	(16)
39	31/08/88	Holland	Amsterdam	0–1	WCQ		
40	19/10/88	Finland	Vetch Field	2–2	WCQ		
41	26/04/89	Sweden	Racecourse	0–2	F		
42	31/05/89	West Germany	Cardiff Arms Park	0–0	WCQ		
43	06/09/89	Finland	Helsinki	0–1	WCQ		
44	28/03/90	Republic of Ireland	Lansdowne Road	0–1	F		
45	11/09/90	Denmark	Copenhagen	0–1	F		
46	17/10/90	Belgium	Cardiff Arms Park	3–1	ECQ	1 Goal	(17)
47	14/11/90	Luxembourg	Luxembourg	1–0	ECQ	1 Goal	(18)
48	06/02/91	Republic of Ireland	Racecourse	0–3	F		
49	27/03/91	Belgium	Brussels	1–1	ECQ		
50	29/05/91	Poland	Radom	0–0	F		
51	05/06/91	Germany	Cardiff Arms Park	1–0	ECQ	1 Goal	(19)
52	16/10/91	Germany	Nuremberg	1–4	ECQ		
53	13/11/91	Luxembourg	Cardiff Arms Park	1–0	ECQ		
54	20/05/92	Romania	Bucharest	1–5	WCQ	1 Goal	(20)
55	09/09/92	Faroe Islands	Cardiff Arms Park	6–0	WCQ	3 Goals	(23)
56	14/10/92	Cyprus	Nicosia	1–0	WCQ		
57	18/11/92	Belgium	Brussels	0–2	WCQ		
58	31/03/93	Belgium	Cardiff Arms Park	2–0	WCQ	1 Goal	(24)
59	28/04/93	Czechoslovakia	Ostrava	1–1	WCQ		
60	06/06/93	Faroe Islands	Toftir	3–0	WCQ	1 Goal	(25)
61	08/09/93	Czechoslovakia	Cardiff Arms Park	2–2	WCQ	1 Goal	(26)
62	13/10/93	Cyprus	Cardiff Arms Park	2–0	WCQ	1 Goal	(27)
63	17/10/93	Romania	Cardiff Arms Park	1–2	WCQ		
64	09/03/94	Norway	Ninian Park	1–3	F		
65	20/04/94	Sweden	Racecourse	0–2	F		
66	23/05/94	Estonia	Tallinn	2–1	F	1 Goal	(28)
67	07/09/94	Albania	Cardiff Arms Park	2–0	ECQ		
68	16/11/94	Georgia	Tbilisi	0–5	ECQ		
69	14/12/94	Bulgaria	Cardiff Arms Park	0–3	ECQ		
70	26/04/95	Germany	Dusseldorf	1–1	ECQ		
71	07/06/95	Georgia	Cardiff Arms Park	0–1	ECQ		
72	06/09/95	Moldova	Cardiff Arms Park	1–0	ECQ		
73	24/01/96	Italy	Terni	0–3	F		

APPEARANCES AND GOALS PER SEASON

SEASON 78–79	GAMES	GOALS
League	1	0
TOTAL	**1**	**0**

SEASON 79–80	GAMES	GOALS
League	32+1	14
FA Cup	5	3
Welsh Cup	2	1
TOTAL	**39+1**	**18**

SEASON 80–81	GAMES	GOALS
League	7	0
League Cup	1	0
European Cup	1	0
TOTAL	**9**	**0**

SEASON 81–82	GAMES	GOALS
League	32	17
FA Cup	3	3
League Cup	10	8
European Cup	3+1	2
TOTAL	**48+1**	**30**

SEASON 82–83	GAMES	GOALS
League	34	24
FA Cup	3	2
League Cup	8	2
European Cup	5	2
FA Charity Shield	1	1
TOTAL	**51**	**31**

SEASON 83–84	GAMES	GOALS
League	41	32
FA Cup	2	2
League Cup	12	8
European Cup	9	5
FA Charity Shield	1	0
TOTAL	**65**	**47**

SEASON 84–85	GAMES	GOALS
League	28	14
FA Cup	6	7
League Cup	1	0
European Cup	6	5
European Super Cup	1	0
World Club Championship	1	0
FA Charity Shield	1	0
TOTAL	**44**	**26**

SEASON 85–86	GAMES	GOALS
League	40	22
FA Cup	8	6
League Cup	6	3
Screen Sport Super Cup	2	2
TOTAL	**56**	**33**

SEASON 86–87	GAMES	GOALS
League	42	30
FA Cup	3	0
League Cup	9	4
Screen Sport Super Cup	2	5
FA Charity Shield	1	1
TOTAL	**57**	**40**

SEASON 87–88	GAMES	GOALS
Italian League	29	7
Italian League Play–off	1	0
Italian Cup	6+1	5
UEFA Cup	3	1
TOTAL	**39+1**	**13**

SEASON 88–89	GAMES	GOALS
League	16+8	7
FA Cup	1+1	3
League Cup	4	1
Mercantile Credit Centenary Trophy	2	0
TOTAL	**23+9**	**11**

SEASON 89–90	GAMES	GOALS
League	36	18
FA Cup	8	6
League Cup	3	2
FA Charity Shield	1	0
TOTAL	**48**	**26**

SEASON 90–91	GAMES	GOALS
League	37	16
FA Cup	7	5
League Cup	3	5
FA Charity Shield	1	0
TOTAL	**48**	**26**

SEASON 91–92	GAMES	GOALS
League	16+2	4
FA Cup	4+1	1
League Cup	3	3
UEFA Cup	5	1
TOTAL	**28+3**	**9**

SEASON 92–93	GAMES	GOALS
League	31+1	14
FA Cup	1	1
League Cup	4	1
European Cup Winners Cup	4	5
FA Charity Shield	1	1
TOTAL	**41+1**	**22**

SEASON 93–94	GAMES	GOALS
League	41+1	14
FA Cup	2	1
League Cup	5	4
TOTAL	**48+1**	**19**

SEASON 94–95	GAMES	GOALS
League	36	12
FA Cup	7	1
League Cup	7	6
TOTAL	**50**	**19**

SEASON 95–96	GAMES	GOALS
League	10+10	5
FA Cup	0+4	1
League Cup	2	1
UEFA Cup	2+1	0
TOTAL	**14+15**	**7**

SEASON 96–97	GAMES	GOALS
League	34+2	3
FA Cup	2+2	0
League Cup	2	0
TOTAL	**38+4**	**3**

CAREER APPEARANCES AND GOALS

COMPETITION	GAMES	TOTAL	GOALS
League	514+25	539	246
FA Cup	62+8	70	42
League Cup	80	80	48
Screen Sport Super Cup	4	4	7
Mercantile Credit Centenary Trophy	2	2	0
FA Charity Shield	7	7	3
Welsh Cup	2	2	1
European Cup	24+1	25	14
European Cup Winners Cup	4	4	5
UEFA Cup	10+1	11	2
European Super Cup	1	1	0
World Club Championship	1	1	0
Italian League	29	29	7
Italian League Play–off	1	1	0
Italian Cup	6+1	7	5
Internationals	70+3	73	28
TOTAL	**817+39**	**856**	**408**

HAT-TRICKS

Liverpool

1	3	Notts County	26/01/82	Away	League	4–0
2	4	Everton	06/11/82	Away	League	5–0
3	3	Coventry City	13/11/82	Home	League	4–0
4	3	Notts County	01/01/83	Home	League	5–1
5	5	Luton Town	29/10/83	Home	League	6–0
6	3	Aston Villa	20/01/84	Away	League	3–1
7	4	Coventry City	07/05/84	Home	League	5–0
8	3	Sport Lisboa E Benfica	24/10/84	Home	Eur Cup	3–1
9	3	Barnsley	10/03/85	Away	FA Cup	4–0
10	3	Everton	30/09/86	Away	SSS Cup	4–1
11	3	Leicester City	14/02/87	Home	League	4–3

Juventus FC

1	4	Pescara Calcio	20/01/88	Away	It Cup	6–2

Liverpool

1	3	Swansea City	09/01/90	Home	FA Cup	8–0
2	3	Crewe Alexandra	09/10/90	Away	Lge Cup	4–1

3	4	Apollon FC Lemesos	16/09/92	Home	ECW Cup	6–1
4	3	Ipswich Town	27/10/93	Home	Lge Cup	3–2
5	3	Blackburn Rovers	30/11/94	Away	Lge Cup	3–1

Wales

| 1 | 3 | Faroe Islands | 09/09/92 | Cardiff Arms Park | WCQ | 6–0 |

League: 8
FA Cup: 2
League Cup: 3
European Cup: 1
European Cup Winners Cup: 1
Screen Sport Super Cup: 1
Italian Cup: 1
International: 1
TOTAL: 18

HONOURS

Winners medals
League Division One Championship: 81/82, 82/83, 83/84, 85/86, 89/90
FA Cup: 85/86, 88/89, 91/92
League Cup: 80/81, 81/82, 82/83, 83/84, 94/95
European Cup: 83/84
Screen Sport Super Cup: 85/86
FA Charity Shield: 82/83, 86/87, 89/90, 90/91

Runner-up medals
League Division One Championship: 84/85, 86/87, 88/89, 90/91
FA Cup: 95/96
League Cup: 86/87
European Cup: 84/85
World Club Championship: 84/85
European Super Cup: 84/85
FA Charity Shield: 83/84, 84/85, 92/93

DEAN SAUNDERS

Born: 21/06/64 – Swansea
Height: 5.8
Weight: 10.06 (96–97)

Clubs
Swansea City: **1983–85** – Matches: **53+9** – Goals: **16**
Cardiff City (loan): **1985** – Matches: **3+1** – Goals: **0**
Brighton & Hove Albion: **1985–87** – Matches: **80+6** – Goals: **25**
Oxford United: **1987–88** – Matches: **70+3** – Goals: **33**
Derby County: **1988–91** – Matches: **131** – Goals: **57**
Liverpool: **1991–92** – Matches: **61** – Goals: **25**
Aston Villa: **1992–95** – Matches: **143+1** – Goals: **48**
Galatasaray SK: **1995–96** – Matches: **25+6** – Goals: **19**
Nottingham Forest: **1996–97** – Matches: **38+1** – Goals: **5**

Country
Wales: **1986–97** – Matches: **53+5** – Goals: **20**

SEASON 1983–84

Swansea City – League Division Two

Sub+1	22/10/83	Charlton Athletic	Away	League	2–2		
Sub+2	25/10/83	Colchester United	Away	Lge Cup	0–1		
Sub+3	17/12/83	Portsmouth	Home	League	1–2		
Sub+4	27/12/83	Shrewsbury Town	Home	League	0–2		
1	18/01/84	Huddersfield Town	Home	League	2–2		
2	15/02/84	Leeds United	Away	League	0–1		
3	21/02/84	Barry Town	Home	Welsh Cup	2–1*	1 Goal	(1)
4	25/02/84	Charlton Athletic	Home	League	1–0		
Sub+5	03/03/84	Carlisle United	Away	League	0–2		
Sub+6	07/03/84	Blackburn Rovers	Away	League	1–4		

5	10/03/84	Barnsley	Home	League	1–0		
6	17/03/84	Oldham Athletic	Away	League	3–3	1 Goal	(2)
7	20/03/84	Shrewsbury Town	Away	Welsh Cup	0–2		
8	31/03/84	Newcastle United	Away	League	0–2		
9	03/04/84	Shrewsbury Town	Home	Welsh Cup	1–0		
10	07/04/84	Manchester City	Home	League	0–2		
11	14/04/84	Grimsby Town	Away	League	0–3		
12	21/04/84	Cardiff City	Home	League	3–2	2 Goals	(4)
13	24/04/84	Shrewsbury Town	Away	League	0–2		
14	27/04/84	Middlesbrough	Home	League	2–1		
15	05/05/84	Crystal Palace	Away	League	0–2		
16	07/05/84	Leeds United	Home	League	2–2		
17	12/05/84	Portsmouth	Away	League	0–5		

SEASON 1984–85

League Division Three

18	25/08/84	Millwall	Away	League	0–2		
19	28/08/84	Walsall	Home	Lge Cup	0–2		
20	01/09/84	York City	Home	League	1–3		
21	04/09/84	Walsall	Away	Lge Cup	1–3		
22	08/09/84	Bristol City	Away	League	2–2	1 Goal	(5)
23	15/09/84	Bradford City	Home	League	1–2	1 Goal	(6)
24	18/09/84	Bolton Wanderers	Home	League	2–1		
Sub+7	22/09/84	Brentford	Away	League	0–3		
25	29/09/84	Gillingham	Home	League	0–1		
26	20/10/84	Walsall	Home	League	1–2		
27	23/10/84	Hull City	Away	League	1–4	1 Goal	(7)
28	27/10/84	Cambridge United	Away	League	2–0		
29	03/11/84	Wigan Athletic	Home	League	2–2		
30	06/11/84	Preston North End	Away	League	2–3	1 Goal	(8)
31	10/11/84	Reading	Home	League	1–2	1 Goal	(9)
32	21/11/84	Bognor Regis Town	Away	FA Cup	1–3		
33	24/11/84	Doncaster Rovers	Away	League	1–4		
34	01/12/84	Plymouth Argyle	Home	League	0–2		
35	04/12/84	Spencer Works	Home	Welsh Cup	1–1		
36	12/12/84	Spencer Works	Away	Welsh Cup	5–0	1 Goal	(10)
37	15/12/84	Burnley	Away	League	1–1		
38	22/12/84	Bristol Rovers	Away	League	2–4	1 Goal	(11)
39	26/12/84	Rotherham United	Home	League	1–0	1 Goal	(12)
40	29/12/84	Derby County	Home	League	1–5	1 Goal	(13)
41	01/01/85	Lincoln City	Away	League	0–1		
42	12/01/85	York City	Away	League	0–1		
Sub+8	22/01/85	Bristol Rovers	Home	FR Trophy	2–0	1 Goal	(14)
Sub+9	26/01/85	Bradford City	Away	League	1–1		
43	29/01/85	Sully	Home	Welsh Cup	7–1	1 Goal	(15)
44	02/02/85	Gillingham	Away	League	1–1		
45	09/02/85	Brentford	Home	League	3–2	1 Goal	(16)
46	12/02/85	AFC Bournemouth	Home	League	0–0		
47	16/02/85	Bolton Wanderers	Away	League	0–0		
48	27/02/85	Hereford United	Home	Welsh Cup	2–0		
49	01/03/85	Cambridge United	Home	League	2–2		
50	09/03/85	Walsall	Away	League	0–3		
51	17/03/85	Newport County	Home	League	0–3		
52	19/03/85	Bristol Rovers	Away	FR Trophy	0–0		
53	26/03/85	Millwall	Home	League	1–2		

Cardiff City (loan) – League Division Two

1	30/03/85	Manchester City	Away	League	2–2		
2	06/04/85	Oxford United	Home	League	0–2		
3	09/04/85	Shrewsbury Town	Away	League	0–0		
Sub+1	13/04/85	Blackburn Rovers	Home	League	1–2		

SEASON 1985–86

Brighton & Hove Albion – League Division Two

Sub+1	17/08/85	Grimsby Town	Home	League	2–2		
Sub+2	20/08/85	Barnsley	Away	League	2–3	1 Goal	(1)
1	24/08/85	Bradford City	Home	League	2–1		
2	27/08/85	Sheffield United	Home	League	0–0		
Sub+3	31/08/85	Middlesbrough	Away	League	1–0		
3	04/09/85	Leeds United	Home	League	0–1		
4	07/09/85	Blackburn Rovers	Home	League	3–1	1 Goal	(2)
5	14/09/85	Millwall	Away	League	1–0		
6	21/09/85	Wimbledon	Home	League	2–0		

7	28/09/85	Fulham	Away	League	0–1		
8	02/10/85	West Bromwich Albion	Home	FM Cup	1–2		
9	05/10/85	Carlisle United	Home	League	6–1	1 Goal	(3)
10	08/10/85	Bradford City	Away	Lge Cup	2–0		
11	12/10/85	Stoke City	Away	League	1–1		
12	16/10/85	Crystal Palace	Away	FM Cup	3–1		
13	19/10/85	Charlton Athletic	Home	League	3–5	1 Goal	(4)
14	26/10/85	Oldham Athletic	Away	League	0–4		
15	29/10/85	Liverpool	Away	Lge Cup	0–4		
16	02/11/85	Norwich	Home	League	1–1	1 Goal	(5)
17	09/11/85	Shrewsbury Town	Away	League	1–2		
18	16/11/85	Huddersfield Town	Home	League	4–3	1 Goal	(6)
19	23/11/85	Sunderland	Away	League	1–2		
20	30/11/85	Hull City	Home	League	3–1		
21	07/12/85	Barnsley	Home	League	0–1		
22	14/12/85	Grimsby Town	Away	League	2–0		
23	20/12/85	Bradford City	Away	League	2–3	1 Goal	(7)
24	26/12/85	Portsmouth	Away	League	2–1	1 Goal	(8)
25	28/12/85	Leeds United	Away	League	3–2		
26	01/01/86	Crystal Palace	Home	League	2–0	1 Goal	(9)
27	04/01/86	Newcastle United	Away	FA Cup	2–0	1 Goal	(10)
28	18/01/86	Middlesbrough	Home	League	3–3	1 Goal	(11)
29	25/01/86	Hull City	Away	FA Cup	3–2	1 Goal	(12)
30	01/02/86	Sheffield United	Away	League	0–3		
31	04/02/86	Charlton Athletic	Away	League	2–2	1 Goal	(13)
32	15/02/86	Peterborough United	Away	FA Cup	2–2	1 Goal	(14)
33	22/02/86	Wimbledon	Away	League	0–0		
34	03/03/86	Peterborough United	Home	FA Cup	1–0	1 Goal	(15)
35	08/03/86	Southampton	Home	FA Cup	0–2		
36	15/03/86	Stoke City	Home	League	2–0		
37	18/03/86	Blackburn Rovers	Away	League	4–1	1 Goal	(16)
38	22/03/86	Millwall	Home	League	1–0		
39	29/03/86	Crystal Palace	Away	League	0–1		
40	31/03/86	Portsmouth	Home	League	2–3	1 Goal	(17)
41	02/04/86	Oldham Athletic	Home	League	1–1	1 Goal	(18)
42	05/04/86	Norwich City	Away	League	0–3		
43	12/04/86	Shrewsbury Town	Home	League	0–2		
44	16/04/86	Fulham	Home	League	2–3		
45	19/04/86	Huddersfield Town	Away	League	0–1		
46	26/04/86	Sunderland	Home	League	3–1	1 Goal	(19)
47	29/04/86	Carlisle United	Away	League	0–2		
48	02/05/86	Hull City	Away	League	0–2		

SEASON 1986–87

League Division Two

49	23/08/86	Portsmouth	Home	League	0–0		
50	30/08/86	Sunderland	Away	League	1–1		
51	03/09/86	Birmingham City	Home	League	2–0	1 Goal	(20)
52	06/09/86	Grimsby Town	Home	League	0–1		
53	13/09/86	Plymouth Argyle	Away	League	2–2		
54	16/09/86	Shrewsbury Town	Away	League	0–1		
55	20/09/86	West Bromwich Albion	Home	League	2–0		
56	24/09/86	Nottingham Forest	Home	Lge Cup	0–0		
57	27/09/86	Oldham Athletic	Away	League	1–1		
58	01/10/86	Birmingham City	Home	FM Cup	0–3		
59	04/10/86	Stoke City	Home	League	1–0		
60	08/10/86	Nottingham Forest	Away	Lge Cup	0–3		
61	11/10/86	Ipswich Town	Away	League	0–1		
62	18/10/86	Barnsley	Home	League	1–1		
63	25/10/86	Derby County	Away	League	1–4		
64	01/11/86	Hull City	Home	League	2–1		
65	08/11/86	Huddersfield Town	Away	League	1–2		
66	15/11/86	Reading	Away	League	1–2		
67	22/11/86	Blackburn Rovers	Home	League	0–2		
68	29/11/86	Sheffield United	Away	League	1–0	1 Goal	(21)
69	06/12/86	Bradford City	Home	League	2–2	1 Goal	(22)
70	13/12/86	Leeds United	Away	League	1–3		
71	21/12/86	Shrewsbury Town	Home	League	3–0	2 Goals	(24)
72	26/12/86	Crystal Palace	Away	League	0–2		
73	27/12/86	Reading	Home	League	1–1		
74	01/01/87	Millwall	Home	League	0–1		
75	03/01/87	Grimsby Town	Away	League	2–1	1 Goal	(25)
76	10/01/87	Sheffield United	Away	FA Cup	0–0		

77	24/01/87	Portsmouth	Away	League	0–1		
78	21/01/87	Sheffield United	Home	FA Cup	1–2		
Sub+4	07/02/87	Sunderland	Home	League	0–3		
Sub+5	14/02/87	Birmingham City	Away	League	0–2		
Sub+6	21/02/87	Oldham Athletic	Home	League	1–2		
79	28/02/87	West Bromwich Albion	Away	League	0–0		
80	07/03/87	Derby County	Home	League	0–1		

Oxford United – League Division One

1	14/03/87	Liverpool	Home	League	1–3		
2	20/03/87	Coventry City	Away	League	0–3		
3	24/03/87	Charlton Athletic	Away	League	0–0		
4	28/03/87	Sheffield Wednesday	Home	League	2–1	1 Goal	(1)
5	04/04/87	Manchester United	Away	League	2–3		
6	11/04/87	Newcastle United	Home	League	1–1		
7	18/04/87	Southampton	Away	League	0–3		
8	20/04/87	Wimbledon	Home	League	3–1	2 Goals	(3)
9	25/04/87	Tottenham Hotspur	Away	League	1–3	1 Goal	(4)
10	02/05/87	Norwich City	Home	League	0–1		
11	05/05/87	Luton Town	Away	League	3–2	2 Goals	(6)
12	09/05/87	Leicester City	Home	League	0–0		

SEASON 1987–88

League Division One

Sub+1	01/09/87	Tottenham Hotspur	Away	League	0–3		
13	05/09/87	Luton Town	Home	League	2–5		
14	12/09/87	Liverpool	Away	League	0–2		
Sub+2	19/09/87	Queens Park Rangers	Home	League	2–0		
Sub+3	23/09/87	Mansfield Town	Home	Lge Cup	1–1	1 Goal	(7)
15	26/09/87	Derby County	Away	League	1–0		
16	03/10/87	Norwich City	Home	League	3–0		
17	06/10/87	Mansfield Town	Away	Lge Cup	2–0	1 Goal	(8)
18	10/10/87	Arsenal	Away	League	0–2		
19	17/10/87	West Ham United	Home	League	1–2	1 Goal	(9)
20	24/10/87	Charlton Athletic	Home	League	2–1	1 Goal	(10)
21	28/10/87	Leicester City	Home	Lge Cup	0–0		
22	31/10/87	Chelsea	Away	League	1–2		
23	04/11/87	Leicester City	Away	Lge Cup	3–2	1 Goal	(11)
24	07/11/87	Coventry City	Home	League	1–0	1 Goal	(12)
25	11/11/87	Crystal Palace	Home	Simod Cup	1–0	1 Goal	(13)
26	14/11/87	Southampton	Away	League	0–3		
27	18/11/87	Wimbledon	Home	Lge Cup	2–1	1 Goal	(14)
28	21/11/87	Watford	Home	League	1–1		
29	28/11/87	Everton	Away	League	0–0		
30	05/12/87	Newcastle United	Home	League	1–3	1 Goal	(15)
31	12/12/87	Manchester United	Away	League	1–3	1 Goal	(16)
32	19/12/87	Nottingham Forest	Home	League	0–2		
33	26/12/87	Liverpool	Home	League	0–3		
34	28/12/87	Queens Park Rangers	Away	League	2–3	1 Goal	(17)
35	02/01/88	Wimbledon	Home	League	2–5	1 Goal	(18)
36	09/01/88	Leicester City	Home	FA Cup	2–0	1 Goal	(19)
37	13/01/88	Reading	Away	Simod Cup	0–1		
38	16/01/88	Portsmouth	Away	League	2–2	1 Goal	(20)
39	20/01/88	Manchester United	Home	Lge Cup	2–0	1 Goal	(21)
40	30/01/88	Bradford City	Away	FA Cup	2–4	1 Goal	(22)
41	06/02/88	Luton Town	Away	League	4–7	1 Goal	(23)
42	10/02/88	Luton Town	Home	Lge Cup	1–1	1 Goal	(24)
43	13/02/88	Tottenham Hotspur	Home	League	0–0		
44	20/02/88	Derby County	Home	League	0–0		
45	28/02/88	Luton Town	Away	Lge Cup	0–2		
46	05/03/88	West Ham United	Away	League	1–1		
47	16/03/88	Norwich City	Away	League	2–4		
48	19/03/88	Chelsea	Home	League	4–4	2 Goals	(26)
49	26/03/88	Charlton Athletic	Away	League	0–0		
50	30/03/88	Arsenal	Away	League	0–0		
51	02/04/88	Coventry City	Away	League	0–1		
52	04/04/88	Southampton	Home	League	0–0		
53	09/04/88	Watford	Away	League	0–3		
54	13/04/88	Sheffield Wednesday	Home	League	0–3		
55	23/04/88	Everton	Home	League	1–1	1 Goal	(27)
56	30/04/88	Newcastle United	Away	League	1–3		
57	02/05/88	Manchester United	Home	League	0–2		
58	07/05/88	Nottingham Forest	Away	League	3–5		

SEASON 1988–89

League Division Two

59	27/08/88	Leeds United	Away	League	1–1		
60	29/08/88	Hull City	Home	League	1–0	1 Goal	(28)
61	03/09/88	Brighton & Hove Albion	Away	League	3–2	1 Goal	(29)
62	20/09/88	Oldham Athletic	Away	League	0–3		
63	24/09/88	AFC Bournemouth	Away	League	1–2		
64	28/09/88	Bristol City	Home	Lge Cup	2–4	2 Goals	(31)
65	01/10/88	Shrewsbury Town	Home	League	4–1	1 Goal	(32)
66	05/10/88	Swindon Town	Home	League	1–1	1 Goal	(33)
67	08/10/88	Portsmouth	Away	League	1–2		
68	11/10/88	Bristol City	Away	Lge Cup	0–2		
69	15/10/88	Ipswich Town	Away	League	2–1		
70	22/10/88	Blackburn Rovers	Home	League	1–1		

Derby County – League Division One

1	29/10/88	Wimbledon	Home	League	4–1	2 Goals	(2)
2	05/11/88	Tottenham Hotspur	Away	League	3–1	1 Goal	(3)
3	09/11/88	AFC Bournemouth	Home	Simod Cup	1–0	1 Goal	(4)
4	12/11/88	Manchester United	Home	League	2–2	1 Goal	(5)
5	19/11/88	Aston Villa	Away	League	2–1	1 Goal	(6)
6	23/11/88	Aston Villa	Home	Simod Cup	2–1		
7	26/11/88	Arsenal	Home	League	2–1		
8	03/12/88	Sheffield Wednesday	Away	League	1–1		
9	10/12/88	Luton Town	Home	League	0–1		
10	17/12/88	Coventry City	Away	League	2–0	1 Goal	(7)
11	21/12/88	Wimbledon	Away	Simod Cup	0–0+		
12	26/12/88	Liverpool	Home	League	0–1		
13	31/12/88	Millwall	Home	League	0–1		
14	02/01/89	Newcastle United	Away	League	1–0		
15	07/01/89	Southampton	Home	FA Cup	1–1		
16	10/01/89	Southampton	Away	FA Cup	2–1*		
17	14/01/89	West Ham United	Home	League	1–2	1 Goal	(8)
18	21/01/89	Queens Park Rangers	Away	League	1–0		
19	28/01/89	Watford	Away	FA Cup	1–2		
20	04/02/89	Southampton	Home	League	3–1	1 Goal	(9)
21	11/02/89	Norwich City	Away	League	0–1		
22	25/02/89	Everton	Home	League	3–2	1 Goal	(10)
23	01/03/89	Wimbledon	Away	League	0–4		
24	11/03/89	Tottenham Hotspur	Home	League	1–1	1 Goal	(11)
25	18/03/89	Middlesbrough	Away	League	1–0		
26	25/03/89	Nottingham Forest	Home	League	0–2		
27	29/03/89	Liverpool	Away	League	0–1		
28	01/04/89	Coventry City	Home	League	1–0		
29	08/04/89	West Ham United	Away	League	1–1		
30	15/04/89	Manchester United	Away	League	2–0		
31	22/04/89	Sheffield Wednesday	Home	League	1–0	1 Goal	(12)
32	29/04/89	Luton Town	Away	League	0–3		
33	06/05/89	Aston Villa	Home	League	2–1	1 Goal	(13)
34	10/05/89	Charlton Athletic	Away	League	0–3		
35	13/05/89	Arsenal	Away	League	2–1	2 Goals	(15)
36	15/05/89	Everton	Away	League	0–1		

+ AET Wimbledon won 4–3 on penalties

SEASON 1989–90

League Division One

37	19/08/89	Charlton Athletic	Away	League	0–0		
38	23/08/89	Wimbledon	Home	League	1–1		
39	26/08/89	Manchester United	Home	League	2–0	1 Goal	(16)
40	30/08/89	Nottingham Forest	Away	League	1–2		
41	09/09/89	Liverpool	Home	League	0–3		
42	16/09/89	Queens Park Rangers	Away	League	1–0	1 Goal	(17)
43	19/09/89	Cambridge United	Away	Lge Cup	1–2		
44	23/09/89	Southampton	Home	League	0–1		
45	30/09/89	Aston Villa	Away	League	0–1		
46	04/10/89	Cambridge United	Home	Lge Cup	5–0	3 Goals	(20)
47	14/10/89	Crystal Palace	Home	League	3–1	1 Goal	(21)
48	21/10/89	Chelsea	Home	League	0–1		
49	25/10/89	Sheffield Wednesday	Home	Lge Cup	2–1	2 Goals	(23)
50	28/10/89	Arsenal	Away	League	1–1		
51	04/11/89	Luton Town	Away	League	0–1		
52	11/11/89	Manchester City	Home	League	6–0	2 Goals	(25)

53	18/11/89	Sheffield Wednesday	Home	League	2–0	1 Goal	(26)
54	22/11/89	West Bromwich Albion	Home	Lge Cup	2–0		
55	25/11/89	Tottenham Hotspur	Away	League	2–1	1 Goal	(27)
56	29/11/89	West Bromwich Albion	Away	ZDS Cup	5–0	3 Goals	(30)
57	02/12/89	Charlton Athletic	Home	League	2–0	1 Goal	(31)
58	09/12/89	Wimbledon	Away	League	1–1		
59	16/12/89	Norwich City	Away	League	0–1		
60	20/12/89	Newcastle United	Away	ZDS Cup	2–3*		
61	26/12/89	Everton	Home	League	0–1		
62	30/12/89	Coventry City	Home	League	4–1		
63	01/01/90	Millwall	Away	League	1–1		
64	07/01/90	Port Vale	Away	FA Cup	1–1		
65	10/01/90	Port Vale	Home	FA Cup	2–3		
66	13/01/90	Manchester United	Away	League	2–1		
67	17/01/90	West Ham United	Away	Lge Cup	1–1	1 Goal	(32)
68	20/01/90	Nottingham Forest	Home	League	0–2		
69	24/01/90	West Ham United	Home	Lge Cup	0–0*		
70	31/01/90	West Ham United	Away	Lge Cup	1–2	1 Goal	(33)
71	10/02/90	Queens Park Rangers	Home	League	2–0	1 Goal	(34)
72	24/02/90	Tottenham Hotspur	Home	League	2–1	1 Goal	(35)
73	03/03/90	Sheffield Wednesday	Away	League	0–1		
74	10/03/90	Southampton	Away	League	1–2	1 Goal	(36)
75	17/03/90	Aston Villa	Home	League	0–1		
76	20/03/90	Crystal Palace	Away	League	1–1		
77	24/03/90	Arsenal	Home	League	1–3		
78	31/03/90	Chelsea	Away	League	1–1		
79	07/04/90	Coventry City	Away	League	0–1		
80	14/04/90	Millwall	Home	League	2–0		
81	16/04/90	Everton	Away	League	1–2		
82	21/04/90	Norwich City	Home	League	0–2		
83	28/04/90	Manchester City	Away	League	1–0		
84	01/05/90	Liverpool	Away	League	0–1		
85	05/05/90	Luton Town	Home	League	2–3		

SEASON 1990–91

League Division One

86	25/08/90	Chelsea	Away	League	1–2	1 Goal	(37)
87	29/08/90	Sheffield United	Home	League	1–1	1 Goal	(38)
88	01/09/90	Wimbledon	Home	League	1–1	1 Goal	(39)
89	08/09/90	Tottenham Hotspur	Away	League	0–3		
90	15/09/90	Aston Villa	Home	League	0–2		
91	22/09/90	Norwich City	Away	League	1–2		
92	25/09/90	Carlisle United	Away	Lge Cup	1–1	1 Goal	(40)
93	29/09/90	Crystal Palace	Home	League	0–2		
94	06/10/90	Liverpool	Away	League	0–2		
95	10/10/90	Carlisle United	Home	Lge Cup	1–0	1 Goal	(41)
96	20/10/90	Manchester City	Home	League	1–1	1 Goal	(42)
97	27/10/90	Southampton	Away	League	1–0		
98	31/10/90	Sunderland	Home	Lge Cup	6–0		
99	03/11/90	Luton Town	Home	League	2–1	1 Goal	(43)
100	10/11/90	Manchester United	Home	League	0–0		
101	17/11/90	Leeds United	Away	League	0–3		
102	24/11/90	Nottingham Forest	Home	League	2–1	1 Goal	(44)
103	28/11/90	Sheffield Wednesday	Home	Lge Cup	1–1	1 Goal	(45)
104	01/12/90	Sunderland	Away	League	2–1	1 Goal	(46)
105	12/12/90	Sheffield Wednesday	Away	Lge Cup	1–2		
106	15/12/90	Chelsea	Home	League	4–6	2 Goals	(48)
107	19/12/90	Coventry City	Home	ZDS Cup	1–0		
108	23/12/90	Queens Park Rangers	Home	League	1–1	1 Goal	(49)
109	26/12/90	Arsenal	Away	League	0–3		
110	29/12/90	Everton	Away	League	0–2		
111	01/01/91	Coventry City	Home	League	1–1		
112	05/01/91	Newcastle United	Away	FA Cup	0–2		
113	12/01/91	Wimbledon	Away	League	1–3		
114	20/01/91	Tottenham Hotspur	Home	League	0–1		
115	22/01/91	Leeds United	Away	ZDS Cup	1–2	1 Goal	(50)
116	26/01/91	Sheffield United	Away	League	0–1		
117	02/02/91	Aston Villa	Away	League	2–3		
118	23/02/91	Norwich City	Home	League	0–0		
119	02/03/91	Sunderland	Home	League	3–3	3 Goals	(53)
120	16/03/91	Crystal Palace	Away	League	1–2		
121	23/03/91	Liverpool	Home	League	1–7	1 Goal	(54)
122	30/03/91	Arsenal	Home	League	0–2		
123	01/04/91	Queens Park Rangers	Away	League	1–1		

124	10/04/91	Nottingham Forest	Away	League	0–1		
125	13/04/91	Coventry City	Away	League	0–3		
126	16/04/91	Manchester United	Away	League	1–3		
127	20/04/91	Manchester City	Away	League	1–2		
128	23/04/91	Leeds United	Home	League	0–1		
129	04/05/91	Southampton	Home	League	6–2	2 Goals	(56)
130	08/05/91	Everton	Home	League	2–3	1 Goal	(57)
131	11/05/91	Luton Town	Away	League	0–2		

SEASON 1991–92

Liverpool – League Division One

1	17/08/91	Oldham Athletic	Home	League	2–1		
2	21/08/91	Manchester City	Away	League	1–2		
3	24/08/91	Luton Town	Away	League	0–0		
4	27/08/91	Queens Park Rangers	Home	League	1–0	1 Goal	(1)
5	31/08/91	Everton	Home	League	3–1	1 Goal	(2)
6	07/09/91	Notts County	Away	League	2–1		
7	14/09/91	Aston Villa	Home	League	1–1		
8	18/09/91	FC Kuusysi Lahti	Home	UEFA Cup	6–2	4 Goals	(6)
9	21/09/91	Leeds United	Away	League	0–1		
10	25/09/91	Stoke City	Home	Lge Cup	2–2		
11	28/09/91	Sheffield Wednesday	Home	League	1–1		
12	06/10/91	Manchester United	Away	League	0–0		
13	09/10/91	Stoke City	Away	Lge Cup	3–2	1 Goal	(7)
14	19/10/91	Chelsea	Away	League	2–2		
15	26/10/91	Coventry City	Home	League	1–0		
16	29/10/91	Port Vale	Home	Lge Cup	2–2		
17	02/11/91	Crystal Palace	Home	League	1–2		
18	20/11/91	Port Vale	Away	Lge Cup	4–1	1 Goal	(8)
19	23/11/91	Wimbledon	Away	League	0–0		
20	27/11/91	FCS Tirol Innsbruck	Away	UEFA Cup	2–0	2 Goals	(10)
21	30/11/91	Norwich City	Home	League	2–1		
22	03/12/91	Peterborough United	Away	Lge Cup	0–1		
23	07/12/91	Southampton	Away	League	1–1		
24	11/12/91	FCS Tirol Innsbruck	Home	UEFA Cup	4–0	3 Goals	(13)
25	13/12/91	Nottingham Forest	Home	League	2–0		
26	18/12/91	Tottenham Hotspur	Away	League	2–1	1 Goal	(14)
27	20/12/91	Manchester City	Home	League	2–2	1 Goal	(15)
28	26/12/91	Queens Park Rangers	Away	League	0–0		
29	28/12/91	Everton	Away	League	1–1		
30	01/01/92	Sheffield United	Home	League	2–0	1 Goal	(16)
31	06/01/92	Crewe Alexandra	Away	FA Cup	4–0		
32	11/01/92	Luton Town	Home	League	2–1	1 Goal	(17)
33	18/01/92	Oldham Athletic	Away	League	3–2	1 Goal	(18)
34	29/01/92	Arsenal	Home	League	2–0		
35	01/02/92	Chelsea	Home	League	1–2		
36	05/02/92	Bristol Rovers	Away	FA Cup	1–1	1 Goal	(19)
37	08/02/92	Coventry City	Away	League	0–0		
38	11/02/92	Bristol Rovers	Home	FA Cup	2–1	1 Goal	(20)
39	16/02/92	Ipswich Town	Away	FA Cup	0–0		
40	22/02/92	Norwich City	Away	League	0–3		
41	26/02/92	Ipswich Town	Home	FA Cup	3–2		
42	29/02/92	Southampton	Home	League	0–0		
43	04/03/92	Genoa 1893	Away	UEFA Cup	0–2		
44	08/03/92	Aston Villa	Home	FA Cup	1–1		
45	11/03/92	West Ham United	Home	League	1–0	1 Goal	(21)
46	18/03/92	Genoa 1893	Home	UEFA Cup	1–2		
47	21/03/92	Tottenham Hotspur	Home	League	2–1	2 Goals	(23)
48	08/04/92	Wimbledon	Home	League	2–3		
49	11/04/92	Aston Villa	Away	League	0–1		
50	13/04/92	Portsmouth	Neutral	FA Cup	0–0+		
51	18/04/92	Leeds United	Home	League	0–0		
52	20/04/92	Arsenal	Away	League	0–4		
53	26/04/92	Manchester United	Home	League	2–0		
54	09/05/92	Sunderland	Wembley	FA Cup	2–0		

+ AET Liverpool won 3–1 on penalties

SEASON 1992–93

Premier League

55	08/08/92	Leeds United	Wembley	FA C/S	3–4	1 Goal	(24)
56	16/08/92	Nottingham Forest	Away	League	0–1		
57	19/08/92	Sheffield United	Home	League	2–1		

58	23/08/92	Arsenal	Home	League	0–2		
59	25/08/92	Ipswich Town	Away	League	2–2		
60	29/08/92	Leeds United	Away	League	2–2		
61	05/09/92	Chelsea	Home	League	2–1	1 Goal	(25)

Aston Villa – Premier League

1	13/09/92	Leeds United	Away	League	1–1		
2	19/09/92	Liverpool	Home	League	4–2	2 Goals	(2)
3	23/09/92	Oxford United	Away	Lge Cup	2–1		
4	26/09/92	Middlesbrough	Away	League	3–2	2 Goals	(4)
5	03/10/92	Wimbledon	Away	League	3–2	2 Goals	(6)
6	07/10/92	Oxford United	Home	Lge Cup	2–1		
7	19/10/92	Blackburn Rovers	Home	League	0–0		
8	24/10/92	Oldham Athletic	Away	League	1–1		
9	28/10/92	Manchester United	Home	Lge Cup	1–0	1 Goal	(7)
10	01/11/92	Queens Park Rangers	Home	League	2–0	1 Goal	(8)
11	07/11/92	Manchester United	Home	League	1–0		
12	21/11/92	Tottenham Hotspur	Away	League	0–0		
13	28/11/92	Norwich City	Home	League	2–3		
14	02/12/92	Ipswich Town	Home	Lge Cup	2–2	1 Goal	(9)
15	05/12/92	Sheffield Wednesday	Away	League	2–1		
16	12/12/92	Nottingham Forest	Home	League	2–1		
17	15/12/92	Ipswich Town	Away	Lge Cup	0–1		
18	19/12/92	Manchester City	Away	League	1–1		
19	26/12/92	Coventry City	Away	League	0–3		
20	28/12/92	Arsenal	Home	League	1–0	1 Goal	(10)
21	02/01/93	Bristol Rovers	Home	FA Cup	1–1		
22	09/01/93	Liverpool	Away	League	2–1	1 Goal	(11)
23	17/01/93	Middlesbrough	Home	League	5–1	1 Goal	(12)
24	20/01/93	Bristol Rovers	Away	FA Cup	3–0	2 Goals	(14)
25	23/01/93	Wimbledon	Home	FA Cup	1–1		
26	27/01/93	Sheffield United	Home	League	3–1		
27	30/01/93	Southampton	Away	League	0–2		
28	03/02/93	Wimbledon	Away	FA Cup	0–0+		
29	06/02/93	Ipswich Town	Home	League	2–0	1 Goal	(15)
30	10/02/93	Crystal Palace	Away	League	0–1		
31	13/02/93	Chelsea	Away	League	1–0		
32	20/02/93	Everton	Home	League	2–1		
33	27/02/93	Wimbledon	Home	League	1–0		
34	10/03/93	Tottenham Hotspur	Home	League	0–0		
35	14/03/93	Manchester United	Away	League	1–1		
36	20/03/93	Sheffield Wednesday	Home	League	2–0		
37	24/03/93	Norwich City	Away	League	0–1		
38	04/04/93	Nottingham Forest	Away	League	1–0		
39	10/04/93	Coventry City	Home	League	0–0		
40	12/04/93	Arsenal	Away	League	1–0		
41	18/04/93	Manchester City	Home	League	3–1	1 Goal	(16)
42	21/04/93	Blackburn Rovers	Away	League	0–3		
43	02/05/93	Oldham Athletic	Home	League	0–1		
44	09/05/93	Queens Park Rangers	Away	League	1–2		

+ AET Wimbledon won 6–5 on penalties

SEASON 1993–94

Premier League

45	14/08/93	Queens Park Rangers	Home	League	4–1	1 Goal	(17)
46	18/08/93	Sheffield Wednesday	Away	League	0–0		
47	21/08/93	Wimbledon	Away	League	2–2		
48	23/08/93	Manchester United	Home	League	1–2		
49	28/08/93	Tottenham Hotspur	Home	League	1–0		
50	31/08/93	Everton	Away	League	1–0		
51	11/09/93	Coventry City	Home	League	0–0		
52	15/09/93	SK Slovan Bratislava	Away	UEFA Cup	0–0		
53	18/09/93	Ipswich Town	Away	League	2–1	1 Goal	(18)
54	21/09/93	Birmingham City	Away	Lge Cup	1–0		
55	25/09/93	Oldham Athletic	Away	League	1–1	1 Goal	(19)
56	29/09/93	SK Slovan Bratislava	Home	UEFA Cup	2–1		
57	02/10/93	Newcastle United	Home	League	0–2		
58	06/10/93	Birmingham City	Home	Lge Cup	1–0	1 Goal	(20)
59	16/10/93	West Ham United	Away	League	0–0		
60	19/10/93	Deportivo La Coruna	Away	UEFA Cup	1–1	1 Goal	(21)
61	23/10/93	Chelsea	Home	League	1–0		

62	03/11/93	Deportivo La Coruna	Home	UEFA Cup	0–1		
63	06/11/93	Arsenal	Away	League	2–1		
64	20/11/93	Sheffield United	Home	League	1–0		
65	24/11/93	Southampton	Home	League	0–2		
66	28/11/93	Liverpool	Away	League	1–2		
67	30/11/93	Arsenal	Away	Lge Cup	1–0		
68	04/12/93	Queens Park Rangers	Away	League	2–2		
69	08/12/93	Sheffield Wednesday	Home	League	2–2	1 Goal	(22)
70	11/12/93	Wimbledon	Home	League	0–1		
71	19/12/93	Manchester United	Away	League	1–3		
72	29/12/93	Norwich City	Away	League	2–1	1 Goal	(23)
73	01/01/94	Blackburn Rovers	Home	League	0–1		
74	08/01/94	Exeter City	Away	FA Cup	1–0	1 Goal	(24)
75	12/01/94	Tottenham Hotspur	Away	Lge Cup	2–1		
76	15/01/94	West Ham United	Home	League	3–1		
77	22/01/94	Chelsea	Away	League	1–1	1 Goal	(25)
78	29/01/94	Grimsby Town	Away	FA Cup	2–1		
79	06/02/94	Leeds United	Home	League	1–0		
80	12/02/94	Swindon Town	Home	League	5–0	3 Goals	(28)
81	16/02/94	Tranmere Rovers	Away	Lge Cup	1–3		
82	20/02/94	Bolton Wanderers	Away	FA Cup	0–1		
Sub+1	22/02/94	Manchester City	Home	League	0–0		
83	27/02/94	Tranmere Rovers	Home	Lge Cup	3–1+	1 Goal	(29)
84	02/03/94	Tottenham Hotspur	Away	League	1–1		
85	06/03/94	Coventry City	Away	League	1–0		
86	12/03/94	Ipswich Town	Home	League	0–1		
87	16/03/94	Leeds United	Away	League	0–2		
88	19/03/94	Oldham Athletic	Home	League	0–0		
89	27/03/94	Manchester United	Wembley	Lge Cup	3–1	2 Goals	(31)
90	30/03/94	Everton	Home	League	0–0		
91	02/04/94	Manchester City	Away	League	0–3		
92	04/04/94	Norwich City	Home	League	0–0		
93	11/04/94	Blackburn Rovers	Away	League	0–1		
94	30/04/94	Southampton	Away	League	1–4		
95	07/05/94	Liverpool	Home	League	2–1		

+ AET Aston Villa won 5–4 on penalties

SEASON 1994–95

Premier League

96	20/08/94	Everton	Away	League	2–2	1 Goal	(32)
97	24/08/94	Southampton	Home	League	1–1	1 Goal	(33)
98	27/08/94	Crystal Palace	Home	League	1–1		
99	29/08/94	Coventry City	Away	League	1–0		
100	10/09/94	Ipswich Town	Home	League	2–0	1 Goal	(34)
101	15/09/94	Internazionale Milano	Away	UEFA Cup	0–1		
102	17/09/94	West Ham United	Away	League	0–1		
103	21/09/94	Wigan Athletic	Home	Lge Cup	5–0	1 Goal	(35)
104	24/09/94	Blackburn Rovers	Away	League	1–3		
105	29/09/94	Internazionale Milano	Home	UEFA Cup	1–0+		
106	08/10/94	Liverpool	Away	League	2–3		
107	15/10/94	Norwich City	Home	League	1–1	1 Goal	(36)
108	18/10/94	Trabzonspor K	Away	UEFA Cup	0–1		
109	22/10/94	Nottingham Forest	Home	League	0–2		
110	26/10/94	Middlesbrough	Home	Lge Cup	1–0		
111	29/10/94	Queens Park Rangers	Away	League	0–2		
112	01/11/94	Trabzonspor K	Home	UEFA Cup	2–1		
113	06/11/94	Manchester United	Home	League	1–2		
114	09/11/94	Wimbledon	Away	League	3–4	2 Goals	(38)
115	19/11/94	Tottenham Hotspur	Away	League	4–3	1 Goal	(39)
116	27/11/94	Sheffield Wednesday	Home	League	1–1		
117	30/11/94	Crystal Palace	Away	Lge Cup	1–4		
118	03/12/94	Leicester City	Away	League	1–1		
119	19/12/94	Southampton	Away	League	1–2		
120	26/12/94	Arsenal	Away	League	0–0		
121	28/12/94	Chelsea	Home	League	3–0		
122	31/12/94	Manchester City	Away	League	2–2	1 Goal	(40)
123	02/01/95	Leeds United	Home	League	0–0		
124	07/01/95	Barnsley	Away	FA Cup	2–0	1 Goal	(41)
125	14/01/95	Queens Park Rangers	Home	League	2–1		
126	21/01/95	Nottingham Forest	Away	League	2–1	1 Goal	(42)
127	25/01/95	Tottenham Hotspur	Home	League	1–0	1 Goal	(43)
128	28/01/95	Manchester City	Away	FA Cup	0–1		

129	04/02/95	Manchester United	Away	League	0–1		
130	11/02/95	Wimbledon	Home	League	7–1	2 Goals	(45)
131	18/02/95	Sheffield Wednesday	Away	League	2–1	2 Goals	(47)
132	22/02/95	Leicester City	Home	League	4–4	1 Goal	(48)
133	25/02/95	Newcastle United	Away	League	1–3		
134	04/03/95	Blackburn Rovers	Home	League	0–1		
135	06/03/95	Coventry City	Home	League	0–0		
136	18/03/95	West Ham United	Home	League	0–2		
137	01/04/95	Ipswich Town	Away	League	1–0		
138	15/04/95	Chelsea	Away	League	0–1		
139	17/04/95	Arsenal	Home	League	0–4		
140	29/04/95	Leeds United	Away	League	0–1		
141	03/05/95	Manchester City	Home	League	1–1		
142	06/05/95	Liverpool	Home	League	2–0		
143	14/05/95	Norwich City	Away	League	1–1		

+ AET Aston Villa won 4–3 on penalties

SEASON 1995–96

Galatasaray SK – Turkish League Division One
Turkish League: Matches: 21+6 – Goals: 15
Turkish Cup: Matches: 2 – Goals: 2
UEFA Cup: Matches: 2 – Goals: 2
Full match details not available – Turkish Cup details include final only

1995–96 Goals

	08/08/95	AC Sparta Praha	Away	UEFA Cup	1–3	1 Goal	(1)
	19/08/95	Altay SK	Home	League	3–1	2 Goals	(3)
	22/08/95	AC Sparta Praha	Home	UEFA Cup	1–1	1 Goal	(4)
	17/09/95	Antalyaspor K	Away	League	2–0	1 Goal	(5)
	14/10/95	Istanbulspor K	Home	League	4–2	2 Goals	(7)
	28/10/95	Karsiyaka K	Home	League	3–0	1 Goal	(8)
	04/11/95	Eskisehirspor K	Away	League	2–1	1 Goal	(9)
	17/02/96	Genclerbirligi SK	Away	League	2–1	2 Goals	(11)
	30/03/96	Karsiyaka K	Away	League	3–0	1 Goal	(12)
	07/04/96	Eskisehirspor K	Home	League	3–0	2 Goals	(14)
	11/04/96	Fenerbahce SK	Home	T Cup	1–0	1 Goal	(15)
	14/04/96	MKE Ankaragucu K	Away	League	2–2	1 Goal	(16)
	20/04/96	Gaziantepspor K	Home	League	2–0	1 Goal	(17)
	24/04/96	Fenerbahce SK	Away	T Cup	1–1*	1 Goal	(18)
	19/05/96	Denizlispor K	Home	League	1–0	1 Goal	(19)

SEASON 1996–97

Nottingham Forest – Premier League

1	17/08/96	Coventry City	Away	League	3–0		
2	21/08/96	Sunderland	Home	League	1–4		
3	24/08/96	Middlesbrough	Home	League	1–1		
4	04/09/96	Southampton	Away	League	2–2	1 Goal	(1)
5	07/09/96	Leicester City	Home	League	0–0		
6	14/09/96	Manchester United	Away	League	1–4		
7	18/09/96	Wycombe Wanderers	Home	Lge Cup	1–0		
8	21/09/96	West Ham United	Home	League	0–2		
9	24/09/96	Wycombe Wanderers	Away	Lge Cup	1–1*		
10	28/09/96	Chelsea	Away	League	1–1		
11	12/10/96	Leeds United	Away	League	0–2		
12	19/10/96	Derby County	Home	League	1–1	1 Goal	(2)
13	23/10/96	West Ham United	Away	Lge Cup	1–4		
14	28/10/96	Everton	Home	League	0–1		
15	02/11/96	Aston Villa	Away	League	0–2		
16	18/11/96	Sheffield Wednesday	Away	League	0–2		
17	25/11/96	Blackburn Rovers	Home	League	2–2		
18	30/11/96	Wimbledon	Away	League	0–1		
19	09/12/96	Newcastle United	Home	League	0–0		
20	17/12/96	Liverpool	Away	League	2–4		
21	21/12/96	Arsenal	Home	League	2–1		
22	26/12/96	Manchester United	Home	League	0–4		
23	28/12/96	Leicester City	Away	League	2–2		
24	01/01/97	West Ham United	Away	League	1–0		
25	04/01/97	Ipswich Town	Home	FA Cup	3–0	2 Goals	(4)
26	11/01/97	Chelsea	Home	League	2–0		
27	15/02/97	Chesterfield	Away	FA Cup	0–1		

28	22/02/97	Aston Villa	Home	League	0–0		
29	01/03/97	Tottenham Hotspur	Away	League	1–0	1 Goal	(5)
30	05/03/97	Sheffield Wednesday	Home	League	0–3		
31	08/03/97	Arsenal	Away	League	0–2		
32	11/03/97	Blackburn Rovers	Away	League	1–1		
33	15/03/97	Liverpool	Home	League	1–1		
34	22/03/97	Sunderland	Away	League	1–1		
35	24/03/97	Middlesbrough	Away	League	1–1		
36	05/04/97	Southampton	Home	League	1–3		
37	23/04/97	Derby County	Away	League	0–0		
38	03/05/97	Wimbledon	Home	League	1–1		
Sub+1	11/05/97	Newcastle United	Away	League	0–5		

INTERNATIONAL APPEARANCES – WALES

Sub 1	26/03/86	Republic of Ireland	Lansdowne Road	1–0	F		
2	10/05/86	Canada	Toronto	0–2	F		
3	20/05/86	Canada	Vancouver	3–0	F	2 Goals	(2)
4	10/09/86	Finland	Helsinki	1–1	WCQ		
Sub 5	18/02/87	USSR	Vetch Field	0–0	F		
6	23/03/88	Yugoslavia	Vetch Field	1–2	F	1 Goal	(3)
7	27/04/88	Sweden	Stockholm	1–4	F		
8	01/06/88	Malta	Valletta	3–2	F		
Sub 9	04/06/88	Italy	Brescia	1–0	F		
Sub 10	14/09/88	Holland	Amsterdam	0–1	WCQ		
11	19/10/88	Finland	Vetch Field	2–2	WCQ	1 Goal	(4)
12	08/02/89	Israel	Tel Aviv	3–3	F		
13	26/04/89	Sweden	Racecourse	0–2	F		
14	31/05/89	West Germany	Ninian Park	0–0	WCQ		
15	06/09/89	Finland	Helsinki	0–1	WCQ		
16	11/10/89	Holland	Racecourse	1–2	WCQ		
17	15/11/89	West Germany	Cologne	1–2	WCQ		
18	25/04/90	Sweden	Stockholm	2–4	F	2 Goals	(6)
19	20/05/90	Costa Rica	Ninian Park	1–0	F	1 Goal	(7)
20	11/09/90	Denmark	Copenhagen	0–1	F		
21	17/10/90	Belgium	Ninian Park	3–1	ECQ	1 Goal	(8)
22	14/11/90	Luxembourg	Luxembourg	1–0	ECQ		
23	06/02/91	Republic of Ireland	Racecourse	0–3	F		
24	27/03/91	Belgium	Brussels	1–1	ECQ	1 Goal	(9)
25	01/05/91	Iceland	Ninian Park	1–0	F		
26	29/05/91	Poland	Radom	0–0	F		
27	05/06/91	Germany	Cardiff Arms Park	1–0	ECQ		
28	11/09/91	Brazil	Cardiff Arms Park	1–0	F	1 Goal	(10)
29	16/10/91	Germany	Nuremberg	1–4	ECQ		
30	19/02/92	Republic of Ireland	RS Showground	1–0	F		
31	20/05/92	Romania	Bucharest	1–5	WCQ		
32	30/05/92	Holland	Utrecht	0–4	F		
33	03/06/92	Argentina	Tokyo	0–1	F		
34	07/06/92	Japan	Matsuyama	1–0	F		
35	09/09/92	Faroe Islands	Cardiff Arms Park	6–0	WCQ	1 Goal	(11)
36	14/10/92	Cyprus	Nicosia	1–0	WCQ		
37	18/11/92	Belgium	Brussels	0–2	WCQ		
38	31/03/93	Belgium	Cardiff Arms Park	2–0	WCQ		
39	28/04/93	Czechoslovakia	Ostrava	1–1	WCQ		
40	06/06/93	Faroe Islands	Toftir	3–0	WCQ	1 Goal	(12)
41	08/09/93	Czechoslovakia	Cardiff Arms Park	2–2	WCQ		
42	13/10/93	Cyprus	Cardiff Arms Park	2–0	WCQ	1 Goal	(13)
43	17/11/93	Romania	Cardiff Arms Park	1–2	WCQ	1 Goal	(14)
Sub 44	09/03/94	Norway	Ninian Park	1–3	F		
45	16/11/94	Georgia	Tblisi	0–5	ECQ		
46	14/12/94	Bulgaria	Cardiff Arms Park	0–3	ECQ		
47	29/03/95	Bulgaria	Sofia	1–3	ECQ	1 Goal	(15)
48	26/04/95	Germany	Dusseldorf	1–1	ECQ	1 Goal	(16)
49	07/06/95	Georgia	Cardiff Arms Park	0–1	ECQ		
50	11/10/95	Germany	Cardiff Arms Park	1–2	ECQ		
51	15/11/95	Albania	Tirana	1–1	ECQ		
52	02/06/96	San Marino	Serravalle	5–0	WCQ		
53	31/08/96	San Marino	Cardiff Arms Park	6–0	WCQ	2 Goals	(18)
54	05/10/96	Holland	Cardiff Arms Park	1–3	WCQ	1 Goal	(19)
55	09/11/96	Holland	Eindhoven	1–7	WCQ	1 Goal	(20)
56	14/12/96	Turkey	Cardiff Arms Park	0–0	WCQ		
57	29/03/97	Belgium	Cardiff Arms Park	1–2	WCQ		
58	27/05/97	Scotland	Rugby Park	1–0	F		

APPEARANCES AND GOALS PER SEASON

SEASON 83–84	GAMES	GOALS
League	14+5	3
League Cup	0+1	0
Welsh Cup	3	1
TOTAL	**17+6**	**4**

SEASON 84–85	GAMES	GOALS
League	31+3	9
FA Cup	1	0
League Cup	2	0
Freight Rover Trophy	1+1	1
Welsh Cup	4	2
TOTAL	**39+4**	**12**

SEASON 85–86	GAMES	GOALS
League	39+3	15
FA Cup	5	4
League Cup	2	0
Full Members Cup	2	0
TOTAL	**48+3**	**19**

SEASON 86–87	GAMES	GOALS
League	39+3	12
FA Cup	2	0
League Cup	2	0
Full Members Cup	1	0
TOTAL	**44+3**	**12**

SEASON 87–88	GAMES	GOALS
League	35+2	12
FA Cup	2	2
League Cup	7+1	6
Simod Cup	2	1
TOTAL	**46+3**	**21**

SEASON 88–89	GAMES	GOALS
League	40	18
FA Cup	3	0
League Cup	2	2
Simod Cup	3	1
TOTAL	**48**	**21**

SEASON 89–90	GAMES	GOALS
League	38	11
FA Cup	2	0
League Cup	7	7
Zenith Data Systems Cup	2	3
TOTAL	**49**	**21**

SEASON 90–91	GAMES	GOALS
League	38	17
FA Cup	1	0
League Cup	5	3
Zenith Data Systems Cup	2	1
TOTAL	**46**	**21**

SEASON 91–92	GAMES	GOALS
League	36	10
FA Cup	8	2
League Cup	5	2
UEFA Cup	5	9
TOTAL	**54**	**23**

SEASON 92–93	GAMES	GOALS
League	41	13
FA Cup	4	2
League Cup	5	2
FA Charity Shield	1	1
TOTAL	**51**	**18**

SEASON 93–94	GAMES	GOALS
League	37+1	9
FA Cup	3	1
League Cup	7	4
UEFA Cup	4	1
TOTAL	**51+1**	**15**

SEASON 94–95	GAMES	GOALS
League	39	15
FA Cup	2	1
League Cup	3	1
UEFA Cup	4	0
TOTAL	**48**	**17**

SEASON 95–96	GAMES	GOALS
Turkish League	21+6	15
Turkish Cup	2	2
UEFA Cup	2	2
TOTAL	**25+6**	**19**

SEASON 96–97	GAMES	GOALS
League	33+1	3
FA Cup	2	2
League Cup	3	0
TOTAL	**38+1**	**5**

CAREER APPEARANCES AND GOALS

COMPETITION	GAMES	TOTAL	GOALS
League	460+18	478	147
FA Cup	35	35	14
League Cup	50+2	52	27
Freight Rover Trophy	1+1	2	1
Full Members Cup	3	3	0
Simod Cup	5	5	2
Zenith Data Systems Cup	4	4	4
FA Charity Shield	1	1	1
Welsh Cup	7	7	3
UEFA Cup	15	15	12
Turkish League	21+6	27	15
Turkish Cup	2	2	2
Internationals	53+5	58	20
TOTAL	**657+32**	**689**	**248**

HAT-TRICKS

Derby County

1	3	Cambridge United	04/10/89	Home	Lge Cup	5–0
2	3	West Bromwich Albion	29/11/89	Away	ZDS Cup	5–0
3	3	Sunderland	02/03/91	Home	League	3–3

Liverpool

1	4	FC Kuusysi Lahti	18/09/91	Home	UEFA Cup	6–2
2	3	FCS Tirol Innsbruck	11/12/91	Home	UEFA Cup	4–0

Aston Villa

1	3	Swindon Town	12/02/94	Home	League	5–0

League: 2
League Cup: 1
UEFA Cup: 2
Zenith Data Systems Cup: 1
TOTAL: 6

HONOURS

Winners medals
FA Cup: 91/92
League Cup: 93/94
Turkish Cup: 95/96

Runner-up medals
Premier League Championship: 92/93
FA Charity Shield: 92/93

TREVOR SENIOR

Born: 28/11/61 – Dorchester
Height: 6.1
Weight: 12.08 (91/92)

Clubs
Portsmouth: **1982–83** – Matches: **11+2** – Goals: **2**
Aldershot (loan): **1983** – Matches: **10** – Goals: **6**
Reading: **1983–87** – Matches: **191** – Goals: **123**
Watford: **1987–88** – Matches: **29+4** – Goals: **5**
Middlesbrough: **1988** – Matches: **14+1** – Goals: **4**
Reading: **1988–92** – Matches: **160+11** – Goals: **68**

SEASON 1981–82

Portsmouth – League Division Three

1	20/03/82	Fulham	Home	League	1–1		
2	27/03/82	Plymouth Argyle	Home	League	1–0		
3	03/04/82	Carlisle United	Away	League	0–2		
4	06/04/82	Preston North End	Home	League	1–1		
5	12/04/82	Reading	Home	League	3–0	2 Goals	(2)
6	17/04/82	Doncaster Rovers	Home	League	0–0		
7	24/04/82	Huddersfield Town	Away	League	1–0		
8	15/05/82	Swindon Town	Home	League	3–0		
9	21/05/82	Millwall	Home	League	2–2		

SEASON 1982–83

League Division Three

Sub+1	31/08/82	Crystal Palace	Away	Lge Cup	0–2		
Sub+2	14/09/82	Crystal Palace	Home	Lge Cup	1–1		
10	16/10/82	AFC Bournemouth	Home	League	0–2		
11	01/03/83	Wigan Athletic	Home	League	0–0		

Aldershot (loan) – League Division Four

1	26/03/83	Chester	Away	League	1–1		
2	02/04/83	Colchester United	Home	League	0–1		
3	04/04/83	Swindon Town	Away	League	0–2		
4	09/04/83	Bury	Home	League	1–1		
5	16/04/83	Port Vale	Away	League	1–2	1 Goal	(1)
6	23/04/83	Rochdale	Home	League	6–4	3 Goals	(4)
7	30/04/83	Blackpool	Away	League	1–4		
8	02/05/83	Hereford United	Home	League	2–1	2 Goals	(6)
9	07/05/83	Halifax Town	Home	League	6–1		
10	14/05/83	Mansfield Town	Away	League	1–4		

SEASON 1983–84

Reading – League Division Four

1	27/08/83	Blackpool	Away	League	0–1		
2	30/08/83	Colchester United	Away	Lge Cup	2–3	1 Goal	(1)
3	03/09/83	Stockport County	Home	League	6–2	3 Goals	(4)
4	07/09/83	Doncaster Rovers	Home	League	3–2	1 Goal	(5)
5	10/09/83	Rochdale	Away	League	1–4		
6	14/09/83	Colchester United	Home	Lge Cup	4–3*	3 Goals	(8)
7	17/09/83	Chesterfield	Home	League	1–1	1 Goal	(9)
8	24/09/83	Chester City	Away	League	1–2	1 Goal	(10)
9	27/09/83	Bristol City	Away	League	1–3	1 Goal	(11)
10	01/10/83	Darlington	Home	League	1–0		
11	09/10/83	Northampton Town	Away	League	2–2	2 Goals	(13)
12	14/10/83	Crewe Alexandra	Home	League	5–0	2 Goals	(15)
13	19/10/83	Mansfield Town	Home	League	4–0	2 Goals	(17)
14	22/10/83	York City	Away	League	2–2		
15	29/10/83	Swindon Town	Home	League	2–2	2 Goals	(19)
16	02/11/83	Peterborough United	Away	League	3–3	2 Goals	(21)
17	05/11/83	Colchester United	Away	League	0–3		
18	12/11/83	Wrexham	Home	League	4–1	2 Goals	(23)

19	19/11/83	Hereford United	Home	FA Cup	2–0	1 Goal	(24)
20	26/11/83	Bury	Away	League	3–2		
21	02/12/83	Halifax Town	Home	League	1–0		
22	10/12/83	Oxford United	Home	FA Cup	1–1		
23	14/12/83	Oxford United	Away	FA Cup	0–2		
24	26/12/83	Aldershot	Away	League	0–0		
25	27/12/83	Torquay United	Home	League	2–2	1 Goal	(25)
26	30/12/83	Tranmere Rovers	Away	League	3–2	1 Goal	(26)
27	02/01/84	Hereford United	Home	League	3–1	1 Goal	(27)
28	06/01/84	Stockport County	Away	League	0–3		
29	14/01/84	Blackpool	Home	League	2–0	1 Goal	(28)
30	21/01/84	Chesterfield	Away	League	1–2	1 Goal	(29)
31	28/01/84	Rochdale	Home	League	0–0		
32	04/02/84	Darlington	Away	League	1–1		
33	11/02/84	Chester City	Home	League	1–0		
34	15/02/84	Peterborough United	Home	League	1–1	1 Goal	(30)
35	18/02/84	Swindon Town	Away	League	1–1	1 Goal	(31)
36	25/02/84	York City	Home	League	1–0		
37	03/03/84	Mansfield Town	Away	League	0–2		
38	07/03/84	Colchester United	Home	League	1–0	1 Goal	(32)
39	10/03/84	Wrexham	Away	League	3–0	1 Goal	(33)
40	17/03/84	Northampton Town	Home	League	3–0	2 Goals	(35)
41	23/03/84	Crewe Alexandra	Away	League	1–1		
42	07/04/84	Bristol City	Home	League	2–0		
43	13/04/84	Halifax Town	Away	League	1–0		
44	21/04/84	Aldershot	Home	League	1–0	1 Goal	(36)
45	23/04/84	Torquay United	Away	League	2–2	1 Goal	(37)
46	28/04/84	Bury	Home	League	1–1	1 Goal	(38)
47	01/05/84	Doncaster Rovers	Away	League	3–2	1 Goal	(39)
48	05/05/84	Hereford United	Away	League	1–1		
49	07/05/84	Tranmere Rovers	Home	League	1–0		
50	12/05/84	Hartlepool United	Away	League	3–3	2 Goals	(41)

SEASON 1984–85

League Division Three

51	25/08/84	Rotherham United	Home	League	1–0	1 Goal	(42)
52	29/08/84	Millwall	Home	Lge Cup	1–1		
53	01/09/84	Plymouth Argyle	Away	League	2–1	1 Goal	(43)
54	04/09/84	Millwall	Away	Lge Cup	3–4	1 Goal	(44)
55	08/09/84	Doncaster Rovers	Home	League	1–4		
56	15/09/84	Bristol Rovers	Away	League	0–1		
57	18/09/84	Walsall	Away	League	1–3		
58	22/09/84	Derby County	Home	League	0–0		
59	29/09/84	Hull City	Away	League	0–0		
60	03/10/84	Wigan Athletic	Home	League	0–1		
61	06/10/84	Bolton Wanderers	Home	League	3–1	1 Goal	(45)
62	13/10/84	Preston North End	Away	League	2–0		
63	20/10/84	Burnley	Home	League	5–1	2 Goals	(47)
64	23/10/84	Gillingham	Away	League	1–4		
65	27/10/84	Lincoln City	Away	League	1–5	1 Goal	(48)
66	03/11/84	AFC Bournemouth	Home	League	0–2		
67	07/11/84	Orient	Home	League	1–1		
68	10/11/84	Swansea City	Away	League	2–1	1 Goal	(49)
69	17/11/84	Barry Town	Away	FA Cup	2–1	1 Goal	(50)
70	24/11/84	Cambridge United	Home	League	3–1	3 Goals	(53)
71	01/12/84	York City	Away	League	2–2	1 Goal	(54)
72	08/12/84	Bognor Regis Town	Home	FA Cup	6–2	2 Goals	(56)
73	15/12/84	Bradford City	Home	League	0–3		
74	22/12/84	Bristol City	Home	League	1–0		
75	26/12/84	Newport County	Away	League	2–1	1 Goal	(57)
76	29/12/84	Brentford	Away	League	1–2		
77	01/01/85	Millwall	Home	League	2–2	1 Goal	(58)
78	05/01/85	Barnsley	Away	FA Cup	3–4	1 Goal	(59)
79	19/01/85	Doncaster Rovers	Away	League	4–0	1 Goal	(60)
80	26/01/85	Bristol Rovers	Home	League	3–2	1 Goal	(61)
81	02/02/85	Hull City	Home	League	4–2	2 Goals	(63)
82	06/02/85	Brentford	Home	FR Trophy	1–3		
83	23/02/85	AFC Bournemouth	Away	League	3–0	2 Goals	(65)
84	26/02/85	Brentford	Away	FR Trophy	0–2		
85	02/03/85	Lincoln City	Home	League	1–1	1 Goal	(66)
86	09/03/85	Burnley	Away	League	2–0	1 Goal	(67)
87	01/05/85	Walsall	Home	League	1–1	1 Goal	(68)
88	04/05/85	Bradford City	Away	League	5–2		

SEASON 1985–86

League Division Three

89	17/08/85	Blackpool	Home	League	1–0		
90	21/08/85	AFC Bournemouth	Home	Lge Cup	1–3		
91	24/08/85	Plymouth Argyle	Away	League	1–0	1 Goal	(69)
92	26/08/85	Bristol Rovers	Home	League	3–2		
93	31/08/85	Cardiff City	Away	League	3–1	3 Goals	(72)
94	03/09/85	AFC Bournemouth	Away	Lge Cup	0–2		
95	07/09/85	Walsall	Home	League	2–1	1 Goal	(73)
96	14/09/85	Rotherham United	Away	League	2–1		
97	17/09/85	Brentford	Away	League	2–1	1 Goal	(74)
98	21/09/85	Swansea City	Home	League	2–0	1 Goal	(75)
99	28/09/85	Doncaster Rovers	Away	League	1–0		
100	02/10/85	Chesterfield	Home	League	4–2	3 Goals	(78)
101	05/10/85	Bolton Wanderers	Home	League	1–0		
102	12/10/85	Newport County	Away	League	2–0		
103	19/10/85	Lincoln City	Away	League	1–0	1 Goal	(79)
104	23/10/85	Wolverhampton Wanderers	Home	League	2–2	1 Goal	(80)
105	26/10/85	Bury	Away	League	1–3		
106	02/11/85	Wigan Athletic	Home	League	1–0		
107	06/11/85	Notts County	Home	League	3–1	1 Goal	(81)
108	09/11/85	York City	Away	League	1–0		
109	16/11/85	Wealdstone	Home	FA Cup	1–0		
110	23/11/85	Darlington	Home	League	0–2		
111	30/11/85	Derby County	Away	League	1–1		
112	07/12/85	Hereford United	Home	FA Cup	2–0	1 Goal	(82)
113	14/12/85	Bristol City	Home	League	1–0		
114	21/12/85	Plymouth Argyle	Home	League	4–3	2 Goals	(84)
115	26/12/85	AFC Bournemouth	Away	League	1–0		
116	28/12/85	Bristol Rovers	Away	League	2–0	1 Goal	(85)
117	01/01/86	Gillingham	Home	League	1–2		
118	04/01/86	Huddersfield Town	Away	FA Cup	0–0		
119	13/01/86	Huddersfield Town	Home	FA Cup	2–1*	2 Goals	(87)
120	11/01/86	Cardiff City	Home	League	1–1		
121	18/01/86	Blackpool	Away	League	0–0		
122	25/01/86	Bury	Home	FA Cup	1–1	1 Goal	(88)
123	28/01/86	Bury	Away	FA Cup	0–3		
124	01/02/86	Walsall	Away	League	0–6		
125	22/02/86	Swansea City	Away	League	3–2	1 Goal	(89)
126	04/03/86	Chesterfield	Away	League	4–3	2 Goals	(91)
127	06/03/86	Orient	Home	FR Trophy	0–3		
128	08/03/86	Bolton Wanderers	Away	League	0–2		
129	12/03/86	Lincoln City	Home	League	0–2		
130	15/03/86	Newport County	Home	League	2–0		
131	19/03/86	Rotherham United	Home	League	2–1	1 Goal	(92)
132	22/03/86	Bury	Home	League	2–0	1 Goal	(93)
133	29/03/86	Gillingham	Away	League	0–3		
134	31/03/86	AFC Bournemouth	Home	League	1–2	1 Goal	(94)
135	05/04/86	Notts County	Away	League	0–0		
136	08/04/86	Wolverhampton Wanderers	Away	League	3–2		
137	12/04/86	York City	Home	League	0–0		
138	16/04/86	Brentford	Home	League	3–1	2 Goals	(96)
139	19/04/86	Darlington	Away	League	0–0		
140	22/04/86	Wigan Athletic	Away	League	0–1		
141	26/04/86	Derby County	Home	League	1–0	1 Goal	(97)
142	03/05/86	Bristol City	Away	League	0–3		
143	05/05/86	Doncaster Rovers	Home	League	2–0	2 Goals	(99)

SEASON 1986–87

League Division Two

144	23/08/86	Millwall	Home	League	0–1		
145	27/08/86	Bristol Rovers	Away	Lge Cup	2–1	2 Goals	(101)
146	30/08/86	Plymouth Argyle	Away	League	0–1		
147	03/09/86	Bristol Rovers	Home	Lge Cup	4–0	3 Goals	(104)
148	06/09/86	West Bromwich Albion	Home	League	1–1		
149	13/09/86	Leeds United	Away	League	2–3	1 Goal	(105)
150	20/09/86	Shrewsbury Town	Home	League	3–1		
151	24/09/86	Aston Villa	Home	Lge Cup	1–1		
152	27/09/86	Crystal Palace	Away	League	3–1	1 Goal	(106)
153	01/10/86	Grimsby Town	Home	League	2–3		
154	04/10/86	Blackburn Rovers	Home	League	4–0	1 Goal	(107)
155	08/10/86	Aston Villa	Away	Lge Cup	1–4	1 Goal	(108)
156	11/10/86	Sheffield United	Away	League	3–3	1 Goal	(109)

157	18/10/86	Hull City	Away	League	2–0	2 Goals	(111)
158	21/10/86	Sunderland	Away	League	1–1		
159	25/10/86	Oldham Athletic	Home	League	2–3	1 Goal	(112)
160	01/11/86	Bradford City	Away	League	0–3		
161	08/11/86	Barnsley	Home	League	0–0		
162	15/11/86	Brighton & Hove Albion	Home	League	2–1		
163	22/11/86	Stoke City	Away	League	0–3		
164	25/11/86	Ipswich Town	Home	FM Cup	0–2		
165	06/12/86	Derby County	Away	League	0–3		
166	13/12/86	Ipswich Town	Home	League	1–4		
167	19/12/86	West Bromwich Albion	Away	League	2–1	1 Goal	(113)
168	26/12/86	Birmingham City	Home	League	2–2		
169	27/12/86	Brighton & Hove Albion	Away	League	1–1		
170	01/01/87	Portsmouth	Away	League	0–1		
171	10/01/87	Arsenal	Home	FA Cup	1–3	1 Goal	(114)
172	24/01/87	Millwall	Away	League	1–2		
173	31/01/87	Sunderland	Home	League	1–0		
174	07/02/87	Plymouth Argyle	Home	League	2–0	2 Goals	(116)
175	14/02/87	Grimsby Town	Away	League	2–3		
176	17/02/87	Huddersfield Town	Home	League	3–2	2 Goals	(118)
177	21/02/87	Crystal Palace	Home	League	1–0	1 Goal	(119)
178	28/02/87	Shrewsbury Town	Away	League	0–0		
179	06/03/87	Oldham Athletic	Away	League	0–4		
180	14/03/87	Hull City	Home	League	1–0		
181	21/03/87	Sheffield United	Home	League	2–0	1 Goal	(120)
182	04/04/87	Barnsley	Away	League	0–2		
183	11/04/87	Bradford City	Home	League	0–1		
184	14/04/87	Blackburn Rovers	Away	League	0–0		
185	18/04/87	Portsmouth	Home	League	2–2		
186	20/04/87	Birmingham City	Away	League	1–1		
187	22/04/87	Leeds United	Home	League	2–1	1 Goal	(121)
188	25/04/87	Stoke City	Home	League	0–1		
189	02/05/87	Huddersfield Town	Away	League	0–2		
190	04/05/87	Derby County	Home	League	2–0	2 Goals	(123)
191	09/05/87	Ipswich Town	Away	League	1–1		

SEASON 1987–88

Watford – League Division One

1	15/08/87	Wimbledon	Home	League	1–0		
2	19/08/87	Nottingham Forest	Away	League	0–1		
3	22/08/87	Manchester United	Away	League	0–2		
4	29/08/87	Tottenham Hotspur	Home	League	1–1		
5	05/09/87	Norwich City	Home	League	0–1		
6	12/09/87	Sheffield Wednesday	Away	League	3–2	1 Goal	(1)
7	19/09/87	Portsmouth	Home	League	0–0		
8	22/09/87	Darlington	Away	Lge Cup	3–0	1 Goal	(2)
9	26/09/87	Chelsea	Home	League	0–3		
10	03/10/87	Coventry City	Away	League	0–1		
11	24/10/87	Everton	Away	League	0–2		
12	28/10/87	Swindon Town	Away	Lge Cup	1–1		
13	31/10/87	West Ham United	Home	League	1–2		
14	03/11/87	Swindon Town	Home	Lge Cup	4–2		
Sub+1	17/11/87	Manchester City	Away	Lge Cup	1–3		
Sub+2	21/11/87	Oxford United	Away	League	1–1		
15	24/11/87	Liverpool	Away	League	0–4		
16	28/11/87	Arsenal	Home	League	2–0		
17	05/12/87	Derby County	Away	League	1–1		
18	12/12/87	Luton Town	Home	League	0–1		
Sub+3	26/12/87	Sheffield Wednesday	Home	League	1–3		
19	28/12/87	Portsmouth	Away	League	1–1		
20	01/01/88	Tottenham Hotspur	Away	League	1–2		
21	02/01/88	Manchester United	Home	League	0–1		
22	09/01/88	Hull City	Away	FA Cup	1–1		
23	25/01/88	Ipswich Town	Away	Simod Cup	2–5*	1 Goal	(3)
Sub+4	30/01/88	Coventry City	Away	FA Cup	1–0	1 Goal	(4)
24	06/02/88	Norwich City	Away	League	0–0		
25	13/02/88	Liverpool	Home	League	1–4		
26	20/02/88	Port Vale	Away	FA Cup	0–0		
27	23/02/88	Port Vale	Home	FA Cup	2–0	1 Goal	(5)
28	27/02/88	Coventry City	Home	League	0–1		
29	05/03/88	Southampton	Home	League	0–1		

Middlesbrough – League Division Two

| 1 | 26/03/88 | Birmingham City | Home | League | 1–1 | | |

2	02/04/88	Sheffield United	Home	League	6–0	2 Goals	(2)
3	04/04/88	Hull City	Away	League	0–0		
4	09/04/88	Manchester City	Home	League	2–1		
5	23/04/88	Ipswich Town	Away	League	0–4		
Sub+1	07/05/88	Leicester City	Home	League	1–2		
6	15/05/88	Bradford City	Away	Lge P/O	1–2	1 Goal	(3)
7	18/05/88	Bradford City	Home	Lge P/O	2–0		
8	25/05/88	Chelsea	Home	Lge P/O	2–0	1 Goal	(4)
9	28/05/88	Chelsea	Away	Lge P/O	0–1		

SEASON 1988–89

League Division One

10	27/08/88	Derby County	Away	League	0–1
11	03/09/88	Norwich City	Home	League	2–3
12	17/09/88	Wimbledon	Home	League	1–0
13	24/09/88	Tottenham Hotspur	Away	League	2–3
14	28/09/88	Tranmere Rovers	Home	Lge Cup	0–0

Reading – League Division Three

1	15/10/88	Mansfield Town	Home	League	1–0		
2	22/10/88	Notts County	Away	League	3–3	1 Goal	(1)
3	26/10/88	Bristol Rovers	Home	League	3–1		
4	29/10/88	Northampton Town	Away	League	3–1		
5	05/11/88	Brentford	Home	League	2–2		
6	08/11/88	Fulham	Away	League	1–2	1 Goal	(2)
7	12/11/88	Preston North End	Home	League	2–2	1 Goal	(3)
8	19/11/88	Hendon	Home	FA Cup	4–0	1 Goal	(4)
9	26/11/88	Chesterfield	Home	League	0–0		
10	30/11/88	Aldershot	Home	SV Trophy	5–2	2 Goals	(6)
11	03/12/88	Bristol City	Away	League	1–2	1 Goal	(7)
12	06/12/88	Leyton Orient	Away	SV Trophy	1–1	1 Goal	(8)
13	10/12/88	Maidstone United	Home	FA Cup	1–1	1 Goal	(9)
14	14/12/88	Maidstone United	Away	FA Cup	2–1	1 Goal	(10)
15	17/12/88	Port Vale	Away	League	0–3		
16	26/12/88	Aldershot	Home	League	3–1		
17	30/12/88	Blackpool	Home	League	2–1	1 Goal	(11)
18	02/01/89	Swansea City	Away	League	0–2		
19	07/01/89	Tranmere Rovers	Away	FA Cup	1–1		
20	11/01/89	Tranmere Rovers	Home	FA Cup	2–1	1 Goal	(12)
21	14/01/89	Wolverhampton Wanderers	Home	League	0–2		
22	18/01/89	Hereford United	Home	SV Trophy	2–3	1 Goal	(13)
23	21/01/89	Bolton Wanderers	Away	League	1–1		
24	28/01/89	Grimsby Town	Away	FA Cup	1–1		
25	01/02/89	Grimsby Town	Home	FA Cup	1–2		
26	04/02/89	Chester City	Away	League	0–3		
27	11/02/89	Bury	Home	League	1–1		
28	18/02/89	Cardiff City	Home	League	3–1	1 Goal	(14)
29	25/02/89	Mansfield Town	Away	League	1–2	1 Goal	(15)
30	01/03/89	Bristol Rovers	Away	League	1–1		
31	04/03/89	Notts County	Home	League	1–3		
32	07/03/89	Huddersfield Town	Away	League	2–2	2 Goals	(17)
33	11/03/89	Brentford	Away	League	2–3	1 Goal	(18)
34	15/03/89	Northampton Town	Home	League	1–1		
35	18/03/89	Sheffield United	Away	League	0–1		
36	25/03/89	Swansea City	Home	League	2–0	2 Goals	(20)
37	27/03/89	Aldershot	Away	League	1–1		
38	01/04/89	Port Vale	Home	League	3–0	1 Goal	(21)
39	05/04/89	Huddersfield Town	Home	League	2–1	2 Goals	(23)
40	08/04/89	Blackpool	Away	League	4–2		
41	14/04/89	Southend United	Away	League	1–2		
42	19/04/89	Wigan Athletic	Home	League	0–3		
43	22/04/89	Gillingham	Home	League	1–2		
44	29/04/89	Preston North End	Away	League	1–2		
45	01/05/89	Fulham	Home	League	0–1		
46	05/05/89	Bristol City	Home	League	1–2		
47	13/05/89	Chesterfield	Away	League	4–2	1 Goal	(24)

SEASON 1989–90

League Division Three

48	19/08/89	Shrewsbury Town	Home	League	3–3
49	22/08/89	Bristol City	Away	Lge Cup	3–2
50	25/08/89	Crewe Alexandra	Away	League	1–1

51	29/08/89	Bristol City	Home	Lge Cup	2–2	1 Goal	(25)
52	02/09/89	Tranmere Rovers	Home	League	1–0		
53	09/09/89	Notts County	Away	League	0–0		
54	16/09/89	Walsall	Home	League	0–1		
55	19/09/89	Newcastle United	Home	Lge Cup	3–1	2 Goals	(27)
56	23/09/89	Swansea City	Away	League	6–1	3 Goals	(30)
57	26/09/89	Chester City	Home	League	1–1		
58	30/09/89	Bristol Rovers	Away	League	0–0		
59	04/10/89	Newcastle United	Away	Lge Cup	0–4		
60	06/10/89	Blackpool	Away	League	0–0		
61	14/10/89	Huddersfield Town	Home	League	0–0		
62	17/10/89	Fulham	Home	League	3–2	1 Goal	(31)
63	21/10/89	Leyton Orient	Away	League	1–4		
64	28/10/89	Mansfield Town	Home	League	1–0		
65	31/10/89	Wigan Athletic	Away	League	1–3	1 Goal	(32)
66	04/11/89	Birmingham City	Home	League	0–2		
67	11/11/89	Bury	Away	League	0–4		
68	17/11/89	Bristol Rovers	Away	FA Cup	1–1		
69	21/11/89	Bristol Rovers	Home	FA Cup	1–1*	1 Goal	(33)
70	25/11/89	Bristol City	Home	League	1–1	1 Goal	(34)
71	27/11/89	Bristol Rovers	Away	FA Cup	1–0	1 Goal	(35)
72	02/12/89	Preston North End	Away	League	0–1		
73	09/12/89	Welling United	Home	FA Cup	0–0		
74	13/12/89	Welling United	Away	FA Cup	1–1*		
75	17/12/89	Northampton Town	Away	League	1–2		
76	19/12/89	Welling United	Home	FA Cup	0–0*		
77	22/12/89	Welling United	Away	FA Cup	2–1		
78	26/12/89	Brentford	Home	League	1–0	1 Goal	(36)
79	30/12/89	Rotherham United	Home	League	3–2	1 Goal	(37)
80	06/01/90	Sunderland	Home	FA Cup	2–1		
81	13/01/90	Crewe Alexandra	Home	League	1–1		
82	17/01/90	Swansea City	Away	LD Cup	2–1	1 Goal	(38)
83	20/01/90	Shrewsbury Town	Away	League	1–1		
84	23/01/90	Brentford	Away	LD Cup	1–2		
85	27/01/90	Newcastle United	Home	FA Cup	3–3	1 Goal	(39)
86	31/01/90	Newcastle United	Away	FA Cup	1–4	1 Goal	(40)
87	11/02/90	Walsall	Away	League	1–1	1 Goal	(41)
88	12/02/90	Tranmere Rovers	Away	League	1–3		
89	17/02/90	Preston North End	Home	League	6–0	2 Goals	(43)
90	20/02/90	Swansea City	Home	League	1–1		
91	24/02/90	Bristol City	Away	League	1–0		
92	16/04/90	Brentford	Away	League	1–1		
93	21/04/90	Northampton Town	Home	League	3–2	1 Goal	(44)
94	24/04/90	Rotherham United	Away	League	1–1	1 Goal	(45)
95	28/04/90	Bury	Home	League	1–0		
96	01/05/90	Cardiff City	Away	League	2–3	1 Goal	(46)
97	03/05/90	Notts County	Home	League	1–1		
98	05/05/90	Birmingham City	Away	League	1–0		

SEASON 1990–91

League Division Three

99	25/08/90	Exeter City	Away	League	3–1	1 Goal	(47)
100	28/08/90	Oxford United	Home	Lge Cup	0–1		
101	01/09/90	Preston North End	Home	League	3–3		
102	05/09/90	Oxford United	Away	Lge Cup	1–2		
103	08/09/90	Bradford City	Away	League	1–2		
104	15/09/90	Cambridge United	Home	League	2–2	1 Goal	(48)
105	18/09/90	Crewe Alexandra	Home	League	2–1		
106	22/09/90	Huddersfield Town	Away	League	2–0	2 Goals	(50)
107	29/09/90	Rotherham United	Away	League	2–0	1 Goal	(51)
108	02/10/90	AFC Bournemouth	Home	League	2–1	1 Goal	(52)
109	06/10/90	Birmingham City	Home	League	2–2	1 Goal	(53)
110	13/10/90	Wigan Athletic	Away	League	0–1		
111	20/10/90	Bury	Away	League	1–2		
112	23/10/90	Brentford	Home	League	1–2	1 Goal	(54)
113	27/10/90	Leyton Orient	Home	League	1–2	1 Goal	(55)
114	03/11/90	Stoke City	Away	League	1–0		
115	10/11/90	Bolton Wanderers	Away	League	1–3		
116	17/11/90	Colchester United	Away	FA Cup	1–2		
Sub+1	24/11/90	Southend United	Home	League	2–4	1 Goal	(56)
117	27/11/90	Aldershot	Away	LD Cup	1–3		
118	07/12/90	Southend United	Home	LD Cup	1–4		
119	14/12/90	Tranmere Rovers	Away	League	0–0		

120	22/12/90	Swansea City	Away	League	1–3		
121	26/12/90	Grimsby Town	Home	League	2–0		
122	29/12/90	Mansfield Town	Home	League	2–1	1 Goal	(57)
123	12/01/91	Preston North End	Away	League	2–1		
124	19/01/91	Exeter City	Home	League	1–0		
125	26/01/91	Wigan Athletic	Home	League	3–1	2 Goals	(59)
126	01/02/91	Crewe Alexandra	Away	League	0–1		
127	19/02/91	Southend United	Away	League	2–1		
128	23/02/91	Bolton Wanderers	Home	League	0–1		
129	02/03/91	Fulham	Away	League	1–1		
130	05/03/91	Chester City	Away	League	0–1		
Sub+2	16/03/91	Rotherham United	Home	League	2–0		
131	23/03/91	Birmingham City	Away	League	1–1		
132	26/03/91	Huddersfield Town	Home	League	1–2		
Sub+3	30/03/91	Grimsby Town	Away	League	0–3		
Sub+4	01/04/91	Swansea City	Home	League	0–0		
Sub+5	06/04/91	Mansfield Town	Away	League	0–2		
133	09/04/91	Cambridge United	Away	League	0–3		
134	13/04/91	Chester City	Home	League	2–2		
135	27/04/91	Brentford	Away	League	0–1		
136	30/04/91	Bradford City	Home	League	1–2		
137	07/05/91	Shrewsbury Town	Away	League	1–5	1 Goal	(60)
138	11/05/91	Stoke City	Home	League	1–0	1 Goal	(61)

SEASON 1991–92

League Division Three

Sub+6	17/08/91	Hull City	Home	League	0–1		
139	24/08/91	Hartlepool United	Away	League	0–2		
Sub+7	28/08/91	Cambridge United	Home	Lge Cup	0–3		
140	31/08/91	Bury	Home	League	3–2	1 Goal	(62)
141	03/09/91	Swansea City	Away	League	2–1	1 Goal	(63)
142	07/09/91	Birmingham City	Home	League	1–1		
143	14/09/91	Brentford	Away	League	0–1		
144	17/09/91	Torquay United	Away	League	2–1	1 Goal	(64)
145	21/09/91	Bradford City	Home	League	1–2		
146	28/09/91	Exeter City	Away	League	1–2		
147	05/10/91	AFC Bournemouth	Home	League	0–0		
148	11/10/91	Wigan Athletic	Away	League	1–1		
Sub+8	19/10/91	Peterborough United	Home	League	1–1		
149	22/10/91	Leyton Orient	Away	A Trophy	0–1		
Sub+9	26/10/91	Shrewsbury Town	Away	League	2–1		
150	28/12/91	Hull City	Away	League	1–0	1 Goal	(65)
151	01/01/92	Swansea City	Home	League	1–0	1 Goal	(66)
152	04/01/92	Bolton Wanderers	Away	FA Cup	0–2		
153	11/01/92	Huddersfield Town	Home	League	1–0	1 Goal	(67)
154	18/01/92	Stoke City	Away	League	0–3		
155	01/02/92	Peterborough United	Away	League	3–5		
156	08/02/92	Shrewsbury Town	Home	League	2–1	1 Goal	(68)
157	11/02/92	Stockport County	Away	League	0–1		
158	15/02/92	Fulham	Home	League	0–2		
Sub+10	29/02/92	Preston North End	Home	League	2–2		
Sub+11	28/03/92	Chester City	Home	League	0–0		
159	01/04/92	Brentford	Home	League	0–0		
160	02/05/92	Wigan Athletic	Home	League	3–2		

APPEARANCES AND GOALS PER SEASON

SEASON 81–82	**GAMES**	**GOALS**
League	9	2
TOTAL	**9**	**2**

SEASON 82–83	**GAMES**	**GOALS**
League	12	6
League Cup	0+2	0
TOTAL	**12+2**	**6**

SEASON 83–84	**GAMES**	**GOALS**
League	45	36
FA Cup	3	1
League Cup	2	4
TOTAL	**50**	**41**

SEASON 84–85	GAMES	GOALS
League	31	22
FA Cup	3	4
League Cup	2	1
Freight Rover Trophy	2	0
TOTAL	**38**	**27**

SEASON 85–86	GAMES	GOALS
League	46	27
FA Cup	6	4
League Cup	2	0
Freight Rover Trophy	1	0
TOTAL	**55**	**31**

SEASON 86–87	GAMES	GOALS
League	42	17
FA Cup	1	1
League Cup	4	6
Full Members Cup	1	0
TOTAL	**48**	**24**

SEASON 87–88	GAMES	GOALS
League	27+3	3
League Play–offs	4	2
FA Cup	3+1	2
League Cup	3+1	1
Simod Cup	1	1
TOTAL	**38+5**	**9**

SEASON 88–89	GAMES	GOALS
League	41	16
FA Cup	7	4
League Cup	1	0
Sherpa Van Trophy	3	4
TOTAL	**52**	**24**

SEASON 89–90	GAMES	GOALS
League	35	14
FA Cup	10	4
League Cup	4	3
Leyland Daf Cup	2	1
TOTAL	**51**	**22**

SEASON 90–91	GAMES	GOALS
League	35+5	15
FA Cup	1	0
League Cup	2	0
Leyland Daf Cup	2	0
TOTAL	**40+5**	**15**

SEASON 91–92	GAMES	GOALS
League	20+5	7
FA Cup	1	0
League Cup	0+1	0
Autoglass Trophy	1	0
TOTAL	**22+6**	**7**

CAREER APPEARANCES AND GOALS

COMPETITION	GAMES	TOTAL	GOALS
League	343+13	356	165
League Play–offs	4	4	2
FA Cup	35+1	36	20
League Cup	20+4	24	15
Freight Rover Trophy	3	3	0
Full Members Cup	1	1	0
Simod Cup	1	1	1
Sherpa Van Trophy	3	3	4
Leyland Daf Cup	4	4	1
Autoglass Trophy	1	1	0
TOTAL	**415+18**	**433**	**208**

HAT-TRICKS

Aldershot (loan)

1	3	Rochdale	23/04/83	Home	League	6–4

Reading

1	3	Stockport County	03/09/83	Home	League	6–2
2	3	Colchester United	14/09/83	Home	Lge Cup	4–3
3	3	Cambridge United	24/11/84	Home	League	3–1
4	3	Cardiff City	31/08/85	Away	League	3–1
5	3	Chesterfield	02/10/85	Home	League	4–2
6	3	Bristol Rovers	03/09/86	Home	Lge Cup	4–0
7	3	Swansea City	23/09/89	Away	League	6–1

League: 6
League Cup: 2
TOTAL: 8

HONOURS

Winners medals
League Division Three Championship: 85/86

Runner-up medals
Promoted to League Division One: 87/88
Promoted to League Division Two: 82/83*
Promoted to League Division Three: 83/84

* Played two (2+0/0) League matches in the Portsmouth team that won the 1982/83 League Division Three Championship.

GRAEME SHARP

Born: 16/10/60 – Glasgow
Height: 6.1
Weight: 11.08 (94–95)

Clubs
Dumbarton: **1978–80** – Matches: **42+3** – Goals: **18**
Everton: **1980–91** – Matches: **425+21** – Goals: **157**
Oldham Athletic: **1991–95** – Matches: **127+8** – Goals: **36**

Country
Scotland: **1985–88** – Matches: **9+3** – Goals: **1**

SEASON 1978–79

Dumbarton – Scottish League Division One

Sub+1	11/11/78	Airdrieonians	Away	League	6–3		
Sub+2	18/11/78	Ayr United	Home	League	2–0		
Sub+3	25/11/78	Hamilton Academical	Away	League	0–5		
1	09/12/78	Raith Rovers	Home	League	1–3		
2	16/12/78	St Johnstone	Away	League	2–2	1 Goal	(1)
3	24/02/79	Clydebank	Home	S Cup	3–1	2 Goals	(3)
4	03/03/79	Arbroath	Away	League	1–1		
5	10/03/79	Partick Thistle	Home	S Cup	0–1		
6	13/03/79	Kilmarnock	Home	League	0–3		

SEASON 1979–80

Scottish League Division One

7	11/08/79	Ayr United	Away	League	2–1	1 Goal	(4)
8	15/08/79	St Johnstone	Home	S Lge Cup	1–1		
9	18/08/79	Hamilton Academical	Home	League	3–2	1 Goal	(5)
10	22/08/79	St Johnstone	Away	S Lge Cup	2–3		
11	25/08/79	Clydebank	Away	League	1–2		
12	01/09/79	Berwick Rangers	Home	League	4–1	2 Goals	(7)
13	05/09/79	Clyde	Away	League	2–0		

14	08/09/79	Stirling Albion	Home	League	1–2		
15	15/09/79	Airdrieonians	Away	League	0–1		
16	19/09/79	Dunfermline Athletic	Away	League	3–1	2 Goals	(9)
17	22/09/79	Arbroath	Home	League	1–0		
18	29/09/79	Motherwell	Away	League	0–3		
19	06/10/79	Heart of Midlothian	Home	League	1–1		
20	13/10/79	Raith Rovers	Home	League	4–2		
21	20/10/79	St Johnstone	Away	League	4–2	1 Goal	(10)
22	27/10/79	Hamilton Academical	Away	League	0–1		
23	03/11/79	Clydebank	Home	League	1–0	1 Goal	(11)
24	10/11/79	Stirling Albion	Away	League	3–2	1 Goal	(12)
25	17/11/79	Airdrieonians	Away	League	0–0		
26	24/11/79	Dunfermline Athletic	Home	League	2–1	1 Goal	(13)
27	01/12/79	Motherwell	Home	League	1–1		
28	08/12/79	Heart of Midlothian	Away	League	0–1		
29	15/12/79	Raith Rovers	Away	League	1–0	1 Goal	(14)
30	29/12/79	Hamilton Academical	Home	League	4–0	1 Goal	(15)
31	05/01/80	Stirling Albion	Home	League	0–1		
32	12/01/80	Airdrieonians	Home	League	0–0		
33	26/01/80	Ayr United	Home	S Cup	1–2		
34	02/02/80	Berwick Rangers	Away	League	2–2	2 Goals	(17)
35	09/02/80	Heart of Midlothian	Home	League	1–1		
36	16/02/80	St Johnstone	Home	League	0–1		
37	23/02/80	Raith Rovers	Away	League	0–4		
38	01/03/80	Ayr United	Home	League	0–3		
39	08/03/80	Clyde	Home	League	3–1		
40	12/03/80	Dunfermline Athletic	Away	League	2–0		
41	15/03/80	Berwick Rangers	Away	League	0–3		
42	25/03/80	Arbroath	Home	League	2–3	1 Goal	(18)

Everton – League Division One

Sub+1	03/05/80	Brighton & Hove Albion	Away	League	0–0
1	09/05/80	Nottingham Forest	Away	League	0–1

SEASON 1980–81

League Division One

2	16/08/80	Sunderland	Away	League	1–3
Sub+2	18/04/81	Middlesbrough	Home	League	4–1
Sub+3	20/04/81	Manchester City	Away	League	1–3
3	25/04/81	Stoke City	Home	League	0–1

SEASON 1981–82

League Division One

Sub+4	03/10/81	Stoke City	Away	League	1–3		
Sub+5	31/10/81	Manchester City	Home	League	0–1		
4	24/11/81	Notts County	Away	League	2–2	1 Goal	(1)
5	28/11/81	Arsenal	Away	League	0–1		
6	05/12/81	Swansea City	Home	League	3–1	1 Goal	(2)
7	15/12/81	Ipswich Town	Away	Lge Cup	2–3		
8	19/12/81	Aston Villa	Home	League	2–0		
9	28/12/81	Coventry City	Home	League	3–2	1 Goal	(3)
10	02/01/82	West Ham United	Away	FA Cup	1–2		
11	06/01/82	Manchester United	Away	League	1–1	1 Goal	(4)
12	19/01/82	Southampton	Home	League	1–1		
13	23/01/82	Wolverhampton Wanderers	Away	League	3–0		
14	30/01/82	Tottenham Hotspur	Home	League	1–1	1 Goal	(5)
15	06/02/82	Brighton & Hove Albion	Away	League	1–3		
16	13/02/82	Stoke City	Home	League	0–0		
17	20/02/82	West Bromwich Albion	Away	League	0–0		
18	27/02/82	West Ham United	Home	League	0–0		
19	06/03/82	Ipswich Town	Away	League	0–3		
20	13/03/82	Middlesbrough	Home	League	2–0	1 Goal	(6)
21	20/03/82	Manchester City	Away	League	1–1		
22	27/03/82	Liverpool	Home	League	1–3	1 Goal	(7)
23	03/04/82	Nottingham Forest	Away	League	1–0		
24	06/04/82	Birmingham City	Away	League	2–0		
25	10/04/82	Manchester United	Home	League	3–3	1 Goal	(8)
26	13/04/82	Coventry City	Away	League	0–1		
27	20/04/82	Nottingham Forest	Home	League	2–1	2 Goals	(10)
28	24/04/82	Arsenal	Home	League	2–1		
29	01/05/82	Swansea City	Away	League	3–1	2 Goals	(12)

30	04/05/82	Leeds United	Home	League	1–0	1 Goal	(13)
31	08/05/82	Wolverhampton Wanderers	Home	League	1–1		
32	15/05/82	Aston Villa	Away	League	2–1	2 Goals	(15)

SEASON 1982–83

League Division One

33	28/08/82	Watford	Away	League	0–2		
34	31/08/82	Aston Villa	Home	League	5–0	2 Goals	(17)
35	04/09/82	Tottenham Hotspur	Home	League	3–1		
36	08/09/82	Manchester United	Away	League	1–2		
37	11/09/82	Notts County	Away	League	0–1		
38	18/09/82	Norwich City	Home	League	1–1		
39	25/09/82	Coventry City	Away	League	2–4		
40	02/10/82	Brighton & Hove Albion	Home	League	2–2		
41	05/10/82	Newport County	Away	Lge Cup	2–0		
42	09/10/82	Manchester City	Home	League	2–1		
43	16/10/82	Swansea City	Away	League	3–0		
44	23/10/82	Sunderland	Home	League	3–1	1 Goal	(18)
45	27/10/82	Newport County	Home	Lge Cup	2–2		
46	30/10/82	Southampton	Away	League	2–3		
47	06/11/82	Liverpool	Home	League	0–5		
48	09/11/82	Arsenal	Home	Lge Cup	1–1		
49	13/11/82	Arsenal	Away	League	1–1		
50	20/11/82	West Bromwich Albion	Home	League	0–0		
51	23/11/82	Arsenal	Away	Lge Cup	0–3		
52	27/11/82	West Ham United	Away	League	0–2		
53	04/12/82	Birmingham City	Home	League	0–0		
Sub+6	18/12/82	Luton Town	Home	League	5–0		
Sub+7	27/12/82	Stoke City	Away	League	0–1		
54	28/12/82	Nottingham Forest	Home	League	3–1	2 Goals	(20)
55	01/01/83	West Bromwich Albion	Away	League	2–2	1 Goal	(21)
56	03/01/83	Tottenham Hotspur	Away	League	1–2	1 Goal	(22)
57	08/01/83	Newport County	Away	FA Cup	1–1		
58	11/01/83	Newport County	Home	FA Cup	2–1	1 Goal	(23)
59	15/01/83	Watford	Home	League	1–0		
60	22/01/83	Norwich City	Away	League	1–0		
61	30/01/83	Shrewsbury Town	Home	FA Cup	2–1		
62	05/02/83	Notts County	Home	League	3–0		
63	12/02/83	Aston Villa	Away	League	0–2		
64	19/02/83	Tottenham Hotspur	Home	FA Cup	2–0	1 Goal	(24)
65	26/02/83	Swansea City	Home	League	2–2		
66	02/03/83	Manchester City	Away	League	0–0		
67	05/03/83	Sunderland	Away	League	1–2	1 Goal	(25)
68	12/03/83	Manchester United	Away	FA Cup	0–1		
69	15/03/83	Southampton	Home	League	2–0		
70	19/03/83	Liverpool	Away	League	0–0		
71	26/03/83	Arsenal	Home	League	2–3		
72	02/04/83	Nottingham Forest	Away	League	0–2		
73	04/04/83	Stoke City	Home	League	3–1	1 Goal	(26)
74	09/04/83	Brighton & Hove Albion	Away	League	2–1		
75	19/04/83	Manchester United	Home	League	2–0	1 Goal	(27)
76	23/04/83	Birmingham City	Away	League	0–1		
77	30/04/83	West Ham United	Home	League	2–0	2 Goals	(29)
78	02/05/83	Coventry City	Home	League	1–0	1 Goal	(30)
79	07/05/83	Luton Town	Away	League	5–1	2 Goals	(32)
80	14/05/83	Ipswich Town	Home	League	1–1		

SEASON 1983–84

League Division One

81	27/08/83	Stoke City	Home	League	1–0	1 Goal	(33)
82	29/08/83	West Ham United	Home	League	0–1		
83	03/09/83	Coventry City	Away	League	1–1		
84	06/09/83	Ipswich Town	Away	League	0–3		
85	10/09/83	West Bromwich Albion	Home	League	0–0		
86	17/09/83	Tottenham Hotspur	Away	League	2–1		
87	24/09/83	Birmingham City	Home	League	1–1	1 Goal	(34)
88	01/10/83	Notts County	Away	League	1–0		
89	04/10/83	Chesterfield	Away	Lge Cup	1–0	1 Goal	(35)
90	15/10/83	Luton Town	Home	League	0–1		
91	22/10/83	Watford	Home	League	1–0		
92	26/10/83	Chesterfield	Home	Lge Cup	2–2		
93	29/10/83	Leicester City	Away	League	0–2		
94	06/11/83	Liverpool	Away	League	0–3		

95	09/11/83	Coventry City	Home	Lge Cup	2–1	1 Goal	(36)
96	30/11/83	West Ham United	Away	Lge Cup	2–2		
97	03/12/83	Manchester United	Away	League	1–0		
98	06/12/83	West Ham United	Home	Lge Cup	2–0*		
99	07/01/84	Stoke City	Away	FA Cup	2–0		
100	14/01/84	Stoke City	Away	League	1–1		
101	18/01/84	Oxford United	Away	Lge Cup	1–1		
102	21/01/84	Tottenham Hotspur	Home	League	2–1		
103	24/01/84	Oxford United	Home	Lge Cup	4–1	1 Goal	(37)
104	28/01/84	Gillingham	Home	FA Cup	0–0		
105	31/01/84	Gillingham	Away	FA Cup	0–0*		
106	15/02/84	Aston Villa	Home	Lge Cup	2–0		
Sub+8	18/02/84	Shrewsbury Town	Home	FA Cup	3–0		
107	22/02/84	Aston Villa	Away	Lge Cup	0–1		
108	25/02/84	Watford	Away	League	4–4	2 Goals	(39)
109	03/03/84	Liverpool	Home	League	1–1		
110	10/03/84	Notts County	Away	FA Cup	1–2		
111	13/03/84	Nottingham Forest	Away	League	0–1		
112	17/03/84	Ipswich Town	Home	League	1–0		
113	25/03/84	Liverpool	Wembley	Lge Cup	0–0*		
114	28/03/84	Liverpool	Neutral	Lge Cup	0–1		
115	31/03/84	Southampton	Home	League	1–0		
116	07/04/84	Luton Town	Away	League	3–0		
117	09/04/84	Arsenal	Home	League	0–0		
Sub+9	14/04/84	Southampton	Neutral	FA Cup	1–0*		
118	21/04/84	Sunderland	Away	League	1–2		
Sub+10	28/04/84	Norwich City	Away	League	1–1		
119	05/05/84	Manchester United	Home	League	1–1		
120	07/05/84	Aston Villa	Away	League	2–0	1 Goal	(40)
121	12/05/84	Queens Park Rangers	Home	League	3–1	2 Goals	(42)
122	14/05/84	West Ham United	Away	League	1–0		
123	19/05/84	Watford	Wembley	FA Cup	2–0	1 Goal	(43)

SEASON 1984–85

League Division One

124	18/08/84	Liverpool	Wembley	FA C/S	1–0		
125	25/08/84	Tottenham Hotspur	Home	League	1–4		
126	27/08/84	West Bromwich Albion	Away	League	1–2		
127	31/08/84	Chelsea	Away	League	1–0		
128	04/09/84	Ipswich Town	Home	League	1–1		
129	08/09/84	Coventry City	Home	League	2–1	1 Goal	(44)
130	19/09/84	University College Dublin	Away	ECW Cup	0–0		
131	22/09/84	Southampton	Home	League	2–2	1 Goal	(45)
132	26/09/84	Sheffield United	Away	Lge Cup	2–2	1 Goal	(46)
133	29/09/84	Watford	Away	League	5–4	1 Goal	(47)
134	02/10/84	University College Dublin	Home	ECW Cup	1–0	1 Goal	(48)
135	06/10/84	Arsenal	Away	League	0–1		
136	10/10/84	Sheffield United	Home	Lge Cup	4–0	1 Goal	(49)
137	13/10/84	Aston Villa	Home	League	2–1	1 Goal	(50)
138	20/10/84	Liverpool	Away	League	1–0	1 Goal	(51)
139	24/10/84	TJ Internacional Slovnaft	Away	ECW Cup	1–0		
140	27/10/84	Manchester United	Home	League	5–0	1 Goal	(52)
141	30/10/84	Manchester United	Away	Lge Cup	2–1	1 Goal	(53)
142	03/11/84	Leicester City	Home	League	3–0		
143	07/11/84	TJ Internacional Slovnaft	Home	ECW Cup	3–0	1 Goal	(54)
144	10/11/84	West Ham United	Away	League	1–0		
145	17/11/84	Stoke City	Home	League	4–0		
146	20/11/84	Grimsby Town	Home	Lge Cup	0–1		
147	24/11/84	Norwich City	Away	League	2–4	1 Goal	(55)
148	01/12/84	Sheffield Wednesday	Home	League	1–1	1 Goal	(56)
149	08/12/84	Queens Park Rangers	Away	League	0–0		
150	15/12/84	Nottingham Forest	Home	League	5–0	2 Goals	(58)
151	22/12/84	Chelsea	Home	League	3–4	2 Goals	(60)
152	26/12/84	Sunderland	Away	League	2–1		
153	29/12/84	Ipswich Town	Away	League	2–0	2 Goals	(62)
154	01/01/85	Luton Town	Home	League	2–1		
155	04/01/85	Leeds United	Away	FA Cup	2–0	1 Goal	(63)
156	12/01/85	Newcastle United	Home	League	4–0	1 Goal	(64)
157	26/01/85	Doncaster Rovers	Home	FA Cup	2–0		
158	02/02/85	Watford	Home	League	4–0		
159	16/02/85	Telford United	Home	FA Cup	3–0		
160	13/03/85	Ipswich Town	Away	FA Cup	1–0	1 Goal	(65)
161	16/03/85	Aston Villa	Away	League	1–1		
162	20/03/85	SC Fortuna Sittard	Away	ECW Cup	2–0	1 Goal	(66)

163	23/03/85	Arsenal	Home	League	2–0	1 Goal	(67)
164	30/03/85	Southampton	Away	League	2–1		
165	03/04/85	Tottenham Hotspur	Away	League	2–1		
166	06/04/85	Sunderland	Home	League	4–1	1 Goal	(68)
167	10/04/85	FC Bayern Munchen	Away	ECW Cup	0–0		
168	13/04/85	Luton Town	Neutral	FA Cup	2–1*		
169	16/04/85	West Bromwich Albion	Home	League	4–1	2 Goals	(70)
170	20/04/85	Stoke City	Away	League	2–0	1 Goal	(71)
171	24/04/85	FC Bayern Munchen	Home	ECW Cup	3–1	1 Goal	(72)
172	27/04/85	Norwich City	Home	League	3–0		
173	04/05/85	Sheffield Wednesday	Away	League	1–0		
174	06/05/85	Queens Park Rangers	Home	League	2–0	1 Goal	(73)
175	08/05/85	West Ham United	Home	League	3–0		
176	15/05/85	SK Rapid Wien	Neutral	ECW Cup	3–1		
177	18/05/85	Manchester United	Wembley	FA Cup	0–1		
178	26/05/85	Coventry City	Away	League	1–4		

SEASON 1985–86

League Division One

179	10/08/85	Manchester United	Wembley	FA C/S	2–0		
180	17/08/85	Leicester City	Away	League	1–3		
181	24/08/85	Coventry City	Home	League	1–1	1 Goal	(74)
Sub+11	26/08/85	Tottenham Hotspur	Away	League	1–0		
182	03/09/85	Sheffield Wednesday	Away	League	5–1		
183	07/09/85	Queens Park Rangers	Away	League	0–3		
Sub+12	14/09/85	Luton Town	Home	League	2–0	1 Goal	(75)
184	18/09/85	Manchester United	Away	SSS Cup	4–2	1 Goal	(76)
185	21/09/85	Liverpool	Home	League	2–3	1 Goal	(77)
186	25/09/85	AFC Bournemouth	Home	Lge Cup	3–2		
187	28/09/85	Aston Villa	Away	League	0–0		
188	02/10/85	Norwich City	Home	SSS Cup	1–0		
189	05/10/85	Oxford United	Home	League	2–0	1 Goal	(78)
190	08/10/85	AFC Bournemouth	Away	Lge Cup	2–0		
191	12/10/85	Chelsea	Away	League	1–2		
192	19/10/85	Watford	Home	League	4–1	2 Goals	(80)
193	23/10/85	Norwich City	Away	SSS Cup	0–1		
194	26/10/85	Manchester City	Away	League	1–1		
195	29/10/85	Shrewsbury Town	Away	Lge Cup	4–1	1 Goal	(81)
196	02/11/85	West Ham United	Away	League	1–2		
197	09/11/85	Arsenal	Home	League	6–1	1 Goal	(82)
198	16/11/85	Ipswich Town	Away	League	4–3	1 Goal	(83)
199	23/11/85	Nottingham Forest	Home	League	1–1		
200	26/11/85	Chelsea	Away	Lge Cup	2–2		
201	10/12/85	Chelsea	Home	Lge Cup	1–2		
202	14/12/85	Leicester City	Home	League	1–2		
203	21/12/85	Coventry City	Away	League	3–1	1 Goal	(84)
204	26/12/85	Manchester United	Home	League	3–1	2 Goals	(86)
205	28/12/85	Sheffield Wednesday	Home	League	3–1		
206	01/01/86	Newcastle United	Away	League	2–2	1 Goal	(87)
207	05/01/86	Exeter City	Home	FA Cup	1–0		
208	11/01/86	Queens Park Rangers	Home	League	4–3	2 Goals	(89)
209	18/01/86	Birmingham City	Away	League	2–0		
210	25/01/86	Blackburn Rovers	Home	FA Cup	3–1		
211	01/02/86	Tottenham Hotspur	Home	League	1–0		
212	11/02/86	Manchester City	Home	League	4–0	1 Goal	(90)
213	22/02/86	Liverpool	Away	League	2–0		
214	01/03/86	Aston Villa	Home	League	2–0	1 Goal	(91)
215	04/03/86	Tottenham Hotspur	Away	FA Cup	2–1		
216	08/03/86	Luton Town	Away	FA Cup	2–2		
217	12/03/86	Luton Town	Home	FA Cup	1–0		
218	16/03/86	Chelsea	Home	League	1–1		
Sub+13	19/03/86	Tottenham Hotspur	Home	SSS Cup	3–1	1 Goal	(92)
219	22/03/86	Luton Town	Away	League	1–2		
220	29/03/86	Newcastle United	Home	League	1–0		
221	31/03/86	Manchester United	Away	League	0–0		
222	05/04/86	Sheffield Wednesday	Neutral	FA Cup	2–1*	1 Goal	(93)
223	12/04/86	Arsenal	Away	League	1–0		
224	15/04/86	Watford	Away	League	2–0	1 Goal	(94)
225	19/04/86	Ipswich Town	Home	League	1–0	1 Goal	(95)
226	26/04/86	Nottingham Forest	Away	League	0–0		
227	30/04/86	Oxford United	Away	League	0–1		
228	03/05/86	Southampton	Home	League	6–1	1 Goal	(96)
229	10/05/86	Liverpool	Wembley	FA Cup	1–3		

SEASON 1986–87

League Division One

230	16/08/86	Liverpool	Wembley	FA C/S	1–0		
231	23/08/86	Nottingham Forest	Home	League	2–0		
232	25/08/86	Sheffield Wednesday	Away	League	2–2	1 Goal	(97)
233	30/08/86	Coventry City	Away	League	1–1		
234	02/09/86	Oxford United	Home	League	3–1		
235	06/09/86	Queens Park Rangers	Home	League	0–0		
236	13/09/86	Wimbledon	Away	League	2–1	1 Goal	(98)
237	16/09/86	Liverpool	Away	SSS Cup	1–3		
238	21/09/86	Manchester United	Home	League	3–1	1 Goal	(99)
239	24/09/86	Newport County	Home	Lge Cup	4–0		
240	27/09/86	Tottenham Hotspur	Away	League	0–2		
241	30/09/86	Liverpool	Home	SSS Cup	1–4	1 Goal	(100)
242	04/10/86	Arsenal	Home	League	0–1		
243	07/10/86	Newport County	Away	Lge Cup	5–1	1 Goal	(101)
244	11/10/86	Charlton Athletic	Away	League	2–3		
245	18/10/86	Southampton	Away	League	2–0		
246	25/10/86	Watford	Home	League	3–2		
247	28/10/86	Sheffield Wednesday	Home	Lge Cup	4–0		
248	02/11/86	West Ham United	Away	League	0–1		
249	08/11/86	Chelsea	Home	League	2–2		
250	15/11/86	Leicester City	Away	League	2–0		
251	19/11/86	Norwich City	Away	Lge Cup	4–1	1 Goal	(102)
252	23/11/86	Liverpool	Home	League	0–0		
253	29/11/86	Manchester City	Away	League	3–1		
254	03/12/86	Newcastle United	Home	FM Cup	5–2	3 Goals	(105)
255	06/12/86	Norwich City	Home	League	4–0		
256	13/12/86	Luton Town	Away	League	0–1		
257	20/12/86	Wimbledon	Home	League	3–0		
258	26/12/86	Newcastle United	Away	League	4–0		
259	03/01/87	Queens Park Rangers	Away	League	1–0	1 Goal	(106)
260	10/01/87	Southampton	Home	FA Cup	2–1	2 Goals	(108)
261	17/01/87	Sheffield Wednesday	Home	League	2–0		
262	21/01/87	Liverpool	Home	Lge Cup	0–1		
263	07/02/87	Coventry City	Home	League	3–1		
264	04/05/87	Norwich City	Away	League	1–0		
265	09/05/87	Luton Town	Home	League	3–1	1 Goal	(109)
266	11/05/87	Tottenham Hotspur	Home	League	1–0		

SEASON 1987–88

League Division One

267	01/08/87	Coventry City	Wembley	FA C/S	1–0		
268	15/08/87	Norwich City	Home	League	1–0		
269	18/08/87	Wimbledon	Away	League	1–1	1 Goal	(110)
270	22/08/87	Nottingham Forest	Away	League	0–0		
271	29/08/87	Sheffield Wednesday	Home	League	4–0		
272	02/09/87	Queens Park Rangers	Away	League	0–1		
273	05/09/87	Tottenham Hotspur	Home	League	0–0		
Sub+14	22/09/87	Rotherham United	Home	Lge Cup	3–2		
274	26/09/87	Coventry City	Home	League	1–2		
275	03/10/87	Southampton	Away	League	4–0	4 Goals	(114)
276	06/10/87	Rotherham United	Away	Lge Cup	0–0		
277	10/10/87	Chelsea	Home	League	4–1	2 Goals	(116)
278	17/10/87	Newcastle United	Away	League	1–1		
279	24/10/87	Watford	Home	League	2–0	1 Goal	(117)
280	28/10/87	Liverpool	Away	Lge Cup	1–0		
281	01/11/87	Liverpool	Away	League	0–2		
282	14/11/87	West Ham United	Home	League	3–1	1 Goal	(118)
283	17/11/87	Oldham Athletic	Home	Lge Cup	2–1		
284	21/11/87	Portsmouth	Away	League	1–0	1 Goal	(119)
285	28/11/87	Oxford United	Home	League	0–0		
286	05/12/87	Charlton Athletic	Away	League	0–0		
287	12/12/87	Derby County	Home	League	3–0		
288	19/12/87	Arsenal	Away	League	1–1		
289	26/12/87	Luton Town	Home	League	2–0		
290	28/12/87	Manchester United	Away	League	1–2		
291	01/01/88	Sheffield Wednesday	Away	League	0–1		
292	09/01/88	Sheffield Wednesday	Away	FA Cup	1–1		
293	13/01/88	Sheffield Wednesday	Home	FA Cup	1–1*	1 Goal	(120)
294	16/01/88	Norwich City	Away	League	3–0	2 Goals	(122)
295	20/01/88	Manchester City	Away	Lge Cup	2–0	1 Goal	(123)
296	25/01/88	Sheffield Wednesday	Home	FA Cup	1–1*		

297	27/01/88	Sheffield Wednesday	Away	FA Cup	5–0	3 Goals	(126)
298	30/01/88	Middlesbrough	Home	FA Cup	1–1	1 Goal	(127)
299	03/02/88	Middlesbrough	Away	FA Cup	2–2*		
300	07/02/88	Arsenal	Home	Lge Cup	0–1		
301	09/02/88	Middlesbrough	Home	FA Cup	2–1	1 Goal	(128)
302	13/02/88	Queens Park Rangers	Home	League	2–0		
303	21/02/88	Liverpool	Home	FA Cup	0–1		
304	24/02/88	Arsenal	Away	Lge Cup	1–3		
305	27/02/88	Southampton	Home	League	1–0		
306	05/03/88	Newcastle United	Home	League	1–0		
307	09/03/88	Tottenham Hotspur	Away	League	1–2		
308	12/03/88	Chelsea	Away	League	0–0		
309	20/03/88	Liverpool	Home	League	1–0		
310	26/03/88	Watford	Away	League	2–1		
311	19/04/88	Coventry City	Away	League	2–1	1 Goal	(129)
312	23/04/88	Oxford United	Away	League	1–1		
313	07/05/88	Arsenal	Home	League	1–2		

SEASON 1988–89

League Division One

314	27/08/88	Newcastle United	Home	League	4–0	1 Goal	(130)
315	29/08/88	Manchester United	Away	MCC Trophy	0–1		
316	03/09/88	Coventry City	Away	League	1–0		
317	10/09/88	Nottingham Forest	Home	League	1–1		
318	17/09/88	Millwall	Away	League	1–2		
319	24/09/88	Luton Town	Home	League	0–2		
320	27/09/88	Bury	Home	Lge Cup	3–0	1 Goal	(131)
321	01/10/88	Wimbledon	Away	League	1–2		
322	08/10/88	Southampton	Home	League	4–1		
323	11/10/88	Bury	Away	Lge Cup	2–2	1 Goal	(132)
324	22/10/88	Aston Villa	Away	League	0–2		
325	30/10/88	Manchester United	Home	League	1–1		
326	05/11/88	Sheffield Wednesday	Away	League	1–1		
327	08/11/88	Oldham Athletic	Home	Lge Cup	1–1		
328	12/11/88	Charlton Athletic	Away	League	2–1	1 Goal	(133)
329	19/11/88	Norwich City	Home	League	1–1		
330	26/11/88	West Ham United	Away	League	1–0		
331	29/11/88	Oldham Athletic	Away	Lge Cup	2–0		
332	03/12/88	Tottenham Hotspur	Home	League	1–0		
333	28/01/89	Plymouth Argyle	Away	FA Cup	1–1		
334	31/01/89	Plymouth Argyle	Home	FA Cup	4–0	2 Goals	(135)
335	04/02/89	Wimbledon	Home	League	1–1	1 Goal	(136)
336	11/02/89	Southampton	Away	League	1–1		
337	14/02/89	Aston Villa	Home	League	1–1		
338	18/02/89	Barnsley	Away	FA Cup	1–0	1 Goal	(137)
339	25/02/89	Derby County	Away	League	2–3	1 Goal	(138)
340	19/03/89	Wimbledon	Home	FA Cup	1–0		
341	22/03/89	Newcastle United	Away	League	0–2		
342	25/03/89	Millwall	Home	League	1–1		
343	10/04/89	Charlton Athletic	Home	League	3–2	1 Goal	(139)
344	15/04/89	Norwich City	Neutral	FA Cup	1–0		
345	22/04/89	Tottenham Hotspur	Away	League	1–2		
346	30/04/89	Nottingham Forest	Wembley	Simod Cup	3–4*	1 Goal	(140)
347	03/05/89	Liverpool	Home	League	0–0		
348	10/05/89	Manchester United	Away	League	2–1	2 Goals	(142)
349	13/05/89	West Ham United	Home	League	3–1		
350	15/05/89	Derby County	Home	League	1–0		
351	20/05/89	Liverpool	Wembley	FA Cup	2–3*		

SEASON 1989–90

League Division One

352	19/08/89	Coventry City	Away	League	0–2		
353	22/08/89	Tottenham Hotspur	Home	League	2–1		
354	26/08/89	Southampton	Home	League	3–0		
355	09/09/89	Manchester United	Home	League	3–2	1 Goal	(143)
356	16/09/89	Charlton Athletic	Away	League	1–0		
357	19/09/89	Leyton Orient	Away	Lge Cup	2–0		
358	23/09/89	Liverpool	Home	League	1–3		
359	30/09/89	Crystal Palace	Away	League	1–2		
360	03/10/89	Leyton Orient	Home	Lge Cup	2–2		
Sub+15	14/10/89	Millwall	Home	League	2–1		
Sub+16	24/10/89	Luton Town	Home	Lge Cup	3–0		

Sub+17	05/11/89	Aston Villa	Away	League	2–6		
Sub+18	11/11/89	Chelsea	Home	League	0–1		
361	18/11/89	Wimbledon	Home	League	1–1		
362	22/11/89	Nottingham Forest	Away	Lge Cup	0–1		
363	25/11/89	Nottingham Forest	Away	League	0–1		
364	02/12/89	Coventry City	Home	League	2–0		
365	09/12/89	Tottenham Hotspur	Away	League	1–2		
366	17/12/89	Manchester City	Home	League	0–0		
367	26/12/89	Derby County	Away	League	1–0		
368	30/12/89	Queens Park Rangers	Away	League	0–1		
369	01/01/90	Luton Town	Home	League	2–1	1 Goal	(144)
370	06/01/90	Middlesbrough	Away	FA Cup	0–0		
371	10/01/90	Middlesbrough	Home	FA Cup	1–1*		
372	13/01/90	Southampton	Away	League	2–2		
373	17/01/90	Middlesbrough	Home	FA Cup	1–0		
374	20/01/90	Sheffield Wednesday	Home	League	2–0		
375	28/01/90	Sheffield Wednesday	Away	FA Cup	2–1		
376	03/02/90	Liverpool	Away	League	1–2	1 Goal	(145)
377	10/02/90	Charlton Athletic	Home	League	2–1		
378	17/02/90	Oldham Athletic	Away	FA Cup	2–2	1 Goal	(146)
379	21/02/90	Oldham Athletic	Home	FA Cup	1–1*		
380	03/03/90	Wimbledon	Away	League	1–3		
381	10/03/90	Oldham Athletic	Away	FA Cup	1–2*		
382	14/03/90	Manchester United	Away	League	0–0		
383	17/03/90	Crystal Palace	Home	League	4–0	1 Goal	(147)
384	21/03/90	Millwall	Away	League	2–1		
385	24/03/90	Norwich City	Home	League	3–1	1 Goal	(148)
386	31/03/90	Arsenal	Away	League	0–1		
387	04/04/90	Nottingham Forest	Home	League	4–0		
388	07/04/90	Queens Park Rangers	Home	League	1–0		
389	14/04/90	Luton Town	Away	League	2–2	1 Goal	(149)
390	16/04/90	Derby County	Home	League	2–1		
391	21/04/90	Manchester City	Away	League	0–1		

SEASON 1990–91

League Division One

392	25/08/90	Leeds United	Home	League	2–3		
393	29/08/90	Coventry City	Away	League	1–3		
394	01/09/90	Manchester City	Away	League	0–1		
395	08/09/90	Arsenal	Home	League	1–1		
396	15/09/90	Sunderland	Away	League	2–2	1 Goal	(150)
397	22/09/90	Liverpool	Home	League	2–3		
398	25/09/90	Wrexham	Away	Lge Cup	5–0		
399	29/09/90	Southampton	Home	League	3–0		
400	07/10/90	Nottingham Forest	Away	League	1–3		
401	09/10/90	Wrexham	Home	Lge Cup	6–0	3 Goals	(153)
402	20/10/90	Crystal Palace	Home	League	0–0		
403	27/10/90	Luton Town	Away	League	1–1		
404	30/10/90	Sheffield United	Away	Lge Cup	1–2		
405	18/11/90	Tottenham Hotspur	Home	League	1–1		
406	24/11/90	Wimbledon	Away	League	1–2		
Sub+19	01/12/90	Manchester City	Home	League	0–1		
Sub+20	08/12/90	Coventry City	Home	League	1–0		
407	16/12/90	Leeds United	Away	League	0–2		
Sub+21	22/12/90	Norwich City	Away	League	0–1		
408	26/12/90	Aston Villa	Home	League	1–0	1 Goal	(154)
409	29/12/90	Derby County	Home	League	2–0		
410	01/01/91	Chelsea	Away	League	2–1	1 Goal	(155)
411	05/01/91	Charlton Athletic	Away	FA Cup	2–1		
412	13/01/91	Manchester City	Home	League	2–0		
413	19/01/91	Arsenal	Away	League	0–1		
414	22/01/91	Sunderland	Away	ZDS Cup	4–1		
415	27/01/91	Woking	Away	FA Cup	1–0		
416	02/02/91	Sunderland	Home	League	2–0		
417	09/02/91	Liverpool	Away	League	1–3		
418	17/02/91	Liverpool	Away	FA Cup	0–0		
419	20/02/91	Liverpool	Home	FA Cup	4–4	2 Goals	(157)
420	23/02/91	Sheffield United	Home	League	1–2		
421	27/02/91	Liverpool	Home	FA Cup	1–0		
422	02/03/91	Manchester United	Away	League	2–0		
423	11/03/91	West Ham United	Away	FA Cup	1–2		
424	23/03/91	Nottingham Forest	Home	League	0–0		
425	30/03/91	Aston Villa	Away	League	2–2		

SEASON 1991–92

Oldham Athletic – League Division One

1	17/08/91	Liverpool	Away	League	1–2		
2	21/08/91	Chelsea	Home	League	3–0		
3	24/08/91	Norwich City	Home	League	2–2		
4	28/08/91	Manchester United	Away	League	0–1		
5	31/08/91	Nottingham Forest	Away	League	1–3		
6	03/09/91	Coventry City	Home	League	2–1		
7	07/09/91	Sheffield United	Home	League	2–1		
8	14/09/91	Luton Town	Away	League	1–2		
9	21/09/91	Crystal Palace	Home	League	2–3		
10	24/09/91	Torquay United	Home	Lge Cup	7–1	1 Goal	(1)
11	28/09/91	Manchester City	Away	League	2–1	2 Goals	(3)
12	01/10/91	Everton	Away	ZDS Cup	2–3		
13	05/10/91	Southampton	Home	League	1–1		
14	09/10/91	Torquay United	Away	Lge Cup	2–0		
15	19/10/91	West Ham United	Home	League	2–2		
16	26/10/91	Leeds United	Away	League	0–1		
17	29/10/91	Derby County	Home	Lge Cup	2–1	1 Goal	(4)
18	02/11/91	Notts County	Away	League	0–2		
19	16/11/91	Arsenal	Home	League	1–1		
20	23/11/91	Queens Park Rangers	Away	League	3–1	1 Goal	(5)
21	30/11/91	Aston Villa	Home	League	3–2	2 Goals	(7)
22	04/12/91	Manchester United	Away	Lge Cup	0–2		
23	07/12/91	Wimbledon	Away	League	1–2		
24	14/12/91	Everton	Home	League	2–2		
25	21/12/91	Chelsea	Away	League	2–4		
26	26/12/91	Manchester United	Home	League	3–6	1 Goal	(8)
27	28/12/91	Nottingham Forest	Home	League	2–1	1 Goal	(9)
28	01/01/92	Sheffield Wednesday	Away	League	1–1		
29	04/01/92	Leyton Orient	Home	FA Cup	1–1	1 Goal	(10)
30	11/01/92	Norwich City	Away	League	2–1		
31	15/01/92	Leyton Orient	Away	FA Cup	2–4		
32	18/01/92	Liverpool	Home	League	2–3		
33	25/01/92	Tottenham Hotspur	Away	League	0–0		
34	01/02/92	West Ham United	Away	League	0–1		
35	08/02/92	Leeds United	Home	League	2–0		
36	15/02/92	Queens Park Rangers	Home	League	2–1		
37	22/02/92	Aston Villa	Away	League	0–1		
38	29/02/92	Wimbledon	Home	League	0–1		
39	07/03/92	Everton	Away	League	1–2		
40	10/03/92	Arsenal	Away	League	1–2		
41	14/03/92	Notts County	Home	League	4–3		
42	21/03/92	Coventry City	Away	League	1–1		
43	28/03/92	Sheffield Wednesday	Home	League	3–0	1 Goal	(11)
44	04/04/92	Sheffield United	Away	League	0–2		
45	11/04/92	Luton Town	Home	League	5–1	4 Goals	(15)
46	18/04/92	Crystal Palace	Away	League	0–0		
47	20/04/92	Tottenham Hotspur	Home	League	1–0		
48	25/04/92	Southampton	Away	League	0–1		
49	02/05/92	Manchester City	Home	League	2–5		

SEASON 1992–93

Premier League

50	15/08/92	Chelsea	Away	League	1–1		
51	19/08/92	Crystal Palace	Home	League	1–1	1 Goal	(16)
52	22/08/92	Nottingham Forest	Home	League	5–3	1 Goal	(17)
53	26/08/92	Arsenal	Away	League	0–2		
54	29/08/92	Manchester City	Away	League	3–3		
55	01/09/92	Leeds United	Home	League	2–2		
56	05/09/92	Coventry City	Home	League	0–1		
57	12/09/92	Crystal Palace	Away	League	2–2	1 Goal	(18)
58	19/09/92	Ipswich Town	Home	League	4–2	1 Goal	(19)
59	22/09/92	Exeter City	Away	Lge Cup	1–0		
60	26/09/92	Blackburn Rovers	Away	League	0–2		
61	04/10/92	Everton	Home	League	1–0		
62	07/10/92	Exeter City	Home	Lge Cup	0–0		
63	17/10/92	Sheffield Wednesday	Away	League	1–2		
64	24/10/92	Aston Villa	Home	League	1–1		
65	27/10/92	Swindon Town	Away	Lge Cup	1–0		
66	31/10/92	Southampton	Away	League	0–1		
67	09/11/92	Norwich City	Home	League	2–3	1 Goal	(20)
68	21/11/92	Manchester United	Away	League	0–3		

69	28/11/92	Middlesbrough	Home	League	4–1	1 Goal	(21)
70	01/12/92	Cambridge United	Away	Lge Cup	0–1		
71	05/12/92	Queens Park Rangers	Away	League	2–3		
72	12/12/92	Wimbledon	Away	League	2–5		
73	19/12/92	Tottenham Hotspur	Home	League	2–1	1 Goal	(22)
74	02/01/93	Tranmere Rovers	Home	FA Cup	2–2		
Sub+1	09/01/93	Ipswich Town	Away	League	2–1		
Sub+2	12/01/93	Tranmere Rovers	Away	FA Cup	0–3		

SEASON 1993–94

Premier League

Sub+3	14/08/93	Ipswich Town	Home	League	0–3		
Sub+4	11/09/93	Everton	Home	League	0–1		
Sub+5	18/09/93	Tottenham Hotspur	Away	League	0–5		
75	21/09/93	Swansea City	Away	Lge Cup	1–2	1 Goal	(23)
76	25/09/93	Aston Villa	Home	League	1–1		
77	04/10/93	Manchester City	Away	League	1–1	1 Goal	(24)
78	06/10/93	Swansea City	Home	Lge Cup	2–0		
79	16/10/93	Liverpool	Away	League	1–2		
80	23/10/93	Arsenal	Home	League	0–0		
81	26/10/93	Coventry City	Home	Lge Cup	2–0	1 Goal	(25)
82	30/10/93	Chelsea	Away	League	1–0		
83	08/11/93	Newcastle United	Home	League	1–3		
84	20/11/93	West Ham United	Away	League	0–2		
85	24/11/93	Sheffield Wednesday	Away	League	0–3		
86	27/11/93	Norwich City	Home	League	2–1	1 Goal	(26)
87	30/11/93	Tranmere Rovers	Away	Lge Cup	0–3		
88	04/12/93	Ipswich Town	Away	League	0–0		
89	07/12/93	Swindon Town	Home	League	2–1		
90	11/12/93	Blackburn Rovers	Home	League	1–2		
91	18/12/93	Coventry City	Away	League	1–1		
92	27/12/93	Queens Park Rangers	Away	League	0–2		
93	29/12/93	Manchester United	Home	League	2–5	1 Goal	(27)
94	01/01/94	Sheffield United	Away	League	1–2		
95	08/01/94	Derby County	Home	FA Cup	2–1		
96	15/01/94	Liverpool	Home	League	0–3		
97	22/01/94	Arsenal	Away	League	1–1	1 Goal	(28)
98	29/01/94	Stoke City	Home	FA Cup	0–0		
99	05/02/94	Southampton	Home	League	2–1		
100	09/02/94	Stoke City	Away	FA Cup	1–0		
101	12/02/94	Chelsea	Home	League	2–1	1 Goal	(29)
102	19/02/94	Barnsley	Home	FA Cup	1–0		
103	28/02/94	Leeds United	Home	League	1–1		
104	05/03/94	Everton	Away	League	1–2	1 Goal	(30)
105	12/03/94	Bolton Wanderers	Away	FA Cup	1–0		
106	30/03/94	Southampton	Away	League	3–1	1 Goal	(31)
107	02/04/94	Queens Park Rangers	Home	League	4–1		
108	04/04/94	Manchester United	Away	League	2–3	1 Goal	(32)
109	10/04/94	Manchester United	Wembley	FA Cup	1–1*		
110	13/04/94	Manchester United	Neutral	FA Cup	1–4		
111	16/04/94	West Ham United	Home	League	1–2		
112	23/04/94	Newcastle United	Away	League	2–3	1 Goal	(33)
113	26/04/94	Wimbledon	Away	League	0–3		
114	30/04/94	Sheffield Wednesday	Home	League	0–0		
115	03/05/94	Sheffield United	Home	League	1–1		
116	05/05/94	Tottenham Hotspur	Home	League	0–2		

SEASON 1994–95

Football League Division One

117	13/08/94	Charlton Athletic	Home	League	5–2	1 Goal	(34)
118	20/08/94	Port Vale	Away	League	1–3	1 Goal	(35)
119	27/08/94	Burnley	Home	League	3–0		
120	30/08/94	Notts County	Away	League	3–1		
121	03/09/94	Southend United	Away	League	0–1		
122	10/09/94	Reading	Home	League	1–3		
123	13/09/94	Watford	Home	League	0–2		
Sub+6	24/09/94	Barnsley	Home	League	1–0		
124	01/10/94	Sheffield United	Away	League	0–2		
Sub+7	04/10/94	Oxford United	Home	Lge Cup	1–0		
Sub+8	08/10/94	Portsmouth	Home	League	3–2		
125	03/01/95	Millwall	Away	League	1–1		
126	07/01/95	Reading	Away	FA Cup	3–1	1 Goal	(36)
127	14/01/95	Sunderland	Home	League	0–0		

INTERNATIONAL APPEARANCES – SCOTLAND

1	28/05/85	Iceland	Reykjavik	1–0	WCQ		
2	10/09/85	Wales	Ninian Park	1–1	WCQ		
Sub 3	20/11/85	Australia	Hampden Park	2–0	WCQ		
Sub 4	04/12/85	Australia	Melbourne	0–0	WCQ		
5	28/01/86	Israel	Tel Aviv	1–0	F		
6	26/03/86	Rumania	Hampden Park	3–0	F		
7	13/06/86	Uruguay	Nezahualcoyotl	0–0	WC		
8	15/10/86	Republic of Ireland	Lansdowne Road	0–0	ECQ		
Sub 9	14/10/87	Belgium	Hampden Park	2–0	ECQ		
10	11/11/87	Bulgaria	Sofia	1–0	ECQ		
11	02/12/87	Luxembourg	Esch sur Alzette	0–0	ECQ		
12	22/03/88	Malta	Valletta	1–1	F	1 Goal	(1)

APPEARANCES AND GOALS PER SEASON

SEASON 78–79	GAMES	GOALS
Scottish League	4+3	1
Scottish Cup	2	2
TOTAL	**6+3**	**3**

SEASON 79–80	GAMES	GOALS
League	1+1	0
Scottish League	33	15
Scottish Cup	1	0
Scottish League Cup	2	0
TOTAL	**37+1**	**15**

SEASON 80–81	GAMES	GOALS
League	2+2	0
TOTAL	**2+2**	**0**

SEASON 81–82	GAMES	GOALS
League	27+2	15
FA Cup	1	0
League Cup	1	0
TOTAL	**29+2**	**15**

SEASON 82–83	GAMES	GOALS
League	39+2	15
FA Cup	5	2
League Cup	4	0
TOTAL	**48+2**	**17**

SEASON 83–84	GAMES	GOALS
League	27+1	7
FA Cup	5+2	1
League Cup	11	3
TOTAL	**43+3**	**11**

SEASON 84–85	GAMES	GOALS
League	36	21
FA Cup	6	2
League Cup	4	3
European Cup Winners Cup	8	4
FA Charity Shield	1	0
TOTAL	**55**	**30**

SEASON 85–86	GAMES	GOALS
League	35+2	19
FA Cup	7	1
League Cup	5	1
Screen Sport Super Cup	3+1	2
FA Charity Shield	1	0
TOTAL	**51+3**	**23**

SEASON 86–87	GAMES	GOALS
League	27	5
FA Cup	1	2
League Cup	5	2
Screen Sport Super Cup	2	1
Full Members Cup	1	3
FA Charity Shield	1	0
TOTAL	**37**	**13**

SEASON 87–88	GAMES	GOALS
League	32	13
FA Cup	8	6
League Cup	6+1	1
FA Charity Shield	1	0
TOTAL	**47+1**	**20**

SEASON 88–89	GAMES	GOALS
League	26	7
FA Cup	6	3
League Cup	4	2
Simod Cup	1	1
Mercantile Credit Centenary Trophy	1	0
TOTAL	**38**	**13**

SEASON 89–90	GAMES	GOALS
League	30+3	6
FA Cup	7	1
League Cup	3+1	0
TOTAL	**40+4**	**7**

SEASON 90–91	GAMES	GOALS
League	24+3	3
FA Cup	6	2
League Cup	3	3
Zenith Data Systems Cup	1	0
TOTAL	**34+3**	**8**

SEASON 91–92	GAMES	GOALS
League	42	12
FA Cup	2	1
League Cup	4	2
Zenith Data Systems Cup	1	0
TOTAL	**49**	**15**

SEASON 92–93	GAMES	GOALS
League	20+1	7
FA Cup	1+1	0
League Cup	4	0
TOTAL	**25+2**	**7**

SEASON 93–94	GAMES	GOALS
League	31+3	9
FA Cup	7	0
League Cup	4	2
TOTAL	**42+3**	**11**

SEASON 94–95	GAMES	GOALS
League	10+2	2
FA Cup	1	1
League Cup	0+1	0
TOTAL	**11+3**	**3**

CAREER APPEARANCES AND GOALS

COMPETITION	GAMES	TOTAL	GOALS
League	409+22	431	141
FA Cup	63+3	66	22
League Cup	58+3	61	19
Screen Sport Super Cup	5+1	6	3
Full Members Cup	1	1	3
Simod Cup	1	1	1
Mercantile Credit Centenary Trophy	1	1	0
Zenith Data Systems Cup	2	2	0
FA Charity Shield	4	4	0
European Cup Winners Cup	8	8	4
Scottish League	37+3	40	16
Scottish Cup	3	3	2
Scottish League Cup	2	2	0
Internationals	9+3	12	1
TOTAL	**603+35**	**638**	**212**

HAT-TRICKS

Everton

1	3	Newcastle United	03/12/86	Home	FM Cup	5–2
2	4	Southampton	03/10/87	Away	League	4–0
3	3	Sheffield Wednesday	27/01/88	Away	FA Cup	5–0
4	3	Wrexham	09/10/90	Home	Lge Cup	6–0

Oldham Athletic

1	4	Luton Town	11/04/92	Home	League	5–1

League: 2
FA Cup: 1
League Cup: 1
Full Members Cup: 1
TOTAL: 5

HONOURS

Winners medals
League Division One Championship: 84/85, 86/87
FA Cup: 83/84
European Cup Winners Cup: 84/85
FA Charity Shield: 84/85, 85/86, 86/87, 87/88

Runner-up medals
League Division One Championship: 85/86
FA Cup: 84/85, 85/86, 88/89
League Cup: 83/84
Simod Cup: 88/89
Screen Sport Super Cup: 85/86

ALAN SHEARER

Born: 13/08/70 – Newcastle
Height: 5.11
Weight: 12.06 (96–97)

Clubs
Southampton: **1988–92** – Matches: **140+18** – Goals: **43**
Blackburn Rovers: **1992–96** – Matches: **165+6** – Goals: **130**
Newcastle United: **1996–97** – Matches: **40** – Goals: **28**

Country
England: **1992–97** – Matches: **34+1** – Goals: **16**

SEASON 1987–88

Southampton – League Division One

Sub+1	26/03/88	Chelsea	Away	League	1–0		
Sub+2	04/04/88	Oxford United	Away	League	0–0		
1	09/04/88	Arsenal	Home	League	4–2	3 Goals	(3)
2	23/04/88	Derby County	Away	League	0–2		
3	30/04/88	West Ham United	Home	League	2–1		

SEASON 1988–89

League Division One

Sub+3	03/09/88	Queens Park Rangers	Away	League	1–0
Sub+4	24/09/88	Liverpool	Home	League	1–3
4	11/02/89	Everton	Home	League	1–1
5	18/02/89	Sheffield Wednesday	Away	League	1–1
6	25/02/89	Tottenham Hotspur	Home	League	0–2
7	11/03/89	Charlton Athletic	Away	League	2–2
8	25/03/89	Arsenal	Home	League	1–3
9	27/03/89	Coventry City	Away	League	1–2
10	01/04/89	Newcastle United	Home	League	1–0
11	08/04/89	Middlesbrough	Away	League	3–3

SEASON 1989–90

League Division One

Sub+5	16/09/89	Crystal Palace	Home	League	1–1		
12	20/09/89	York City	Away	Lge Cup	1–0		
13	23/09/89	Derby County	Away	League	1–0		
14	30/09/89	Wimbledon	Home	League	2–2		
15	03/10/89	York City	Home	Lge Cup	2–0	2 Goals	(5)
16	14/10/89	Queens Park Rangers	Away	League	4–1	1 Goal	(6)
17	21/10/89	Liverpool	Home	League	4–1		
18	24/10/89	Charlton Athletic	Home	Lge Cup	1–0		
19	28/10/89	Manchester United	Away	League	1–2		
20	04/11/89	Tottenham Hotspur	Home	League	1–1		
21	11/11/89	Coventry City	Away	League	0–1		
22	18/11/89	Chelsea	Away	League	2–2		
23	25/11/89	Luton Town	Home	League	6–3	1 Goal	(7)
24	29/11/89	Swindon Town	Away	Lge Cup	0–0		
25	02/12/89	Millwall	Away	League	2–2		
26	09/12/89	Manchester City	Home	League	2–1		
Sub+6	17/12/89	Nottingham Forest	Away	League	0–2		
Sub+7	30/12/89	Sheffield Wednesday	Home	League	2–2		
Sub+8	06/01/90	Tottenham Hotspur	Away	FA Cup	3–1		
Sub+9	16/01/90	Swindon Town	Home	Lge Cup	4–2*		
Sub+10	27/01/90	Oxford United	Home	FA Cup	1–0		
Sub+11	31/01/90	Oldham Athletic	Away	Lge Cup	0–2		
27	10/02/90	Crystal Palace	Away	League	1–3		
28	17/02/90	Liverpool	Away	FA Cup	0–3		
29	24/02/90	Luton Town	Away	League	1–1	1 Goal	(8)
30	27/02/90	Norwich City	Home	League	4–1		
31	03/03/90	Chelsea	Home	League	2–3		
32	10/03/90	Derby County	Home	League	2–1		
33	17/03/90	Wimbledon	Away	League	3–3		
34	24/03/90	Manchester United	Home	League	0–2		
Sub+12	07/04/90	Sheffield Wednesday	Away	League	1–0		
Sub+13	14/04/90	Charlton Athletic	Home	League	3–2		
Sub+14	28/04/90	Coventry City	Home	League	3–0		
Sub+15	02/05/90	Arsenal	Away	League	1–2		
35	05/05/90	Tottenham Hotspur	Away	League	1–2		

SEASON 1990–91

League Division One

Sub+16	25/08/90	Aston Villa	Away	League	1–1		
Sub+17	01/09/90	Luton Town	Home	League	1–2		
36	15/09/90	Sheffield United	Home	League	2–0		
37	22/09/90	Manchester United	Away	League	2–3		
38	25/09/90	Rochdale	Away	Lge Cup	5–0	2 Goals	(10)
39	29/09/90	Everton	Away	League	0–3		
40	06/10/90	Chelsea	Home	League	3–3	1 Goal	(11)
41	09/10/90	Rochdale	Home	Lge Cup	3–0		
42	20/10/90	Coventry City	Away	League	2–1		
43	27/10/90	Derby County	Home	League	0–1		
44	30/10/90	Ipswich Town	Away	Lge Cup	2–0		
45	03/11/90	Wimbledon	Away	League	1–1		
46	10/11/90	Queens Park Rangers	Home	League	3–1		
47	17/11/90	Arsenal	Away	League	0–4		
48	20/11/90	Queens Park Rangers	Home	ZDS Cup	4–0	2 Goals	(13)
49	24/11/90	Crystal Palace	Home	League	2–3		
50	27/11/90	Crystal Palace	Home	Lge Cup	2–0	1 Goal	(14)
51	01/12/90	Leeds United	Away	League	1–2		
52	08/12/90	Norwich City	Away	League	1–3		
53	15/12/90	Aston Villa	Home	League	1–1		
54	22/12/90	Liverpool	Away	League	2–3		
55	26/12/90	Manchester City	Home	League	2–1		
56	29/12/90	Tottenham Hotspur	Home	League	3–0		
57	01/01/91	Sunderland	Away	League	0–1		
58	05/01/91	Ipswich Town	Home	FA Cup	3–2	1 Goal	(15)
59	12/01/91	Luton Town	Away	League	4–3		
60	16/01/91	Manchester United	Home	Lge Cup	1–1	1 Goal	(16)
61	19/01/91	Nottingham Forest	Home	League	1–1		
62	23/01/91	Manchester United	Away	Lge Cup	2–3	2 Goals	(18)
63	26/01/91	Coventry City	Away	FA Cup	1–1	1 Goal	(19)
64	29/01/91	Coventry City	Home	FA Cup	2–0		
65	02/02/91	Sheffield United	Away	League	1–4		
66	20/02/91	Norwich City	Away	ZDS Cup	1–2		

67	23/02/91	Queens Park Rangers	Away	League	1–2		
68	02/03/91	Leeds United	Home	League	2–0		
Sub+18	04/03/91	Nottingham Forest	Away	FA Cup	1–3		
69	09/03/91	Crystal Palace	Away	League	1–2		
70	13/03/91	Manchester United	Home	League	1–1		
71	16/03/91	Everton	Home	League	3–4	1 Goal	(20)
72	23/03/91	Chelsea	Away	League	2–0	1 Goal	(21)
73	30/03/91	Manchester City	Away	League	3–3		
74	01/04/91	Liverpool	Home	League	1–0		
75	06/04/91	Tottenham Hotspur	Away	League	0–2		
76	09/04/91	Arsenal	Home	League	1–1		
77	13/04/91	Sunderland	Home	League	3–1	1 Goal	(22)
78	20/04/91	Coventry City	Home	League	2–1		
79	04/05/91	Derby County	Away	League	2–6		
80	11/05/91	Wimbledon	Home	League	1–1		

SEASON 1991–92

League Division One

81	17/08/91	Tottenham Hotspur	Home	League	2–3	1 Goal	(23)
82	20/08/91	Notts County	Away	League	0–1		
83	24/08/91	Sheffield United	Away	League	2–0	1 Goal	(24)
84	28/08/91	Leeds United	Home	League	0–4		
85	31/08/91	Aston Villa	Home	League	1–1	1 Goal	(25)
86	04/09/91	Luton Town	Away	League	1–2		
87	07/09/91	Queens Park Rangers	Away	League	2–2	1 Goal	(26)
88	14/09/91	Manchester United	Home	League	0–1		
89	18/09/91	Wimbledon	Home	League	1–0		
90	21/09/91	Sheffield Wednesday	Away	League	0–2		
91	24/09/91	Scarborough	Away	Lge Cup	3–1	2 Goals	(28)
92	28/09/91	Arsenal	Home	League	0–4		
93	05/10/91	Oldham Athletic	Away	League	1–1	1 Goal	(29)
94	09/10/91	Scarborough	Home	Lge Cup	2–0		
95	19/10/91	Norwich City	Home	League	0–0		
96	22/10/91	Bristol City	Away	ZDS Cup	2–1	1 Goal	(30)
97	26/10/91	Nottingham Forest	Away	League	3–1	1 Goal	(31)
98	30/10/91	Sheffield Wednesday	Away	Lge Cup	1–1	1 Goal	(32)
99	02/11/91	Manchester City	Home	League	0–3		
100	16/11/91	Crystal Palace	Away	League	0–1		
101	20/11/91	Sheffield Wednesday	Home	Lge Cup	1–0		
102	23/11/91	Chelsea	Home	League	2–0	1 Goal	(33)
103	26/11/91	Plymouth Argyle	Away	ZDS Cup	1–0		
104	30/11/91	Coventry City	Away	League	0–2		
105	04/12/91	Nottingham Forest	Away	Lge Cup	0–0		
106	07/12/91	Liverpool	Home	League	1–1	1 Goal	(34)
107	17/12/91	Nottingham Forest	Home	Lge Cup	0–1		
108	20/12/91	Notts County	Home	League	1–1		
109	26/12/91	Leeds United	Away	League	3–3	1 Goal	(35)
110	28/12/91	Aston Villa	Away	League	1–2	1 Goal	(36)
111	01/01/92	Everton	Home	League	1–2		
112	04/01/92	Queens Park Rangers	Home	FA Cup	2–0		
113	07/01/92	West Ham United	Home	ZDS Cup	2–1	1 Goal	(37)
114	11/01/92	Sheffield United	Home	League	2–4		
115	18/01/92	Tottenham Hotspur	Away	League	2–1		
116	21/01/92	Chelsea	Home	ZDS Cup	2–0	1 Goal	(38)
117	27/01/92	Manchester United	Home	FA Cup	0–0		
118	29/01/92	Chelsea	Away	ZDS Cup	3–0		
119	01/02/92	Norwich City	Away	League	1–2		
120	05/02/92	Manchester United	Away	FA Cup	2–2+	1 Goal	(39)
121	12/02/92	Chelsea	Away	League	1–1		
122	16/02/92	Bolton Wanderers	Away	FA Cup	2–2		
123	22/02/92	Coventry City	Home	League	0–0		
124	26/02/92	Bolton Wanderers	Home	FA Cup	3–2*	1 Goal	(40)
125	29/02/92	Liverpool	Away	League	0–0		
126	03/03/92	West Ham United	Home	League	1–0		
127	07/03/92	Norwich City	Home	FA Cup	0–0		
128	11/03/92	Crystal Palace	Home	League	1–0		
129	15/03/92	Manchester City	Away	League	1–0		
130	18/03/92	Norwich City	Away	FA Cup	1–2*		
131	21/03/92	Luton Town	Home	League	2–1	1 Goal	(41)
132	29/03/92	Nottingham Forest	Wembley	ZDS Cup	2–3*		
133	04/04/92	Queens Park Rangers	Home	League	2–1	1 Goal	(42)
134	08/04/92	Nottingham Forest	Home	League	0–1		
135	14/04/92	West Ham United	Away	League	1–0		
136	16/04/92	Manchester United	Away	League	0–1		

137	18/04/92	Sheffield Wednesday	Home	League	0–1		
138	20/04/92	Wimbledon	Away	League	1–0		
139	25/04/92	Oldham Athletic	Home	League	1–0	1 Goal	(43)
140	02/05/92	Arsenal	Away	League	1–5		

+ AET Southampton won 4–2 on penalties

SEASON 1992–93

Blackburn Rovers – Premier League

1	15/08/92	Crystal Palace	Away	League	3–3	2 Goals	(2)
2	18/08/92	Arsenal	Home	League	1–0	1 Goal	(3)
3	22/08/92	Manchester City	Home	League	1–0		
4	26/08/92	Chelsea	Away	League	0–0		
5	29/08/92	Coventry City	Away	League	2–0	1 Goal	(4)
6	05/09/92	Nottingham Forest	Home	League	4–1	2 Goals	(6)
7	12/09/92	Arsenal	Away	League	1–0		
8	15/09/92	Everton	Home	League	2–3	2 Goals	(8)
9	19/09/92	Wimbledon	Away	League	1–1	1 Goal	(9)
10	23/09/92	Huddersfield Town	Away	Lge Cup	1–1	1 Goal	(10)
11	26/09/92	Oldham Athletic	Home	League	2–0	1 Goal	(11)
12	03/10/92	Norwich City	Home	League	7–1	2 Goals	(13)
13	06/10/92	Huddersfield Town	Home	Lge Cup	4–3	2 Goals	(15)
14	19/10/92	Aston Villa	Away	League	0–0		
15	24/10/92	Manchester United	Home	League	0–0		
16	28/10/92	Norwich City	Home	Lge Cup	2–0	1 Goal	(16)
17	31/10/92	Sheffield Wednesday	Away	League	0–0		
18	07/11/92	Tottenham Hotspur	Home	League	0–2		
19	22/11/92	Southampton	Away	League	1–1		
20	28/11/92	Queens Park Rangers	Home	League	1–0	1 Goal	(17)
21	05/12/92	Middlesbrough	Away	League	2–3		
22	09/12/92	Watford	Home	Lge Cup	6–1	2 Goals	(19)
23	13/12/92	Liverpool	Away	League	1–2	1 Goal	(20)
24	19/12/92	Sheffield United	Home	League	1–0		
25	26/12/92	Leeds United	Home	League	3–1	2 Goals	(22)
26	06/01/93	Cambridge United	Home	Lge Cup	3–2		

SEASON 1993–94

Premier League

Sub+1	18/08/93	Norwich City	Home	League	2–3		
Sub+2	21/08/93	Oldham Athletic	Home	League	1–0		
Sub+3	24/08/93	Manchester City	Away	League	2–0		
Sub+4	29/08/93	Newcastle United	Away	League	1–1	1 Goal	(23)
Sub+5	01/09/93	Arsenal	Home	League	1–1		
Sub+6	18/09/93	West Ham United	Home	League	0–2		
27	21/09/93	AFC Bournemouth	Home	Lge Cup	1–0	1 Goal	(24)
28	25/09/93	Sheffield Wednesday	Home	League	1–1	1 Goal	(25)
29	02/10/93	Swindon Town	Away	League	3–1	2 Goals	(27)
30	05/10/93	AFC Bournemouth	Away	Lge Cup	0–0		
31	18/10/93	Sheffield United	Home	League	0–0		
32	23/10/93	Leeds United	Away	League	3–3	3 Goals	(30)
33	26/10/93	Shrewsbury Town	Home	Lge Cup	0–0		
34	30/10/93	Tottenham Hotspur	Home	League	1–0	1 Goal	(31)
35	06/11/93	Queens Park Rangers	Away	League	0–1		
36	20/11/93	Southampton	Home	League	2–0	2 Goals	(33)
37	23/11/93	Coventry City	Home	League	2–1	2 Goals	(35)
38	27/11/93	Ipswich Town	Away	League	0–1		
39	30/11/93	Tottenham Hotspur	Away	Lge Cup	0–1		
40	05/12/93	Chelsea	Home	League	2–0	1 Goal	(36)
41	11/12/93	Oldham Athletic	Away	League	2–1	2 Goals	(38)
42	18/12/93	Manchester City	Home	League	2–0	1 Goal	(39)
43	26/12/93	Manchester United	Away	League	1–1		
44	29/12/93	Everton	Home	League	2–0	2 Goals	(41)
45	01/01/94	Aston Villa	Away	League	1–0	1 Goal	(42)
46	08/01/94	Portsmouth	Home	FA Cup	3–3	1 Goal	(43)
47	15/01/94	Sheffield United	Away	League	2–1	2 Goals	(45)
48	19/01/94	Portsmouth	Away	FA Cup	3–1	1 Goal	(46)
49	23/01/94	Leeds United	Home	League	2–1	2 Goals	(48)
50	29/01/94	Charlton Athletic	Away	FA Cup	0–0		
51	05/02/94	Wimbledon	Home	League	3–0	1 Goal	(49)
52	08/02/94	Charlton Athletic	Home	FA Cup	0–1		
53	12/02/94	Tottenham Hotspur	Away	League	2–0	1 Goal	(50)
54	19/02/94	Newcastle United	Home	League	1–0		
55	22/02/94	Norwich City	Away	League	2–2		
56	25/02/94	Arsenal	Away	League	0–1		

57	05/03/94	Liverpool	Home	League	2–0		
58	20/03/94	Sheffield Wednesday	Away	League	2–1		
59	26/03/94	Swindon Town	Home	League	3–1	2 Goals	(52)
60	29/03/94	Wimbledon	Away	League	1–4		
61	02/04/94	Manchester United	Home	League	2–0	2 Goals	(54)
62	04/04/94	Everton	Away	League	3–0		
63	11/04/94	Aston Villa	Home	League	1–0	1 Goal	(55)
64	16/04/94	Southampton	Away	League	1–3		
65	24/04/94	Queens Park Rangers	Home	League	1–1	1 Goal	(56)
66	27/04/94	West Ham United	Away	League	2–1		
67	02/05/94	Coventry City	Away	League	1–2		
68	07/05/94	Ipswich Town	Home	League	0–0		

SEASON 1994–95

Premier League

69	20/08/94	Southampton	Away	League	1–1	1 Goal	(57)
70	23/08/94	Leicester City	Home	League	3–0	1 Goal	(58)
71	27/08/94	Coventry City	Home	League	4–0		
72	31/08/94	Arsenal	Away	League	0–0		
73	10/09/94	Everton	Home	League	3–0	2 Goals	(60)
74	13/09/94	Trelleborgs FF	Home	UEFA Cup	0–1		
75	18/09/94	Chelsea	Away	League	2–1		
76	24/09/94	Aston Villa	Home	League	3–1	2 Goals	(62)
77	27/09/94	Trelleborgs FF	Away	UEFA Cup	2–2	1 Goal	(63)
78	01/10/94	Norwich City	Away	League	1–2		
79	04/10/94	Birmingham City	Away	Lge Cup	1–1		
80	09/10/94	Newcastle United	Away	League	1–1	1 Goal	(64)
81	15/10/94	Liverpool	Home	League	3–2		
82	23/10/94	Manchester United	Home	League	2–4		
83	26/10/94	Coventry City	Home	Lge Cup	2–0	2 Goals	(66)
84	29/10/94	Nottingham Forest	Away	League	2–0		
85	02/11/94	Sheffield Wednesday	Away	League	1–0	1 Goal	(67)
86	05/11/94	Tottenham Hotspur	Home	League	2–0	1 Goal	(68)
87	19/11/94	Ipswich Town	Away	League	3–1	1 Goal	(69)
88	26/11/94	Queens Park Rangers	Home	League	4–0	3 Goals	(72)
89	30/11/94	Liverpool	Home	Lge Cup	1–3		
90	03/12/94	Wimbledon	Away	League	3–0	1 Goal	(73)
91	10/12/94	Southampton	Home	League	3–2	2 Goals	(75)
92	17/12/94	Leicester City	Away	League	0–0		
93	26/12/94	Manchester City	Away	League	3–1	1 Goal	(76)
94	31/12/94	Crystal Palace	Away	League	1–0		
95	02/01/95	West Ham United	Home	League	4–2	3 Goals	(79)
96	08/01/95	Newcastle United	Away	FA Cup	1–1		
97	14/01/95	Nottingham Forest	Home	League	3–0		
98	18/01/95	Newcastle United	Home	FA Cup	1–2		
99	22/01/95	Manchester United	Away	League	0–1		
100	28/01/95	Ipswich Town	Home	League	4–1	3 Goals	(82)
101	01/02/95	Leeds United	Home	League	1–1	1 Goal	(83)
102	05/02/95	Tottenham Hotspur	Away	League	1–3		
103	12/02/95	Sheffield Wednesday	Home	League	3–1	1 Goal	(84)
104	22/02/95	Wimbledon	Home	League	2–1	1 Goal	(85)
105	25/02/95	Norwich City	Home	League	0–0		
106	04/03/95	Aston Villa	Away	League	1–0		
107	08/03/95	Arsenal	Home	League	3–1	2 Goals	(87)
108	11/03/95	Coventry City	Away	League	1–1	1 Goal	(88)
109	18/03/95	Chelsea	Home	League	2–1	1 Goal	(89)
110	01/04/95	Everton	Away	League	2–1	1 Goal	(90)
111	04/04/95	Queens Park Rangers	Away	League	1–0		
112	15/04/95	Leeds United	Away	League	1–1		
113	17/04/95	Manchester City	Home	League	2–3	1 Goal	(91)
114	20/04/95	Crystal Palace	Home	League	2–1		
115	30/04/95	West Ham United	Away	League	0–2		
116	08/05/95	Newcastle United	Home	League	1–0	1 Goal	(92)
117	14/05/95	Liverpool	Away	League	1–2	1 Goal	(93)

SEASON 1995–96

Premier League

118	13/08/95	Everton	Wembley	FA C/S	0–1		
119	19/08/95	Queens Park Rangers	Home	League	1–0	1 Goal	(94)
120	23/08/95	Sheffield Wednesday	Away	League	1–2	1 Goal	(95)
121	26/08/95	Bolton Wanderers	Away	League	1–2		
122	28/08/95	Manchester United	Home	League	1–2	1 Goal	(96)
123	09/09/95	Aston Villa	Home	League	1–1	1 Goal	(97)

124	13/09/95	Spartak Moskva	Home	Eur Cup	0–1		
125	16/09/95	Liverpool	Away	League	0–3		
126	20/09/95	Swindon Town	Away	Lge Cup	3–2	2 Goals	(99)
127	23/09/95	Coventry City	Home	League	5–1	3 Goals	(102)
128	27/09/95	Rosenborg BK	Away	Eur Cup	1–2		
129	30/09/95	Middlesbrough	Away	League	0–2		
130	04/10/95	Swindon Town	Home	Lge Cup	2–0	2 Goals	(104)
131	14/10/95	Southampton	Home	League	2–1	1 Goal	(105)
132	18/10/95	Legia Warszawa	Away	Eur Cup	0–1		
133	21/10/95	West Ham United	Away	League	1–1	1 Goal	(106)
134	24/10/95	Watford	Away	Lge Cup	2–1	1 Goal	(107)
135	28/10/95	Chelsea	Home	League	3–0	1 Goal	(108)
136	01/11/95	Legia Warszawa	Home	Eur Cup	0–0		
137	05/11/95	Everton	Away	League	0–1		
138	08/11/95	Newcastle United	Away	League	0–1		
139	18/11/95	Nottingham Forest	Home	League	7–0	3 Goals	(111)
140	22/11/95	Spartak Moskva	Away	Eur Cup	0–3		
141	26/11/95	Arsenal	Away	League	0–0		
142	29/11/95	Leeds United	Away	Lge Cup	1–2		
143	02/12/95	West Ham United	Home	League	4–2	3 Goals	(114)
144	06/12/95	Rosenborg BK	Home	Eur Cup	4–1	1 Goal	(115)
145	09/12/95	Coventry City	Away	League	0–5		
146	16/12/95	Middlesbrough	Home	League	1–0	1 Goal	(116)
147	23/12/95	Wimbledon	Away	League	1–1		
148	26/12/95	Manchester City	Home	League	2–0	1 Goal	(117)
149	30/12/95	Tottenham Hotspur	Home	League	2–1	1 Goal	(118)
150	01/01/96	Leeds United	Away	League	0–0		
151	06/01/96	Ipswich Town	Away	FA Cup	0–0		
152	13/01/96	Queens Park Rangers	Away	League	1–0	1 Goal	(119)
153	16/01/96	Ipswich Town	Home	FA Cup	0–1*		
154	20/01/96	Sheffield Wednesday	Home	League	3–0	1 Goal	(120)
155	03/02/96	Bolton Wanderers	Home	League	3–1	3 Goals	(123)
156	10/02/96	Manchester United	Away	League	0–1		
157	24/02/96	Liverpool	Home	League	2–3		
158	28/02/96	Aston Villa	Away	League	0–2		
159	02/03/96	Manchester City	Away	League	1–1	1 Goal	(124)
160	13/03/96	Leeds United	Home	League	1–0		
161	16/03/96	Tottenham Hotspur	Away	League	3–2	3 Goals	(127)
162	06/04/96	Southampton	Away	League	0–1		
163	08/04/96	Newcastle United	Home	League	2–1		
164	13/04/96	Nottingham Forest	Away	League	5–1	1 Goal	(128)
165	17/04/96	Wimbledon	Home	League	3–2	2 Goals	(130)

SEASON 1996–97

Newcastle United – Premier League

1	11/08/96	Manchester United	Wembley	FA C/S	0–4		
2	17/08/96	Everton	Away	League	0–2		
3	21/08/96	Wimbledon	Home	League	2–0	1 Goal	(1)
4	24/08/96	Sheffield Wednesday	Home	League	1–2	1 Goal	(2)
5	04/09/96	Sunderland	Away	League	2–1		
6	07/09/96	Tottenham Hotspur	Away	League	2–1		
7	10/09/96	Halmstads BK	Home	UEFA Cup	4–0		
8	14/09/96	Blackburn Rovers	Home	League	2–1	1 Goal	(3)
9	21/09/96	Leeds United	Away	League	1–0	1 Goal	(4)
10	24/09/96	Halmstads BK	Away	UEFA Cup	1–2		
11	30/09/96	Aston Villa	Home	League	4–3	1 Goal	(5)
12	12/10/96	Derby County	Away	League	1–0	1 Goal	(6)
13	15/10/96	Ferencvarosi TC	Away	UEFA Cup	2–3	1 Goal	(7)
14	20/10/96	Manchester United	Home	League	5–0	1 Goal	(8)
15	23/11/96	Chelsea	Away	League	1–1	1 Goal	(9)
16	27/11/96	Middlesbrough	Away	Lge Cup	1–3	1 Goal	(10)
17	30/11/96	Arsenal	Home	League	1–2	1 Goal	(11)
18	03/12/96	FC Metz	Home	UEFA Cup	2–0		
19	09/12/96	Nottingham Forest	Away	League	0–0		
20	17/12/96	Coventry City	Away	League	1–2	1 Goal	(12)
21	23/12/96	Liverpool	Home	League	1–1	1 Goal	(13)
22	26/12/96	Blackburn Rovers	Away	League	0–1		
23	28/12/96	Tottenham Hotspur	Home	League	7–1	2 Goals	(15)
24	01/01/97	Leeds United	Home	League	3–0	2 Goals	(17)
25	05/01/97	Charlton Athletic	Away	FA Cup	1–1		
26	11/01/97	Aston Villa	Away	League	2–2	1 Goal	(18)
27	15/01/97	Charlton Athletic	Home	FA Cup	2–1*	1 Goal	(19)
28	18/01/97	Southampton	Away	League	2–2		
29	26/01/97	Nottingham Forest	Home	FA Cup	1–2		

30	29/01/97	Everton	Home	League	4–1	1 Goal	(20)
31	02/02/97	Leicester City	Home	League	4–3	3 Goals	(23)
32	22/02/97	Middlesbrough	Away	League	1–0		
33	05/04/97	Sunderland	Home	League	1–1	1 Goal	(24)
34	13/04/97	Sheffield Wednesday	Away	League	1–1		
35	16/04/97	Chelsea	Home	League	3–1	2 Goals	(26)
36	19/04/97	Derby County	Home	League	3–1	1 Goal	(27)
37	03/05/97	Arsenal	Away	League	1–0		
38	06/05/97	West Ham United	Away	League	0–0		
39	08/05/97	Manchester United	Away	League	0–0		
40	11/05/97	Nottingham Forest	Home	League	5–0	1 Goal	(28)

INTERNATIONAL APPEARANCES – ENGLAND

1	19/02/92	France	Wembley	2–0	F	1 Goal	(1)
2	29/04/92	CIS	Moscow	2–2	F		
3	14/06/92	France	Malmo	0–0	EC		
4	09/09/92	Spain	Santander	0–1	F		
5	14/10/92	Norway	Wembley	1–1	WCQ		
6	18/11/92	Turkey	Wembley	4–0	WCQ	1 Goal	(2)
7	13/10/93	Holland	Rotterdam	0–2	WCQ		
8	09/03/94	Denmark	Wembley	1–0	F		
9	17/05/94	Greece	Wembley	5–0	F	1 Goal	(3)
10	22/05/94	Norway	Wembley	0–0	F		
11	07/09/94	USA	Wembley	2–0	F	2 Goals	(5)
12	12/10/94	Romania	Wembley	1–1	F		
13	16/11/94	Nigeria	Wembley	1–0	F		
14	15/02/95	Republic of Ireland	Lansdowne Road	Aba	F		
15	03/06/95	Japan	Wembley	2–1	UC		
16	08/06/95	Sweden	Elland Road	3–3	UC		
17	11/06/95	Brazil	Wembley	1–3	UC		
18	06/09/95	Colombia	Wembley	0–0	F		
19	11/10/95	Norway	Oslo	0–0	F		
20	15/11/95	Switzerland	Wembley	3–1	F		
21	12/12/95	Portugal	Wembley	1–1	F		
Sub 22	18/05/96	Hungary	Wembley	3–0	F		
23	23/05/96	China	Beijing	3–0	F		
24	08/06/96	Switzerland	Wembley	1–1	EC	1 Goal	(6)
25	15/06/96	Scotland	Wembley	2–0	EC	1 Goal	(7)
26	18/06/96	Holland	Wembley	4–1	EC	2 Goals	(9)
27	22/06/96	Spain	Wembley	0–0+	EC		
28	26/06/96	Germany	Wembley	1–1#	EC	1 Goal	(10)
29	01/09/96	Moldova	Kishinev	3–0	WCQ	1 Goal	(11)
30	09/10/96	Poland	Wembley	2–1	WCQ	2 Goals	(13)
31	12/02/97	Italy	Wembley	0–1	WCQ		
32	30/04/97	Georgia	Wembley	2–0	WCQ	1 Goal	(14)
33	31/05/97	Poland	Katowice	2–0	WCQ	1 Goal	(15)
34	07/06/97	France	Montpellier	1–0	LTDF	1 Goal	(16)
35	10/06/97	Brazil	Paris	0–1	LTDF		

+ AET England won 4–2 on penalties
# AET Germany won 6–5 on penalties

APPEARANCES AND GOALS PER SEASON

SEASON 87–88	GAMES	GOALS
League	3+2	3
TOTAL	**3+2**	**3**

SEASON 88–89	GAMES	GOALS
League	8+2	0
TOTAL	**8+2**	**0**

SEASON 89–90	GAMES	GOALS
League	19+7	3
FA Cup	1+2	0
League Cup	4+2	2
TOTAL	**24+11**	**5**

SEASON 90–91	GAMES	GOALS
League	34+2	4
FA Cup	3+1	2
League Cup	6	6
Zenith Data Systems Cup	2	2
TOTAL	**45+3**	**14**

SEASON 91–92	GAMES	GOALS
League	41	13
FA Cup	7	2
League Cup	6	3
Zenith Data Systems Cup	6	3
TOTAL	**60**	**21**

SEASON 92–93	GAMES	GOALS
League	21	16
League Cup	5	6
TOTAL	**26**	**22**

SEASON 93–94	GAMES	GOALS
League	34+6	31
FA Cup	4	2
League Cup	4	1
TOTAL	**42+6**	**34**

SEASON 94–95	GAMES	GOALS
League	42	34
FA Cup	2	0
League Cup	3	2
UEFA Cup	2	1
TOTAL	**49**	**37**

SEASON 95–96	GAMES	GOALS
League	35	31
FA Cup	2	0
League Cup	4	5
European Cup	6	1
FA Charity Shield	1	0
TOTAL	**48**	**37**

SEASON 96–97	GAMES	GOALS
League	31	25
FA Cup	3	1
League Cup	1	1
UEFA Cup	4	1
FA Charity Shield	1	0
TOTAL	**40**	**28**

CAREER APPEARANCES AND GOALS

COMPETITION	GAMES	TOTAL	GOALS
League	268+19	287	160
FA Cup	22+3	25	7
League Cup	33+2	35	26
Zenith Data Systems Cup	8	8	5
FA Charity Shield	2	2	0
European Cup	6	6	1
UEFA Cup	6	6	2
Internationals	34+1	35	16
TOTAL	**379+25**	**404**	**217**

HAT-TRICKS

Southampton

1	3	Arsenal	09/04/88	Home	League	4–2

Blackburn Rovers

1	3	Leeds United	23/10/93	Away	League	3–3
2	3	Queens Park Rangers	26/11/94	Home	League	4–0
3	3	West Ham United	02/01/95	Home	League	4–2
4	3	Ipswich Town	28/01/95	Home	League	4–1
5	3	Coventry City	23/09/95	Home	League	5–1
6	3	Nottingham Forest	18/11/95	Home	League	7–0
7	3	West Ham United	02/12/95	Home	League	4–2
8	3	Bolton Wanderers	03/02/96	Home	League	3–1
9	3	Tottenham Hotspur	16/03/96	Away	League	3–2

Newcastle United

1	3	Leicester City	02/02/97	Home	League	4–3

League: 11
TOTAL: 11

HONOURS

Winners medals
Premier League Championship: 94/95

Runner-up medals
Premier League Championship: 93/94, 96/97
Zenith Data Systems Cup: 91/92
FA Charity Shield: 95/96, 96/97

DUNCAN SHEARER

Born: 28/08/62 – Fort William
Height: 5.10
Weight: 10.10 (96–97)

Clubs
Chelsea: **1986** – Matches: **2** – Goals: **1**
Huddersfield Town: **1986–88** – Matches: **93+3** – Goals: **48**
Swindon Town: **1988–92** – Matches: **195+4** – Goals: **98**
Blackburn Rovers: **1992** – Matches: **5+2** – Goals: **1**
Aberdeen: **1992–97** – Matches: **137+58** – Goals: **79**

Country
Scotland: **1994–95** – Matches: **4+3** – Goals: **2**

SEASON 1985–86

Chelsea – League Division One

1	01/02/86	Leicester City	Home	League	2–2	1 Goal	(1)
2	08/02/86	Oxford United	Home	League	1–4		

Huddersfield Town – League Division Two

Sub+1	29/03/86	Middlesbrough	Home	League	0–3		
1	31/03/86	Barnsley	Away	League	3–1	3 Goals	(3)
2	05/04/86	Stoke City	Home	League	2–0	2 Goals	(5)
3	12/04/86	Charlton Athletic	Away	League	0–3		
4	15/04/86	Blackburn Rovers	Away	League	1–0		
5	19/04/86	Brighton & Hove Albion	Home	League	1–0	1 Goal	(6)
6	26/04/86	Fulham	Away	League	1–2	1 Goal	(7)
7	03/05/86	Wimbledon	Home	League	0–1		

SEASON 1986–87

League Division Two

8	23/08/86	Sunderland	Home	League	0–2		
9	26/08/86	Halifax Town	Home	Lge Cup	3–1	1 Goal	(8)
10	30/08/86	West Bromwich Albion	Away	League	0–1		
11	02/09/86	Halifax Town	Away	Lge Cup	2–2*	1 Goal	(9)
12	06/09/86	Leeds United	Home	League	1–1	1 Goal	(10)
13	09/09/86	Crystal Palace	Away	League	0–1		
14	13/09/86	Birmingham City	Away	League	1–1		
15	16/09/86	Blackburn Rovers	Home	FM Cup	1–2*	1 Goal	(11)
16	20/09/86	Oldham Athletic	Home	League	5–4	2 Goals	(13)
17	23/09/86	Arsenal	Away	Lge Cup	0–2		
18	27/09/86	Portsmouth	Away	League	0–1		
19	04/10/86	Derby County	Home	League	2–0		
20	07/10/86	Arsenal	Home	Lge Cup	1–1		
21	11/10/86	Stoke City	Away	League	0–2		
22	18/10/86	Sheffield United	Away	League	0–0		
23	21/10/86	Shrewsbury Town	Home	League	2–1	2 Goals	(15)
24	25/10/86	Hull City	Home	League	1–3		
25	01/11/86	Ipswich Town	Away	League	0–3		
26	08/11/86	Brighton & Hove Albion	Home	League	2–1	1 Goal	(16)
27	15/11/86	Bradford City	Away	League	3–4		
28	22/11/86	Plymouth Argyle	Home	League	1–2		
29	13/12/86	Millwall	Away	League	0–4		
30	20/12/86	Crystal Palace	Home	League	1–2	1 Goal	(17)

31	26/12/86	Blackburn Rovers	Away	League	2–1	1 Goal	(18)
32	27/12/86	Bradford City	Home	League	5–2	4 Goals	(22)
33	01/01/87	Grimsby Town	Home	League	0–0		
34	03/01/87	Leeds United	Away	League	1–1		
35	10/01/87	Norwich City	Away	FA Cup	1–1	1 Goal	(23)
36	21/01/87	Norwich City	Home	FA Cup	2–4		
37	24/01/87	Sunderland	Away	League	1–2		
38	07/02/87	West Bromwich Albion	Home	League	2–1	1 Goal	(24)
39	14/02/87	Shrewsbury Town	Away	League	2–1	1 Goal	(25)
40	17/02/87	Reading	Away	League	2–3	1 Goal	(26)
41	21/02/87	Portsmouth	Home	League	2–0	1 Goal	(27)
42	28/02/87	Oldham Athletic	Away	League	0–2		
43	03/03/87	Birmingham City	Home	League	2–2		
44	07/03/87	Hull City	Away	League	0–0		
45	14/03/87	Sheffield United	Home	League	1–1		
46	21/03/87	Stoke City	Home	League	2–2	1 Goal	(28)
47	31/03/87	Barnsley	Home	League	2–2	2 Goals	(30)
48	03/04/87	Brighton & Hove Albion	Away	League	1–1	1 Goal	(31)
49	08/04/87	Derby County	Away	League	0–2		
50	11/04/87	Ipswich Town	Home	League	1–2		
51	18/04/87	Grimsby Town	Away	League	1–0		
52	20/04/87	Blackburn Rovers	Home	League	1–2		
53	25/04/87	Plymouth Argyle	Away	League	1–1		
54	02/05/87	Reading	Home	League	2–0	1 Goal	(32)
55	04/05/87	Barnsley	Away	League	1–0		
56	09/05/87	Millwall	Home	League	3–0		

SEASON 1987–88

League Division Two

57	15/08/87	Crystal Palace	Home	League	2–2	1 Goal	(33)
58	18/08/87	Rotherham United	Away	Lge Cup	4–4	3 Goals	(36)
59	22/08/87	Plymouth Argyle	Away	League	1–6		
60	25/08/87	Rotherham United	Home	Lge Cup	1–3	1 Goal	(37)
61	29/08/87	Shrewsbury Town	Home	League	0–0		
62	31/08/87	Oldham Athletic	Away	League	2–3	1 Goal	(38)
63	12/09/87	Blackburn Rovers	Away	League	2–2		
64	15/09/87	Leeds United	Home	League	0–0		
65	19/09/87	Aston Villa	Home	League	0–1		
66	29/09/87	Bradford City	Home	League	1–2	1 Goal	(39)
67	03/10/87	Birmingham City	Away	League	0–2		
68	10/10/87	Middlesbrough	Home	League	1–4	1 Goal	(40)
69	17/10/87	Reading	Away	League	2–3	2 Goals	(42)
70	20/10/87	Hull City	Home	League	0–2		
71	24/10/87	West Bromwich Albion	Away	League	2–3	1 Goal	(43)
72	31/10/87	Millwall	Home	League	2–1		
73	03/11/87	Ipswich Town	Away	League	0–3		
74	07/11/87	Manchester City	Away	League	1–10		
75	10/11/87	Leicester City	Away	Simod Cup	0–1		
76	14/11/87	Barnsley	Home	League	2–2		
Sub+2	19/12/87	Leeds United	Away	League	0–3		
Sub+3	26/12/87	Stoke City	Home	League	0–3		
77	28/12/87	Aston Villa	Away	League	1–1	1 Goal	(44)
78	01/01/88	Shrewsbury Town	Away	League	1–3		
79	02/01/88	Blackburn Rovers	Home	League	1–2		
80	09/01/88	Manchester City	Home	FA Cup	2–2	2 Goals	(46)
81	12/01/88	Manchester City	Away	FA Cup	0–0*		
82	16/01/88	Crystal Palace	Away	League	1–2	1 Goal	(47)
83	25/01/88	Manchester City	Home	FA Cup	0–3		
84	13/02/88	Swindon Town	Home	League	0–3		
85	27/02/88	Birmingham City	Home	League	2–2		
86	01/03/88	Bradford City	Away	League	1–0		
87	05/03/88	Reading	Home	League	0–2		
88	19/03/88	Millwall	Away	League	1–4		
89	26/03/88	West Bromwich Albion	Home	League	1–3		
90	02/04/88	Manchester City	Home	League	1–0		
91	04/04/88	Barnsley	Away	League	0–1		
92	08/04/88	Ipswich Town	Home	League	1–2		
93	19/04/88	Oldham Athletic	Home	League	2–2	1 Goal	(48)

SEASON 1988–89

Swindon Town – League Division Two

| 1 | 29/08/88 | Barnsley | Away | League | 1–1 | | |
| 2 | 03/09/88 | West Bromwich Albion | Away | League | 1–3 | | |

3	11/09/88	Portsmouth	Home	League	1–1		
4	17/09/88	Blackburn Rovers	Away	League	0–0		
5	20/09/88	AFC Bournemouth	Home	League	3–1		
6	24/09/88	Brighton & Hove Albion	Home	League	3–0		
7	27/09/88	Crystal Palace	Home	Lge Cup	1–2	1 Goal	(1)
8	01/10/88	Watford	Away	League	3–2	1 Goal	(2)
9	05/10/88	Oxford United	Away	League	1–1		
10	09/10/88	Chelsea	Home	League	1–1	1 Goal	(3)
11	12/10/88	Crystal Palace	Away	Lge Cup	0–2		
12	16/10/88	Leeds United	Home	League	0–0		
Sub+1	05/11/88	Hull City	Away	League	0–1		
Sub+2	09/11/88	Norwich City	Away	Simod Cup	1–2		
Sub+3	19/11/88	Stoke City	Away	League	1–2		
Sub+4	03/12/88	Shrewsbury Town	Away	League	1–0		
13	17/12/88	Bradford City	Away	League	2–2	1 Goal	(4)
14	26/12/88	Plymouth Argyle	Home	League	1–0	1 Goal	(5)
15	31/12/88	Manchester City	Home	League	1–2		
16	02/01/89	Portsmouth	Away	League	2–0	1 Goal	(6)
17	07/01/89	Portsmouth	Away	FA Cup	1–1		
18	10/01/89	Portsmouth	Home	FA Cup	2–0	1 Goal	(7)
19	18/02/89	Sunderland	Home	League	4–1	2 Goals	(9)
20	25/02/89	Leeds United	Away	League	0–0		
21	28/02/89	Leicester City	Home	League	2–1	1 Goal	(10)
22	04/03/89	Ipswich Town	Away	League	2–1		
23	11/03/89	Hull City	Home	League	1–0	1 Goal	(11)
24	18/03/89	AFC Bournemouth	Away	League	3–2		
25	25/03/89	West Bromwich Albion	Home	League	0–0		
26	27/03/89	Plymouth Argyle	Away	League	1–4		
27	01/04/89	Blackburn Rovers	Home	League	1–1		
28	04/04/89	Bradford City	Home	League	1–0	1 Goal	(12)
29	08/04/89	Manchester City	Away	League	1–2	1 Goal	(13)
30	15/04/89	Watford	Home	League	1–1		
31	18/04/89	Birmingham City	Away	League	2–1		
32	22/04/89	Brighton & Hove Albion	Away	League	2–0		
33	25/04/89	Crystal Palace	Home	League	1–0		
34	29/04/89	Walsall	Away	League	2–2	1 Goal	(14)
35	01/05/89	Shrewsbury Town	Home	League	1–0		
36	06/05/89	Stoke City	Home	League	3–0	2 Goals	(16)
37	13/05/89	Oldham Athletic	Away	League	2–2		
38	21/05/89	Crystal Palace	Home	Lge P/O	1–0		
39	24/05/89	Crystal Palace	Away	Lge P/O	0–2		

SEASON 1989–90

League Division Two

40	19/08/89	Sunderland	Home	League	0–2		
41	26/08/89	Oldham Athletic	Away	League	2–2	1 Goal	(17)
42	03/09/89	Wolverhampton Wanderers	Home	League	3–1	1 Goal	(18)
43	16/09/89	Barnsley	Home	League	0–0		
44	19/09/89	Shrewsbury Town	Away	Lge Cup	3–0	1 Goal	(19)
45	23/09/89	Leeds United	Away	League	0–4		
46	26/09/89	Plymouth Argyle	Home	League	3–0		
47	30/09/89	Bradford City	Away	League	1–1		
48	03/10/89	Shrewsbury Town	Home	Lge Cup	3–1	1 Goal	(20)
49	07/10/89	Hull City	Away	League	3–2		
50	14/10/89	Ipswich Town	Home	League	3–0	1 Goal	(21)
51	24/10/89	Bolton Wanderers	Home	Lge Cup	3–3	1 Goal	(22)
52	01/11/89	Brighton & Hove Albion	Away	League	2–1		
53	04/11/89	Stoke City	Home	League	6–0	2 Goals	(24)
54	07/11/89	Bolton Wanderers	Away	Lge Cup	1–1*	1 Goal	(25)
55	11/11/89	Middlesbrough	Away	League	2–0	1 Goal	(26)
56	14/11/89	Bolton Wanderers	Away	Lge Cup	1–1*		
57	18/11/89	Port Vale	Away	League	0–2		
58	21/11/89	Bolton Wanderers	Home	Lge Cup	2–1*		
59	26/11/89	Portsmouth	Home	League	2–2	2 Goals	(28)
60	29/11/89	Southampton	Home	Lge Cup	0–0		
61	02/12/89	Sunderland	Away	League	2–2	1 Goal	(29)
62	05/12/89	AFC Bournemouth	Home	League	2–3		
63	10/12/89	Sheffield United	Home	League	0–2		
64	13/12/89	Millwall	Home	ZDS Cup	2–1		
65	17/12/89	West Bromwich Albion	Away	League	2–1	1 Goal	(30)
66	26/12/89	Blackburn Rovers	Home	League	4–3	2 Goals	(32)
67	30/12/89	Newcastle United	Home	League	1–1	1 Goal	(33)
68	01/01/90	Watford	Away	League	2–0		

69	06/01/90	Bristol City	Away	FA Cup	1–2	1 Goal	(34)
70	13/01/90	Oldham Athletic	Home	League	3–2		
71	24/01/90	Norwich City	Home	ZDS Cup	4–1	1 Goal	(35)
72	16/01/90	Southampton	Away	Lge Cup	2–4*		
73	20/01/90	Wolverhampton Wanderers	Away	League	1–2		
74	04/02/90	Leeds United	Home	League	3–2		
75	10/02/90	Barnsley	Away	League	1–0		
76	13/02/90	Crystal Palace	Away	ZDS Cup	0–1		
77	18/02/90	West Ham United	Home	League	2–2		
78	24/02/90	Portsmouth	Away	League	1–1		
79	03/03/90	Port Vale	Home	League	3–0	1 Goal	(36)
80	06/03/90	Bradford City	Home	League	3–1	2 Goals	(38)
81	10/03/90	Plymouth Argyle	Away	League	3–0	1 Goal	(39)
82	17/03/90	Hull City	Home	League	1–3	1 Goal	(40)
83	20/03/90	Ipswich Town	Away	League	0–1		
84	24/03/90	Oxford United	Away	League	2–2		
85	31/03/90	Leicester City	Home	League	1–1		
86	07/04/90	AFC Bournemouth	Away	League	2–1		
87	10/04/90	Brighton & Hove Albion	Home	League	1–2		
88	14/04/90	Watford	Home	League	2–0	1 Goal	(41)
89	16/04/90	Blackburn Rovers	Away	League	1–2		
90	21/04/90	West Bromwich Albion	Home	League	2–1		
91	25/04/90	Newcastle United	Away	League	0–0		
92	28/04/90	Middlesbrough	Home	League	1–1		
93	05/05/90	Stoke City	Away	League	1–1	1 Goal	(42)
94	13/05/90	Blackburn Rovers	Away	Lge P/O	2–1		
95	16/05/90	Blackburn Rovers	Home	Lge P/O	2–1	1 Goal	(43)
96	28/05/90	Sunderland	Wembley	Lge P/O	1–0		

SEASON 1990–91

League Division Two

97	25/08/90	Charlton Athletic	Away	League	2–1	1 Goal	(44)
98	28/08/90	Ipswich Town	Home	League	1–0	1 Goal	(45)
99	02/09/90	Bristol City	Home	League	0–1		
100	08/09/90	Hull City	Away	League	1–1		
101	15/09/90	Middlesbrough	Home	League	1–3	1 Goal	(46)
102	18/09/90	Wolverhampton Wanderers	Home	League	1–0		
103	22/09/90	Oxford United	Away	League	4–2	2 Goals	(48)
104	25/09/90	Darlington	Away	Lge Cup	0–3		
105	30/09/90	Millwall	Home	League	0–0		
106	02/10/90	Oldham Athletic	Away	League	2–3		
107	06/10/90	Brighton & Hove Albion	Away	League	3–3		
108	24/10/90	Leicester City	Away	League	2–2	1 Goal	(49)
109	27/10/90	Barnsley	Away	League	1–5		
110	31/10/90	Sheffield Wednesday	Away	Lge Cup	0–0		
111	03/11/90	Port Vale	Home	League	1–2		
112	06/11/90	Sheffield Wednesday	Home	Lge Cup	0–1		
113	10/11/90	Portsmouth	Home	League	3–0	1 Goal	(50)
114	17/11/90	Sheffield Wednesday	Away	League	1–2		
115	24/11/90	Notts County	Away	League	0–0		
116	01/12/90	Blackburn Rovers	Home	League	1–1	1 Goal	(51)
117	08/12/90	Ipswich Town	Away	League	1–1	1 Goal	(52)
118	12/12/90	Chelsea	Away	ZDS Cup	0–1		
119	15/12/90	Charlton Athletic	Home	League	1–1		
120	22/12/90	West Bromwich Albion	Home	League	2–1	1 Goal	(53)
121	26/12/90	Newcastle United	Away	League	1–1		
122	29/12/90	Watford	Away	League	2–2	1 Goal	(54)
123	01/01/91	Plymouth Argyle	Home	League	1–1		
124	05/01/91	Leyton Orient	Away	FA Cup	1–1	1 Goal	(55)
125	12/01/91	Bristol City	Away	League	4–0	1 Goal	(56)
126	19/01/91	Hull City	Home	League	3–1	2 Goals	(58)
127	21/01/91	Leyton Orient	Home	FA Cup	1–0		
128	26/01/91	Norwich City	Away	FA Cup	1–3		
129	02/02/91	Middlesbrough	Away	League	0–2		
130	19/02/91	Sheffield Wednesday	Home	League	2–1		
131	23/02/91	Portsmouth	Away	League	1–2		
132	02/03/91	Blackburn Rovers	Away	League	1–2		
133	05/03/91	Oxford United	Home	League	0–0		
134	12/03/91	Oldham Athletic	Home	League	2–2	1 Goal	(59)
135	16/03/91	Millwall	Away	League	0–1		
136	20/03/91	Bristol Rovers	Away	League	1–2	1 Goal	(60)
137	23/03/91	Brighton & Hove Albion	Home	League	1–3	1 Goal	(61)
138	30/03/91	Newcastle United	Home	League	3–2	1 Goal	(62)

139	01/04/91	West Bromwich Albion	Away	League	1–2		
140	06/04/91	Watford	Home	League	1–2		
141	13/04/91	Plymouth Argyle	Away	League	3–3	2 Goals	(64)
142	16/04/91	Wolverhampton Wanderers	Away	League	2–1	1 Goal	(65)
143	20/04/91	West Ham United	Away	League	0–2		
144	23/04/91	Notts County	Home	League	1–2	1 Goal	(66)
145	27/04/91	Leicester City	Home	League	5–2		
146	04/05/91	Barnsley	Home	League	1–2		
147	11/05/91	Port Vale	Away	League	1–3		

SEASON 1991–92

League Division Two

148	17/08/91	Leicester City	Home	League	0–0		
149	20/08/91	West Bromwich Albion	Home	Lge Cup	2–0		
150	24/08/91	Cambridge United	Home	League	2–3	1 Goal	(67)
151	28/08/91	West Bromwich Albion	Away	Lge Cup	2–2	2 Goals	(69)
152	31/08/91	Barnsley	Home	League	3–1	1 Goal	(70)
153	03/09/91	Ipswich Town	Home	League	4–1		
154	07/09/91	Port Vale	Home	League	2–2		
155	14/09/91	Sunderland	Home	League	5–3	1 Goal	(71)
156	17/09/91	Bristol Rovers	Home	League	1–0		
157	21/09/91	Wolverhampton Wanderers	Home	League	1–2		
158	25/09/91	Millwall	Away	Lge Cup	2–2		
159	28/09/91	Watford	Home	League	3–1	1 Goal	(72)
160	01/10/91	Oxford United	Home	ZDS Cup	3–3+		
161	05/10/91	Plymouth Argyle	Home	League	4–0	4 Goals	(76)
162	08/10/91	Millwall	Home	Lge Cup	3–1	2 Goals	(78)
163	12/10/91	Derby County	Home	League	1–2		
164	19/10/91	Blackburn Rovers	Home	League	2–1		
165	23/10/91	Chelsea	Away	ZDS Cup	0–1		
166	26/10/91	Brighton & Hove Albion	Home	League	2–0	2 Goals	(80)
167	29/10/91	Huddersfield Town	Away	Lge Cup	4–1	2 Goals	(82)
168	02/11/91	Newcastle United	Home	League	2–1		
169	06/11/91	Charlton Athletic	Home	League	0–0		
170	09/11/91	Southend United	Home	League	2–3	1 Goal	(83)
171	16/11/91	Portsmouth	Home	League	2–3		
172	22/11/91	Tranmere Rovers	Home	League	0–0		
173	30/11/91	Grimsby Town	Home	League	1–1		
174	07/12/91	Middlesbrough	Home	League	2–2	1 Goal	(84)
175	17/12/91	Crystal Palace	Home	Lge Cup	0–1		
176	20/12/91	Ipswich Town	Home	League	0–0		
177	26/12/91	Bristol City	Home	League	1–1	1 Goal	(85)
178	28/12/91	Barnsley	Home	League	1–1	1 Goal	(86)
179	01/01/92	Millwall	Home	League	3–1	2 Goals	(88)
180	04/01/92	Watford	Home	FA Cup	3–2	2 Goals	(90)
181	11/01/92	Cambridge United	Home	League	0–2		
182	18/01/92	Leicester City	Home	League	1–3		
183	25/01/92	Cambridge United	Away	FA Cup	3–0	2 Goals	(92)
184	28/01/92	Oxford United	Home	League	2–1	1 Goal	(93)
185	01/02/92	Blackburn Rovers	Home	League	1–2		
186	04/02/92	Bristol City	Home	League	2–0	1 Goal	(94)
187	08/02/92	Brighton & Hove Albion	Home	League	2–1		
188	16/02/92	Aston Villa	Home	FA Cup	1–2		
189	22/02/92	Grimsby Town	Home	League	0–0		
190	29/02/92	Middlesbrough	Home	League	0–1		
191	07/03/92	Oxford United	Home	League	3–5		
192	10/03/92	Charlton Athletic	Home	League	1–2	1 Goal	(95)
193	14/03/92	Newcastle United	Home	League	1–3		
194	17/03/92	Tranmere Rovers	Home	League	2–0	2 Goals	(97)
195	21/03/92	Southend United	Home	League	3–1	1 Goal	(98)

+ AET Swindon Town won 4–3 on penalties

Blackburn Rovers – League Division Two

1	28/03/92	Barnsley	Away	League	1–2	1 Goal	(1)
2	31/03/92	Port Vale	Away	League	0–2		
3	11/04/92	Watford	Away	League	1–2		
4	14/04/92	Wolverhampton Wanderers	Home	League	1–2		
5	18/04/92	Leicester City	Home	League	0–1		
Sub+1	20/04/92	Tranmere Rovers	Away	League	2–2		
Sub+2	10/05/92	Derby County	Home	Lge P/O	4–2		

SEASON 1992–93

Aberdeen – Scottish League Premier Division

1	01/08/92	Hibernian	Home	League	3–0	2 Goals	(2)
2	05/08/92	Celtic	Home	League	1–1	1 Goal	(3)
3	08/08/92	Falkirk	Away	League	1–0		
4	12/08/92	Arbroath	Away	S Lge Cup	4–0	1 Goal	(4)
5	15/08/92	Motherwell	Away	League	1–2		
6	19/08/92	Dunfermline Athletic	Home	S Lge Cup	1–0*		
7	22/08/92	Dundee	Home	League	2–1	1 Goal	(5)
8	26/08/92	Falkirk	Away	S Lge Cup	4–1	3 Goals	(8)
9	29/08/92	Rangers	Away	League	1–3		
10	12/09/92	Heart of Midlothian	Away	League	0–1		
11	19/09/92	Partick Thistle	Home	League	2–0		
12	23/09/92	Celtic	Hampden	S Lge Cup	1–0		
13	26/09/92	St Johnstone	Away	League	3–0	2 Goals	(10)
14	03/10/92	Dundee United	Home	League	0–1		
15	07/10/92	Hibernian	Away	League	3–1	1 Goal	(11)
16	17/10/92	Falkirk	Home	League	3–1		
17	25/10/92	Rangers	Hampden	S Lge Cup	1–2*	1 Goal	(12)
18	31/10/92	Airdrieonians	Away	League	2–1	1 Goal	(13)
19	07/11/92	Dundee	Away	League	2–1	1 Goal	(14)
20	11/11/92	Motherwell	Home	League	2–0	1 Goal	(15)
21	24/11/92	Partick Thistle	Away	League	7–0	3 Goals	(18)
22	28/11/92	Heart of Midlothian	Home	League	6–2	3 Goals	(21)
23	30/01/93	Falkirk	Away	League	4–1	2 Goals	(23)
Sub+1	02/02/93	Rangers	Home	League	0–1		
24	07/02/93	Dundee United	Home	S Cup	2–0		
25	13/02/93	Celtic	Home	League	1–1		
26	20/02/93	St Johnstone	Away	League	2–0		
27	24/02/93	Dundee United	Home	League	0–0		
28	02/03/93	Partick Thistle	Home	League	1–0		
29	06/03/93	Clydebank	Home	S Cup	1–1	1 Goal	(24)
30	09/03/93	Hibernian	Away	League	2–1		
31	13/03/93	Falkirk	Home	League	2–2		
Sub+2	20/03/93	Dundee	Away	League	2–1		
32	30/03/93	Rangers	Away	League	0–2		
Sub+3	03/04/93	Hibernian	Neutral	S Cup	1–0		
33	10/04/93	Airdrieonians	Away	League	1–1	1 Goal	(25)
34	17/04/93	Heart of Midlothian	Home	League	3–2	1 Goal	(26)
35	20/04/93	Partick Thistle	Away	League	3–1		
36	01/05/93	Celtic	Away	League	0–1		
37	05/05/93	Heart of Midlothian	Away	League	2–1	1 Goal	(27)
38	08/05/93	St Johnstone	Home	League	1–1		
39	12/05/93	Rangers	Home	League	1–0	1 Goal	(28)
40	29/05/93	Rangers	Hampden	S Cup	1–2		

SEASON 1993–94

Scottish League Premier Division

Sub+4	07/08/93	Dundee United	Away	League	1–1		
41	10/08/93	Clydebank	Home	S Lge Cup	5–0	3 Goals	(31)
42	14/08/93	Kilmarnock	Home	League	1–0		
43	21/08/93	Dundee	Away	League	1–1	1 Goal	(32)
44	24/08/93	Motherwell	Home	S Lge Cup	5–2	1 Goal	(33)
45	28/08/93	St Johnstone	Home	League	0–0		
Sub+5	01/09/93	Rangers	Away	S Lge Cup	1–2		
46	04/09/93	Celtic	Away	League	1–0		
47	11/09/93	Hibernian	Away	League	1–2	1 Goal	(34)
48	14/09/93	Valur Reykjavik	Away	ECW Cup	3–0	1 Goal	(35)
49	18/09/93	Rangers	Home	League	2–0	1 Goal	(36)
50	25/09/93	Raith Rovers	Home	League	4–1	1 Goal	(37)
51	02/10/93	Motherwell	Away	League	0–0		
52	05/10/93	Heart of Midlothian	Home	League	0–0		
53	09/10/93	Partick Thistle	Away	League	2–3	1 Goal	(38)
54	16/10/93	Kilmarnock	Away	League	1–1		
55	23/10/93	Dundee United	Home	League	2–0	1 Goal	(39)
56	30/10/93	Dundee	Home	League	1–0	1 Goal	(40)
57	03/11/93	Torino Calcio	Home	ECW Cup	1–2		
58	06/11/93	St Johnstone	Away	League	1–1		
Sub+6	09/11/93	Celtic	Home	League	1–1		
Sub+7	13/11/93	Motherwell	Home	League	1–1		
59	27/11/93	Hibernian	Home	League	4–0	1 Goal	(41)
60	01/12/94	Rangers	Away	League	0–2		
Sub+8	04/12/94	Heart of Midlothian	Away	League	1–1	1 Goal	(42)

61	07/12/94	Raith Rovers	Away	League	1–1		
62	14/12/94	Partick Thistle	Home	League	2–1	1 Goal	(43)
63	18/12/94	Kilmarnock	Home	League	3–1	1 Goal	(44)
64	27/12/94	Dundee United	Away	League	1–0		
65	08/01/94	St Johnstone	Home	League	1–1	1 Goal	(45)
66	11/01/94	Dundee	Away	League	1–0		
67	19/01/94	Celtic	Away	League	2–2		
68	22/01/94	Rangers	Home	League	0–0		
69	05/02/94	Hibernian	Away	League	1–3		
70	08/02/94	East Stirling	Away	S Cup	3–1	2 Goals	(47)
71	12/02/94	Raith Rovers	Home	League	4–0	1 Goal	(48)
72	19/02/94	Raith Rovers	Home	S Cup	1–0		
73	05/03/94	Heart of Midlothian	Home	League	0–1		
74	08/03/94	Motherwell	Away	League	1–1	1 Goal	(49)
75	12/03/94	St Johnstone	Away	S Cup	1–1		
76	15/03/94	St Johnstone	Home	S Cup	2–0	1 Goal	(50)
77	19/03/94	Kilmarnock	Away	League	3–2	1 Goal	(51)
78	26/03/94	Dundee United	Home	League	1–0	1 Goal	(52)
79	29/03/94	Hibernian	Home	League	2–3		
80	02/04/94	Rangers	Away	League	1–1		
81	09/04/94	Dundee United	Hampden	S Cup	1–1	1 Goal	(53)
82	12/04/94	Dundee United	Hampden	S Cup	0–1		
83	16/04/94	Motherwell	Home	League	0–0		
84	23/04/94	Partick Thistle	Home	League	2–0		
85	27/04/94	Heart of Midlothian	Away	League	1–1		
86	30/04/94	Dundee	Home	League	1–1		
87	03/05/94	Raith Rovers	Away	League	2–0	1 Goal	(54)
88	07/05/94	St Johnstone	Away	League	1–0		
89	14/05/94	Celtic	Home	League	1–1		

SEASON 1994–95

Scottish League Premier Division

90	09/08/94	Skonto Riga	Away	UEFA Cup	0–0		
91	13/08/94	Heart of Midlothian	Home	League	3–1		
92	17/08/94	Stranraer	Home	S Lge Cup	1–0	1 Goal	(55)
93	20/08/94	Falkirk	Home	League	2–2		
Sub+9	23/08/94	Skonto Riga	Home	UEFA Cup	1–1		
94	27/08/94	Dundee United	Away	League	1–2		
95	31/08/94	Partick Thistle	Away	S Lge Cup	5–0	3 Goals	(58)
Sub+10	05/11/94	Falkirk	Away	League	1–2		
96	09/11/94	Hibernian	Home	League	0–0		
Sub+11	26/12/94	Celtic	Home	League	0–0		
97	31/12/94	Hearts	Home	League	3–1	2 Goals	(60)
98	02/01/95	Dundee United	Away	League	0–0		
99	07/01/95	Falkirk	Home	League	0–0		
100	14/01/95	Partick Thistle	Home	League	3–1	1 Goal	(61)
101	21/01/95	Hibernian	Away	League	2–4		
102	28/01/95	Stranraer	Home	S Cup	1–0		
Sub+12	04/02/95	Kilmarnock	Away	League	1–3		
103	12/02/95	Rangers	Home	League	2–0	1 Goal	(62)
104	18/02/95	Stenhousemuir	Away	S Cup	0–2		
105	25/02/95	Motherwell	Home	League	0–2		
Sub+13	05/03/95	Celtic	Away	League	0–2		
106	18/03/95	Hibernian	Home	League	0–0		
107	01/04/95	Kilmarnock	Home	League	0–1		
108	08/04/95	Rangers	Away	League	2–3	1 Goal	(63)
109	15/04/95	Celtic	Home	League	2–0	1 Goal	(64)
110	18/04/95	Motherwell	Away	League	1–2		
111	29/04/95	Heart of Midlothian	Away	League	2–1		
112	06/05/95	Dundee United	Home	League	2–1	1 Goal	(65)
113	13/05/95	Falkirk	Away	League	2–0		
114	20/05/95	Dunfermline Athletic	Home	Lge P/O	3–1	2 Goals	(67)
115	24/05/95	Dunfermline Athletic	Away	Lge P/O	3–1		

SEASON 1995–96

Scottish League Premier Division

Sub+14	10/09/95	Celtic	Home	League	2–3		
Sub+15	16/09/95	Hibernian	Away	League	1–1	1 Goal	(68)
Sub+16	20/09/95	Motherwell	Away	S Lge Cup	2–1*		
Sub+17	23/09/95	Kilmarnock	Away	League	2–1		
Sub+18	30/09/95	Raith Rovers	Home	League	3–0		
Sub+19	04/10/95	Heart of Midlothian	Away	League	2–1		
Sub+20	07/10/95	Rangers	Home	League	0–1		
Sub+21	14/10/95	Motherwell	Away	League	1–2		

116	21/10/95	Partick Thistle	Home	League	3–0		
Sub+22	28/10/95	Celtic	Away	League	0–2		
Sub+23	04/11/95	Hibernian	Home	League	1–2		
117	08/11/95	Falkirk	Home	League	3–1		
Sub+24	11/11/95	Rangers	Away	League	1–1		
Sub+25	18/11/95	Raith Rovers	Away	League	0–1		
118	26/11/95	Dundee	Hampden	S Lge Cup	2–0	1 Goal	(69)
119	02/12/95	Partick Thistle	Away	League	0–1		
120	09/12/95	Motherwell	Home	League	1–0	1 Goal	(70)
121	13/12/95	Kilmarnock	Home	League	4–1		
122	16/12/95	Heart of Midlothian	Home	League	1–2		
Sub+26	14/01/96	Celtic	Home	League	1–2		
Sub+27	16/01/96	Falkirk	Away	League	1–1		
Sub+28	20/01/96	Partick Thistle	Home	League	1–0		
123	23/01/96	Kilmarnock	Away	League	1–1		
124	30/01/96	Motherwell	Away	S Cup	2–0	1 Goal	(71)
125	07/02/96	Raith Rovers	Home	League	1–0		
126	10/02/96	Heart of Midlothian	Away	League	3–1	1 Goal	(72)
127	13/02/96	Motherwell	Away	League	0–1		
128	17/02/96	Stirling Albion	Away	S Cup	2–0	1 Goal	(73)
129	25/02/96	Rangers	Home	League	0–1		
Sub+29	09/03/96	Airdrieonians	Home	S Cup	2–1		
130	16/03/96	Raith Rovers	Away	League	2–2		
131	23/03/96	Hibernian	Home	League	2–1		
Sub+30	06/04/96	Heart of Midlothian	Neutral	S Cup	1–2	1 Goal	(74)
132	13/04/96	Motherwell	Home	League	2–1		
Sub+31	16/04/96	Partick Thistle	Away	League	1–1		
133	20/04/96	Heart of Midlothian	Home	League	1–1		

SEASON 1996–97

Scottish League Premier Division

Sub+32	06/08/96	Zalgiris Vilnius	Away	UEFA Cup	4–1	1 Goal	(75)
Sub+33	10/08/96	Celtic	Home	League	2–2	1 Goal	(76)
134	14/08/96	Queen's Park	Away	S Lge Cup	2–0		
Sub+34	17/08/96	Motherwell	Away	League	2–2	1 Goal	(77)
135	20/08/96	Zalgiris Vilnius	Home	UEFA Cup	1–3		
Sub+35	04/09/96	Greenock Morton	Away	S Lge Cup	7–3*		
Sub+36	10/09/96	Barry Town	Home	UEFA Cup	3–1		
Sub+37	14/09/96	Kilmarnock	Home	League	3–0		
Sub+38	18/09/96	Dundee	Away	S Lge Cup	1–2		
136	21/09/96	Hibernian	Home	League	0–2		
Sub+39	24/09/96	Barry Town	Away	UEFA Cup	3–3		
Sub+40	28/09/96	Dundee United	Away	League	0–1		
137	12/10/96	Dunfermline Athletic	Home	League	3–0		
Sub+41	15/10/96	Brondby IF	Home	UEFA Cup	0–2		
Sub+42	19/10/96	Rangers	Away	League	2–2		
Sub+43	16/11/96	Dundee United	Home	League	3–3		
Sub+44	11/12/96	Heart of Midlothian	Away	League	2–1	1 Goal	(78)
Sub+45	14/12/96	Motherwell	Home	League	0–0		
Sub+46	21/12/96	Kilmarnock	Away	League	0–3		
Sub+47	26/12/96	Celtic	Home	League	1–2		
Sub+48	28/12/96	Hibernian	Home	League	1–1	1 Goal	(79)
Sub+49	01/01/97	Dundee United	Away	League	0–4		
Sub+50	04/01/97	Dunfermline Athletic	Home	League	0–2		
Sub+51	23/01/97	Hibernian	Away	S Cup	2–2		
Sub+52	28/01/97	Hibernian	Home	S Cup	0–0+		
Sub+53	10/02/97	Heart of Midlothian	Home	League	0–0		
Sub+54	05/04/97	Motherwell	Home	League	0–0		
Sub+55	12/04/97	Heart of Midlothian	Away	League	0–0		
Sub+56	20/04/97	Celtic	Away	League	0–3		
Sub+57	03/05/97	Raith Rovers	Home	League	2–0		
Sub+58	10/05/97	Kilmarnock	Away	League	1–1		

+ AET Hibernian won 5–3 on penalties

INTERNATIONAL APPEARANCES – SCOTLAND

Sub 1	20/04/94	Austria	Vienna	2–1	F		
Sub 2	27/05/94	Holland	Utrecht	1–3	F	1 Goal	(1)
3	07/09/94	Finland	Helsinki	2–0	ECQ	1 Goal	(2)
Sub 4	29/03/95	Russia	Moscow	0–0	ECQ		
5	26/04/95	San Marino	Serravalle	2–0	ECQ		
6	07/06/95	Faroe Islands	Toftir	2–0	ECQ		
7	16/08/95	Greece	Hampden Park	1–0	ECQ		

APPEARANCES AND GOALS PER SEASON

SEASON 85–86	GAMES	GOALS
League	9+1	8
TOTAL	**9+1**	**8**

SEASON 86–87	GAMES	GOALS
League	42	21
FA Cup	2	1
League Cup	4	2
Full Members Cup	1	1
TOTAL	**49**	**25**

SEASON 87–88	GAMES	GOALS
League	31+2	10
FA Cup	3	2
League Cup	2	4
Simod Cup	1	0
TOTAL	**37+2**	**16**

SEASON 88–89	GAMES	GOALS
League	33+3	14
League Play–offs	2	0
FA Cup	2	1
League Cup	2	1
Simod Cup	0+1	0
TOTAL	**39+4**	**16**

SEASON 89–90	GAMES	GOALS
League	42	20
League Play–offs	3	1
FA Cup	1	1
League Cup	8	4
Zenith Data Systems Cup	3	1
TOTAL	**57**	**27**

SEASON 90–91	GAMES	GOALS
League	44	22
FA Cup	3	1
League Cup	3	0
Zenith Data Systems Cup	1	0
TOTAL	**51**	**23**

SEASON 91–92	GAMES	GOALS
League	42+1	23
League Play–offs	0+1	0
FA Cup	3	4
League Cup	6	6
Zenith Data Systems Cup	2	0
TOTAL	**53+2**	**33**

SEASON 92–93	GAMES	GOALS
Scottish League	32+2	22
Scottish Cup	3+1	1
Scottish League Cup	5	5
TOTAL	**40+3**	**28**

SEASON 93–94	GAMES	GOALS
Scottish League	39+4	17
Scottish Cup	6	4
Scottish League Cup	2+1	4
European Cup Winners Cup	2	1
TOTAL	**49+5**	**26**

SEASON 94–95	GAMES	GOALS
Scottish League	19+4	7
Scottish League Play–offs	2	2
Scottish Cup	2	0
Scottish League Cup	2	4
UEFA Cup	1+1	0
TOTAL	**26+5**	**13**

SEASON 95–96	GAMES	GOALS
Scottish League	15+15	3
Scottish Cup	2+2	3
Scottish League Cup	1+1	1
TOTAL	**18+18**	**7**

SEASON 96–97	GAMES	GOALS
Scottish League	2+19	4
Scottish Cup	0+2	0
Scottish League Cup	1+2	0
UEFA Cup	1+4	1
TOTAL	**4+27**	**5**

CAREER APPEARANCES AND GOALS

COMPETITION	GAMES	TOTAL	GOALS
League	243+7	250	118
League Play–offs	5+1	6	1
FA Cup	14	14	10
League Cup	25	25	17
Full Members Cup	1	1	1
Simod Cup	1+1	2	0
Zenith Data Systems Cup	6	6	1
Scottish League	107+44	151	53
Scottish League Play–offs	2	2	2
Scottish Cup	13+5	18	8
Scottish League Cup	11+4	15	14
European Cup Winners Cup	2	2	1
UEFA Cup	2+5	7	1
Internationals	4+3	7	2
TOTAL	**436+70**	**506**	**229**

HAT-TRICKS

Huddersfield Town

1	3	Barnsley	31/03/86	Away	League	3–1
2	4	Bradford City	27/12/86	Home	League	5–2
3	3	Rotherham United	18/08/87	Away	Lge Cup	4–4

Swindon Town

1	4	Plymouth Argyle	05/10/91	Home	League	4–0

Aberdeen

1	3	Falkirk	26/08/92	Away	S Lge Cup	4–1
2	3	Partick Thistle	24/11/92	Away	League	7–0
3	3	Heart of Midlothian	28/11/92	Home	League	6–2
4	3	Clydebank	10/08/93	Home	S Lge Cup	5–0
5	3	Partick Thistle	31/08/94	Away	S Lge Cup	5–0

League: 3
League Cup: 1
Scottish League: 2
Scottish League Cup: 3
TOTAL: 9

HONOURS

Winners medals
Scottish League Cup: 95/96

Runner-up medals
Promoted to the Premier League: 91/92
Promoted to League Division One: 89/90*
Scottish Premier Division Championship: 92/93, 93/94
Scottish Cup: 92/93
Scottish League Cup: 92/93

* Later negated by the Football League after Swindon Town were found guilty of making irregular financial payments to players.

TEDDY SHERINGHAM

Born: 02/04/66 – Highams Park
Height: 5.11
Weight: 12.05 (96–97)

Clubs
Millwall: **1984–91** – Matches: **244+18** – Goals: **111**
Aldershot (loan): **1985** – Matches: **5+1** – Goals: **0**
Nottingham Forest: **1991–92** – Matches: **62** – Goals: **23**
Tottenham Hotspur: **1992–97** – Matches: **194+3** – Goals: **99**

Country
England: **1993–97** – Matches: **22+6** – Goals: **8**

SEASON 1983–84

Millwall – League Division Three

1	15/01/84	Brentford	Home	League	1–2		
2	21/01/84	AFC Bournemouth	Away	League	1–1	1 Goal	(1)
3	28/01/84	Hull City	Home	League	1–0		
Sub+1	20/02/84	Gillingham	Home	AM Cup	4–3*	1 Goal	(2)
4	25/02/84	Preston North End	Away	League	0–0		
Sub+2	17/03/84	Burnley	Away	League	0–1		
Sub+3	27/03/84	Swindon Town	Home	AM Cup	3–1		
Sub+4	14/04/84	Walsall	Home	League	2–0		
Sub+5	23/04/84	Wimbledon	Home	League	1–1		
5	17/05/84	Plymouth Argyle	Away	AM Cup	1–0		

SEASON 1984–85

League Division Three

Sub+6	09/10/84	Chelsea	Home	Lge Cup	1–1	

Aldershot (loan) – League Division Four

1	05/02/85	Orient	Home	FR Trophy	0–1	
2	23/02/85	Scunthorpe United	Home	League	1–2	
Sub+1	25/02/85	Stockport County	Away	League	0–6	
3	02/03/85	Southend United	Away	League	0–1	
4	06/03/85	Mansfield Town	Away	League	2–1	
5	09/03/85	Northampton Town	Home	League	0–0	

SEASON 1985–86

Millwall – League Division Two

Sub+7	23/11/85	Middlesbrough	Home	League	3–0		
Sub+8	07/12/85	Carlisle United	Away	League	0–1		
6	14/12/85	Huddersfield Town	Home	League	2–1		
7	21/12/85	Norwich City	Away	League	1–6	1 Goal	(3)
Sub+9	08/03/86	Sheffield United	Home	League	3–0		
Sub+10	15/03/86	Blackburn Rovers	Away	League	2–1		
Sub+11	18/03/86	Fulham	Home	League	1–1		
Sub+12	22/03/86	Brighton & Hove Albion	Away	League	0–1		
Sub+13	25/03/86	Portsmouth	Away	League	1–2		
Sub+14	31/03/86	Fulham	Away	League	2–1		
Sub+15	05/04/86	Grimsby Town	Home	League	1–0		
8	12/04/86	Leeds United	Away	League	1–3		
9	15/04/86	Charlton Athletic	Away	League	3–3		
10	19/04/86	Bradford City	Home	League	2–1	2 Goals	(5)
11	22/04/86	Crystal Palace	Home	League	3–2	1 Goal	(6)
12	26/04/86	Middlesbrough	Away	League	0–3		
13	30/04/86	Bradford City	Away	League	2–0		
14	03/05/86	Barnsley	Home	League	2–2		

SEASON 1986–87

League Division Two

15	23/08/86	Reading	Away	League	1–0
16	26/08/86	Hull City	Home	League	0–1

17	30/08/86	Barnsley	Home	League	1–0		
18	02/09/86	Sheffield United	Away	League	1–2	1 Goal	(7)
19	06/09/86	Stoke City	Away	League	0–2		
20	13/09/86	Bradford City	Home	League	1–2		
21	20/09/86	Derby County	Away	League	1–1		
22	27/09/86	Blackburn Rovers	Home	League	2–2	1 Goal	(8)
23	04/10/86	Crystal Palace	Away	League	1–2	1 Goal	(9)
24	07/10/86	Walsall	Away	Lge Cup	1–0	1 Goal	(10)
25	11/10/86	Shrewsbury Town	Home	League	4–0		
26	14/10/86	Walsall	Home	Lge Cup	3–2	1 Goal	(11)
27	17/10/86	Oldham Athletic	Away	League	1–2		
28	21/10/86	West Bromwich Albion	Home	FM Cup	2–0	1 Goal	(12)
29	25/10/86	Plymouth Argyle	Home	League	3–1	1 Goal	(13)
30	29/10/86	Norwich City	Away	Lge Cup	1–4		
31	01/11/86	Grimsby Town	Away	League	0–1		
32	04/11/86	Portsmouth	Away	FM Cup	2–3*		
33	08/11/86	Leeds United	Home	League	1–0	1 Goal	(14)
34	15/11/86	Birmingham City	Home	League	0–2		
35	22/11/86	West Bromwich Albion	Away	League	1–0	1 Goal	(15)
36	29/11/86	Portsmouth	Home	League	1–1	1 Goal	(16)
37	06/12/86	Sunderland	Away	League	1–1		
38	13/12/86	Huddersfield Town	Home	League	4–0	3 Goals	(19)
39	26/12/86	Ipswich Town	Home	League	1–0		
40	29/12/86	Birmingham City	Away	League	1–1		
41	01/01/87	Brighton & Hove Albion	Away	League	1–0		
42	03/01/87	Stoke City	Home	League	1–1		
43	10/01/87	Cardiff City	Home	FA Cup	0–0		
44	17/01/87	Bradford City	Away	League	0–4		
45	20/01/87	Cardiff City	Away	FA Cup	2–2*		
46	24/01/87	Reading	Home	League	2–1		
47	26/01/87	Cardiff City	Away	FA Cup	0–1		
48	07/02/87	Barnsley	Away	League	0–1		
49	14/02/87	Sheffield United	Home	League	1–0		
50	21/02/87	Blackburn Rovers	Away	League	0–1		
51	28/02/87	Derby County	Home	League	0–1		
52	07/03/87	Plymouth Argyle	Away	League	0–1		
53	14/03/87	Oldham Athletic	Home	League	0–0		
54	21/03/87	Shrewsbury Town	Away	League	2–1	1 Goal	(20)
55	28/03/87	Crystal Palace	Home	League	0–1		
56	04/04/87	Leeds United	Away	League	0–2		
57	11/04/87	Grimsby Town	Home	League	1–0	1 Goal	(21)
58	14/04/87	Hull City	Away	League	1–2	1 Goal	(22)
59	18/04/87	Brighton & Hove Albion	Home	League	3–1		
60	21/04/87	Ipswich Town	Away	League	0–0		
61	25/04/87	West Bromwich Albion	Home	League	0–1		
62	02/05/87	Portsmouth	Away	League	0–2		
63	05/05/87	Sunderland	Home	League	1–1		
64	09/05/87	Huddersfield Town	Away	League	0–3		

SEASON 1987–88

League Division Two

65	15/08/87	Middlesbrough	Away	League	1–1	1 Goal	(23)
66	18/08/87	Leyton Orient	Away	Lge Cup	1–1		
67	22/08/87	Barnsley	Home	League	3–1	1 Goal	(24)
68	25/08/87	Leyton Orient	Home	Lge Cup	1–0		
69	29/08/87	Leicester City	Away	League	0–1		
70	01/09/87	Birmingham City	Home	League	3–1		
71	05/09/87	Bradford City	Away	League	1–3		
72	12/09/87	Ipswich Town	Home	League	2–1		
73	19/09/87	Sheffield United	Away	League	2–1		
74	23/09/87	Queens Park Rangers	Away	Lge Cup	1–2		
75	26/09/87	West Bromwich Albion	Home	League	2–0	1 Goal	(25)
76	29/09/87	Oldham Athletic	Away	League	0–0		
77	03/10/87	Swindon Town	Home	League	2–2	1 Goal	(26)
78	06/10/87	Queens Park Rangers	Home	Lge Cup	0–0		
79	10/10/87	Crystal Palace	Away	League	0–1		
80	17/10/87	Shrewsbury Town	Home	League	4–1	1 Goal	(27)
81	20/10/87	Plymouth Argyle	Away	League	2–1	1 Goal	(28)
82	31/10/87	Huddersfield Town	Away	League	1–2		
83	03/11/87	AFC Bournemouth	Home	League	1–2		
84	07/11/87	Aston Villa	Away	League	2–1		
85	10/11/87	West Ham United	Away	Simod Cup	2–1	1 Goal	(29)
86	14/11/87	Leeds United	Home	League	3–1		

87	21/11/87	Stoke City	Away	League	2–1		
88	28/11/87	Hull City	Home	League	2–0	1 Goal	(30)
89	01/12/87	Reading	Home	League	3–0		
90	05/12/87	Blackburn Rovers	Away	League	1–2		
91	08/12/87	Leeds United	Home	Simod Cup	2–0	1 Goal	(31)
92	12/12/87	Manchester City	Home	League	0–1		
93	19/12/87	Barnsley	Away	League	1–4	1 Goal	(32)
94	26/12/87	West Bromwich Albion	Away	League	4–1	3 Goals	(35)
95	28/12/87	Sheffield Wednesday	Home	League	3–1	1 Goal	(36)
96	01/01/88	Leicester City	Home	League	1–0		
97	02/01/88	Ipswich Town	Away	League	1–1		
98	09/01/88	Arsenal	Away	FA Cup	0–2		
99	13/01/88	Norwich City	Home	Simod Cup	2–3		
100	16/01/88	Middlesbrough	Home	League	2–1	1 Goal	(37)
101	06/02/88	Bradford City	Home	League	0–1		
102	09/02/88	Birmingham City	Away	League	0–1		
103	13/02/88	Reading	Away	League	3–2	2 Goals	(39)
104	20/02/88	Oldham Athletic	Home	League	1–1		
105	27/02/88	Swindon Town	Away	League	1–0		
106	05/03/88	Shrewsbury Town	Away	League	0–0		
107	12/03/88	Crystal Palace	Home	League	1–1	1 Goal	(40)
108	19/03/88	Huddersfield Town	Home	League	4–1	2 Goals	(42)
109	02/04/88	Aston Villa	Home	League	2–1	1 Goal	(43)
110	06/04/88	Leeds United	Away	League	2–1		
111	09/04/88	Plymouth Argyle	Home	League	3–2	1 Goal	(44)
112	19/04/88	AFC Bournemouth	Away	League	2–1		
113	30/04/88	Stoke City	Home	League	2–1	1 Goal	(45)
114	02/05/88	Hull City	Away	League	1–0		
115	07/05/88	Blackburn Rovers	Home	League	1–4	1 Goal	(46)

SEASON 1988–89

League Division One

116	27/08/88	Aston Villa	Away	League	2–2		
117	03/09/88	Derby County	Home	League	1–0	1 Goal	(47)
118	10/09/88	Charlton Athletic	Away	League	3–0	1 Goal	(48)
119	17/09/88	Everton	Home	League	2–1		
120	24/09/88	Norwich City	Away	League	2–2		
121	27/09/88	Gillingham	Home	Lge Cup	3–0	1 Goal	(49)
122	01/10/88	Queens Park Rangers	Home	League	3–2		
123	11/10/88	Gillingham	Away	Lge Cup	3–1	2 Goals	(51)
124	15/10/88	Coventry City	Away	League	0–0		
125	22/10/88	Nottingham Forest	Home	League	2–2	1 Goal	(52)
126	29/10/88	Middlesbrough	Away	League	2–4	1 Goal	(53)
127	02/11/88	Aston Villa	Away	Lge Cup	1–3		
128	05/11/88	Luton Town	Home	League	3–1	1 Goal	(54)
129	12/11/88	Liverpool	Away	League	1–1		
130	19/11/88	Newcastle United	Home	League	4–0		
131	26/11/88	Southampton	Away	League	2–2	1 Goal	(55)
132	29/11/88	Leeds United	Home	Simod Cup	2–0		
133	03/12/88	West Ham United	Home	League	0–1		
134	10/12/88	Tottenham Hotspur	Away	League	0–2		
135	17/12/88	Sheffield Wednesday	Home	League	1–0	1 Goal	(56)
136	20/12/88	Everton	Away	Simod Cup	0–2		
137	26/12/88	Wimbledon	Away	League	0–1		
138	31/12/88	Derby County	Away	League	1–0	1 Goal	(57)
139	02/01/89	Charlton Athletic	Home	League	1–0		
140	07/01/89	Luton Town	Home	FA Cup	3–2	1 Goal	(58)
141	14/01/89	Manchester United	Away	League	0–3		
142	22/01/89	Norwich City	Home	League	2–3		
143	29/01/89	Liverpool	Home	FA Cup	0–2		
144	11/02/89	Arsenal	Home	League	1–2		
145	21/02/89	Middlesbrough	Home	League	2–0		
146	25/02/89	Coventry City	Home	League	1–0		
147	28/02/89	Arsenal	Away	League	0–0		
148	11/03/89	Luton Town	Away	League	2–1		
149	18/03/89	Aston Villa	Home	League	2–0		
150	25/03/89	Everton	Away	League	1–1	1 Goal	(59)
151	27/03/89	Wimbledon	Home	League	0–1		
152	01/04/89	Sheffield Wednesday	Away	League	0–3		
153	03/05/89	Nottingham Forest	Away	League	1–4		
154	06/05/89	Newcastle United	Away	League	1–1	1 Goal	(60)
155	13/05/89	Southampton	Home	League	1–1	1 Goal	(61)

SEASON 1989-90

League Division One

156	19/08/89	Southampton	Away	League	2–1		
157	22/08/89	Charlton Athletic	Home	League	2–2	1 Goal	(62)
158	26/08/89	Nottingham Forest	Home	League	1–0		
159	29/08/89	Wimbledon	Away	League	2–2		
160	09/09/89	Coventry City	Home	League	4–1	2 Goals	(64)
161	16/09/89	Manchester United	Away	League	1–5	1 Goal	(65)
162	19/09/89	Stoke City	Away	Lge Cup	0–1		
163	23/09/89	Sheffield Wednesday	Home	League	2–0		
164	30/09/89	Norwich City	Home	League	0–1		
165	03/10/89	Stoke City	Home	Lge Cup	2–0*	1 Goal	(66)
166	14/10/89	Everton	Away	League	1–2	1 Goal	(67)
167	21/10/89	Crystal Palace	Away	League	3–4		
168	23/10/89	Tranmere Rovers	Away	Lge Cup	2–3		
169	28/10/89	Luton Town	Home	League	1–1		
170	04/11/89	Chelsea	Away	League	0–4		
171	11/11/89	Arsenal	Home	League	1–2	1 Goal	(68)
172	19/11/89	Liverpool	Home	League	1–2		
173	25/11/89	Queens Park Rangers	Away	League	0–0		
Sub+16	13/01/90	Nottingham Forest	Away	League	1–3	1 Goal	(69)
174	15/01/90	Manchester City	Home	FA Cup	3–1	2 Goals	(71)
175	20/01/90	Wimbledon	Home	League	0–0		
176	27/01/90	Cambridge United	Home	FA Cup	1–1		
177	30/01/90	Cambridge United	Away	FA Cup	0–1*		
178	03/02/90	Sheffield Wednesday	Away	League	1–1	1 Goal	(72)
179	17/02/90	Coventry City	Away	League	1–3		
180	24/02/90	Queens Park Rangers	Home	League	1–2		
181	03/03/90	Liverpool	Away	League	0–1		
182	17/03/90	Norwich City	Away	League	1–1	1 Goal	(73)
183	21/03/90	Everton	Home	League	1–2		
Sub+17	24/03/90	Luton Town	Away	League	1–2		
Sub+18	31/03/90	Crystal Palace	Home	League	1–2		
184	07/04/90	Manchester City	Home	League	1–1		
185	14/04/90	Derby County	Away	League	0–2		
186	16/04/90	Tottenham Hotspur	Home	League	0–1		
187	21/04/90	Aston Villa	Away	League	0–1		
188	28/04/90	Arsenal	Away	League	0–2		
189	05/05/90	Chelsea	Home	League	1–3		

SEASON 1990-91

League Division Two

190	25/08/90	Watford	Away	League	2–1		
191	01/09/90	Barnsley	Home	League	4–1	1 Goal	(74)
192	08/09/90	Newcastle United	Away	League	2–1	1 Goal	(75)
193	15/09/90	Ipswich Town	Home	League	1–1		
194	19/09/90	Hull City	Home	League	3–3	1 Goal	(76)
195	22/09/90	Charlton Athletic	Away	League	0–0		
196	25/09/90	AFC Bournemouth	Away	Lge Cup	0–0		
197	30/09/90	Swindon Town	Away	League	0–0		
198	03/10/90	Portsmouth	Home	League	2–0	1 Goal	(77)
199	06/10/90	West Bromwich Albion	Home	League	4–1	3 Goals	(80)
200	10/10/90	AFC Bournemouth	Home	Lge Cup	2–1	2 Goals	(82)
201	13/10/90	Middlesbrough	Away	League	1–2		
202	20/10/90	Notts County	Away	League	1–0		
203	24/10/90	Bristol City	Home	League	1–2		
204	27/10/90	Sheffield Wednesday	Home	League	4–2	1 Goal	(83)
205	31/10/90	Aston Villa	Away	Lge Cup	0–2		
206	03/11/90	Blackburn Rovers	Away	League	0–1		
207	07/11/90	Oxford United	Home	League	1–2		
208	10/11/90	West Ham United	Home	League	1–1		
209	17/11/90	Plymouth Argyle	Away	League	2–3	1 Goal	(84)
210	24/11/90	Brighton & Hove Albion	Away	League	0–0		
211	01/12/90	Bristol Rovers	Home	League	1–1	1 Goal	(85)
212	15/12/90	Watford	Home	League	0–2		
213	19/12/90	Norwich City	Away	ZDS Cup	1–1+	1 Goal	(86)
214	22/12/90	Wolverhampton Wanderers	Away	League	1–4	1 Goal	(87)
215	26/12/90	Leicester City	Home	League	2–1	2 Goals	(89)
216	29/12/90	Oldham Athletic	Home	League	0–0		
217	01/01/91	Port Vale	Away	League	2–0	1 Goal	(90)
218	05/01/91	Leicester City	Home	FA Cup	2–1	1 Goal	(91)
219	12/01/91	Barnsley	Away	League	2–1	1 Goal	(92)

220	19/01/91	Newcastle United	Home	League	0–1		
221	26/01/91	Sheffield Wednesday	Home	FA Cup	4–4	1 Goal	(93)
222	30/01/91	Sheffield Wednesday	Away	FA Cup	0–2		
223	02/02/91	Ipswich Town	Away	League	3–0	1 Goal	(94)
224	16/02/91	Plymouth Argyle	Home	League	4–1	4 Goals	(98)
225	24/02/91	West Ham United	Away	League	1–3		
226	27/02/91	Oxford United	Away	League	0–0		
227	02/03/91	Bristol Rovers	Away	League	0–1		
228	09/03/91	Brighton & Hove Albion	Home	League	3–0	1 Goal	(99)
229	12/03/91	Portsmouth	Away	League	0–0		
230	16/03/91	Swindon Town	Home	League	1–0		
231	20/03/91	Middlesbrough	Home	League	2–2		
232	23/03/91	West Bromwich Albion	Away	League	1–0	1 Goal	(100)
233	30/03/91	Leicester City	Away	League	2–1	2 Goals	(102)
234	03/04/91	Wolverhampton Wanderers	Home	League	2–1	1 Goal	(103)
235	06/04/91	Oldham Athletic	Away	League	1–1		
236	10/04/91	Charlton Athletic	Home	League	3–1	3 Goals	(106)
237	13/04/91	Port Vale	Home	League	1–2		
238	16/04/91	Hull City	Away	League	1–1		
239	20/04/91	Notts County	Home	League	1–2		
240	27/04/91	Bristol City	Away	League	4–1	3 Goals	(109)
241	04/05/91	Sheffield Wednesday	Away	League	1–2	1 Goal	(110)
242	11/05/91	Blackburn Rovers	Home	League	1–2	1 Goal	(111)
243	19/05/91	Brighton & Hove Albion	Away	Lge P/O	1–4		
244	22/05/91	Brighton & Hove Albion	Home	Lge P/O	1–2		

+ AET Norwich City won 6–5 on penalties

SEASON 1991–92

Nottingham Forest – League Division One

1	17/08/91	Everton	Home	League	2–1		
2	20/08/91	Leeds United	Away	League	0–1		
3	24/08/91	Notts County	Away	League	4–0	1 Goal	(1)
4	28/08/91	Tottenham Hotspur	Home	League	1–3		
5	31/08/91	Oldham Athletic	Home	League	3–1		
6	04/09/91	Manchester City	Away	League	1–2	1 Goal	(2)
7	07/09/91	Sheffield Wednesday	Away	League	1–2		
8	14/09/91	Wimbledon	Home	League	4–2		
9	21/09/91	Aston Villa	Away	League	1–3		
10	25/09/91	Bolton Wanderers	Home	Lge Cup	4–0		
11	28/09/91	West Ham United	Home	League	2–2	1 Goal	(3)
12	05/10/91	Queens Park Rangers	Away	League	2–0	2 Goals	(5)
13	08/10/91	Bolton Wanderers	Away	Lge Cup	5–2	1 Goal	(6)
14	19/10/91	Sheffield United	Away	League	2–4		
15	22/10/91	Leeds United	Away	ZDS Cup	3–1	2 Goals	(8)
16	26/10/91	Southampton	Home	League	1–3		
17	30/10/91	Bristol Rovers	Home	Lge Cup	2–0		
18	02/11/91	Norwich City	Away	League	0–0		
19	16/11/91	Coventry City	Home	League	1–0	1 Goal	(9)
20	19/11/91	Aston Villa	Away	ZDS Cup	2–0		
21	23/11/91	Crystal Palace	Home	League	5–1	2 Goals	(11)
22	30/11/91	Chelsea	Away	League	0–1		
23	04/12/91	Southampton	Home	Lge Cup	0–0		
24	08/12/91	Arsenal	Home	League	3–2	1 Goal	(12)
25	10/12/91	Tranmere Rovers	Away	ZDS Cup	2–0		
26	13/12/91	Liverpool	Away	League	0–2		
27	17/12/91	Southampton	Away	Lge Cup	1–0		
28	22/12/91	Leeds United	Home	League	0–0		
29	26/12/91	Tottenham Hotspur	Away	League	2–1		
30	28/12/91	Oldham Athletic	Away	League	1–2		
31	01/01/92	Luton Town	Home	League	1–1		
32	04/01/92	Wolverhampton Wanderers	Home	FA Cup	1–0		
33	08/01/92	Crystal Palace	Away	Lge Cup	1–1		
34	11/01/92	Notts County	Home	League	1–1		
35	19/01/92	Everton	Away	League	1–1		
36	26/01/92	Hereford United	Home	FA Cup	2–0	1 Goal	(13)
37	05/02/92	Crystal Palace	Home	Lge Cup	4–2	3 Goals	(16)
38	09/02/92	Tottenham Hotspur	Home	Lge Cup	1–1	1 Goal	(17)
39	12/02/92	Leicester City	Away	ZDS Cup	1–1		
40	15/02/92	Bristol City	Home	FA Cup	4–1	1 Goal	(18)
41	22/02/92	Chelsea	Home	League	1–1	1 Goal	(19)
42	26/02/92	Leicester City	Home	ZDS Cup	2–0		
43	01/03/92	Tottenham Hotspur	Away	Lge Cup	2–1*		

44	03/03/92	Crystal Palace	Away	League	0–0		
45	07/03/92	Portsmouth	Away	FA Cup	0–1		
46	11/03/92	Coventry City	Away	League	2–0	1 Goal	(20)
47	14/03/92	Norwich City	Home	League	2–0		
48	18/03/92	Manchester United	Home	League	1–0		
49	21/03/92	Manchester City	Home	League	2–0		
50	29/03/92	Southampton	Wembley	ZDS Cup	3–2		
51	31/03/92	Arsenal	Away	League	3–3		
52	08/04/92	Southampton	Away	League	1–0		
53	12/04/92	Manchester United	Wembley	Lge Cup	0–1		
54	14/04/92	Luton Town	Away	League	1–2		
55	18/04/92	Aston Villa	Home	League	2–0	1 Goal	(21)
56	20/04/92	Manchester United	Away	League	2–1		
57	22/04/92	Liverpool	Home	League	1–1	1 Goal	(22)
58	25/04/92	Queens Park Rangers	Home	League	1–1		
59	02/05/92	West Ham United	Away	League	0–3		

SEASON 1992–93

Premier League

60	16/08/92	Liverpool	Home	League	1–0	1 Goal	(23)
61	19/08/92	Sheffield Wednesday	Away	League	0–2		
62	22/08/92	Oldham Athletic	Away	League	3–5		

Tottenham Hotspur – Premier League

1	30/08/92	Ipswich Town	Away	League	1–1		
2	02/09/92	Sheffield United	Home	League	2–0	1 Goal	(1)
3	05/09/92	Everton	Home	League	2–1		
4	14/09/92	Coventry City	Away	League	0–1		
5	19/09/92	Manchester United	Home	League	1–1		
6	21/09/92	Brentford	Home	Lge Cup	3–1	1 Goal	(2)
7	27/09/92	Sheffield Wednesday	Away	League	0–2		
8	03/10/92	Queens Park Rangers	Away	League	1–4	1 Goal	(3)
9	07/10/92	Brentford	Away	Lge Cup	4–2	2 Goals	(5)
10	17/10/92	Middlesbrough	Home	League	2–2	1 Goal	(6)
11	25/10/92	Wimbledon	Away	League	1–1		
12	28/10/92	Manchester City	Away	Lge Cup	1–0		
13	31/10/92	Liverpool	Home	League	2–0		
14	07/11/92	Blackburn Rovers	Away	League	2–0	1 Goal	(7)
15	21/11/92	Aston Villa	Home	League	0–0		
16	28/11/92	Manchester City	Away	League	1–0		
17	02/12/92	Nottingham Forest	Away	Lge Cup	0–2		
18	05/12/92	Chelsea	Home	League	1–2		
19	12/12/92	Arsenal	Home	League	1–0		
20	19/12/92	Oldham Athletic	Away	League	1–2	1 Goal	(8)
21	26/12/92	Norwich City	Away	League	0–0		
22	28/12/92	Nottingham Forest	Home	League	2–1		
23	02/01/93	Marlow	Away	FA Cup	5–1+	1 Goal	(9)
24	09/01/93	Manchester United	Away	League	1–4		
25	16/01/93	Sheffield Wednesday	Home	League	0–2		
26	24/01/93	Norwich City	Away	FA Cup	2–0	2 Goals	(11)
27	27/01/93	Ipswich Town	Home	League	0–2		
28	30/01/93	Crystal Palace	Away	League	3–1	2 Goals	(13)
29	06/02/93	Southampton	Home	League	4–2	2 Goals	(15)
30	10/02/93	Everton	Away	League	2–1		
31	14/02/93	Wimbledon	Home	FA Cup	3–2	1 Goal	(16)
32	20/02/93	Leeds United	Home	League	4–0	3 Goals	(19)
33	27/02/93	Queens Park Rangers	Home	League	3–2	2 Goals	(21)
34	02/03/93	Sheffield United	Away	League	0–6		
35	07/03/93	Manchester City	Away	FA Cup	4–2		
36	10/03/93	Aston Villa	Away	League	0–0		
37	20/03/93	Chelsea	Away	League	1–1	1 Goal	(22)
38	24/03/93	Manchester City	Home	League	3–1		
39	04/04/93	Arsenal	Wembley	FA Cup	0–1		
40	09/04/93	Norwich City	Home	League	5–1	2 Goals	(24)
41	12/04/93	Nottingham Forest	Away	League	1–2		
42	17/04/93	Oldham Athletic	Home	League	4–1	2 Goals	(26)
43	20/04/93	Middlesbrough	Away	League	0–3		
44	01/05/93	Wimbledon	Home	League	1–1		
45	05/05/93	Blackburn Rovers	Home	League	1–2		
46	08/05/93	Liverpool	Away	League	2–6	1 Goal	(27)
47	11/05/93	Arsenal	Away	League	3–1	1 Goal	(28)

+ Played at Tottenham Hotspur

SEASON 1993–94

Premier League

48	14/08/93	Newcastle United	Away	League	1–0	1 Goal	(29)
49	16/08/93	Arsenal	Home	League	0–1		
50	21/08/93	Manchester City	Home	League	1–0		
51	25/08/93	Liverpool	Away	League	2–1	2 Goals	(31)
52	28/08/93	Aston Villa	Away	League	0–1		
53	01/09/93	Chelsea	Home	League	1–1	1 Goal	(32)
54	11/09/93	Sheffield United	Away	League	2–2	2 Goals	(34)
55	18/09/93	Oldham Athletic	Home	League	5–0	2 Goals	(36)
56	22/09/93	Burnley	Away	Lge Cup	0–0		
57	26/09/93	Ipswich Town	Away	League	2–2	1 Goal	(37)
58	03/10/93	Everton	Home	League	3–2	1 Goal	(38)
59	06/10/93	Burnley	Home	Lge Cup	3–1	2 Goals	(40)
60	16/10/93	Manchester United	Away	League	1–2		
Sub+1	02/04/94	Norwich City	Away	League	2–1	1 Goal	(41)
Sub+2	04/04/94	West Ham United	Home	League	1–4	1 Goal	(42)
61	09/04/94	Coventry City	Away	League	0–1		
62	17/04/94	Leeds United	Away	League	0–2		
63	23/04/94	Southampton	Home	League	3–0		
64	30/04/94	Wimbledon	Away	League	1–2	1 Goal	(43)
65	05/05/94	Oldham Athletic	Away	League	2–0		
66	07/05/94	Queens Park Rangers	Home	League	1–2	1 Goal	(44)

SEASON 1994–95

Premier League

67	20/08/94	Sheffield Wednesday	Away	League	4–3	1 Goal	(45)
68	24/08/94	Everton	Home	League	2–1		
69	27/08/94	Manchester United	Home	League	0–1		
70	30/08/94	Ipswich Town	Away	League	3–1		
71	12/09/94	Southampton	Home	League	1–2		
72	17/09/94	Leicester City	Away	League	1–3		
73	21/09/94	Watford	Away	Lge Cup	6–3	1 Goal	(46)
74	24/09/94	Nottingham Forest	Home	League	1–4		
75	01/10/94	Wimbledon	Away	League	2–1	1 Goal	(47)
76	08/10/94	Queens Park Rangers	Home	League	1–1		
77	15/10/94	Leeds United	Away	League	1–1	1 Goal	(48)
78	22/10/94	Manchester City	Away	League	2–5		
79	26/10/94	Notts County	Away	Lge Cup	0–3		
Sub+3	29/10/94	West Ham United	Home	League	3–1	1 Goal	(49)
80	05/11/94	Blackburn Rovers	Away	League	0–2		
81	19/11/94	Aston Villa	Home	League	3–4	1 Goal	(50)
82	23/11/94	Chelsea	Home	League	0–0		
83	26/11/94	Liverpool	Away	League	1–1		
84	03/12/94	Newcastle United	Home	League	4–2	3 Goals	(53)
85	10/12/94	Sheffield Wednesday	Home	League	3–1		
86	17/12/94	Everton	Away	League	0–0		
87	26/12/94	Norwich City	Away	League	2–0	1 Goal	(54)
88	27/12/94	Crystal Palace	Home	League	0–0		
89	31/12/94	Coventry City	Away	League	4–0	1 Goal	(55)
90	02/01/95	Arsenal	Home	League	1–0		
91	07/01/95	Altrincham	Home	FA Cup	3–0	1 Goal	(56)
92	14/01/95	West Ham United	Away	League	2–1	1 Goal	(57)
93	25/01/95	Aston Villa	Away	League	0–1		
94	29/01/95	Sunderland	Away	FA Cup	4–1	1 Goal	(58)
95	05/02/95	Blackburn Rovers	Home	League	3–1		
96	11/02/95	Chelsea	Away	League	1–1	1 Goal	(59)
97	18/02/95	Southampton	Home	FA Cup	1–1		
98	25/02/95	Wimbledon	Home	League	1–2		
99	01/03/95	Southampton	Away	FA Cup	6–2*	1 Goal	(60)
100	04/03/95	Nottingham Forest	Away	League	2–2	1 Goal	(61)
101	08/03/95	Ipswich Town	Home	League	3–0		
102	11/03/95	Liverpool	Away	FA Cup	2–1	1 Goal	(62)
103	15/03/95	Manchester United	Away	League	0–0		
104	18/03/95	Leicester City	Home	League	1–0		
105	22/03/95	Liverpool	Home	League	0–0		
106	03/04/95	Southampton	Away	League	3–4	2 Goals	(64)
107	09/04/95	Everton	Neutral	FA Cup	1–4		
108	11/04/95	Manchester City	Home	League	2–1		
109	14/04/95	Crystal Palace	Away	League	1–1		
110	17/04/95	Norwich City	Home	League	1–0	1 Goal	(65)
111	29/04/95	Arsenal	Away	League	1–1		
112	03/05/95	Newcastle United	Away	League	3–3		

113	06/05/95	Queens Park Rangers	Away	League	1–2	1 Goal	(66)
114	09/05/95	Coventry City	Home	League	1–3		
115	14/05/95	Leeds United	Home	League	1–1	1 Goal	(67)

SEASON 1995–96

Premier League

116	19/08/95	Manchester City	Away	League	1–1	1 Goal	(68)
117	23/08/95	Aston Villa	Home	League	0–1		
118	26/08/95	Liverpool	Home	League	1–3		
119	30/08/95	West Ham United	Away	League	1–1		
120	09/09/95	Leeds United	Home	League	2–1	1 Goal	(69)
121	16/09/95	Sheffield Wednesday	Away	League	3–1	2 Goals	(71)
122	20/09/95	Chester City	Home	Lge Cup	4–0	1 Goal	(72)
123	25/09/95	Queens Park Rangers	Away	League	3–2	2 Goals	(74)
124	30/09/95	Wimbledon	Home	League	3–1	2 Goals	(76)
125	04/10/95	Chester City	Away	Lge Cup	3–1	2 Goals	(78)
126	14/10/95	Nottingham Forest	Home	League	0–1		
127	22/10/95	Everton	Away	League	1–1		
128	25/10/95	Coventry City	Away	Lge Cup	2–3		
129	29/10/95	Newcastle United	Home	League	1–1		
130	04/11/95	Coventry City	Away	League	3–2	1 Goal	(79)
131	18/11/95	Arsenal	Home	League	2–1	1 Goal	(80)
132	21/11/95	Middlesbrough	Away	League	1–0		
133	25/11/95	Chelsea	Away	League	0–0		
134	02/12/95	Everton	Home	League	0–0		
135	09/12/95	Queens Park Rangers	Home	League	1–0	1 Goal	(81)
136	16/12/95	Wimbledon	Away	League	1–0		
137	23/12/95	Bolton Wanderers	Home	League	2–2	1 Goal	(82)
138	26/12/95	Southampton	Away	League	0–0		
139	30/12/95	Blackburn Rovers	Away	League	1–2	1 Goal	(83)
140	01/01/96	Manchester United	Home	League	4–1	1 Goal	(84)
141	06/01/96	Hereford United	Away	FA Cup	1–1		
142	13/01/96	Manchester City	Home	League	1–0		
143	17/01/96	Hereford United	Home	FA Cup	5–1	3 Goals	(87)
144	21/01/96	Aston Villa	Away	League	1–2		
145	27/01/96	Wolverhampton Wanderers	Home	FA Cup	1–1		
146	03/02/96	Liverpool	Away	League	0–0		
147	07/02/96	Wolverhampton Wanderers	Away	FA Cup	2–0	1 Goal	(88)
148	12/02/96	West Ham United	Home	League	0–1		
149	24/02/96	Sheffield Wednesday	Home	League	1–0		
150	28/02/96	Nottingham Forest	Away	FA Cup	2–2		
151	02/03/96	Southampton	Home	League	1–0		
152	09/03/96	Nottingham Forest	Home	FA Cup	1–1+	1 Goal	(89)
153	16/03/96	Blackburn Rovers	Home	League	2–3	1 Goal	(90)
154	20/03/96	Bolton Wanderers	Away	League	3–2		
155	24/03/96	Manchester United	Away	League	0–1		
156	30/03/96	Coventry City	Home	League	3–1	1 Goal	(91)
157	06/04/96	Nottingham Forest	Away	League	1–2		
158	08/04/96	Middlesbrough	Home	League	1–1		
159	15/04/96	Arsenal	Away	League	0–0		
160	27/04/96	Chelsea	Home	League	1–1		
161	02/05/96	Leeds United	Away	League	3–1		
162	05/05/96	Newcastle United	Away	League	1–1		

+ AET Nottingham Forest won 3–1 on penalties

SEASON 1996–97

Premier League

163	17/08/96	Blackburn Rovers	Away	League	2–0		
164	21/08/96	Derby County	Home	League	1–1	1 Goal	(92)
165	24/08/96	Everton	Home	League	0–0		
166	25/09/96	Preston North End	Home	Lge Cup	3–0		
167	29/09/96	Manchester United	Away	League	0–2		
168	12/10/96	Aston Villa	Home	League	1–0		
169	19/10/96	Middlesbrough	Away	League	3–0	2 Goals	(94)
170	23/10/96	Sunderland	Home	Lge Cup	2–1		
171	26/10/96	Chelsea	Away	League	1–3		
172	02/11/96	West Ham United	Home	League	1–0		
173	16/11/96	Sunderland	Home	League	2–0	1 Goal	(95)
174	24/11/96	Arsenal	Away	League	1–3		
175	27/11/96	Bolton Wanderers	Away	Lge Cup	1–6	1 Goal	(96)
176	02/12/96	Liverpool	Home	League	0–2		
177	07/12/96	Coventry City	Away	League	2–1	1 Goal	(97)

178	14/12/96	Leeds United	Away	League	0–0		
179	21/12/96	Sheffield Wednesday	Home	League	1–1		
180	26/12/96	Southampton	Home	League	3–1		
181	28/12/96	Newcastle United	Away	League	1–7		
182	24/02/97	West Ham United	Away	League	3–4	1 Goal	(98)
183	01/03/97	Nottingham Forest	Home	League	0–1		
184	04/03/97	Sunderland	Away	League	4–0		
185	15/03/97	Leeds United	Home	League	1–0		
186	19/03/97	Leicester City	Away	League	1–1	1 Goal	(99)
187	22/03/97	Derby County	Away	League	2–4		
188	05/04/97	Wimbledon	Home	League	1–0		
189	09/04/97	Sheffield Wednesday	Away	League	1–2		
190	12/04/97	Everton	Away	League	0–1		
191	19/04/97	Aston Villa	Away	League	1–1		
192	24/04/97	Middlesbrough	Home	League	1–0		
193	03/05/97	Liverpool	Away	League	1–2		
194	11/05/97	Coventry City	Home	League	1–2		

INTERNATIONAL APPEARANCES – ENGLAND

1	29/05/93	Poland	Katowice	1–1	WCQ		
2	02/06/93	Norway	Oslo	0–2	WCQ		
3	07/09/94	USA	Wembley	2–0	F		
Sub 4	12/10/94	Romania	Wembley	1–1	F		
Sub 5	16/11/94	Nigeria	Wembley	1–0	F		
6	29/03/95	Uruguay	Wembley	0–0	F		
Sub 7	03/06/95	Japan	Wembley	2–1	UC		
8	08/06/95	Sweden	Elland Road	3–3	UC	1 Goal	(1)
9	11/06/95	Brazil	Wembley	1–3	UC		
Sub 10	06/09/95	Colombia	Wembley	0–0	F		
Sub 11	11/10/95	Norway	Oslo	0–0	F		
12	15/11/95	Switzerland	Wembley	3–1	F	1 Goal	(2)
13	27/03/96	Bulgaria	Wembley	1–0	F		
14	24/04/96	Croatia	Wembley	0–0	F		
15	18/05/96	Hungary	Wembley	3–0	F		
16	08/06/96	Switzerland	Wembley	1–1	EC		
17	15/06/96	Scotland	Wembley	2–0	EC		
18	18/06/96	Holland	Wembley	4–1	EC	2 Goals	(4)
19	22/06/96	Spain	Wembley	0–0+	EC		
20	26/06/96	Germany	Wembley	1–1#	EC		
21	09/11/96	Georgia	Tblisi	2–0	WCQ	1 Goal	(5)
22	29/03/97	Mexico	Wembley	2–0	F	1 Goal	(6)
23	30/04/97	Georgia	Wembley	2–0	WCQ	1 Goal	(7)
24	24/05/97	South Africa	Old Trafford	2–1	F		
25	31/05/97	Poland	Katowice	2–0	WCQ	1 Goal	(8)
26	04/06/97	Italy	Nantes	2–0	LTDF		
Sub 27	07/06/97	France	Montpellier	1–0	LTDF		
28	10/06/97	Brazil	Paris	0–1	LTDF		

+ AET England won 4–2 on penalties
# AET Germany won 6–5 on penalties

APPEARANCES AND GOALS PER SEASON

SEASON 83–84	GAMES	GOALS
League	4+3	1
Associate Members Cup	1+2	1
TOTAL	**5+5**	**2**

SEASON 84–85	GAMES	GOALS
League	4+1	0
League Cup	0+1	0
Freight Rover Trophy	1	0
TOTAL	**5+2**	**0**

SEASON 85–86	GAMES	GOALS
League	9+9	4
TOTAL	**9+9**	**4**

SEASON 86–87	GAMES	GOALS
League	42	13
FA Cup	3	0
League Cup	3	2
Full Members Cup	2	1
TOTAL	**50**	**16**

SEASON 87–88	GAMES	GOALS
League	43	22
FA Cup	1	0
League Cup	4	0
Simod Cup	3	2
TOTAL	**51**	**24**

SEASON 88–89	GAMES	GOALS
League	33	11
FA Cup	2	1
League Cup	3	3
Simod Cup	2	0
TOTAL	**40**	**15**

SEASON 89–90	GAMES	GOALS
League	28+3	9
FA Cup	3	2
League Cup	3	1
TOTAL	**34+3**	**12**

SEASON 90–91	GAMES	GOALS
League	46	33
League Play–offs	2	0
FA Cup	3	2
League Cup	3	2
Zenith Data Systems Cup	1	1
TOTAL	**55**	**38**

SEASON 91–92	GAMES	GOALS
League	39	13
FA Cup	4	2
League Cup	10	5
Zenith Data Systems Cup	6	2
TOTAL	**59**	**22**

SEASON 92–93	GAMES	GOALS
League	41	22
FA Cup	5	4
League Cup	4	3
TOTAL	**50**	**29**

SEASON 93–94	GAMES	GOALS
League	17+2	14
League Cup	2	2
TOTAL	**19+2**	**16**

SEASON 94–95	GAMES	GOALS
League	41+1	18
FA Cup	6	4
League Cup	2	1
TOTAL	**49+1**	**23**

SEASON 95–96	GAMES	GOALS
League	38	16
FA Cup	6	5
League Cup	3	3
TOTAL	**47**	**24**

SEASON 96–97	GAMES	GOALS
League	29	7
League Cup	3	1
TOTAL	**32**	**8**

CAREER APPEARANCES AND GOALS

COMPETITION	GAMES	TOTAL	GOALS
League	414+19	433	183
League Play–offs	2	2	0
FA Cup	33	33	20
League Cup	40+1	41	23
Freight Rover Trophy	1	1	0
Associate Members Cup	1+2	3	1
Full Members Cup	2	2	1
Simod Cup	5	5	2
Zenith Data Systems Cup	7	7	3
Internationals	22+6	28	8
TOTAL	**527+28**	**555**	**241**

HAT-TRICKS

Millwall

1	3	Huddersfield Town	13/12/86	Home	League	4–0	
2	3	West Bromwich Albion	26/12/87	Away	League	4–1	
3	3	West Bromwich Albion	06/10/90	Home	League	4–1	
4	4	Plymouth Argyle	16/02/91	Home	League	4–1	
5	3	Charlton Athletic	10/04/91	Home	League	3–1	
6	3	Bristol City	27/04/91	Away	League	4–1	

Nottingham Forest

1	3	Crystal Palace	05/02/92	Home	Lge Cup	4–2	

Tottenham Hotspur

1	3	Leeds United	20/02/93	Home	League	4–0	
2	3	Newcastle United	03/12/94	Home	League	4–2	
3	3	Hereford United	17/01/96	Home	FA Cup	5–1	

League: 8
FA Cup: 1
League Cup: 1
TOTAL: 10

HONOURS

Winners medals
League Division Two Championship: 87/88
Zenith Data Systems Cup: 91/92

Runner-up medals
League Cup: 91/92
Promoted to League Division Two: 84/85*

* Promoted in the Millwall team that were runners–up in the League Division Three Championship without playing a League match.

BERNIE SLAVEN

Born: 13/11/60 – Paisley
Height: 5.10
Weight: 12.00 (95–96)

Clubs
Morton: **1981–83** – Matches: **13+11** – Goals: **1**
Airdrieonians: **1983** – Matches: **5+1** – Goals: **0**
Queen of the South: **1983** – Matches: **2** – Goals: **0**
Albion Rovers: **1984–85** – Matches: **45** – Goals: **30**
Middlesbrough: **1985–93** – Matches: **355+26** – Goals: **146**
Port Vale: **1993–94** – Matches: **40+6** – Goals: **13**
Darlington: **1994–95** – Matches: **39+3** – Goals: **9**

Country
Republic of Ireland: **1990–93** – Matches: **4+3** – Goals: **1**

SEASON 1981–82

Morton – Scottish League Premier Division

Sub+1	17/10/81	Airdrieonians	Home	League	3–0		
Sub+2	24/10/81	Rangers	Away	League	1–1		
Sub+3	07/11/81	Dundee United	Away	League	0–3		
1	14/11/81	Celtic	Home	League	1–1		
2	21/11/81	Partick Thistle	Away	League	2–2		
3	28/11/81	Dundee	Away	League	1–4		
4	23/01/82	St Mirren	Away	S Cup	1–2		
5	30/01/82	Partick Thistle	Home	League	0–0		
6	06/02/82	Aberdeen	Away	League	0–0		
7	13/02/82	Airdrieonians	Away	League	1–1	1 Goal	(1)
8	20/02/82	Dundee	Home	League	2–0		
9	27/02/82	Rangers	Away	League	0–3		

Sub+4	17/04/82	Aberdeen	Home	League	2–1
Sub+5	15/05/82	Hibernian	Home	League	0–0

SEASON 1982–83

Scottish League Premier Division

Sub+6	20/11/82	Dundee	Home	League	1–2
10	27/11/82	Motherwell	Away	League	1–3
11	27/12/82	Celtic	Away	League	1–5
Sub+7	03/01/83	Kilmarnock	Home	League	1–3
Sub+8	08/01/83	Aberdeen	Away	League	0–2
Sub+9	15/01/83	Dundee	Away	League	3–3
Sub+10	22/01/83	Motherwell	Home	League	0–1
Sub+11	12/02/83	Rangers	Home	League	0–5
12	19/02/83	St Mirren	Home	S Cup	0–2
13	30/04/83	Dundee United	Home	League	0–4

SEASON 1983–84

Airdrieonians – Scottish League Division One

1	20/08/83	Hamilton Academical	Away	League	1–1
2	24/08/83	Clyde	Home	S Lge Cup	2–0
Sub+1	27/08/83	Clyde	Away	S Lge Cup	0–1
3	31/08/83	Celtic	Home	S Lge Cup	1–6
4	03/09/83	Brechin City	Home	League	1–0
5	07/09/83	Kilmarnock	Away	S Lge Cup	0–3

Queen of the South – Scottish League Division Two

1	26/11/83	Cowdenbeath	Home	League	1–0
2	10/12/83	East Fife	Home	League	0–0

Albion Rovers – Scottish League Division Two

1	14/04/84	Berwick Rangers	Home	League	0–0
2	21/04/84	Stenhousemuir	Away	League	1–1
3	28/04/84	Dunfermline Athletic	Home	League	0–5

SEASON 1984–85

Scottish League Division Two

4	11/08/84	Cowdenbeath	Home	League	1–0		
5	14/08/84	Montrose	Home	S Lge Cup	2–0	2 Goals	(2)
6	18/08/84	Stenhousemuir	Away	League	1–1	1 Goal	(3)
7	22/08/84	St Johnstone	Away	S Lge Cup	1–2	1 Goal	(4)
8	25/08/84	Queen of the South	Home	League	3–4	1 Goal	(5)
9	01/09/84	Queen's Park	Away	League	1–5		
10	08/09/84	Arbroath	Away	League	2–1	1 Goal	(6)
11	15/09/84	Alloa	Home	League	0–1		
12	22/09/84	East Stirling	Away	League	3–2	3 Goals	(9)
13	29/09/84	Stranraer	Home	League	1–2		
14	06/10/84	Stirling Albion	Away	League	3–2	2 Goals	(11)
15	13/10/84	Montrose	Away	League	0–1		
16	20/10/84	Dunfermline Athletic	Home	League	0–2		
17	27/10/84	Raith Rovers	Away	League	0–3		
18	06/11/84	Berwick Rangers	Home	League	1–0		
19	10/11/84	Arbroath	Home	League	1–0		
20	17/11/84	Alloa	Away	League	0–4		
21	01/12/84	Stirling Albion	Home	League	0–4		
22	08/12/84	Berwick Rangers	Away	S Cup	1–3		
23	22/12/84	Queen of the South	Away	League	2–3	1 Goal	(12)
24	01/01/85	Stenhousemuir	Home	League	0–1		
25	12/01/85	Cowdenbeath	Away	League	0–0		
26	02/02/85	Montrose	Home	League	1–4	1 Goal	(13)
27	09/02/85	Dunfermline Athletic	Away	League	1–1	1 Goal	(14)
28	16/02/85	Arbroath	Home	League	3–0	3 Goals	(17)
29	19/02/85	East Stirling	Home	League	1–0		
30	23/02/85	Queen's Park	Away	League	1–1		
31	02/03/85	Stenhousemuir	Away	League	1–2	1 Goal	(18)
32	05/03/85	Queen's Park	Home	League	3–3	1 Goal	(19)
33	09/03/85	Stranraer	Home	League	1–2	1 Goal	(20)
34	16/03/85	Berwick Rangers	Home	League	3–2	2 Goals	(22)
35	23/03/85	Stirling Albion	Away	League	1–4	1 Goal	(23)
36	26/03/85	Stranraer	Away	League	3–2	2 Goals	(25)
37	02/04/85	Raith Rovers	Home	League	0–6		
38	10/04/85	Berwick Rangers	Away	League	1–0	1 Goal	(26)
39	13/04/85	Alloa	Home	League	4–1	2 Goals	(28)

40	16/04/85	Dunfermline Athletic	Home	League	1–1		
41	20/04/85	Queen of the South	Away	League	2–1	1 Goal	(29)
42	23/04/85	Montrose	Away	League	0–0		
43	27/04/85	Raith Rovers	Home	League	2–4	1 Goal	(30)
44	04/05/85	East Stirling	Away	League	0–0		
45	11/05/85	Cowdenbeath	Home	League	1–2		

SEASON 1985–86

Middlesbrough – League Division Two

1	12/10/85	Leeds United	Away	League	0–1		
2	19/10/85	Bradford City	Home	League	1–1	1 Goal	(1)
3	22/10/85	Sunderland	Away	League	0–1		
4	26/10/85	Grimsby Town	Away	League	2–3		
5	02/11/85	Blackburn Rovers	Home	League	0–0		
6	05/11/85	Hull City	Away	FM Cup	1–3*	1 Goal	(2)
7	16/11/85	Oldham Athletic	Home	League	3–2		
8	23/11/85	Millwall	Away	League	0–3		
9	30/11/85	Shrewsbury Town	Home	League	3–1		
10	07/12/85	Stoke City	Away	League	2–3		
11	14/12/85	Wimbledon	Home	League	1–0		
12	21/12/85	Fulham	Away	League	3–0	1 Goal	(3)
13	26/12/85	Carlisle United	Away	League	0–1		
14	28/12/85	Sunderland	Home	League	2–0		
15	01/01/86	Huddersfield Town	Home	League	0–1		
16	11/01/86	Norwich City	Away	League	0–2		
17	13/01/86	Southampton	Home	FA Cup	1–3		
18	18/01/86	Brighton & Hove Albion	Away	League	3–3	1 Goal	(4)
19	25/01/86	Portsmouth	Away	League	0–1		
20	01/02/86	Charlton Athletic	Home	League	1–3		
21	04/03/86	Grimsby Town	Home	League	3–1	2 Goals	(6)
22	08/03/86	Crystal Palace	Away	League	1–2	1 Goal	(7)
23	15/03/86	Leeds United	Home	League	2–2		
24	18/03/86	Sheffield United	Home	League	1–2		
25	22/03/86	Hull City	Home	League	1–2		
26	25/03/86	Barnsley	Away	League	0–0		
27	29/03/86	Huddersfield Town	Away	League	3–0	1 Goal	(8)
28	31/03/86	Carlisle United	Home	League	1–3		
29	05/04/86	Blackburn Rovers	Away	League	1–0		
30	12/04/86	Portsmouth	Home	League	1–0		
31	19/04/86	Oldham Athletic	Away	League	0–1		
32	23/04/86	Bradford City	Away	League	1–2		
33	26/04/86	Millwall	Home	League	3–0	1 Goal	(9)
34	03/05/86	Shrewsbury Town	Away	League	1–2		

SEASON 1986–87

League Division Three

35	23/08/86	Port Vale	Home	League	2–2		
36	26/08/86	Hartlepool United	Away	Lge Cup	1–1	1 Goal	(10)
37	30/08/86	Wigan Athletic	Away	Lge Cup	2–0		
38	02/09/86	Hartlepool United	Home	Lge Cup	2–0		
39	06/09/86	Bury	Home	League	3–1	1 Goal	(11)
40	13/09/86	Gillingham	Away	League	0–0		
41	17/09/86	Bristol Rovers	Away	League	2–1	2 Goals	(13)
42	20/09/86	Chesterfield	Home	League	2–0		
43	23/09/86	Birmingham City	Home	Lge Cup	2–2		
44	27/09/86	Fulham	Away	League	2–2		
45	30/09/86	Swindon Town	Home	League	1–0		
46	04/10/86	Rotherham United	Away	League	4–1		
47	07/10/86	Birmingham City	Away	Lge Cup	2–3*		
48	11/10/86	Blackpool	Home	League	1–3		
49	18/10/86	Walsall	Home	League	3–1		
50	21/10/86	Notts County	Away	League	0–1		
51	25/10/86	Bristol City	Away	League	2–2	1 Goal	(14)
52	01/11/86	AFC Bournemouth	Home	League	4–0	1 Goal	(15)
53	04/11/86	Bolton Wanderers	Home	League	0–0		
54	08/11/86	Darlington	Away	League	1–0		
55	15/11/86	Blackpool	Home	FA Cup	3–0	3 Goals	(18)
56	22/11/86	Newport County	Away	League	1–0		
57	24/11/86	Doncaster Rovers	Home	FR Trophy	3–0		
58	29/11/86	Chester City	Home	League	1–2	1 Goal	(19)
59	02/12/86	Chesterfield	Away	FR Trophy	1–2		
60	07/12/86	Notts County	Away	FA Cup	1–0		
61	13/12/86	Doncaster Rovers	Home	League	1–0		

62	21/12/86	Brentford	Away	League	1–0	1 Goal	(20)
63	26/12/86	Carlisle United	Home	League	1–0		
64	27/12/86	Mansfield Town	Away	League	1–1		
65	01/01/87	York City	Away	League	1–3		
66	03/01/87	Newport County	Home	League	2–0		
67	10/01/87	Preston North End	Home	FA Cup	0–1		
68	21/01/87	Halifax Town	Away	FR Trophy	2–1		
69	24/01/87	Bury	Away	League	3–0	2 Goals	(22)
70	07/02/87	Bristol Rovers	Home	League	1–0		
71	10/02/87	Rochdale	Away	FR Trophy	0–0+		
72	14/02/87	Chesterfield	Away	League	1–2	1 Goal	(23)
73	17/02/87	Port Vale	Away	League	0–0		
74	21/02/87	Fulham	Home	League	3–0	1 Goal	(24)
75	28/02/87	Swindon Town	Away	League	0–1		
76	03/03/87	AFC Bournemouth	Away	League	1–3	1 Goal	(25)
77	07/03/87	Bristol City	Home	League	1–0		
78	10/03/87	Mansfield Town	Home	FR Trophy	0–1		
79	14/03/87	Walsall	Away	League	0–1		
80	17/03/87	Notts County	Home	League	2–0	1 Goal	(26)
81	21/03/87	Blackpool	Away	League	1–0		
82	28/03/87	Rotherham United	Home	League	0–0		
83	05/04/87	Darlington	Home	League	1–1	1 Goal	(27)
84	11/04/87	Bolton Wanderers	Away	League	1–0	1 Goal	(28)
85	18/04/87	York City	Home	League	3–1		
86	20/04/87	Carlisle United	Away	League	1–0		
87	25/04/87	Brentford	Home	League	2–0	1 Goal	(29)
88	28/04/87	Gillingham	Home	League	3–0	1 Goal	(30)
89	02/05/87	Chester City	Away	League	2–1		
90	04/05/87	Mansfield Town	Home	League	1–0		
91	06/05/87	Wigan Athletic	Home	League	0–0		
92	09/05/87	Doncaster Rovers	Away	League	2–0		

+ AET Middlesbrough won 4–3 on penalties

SEASON 1987–88

League Division Two

93	15/08/87	Millwall	Home	League	1–1		
94	18/08/87	Sunderland	Away	Lge Cup	0–1		
95	22/08/87	Stoke City	Away	League	0–1		
96	25/08/87	Sunderland	Home	Lge Cup	2–0	1 Goal	(31)
97	29/08/87	Oldham Athletic	Home	League	1–0	1 Goal	(32)
98	01/09/87	Crystal Palace	Away	League	1–3	1 Goal	(33)
99	05/09/87	Swindon Town	Home	League	2–3	1 Goal	(34)
100	08/09/87	Aston Villa	Away	League	1–0		
101	15/09/87	AFC Bournemouth	Home	League	3–0	1 Goal	(35)
102	19/09/87	Leeds United	Home	League	2–0		
103	23/09/87	Aston Villa	Home	Lge Cup	0–1		
104	26/09/87	Blackburn Rovers	Away	League	2–0		
105	29/09/87	Reading	Home	League	0–0		
106	03/10/87	Bradford City	Away	League	0–2		
107	07/10/87	Aston Villa	Away	Lge Cup	0–1		
108	10/10/87	Huddersfield Town	Away	League	4–1	3 Goals	(38)
109	17/10/87	West Bromwich Albion	Home	League	2–1	1 Goal	(39)
110	20/10/87	Ipswich Town	Home	League	3–1	1 Goal	(40)
111	24/10/87	Birmingham City	Away	League	0–0		
112	31/10/87	Shrewsbury Town	Home	League	4–0	3 Goals	(43)
113	04/11/87	Manchester City	Away	League	1–1		
114	07/11/87	Sheffield United	Away	League	2–0	1 Goal	(44)
115	10/11/87	Ipswich Town	Away	Simod Cup	0–1		
116	14/11/87	Hull City	Home	League	1–0		
117	21/11/87	Plymouth Argyle	Away	League	1–0		
118	28/11/87	Barnsley	Home	League	2–0	1 Goal	(45)
119	05/12/87	Leicester City	Away	League	0–0		
120	12/12/87	Stoke City	Home	League	2–0	1 Goal	(46)
121	19/12/87	AFC Bournemouth	Away	League	0–0		
122	26/12/87	Blackburn Rovers	Home	League	1–1	1 Goal	(47)
123	28/12/87	Leeds United	Away	League	0–2		
124	01/01/88	Oldham Athletic	Away	League	1–3		
125	09/01/88	Sutton United	Away	FA Cup	1–1		
126	12/01/88	Sutton United	Home	FA Cup	1–0*		
127	16/01/88	Millwall	Away	League	1–2	1 Goal	(48)
128	23/01/88	Crystal Palace	Home	League	2–1		
129	30/01/88	Everton	Away	FA Cup	1–1		
130	03/02/88	Everton	Home	FA Cup	2–2*		

131	06/02/88	Swindon Town	Away	League	1–1		
132	09/02/88	Everton	Away	FA Cup	1–2		
133	14/02/88	Aston Villa	Home	League	2–1		
134	20/02/88	Reading	Away	League	0–0		
135	27/02/88	Bradford City	Home	League	1–2		
136	05/03/88	West Bromwich Albion	Away	League	0–0		
137	12/03/88	Huddersfield Town	Home	League	2–0		
138	19/03/88	Shrewsbury Town	Away	League	1–0		
139	26/03/88	Birmingham City	Home	League	1–1		
140	02/04/88	Sheffield United	Home	League	6–0	1 Goal	(49)
141	04/04/88	Hull City	Away	League	0–0		
142	09/04/88	Manchester City	Home	League	2–1		
143	23/04/88	Ipswich Town	Away	League	0–4		
144	30/04/88	Plymouth Argyle	Home	League	3–1		
145	02/05/88	Barnsley	Away	League	3–0	2 Goals	(51)
146	07/05/88	Leicester City	Home	League	1–2	1 Goal	(52)
147	15/05/88	Bradford City	Away	Lge P/O	1–2		
148	18/05/88	Bradford City	Home	Lge P/O	2–0	1 Goal	(53)
149	25/05/88	Chelsea	Home	Lge P/O	2–0	1 Goal	(54)
150	28/05/88	Chelsea	Away	Lge P/O	0–1		

SEASON 1988–89

League Division One

151	27/08/88	Derby County	Away	League	0–1		
152	03/09/88	Norwich City	Home	League	2–3		
153	10/09/88	Manchester United	Away	League	0–1		
154	17/09/88	Wimbledon	Home	League	1–0		
155	24/09/88	Tottenham Hotspur	Away	League	2–3	1 Goal	(55)
156	28/09/88	Tranmere Rovers	Home	Lge Cup	0–0		
157	01/10/88	Coventry City	Away	League	4–3	3 Goals	(58)
158	08/10/88	West Ham United	Home	League	1–0		
159	11/10/88	Tranmere Rovers	Away	Lge Cup	0–1		
160	22/10/88	Luton Town	Home	League	2–1	1 Goal	(59)
161	26/10/88	Newcastle United	Away	League	0–3		
162	29/10/88	Millwall	Home	League	4–2	1 Goal	(60)
163	05/11/88	Liverpool	Away	League	0–3		
164	12/11/88	Queens Park Rangers	Home	League	1–0		
165	19/11/88	Arsenal	Away	League	0–3		
166	26/11/88	Sheffield Wednesday	Home	League	0–1		
Sub+1	10/12/88	Aston Villa	Home	League	3–3		
167	14/12/88	Oldham Athletic	Home	Simod Cup	1–0		
168	17/12/88	Charlton Athletic	Home	League	0–0		
169	21/12/88	Portsmouth	Home	Simod Cup	2–1*	1 Goal	(61)
170	26/12/88	Everton	Away	League	1–2		
171	31/12/88	Norwich City	Away	League	0–0		
172	02/01/89	Manchester United	Home	League	1–0		
173	07/01/89	Grimsby Town	Home	FA Cup	1–2	1 Goal	(62)
174	11/01/89	Coventry City	Home	Simod Cup	1–0		
175	14/01/89	Southampton	Away	League	3–1	1 Goal	(63)
176	21/01/89	Tottenham Hotspur	Home	League	2–2		
177	28/01/89	Crystal Palace	Home	Simod Cup	2–3	1 Goal	(64)
178	04/02/89	Coventry City	Home	League	1–1	1 Goal	(65)
179	18/02/89	Luton Town	Away	League	0–1		
180	21/02/89	Millwall	Away	League	0–2		
181	26/02/89	Newcastle United	Home	League	1–1	1 Goal	(66)
182	11/03/89	Liverpool	Home	League	0–4		
183	18/03/89	Derby County	Home	League	0–1		
184	25/03/89	Wimbledon	Away	League	1–1	1 Goal	(67)
185	27/03/89	Everton	Home	League	3–3	1 Goal	(68)
186	01/04/89	Charlton Athletic	Away	League	0–2		
187	08/04/89	Southampton	Home	League	3–3	1 Goal	(69)
188	11/04/89	West Ham United	Away	League	2–1	2 Goals	(71)
189	15/04/89	Queens Park Rangers	Away	League	0–0		
190	22/04/89	Nottingham Forest	Home	League	3–4	1 Goal	(72)
191	29/04/89	Aston Villa	Away	League	1–1		
192	06/05/89	Arsenal	Home	League	0–1		
193	13/05/89	Sheffield Wednesday	Away	League	0–1		

SEASON 1989–90

League Division Two

194	19/08/89	Wolverhampton Wanderers	Home	League	4–2	2 Goals	(74)
195	23/08/89	Leeds United	Away	League	1–2		
196	27/08/89	Sunderland	Away	League	1–2	1 Goal	(75)

197	02/09/89	Sheffield United	Home	League	3–3	2 Goals	(77)
198	09/09/89	Barnsley	Away	League	1–1		
199	16/09/89	AFC Bournemouth	Home	League	2–1	1 Goal	(78)
200	20/09/89	Halifax Town	Home	Lge Cup	4–0	2 Goals	(80)
201	23/09/89	Portsmouth	Away	League	1–3	1 Goal	(81)
202	27/09/89	Hull City	Home	League	1–0		
203	30/09/89	Watford	Away	League	0–1		
204	03/10/89	Halifax Town	Away	Lge Cup	1–0	1 Goal	(82)
205	14/10/89	Plymouth Argyle	Home	League	0–2		
206	18/10/89	Brighton & Hove Albion	Home	League	2–2		
207	21/10/89	Oldham Athletic	Away	League	0–2		
208	25/10/89	Wimbledon	Home	Lge Cup	1–1	1 Goal	(83)
209	28/10/89	West Bromwich Albion	Home	League	0–0		
210	30/10/89	Port Vale	Away	League	1–1		
211	04/11/89	Newcastle United	Away	League	2–2		
212	08/11/89	Wimbledon	Away	Lge Cup	0–1		
213	11/11/89	Swindon Town	Home	League	0–2		
214	18/11/89	West Ham United	Away	League	0–2		
215	21/11/89	Blackburn Rovers	Away	League	4–2	1 Goal	(84)
216	25/11/89	Oxford United	Home	League	1–0	1 Goal	(85)
217	29/11/89	Port Vale	Home	ZDS Cup	3–1	2 Goals	(87)
218	02/12/89	Wolverhampton Wanderers	Away	League	0–2		
219	09/12/89	Leeds United	Home	League	0–2		
220	16/12/89	Leicester City	Home	League	4–1	1 Goal	(88)
221	20/12/89	Sheffield Wednesday	Home	ZDS Cup	4–1	3 Goals	(91)
222	26/12/89	Bradford City	Away	League	1–0	1 Goal	(92)
223	30/12/89	Ipswich Town	Away	League	0–3		
224	01/01/90	Stoke City	Home	League	0–1		
225	06/01/90	Everton	Home	FA Cup	0–0		
226	10/01/90	Everton	Away	FA Cup	1–1*		
227	14/01/90	Sunderland	Home	League	3–0	1 Goal	(93)
228	17/01/90	Everton	Away	FA Cup	0–1		
229	20/01/90	Sheffield United	Away	League	0–1		
230	23/01/90	Newcastle United	Home	ZDS Cup	1–0		
231	30/01/90	Aston Villa	Away	ZDS Cup	2–1	1 Goal	(94)
232	03/02/90	Portsmouth	Home	League	2–0	1 Goal	(95)
233	06/02/90	Aston Villa	Home	ZDS Cup	2–1*	1 Goal	(96)
234	10/02/90	AFC Bournemouth	Away	League	2–2	1 Goal	(97)
235	24/02/90	Oxford United	Away	League	1–3		
236	28/02/90	Brighton & Hove Albion	Away	League	0–1		
237	03/03/90	West Ham United	Home	League	0–1		
238	07/03/90	Watford	Home	League	1–2		
239	10/03/90	Hull City	Away	League	0–0		
240	17/03/90	Blackburn Rovers	Home	League	0–3		
241	20/03/90	Plymouth Argyle	Away	League	2–1		
242	25/03/90	Chelsea	Wembley	ZDS Cup	0–1		
243	31/03/90	Oldham Athletic	Home	League	1–0	1 Goal	(98)
244	07/04/90	West Bromwich Albion	Away	League	0–0		
245	11/04/90	Port Vale	Home	League	2–3	1 Goal	(99)
246	14/04/90	Stoke City	Away	League	0–0		
247	16/04/90	Bradford City	Home	League	2–0	1 Goal	(100)
248	21/04/90	Leicester City	Away	League	1–2	1 Goal	(101)
249	25/04/90	Ipswich Town	Home	League	1–2		
250	28/04/90	Swindon Town	Away	League	1–1	1 Goal	(102)
251	02/05/90	Barnsley	Home	League	0–1		
252	05/05/90	Newcastle United	Home	League	4–1	2 Goals	(104)

SEASON 1990–91

League Division Two

253	25/08/90	West Ham United	Home	League	0–0		
254	28/08/90	Tranmere Rovers	Home	Lge Cup	1–1		
255	01/09/90	Plymouth Argyle	Away	League	1–1	1 Goal	(105)
256	03/09/90	Tranmere Rovers	Away	Lge Cup	2–1	1 Goal	(106)
257	08/09/90	Notts County	Home	League	1–0		
258	15/09/90	Swindon Town	Away	League	3–1	2 Goals	(108)
259	17/09/90	Port Vale	Away	League	1–3		
260	22/09/90	Oldham Athletic	Home	League	0–1		
Sub+2	29/09/90	Leicester City	Home	League	6–0	1 Goal	(109)
261	03/10/90	Newcastle United	Away	League	0–0		
262	06/10/90	Watford	Away	League	3–0		
263	10/10/90	Newcastle United	Away	Lge Cup	0–1		
264	13/10/90	Millwall	Home	League	2–1		
265	20/10/90	Bristol Rovers	Home	League	1–2		
266	23/10/90	Wolverhampton Wanderers	Away	League	0–1		

267	27/10/90	Brighton & Hove Albion	Away	League	4–2	3 Goals	(112)
268	30/10/90	Norwich City	Home	Lge Cup	2–0		
269	03/11/90	Barnsley	Home	League	1–0		
270	06/11/90	West Bromwich Albion	Away	League	1–0	1 Goal	(113)
271	10/11/90	Charlton Athletic	Home	League	1–2		
272	17/11/90	Portsmouth	Away	League	3–0	1 Goal	(114)
273	20/11/90	Hull City	Home	ZDS Cup	3–1*	1 Goal	(115)
274	24/11/90	Oxford United	Away	League	5–2	1 Goal	(116)
275	28/11/90	Aston Villa	Away	Lge Cup	2–3	2 Goals	(118)
276	01/12/90	Hull City	Home	League	3–0	1 Goal	(119)
277	15/12/90	West Ham United	Away	League	0–0		
278	19/12/90	Manchester City	Away	ZDS Cup	1–2		
279	22/12/90	Blackburn Rovers	Home	League	0–1		
280	26/12/90	Ipswich Town	Away	League	1–0		
281	29/12/90	Bristol City	Away	League	0–3		
282	01/01/91	Sheffield Wednesday	Home	League	0–2		
283	05/01/91	Plymouth Argyle	Home	FA Cup	0–0		
284	12/01/91	Plymouth Argyle	Home	League	0–0		
285	14/01/91	Plymouth Argyle	Away	FA Cup	2–1		
Sub+3	19/01/91	Notts County	Away	League	2–3		
Sub+4	26/01/91	Cambridge United	Away	FA Cup	0–2		
286	02/02/91	Swindon Town	Home	League	2–0	1 Goal	(120)
287	19/02/91	West Bromwich Albion	Home	League	3–2	1 Goal	(121)
288	23/02/91	Charlton Athletic	Away	League	1–0	1 Goal	(122)
289	26/02/91	Portsmouth	Home	League	1–2		
290	02/03/91	Hull City	Away	League	0–0		
291	09/03/91	Oxford United	Home	League	0–0		
292	12/03/91	Newcastle United	Home	League	3–0	2 Goals	(124)
293	16/03/91	Leicester City	Away	League	3–4		
294	20/03/91	Millwall	Away	League	2–2		
295	23/03/91	Watford	Home	League	1–2		
296	30/03/91	Ipswich Town	Home	League	1–1		
297	01/04/91	Blackburn Rovers	Away	League	0–1		
298	06/04/91	Bristol City	Home	League	2–1		
Sub+5	09/04/91	Port Vale	Home	League	4–0		
Sub+6	13/04/91	Sheffield Wednesday	Away	League	0–2		
Sub+7	20/04/91	Bristol Rovers	Away	League	0–2		
299	27/04/91	Wolverhampton Wanderers	Home	League	2–0		
300	04/05/91	Brighton & Hove Albion	Home	League	2–0		
301	07/05/91	Oldham Athletic	Away	League	0–2		
302	11/05/91	Barnsley	Away	League	0–1		
303	19/05/91	Notts County	Home	Lge P/O	1–1		
304	22/05/91	Notts County	Away	Lge P/O	0–1		

SEASON 1991–92

League Division Two

Sub+8	21/08/91	Derby County	Away	League	0–2		
Sub+9	24/08/91	Ipswich Town	Away	League	1–2		
Sub+10	31/08/91	Portsmouth	Home	League	2–0	1 Goal	(125)
Sub+11	04/09/91	Oxford United	Away	League	2–1	2 Goals	(127)
305	07/09/91	Watford	Away	League	2–1		
306	14/09/91	Leicester City	Home	League	3–0	1 Goal	(128)
307	17/09/91	Tranmere Rovers	Home	League	1–0		
308	21/09/91	Plymouth Argyle	Away	League	1–1		
309	24/09/91	AFC Bournemouth	Home	Lge Cup	1–1		
310	28/09/91	Sunderland	Home	League	2–1	1 Goal	(129)
311	05/10/91	Bristol Rovers	Away	League	1–2		
Sub+12	08/10/91	AFC Bournemouth	Away	Lge Cup	2–1*		
312	12/10/91	Wolverhampton Wanderers	Home	League	0–0		
313	19/10/91	Grimsby Town	Away	League	0–1		
314	22/10/91	Derby County	Home	ZDS Cup	4–2*	1 Goal	(130)
315	26/10/91	Port Vale	Home	League	1–0		
316	29/10/91	Barnsley	Home	Lge Cup	1–0		
317	02/11/91	Southend United	Home	League	1–1		
318	05/11/91	Barnsley	Away	League	1–2	1 Goal	(131)
Sub+13	09/11/91	Brighton & Hove Albion	Away	League	1–1	1 Goal	(132)
319	16/11/91	Charlton Athletic	Home	League	2–0	1 Goal	(133)
320	23/11/91	Bristol City	Home	League	3–1	2 Goals	(135)
321	26/11/91	Tranmere Rovers	Home	ZDS Cup	0–1		
322	30/11/91	Blackburn Rovers	Away	League	1–2	1 Goal	(136)
323	03/12/91	Manchester City	Home	Lge Cup	2–1		
324	07/12/91	Swindon Town	Home	League	2–2	1 Goal	(137)
325	26/12/91	Newcastle United	Away	League	1–0		
326	28/12/91	Portsmouth	Away	League	0–4		

327	01/01/92	Derby County	Home	League	1–1		
328	04/01/92	Manchester City	Home	FA Cup	2–1		
329	08/01/92	Peterborough United	Away	Lge Cup	0–0		
330	11/01/92	Ipswich Town	Home	League	1–0		
Sub+14	22/02/92	Blackburn Rovers	Home	League	0–0		
Sub+15	26/02/92	Portsmouth	Home	FA Cup	2–4		
331	04/03/92	Manchester United	Home	Lge Cup	0–0		
332	07/03/92	Cambridge United	Home	League	1–1		
333	11/03/92	Manchester United	Away	Lge Cup	1–2*	1 Goal	(138)
334	14/03/92	Southend United	Away	League	1–0	1 Goal	(139)
335	17/03/92	Cambridge United	Away	League	0–0		
336	21/03/92	Brighton & Hove Albion	Home	League	4–0	3 Goals	(142)
337	28/03/92	Charlton Athletic	Away	League	0–0		
338	01/04/92	Leicester City	Away	League	1–2		
339	04/04/92	Watford	Home	League	1–2		
Sub+16	13/04/92	Barnsley	Home	League	0–1		
340	15/04/92	Oxford United	Home	League	2–1		
Sub+17	18/04/92	Plymouth Argyle	Home	League	2–1		
Sub+18	20/04/92	Sunderland	Away	League	0–1		
Sub+19	25/04/92	Bristol Rovers	Home	League	2–1		
341	02/05/92	Wolverhampton Wanderers	Away	League	2–1		

SEASON 1992–93

Premier League

Sub+20	15/08/92	Coventry City	Away	League	1–2		
342	19/08/92	Manchester City	Home	League	2–0	2 Goals	(144)
343	22/08/92	Leeds United	Home	League	4–1		
344	29/08/92	Southampton	Away	League	1–2		
345	01/09/92	Ipswich Town	Home	League	2–2		
346	05/09/92	Sheffield United	Home	League	2–0		
Sub+21	19/09/92	Queens Park Rangers	Away	League	3–3		
Sub+22	23/09/92	Newcastle United	Away	Lge Cup	0–0		
347	26/09/92	Aston Villa	Home	League	2–3	1 Goal	(145)
348	03/10/92	Manchester United	Home	League	1–1	1 Goal	(146)
349	07/10/92	Newcastle United	Home	Lge Cup	1–3		
350	17/10/92	Tottenham Hotspur	Away	League	2–2		
351	21/10/92	Nottingham Forest	Away	League	0–1		
352	24/10/92	Sheffield Wednesday	Home	League	1–1		
Sub+23	07/11/92	Liverpool	Away	League	1–4		
Sub+24	03/02/93	Nottingham Forest	Home	FA Cup	0–3		
353	06/02/93	Coventry City	Home	League	0–2		
354	09/02/93	Sheffield United	Away	League	0–2		
355	20/02/93	Nottingham Forest	Home	League	1–2		
Sub+25	27/02/93	Manchester United	Away	League	0–3		
Sub+26	09/03/93	Wimbledon	Away	League	0–2		

Port Vale – Football League Division Two

1	20/03/93	Leyton Orient	Away	League	1–0		
2	23/03/93	Huddersfield Town	Home	League	1–0		
3	27/03/93	Hull City	Away	League	1–0		
4	31/03/93	Stoke City	Home	League	0–2		
Sub+1	13/04/93	Bradford City	Home	League	1–2		
5	17/04/93	Wigan Athletic	Away	League	4–0	1 Goal	(1)
6	21/04/93	Exeter City	Away	A Trophy	1–1	1 Goal	(2)
7	24/04/93	Plymouth Argyle	Away	League	1–0		
8	27/04/93	Mansfield Town	Home	League	3–0		
9	04/05/93	Exeter City	Away	League	1–1		
10	08/05/93	Blackpool	Away	League	4–2	1 Goal	(3)
11	16/05/93	Stockport County	Away	Lge P/O	1–1		
12	19/05/93	Stockport County	Home	Lge P/O	1–0		
13	22/05/93	Stockport County	Wembley	A Trophy	2–1	1 Goal	(4)
14	30/05/93	West Bromwich Albion	Wembley	Lge P/O	0–3		

SEASON 1993–94

Football League Division Two

15	14/08/93	Burnley	Away	League	1–2		
16	17/08/93	Lincoln City	Home	Lge Cup	2–2	1 Goal	(5)
17	21/08/93	Barnet	Home	League	6–0	3 Goals	(8)
18	24/08/93	Lincoln City	Away	Lge Cup	0–0		
19	28/08/93	Plymouth Argyle	Away	League	0–2		
20	31/08/93	Cambridge United	Home	League	2–2		

21	04/09/93	Cardiff City	Home	League	2–2	2 Goals	(10)
22	11/09/93	Bristol Rovers	Away	League	0–2		
23	14/09/93	Huddersfield Town	Away	League	1–1	1 Goal	(11)
24	18/09/93	Hartlepool United	Home	League	1–0		
25	25/09/93	Brentford	Away	League	2–1		
26	02/10/93	Wrexham	Home	League	3–0		
27	30/10/93	Rotherham United	Away	League	2–0		
28	06/11/93	Swansea City	Home	League	3–0		
29	09/11/93	Wrexham	Home	A Trophy	0–0		
Sub+2	20/11/93	Exeter City	Away	League	1–1		
Sub+3	27/11/93	Brighton & Hove Albion	Home	League	4–0		
Sub+4	03/12/93	Huddersfield Town	Home	FA Cup	1–0		
Sub+5	07/12/93	AFC Bournemouth	Away	League	1–2		
30	11/12/93	Barnet	Away	League	3–2		
31	18/12/93	Burnley	Home	League	1–1	1 Goal	(12)
32	27/12/93	Fulham	Away	League	0–0		
33	29/12/93	Leyton Orient	Home	League	2–1		
34	01/01/94	York City	Away	League	0–1		
Sub+6	08/01/94	Southampton	Away	FA Cup	1–1		
35	11/01/94	Swansea City	Away	A Trophy	0–1		
36	18/01/94	Southampton	Home	FA Cup	1–0	1 Goal	(13)
37	22/01/94	Hull City	Away	League	0–0		
38	29/01/94	Wolverhampton Wanderers	Home	FA Cup	0–2		
39	05/02/94	Reading	Away	League	2–1		
40	12/02/94	Stockport County	Home	League	1–1		

Darlington – Football League Division Three

1	05/03/94	Shrewsbury Town	Away	League	1–1		
2	08/03/94	Chesterfield	Home	League	0–0		
3	12/03/94	Crewe Alexandra	Home	League	1–0		
4	19/03/94	Walsall	Away	League	0–3		
5	26/03/94	Northampton Town	Home	League	0–1		
6	04/04/94	Doncaster Rovers	Home	League	1–3	1 Goal	(1)
7	09/04/94	Wigan Athletic	Away	League	0–2		
8	16/04/94	Colchester United	Away	League	2–1		
9	23/04/94	Preston North End	Home	League	0–2		
10	30/04/94	Mansfield Town	Away	League	3–0		
11	07/05/94	Bury	Home	League	1–0	1 Goal	(2)

SEASON 1994–95

Football League Division Three

12	14/08/94	Preston North End	Home	League	0–0		
13	17/08/94	Barnsley	Home	Lge Cup	2–2	1 Goal	(3)
14	20/08/94	Hartlepool United	Away	League	0–1		
15	23/08/94	Barnsley	Away	Lge Cup	0–0*		
16	27/08/94	Exeter City	Home	League	2–0		
17	30/08/94	Mansfield Town	Away	League	1–0		
18	03/09/94	Doncaster Rovers	Away	League	0–0		
19	10/09/94	Torquay United	Home	League	2–1		
20	13/09/94	Scunthorpe United	Home	League	1–3		
Sub+1	24/09/94	Colchester United	Home	League	2–3		
Sub+2	27/09/94	Carlisle United	Home	AW Shield	2–3		
21	01/10/94	Carlisle United	Away	League	1–2		
22	08/10/94	Bury	Home	League	0–2		
Sub+3	22/10/94	Hereford United	Home	League	3–1		
23	29/10/94	Gillingham	Away	League	1–2		
24	12/11/94	Hyde United	Away	FA Cup	3–1	1 Goal	(4)
25	26/11/94	Barnet	Home	League	0–1		
26	04/12/94	Carlisle United	Away	FA Cup	0–2		
27	10/12/94	Hartlepool United	Home	League	1–2		
28	17/12/94	Exeter City	Away	League	2–0		
29	26/12/94	Scarborough	Home	League	1–0	1 Goal	(5)
30	27/12/94	Lincoln City	Away	League	1–3	1 Goal	(6)
31	31/12/94	Northampton Town	Home	League	4–1	1 Goal	(7)
32	07/01/95	Hereford United	Away	League	0–0		
33	04/02/95	Barnet	Away	League	3–2		
34	11/02/95	Wigan Athletic	Home	League	1–3		
35	18/02/95	Fulham	Away	League	1–3	1 Goal	(8)
36	21/02/95	Gillingham	Home	League	2–0	1 Goal	(9)
37	25/02/95	Carlisle United	Home	League	0–2		
38	04/03/95	Colchester United	Away	League	0–1		
39	21/03/95	Rochdale	Away	League	0–2		

INTERNATIONAL APPEARANCES – REPUBLIC OF IRELAND

1	28/03/90	Wales	Lansdowne Road	1–0	F	1 Goal	(1)
2	16/05/90	Finland	Lansdowne Road	1–1	F		
Sub 3	27/05/90	Turkey	Izmir	0–0	F		
4	02/06/90	Malta	Valletta	3–0	F		
5	06/02/91	Wales	Racecourse	3–0	F		
Sub 6	01/05/91	Poland	Lansdowne Road	0–0	ECQ		
Sub 7	17/02/93	Wales	Tolka Park	2–1	F		

APPEARANCES AND GOALS PER SEASON

SEASON 81–82	GAMES	GOALS
Scottish League	8+5	1
Scottish Cup	1	0
TOTAL	**9+5**	**1**

SEASON 82–83	GAMES	GOALS
Scottish League	3+6	0
Scottish Cup	1	0
TOTAL	**4+6**	**0**

SEASON 83–84	GAMES	GOALS
Scottish League	7	0
Scottish League Cup	3+1	0
TOTAL	**10+1**	**0**

SEASON 84–85	GAMES	GOALS
Scottish League	39	27
Scottish Cup	1	0
Scottish League Cup	2	3
TOTAL	**42**	**30**

SEASON 85–86	GAMES	GOALS
League	32	8
FA Cup	1	0
Full Members Cup	1	1
TOTAL	**34**	**9**

SEASON 86–87	GAMES	GOALS
League	46	17
FA Cup	3	3
League Cup	4	1
Freight Rover Trophy	5	0
TOTAL	**58**	**21**

SEASON 87–88	GAMES	GOALS
League	44	21
League Play–offs	4	2
FA Cup	5	0
League Cup	4	1
Simod Cup	1	0
TOTAL	**58**	**24**

SEASON 88–89	GAMES	GOALS
League	36+1	15
FA Cup	1	1
League Cup	2	0
Simod Cup	4	2
TOTAL	**43+1**	**18**

SEASON 89–90	GAMES	GOALS
League	46	21
FA Cup	3	0
League Cup	4	4
Zenith Data Systems Cup	6	7
TOTAL	**59**	**32**

SEASON 90–91	GAMES	GOALS
League	41+5	16
League Play–offs	2	0
FA Cup	2+1	0
League Cup	5	3
Zenith Data Systems Cup	2	1
TOTAL	**52+6**	**20**

SEASON 91–92	GAMES	GOALS
League	28+10	16
FA Cup	1+1	0
League Cup	6+1	1
Zenith Data Systems Cup	2	1
TOTAL	**37+12**	**18**

SEASON 92–93	GAMES	GOALS
League	22+6	6
League Play–offs	3	0
FA Cup	0+1	0
League Cup	1+1	0
Autoglass Trophy	2	2
TOTAL	**28+8**	**8**

SEASON 93–94	GAMES	GOALS
League	31+3	9
FA Cup	2+2	1
League Cup	2	1
Autoglass Trophy	2	0
TOTAL	**37+5**	**11**

SEASON 94–95	GAMES	GOALS
League	24+2	5
FA Cup	2	1
League Cup	2	1
Auto Windscreen Shields	0+1	0
TOTAL	**28+3**	**7**

CAREER APPEARANCES AND GOALS

COMPETITION	GAMES	TOTAL	GOALS
League	350+27	377	134
League Play–offs	9	9	2
FA Cup	20+5	25	6
League Cup	30+2	32	12
Full Members Cup	1	1	1
Freight Rover Trophy	5	5	0
Simod Cup	5	5	2
Zenith Data Systems Cup	10	10	9
Autoglass Trophy	4	4	2
Auto Windscreens Shield	0+1	1	0
Scottish League	57+11	68	28
Scottish Cup	3	3	0
Scottish League Cup	5+1	6	3
Internationals	4+3	7	1
TOTAL	**503+50**	**553**	**200**

HAT-TRICKS

Albion Rovers

1	3	East Stirling	22/09/84	Away	League	3–2
2	3	Arbroath	16/02/85	Home	League	3–0

Middlesbrough

1	3	Blackpool	15/11/86	Home	FA Cup	3–0
2	3	Huddersfield Town	10/10/87	Away	League	4–1
3	3	Shrewsbury Town	31/10/87	Home	League	4–0
4	3	Coventry City	01/10/88	Away	League	4–3
5	3	Sheffield Wednesday	20/12/89	Home	ZDS Cup	4–1
6	3	Brighton & Hove Albion	27/10/90	Away	League	4–2
7	3	Brighton & Hove Albion	21/03/92	Home	League	4–0

Port Vale

1	3	Barnet	21/08/93	Home	League	6–0

League: 6
Scottish League: 2
FA Cup: 1
Zenith Data Systems Cup: 1
TOTAL: 10

HONOURS

Winners medals
Autoglass Trophy: 92/93

Runner-up medals
League Division Two Championship: 91/92
Football League Division Two Championship: 93/94
League Division Three Championship: 86/87
Promoted to League Division One: 87/88
Zenith Data Systems Cup: 89/90

ALAN SMITH

Born: 21/11/62 – Bromsgrove
Height: 6.3
Weight: 12.10 (95–96)

Clubs
Leicester City: **1982–87** – Matches: **206+11** – Goals: **84**
Arsenal: **1987–95** – Matches: **321+29** – Goals: **115**

Country
England: **1988–92** – Matches: **8+5** – Goals: **2**

SEASON 1982–83

Leicester City – League Division Two

1	27/08/82	Charlton Athletic	Home	League	1–2		
2	31/08/82	Rotherham United	Away	League	3–1	1 Goal	(1)
3	04/09/82	Chelsea	Away	League	1–1		
4	08/09/82	Leeds United	Home	League	0–1		
5	11/09/82	Carlisle United	Home	League	6–0		
6	18/09/82	Blackburn Rovers	Away	League	1–3	1 Goal	(2)
7	25/09/82	Queens Park Rangers	Home	League	0–1		
Sub+1	16/10/82	Wolverhampton Wanderers	Away	League	3–0		
Sub+2	23/10/82	Derby County	Away	League	4–0	1 Goal	(3)
8	27/10/82	Lincoln City	Home	Lge Cup	0–1		
9	30/10/82	Sheffield Wednesday	Home	League	0–2		
10	06/11/82	Cambridge United	Away	League	1–3		
Sub+3	20/11/82	Crystal Palace	Home	League	0–1		
Sub+4	27/11/82	Bolton Wanderers	Away	League	1–3		
11	04/12/82	Fulham	Home	League	2–0		
12	11/12/82	Burnley	Away	League	4–2	2 Goals	(5)
13	18/12/82	Oldham Athletic	Home	League	2–1	1 Goal	(6)
14	27/12/82	Middlesbrough	Away	League	1–1		
15	28/12/82	Barnsley	Home	League	1–0	1 Goal	(7)
16	01/01/83	Crystal Palace	Away	League	0–1		
17	03/01/83	Chelsea	Home	League	3–0	1 Goal	(8)
18	08/01/83	Notts County	Home	FA Cup	2–3	1 Goal	(9)
19	15/01/83	Charlton Athletic	Away	League	1–2		
20	22/01/83	Blackburn Rovers	Home	League	0–1		
21	05/02/83	Carlisle United	Away	League	1–0		
22	19/02/83	Grimsby Town	Away	League	0–2		
23	22/02/83	Shrewsbury Town	Home	League	3–2		
24	26/02/83	Wolverhampton Wanderers	Home	League	5–0	1 Goal	(10)
25	05/03/83	Derby County	Home	League	1–1		
26	19/03/83	Cambridge United	Home	League	4–0	2 Goals	(12)
27	22/03/83	Sheffield Wednesday	Away	League	2–2	1 Goal	(13)
28	26/03/83	Newcastle United	Away	League	2–2		
29	02/04/83	Barnsley	Away	League	2–1		
30	05/04/83	Middlesbrough	Home	League	1–0		
31	09/04/83	Queens Park Rangers	Away	League	2–2		
32	16/04/83	Rotherham United	Home	League	3–1		
33	23/04/83	Fulham	Away	League	1–0		
34	30/04/83	Bolton Wanderers	Home	League	0–0		
35	02/05/83	Leeds United	Away	League	2–2	1 Goal	(14)
36	07/05/83	Oldham Athletic	Away	League	2–1		
37	14/05/83	Barnsley	Home	League	0–0		

SEASON 1983–84

League Division One

38	27/08/83	Notts County	Home	League	0–4			
39	31/08/83	Luton Town	Home	League	0–3			
40	03/09/83	West Bromwich Albion	Away	League	0–1			
41	06/09/83	West Ham United	Away	League	1–3			
42	10/09/83	Tottenham Hotspur	Home	League	0–3			
43	17/09/83	Coventry City	Away	League	1–2			
44	24/09/83	Stoke City	Home	League	2–2			
Sub+5	05/10/83	Chelsea	Home	Lge Cup	0–2			
Sub+6	22/10/83	Ipswich Town	Away	League	0–0			
45	25/10/83	Chelsea	Away	Lge Cup	2–0+	1 Goal	(15)	
46	29/10/83	Everton	Home	League	2–0	1 Goal	(16)	
47	05/11/83	Watford	Away	League	3–3			
48	12/11/83	Manchester United	Home	League	1–1			
49	19/11/83	Aston Villa	Away	League	1–3			
50	26/11/83	Arsenal	Home	League	3–0	1 Goal	(17)	
51	30/11/83	Southampton	Home	League	2–1	1 Goal	(18)	
52	04/12/83	Nottingham Forest	Away	League	2–3	1 Goal	(19)	
53	10/12/83	Wolverhampton Wanderers	Home	League	5–1	3 Goals	(22)	
54	18/12/83	Sunderland	Away	League	1–1			
55	26/12/83	Queens Park Rangers	Home	League	2–1			
56	27/12/83	Liverpool	Away	League	2–2	1 Goal	(23)	
57	31/12/83	West Bromwich Albion	Home	League	1–1			
58	02/01/84	Stoke City	Away	League	1–0	1 Goal	(24)	
59	07/01/84	Crystal Palace	Away	FA Cup	0–1			
60	14/01/84	Notts County	Away	League	5–2			
61	21/01/84	Coventry City	Home	League	1–1			
62	04/02/84	Birmingham City	Home	League	2–3	2 Goals	(26)	
63	11/02/84	Tottenham Hotspur	Away	League	2–3			
64	25/02/84	Ipswich Town	Home	League	2–0	1 Goal	(27)	
65	03/03/84	Watford	Home	League	4–1	1 Goal	(28)	
66	10/03/84	Manchester United	Away	League	0–2			
67	17/03/84	West Ham United	Home	League	4–1			
68	20/03/84	Everton	Away	League	1–1			
69	24/03/84	Luton Town	Away	League	0–0			
70	31/03/84	Norwich City	Home	League	2–1	2 Goals	(30)	
71	07/04/84	Southampton	Away	League	2–2			
72	14/04/84	Aston Villa	Home	League	2–0			
73	18/04/84	Liverpool	Home	League	3–3			
74	21/04/84	Queens Park Rangers	Away	League	0–2			
75	28/04/84	Arsenal	Away	League	1–2			
76	05/05/84	Nottingham Forest	Home	League	2–1			
77	07/05/84	Wolverhampton Wanderers	Away	League	0–1			
78	12/05/84	Sunderland	Home	League	0–2			

+ AET Chelsea won 4–3 on penalties

SEASON 1984–85

League Division One

79	25/08/84	Newcastle United	Home	League	2–3			
80	27/08/84	Tottenham Hotspur	Away	League	2–2	1 Goal	(31)	
81	01/09/84	Coventry City	Away	League	0–2			
82	05/09/84	Watford	Home	League	1–1			
83	08/09/84	Ipswich Town	Home	League	2–1			
84	15/09/84	Stoke City	Away	League	2–2			
85	22/09/84	West Bromwich Albion	Home	League	2–1			
86	06/10/84	West Ham United	Away	League	1–3			
87	09/10/84	Brentford	Away	Lge Cup	2–0	1 Goal	(32)	
88	13/10/84	Arsenal	Home	League	1–4			
89	20/10/84	Sheffield Wednesday	Away	League	0–5			
90	30/10/84	Luton Town	Away	Lge Cup	1–3			
Sub+7	10/11/84	Manchester United	Home	League	2–3			
Sub+8	17/11/84	Norwich City	Home	League	2–0			
Sub+9	25/11/84	Nottingham Forest	Away	League	1–2			
91	01/12/84	Queens Park Rangers	Home	League	4–0	1 Goal	(33)	
92	08/12/84	Sunderland	Away	League	4–0	2 Goals	(35)	
93	15/12/84	Luton Town	Home	League	2–2	1 Goal	(36)	
94	23/12/84	Coventry City	Home	League	5–1	1 Goal	(37)	
95	26/12/84	Liverpool	Away	League	2–1	1 Goal	(38)	
96	29/12/84	Watford	Away	League	1–4			
97	01/01/85	Southampton	Home	League	1–2			

98	05/01/85	Burton Albion	Away	FA Cup	6–1+	2 Goals	(40)
99	12/01/85	Stoke City	Home	League	0–0		
100	16/01/85	Burton Albion	Neutral	FA Cup	1–0#		
101	26/01/85	Carlisle United	Home	FA Cup	1–0		
102	02/02/85	Chelsea	Home	League	1–1		
103	16/02/85	Millwall	Away	FA Cup	0–2		
104	23/02/85	Everton	Home	League	1–2		
105	02/03/85	Aston Villa	Away	League	1–0	1 Goal	(41)
106	09/03/85	Sheffield Wednesday	Home	League	3–1	1 Goal	(42)
107	16/03/85	Arsenal	Away	League	0–2		
108	20/03/85	Newcastle United	Away	League	4–1	1 Goal	(43)
109	23/03/85	West Ham United	Home	League	1–0		
110	30/03/85	West Bromwich Albion	Away	League	0–2		
111	03/04/85	Manchester United	Away	League	1–2		
112	06/04/85	Liverpool	Home	League	0–1		
113	09/04/85	Southampton	Away	League	1–3		
114	13/04/85	Tottenham Hotspur	Home	League	1–2		
115	20/04/85	Norwich City	Away	League	3–1	2 Goals	(45)
116	23/04/85	Ipswich Town	Away	League	0–2		
117	27/04/85	Nottingham Forest	Home	League	1–0		
118	04/05/85	Queens Park Rangers	Away	League	3–4		
119	06/05/85	Sunderland	Home	League	2–0		
120	11/05/85	Luton Town	Away	League	0–4		

+ The FA ordered the match to be replayed after the Burton Albion keeper Evans was struck by a missile
# Played behind closed doors at Highfield Road, Coventry City

SEASON 1985–86

League Division One

121	17/08/85	Everton	Home	League	3–1		
122	21/08/85	Manchester City	Away	League	1–1		
123	24/08/85	Oxford United	Away	League	0–5		
124	28/08/85	Chelsea	Home	League	0–0		
125	31/08/85	Arsenal	Away	League	0–1		
126	04/09/85	Watford	Home	League	2–2		
Sub+10	08/09/85	Nottingham Forest	Home	League	0–3		
127	14/09/85	West Ham United	Away	League	0–3		
128	21/09/85	Birmingham City	Away	League	1–2		
Sub+11	28/09/85	Ipswich Town	Home	League	1–0	1 Goal	(46)
129	02/10/85	Oxford United	Home	League	4–4	1 Goal	(47)
130	06/10/85	Coventry City	Away	League	0–3		
131	09/10/85	Derby County	Home	Lge Cup	1–1		
132	12/10/85	West Bromwich Albion	Home	League	2–2	1 Goal	(48)
133	19/10/85	Sheffield Wednesday	Home	League	2–3	1 Goal	(49)
134	26/10/85	Tottenham Hotspur	Away	League	3–1	1 Goal	(50)
135	02/11/85	Liverpool	Away	League	0–1		
136	09/11/85	Southampton	Home	League	2–2	1 Goal	(51)
137	16/11/85	Queens Park Rangers	Away	League	0–2		
138	23/11/85	Manchester United	Home	League	3–0	2 Goals	(53)
139	30/11/85	Newcastle United	Away	League	1–2	1 Goal	(54)
140	07/12/85	Manchester City	Home	League	1–1	1 Goal	(55)
141	14/12/85	Everton	Away	League	2–1	1 Goal	(56)
142	26/12/85	Aston Villa	Home	League	3–1	2 Goals	(58)
143	28/12/85	Watford	Away	League	1–2	1 Goal	(59)
144	01/01/86	Luton Town	Away	League	1–3		
145	04/01/86	Bristol Rovers	Away	FA Cup	1–3		
146	11/01/86	West Ham United	Home	League	0–1		
147	18/01/86	Arsenal	Home	League	2–2		
148	01/02/86	Chelsea	Away	League	2–2		
149	08/03/86	Coventry City	Home	League	2–1	1 Goal	(60)
150	12/03/86	Birmingham City	Home	League	4–2	1 Goal	(61)
151	15/03/86	West Bromwich Albion	Away	League	2–2		
152	18/03/86	Sheffield Wednesday	Away	League	0–1		
153	22/03/86	Nottingham Forest	Away	League	3–4	2 Goals	(63)
154	29/03/86	Luton Town	Home	League	0–0		
155	31/03/86	Aston Villa	Away	League	0–1		
156	05/04/86	Tottenham Hotspur	Home	League	1–4		
157	08/04/86	Ipswich Town	Away	League	2–0	1 Goal	(64)
158	12/04/86	Southampton	Away	League	0–0		
159	30/04/86	Liverpool	Home	League	0–2		
160	03/05/86	Newcastle United	Home	League	2–0		

SEASON 1986–87

League Division One

161	23/08/86	Luton Town	Home	League	1–1	1 Goal	(65)
162	30/08/86	Wimbledon	Away	League	0–1		
163	03/09/86	Liverpool	Home	League	2–1		
164	06/09/86	Manchester United	Home	League	1–1		
165	13/09/86	Sheffield Wednesday	Away	League	2–2		
166	17/09/86	Norwich City	Away	League	1–2	1 Goal	(66)
167	20/09/86	Tottenham Hotspur	Home	League	1–2		
168	23/09/86	Swansea City	Away	Lge Cup	2–0	1 Goal	(67)
169	27/09/86	Queens Park Rangers	Away	League	1–0	1 Goal	(68)
170	04/10/86	Manchester City	Away	League	2–1	1 Goal	(69)
171	08/10/86	Swansea City	Home	Lge Cup	4–2	1 Goal	(70)
172	11/10/86	Nottingham Forest	Home	League	3–1	1 Goal	(71)
173	18/10/86	Charlton Athletic	Away	League	0–2		
174	25/10/86	Southampton	Home	League	2–3		
175	29/10/86	Liverpool	Away	Lge Cup	1–4		
176	01/11/86	Aston Villa	Away	League	0–2		
177	08/11/86	Newcastle United	Home	League	1–1	1 Goal	(72)
178	15/11/86	Everton	Home	League	0–2		
179	22/11/86	Watford	Away	League	1–5	1 Goal	(73)
180	29/11/86	Chelsea	Home	League	2–2		
181	06/12/86	Coventry City	Away	League	0–1		
182	14/12/86	Oxford United	Home	League	2–0	1 Goal	(74)
183	20/12/86	Manchester United	Away	League	0–2		
184	26/12/86	Arsenal	Home	League	1–1		
185	28/12/86	Everton	Away	League	1–5		
186	01/01/87	West Ham United	Away	League	1–4		
187	03/01/87	Sheffield Wednesday	Home	League	6–1	2 Goals	(76)
188	10/01/87	Queens Park Rangers	Away	FA Cup	2–5	1 Goal	(77)
189	24/01/87	Luton Town	Away	League	0–1		
190	07/02/87	Wimbledon	Home	League	3–1	1 Goal	(78)
191	14/02/87	Liverpool	Away	League	3–4	2 Goals	(80)
192	21/02/87	Norwich City	Home	League	0–2		
193	25/02/87	Tottenham Hotspur	Away	League	0–5		
194	07/03/87	Southampton	Away	League	0–4		
195	14/03/87	Charlton Athletic	Home	League	1–0	1 Goal	(81)
196	22/03/87	Nottingham Forest	Away	League	1–2		
197	25/03/87	Queens Park Rangers	Home	League	4–1		

Arsenal – League Division One
No Competitive Matches

Leicester City (loan) – League Division One

198	28/03/87	Manchester City	Home	League	4–0	1 Goal	(82)
199	04/04/87	Newcastle United	Away	League	0–2		
200	11/04/87	Aston Villa	Home	League	1–1		
201	18/04/87	West Ham United	Home	League	2–0	1 Goal	(83)
202	20/04/87	Arsenal	Away	League	1–4		
203	25/04/87	Watford	Home	League	1–2		
204	02/05/87	Chelsea	Away	League	1–3	1 Goal	(84)
205	04/05/87	Coventry City	Home	League	1–1		
206	09/05/87	Oxford United	Away	League	0–0		

SEASON 1987–88

Arsenal – League Division One

1	15/08/87	Liverpool	Home	League	1–2		
2	19/08/87	Manchester United	Away	League	0–0		
3	22/08/87	Queens Park Rangers	Away	League	0–2		
4	29/08/87	Portsmouth	Home	League	6–0	3 Goals	(3)
5	31/08/87	Luton Town	Away	League	1–1		
6	12/09/87	Nottingham Forest	Away	League	1–0	1 Goal	(4)
7	19/09/87	Wimbledon	Home	League	3–0	1 Goal	(5)
8	23/09/87	Doncaster Rovers	Away	Lge Cup	3–0	1 Goal	(6)
9	26/09/87	West Ham United	Home	League	1–0		
10	03/10/87	Charlton Athletic	Away	League	3–0		
11	06/10/87	Doncaster Rovers	Home	Lge Cup	1–0		
12	10/10/87	Oxford United	Home	League	2–0		
13	18/10/87	Tottenham Hotspur	Away	League	2–1		
14	24/10/87	Derby County	Home	League	2–1		
15	27/10/87	AFC Bournemouth	Home	Lge Cup	3–0	1 Goal	(7)
16	31/10/87	Newcastle United	Away	League	1–0	1 Goal	(8)
17	03/11/87	Chelsea	Home	League	3–1		

18	14/11/87	Norwich City	Away	League	4–2		
19	17/11/87	Stoke City	Home	Lge Cup	3–0		
20	21/11/87	Southampton	Home	League	0–1		
21	28/11/87	Watford	Away	League	0–2		
22	05/12/87	Sheffield Wednesday	Home	League	3–1		
23	13/12/87	Coventry City	Away	League	0–0		
24	19/12/87	Everton	Home	League	1–1		
Sub+1	26/12/87	Nottingham Forest	Home	League	0–2		
Sub+2	28/12/87	Wimbledon	Away	League	1–3		
Sub+3	01/01/88	Portsmouth	Away	League	1–1	1 Goal	(9)
25	02/01/88	Queens Park Rangers	Home	League	0–0		
26	09/01/88	Millwall	Home	FA Cup	2–0		
27	16/01/88	Liverpool	Away	League	0–2		
28	20/01/88	Sheffield Wednesday	Away	Lge Cup	1–0		
29	24/01/88	Manchester United	Home	League	1–2		
30	07/02/88	Everton	Away	Lge Cup	1–0		
31	13/02/88	Luton Town	Home	League	2–1		
32	20/02/88	Manchester United	Home	FA Cup	2–1	1 Goal	(10)
33	24/02/88	Everton	Home	Lge Cup	3–1	1 Goal	(11)
34	27/02/88	Charlton Athletic	Home	League	4–0	1 Goal	(12)
35	06/03/88	Tottenham Hotspur	Home	League	2–1	1 Goal	(13)
36	12/03/88	Nottingham Forest	Home	FA Cup	1–2		
37	19/03/88	Newcastle United	Home	League	1–1		
38	26/03/88	Derby County	Away	League	0–0		
39	30/03/88	Oxford United	Away	League	0–0		
40	04/04/88	Norwich City	Home	League	2–0	1 Goal	(14)
41	09/04/88	Southampton	Away	League	2–4		
42	12/04/88	West Ham United	Away	League	1–0		
43	15/04/88	Watford	Home	League	0–1		
44	24/04/88	Luton Town	Wembley	Lge Cup	2–3	1 Goal	(15)
45	30/04/88	Sheffield Wednesday	Away	League	3–3	1 Goal	(16)
46	02/05/88	Coventry City	Home	League	1–1		
47	07/05/88	Everton	Away	League	2–1		

SEASON 1988–89

League Division One

48	27/08/88	Wimbledon	Away	League	5–1	3 Goals	(19)
49	31/08/88	Queens Park Rangers	Away	MCC Trophy	2–0		
50	03/09/88	Aston Villa	Home	League	2–3	1 Goal	(20)
51	10/09/88	Tottenham Hotspur	Away	League	3–2	1 Goal	(21)
52	17/09/88	Southampton	Home	League	2–2	1 Goal	(22)
53	20/09/88	Liverpool	Home	MCC Trophy	2–1		
54	24/09/88	Sheffield Wednesday	Away	League	1–2	1 Goal	(23)
55	28/09/88	Hull City	Away	Lge Cup	2–1		
56	01/10/88	West Ham United	Away	League	4–1	2 Goals	(25)
57	09/10/88	Manchester United	Neutral	MCC Trophy	2–1		
58	12/10/88	Hull City	Home	Lge Cup	3–0	2 Goals	(27)
59	22/10/88	Queens Park Rangers	Home	League	2–1	1 Goal	(28)
60	25/10/88	Luton Town	Away	League	1–1	1 Goal	(29)
61	29/10/88	Coventry City	Home	League	2–0		
62	02/11/88	Liverpool	Away	Lge Cup	1–1		
63	06/11/88	Nottingham Forest	Away	League	4–1	1 Goal	(30)
64	09/11/88	Liverpool	Home	Lge Cup	0–0*		
65	12/11/88	Newcastle United	Away	League	1–0		
66	19/11/88	Middlesbrough	Home	League	3–0		
67	23/11/88	Liverpool	Neutral	Lge Cup	1–2		
68	26/11/88	Derby County	Away	League	1–2		
69	04/12/88	Liverpool	Home	League	1–1	1 Goal	(31)
70	10/12/88	Norwich City	Away	League	0–0		
71	17/12/88	Manchester United	Home	League	2–1		
72	26/12/88	Charlton Athletic	Away	League	3–2		
73	31/12/88	Aston Villa	Away	League	3–0	1 Goal	(32)
74	02/01/89	Tottenham Hotspur	Home	League	2–0		
75	08/01/89	West Ham United	Away	FA Cup	2–2		
76	11/01/89	West Ham United	Home	FA Cup	0–1		
77	14/01/89	Everton	Away	League	3–1	1 Goal	(33)
78	21/01/89	Sheffield Wednesday	Home	League	1–1		
79	04/02/89	West Ham United	Home	League	2–1	1 Goal	(34)
80	11/02/89	Millwall	Away	League	2–1	1 Goal	(35)
81	18/02/89	Queens Park Rangers	Away	League	0–0		
82	21/02/89	Coventry City	Away	League	0–1		
83	25/02/89	Luton Town	Home	League	2–0	1 Goal	(36)
84	28/02/89	Millwall	Home	League	0–0		
85	11/03/89	Nottingham Forest	Home	League	1–3	1 Goal	(37)

86	21/03/89	Charlton Athletic	Home	League	2–2		
87	25/03/89	Southampton	Away	League	3–1		
88	02/04/89	Manchester United	Away	League	1–1		
89	01/05/89	Norwich City	Home	League	5–0	2 Goals	(39)
90	06/05/89	Middlesbrough	Away	League	1–0		
91	13/05/89	Derby County	Home	League	1–2	1 Goal	(40)
92	17/05/89	Wimbledon	Home	League	2–2		
93	26/05/89	Liverpool	Away	League	2–0	1 Goal	(41)

SEASON 1989–90

League Division One

94	12/08/89	Liverpool	Wembley	FA C/S	0–1		
95	19/08/89	Manchester United	Away	League	1–4		
96	22/08/89	Coventry City	Home	League	2–0		
97	26/08/89	Wimbledon	Home	League	0–0		
98	09/09/89	Sheffield Wednesday	Home	League	5–0	1 Goal	(42)
99	16/09/89	Nottingham Forest	Away	League	2–1		
100	19/09/89	Plymouth Argyle	Home	Lge Cup	2–0	1 Goal	(43)
101	23/09/89	Charlton Athletic	Home	League	1–0		
102	30/09/89	Chelsea	Away	League	0–0		
103	03/10/89	Plymouth Argyle	Away	Lge Cup	6–1	1 Goal	(44)
104	14/10/89	Manchester City	Home	League	4–0		
105	18/10/89	Tottenham Hotspur	Away	League	1–2		
Sub+4	21/10/89	Everton	Away	League	0–3		
Sub+5	25/10/89	Liverpool	Home	Lge Cup	1–0	1 Goal	(45)
106	28/10/89	Derby County	Home	League	1–1	1 Goal	(46)
107	04/11/89	Norwich City	Home	League	4–3		
108	11/11/89	Millwall	Away	League	2–1		
109	18/11/89	Queens Park Rangers	Home	League	3–0	1 Goal	(47)
110	22/11/89	Oldham Athletic	Away	Lge Cup	1–3		
111	26/11/89	Liverpool	Away	League	1–2	1 Goal	(48)
112	03/12/89	Manchester United	Home	League	1–0		
113	09/12/89	Coventry City	Away	League	1–0		
114	16/12/89	Luton Town	Home	League	3–2	1 Goal	(49)
115	26/12/89	Southampton	Away	League	0–1		
116	30/12/89	Aston Villa	Away	League	1–2		
117	01/01/90	Crystal Palace	Home	League	4–1	2 Goals	(51)
118	13/01/90	Wimbledon	Away	League	0–1		
119	20/01/90	Tottenham Hotspur	Home	League	1–0		
120	27/01/90	Queens Park Rangers	Home	FA Cup	0–0		
121	31/01/90	Queens Park Rangers	Away	FA Cup	0–2		
122	17/02/90	Sheffield Wednesday	Away	League	0–1		
123	27/02/90	Charlton Athletic	Away	League	0–0		
124	03/03/90	Queens Park Rangers	Away	League	0–2		
125	07/03/90	Nottingham Forest	Home	League	3–0		
126	10/03/90	Manchester City	Away	League	1–1		
127	17/03/90	Chelsea	Home	League	0–1		
128	24/03/90	Derby County	Away	League	3–1		
129	31/03/90	Everton	Home	League	1–0	1 Goal	(52)
130	11/04/90	Aston Villa	Home	League	0–1		
131	14/04/90	Crystal Palace	Away	League	1–1		
132	18/04/90	Liverpool	Home	League	1–1		
133	21/04/90	Luton Town	Away	League	0–2		
134	28/04/90	Millwall	Home	League	2–0		
135	02/05/90	Southampton	Home	League	2–1		
136	05/05/90	Norwich City	Away	League	2–2	2 Goals	(54)

SEASON 1990–91

League Division One

137	25/08/90	Wimbledon	Away	League	3–0	1 Goal	(55)
138	29/08/90	Luton Town	Home	League	2–1		
139	01/09/90	Tottenham Hotspur	Home	League	0–0		
140	08/09/90	Everton	Away	League	1–1		
Sub+6	22/09/90	Nottingham Forest	Away	League	2–0		
141	25/09/90	Chester City	Away	Lge Cup	1–0		
142	29/09/90	Leeds United	Away	League	2–2		
143	06/10/90	Norwich City	Home	League	2–0		
144	09/10/90	Chester City	Home	Lge Cup	5–0	1 Goal	(56)
145	20/10/90	Manchester United	Away	League	1–0		
146	27/10/90	Sunderland	Home	League	1–0		
147	30/10/90	Manchester City	Away	Lge Cup	2–1		
148	03/11/90	Coventry City	Away	League	2–0		
Sub+7	10/11/90	Crystal Palace	Away	League	0–0		

149	17/11/90	Southampton	Home	League	4–0	2 Goals	(58)
150	24/11/90	Queens Park Rangers	Away	League	3–1	1 Goal	(59)
151	28/11/90	Manchester United	Home	Lge Cup	2–6	2 Goals	(61)
152	02/12/90	Liverpool	Home	League	3–0	1 Goal	(62)
153	08/12/90	Luton Town	Away	League	1–1	1 Goal	(63)
154	15/12/90	Wimbledon	Home	League	2–2		
155	23/12/90	Aston Villa	Away	League	0–0		
156	26/12/90	Derby County	Home	League	3–0	2 Goals	(65)
157	29/12/90	Sheffield United	Home	League	4–1	2 Goals	(67)
158	01/01/91	Manchester City	Away	League	1–0	1 Goal	(68)
159	05/01/91	Sunderland	Home	FA Cup	2–1	1 Goal	(69)
160	12/01/91	Tottenham Hotspur	Away	League	0–0		
161	19/01/91	Everton	Home	League	1–0		
162	27/01/91	Leeds United	Home	FA Cup	0–0		
163	30/01/91	Leeds United	Away	FA Cup	1–1*		
164	02/02/91	Chelsea	Away	League	1–2	1 Goal	(70)
165	13/02/91	Leeds United	Home	FA Cup	0–0*		
166	16/02/91	Leeds United	Away	FA Cup	2–1		
167	23/02/91	Crystal Palace	Home	League	4–0	1 Goal	(71)
168	27/02/91	Shrewsbury Town	Away	FA Cup	1–0		
169	03/03/91	Liverpool	Away	League	1–0		
170	09/03/91	Cambridge United	Home	FA Cup	2–1		
171	17/03/91	Leeds United	Home	League	2–0		
172	20/03/91	Nottingham Forest	Home	League	1–1		
173	23/03/91	Norwich City	Away	League	0–0		
174	30/03/91	Derby County	Away	League	2–0	2 Goals	(73)
175	03/04/91	Aston Villa	Home	League	5–0	2 Goals	(75)
176	06/04/91	Sheffield United	Away	League	2–0	1 Goal	(76)
177	09/04/91	Southampton	Away	League	1–1		
178	14/04/91	Tottenham Hotspur	Wembley	FA Cup	1–3	1 Goal	(77)
179	17/04/91	Manchester City	Home	League	2–2		
180	23/04/91	Queens Park Rangers	Home	League	2–0		
181	04/05/91	Sunderland	Away	League	0–0		
182	06/05/91	Manchester United	Home	League	3–1	3 Goals	(80)
183	11/05/91	Coventry City	Home	League	6–1	1 Goal	(81)

SEASON 1991–92

League Division One

184	10/08/91	Tottenham Hotspur	Wembley	FA C/S	0–0		
185	17/08/91	Queens Park Rangers	Home	League	1–1		
186	20/08/91	Everton	Away	League	1–3		
187	24/08/91	Aston Villa	Away	League	1–3	1 Goal	(82)
188	27/08/91	Luton Town	Home	League	2–0	1 Goal	(83)
189	31/08/91	Manchester City	Home	League	2–1	1 Goal	(84)
190	03/09/91	Leeds United	Away	League	2–2	2 Goals	(86)
191	07/09/91	Coventry City	Home	League	1–2		
192	14/09/91	Crystal Palace	Away	League	4–1	1 Goal	(87)
193	18/09/91	FK Austria Wien	Home	Eur Cup	6–1	4 Goals	(91)
194	21/09/91	Sheffield United	Home	League	5–2	1 Goal	(92)
195	28/09/91	Southampton	Away	League	4–0		
196	02/10/91	FK Austria Wien	Away	Eur Cup	0–1		
197	05/10/91	Chelsea	Home	League	3–2		
198	08/10/91	Leicester City	Home	Lge Cup	2–0		
199	19/10/91	Manchester United	Away	League	1–1		
200	23/10/91	Sport Lisboa E Benfica	Away	Eur Cup	1–1		
201	26/10/91	Notts County	Home	League	2–0	1 Goal	(93)
202	30/10/91	Coventry City	Away	Lge Cup	0–1		
203	02/11/91	West Ham United	Home	League	0–1		
204	06/11/91	Sport Lisboa E Benfica	Home	Eur Cup	1–3*		
205	16/11/91	Oldham Athletic	Away	League	1–1		
206	23/11/91	Sheffield Wednesday	Away	League	1–1		
207	01/12/91	Tottenham Hotspur	Home	League	2–0		
208	08/12/91	Nottingham Forest	Away	League	2–3	1 Goal	(94)
209	21/12/91	Everton	Home	League	4–2		
210	26/12/91	Luton Town	Away	League	0–1		
211	28/12/91	Manchester City	Away	League	0–1		
212	01/01/92	Wimbledon	Home	League	1–1		
213	04/01/92	Wrexham	Away	FA Cup	1–2	1 Goal	(95)
214	11/01/92	Aston Villa	Home	League	0–0		
215	18/01/92	Queens Park Rangers	Away	League	0–0		
216	29/01/92	Liverpool	Away	League	0–2		
217	01/02/92	Manchester United	Home	League	1–1		
218	08/02/92	Notts County	Away	League	1–0	1 Goal	(96)
219	11/02/92	Norwich City	Home	League	1–1		

220	15/02/92	Sheffield Wednesday	Home	League	7–1	1 Goal	(97)
221	22/02/92	Tottenham Hotspur	Away	League	1–1		
222	10/03/92	Oldham Athletic	Home	League	2–1		
223	14/03/92	West Ham United	Away	League	2–0		
Sub+8	31/03/92	Nottingham Forest	Home	League	3–3		
Sub+9	04/04/92	Coventry City	Away	League	1–0		
Sub+10	08/04/92	Norwich City	Away	League	3–1		
Sub+11	11/04/92	Crystal Palace	Home	League	4–1		
224	18/04/92	Sheffield United	Away	League	1–1		
Sub+12	25/04/92	Chelsea	Away	League	1–1		
Sub+13	02/05/92	Southampton	Home	League	5–1	1 Goal	(98)

SEASON 1992–93

Premier League

225	15/08/92	Norwich City	Home	League	2–4		
226	18/08/92	Blackburn Rovers	Away	League	0–1		
Sub+14	26/08/92	Oldham Athletic	Home	League	2–0		
Sub+15	29/08/92	Sheffield Wednesday	Home	League	2–1		
Sub+16	02/09/92	Queens Park Rangers	Away	League	0–0		
Sub+17	05/09/92	Wimbledon	Away	League	2–3		
227	12/09/92	Blackburn Rovers	Home	League	0–1		
228	19/09/92	Sheffield United	Away	League	1–1		
229	22/09/92	Millwall	Home	Lge Cup	1–1		
230	28/09/92	Manchester City	Home	League	1–0		
231	03/10/92	Chelsea	Home	League	2–1		
232	07/10/92	Millwall	Away	Lge Cup	1–1+		
233	17/10/92	Nottingham Forest	Away	League	1–0	1 Goal	(99)
234	24/10/92	Everton	Home	League	2–0		
235	28/10/92	Derby County	Away	Lge Cup	1–1		
236	02/11/92	Crystal Palace	Away	League	2–1		
237	07/11/92	Coventry City	Home	League	3–0	1 Goal	(100)
238	19/12/92	Middlesbrough	Home	League	1–1		
239	26/12/92	Ipswich Town	Home	League	0–0		
240	28/12/92	Aston Villa	Away	League	0–1		
241	02/01/93	Yeovil Town	Away	FA Cup	3–1		
242	06/01/93	Scarborough	Away	Lge Cup	1–0		
243	09/01/93	Sheffield United	Home	League	1–1		
244	12/01/93	Nottingham Forest	Home	Lge Cup	2–0		
245	16/01/93	Manchester City	Away	League	1–0		
246	25/01/93	Leeds United	Home	FA Cup	2–2		
247	31/01/93	Liverpool	Home	League	0–1		
248	03/02/93	Leeds United	Away	FA Cup	3–2*	1 Goal	(101)
249	07/02/93	Crystal Palace	Away	Lge Cup	3–1	2 Goals	(103)
250	10/02/93	Wimbledon	Home	League	0–1		
251	24/02/93	Leeds United	Home	League	0–0		
252	01/03/93	Chelsea	Away	League	0–1		
253	06/03/93	Ipswich Town	Away	FA Cup	4–2		
254	10/03/93	Crystal Palace	Home	Lge Cup	2–0		
Sub+18	04/04/93	Tottenham Hotspur	Wembley	FA Cup	1–0		
255	06/04/93	Middlesbrough	Away	League	0–1		
256	10/04/93	Ipswich Town	Away	League	2–1	1 Goal	(104)
257	12/04/93	Aston Villa	Home	League	0–1		
258	21/04/93	Nottingham Forest	Home	League	1–1		
259	01/05/93	Everton	Away	League	0–0		
260	04/05/93	Queens Park Rangers	Home	League	0–0		
261	06/05/93	Sheffield Wednesday	Away	League	0–1		
262	11/05/93	Tottenham Hotspur	Home	League	1–3		
Sub+19	15/05/93	Sheffield Wednesday	Wembley	FA Cup	1–1*		
263	20/05/93	Sheffield Wednesday	Wembley	FA Cup	2–1*		

+ AET Arsenal won 3–1 on penalties

SEASON 1993–94

Premier League

Sub+20	15/09/93	Odense BK	Away	ECW Cup	2–1		
Sub+21	19/09/93	Manchester United	Away	League	0–1		
Sub+22	21/09/93	Huddersfield Town	Away	Lge Cup	5–0		
Sub+23	29/09/93	Odense BK	Home	ECW Cup	1–1		
264	05/10/93	Huddersfield Town	Home	Lge Cup	1–1	1 Goal	(105)
265	16/10/93	Manchester City	Home	League	0–0		
266	23/10/93	Oldham Athletic	Away	League	0–0		
267	20/10/93	R Standard Liege	Home	ECW Cup	3–0		
268	26/10/93	Norwich City	Home	Lge Cup	1–1		

269	30/10/93	Norwich City	Home	League	0–0		
270	03/11/93	R Standard Liege	Away	ECW Cup	7–0	1 Goal	(106)
271	10/11/93	Norwich City	Away	Lge Cup	3–0		
272	20/11/93	Chelsea	Away	League	2–0	1 Goal	(107)
273	24/11/93	West Ham United	Away	League	0–0		
274	27/11/93	Newcastle United	Home	League	2–1	1 Goal	(108)
275	30/11/93	Aston Villa	Home	Lge Cup	0–1		
276	04/12/93	Coventry City	Away	League	0–1		
277	06/12/93	Tottenham Hotspur	Home	League	1–1		
278	12/12/93	Sheffield Wednesday	Home	League	1–0		
279	18/12/93	Leeds United	Away	League	1–2		
Sub+24	31/01/94	Bolton Wanderers	Away	FA Cup	2–2		
280	09/02/94	Bolton Wanderers	Home	FA Cup	1–3*	1 Goal	(109)
281	13/02/94	Norwich City	Away	League	1–1		
282	19/02/94	Everton	Away	League	1–1		
283	26/02/94	Blackburn Rovers	Home	League	1–0		
284	02/03/94	Torino Calcio	Away	ECW Cup	0–0		
285	05/03/94	Ipswich Town	Away	League	5–1		
286	15/03/94	Torino Calcio	Home	ECW Cup	1–0		
Sub+25	19/03/94	Southampton	Away	League	4–0		
287	22/03/94	Manchester United	Home	League	2–2		
Sub+26	26/03/94	Liverpool	Home	League	1–0		
288	29/03/94	Paris Saint–Germain FC	Away	ECW Cup	1–1		
289	02/04/94	Swindon Town	Home	League	1–1	1 Goal	(110)
290	04/04/94	Sheffield United	Away	League	1–1		
291	12/04/94	Paris Saint–Germain FC	Home	ECW Cup	1–0		
Sub+27	16/04/94	Chelsea	Home	League	1–0		
292	19/04/94	Wimbledon	Home	League	1–1		
293	23/04/94	Aston Villa	Away	League	2–1		
294	27/04/94	Queens Park Rangers	Away	League	1–1		
295	04/05/94	Parma AC	Neutral	ECW Cup	1–0	1 Goal	(111)
296	07/05/94	Newcastle United	Away	League	0–2		

SEASON 1994–95

Premier League

297	20/08/94	Manchester City	Home	League	3–0		
298	23/08/94	Leeds United	Away	League	0–1		
299	28/08/94	Liverpool	Away	League	0–3		
300	31/08/94	Blackburn Rovers	Home	League	0–0		
Sub+28	10/09/94	Norwich City	Away	League	0–0		
301	15/09/94	Omonia Nicosia	Away	ECW Cup	3–1		
302	18/09/94	Newcastle United	Home	League	2–3		
303	21/09/94	Hartlepool United	Away	Lge Cup	5–0	1 Goal	(112)
304	25/09/94	West Ham United	Away	League	2–0		
305	29/09/94	Omonia Nicosia	Home	ECW Cup	3–0		
306	01/10/94	Crystal Palace	Home	League	1–2		
307	08/10/94	Wimbledon	Away	League	3–1	1 Goal	(113)
308	15/10/94	Chelsea	Home	League	3–1		
309	20/10/94	Brondby IF	Away	ECW Cup	2–1	1 Goal	(114)
310	23/10/94	Coventry City	Home	League	2–1		
311	26/10/94	Oldham Athletic	Away	Lge Cup	0–0		
312	29/10/94	Everton	Away	League	1–1		
313	03/11/94	Brondby IF	Home	ECW Cup	2–2		
314	06/11/94	Sheffield Wednesday	Home	League	0–0		
315	26/11/94	Manchester United	Home	League	0–0		
316	30/11/94	Sheffield Wednesday	Home	Lge Cup	2–0		
317	12/12/94	Manchester City	Away	League	2–1	1 Goal	(115)
318	17/12/94	Leeds United	Home	League	1–3		
319	28/12/94	Ipswich Town	Away	League	2–0		
320	31/12/94	Queens Park Rangers	Home	League	1–3		
Sub+29	02/01/95	Tottenham Hotspur	Away	League	0–1		
321	07/01/95	Millwall	Away	FA Cup	0–0		

INTERNATIONAL APPEARANCES – ENGLAND

Sub 1	15/11/88	Saudi Arabia	Riyadh	1–0	F		
2	08/02/89	Greece	Athens	2–1	F		
Sub 3	08/03/89	Albania	Tirana	2–0	WCQ		
Sub 4	03/06/89	Poland	Wembley	3–0	WCQ		
5	01/05/91	Turkey	Izmir	1–0	ECQ		
6	21/05/91	USSR	Wembley	3–1	F		
7	25/05/91	Argentina	Wembley	2–2	F	1 Goal	(1)

8	11/09/91	Germany	Wembley	0–1	F		
9	16/10/91	Turkey	Wembley	1–0	ECQ	1 Goal	(2)
Sub 10	13/11/91	Poland	Poznan	1–1	ECQ		
Sub 11	12/05/92	Hungary	Budapest	1–0	F		
12	11/06/92	Denmark	Malmo	0–0	EC		
13	17/06/92	Sweden	Solna	0–0	EC		

APPEARANCES AND GOALS PER SEASON

SEASON 82–83	**GAMES**	**GOALS**
League	35+4	13
FA Cup	1	1
League Cup	1	0
TOTAL	**37+4**	**14**

SEASON 83–84	**GAMES**	**GOALS**
League	39+1	15
FA Cup	1	0
League Cup	1+1	1
TOTAL	**41+2**	**16**

SEASON 84–85	**GAMES**	**GOALS**
League	36+3	12
FA Cup	4	2
League Cup	2	1
TOTAL	**42+3**	**15**

SEASON 85–86	**GAMES**	**GOALS**
League	38+2	19
FA Cup	1	0
League Cup	1	0
TOTAL	**40+2**	**19**

SEASON 86–87	**GAMES**	**GOALS**
League	42	17
FA Cup	1	1
League Cup	3	2
TOTAL	**46**	**20**

SEASON 87–88	**GAMES**	**GOALS**
League	36+3	11
FA Cup	3	1
League Cup	8	4
TOTAL	**47+3**	**16**

SEASON 88–89	**GAMES**	**GOALS**
League	36	23
FA Cup	2	0
League Cup	5	2
Mercantile Credit Centenary Trophy	3	0
TOTAL	**46**	**25**

SEASON 89–90	**GAMES**	**GOALS**
League	37+1	10
FA Cup	2	0
League Cup	3+1	3
FA Charity Shield	1	0
TOTAL	**43+2**	**13**

SEASON 90–91	**GAMES**	**GOALS**
League	35+2	22
FA Cup	8	2
League Cup	4	3
TOTAL	**47+2**	**27**

SEASON 91–92	**GAMES**	**GOALS**
League	33+6	12
FA Cup	1	1
League Cup	2	0
European Cup	4	4
FA Charity Shield	1	0
TOTAL	**41+6**	**17**

SEASON 92–93	GAMES	GOALS
League	27+4	3
FA Cup	5+2	1
League Cup	7	2
TOTAL	**39+6**	**6**

SEASON 93–94	GAMES	GOALS
League	21+4	3
FA Cup	1+1	1
League Cup	4+1	1
European Cup Winners Cup	7+2	2
TOTAL	**33+8**	**7**

SEASON 94–95	GAMES	GOALS
League	17+2	2
FA Cup	1	0
League Cup	3	1
European Cup Winners Cup	4	1
TOTAL	**25+2**	**4**

CAREER APPEARANCES AND GOALS

COMPETITION	GAMES	TOTAL	GOALS
League	432+32	464	162
FA Cup	31+3	34	10
League Cup	44+3	47	20
Mercantile Credit Centenary Trophy	3	3	0
FA Charity Shield	2	2	0
European Cup	4	4	4
European Cup Winners Cup	11+2	13	3
Internationals	8+5	13	2
TOTAL	**535+45**	**580**	**201**

HAT-TRICKS

Leicester City

1	3	Wolverhampton Wanderers	10/12/83	Home	League	5–1

Arsenal

1	3	Portsmouth	29/08/87	Home	League	6–0
2	3	Wimbledon	27/08/88	Away	League	5–1
3	3	Manchester United	06/05/91	Home	League	3–1
4	4	FK Austria Wien	18/09/91	Home	Eur Cup	6–1

League: 4
European Cup: 1
TOTAL: 5

HONOURS

Winners medals
League Division One Championship: 88/89, 90/91
FA Cup: 92/93
European Cup Winners Cup: 93/94
Mercantile Centenary Credit Trophy: 88/89
FA Charity Shield: 91/92

Runner-up medals
League Cup: 87/88
FA Charity Shield: 89/90

PHIL STANT

Born: 13/10/62 – Bolton
Height: 6.1
Weight: 12.07 (96–97)

Clubs
Reading: **1982–83** – Matches: **4+1** – Goals: **2**
Hereford United: **1986–89** – Matches: **106+6** – Goals: **51**
Notts County: **1989–90** – Matches: **19+11** – Goals: **7**
Blackpool (loan): **1990** – Matches: **12** – Goals: **5**
Lincoln City (loan): **1990** – Matches: **4** – Goals: **0**

Huddersfield Town (loan): **1991** – Matches: **5** – Goals: **1**
Fulham: **1991** – Matches: **20** – Goals: **5**
Mansfield Town: **1991–92** – Matches: **64+1** – Goals: **33**
Cardiff City: **1992–95** – Matches: **105+3** – Goals: **56**
Mansfield Town (loan): **1993** – Matches: **5** – Goals: **2**
Bury: **1995–96** – Matches: **60+14** – Goals: **27**
Northampton Town (loan): **1996** – Matches: **4+1** – Goals: **2**
Lincoln City: **1996–97** – Matches: **23** – Goals: **16**

SEASON 1982–83

Reading – League Division Three

1	06/11/82	Newport County	Home	League	4–2	1 Goal	(1)
2	13/11/82	Walsall	Away	League	1–2	1 Goal	(2)
3	20/11/82	Bishop's Stortford	Home	FA Cup	1–2		
Sub+1	03/01/83	Oxford United	Home	League	0–3		
4	01/02/83	Plymouth Argyle	Away	League	0–3		

SEASON 1986–87

Hereford United – League Division Four

1	10/12/86	Newport County	Home	FR Trophy	4–0	3 Goals	(3)
2	13/12/86	Cambridge United	Home	League	2–3	1 Goal	(4)
3	19/12/86	Halifax Town	Away	League	1–2		
4	22/12/86	Port Vale	Away	FR Trophy	0–1		
5	03/01/87	Torquay United	Home	League	2–2		
Sub+1	28/01/87	Crewe Alexandra	Home	League	2–0		
Sub+2	07/02/87	Southend United	Home	League	0–1		
6	14/02/87	Orient	Away	League	0–2		
7	21/02/87	Cardiff City	Home	League	0–2		
8	03/03/87	Aldershot	Away	League	0–1		
9	14/03/87	Exeter City	Away	League	0–1		

SEASON 1987–88

League Division Four

Sub+3	29/08/87	Wolverhampton Wanderers	Home	League	1–2	1 Goal	(5)
Sub+4	12/09/87	Swansea City	Away	League	0–3		
10	16/09/87	Colchester United	Home	League	1–0	1 Goal	(6)
11	19/09/87	Darlington	Home	League	1–0		
Sub+5	27/09/87	Newport County	Away	League	0–0		
12	03/10/87	Halifax Town	Away	League	1–2		
13	07/10/87	Nottingham Forest	Home	Lge Cup	1–1	1 Goal	(7)
14	10/10/87	Cardiff City	Away	League	1–0		
15	28/10/87	Bristol Rovers	Away	SV Trophy	2–0		
16	17/10/87	Scunthorpe United	Home	League	2–3		
17	21/10/87	Scarborough	Home	League	1–1		
18	23/10/87	Stockport County	Away	League	2–0	1 Goal	(8)
19	03/11/87	Cambridge United	Away	League	1–0		
20	07/11/87	Crewe Alexandra	Home	League	1–1		
21	14/11/87	Barnet	Away	FA Cup	1–0	1 Goal	(9)
22	21/11/87	Torquay United	Away	League	0–1		
23	25/11/87	Torquay United	Home	SV Trophy	0–2		
24	28/11/87	Leyton Orient	Home	League	0–3		
25	30/11/87	Kidderminster Harriers	Home	Welsh Cup	0–3		
26	05/12/87	Colchester United	Away	FA Cup	2–3	1 Goal	(10)
27	12/12/87	Burnley	Away	League	0–0		
28	19/12/87	Hartlepool United	Home	League	4–2	2 Goals	(12)
29	26/12/87	Newport County	Home	League	4–2		
30	28/12/87	Wrexham	Away	League	0–0		
31	01/01/88	Wolverhampton Wanderers	Away	League	0–2		
32	02/01/88	Swansea City	Home	League	0–0		
33	09/01/88	Tranmere Rovers	Home	League	1–1		
34	17/01/88	Darlington	Away	League	1–3		
35	19/01/88	Newport County	Away	SV Trophy	3–2	1 Goal	(13)
36	30/01/88	Carlisle United	Home	League	2–0		
37	06/02/88	Bolton Wanderers	Away	League	0–1		
38	10/02/88	Brighton & Hove Albion	Home	SV Trophy	0–1*		
39	13/02/88	Wrexham	Home	League	0–2		
40	20/02/88	Rochdale	Away	League	1–3		
41	24/02/88	Peterborough United	Away	League	2–1	1 Goal	(14)
42	27/02/88	Halifax Town	Home	League	2–1		
43	05/03/88	Scunthorpe United	Away	League	0–3		
44	13/03/88	Cardiff City	Home	League	1–2	1 Goal	(15)
45	19/03/88	Exeter City	Away	League	2–2	1 Goal	(16)

46	26/03/88	Stockport County	Home	League	0–1		
47	01/04/88	Crewe Alexandra	Away	League	0–0		
48	04/04/88	Torquay United	Home	League	0–0		
49	09/04/88	Scarborough	Away	League	1–2		
50	19/04/88	Colchester United	Away	League	0–1		
51	30/04/88	Leyton Orient	Away	League	0–4		
52	02/05/88	Burnley	Home	League	2–1		
53	07/05/88	Hartlepool United ·	Away	League	2–1	1 Goal	(17)

SEASON 1988–89

League Division Four

54	27/08/88	Scunthorpe United	Away	League	1–3		
55	29/08/88	Plymouth Argyle	Home	Lge Cup	0–3		
56	03/09/88	Cambridge United	Home	League	4–2	1 Goal	(18)
57	06/09/88	Plymouth Argyle	Away	Lge Cup	2–3	1 Goal	(19)
58	10/09/88	Leyton Orient	Away	League	3–1	2 Goals	(21)
59	17/09/88	Scarborough	Home	League	1–3	1 Goal	(22)
60	21/09/88	Crewe Alexandra	Home	League	0–1		
61	24/09/88	Lincoln City	Away	League	0–2		
62	01/10/88	Grimsby Town	Home	League	2–1	1 Goal	(23)
63	04/10/88	Doncaster Rovers	Away	League	2–3	2 Goals	(25)
64	26/10/88	Rochdale	Home	League	4–4	3 Goals	(28)
65	29/10/88	Hartlepool United	Home	League	1–1		
66	05/11/88	Wrexham	Home	League	0–0		
67	07/11/88	Tranmere Rovers	Away	League	0–1		
68	12/11/88	Halifax Town	Home	League	3–1	1 Goal	(29)
69	15/11/88	Rhos Aelwyd	Away	Welsh Cup	4–0	2 Goals	(31)
70	19/11/88	Cardiff City	Away	FA Cup	0–3		
71	21/11/88	Port Vale	Away	SV Trophy	1–1		
72	26/11/88	Rotherham United	Home	League	1–1	1 Goal	(32)
73	30/11/88	Wolverhampton Wanderers	Home	SV Trophy	2–2		
74	03/12/88	York City	Away	League	1–4	1 Goal	(33)
75	17/12/88	Burnley	Home	League	0–0		
76	26/12/88	Exeter City	Away	League	1–3	1 Goal	(34)
77	31/12/88	Darlington	Away	League	0–0		
78	02/01/89	Torquay United	Home	League	1–1	1 Goal	(35)
79	07/01/89	Bethesda Athletic	Away	Welsh Cup	2–0		
80	14/01/89	Cambridge United	Away	League	1–2	1 Goal	(36)
81	18/01/89	Reading	Away	SV Trophy	3–2	2 Goals	(38)
82	21/01/89	Scunthorpe United	Home	League	1–2		
83	28/01/89	Scarborough	Away	League	2–0		
84	04/02/89	Crewe Alexandra	Away	League	1–2	1 Goal	(39)
85	07/02/89	Newport County	Away	Welsh Cup	1–0		
86	11/02/89	Lincoln City	Home	League	3–2	1 Goal	(40)
87	14/02/89	Colchester United	Away	SV Trophy	1–0	1 Goal	(41)
88	18/02/89	Carlisle United	Away	League	0–3		
89	25/02/89	Stockport County	Home	League	2–1	1 Goal	(42)
90	28/02/89	Rochdale	Away	League	2–2		
91	04/03/89	Peterborough United	Home	League	4–0	3 Goals	(45)
92	06/03/89	Kidderminster Harriers	Away	Welsh Cup	0–1		
93	11/03/89	Wrexham	Away	League	1–1		
94	15/03/89	Hartlepool United	Home	League	2–0	1 Goal	(46)
95	18/03/89	Leyton Orient	Home	League	1–1		
96	22/03/89	Wolverhampton Wanderers	Home	SV Trophy	0–2		
97	25/03/89	Torquay United	Away	League	0–1		
98	27/03/89	Exeter City	Home	League	1–0		
99	01/04/89	Burnley	Away	League	3–3		
100	08/04/89	Darlington	Home	League	1–1	1 Goal	(47)
101	12/04/89	Colchester United	Home	League	1–1		
102	15/04/89	Grimsby Town	Away	League	1–1		
103	19/04/89	Kidderminster Harriers	Home	Welsh Cup	0–1		
Sub+6	22/04/89	Doncaster Rovers	Home	League	3–1	1 Goal	(48)
104	01/05/89	Tranmere Rovers	Home	League	2–1	1 Goal	(49)
105	06/05/89	York City	Home	League	1–2	1 Goal	(50)
106	13/05/89	Halifax Town	Away	League	2–2	1 Goal	(51)

SEASON 1989–90

Notts County – League Division Three

1	19/08/89	Leyton Orient	Away	League	1–0	1 Goal	(1)
2	22/08/89	Shrewsbury Town	Away	Lge Cup	0–3		
3	26/08/89	Blackpool	Home	League	0–1		
4	29/08/89	Shrewsbury Town	Home	Lge Cup	3–1	1 Goal	(2)
5	02/09/89	Bristol Rovers	Away	League	2–3		

6	09/09/89	Reading	Home	League	0–0		
7	15/09/89	Chester City	Away	League	3–3		
Sub+1	30/09/89	Swansea City	Away	League	0–0		
Sub+2	17/10/89	Bristol City	Away	League	0–2		
Sub+3	28/10/89	Northampton Town	Away	League	0–0		
Sub+4	31/10/89	Brentford	Home	League	3–1		
Sub+5	04/11/89	Mansfield Town	Away	League	3–1		
Sub+6	11/11/89	Wigan Athletic	Home	League	1–1		
Sub+7	18/11/89	Doncaster Rovers	Away	FA Cup	0–1		
8	25/11/89	Huddersfield Town	Away	League	2–1		
9	28/11/89	Fulham	Away	LD Cup	1–0		
10	02/12/89	Fulham	Home	League	2–0		
11	12/12/89	Peterborough United	Home	LD Cup	2–2		
12	16/12/89	Cardiff City	Away	League	3–1	2 Goals	(4)
13	26/12/89	Shrewsbury Town	Home	League	4–0	2 Goals	(6)
14	30/12/89	Birmingham City	Home	League	3–2		
15	01/01/90	Crewe Alexandra	Away	League	0–1		
16	06/01/90	Bury	Home	League	0–4		
17	21/02/90	Hereford United	Away	LD Cup	1–1+		
Sub+8	28/03/90	Bristol Rovers	Away	LD Cup	0–1		
Sub+9	31/03/90	Preston North End	Away	League	4–2		
Sub+10	02/04/90	Bristol Rovers	Home	LD Cup	0–0		
Sub+11	07/04/90	Brentford	Away	League	1–0		
18	10/04/90	Northampton Town	Home	League	3–2	1 Goal	(7)
19	14/04/90	Crewe Alexandra	Home	League	2–0		

+ AET Notts County won 4–3 on penalties

SEASON 1990–91

Blackpool (loan) – League Division Four

1	08/09/90	Northampton Town	Away	League	0–1		
2	15/09/90	Wrexham	Home	League	4–1	1 Goal	(1)
3	18/09/90	Burnley	Home	League	1–2	1 Goal	(2)
4	22/09/90	Chesterfield	Away	League	2–2		
5	29/09/90	Hartlepool United	Home	League	2–0		
6	03/10/90	Scarborough	Away	League	1–0		
7	06/10/90	Torquay United	Away	League	1–2	1 Goal	(3)
8	13/10/90	Darlington	Home	League	1–2		
9	20/10/90	Gillingham	Home	League	2–0	1 Goal	(4)
10	22/10/90	Stockport County	Away	League	0–0		
11	27/10/90	Halifax Town	Away	League	3–5	1 Goal	(5)
12	03/11/90	Walsall	Home	League	1–2		

Lincoln City (loan) – League Division Four

1	24/11/90	Darlington	Home	League	0–3	
2	01/12/90	Scarborough	Home	League	2–0	
3	15/12/90	Hartlepool United	Away	League	0–2	
4	22/12/90	Gillingham	Home	League	1–1	

Huddersfield Town (loan) – League Division Three

1	05/01/91	Tranmere Rovers	Away	League	0–2		
2	12/01/91	Swansea City	Home	League	1–2	1 Goal	(1)
3	19/01/91	Southend United	Away	League	1–0		
4	26/01/91	Fulham	Home	League	1–0		
5	02/02/91	Grimsby Town	Home	League	1–1		

Fulham – League Division Three

1	05/02/91	Preston North End	Home	League	1–0	1 Goal	(1)
2	16/02/91	Tranmere Rovers	Away	League	1–1	1 Goal	(2)
3	19/02/91	Mansfield Town	Away	LD Cup	1–2		
4	23/02/91	Southend United	Home	League	0–3		
5	02/03/91	Reading	Home	League	1–1	1 Goal	(3)
6	09/03/91	Bolton Wanderers	Away	League	0–3		
7	12/03/91	Birmingham City	Away	League	0–2		
8	16/03/91	AFC Bournemouth	Home	League	1–1		
9	19/03/91	Stoke City	Home	League	0–1		
10	30/03/91	Bradford City	Away	League	0–0		
11	01/04/91	Mansfield Town	Home	League	1–0	1 Goal	(4)
12	06/04/91	Chester City	Away	League	0–1		
13	09/04/91	Shrewsbury Town	Home	League	4–0		
14	13/04/91	Grimsby Town	Home	League	0–0		
15	16/04/91	Brentford	Away	League	2–1	1 Goal	(5)
16	20/04/91	Swansea City	Home	League	1–1		
17	23/04/91	Brentford	Home	League	0–1		

18	27/04/91	Bury	Away	League	1–1		
19	04/05/91	Exeter City	Away	League	1–0		
20	11/05/91	Leyton Orient	Home	League	1–1		

SEASON 1991–92

Mansfield Town – League Division Four

1	17/08/91	Scarborough	Away	League	0–0		
2	20/08/91	Blackpool	Home	Lge Cup	0–3		
3	24/08/91	Barnet	Home	League	1–2		
4	27/08/91	Blackpool	Away	Lge Cup	2–4		
5	31/08/91	Chesterfield	Away	League	2–0		
Sub+1	07/09/91	Blackpool	Home	League	1–1		
6	13/09/91	Crewe Alexandra	Away	League	2–1	1 Goal	(1)
7	17/09/91	Carlisle United	Away	League	2–1	1 Goal	(2)
8	27/09/91	Halifax Town	Away	League	3–1	1 Goal	(3)
9	05/10/91	Maidstone United	Home	League	2–0	1 Goal	(4)
10	12/10/91	Rochdale	Away	League	2–0	1 Goal	(5)
11	15/10/91	Wrexham	Away	A Trophy	0–1		
12	19/10/91	Cardiff City	Home	League	3–0		
13	26/10/91	Scunthorpe United	Away	League	4–1	1 Goal	(6)
14	02/11/91	Doncaster Rovers	Home	League	2–2	2 Goals	(8)
15	05/11/91	Northampton Town	Away	League	2–1		
16	09/11/91	Burnley	Away	League	2–3		
17	23/11/91	Gillingham	Home	League	4–3	2 Goals	(10)
18	27/11/91	Preston North End	Home	FA Cup	0–1		
19	30/11/91	Walsall	Home	League	3–1	2 Goals	(12)
20	21/12/91	Barnet	Away	League	0–2		
21	26/12/91	Scarborough	Home	League	1–2		
22	28/12/91	Chesterfield	Home	League	2–1	1 Goal	(13)
23	01/01/92	Wrexham	Away	League	2–3		
24	04/01/92	York City	Away	League	2–1		
25	18/01/92	Rotherham United	Away	League	1–1		
26	31/01/92	Cardiff City	Away	League	2–3	1 Goal	(14)
27	04/02/92	Peterborough United	Home	A Trophy	0–3		
28	08/02/92	Scunthorpe United	Home	League	1–3		
29	11/02/92	Walsall	Away	League	3–3	1 Goal	(15)
30	15/02/92	Hereford United	Home	League	1–1		
31	29/02/92	York City	Home	League	5–2	2 Goals	(17)
32	03/03/92	Rotherham United	Home	League	1–0	1 Goal	(18)
33	07/03/92	Lincoln City	Away	League	0–2		
34	10/03/92	Northampton Town	Home	League	2–0	1 Goal	(19)
35	14/03/92	Doncaster Rovers	Away	League	1–0		
36	21/03/92	Burnley	Home	League	0–1		
37	24/03/92	Lincoln City	Home	League	0–0		
38	28/03/92	Gillingham	Away	League	0–2		
39	31/03/92	Crewe Alexandra	Home	League	4–3	2 Goals	(21)
40	04/04/92	Blackpool	Away	League	1–2	1 Goal	(22)
41	11/04/92	Carlisle United	Home	League	2–1		
42	21/04/92	Halifax Town	Home	League	3–2	3 Goals	(25)
43	25/04/92	Maidstone United	Away	League	0–0		
44	02/05/92	Rochdale	Home	League	2–1	1 Goal	(26)

SEASON 1992–93

Football League Division Two

45	15/08/92	Plymouth Argyle	Home	League	0–0		
46	19/08/92	Newcastle United	Away	Lge Cup	1–2	1 Goal	(27)
47	22/08/92	Swansea City	Away	League	0–4		
48	25/08/92	Newcastle United	Home	Lge Cup	0–0		
49	29/08/92	Fulham	Home	League	2–3	2 Goals	(29)
50	01/09/92	AFC Bournemouth	Home	League	0–2		
51	05/09/92	Blackpool	Away	League	1–1		
52	12/09/92	Bradford City	Home	League	5–2		
53	15/09/92	Chester City	Away	League	2–1	1 Goal	(30)
54	19/09/92	Burnley	Away	League	0–1		
55	26/09/92	Stoke City	Home	League	0–4		
56	03/10/92	Wigan Athletic	Away	League	0–2		
57	10/10/92	Stockport County	Home	League	2–0		
58	17/10/92	Exeter City	Away	League	0–2		
59	24/10/92	Preston North End	Home	League	2–2	1 Goal	(31)
60	31/10/92	Rotherham United	Away	League	0–2		
61	03/11/92	Hull City	Home	League	3–1	1 Goal	(32)

62	07/11/92	Huddersfield Town	Away	League	1–2	1 Goal	(33)
63	14/11/92	Shrewsbury Town	Away	FA Cup	1–3		
64	28/11/92	Leyton Orient	Away	League	1–5		

Cardiff City – Football League Division Three

1	08/12/92	Hereford United	Home	A Trophy	3–2	1 Goal	(1)
2	11/12/92	Doncaster Rovers	Away	League	1–0		
3	18/12/92	Wrexham	Home	League	1–2		
4	26/12/92	York City	Home	League	3–3	2 Goals	(3)
5	28/12/92	Lincoln City	Away	League	2–3		
6	02/01/93	Hereford United	Home	League	2–1	1 Goal	(4)
7	09/01/93	Carlisle United	Away	League	2–1		
8	16/01/93	Maesteg Park Athletic	Home	Welsh Cup	4–0	3 Goals	(7)
9	18/01/93	Swansea City	Home	A Trophy	1–2*		
10	23/01/93	Gillingham	Away	League	1–0		
11	26/01/93	Halifax Town	Away	League	1–0	1 Goal	(8)
12	30/01/93	Walsall	Home	League	2–1	1 Goal	(9)
13	06/02/93	Darlington	Away	League	2–0		
14	13/02/93	Torquay United	Home	League	4–0	2 Goals	(11)
15	19/02/93	Northampton Town	Away	League	2–1	1 Goal	(12)
16	27/02/93	Crewe Alexandra	Home	League	1–1		
17	09/03/93	Scarborough	Home	League	1–0	1 Goal	(13)
18	12/03/93	Colchester United	Away	League	4–2		
19	16/03/93	Wrexham	Home	Welsh Cup	2–0		
20	20/03/93	Chesterfield	Home	League	2–1		
21	23/03/93	Bury	Away	League	0–1		
22	27/03/93	Barnet	Home	League	1–1		
23	03/04/93	Scarborough	Away	League	3–1	1 Goal	(14)
24	06/04/93	Doncaster Rovers	Home	League	1–1		
25	10/04/93	York City	Away	League	1–3		
26	12/04/93	Lincoln City	Home	League	3–1	1 Goal	(15)
27	17/04/93	Wrexham	Away	League	2–0		
28	20/04/93	Wrexham	Away	Welsh Cup	0–1		
29	08/05/93	Scunthorpe United	Away	League	3–0	1 Goal	(16)
30	16/05/93	Rhyl	Neutral	Welsh Cup	5–0	3 Goals	(19)

SEASON 1993–94

Mansfield Town (loan) – Football League Division Three

1	14/08/93	Shrewsbury Town	Home	League	1–0		
2	24/08/93	Stoke City	Home	Lge Cup	1–3	1 Goal	(1)
3	28/08/93	Scunthorpe United	Home	League	0–1		
4	31/08/93	Chesterfield	Away	League	2–0		
5	04/09/93	Crewe Alexandra	Away	League	1–2	1 Goal	(2)

Cardiff City – Football League Division Two

31	11/09/93	Hull City	Home	League	3–4		
32	15/09/93	Standard Liege	Away	ECW Cup	2–5		
33	18/09/93	Blackpool	Away	League	0–1		
34	25/09/93	Plymouth Argyle	Home	League	2–3	1 Goal	(20)
35	28/09/93	Standard Liege	Home	ECW Cup	1–3		
36	02/10/93	York City	Away	League	0–5		
37	10/10/93	Barnet	Away	League	0–0		
Sub+1	16/10/93	Bristol Rovers	Home	League	1–2		
Sub+2	23/10/93	Wrexham	Away	League	1–3		
38	26/10/93	Afan Lido	Home	Welsh Cup	2–0		
39	30/10/93	Hartlepool United	Home	League	2–2		
40	02/11/93	Brentford	Away	League	1–1		
41	06/11/93	Stockport County	Home	League	3–1		
42	09/11/93	Torquay United	Home	A Trophy	2–0	1 Goal	(21)
43	13/11/93	Enfield	Away	FA Cup	0–0		
44	19/11/93	Cambridge United	Away	League	1–1		
45	27/11/93	Bradford City	Home	League	1–1	1 Goal	(22)
46	30/11/93	Enfield	Home	FA Cup	1–0		
47	04/12/93	Brentford	Away	FA Cup	3–1	1 Goal	(23)
48	07/12/93	Wrexham	Away	Welsh Cup	2–0	1 Goal	(24)
49	11/12/93	Fulham	Home	League	1–0		
50	14/12/93	Wycombe Wanderers	Away	A Trophy	2–3*	1 Goal	(25)
51	18/12/93	Leyton Orient	Away	League	2–2	1 Goal	(26)
52	22/12/93	Swansea City	Home	League	1–0		
53	01/01/94	Reading	Home	League	3–0		
54	03/01/94	Rotherham United	Away	League	2–5		
55	08/01/94	Middlesbrough	Home	FA Cup	2–2	1 Goal	(27)
56	15/01/94	Bristol Rovers	Away	League	1–2		

57	19/01/94	Middlesbrough	Away	FA Cup	2–1*	1 Goal	(28)
Sub+3	20/02/94	Luton Town	Home	FA Cup	1–2	1 Goal	(29)
58	22/02/94	Ebbw Vale	Home	Welsh Cup	3–0	1 Goal	(30)
59	01/03/94	Burnley	Home	League	2–1	1 Goal	(31)
60	05/03/94	Hull City	Away	League	0–1		
61	12/03/94	Blackpool	Home	League	0–2		
62	19/03/94	Plymouth Argyle	Away	League	2–1	2 Goals	(33)
63	22/03/94	Hartlepool United	Away	League	0–3		
64	26/03/94	York City	Home	League	0–0		
65	29/03/94	Rotherham United	Home	League	1–0		
66	04/04/94	Huddersfield Town	Home	League	2–2		
67	09/04/94	Reading	Away	League	1–1		
68	12/04/94	Brighton & Hove Albion	Away	League	5–3	1 Goal	(34)
69	14/04/94	Swansea City	Away	Welsh Cup	2–1	2 Goals	(36)
70	16/04/94	Brentford	Home	League	1–1		
71	19/04/94	Huddersfield Town	Away	League	0–2		
72	21/04/94	AFC Bournemouth	Home	League	2–1	1 Goal	(37)
73	23/04/94	Stockport County	Away	League	2–2	1 Goal	(38)
74	26/04/94	Exeter City	Home	League	2–0		
75	28/04/94	Swansea City	Home	Welsh Cup	4–1	1 Goal	(39)
76	30/04/94	Cambridge United	Home	League	2–7		
77	03/05/94	Port Vale	Home	League	1–3	1 Goal	(40)
78	07/05/94	Bradford City	Away	League	0–2		
79	15/05/94	Barry Town	Neutral	Welsh Cup	1–2	1 Goal	(41)

SEASON 1994–95

Football League Division Two

80	13/08/94	Stockport County	Away	League	1–4	1 Goal	(42)
81	16/08/94	Torquay United	Home	Lge Cup	1–0		
82	20/08/94	Oxford United	Home	Lge	1–3	1 Goal	(43)
83	23/08/94	Torquay United	Away	Lge Cup	2–4	2 Goals	(45)
84	10/09/94	Blackpool	Away	League	1–2		
85	13/09/94	Chester City	Away	League	2–0	1 Goal	(46)
86	01/10/94	Peterborough United	Home	League	1–2		
87	08/10/94	Crewe Alexandra	Home	League	1–2	1 Goal	(47)
88	15/10/94	Bristol Rovers	Away	League	2–2		
89	22/10/94	Cambridge United	Home	League	3–1	3 Goals	(50)
90	30/10/94	Bradford City	Away	League	3–2	1 Goal	(51)
91	01/11/94	Leyton Orient	Away	League	0–2		
92	05/11/94	Brighton & Hove Albion	Home	League	3–0	2 Goals	(53)
93	07/11/94	Ebbw Vale	Away	Welsh Cup	1–1		
94	12/11/94	Enfield	Away	FA Cup	0–1		
95	15/11/94	Exeter City	Away	AW Shield	1–1		
96	19/11/94	Wycombe Wanderers	Away	League	1–3	1 Goal	(54)
97	22/11/94	Ebbw Vale	Home	Welsh Cup	2–0+		
98	25/11/94	Hull City	Home	League	0–2		
99	29/11/94	Exeter City	Away	AW Shield	0–1		
100	10/12/94	Oxford United	Away	League	0–1		
101	17/12/94	Stockport County	Home	League	1–1		
102	26/12/94	Shrewsbury Town	Away	League	1–0	1 Goal	(55)
103	28/12/94	Birmingham City	Home	League	0–1		
104	31/12/94	Rotherham United	Away	League	0–2		
105	02/01/95	Brentford	Home	League	2–3	1 Goal	(56)

+ Match replayed after Cardiff City fielded an ineligible player

Bury – Football League Division Three

Sub+1	04/02/95	Fulham	Away	League	0–1		
1	18/02/95	Hereford United	Away	League	0–1		
2	25/02/95	Colchester United	Home	League	4–1	1 Goal	(1)
3	28/02/95	Torquay United	Home	League	3–1	1 Goal	(2)
4	04/03/95	Chesterfield	Away	League	0–0		
5	07/03/95	Northampton Town	Away	League	5–0	1 Goal	(3)
6	11/03/95	Scunthorpe United	Away	League	2–3		
7	14/03/95	Barnet	Home	League	3–0	1 Goal	(4)
8	18/03/95	Preston North End	Away	League	0–5		
9	21/03/95	Scarborough	Away	League	2–1		
10	25/03/95	Mansfield Town	Home	League	2–2		
11	01/04/95	Doncaster Rovers	Away	League	2–1	2 Goals	(6)
12	04/04/95	Gillingham	Away	League	1–1		
13	08/04/95	Torquay United	Away	League	2–2	2 Goals	(8)
14	15/04/95	Carlisle United	Home	League	2–0	1 Goal	(9)
15	18/04/95	Wigan Athletic	Away	League	3–0	2 Goals	(11)

16	22/04/95	Northampton Town	Home	League	5–0		
17	29/04/95	Lincoln City	Away	League	3–0	1 Goal	(12)
18	04/05/95	Walsall	Home	League	0–0		
19	06/05/95	Darlington	Home	League	2–1	1 Goal	(13)
20	14/05/95	Preston North End	Away	Lge P/O	1–0		
21	17/05/95	Preston North End	Home	Lge P/O	1–0		
22	27/05/95	Chesterfield	Wembley	Lge P/O	0–2		

SEASON 1995–96

Football League Division Three

23	12/08/95	Northampton Town	Away	League	1–4	1 Goal	(14)
24	15/08/95	Chesterfield	Away	Lge Cup	1–0	1 Goal	(15)
25	19/08/95	Chester City	Home	League	1–1	1 Goal	(16)
26	26/08/95	Hereford United	Away	League	4–3		
27	29/08/95	Preston North End	Home	League	0–0		
28	02/09/95	Plymouth Argyle	Home	League	0–5		
29	05/09/95	Chesterfield	Home	Lge Cup	2–1		
30	09/09/95	Wigan Athletic	Away	League	2–1	1 Goal	(17)
31	12/09/95	Lincoln City	Away	League	2–2		
32	16/09/95	Cambridge United	Home	League	1–2		
33	20/09/95	Sheffield United	Away	Lge Cup	1–2	1 Goal	(18)
34	23/09/95	Barnet	Home	League	0–0		
35	30/09/95	Gillingham	Away	League	0–3		
36	03/10/95	Sheffield United	Home	Lge Cup	4–2	2 Goals	(20)
37	07/10/95	Leyton Orient	Home	League	2–1		
38	14/10/95	Fulham	Away	League	0–0		
39	17/10/95	Scunthorpe United	Away	AW Shield	0–4		
40	21/10/95	Scarborough	Home	League	0–2		
41	28/10/95	Mansfield Town	Away	League	5–1	4 Goals	(24)
42	31/10/95	Torquay United	Away	League	2–0	1 Goal	(25)
43	04/11/95	Darlington	Home	League	0–0		
44	07/11/95	Reading	Away	Lge Cup	1–2		
45	11/11/95	Blyth Spartans	Home	FA Cup	0–2		
46	14/11/95	Wigan Athletic	Home	AW Shield	0–0		
47	18/11/95	Cardiff City	Away	League	1–0		
48	25/11/95	Exeter City	Home	League	2–0		
49	09/12/95	Barnet	Away	League	0–0		
50	16/12/95	Gillingham	Home	League	1–0		
51	23/12/95	Colchester United	Home	League	0–0		
52	01/01/96	Hartlepool United	Home	League	0–3		
53	06/01/96	Doncaster Rovers	Home	League	4–1	1 Goal	(26)
54	13/01/96	Chester City	Away	League	1–1		
55	20/01/96	Northampton Town	Home	League	0–1		
Sub+2	16/03/96	Rochdale	Home	League	1–1		
56	19/03/96	Hereford United	Home	League	2–0		
Sub+3	02/04/96	Fulham	Home	League	3–0		
Sub+4	06/04/96	Mansfield Town	Home	League	0–2		
Sub+5	09/04/96	Scarborough	Away	League	2–0		
Sub+6	13/04/96	Torquay United	Home	League	1–0		
Sub+7	20/04/96	Darlington	Away	League	0–4		
57	27/04/96	Exeter City	Away	League	1–1		
Sub+8	04/05/96	Cardiff City	Home	League	3–0		

SEASON 1996–97

Football League Division Two

Sub+9	31/08/96	Bristol City	Home	League	4–0		
Sub+10	14/09/96	Shrewsbury Town	Away	League	1–1		
Sub+11	17/09/96	Crystal Palace	Home	Lge Cup	1–3		
Sub+12	21/09/96	Luton Town	Home	League	0–0		
Sub+13	05/10/96	Blackpool	Home	League	1–0		
Sub+14	19/10/96	Watford	Home	League	1–1		
58	26/10/96	Bristol Rovers	Home	League	2–1	1 Goal	(27)
59	29/10/96	Wrexham	Away	League	1–1		
60	02/11/96	AFC Bournemouth	Away	League	1–1		

Northampton Town (loan) – Football League Division Three

1	23/11/96	Rochdale	Home	League	2–2		
Sub+1	30/11/96	Darlington	Away	League	1–3		
2	03/12/96	Hull City	Home	League	2–1	2 Goals	(2)
3	14/12/96	Lincoln City	Away	League	1–1		
4	20/12/96	Hereford United	Home	League	1–0		

Lincoln City – Football League Division Three

1	26/12/96	Hull City	Away	League	1–2	1 Goal	(1)
2	11/01/97	Cardiff City	Away	League	3–1	1 Goal	(2)
3	14/01/97	Blackpool	Away	AW Shield	0–4		
4	18/01/97	Brighton & Hove Albion	Home	League	2–1	1 Goal	(3)
5	25/01/97	Doncaster Rovers	Home	League	3–2	2 Goals	(5)
6	28/01/97	Chester City	Home	League	0–0		
7	01/02/97	Darlington	Away	League	2–5		
8	04/02/96	Wigan Athletic	Home	League	1–3		
9	08/02/97	Fulham	Home	League	2–0	1 Goal	(6)
10	15/02/97	Mansfield Town	Away	League	2–2	1 Goal	(7)
11	22/02/97	Hereford United	Home	League	3–3	1 Goal	(8)
12	25/02/97	Barnet	Away	League	0–1		
13	01/03/97	Carlisle United	Away	League	0–1		
14	08/03/97	Hartlepool United	Home	League	2–1		
15	15/03/97	Northampton Town	Away	League	1–1		
16	22/03/97	Leyton Orient	Away	League	3–2	1 Goal	(9)
17	29/03/97	Torquay United	Home	League	1–2		
18	31/03/97	Cambridge United	Away	League	3–1	1 Goal	(10)
19	05/04/97	Swansea City	Home	League	4–0	2 Goals	(12)
20	12/04/97	Exeter City	Away	League	3–3	1 Goal	(13)
21	19/04/97	Scunthorpe United	Home	League	2–0	1 Goal	(14)
22	26/04/97	Scarborough	Away	League	2–0	2 Goals	(16)
23	03/05/97	Rochdale	Home	League	0–2		

APPEARANCES AND GOALS PER SEASON

SEASON 82–83	**GAMES**	**GOALS**
League	3+1	2
FA Cup	1	0
TOTAL	**4+1**	**2**

SEASON 83–84
No Competitive Matches

SEASON 84–85
No Competitive Matches

SEASON 85–86
No Competitive Matches

SEASON 86–87	**GAMES**	**GOALS**
League	7+2	1
Freight Rover Trophy	2	3
TOTAL	**9+2**	**4**

SEASON 87–88	**GAMES**	**GOALS**
League	36+3	9
FA Cup	2	2
League Cup	1	1
Sherpa Van Trophy	4	1
Welsh Cup	1	0
TOTAL	**44+3**	**13**

SEASON 88–89	**GAMES**	**GOALS**
League	40+1	28
FA Cup	1	0
League Cup	2	1
Sherpa Van Trophy	5	3
Welsh Cup	5	2
TOTAL	**53+1**	**34**

SEASON 89–90	**GAMES**	**GOALS**
League	14+8	6
FA Cup	0+1	0
League Cup	2	1
Leyland Daf Cup	3+2	0
TOTAL	**19+11**	**7**

SEASON 90–91	**GAMES**	**GOALS**
League	40	11
Leyland Daf Cup	1	0
TOTAL	**41**	**11**

SEASON 91–92	GAMES	GOALS
League	39+1	26
FA Cup	1	0
League Cup	2	0
Autoglass Trophy	2	0
TOTAL	**44+1**	**26**

SEASON 92–93	GAMES	GOALS
League	41	18
FA Cup	1	0
League Cup	2	1
Autoglass Trophy	2	1
Welsh Cup	4	6
TOTAL	**50**	**26**

SEASON 93–94	GAMES	GOALS
League	38+2	11
FA Cup	5+1	4
League Cup	1	1
Autoglass Trophy	2	2
Welsh Cup	6	6
European Cup Winners Cup	2	0
TOTAL	**54+3**	**24**

SEASON 94–95	GAMES	GOALS
League	38+1	26
League Play–offs	3	0
FA Cup	1	0
League Cup	2	2
Auto Windscreens Shield	2	0
Welsh Cup	2	0
TOTAL	**48+1**	**28**

SEASON 95–96	GAMES	GOALS
League	27+7	9
FA Cup	1	0
League Cup	5	4
Auto Windscreens Shield	2	0
TOTAL	**35+7**	**13**

SEASON 96–97	GAMES	GOALS
League	29+6	19
League Cup	0+1	0
Auto Windscreens Shield	1	0
TOTAL	**30+7**	**19**

CAREER APPEARANCES AND GOALS

COMPETITION	GAMES	TOTAL	GOALS
League	352+32	384	166
League Play–offs	3	3	0
FA Cup	13+2	15	6
League Cup	17+1	18	11
Freight Rover Trophy	2	2	3
Sherpa Van Trophy	9	9	4
Leyland Daf Cup	4+2	6	0
Autoglass Trophy	6	6	3
Auto Windscreens Shield	5	5	0
Welsh Cup	18	18	14
European Cup Winners Cup	2	2	0
TOTAL	**431+37**	**468**	**207**

HAT-TRICKS

Hereford United

1	3	Newport County	10/12/86	Home	FR Trophy	4–0
2	3	Rochdale	26/10/88	Home	League	4–4
3	3	Peterborough United	04/03/89	Home	League	4–0

Mansfield Town

1	3	Halifax Town	21/04/92	Home	League	3–2

Cardiff City

1	3	Maesteg Park Athletic	16/01/93	Home	Welsh Cup	4–0
2	3	Rhyl	16/05/93	Neutral	Welsh Cup	5–0
3	3	Cambridge United	22/10/94	Home	League	3–1

Bury

1	4	Mansfield Town	28/10/95	Away	League	5–1

League: 5
Freight Rover Trophy: 1
Welsh Cup: 2
TOTAL: 8

HONOURS

Winners medals
Football League Division Three Championship: 92/93
Welsh Cup: 92/93

Runner-up medals
Welsh Cup 93/94
Promoted to League Division Two: 89/90
Promoted to League Division Three: 91/92
Promoted to Football League Division Two: 95/96

BOB TAYLOR

Born: 03/02/67 – Horden
Height: 5.10
Weight: 12.00 (96–97)

Clubs
Leeds United: **1986–89** – Matches: **43+11** – Goals: **13**
Bristol City: **1989–92** – Matches: **114+12** – Goals: **58**
West Bromwich Albion: **1992–97** – Matches: **235+28** – Goals: **110**

SEASON 1985–86

Leeds United – League Division Two

1	12/04/86	Millwall	Home	League	3–1	
2	19/04/86	Crystal Palace	Away	League	0–3	

SEASON 1986–87

League Division Two

3	23/09/86	Oldham Athletic	Away	Lge Cup	2–3	1 Goal	(1)
4	01/10/86	Bradford City	Home	FM Cup	0–1*		
Sub+1	08/10/86	Oldham Athletic	Home	Lge Cup	0–1		
5	15/11/86	Oldham Athletic	Home	League	0–2		
6	21/11/86	Birmingham City	Away	League	1–2		
7	25/05/87	Charlton Athletic	Home	Lge P/O	1–0		

SEASON 1987–88

League Division Two

8	16/08/87	Barnsley	Away	League	1–1	1 Goal	(2)
9	19/08/87	Leicester City	Home	League	1–0		
10	29/08/87	Bradford City	Away	League	0–0		
11	31/08/87	West Bromwich Albion	Home	League	0–0		
12	05/09/87	Ipswich Town	Away	League	0–1		
13	19/09/87	Middlesbrough	Away	League	0–2		
14	23/09/87	York City	Home	Lge Cup	1–1		
15	26/09/87	Manchester City	Home	League	2–0		
16	30/09/87	Stoke City	Home	League	0–0		
Sub+2	03/10/87	Blackburn Rovers	Away	League	1–1	1 Goal	(3)

17	06/10/87	York City	Away	Lge Cup	4–0	1 Goal	(4)
18	10/10/87	Aston Villa	Home	League	1–3	1 Goal	(5)
19	17/10/87	Plymouth Argyle	Away	League	3–6	1 Goal	(6)
20	20/10/87	Oldham Athletic	Away	League	1–1		
21	24/10/87	AFC Bournemouth	Home	League	3–2	1 Goal	(7)
22	28/10/87	Oldham Athletic	Home	Lge Cup	2–2		
23	31/10/87	Sheffield United	Away	League	2–2		
24	04/11/87	Oldham Athletic	Away	Lge Cup	2–4	1 Goal	(8)
25	07/11/87	Shrewsbury Town	Home	League	2–1	1 Goal	(9)
26	14/11/87	Millwall	Away	League	1–3		
27	21/11/87	Swindon Town	Home	League	4–2	1 Goal	(10)
28	25/11/87	Sheffield United	Home	Simod Cup	3–0	1 Goal	(11)
29	28/11/87	Crystal Palace	Away	League	0–3		
30	05/12/87	Birmingham City	Home	League	4–1	1 Goal	(12)
31	08/12/87	Millwall	Away	Simod Cup	0–2		
32	12/12/87	Reading	Away	League	1–0		
33	19/12/87	Huddersfield Town	Home	League	3–0		
Sub+3	03/01/88	Hull City	Away	League	1–3		
34	09/01/88	Aston Villa	Home	FA Cup	1–2		
35	16/01/88	Barnsley	Home	League	0–2		
Sub+4	30/01/88	West Bromwich Albion	Away	League	4–1		
Sub+5	13/02/88	Leicester City	Away	League	2–3		
36	27/02/88	Blackburn Rovers	Home	League	2–2		
37	12/03/88	Aston Villa	Away	League	2–1	1 Goal	(13)
38	19/03/88	Sheffield United	Home	League	5–0		
39	02/04/88	Shrewsbury Town	Away	League	0–1		
40	06/04/88	Millwall	Home	League	1–2		
Sub+6	23/04/88	Oldham Athletic	Home	League	1–1		
41	30/04/88	Swindon Town	Away	League	2–1		

SEASON 1988–89

League Division Two

42	03/09/88	Portsmouth	Away	League	0–4		
43	17/09/88	AFC Bournemouth	Away	League	0–0		
Sub+7	09/11/88	Shrewsbury Town	Home	Simod Cup	3–1		
Sub+8	22/11/88	Birmingham City	Away	League	0–0		
Sub+9	10/12/88	Shrewsbury Town	Home	League	2–3		
Sub+10	17/12/88	Crystal Palace	Away	League	0–0		
Sub+11	19/03/89	Barnsley	Away	League	2–2		

Bristol City – League Division Three

1	25/03/89	Bristol Rovers	Away	League	1–1		
2	27/03/89	Bury	Home	League	3–0	1 Goal	(1)
3	01/04/89	Cardiff City	Away	League	1–1	1 Goal	(2)
4	04/04/89	Brentford	Away	League	0–3		
5	11/04/89	Brentford	Home	League	0–1		
6	15/04/89	Blackpool	Home	League	1–2	1 Goal	(3)
7	18/04/89	Huddersfield Town	Home	League	6–1	3 Goals	(6)
8	21/04/89	Port Vale	Away	League	1–0	1 Goal	(7)
9	29/04/89	Wigan Athletic	Home	League	0–1		
10	01/05/89	Wolverhampton Wanderers	Away	League	0–2		
11	05/05/89	Reading	Away	League	2–1		
12	13/05/89	Sheffield United	Home	League	2–0	1 Goal	(8)

SEASON 1989–90

League Division Three

13	19/08/89	Bury	Away	League	1–1	1 Goal	(9)
14	22/08/89	Reading	Home	Lge Cup	2–3		
15	26/08/89	Birmingham City	Home	League	1–0	1 Goal	(10)
16	29/08/89	Reading	Away	Lge Cup	2–2	2 Goals	(12)
17	02/09/89	Northampton Town	Away	League	0–2		
18	09/09/89	Blackpool	Home	League	2–0		
19	16/09/89	Cardiff City	Away	League	3–0	1 Goal	(13)
20	23/09/89	Bristol Rovers	Home	League	0–0		
21	26/09/89	Shrewsbury Town	Home	League	2–1	2 Goals	(15)
22	29/09/89	Tranmere Rovers	Away	League	0–6		
23	07/10/89	Brentford	Away	League	2–0		
24	14/10/89	Swansea City	Home	League	1–3	1 Goal	(16)
25	17/10/89	Notts County	Home	League	2–0		
26	21/10/89	Mansfield Town	Away	League	0–1		
27	31/10/89	Crewe Alexandra	Away	League	1–0		

28	04/11/89	Walsall	Away	League	2–0	1 Goal	(17)
29	11/11/89	Bolton Wanderers	Home	League	1–1		
30	18/11/89	Barnet	Home	FA Cup	2–0	1 Goal	(18)
31	09/12/89	Fulham	Home	FA Cup	2–1	1 Goal	(19)
32	16/12/89	Leyton Orient	Home	League	2–1	2 Goals	(21)
33	26/12/89	Fulham	Away	League	1–0	1 Goal	(22)
34	30/12/89	Huddersfield Town	Away	League	1–2		
35	01/01/90	Preston North End	Home	League	2–1		
36	06/01/90	Swindon Town	Home	FA Cup	2–1	1 Goal	(23)
37	13/01/90	Birmingham City	Away	League	4–0	2 Goals	(25)
38	20/01/90	Bury	Home	League	1–0		
39	23/01/90	Notts County	Home	LD Cup	0–1		
40	27/01/90	Chelsea	Home	FA Cup	3–1		
41	30/01/90	Chester City	Home	League	1–0		
42	10/02/90	Cardiff City	Home	League	1–0		
43	17/02/90	Cambridge United	Home	FA Cup	0–0		
44	21/02/90	Cambridge United	Away	FA Cup	1–1*	1 Goal	(26)
45	24/02/90	Reading	Home	League	0–1		
46	27/02/90	Cambridge United	Away	FA Cup	1–5	1 Goal	(27)
47	03/03/90	Chester City	Away	League	3–0	3 Goals	(30)
48	06/03/90	Tranmere Rovers	Home	League	1–3		
49	10/03/90	Shrewsbury Town	Away	League	1–0		
50	13/03/90	Blackpool	Away	League	3–1	2 Goals	(32)
51	17/03/90	Brentford	Home	League	2–0		
52	20/03/90	Swansea City	Away	League	5–0	3 Goals	(35)
53	24/03/90	Notts County	Away	League	0–0		
54	27/03/90	Northampton Town	Home	League	3–1	1 Goal	(36)
55	31/03/90	Mansfield Town	Home	League	1–1	1 Goal	(37)
56	03/04/90	Rotherham United	Away	League	2–1	1 Goal	(38)
57	07/04/90	Wigan Athletic	Away	League	3–2	1 Goal	(39)
58	10/04/90	Crewe Alexandra	Home	League	4–1	3 Goals	(42)
59	28/04/90	Bolton Wanderers	Away	League	0–1		

SEASON 1990–91

League Division Two

60	25/08/90	Blackburn Rovers	Home	League	4–2	2 Goals	(44)
61	29/08/90	West Bromwich Albion	Away	Lge Cup	2–2		
62	02/09/90	Swindon Town	Away	League	1–0		
63	05/09/90	West Bromwich Albion	Home	Lge Cup	1–0*		
64	08/09/90	Plymouth Argyle	Home	League	1–1		
65	15/09/90	West Bromwich Albion	Away	League	1–2		
66	22/09/90	Brighton & Hove Albion	Home	League	3–1	2 Goals	(46)
67	25/09/90	Sunderland	Away	Lge Cup	1–0		
68	29/09/90	Newcastle United	Home	League	1–0		
69	03/10/90	Leicester City	Away	League	0–3		
70	06/10/90	Wolverhampton Wanderers	Away	League	0–4		
71	09/10/90	Sunderland	Home	Lge Cup	1–6		
72	13/10/90	West Ham United	Home	League	1–1		
73	20/10/90	Oldham Athletic	Home	League	1–2		
Sub+1	24/10/90	Millwall	Away	League	2–1		
Sub+2	10/11/90	Oxford United	Away	League	1–3		
74	21/11/90	Oxford United	Away	ZDS Cup	2–2+		
Sub+3	24/11/90	Ipswich Town	Away	League	1–1	1 Goal	(47)
75	01/12/90	Charlton Athletic	Home	League	0–1		
76	08/12/90	Sheffield Wednesday	Home	League	1–1		
77	15/12/90	Blackburn Rovers	Away	League	1–0		
78	22/12/90	Notts County	Away	League	2–3		
79	26/12/90	Portsmouth	Home	League	4–1		
Sub+4	01/01/91	Barnsley	Away	League	0–2		
80	05/01/91	Norwich City	Away	FA Cup	1–2		
Sub+5	12/01/91	Swindon Town	Home	League	0–4		
81	26/01/91	Bristol Rovers	Away	League	2–3		
82	02/02/91	West Bromwich Albion	Home	League	2–0	1 Goal	(48)
83	16/02/91	Hull City	Away	League	2–1		
84	23/02/91	Oxford United	Home	League	3–1	1 Goal	(49)
85	02/03/91	Charlton Athletic	Away	League	1–2		
86	05/03/91	Bristol Rovers	Home	League	1–0		
87	09/03/91	Ipswich Town	Home	League	4–2	2 Goals	(51)
88	12/03/91	Leicester City	Home	League	1–0	1 Goal	(52)
89	16/03/91	Newcastle United	Away	League	0–0		
90	20/03/91	West Ham United	Away	League	0–1		
91	23/03/91	Wolverhampton Wanderers	Home	League	1–1		
92	30/03/91	Portsmouth	Away	League	1–4		

93	01/04/91	Notts County	Home	League	3–2		
94	06/04/91	Middlesbrough	Away	League	1–2	1 Goal	(53)
95	13/04/91	Barnsley	Home	League	1–0		
96	20/04/91	Oldham Athletic	Away	League	1–2		
97	23/04/91	Brighton & Hove Albion	Away	League	1–0		
98	27/04/91	Millwall	Home	League	1–4		
99	04/05/91	Port Vale	Home	League	1–1		

+ AET Oxford United won 3–2 on penalties

SEASON 1991–92

League Division Two

100	17/08/91	Southend United	Away	League	1–1	1 Goal	(54)
101	20/08/91	Brighton & Hove Albion	Home	League	2–1		
102	24/08/91	Blackburn Rovers	Home	League	1–0		
103	31/08/91	Port Vale	Away	League	1–1		
Sub+6	17/09/91	Millwall	Home	League	2–2		
Sub+7	08/10/91	Bristol Rovers	Away	Lge Cup	2–4*		
Sub+8	12/10/91	Watford	Home	League	1–0		
Sub+9	19/10/91	Barnsley	Away	League	2–1		
104	22/10/91	Southampton	Home	ZDS Cup	1–2	1 Goal	(55)
105	26/10/91	Newcastle United	Home	League	1–1	1 Goal	(56)
106	02/11/91	Cambridge United	Away	League	0–0		
Sub+10	16/11/91	Oxford United	Away	League	1–1		
Sub+11	23/11/91	Middlesbrough	Away	League	1–3	1 Goal	(57)
107	30/11/91	Charlton Athletic	Home	League	0–2		
108	07/12/91	Grimsby Town	Away	League	1–3		
109	21/12/91	Bristol Rovers	Away	League	2–3		
110	26/12/91	Swindon Town	Home	League	1–1	1 Goal	(58)
111	28/12/91	Port Vale	Home	League	3–0		
112	01/01/92	Brighton & Hove Albion	Away	League	0–0		
113	04/01/92	Wimbledon	Home	FA Cup	1–1		
114	11/01/92	Blackburn Rovers	Away	League	0–4		
Sub+12	14/01/92	Wimbledon	Away	FA Cup	1–0		

West Bromwich Albion – League Division Three

1	01/02/92	Brentford	Home	League	2–0	1 Goal	(1)
2	08/02/92	Birmingham City	Away	League	3–0	2 Goals	(3)
3	12/02/92	Stoke City	Away	League	0–1		
4	15/02/92	Bradford City	Home	League	1–1		
5	22/02/92	AFC Bournemouth	Away	League	1–2	1 Goal	(4)
6	29/02/92	Torquay United	Home	League	1–0		
7	03/03/92	Leyton Orient	Home	League	1–3		
8	06/03/92	Swansea City	Away	League	0–0		
9	11/03/92	Hartlepool United	Home	League	1–2		
10	14/03/92	Bury	Away	League	1–1	1 Goal	(5)
11	21/03/92	Reading	Home	League	2–0		
12	28/03/92	Huddersfield Town	Away	League	0–3		
13	31/03/92	Stockport County	Away	League	0–3		
14	04/04/92	Bolton Wanderers	Home	League	2–2	1 Goal	(6)
15	11/04/92	Peterborough United	Away	League	0–0		
16	18/04/92	Chester City	Home	League	1–1		
17	20/04/92	Hull City	Away	League	0–1		
18	25/04/92	Preston North End	Home	League	3–0	1 Goal	(7)
19	02/05/92	Shrewsbury Town	Away	League	3–1	1 Goal	(8)

SEASON 1992–93

Football League Division Two

20	15/08/92	Blackpool	Home	League	3–1	2 Goals	(10)
21	19/08/92	Plymouth Argyle	Home	Lge Cup	1–0	1 Goal	(11)
22	22/08/92	Huddersfield Town	Away	League	1–0		
23	25/08/92	Plymouth Argyle	Away	Lge Cup	0–2		
24	29/08/92	AFC Bournemouth	Home	League	2–1	1 Goal	(12)
25	02/09/92	Stockport County	Home	League	3–0		
26	05/09/92	Fulham	Away	League	1–1	1 Goal	(13)
27	09/09/92	Reading	Home	League	3–0	1 Goal	(14)
28	15/09/92	Bolton Wanderers	Away	League	2–0	2 Goals	(16)
29	19/09/92	Stoke City	Away	League	3–4	2 Goals	(18)
30	26/09/92	Exeter City	Home	League	2–0		
31	03/10/92	Burnley	Away	League	1–2		
32	10/10/92	Port Vale	Home	League	0–1		

33	17/10/92	Wigan Athletic	Away	League	0–1		
34	24/10/92	Rotherham United	Home	League	2–2	1 Goal	(19)
35	31/10/92	Hull City	Away	League	2–1		
36	03/11/92	Hartlepool United	Home	League	3–1	1 Goal	(20)
37	07/11/92	Leyton Orient	Away	League	0–2		
38	14/11/92	Aylesbury United	Home	FA Cup	8–0	1 Goal	(21)
39	21/11/92	Bradford City	Home	League	1–1		
40	28/11/92	Preston North End	Away	League	1–1		
41	06/12/92	Wycombe Wanderers	Away	FA Cup	2–2	1 Goal	(22)
42	12/12/92	Swansea City	Away	League	0–0		
43	15/12/92	Wycombe Wanderers	Home	FA Cup	1–0	1 Goal	(23)
44	20/12/92	Mansfield Town	home	League	2–0		
45	26/12/92	Chester City	Home	League	2–0		
46	28/12/92	Plymouth Argyle	Away	League	0–0		
47	02/01/93	West Ham United	Home	FA Cup	0–2		
48	05/01/93	Walsall	Home	A Trophy	4–0	1 Goal	(24)
49	09/01/93	Bolton Wanderers	Home	League	3–1	1 Goal	(25)
50	12/01/93	Mansfield Town	Away	A Trophy	1–0	1 Goal	(26)
51	16/01/93	Exeter City	Away	League	3–2		
52	23/01/93	Stoke City	Home	League	1–2	1 Goal	(27)
53	26/01/93	AFC Bournemouth	Away	League	1–0		
54	30/01/93	Huddersfield Town	Home	League	2–2		
55	06/02/93	Blackpool	Away	League	1–2	1 Goal	(28)
56	09/02/93	Torquay United	Home	A Trophy	2–1		
57	13/02/93	Fulham	Home	League	4–0	1 Goal	(29)
58	16/02/93	Stoke City	Away	A Trophy	1–2	1 Goal	(30)
59	20/02/93	Stockport County	Away	League	1–5	1 Goal	(31)
60	27/02/93	Port Vale	Away	League	1–2		
61	06/03/93	Burnley	Home	League	2–0	1 Goal	(32)
62	10/03/93	Brighton & Hove Albion	Away	League	1–3	1 Goal	(33)
63	13/03/93	Leyton Orient	Home	League	2–0		
64	20/03/93	Hartlepool United	Away	League	2–2		
65	24/03/93	Preston North End	Home	League	3–2	2 Goals	(35)
66	28/03/93	Bradford City	Away	League	2–2	1 Goal	(36)
67	03/04/93	Brighton & Hove Albion	Home	League	3–1		
68	07/04/93	Swansea City	Home	League	3–0	2 Goals	(38)
69	10/04/93	Chester City	Away	League	3–1		
70	12/04/93	Plymouth Argyle	Home	League	2–5	1 Goal	(39)
71	17/04/93	Mansfield Town	Away	League	3–0	1 Goal	(40)
72	21/04/93	Reading	Away	League	1–1	1 Goal	(41)
73	24/04/93	Wigan Athletic	Home	League	5–1	2 Goals	(43)
74	01/05/93	Rotherham United	Away	League	2–0	1 Goal	(44)
75	08/05/93	Hull City	Home	League	3–1	1 Goal	(45)
76	16/05/93	Swansea City	Away	Lge P/O	1–2		
77	19/05/93	Swansea City	Home	Lge P/O	2–0		
78	31/05/93	Port Vale	Wembley	Lge P/O	3–0		

SEASON 1993–94

Football League Division One

79	14/08/93	Barnsley	Away	League	1–1		
80	18/08/93	Bristol Rovers	Away	Lge Cup	4–1		
81	21/08/93	Oxford United	Home	League	3–1		
82	25/08/93	Bristol Rovers	Home	Lge Cup	0–0		
83	28/08/93	Stoke City	Away	League	0–1		
84	01/09/93	Southend United	Home	League	2–2	2 Goals	(47)
Sub+1	15/09/93	Peterborough United	Home	AI Cup	3–1		
85	18/09/93	Crystal Palace	Home	League	1–4	1 Goal	(48)
86	22/09/93	Chelsea	Home	Lge Cup	1–1		
87	25/09/93	Middlesbrough	Home	League	1–1	1 Goal	(49)
88	03/10/93	Derby County	Away	League	3–5	1 Goal	(50)
89	06/10/93	Chelsea	Away	Lge Cup	1–2	1 Goal	(51)
90	09/10/93	Millwall	Away	League	1–2		
91	12/10/93	Pescara Calcio	Home	AI Cup	1–2	1 Goal	(52)
92	16/10/93	Peterborough United	Home	League	3–0	2 Goals	(54)
93	23/10/93	Sunderland	Away	League	0–1		
94	30/10/93	Watford	Home	League	4–1	1 Goal	(55)
95	02/11/93	Tranmere Rovers	Away	League	0–3		
96	06/11/93	Bolton Wanderers	Home	League	2–2	1 Goal	(56)
97	09/11/93	Padova Calcio	Home	AI Cup	3–4		
98	13/11/93	Halifax Town	Away	FA Cup	1–2		
99	16/11/93	AC Fiorentina	Away	AI Cup	0–2		
100	21/11/93	Nottingham Forest	Home	League	0–2		
101	27/11/93	Portsmouth	Home	League	4–1	1 Goal	(57)

102	07/12/93	Bolton Wanderers	Away	League	1–1		
103	11/12/93	Southend United	Away	League	3–0	1 Goal	(58)
104	19/12/93	Barnsley	Home	League	1–1		
105	22/12/93	Cosenza Calcio	Away	AI Cup	1–2	1 Goal	(59)
106	27/12/93	Bristol City	Home	League	0–1		
107	28/12/93	Birmingham City	Away	League	0–2		
108	01/01/94	Luton Town	Home	League	1–1		
109	03/01/94	Charlton Athletic	Away	League	1–2		
110	22/01/94	Millwall	Home	League	0–0		
111	01/02/94	Grimsby Town	Away	League	2–2	1 Goal	(60)
112	05/02/94	Sunderland	Home	League	2–1		
113	12/02/94	Watford	Away	League	1–0		
114	19/02/94	Leicester City	Home	League	1–2		
115	25/02/94	Wolverhampton Wanderers	Away	League	2–1	1 Goal	(61)
116	05/03/94	Stoke City	Home	League	0–0		
117	12/03/94	Crystal Palace	Away	League	0–1		
118	16/03/94	Notts County	Home	League	3–0	2 Goals	(63)
119	19/03/94	Middlesbrough	Away	League	0–3		
120	26/03/94	Derby County	Home	League	1–2		
121	30/03/94	Charlton Athletic	Home	League	2–0		
122	02/04/94	Bristol City	Away	League	0–0		
123	12/04/94	Oxford United	Away	League	1–1	1 Goal	(64)
124	16/04/94	Tranmere Rovers	Home	League	1–3		
125	24/04/94	Nottingham Forest	Away	League	1–2	1 Goal	(65)
126	27/04/94	Birmingham City	Home	League	2–4		
127	30/04/94	Grimsby Town	Home	League	1–0		
128	03/05/94	Luton Town	Away	League	2–3	1 Goal	(66)
129	08/05/94	Portsmouth	Away	League	1–0		

SEASON 1994–95

Football League Division One

130	13/08/94	Luton Town	Away	League	1–1	1 Goal	(67)
131	16/08/94	Hereford United	Away	Lge Cup	0–0		
132	28/08/94	Wolverhampton Wanderers	Away	League	0–2		
133	31/08/94	Swindon Town	Away	League	0–0		
134	10/09/94	Millwall	Away	League	2–2	2 Goals	(69)
135	14/09/94	Middlesbrough	Away	League	1–2		
136	17/09/94	Grimsby Town	Home	League	1–1		
137	24/09/94	Burnley	Home	League	1–0	1 Goal	(70)
138	28/09/94	Portsmouth	Home	League	0–2		
139	02/10/94	Stoke City	Away	League	1–4	1 Goal	(71)
140	08/10/94	Sunderland	Home	League	1–3		
141	15/10/94	Tranmere Rovers	Away	League	1–3		
142	18/10/94	Sheffield United	Home	League	1–0		
143	22/10/94	Barnsley	Away	League	0–2		
144	29/10/94	Reading	Home	League	2–0		
145	02/11/94	Port Vale	Home	League	0–0		
146	05/11/94	Watford	Away	League	0–1		
147	13/11/94	Charlton Athletic	Away	League	1–1	1 Goal	(72)
148	19/11/94	Oldham Athletic	Home	League	3–1	1 Goal	(73)
149	26/11/94	Notts County	Away	League	0–2		
150	03/12/94	Barnsley	Home	League	2–1		
151	10/12/94	Sheffield United	Away	League	0–2		
152	18/12/94	Luton Town	Home	League	1–0		
Sub+2	26/12/94	Bristol City	Home	League	1–0		
153	27/12/94	Southend United	Away	League	1–2		
154	31/12/94	Bolton Wanderers	Home	League	1–0		
155	02/01/95	Derby County	Away	League	1–1		
Sub+3	18/01/95	Coventry City	Home	FA Cup	1–2		
156	01/02/95	Watford	Home	League	0–1		
Sub+4	05/02/95	Charlton Athletic	Home	League	0–1		
157	11/02/95	Port Vale	Away	League	0–1		
158	18/02/95	Notts County	Home	League	3–2		
159	21/02/95	Oldham Athletic	Away	League	0–1		
160	25/02/95	Stoke City	Home	League	1–3		
161	08/03/95	Portsmouth	Away	League	2–1	2 Goals	(75)
162	15/03/95	Wolverhampton Wanderers	Home	League	2–0	1 Goal	(76)
163	19/03/95	Swindon Town	Home	League	2–5		
Sub+5	01/04/95	Middlesbrough	Home	League	1–3		
Sub+6	08/04/95	Bolton Wanderers	Home	League	0–1		
164	15/04/95	Southend United	Home	League	2–0		
165	17/04/95	Bristol City	Home	League	0–1		
166	22/04/95	Derby County	Home	League	0–0		

| 167 | 30/04/95 | Tranmere Rovers | Home | League | 5–1 | 1 Goal | (77) |
| 168 | 07/05/95 | Sunderland | Home | League | 2–2 | | |

SEASON 1995–96

Football League Division One

169	12/08/95	Charlton Athletic	Home	League	1–0		
170	15/08/95	Northampton Town	Home	Lge Cup	1–1	1 Goal	(78)
171	20/08/95	Wolverhampton Wanderers	Away	League	1–1	1 Goal	(79)
172	22/08/95	Northampton Town	Away	Lge Cup	4–2	2 Goals	(81)
173	26/08/95	Ipswich Town	Home	League	0–0		
174	29/08/95	Southend United	Away	League	1–2		
175	02/09/95	Sheffield United	Home	League	3–1		
176	05/09/95	US Salernitana	Away	AI Cup	0–0		
177	09/09/95	Oldham Athletic	Away	League	2–1	1 Goal	(82)
178	12/09/95	Tranmere Rovers	Away	League	2–2		
179	17/09/95	Birmingham City	Home	League	1–0		
180	20/09/95	Reading	Away	Lge Cup	1–1		
181	24/09/95	Stoke City	Away	League	1–2		
182	30/09/95	Huddersfield Town	Home	League	1–2	1 Goal	(83)
183	03/10/95	Reading	Home	Lge Cup	2–4		
184	07/10/95	Reading	Home	League	2–0	1 Goal	(84)
185	11/10/95	Foggia Calcio	Home	AI Cup	1–2		
186	14/10/95	Luton Town	Away	League	2–1		
187	21/10/95	Portsmouth	Home	League	2–1		
188	28/10/95	Millwall	Away	League	1–2		
189	05/11/95	Leicester City	Home	League	2–3		
Sub+7	08/11/95	AC Reggiana	Home	AI Cup	2–1	1 Goal	(85)
190	11/11/95	Derby County	Away	League	0–3		
Sub+8	18/11/95	Grimsby Town	Away	League	0–1		
191	21/11/95	Norwich City	Home	League	1–4		
192	09/12/95	Stoke City	Home	League	0–1		
193	13/12/95	Brescia Calcio	Away	AI Cup	1–0	1 Goal	(86)
194	16/12/95	Huddersfield Town	Away	League	1–4		
Sub+9	23/12/95	Crystal Palace	Home	League	2–3		
195	26/12/95	Port Vale	Away	League	1–3		
196	06/01/96	Crewe Alexandra	Away	FA Cup	3–4		
197	13/01/96	Wolverhampton Wanderers	Home	League	0–0		
198	20/01/96	Charlton Athletic	Away	League	1–4		
Sub+10	30/01/96	Birmingham City	Away	AI Cup	2–2+		
Sub+11	03/02/96	Ipswich Town	Away	League	1–2	1 Goal	(87)
199	10/02/96	Southend United	Home	League	3–1	2 Goals	(89)
200	17/02/96	Tranmere Rovers	Home	League	1–1		
201	20/02/96	Sheffield United	Away	League	2–1		
202	24/02/96	Port Vale	Home	AI Cup	0–0		
203	27/02/96	Oldham Athletic	Home	League	1–0	1 Goal	(90)
204	02/03/96	Port Vale	Home	League	1–1	1 Goal	(91)
205	05/03/96	Port Vale	Away	AI Cup	1–3	1 Goal	(92)
206	09/03/96	Crystal Palace	Away	League	0–1		
207	12/03/96	Watford	Home	League	4–4	3 Goals	(95)
208	16/03/96	Barnsley	Home	League	2–1		
209	20/03/96	Birmingham City	Away	League	1–1		
210	23/03/96	Watford	Away	League	1–1	1 Goal	(96)
211	30/03/96	Portsmouth	Away	League	2–0		
212	02/04/96	Luton Town	Home	League	0–2		
213	06/04/96	Millwall	Home	League	1–0		
214	09/04/96	Leicester City	Away	League	2–1		
215	13/04/96	Grimsby Town	Home	League	3–1	2 Goals	(98)
216	20/04/96	Norwich City	Away	League	2–2	1 Goal	(99)
217	05/05/96	Derby County	Home	League	3–2	1 Goal	(100)

+ AET West Bromwich Albion won 4–1 on penalties

SEASON 1996–97

Football League Division One

218	17/08/96	Barnsley	Home	League	1–2		
219	20/08/96	Colchester United	Away	Lge Cup	3–2		
220	24/08/96	Charlton Athletic	Away	League	1–1	1 Goal	(101)
221	27/08/96	Crystal Palace	Away	League	0–0		
222	03/09/96	Colchester United	Home	Lge Cup	1–3		
Sub+12	07/09/96	Queens Park Rangers	Away	League	2–0	1 Goal	(102)
Sub+13	10/09/96	Reading	Home	League	3–2		

Sub+14	15/09/96	Wolverhampton Wanderers	Home	League	2–4	1 Goal	(103)
Sub+15	16/10/96	Stoke City	Home	League	0–2		
Sub+16	19/10/96	Grimsby Town	Away	League	1–1		
Sub+17	02/11/96	Portsmouth	Away	League	0–4		
223	09/11/96	Port Vale	Home	League	1–1	1 Goal	(104)
224	13/11/96	Sheffield United	Home	League	1–2		
Sub+18	27/11/96	Manchester City	Away	League	2–3		
Sub+19	08/12/96	Bolton Wanderers	Home	League	2–2	1 Goal	(105)
Sub+20	21/12/96	Oxford United	Home	League	3–3	1 Goal	(106)
Sub+21	26/12/96	Reading	Away	League	2–2		
Sub+22	01/01/97	Tranmere Rovers	Home	League	1–2		
Sub+23	04/01/97	Chelsea	Away	FA Cup	0–3		
Sub+24	12/01/97	Wolverhampton Wanderers	Away	League	0–2		
225	18/01/97	Oldham Athletic	Home	League	1–1	1 Goal	(107)
226	25/01/97	Ipswich Town	Away	League	0–5		
Sub+25	01/02/97	Port Vale	Away	League	2–2		
227	04/02/97	Birmingham City	Away	League	3–2	2 Goals	(109)
228	08/02/97	Swindon Town	Home	League	1–2		
229	02/03/97	Bolton Wanderers	Away	League	0–1		
230	05/03/97	Southend United	Home	League	4–0		
Sub+26	08/03/97	Oxford United	Away	League	0–1		
231	16/03/97	Birmingham City	Home	League	2–0		
Sub+27	22/03/97	Charlton Athletic	Home	League	1–2		
Sub+28	28/03/97	Barnsley	Away	League	0–2		
232	05/04/97	Sheffield United	Away	League	2–1	1 Goal	(110)
233	09/04/97	Crystal Palace	Home	League	1–0		
234	12/04/97	Manchester City	Home	League	1–3		
235	19/04/97	Huddersfield Town	Away	League	0–0		

APPEARANCES AND GOALS PER SEASON

SEASON 85–86	GAMES	GOALS
League	2	0
TOTAL	**2**	**0**

SEASON 86–87	GAMES	GOALS
League	2	0
League Play–offs	1	0
League Cup	1+1	1
Full Members Cup	1	0
TOTAL	**5+1**	**1**

SEASON 87–88	GAMES	GOALS
League	27+5	9
FA Cup	1	0
League Cup	4	2
Simod Cup	2	1
TOTAL	**34+5**	**12**

SEASON 88–89	GAMES	GOALS
League	14+4	8
Simod Cup	0+1	0
TOTAL	**14+5**	**8**

SEASON 89–90	GAMES	GOALS
League	37	27
FA Cup	7	5
League Cup	2	2
Leyland Daf Cup	1	0
TOTAL	**47**	**34**

SEASON 90–91	GAMES	GOALS
League	34+5	11
FA Cup	1	0
League Cup	4	0
Zenith Data Systems Cup	1	0
TOTAL	**40+5**	**11**

SEASON 91–92	GAMES	GOALS
League	32+5	12
FA Cup	1+1	0
League Cup	0+1	0
Zenith Data Systems Cup	1	1
TOTAL	**34+7**	**13**

SEASON 92–93	GAMES	GOALS
League	46	30
League Play–offs	3	0
FA Cup	4	3
League Cup	2	1
Autoglass Trophy	4	3
TOTAL	**59**	**37**

SEASON 93–94	GAMES	GOALS
League	42	18
FA Cup	1	0
League Cup	4	1
Anglo–Italian Cup	4+1	2
TOTAL	**51+1**	**21**

SEASON 94–95	GAMES	GOALS
League	38+4	11
FA Cup	0+1	0
League Cup	1	0
TOTAL	**39+5**	**11**

SEASON 95–96	GAMES	GOALS
League	39+3	17
FA Cup	1	0
League Cup	4	3
Anglo–Italian Cup	5+2	3
TOTAL	**49+5**	**23**

SEASON 96–97	GAMES	GOALS
League	16+16	10
FA Cup	0+1	0
League Cup	2	0
TOTAL	**18+17**	**10**

CAREER APPEARANCES AND GOALS

COMPETITION	GAMES	TOTAL	GOALS
League	329+42	371	153
League Play–offs	4	4	0
FA Cup	16+3	19	8
League Cup	24+2	26	10
Full Members Cup	1	1	0
Simod Cup	2+1	3	1
Leyland Daf Cup	1	1	0
Zenith Data Systems Cup	2	2	1
Autoglass Trophy	4	4	3
Anglo–Italian Cup	9+3	12	5
TOTAL	**392+51**	**443**	**181**

HAT-TRICKS

Bristol City

1	3	Huddersfield Town	18/04/89	Home	League	6–1
2	3	Chester City	03/03/90	Away	League	3–0
3	3	Swansea City	20/03/90	Away	League	5–0
4	3	Crewe Alexandra	10/04/90	Home	League	4–1

West Bromwich Albion

1	3	Watford	12/03/96	Home	League	4–4

League: 5
TOTAL: 5

HONOURS

Winners medals
None

Runner-up medals
League Division Three Championship: 89/90
Promoted to Football League Division One: 92/93

TOMMY TYNAN

Born: 17/11/55 – Liverpool
Height: 5.10
Weight: 12.09 (91–92)

Clubs
Liverpool: **1975** – No Competitive Matches
Swansea City (loan): **1975** – Matches: **6** – Goals: **2**
Dallas Tornado: **1976** – Matches: **17+2** – Goals: **2**
Sheffield Wednesday: **1976–78** – Matches: **105+2** – Goals: **37**
Lincoln City: **1978** – Matches: **9** – Goals: **1**
Newport County: **1979–83** – Matches: **209+20** – Goals: **88**
Plymouth Argyle: **1983–85** – Matches: **104+1** – Goals: **52**
Rotherham United: **1985–86** – Matches: **43** – Goals: **19**
Plymouth Argyle (loan): **1986** – Matches: **9** – Goals: **10**
Plymouth Argyle: **1986–90** – Matches: **195+1** – Goals: **83**
Torquay United: **1990–91** – Matches: **45+1** – Goals: **19**
Doncaster Rovers: **1991–92** – Matches: **7+7** – Goals: **1**

SEASON 1975–76

Liverpool – League Division One
No Competitive Matches

Swansea City (loan) – League Division Four

1	18/10/75	Doncaster Rovers	Away	League	1–2	1 Goal	(1)
2	21/10/75	Darlington	Home	League	2–0		
3	25/10/75	Bradford City	Home	League	3–1	1 Goal	(2)
4	01/11/75	Barnsley	Away	League	0–0		
5	05/11/75	Reading	Away	League	0–1		
6	08/11/75	Torquay United	Home	League	3–0		

Liverpool – League Division One
No Competitive Matches

Dallas Tornado – North American Soccer League – Season 1976

1	17/04/76	Washington Diplomats	Home	League	1–0		
2	24/04/76	San Antonio Thunder	Home	League	1–0		
Sub+1	02/05/76	San Jose Earthquakes	Home	League	3–1		
3	07/05/76	Vancouver Whitecaps	Away	League	0–2		
Sub+2	08/05/76	Portland Timbers	Away	League	2–0		
4	15/05/76	St Louis Stars	Home	League	3–2		
5	16/05/76	Minnesota Kicks	Away	League	0–3		
6	05/06/76	Philadelphia Atoms	Home	League	3–1		
7	06/06/76	St Louis Stars	Away	League	2–0	1 Goal	(1)
8	12/06/76	Minnesota Kicks	Home	League	2–1+		
9	10/07/76	Seattle Sounders	Home	League	4–2	1 Goal	(2)
10	18/07/76	Rochester Lancers	Away	League	0–2		
11	24/07/76	Portland Timbers	Home	League	3–0		
12	28/07/76	New York Cosmos	Away	League	0–4		
13	07/08/76	San Antonio Thunder	Away	League	2–3		
14	08/08/76	San Diego Jaws	Home	League	4–3		
15	14/08/76	Los Angeles Aztecs	Away	League	1–4		
16	18/08/76	Los Angeles Aztecs	Home	Lge P/O	2–0		
17	20/08/76	San Jose Earthquakes	Away	Lge P/O	0–2		

+ Decided on penalties

SEASON 1976–77

Sheffield Wednesday – League Division Three

1	11/09/76	Swindon Town	Away	League	2–5	1 Goal	(1)
2	18/09/76	Chesterfield	Home	League	4–1	1 Goal	(2)
3	21/09/76	Watford	Home	Lge Cup	3–1		
4	25/09/76	Wrexham	Away	League	2–2		
5	02/10/76	Lincoln City	Away	League	1–1		
6	05/10/76	Chester	Home	League	3–0	1 Goal	(3)

7	09/10/76	Gillingham	Home	League	2–0		
8	16/10/76	Reading	Away	League	1–0		
9	23/10/76	Shrewsbury Town	Home	League	0–1		
10	27/10/76	Millwall	Away	Lge Cup	0–3		
11	02/11/76	Rotherham United	Home	League	1–3		
12	06/11/76	Bury	Away	League	3–1	2 Goals	(5)
13	09/11/76	Crystal Palace	Home	League	1–0		
14	20/11/76	Stockport County	Home	FA Cup	2–0	1 Goal	(6)
15	27/11/76	Peterborough United	Away	League	2–1	2 Goals	(8)
16	04/12/76	Tranmere Rovers	Home	League	3–1		
17	15/12/76	Darlington	Away	FA Cup	0–1		
18	18/12/76	Oxford United	Away	League	1–1	1 Goal	(9)
19	27/12/76	York City	Home	League	3–2	1 Goal	(10)
20	28/12/76	Grimsby Town	Away	League	1–1		
21	08/01/77	Brighton & Hove Albion	Home	League	0–0		
22	11/01/77	Mansfield Town	Away	League	0–1		
23	15/01/77	Northampton Town	Away	League	2–0		
24	22/01/77	Walsall	Away	League	1–5		
25	25/01/77	Bury	Home	League	1–0		
26	05/02/77	Port Vale	Home	League	1–2		
27	12/02/77	Portsmouth	Away	League	3–0	2 Goals	(12)
28	15/02/77	Chester	Away	League	0–1		
29	19/02/77	Swindon Town	Home	League	3–1		
30	26/02/77	Chesterfield	Away	League	0–2		
31	05/03/77	Wrexham	Home	League	3–1		
32	12/03/77	Lincoln City	Home	League	1–1		
33	19/03/77	Gillingham	Away	League	0–1		
34	26/03/77	Reading	Home	League	2–1		
Sub+1	02/04/77	Shrewsbury Town	Away	League	1–1		
35	11/04/77	York City	Away	League	2–0	1 Goal	(13)
36	12/04/77	Rotherham United	Away	League	1–0		
37	16/04/77	Preston North End	Home	League	1–0	1 Goal	(14)
38	23/04/77	Crystal Palace	Away	League	0–4		
39	30/04/77	Peterborough United	Home	League	4–0		
40	03/05/77	Brighton & Hove Albion	Away	League	2–3		
41	06/05/77	Tranmere Rovers	Away	League	0–1		
42	14/05/77	Oxford United	Home	League	2–0	1 Goal	(15)

SEASON 1977–78

League Division Three

43	13/08/77	Doncaster Rovers	Home	Lge Cup	5–3		
44	16/08/77	Doncaster Rovers	Away	Lge Cup	3–0	1 Goal	(16)
45	20/08/77	Swindon Town	Home	League	1–1	1 Goal	(17)
46	27/08/77	Walsall	Home	League	0–0		
47	30/08/77	Blackpool	Away	Lge Cup	2–2	1 Goal	(18)
48	03/09/77	Bury	Away	League	0–3		
49	05/09/77	Blackpool	Home	Lge Cup	3–1	1 Goal	(19)
50	10/09/77	Shrewsbury Town	Home	League	0–1		
51	14/09/77	Chester	Away	League	1–2	1 Goal	(20)
52	17/09/77	Port Vale	Away	League	0–0		
53	24/09/77	Peterborough United	Home	League	0–1		
Sub+2	01/10/77	Portsmouth	Away	League	2–2	1 Goal	(21)
54	04/10/77	Preston North End	Away	League	1–2		
55	08/10/77	Chesterfield	Home	League	1–0	1 Goal	(22)
56	12/10/77	Exeter City	Away	League	1–2		
57	15/10/77	Wrexham	Away	League	1–1	1 Goal	(23)
58	22/10/77	Lincoln City	Home	League	2–0		
59	25/10/77	Walsall	Home	Lge Cup	2–1	1 Goal	(24)
60	29/10/77	Bradford City	Away	League	2–3	1 Goal	(25)
61	05/11/77	Carlisle United	Home	League	3–1	1 Goal	(26)
62	12/11/77	Oxford United	Away	League	0–1		
63	19/11/77	Gillingham	Home	League	0–0		
64	26/11/77	Bury	Home	FA Cup	1–0		
65	29/11/77	Everton	Away	Lge Cup	1–3	1 Goal	(27)
66	03/12/77	Colchester United	Home	League	1–2		
67	10/12/77	Cambridge United	Away	League	0–3		
68	17/12/77	Wigan Athletic	Away	FA Cup	0–1		
69	26/12/77	Tranmere Rovers	Away	League	1–3	1 Goal	(28)
70	27/12/77	Rotherham United	Home	League	1–0		
71	31/12/77	Hereford United	Home	League	1–0		
72	02/01/78	Carlisle United	Away	League	0–1		
73	14/01/78	Swindon Town	Away	League	2–2		
74	17/01/78	Exeter City	Home	League	2–1		
75	28/01/78	Bury	Home	League	3–2	1 Goal	(29)

76	11/02/78	Port Vale	Home	League	3–1	1 Goal	(30)
77	22/02/78	Peterborough United	Away	League	1–2		
78	25/02/78	Portsmouth	Home	League	0–0		
79	28/02/78	Shrewsbury Town	Away	League	0–0		
80	04/03/78	Chesterfield	Away	League	2–2	1 Goal	(31)
81	07/03/78	Chester	Home	League	1–1		
82	18/03/78	Lincoln City	Away	League	1–3		
83	21/03/78	Bradford City	Home	League	2–0	1 Goal	(32)
84	25/03/78	Rotherham United	Away	League	2–1		
85	27/03/78	Tranmere Rovers	Home	League	1–0	1 Goal	(33)
86	01/04/78	Hereford United	Away	League	1–0		
87	04/04/78	Plymouth Argyle	Away	League	1–1		
88	08/04/78	Oxford United	Home	League	2–1		
89	15/04/78	Gillingham	Away	League	1–2		
90	18/04/78	Preston North End	Home	League	1–0	1 Goal	(34)
91	22/04/78	Cambridge United	Home	League	0–0		
92	25/04/78	Walsall	Away	League	1–1	1 Goal	(35)
93	03/05/78	Wrexham	Home	League	2–1	1 Goal	(36)

SEASON 1978–79

League Division Three

94	12/08/78	Doncaster Rovers	Away	Lge Cup	1–0		
95	15/08/78	Doncaster Rovers	Home	Lge Cup	0–1		
96	19/08/78	Peterborough United	Away	League	0–2		
97	22/08/78	Doncaster Rovers	Away	Lge Cup	1–0		
98	26/08/78	Colchester United	Home	League	0–0		
99	30/08/78	Aston Villa	Away	Lge Cup	0–1		
100	02/09/78	Lincoln City	Away	League	2–1	1 Goal	(37)
101	09/09/78	Southend United	Home	League	3–2		
102	12/09/78	Gillingham	Away	League	0–0		
103	16/09/78	Mansfield Town	Away	League	1–1		
104	23/09/78	Plymouth Argyle	Home	League	2–3		
105	26/09/78	Bury	Home	League	0–0		

Lincoln City – League Division Three

1	13/10/78	Colchester United	Home	League	0–0		
2	17/10/78	Gillingham	Away	League	2–4		
3	21/10/78	Swindon Town	Home	League	0–3		
4	04/11/78	Mansfield Town	Home	League	0–1		
5	11/11/78	Sheffield Wednesday	Away	League	0–0		
6	18/11/78	Plymouth Argyle	Home	League	3–3		
7	09/12/78	Oxford United	Home	League	2–2	1 Goal	(1)
8	23/12/78	Chesterfield	Home	League	0–1		
9	26/12/78	Peterborough United	Away	League	1–0		

Newport County – League Division Four

1	24/02/79	Huddersfield Town	Away	League	1–0		
2	27/02/79	Bradford City	Home	League	2–4	1 Goal	(1)
3	03/03/79	Doncaster Rovers	Home	League	3–0	1 Goal	(2)
4	06/03/79	Wimbledon	Away	League	0–0		
5	10/03/79	Barnsley	Away	League	0–1		
6	13/03/79	Crewe Alexandra	Away	League	1–0	1 Goal	(3)
7	16/03/79	Northampton Town	Home	League	2–1		
8	20/03/79	York City	Away	League	2–1	1 Goal	(4)
9	24/03/79	Aldershot	Away	League	3–2	1 Goal	(5)
10	31/03/79	Halifax Town	Home	League	2–0		
11	07/04/79	Darlington	Away	League	0–1		
12	11/04/79	Hereford United	Home	League	4–1		
13	14/04/79	Torquay United	Away	League	0–2		
14	16/04/79	Portsmouth	Home	League	1–2		
15	18/04/79	Scunthorpe United	Home	League	2–0		
16	21/04/79	Port Vale	Away	League	1–1	1 Goal	(6)
17	23/04/79	Rochdale	Away	League	0–1		
18	28/04/79	Grimsby Town	Home	League	1–1		
19	01/05/79	AFC Bournemouth	Home	League	2–0	1 Goal	(7)
20	05/05/79	Halifax Town	Away	League	2–1		

SEASON 1979–80

League Division Four

21	01/08/79	Plymouth Argyle	Home	Lge Cup	1–0	1 Goal	(8)
22	14/08/79	Plymouth Argyle	Away	Lge Cup	0–2		

23	18/08/79	Port Vale	Home	League	2–1		
24	21/08/79	Aldershot	Away	League	1–0		
25	25/08/79	AFC Bournemouth	Away	League	2–3		
26	01/09/79	York City	Home	League	2–0		
27	08/09/79	Huddersfield Town	Away	League	1–2		
28	15/09/79	Bradford City	Home	League	1–2		
29	18/09/79	Northampton Town	Home	League	2–1	1 Goal	(9)
30	22/09/79	Doncaster Rovers	Away	League	3–1	1 Goal	(10)
31	29/09/79	Lincoln City	Home	League	1–1		
32	02/10/79	Northampton Town	Away	League	2–3		
33	06/10/79	Halifax Town	Away	League	1–2		
34	27/10/79	Wigan Athletic	Home	League	3–2	2 Goals	(12)
35	03/11/79	Port Vale	Away	League	0–2		
36	06/11/79	Portsmouth	Home	League	4–3	2 Goals	(14)
37	10/11/79	Crewe Alexandra	Home	League	1–1		
38	17/11/79	Stockport County	Away	League	5–0		
39	24/11/79	Portsmouth	Away	FA Cup	0–1		
40	01/12/79	Darlington	Home	League	4–0		
Sub+1	08/12/79	Hartlepool United	Away	League	0–0		
41	15/12/79	Scunthorpe United	Home	League	2–1		
42	21/12/79	Peterborough United	Home	League	1–1	1 Goal	(15)
43	26/12/79	Torquay United	Away	League	0–2		
44	29/12/79	Walsall	Home	League	0–1		
45	01/01/80	Hereford United	Home	League	1–0		
46	12/01/80	York City	Away	League	1–2		
Sub+2	22/01/80	Cardiff City	Home	Welsh Cup	2–0	1 Goal	(16)
Sub+3	26/01/80	AFC Bournemouth	Home	League	0–0		
47	16/02/80	Lincoln City	Away	League	1–2		
Sub+4	26/02/80	Doncaster Rovers	Home	League	2–1		
Sub+5	04/03/80	Wrexham	Away	Welsh Cup	1–0		
Sub+6	08/03/80	Wigan Athletic	Away	League	1–0		
Sub+7	14/03/80	Halifax Town	Home	League	5–2		
Sub+8	25/03/80	Merthyr Tydfil	Home	Welsh Cup	3–1		
Sub+9	29/03/80	Stockport County	Home	League	3–1		
48	08/04/80	Peterborough United	Away	League	1–0		
Sub+10	12/04/80	Rochdale	Home	League	1–0		
Sub+11	29/04/80	Rochdale	Away	League	0–2		
49	03/05/80	Walsall	Away	League	4–2	1 Goal	(17)
50	06/05/80	Shrewsbury Town	Home	Welsh Cup	2–1	2 Goals	(19)
51	12/05/80	Shrewsbury Town	Away	Welsh Cup	3–0	1 Goal	(20)

SEASON 1980–81

League Division Three

52	09/08/80	Hereford United	Away	Lge Cup	0–1		
53	12/08/80	Hereford United	Home	Lge Cup	5–0	2 Goals	(22)
54	16/08/80	Burnley	Away	League	1–1		
55	19/08/80	Charlton Athletic	Home	League	1–2	1 Goal	(23)
56	23/08/80	Millwall	Home	League	2–1	2 Goals	(25)
57	26/08/80	Notts County	Home	Lge Cup	1–1		
58	30/08/80	Carlisle United	Away	League	4–1		
59	02/09/80	Notts County	Away	Lge Cup	0–2		
60	06/09/80	Gillingham	Away	League	2–3		
61	13/09/80	Oxford United	Home	League	2–1		
62	16/09/80	Crusaders	Home	ECW Cup	4–0		
63	20/09/80	Chesterfield	Away	League	2–3	1 Goal	(26)
64	27/09/80	Plymouth Argyle	Home	League	0–2		
65	01/10/80	Crusaders	Away	ECW Cup	0–0		
66	04/10/80	Brentford	Away	League	1–0		
67	07/10/80	Reading	Home	League	0–0		
68	11/10/80	Portsmouth	Home	League	2–1		
69	14/10/80	Sheffield United	Away	League	0–2		
Sub+12	18/10/80	Walsall	Away	League	0–1		
70	25/10/80	Huddersfield Town	Home	League	3–2		
71	28/10/80	Fulham	Home	League	2–1		
72	01/11/80	Blackpool	Away	League	4–2		
73	04/11/80	SK Haugar Haugesund	Home	ECW Cup	6–0	2 Goals	(28)
74	08/11/80	Hull City	Home	League	4–0		
75	11/11/80	Charlton Athletic	Away	League	0–3		
76	15/11/80	Burnley	Home	League	1–2	1 Goal	(29)
77	17/11/80	Worcester City	Home	Welsh Cup	2–2		
78	22/11/80	Plymouth Argyle	Away	FA Cup	0–2		
79	29/11/80	Rotherham United	Away	League	0–1		
80	03/12/80	Chester	Away	League	1–1		

81	06/12/80	Barnsley	Home	League	0–0		
82	13/12/80	Chester	Home	League	1–1		
83	20/12/80	Colchester United	Away	League	0–1		
84	26/12/80	Swindon Town	Home	League	0–2		
85	27/12/80	Exeter City	Away	League	2–2	1 Goal	(30)
86	03/01/81	Sheffield United	Home	League	4–0	1 Goal	(31)
87	06/01/81	Ton Pentre	Home	Welsh Cup	3–0		
88	10/01/81	Huddersfield Town	Away	League	1–4		
89	16/01/81	Rotherham United	Home	League	0–1		
90	31/01/81	Millwall	Away	League	0–0		
91	07/02/81	Oxford United	Away	League	1–0		
92	10/02/81	Bangor City	Home	Welsh Cup	3–1	1 Goal	(32)
93	14/02/81	Gillingham	Home	League	1–1		
94	18/02/81	Reading	Away	League	1–1		
95	21/02/81	Plymouth Argyle	Away	League	2–3	1 Goal	(33)
96	28/02/81	Chesterfield	Home	League	5–1	2 Goals	(35)
97	04/03/81	FC Carl Zeiss Jena	Away	ECW Cup	2–2	2 Goals	(37)
98	07/03/81	Brentford	Home	League	1–1	1 Goal	(38)
99	14/03/81	Portsmouth	Away	League	0–0		
100	18/03/81	FC Carl Zeiss Jena	Home	ECW Cup	0–1		
101	25/03/81	Hereford United	Away	Welsh Cup	1–2		
102	28/03/81	Fulham	Away	League	1–2		
103	31/03/81	Hereford United	Home	Welsh Cup	1–1		
104	07/04/81	Walsall	Home	League	1–1		
105	18/04/81	Exeter City	Home	League	2–1	1 Goal	(39)
106	20/04/81	Swindon Town	Away	League	1–1		
107	25/04/81	Colchester United	Home	League	1–0		
108	02/05/81	Barnsley	Away	League	1–4		
109	05/05/81	Carlisle United	Home	League	4–0	1 Goal	(40)
110	07/05/81	Hull City	Away	League	1–3		

SEASON 1981–82

League Division Three

111	15/08/81	Torquay United	Home	FLG Cup	0–0		
112	18/08/81	Plymouth Argyle	Home	FLG Cup	2–1		
113	22/08/81	AFC Bournemouth	Away	FLG Cup	0–0		
Sub+13	04/09/81	Southend United	Away	League	4–0	1 Goal	(41)
Sub+14	15/09/81	Torquay United	Away	Lge Cup	0–0		
Sub+15	19/09/81	Bristol City	Away	League	1–2		
114	26/09/81	Preston North End	Home	League	1–1		
115	29/09/81	Brentford	Home	League	0–1		
116	03/10/81	Lincoln City	Away	League	2–2	2 Goals	(43)
117	06/10/81	Oldham Athletic	Away	Lge Cup	0–1		
118	10/10/81	Doncaster Rovers	Home	League	1–0		
119	17/10/81	Fulham	Away	League	1–3	1 Goal	(44)
120	20/10/81	Millwall	Home	League	1–1		
Sub+16	24/10/81	Portsmouth	Away	League	0–0		
121	07/11/81	Walsall	Away	League	1–3		
Sub+17	14/11/81	Plymouth Argyle	Home	League	0–1		
Sub+18	21/11/81	Colchester United	Away	FA Cup	0–2		
122	28/11/81	Exeter City	Home	League	1–1		
123	01/12/81	Taffs Well	Home	Welsh Cup	5–0	2 Goals	(46)
124	05/12/81	Wimbledon	Away	League	3–2	1 Goal	(47)
125	08/12/81	Grimsby Town	Home	FLG Cup	0–2		
126	28/12/81	Gillingham	Away	League	1–1		
127	02/01/82	Reading	Home	League	3–1		
128	16/01/82	Burnley	Away	League	1–2		
129	23/01/82	Chesterfield	Away	League	0–1		
Sub+19	30/01/82	Bristol City	Home	League	1–1		
130	06/02/82	Oxford United	Away	League	1–1	1 Goal	(48)
131	13/02/82	Lincoln City	Home	League	0–0		
132	20/02/82	Brentford	Away	League	0–2		
Sub+20	27/02/82	Doncaster Rovers	Away	League	2–0		
133	13/03/82	Portsmouth	Home	League	1–1		
134	16/03/82	Bristol Rovers	Home	League	1–1	1 Goal	(49)
135	20/03/82	Carlisle United	Away	League	2–2	1 Goal	(50)
136	27/03/82	Walsall	Home	League	2–2	1 Goal	(51)
137	30/03/82	Huddersfield Town	Away	League	0–2		
138	02/04/82	Plymouth Argyle	Away	League	2–1		
139	10/04/82	Chester	Away	League	2–0		
140	12/04/82	Gillingham	Home	League	4–2	1 Goal	(52)
141	17/04/82	Wimbledon	Home	League	0–0		
142	24/04/82	Exeter City	Away	League	0–1		

143	01/05/82	Burnley	Home	League	0–0		
144	04/05/82	Preston North End	Away	League	1–2		
145	08/05/82	Swindon Town	Away	League	1–1		
146	11/05/82	Southend United	Home	League	3–2	2 Goals	(54)
147	15/05/82	Huddersfield Town	Home	League	1–0		
148	18/05/82	Swindon Town	Home	League	1–0	1 Goal	(55)

SEASON 1982–83

League Division Three

149	14/08/82	Torquay United	Home	FL Trophy	0–1		
150	18/08/82	Exeter City	Home	FL Trophy	5–1	1 Goal	(56)
151	21/08/82	Bristol City	Away	FL Trophy	4–1	1 Goal	(57)
152	28/08/82	Doncaster Rovers	Away	League	0–0		
153	01/09/82	Exeter City	Away	Lge Cup	2–1		
154	04/09/82	Chesterfield	Home	League	1–0	1 Goal	(58)
155	07/09/82	Plymouth Argyle	Home	League	2–2	1 Goal	(59)
156	11/09/82	Bradford city	Away	League	2–4	1 Goal	(60)
157	14/09/82	Exeter City	Home	Lge Cup	6–0	1 Goal	(61)
158	18/09/82	Huddersfield Town	Home	League	2–1		
159	25/09/82	Portsmouth	Away	League	2–1		
160	28/09/82	Brentford	Away	League	0–2		
161	02/10/82	Lincoln City	Home	League	1–0	1 Goal	(62)
162	05/10/82	Everton	Home	Lge Cup	0–2		
163	09/10/82	Bristol Rovers	Home	League	2–0	1 Goal	(63)
164	16/10/82	Orient	Away	League	5–1	2 Goals	(65)
165	19/10/82	Preston North End	Away	League	0–0		
166	23/10/82	Southend United	Home	League	1–1		
167	27/10/82	Everton	Away	Lge Cup	2–2	1 Goal	(66)
168	30/10/82	Wigan Athletic	Away	League	1–0		
169	02/11/82	Sheffield United	Home	League	3–1	1 Goal	(67)
170	06/11/82	Reading	Away	League	2–4	1 Goal	(68)
171	13/11/82	AFC Bournemouth	Home	League	5–1		
172	20/11/82	Enfield	Away	FA Cup	0–0		
173	23/11/82	Enfield	Home	FA Cup	4–2	3 Goals	(71)
174	27/11/82	Wrexham	Away	League	0–1		
175	30/11/82	Cardiff City	Home	Welsh Cup	1–0		
176	04/12/82	Gillingham	Home	League	2–1		
177	11/12/82	Orient	Home	FA Cup	1–0	1 Goal	(72)
178	18/12/82	Walsall	Home	League	1–1		
179	27/12/82	Cardiff City	Away	League	2–3		
180	28/12/82	Oxford United	Home	League	1–2	1 Goal	(73)
181	01/01/83	Exeter City	Away	League	1–0		
182	03/01/83	Millwall	Home	League	2–2		
183	08/01/83	Everton	Home	FA Cup	1–1		
184	11/01/83	Everton	Away	FA Cup	1–2		
185	15/01/83	Doncaster Rovers	Home	League	1–2		
186	19/01/83	Wrexham	Away	Welsh Cup	1–4		
187	22/01/83	Plymouth Argyle	Away	League	4–2	2 Goals	(75)
188	26/01/83	Chester City	Away	FL Trophy	0–0+		
189	29/01/83	Bradford City	Home	League	1–1		
190	01/02/83	Chesterfield	Away	League	1–3	1 Goal	(76)
191	06/02/83	Brentford	Home	League	0–0		
192	15/02/83	Preston North End	Home	League	3–0	2 Goals	(78)
193	19/02/83	Bristol Rovers	Away	League	3–1	2 Goals	(80)
194	26/02/83	Orient	Home	League	4–1		
195	01/03/83	Sheffield United	Away	League	0–2		
196	04/03/83	Southend United	Away	League	4–1		
197	12/03/83	Wigan Athletic	Home	League	1–0		
198	19/03/83	Reading	Home	League	1–0	1 Goal	(81)
199	23/03/83	Lincoln City	Away	League	4–1	2 Goals	(83)
200	26/03/83	AFC Bournemouth	Away	League	1–0		
201	02/04/83	Oxford United	Away	League	3–0	1 Goal	(84)
202	04/04/83	Cardiff City	Home	League	1–0		
203	09/04/83	Gillingham	Away	League	0–2		
204	16/04/83	Portsmouth	Home	League	0–3		
205	23/04/83	Walsall	Away	League	1–2	1 Goal	(85)
206	30/04/83	Wrexham	Home	League	4–0	3 Goals	(88)
207	02/05/83	Millwall	Away	League	0–3		
208	07/05/83	Huddersfield Town	Away	League	0–1		
209	14/05/83	Exeter City	Home	League	1–1		

+ AET Chester City won 5–4 on penalties

SEASON 1983–84

Plymouth Argyle – League Division Three

1	27/08/83	Wigan Athletic	Home	League	0–0		
2	30/08/83	Swindon Town	Away	Lge Cup	0–1		
3	03/09/83	Millwall	Away	League	0–1		
4	06/09/83	Rotherham United	Away	League	0–2		
5	10/09/83	Gillingham	Home	League	1–1		
6	13/09/83	Swindon Town	Home	Lge Cup	4–1	1 Goal	(1)
7	17/09/83	Lincoln City	Away	League	1–3	1 Goal	(2)
8	24/09/83	Preston North End	Home	League	1–0		
9	27/09/83	Scunthorpe United	Home	League	4–0		
10	01/10/83	Burnley	Away	League	1–2		
11	04/10/83	Arsenal	Home	Lge Cup	1–1		
12	08/10/83	AFC Bournemouth	Away	League	1–2		
13	15/10/83	Oxford United	Home	League	2–1		
14	18/10/83	Bristol Rovers	Home	League	1–1		
15	22/10/83	Hull City	Away	League	2–1	1 Goal	(3)
16	25/10/83	Arsenal	Away	Lge Cup	0–1		
17	29/10/83	Sheffield United	Home	League	0–1		
18	31/10/83	Port Vale	Away	League	1–0		
19	05/11/83	Brentford	Away	League	2–2	1 Goal	(4)
20	12/11/83	Bolton Wanderers	Home	League	2–0		
21	19/11/83	Southend United	Away	FA Cup	0–0		
22	22/11/83	Southend United	Home	FA Cup	2–0*	1 Goal	(5)
23	03/12/83	Bradford City	Away	League	0–2		
24	10/12/83	Barking	Home	FA Cup	2–1		
25	31/12/83	Southend United	Home	League	4–0	1 Goal	(6)
26	02/01/84	Walsall	Away	League	2–3	1 Goal	(7)
27	07/01/84	Newport County	Home	FA Cup	2–2	1 Goal	(8)
28	10/01/84	Newport County	Away	FA Cup	1–0		
29	21/01/84	Lincoln City	Home	League	2–2		
30	28/01/84	Darlington	Home	FA Cup	2–1		
31	14/02/84	Port Vale	Home	League	3–0	2 Goals	(10)
32	18/02/84	West Bromwich Albion	Away	FA Cup	1–0	1 Goal	(11)
33	21/02/84	Torquay United	Home	AM Cup	5–1	2 Goals	(13)
34	25/02/84	Hull City	Home	League	2–0	1 Goal	(14)
35	28/02/84	Sheffield United	Away	League	0–2		
36	03/03/84	Bristol Rovers	Away	League	0–2		
37	06/03/84	Brentford	Home	League	1–1		
38	10/03/84	Derby County	Home	FA Cup	0–0		
39	14/03/84	Derby County	Away	FA Cup	1–0		
40	17/03/84	AFC Bournemouth	Home	League	1–0		
41	20/03/84	Millwall	Home	League	0–1		
42	24/03/84	Oxford United	Away	League	0–5		
43	26/03/84	Brentford	Home	AM Cup	2–0*	2 Goals	(16)
44	30/03/84	Rotherham United	Home	League	1–1	1 Goal	(17)
45	03/04/84	Wigan Athletic	Away	League	1–1	1 Goal	(18)
46	07/04/84	Scunthorpe United	Away	League	0–3		
47	10/04/84	Wimbledon	Home	League	1–2	1 Goal	(19)
48	14/04/84	Watford	Neutral	FA Cup	0–1		
49	16/04/84	Bolton Wanderers	Away	League	1–2	1 Goal	(20)
50	20/04/84	Newport County	Home	League	0–1		
51	21/04/84	Exeter City	Away	League	1–1		
Sub+1	17/05/84	Millwall	Home	AM Cup	0–1		

SEASON 1984–85

League Division Three

52	25/08/84	Burnley	Away	League	1–1		
53	27/08/84	Torquay United	Home	Lge Cup	1–0		
54	01/09/84	Reading	Home	League	1–2		
55	04/09/84	Torquay United	Away	Lge Cup	1–0		
56	08/09/84	Lincoln City	Away	League	2–2	1 Goal	(21)
57	15/09/84	AFC Bournemouth	Home	League	0–0		
58	18/09/84	York City	Home	League	1–1		
59	22/09/84	Bolton Wanderers	Away	League	2–7	1 Goal	(22)
60	25/09/84	Birmingham City	Away	Lge Cup	1–4		
61	29/09/84	Preston North End	Home	League	6–4	1 Goal	(23)
62	02/10/84	Gillingham	Away	League	3–3	1 Goal	(24)
63	06/10/84	Hull City	Home	League	0–1		
64	09/10/84	Birmingham City	Home	Lge Cup	0–1		
65	13/10/84	Derby County	Away	League	1–3	1 Goal	(25)
66	20/10/84	Rotherham United	Home	League	1–0		

67	23/10/84	Orient	Away	League	0–3		
68	26/10/84	Doncaster Rovers	Away	League	3–4	2 Goals	(27)
69	03/11/84	Bristol Rovers	Home	League	3–2	1 Goal	(28)
70	06/11/84	Bradford City	Home	League	0–0		
71	10/11/84	Wigan Athletic	Away	League	0–1		
72	17/11/84	Barnet	Home	FA Cup	3–0	1 Goal	(29)
73	24/11/84	Walsall	Home	League	1–3	1 Goal	(30)
74	01/12/84	Swansea City	Away	League	2–0	1 Goal	(31)
75	08/12/84	Hereford United	Home	FA Cup	0–0		
76	12/12/84	Hereford United	Away	FA Cup	0–2		
77	15/12/84	Cambridge United	Home	League	2–0	1 Goal	(32)
78	22/12/84	Millwall	Home	League	3–1	1 Goal	(33)
79	26/12/84	Bristol City	Away	League	3–4	3 Goals	(36)
80	29/12/84	Newport County	Home	League	0–1		
81	01/01/85	Brentford	Home	League	1–1	1 Goal	(37)
82	02/02/85	Preston North End	Away	League	2–1		
83	05/02/85	AFC Bournemouth	Away	FR Trophy	0–2		
84	09/02/85	Bolton Wanderers	Home	League	2–0	1 Goal	(38)
85	12/02/85	York City	Away	League	0–0		
86	23/02/85	Bristol Rovers	Away	League	0–1		
87	02/03/85	Doncaster Rovers	Home	League	2–1	1 Goal	(39)
88	05/03/85	Orient	Home	League	1–1		
89	09/03/85	Rotherham United	Away	League	2–0	1 Goal	(40)
90	16/03/85	Derby County	Home	League	0–1		
91	19/03/85	Gillingham	Home	League	1–1	1 Goal	(41)
92	23/03/85	Hull City	Away	League	2–2	2 Goals	(43)
93	26/03/85	Burnley	Home	League	2–2	2 Goals	(45)
94	30/03/85	Bradford City	Away	League	0–1		
95	05/04/85	Bristol City	Home	League	1–0		
96	08/04/85	Brentford	Away	League	1–3	1 Goal	(46)
97	13/04/85	Wigan Athletic	Home	League	1–0	1 Goal	(47)
98	16/04/85	Lincoln City	Home	League	2–0	2 Goals	(49)
99	20/04/85	Walsall	Away	League	3–0	1 Goal	(50)
100	24/04/85	Reading	Away	League	1–1		
101	27/04/85	Swansea City	Home	League	1–2	1 Goal	(51)
102	04/05/85	Cambridge United	Away	League	1–1	1 Goal	(52)
103	06/05/85	Newport County	Home	League	1–0		
104	11/05/85	Millwall	Away	League	0–2		

SEASON 1985–86

Rotherham United – League Division Three

1	17/08/85	Bolton Wanderers	Away	League	1–1		
2	20/08/85	Sheffield United	Home	Lge Cup	1–3		
3	24/08/85	Lincoln City	Home	League	1–0		
4	27/08/85	Chesterfield	Away	League	0–2		
5	31/08/85	Bristol City	Home	League	2–0	1 Goal	(1)
6	03/09/85	Sheffield United	Away	Lge Cup	1–5		
7	07/09/85	Swansea City	Away	League	0–1		
8	14/09/85	Reading	Home	League	1–2		
9	17/09/85	Walsall	Away	League	1–3		
10	21/09/85	Doncaster Rovers	Home	League	2–1		
11	28/09/85	Brentford	Away	League	1–1		
12	01/10/85	Cardiff City	Home	League	3–0		
13	05/10/85	Wolverhampton Wanderers	Home	League	1–2	1 Goal	(2)
14	12/10/85	Bristol Rovers	Away	League	2–5	1 Goal	(3)
15	19/10/85	Plymouth Argyle	Home	League	1–1	1 Goal	(4)
16	22/10/85	Newport County	Away	League	0–0		
17	26/10/85	York City	Away	League	1–2		
18	06/11/85	Gillingham	Home	League	1–1		
19	09/11/85	Wigan Athletic	Away	League	0–2		
20	16/11/85	Wolverhampton Wanderers	Home	FA Cup	6–0	1 Goal	(5)
21	23/11/85	Bury	Home	League	2–0	1 Goal	(6)
22	07/12/85	Burnley	Home	FA Cup	4–1	1 Goal	(7)
23	14/12/85	Notts County	Home	League	1–0		
24	17/12/85	AFC Bournemouth	Away	League	2–1	1 Goal	(8)
25	22/12/85	Lincoln City	Away	League	0–0		
26	26/12/85	Darlington	Away	League	2–2		
27	28/12/85	Chesterfield	Home	League	1–2		
28	01/01/86	Blackpool	Home	League	4–1		
29	04/01/86	Frickley Athletic	Away	FA Cup	3–1	1 Goal	(9)
30	11/01/86	Bristol City	Away	League	1–3	1 Goal	(10)
31	14/01/86	York City	Away	FR Trophy	0–0		
32	18/01/86	Bolton Wanderers	Home	League	4–0	2 Goals	(12)

33	21/01/86	Hartlepool	Home	FR Trophy	3–0		
34	25/01/86	Arsenal	Away	FA Cup	1–5	1 Goal	(13)
35	01/02/86	Swansea City	Home	League	4–1	3 Goals	(16)
36	04/02/86	Newport County	Home	League	0–0		
37	15/02/86	Walsall	Home	League	3–0	1 Goal	(17)
38	18/02/86	Wigan Athletic	Away	FR Trophy	0–3		
39	01/03/86	Brentford	Home	League	1–2		

Plymouth Argyle (loan) – League Division Three

1	05/04/86	AFC Bournemouth	Away	League	3–1		
2	08/04/86	Rotherham United	Home	League	4–0	2 Goals	(2)
3	12/04/86	Bury	Home	League	3–0	2 Goals	(4)
4	16/04/86	Lincoln City	Away	League	1–1	1 Goal	(5)
5	19/04/86	Wigan Athletic	Away	League	0–3		
6	22/04/86	Bolton Wanderers	Home	League	4–1	1 Goal	(6)
7	26/04/86	Blackpool	Home	League	3–1	1 Goal	(7)
8	29/04/86	Bristol City	Home	League	4–0	2 Goals	(9)
9	03/05/86	Darlington	Away	League	2–0	1 Goal	(10)

SEASON 1986–87

Rotherham United – League Division Three

40	23/08/86	Fulham	Home	League	0–0		
41	26/08/86	Doncaster Rovers	Away	Lge Cup	1–1	1 Goal	(18)
42	30/08/86	Port Vale	Away	League	1–1		
43	02/09/86	Doncaster Rovers	Home	Lge Cup	4–0	1 Goal	(19)

Plymouth Argyle – League Division Two

1	06/09/86	Hull City	Away	League	3–0		
2	13/09/86	Brighton & Hove Albion	Home	League	2–2		
3	16/09/86	Ipswich Town	Away	FM Cup	2–3	1 Goal	(1)
4	20/09/86	Barnsley	Away	League	1–1		
5	30/09/86	Blackburn Rovers	Away	League	2–1		
6	04/10/86	Leeds United	Home	League	1–1		
7	11/10/86	Grimsby Town	Away	League	1–1		
8	14/10/86	Sheffield United	Home	League	1–0	1 Goal	(2)
9	18/10/86	Sunderland	Home	League	2–4	1 Goal	(3)
10	21/10/86	Ipswich Town	Home	League	2–0		
11	25/10/86	Millwall	Away	League	1–3		
12	01/11/86	Crystal Palace	Home	League	3–1	2 Goals	(5)
13	08/11/86	Shrewsbury Town	Away	League	1–1		
14	15/11/86	West Bromwich Albion	Home	League	1–0		
15	22/11/86	Huddersfield Town	Away	League	2–1	1 Goal	(6)
16	29/11/86	Oldham Athletic	Home	League	3–2	1 Goal	(7)
17	06/12/86	Stoke City	Away	League	0–1		
18	13/12/86	Derby County	Home	League	1–1	1 Goal	(8)
19	19/12/86	Ipswich Town	Away	League	0–3		
20	26/12/86	Portsmouth	Home	League	2–3		
21	27/12/86	West Bromwich Albion	Away	League	0–0		
22	01/01/87	Birmingham City	Away	League	2–3	1 Goal	(9)
23	03/01/87	Hull City	Home	League	4–0	2 Goals	(11)
24	10/01/87	Bristol City	Away	FA Cup	1–1		
25	19/01/87	Bristol City	Home	FA Cup	3–1*	1 Goal	(12)
26	24/01/87	Bradford City	Home	League	3–2	1 Goal	(13)
27	31/01/87	Arsenal	Away	FA Cup	1–6		
28	07/02/87	Reading	Away	League	0–2		
29	14/02/87	Blackburn Rovers	Home	League	1–1		
30	21/02/87	Sheffield United	Away	League	1–2		
31	28/02/87	Barnsley	Home	League	2–0		
32	07/03/87	Millwall	Home	League	1–0	1 Goal	(14)
33	14/03/87	Sunderland	Away	League	1–2	1 Goal	(15)
34	21/03/87	Grimsby Town	Home	League	5–0	2 Goals	(17)
35	28/03/87	Leeds United	Away	League	0–4		
36	04/04/87	Shrewsbury Town	Home	League	3–2	2 Goals	(19)
37	07/04/87	Brighton & Hove Albion	Away	League	1–1	1 Goal	(20)
38	11/04/87	Crystal Palace	Away	League	0–0		
39	18/04/87	Birmingham City	Home	League	0–0		
40	20/04/87	Portsmouth	Away	League	1–0		
41	25/04/87	Huddersfield Town	Home	League	1–1		
42	02/05/87	Oldham Athletic	Away	League	1–2		
43	04/05/87	Stoke City	Home	League	1–3		
44	09/05/87	Derby County	Away	League	2–4		

SEASON 1987–88

League Division Two

45	15/08/87	Manchester City	Away	League	1–2		
46	18/08/87	Ipswich Town	Home	League	0–0		
47	22/08/87	Huddersfield Town	Home	League	6–1	2 Goals	(22)
48	29/08/87	Reading	Away	League	1–0		
49	31/08/87	Sheffield United	Home	League	1–0		
50	05/09/87	Barnsley	Away	League	1–2	1 Goal	(23)
51	12/09/87	West Bromwich Albion	Home	League	3–3	2 Goals	(25)
52	16/09/87	Bradford City	Away	League	1–3		
53	19/09/87	Leicester City	Away	League	0–4		
54	23/09/87	Peterborough United	Away	Lge Cup	1–4	1 Goal	(26)
55	26/09/87	Birmingham City	Home	League	1–1	1 Goal	(27)
56	29/09/87	AFC Bournemouth	Away	League	2–2		
57	10/10/87	Stoke City	Away	League	0–1		
58	17/10/87	Leeds United	Home	League	6–3	1 Goal	(28)
59	20/10/87	Millwall	Home	League	1–2		
60	24/10/87	Blackburn Rovers	Away	League	1–1		
61	31/10/87	Hull City	Home	League	3–1	1 Goal	(29)
62	03/11/87	Crystal Palace	Away	League	1–5		
63	10/11/87	Manchester City	Away	Simod Cup	2–6	1 Goal	(30)
64	14/11/87	Swindon Town	Away	League	1–1		
65	21/11/87	Middlesbrough	Home	League	0–1		
66	28/11/87	Oldham Athletic	Away	League	1–0	1 Goal	(31)
67	05/12/87	Shrewsbury Town	Home	League	2–0		
68	12/12/87	Huddersfield Town	Away	League	1–2		
69	20/12/87	Bradford City	Home	League	2–1		
70	26/12/87	Birmingham City	Away	League	1–0	1 Goal	(32)
71	28/12/87	Leicester City	Home	League	4–0	1 Goal	(33)
72	01/01/88	Reading	Home	League	1–3	1 Goal	(34)
73	02/01/88	West Bromwich Albion	Away	League	0–1		
74	11/01/88	Colchester United	Home	FA Cup	2–0		
75	16/01/88	Manchester City	Home	League	3–2	1 Goal	(35)
76	30/01/88	Shrewsbury Town	Home	FA Cup	1–0		
77	13/02/88	Ipswich Town	Away	League	2–1		
78	20/02/88	Manchester City	Away	FA Cup	1–3	1 Goal	(36)
79	27/02/88	Aston Villa	Away	League	2–5	1 Goal	(37)
80	05/03/88	Leeds United	Away	League	0–1		
81	12/03/88	Stoke City	Home	League	3–0	2 Goals	(39)
82	19/03/88	Hull City	Away	League	1–1		
83	26/03/88	Blackburn Rovers	Home	League	3–0		
84	04/04/88	Swindon Town	Home	League	1–0		
85	09/04/88	Millwall	Away	League	2–3		
86	15/04/88	Barnsley	Home	League	0–0		
87	19/04/88	Sheffield United	Away	League	0–1		
88	23/04/88	Crystal Palace	Home	League	1–3		
89	26/04/88	AFC Bournemouth	Home	League	1–2		
90	30/04/88	Middlesbrough	Away	League	1–3		
91	02/05/88	Oldham Athletic	Home	League	1–0		
Sub+1	07/05/88	Shrewsbury Town	Away	League	1–2		

SEASON 1988–89

League Division Two

92	27/08/88	Walsall	Away	League	2–2	1 Goal	(40)
93	29/08/88	Hereford United	Away	Lge Cup	3–0		
94	03/09/88	Hull City	Home	League	2–0	1 Goal	(41)
95	06/09/88	Hereford United	Home	Lge Cup	3–2		
96	10/09/88	Watford	Away	League	0–3		
97	17/09/88	Stoke City	Home	League	4–0	3 Goals	(44)
98	21/09/88	Leicester City	Away	League	0–1		
99	24/09/88	West Bromwich Albion	Home	League	1–1	1 Goal	(45)
100	28/09/88	Manchester City	Away	Lge Cup	0–1		
101	01/10/88	Crystal Palace	Away	League	1–4		
102	04/10/88	Birmingham City	Away	League	1–0	1 Goal	(46)
103	08/10/88	Bradford City	Home	League	3–1	2 Goals	(48)
104	12/10/88	Manchester City	Home	Lge Cup	3–6	1 Goal	(49)
105	15/10/88	Manchester City	Home	League	0–1		
106	22/10/88	Chelsea	Away	League	0–5		
107	25/10/88	Shrewsbury Town	Home	League	0–0		
108	29/10/88	Barnsley	Away	League	1–3		
109	05/11/88	Blackburn Rovers	Home	League	4–3	4 Goals	(53)
110	09/11/88	Chelsea	Away	Simod Cup	2–6		
111	12/11/88	Portsmouth	Away	League	0–2		

112	19/11/88	Oxford United	Away	League	1–0	1 Goal	(54)
113	26/11/88	Oldham Athletic	Home	League	3–0	1 Goal	(55)
114	03/12/88	Ipswich Town	Away	League	2–2		
115	06/12/88	Brighton & Hove Albion	Home	League	3–0	2 Goals	(57)
116	10/12/88	AFC Bournemouth	Home	League	1–1		
117	18/12/88	Sunderland	Home	League	1–4	1 Goal	(58)
118	26/12/88	Swindon Town	Away	League	0–1		
119	31/12/88	Leeds United	Away	League	0–2		
120	02/01/89	Watford	Home	League	1–0		
121	07/01/89	Cambridge United	Home	FA Cup	2–0	1 Goal	(59)
122	14/01/89	Brighton & Hove Albion	Away	League	2–2	1 Goal	(60)
123	21/01/89	Walsall	Home	League	2–0	1 Goal	(61)
124	28/01/89	Everton	Home	FA Cup	1–1		
125	31/01/89	Everton	Away	FA Cup	0–4		
126	04/02/89	Birmingham City	Home	League	0–1		
127	11/02/89	Bradford City	Away	League	1–1		
128	18/02/89	Chelsea	Home	League	0–1		
129	25/02/89	Manchester City	Away	League	0–2		
130	28/02/89	Shrewsbury Town	Away	League	0–2		
131	04/03/89	Portsmouth	Home	League	0–1		
132	11/03/89	Blackburn Rovers	Away	League	2–1	1 Goal	(62)
133	18/03/89	Leicester City	Home	League	1–1		
134	25/03/89	Hull City	Away	League	0–3		
135	27/03/89	Swindon Town	Home	League	4–1	1 Goal	(63)
136	01/04/89	Stoke City	Away	League	2–2	1 Goal	(64)
137	04/04/89	Sunderland	Away	League	1–2	1 Goal	(65)
138	09/04/89	Leeds United	Home	League	1–0		
139	15/04/89	West Bromwich Albion	Away	League	2–2		
140	22/04/89	Crystal Palace	Home	League	0–2		
141	25/04/89	Barnsley	Home	League	1–2		
142	29/04/89	Oldham Athletic	Away	League	2–2		
143	01/05/89	Ipswich Town	Home	League	0–1		
144	06/05/89	Oxford United	Home	League	3–1		
145	13/05/89	AFC Bournemouth	Away	League	0–0		

SEASON 1989–90

League Division Two

146	19/08/89	Oxford United	Home	League	2–0		
147	22/08/89	Cardiff City	Away	Lge Cup	3–0	2 Goals	(67)
148	26/08/89	West Ham United	Away	Lge Cup	2–3		
149	29/08/89	Cardiff City	Home	Lge Cup	0–2		
150	02/09/89	Barnsley	Home	League	2–1		
151	09/09/89	Oldham Athletic	Away	League	2–3		
152	12/09/89	Portsmouth	Away	League	3–0	2 Goals	(69)
153	16/09/89	Sheffield United	Home	League	0–0		
154	19/09/89	Arsenal	Away	Lge Cup	0–2		
155	23/09/89	Wolverhampton Wanderers	Away	League	0–1		
156	26/09/89	Swindon Town	Away	League	0–3		
157	30/09/89	Brighton & Hove Albion	Home	League	2–1	1 Goal	(70)
158	03/10/89	Arsenal	Home	Lge Cup	1–6	1 Goal	(71)
159	07/10/89	Stoke City	Home	League	3–0	1 Goal	(72)
160	14/10/89	Middlesbrough	Away	League	2–0		
161	17/10/89	Leicester City	Home	League	3–1		
162	21/10/89	Ipswich Town	Away	League	0–3		
163	28/10/89	Blackburn Rovers	Home	League	2–2		
164	01/11/89	Leeds United	Away	League	1–2		
165	04/11/89	Bradford City	Home	League	1–1	1 Goal	(73)
166	11/11/89	Watford	Away	League	2–1	1 Goal	(74)
167	18/11/89	Sunderland	Away	League	1–3		
168	25/11/89	Port Vale	Home	League	1–2	1 Goal	(75)
169	29/11/89	West Ham United	Away	ZDS Cup	2–5*		
170	02/12/89	Oxford United	Away	League	2–3	1 Goal	(76)
171	10/12/89	Portsmouth	Home	League	0–2		
172	26/12/89	West Bromwich Albion	Home	League	2–2		
173	01/01/90	AFC Bournemouth	Away	League	2–2	1 Goal	(77)
174	06/01/90	Oxford United	Home	FA Cup	0–1		
175	13/01/90	West Ham United	Home	League	1–1	1 Goal	(78)
176	20/01/90	Barnsley	Away	League	1–1		
177	03/02/90	Wolverhampton Wanderers	Home	League	0–1		
178	10/02/90	Sheffield United	Away	League	0–1		
179	24/02/90	Port Vale	Away	League	0–3		
180	03/03/90	Sunderland	Home	League	3–0	2 Goals	(80)
181	07/03/90	Brighton & Hove Albion	Away	League	1–2		
182	10/03/90	Swindon Town	Home	League	0–3		

183	17/03/90	Stoke City	Away	League	0–0		
184	20/03/90	Middlesbrough	Home	League	1–2		
185	24/03/90	Leicester City	Away	League	1–1		
186	31/03/90	Ipswich Town	Home	League	1–0		
187	03/04/90	Newcastle United	Away	League	1–3		
188	07/04/90	Blackburn Rovers	Away	League	0–2		
189	10/04/90	Leeds United	Home	League	1–1	1 Goal	(81)
190	14/04/90	AFC Bournemouth	Home	League	1–0	1 Goal	(82)
191	16/04/90	West Bromwich Albion	Away	League	3–0		
192	18/04/90	Oldham Athletic	Home	League	2–0		
193	21/04/90	Newcastle United	Home	League	1–1	1 Goal	(83)
194	24/04/90	Hull City	Away	League	3–3		
195	28/04/90	Watford	Home	League	0–0		

SEASON 1990–91

Torquay United – League Division Four

1	25/08/90	Walsall	Away	League	2–2		
2	29/08/90	Bristol Rovers	Away	Lge Cup	2–1	1 Goal	(1)
3	31/08/90	Gillingham	Home	League	3–1	1 Goal	(2)
4	04/09/90	Bristol Rovers	Home	Lge Cup	1–1		
5	08/09/90	Cardiff City	Away	League	3–3	1 Goal	(3)
6	15/09/90	Chesterfield	Home	League	2–0	1 Goal	(4)
7	18/09/90	Scunthorpe United	Home	League	1–1		
8	21/09/90	Halifax Town	Away	League	1–0		
9	26/09/90	Manchester City	Home	Lge Cup	0–4		
10	29/09/90	Peterborough United	Away	League	2–1	1 Goal	(5)
11	02/10/90	Doncaster Rovers	Home	League	1–0		
12	06/10/90	Blackpool	Home	League	2–1	1 Goal	(6)
13	10/10/90	Manchester City	Away	Lge Cup	0–0		
14	12/10/90	Aldershot	Away	League	3–2	1 Goal	(7)
15	16/10/90	Wrexham	Home	League	1–0	1 Goal	(8)
16	20/10/90	Rochdale	Away	League	0–0		
17	27/10/90	Carlisle United	Home	League	3–0	2 Goals	(10)
18	03/11/90	York City	Away	League	0–0		
19	06/11/90	Swansea City	Home	LD Cup	1–1		
20	09/11/90	Scarborough	Away	League	0–1		
21	17/11/90	Maidstone United	Away	FA Cup	1–4	1 Goal	(11)
22	01/12/90	Hartlepool United	Home	League	0–1		
23	07/12/90	Stockport County	Home	League	1–1		
24	15/12/90	Darlington	Away	League	0–3		
25	18/12/90	Shrewsbury Town	Away	LD Cup	1–1		
26	22/12/90	Maidstone United	Away	League	2–2	1 Goal	(12)
27	29/12/90	Burnley	Home	League	2–0		
28	01/01/91	Hereford United	Away	League	0–0		
29	11/01/91	Gillingham	Away	League	2–2	1 Goal	(13)
30	16/01/91	Shrewsbury Town	Away	LD Cup	6–2	3 Goals	(16)
31	19/01/91	Walsall	Home	League	0–0		
32	26/01/91	Chesterfield	Away	League	1–1		
33	28/01/91	Swansea City	Home	LD Cup	2–0	1 Goal	(17)
34	02/02/91	Scunthorpe United	Away	League	0–3		
35	05/02/91	Halifax Town	Home	League	3–1	1 Goal	(18)
36	19/02/91	Northampton Town	Home	LD Cup	2–0		
37	26/02/91	Southend United	Away	LD Cup	0–7		
38	02/03/91	Hartlepool United	Away	League	0–0		
39	05/03/91	Lincoln City	Home	League	0–1		
40	09/03/91	Darlington	Home	League	2–1	1 Goal	(19)
41	15/03/91	Peterborough United	Home	League	0–0		
42	23/03/91	Blackpool	Away	League	0–1		
43	26/03/91	Northampton Town	Home	League	0–0		
44	30/03/91	Lincoln City	Away	League	2–3		
45	02/04/91	Maidstone United	Home	League	1–1		
Sub+1	11/05/91	York City	Home	League	2–1		

SEASON 1991–92

Doncaster Rovers – League Division Four

1	17/08/91	Carlisle United	Home	League	0–3		
2	20/08/91	Crewe Alexandra	Away	Lge Cup	2–5		
3	24/08/91	Scunthorpe United	Away	League	2–3	1 Goal	(1)
4	27/08/91	Crewe Alexandra	Home	Lge Cup	2–4		
Sub+1	31/08/91	Burnley	Home	League	1–4		
Sub+2	03/09/91	Northampton Town	Away	League	1–3		
5	07/09/91	Wrexham	Home	League	3–1		
6	14/09/91	Barnet	Away	League	0–1		

Sub+3	18/09/91	Scarborough	Away	League	0–1
7	20/09/91	Blackpool	Home	League	0–2
Sub+4	06/11/91	Rotherham United	Home	League	1–1
Sub+5	08/11/91	York City	Home	League	0–1
Sub+6	19/11/91	Burnley	Away	A Trophy	0–2
Sub+7	01/02/92	Gillingham	Away	League	1–2

APPEARANCES AND GOALS PER SEASON

SEASON 75–76	GAMES	GOALS
League	6	2
North American Soccer League	15+2	2
North American Soccer League Play–offs	2	0
TOTAL	**23+2**	**4**

SEASON 76–77	GAMES	GOALS
League	38+1	14
FA Cup	2	1
League Cup	2	0
TOTAL	**42+1**	**15**

SEASON 77–78	GAMES	GOALS
League	43+1	16
FA Cup	2	0
League Cup	6	5
TOTAL	**51+1**	**21**

SEASON 78–79	GAMES	GOALS
League	37	9
League Cup	4	0
TOTAL	**41**	**9**

SEASON 79–80	GAMES	GOALS
League	26+8	8
FA Cup	1	0
League Cup	2	1
Welsh Cup	2+3	4
TOTAL	**31+11**	**13**

SEASON 80–81	GAMES	GOALS
League	44+1	13
FA Cup	1	0
League Cup	4	2
European Cup Winners Cup	5	4
Welsh Cup	5	1
TOTAL	**59+1**	**20**

SEASON 81–82	GAMES	GOALS
League	32+6	13
FA Cup	0+1	0
League Cup	1+1	0
Football League Group Cup	4	0
Welsh Cup	1	2
TOTAL	**38+8**	**15**

SEASON 82–83	GAMES	GOALS
League	46	25
FA Cup	5	4
League Cup	4	2
Football League Trophy	4	2
Welsh Cup	2	0
TOTAL	**61**	**33**

SEASON 83–84	GAMES	GOALS
League	35	12
FA Cup	10	3
League Cup	4	1
Associate Members Cup	2+1	4
TOTAL	**51+1**	**20**

SEASON 84–85	GAMES	GOALS
League	45	31
FA Cup	3	1
League Cup	4	0
Freight Rover Trophy	1	0
TOTAL	**53**	**32**

SEASON 85–86	GAMES	GOALS
League	39	23
FA Cup	4	4
League Cup	2	0
Freight Rover Trophy	3	0
TOTAL	48	27

SEASON 86–87	GAMES	GOALS
League	42	18
FA Cup	3	1
League Cup	2	2
Full Members Cup	1	1
TOTAL	48	22

SEASON 87–88	GAMES	GOALS
League	42+1	16
FA Cup	3	1
League Cup	1	1
Simod Cup	1	1
TOTAL	47+1	19

SEASON 88–89	GAMES	GOALS
League	46	24
FA Cup	3	1
League Cup	4	1
Simod Cup	1	0
TOTAL	54	26

SEASON 89–90	GAMES	GOALS
League	44	15
FA Cup	1	0
League Cup	4	3
Zenith Data Systems Cup	1	0
TOTAL	50	18

SEASON 90–91	GAMES	GOALS
League	34+1	13
FA Cup	1	1
League Cup	4	1
Leyland Daf Cup	6	4
TOTAL	45+1	19

SEASON 91–92	GAMES	GOALS
League	5+6	1
League Cup	2	0
Autoglass Trophy	0+1	0
TOTAL	7+7	1

CAREER APPEARANCES AND GOALS

COMPETITION	GAMES	TOTAL	GOALS
League	604+25	629	253
FA Cup	39+1	40	17
League Cup	50+1	51	19
Football League Group Cup	4	4	0
Football League Trophy	4	4	2
Associate Members Cup	2+1	3	4
Freight Rover Trophy	4	4	0
Full Members Cup	1	1	1
Simod Cup	2	2	1
Zenith Data Systems Cup	1	1	0
Leyland Daf Cup	6	6	4
Autoglass Trophy	0+1	1	0
European Cup Winners Cup	5	5	4
Welsh Cup	10+3	13	7
North American Soccer League	15+2	17	2
North American Soccer League Play–offs	2	2	0
TOTAL	749+34	783	314

HAT-TRICKS

Newport County

1	3	Enfield	23/11/82	Home	FA Cup	4–2
2	3	Wrexham	30/04/83	Home	League	4–0

Plymouth Argyle							
1	3	Bristol City	26/12/84	Away	League	3–4	
Rotherham United							
1	3	Swansea City	01/02/86	Home	League	4–1	
Plymouth Argyle							
1	3	Stoke City	17/09/88	Home	League	4–0	
2	4	Blackburn Rovers	05/11/88	Home	League	4–3	
Torquay United							
1	3	Shrewsbury Town	16/01/91	Away	LD Cup	6–2	

League: 5
FA Cup: 1
Leyland Daf Cup: 1
TOTAL: 7

HONOURS

Winners medals
Welsh Cup: 79/80

Runner-up medals
Promoted to League Division Two: 85/86*
Promoted to League Division Three: 79/80, 90/91

* Played nine (9+0/10) League matches, while on loan from Rotherham United, in the Plymouth Argyle team that were runners–up in the League Division Three Championship.

CHRIS WADDLE

Born: 14/12/60 – Felling
Height: 6.0
Weight: 11.05 (96–97)

Clubs
Newcastle United: **1980–85** – Matches: **189+1** – Goals: **52**
Tottenham Hotspur: **1985–89** – Matches: **176+1** – Goals: **42**
Olympique de Marseille: **1989–92** – Matches: **131+9** – Goals: **28**
Sheffield Wednesday: **1992–96** – Matches: **130+17** – Goals: **15**
Falkirk: **1996** – Matches: **4** – Goals: **1**
Bradford City: **1996–97** – Matches: **28** – Goals: **7**
Sunderland: **1997** – Matches: **7** – Goals: **1**

Country
England: **1985–91** – Matches: **49+13** – Goals: **6**

SEASON 1980–81

Newcastle United – League Division Two

1	22/10/80	Shrewsbury Town	Home	League	1–0		
2	25/10/80	Chelsea	Away	League	0–6		
3	20/12/80	Bristol City	Home	League	0–0		
4	26/12/80	Grimsby Town	Away	League	0–0		
5	27/12/80	Derby County	Home	League	0–2		
6	03/01/81	Sheffield Wednesday	Home	FA Cup	2–1	2 Goals	(2)
7	10/01/81	Wrexham	Away	League	0–0		
8	17/01/81	Luton Town	Away	League	1–0		
9	24/01/81	Luton Town	Home	FA Cup	2–1		
10	31/01/81	Bolton Wanderers	Home	League	2–1		
11	07/02/81	Queens Park Rangers	Home	League	1–0	1 Goal	(3)
12	14/02/81	Exeter City	Home	FA Cup	1–1		
13	18/02/81	Exeter City	Away	FA Cup	0–4		
14	21/02/81	Bristol Rovers	Home	League	0–0		
15	25/02/81	Cardiff City	Away	League	0–1		
16	28/02/81	Oldham Athletic	Away	League	0–0		
17	07/03/81	West Ham United	Away	League	0–1		

SEASON 1981–82

League Division Two

18	29/08/81	Watford	Home	League	0–1		
19	05/09/81	Queens Park Rangers	Away	League	0–3		
20	12/09/81	Cambridge United	Home	League	1–0		
21	19/09/81	Norwich City	Away	League	1–2	1 Goal	(4)
22	23/09/81	Shrewsbury Town	Home	League	2–0		
23	26/09/81	Orient	Home	League	1–0		
24	29/09/81	Bolton Wanderers	Away	League	0–1		
25	03/10/81	Cardiff City	Away	League	4–0		
26	07/10/81	Fulham	Home	Lge Cup	1–2		
27	10/10/81	Derby County	Home	League	3–0		
28	17/10/81	Barnsley	Away	League	0–1		
29	24/10/81	Rotherham United	Home	League	1–1		
30	27/10/81	Fulham	Away	Lge Cup	0–2		
31	31/10/81	Oldham Athletic	Away	League	1–3		
32	07/11/81	Chelsea	Away	League	1–2	1 Goal	(5)
33	14/11/81	Charlton Athletic	Home	League	4–1		
34	21/11/81	Luton Town	Home	League	3–2		
35	24/11/81	Orient	Away	League	0–1		
36	28/11/81	Grimsby Town	Away	League	1–1		
37	05/12/81	Blackburn Rovers	Home	League	0–0		
38	04/01/82	Colchester United	Home	FA Cup	1–1		
39	16/01/82	Watford	Away	League	3–2		
40	18/01/82	Colchester United	Away	FA Cup	4–3*	1 Goal	(6)
41	23/01/82	Grimsby Town	Home	FA Cup	1–2		
42	30/01/82	Norwich City	Home	League	2–1		
43	03/02/82	Bolton Wanderers	Home	League	2–0		
44	06/02/82	Cambridge United	Away	League	0–1		
45	13/02/82	Cardiff City	Home	League	2–1		
46	20/02/82	Shrewsbury Town	Away	League	0–0		
47	24/02/82	Sheffield Wednesday	Home	League	1–0		
48	27/02/82	Derby County	Away	League	2–2	1 Goal	(7)
49	02/03/82	Leicester City	Away	League	0–3		
50	06/03/82	Barnsley	Home	League	1–0		
51	13/03/82	Rotherham United	Away	League	0–0		
52	20/03/82	Oldham Athletic	Home	League	2–0		
53	27/03/82	Chelsea	Home	League	1–0	1 Goal	(8)
54	31/03/82	Crystal Palace	Home	League	0–0		
55	03/04/82	Charlton Athletic	Away	League	1–0	1 Goal	(9)
56	06/04/82	Wrexham	Away	League	2–4		
57	10/04/82	Leicester City	Home	League	0–0		
58	12/04/82	Sheffield Wednesday	Away	League	1–2		
59	17/04/82	Luton Town	Away	League	2–3		
60	24/04/82	Grimsby Town	Home	League	0–1		
61	01/05/82	Blackburn Rovers	Away	League	1–4		
62	05/05/82	Queens Park Rangers	Home	League	0–4		
63	08/05/82	Wrexham	Home	League	4–2	1 Goal	(10)
64	15/05/82	Crystal Palace	Away	League	2–1	1 Goal	(11)

SEASON 1982–83

League Division Two

65	28/08/82	Queens Park Rangers	Home	League	1–0		
66	01/09/82	Blackburn Rovers	Away	League	2–1		
67	04/09/82	Bolton Wanderers	Away	League	1–3		
68	08/09/82	Middlesbrough	Home	League	1–1		
69	11/09/82	Chelsea	Home	League	1–1		
70	23/10/82	Crystal Palace	Home	League	1–0	1 Goal	(12)
71	27/10/82	Leeds United	Home	Lge Cup	1–4		
72	30/10/82	Leeds United	Away	League	1–3		
73	06/11/82	Burnley	Home	League	3–0	1 Goal	(13)
74	13/11/82	Leicester City	Away	League	2–2		
75	20/11/82	Carlisle United	Away	League	0–2		
76	27/11/82	Cambridge United	Home	League	2–0		
77	04/12/82	Charlton Athletic	Away	League	0–2		
78	11/12/82	Wolverhampton Wanderers	Home	League	1–1		
79	18/12/82	Sheffield Wednesday	Away	League	1–1		
80	27/12/82	Derby County	Home	League	1–0		
81	28/12/82	Grimsby Town	Away	League	2–2		
82	01/01/83	Carlisle United	Home	League	2–2		
83	03/01/83	Bolton Wanderers	Home	League	2–2	1 Goal	(14)
84	08/01/83	Brighton & Hove Albion	Away	FA Cup	1–1		
85	12/01/83	Brighton & Hove Albion	Home	FA Cup	0–1		

86	15/01/83	Queens Park Rangers	Away	League	0–2		
87	22/01/83	Shrewsbury Town	Home	League	4–0		
88	05/02/83	Middlesbrough	Away	League	1–1		
89	19/02/83	Oldham Athletic	Home	League	1–0		
90	26/02/83	Fulham	Away	League	2–2		
91	05/03/83	Crystal Palace	Away	League	2–0	1 Goal	(15)
92	12/03/83	Leeds United	Home	League	2–1	1 Goal	(16)
93	19/03/83	Barnsley	Away	League	0–1		
94	26/03/83	Leicester City	Home	League	2–2		
95	02/04/83	Grimsby Town	Home	League	4–0		
96	04/04/83	Derby County	Away	League	1–2	1 Goal	(17)
97	09/04/83	Blackburn Rovers	Home	League	3–2	1 Goal	(18)
98	16/04/83	Chelsea	Away	League	2–0		
99	20/04/83	Rotherham United	Home	League	4–0		
100	23/04/83	Charlton Athletic	Home	League	4–2		
101	30/04/83	Cambridge United	Away	League	0–1		
102	04/05/83	Barnsley	Away	League	5–0		
103	07/05/83	Sheffield Wednesday	Home	League	2–1		
104	14/05/83	Wolverhampton Wanderers	Away	League	2–2		

SEASON 1983–84

League Division Two

105	27/08/83	Leeds United	Away	League	1–0		
106	29/08/83	Shrewsbury Town	Home	League	0–1		
107	03/09/83	Oldham Athletic	Home	League	3–0	1 Goal	(19)
108	06/09/83	Middlesbrough	Away	League	2–3		
109	10/09/83	Grimsby Town	Away	League	1–1		
110	17/09/83	Crystal Palace	Home	League	3–1	1 Goal	(20)
111	24/09/83	Barnsley	Away	League	1–1	1 Goal	(21)
112	01/10/83	Portsmouth	Home	League	4–2	2 Goals	(23)
113	05/10/83	Oxford United	Home	Lge Cup	1–1		
114	08/10/83	Charlton Athletic	Home	League	2–1		
115	16/10/83	Swansea City	Away	League	2–1		
116	19/10/83	Cardiff City	Away	League	2–0		
117	29/10/83	Manchester City	Home	League	5–0	1 Goal	(24)
118	05/11/83	Fulham	Home	League	3–2		
119	12/11/83	Chelsea	Away	League	0–4		
120	19/11/83	Sheffield Wednesday	Away	League	2–4		
121	26/11/83	Cambridge United	Home	League	2–1		
122	03/12/83	Derby County	Away	League	2–3	1 Goal	(25)
123	10/12/83	Huddersfield Town	Home	League	5–2	2 Goals	(27)
124	17/12/83	Brighton & Hove Albion	Away	League	1–0	1 Goal	(28)
125	26/12/83	Blackburn Rovers	Home	League	1–1	1 Goal	(29)
126	27/12/83	Carlisle United	Away	League	1–3	1 Goal	(30)
127	31/12/83	Oldham Athletic	Away	League	2–1		
128	02/01/84	Barnsley	Home	League	1–0	1 Goal	(31)
129	06/01/84	Liverpool	Away	FA Cup	0–4		
130	21/01/84	Crystal Palace	Away	League	1–3		
131	04/02/84	Portsmouth	Away	League	4–1		
132	11/02/84	Grimsby Town	Home	League	0–1		
133	18/02/84	Manchester City	Away	League	2–1		
134	25/02/84	Cardiff City	Home	League	3–1	1 Goal	(32)
135	03/03/84	Fulham	Away	League	2–2		
136	10/03/84	Chelsea	Home	League	1–1		
137	17/03/84	Middlesbrough	Home	League	3–1		
138	24/03/84	Shrewsbury Town	Away	League	2–2		
139	28/03/84	Leeds United	Home	League	1–0		
140	31/03/84	Swansea City	Home	League	2–0		
141	07/04/84	Charlton Athletic	Away	League	3–1	1 Goal	(33)
142	14/04/84	Sheffield Wednesday	Home	League	0–1		
143	20/04/84	Blackburn Rovers	Away	League	1–1		
144	23/04/84	Carlisle United	Home	League	5–1	1 Goal	(34)
145	28/04/84	Cambridge United	Away	League	0–1		
146	05/05/84	Derby County	Home	League	4–0	1 Goal	(35)
147	07/05/84	Huddersfield Town	Away	League	2–2		
148	12/05/84	Brighton & Hove Albion	Home	League	3–1	1 Goal	(36)

SEASON 1984–85

League Division One

149	25/08/84	Leicester City	Away	League	3–2	1 Goal	(37)
150	27/08/84	Sheffield Wednesday	Home	League	2–1		
151	01/09/84	Aston Villa	Home	League	3–0	2 Goals	(39)
152	04/09/84	Arsenal	Away	League	0–2		

153	08/09/84	Manchester United	Away	League	0–5		
154	15/09/84	Everton	Home	League	2–3		
155	22/09/84	Queens Park Rangers	Away	League	5–5	3 Goals	(42)
156	26/09/84	Bradford City	Home	Lge Cup	3–1		
157	29/09/84	West Ham United	Home	League	1–1		
158	06/10/84	Ipswich Town	Home	League	3–0	1 Goal	(43)
159	10/10/84	Bradford City	Away	Lge Cup	1–0	1 Goal	(44)
160	13/10/84	Coventry City	Away	League	1–1		
161	20/10/84	Nottingham Forest	Home	League	1–1		
162	27/10/84	Watford	Away	League	3–3		
163	30/10/84	Ipswich Town	Away	Lge Cup	1–1		
164	03/11/84	Luton Town	Away	League	2–2		
165	07/11/84	Ipswich Town	Home	Lge Cup	1–2	1 Goal	(45)
166	10/11/84	Chelsea	Home	League	2–1	1 Goal	(46)
167	18/11/84	Liverpool	Home	League	0–2		
168	24/11/84	Southampton	Away	League	0–1		
169	01/12/84	Stoke City	Home	League	2–1	1 Goal	(47)
170	08/12/84	Tottenham Hotspur	Away	League	1–3	1 Goal	(48)
171	15/12/84	Norwich City	Home	League	1–1	1 Goal	(49)
172	22/12/84	Aston Villa	Away	League	0–4		
173	26/12/84	West Bromwich Albion	Away	League	1–2		
174	29/12/84	Arsenal	Home	League	1–3		
175	06/01/85	Nottingham Forest	Away	FA Cup	1–1		
176	09/01/85	Nottingham Forest	Home	FA Cup	1–3*	1 Goal	(50)
177	12/01/85	Everton	Away	League	0–4		
178	02/02/85	West Ham United	Away	League	1–1	1 Goal	(51)
179	09/02/85	Manchester United	Home	League	1–1		
180	23/02/85	Luton Town	Home	League	1–0		
181	02/03/85	Watford	Home	League	3–1		
182	09/03/85	Nottingham Forest	Away	League	0–0		
183	20/03/85	Leicester City	Home	League	1–4		
Sub+1	23/03/85	Ipswich Town	Away	League	1–1		
184	30/03/85	Sheffield Wednesday	Away	League	2–4	1 Goal	(52)
185	20/04/85	Liverpool	Away	League	1–3		
186	27/04/85	Southampton	Home	League	2–1		
187	04/05/85	Stoke City	Away	League	1–0		
188	06/05/85	Tottenham Hotspur	Home	League	2–3		
189	11/05/85	Norwich City	Away	League	0–0		

SEASON 1985–86

Tottenham Hotspur – League Division One

1	17/08/85	Watford	Home	League	4–0	2 Goals	(2)
2	21/08/85	Oxford United	Away	League	1–1		
3	24/08/85	Ipswich Town	Away	League	0–1		
4	26/08/85	Everton	Home	League	0–1		
5	31/08/85	Manchester City	Away	League	1–2		
6	04/09/85	Chelsea	Home	League	4–1		
7	07/09/85	Newcastle United	Home	League	5–1		
8	14/09/85	Nottingham Forest	Away	League	1–0		
9	21/09/85	Sheffield Wednesday	Home	League	5–1	2 Goals	(4)
10	23/09/85	Orient	Away	Lge Cup	0–2		
11	28/09/85	Liverpool	Away	League	1–4		
12	02/10/85	Southampton	Home	SSS Cup	2–1		
13	05/10/85	West Bromwich Albion	Away	League	1–1	1 Goal	(5)
14	20/10/85	Coventry City	Away	League	3–2		
15	26/10/85	Leicester City	Home	League	1–3		
16	30/10/85	Orient	Home	Lge Cup	4–0	1 Goal	(6)
17	02/11/85	Southampton	Away	League	0–1		
18	06/11/85	Wimbledon	Home	Lge Cup	2–0		
19	09/11/85	Luton Town	Home	League	1–3		
20	16/11/85	Manchester United	Away	League	0–0		
21	19/11/85	Portsmouth	Home	Lge Cup	0–0		
22	23/11/85	Queens Park Rangers	Home	League	1–1		
23	26/11/85	Portsmouth	Away	Lge Cup	0–0*		
24	30/11/85	Aston Villa	Away	League	2–1		
25	03/12/85	Liverpool	Away	SSS Cup	0–2		
26	07/12/85	Oxford United	Home	League	5–1	1 Goal	(7)
27	10/12/85	Portsmouth	Away	Lge Cup	0–1		
28	21/12/85	Ipswich Town	Home	League	2–0		
29	26/12/85	West Ham United	Home	League	1–0		
30	28/12/85	Chelsea	Away	League	0–2		
31	01/01/86	Arsenal	Away	League	0–0		
32	04/01/86	Oxford United	Away	FA Cup	1–1		
33	08/01/86	Oxford United	Home	FA Cup	2–1	1 Goal	(8)

34	11/01/86	Nottingham Forest	Home	League	0–3		
35	18/01/86	Manchester City	Home	League	0–2		
36	25/01/86	Notts County	Away	FA Cup	1–1		
37	29/01/86	Notts County	Home	FA Cup	5–0	1 Goal	(9)
38	01/02/86	Everton	Away	League	0–1		
39	05/02/86	Everton	Home	SSS Cup	0–0		
40	08/02/86	Coventry City	Home	League	0–1		
41	22/02/86	Sheffield Wednesday	Away	League	2–1		
42	02/03/86	Liverpool	Home	League	1–2	1 Goal	(10)
43	04/03/86	Everton	Home	FA Cup	1–2		
44	08/03/86	West Bromwich Albion	Home	League	5–0	1 Goal	(11)
45	15/03/86	Birmingham City	Away	League	2–1	1 Goal	(12)
46	19/03/86	Everton	Away	SSS Cup	1–3*		
47	22/03/86	Newcastle United	Away	League	2–2	1 Goal	(13)
48	29/03/86	Arsenal	Home	League	1–0		
49	31/03/86	West Ham United	Away	League	1–2		
50	05/04/86	Leicester City	Away	League	4–1		
51	12/04/86	Luton Town	Away	League	1–1		
52	26/04/86	Queens Park Rangers	Away	League	5–2		
53	03/05/86	Aston Villa	Home	League	4–2		
54	05/05/86	Southampton	Home	League	5–3	1 Goal	(14)

SEASON 1986–87

League Division One

55	23/08/86	Aston Villa	Away	League	3–0		
56	25/08/86	Newcastle United	Home	League	1–1		
57	30/08/86	Manchester City	Home	League	1–0		
58	02/09/86	Southampton	Away	League	0–2		
59	06/09/86	Arsenal	Away	League	0–0		
60	13/09/86	Chelsea	Home	League	1–3		
61	20/09/86	Leicester City	Away	League	2–1		
62	23/09/86	Barnsley	Away	Lge Cup	3–2	1 Goal	(15)
63	27/09/86	Everton	Home	League	2–0		
64	04/10/86	Luton Town	Home	League	0–0		
65	08/10/86	Barnsley	Home	Lge Cup	5–3		
66	11/10/86	Liverpool	Away	League	1–0		
67	18/10/86	Sheffield Wednesday	Home	League	1–1		
68	25/10/86	Queens Park Rangers	Away	League	0–2		
69	29/10/86	Birmingham City	Home	Lge Cup	5–0	1 Goal	(16)
70	01/11/86	Wimbledon	Home	League	1–2		
71	08/11/86	Norwich City	Away	League	1–2		
72	15/11/86	Coventry City	Home	League	1–0		
73	22/11/86	Oxford United	Away	League	4–2	2 Goals	(18)
74	26/11/86	Cambridge United	Away	Lge Cup	3–1	1 Goal	(19)
75	29/11/86	Nottingham Forest	Home	League	2–3		
76	07/12/86	Manchester United	Away	League	3–3		
77	13/12/86	Watford	Home	League	2–1		
78	20/12/86	Chelsea	Away	League	2–0		
79	26/12/86	West Ham United	Home	League	4–0	1 Goal	(20)
80	27/12/86	Coventry City	Away	League	3–4		
81	01/01/87	Charlton Athletic	Away	League	2–0		
82	04/01/87	Arsenal	Home	League	1–2		
83	10/01/87	Scunthorpe United	Home	FA Cup	3–2	1 Goal	(21)
84	24/01/87	Aston Villa	Home	League	3–0		
85	27/01/87	West Ham United	Away	Lge Cup	1–1		
86	31/01/87	Crystal Palace	Home	FA Cup	4–0		
87	02/02/87	West Ham United	Home	Lge Cup	5–0		
88	08/02/87	Arsenal	Away	Lge Cup	1–0		
89	14/02/87	Southampton	Home	League	2–0		
90	21/02/87	Newcastle United	Home	FA Cup	1–0		
91	25/02/87	Leicester City	Home	League	5–0		
92	01/03/87	Arsenal	Home	Lge Cup	1–2*		
93	04/03/87	Arsenal	Home	Lge Cup	1–2		
94	07/03/87	Queens Park Rangers	Home	League	1–0		
95	14/03/87	Wimbledon	Away	FA Cup	2–0	1 Goal	(22)
96	22/03/87	Liverpool	Home	League	1–0	1 Goal	(23)
97	25/03/87	Newcastle United	Away	League	1–1		
98	28/03/87	Luton Town	Away	League	1–3	1 Goal	(24)
99	04/04/87	Norwich City	Home	League	3–0		
100	07/04/87	Sheffield Wednesday	Away	League	1–0		
101	11/04/87	Watford	Neutral	FA Cup	4–1		
102	15/04/87	Manchester City	Away	League	1–1		
103	20/04/87	West Ham United	Away	League	1–2		
104	25/04/87	Oxford United	Home	League	3–1	1 Goal	(25)

105	02/05/87	Nottingham Forest	Away	League	0–2		
106	04/05/87	Manchester United	Home	League	4–0		
107	09/05/87	Watford	Away	League	0–1		
108	16/05/87	Coventry City	Wembley	FA Cup	2–3*		

SEASON 1987–88

League Division One

109	15/08/87	Coventry City	Away	League	1–2		
110	19/08/87	Newcastle United	Home	League	3–1	1 Goal	(26)
111	22/08/87	Chelsea	Home	League	1–0		
112	29/08/87	Watford	Away	League	1–1		
113	01/09/87	Oxford United	Home	League	3–0		
114	05/09/87	Everton	Away	League	0–0		
115	23/09/87	Torquay United	Away	Lge Cup	0–1		
116	18/10/87	Arsenal	Home	League	1–2		
117	28/11/87	Liverpool	Home	League	0–2		
118	13/12/87	Charlton Athletic	Home	League	0–1		
119	20/12/87	Derby County	Away	League	2–1		
120	26/12/87	Southampton	Away	League	1–2		
121	28/12/87	West Ham United	Home	League	2–1	1 Goal	(27)
122	01/01/88	Watford	Home	League	2–1		
123	02/01/88	Chelsea	Away	League	0–0		
124	09/01/88	Oldham Athletic	Away	FA Cup	4–2	1 Goal	(28)
125	16/01/88	Coventry City	Home	League	2–2		
126	23/01/88	Newcastle United	Away	League	0–2		
127	30/01/88	Port Vale	Away	FA Cup	1–2		
128	13/02/88	Oxford United	Away	League	0–0		
129	23/02/88	Manchester United	Home	League	1–1		
Sub+1	04/04/88	Queens Park Rangers	Away	League	0–2		
130	23/04/88	Liverpool	Away	League	0–1		
131	02/05/88	Charlton Athletic	Away	League	1–1		
132	04/05/88	Luton Town	Home	League	2–1		

SEASON 1988–89

League Division One

133	03/09/88	Newcastle United	Away	League	2–2	1 Goal	(29)
134	10/09/88	Arsenal	Home	League	2–3	1 Goal	(30)
135	17/09/88	Liverpool	Away	League	1–1		
136	24/09/88	Middlesbrough	Home	League	3–2	1 Goal	(31)
137	27/09/88	Notts County	Away	Lge Cup	1–1		
138	01/10/88	Manchester United	Home	League	2–2	1 Goal	(32)
139	08/10/88	Charlton Athletic	Away	League	2–2		
140	11/10/88	Notts County	Home	Lge Cup	2–1		
141	22/10/88	Norwich City	Away	League	1–3		
142	25/10/88	Southampton	Home	League	1–2		
143	29/10/88	Aston Villa	Away	League	1–2		
144	01/11/88	Blackburn Rovers	Home	Lge Cup	0–0		
145	05/11/88	Derby County	Home	League	1–3		
146	09/11/88	Blackburn Rovers	Away	Lge Cup	2–1*		
147	12/11/88	Wimbledon	Home	League	3–2		
148	20/11/88	Sheffield Wednesday	Away	League	2–0		
149	23/11/88	Coventry City	Home	League	1–1		
150	26/11/88	Queens Park Rangers	Home	League	2–2	1 Goal	(33)
151	29/11/88	Southampton	Away	Lge Cup	1–2		
152	03/12/88	Everton	Away	League	0–1		
153	10/12/88	Millwall	Home	League	2–0	1 Goal	(34)
154	17/12/88	West Ham United	Away	League	2–0		
155	26/12/88	Luton Town	Home	League	0–0		
156	31/12/88	Newcastle United	Home	League	2–0	1 Goal	(35)
157	02/01/89	Arsenal	Away	League	0–2		
158	07/01/89	Bradford City	Away	FA Cup	0–1		
159	15/01/89	Nottingham Forest	Home	League	1–2	1 Goal	(36)
160	21/01/89	Middlesbrough	Away	League	2–2		
161	05/02/89	Manchester United	Away	League	0–1		
162	11/02/89	Charlton Athletic	Home	League	1–1		
163	21/02/89	Norwich City	Home	League	2–1	1 Goal	(37)
164	25/02/89	Southampton	Away	League	2–0	1 Goal	(38)
165	01/03/89	Aston Villa	Home	League	2–0	2 Goals	(40)
166	11/03/89	Derby County	Away	League	1–1		
167	18/03/89	Coventry City	Away	League	1–1	1 Goal	(41)
168	22/03/89	Nottingham Forest	Away	League	2–1		

169	26/03/89	Liverpool	Home	League	1–2		
170	28/03/89	Luton Town	Away	League	3–1		
171	01/04/89	West Ham United	Home	League	3–0		
172	12/04/89	Sheffield Wednesday	Home	League	0–0		
173	15/04/89	Wimbledon	Away	League	2–1	1 Goal	(42)
174	22/04/89	Everton	Home	League	2–1		
175	29/04/89	Millwall	Away	League	5–0		
176	13/05/89	Queens Park Rangers	Away	League	0–1		

SEASON 1989–90

Olympique de Marseille – French League Division One

Sub+1	21/07/89	Olympique Lyonnais	Away	League	4–1		
Sub+2	29/07/89	FC Nantes	Home	League	1–0		
1	02/08/89	Toulouse FC	Away	League	1–2	1 Goal	(1)
2	05/08/89	FC Metz	Home	League	2–1		
3	12/08/89	OGC Nice	Away	League	1–1		
4	19/08/89	Montpellier HSC	Home	League	2–0		
5	26/08/89	Racing Club de Paris	Away	League	1–1		
6	30/08/89	FC Sochaux–Montbeliard	Home	League	6–1		
7	13/09/89	Brondby IF Kobenhavn	Home	Eur Cup	3–0		
8	16/09/89	AS Saint–Etienne	Home	League	2–0		
9	23/09/89	SC Toulon	Away	League	4–0	1 Goal	(2)
10	27/09/89	Brondby IF Kobenhavn	Away	Eur Cup	1–1		
11	30/09/89	Brest–Armorique	Home	League	1–0		
12	04/10/89	Lille OSC	Away	League	0–2		
Sub+3	14/10/89	AS Cannes	Home	League	1–1		
13	18/10/89	AEK Athina	Home	Eur Cup	2–0		
Sub+4	21/10/89	Girondins de Bordeaux	Away	League	0–3		
14	28/10/89	Paris Saint–Germain FC	Home	League	2–1	1 Goal	(3)
15	01/11/89	AEK Athina	Away	Eur Cup	1–1		
16	04/11/89	FC Mulhouse	Away	League	2–1	1 Goal	(4)
17	08/11/89	AJ Auxerre	Home	League	1–1		
18	11/11/89	SM Caen	Away	League	2–0		
19	22/11/89	AS Monaco	Away	League	3–1		
20	25/11/89	FC Nantes	Away	League	0–0		
21	03/12/89	Toulouse FC	Home	League	6–1		
22	10/12/89	FC Metz	Away	League	2–3	1 Goal	(5)
23	17/12/89	OGC Nice	Home	League	3–0		
24	04/02/90	Montpellier HSC	Away	League	1–1		
25	11/02/90	Racing Club de Paris	Home	League	4–1	1 Goal	(6)
26	17/02/90	FC Tours	Away	FR Cup	4–0	1 Goal	(7)
27	25/02/90	AS Monaco	Home	League	2–2		
28	07/03/90	CSKA Sofija	Away	Eur Cup	1–0		
29	10/03/90	AC Ajaccio	Away	FR Cup	3–1		
30	14/03/90	FC Sochaux–Montbeliard	Away	League	2–0		
31	17/03/90	SC Toulon	Home	League	3–0		
32	21/03/90	CSKA Sofija	Home	Eur Cup	3–1	1 Goal	(8)
33	24/03/90	Brest–Armorique	Away	League	1–2		
34	31/03/90	Lille OSC	Home	League	4–1	1 Goal	(9)
35	04/04/90	Sport Lisboa E Benfica	Home	Eur Cup	2–1		
36	07/04/90	AS Cannes	Away	League	2–2		
Sub+5	11/04/90	Nimes Olympique	Home	FR Cup	2–0		
37	14/04/90	Girondins de Bordeaux	Home	League	2–0	2 Goals	(11)
38	18/04/90	Sport Lisboa E Benfica	Away	Eur Cup	0–1		
39	21/04/90	Paris Saint–Germain FC	Away	League	1–2		
40	25/04/90	AS Saint–Etienne	Away	League	0–0		
41	28/04/90	FC Mulhouse	Home	League	3–1		
42	02/05/90	AS Cannes	Away	FR Cup	3–0*	1 Goal	(12)
43	05/05/90	AJ Auxerre	Away	League	2–0		
44	12/05/90	SM Caen	Home	League	1–0		
45	24/05/90	Racing Club de Paris	Home	FR Cup	2–3		

SEASON 1990–91

French League Division One

Sub+6	04/08/90	SM Caen	Home	League	2–1		
46	11/08/90	Olympique Lyonnais	Away	League	2–2		
47	18/08/90	Lille OSC	Home	League	2–0		
48	25/08/90	FC Nantes	Away	League	1–1		
49	29/08/90	Girondins de Bordeaux	Home	League	2–0		
50	08/09/90	Paris Saint–Germain FC	Home	League	2–1	1 Goal	(13)
51	15/09/90	Toulouse FC	Away	League	2–0	1 Goal	(14)

52	19/09/90	KS Dinamo Tirane	Home	Eur Cup	5–1		
53	22/09/90	AS Cannes	Home	League	0–1		
54	28/09/90	AS Monaco	Away	League	3–1		
55	03/10/90	KS Dinamo Tirane	Away	Eur Cup	0–0		
56	06/10/90	AS Saint–Etienne	Home	League	3–1		
57	20/10/90	FC Sochaux–Montbeliard	Away	League	1–2		
58	25/10/90	KKS Lech Poznan	Away	Eur Cup	2–3	1 Goal	(15)
59	28/10/90	Brest–Armorique	Home	League	3–1		
60	03/11/90	AS Nancy–Lorraine	Away	League	0–2		
61	07/11/90	KKS Lech Poznan	Home	Eur Cup	6–1		
62	11/11/90	Stade Rennais	Home	League	4–1	1 Goal	(16)
63	24/11/90	SC Toulon	Away	League	1–0		
64	02/12/90	Montpellier HSC	Home	League	2–0		
65	09/12/90	AJ Auxerre	Away	League	0–4		
66	16/12/90	FC Metz	Home	League	3–0	1 Goal	(17)
67	23/12/90	SM Caen	Away	League	0–0		
68	13/01/91	Olympique Lyonnais	Home	League	7–0		
69	20/01/91	Lille OSC	Away	League	0–1		
70	27/01/91	FC Nantes	Home	League	6–0		
71	01/02/91	Girondins de Bordeaux	Away	League	1–1	1 Goal	(18)
72	10/02/91	Paris Saint–Germain	Away	League	1–0		
73	13/02/91	Toulouse FC	Home	League	1–0		
74	24/02/91	AS Cannes	Away	League	0–0		
75	01/03/91	AS Monaco	Home	League	1–0		
76	06/03/91	Milan AC	Away	Eur Cup	1–1		
77	09/03/91	RC Strasbourg	Home	FR Cup	4–1		
78	15/03/91	AS Saint–Etienne	Away	League	1–1		
79	20/03/91	Milan AC	Home	Eur Cup	1–0	1 Goal	(19)
80	10/04/91	Spartak Moskva	Away	Eur Cup	3–1		
81	13/04/91	AS Nancy–Lorraine	Home	League	6–2	1 Goal	(20)
82	19/04/91	Stade Rennais FC	Away	League	1–1		
83	24/04/91	Spartak Moskva	Home	Eur Cup	2–1		
84	27/04/91	Paris Saint–Germain	Away	FR Cup	2–0		
85	01/05/91	Brest–Armorique	Away	League	1–1		
86	04/05/91	SC Toulon	Home	League	3–3		
87	10/05/91	Montpellier HSC	Away	League	0–0		
88	14/05/91	FC Nantes	Away	FR Cup	2–1		
89	17/05/91	AJ Auxerre	Home	League	1–0		
Sub+7	22/05/91	OGC Nice	Away	League	1–0		
90	29/05/91	Crvena Zvezda Beograd	Neutral	Eur Cup	0–0+		
91	31/05/91	Stade Rodez	Home	FR Cup	4–1		
92	08/06/91	AS Monaco	Neutral	FR Cup	0–1		

+ AET Crvena Zvezda Beograd won 5–3 on penalties

SEASON 1991–92

French League Division One

93	20/07/91	Lille OSC	Home	League	1–0		
94	27/07/91	Olympique Lyonnais	Away	League	1–1		
95	31/07/91	FC Metz	Home	League	2–0		
96	03/08/91	Stade Rennais FC	Away	League	2–1		
97	09/08/91	Paris–Saint–Germain	Home	League	0–0		
98	18/08/91	SM Caen	Away	League	3–1		
99	24/08/91	Nimes Olympique	Home	League	4–2		
Sub+8	28/08/91	SC Toulon	Away	League	0–1		
100	14/09/91	FC Sochaux–Montbeliard	Away	League	3–2	1 Goal	(21)
101	18/09/91	Union Sportive Luxembourg	Away	Eur Cup	5–0		
102	21/09/91	RC Lens	Home	League	1–1		
103	05/10/91	FC Nantes	Home	League	4–0		
104	23/10/91	AC Sparta Praha	Home	Eur Cup	3–2	1 Goal	(22)
105	26/10/91	Le Havre AC	Away	League	2–0	1 Goal	(23)
106	01/11/91	AS Nancy–Lorraine	Home	League	4–0	1 Goal	(24)
107	06/11/91	AC Sparta Praha	Away	Eur Cup	1–2		
108	09/11/91	Montpellier HSC	Away	League	0–0		
109	14/11/91	AS Monaco	Home	League	1–1		
110	24/11/91	AS Cannes	Away	League	2–1	1 Goal	(25)
111	30/11/91	Olympique Lyonnais	Home	League	0–0		
112	07/12/91	FC Metz	Away	League	0–0		
113	14/12/91	Stade Rennais FC	Home	League	5–1		
114	17/12/91	Paris–Saint–Germain	Away	League	0–0		
115	21/12/91	SM Caen	Home	League	5–0	1 Goal	(26)
116	19/01/92	Nimes Olympique	Away	League	2–1		
117	25/01/92	SC Toulon	Home	League	0–1		
118	29/01/92	AS Saint–Etienne	Away	League	1–1+		

119	01/02/92	Toulouse FC	Away	League	2–0	
120	09/02/92	FC Sochaux–Montbeliard	Home	League	2–2	
121	15/02/92	RC Lens	Away	League	1–2	
122	23/02/92	ANG Bordeaux FC	Home	FR Cup	1–0	
123	29/02/92	AJ Auxerre	Home	League	2–0	1 Goal (27)
124	07/03/92	FC Nantes	Away	League	1–0	
125	14/03/92	Istres SF	Away	FR Cup	2–1	
126	21/03/92	AS Saint–Etienne	Home	League	2–0	
127	28/03/92	Le Havre AC	Home	League	2–0	1 Goal (28)
128	04/04/92	AS Nancy–Lorraine	Away	League	3–1	
129	08/04/92	US Valenciennes–Anzin	Away	FR Cup	2–0	
130	11/04/92	Montpellier HSC	Home	League	0–0	
131	18/04/92	AS Monaco	Away	League	3–0	
Sub+9	25/04/92	AS Cannes	Home	League	2–0	

+ Match abandoned after Papin was struck by a missile

SEASON 1992–93

Sheffield Wednesday – Premier League

1	15/08/92	Everton	Away	League	1–1	
2	02/09/92	Coventry City	Home	League	1–2	
3	05/09/92	Manchester City	Home	League	0–3	
4	12/09/92	Nottingham Forest	Away	League	2–1	
5	16/09/92	CA Spora Luxembourg	Home	UEFA Cup	8–1	1 Goal (1)
6	19/09/92	Norwich City	Away	League	0–1	
7	23/09/92	Hartlepool United	Home	Lge Cup	3–0	
8	27/09/92	Tottenham Hotspur	Home	League	2–0	
Sub+1	01/10/92	CA Spora Luxembourg	Away	UEFA Cup	2–1	
9	03/10/92	Liverpool	Away	League	0–1	
10	06/10/92	Hartlepool United	Away	Lge Cup	2–2	
11	17/10/92	Oldham Athletic	Home	League	2–1	
12	20/10/92	1.FC Kaiserslautern	Away	UEFA Cup	1–3	
13	24/10/92	Middlesbrough	Away	League	1–1	
14	27/10/92	Leicester City	Home	Lge Cup	7–1	
15	31/10/92	Blackburn Rovers	Home	League	0–0	
16	04/11/92	1.FC Kaiserslautern	Home	UEFA Cup	2–2	
17	08/11/92	Sheffield United	Away	League	1–1	
18	21/11/92	Ipswich Town	Home	League	1–1	
19	28/11/92	Wimbledon	Away	League	1–1	
20	02/12/92	Queens Park Rangers	Home	Lge Cup	4–0	
21	05/12/92	Aston Villa	Home	League	1–2	
22	12/12/92	Leeds United	Away	League	1–3	
23	19/12/92	Queens Park Rangers	Home	League	1–0	
24	26/12/92	Manchester United	Home	League	3–3	
25	28/12/92	Southampton	Away	League	2–1	
26	10/01/93	Norwich City	Home	League	1–0	
27	13/01/93	Cambridge United	Away	FA Cup	2–1	
28	16/01/93	Tottenham Hotspur	Away	League	2–0	
29	19/01/93	Ipswich Town	Away	Lge Cup	1–1	
30	24/01/93	Sunderland	Home	FA Cup	1–0	
31	30/01/93	Chelsea	Away	League	2–0	
32	03/02/93	Ipswich Town	Home	Lge Cup	1–0	
33	06/02/93	Everton	Home	League	3–1	1 Goal (2)
34	10/02/93	Blackburn Rovers	Away	Lge Cup	4–2	
35	13/02/93	Southend United	Home	FA Cup	2–0	
36	20/02/93	Crystal Palace	Home	League	2–1	
37	23/02/93	Manchester City	Away	League	2–1	
38	27/02/93	Liverpool	Home	League	1–1	
39	03/03/93	Coventry City	Away	League	0–1	
40	08/03/93	Derby County	Away	FA Cup	3–3	
41	14/03/93	Blackburn Rovers	Home	Lge Cup	2–1	
42	17/03/93	Derby County	Home	FA Cup	1–0	
43	20/03/93	Aston Villa	Away	League	0–2	
44	24/03/93	Wimbledon	Home	League	1–1	
45	03/04/93	Sheffield United	Wembley	FA Cup	2–1	1 Goal (3)
46	07/04/93	Oldham Athletic	Away	League	1–1	
47	10/04/93	Manchester United	Away	League	1–2	
48	18/04/93	Arsenal	Wembley	Lge Cup	1–2	
49	21/04/93	Sheffield United	Home	League	1–1	
Sub+2	06/05/93	Arsenal	Home	League	1–0	
50	08/05/93	Blackburn Rovers	Away	League	0–1	
51	15/05/93	Arsenal	Wembley	FA Cup	1–1*	
52	20/05/93	Arsenal	Wembley	FA Cup	1–2*	1 Goal (4)

SEASON 1993–94

Premier League

53	25/08/93	West Ham United	Away	League	0–2		
54	28/08/93	Chelsea	Away	League	1–1		
55	01/09/93	Norwich City	Home	League	3–3		
56	13/09/93	Newcastle United	Away	League	2–4		
57	18/09/93	Southampton	Home	League	2–0		
58	21/09/93	Bolton Wanderers	Away	Lge Cup	1–1		
59	25/09/93	Blackburn Rovers	Away	League	1–1		
60	02/10/93	Manchester United	Home	League	2–3		
61	06/10/93	Bolton Wanderers	Home	Lge Cup	1–0		
62	16/10/93	Wimbledon	Home	League	2–2	1 Goal	(5)
63	23/10/93	Sheffield United	Away	League	1–1		
64	27/10/93	Middlesbrough	Away	Lge Cup	1–1		
65	30/10/93	Leeds United	Home	League	3–3	1 Goal	(6)
66	06/11/93	Ipswich Town	Away	League	4–1		
67	10/11/93	Middlesbrough	Home	Lge Cup	2–1		
68	20/11/93	Coventry City	Home	League	0–0		
69	24/11/93	Oldham Athletic	Home	League	3–0		
70	27/11/93	Manchester City	Away	League	3–1		
71	01/12/93	Queens Park Rangers	Away	Lge Cup	2–1		
72	04/12/93	Liverpool	Home	League	3–1		
73	08/12/93	Aston Villa	Away	League	2–2		
74	18/12/93	West Ham United	Home	League	5–0	1 Goal	(7)
75	27/12/93	Everton	Away	League	2–0		
76	29/12/93	Swindon Town	Home	League	3–3		
Sub+3	09/02/94	Chelsea	Home	FA Cup	1–3*		
77	13/02/94	Manchester United	Away	Lge Cup	0–1		

SEASON 1994–95

Premier League

Sub+4	03/12/94	Crystal Palace	Home	League	1–0		
78	10/12/94	Tottenham Hotspur	Away	League	1–3		
79	17/12/94	Queens Park Rangers	Home	League	0–2		
Sub+5	28/12/94	Coventry City	Home	League	5–1	1 Goal	(8)
80	31/12/94	Leicester City	Away	League	1–0		
81	02/01/95	Southampton	Home	League	1–1		
82	07/01/95	Gillingham	Away	FA Cup	2–1	1 Goal	(9)
83	14/01/95	Chelsea	Away	League	1–1		
84	21/01/95	Newcastle United	Home	League	0–0		
85	23/01/95	West Ham United	Away	League	2–0	1 Goal	(10)
86	30/01/95	Wolverhampton Wanderers	Home	FA Cup	0–0		
87	04/02/95	Arsenal	Home	League	3–1		
88	08/02/95	Wolverhampton Wanderers	Away	FA Cup	1–1+		
89	12/02/95	Blackburn Rovers	Away	League	1–3	1 Goal	(11)
90	18/02/95	Aston Villa	Home	League	1–2		
91	25/02/95	Liverpool	Home	League	1–2		
92	04/03/95	Leeds United	Away	League	1–0	1 Goal	(12)
93	08/03/95	Norwich City	Away	League	0–0		
94	11/03/95	Wimbledon	Home	League	0–1		
Sub+6	14/03/95	Crystal Palace	Away	League	1–2		
95	18/03/95	Manchester City	Away	League	2–3		
96	01/04/95	Nottingham Forest	Home	League	1–7		
97	08/04/95	Leicester City	Home	League	1–0		
Sub+7	15/04/95	Coventry City	Away	League	0–2		
98	17/04/95	Everton	Home	League	0–0		
99	29/04/95	Southampton	Away	League	0–0		
Sub+8	07/05/95	Manchester United	Away	League	0–1		
100	14/05/95	Ipswich Town	Home	League	4–1		

+ AET Wolverhampton Wanderers won 4–3 on penalties

SEASON 1995–96

Premier League

101	08/07/95	Gornik Zabrze	Home	IT Cup	3–2+	1 Goal	(13)
102	15/07/95	Karlsruhe	Away	IT Cup	1–1		
103	19/08/95	Liverpool	Away	League	0–1		
104	23/08/95	Blackburn Rovers	Home	League	2–1	1 Goal	(14)
Sub+9	16/09/95	Tottenham Hotspur	Home	League	1–3		
105	19/09/95	Crewe Alexandra	Away	Lge Cup	2–2		

106	23/09/95	Manchester United	Home	League	0–0			
107	30/09/95	Leeds United	Away	League	0–2			
108	04/10/95	Crewe Alexandra	Home	Lge Cup	5–2			
109	15/10/95	Middlesbrough	Home	League	0–1			
110	21/10/95	Coventry City	Away	League	1–0			
111	25/10/95	Millwall	Away	Lge Cup	2–0			
112	28/10/95	West Ham United	Home	League	0–1			
113	04/11/95	Chelsea	Away	League	0–0			
114	18/11/95	Manchester City	Home	League	1–1			
115	21/11/95	Arsenal	Away	League	2–4	1 Goal	(15)	
116	25/11/95	Everton	Away	League	2–2			
117	29/11/95	Arsenal	Away	Lge Cup	1–2			
118	04/12/95	Coventry City	Home	League	4–3			
119	09/12/95	Manchester United	Away	League	2–2			
120	16/12/95	Leeds United	Home	League	6–2			
121	23/12/95	Southampton	Home	League	2–2			
122	26/12/95	Nottingham Forest	Away	League	0–1			
123	01/01/96	Bolton Wanderers	Home	League	4–2			
124	06/01/96	Charlton Athletic	Away	FA Cup	0–2			
125	13/01/96	Liverpool	Home	League	1–1			
126	20/01/96	Blackburn Rovers	Away	League	0–3			
127	03/02/96	Newcastle United	Away	League	0–2			
128	10/02/96	Wimbledon	Home	League	2–1			
129	17/02/96	Queens Park Rangers	Home	League	1–3			
Sub+10	24/02/96	Tottenham Hotspur	Away	League	0–1			
Sub+11	02/03/96	Nottingham Forest	Home	League	1–3			
130	06/03/96	Aston Villa	Away	League	2–3			
Sub+12	23/03/96	Bolton Wanderers	Away	League	1–2			
Sub+13	08/04/96	Arsenal	Home	League	1–0			
Sub+14	13/04/96	Manchester City	Away	League	0–1			
Sub+15	17/04/96	Chelsea	Home	League	0–0			
Sub+16	27/04/96	Everton	Home	League	2–5			
Sub+17	05/05/96	West Ham United	Away	League	1–1			

+ Played at Millmoor Ground, Rotherham United

SEASON 1996–97

Falkirk – Scottish League Division One

1	14/09/96	Clydebank	Home	League	2–0	1 Goal	(1)	
2	21/09/96	St Mirren	Away	League	1–0			
3	28/09/96	Airdrieonians	Home	League	1–1			
4	05/10/96	East Fife	Away	League	1–3			

Bradford City – Football League Division One

1	12/10/96	Birmingham City	Away	League	0–3			
2	16/10/96	Queens Park Rangers	Away	League	0–1			
3	19/10/96	Barnsley	Home	League	2–2	1 Goal	(1)	
4	26/10/96	West Bromwich Albion	Away	League	0–0			
5	29/10/96	Crystal Palace	Home	League	0–4			
6	02/11/96	Oldham Athletic	Home	League	0–3			
7	08/11/96	Huddersfield Town	Away	League	3–3	1 Goal	(2)	
8	16/11/96	Ipswich Town	Home	League	2–1			
9	23/11/96	Charlton Athletic	Away	League	2–0	1 Goal	(3)	
10	30/11/96	West Bromwich Albion	Home	League	1–1			
11	07/12/96	Manchester City	Away	League	2–3	1 Goal	(4)	
12	17/12/96	Reading	Home	League	0–0			
13	21/12/96	Grimsby Town	Away	League	1–1			
14	26/12/96	Sheffield United	Home	League	1–2			
15	28/12/96	Norwich City	Away	League	0–2			
16	01/01/97	Bolton Wanderers	Away	League	1–2			
17	05/01/97	Wycombe Wanderers	Away	FA Cup	2–0			
18	11/01/97	Oxford United	Home	League	2–0			
19	18/01/97	Swindon Town	Away	League	1–1			
20	25/01/97	Everton	Away	FA Cup	3–2	1 Goal	(5)	
21	28/01/97	Port Vale	Home	League	1–0			
22	01/02/97	Huddersfield Town	Home	League	1–1	1 Goal	(6)	
23	08/02/97	Crystal Palace	Away	League	1–3	1 Goal	(7)	
24	16/02/97	Sheffield Wednesday	Home	FA Cup	0–1			
25	22/02/97	Oldham Athletic	Away	League	2–1			
26	01/03/97	Manchester City	Home	League	1–3			
27	04/03/97	Ipswich Town	Away	League	2–3			
28	08/03/97	Grimsby Town	Home	League	3–4			

Sunderland – Premier League

1	22/03/97	Nottingham Forest	Home	League	1–1		
2	05/04/97	Newcastle United	Away	League	1–1		
3	13/04/97	Liverpool	Home	League	1–2		
4	19/04/97	Middlesbrough	Away	League	1–0		
5	22/04/97	Southampton	Home	League	0–1		
6	03/05/97	Everton	Home	League	3–0	1 Goal	(1)
7	11/05/97	Wimbledon	Away	League	0–1		

INTERNATIONAL APPEARANCES – ENGLAND

1	26/03/85	Republic of Ireland	Wembley	2–1	F		
Sub 2	01/05/85	Romania	Bucharest	0–0	WCQ		
Sub 3	22/05/85	Finland	Helsinki	1–1	WCQ		
Sub 4	25/05/85	Scotland	Hampden Park	0–1	RC		
5	06/06/85	Italy	Mexico City	1–2	F		
Sub 6	09/06/85	Mexico	Mexico City	0–1	F		
7	12/06/85	West Germany	Mexico City	3–0	F		
8	16/06/85	USA	Los Angeles	5–0	F		
9	11/09/85	Romania	Wembley	1–1	WCQ		
10	16/10/85	Turkey	Wembley	5–0	WCQ	1 Goal	(1)
11	13/11/85	Northern Ireland	Wembley	0–0	WCQ		
12	26/02/86	Israel	Tel Aviv	2–1	F		
13	26/03/86	USSR	Tbilisi	1–0	F	1 Goal	(2)
14	23/04/86	Scotland	Wembley	2–1	RC		
15	17/05/86	Mexico	Los Angeles	3–0	F		
16	24/05/86	Canada	Vancouver	1–0	F		
17	03/06/86	Portugal	Monterrey	0–1	WC		
18	06/06/86	Morocco	Monterrey	0–0	WC		
Sub 19	11/06/86	Poland	Monterrey	3–0	WC		
Sub 20	22/06/86	Argentina	Mexico City	1–2	WC		
21	10/09/86	Sweden	Stockholm	0–1	F		
22	15/10/86	Northern Ireland	Wembley	3–0	ECQ	1 Goal	(3)
23	12/11/86	Yugoslavia	Wembley	2–0	ECQ		
24	18/02/87	Spain	Madrid	4–2	F		
25	01/04/87	Northern Ireland	Windsor Park	2–0	ECQ	1 Goal	(4)
26	29/04/87	Turkey	Izmir	0–0	ECQ		
27	19/05/87	Brazil	Wembley	1–1	RC		
28	23/05/87	Scotland	Hampden Park	0–0	RC		
29	09/09/87	West Germany	Dusseldorf	1–3	F		
30	17/02/88	Israel	Tel Aviv	0–0	F		
31	27/04/88	Hungary	Budapest	0–0	F		
Sub 32	21/05/88	Scotland	Wembley	1–0	RC		
33	24/05/88	Colombia	Wembley	1–1	RC		
Sub 34	28/05/88	Switzerland	Lausanne	1–0	F		
35	12/06/88	Republic of Ireland	Stuttgart	0–1	EC		
Sub 36	15/06/88	Holland	Dusseldorf	1–3	EC		
37	19/10/88	Sweden	Wembley	0–0	WCQ		
38	16/11/88	Saudi Arabia	Riyadh	1–1	F		
39	08/03/89	Albania	Tirana	2–0	WCQ		
40	26/04/89	Albania	Wembley	5–0	WCQ	1 Goal	(5)
41	23/05/89	Chile	Wembley	0–0	RC		
42	27/05/89	Scotland	Hampden Park	2–0	RC	1 Goal	(6)
43	03/06/89	Poland	Wembley	3–0	WCQ		
Sub 44	07/06/89	Denmark	Copenhagen	1–1	F		
45	06/09/89	Sweden	Solna	0–0	WCQ		
46	11/10/89	Poland	Katowice	0–0	WCQ		
47	15/11/89	Italy	Wembley	0–0	F		
48	13/12/89	Yugoslavia	Wembley	2–1	F		
49	28/03/90	Brazil	Wembley	1–0	F		
50	15/05/90	Denmark	Wembley	1–0	F		
51	22/05/90	Uruguay	Wembley	1–2	F		
52	02/06/90	Tunisia	Tunis	1–1	F		
53	11/06/90	Republic of Ireland	Cagliari	1–1	WC		
54	16/06/90	Holland	Cagliari	0–0	WC		
55	21/06/90	Egypt	Cagliari	1–0	WC		
56	26/06/90	Belgium	Bologna	1–0*	WC		
57	01/07/90	Cameroon	Naples	3–2*	WC		
58	04/07/90	West Germany	Turin	1–1+	WC		
Sub 59	07/07/90	Italy	Bari	1–2	WC		
Sub 60	12/09/90	Hungary	Wembley	1–0	F		
Sub 61	17/10/90	Poland	Wembley	2–0	ECQ		
62	16/10/91	Turkey	Wembley	1–0	ECQ		

+ AET West Germany won 4–3 on penalties

APPEARANCES AND GOALS PER SEASON

SEASON 80–81	GAMES	GOALS
League	13	1
FA Cup	4	2
TOTAL	17	3

SEASON 81–82	GAMES	GOALS
League	42	7
FA Cup	3	1
League Cup	2	0
TOTAL	47	8

SEASON 82–83	GAMES	GOALS
League	37	7
FA Cup	2	0
League Cup	1	0
TOTAL	40	7

SEASON 83–84	GAMES	GOALS
League	42	18
FA Cup	1	0
League Cup	1	0
TOTAL	44	18

SEASON 84–85	GAMES	GOALS
League	35+1	13
FA Cup	2	1
League Cup	4	2
TOTAL	41+1	16

SEASON 85–86	GAMES	GOALS
League	39	11
FA Cup	5	2
League Cup	6	1
Screen Sport Super Cup	4	0
TOTAL	54	14

SEASON 86–87	GAMES	GOALS
League	39	6
FA Cup	6	2
League Cup	9	3
TOTAL	54	11

SEASON 87–88	GAMES	GOALS
League	21+1	2
FA Cup	2	1
League Cup	1	0
TOTAL	24+1	3

SEASON 88–89	GAMES	GOALS
League	38	14
FA Cup	1	0
League Cup	5	0
TOTAL	44	14

SEASON 89–90	GAMES	GOALS
French League	33+4	9
French Cup	4+1	2
European Cup	8	1
TOTAL	45+5	12

SEASON 90–91	GAMES	GOALS
French League	33+2	6
French Cup	5	0
European Cup	9	2
TOTAL	47+2	8

SEASON 91–92	GAMES	GOALS
French League	33+2	7
French Cup	3	0
European Cup	3	1
TOTAL	39+2	8

SEASON 92–93	GAMES	GOALS
League	32+1	1
FA Cup	8	2
League Cup	9	0
UEFA Cup	3+1	1
TOTAL	**52+2**	**4**

SEASON 93–94	GAMES	GOALS
League	19	3
FA Cup	0+1	0
League Cup	6	0
TOTAL	**25+1**	**3**

SEASON 94–95	GAMES	GOALS
League	20+5	4
FA Cup	3	1
TOTAL	**23+5**	**5**

SEASON 95–96	GAMES	GOALS
League	23+9	2
FA Cup	1	0
League Cup	4	0
Inter–Toto Cup	2	1
TOTAL	**30+9**	**3**

SEASON 96–97	GAMES	GOALS
League	32	7
FA Cup	3	1
Scottish League	4	1
TOTAL	**39**	**9**

CAREER APPEARANCES AND GOALS

COMPETITION	GAMES	TOTAL	GOALS
League	432+17	449	96
FA Cup	41+1	42	13
League Cup	48	48	6
Screen Sport Super Cup	4	4	0
European Cup	20	20	4
UEFA Cup	3+1	4	1
Inter–Toto Cup	2	2	1
French League	99+8	107	22
French Cup	12+1	13	2
Scottish League	4	4	1
Internationals	49+13	62	6
TOTAL	**714+41**	**755**	**152**

HAT-TRICKS

Newcastle United

1	3	Queens Park Rangers	22/09/84	Away	League	5–5

League: 1
TOTAL: 1

HONOURS

Winners medals
French League Championship: 89/90, 90/91, 91/92

Runner-up medals
FA Cup: 86/87, 92/93
League Cup: 92/93
European Cup: 90/91
French Cup: 90/91

STEVE WHITE

Born: 02/01/59 – Chipping Sodbury
Height: 5.10
Weight: 11.04 (96–97)

Clubs
Bristol Rovers: **1978–79** – Matches: **51+4** – Goals: **24**
Luton Town: **1979–82** – Matches: **68+11** – Goals: **26**
Charlton Athletic: **1982–83** – Matches: **31** – Goals: **12**
Lincoln City (loan): **1983** – Matches: **3+1** – Goals: **0**
Luton Town (loan): **1983** – Matches: **4** – Goals: **0**
Bristol Rovers: **1983–86** – Matches: **109+15** – Goals: **29**
Swindon Town: **1986–94** – Matches: **252+60** – Goals: **111**
Hereford United: **1994–96** – Matches: **90+8** – Goals: **52**
Cardiff City: **1996–97** – Matches: **38+8** – Goals: **14**

SEASON 1977–78

Bristol Rovers – League Division Two

1	27/03/78	Southampton	Away	League	1–3		
2	01/04/78	Millwall	Away	League	3–1+	1 Goal	(1)
3	04/04/78	Oldham Athletic	Away	League	1–4		
4	08/04/78	Sheffield United	Home	League	4–1	2 Goals	(3)
5	15/04/78	Bolton Wanderers	Away	League	0–3		
6	18/04/78	Brighton & Hove Albion	Home	League	0–4		
7	22/04/78	Stoke City	Home	League	4–1	1 Goal	(4)
8	24/04/78	Mansfield Town	Away	League	0–3		

+ Played at Fratton Park, Portsmouth

SEASON 1978–79

League Division Two

9	14/10/78	Notts County	Away	League	1–2	1 Goal	(5)
Sub+1	10/11/78	Fulham	Away	League	0–3		
Sub+2	25/11/78	Sheffield United	Home	League	2–1		
Sub+3	02/12/78	Sunderland	Away	League	0–5		
Sub+4	23/12/78	Stoke City	Home	League	0–0		
10	26/12/78	Crystal Palace	Away	League	1–0	1 Goal	(6)
11	30/12/78	Preston North End	Away	League	1–1		
12	08/01/79	Swansea City	Away	FA Cup	1–0	1 Goal	(7)
13	16/01/79	Luton Town	Away	League	2–3	2 Goals	(9)
14	20/01/79	West Ham United	Home	League	0–1		
15	05/02/79	Charlton Athletic	Home	FA Cup	1–0	1 Goal	(10)
16	10/02/79	Cambridge United	Home	League	2–0	1 Goal	(11)
17	24/02/79	Notts County	Home	League	2–2		
18	26/02/79	Ipswich Town	Away	FA Cup	1–6	1 Goal	(12)
19	03/03/79	Orient	Away	League	1–1	1 Goal	(13)
20	10/03/79	Leicester City	Home	League	1–1		
21	20/03/79	Brighton & Hove Albion	Home	League	1–2		
22	24/03/79	Oldham Athletic	Home	League	0–0		
23	31/03/79	Sheffield United	Away	League	0–1		
24	04/04/79	Blackburn Rovers	Away	League	2–0	1 Goal	(14)
25	07/04/79	Sunderland	Home	League	0–0		
26	14/04/79	Crystal Palace	Home	League	0–1		
27	16/04/79	Brighton & Hove Albion	Away	League	0–3		
28	17/04/79	Stoke City	Away	League	0–2		
29	21/04/79	Burnley	Home	League	2–0	1 Goal	(15)
30	28/04/79	Millwall	Away	League	3–0	2 Goals	(17)
31	02/05/79	Newcastle united	Away	League	0–3		
32	05/05/79	Preston North End	Home	League	0–1		
33	07/05/79	Cardiff City	Away	League	0–2		
34	10/05/79	Wrexham	Away	League	1–0		

SEASON 1979–80

League Division Two

35	11/08/79	Torquay United	Away	Lge Cup	2–1	1 Goal	(18)
36	14/08/79	Torquay United	Home	Lge Cup	1–3*		
37	18/08/79	Queens Park Rangers	Away	League	0–2		
38	21/08/79	Luton Town	Home	League	3–2	2 Goals	(20)
39	25/08/79	Shrewsbury Town	Home	League	2–1		
40	01/09/79	Birmingham City	Away	League	1–1		
41	08/09/79	Watford	Home	League	1–1		
42	15/09/79	Cambridge United	Away	League	1–4		
43	22/09/79	Preston North End	Away	League	2–3		
44	13/10/79	Chelsea	Away	League	0–1		
45	20/10/79	Charlton Athletic	Home	League	3–0	1 Goal	(21)
46	27/10/79	Orient	Away	League	1–2		
47	10/11/79	Wrexham	Away	League	2–1	1 Goal	(22)
48	17/11/79	Newcastle United	Home	League	1–1	1 Goal	(23)
49	24/11/79	Sunderland	Away	League	2–3	1 Goal	(24)
50	01/12/79	Burnley	Home	League	0–0		
51	15/12/79	Oldham Athletic	Home	League	2–0		

Luton Town – League Division Two

Sub+1	29/12/79	Orient	Away	League	2–2	
Sub+2	05/01/80	Swindon Town	Home	FA Cup	0–2	
Sub+3	02/02/80	Notts County	Home	League	2–1	
Sub+4	09/02/80	Oldham Athletic	Away	League	1–2	
Sub+5	01/03/80	West Ham United	Home	League	1–1	
1	08/03/80	Preston North End	Away	League	1–1	
Sub+6	14/03/80	Cardiff City	Home	League	1–2	
2	22/03/80	Queens Park Rangers	Away	League	2–2	
Sub+7	12/04/80	Shrewsbury Town	Home	League	0–0	
Sub+8	19/04/80	Birmingham City	Away	League	0–1	

SEASON 1980–81

League Division Two

3	16/08/80	West Ham United	Away	League	2–1		
4	19/08/80	Watford	Home	League	1–0	1 Goal	(1)
Sub+9	27/08/80	Reading	Away	Lge Cup	2–0		
5	02/09/80	Reading	Home	Lge Cup	1–1		
Sub+10	13/09/80	Blackburn Rovers	Away	League	0–3		
6	11/10/80	Preston North End	Away	League	0–1		
7	18/10/80	Shrewsbury Town	Home	League	1–1	1 Goal	(2)
8	21/10/80	Swansea City	Home	League	2–2		
9	25/10/80	Cambridge United	Away	League	3–1		
10	01/11/80	Sheffield Wednesday	Home	League	3–0	1 Goal	(3)
11	08/11/80	Queens Park Rangers	Away	League	2–3		
12	11/11/80	Watford	Away	League	1–0	1 Goal	(4)
13	15/11/80	West Ham United	Home	League	3–2		
14	22/11/80	Cardiff City	Away	League	0–1		
15	29/11/80	Bolton Wanderers	Home	League	2–2		
16	06/12/80	Oldham Athletic	Away	League	0–0		
Sub+11	21/02/81	Grimsby Town	Home	League	0–2		
17	07/03/81	Notts County	Away	League	1–0		
18	14/03/81	Bristol City	Home	League	3–1	2 Goals	(6)
19	28/03/81	Cambridge United	Home	League	0–0		
20	31/03/81	Wrexham	Away	League	0–0		
21	27/04/81	Swansea City	Away	League	2–2		
22	02/05/81	Bolton Wanderers	Away	League	3–0	1 Goal	(7)

SEASON 1981–82

League Division Two

23	29/08/81	Charlton Athletic	Home	League	3–0	1 Goal	(8)
24	01/09/81	Queens Park Rangers	Away	League	2–1		
25	05/09/81	Bolton Wanderers	Away	League	2–1		
26	12/09/81	Sheffield Wednesday	Home	League	0–3		
27	19/09/81	Leicester City	Away	League	2–1	2 Goals	(10)
28	22/09/81	Cardiff City	Home	League	2–3		
29	26/09/81	Watford	Home	League	4–1		
30	03/10/81	Orient	Away	League	3–0	1 Goal	(11)
31	06/10/81	Wrexham	Home	Lge Cup	0–2		
32	10/10/81	Oldham Athletic	Away	League	1–1	1 Goal	(12)

33	17/10/81	Grimsby Town	Home	League	6–0	4 Goals	(16)
34	24/10/81	Wrexham	Away	League	2–0	1 Goal	(17)
35	27/10/81	Wrexham	Away	Lge Cup	1–0	1 Goal	(18)
36	31/10/81	Crystal Palace	Home	League	1–0		
37	07/11/81	Derby County	Home	League	3–2		
38	14/11/81	Blackburn Rovers	Away	League	1–0		
39	21/11/81	Newcastle United	Away	League	2–3		
40	24/11/81	Bolton Wanderers	Home	League	2–0		
41	28/11/81	Rotherham United	Home	League	3–1	1 Goal	(19)
42	05/12/81	Shrewsbury Town	Away	League	2–2	1 Goal	(20)
43	28/12/81	Norwich City	Away	League	3–1	1 Goal	(21)
44	02/01/82	Swindon Town	Home	FA Cup	2–1		
45	19/01/82	Charlton Athletic	Away	League	0–0		
46	23/01/82	Ipswich Town	Home	FA Cup	0–3		
47	30/01/82	Leicester City	Home	League	2–1	1 Goal	(22)
48	06/02/82	Sheffield Wednesday	Away	League	3–3	1 Goal	(23)
49	20/02/82	Watford	Away	League	1–1		
50	27/02/82	Oldham Athletic	Home	League	2–0		
51	02/03/82	Cambridge United	Home	League	1–0		
52	06/03/82	Grimsby Town	Away	League	0–0		
53	12/03/82	Wrexham	Home	League	0–0		
54	16/03/82	Barnsley	Away	League	3–4		
55	20/03/82	Crystal Palace	Away	League	3–3		
56	27/03/82	Derby County	Away	League	0–0		
57	30/03/82	Orient	Home	League	2–0		
58	03/04/82	Blackburn Rovers	Home	League	2–0	1 Goal	(24)
59	10/04/82	Cambridge United	Away	League	1–1		
60	12/04/82	Norwich City	Home	League	2–0		
61	17/04/82	Newcastle United	Home	League	3–2		
62	20/04/82	Chelsea	Home	League	2–2		
63	24/04/82	Rotherham United	Away	League	2–2		
64	30/04/82	Shrewsbury Town	Home	League	4–1	1 Goal	(25)
65	08/05/82	Chelsea	Away	League	2–1		
66	11/05/82	Queens Park Rangers	Home	League	3–2	1 Goal	(26)
67	15/05/82	Barnsley	Home	League	1–1		
68	17/05/82	Cardiff City	Away	League	3–2		

SEASON 1982–83

Charlton Athletic – League Division Two

1	28/08/82	Leicester City	Away	League	2–1		
2	04/09/82	Sheffield Wednesday	Home	League	0–3		
3	07/09/82	Wolverhampton Wanderers	Away	League	0–5		
4	11/09/82	Cambridge United	Away	League	2–3		
5	18/09/82	Grimsby Town	Home	League	0–1		
6	25/09/82	Oldham Athletic	Away	League	2–2		
7	28/09/82	Fulham	Home	League	3–0		
8	02/10/82	Derby County	Home	League	1–1	1 Goal	(1)
9	05/10/82	Luton Town	Away	Lge Cup	0–3		
10	09/10/82	Carlisle United	Away	League	1–4		
11	16/10/82	Burnley	Home	League	2–1	1 Goal	(2)
12	23/10/82	Chelsea	Away	League	1–3		
13	26/10/82	Luton Town	Home	Lge Cup	2–0		
14	30/10/82	Blackburn Rovers	Home	League	3–0	2 Goals	(4)
15	06/11/82	Leeds United	Away	League	2–1	1 Goal	(5)
16	13/11/82	Middlesbrough	Home	League	2–3		
17	20/11/82	Rotherham United	Home	League	1–5		
18	27/11/82	Shrewsbury Town	Away	League	0–0		
19	27/12/82	Crystal Palace	Away	League	1–1	1 Goal	(6)
20	29/12/82	Queens Park Rangers	Home	League	1–3	1 Goal	(7)
21	01/01/83	Rotherham United	Away	League	0–1		
22	03/01/83	Sheffield Wednesday	Away	League	4–5	1 Goal	(8)

Lincoln City (loan) – League Division Three

1	29/01/83	Reading	Away	League	1–1	
2	05/02/83	Orient	Away	League	1–1	
3	08/02/83	Chester	Away	FL Trophy	3–1	
Sub+1	16/02/83	Portsmouth	Home	League	0–3	

Luton Town (loan) – League Division One

1	26/02/83	Ipswich Town	Away	League	0–3	
2	05/03/83	West Bromwich Albion	Home	League	0–0	
3	12/03/83	Nottingham Forest	Away	League	1–0	
4	19/03/83	Arsenal	Away	League	1–4	

Charlton Athletic – League Division Two

23	04/04/83	Crystal Palace	Home	League	2–1	1 Goal	(9)
24	09/04/83	Fulham	Away	League	1–2	1 Goal	(10)
25	13/04/83	Derby County	Away	League	1–1		
26	17/04/83	Oldham Athletic	Home	League	4–1	1 Goal	(11)
27	23/04/83	Newcastle United	Away	League	2–4		
28	29/04/83	Shrewsbury Town	Home	League	0–1		
29	02/05/83	Wolverhampton Wanderers	Home	League	3–3	1 Goal	(12)
30	07/05/83	Barnsley	Away	League	0–0		
31	14/05/83	Bolton Wanderers	Home	League	4–1		

SEASON 1983–84

Bristol Rovers – League Division Three

1	27/08/83	Newport County	Away	League	1–2		
2	30/08/83	AFC Bournemouth	Away	Lge Cup	2–1		
3	03/09/83	Southend United	Home	League	2–1		
4	06/09/83	Brentford	Home	League	3–1	1 Goal	(1)
5	10/09/83	Port Vale	Away	League	0–2		
6	13/09/83	AFC Bournemouth	Home	Lge Cup	2–2		
7	17/09/83	Exeter City	Home	League	2–0		
8	23/09/83	Orient	Away	League	1–0		
9	27/09/83	AFC Bournemouth	Away	League	1–0	1 Goal	(2)
10	01/10/83	Bolton Wanderers	Home	League	2–1		
11	04/10/83	Brighton & Hove Albion	Away	Lge Cup	2–4		
12	08/10/83	Wimbledon	Away	League	1–1		
Sub+1	15/10/83	Bradford City	Home	League	1–0		
Sub+2	18/10/83	Plymouth Argyle	Away	League	1–1		
Sub+3	22/10/83	Scunthorpe United	Home	League	4–1		
13	25/10/83	Brighton & Hove Albion	Home	Lge Cup	2–1*	1 Goal	(3)
14	29/10/83	Walsall	Away	League	1–2		
15	01/11/83	Preston North End	Home	League	3–1		
16	05/11/83	Rotherham United	Away	League	2–2		
17	12/11/83	Burnley	Home	League	2–1		
18	19/11/83	Barnet	Away	FA Cup	0–0		
19	22/11/83	Barnet	Home	FA Cup	3–1		
20	26/11/83	Lincoln City	Away	League	0–4		
Sub+4	03/12/83	Sheffield United	Home	League	1–1		
Sub+5	10/12/83	Bristol City	Home	FA Cup	1–2		
Sub+6	17/12/83	Hull City	Home	League	1–3		
21	26/12/83	Oxford United	Away	League	2–3		
22	27/12/83	Gillingham	Home	League	3–0	1 Goal	(4)
23	30/12/83	Millwall	Away	League	0–1		
24	09/01/84	Southend United	Away	League	2–1		
25	14/01/84	Newport County	Home	League	4–0		
26	21/01/84	Exeter City	Away	League	2–1		
27	28/01/84	Port Vale	Home	League	0–0		
28	04/02/84	Bolton Wanderers	Away	League	0–3		
29	25/02/84	Scunthorpe United	Away	League	2–2	2 Goals	(6)
30	28/02/84	Newport County	Away	AM Cup	1–0		
31	03/03/84	Plymouth Argyle	Home	League	2–0	1 Goal	(7)
32	06/03/84	Rotherham United	Home	League	2–0		
33	10/03/84	Burnley	Away	League	0–0		
Sub+7	13/03/84	Port Vale	Home	AM Cup	2–0		
34	17/03/84	Wimbledon	Home	League	1–1	1 Goal	(8)
35	27/03/84	Wigan Athletic	Home	League	2–1		
36	31/03/84	Brentford	Away	League	2–2	1 Goal	(9)
37	07/04/84	AFC Bournemouth	Home	League	1–3		
38	14/04/84	Sheffield United	Away	League	0–4		
39	17/04/84	Wigan Athletic	Away	League	0–0		
40	21/04/84	Oxford United	Home	League	1–1		
41	23/04/84	Gillingham	Away	League	2–1		
42	28/04/84	Lincoln City	Home	League	3–1	1 Goal	(10)
43	02/05/84	Bradford City	Away	League	1–0		
44	08/05/84	Millwall	Home	League	3–2		
45	12/05/84	Hull City	Away	League	0–0		
46	14/05/84	AFC Bournemouth	Away	AM Cup	0–1		

SEASON 1984–85

League Division Three

47	29/09/84	AFC Bournemouth	Home	League	1–0	1 Goal	(11)
48	02/10/84	York City	Away	League	0–1		

49	09/10/84	Arsenal	Home	Lge Cup	1–1	1 Goal	(12)
50	06/10/84	Derby County	Home	League	2–1		
51	13/10/84	Rotherham United	Away	League	3–3		
52	20/10/84	Doncaster Rovers	Home	League	1–1		
53	17/11/84	King's Lynn	Home	FA Cup	2–1		
Sub+8	15/12/84	Newport County	Home	League	2–0		
Sub+9	22/12/84	Swansea City	Home	League	4–2		
Sub+10	26/12/84	Brentford	Away	League	3–0		
54	12/01/85	Preston North End	Away	League	2–2	1 Goal	(13)
55	22/01/85	Swansea City	Away	FR Trophy	0–2		
56	26/01/85	Reading	Away	League	2–3		
57	29/01/85	Bolton Wanderers	Home	League	1–2		
58	02/02/85	AFC Bournemouth	Away	League	0–1		
Sub+11	19/03/85	Swansea City	Home	FR Trophy	0–0		
Sub+12	06/04/85	Brentford	Home	League	3–0		
59	20/04/85	Millwall	Away	League	0–1		
60	23/04/85	Walsall	Home	League	0–0		
61	04/05/85	Newport County	Away	League	1–1		
62	07/05/85	Gillingham	Home	League	3–2	1 Goal	(14)
63	11/05/85	Swansea City	Away	League	2–3		

SEASON 1985–86

League Division Three

Sub+13	18/08/85	Darlington	Away	League	3–3	1 Goal	(15)
Sub+14	24/08/85	Brentford	Home	League	0–1		
64	26/08/85	Reading	Away	League	2–3		
65	31/08/85	Derby County	Home	League	0–0		
66	03/09/85	Newport County	Away	Lge Cup	0–1		
67	07/09/85	Newport County	Away	League	0–3		
68	17/09/85	Wolverhampton Wanderers	Away	League	4–3	1 Goal	(16)
69	21/09/85	Walsall	Home	League	0–1		
70	24/09/85	Birmingham City	Home	Lge Cup	2–3		
Sub+15	05/10/85	Plymouth Argyle	Away	League	2–4		
71	07/10/85	Birmingham City	Away	Lge Cup	1–2		
72	12/10/85	Rotherham United	Home	League	5–2	1 Goal	(17)
73	19/10/85	Doncaster Rovers	Away	League	2–0		
74	22/10/85	Bolton Wanderers	Home	League	2–1	1 Goal	(18)
75	26/10/85	AFC Bournemouth	Away	League	1–6		
76	02/11/85	York City	Home	League	0–1		
77	05/11/85	Bury	Home	League	2–1	1 Goal	(19)
78	09/11/85	Blackpool	Away	League	2–4		
79	16/11/85	Brentford	Away	FA Cup	3–1	1 Goal	(20)
80	23/11/85	Cardiff City	Home	League	2–1		
81	07/12/85	Swansea City	Away	FA Cup	2–1	1 Goal	(21)
82	14/12/85	Gillingham	Home	League	1–0		
83	22/12/85	Brentford	Away	League	0–1		
84	26/12/85	Wigan Athletic	Away	League	0–4		
85	28/12/85	Reading	Home	League	0–2		
86	04/01/86	Leicester City	Home	FA Cup	3–1		
87	15/01/86	Hereford United	Away	FR Trophy	0–2		
88	18/01/86	Darlington	Home	League	3–1	3 Goals	(24)
89	21/01/86	Swindon Town	Home	FR Trophy	2–1	1 Goal	(25)
90	25/01/86	Luton Town	Away	FA Cup	0–4		
91	01/02/86	Newport County	Home	League	2–0		
92	04/02/86	Bolton Wanderers	Away	League	2–0	1 Goal	(26)
93	08/02/86	Doncaster Rovers	Home	League	1–0	1 Goal	(27)
94	01/03/86	Swansea City	Home	League	0–0		
95	04/03/86	Notts County	Away	League	0–0		
96	08/03/86	Plymouth Argyle	Home	League	1–2		
97	12/03/86	York City	Away	League	0–4		
98	15/03/86	Rotherham United	Away	League	0–2		
99	18/03/86	Walsall	Away	League	0–6		
100	22/03/86	AFC Bournemouth	Home	League	2–3	1 Goal	(28)
101	25/03/86	Wolverhampton Wanderers	Home	League	1–1		
102	29/03/86	Bristol City	Away	League	0–2		
103	09/04/86	Derby County	Away	League	2–0	1 Goal	(29)
104	15/04/86	Chesterfield	Away	League	0–2		
105	19/04/86	Cardiff City	Away	League	0–2		
106	22/04/86	Bristol City	Home	League	1–1		
107	26/04/86	Chesterfield	Home	League	1–1		
108	30/04/86	Lincoln City	Away	League	2–2		
109	03/05/86	Gillingham	Away	League	0–2		

SEASON 1986–87

Swindon Town – League Division Three

Sub+1	31/08/86	Notts County	Home	League	1–2	1 Goal	(1)
Sub+2	13/09/86	Chester City	Home	League	1–1	1 Goal	(2)
1	16/09/86	Blackpool	Home	League	2–6		
2	05/10/86	Wigan Athletic	Home	League	3–1		
Sub+3	08/10/86	Southampton	Home	Lge Cup	0–0		
Sub+4	11/10/86	Fulham	Away	League	2–0	1 Goal	(3)
Sub+5	18/10/86	Chesterfield	Home	League	2–1		
3	21/10/86	Port Vale	Away	League	4–3	1 Goal	(4)
4	25/10/86	Darlington	Away	League	0–0		
5	01/11/86	York City	Home	League	3–1		
6	04/11/86	Bristol Rovers	Home	League	1–2		
7	08/11/86	Mansfield Town	Away	League	0–0		
8	15/11/86	Farnborough Town	Away	FA Cup	4–0+		
9	09/12/86	Orient	Home	FR Trophy	3–0	1 Goal	(5)
10	14/12/86	Bristol City	Home	League	1–2	1 Goal	(6)
11	21/12/86	Doncaster Rovers	Away	League	2–2	1 Goal	(7)
12	26/12/86	Brentford	Home	League	2–0	1 Goal	(8)
13	27/12/86	Gillingham	Away	League	3–1		
14	01/01/87	AFC Bournemouth	Away	League	0–1		
15	03/01/87	Bury	Home	League	1–0		
16	06/01/87	Brentford	Away	FR Trophy	2–4	1 Goal	(9)
17	10/01/87	Fulham	Away	FA Cup	1–0		
18	28/01/87	AFC Bournemouth	Home	FR Trophy	2–2#		
Sub+6	03/02/87	Leeds United	Home	FA Cup	1–2		
19	07/02/87	Blackpool	Away	League	1–1		
20	10/02/87	Hereford United	Home	FR Trophy	4–2	1 Goal	(10)
21	21/02/87	Rotherham United	Away	League	2–1		
22	28/02/87	Middlesbrough	Home	League	1–0	1 Goal	(11)
23	03/03/87	York City	Away	League	3–0		
24	10/03/87	Aldershot	Home	FR Trophy	2–3	1 Goal	(12)
25	14/03/87	Chesterfield	Away	League	3–1	2 Goals	(14)
26	17/03/87	Port Vale	Home	League	1–0		
27	21/03/87	Fulham	Home	League	2–0		
28	24/03/87	Bolton Wanderers	Home	League	2–0	1 Goal	(15)
29	28/03/87	Wigan Athletic	Away	League	2–3		
30	01/04/87	Chester City	Away	League	0–2		
31	03/04/87	Mansfield Town	Home	League	3–0	3 Goals	(18)
32	11/04/87	Bristol Rovers	Away	League	4–3	1 Goal	(19)
33	18/04/87	AFC Bournemouth	Home	League	1–1		
34	22/04/87	Darlington	Home	League	1–0		
35	25/04/87	Doncaster Rovers	Home	League	1–1		
36	28/04/87	Notts County	Away	League	3–2		
Sub+7	02/05/87	Carlisle United	Away	League	3–0		
Sub+8	04/05/87	Gillingham	Home	League	1–1		
37	25/05/87	Gillingham	Home	Lge P/O	2–1		
38	29/05/87	Gillingham	Home	Lge P/O	2–0	2 Goals	(21)

+ Match played at Swindon Town
# AET Swindon Town won 4–2 on penalties

SEASON 1987–88

League Division Two

39	22/09/87	Portsmouth	Home	Lge Cup	3–1		
Sub+9	26/09/87	Reading	Home	League	4–0		
Sub+10	07/10/87	Portsmouth	Away	Lge Cup	3–1	1 Goal	(22)
40	10/10/87	Oldham Athletic	Home	League	2–0	1 Goal	(23)
41	20/10/87	Stoke City	Home	League	3–0	2 Goals	(25)
42	24/10/87	Crystal Palace	Away	League	1–2	1 Goal	(26)
43	27/10/87	Watford	Home	Lge Cup	1–1		
44	31/10/87	Manchester City	Home	League	3–4		
Sub+11	03/11/87	Watford	Away	Lge Cup	2–4		
45	10/11/87	Blackburn Rovers	Away	Simod Cup	2–1		
Sub+12	14/11/87	Plymouth Argyle	Home	League	1–1		
46	28/11/87	AFC Bournemouth	Home	League	4–2	2 Goals	(28)
47	01/12/87	Huddersfield Town	Home	League	4–1		
48	05/12/87	Aston Villa	Away	League	1–2		
49	20/12/87	Sheffield United	Away	League	0–1		
Sub+13	01/01/88	West Bromwich Albion	Home	League	2–0	2 Goals	(30)
Sub+14	02/01/88	Birmingham City	Away	League	1–1		
50	09/01/88	Norwich City	Home	FA Cup	0–0		
51	19/01/88	Chelsea	Home	Simod Cup	4–0	2 Goals	(32)
52	06/02/88	Middlesbrough	Home	League	1–1		

Sub+15	20/02/88	Shrewsbury Town	Away	League	1–2		
53	23/02/88	Norwich City	Home	Simod Cup	2–0		
54	27/02/88	Millwall	Home	League	0–1		
Sub+16	08/03/88	Luton Town	Away	Simod Cup	1–2		
55	12/03/88	Oldham Athletic	Away	League	3–4		
56	15/03/88	Barnsley	Home	League	3–0	2 Goals	(34)
57	19/03/88	Manchester City	Away	League	1–1		
58	27/03/88	Crystal Palace	Home	League	2–2	1 Goal	(35)
Sub+17	04/04/88	Plymouth Argyle	Away	League	0–1		
59	09/04/88	Blackburn Rovers	Home	League	1–2		
Sub+18	23/04/88	Stoke City	Away	League	0–1		
60	25/04/88	Blackburn Rovers	Away	League	0–0		
Sub+19	02/05/88	AFC Bournemouth	Away	League	0–2		
61	07/05/88	Aston Villa	Home	League	0–0		

SEASON 1988–89

League Division Two

62	29/08/88	Barnsley	Away	League	1–1	1 Goal	(36)
63	03/09/88	West Bromwich Albion	Away	League	1–3	1 Goal	(37)
64	11/09/88	Portsmouth	Home	League	1–1		
65	17/09/88	Blackburn Rovers	Away	League	0–0		
66	20/09/88	AFC Bournemouth	Home	League	3–1		
67	24/09/88	Brighton & Hove Albion	Home	League	3–0	1 Goal	(38)
68	27/09/88	Crystal Palace	Home	Lge Cup	1–2		
69	01/10/88	Watford	Away	League	3–2		
70	05/10/88	Oxford United	Away	League	1–1		
71	09/10/88	Chelsea	Home	League	1–1		
72	12/10/88	Crystal Palace	Away	Lge Cup	0–2		
73	16/10/88	Leeds United	Home	League	0–0		
74	22/10/88	Sunderland	Away	League	0–4		
75	26/10/88	Leicester City	Away	League	3–3	1 Goal	(39)
76	29/10/88	Birmingham City	Home	League	2–1	2 Goals	(41)
77	05/11/88	Hull City	Away	League	0–1		
78	09/11/88	Norwich City	Away	Simod Cup	1–2	1 Goal	(42)
79	12/11/88	Ipswich Town	Home	League	2–3		
80	19/11/88	Stoke City	Away	League	1–2		
81	26/11/88	Walsall	Home	League	1–0		
82	03/12/88	Shrewsbury Town	Away	League	1–0		
Sub+20	10/12/88	Oldham Athletic	Home	League	2–2		
83	31/12/88	Manchester City	Home	League	1–2	1 Goal	(43)
Sub+21	02/01/89	Portsmouth	Away	League	2–0		
Sub+22	07/01/89	Portsmouth	Away	FA Cup	1–1		
84	10/01/89	Portsmouth	Home	FA Cup	2–0		
85	14/01/89	Barnsley	Home	League	0–0		
86	05/02/89	Oxford United	Home	League	3–0		
87	11/02/89	Chelsea	Away	League	2–3		
88	18/02/89	Sunderland	Home	League	4–1	1 Goal	(44)
89	25/02/89	Leeds United	Away	League	0–0		
90	28/02/89	Leicester City	Home	League	2–1		
91	04/03/89	Ipswich Town	Away	League	2–1	2 Goals	(46)
92	11/03/89	Hull City	Home	League	1–0		
93	18/03/89	AFC Bournemouth	Away	League	3–2		
94	25/03/89	West Bromwich Albion	Home	League	0–0		
95	27/03/89	Plymouth Argyle	Away	League	1–4		
96	01/04/89	Blackburn Rovers	Home	League	1–1		
97	04/04/89	Bradford City	Home	League	1–0		
98	08/04/89	Manchester City	Away	League	1–2		
99	15/04/89	Watford	Home	League	1–1	1 Goal	(47)
100	18/04/89	Birmingham City	Away	League	2–1		
101	22/04/89	Brighton & Hove Albion	Away	League	2–0		
102	25/04/89	Crystal Palace	Home	League	1–0	1 Goal	(48)
103	29/04/89	Walsall	Away	League	2–2		
104	01/05/89	Shrewsbury Town	Home	League	1–0		
105	06/05/89	Stoke City	Home	League	3–0		
106	13/05/89	Oldham Athletic	Away	League	2–2	1 Goal	(49)
107	21/05/89	Crystal Palace	Home	Lge P/O	1–0		
108	24/05/89	Crystal Palace	Away	Lge P/O	0–2		

SEASON 1989–90

League Division Two

109	19/08/89	Sunderland	Home	League	0–2		
110	26/08/89	Oldham Athletic	Away	League	2–2		
111	03/09/89	Wolverhampton Wanderers	Home	League	3–1		

112	09/09/89	West Ham United	Away	League	1–1		
113	12/09/89	Sheffield United	Away	League	0–2		
Sub+23	30/09/89	Bradford City	Away	League	1–1	1 Goal	(50)
114	03/10/89	Shrewsbury Town	Home	Lge Cup	3–1	2 Goals	(52)
115	07/10/89	Hull City	Away	League	3–2		
116	14/10/89	Ipswich Town	Home	League	3–0		
117	17/10/89	Oxford United	Home	League	3–0	2 Goals	(54)
118	21/10/89	Leicester City	Away	League	1–2		
119	24/10/89	Bolton Wanderers	Home	Lge Cup	3–3		
120	01/11/89	Brighton & Hove Albion	Away	League	2–1		
121	04/11/89	Stoke City	Home	League	6–0	2 Goals	(56)
122	07/11/89	Bolton Wanderers	Away	Lge Cup	1–1*		
123	11/11/89	Middlesbrough	Away	League	2–0		
124	14/11/89	Bolton Wanderers	Away	Lge Cup	1–1*	1 Goal	(57)
125	18/11/89	Port Vale	Away	League	0–2		
126	21/11/89	Bolton Wanderers	Home	Lge Cup	2–1*	1 Goal	(58)
127	26/11/89	Portsmouth	Home	League	2–2		
128	29/11/89	Southampton	Home	Lge Cup	0–0		
129	02/12/89	Sunderland	Away	League	2–2		
130	05/12/89	AFC Bournemouth	Home	League	2–3	1 Goal	(59)
131	10/12/89	Sheffield United	Home	League	0–2		
132	13/12/89	Millwall	Home	ZDS Cup	2–1	1 Goal	(60)
133	17/12/89	West Bromwich Albion	Away	League	2–1	1 Goal	(61)
134	26/12/89	Blackburn Rovers	Home	League	4–3		
135	30/12/89	Newcastle United	Home	League	1–1		
136	01/01/90	Watford	Away	League	2–0		
137	06/01/90	Bristol City	Away	FA Cup	1–2		
138	13/01/90	Oldham Athletic	Home	League	3–2	2 Goals	(63)
139	24/01/90	Norwich City	Home	ZDS Cup	4–1	1 Goal	(64)
140	16/01/90	Southampton	Away	Lge Cup	2–4*	1 Goal	(65)
141	20/01/90	Wolverhampton Wanderers	Away	League	1–2	1 Goal	(66)
142	04/02/90	Leeds United	Home	League	3–2		
143	10/02/90	Barnsley	Away	League	1–0		
144	13/02/90	Crystal Palace	Away	ZDS Cup	0–1		
145	18/02/90	West Ham United	Home	League	2–2	1 Goal	(67)
146	24/02/90	Portsmouth	Away	League	1–1		
147	03/03/90	Port Vale	Home	League	3–0	1 Goal	(68)
148	06/03/90	Bradford City	Home	League	3–1		
149	10/03/90	Plymouth Argyle	Away	League	3–0	2 Goals	(70)
150	17/03/90	Hull City	Home	League	1–3		
151	20/03/90	Ipswich Town	Away	League	0–1		
152	24/03/90	Oxford United	Away	League	2–2	1 Goal	(71)
153	31/03/90	Leicester City	Home	League	1–1		
154	07/04/90	AFC Bournemouth	Away	League	2–1		
155	10/04/90	Brighton & Hove Albion	Home	League	1–2	1 Goal	(72)
156	14/04/90	Watford	Home	League	2–0	1 Goal	(73)
157	16/04/90	Blackburn Rovers	Away	League	1–2		
158	21/04/90	West Bromwich Albion	Home	League	2–1	1 Goal	(74)
159	25/04/90	Newcastle United	Away	League	0–0		
160	28/04/90	Middlesbrough	Home	League	1–1		
161	05/05/90	Stoke City	Away	League	1–1		
162	13/05/90	Blackburn Rovers	Away	Lge P/O	2–1	1 Goal	(75)
163	16/05/90	Blackburn Rovers	Home	Lge P/O	2–1	1 Goal	(76)
164	28/05/90	Sunderland	Wembley	Lge P/O	1–0		

SEASON 1990–91

League Division Two

Sub+24	22/09/90	Oxford United	Away	League	4–2		
Sub+25	25/09/90	Darlington	Away	Lge Cup	0–3		
Sub+26	30/09/90	Millwall	Home	League	0–0		
165	02/10/90	Oldham Athletic	Away	League	2–3		
166	06/10/90	Brighton & Hove Albion	Away	League	3–3	1 Goal	(77)
167	09/10/90	Darlington	Home	Lge Cup	4–0		
168	13/10/90	Bristol Rovers	Home	League	0–2		
169	20/10/90	West Ham United	Home	League	0–1		
170	24/10/90	Leicester City	Away	League	2–2	1 Goal	(78)
171	27/10/90	Barnsley	Away	League	1–5	1 Goal	(79)
172	31/10/90	Sheffield Wednesday	Away	Lge Cup	0–0		
173	03/11/90	Port Vale	Home	League	1–2		
174	06/11/90	Sheffield Wednesday	Home	Lge Cup	0–1		
175	10/11/90	Portsmouth	Home	League	3–0		
176	17/11/90	Sheffield Wednesday	Away	League	1–2		
177	24/11/90	Notts County	Away	League	0–0		
178	01/12/90	Blackburn Rovers	Home	League	1–1		

179	08/12/90	Ipswich Town	Away	League	1–1		
Sub+27	15/12/90	Charlton Athletic	Home	League	1–1		
180	22/12/90	West Bromwich Albion	Home	League	2–1		
181	26/12/90	Newcastle United	Away	League	1–1		
182	29/12/90	Watford	Away	League	2–2		
183	01/01/91	Plymouth Argyle	Home	League	1–1		
184	05/01/91	Leyton Orient	Away	FA Cup	1–1		
185	12/01/91	Bristol City	Away	League	4–0	2 Goals	(81)
186	19/01/91	Hull City	Home	League	3–1	1 Goal	(82)
187	21/01/91	Leyton Orient	Home	FA Cup	1–0	1 Goal	(83)
188	26/01/91	Norwich City	Away	FA Cup	1–3	1 Goal	(84)
189	02/02/91	Middlesbrough	Away	League	0–2		
190	19/02/91	Sheffield Wednesday	Home	League	2–1		
191	23/02/91	Portsmouth	Away	League	1–2	1 Goal	(85)
192	02/03/91	Blackburn Rovers	Away	League	1–2	1 Goal	(86)
193	05/03/91	Oxford United	Home	League	0–0		
194	12/03/91	Oldham Athletic	Home	League	2–2		
195	16/03/91	Millwall	Away	League	0–1		
196	20/03/91	Bristol Rovers	Away	League	1–2		
197	23/03/91	Brighton & Hove Albion	Home	League	1–3		
Sub+28	30/03/91	Newcastle United	Home	League	3–2		
Sub+29	06/04/91	Watford	Home	League	1–2	1 Goal	(87)
Sub+30	20/04/91	West Ham United	Away	League	0–2		
198	23/04/91	Notts County	Home	League	1–2		
Sub+31	27/04/91	Leicester City	Home	League	5–2		

SEASON 1991–92

League Division Two

Sub+32	17/08/91	Leicester City	Home	League	0–0		
Sub+33	20/08/91	West Bromwich Albion	Home	Lge Cup	2–0		
199	28/08/91	West Bromwich Albion	Away	Lge Cup	2–2		
200	31/08/91	Barnsley	Home	League	3–1	1 Goal	(88)
201	03/09/91	Ipswich Town	Home	League	4–1	1 Goal	(89)
202	07/09/91	Port Vale	Home	League	2–2	1 Goal	(90)
203	14/09/91	Sunderland	Home	League	5–3	1 Goal	(91)
204	17/09/91	Bristol Rovers	Home	League	1–0		
205	21/09/91	Wolverhampton Wanderers	Home	League	1–2	1 Goal	(92)
206	25/09/91	Millwall	Away	Lge Cup	2–2	2 Goals	(94)
207	28/09/91	Watford	Home	League	3–1		
208	01/10/91	Oxford United	Home	ZDS Cup	3–3+	2 Goals	(96)
209	05/10/91	Plymouth Argyle	Home	League	4–0		
210	08/10/91	Millwall	Home	Lge Cup	3–1	1 Goal	(97)
211	12/10/91	Derby County	Home	League	1–2		
212	19/10/91	Blackburn Rovers	Home	League	2–1	1 Goal	(98)
213	23/10/91	Chelsea	Away	ZDS Cup	0–1		
214	26/10/91	Brighton & Hove Albion	Home	League	2–0		
215	29/10/91	Huddersfield Town	Away	Lge Cup	4–1		
216	02/11/91	Newcastle United	Home	League	2–1	1 Goal	(99)
217	06/11/91	Charlton Athletic	Home	League	0–0		
218	09/11/91	Southend United	Home	League	2–3	1 Goal	(100)
219	16/11/91	Portsmouth	Home	League	2–3	2 Goals	(102)
220	22/11/91	Tranmere Rovers	Home	League	0–0		
221	30/11/91	Grimsby Town	Home	League	1–1		
222	07/12/91	Middlesbrough	Home	League	2–2		
223	17/12/91	Crystal Palace	Home	Lge Cup	0–1		
224	20/12/91	Ipswich Town	Home	League	0–0		
225	26/12/91	Bristol City	Home	League	1–1		
226	28/12/91	Barnsley	Home	League	1–1		
Sub+34	11/01/92	Cambridge United	Home	League	0–2		

+ AET Swindon Town won 4–3 on penalties

SEASON 1992–93

Football League Division One

Sub+35	19/08/92	Bristol Rovers	Away	League	4–3		
Sub+36	01/09/92	Oxford United	Away	AI Cup	3–1		
Sub+37	05/09/92	Millwall	Away	League	1–2		
Sub+38	16/09/92	Brentford	Home	AI Cup	1–2		
Sub+39	23/09/92	Torquay United	Away	Lge Cup	6–0	1 Goal	(103)
Sub+40	26/09/92	Charlton Athletic	Away	League	0–2		
Sub+41	03/10/92	Watford	Home	League	3–1		
227	06/10/92	Torquay United	Home	Lge Cup	3–2	1 Goal	(104)
Sub+42	10/10/92	Portsmouth	Away	League	1–3	1 Goal	(105)
Sub+43	17/10/92	Notts County	Home	League	5–1		

Sub+44	24/10/92	West Ham United	Away	League	1–0		
Sub+45	27/10/92	Oldham Athletic	Home	Lge Cup	0–1		
Sub+46	31/10/92	Barnsley	Home	League	1–0		
Sub+47	03/11/92	Brentford	Home	League	0–2		
Sub+48	08/11/92	Newcastle United	Away	League	0–0		
Sub+49	21/11/92	Bristol City	Away	League	2–2		
Sub+50	06/12/92	Derby County	Home	League	2–4		
Sub+51	20/12/92	Leicester City	Away	League	2–4		
228	04/01/92	Queens Park Rangers	Away	FA Cup	0–3		
229	09/01/93	Oxford United	Away	League	1–0	1 Goal	(106)
230	12/01/93	Birmingham City	Home	League	0–0		
231	16/01/93	Charlton Athletic	Home	League	2–2		
232	26/01/93	Grimsby Town	Away	League	1–2		
233	30/01/93	Wolverhampton Wanderers	Home	League	1–0		
234	06/02/93	Sunderland	Away	League	1–0		
235	13/02/93	Millwall	Home	League	3–0	1 Goal	(107)
236	20/02/93	Cambridge United	Away	League	0–1		
237	23/02/93	Tranmere Rovers	Home	League	2–0		
238	27/02/93	Portsmouth	Home	League	1–0		
239	06/03/93	Watford	Away	League	4–0	3 Goals	(110)
240	10/03/93	Southend United	Away	League	1–1	1 Goal	(111)
241	13/03/93	Newcastle United	Home	League	2–1		
242	17/03/93	Luton Town	Away	League	0–0		
243	21/03/93	Derby County	Away	League	1–2		
244	24/03/93	Bristol City	Home	League	2–1		
245	27/03/93	Brentford	Away	League	0–0		
246	03/04/93	Peterborough United	Home	League	1–0		
247	06/04/93	Tranmere Rovers	Away	League	1–3		
Sub+52	24/04/93	Notts County	Away	League	1–1		
248	02/05/93	West Ham United	Home	League	1–3		
Sub+53	16/05/93	Tranmere Rovers	Home	Lge P/O	3–1		
249	19/05/93	Tranmere Rovers	Away	Lge P/O	2–3		
Sub+54	31/05/93	Leicester City	Wembley	Lge P/O	4–3		

SEASON 1993–94

Premier League

250	14/08/93	Sheffield United	Away	League	1–3		
Sub+55	11/09/93	West Ham United	Away	League	0–0		
Sub+56	18/09/93	Newcastle United	Home	League	2–2		
251	22/09/93	Wolverhampton Wanderers	Home	Lge Cup	2–0		
Sub+57	25/09/93	Manchester United	Away	League	2–4		
252	02/10/93	Blackburn Rovers	Home	League	1–3		
Sub+58	05/10/93	Wolverhampton Wanderers	Away	Lge Cup	1–2		
Sub+59	06/11/93	Wimbledon	Away	League	0–3		

SEASON 1994–95

Football League Division One

Sub+60	24/08/94	Atalanta BC	Home	AI Cup	0–2		

Hereford United – Football League Division Three

1	27/08/94	Walsall	Home	League	0–0		
2	30/08/94	Scarborough	Away	League	1–3		
3	03/09/94	Rochdale	Away	League	3–1	1 Goal	(1)
4	07/09/94	West Bromwich Albion	Away	Lge Cup	1–0	1 Goal	(2)
5	10/09/94	Wigan Athletic	Home	League	1–2	1 Goal	(3)
6	13/09/94	Torquay United	Home	League	1–1	1 Goal	(4)
7	16/09/94	Doncaster Rovers	Away	League	0–3		
8	21/09/94	Nottingham Forest	Away	Lge Cup	1–2	1 Goal	(5)
9	24/09/94	Fulham	Away	League	1–1	1 Goal	(6)
10	27/09/94	Torquay United	Home	AW Shield	4–2	1 Goal	(7)
11	01/10/94	Scunthorpe United	Home	League	2–1	1 Goal	(8)
12	04/10/94	Nottingham Forest	Home	Lge Cup	0–0		
13	08/10/94	Barnet	Away	League	2–2	1 Goal	(9)
14	15/10/94	Gillingham	Home	League	2–1		
15	22/10/94	Darlington	Away	League	1–3		
16	29/10/94	Lincoln City	Home	League	0–3		
17	05/11/94	Chesterfield	Away	League	0–1		
Sub+1	08/11/94	Swansea City	Away	AW Shield	1–1		
18	12/11/94	Hitchin Town	Home	FA Cup	2–2		
Sub+2	19/11/94	Carlisle United	Home	League	0–1		
19	22/11/94	Hitchin Town	Away	FA Cup	2–4	1 Goal	(10)
20	26/11/94	Northampton Town	Away	League	3–1	1 Goal	(11)
21	29/11/94	Peterborough United	Home	AW Shield	2–0		
22	10/12/94	Preston North End	Away	League	2–4		

23	17/12/94	Walsall	Away	League	3–4	1 Goal	(12)
24	26/12/94	Mansfield Town	Away	League	1–7		
25	07/01/95	Darlington	Home	League	0–0		
26	10/01/94	Birmingham City	Away	AW Shield	1–3		
27	14/01/95	Bury	Away	League	1–1		
Sub+3	24/01/95	Chesterfield	Home	League	0–2		
Sub+4	28/01/95	Lincoln City	Away	League	0–2		
28	04/02/95	Northampton Town	Home	League	2–1	1 Goal	(13)
29	11/02/95	Carlisle United	Away	League	0–1		
Sub+5	18/02/95	Bury	Home	League	1–0		
Sub+6	21/02/95	Hartlepool United	Home	League	1–0	1 Goal	(14)
30	04/03/95	Fulham	Home	League	1–1		
31	25/03/95	Rochdale	Home	League	0–0		
32	29/03/95	Wigan Athletic	Away	League	1–1		
33	01/04/95	Torquay United	Away	League	1–0	1 Goal	(15)
34	08/04/95	Colchester United	Home	League	3–0	2 Goals	(17)
35	15/04/95	Exeter City	Away	League	1–1	1 Goal	(18)
36	17/04/95	Mansfield Town	Home	League	0–0		
37	22/04/95	Hartlepool United	Away	League	0–4		
38	29/04/95	Gillingham	Away	League	0–0		
39	06/05/95	Barnet	Home	League	3–2	1 Goal	(19)

SEASON 1995–96

Football League Division Three

40	12/08/95	Barnet	Home	League	4–1		
41	15/08/95	Oxford United	Home	Lge Cup	0–2		
42	19/08/95	Cambridge United	Away	League	2–2		
43	22/08/95	Oxford United	Away	Lge Cup	2–3		
44	26/08/95	Bury	Home	League	3–4	2 Goals	(21)
45	29/08/95	Plymouth Argyle	Away	League	1–0	1 Goal	(22)
Sub+7	26/09/95	Cardiff City	Home	AW Shield	3–3		
46	30/09/95	Wigan Athletic	Home	League	2–2	1 Goal	(23)
47	07/10/95	Torquay United	Home	League	2–1	1 Goal	(24)
48	14/10/95	Doncaster Rovers	Away	League	0–0		
49	21/10/95	Exeter City	Home	League	2–2	1 Goal	(25)
50	28/10/95	Fulham	Away	League	0–0		
51	31/10/95	Leyton Orient	Away	League	1–0		
52	04/11/95	Mansfield Town	Home	League	0–1		
53	07/11/95	Gillingham	Away	AW Shield	2–2		
54	11/11/95	Stevenage Borough	Home	FA Cup	2–1	1 Goal	(26)
55	18/11/95	Rochdale	Away	League	0–0		
56	26/11/95	Cardiff City	Home	League	1–3	1 Goal	(27)
57	29/11/95	Swindon Town	Away	AW Shield	1–0	1 Goal	(28)
58	02/12/95	Sutton United	Home	FA Cup	2–0	2 Goals	(30)
59	09/12/95	Colchester United	Home	League	1–1		
60	16/12/95	Wigan Athletic	Away	League	1–2		
61	19/12/95	Scunthorpe United	Home	League	3–0	2 Goals	(32)
62	·26/12/95	Northampton Town	Away	League	1–1		
63	06/01/96	Tottenham Hotspur	Home	FA Cup	1–1		
64	09/01/96	Northampton Town	Home	AW Shield	1–0		
65	13/01/96	Cambridge United	Home	League	5–2	4 Goals	(36)
66	17/01/96	Tottenham Hotspur	Away	FA Cup	1–5		
67	20/01/96	Barnet	Away	League	3–1	1 Goal	(37)
68	31/01/96	Shrewsbury Town	Away	AW Shield	1–4		
69	13/02/96	Lincoln City	Away	League	1–2	1 Goal	(38)
70	17/02/96	Gillingham	Away	League	1–1		
71	20/02/96	Chester City	Home	League	1–0	1 Goal	(39)
72	24/02/96	Scarborough	Home	League	0–0		
73	27/02/96	Preston North End	Away	League	2–2		
74	02/03/96	Northampton Town	Home	League	1–0		
75	05/03/96	Hartlepool United	Away	League	1–0		
Sub+8	19/03/96	Bury	Away	League	0–2		
76	23/03/96	Darlington	Home	League	0–1		
77	27/03/96	Lincoln City	Home	League	1–0		
78	30/03/96	Torquay United	Away	League	1–1	1 Goal	(40)
79	02/04/96	Doncaster Rovers	Home	League	1–0	1 Goal	(41)
80	06/04/96	Fulham	Home	League	1–0		
81	08/04/96	Exeter City	Away	League	2–0	2 Goals	(43)
82	13/04/96	Leyton Orient	Home	League	3–2	2 Goals	(45)
83	16/04/96	Plymouth Argyle	Home	League	3–0	3 Goals	(48)
84	20/04/96	Mansfield Town	Away	League	2–1	1 Goal	(49)
85	23/04/96	Darlington	Home	League	0–1		
86	27/04/96	Cardiff City	Away	League	2–3	1 Goal	(50)

87	30/04/96	Hartlepool United	Home	League	4–1	1 Goal	(51)
88	04/05/96	Rochdale	Home	League	2–0	1 Goal	(52)
89	12/05/96	Darlington	Home	Lge P/O	1–2		
90	15/05/96	Darlington	Away	Lge P/O	1–2		

SEASON 1996–97

Cardiff City – Football League Division Three

1	17/08/96	Scarborough	Away	League	0–0		
2	20/08/96	Northampton Town	Home	Lge Cup	1–0		
3	24/08/96	Brighton & Hove Albion	Home	League	1–0		
4	27/08/96	Wigan Athletic	Home	League	0–2		
5	31/08/96	Cambridge United	Away	League	2–0	2 Goals	(2)
6	03/09/96	Northampton Town	Away	Lge Cup	0–2		
7	07/09/96	Exeter City	Home	League	2–1	2 Goals	(4)
8	10/09/96	Torquay United	Away	League	0–2		
9	14/09/96	Scunthorpe United	Away	League	1–0		
10	21/09/96	Northampton Town	Home	League	2–2		
11	28/09/96	Lincoln City	Away	League	0–2		
12	12/10/96	Barnet	Home	League	1–2		
13	15/10/96	Darlington	Home	League	2–0	1 Goal	(5)
14	19/10/96	Carlisle United	Away	League	2–0		
15	26/10/96	Leyton Orient	Home	League	3–0	1 Goal	(6)
16	29/10/96	Hull City	Away	League	1–1		
17	02/11/96	Colchester United	Away	League	1–1	1 Goal	(7)
18	05/11/96	Rochdale	Home	League	2–1		
19	09/11/96	Fulham	Home	League	1–2	1 Goal	(8)
20	16/11/96	Hendon	Home	FA Cup	2–0	1 Goal	(9)
21	23/11/96	Hereford United	Home	League	2–0	2 Goals	(11)
22	26/11/96	Chester City	Away	League	1–0		
23	30/11/96	Leyton Orient	Away	League	0–3		
24	03/12/96	Swansea City	Home	League	1–3	1 Goal	(12)
25	07/12/96	Gillingham	Home	FA Cup	0–2		
26	10/12/96	Gillingham	Away	AW Shield	2–1*		
27	21/12/96	Mansfield Town	Home	League	1–2		
28	26/12/96	Torquay United	Home	League	2–0		
29	28/12/96	Exeter City	Away	League	0–2		
30	01/01/97	Northampton Town	Away	League	0–4		
Sub+1	11/01/97	Lincoln City	Home	League	1–3		
Sub+2	14/01/97	Exeter City	Home	AW Shield	1–1+		
Sub+3	18/01/97	Rochdale	Away	League	0–1		
31	25/01/97	Hull City	Home	League	2–0		
32	31/01/97	Fulham	Away	League	4–1	2 Goals	(14)
33	08/02/97	Colchester United	Home	League	1–2		
34	01/03/97	Swansea City	Away	League	1–0		
35	08/03/97	Mansfield Town	Away	League	3–1		
36	14/03/97	Doncaster Rovers	Home	League	0–2		
37	22/03/97	Brighton & Hove Albion	Away	League	0–2		
Sub+4	05/04/97	Cambridge United	Home	League	0–0		
Sub+5	19/04/97	Barnet	Away	League	1–3		
Sub+6	26/04/97	Carlisle United	Home	League	2–0		
Sub+7	03/05/97	Darlington	Away	League	1–2		
Sub+8	11/05/97	Northampton Town	Home	Lge P/O	0–1		
38	14/05/97	Northampton Town	Away	Lge P/O	2–3		

+ AET Exeter City won 4–2 on penalties

APPEARANCES AND GOALS PER SEASON

SEASON 77–88	**GAMES**	**GOALS**
League	8	4
TOTAL	**8**	**4**

SEASON 78–79	**GAMES**	**GOALS**
League	23+4	10
FA Cup	3	3
TOTAL	**26+4**	**13**

SEASON 79–80	**GAMES**	**GOALS**
League	17+7	6
FA Cup	0+1	0
League Cup	2	1
TOTAL	**19+8**	**7**

SEASON 80–81	GAMES	GOALS
League	19+2	7
League Cup	1+1	0
TOTAL	**20+3**	**7**

SEASON 81–82	GAMES	GOALS
League	42	18
FA Cup	2	0
League Cup	2	1
TOTAL	**46**	**19**

SEASON 82–83	GAMES	GOALS
League	35+1	12
League Cup	2	0
Football League Trophy	1	0
TOTAL	**38+1**	**12**

SEASON 83–84	GAMES	GOALS
League	38+5	9
FA Cup	2+1	0
League Cup	4	1
Associate Members Cup	2+1	0
TOTAL	**46+7**	**10**

SEASON 84–85	GAMES	GOALS
League	14+4	3
FA Cup	1	0
League Cup	1	1
Freight Rover Trophy	1+1	0
TOTAL	**17+5**	**4**

SEASON 85–86	GAMES	GOALS
League	37+3	12
FA Cup	4	2
League Cup	3	0
Freight Rover Trophy	2	1
TOTAL	**46+3**	**15**

SEASON 86–87	GAMES	GOALS
League	29+6	15
League Play–offs	2	2
FA Cup	2+1	0
League Cup	0+1	0
Freight Rover Trophy	5	4
TOTAL	**38+8**	**21**

SEASON 87–88	GAMES	GOALS
League	17+8	11
FA Cup	1	0
League Cup	2+2	1
Simod Cup	3+1	2
TOTAL	**23+11**	**14**

SEASON 88–89	GAMES	GOALS
League	41+2	13
League Play–offs	2	0
FA Cup	1+1	0
League Cup	2	0
Simod Cup	1	1
TOTAL	**47+3**	**14**

SEASON 89–90	GAMES	GOALS
League	42+1	18
League Play–offs	3	2
FA Cup	1	0
League Cup	7	5
Zenith Data Systems Cup	3	2
TOTAL	**56+1**	**27**

SEASON 90–91	GAMES	GOALS
League	28+7	9
FA Cup	3	2
League Cup	3+1	0
TOTAL	**34+8**	**11**

SEASON 91–92	GAMES	GOALS
League	21+2	10
League Cup	5+1	3
Zenith Data Systems Cup	2	2
TOTAL	**28+3**	**15**

SEASON 92–93	GAMES	GOALS
League	20+14	7
League Play–offs	1+2	0
FA Cup	1	0
League Cup	1+2	2
Anglo–Italian Cup	0+2	0
TOTAL	**23+20**	**9**

SEASON 93–94	GAMES	GOALS
League	2+4	0
League Cup	1+1	0
TOTAL	**3+5**	**0**

SEASON 94–95	GAMES	GOALS
League	31+5	15
FA Cup	2	1
League Cup	3	2
Anglo–Italian Cup	0+1	0
Auto Windscreens Shield	3+1	1
TOTAL	**39+7**	**19**

SEASON 95–96	GAMES	GOALS
League	39+1	29
League Play–offs	2	0
FA Cup	4	3
League Cup	2	0
Auto Windscreens Shield	4+1	1
TOTAL	**51+2**	**33**

SEASON 96–97	GAMES	GOALS
League	32+6	13
League Play–offs	1+1	0
FA Cup	2	1
League Cup	2	0
Auto Windscreens Shield	1+1	0
TOTAL	**38+8**	**14**

CAREER APPEARANCES AND GOALS

COMPETITION	GAMES	TOTAL	GOALS
League	535+82	617	221
League Play–offs	11+3	14	4
FA Cup	29+4	33	12
League Cup	43+9	52	17
Football League Trophy	1	1	0
Associate Members Cup	2+1	3	0
Freight Rover Trophy	8+1	9	5
Simod Cup	4+1	5	3
Zenith Data Systems Cup	5	5	4
Anglo–Italian Cup	0+3	3	0
Auto Windscreens Shield	8+3	11	2
TOTAL	**646+107**	**753**	**268**

HAT–TRICKS

Luton Town

1	4	Grimsby Town	17/10/81	Home	League	6–0

Bristol Rovers

1	3	Darlington	18/01/86	Home	League	3–1

Swindon Town

1	3	Mansfield Town	03/04/87	Home	League	3–0
2	3	Watford	06/03/93	Away	League	4–0

Hereford United

1	4	Cambridge United	13/01/96	Home	League	5–2
2	3	Plymouth Argyle	16/04/96	Home	League	3–0

League: 6
TOTAL: 6

HONOURS

Winners medals
League Division Two Championship: 81/82

Runner–up medals
Promoted to the Premier League: 92/93
Promoted to League Division One: 89/90*
Promoted to League Division Two: 86/87

* Later negated by the Football League after Swindon Town were found guilty of making irregular financial payments to players.

IAN WRIGHT

Born: 03/11/63 – Woolwich
Height: 5.10
Weight: 11.08 (96–97)

Clubs
Crystal Palace: **1985–91** – Matches: **253+24** – Goals: **117**
Arsenal: **1991–97** – Matches: **253+7** – Goals: **174**

Country
England: **1991–97** – Matches: **13+14** – Goals: **7**

SEASON 1985–86

Crystal Palace – League Division Two

Sub+1	31/08/85	Huddersfield Town	Home	League	2–3		
1	03/09/85	Charlton Athletic	Home	Lge Cup	1–1		
Sub+2	14/09/85	Fulham	Home	League	0–0		
Sub+3	18/09/85	Norwich City	Away	League	3–4		
Sub+4	28/09/85	Stoke City	Away	League	0–0		
Sub+5	12/10/85	Oldham Athletic	Home	League	3–2	1 Goal	(1)
Sub+6	16/10/85	Brighton & Hove Albion	Home	FM Cup	1–3		
2	19/10/85	Portsmouth	Away	League	0–1		
Sub+7	23/10/85	West Bromwich Albion	Away	FM Cup	1–2		
Sub+8	26/10/85	Blackburn Rovers	Home	League	2–0	1 Goal	(2)
Sub+9	02/11/85	Bradford City	Away	League	0–1		
Sub+10	23/11/85	Barnsley	Home	League	1–0		
Sub+11	07/12/85	Hull City	Away	League	2–1		
Sub+12	15/12/85	Shrewsbury Town	Home	League	0–1		
3	22/12/85	Sunderland	Away	League	1–1		
4	26/12/85	Wimbledon	Home	League	1–3		
Sub+13	01/01/86	Brighton & Hove Albion	Away	League	0–2		
5	06/01/86	Luton Town	Home	FA Cup	1–2		
6	11/01/86	Charlton Athletic	Home	League	2–1		
7	18/01/86	Huddersfield Town	Away	League	0–0		
8	25/01/86	Norwich City	Home	League	1–2		
Sub+14	01/02/86	Carlisle United	Home	League	1–1		
Sub+15	15/02/86	Blackburn Rovers	Away	League	2–1	1 Goal	(3)
Sub+16	08/03/86	Middlesbrough	Home	League	2–1	1 Goal	(4)
Sub+17	15/03/86	Oldham Athletic	Away	League	0–2		
Sub+18	18/03/86	Stoke City	Home	League	0–1		
9	22/03/86	Fulham	Away	League	3–2	1 Goal	(5)
10	29/03/86	Brighton & Hove Albion	Home	League	1–0		
11	01/04/86	Wimbledon	Away	League	1–1	1 Goal	(6)
12	05/04/86	Bradford City	Home	League	2–1		
13	08/04/86	Portsmouth	Home	League	2–1		
14	12/04/86	Grimsby Town	Away	League	0–3		
15	19/04/86	Leeds United	Home	League	3–0	1 Goal	(7)
16	22/04/86	Millwall	Away	League	2–3		
17	26/04/86	Barnsley	Away	League	4–2	2 Goals	(9)
18	03/05/86	Sheffield United	Home	League	1–1		

SEASON 1986–87

League Division Two

19	23/08/86	Barnsley	Away	League	3–2	1 Goal	(10)
20	30/08/86	Stoke City	Home	League	1–0		
21	03/09/86	Bradford City	Away	League	2–1		
22	06/09/86	Derby County	Away	League	0–1		
23	09/09/86	Huddersfield Town	Home	League	1–0		
24	13/09/86	Sheffield United	Home	League	1–2		
25	16/09/86	Portsmouth	Away	FM Cup	0–4		
26	20/09/86	Blackburn Rovers	Away	League	2–0		
27	24/09/86	Bury	Home	Lge Cup	0–0		
28	27/09/86	Reading	Home	League	1–3		
29	04/10/86	Millwall	Home	League	2–1		
30	07/10/86	Bury	Away	Lge Cup	1–0	1 Goal	(11)
31	11/10/86	Leeds United	Away	League	0–3		
32	18/10/86	Birmingham City	Away	League	1–4		
33	25/10/86	Shrewsbury Town	Home	League	2–3	1 Goal	(12)
34	29/10/86	Nottingham Forest	Home	Lge Cup	2–2		
35	01/11/86	Plymouth Argyle	Away	League	1–3		
36	05/11/86	Nottingham Forest	Away	Lge Cup	0–1		
37	08/11/86	Grimsby Town	Home	League	0–3		
38	15/11/86	Ipswich Town	Home	League	3–3	1 Goal	(13)
39	22/11/86	Oldham Athletic	Away	League	0–1		
40	29/11/86	Sunderland	Home	League	2–0		
Sub+19	26/12/86	Brighton & Hove Albion	Home	League	2–0		
41	27/12/86	Ipswich Town	Away	League	0–3		
42	01/01/87	West Bromwich Albion	Away	League	2–1		
43	03/01/87	Derby County	Home	League	1–0		
44	11/01/87	Nottingham Forest	Home	FA Cup	1–0		
45	07/02/87	Stoke City	Away	League	1–3		
46	14/02/87	Bradford City	Home	League	1–1		
47	21/02/87	Reading	Away	League	0–1		
48	28/02/87	Blackburn Rovers	Home	League	2–0	1 Goal	(14)
49	14/03/87	Birmingham City	Home	League	6–0	2 Goals	(16)
50	17/03/87	Sheffield United	Away	League	0–1		
51	21/03/87	Leeds United	Home	League	1–0		
52	24/03/87	Shrewsbury Town	Away	League	0–0		
53	28/03/87	Millwall	Away	League	1–0		
54	04/04/87	Grimsby Town	Away	League	1–0		
55	11/04/87	Plymouth Argyle	Home	League	0–0		
56	18/04/87	West Bromwich Albion	Home	League	1–1		
57	20/04/87	Brighton & Hove Albion	Away	League	0–2		
58	25/04/87	Oldham Athletic	Home	League	2–1	1 Goal	(17)
59	02/05/87	Sunderland	Away	League	0–1		
60	04/05/87	Portsmouth	Home	League	1–0	1 Goal	(18)
61	09/05/87	Hull City	Away	League	0–3		

SEASON 1987–88

League Division Two

62	15/08/87	Huddersfield Town	Away	League	2–2		
63	22/08/87	Hull City	Home	League	2–2		
64	29/08/87	Barnsley	Away	League	1–2		
65	01/09/87	Middlesbrough	Home	League	3–1		
66	05/09/87	Birmingham City	Away	League	6–0		
67	08/09/87	West Bromwich Albion	Home	League	4–1	1 Goal	(19)
68	12/09/87	Leicester City	Home	League	2–1	1 Goal	(20)
69	15/09/87	Sheffield United	Away	League	1–1	1 Goal	(21)
70	19/09/87	Reading	Away	League	3–2	1 Goal	(22)
71	22/09/87	Newport County	Home	Lge Cup	4–0	2 Goals	(24)
72	26/09/87	Ipswich Town	Home	League	1–2		
73	03/10/87	Shrewsbury Town	Away	League	0–2		
74	06/10/87	Newport County	Away	Lge Cup	2–0	1 Goal	(25)
75	10/10/87	Millwall	Home	League	1–0		
76	21/10/87	Aston Villa	Away	League	1–4	1 Goal	(26)
77	24/10/87	Swindon Town	Home	League	2–1		
78	28/10/87	Manchester United	Away	Lge Cup	1–2		
79	31/10/87	Bradford City	Away	League	0–2		
80	03/11/87	Plymouth Argyle	Home	League	5–1	3 Goals	(29)
81	07/11/87	AFC Bournemouth	Away	League	3–2		
82	11/11/87	Oxford United	Away	Simod Cup	0–1		
83	14/11/87	Stoke City	Home	League	2–0	1 Goal	(30)
84	21/11/87	Blackburn Rovers	Away	League	0–2		
85	28/11/87	Leeds United	Home	League	3–0	1 Goal	(31)

86	05/12/87	Manchester City	Away	League	3–1		
87	13/12/87	Sheffield United	Home	League	2–1		
88	19/12/87	Hull City	Away	League	1–2		
89	26/12/87	Ipswich Town	Away	League	3–2	2 Goals	(33)
90	28/12/87	Reading	Home	League	2–3	1 Goal	(34)
91	01/01/88	Barnsley	Home	League	3–2	1 Goal	(35)
92	02/01/88	Leicester City	Away	League	4–4	2 Goals	(37)
93	09/01/88	Newcastle United	Away	FA Cup	0–1		
94	16/01/88	Huddersfield Town	Home	League	2–1		
95	23/01/88	Middlesbrough	Away	League	2–1	1 Goal	(38)
96	29/01/88	Oldham Athletic	Away	League	0–1		
97	27/02/88	Shrewsbury Town	Home	League	1–2		
98	05/03/88	Oldham Athletic	Home	League	3–1	1 Goal	(39)
99	12/03/88	Millwall	Away	League	1–1		
100	19/03/88	Bradford City	Home	League	1–1		
101	27/03/88	Swindon Town	Away	League	2–2	1 Goal	(40)
102	02/04/88	AFC Bournemouth	Home	League	3–0		
103	04/04/88	Stoke City	Away	League	1–1		
104	09/04/88	Aston Villa	Home	League	1–1	1 Goal	(41)
105	30/04/88	Blackburn Rovers	Home	League	2–0		
106	02/05/88	Leeds United	Away	League	0–1		
107	07/05/88	Manchester City	Home	League	2–0		

SEASON 1988–89

League Division Two

108	30/08/88	Chelsea	Home	League	1–1		
109	03/09/88	Watford	Home	League	0–2		
110	10/09/88	Walsall	Away	League	0–0		
111	17/09/88	Shrewsbury Town	Home	League	1–1	1 Goal	(42)
112	20/09/88	Sunderland	Away	League	1–1		
113	24/09/88	Portsmouth	Away	League	1–1	1 Goal	(43)
114	27/09/88	Swindon Town	Away	Lge Cup	2–1	1 Goal	(44)
115	01/10/88	Plymouth Argyle	Home	League	4–1	1 Goal	(45)
116	04/10/88	Ipswich Town	Home	League	2–0	1 Goal	(46)
117	08/10/88	Blackburn Rovers	Away	League	4–5	1 Goal	(47)
118	12/10/88	Swindon Town	Home	Lge Cup	2–0		
119	15/10/88	Bradford City	Away	League	1–0	1 Goal	(48)
120	22/10/88	Hull City	Home	League	3–1	1 Goal	(49)
Sub+20	05/11/88	Barnsley	Home	League	1–1		
121	12/11/88	AFC Bournemouth	Away	League	0–2		
122	19/11/88	Leicester City	Home	League	4–2		
Sub+21	22/11/88	Walsall	Home	Simod Cup	4–2	1 Goal	(50)
123	26/11/88	West Bromwich Albion	Away	League	3–5		
124	03/12/88	Manchester City	Home	League	0–0		
125	10/12/88	Birmingham City	Away	League	1–0		
126	13/12/88	Southampton	Away	Simod Cup	2–1	1 Goal	(51)
127	17/12/88	Leeds United	Home	League	0–0		
128	26/12/88	Brighton & Hove Albion	Away	League	1–3	1 Goal	(52)
129	30/12/88	Oldham Athletic	Away	League	3–2	2 Goals	(54)
130	02/01/89	Walsall	Home	League	4–0	1 Goal	(55)
131	07/01/89	Stoke City	Away	FA Cup	0–1		
132	10/01/89	Luton Town	Home	Simod Cup	4–1	1 Goal	(56)
133	14/01/89	Chelsea	Away	League	0–1		
134	21/01/89	Swindon Town	Home	League	2–1		
135	28/01/89	Middlesbrough	Away	Simod Cup	3–2	1 Goal	(57)
136	04/02/89	Ipswich Town	Away	League	2–1	2 Goals	(59)
137	11/02/89	Blackburn Rovers	Home	League	2–2	1 Goal	(60)
138	22/03/89	Nottingham Forest	Away	Simod Cup	1–3	1 Goal	(61)
139	04/03/89	AFC Bournemouth	Home	League	2–3	1 Goal	(62)
140	11/03/89	Barnsley	Away	League	1–1		
141	18/03/89	Sunderland	Home	League	1–0		
142	24/03/89	Watford	Away	League	1–0		
143	27/03/89	Brighton & Hove Albion	Home	League	2–1	1 Goal	(63)
144	01/04/89	Shrewsbury Town	Away	League	1–2		
145	05/04/89	Leeds United	Away	League	2–1	1 Goal	(64)
146	08/04/89	Oldham Athletic	Home	League	2–0		
147	11/04/89	Hull City	Away	League	1–0	1 Goal	(65)
148	15/04/89	Portsmouth	Home	League	2–0	1 Goal	(66)
149	22/04/89	Plymouth Argyle	Away	League	2–0		
150	25/04/89	Swindon Town	Away	League	0–1		
151	29/04/89	West Bromwich Albion	Home	League	1–0	1 Goal	(67)
152	01/05/89	Manchester City	Away	League	1–1	1 Goal	(68)
153	06/05/89	Leicester City	Away	League	2–2		
154	09/05/89	Stoke City	Home	League	1–0		

155	13/05/89	Birmingham City	Home	League	4–1	3 Goals	(71)
156	21/05/89	Swindon Town	Away	Lge P/O	0–1		
157	24/05/89	Swindon Town	Home	Lge P/O	2–0	1 Goal	(72)
158	31/05/89	Blackburn Rovers	Away	Lge P/O	1–3		
159	03/06/89	Blackburn Rovers	Home	Lge P/O	3–0*	2 Goals	(74)

SEASON 1989–90

League Division One

160	19/08/89	Queens Park Rangers	Away	League	0–2		
161	22/08/89	Manchester United	Home	League	1–1	1 Goal	(75)
162	26/08/89	Coventry City	Home	League	0–1		
163	09/09/89	Wimbledon	Home	League	2–0	1 Goal	(76)
164	12/09/89	Liverpool	Away	League	0–9		
165	16/09/89	Southampton	Away	League	1–1		
166	19/09/89	Leicester City	Home	Lge Cup	1–2	1 Goal	(77)
167	23/09/89	Nottingham Forest	Home	League	1–0	1 Goal	(78)
168	30/09/89	Everton	Home	League	2–1	1 Goal	(79)
169	04/10/89	Leicester City	Away	Lge Cup	3–2*		
170	14/10/89	Derby County	Away	League	1–3		
171	21/10/89	Millwall	Home	League	4–3	2 Goals	(81)
172	24/10/89	Nottingham Forest	Home	Lge Cup	0–0		
173	28/10/89	Aston Villa	Away	League	1–2		
174	01/11/89	Nottingham Forest	Away	Lge Cup	0–5		
175	04/11/89	Manchester City	Away	League	0–3		
176	11/11/89	Luton Town	Home	League	1–1		
177	18/11/89	Tottenham Hotspur	Home	League	2–3		
178	25/11/89	Sheffield Wednesday	Away	League	2–2		
179	27/11/89	Luton Town	Home	ZDS Cup	4–1	1 Goal	(82)
180	02/12/89	Queens Park Rangers	Home	League	0–3		
181	09/12/89	Manchester United	Away	League	2–1		
182	16/12/89	Charlton Athletic	Away	League	2–1		
183	19/12/89	Charlton Athletic	Home	ZDS Cup	2–0	1 Goal	(83)
184	26/12/89	Chelsea	Home	League	2–2	1 Goal	(84)
185	30/12/89	Norwich City	Home	League	1–0	1 Goal	(85)
186	01/01/90	Arsenal	Away	League	1–4		
187	06/01/90	Portsmouth	Home	FA Cup	2–1		
188	13/01/90	Coventry City	Away	League	0–1		
189	20/01/90	Liverpool	Home	League	0–2		
Sub+22	03/03/90	Tottenham Hotspur	Away	League	1–0		
190	10/03/90	Cambridge United	Away	FA Cup	1–0		
191	12/03/90	Chelsea	Away	ZDS Cup	0–2		
192	17/03/90	Everton	Away	League	0–4		
193	20/03/90	Derby County	Home	League	1–1		
Sub+23	12/05/90	Manchester United	Wembley	FA Cup	3–3*	2 Goals	(87)
Sub+24	17/05/90	Manchester United	Wembley	FA Cup	0–1		

SEASON 1990–91

League Division One

194	25/08/90	Luton Town	Away	League	1–1		
195	28/08/90	Chelsea	Home	League	2–1	1 Goal	(88)
196	01/09/90	Sheffield United	Home	League	1–0		
197	08/09/90	Norwich City	Away	League	3–0	1 Goal	(89)
198	15/09/90	Nottingham Forest	Home	League	2–2		
199	22/09/90	Tottenham Hotspur	Away	League	1–1		
200	25/09/90	Southend United	Home	Lge Cup	8–0	3 Goals	(92)
201	29/09/90	Derby County	Away	League	2–0	1 Goal	(93)
202	06/10/90	Leeds United	Home	League	1–1		
203	09/10/90	Southend United	Away	Lge Cup	2–1		
204	20/10/90	Everton	Away	League	0–0		
205	27/10/90	Wimbledon	Home	League	4–3		
206	30/10/90	Leyton Orient	Home	Lge Cup	0–0		
207	03/11/90	Manchester United	Away	League	0–2		
208	07/11/90	Leyton Orient	Away	Lge Cup	1–0		
209	10/11/90	Arsenal	Home	League	0–0		
210	17/11/90	Queens Park Rangers	Away	League	2–1	2 Goals	(95)
211	24/11/90	Southampton	Away	League	3–2	2 Goals	(97)
212	27/11/90	Southampton	Away	Lge Cup	0–2		
213	01/12/90	Coventry City	Home	League	2–1		
214	08/12/90	Chelsea	Away	League	1–2		
215	16/12/90	Luton Town	Home	League	1–0		
216	18/12/90	Bristol Rovers	Home	ZDS Cup	2–1		

217	22/12/90	Manchester City	Away	League	2–0	1 Goal	(98)
218	26/12/90	Sunderland	Home	League	2–1		
219	30/12/90	Liverpool	Home	League	1–0		
220	01/01/91	Aston Villa	Away	League	0–2		
221.	06/01/91	Nottingham Forest	Home	FA Cup	0–0		
222	12/01/91	Sheffield United	Away	League	1–0		
223	19/01/91	Norwich City	Home	League	1–3		
224	21/01/91	Nottingham Forest	Away	FA Cup	2–2*	1 Goal	(99)
225	28/01/91	Nottingham Forest	Away	FA Cup	0–3		
226	02/02/91	Nottingham Forest	Away	League	1–0		
227	16/02/91	Queens Park Rangers	Home	League	0–0		
228	18/02/91	Brighton & Hove Albion	Away	ZDS Cup	2–0*	1 Goal	(100)
229	23/02/91	Arsenal	Away	League	0–4		
230	26/02/91	Luton Town	Home	ZDS Cup	3–1	2 Goals	(102)
231	02/03/91	Coventry City	Away	League	1–3	1 Goal	(103)
232	05/03/91	Norwich City	Away	ZDS Cup	1–1		
233	09/03/91	Southampton	Home	League	2–1		
234	16/03/91	Derby County	Home	League	2–1	1 Goal	(104)
235	19/03/91	Norwich City	Home	ZDS Cup	2–0	1 Goal	(105)
236	23/03/91	Leeds United	Away	League	2–1	1 Goal	(106)
237	30/03/91	Sunderland	Away	League	1–2		
238	01/04/91	Manchester City	Home	League	1–3		
239	07/04/91	Everton	Wembley	ZDS Cup	4–1*	2 Goals	(108)
240	13/04/91	Aston Villa	Home	League	0–0		
241	17/04/91	Tottenham Hotspur	Home	League	1–0		
242	20/04/91	Everton	Home	League	0–0		
243	23/04/91	Liverpool	Away	League	0–3		
244	04/05/91	Wimbledon	Away	League	3–0	3 Goals	(111)
245	11/05/91	Manchester United	Home	League	3–0	1 Goal	(112)

SEASON 1991–92

League Division One

246	24/08/91	Manchester City	Away	League	2–3		
247	27/08/91	Wimbledon	Home	League	3–2	1 Goal	(113)
248	31/08/91	Sheffield United	Home	League	2–1	1 Goal	(114)
249	04/09/91	Aston Villa	Away	League	1–0	1 Goal	(115)
250	07/09/91	Everton	Away	League	2–2		
251	14/09/91	Arsenal	Home	League	1–4		
252	17/09/91	West Ham United	Home	League	2–3	1 Goal	(116)
253	21/09/91	Oldham Athletic	Away	League	3–2	1 Goal	(117)

Arsenal – League Division One

1	25/09/91	Leicester City	Away	Lge Cup	1–1	1 Goal	(1)
2	28/09/91	Southampton	Away	League	4–0	3 Goals	(4)
3	05/10/91	Chelsea	Home	League	3–2	1 Goal	(5)
4	08/10/91	Leicester City	Home	Lge Cup	2–0	1 Goal	(6)
5	19/10/91	Manchester United	Away	League	1–1		
6	26/10/91	Notts County	Home	League	2–0	1 Goal	(7)
7	30/10/91	Coventry City	Away	Lge Cup	0–1		
8	02/11/91	West Ham United	Home	League	0–1		
9	16/11/91	Oldham Athletic	Away	League	1–1	1 Goal	(8)
10	23/11/91	Sheffield Wednesday	Away	League	1–1		
11	01/12/91	Tottenham Hotspur	Home	League	2–0	1 Goal	(9)
12	21/12/91	Everton	Home	League	4–2	4 Goals	(13)
13	26/12/91	Luton Town	Away	League	0–1		
14	28/12/91	Manchester City	Away	League	0–1		
15	01/01/92	Wimbledon	Home	League	1–1		
16	18/01/92	Queens Park Rangers	Away	League	0–0		
17	29/01/92	Liverpool	Away	League	0–2		
18	01/02/92	Manchester United	Home	League	1–1		
19	08/02/92	Notts County	Away	League	1–0		
20	11/02/92	Norwich City	Home	League	1–1		
21	15/02/92	Sheffield Wednesday	Home	League	7–1	1 Goal	(14)
22	22/02/92	Tottenham Hotspur	Away	League	1–1	1 Goal	(15)
23	10/03/92	Oldham Athletic	Home	League	2–1	1 Goal	(16)
24	14/03/92	West Ham United	Away	League	2–0	2 Goals	(18)
25	22/03/92	Leeds United	Home	League	1–1		
26	28/03/92	Wimbledon	Away	League	3–1	1 Goal	(19)
27	31/03/92	Nottingham Forest	Home	League	3–3		
28	04/04/92	Coventry City	Away	League	1–0		
29	08/04/92	Norwich City	Away	League	3–1	2 Goals	(21)
30	11/04/92	Crystal Palace	Home	League	4–1		

31	20/04/92	Liverpool	Home	League	4–0	2 Goals	(23)
32	25/04/92	Chelsea	Away	League	1–1		
33	02/05/92	Southampton	Home	League	5–1	3 Goals	(26)

SEASON 1992–93

Premier League

Sub+1	15/08/92	Norwich City	Home	League	2–4		
34	23/08/92	Liverpool	Away	League	2–0	1 Goal	(27)
35	26/08/92	Oldham Athletic	Home	League	2–0	1 Goal	(28)
36	29/08/92	Sheffield Wednesday	Home	League	2–1		
37	02/09/92	Queens Park Rangers	Away	League	0–0		
38	05/09/92	Wimbledon	Away	League	2–3	2 Goals	(30)
39	12/09/92	Blackburn Rovers	Home	League	0–1		
40	19/09/92	Sheffield United	Away	League	1–1	1 Goal	(31)
41	22/09/92	Millwall	Home	Lge Cup	1–1		
42	28/09/92	Manchester City	Home	League	1–0	1 Goal	(32)
43	03/10/92	Chelsea	Home	League	2–1	1 Goal	(33)
44	07/10/92	Millwall	Away	Lge Cup	1–1+		
45	17/10/92	Nottingham Forest	Away	League	1–0		
46	24/10/92	Everton	Home	League	2–0	1 Goal	(34)
47	02/11/92	Crystal Palace	Away	League	2–1	1 Goal	(35)
48	07/11/92	Coventry City	Home	League	3–0	1 Goal	(36)
49	21/11/92	Leeds United	Away	League	0–3		
50	28/11/92	Manchester United	Home	League	0–1		
51	01/12/92	Derby County	Home	Lge Cup	2–1	1 Goal	(37)
52	05/12/92	Southampton	Away	League	0–2		
53	12/12/92	Tottenham Hotspur	Away	League	0–1		
54	19/12/92	Middlesbrough	Home	League	1–1	1 Goal	(38)
55	26/12/92	Ipswich Town	Home	League	0–0		
56	28/12/92	Aston Villa	Away	League	0–1		
57	02/01/93	Yeovil Town	Away	FA Cup	3–1	3 Goals	(41)
58	06/01/93	Scarborough	Away	Lge Cup	1–0		
59	09/01/93	Sheffield United	Home	League	1–1		
60	12/01/93	Nottingham Forest	Home	Lge Cup	2–0	2 Goals	(43)
61	03/02/93	Leeds United	Away	FA Cup	3–2*	2 Goals	(45)
62	07/02/93	Crystal Palace	Away	Lge Cup	3–1	1 Goal	(46)
63	10/02/93	Wimbledon	Home	League	0–1		
64	13/02/93	Nottingham Forest	Home	FA Cup	2–0	2 Goals	(48)
65	24/02/93	Leeds United	Home	League	0–0		
66	03/03/93	Norwich City	Away	League	1–1	1 Goal	(49)
67	06/03/93	Ipswich Town	Away	FA Cup	4–2	1 Goal	(50)
68	10/03/93	Crystal Palace	Home	Lge Cup	2–0	1 Goal	(51)
69	13/03/93	Coventry City	Away	League	2–0	1 Goal	(52)
70	24/03/93	Manchester United	Away	League	0–0		
71	04/04/93	Tottenham Hotspur	Wembley	FA Cup	1–0		
72	06/04/93	Middlesbrough	Away	League	0–1		
73	12/04/93	Aston Villa	Home	League	0–1		
74	18/04/93	Sheffield Wednesday	Wembley	Lge Cup	2–1		
75	21/04/93	Nottingham Forest	Home	League	1–1	1 Goal	(53)
76	08/05/93	Crystal Palace	Home	League	3–0	1 Goal	(54)
77	15/05/93	Sheffield Wednesday	Wembley	FA Cup	1–1*	1 Goal	(55)
78	20/05/93	Sheffield Wednesday	Wembley	FA Cup	2–1*	1 Goal	(56)

+ AET Arsenal won 3–1 on penalties

SEASON 1993–94

Premier League

79	07/08/93	Manchester United	Wembley	FA C/S	1–1+	1 Goal	(57)
80	14/08/93	Coventry City	Home	League	0–3		
81	16/08/93	Tottenham Hotspur	Away	League	1–0	1 Goal	(58)
82	21/08/93	Sheffield Wednesday	Away	League	1–0	1 Goal	(59)
83	24/08/93	Leeds United	Home	League	2–1		
84	28/08/93	Everton	Home	League	2–0	2 Goals	(61)
85	01/09/93	Blackburn Rovers	Away	League	1–1		
86	11/09/93	Ipswich Town	Home	League	4–0	1 Goal	(62)
87	15/09/93	Odense BK	Away	ECW Cup	2–1	1 Goal	(63)
88	19/09/93	Manchester United	Away	League	0–1		
89	21/09/93	Huddersfield Town	Away	Lge Cup	5–0	3 Goals	(66)
90	25/09/93	Southampton	Home	League	1–0		
91	29/09/93	Odense BK	Home	ECW Cup	1–1		

92	02/10/93	Liverpool	Away	League	0-0		
93	16/10/93	Manchester City	Home	League	0-0		
94	20/10/93	R Standard Liege	Home	ECW Cup	3-0	2 Goals	(68)
95	23/10/93	Oldham Athletic	Away	League	0-0		
96	26/10/93	Norwich City	Home	Lge Cup	1-1	1 Goal	(69)
97	30/10/93	Norwich City	Home	League	0-0		
98	06/11/93	Aston Villa	Home	League	1-2	1 Goal	(70)
99	10/11/93	Norwich City	Away	Lge Cup	3-0	2 Goals	(72)
100	20/11/93	Chelsea	Away	League	2-0	1 Goal	(73)
101	24/11/93	West Ham United	Away	League	0-0		
102	27/11/93	Newcastle United	Home	League	2-1	1 Goal	(74)
103	30/11/93	Aston Villa	Home	Lge Cup	0-1		
104	04/12/93	Coventry City	Away	League	0-1		
105	06/12/93	Tottenham Hotspur	Home	League	1-1	1 Goal	(75)
106	12/12/93	Sheffield Wednesday	Home	League	1-0	1 Goal	(76)
107	18/12/93	Leeds United	Away	League	1-2		
108	27/12/93	Swindon Town	Away	League	4-0	1 Goal	(77)
109	29/12/93	Sheffield United	Home	League	3-0	1 Goal	(78)
110	01/01/94	Wimbledon	Away	League	3-0	1 Goal	(79)
111	03/01/94	Queens Park Rangers	Home	League	0-0		
112	10/01/94	Millwall	Away	FA Cup	1-0		
113	15/01/94	Manchester City	Away	League	0-0		
114	22/01/94	Oldham Athletic	Home	League	1-1	1 Goal	(80)
115	31/01/94	Bolton Wanderers	Away	FA Cup	2-2	1 Goal	(81)
116	09/02/94	Bolton Wanderers	Home	FA Cup	1-3*		
117	05/03/94	Ipswich Town	Away	League	5-1	3 Goals	(84)
118	15/03/94	Torino Calcio	Home	ECW Cup	1-0		
119	19/03/94	Southampton	Away	League	4-0	3 Goals	(87)
120	22/03/94	Manchester United	Home	League	2-2		
121	26/03/94	Liverpool	Home	League	1-0		
122	29/03/94	Paris Saint-Germain FC	Away	ECW Cup	1-1	1 Goal	(88)
123	02/04/94	Swindon Town	Home	League	1-1		
124	04/04/94	Sheffield United	Away	League	1-1		
125	12/04/94	Paris Saint-Germain FC	Home	ECW Cup	1-0		
126	16/04/94	Chelsea	Home	League	1-0	1 Goal	(89)
127	19/04/94	Wimbledon	Home	League	1-1		
128	23/04/94	Aston Villa	Away	League	2-1	2 Goals	(91)
129	27/04/94	Queens Park Rangers	Away	League	1-1		
130	30/04/94	West Ham United	Home	League	0-2		
131	07/05/94	Newcastle United	Away	League	0-2		

+ AET Manchester United won 5-4 on penalties

SEASON 1994-95

Premier League

132	20/08/94	Manchester City	Home	League	3-0	1 Goal	(92)
133	23/08/94	Leeds United	Away	League	0-1		
134	28/08/94	Liverpool	Away	League	0-3		
135	31/08/94	Blackburn Rovers	Home	League	0-0		
136	10/09/94	Norwich City	Away	League	0-0		
137	15/09/94	Omonia Nicosia	Away	ECW Cup	3-1	1 Goal	(93)
138	18/09/94	Newcastle United	Home	League	2-3	1 Goal	(94)
139	21/09/94	Hartlepool United	Away	Lge Cup	5-0	2 Goals	(96)
140	25/09/94	West Ham United	Away	League	2-0	1 Goal	(97)
141	29/09/94	Omonia Nicosia	Home	ECW Cup	3-0	2 Goals	(99)
142	01/10/94	Crystal Palace	Home	League	1-2	1 Goal	(100)
143	08/10/94	Wimbledon	Away	League	3-1	1 Goal	(101)
144	15/10/94	Chelsea	Home	League	3-1	2 Goals	(103)
145	20/10/94	Brondby IF	Away	ECW Cup	2-1	1 Goal	(104)
146	23/10/94	Coventry City	Home	League	2-1	2 Goals	(106)
147	03/11/94	Brondby IF	Home	ECW Cup	2-2	1 Goal	(107)
148	23/11/94	Leicester City	Away	League	1-2	1 Goal	(108)
149	26/11/94	Manchester United	Home	League	0-0		
150	30/11/94	Sheffield Wednesday	Home	Lge Cup	2-0	1 Goal	(109)
151	28/12/94	Ipswich Town	Away	League	2-0	1 Goal	(110)
152	31/12/94	Queens Park Rangers	Home	League	1-3		
153	02/01/95	Tottenham Hotspur	Away	League	0-1		
154	07/01/95	Millwall	Away	FA Cup	0-0		
155	11/01/95	Liverpool	Away	Lge Cup	0-1		
156	14/01/95	Everton	Home	League	1-1	1 Goal	(111)
157	18/01/95	Millwall	Home	FA Cup	0-2		
158	21/01/95	Coventry City	Away	League	1-0		
159	24/01/95	Southampton	Home	League	1-1		

160	01/02/95	Milan AC	Home	ES Cup	0–0		
161	08/02/95	Milan AC	Away	ES Cup	0–2		
162	02/03/95	AJ Auxerre	Home	ECW Cup	1–1	1 Goal	(112)
163	05/03/95	West Ham United	Home	League	0–1		
Sub+2	08/03/95	Blackburn Rovers	Away	League	1–3		
164	16/03/95	AJ Auxerre	Away	ECW Cup	1–0	1 Goal	(113)
165	19/03/95	Newcastle United	Away	League	0–1		
166	22/03/95	Manchester United	Away	League	0–3		
167	01/04/95	Norwich City	Home	League	5–1		
168	06/04/95	Sampdoria UC	Home	ECW Cup	3–2	1 Goal	(114)
169	08/04/95	Queens Park Rangers	Away	League	1–3		
170	12/04/95	Liverpool	Home	League	0–1		
171	15/04/95	Ipswich Town	Home	League	4–1	3 Goals	(117)
172	17/04/95	Aston Villa	Away	League	4–0	2 Goals	(119)
173	20/04/95	Sampdoria UC	Away	ECW Cup	2–3+	1 Goal	(120)
174	29/04/95	Tottenham Hotspur	Home	League	1–1	1 Goal	(121)
175	04/05/95	Wimbledon	Home	League	0–0		
176	10/05/95	Real Zaragoza CD	Neutral	ECW Cup	1–2*		
177	14/05/95	Chelsea	Away	League	1–2		

+ AET Arsenal won 3–2 on penalties

SEASON 1995–96

Premier League

178	20/08/95	Middlesbrough	Home	League	1–1	1 Goal	(122)
179	23/08/95	Everton	Away	League	2–0	1 Goal	(123)
180	26/08/95	Coventry City	Away	League	0–0		
181	29/08/95	Nottingham Forest	Home	League	1–1		
182	10/09/95	Manchester City	Away	League	1–0	1 Goal	(124)
183	16/09/95	West Ham United	Home	League	1–0	1 Goal	(125)
184	19/09/95	Hartlepool United	Away	Lge Cup	3–0	1 Goal	(126)
185	23/09/95	Southampton	Home	League	4–2	1 Goal	(127)
186	30/09/95	Chelsea	Away	League	0–1		
187	03/10/95	Hartlepool United	Home	Lge Cup	5–0	3 Goals	(130)
188	14/10/95	Leeds United	Away	League	3–0	1 Goal	(131)
189	21/10/95	Aston Villa	Home	League	2–0	1 Goal	(132)
190	24/10/95	Barnsley	Away	Lge Cup	3–0		
191	30/10/95	Bolton Wanderers	Away	League	0–1		
192	04/11/95	Manchester United	Home	League	1–0		
193	29/11/95	Sheffield Wednesday	Home	Lge Cup	2–1	1 Goal	(133)
194	02/12/95	Aston Villa	Away	League	1–1		
195	09/12/95	Southampton	Away	League	0–0		
196	16/12/95	Chelsea	Home	League	1–1		
197	23/12/95	Liverpool	Away	League	1–3	1 Goal	(134)
198	26/12/95	Queens Park Rangers	Home	League	3–0	1 Goal	(135)
199	30/12/95	Wimbledon	Home	League	1–3	1 Goal	(136)
200	02/01/96	Newcastle United	Away	League	0–2		
201	06/01/96	Sheffield United	Home	FA Cup	1–1	1 Goal	(137)
202	10/01/96	Newcastle United	Home	Lge Cup	2–0	2 Goals	(139)
203	13/01/96	Middlesbrough	Away	League	3–2		
204	17/01/96	Sheffield United	Away	FA Cup	0–1		
205	20/01/96	Everton	Home	League	1–2	1 Goal	(140)
206	03/02/96	Coventry City	Home	League	1–1		
207	10/02/96	Nottingham Forest	Away	League	1–0		
208	14/02/96	Aston Villa	Home	Lge Cup	2–2		
209	21/02/96	Aston Villa	Away	Lge Cup	0–0*		
210	16/03/96	Wimbledon	Away	League	3–0		
211	20/03/96	Manchester United	Away	League	0–1		
212	23/03/96	Newcastle United	Home	League	2–0	1 Goal	(141)
213	06/04/96	Leeds United	Home	League	2–1	2 Goals	(143)
214	08/04/96	Sheffield Wednesday	Away	League	0–1		
215	15/04/96	Tottenham Hotspur	Home	League	0–0		
216	27/04/96	Blackburn Rovers	Away	League	1–1	1 Goal	(144)
217	05/05/96	Bolton Wanderers	Home	League	2–1		

SEASON 1996–97

Premier League

Sub+3	17/08/96	West Ham United	Home	League	2–0		
Sub+4	19/08/96	Liverpool	Away	League	0–2		
Sub+5	24/08/96	Leicester City	Away	League	2–0	1 Goal	(145)
Sub+6	04/09/96	Chelsea	Home	League	3–3	1 Goal	(146)
218	07/09/96	Aston Villa	Away	League	2–2		
219	10/09/96	Borussia Monchengladbach	Home	UEFA Cup	2–3	1 Goal	(147)
220	16/09/96	Sheffield Wednesday	Home	League	4–1	3 Goals	(150)

221	21/09/96	Middlesbrough	Away	League	2–0	1 Goal	(151)
222	25/09/96	Borussia Monchengladbach	Away	UEFA Cup	2–3	1 Goal	(152)
223	28/09/96	Sunderland	Home	League	2–0		
224	12/10/96	Blackburn Rovers	Away	League	2–0	2 Goals	(154)
225	19/10/96	Coventry City	Home	League	0–0		
226	23/10/96	Stoke City	Away	Lge Cup	1–1	1 Goal	(155)
227	26/10/96	Leeds United	Home	League	3–0	1 Goal	(156)
228	02/11/96	Wimbledon	Away	League	2–2	1 Goal	(157)
229	13/11/96	Stoke City	Home	Lge Cup	5–2	2 Goals	(159)
230	16/11/96	Manchester United	Away	League	0–1		
231	24/11/96	Tottenham Hotspur	Home	League	3–1	1 Goal	(160)
232	27/11/96	Liverpool	Away	Lge Cup	2–4	2 Goals	(162)
233	30/11/96	Newcastle United	Away	League	2–1	1 Goal	(163)
234	04/12/96	Southampton	Home	League	3–1	1 Goal	(164)
235	07/12/96	Derby County	Home	League	2–2		
236	21/12/96	Nottingham Forest	Away	League	1–2	1 Goal	(165)
237	26/12/96	Sheffield Wednesday	Away	League	0–0		
238	28/12/96	Aston Villa	Home	League	2–2	1 Goal	(166)
239	01/01/97	Middlesbrough	Home	League	2–0	1 Goal	(167)
240	19/01/97	Everton	Home	League	3–1		
241	29/01/97	West Ham United	Away	League	2–1	1 Goal	(168)
Sub+7	01/02/97	Leeds United	Away	League	0–0		
242	04/02/97	Leeds United	Home	FA Cup	0–1		
243	15/02/97	Tottenham Hotspur	Away	League	0–0		
244	19/02/97	Manchester United	Home	League	1–2		
245	23/02/97	Wimbledon	Home	League	0–1		
246	01/03/97	Everton	Away	League	2–0	1 Goal	(169)
247	24/03/97	Liverpool	Home	League	1–2	1 Goal	(170)
248	05/04/97	Chelsea	Away	League	3–0	1 Goal	(171)
249	12/04/97	Leicester City	Home	League	2–0		
250	19/04/97	Blackburn Rovers	Home	League	1–1		
251	21/04/97	Coventry City	Away	League	1–1	1 Goal	(172)
252	03/05/97	Newcastle United	Home	League	0–1		
253	11/05/97	Derby County	Away	League	3–1	2 Goals	(174)

INTERNATIONAL APPEARANCES – ENGLAND

1	06/02/91	Cameroon	Wembley	2–0	F		
Sub 2	27/03/91	Republic of Ireland	Wembley	1–1	ECQ		
3	21/05/91	USSR	Wembley	3–1	F		
4	08/06/91	New Zealand	Wellington	2–0	F		
Sub 5	12/05/92	Hungary	Budapest	1–0	F		
6	14/10/92	Norway	Wembley	1–1	WCQ		
7	18/11/92	Turkey	Wembley	4–0	WCQ		
8	31/03/93	Turkey	Izmir	2–0	WCQ		
Sub 9	29/05/93	Poland	Katowice	1–1	WCQ	1 Goal	(1)
Sub 10	02/06/93	Norway	Oslo	0–2	WCQ		
Sub 11	09/06/93	USA	Boston	0–2	USC		
12	13/06/93	Brazil	Washington	1–1	USC		
Sub 13	19/06/93	Germany	Detroit	1–2	USC		
14	08/09/93	Poland	Wembley	3–0	WCQ		
15	13/10/93	Holland	Rotterdam	0–2	WCQ		
16	17/11/93	San Marino	Bologna	7–1	WCQ	4 Goals	(5)
Sub 17	17/05/94	Greece	Wembley	5–0	F		
Sub 18	22/05/94	Norway	Wembley	0–0	F		
Sub 19	07/09/94	USA	Wembley	2–0	F		
Sub 20	12/10/94	Romania	Wembley	1–1	F		
Sub 21	09/11/96	Georgia	Tblisi	2–0	WCQ		
Sub 22	12/02/97	Italy	Wembley	0–1	WCQ		
Sub 23	29/03/97	Mexico	Wembley	2–0	F		
24	24/05/97	South Africa	Old Trafford	2–1	F	1 Goal	(6)
25	04/06/97	Italy	Nantes	2–0	LTDF	1 Goal	(7)
26	07/06/97	France	Montpellier	1–0	LTDF		
Sub 27	10/06/97	Brazil	Paris	0–1	LTDF		

APPEARANCES AND GOALS PER SEASON

SEASON 85–86	GAMES	GOALS
League	16+16	9
FA Cup	1	0
League Cup	1	0
Full Members Cup	0+2	0
TOTAL	**18+18**	**9**

SEASON 86–87	GAMES	GOALS
League	37+1	8
FA Cup	1	0
League Cup	4	1
Full Members Cup	1	0
TOTAL	**43+1**	**9**

SEASON 87–88	GAMES	GOALS
League	41	20
FA Cup	1	0
League Cup	3	3
Simod Cup	1	0
TOTAL	**46**	**23**

SEASON 88–89	GAMES	GOALS
League	41+1	24
League Play–offs	4	3
FA Cup	1	0
League Cup	2	1
Simod Cup	4+1	5
TOTAL	**52+2**	**33**

SEASON 89–90	GAMES	GOALS
League	25+1	8
FA Cup	2+2	2
League Cup	4	1
Zenith Data Systems Cup	3	2
TOTAL	**34+3**	**13**

SEASON 90–91	GAMES	GOALS
League	38	15
FA Cup	3	1
League Cup	5	3
Zenith Data Systems Cup	6	6
TOTAL	**52**	**25**

SEASON 91–92	GAMES	GOALS
League	38	29
League Cup	3	2
TOTAL	**41**	**31**

SEASON 92–93	GAMES	GOALS
League	30+1	15
FA Cup	7	10
League Cup	8	5
TOTAL	**45+1**	**30**

SEASON 93–94	GAMES	GOALS
League	39	23
FA Cup	3	1
League Cup	4	6
European Cup Winners Cup	6	4
FA Charity Shield	1	1
TOTAL	**53**	**35**

SEASON 94–95	GAMES	GOALS
League	30+1	18
FA Cup	2	0
League Cup	3	3
European Cup Winners Cup	9	9
European Super Cup	2	0
TOTAL	**46+1**	**30**

SEASON 95–96	GAMES	GOALS
League	31	15
FA Cup	2	1
League Cup	7	7
TOTAL	**40**	**23**

SEASON 96–97	GAMES	GOALS
League	30+5	23
FA Cup	1	0
League Cup	3	5
UEFA Cup	2	2
TOTAL	**36+5**	**30**

CAREER APPEARANCES AND GOALS

COMPETITION	GAMES	TOTAL	GOALS
League	396+26	422	207
League Play–offs	4	4	3
FA Cup	24+2	26	15
League Cup	47	47	37
Full Members Cup	1+2	3	0
Simod Cup	5+1	6	5
Zenith Data Systems Cup	9	9	8
FA Charity Shield	1	1	1
UEFA Cup	2	2	2
European Cup Winners Cup	15	15	13
European Super Cup	2	2	0
Internationals	13+14	27	7
TOTAL	**519+45**	**564**	**298**

HAT-TRICKS

Crystal Palace

1	3	Plymouth Argyle	03/11/87	Home	League	5–1
2	3	Birmingham City	13/05/89	Home	League	4–1
3	3	Southend United	25/09/90	Home	Lge Cup	8–0
4	3	Wimbledon	04/05/91	Away	League	3–0

Arsenal

1	3	Southampton	28/09/91	Away	League	4–0
2	4	Everton	21/12/91	Home	League	4–2
3	3	Southampton	02/05/92	Home	League	5–1
4	3	Yeovil Town	02/01/93	Away	FA Cup	3–1
5	3	Huddersfield Town	21/09/93	Away	Lge Cup	5–0
6	3	Ipswich Town	05/03/94	Away	League	5–1
7	3	Southampton	19/03/94	Away	League	4–0
8	3	Ipswich Town	15/04/95	Home	League	4–1
9	3	Hartlepool United	03/10/95	Home	Lge Cup	5–0
10	3	Sheffield Wednesday	16/09/96	Home	League	4–1

England

1	4	San Marino	17/11/93	Bologna	WCQ	7–1

League: 10
FA Cup: 1
Lge Cup: 3
International: 1
TOTAL: 15

HONOURS

Winners medals
FA Cup: 92/93
League Cup: 92/93
Zenith Data Systems Cup: 90/91

Runner-up medals
FA Cup: 89/90
European Cup Winners Cup: 94/95
European Super Cup: 94/95
FA Charity Shield: 93/94
Promoted to League Division One: 88/89

KEITH WRIGHT

Born: 17/05/65 – Edinburgh
Height: 5.11
Weight: 11.00 (96–97)

Clubs
Raith Rovers: **1983–86** – Matches: **138+4** – Goals: **61**
Dundee: **1986–91** – Matches: **189+9** – Goals: **75**
Hibernian: **1991–97** – Matches: **219+14** – Goals: **76**

Country
Scotland: **1992** – Matches: **1** – Goals: **0**

SEASON 1983–84

Raith Rovers – Scottish League Division Two

Sub+1	20/08/83	Brechin City	Away	League	1–1			
Sub+2	03/09/83	Falkirk	Away	League	1–2			
1	10/09/83	Clydebank	Home	League	0–0			
2	14/09/83	Hamilton Academical	Home	League	1–2			
Sub+3	17/09/83	Partick Thistle	Away	League	0–2			
3	24/09/83	Morton	Home	League	1–3			
4	28/09/83	Ayr United	Away	League	2–2	1 Goal	(1)
5	01/10/83	Dumbarton	Away	League	1–2			
6	08/10/83	Clyde	Home	League	2–1			
7	15/10/83	Alloa	Away	League	2–1			
8	22/10/83	Airdrieonians	Home	League	0–0			
9	29/10/83	Kilmarnock	Away	League	1–2			
10	05/11/83	Meadowbank Thistle	Home	League	3–1			
11	12/11/83	Hamilton Academical	Away	League	0–0			
12	19/11/83	Partick Thistle	Home	League	1–2			
13	26/11/83	Clyde	Away	League	0–5			
14	03/12/83	Dumbarton	Home	League	1–3			
15	10/12/83	Morton	Away	League	0–0			
16	17/12/83	Ayr United	Home	League	1–3			
17	31/12/83	Falkirk	Home	League	2–2			
18	02/01/84	Brechin City	Home	League	1–1			
19	04/02/84	Meadowbank Thistle	Away	League	3–1	1 Goal	(2)
20	06/02/84	Dumbarton	Home	S Cup	1–4			
21	11/02/84	Airdrieonians	Home	League	2–3			
22	17/02/84	Alloa	Home	League	1–1			
23	25/02/84	Dumbarton	Away	League	1–3			
24	29/02/84	Kilmarnock	Home	League	2–1	1 Goal	(3)
25	03/03/84	Morton	Home	League	0–2			
26	10/03/84	Clydebank	Away	League	3–4			
27	17/03/84	Partick Thistle	Home	League	2–1			
28	24/03/84	Kilmarnock	Away	League	2–1			
29	31/03/84	Clyde	Home	League	2–2			
30	07/04/84	Ayr United	Home	League	5–0	1 Goal	(4)
31	14/04/84	Falkirk	Away	League	0–1			
32	21/04/84	Alloa	Away	League	0–2			
33	28/04/84	Hamilton Academical	Home	League	0–2			
34	05/05/84	Brechin City	Home	League	6–0	1 Goal	(5)
35	12/05/84	Meadowbank Thistle	Away	League	2–1			

SEASON 1984–85

Scottish League Division Two

36	11/08/84	Berwick Rangers	Away	League	1–2	1 Goal	(6)
37	18/08/84	Dunfermline Athletic	Home	League	1–3	1 Goal	(7)
38	21/08/84	Clydebank	Home	S Lge Cup	2–0			
39	25/08/84	Cowdenbeath	Away	League	1–5			
40	29/08/84	Rangers	Away	S Lge Cup	0–4			
41	01/09/84	Arbroath	Home	League	2–0	2 Goals	(9)
42	08/09/84	Stirling Albion	Home	League	1–1	1 Goal	(10)
43	15/09/84	Stranraer	Away	League	2–1			
44	22/09/84	Queen's Park	Home	League	0–2			
45	29/09/84	East Stirling	Home	League	2–0			
46	06/10/84	Stenhousemuir	Away	League	1–1			
47	13/10/84	Alloa	Away	League	1–1	1 Goal	(11)
48	20/10/84	Montrose	Home	League	0–1			
49	27/10/84	Albion Rovers	Home	League	3–0	1 Goal	(12)
50	03/11/84	Queen of the South	Away	League	5–3			
51	10/11/84	Stirling Albion	Away	League	1–1	1 Goal	(13)
52	17/11/84	Stranraer	Home	League	1–2			
53	24/11/84	Queen's Park	Away	League	1–1			
54	01/12/84	Stenhousemuir	Home	League	3–0	1 Goal	(14)
55	15/12/84	East Stirling	Away	League	3–1	1 Goal	(15)
56	22/12/84	Cowdenbeath	Home	League	0–3			
57	29/12/84	Arbroath	Away	League	1–2			
58	02/01/85	Dunfermline Athletic	Away	League	2–1			
59	05/01/85	Queen's Park	Away	S Cup	0–0			
60	21/01/85	Queen's Park	Home	S Cup	1–0			
61	26/01/85	Clyde	Home	S Cup	2–2			
62	02/02/85	Alloa	Home	League	1–2			
63	04/02/85	Clyde	Away	S Cup	2–1			
64	09/02/85	Montrose	Away	League	0–2			
65	16/02/85	Aberdeen	Home	S Cup	1–2			

66	23/02/85	Cowdenbeath	Away	League	0–0		
67	02/03/85	East Stirling	Away	League	1–2		
68	06/03/85	Stenhousemuir	Home	League	1–2	1 Goal	(16)
69	09/03/85	Stirling Albion	Home	League	2–4		
Sub+4	16/03/85	Queen of the South	Away	League	0–3		
70	23/03/85	Stranraer	Away	League	4–1	2 Goals	(18)
71	26/03/85	Queen of the South	Home	League	3–0	1 Goal	(19)
72	02/04/85	Albion Rovers	Away	League	6–0	3 Goals	(22)
73	09/04/85	Alloa	Home	League	2–0		
74	13/04/85	Arbroath	Home	League	2–1	1 Goal	(23)
75	20/04/85	Queen's Park	Away	League	2–1		
76	23/04/85	Dunfermline Athletic	Away	League	3–2		
77	27/04/85	Albion Rovers	Away	League	4–2	3 Goals	(26)
78	04/05/85	Berwick Rangers	Home	League	3–0	1 Goal	(27)
79	11/05/85	Montrose	Home	League	1–3		

SEASON 1985–86

Scottish League Division Two

80	10/08/85	St Johnstone	Home	League	0–2		
81	17/08/85	Stranraer	Away	League	2–3	1 Goal	(28)
82	21/08/85	Clydebank	Away	S Lge Cup	2–7		
83	24/08/85	Cowdenbeath	Away	League	4–1	1 Goal	(29)
84	31/08/85	Stirling Albion	Home	League	1–1		
85	07/09/85	Meadowbank Thistle	Home	League	1–1	1 Goal	(30)
86	14/09/85	Dunfermline Athletic	Away	League	3–3		
87	24/09/85	Queen's Park	Home	League	3–1		
88	28/09/85	Albion Rovers	Away	League	0–2		
89	05/10/85	Arbroath	Home	League	2–1		
90	12/10/85	Berwick Rangers	Away	League	3–4	2 Goals	(32)
91	19/10/85	Queen of the South	Home	League	0–1		
92	26/10/85	East Stirling	Away	League	2–0	1 Goal	(33)
93	02/11/85	Stenhousemuir	Home	League	9–2	5 Goals	(38)
94	09/11/85	Meadowbank Thistle	Away	League	0–6		
95	16/11/85	Dunfermline Athletic	Home	League	1–2		
96	23/11/85	Queen's Park	Away	League	0–0		
97	07/12/85	Dunfermline Athletic	Away	S Cup	0–2		
98	14/12/85	Arbroath	Away	League	2–2		
99	28/12/85	St Johnstone	Away	League	1–4		
100	11/01/86	Cowdenbeath	Home	League	0–1		
101	18/01/86	Queen of the South	Away	League	0–2		
102	01/02/86	Stenhousemuir	Away	League	0–2		
103	04/02/86	Albion Rovers	Home	League	1–0		
104	15/02/86	Dunfermline Athletic	Home	League	3–3	1 Goal	(39)
105	18/02/86	Berwick Rangers	Home	League	3–1	2 Goals	(41)
106	05/03/86	Meadowbank Thistle	Away	League	3–0	2 Goals	(43)
107	08/03/86	St Johnstone	Away	League	3–1		
108	11/03/86	Stranraer	Home	League	1–0	1 Goal	(44)
109	15/03/86	Arbroath	Away	League	1–2		
110	22/03/86	Cowdenbeath	Home	League	2–1		
111	25/03/86	East Stirling	Home	League	1–4	1 Goal	(45)
112	29/03/86	Berwick Rangers	Away	League	0–1		
113	05/04/86	East Stirling	Home	League	2–0		
114	09/04/86	Queen of the South	Home	League	0–2		
115	12/04/86	Stenhousemuir	Away	League	0–1		
116	15/04/86	Stirling Albion	Away	League	1–1		
117	19/04/86	Stirling Albion	Away	League	1–3		
118	22/04/86	Stranraer	Home	League	4–1		
119	26/04/86	Queen's Park	Home	League	2–1	2 Goals	(47)
120	03/05/86	Albion Rovers	Home	League	5–2	1 Goal	(48)

SEASON 1986–87

Scottish League Division Two

121	09/08/86	Stranraer	Away	League	1–1		
122	13/08/86	Arbroath	Away	S Lge Cup	1–2		
123	16/08/86	Ayr United	Home	League	5–0	1 Goal	(49)
124	23/08/86	Meadowbank Thistle	Away	League	1–0	1 Goal	(50)
125	30/08/86	Queen's Park	Home	League	2–2	1 Goal	(51)
126	06/09/86	Stirling Albion	Home	League	0–0		
127	13/09/86	Cowdenbeath	Away	League	2–1		
128	20/09/86	Berwick Rangers	Home	League	1–1	1 Goal	(52)
129	27/09/86	East Stirling	Away	League	5–0	1 Goal	(53)
130	04/10/86	Stenhousemuir	Away	League	2–1		
131	11/10/86	St Johnstone	Home	League	2–2	2 Goals	(55)

132	18/10/86	Alloa	Away	League	2–2	2 Goals	(57)
133	25/10/86	Arbroath	Home	League	3–0	1 Goal	(58)
134	01/11/86	Albion Rovers	Away	League	4–2	1 Goal	(59)
135	08/11/86	Ayr United	Away	League	3–3	1 Goal	(60)
136	15/11/86	Stranraer	Home	League	2–1	1 Goal	(61)
137	22/11/86	Meadowbank Thistle	Home	League	2–3		
138	29/11/86	Queen's Park	Away	League	2–2		

Dundee – Scottish League Premier Division

Sub+1	06/12/86	Celtic	Away	League	0–2		
1	13/12/86	St Mirren	Home	League	6–3	2 Goals	(2)
2	27/12/86	Hibernian	Home	League	2–0		
3	01/01/87	Aberdeen	Away	League	1–2		
Sub+2	24/01/87	Heart of Midlothian	Home	League	0–1		
Sub+3	03/02/87	East Fife	Home	S Cup	2–2		
4	07/02/87	Clydebank	Away	League	1–1		
5	09/02/87	East Fife	Away	S Cup	4–1	1 Goal	(3)
6	14/02/87	Hamilton Academical	Away	League	1–1		
7	21/02/87	Meadowbank Thistle	Home	S Cup	1–1		
Sub+4	28/02/87	Celtic	Home	League	4–1		
Sub+5	02/03/87	Meadowbank Thistle	Home	S Cup	2–0		
8	07/03/87	St Mirren	Away	League	1–0		
Sub+6	10/03/87	Dundee United	Home	League	1–1		
9	14/03/87	Clydebank	Away	S Cup	4–0	1 Goal	(4)
Sub+7	17/03/87	Rangers	Home	League	0–4		
10	25/03/87	Falkirk	Home	League	4–0	1 Goal	(5)
11	28/03/87	Dundee United	Away	League	1–1		
12	04/04/87	Aberdeen	Home	League	1–1		
13	11/04/87	Dundee United	Neutral	S Cup	2–3	1 Goal	(6)
14	14/04/87	Rangers	Away	League	0–2		
15	18/04/87	Motherwell	Home	League	4–1	1 Goal	(7)
16	21/04/87	Falkirk	Away	League	0–0		
17	25/04/87	Clydebank	Home	League	4–1	1 Goal	(8)
18	02/05/87	Heart of Midlothian	Away	League	3–1	2 Goals	(10)
19	09/05/87	Hamilton Academical	Home	League	7–3	3 Goals	(13)

SEASON 1987–88

Scottish League Premier Division

20	08/08/87	Aberdeen	Home	League	1–1		
21	12/08/87	Falkirk	Away	League	3–0	1 Goal	(14)
22	15/08/87	Hibernian	Away	League	4–0	1 Goal	(15)
23	18/08/87	Queen's Park	Away	S Lge Cup	3–0	1 Goal	(16)
24	22/08/87	St Mirren	Home	League	0–2		
25	26/08/87	Meadowbank Thistle	Away	S Lge Cup	3–0	1 Goal	(17)
26	29/08/87	Dunfermline Athletic	Home	League	5–0	1 Goal	(18)
27	02/09/87	Dundee United	Home	S Lge Cup	2–1*	1 Goal	(19)
28	05/09/87	Rangers	Away	League	1–2		
29	12/09/87	Morton	Away	League	3–4		
30	19/09/87	Heart of Midlothian	Home	League	1–3		
31	23/09/87	Aberdeen	Neutral	S Lge Cup	0–2		
32	03/10/87	Dundee United	Home	League	1–1		
33	07/10/87	Celtic	Home	League	1–1		
34	10/10/87	Aberdeen	Away	League	0–0		
35	17/10/87	Dunfermline Athletic	Away	League	1–0		
36	28/10/87	Morton	Home	League	1–0		
37	31/10/87	Heart of Midlothian	Away	League	2–4	1 Goal	(20)
38	07/11/87	Falkirk	Home	League	3–1	1 Goal	(21)
39	14/11/87	Celtic	Away	League	0–5		
40	17/11/87	St Mirren	Away	League	2–1		
41	21/11/87	Hibernian	Home	League	2–1		
42	24/11/87	Motherwell	Home	League	2–0		
43	28/11/87	Dundee United	Away	League	3–1	1 Goal	(22)
44	05/12/87	Aberdeen	Home	League	1–2		
45	12/12/87	Falkirk	Away	League	6–0	2 Goals	(24)
46	16/12/87	Morton	Away	League	7–1	2 Goals	(26)
47	19/12/87	Heart of Midlothian	Home	League	0–0		
48	26/12/87	Rangers	Away	League	0–2		
49	01/01/88	Dunfermline Athletic	Home	League	2–0		
50	06/01/88	Rangers	Home	League	0–1		
51	09/01/88	Motherwell	Away	League	3–3		
52	16/01/88	Dundee United	Home	League	0–2		
53	30/01/88	Brechin City	Home	S Cup	0–0		
54	03/02/88	Brechin City	Away	S Cup	3–0	1 Goal	(27)
55	06/02/88	Hibernian	Away	League	1–2	1 Goal	(28)

56	13/02/88	Celtic	Home	League	1–2	
57	20/02/88	Motherwell	Home	S Cup	2–0	
58	27/02/88	Aberdeen	Away	League	0–1	
59	01/03/88	St Mirren	Home	League	2–1	
60	05/03/88	Morton	Home	League	1–0	
61	12/03/88	Dundee United	Home	S Cup	0–0	
62	15/03/88	Dundee United	Away	S Cup	2–2*	
63	19/03/88	Dunfermline Athletic	Away	League	1–6	1 Goal (29)
64	28/03/88	Dundee United	Neutral	S Cup	0–3	
65	30/03/88	Heart of Midlothian	Away	League	0–2	
Sub+8	02/04/88	Dundee United	Away	League	0–1	
Sub+9	06/04/88	Motherwell	Home	League	1–2	
66	16/04/88	Falkirk	Home	League	4–2	3 Goals (32)
67	23/04/88	Celtic	Away	League	0–3	
68	30/04/88	Hibernian	Home	League	0–0	
69	07/05/88	St Mirren	Away	League	0–1	

SEASON 1988–89

Scottish League Premier Division

70	13/08/88	Aberdeen	Home	League	1–1	
71	17/08/88	Queen of the South	Home	S Lge Cup	5–1	1 Goal (33)
72	20/08/88	Motherwell	Away	League	1–1	1 Goal (34)
73	23/08/88	Falkirk	Home	S Lge Cup	2–1	1 Goal (35)
74	27/08/88	St Mirren	Away	League	0–0	
75	31/08/88	Rangers	Away	S Lge Cup	1–4	
76	03/09/88	Dundee United	Home	League	0–3	
77	17/09/88	Hamilton Academical	Away	League	0–1	
78	24/09/88	Celtic	Home	League	1–0	
79	28/09/88	Heart of Midlothian	Away	League	1–1	
80	01/10/88	Rangers	Away	League	0–2	
81	08/10/88	Hibernian	Home	League	2–1	
82	12/10/88	Motherwell	Home	League	1–1	1 Goal (36)
83	29/10/88	Celtic	Away	League	3–2	
84	02/11/88	Hamilton Academical	Home	League	5–2	1 Goal (37)
85	05/11/88	Dundee United	Away	League	0–2	
86	12/11/88	St Mirren	Home	League	0–1	
87	16/11/88	Aberdeen	Away	League	0–1	
88	19/11/88	Rangers	Home	League	0–0	
89	26/11/88	Hibernian	Away	League	1–1	
90	03/12/88	Heart of Midlothian	Home	League	1–1	
91	10/12/88	Hamilton Academical	Away	League	0–1	
92	17/12/88	Motherwell	Away	League	0–1	
93	31/12/88	Aberdeen	Home	League	2–0	
94	03/01/89	St Mirren	Away	League	1–1	1 Goal (38)
95	07/01/89	Dundee United	Home	League	0–1	
96	14/01/89	Hibernian	Home	League	1–2	
97	21/01/89	Rangers	Away	League	1–3	1 Goal (39)
98	28/01/89	Dundee United	Home	S Cup	1–2	
99	11/02/89	Heart of Midlothian	Away	League	1–3	
100	11/03/89	Aberdeen	Away	League	0–2	
101	25/03/89	Motherwell	Home	League	2–1	
102	01/04/89	St Mirren	Home	League	2–1	
103	08/04/89	Dundee United	Away	League	1–2	
104	15/04/89	Heart of Midlothian	Home	League	2–1	1 Goal (40)
105	22/04/89	Celtic	Away	League	1–2	
106	29/04/89	Hamilton Academical	Home	League	1–0	
107	06/05/89	Rangers	Home	League	1–2	1 Goal (41)
108	13/05/89	Hibernian	Away	League	1–1	1 Goal (42)

SEASON 1989–90

Scottish League Premier Division

109	12/08/89	Dunfermline Athletic	Away	League	1–2	
110	15/08/89	Clyde	Home	S Lge Cup	5–1	1 Goal (43)
111	19/08/89	Dundee United	Home	League	4–3	3 Goals (46)
112	23/08/89	Dunfermline Athletic	Away	S Lge Cup	0–1	
113	26/08/89	Aberdeen	Away	League	0–1	
114	09/09/89	Heart of Midlothian	Home	League	2–2	1 Goal (47)
115	16/09/89	Rangers	Away	League	2–2	1 Goal (48)
116	23/09/89	Hibernian	Home	League	0–0	
117	30/09/89	Motherwell	Away	League	0–3	
118	04/10/89	St Mirren	Away	League	2–3	1 Goal (49)
119	14/10/89	Celtic	Home	League	1–3	
120	21/10/89	Dunfermline Athletic	Home	League	1–2	

121	28/10/89	Dundee United	Away	League	0–0		
122	04/11/89	Aberdeen	Home	League	1–1		
123	11/11/89	Heart of Midlothian	Away	League	3–6		
124	18/11/89	Rangers	Home	League	0–2		
125	25/11/89	Hibernian	Away	League	2–3		
126	02/12/89	Motherwell	Home	League	2–1		
127	09/12/89	St Mirren	Home	League	3–3		
128	16/12/89	Celtic	Away	League	1–4		
129	26/12/89	Dunfermline Athletic	Away	League	0–1		
130	30/12/89	Dundee United	Home	League	1–1		
131	02/01/90	Aberdeen	Away	League	2–5	1 Goal	(50)
132	06/01/90	Heart of Midlothian	Home	League	0–1		
133	13/01/90	Rangers	Away	League	0–3		
134	20/01/90	Dundee United	Home	S Cup	0–0		
135	23/01/90	Dundee United	Away	S Cup	0–1		
136	27/01/90	Hibernian	Home	League	2–0	1 Goal	(51)
137	03/02/90	Celtic	Home	League	0–0		
138	03/03/90	Rangers	Home	League	2–2		
139	10/03/90	Dunfermline Athletic	Home	League	1–0		
140	24/03/90	Dundee United	Away	League	2–1	1 Goal	(52)
141	31/03/90	Aberdeen	Home	League	1–1	1 Goal	(53)
142	04/04/90	Heart of Midlothian	Away	League	0–0		
143	14/04/90	St Mirren	Home	League	1–2		
144	21/04/90	Celtic	Away	League	1–1		
145	28/04/90	Hibernian	Away	League	1–1		
146	05/05/90	Motherwell	Home	League	1–2	1 Goal	(54)

SEASON 1990–91

Scottish League Division One

147	21/08/90	Queen of the South	Away	S Lge Cup	2–2+		
148	25/08/90	Partick Thistle	Home	League	1–1		
149	01/09/90	Morton	Away	League	1–0		
150	08/09/90	Clydebank	Away	League	3–1	2 Goals	(56)
151	15/09/90	Clyde	Home	League	3–1	2 Goals	(58)
152	18/09/90	Hamilton Academical	Away	League	0–1		
153	22/09/90	Forfar Athletic	Away	League	1–1		
154	29/09/90	Kilmarnock	Home	League	1–1		
155	06/10/90	Ayr United	Away	League	4–2	1 Goal	(59)
156	09/10/90	Airdrieonians	Home	League	0–1		
157	13/10/90	Raith Rovers	Away	League	1–1		
158	16/10/90	Alloa	Away	B & Q CC	5–3	1 Goal	(60)
159	20/10/90	Falkirk	Home	League	2–2	1 Goal	(61)
160	23/10/90	Raith Rovers	Away	B & Q CC	1–0*		
161	27/10/90	Brechin City	Away	League	3–1	2 Goals	(63)
162	30/10/90	Kilmarnock	Away	B & Q CC	2–0	2 Goals	(65)
163	03/11/90	Meadowbank Thistle	Home	League	1–2		
164	11/11/90	Ayr United	Neutral	B & Q CC	3–2*		
165	17/11/90	Partick Thistle	Away	League	3–1	1 Goal	(66)
166	20/11/90	Morton	Home	League	1–0		
167	24/11/90	Airdrieonians	Away	League	1–0		
168	01/12/90	Ayr United	Home	League	1–0		
169	08/12/90	Kilmarnock	Away	League	1–2	1 Goal	(67)
170	18/12/90	Forfar Athletic	Home	League	4–1	1 Goal	(68)
171	22/12/90	Brechin City	Home	League	1–2		
172	29/12/90	Meadowbank Thistle	Away	League	1–0		
173	01/01/91	Raith Rovers	Home	League	2–1		
174	05/01/91	Falkirk	Away	League	0–1		
175	26/01/91	Brechin City	Home	S Cup	1–0		
176	02/02/91	Hamilton Academical	Home	League	3–2		
177	05/02/91	Clydebank	Home	League	1–0		
178	23/02/91	Kilmarnock	Home	S Cup	2–0		
179	02/03/91	Airdrieonians	Away	League	1–0		
180	05/03/91	Ayr United	Home	League	4–0	3 Goals	(71)
181	23/03/91	Clyde	Away	League	2–4		
182	30/03/91	Clydebank	Away	League	1–1	1 Goal	(72)
183	06/04/91	Morton	Home	League	1–0	1 Goal	(73)
184	13/04/91	Falkirk	Away	League	0–0		
185	20/04/91	Meadowbank Thistle	Home	League	4–0	1 Goal	(74)
186	27/04/91	Raith Rovers	Home	League	2–0		
187	30/04/91	Clyde	Away	League	1–0	1 Goal	(75)
188	04/05/91	Kilmarnock	Away	League	0–0		
189	11/05/91	Hamilton Academical	Away	League	2–1		

+ AET Queen of the South won 4–1 on penalties

SEASON 1991–92

Hibernian – Scottish League Premier Division

1	10/08/91	St Mirren	Home	League	4–1		
2	13/08/91	St Johnstone	Home	League	2–1		
3	17/08/91	Motherwell	Away	League	1–1	1 Goal	(1)
4	20/08/91	Stirling Albion	Away	S Lge Cup	3–0	1 Goal	(2)
5	24/08/91	Dundee United	Home	League	1–0		
6	28/08/91	Kilmarnock	Away	S Lge Cup	3–2	1 Goal	(3)
7	31/08/91	Heart of Midlothian	Away	League	0–0		
8	03/09/91	Ayr United	Away	S Lge Cup	2–0	1 Goal	(4)
9	07/09/91	Airdrieonians	Away	League	1–0		
10	14/09/91	Falkirk	Home	League	2–2		
11	21/09/91	Aberdeen	Away	League	1–1		
12	25/09/91	Rangers	Hampden	S Lge Cup	1–0	1 Goal	(5)
13	28/09/91	Celtic	Home	League	1–1		
14	05/10/91	Dunfermline Athletic	Home	League	3–0	1 Goal	(6)
15	08/10/91	Rangers	Away	League	2–4		
16	12/10/91	St Mirren	Away	League	1–0		
17	19/10/91	Motherwell	Home	League	0–0		
18	27/10/91	Dunfermline Athletic	Home	S Lge Cup	2–0	1 Goal	(7)
19	02/11/91	Heart of Midlothian	Home	League	1–1	1 Goal	(8)
20	05/11/91	Airdrieonians	Home	League	2–2	1 Goal	(9)
21	09/11/91	Dundee United	Away	League	1–1		
22	12/11/91	Falkirk	Away	League	2–3		
23	16/11/91	Dunfermline Athletic	Away	League	2–1	1 Goal	(10)
24	19/11/91	Rangers	Home	League	0–3		
25	23/11/91	Aberdeen	Home	League	1–0		
26	30/11/91	St Johnstone	Away	League	1–0		
27	04/12/91	Celtic	Away	League	0–0		
28	07/12/91	St Mirren	Home	League	0–0		
29	14/12/91	Airdrieonians	Away	League	3–0		
30	21/12/91	Falkirk	Home	League	0–1		
31	28/12/91	Dundee United	Home	League	3–2	1 Goal	(11)
32	01/01/92	Heart of Midlothian	Away	League	1–1		
33	04/01/92	Dunfermline Athletic	Home	League	5–0	3 Goals	(14)
34	11/01/92	Rangers	Away	League	0–2		
35	18/01/92	St Johnstone	Home	League	0–1		
36	25/01/92	Partick Thistle	Home	S Cup	2–0	2 Goals	(16)
37	01/02/92	Motherwell	Away	League	1–1		
38	08/02/92	Aberdeen	Away	League	1–0		
39	15/02/92	Clydebank	Away	S Cup	5–1	1 Goal	(17)
40	22/02/92	Celtic	Home	League	0–2		
41	29/02/92	Dunfermline Athletic	Away	League	0–0		
42	07/03/92	Airdrieonians	Home	S Cup	0–2		
43	10/03/92	Rangers	Home	League	1–3		
44	14/03/92	Dundee United	Away	League	0–1		
45	21/03/92	Heart of Midlothian	Home	League	1–2		
46	28/03/92	St Mirren	Away	League	1–0		
47	04/04/92	Motherwell	Home	League	0–0		
48	02/05/92	Celtic	Away	League	2–1		

SEASON 1992–93

Scottish League Premier Division

49	01/08/92	Aberdeen	Away	League	0–3		
50	04/08/92	Motherwell	Away	League	2–1	1 Goal	(18)
51	08/08/92	Rangers	Home	League	0–0		
52	12/08/92	Raith Rovers	Home	S Lge Cup	4–1		
53	15/08/92	Falkirk	Away	League	1–2		
54	18/08/92	Kilmarnock	Away	S Lge Cup	1–3*	1 Goal	(19)
55	22/08/92	Heart of Midlothian	Home	League	0–0		
56	29/08/92	St Johnstone	Away	League	1–1		
57	02/09/92	Dundee United	Home	League	2–1		
58	12/09/92	Celtic	Away	League	3–2	1 Goal	(20)
59	15/09/92	RSC Anderlecht	Home	UEFA Cup	2–2		
60	19/09/92	Airdrieonians	Home	League	2–2		
61	26/09/92	Dundee	Home	League	0–0		
62	29/09/92	RSC Anderlecht	Away	UEFA Cup	1–1		
63	03/10/92	Partick Thistle	Away	League	2–2		
64	07/10/92	Aberdeen	Home	League	1–3	1 Goal	(21)
65	17/10/92	Rangers	Away	League	0–1		
66	24/10/92	St Johnstone	Home	League	3–1		
67	31/10/92	Dundee United	Away	League	0–1		
68	07/11/92	Heart of Midlothian	Away	League	0–1		

69	21/11/92	Airdrieonians	Away	League	0–2		
70	28/11/92	Celtic	Home	League	1–2		
71	01/12/92	Motherwell	Home	League	2–2	1 Goal	(22)
72	05/12/92	Dundee	Away	League	1–1		
73	19/12/92	Aberdeen	Away	League	0–2		
74	26/12/92	Falkirk	Away	League	3–3		
75	02/01/93	Heart of Midlothian	Home	League	0–0		
76	09/01/92	St Mirren	Home	S Cup	5–2	1 Goal	(23)
77	16/01/93	Dundee United	Home	League	2–1		
78	23/01/93	St Johnstone	Away	League	0–2		
79	30/01/93	Rangers	Home	League	3–4		
80	06/02/93	Cowdenbeath	Away	S Cup	0–0		
81	10/02/93	Cowdenbeath	Home	S Cup	1–0		
82	13/02/93	Motherwell	Away	League	0–0		
83	16/02/93	Partick Thistle	Away	League	3–0		
84	20/02/93	Dundee	Home	League	1–3		
85	27/02/93	Airdrieonians	Home	League	3–1		
86	06/03/93	St Johnstone	Home	S Cup	2–0	1 Goal	(24)
87	09/03/93	Aberdeen	Home	League	1–2		
88	13/03/93	Rangers	Away	League	0–3		
89	16/03/93	Celtic	Away	League	1–2	1 Goal	(25)
90	20/03/93	Heart of Midlothian	Away	League	0–1		
91	27/03/93	Falkirk	Home	League	1–1	1 Goal	(26)
92	03/04/93	Aberdeen	Neutral	S Cup	0–1		
93	06/04/93	St Johnstone	Home	League	2–2	1 Goal	(27)
94	13/04/93	Dundee United	Away	League	3–0	3 Goals	(30)
95	17/04/93	Celtic	Home	League	3–1	1 Goal	(31)
96	20/04/93	Airdrieonians	Away	League	1–3		
97	01/05/93	Motherwell	Home	League	1–0		
98	08/05/93	Dundee	Away	League	1–3		
99	15/05/93	Partick Thistle	Home	League	0–1		

SEASON 1993–94

Scottish League Premier Division

100	07/08/93	Partick Thistle	Home	League	0–0		
101	10/08/93	Alloa	Home	S Lge Cup	2–0	1 Goal	(32)
102	14/08/93	Celtic	Away	League	1–1		
103	21/08/93	Heart of Midlothian	Away	League	0–1		
104	24/08/93	Dundee	Home	S Lge Cup	2–1	1 Goal	(33)
105	28/08/93	Dundee	Home	League	2–0		
106	31/08/93	Partick Thistle	Away	S Lge Cup	2–2+		
Sub+1	04/09/93	Kilmarnock	Away	League	1–1		
107	11/09/93	Aberdeen	Home	League	2–1	1 Goal	(34)
108	18/09/93	St Johnstone	Away	League	3–1	1 Goal	(35)
109	21/09/93	Dundee United	Neutral	S Lge Cup	1–0		
110	25/09/93	Rangers	Away	League	1–2		
111	02/10/93	Dundee United	Home	League	2–0		
112	05/10/93	Raith Rovers	Home	League	3–2		
113	09/10/93	Motherwell	Away	League	2–0	1 Goal	(36)
114	16/10/93	Celtic	Home	League	1–1		
115	24/10/93	Rangers	Neutral	S Lge Cup	1–2		
116	30/10/93	Heart of Midlothian	Home	League	0–2		
117	02/11/93	Partick Thistle	Away	League	0–0		
118	06/11/93	Dundee	Away	League	2–3	1 Goal	(37)
119	09/11/93	Kilmarnock	Home	League	2–1		
120	13/11/93	Dundee United	Away	League	2–2		
121	20/11/93	Rangers	Home	League	0–1		
122	30/11/93	St Johnstone	Home	League	0–0		
123	04/12/93	Raith Rovers	Away	League	2–1	1 Goal	(38)
124	11/12/93	Motherwell	Home	League	3–2	1 Goal	(39)
125	18/12/93	Celtic	Away	League	0–1		
126	27/12/93	Partick Thistle	Home	League	5–1	1 Goal	(40)
127	08/01/94	Dundee	Home	League	2–0		
128	12/01/94	Heart of Midlothian	Away	League	1–1	1 Goal	(41)
129	15/01/94	Kilmarnock	Away	League	3–0		
130	22/01/94	St Johnstone	Away	League	2–2		
131	29/01/94	Clyde	Home	S Cup	2–1		
132	05/02/94	Aberdeen	Home	League	3–1	2 Goals	(43)
133	20/02/94	Heart of Midlothian	Home	S Cup	1–2	1 Goal	(44)
134	26/02/94	Dundee United	Home	League	0–1		
135	05/03/94	Raith Rovers	Home	League	3–0	2 Goals	(46)
136	12/03/94	Motherwell	Away	League	0–0		
137	19/03/94	Celtic	Home	League	0–0		

138	26/03/94	Partick Thistle	Away	League	0–1		
139	29/03/94	Aberdeen	Away	League	3–2	2 Goals	(48)
140	02/04/94	St Johnstone	Home	League	0–0		
141	16/04/94	Dundee United	Away	League	0–3		
142	23/04/94	Motherwell	Home	League	0–2		
143	26/04/94	Raith Rovers	Away	League	1–1	1 Goal	(49)
144	30/04/94	Heart of Midlothian	Home	League	0–0		
145	03/05/94	Rangers	Home	League	1–0	1 Goal	(50)
146	07/05/94	Dundee	Away	League	0–4		
147	14/05/94	Kilmarnock	Home	League	0–0		

+ AET Hibernian won 3–2 on penalties

SEASON 1994–95

Scottish League Premier Division

148	26/12/94	Rangers	Away	League	0–2		
149	31/12/94	Dundee United	Home	League	4–0	3 Goals	(53)
150	07/01/95	Kilmarnock	Home	League	2–1		
151	13/01/95	Motherwell	Away	League	0–0		
152	18/01/95	Heart of Midlothian	Away	League	0–2		
153	21/01/95	Aberdeen	Home	League	4–2	1 Goal	(54)
154	28/01/95	Montrose	Away	S Cup	2–0		
155	04/02/95	Partick Thistle	Home	League	1–2		
156	11/02/95	Celtic	Away	League	2–2		
157	18/02/95	Motherwell	Home	S Cup	2–0		
158	25/02/95	Falkirk	Away	League	0–1		
159	04/03/95	Rangers	Home	League	1–1	1 Goal	(55)
160	10/03/95	Stenhousemuir	Away	S Cup	4–0		
161	18/03/95	Aberdeen	Away	League	0–0		
162	22/03/95	Motherwell	Home	League	2–0	2 Goals	(57)
163	01/04/95	Partick Thistle	Away	League	2–2	1 Goal	(58)
164	07/04/95	Celtic	Neutral	S Cup	0–0		
165	11/04/95	Celtic	Neutral	S Cup	1–3	1 Goal	(59)
166	16/04/95	Rangers	Away	League	1–3		
167	19/04/95	Falkirk	Home	League	0–2		
168	29/04/95	Dundee United	Away	League	1–0		
169	06/05/95	Heart of Midlothian	Home	League	3–1	1 Goal	(60)
170	09/05/95	Celtic	Home	League	1–1		
171	13/05/95	Kilmarnock	Away	League	2–1	1 Goal	(61)

SEASON 1995–96

Scottish League Premier Division

172	09/09/95	Kilmarnock	Away	League	3–0	2 Goals	(63)
173	16/09/95	Aberdeen	Home	League	1–1		
174	23/09/95	Rangers	Away	League	1–0		
175	01/10/95	Heart of Midlothian	Home	League	2–2		
176	04/10/95	Raith Rovers	Away	League	0–3		
Sub+2	14/10/95	Celtic	Away	League	2–2		
177	21/10/95	Motherwell	Home	League	4–2	1 Goal	(64)
178	28/10/95	Kilmarnock	Home	League	2–0	1 Goal	(65)
179	04/11/95	Aberdeen	Away	League	2–1	1 Goal	(66)
180	11/11/95	Falkirk	Away	League	0–2		
181	02/12/95	Motherwell	Away	League	2–0	2 Goals	(68)
182	09/12/95	Celtic	Home	League	0–4		
183	16/12/95	Raith Rovers	Home	League	1–2		
184	30/12/95	Rangers	Away	League	0–7		
185	01/01/96	Heart of Midlothian	Home	League	2–1		
186	08/01/96	Aberdeen	Home	League	1–2		
187	13/01/96	Kilmarnock	Away	League	2–3	1 Goal	(69)
188	16/01/96	Partick Thistle	Away	League	0–0		
189	20/01/96	Motherwell	Home	League	0–0		
190	27/01/96	Kilmarnock	Home	S Cup	0–2		
Sub+3	03/02/96	Celtic	Away	League	1–2		
191	10/02/96	Raith Rovers	Away	League	0–1		
192	24/02/96	Falkirk	Home	League	2–1	1 Goal	(70)
193	03/03/96	Rangers	Home	League	0–2		
194	16/03/96	Heart of Midlothian	Away	League	1–1		
Sub+4	14/04/96	Celtic	Home	League	1–2		
195	20/04/96	Raith Rovers	Home	League	1–1		
196	27/04/96	Falkirk	Away	League	1–1		
197	04/05/96	Partick Thistle	Home	League	1–0		

SEASON 1996–97

Scottish League Premier Division

198	10/08/96	Kilmarnock	Home	League	1–2			
199	13/08/96	Brechin City	Away	S Lge Cup	2–0			
200	17/08/96	Dundee United	Away	League	1–0			
201	24/08/96	Dunfermline Athletic	Home	League	0–0			
202	04/09/96	Albion Rovers	Away	S Lge Cup	2–0	1 Goal	(71)
Sub+5	07/09/96	Celtic	Away	League	0–5			
203	14/09/96	Raith Rovers	Home	League	1–0			
204	18/09/96	Rangers	Away	S Lge Cup	0–4			
205	21/09/96	Aberdeen	Away	League	2–0	1 Goal	(72)
206	28/09/96	Heart of Midlothian	Home	League	1–3			
Sub+6	23/11/96	Aberdeen	Home	League	0–1			
207	30/11/96	Motherwell	Home	League	2–0			
208	07/12/96	Rangers	Away	League	3–4	1 Goal	(73)
209	11/12/96	Dunfermline Athletic	Away	League	1–2			
210	14/12/96	Dundee United	Home	League	1–1			
211	26/12/96	Kilmarnock	Home	League	0–1			
212	28/12/96	Aberdeen	Away	League	1–1			
213	01/01/97	Heart of Midlothian	Home	League	0–4			
Sub+7	04/01/97	Rangers	Home	League	1–2			
214	11/01/97	Motherwell	Away	League	1–2			
Sub+8	17/02/97	Celtic	Home	S Cup	1–1			
215	26/02/97	Celtic	Away	S Cup	0–2			
216	01/03/97	Motherwell	Home	League	1–1	1 Goal	(74)
217	08/03/97	Dunfermline Athletic	Home	League	1–0	1 Goal	(75)
218	15/03/97	Heart of Midlothian	Away	League	0–1			
Sub+9	22/03/97	Aberdeen	Home	League	3–1			
Sub+10	05/04/97	Dundee United	Home	League	2–0			
Sub+11	12/04/97	Dunfermline Athletic	Away	League	1–1			
Sub+12	19/04/97	Kilmarnock	Away	League	1–1			
Sub+13	10/05/97	Raith Rovers	Away	League	1–1			
219	17/05/97	Airdrieonians	Home	Lge P/O	1–0			
Sub+14	22/05/97	Airdrieonians	Away	Lge P/O	4–2	1 Goal	(76)

INTERNATIONAL APPEARANCES – SCOTLAND

1	19/02/92	Northern Ireland	Hampden Park	1–0	F

APPEARANCES AND GOALS PER SEASON

SEASON 83–84

	GAMES	GOALS
Scottish League	34+3	5
Scottish Cup	1	0
TOTAL	**35+3**	**5**

SEASON 84–85

	GAMES	GOALS
Scottish League	37+1	22
Scottish Cup	5	0
Scottish League Cup	2	0
TOTAL	**44+1**	**22**

SEASON 85–86

	GAMES	GOALS
Scottish League	39	21
Scottish Cup	1	0
Scottish League Cup	1	0
TOTAL	**41**	**21**

SEASON 86–87

	GAMES	GOALS
Scottish League	32+5	23
Scottish Cup	4+2	3
Scottish League Cup	1	0
TOTAL	**37+7**	**26**

SEASON 87–88

	GAMES	GOALS
Scottish League	40+2	15
Scottish Cup	6	1
Scottish League Cup	4	3
TOTAL	**50+2**	**19**

SEASON 88–89	GAMES	GOALS
Scottish League	35	8
Scottish Cup	1	0
Scottish League Cup	3	2
TOTAL	**39**	**10**

SEASON 89–90	GAMES	GOALS
Scottish League	34	11
Scottish Cup	2	0
Scottish League Cup	2	1
TOTAL	**38**	**12**

SEASON 90–91	GAMES	GOALS
Scottish League	36	18
Scottish Cup	2	0
Scottish League Cup	1	0
B & Q Centenary Cup	4	3
TOTAL	**43**	**21**

SEASON 91–92	GAMES	GOALS
Scottish League	40	9
Scottish Cup	3	3
Scottish League Cup	5	5
TOTAL	**48**	**17**

SEASON 92–93	GAMES	GOALS
Scottish League	42	11
Scottish Cup	5	2
Scottish League Cup	2	1
UEFA Cup	2	0
TOTAL	**51**	**14**

SEASON 93–94	GAMES	GOALS
Scottish League	41+1	16
Scottish Cup	2	1
Scottish League Cup	5	2
TOTAL	**48+1**	**19**

SEASON 94–95	GAMES	GOALS
Scottish League	19	10
Scottish Cup	5	1
TOTAL	**24**	**11**

SEASON 95–96	GAMES	GOALS
Scottish League	25+3	9
Scottish Cup	1	0
TOTAL	**26+3**	**9**

SEASON 96–97	GAMES	GOALS
Scottish League	17+8	4
Scottish League Play–offs	1+1	1
Scottish Cup	1+1	0
Scottish League Cup	3	1
TOTAL	**22+10**	**6**

CAREER APPEARANCES AND GOALS

COMPETITION	GAMES	TOTAL	GOALS
Scottish League	471+23	494	182
Scottish League Play–offs	1+1	2	1
Scottish Cup	39+3	42	11
Scottish League Cup	29	29	15
B & Q Centenary Cup	4	4	3
UEFA Cup	2	2	0
Internationals	1	1	0
TOTAL	**547+27**	**574**	**212**

HAT–TRICKS

Raith Rovers

1	3	Albion Rovers	02/04/85	Away	League	6–0
2	3	Albion Rovers	27/04/85	Away	League	4–2
3	5	Stenhousemuir	02/11/85	Home	League	9–2

Dundee

1	3	Hamilton Academical	09/05/87	Home	League	7–3
2	3	Falkirk	16/04/88	Home	League	4–2
3	3	Dundee United	19/08/89	Home	League	4–3
4	3	Ayr United	05/03/91	Home	League	4–0

Hibernian

1	3	Dunfermline Athletic	04/01/92	Home	League	5–0
2	3	Dundee United	13/04/93	Away	League	3–0
3	3	Dundee United	31/12/94	Home	League	4–0

Scottish League: 10
TOTAL: 10

HONOURS

Winners medals
Scottish League Cup: 91/92
B & Q Centenary Cup: 90/91

Runner–up medals
Scottish League Division Two Championship: 86/87
Scottish League Cup: 93/94

RECORDS

MOST GOALS SCORED

Strike Rate One: Games per goal excluding substitute appearances
Strike Rate Two: Games per goal including substitute appearances

No	Player	Matches	Total	Goals	SR 1	SR 2
1	John Aldridge	823+59	882	471	1.74	1.87
2	Ian Rush	817+39	856	408	2.00	2.09
3	Ally McCoist	630+111	741	390	1.61	1.90
4	Gary Lineker	638+19	657	334	1.91	1.96
5	Tommy Tynan	749+34	783	314	2.38	2.49
6	Keith Edwards	599+58	657	301	1.99	2.18
7=	Steve Bull	511+16	527	298	1.71	1.76
7=	Ian Wright	519+45	564	298	1.74	1.89
9	Kerry Dixon	682+46	728	287	2.37	2.53
10	Peter Beardsley	821+44	865	277	2.96	3.12
11	Tony Cascarino	641+73	714	275	2.33	2.59
12	Brian McClair	634+100	734	272	2.33	2.69
13=	Mick Quinn	556+46	602	268	2.07	2.24
13=	John Robertson	565+74	639	268	2.10	2.38
13=	Steve White	646+107	753	268	2.41	2.80
16	Mo Johnston	622+20	642	266	2.33	2.41
17	Luther Blissett	661+62	723	261	2.53	2.77
18=	Jimmy Quinn	549+128	677	256	2.14	2.64
18=	Lee Chapman	645+44	689	256	2.51	2.69
20	Dean Saunders	657+32	689	248	2.64	2.77
21=	Tony Cottee	530+54	584	245	2.16	2.38
21=	Tony Adcock	614+55	669	245	2.50	2.73
23	Clive Allen	457+55	512	244	1.87	2.09
24	Teddy Sheringham	527+28	555	241	2.18	2.30
25	Mark Hately	566+55	621	234	2.41	2.65
26	Mick Harford	660+50	710	232	2.84	3.06
27	Duncan Shearer	436+70	506	229	1.90	2.20
28	Charlie Nicholas	534+61	595	227	2.35	2.62
29	Simon Garner	638+64	702	225	2.83	3.12
30	Tommy Coyne	480+81	561	221	2.17	2.53
31	Mark Hughes	665+18	683	218	3.05	3.13
32	Alan Shearer	379+25	404	217	1.74	1.86
33	Gary Bannister	589+53	642	216	2.72	2.97
34=	Keith Wright	547+27	574	212	2.58	2.70
34=	Graeme Sharp	603+35	638	212	2.84	3.00
36=	Gary Bennett	498+64	562	209	2.38	2.68
36=	Gordon Davies	538+42	580	209	2.57	2.77
38	Trevor Senior	415+18	433	208	1.99	2.08
39=	Phil Stant	431+37	468	207	2.08	2.26
39=	Andy Ritchie	563+78	641	207	2.71	3.09
41	David Platt	556+14	570	206	2.69	2.76
42=	David Kelly	503+75	578	205	2.45	2.81
42=	Cyrille Regis	701+43	744	205	3.41	3.62
44	John Barnes	763+19	782	204	3.74	3.83
45=	Mark Bright	489+58	547	203	2.40	2.69
45=	David Crown	537+11	548	203	2.64	2.69
47	Alan Smith	535+45	580	201	2.66	2.88
48=	Bernie Slaven	503+50	553	200	2.51	2.76
48=	Andy Flounders	494+61	555	200	2.47	2.77
50=	Matthew Le Tissier	400+49	449	184	2.17	2.44
50=	Eric Cantona	466+19	485	184	2.53	2.63
52=	Bob Taylor	392+51	443	181	2.16	2.44
52=	Marco Gabbiadini	463+52	515	181	2.55	2.84
52=	Gordon Durie	481+55	536	181	2.65	2.96
55	John McGinlay	353+33	386	171	2.06	2.25
56	Les Ferdinand	298+18	316	166	1.79	1.90
57	John Fashanu	451+16	467	164	2.75	2.84
58	Dean Holdsworth	322+60	382	159	2.02	2.40
59	Chris Waddle	714+41	755	152	4.69	4.96
60	David Hirst	335+49	384	138	2.42	2.78
61	Kevin Francis	237+44	281	137	1.72	2.05

62	Andy Cole	219+22	241	**129**	1.69	1.86
63	Dion Dublin	295+40	335	**121**	2.43	2.76
64	Robbie Fowler	186+8	194	**117**	1.58	1.65
65	Chris Armstrong	262+48	310	**111**	2.36	2.79
66	Stan Collymore	188+31	219	**105**	1.79	2.08

GREATEST STRIKE RATES – ONE

No	Player	SR	Matches	Goals
1	Robbie Fowler	**1.58**	186	117
2	Ally McCoist	**1.61**	630	390
3	Andy Cole	**1.69**	219	129
4	Steve Bull	**1.71**	511	298
5	Kevin Francis	**1.72**	237	137
6=	John Aldridge	**1.74**	823	471
6=	Ian Wright	**1.74**	519	298
6=	Alan Shearer	**1.74**	379	217
9=	Les Ferdinand	**1.79**	298	166
9=	Stan Collymore	**1.79**	188	105
11	Clive Allen	**1.87**	457	244
12	Duncan Shearer	**1.90**	436	229
13	Gary Lineker	**1.91**	639	334
14=	Keith Edwards	**1.99**	599	301
14=	Trevor Senior	**1.99**	415	208
16	Ian Rush	**2.00**	817	408
17	Dean Holdsworth	**2.02**	322	159
18	John McGinlay	**2.06**	353	171
19	Mick Quinn	**2.07**	556	268
20	Phil Stant	**2.08**	431	207
21	John Robertson	**2.10**	565	268
22	Jimmy Quinn	**2.14**	549	256
23=	Tony Cottee	**2.16**	530	245
23=	Bob Taylor	**2.16**	392	181
25=	Tommy Coyne	**2.17**	480	221
25=	Matthew Le Tissier	**2.17**	400	184
27	Teddy Sheringham	**2.18**	527	241
28=	Tony Cascarino	**2.33**	641	275
28=	Brian McClair	**2.33**	634	272
28=	Mo Johnston	**2.33**	622	266
31	Charlie Nicholas	**2.35**	534	227
32	Chris Armstrong	**2.36**	262	111
33	Kerry Dixon	**2.37**	682	287
34=	Tommy Tynan	**2.38**	749	314
34=	Gary Bennett	**2.38**	498	209
36	Mark Bright	**2.40**	489	203
37=	Steve White	**2.41**	646	268
37=	Mark Hately	**2.41**	566	234
39	David Hirst	**2.42**	335	138
40	Dion Dublin	**2.43**	295	121
41	David Kelly	**2.45**	503	205
42	Andy Flounders	**2.47**	494	200
43	Tony Adcock	**2.50**	614	245
44=	Lee Chapman	**2.51**	645	256
44=	Bernie Slaven	**2.51**	503	200
46=	Luther Blissett	**2.53**	661	261
46=	Eric Cantona	**2.53**	466	184
48	Marco Gabbiadini	**2.55**	463	181
49	Gordon Davies	**2.57**	538	209
50	Keith Wright	**2.58**	547	212
51=	Dean Saunders	**2.64**	657	248
51=	David Crown	**2.64**	537	203
53	Gordon Durie	**2.65**	481	181
54	Alan Smith	**2.66**	535	201
55	David Platt	**2.69**	556	206
56	Andy Ritchie	**2.71**	563	207
57	Gary Bannister	**2.72**	589	216
58	John Fashanu	**2.75**	451	164
59	Simon Garner	**2.83**	638	225
60=	Mick Harford	**2.84**	660	232
60=	Graeme Sharp	**2.84**	603	212
62	Peter Beardsley	**2.96**	821	277
63	Mark Hughes	**3.05**	665	218
64	Cyrille Regis	**3.41**	701	205
65	John Barnes	**3.74**	763	204
66	Chris Waddle	**4.69**	714	152

GREATEST STRIKE RATES – TWO

No	Player	SR	Matches	Goals
1	Robbie Fowler	1.65	194	117
2	Steve Bull	1.76	527	298
3=	Alan Shearer	1.86	404	217
3=	Andy Cole	1.86	241	129
5	John Aldridge	1.87	882	471
6	Ian Wright	1.89	564	298
7=	Ally McCoist	1.90	741	390
7=	Les Ferdinand	1.90	316	166
9	Gary Lineker	1.96	657	334
10	Kevin Francis	2.05	281	137
11=	Trevor Senior	2.08	433	208
11=	Stan Collymore	2.08	219	105
13=	Ian Rush	2.09	856	408
13=	Clive Allen	2.09	512	244
15	Keith Edwards	2.18	657	301
16	Duncan Shearer	2.20	506	229
17	Mick Quinn	2.24	602	268
18	John McGinlay	2.25	386	171
19	Phil Stant	2.26	468	207
20	Teddy Sheringham	2.30	555	241
21=	John Robertson	2.38	639	268
21=	Tony Cottee	2.38	584	245
23	Dean Holdsworth	2.40	382	159
24	Mo Johnston	2.41	642	266
25=	Matthew Le Tissier	2.44	449	184
25=	Bob Taylor	2.44	443	181
27	Tommy Tynan	2.49	783	314
28=	Kerry Dixon	2.53	728	287
28=	Tommy Coyne	2.53	561	221
30	Tony Cascarino	2.59	714	275
31	Charlie Nicholas	2.62	595	227
32	Eric Cantona	2.63	485	184
33	Jimmy Quinn	2.64	677	256
34	Mark Hately	2.65	621	234
35	Gary Bennett	2.68	562	209
36=	Brian McClair	2.69	734	272
36=	Lee Chapman	2.69	689	256
38=	Mark Bright	2.69	547	203
38=	David Crown	2.69	548	203
40	Keith Wright	2.70	574	212
41	Tony Adcock	2.73	669	245
42=	David Platt	2.76	570	206
42=	Bernie Slaven	2.76	553	200
42=	Dion Dublin	2.76	335	121
45=	Luther Blissett	2.77	723	261
45=	Dean Saunders	2.77	689	248
45=	Gordon Davies	2.77	580	209
45=	Andy Flounders	2.77	555	200
49	David Hirst	2.78	384	138
50	Chris Armstrong	2.79	310	111
51	Steve White	2.80	753	268
52	David Kelly	2.81	578	205
53=	Marco Gabbiadini	2.84	515	181
53=	John Fashanu	2.84	467	164
55	Alan Smith	2.88	580	201
56	Gordon Durie	2.96	536	181
57	Gary Bannister	2.97	642	216
58	Graeme Sharp	3.00	638	212
59	Mick Harford	3.06	710	232
60	Andy Ritchie	3.09	641	207
61=	Peter Beardsley	3.12	865	277
61=	Simon Garner	3.12	702	225
63	Mark Hughes	3.13	683	218
64	Cyrille Regis	3.62	744	205
65	John Barnes	3.83	782	204
66	Chris Waddle	4.96	755	152

GOALS PER SEASON

Excluding international goals

Player	Seasons	0–9	10–19	20–29	30–39	40–49	50–59	Highest
Tony Adcock	17	5	8	3	1	0	0	33 – 83/84
John Aldridge	18	0	4	9	4	1	0	40 – 91/92
Clive Allen	17	4	10	1	1	1	0	49 – 86/87
Chris Armstrong	8	3	3	2	0	0	0	25 – 93/94
Gary Bannister	18	6	8	4	0	0	0	28 – 84/85
John Barnes	16	6	9	1	0	0	0	28 – 89/90
Peter Beardsley	18	4	10	4	0	0	0	28 – 80/81*
Gary Bennett	13	4	5	2	1	1	0	47 – 94/95
Luther Blissett	19	8	5	5	1	0	0	33 – 82/83
Mark Bright	16	6	5	5	0	0	0	25 – 87/88 & 88/89
Steve Bull	12	1	4	5	0	0	2	52 – 87/88
Eric Cantona	14	5	7	2	0	0	0	25 – 93/94
Tony Cascarino	16	5	5	3	3	0	0	36 – 94/95
Lee Chapman	18	6	5	6	1	0	0	31 – 90/91
Andy Cole	7	2	2	2	0	1	0	41 – 93/94
Stan Collymore	7	2	3	2	0	0	0	25 – 93/94 & 94/95
Tony Cottee	15	2	9	4	0	0	0	29 – 86/87
Tommy Coyne	16	7	7	1	1	0	0	37 – 87/88
David Crown	13	5	3	5	0	0	0	29 – 87/88 & 88/89
Gordon Davies	15	5	6	4	0	0	0	26 – 83/84
Kerry Dixon	17	4	7	3	3	0	0	35 – 84/85
Dion Dublin	9	3	4	2	0	0	0	25 – 90/91
Gordon Durie	16	7	8	1	0	0	0	23 – 95/96
Keith Edwards	16	4	5	4	2	1	0	42 – 83/84
John Fashanu	14	5	6	3	0	0	0	21 – 87/88
Les Ferdinand	11	3	3	5	0	0	0	29 – 95/96
Andy Flounders	15	4	7	4	0	0	0	27 – 87/88 & 90/91
Robbie Fowler	4	0	1	0	3	0	0	36 – 95/96
Kevin Francis	8	4	0	2	2	0	0	39 – 92/93
Marco Gabbiadini	13	3	7	3	0	0	0	26 – 89/90
Simon Garner	18	8	7	3	0	0	0	25 – 88/89
Mick Harford	20	9	8	3	0	0	0	25 – 85/86
Mark Hately	19	9	6	3	1	0	0	30 – 93/94
David Hirst	12	7	3	1	1	0	0	32 – 90/91
Dean Holdsworth	10	5	2	2	1	0	0	38 – 91/92
Mark Hughes	14	3	8	3	0	0	0	24 – 84/85
Mo Johnston	15	4	6	3	2	0	0	34 – 82/83 & 83/84
David Kelly	14	3	7	3	1	0	0	30 – 87/88
Matthew Le Tissier	11	1	6	3	1	0	0	30 – 94/95
Gary Lineker	16	5	3	6	1	1	0	40 – 85/86
Brian McClair	16	7	2	4	2	1	0	41 – 86/87
Ally McCoist	19	5	5	5	2	2	0	49 – 92/93
John McGinlay	9	3	1	3	2	0	0	33 – 93/94
Charlie Nicholas	16	7	6	2	0	1	0	48 – 82/83
David Platt	13	4	5	4	0	0	0	26 – 87/88
Jimmy Quinn	16	5	6	3	1	1	0	40 – 93/94
Mick Quinn	17	5	4	7	1	0	0	36 – 89/90
Cyrille Regis	19	8	10	1	0	0	0	25 – 81/82
Andy Ritchie	20	9	9	2	0	0	0	28 – 89/90
John Robertson	16	2	8	5	1	0	0	31 – 87/88
Ian Rush	19	5	5	4	3	2	0	47 – 83/84
Dean Saunders	14	2	7	5	0	0	0	23 – 91/92
Trevor Senior	11	4	1	4	1	1	0	41 – 83/84
Graeme Sharp	17	6	8	2	1	0	0	30 – 84/85
Alan Shearer	10	3	1	3	3	0	0	37 – 94/95 & 95/96
Duncan Shearer	12	3	3	5	1	0	0	33 – 91/92
Teddy Sheringham	14	4	4	5	1	0	0	38 – 90/91
Bernie Slaven	14	6	3	3	2	0	0	32 – 89/90
Alan Smith	13	3	7	3	0	0	0	27 – 90/91
Phil Stant	12	3	4	4	1	0	0	34 – 88/89
Bob Taylor	12	3	5	2	2	0	0	37 – 92/93
Tommy Tynan	17	3	6	6	2	0	0	33 – 82/83
Chris Waddle	17	11	6	0	0	0	0	18 – 83/84
Steve White	20	6	11	2	1	0	0	33 – 95/96
Ian Wright	12	2	1	3	6	0	0	35 – 93/94
Keith Wright	14	3	7	4	0	0	0	26 – 86/87

* Including 13 goals scored in the 1981 North American Soccer League Season

AVERAGE NUMBER OF GOALS PER SEASON

Including international goals

No	Player	Seasons	Goals	Average Per Season
1	Robbie Fowler	4	117	29.25
2	John Aldridge	18	471	26.16
3=	Steve Bull	12	298	24.83
3=	Ian Wright	12	298	24.83
5	Alan Shearer	10	217	21.70
6	Ian Rush	19	408	21.47
7	Gary Lineker	16	334	20.87
8	Ally McCoist	19	390	20.52
9	Duncan Shearer	12	229	19.08
10	John McGinlay	9	171	19.00
11	Trevor Senior	11	208	18.90
12	Keith Edwards	16	301	18.81
13	Tommy Tynan	17	314	18.47
14	Andy Cole	7	129	18.42
15	Mo Johnston	15	266	17.73
16	Dean Saunders	14	248	17.71
17	Phil Stant	12	207	17.25
18	Teddy Sheringham	14	241	17.21
19	Tony Cascarino	16	275	17.18
20	Kevin Francis	8	137	17.12
21	Brian McClair	16	272	17.00
22	Kerry Dixon	17	287	16.88
23	John Robertson	16	268	16.75
24	Matthew Le Tissier	11	184	16.72
25	Tony Cottee	15	245	16.33
26	Gary Bennett	13	209	16.07
27	Jimmy Quinn	16	256	16.00
28	Dean Holdsworth	10	159	15.90
29	David Platt	13	206	15.84
30	Mick Quinn	17	268	15.76
31	David Crown	13	203	15.61
32	Mark Hughes	14	218	15.57
33	Alan Smith	13	201	15.46
34	Peter Beardsley	18	277	15.38
35	Keith Wright	14	212	15.14
36	Les Ferdinand	11	166	15.09
37	Bob Taylor	12	181	15.08
38	Stan Collymore	7	105	15.00
39	David Kelly	14	205	14.64
40	Tony Adcock	17	245	14.41
41	Clive Allen	17	244	14.35
42	Bernie Slaven	14	200	14.28
43	Lee Chapman	18	256	14.22
44	Charlie Nicholas	16	227	14.18
45	Gordon Davies	15	209	13.93
46	Marco Gabbiadini	13	181	13.92
47	Chris Armstrong	8	111	13.87
48	Tommy Coyne	16	221	13.81
49	Luther Blissett	19	261	13.73
50	Dion Dublin	9	121	13.44
51	Steve White	20	268	13.40
52	Andy Flounders	15	200	13.33
53	Eric Cantona	14	184	13.14
54	John Barnes	16	204	12.75
55	Mark Bright	16	203	12.68
56	Simon Garner	18	225	12.50
57	Graeme Sharp	17	212	12.47
58	Mark Hateley	19	234	12.31
59	Gary Bannister	18	216	12.00
60	John Fashanu	14	164	11.71
61	Mick Harford	20	232	11.60
62	David Hirst	12	138	11.50
63	Gordon Durie	16	181	11.31
64	Cyrille Regis	19	205	10.78
65	Andy Ritchie	20	207	10.35
66	Chris Waddle	17	152	8.94

HAT-TRICKS

All matches include substitute appearances

No	Player	Hat-tricks	Matches	Matches Per Hat-trick
1	Ally McCoist	24	741	30.87
2	John Aldridge	23	882	38.34
3	Gary Lineker	18	657	36.50
4	Ian Rush	18	856	47.55
5	Steve Bull	17	527	31.00
6	Ian Wright	15	564	37.60
7	Tony Cottee	12	584	48.66
8	Kerry Dixon	12	728	60.66
9	Alan Shearer	11	404	36.72
10	Mick Quinn	11	602	54.72
11	Keith Edwards	11	657	59.72
12	Bernie Slaven	10	553	55.30
13	Teddy Sheringham	10	555	55.50
14	Keith Wright	10	574	57.40
15	Brian McClair	10	734	73.40
16	Andy Cole	9	241	26.77
17	Matthew Le Tissier	9	449	49.88
18	Duncan Shearer	9	506	56.22
19	Clive Allen	9	512	56.88
20	Gordon Durie	9	536	59.55
21	Tommy Coyne	9	561	62.33
22	Tony Cascarino	9	714	79.33
23	Trevor Senior	8	433	54.12
24	Phil Stant	8	468	58.50
25	Tony Adcock	8	669	83.62
26	Mick Harford	8	710	88.75
27	Andy Flounders	7	555	79.28
28	Gary Bennett	7	562	80.28
29	David Kelly	7	578	82.57
30	Andy Ritchie	7	641	91.57
31	Simon Garner	7	702	100.28
32	Luther Blissett	7	723	103.28
33	Tommy Tynan	7	783	111.85
34	Peter Beardsley	7	865	123.57
35	Robbie Fowler	6	194	32.33
36	David Crown	6	548	91.33
37	Gordon Davies	6	580	96.66
38	Mo Johnston	6	642	107.00
39	Mark Hughes	6	683	113.83
40=	Lee Chapman	6	689	114.83
40=	Dean Saunders	6	689	114.83
42	Steve White	6	753	125.50
43	John McGinlay	5	386	77.20
44	Bob Taylor	5	443	88.60
45	Marco Gabbiadini	5	515	103.00
46	Alan Smith	5	580	116.00
47	Charlie Nicholas	5	595	119.00
48	Mark Hateley	5	621	124.20
49	Graeme Sharp	5	638	127.60
50	Kevin Francis	4	281	70.25
51	Dean Holdsworth	4	382	95.50
52	Mark Bright	4	547	136.75
53	David Platt	4	570	142.50
54	John Robertson	4	639	159.75
55	Gary Bannister	4	642	160.50
56	Jimmy Quinn	4	677	169.25
57	Cyrille Regis	4	744	186.00
58	Les Ferdinand	3	316	105.33
59	Eric Cantona	3	485	161.66
60	John Barnes	3	782	260.66
61	Stan Collymore	2	219	109.50
62	Dion Dublin	2	335	167.50
63	David Hirst	2	384	192.00
64	Chris Armstrong	1	310	310.00
65	John Fashanu	1	467	467.00
66	Chris Waddle	1	755	755.00

MATCHES PER HAT-TRICK

All matches include substitute appearances

No	Player	Matches per hat-trick	Hat-tricks	Matches
1	Andy Cole	26.77	9	241
2	Ally McCoist	30.87	24	741
3	Steve Bull	31.00	17	527
4	Robbie Fowler	32.33	6	194
5	Gary Lineker	36.50	18	657
6	Alan Shearer	36.72	11	404
7	Ian Wright	37.60	15	564
8	John Aldridge	38.34	23	882
9	Ian Rush	47.55	18	856
10	Tony Cottee	48.66	12	584
11	Matthew Le Tissier	49.88	9	449
12	Trevor Senior	54.12	8	433
13	Mick Quinn	54.72	11	602
14	Bernie Slaven	55.30	10	553
15	Teddy Sheringham	55.50	10	555
16	Duncan Shearer	56.22	9	506
17	Clive Allen	56.88	9	512
18	Keith Wright	57.40	10	574
19	Phil Stant	58.50	8	468
20	Gordon Durie	59.55	9	536
21	Keith Edwards	59.72	11	657
22	Kerry Dixon	60.66	12	728
23	Tommy Coyne	62.33	9	561
24	Kevin Francis	70.25	4	281
25	Brian McClair	73.40	10	734
26	John McGinlay	77.20	5	386
27	Andy Flounders	79.28	7	555
28	Tony Cascarino	79.33	9	714
29	Gary Bennett	80.28	7	562
30	David Kelly	82.57	7	578
31	Tony Adcock	83.62	8	669
32	Bob Taylor	88.60	5	443
33	Mick Harford	88.75	8	710
34	David Crown	91.33	6	548
35	Andy Ritchie	91.57	7	641
36	Dean Holdsworth	95.50	4	382
37	Gordon Davies	96.66	6	580
38	Simon Garner	100.28	7	702
39	Marco Gabbiadini	103.00	5	515
40	Luther Blissett	103.28	7	723
41	Les Ferdinand	105.33	3	316
42	Mo Johnston	107.00	6	642
43	Stan Collymore	109.50	2	219
44	Tommy Tynan	111.85	7	783
45	Mark Hughes	113.83	6	683
46=	Lee Chapman	114.83	6	689
46=	Dean Saunders	114.83	6	689
48	Alan Smith	116.00	5	580
49	Charlie Nicholas	119.00	5	595
50	Peter Beardsley	123.57	7	865
51	Mark Hateley	124.20	5	621
52	Steve White	125.50	6	753
53	Graeme Sharp	127.60	5	638
54	Mark Bright	136.75	4	547
55	David Platt	142.50	4	570
56	John Robertson	159.75	4	639
57	Gary Bannister	160.50	4	642
58	Eric Cantona	161.66	3	485
59	Dion Dublin	167.50	2	335
60	Jimmy Quinn	169.25	4	677
61	Cyrille Regis	186.00	4	744
62	David Hirst	192.00	2	384
63	John Barnes	260.66	3	782
64	Chris Armstrong	310.00	1	310
65	John Fashanu	467.00	1	467
66	Chris Waddle	755.00	1	755

GOALS PER MATCH

All matches include substitute appearances

No	Player	Matches	Goals	Zero	One	Two	Three	Four	Five	Matches scored in
1	Robbie Fowler	194	117	112	57	19	3	2	1	82 – 42.26%
2	Steve Bull	527	298	308	160	42	14	3	0	219 – 41.55%
3	Andy Cole	241	129	141	82	9	8	0	1	100 – 41.49%
4	Ian Wright	564	298	334	179	36	13	2	0	230 – 40.78%
5	John Aldridge	882	471	530	258	71	21	2	0	352 – 39.90%
6	Les Ferdinand*	284	145	171	84	26	3	0	0	113 – 39.78%
7	Alan Shearer	404	217	244	114	35	11	0	0	160 – 39.60%
8	Ally McCoist	741	390	453	212	52	22	2	0	288 – 38.86%
9	Stan Collymore	219	105	134	67	16	2	0	0	85 – 38.81%
10	Kevin Francis	281	137	175	79	23	4	0	0	106 – 37.72%
11	Gary Lineker	657	334	415	171	53	15	3	0	242 – 36.83%
12	Trevor Senior	433	208	274	118	33	8	0	0	159 – 36.72%
13	Clive Allen	512	244	324	142	37	8	1	0	188 – 36.71%
14	Ian Rush	856	408	546	236	56	13	4	1	310 – 36.21%
15	John McGinlay	386	171	247	112	22	5	0	0	139 – 36.01%
16	Keith Edwards	657	301	422	182	42	9	2	0	235 – 35.76%
17	Duncan Shearer	506	229	326	142	29	7	2	0	180 – 35.57%
18	Phil Stant	468	207	305	128	27	7	1	0	163 – 34.82%
19	John Robertson	639	268	420	174	41	4	0	0	219 – 34.27%
20	Teddy Sheringham	555	241	365	150	30	9	1	0	190 – 34.23%
21	Mick Quinn	602	268	396	156	39	10	1	0	206 – 34.21%
22	Mo Johnston	642	266	424	177	35	5	1	0	218 – 33.95%
23	Bob Taylor	443	181	296	118	24	5	0	0	147 – 33.18%
24	Dean Holdsworth	382	159	257	95	26	4	0	0	125 – 32.72%
25	Tommy Tynan	783	314	527	206	43	6	1	0	256 – 32.69%
26	Dion Dublin	335	121	227	97	9	2	0	0	108 – 32.23%
27	Tony Cottee	584	245	396	145	31	10	2	0	188 – 32.19%
28	John Fashanu	467	164	319	133	14	1	0	0	148 – 31.69%
29	Eric Cantona	485	184	332	125	25	3	0	0	153 – 31.54%
30	Tony Cascarino	714	275	491	180	34	9	0	0	223 – 31.23%
31	Mark Bright	547	203	378	139	26	4	0	0	169 – 30.89%
32	David Platt	570	206	394	152	20	2	2	0	176 – 30.87%
33	Matthew Le Tissier	449	184	311	102	27	8	1	0	138 – 30.73%
34	David Crown	548	203	380	139	23	6	0	0	168 – 30.65%
35	Lee Chapman	689	256	480	169	34	5	1	0	209 – 30.33%
36	Charlie Nicholas	595	227	415	139	36	4	1	0	180 – 30.25%
37	Jimmy Quinn	677	256	473	156	44	4	0	0	204 – 30.13%
38	Marco Gabbiadini	515	181	360	134	16	5	0	0	155 – 30.09%
39	Chris Armstrong	310	111	217	76	16	1	0	0	93 – 30.00%
40	David Hirst	384	138	269	95	18	1	1	0	115 – 29.94%
41	Dean Saunders	689	248	484	169	30	5	1	0	205 – 29.75%
42	Kerry Dixon	728	287	513	159	44	8	4	0	215 – 29.53%
43	Mark Hately	621	234	439	135	42	5	0	0	182 – 29.30%
44	Tony Adcock	669	245	473	155	33	8	0	0	196 – 29.29%
45	Keith Wright	574	212	406	136	22	9	0	1	168 – 29.26%
46	Tommy Coyne	561	221	397	117	38	8	1	0	164 – 29.23%
47	Gordon Davies	580	209	411	136	27	5	1	0	169 – 29.13%
48	Steve White	753	268	535	176	36	4	2	0	218 – 28.95%
49	David Kelly	578	205	411	136	24	7	0	0	167 – 28.89%
50=	Gary Bennett	562	209	400	122	33	7	0	0	162 – 28.82%
50=	Andy Flounders	555	200	395	127	26	7	0	0	160 – 28.82%
52	Bernie Slaven	553	200	395	126	22	10	0	0	158 – 28.57%
53	Gary Bannister	642	216	459	154	25	4	0	0	183 – 28.50%
54	Alan Smith	580	201	415	135	25	4	1	0	165 – 28.44%
55	Luther Blissett	723	261	518	159	39	4	3	0	205 – 28.35%
56	Brian McClair	734	272	529	151	44	7	3	0	205 – 27.92%
57	Mark Hughes	683	218	498	158	21	6	0	0	185 – 27.08%
58	Graeme Sharp	638	212	466	139	28	3	2	0	172 – 26.95%
59	Peter Beardsley	865	277	634	192	32	7	0	0	231 – 26.70%
60	Mick Harford	710	232	521	154	27	8	0	0	189 – 26.61%
61	Andy Ritchie	641	207	473	137	24	6	1	0	168 – 26.20%
62	Simon Garner	702	225	519	151	25	5	1	1	183 – 26.06%
63	Gordon Durie	536	181	400	104	23	6	2	1	136 – 25.37%
64	Cyrille Regis	744	205	568	153	19	3	0	1	176 – 23.65%
65	John Barnes	782	204	607	149	23	3	0	0	175 – 22.37%
66	Chris Waddle	755	152	614	131	9	1	0	0	141 – 18.67%

* Does not include 32 matches and 21 League and Cup goals for Besiktas JK

GOALS PER VENUE

Player	Goals	Home	Away	Neutral	Wembley
Tony Adcock	245	164 – 66.93%	81 – 33.06%	0 – 0.00%	0 – 0.00%
John Aldridge	471	293 – 62.20%	170 – 36.09%	5 – 1.06%	3 – 0.63%
Clive Allen	244	141 – 57.78%	99 – 40.57%	3 – 1.22%	1 – 0.40%
Chris Armstrong	111	63 – 56.75%	47 – 42.34%	1 – 0.90%	0 – 0.00%
Gary Bannister	216	112 – 51.85%	104 – 48.14%	0 – 0.00%	0 – 0.00%
John Barnes	204	95 – 46.56%	102 – 50.00%	1 – 0.49%	6 – 2.94%
Peter Beardsley	277	158 – 57.03%	110 – 39.71%	2 – 0.72%	7 – 2.52%
Gary Bennett	209	128 – 61.24%	79 – 37.79%	2 – 0.95%	0 – 0.00%
Luther Blissett	261	162 – 62.06%	96 – 36.78%	0 – 0.00%	3 – 1.14%
Mark Bright	203	126 – 62.06%	75 – 36.94%	1 – 0.49%	1 – 0.49%
Steve Bull	298	185 – 62.08%	111 – 37.24%	0 – 0.00%	2 – 0.67%
Eric Cantona	184	105 – 57.06%	66 – 35.86%	5 – 2.71%	8 – 4.34%
Tony Cascarino	275	172 – 62.54%	101 – 36.72%	2 – 0.72%	0 – 0.00%
Lee Chapman	256	144 – 56.25%	110 – 42.96%	0 – 0.00%	2 – 0.78%
Andy Cole	129	74 – 57.36%	54 – 41.86%	1 – 0.77%	0 – 0.00%
Stan Collymore	105	64 – 60.95%	41 – 39.04%	0 – 0.00%	0 – 0.00%
Tony Cottee	245	151 – 61.63%	92 – 37.55%	0 – 0.00%	2 – 0.81%
Tommy Coyne	221	123 – 55.65%	95 – 42.98%	3 – 1.35%	0 – 0.00%
David Crown	203	118 – 58.12%	85 – 41.87%	0 – 0.00%	0 – 0.00%
Gordon Davies	209	122 – 58.37%	86 – 41.14%	1 – 0.47%	0 – 0.00%
Kerry Dixon	287	158 – 55.05%	127 – 44.25%	2 – 0.69%	0 – 0.00%
Dion Dublin	121	62 – 51.23%	58 – 47.93%	0 – 0.00%	1 – 0.82%
Gordon Durie	181	104 – 57.45%	74 – 40.88%	3 – 1.65%	0 – 0.00%
Keith Edwards	301	183 – 60.79%	117 – 38.87%	1 – 0.33%	0 – 0.00%
John Fashanu	164	93 – 56.70%	69 – 42.07%	1 – 0.60%	1 – 0.60%
Les Ferdinand*	145	87 – 60.00%	55 – 37.93%	0 – 0.00%	3 – 2.06%
Andy Flounders	200	116 – 58.00%	84 – 42.00%	0 – 0.00%	0 – 0.00%
Robbie Fowler	117	80 – 68.37%	34 – 29.05%	2 – 1.70%	1 – 0.85%
Kevin Francis	137	87 – 63.50%	48 – 35.03%	0 – 0.00%	2 – 1.45%
Marco Gabbiadini	181	95 – 52.48%	85 – 46.96%	0 – 0.00%	1 – 0.55%
Simon Garner	225	140 – 62.22%	84 – 37.33%	0 – 0.00%	1 – 0.44%
Mick Harford	232	145 – 62.50%	84 – 36.20%	1 – 0.43%	2 – 0.86%
Mark Hately	234	126 – 53.84%	98 – 41.88%	8 – 3.41%	2 – 0.85%
David Hirst	138	89 – 64.49%	48 – 34.78%	0 – 0.00%	1 – 0.72%
Dean Holdsworth	159	104 – 65.40%	55 – 34.59%	0 – 0.00%	0 – 0.00%
Mark Hughes	218	133 – 61.00%	73 – 33.48%	6 – 2.75%	6 – 2.75%
Mo Johnston	266	143 – 53.75%	119 – 44.73%	4 – 1.50%	0 – 0.00%
David Kelly	205	129 – 62.92%	76 – 37.07%	0 – 0.00%	0 – 0.00%
Matthew Le Tissier	184	103 – 55.97%	80 – 43.47%	0 – 0.00%	1 – 0.54%
Gary Lineker	334	171 – 51.19%	126 – 37.72%	25 – 7.48%	12 – 3.59%
Brian McClair	272	146 – 53.67%	117 – 43.01%	7 – 2.57%	2 – 0.73%
Ally McCoist	390	213 – 54.61%	158 – 40.51%	19 – 4.87%	0 – 0.00%
John McGinlay	171	103 – 60.23%	68 – 39.76%	0 – 0.00%	0 – 0.00%
Charlie Nicholas	227	119 – 52.42%	101 – 44.49%	5 – 2.20%	2 – 0.88%
David Platt	206	113 – 54.85%	73 – 35.43%	4 – 1.94%	16 – 7.76%
Jimmy Quinn	256	145 – 56.64%	110 – 42.96%	0 – 0.00%	1 – 0.39%
Mick Quinn	268	166 – 61.94%	102 – 38.05%	0 – 0.00%	0 – 0.00%
Cyrille Regis	205	112 – 54.63%	93 – 45.36%	0 – 0.00%	0 – 0.00%
Andy Ritchie	207	132 – 63.76%	74 – 35.74%	1 – 0.48%	0 – 0.00%
John Robertson	268	159 – 59.32%	106 – 39.55%	3 – 1.11%	0 – 0.00%
Ian Rush	408	224 – 54.90%	`170 – 41.66%	3 – 0.73%	11 – 2.69%
Dean Saunders	248	153 – 61.69%	92 – 37.09%	0 – 0.00%	3 – 1.20%
Trevor Senior	208	128 – 61.53%	80 – 38.46%	0 – 0.00%	0 – 0.00%
Graeme Sharp	212	125 – 58.96%	84 – 39.62%	1 – 0.47%	2 – 0.94%
Alan Shearer	217	135 – 62.21%	69 – 31.79%	0 – 0.00%	13 – 5.99%
Duncan Shearer	229	136 – 59.38%	89 – 38.86%	4 – 1.74%	0 – 0.00%
Teddy Sheringham	241	130 – 53.94%	106 – 43.98%	0 – 0.00%	5 – 2.07%
Bernie Slaven	200	115 – 57.50%	84 – 42.00%	0 – 0.00%	1 – 0.50%
Alan Smith	201	110 – 54.72%	86 – 42.78%	1 – 0.49%	4 – 1.99%
Phil Stant	207	114 – 55.07%	89 – 42.99%	4 – 1.93%	0 – 0.00%
Bob Taylor	181	98 – 54.14%	83 – 45.85%	0 – 0.00%	0 – 0.00%
Tommy Tynan	314	190 – 60.50%	124 – 39.49%	0 – 0.00%	0 – 0.00%
Chris Waddle	152	87 – 57.23%	60 – 39.47%	0 – 0.00%	5 – 3.28%
Steve White	268	162 – 60.44%	106 – 39.55%	0 – 0.00%	0 – 0.00%
Ian Wright	298	156 – 52.34%	134 – 44.96%	1 – 0.33%	7 – 2.34%
Keith Wright	212	112 – 52.83%	97 – 45.75%	3 – 1.41%	0 – 0.00%

* Does not include 21 League and Cup goals for Besiktas JK

GOALS IN CONSECUTIVE MATCHES

Goals in six or more consecutive matches or the single best sequence per player
Does not include international matches

	Mat	Goals	Season	Goals in each match											
				1	2	3	4	5	6	7	8	9	10	11	12
Tony Adcock	6	7	83/84	1	1	1	2	1	1	–	–	–	–	–	–
John Aldridge	8	11	88/89	1	1	1	1	2	1	1	3	–	–	–	–
	7	10	89/90	2	1	1	1	1	2	2	–	–	–	–	–
	6	8	93/94	2	1	2	1	1	1	–	–	–	–	–	–
	6	7	88/89	2	1	1	1	1	1	–	–	–	–	–	–
	6	6	87/88	1	1	1	1	1	1	–	–	–	–	–	–
Clive Allen	7	9	86/87	1	2	1	2	1	1	1	–	–	–	–	–
	6	8	92/93	1	2	2	1	1	1	–	–	–	–	–	–
Chris Armstrong	4	4	93/94	1	1	1	1	–	–	–	–	–	–	–	–
Gary Bannister	5	6	81/82	1	1	2	1	1	–	–	–	–	–	–	–
John Barnes	4	4	90/91	1	1	1	1	–	–	–	–	–	–	–	–
Peter Beardsley	6	8	91/92	1	1	1	3	1	1	–	–	–	–	–	–
Gary Bennett	7	11	94/95	1	2	1	2	1	1	3	–	–	–	–	–
Luther Blissett	5	9	78/79	2	2	2	1	2	–	–	–	–	–	–	–
	5	8	88/89	1	4	1	1	1	–	–	–	–	–	–	–
	5	6	80/81–81/82	2	1	1	1	1	–	–	–	–	–	–	–
Mark Bright	8	9	91/92	1	1	1	1	1	2	1	1	–	–	–	–
	7	7	93/94	1	1	1	1	1	1	1	–	–	–	–	–
Steve Bull	6	8	87/88	2	1	2	1	1	1	–	–	–	–	–	–
Eric Cantona	5	5	95/96	1	1	1	1	1	–	–	–	–	–	–	–
Tony Cascarino	6	7	94/95	1	1	1	1	1	2	–	–	–	–	–	–
Lee Chapman	6	6	90/91	1	1	1	1	1	1	–	–	–	–	–	–
Andy Cole	5	8	93/94	1	1	2	3	1	–	–	–	–	–	–	–
	5	5	91/92	1	1	1	1	1	–	–	–	–	–	–	–
	5	5	92/93	1	1	1	1	1	–	–	–	–	–	–	–
Stan Collymore	6	7	94/95	1	1	1	2	1	1	–	–	–	–	–	–
Tony Cottee	7	7	85/86	1	1	1	1	1	1	1	–	–	–	–	–
Tommy Coyne	5	6	90/91–91/92	1	1	1	1	2	–	–	–	–	–	–	–
	5	5	94/95	1	1	1	1	1	–	–	–	–	–	–	–
David Crown	7	9	85/86	1	3	1	1	1	1	1	–	–	–	–	–
Gordon Davies	5	6	86/87	1	2	1	1	1	–	–	–	–	–	–	–
	5	5	84/85	1	1	1	1	1	–	–	–	–	–	–	–
Kerry Dixon	6	7	85/86	1	1	2	1	1	1	–	–	–	–	–	–
Dion Dublin	4	5	89/90	2	1	1	1	–	–	–	–	–	–	–	–
	4	4	90/91	1	1	1	1	–	–	–	–	–	–	–	–
Gordon Durie	8	9	83/84	1	1	1	1	1	1	2	1	–	–	–	–
Keith Edwards	8	13	88/89	2	1	3	1	1	2	2	1	–	–	–	–
	8	11	76/77	2	2	1	2	1	1	1	1	–	–	–	–
	7	9	83/84	1	2	1	1	1	1	2	–	–	–	–	–
John Fashanu	5	7	90/91	2	2	1	1	1	–	–	–	–	–	–	–
Les Ferdinand	8	12	95/96	2	1	2	1	1	1	3	1	–	–	–	–
	6	8	96/97	1	2	1	1	1	2	–	–	–	–	–	–
Andy Flounders	4	4	91/92	1	1	1	1	–	–	–	–	–	–	–	–
Robbie Fowler	5	7	96/97	1	1	1	2	2	–	–	–	–	–	–	–
Kevin Francis	5	7	92/93	2	2	1	1	1	–	–	–	–	–	–	–
Marco Gabbiadini	3	6	87/88	2	2	2	–	–	–	–	–	–	–	–	–
	3	5	93/94	1	1	3	–	–	–	–	–	–	–	–	–
	3	4	95/96	2	1	1	–	–	–	–	–	–	–	–	–
	3	3	87/88	1	1	1	–	–	–	–	–	–	–	–	–
	3	3	89/90	1	1	1	–	–	–	–	–	–	–	–	–
	3	3	91/92	1	1	1	–	–	–	–	–	–	–	–	–
	3	3	94/95	1	1	1	–	–	–	–	–	–	–	–	–
	3	3	95/96	1	1	1	–	–	–	–	–	–	–	–	–
Simon Garner	5	5	84/85	1	1	1	1	1	–	–	–	–	–	–	–
Mick Harford	6	10	79/80–80/81	1	1	3	2	1	2	–	–	–	–	–	–
Mark Hately	4	7	93/94	2	2	1	2	–	–	–	–	–	–	–	–
	4	5	93/94	1	1	1	2	–	–	–	–	–	–	–	–
	4	5	94/95	2	1	1	1	–	–	–	–	–	–	–	–
	4	4	87/88	1	1	1	1	–	–	–	–	–	–	–	–
	4	4	93/94	1	1	1	1	–	–	–	–	–	–	–	–
David Hirst	5	7	90/91	1	2	1	2	1	–	–	–	–	–	–	–
Dean Holdsworth	5	8	92/93	2	1	2	2	1	–	–	–	–	–	–	–
	5	7	91/92	1	1	2	2	1	–	–	–	–	–	–	–
	5	5	93/94	1	1	1	1	1	–	–	–	–	–	–	–
Mark Hughes	4	4	85/86	1	1	1	1	–	–	–	–	–	–	–	–
	4	4	92/93	1	1	1	1	–	–	–	–	–	–	–	–
Mo Johnston	5	7	82/83	1	1	1	1	3	–	–	–	–	–	–	–

	Mat	Goals	Season	1	2	3	4	5	6	7	8	9	10	11	12
	5	7	86/87	1	2	1	1	2	–	–	–	–	–	–	–
	5	5	83/84	1	1	1	1	1	–	–	–	–	–	–	–
David Kelly	5	6	92/93	1	1	1	1	2	–	–	–	–	–	–	–
	5	5	86/87	1	1	1	1	1	–	–	–	–	–	–	–
Matthew Le Tissier	4	6	93/94	1	1	3	1	–	–	–	–	–	–	–	–
Gary Lineker	4	8	85/86–86/87	3	2	1	2	–	–	–	–	–	–	–	–
	4	7	91/92	1	3	1	2	–	–	–	–	–	–	–	–
	4	6	85/86	3	1	1	1	–	–	–	–	–	–	–	–
	4	5	84/85	1	1	2	1	–	–	–	–	–	–	–	–
	4	5	89/90	1	1	1	2	–	–	–	–	–	–	–	–
Brian McClair	7	10	86/87	2	1	2	1	1	2	1	–	–	–	–	–
Ally McCoist	5	8	86/87	1	1	1	2	3	–	–	–	–	–	–	–
	5	7	85/86	1	3	1	1	1	–	–	–	–	–	–	–
	5	7	91/92	2	1	1	1	2	–	–	–	–	–	–	–
	5	6	85/86–86/87	1	1	1	2	1	–	–	–	–	–	–	–
	5	5	91/92	1	1	1	1	1	–	–	–	–	–	–	–
John McGinlay	5	6	94/95	1	1	2	1	1	–	–	–	–	–	–	–
	5	6	96/97	2	1	1	1	1	–	–	–	–	–	–	–
	5	5	96/97	1	1	1	1	1	–	–	–	–	–	–	–
Charlie Nicholas	9	12	80/81	2	1	2	1	2	1	1	1	1	–	–	–
David Platt	5	6	87/88	1	1	2	1	1	–	–	–	–	–	–	–
	5	5	90/91	1	1	1	1	1	–	–	–	–	–	–	–
Jimmy Quinn	6	10	93/94	1	2	2	2	2	1	–	–	–	–	–	–
Mick Quinn	6	10	88/89–89/90	1	4	1	2	1	1	–	–	–	–	–	–
	6	10	92/93	2	1	1	2	2	2	–	–	–	–	–	–
Cyrille Regis	7	9	81/82	1	1	1	1	2	2	1	–	–	–	–	–
Andy Ritchie	8	10	89/90	1	2	1	1	1	1	2	1	–	–	–	–
John Robertson	8	10	85/86	1	1	1	2	1	1	1	2	–	–	–	–
	6	6	94/95	1	1	1	1	1	1	–	–	–	–	–	–
Ian Rush	6	10	83/84	5	1	1	1	1	1	–	–	–	–	–	–
	6	8	81/82	1	3	1	1	1	1	–	–	–	–	–	–
Dean Saunders	6	7	95/96	1	2	1	1	1	1	–	–	–	–	–	–
Trevor Senior	5	8	84/85	1	1	3	1	2	–	–	–	–	–	–	–
	5	6	84/85	1	1	1	1	2	–	–	–	–	–	–	–
	5	6	88/89	2	1	1	1	1	–	–	–	–	–	–	–
Graeme Sharp	4	4	84/85	1	1	1	1	–	–	–	–	–	–	–	–
Alan Shearer	7	7	96/97	1	1	1	1	1	1	1	–	–	–	–	–
	6	9	92/93	2	1	1	1	2	2	–	–	–	–	–	–
	6	9	93/94	2	1	1	2	1	2	–	–	–	–	–	–
Duncan Shearer	7	12	92/93	1	1	1	1	3	3	2	–	–	–	–	–
Teddy Sheringham	6	10	95/96	1	2	1	2	2	2	–	–	–	–	–	–
Bernie Slaven	6	8	84/85	1	1	1	2	1	2	–	–	–	–	–	–
Alan Smith	6	8	85/86	2	1	1	1	2	1	–	–	–	–	–	–
Phil Stant	5	7	96/97	1	2	1	1	2	–	–	–	–	–	–	–
	5	5	88/89–89/90	1	1	1	1	1	–	–	–	–	–	–	–
	5	5	91/92	1	1	1	1	1	–	–	–	–	–	–	–
Bob Taylor	6	7	92/93	1	1	1	2	1	1	–	–	–	–	–	–
Tommy Tynan	4	6	80/81	1	2	2	1	–	–	–	–	–	–	–	–
	4	6	83/84	2	1	2	1	–	–	–	–	–	–	–	–
	4	5	84/85	1	1	2	1	–	–	–	–	–	–	–	–
	4	5	85/86	1	1	2	1	–	–	–	–	–	–	–	–
	4	4	82/83	1	1	1	1	–	–	–	–	–	–	–	–
Chris Waddle	5	6	83/84	1	2	1	1	1	–	–	–	–	–	–	–
Steve White	4	8	95/96	2	2	3	1	–	–	–	–	–	–	–	–
	4	7	81/82	1	4	1	1	–	–	–	–	–	–	–	–
	4	5	87/88	1	1	2	1	–	–	–	–	–	–	–	–
	4	5	89/90	2	1	1	1	–	–	–	–	–	–	–	–
	4	5	90/91	2	1	1	1	–	–	–	–	–	–	–	–
	4	4	86/87	1	1	1	1	–	–	–	–	–	–	–	–
	4	4	91/92	1	1	1	1	–	–	–	–	–	–	–	–
	4	4	94/95	1	1	1	1	–	–	–	–	–	–	–	–
	4	4	94/95	1	1	1	1	–	–	–	–	–	–	–	–
Ian Wright	12	16	94/95	1	1	2	1	2	1	1	2	1	2	1	1
Keith Wright	6	8	86/87	2	2	1	1	1	1	–	–	–	–	–	–